P9-ELQ-150

Home Improvement 1-2-3®

THE HOME DEPOT®

Meredith® BOOKS
Des Moines, Iowa

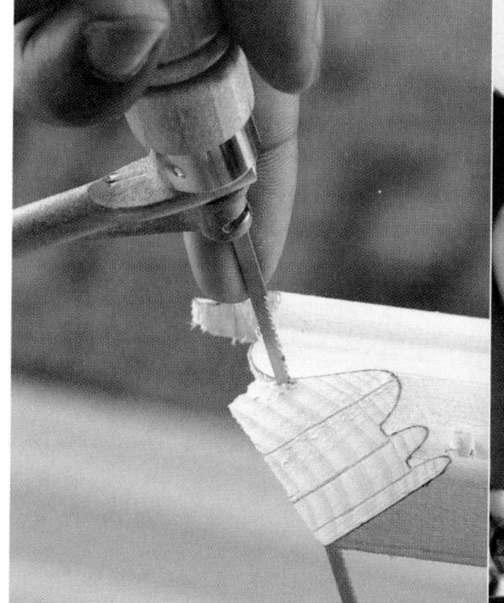

HOME IMPROVEMENT 1-2-3®
Editor: Benjamin W. Allen
Senior Associate Design Director: Tom Wegner
Copy Chief: Doug Kouma
Copy Editor: Kevin Cox
Publishing Operations Manager: Karen Schirm
Edit and Design Coordinator: Mary Lee Gavin
Editorial Assistant: Diana Meinders
Book Production Managers: Marjorie J. Schenkelberg, Mark Weaver
Imaging Center Operator: Tony Jungweber
Contributing Copy Editors: Charles DeLaFuente, Ira Lacher, Ro Sila
Contributing Proofreaders: Steve Hallam, David Krause, Kristin McCullough, Cheri Madison, Linda Wagner
Contributing Indexer: Donald Glassman

Additional editorial and design contributions from Abramowitz Creative Studios
Publishing Director/Designer: Tim Abramowitz
Graphic Designers: Kelly Bailey, Adam White
Illustration: Kelly Bailey, Abramowitz Creative Studios; Jim Swanson, Performance Marketing
Photography: Image Studios, Inc.
Account Executive: Lisa Egan
Photographers: Bill Rein, John von Dorn
Assistants: Rob Resnick, Scott Verber
Technical Advisor: Rick Nadke

Meredith® Books
Editorial Director: Gregory H. Kayko
Art Director: Gene Rauch
Managing Editor: Kathleen Armentrout
Brand Manager: Mark Hetrick

Editorial Director, Marketing and Publicity: Amy Nichols
Director, Sales—Home Depot: Robb Morris
Executive Director, Sales: Ken Zagor
Director, Operations: George A. Susral
Director, Production: Douglas M. Johnston
Business Director: Janice Croat

Vice President and General Manager, SIM: Jeff Myers

Meredith Publishing Group
President: Jack Griffin
Executive Vice President: Doug Olson

Meredith Corporation
Chairman of the Board: William T. Kerr
President and Chief Executive Officer: Stephen M. Lacy

In Memoriam: E.T. Meredith III (1933–2003)

The Home Depot®
Marketing Manager: Nathan Ehrlich

Third Edition.

Printed in the United States of America.
Library of Congress Control Number: 2008924090
ISBN: 978-0-696-23850-5

Distributed by Meredith Corporation.
Meredith Corporation is not affiliated with The Home Depot®.

Special thanks to:
FLIR Systems, 25 Esquire Road, N. Billerica, MA 01862
978/901-8866; www.goinfrared.com
(Photo: top left, page 507)

The Energy Conservatory, 2801 21st Avenue S, Suite 160, Minneapolis, MN 55407
612/827-1117; www.energyconservatory.com
(Photo: bottom right, page 507)

Intermatic, Inc., Intermatic Plaza, Spring Grove, IL 60081
815/675-7000; www.intermatic.com
(Photo: top left, page 439)

Note to the reader: Due to differing conditions, tools, and individual skills, Meredith Corporation and The Home Depot® assume no responsibility for any damages, injuries suffered, or losses incurred as a result of following the information published in this book. Before beginning any project, review the instructions carefully, and if any doubts or questions remain, consult local experts or authorities. Because codes and regulations vary greatly, you always should check with authorities to ensure that your project complies with all applicable local codes and regulations. Always read and observe all of the safety precautions provided by any tool or equipment manufacturer, and follow all accepted safety procedures.

We are dedicated to providing accurate and helpful do-it-yourself information. We welcome your comments about improving this book and ideas for other books we might offer to home-improvement enthusiasts. Contact us by any of these methods:
Leave a voice message at: 800/678-2093
Write to: Meredith Books, Home Depot Books
1716 Locust St.
Des Moines, IA 50309–3023
Send e-mail to: hi123@mdp.com.

Home Improvement 1-2-3®

THE HOME DEPOT®

Table of contents

Chapter 1: Painting and Wallpapering

Field guide to paint 12
The color wheel 14
Choosing a color scheme 15
The painting tool kit 16
Brushes and rollers 17
Power rollers 18
Spraying paint 19
Protection 20
Priming is essential 22
Preparing to paint 24
Cleaning and deglossing 25
Treating stains, mold, and mildew 26
Painting over wallpaper 27
Removing wallpaper 28
Priming and painting walls 30
Using a brush 33
Painting doors and trim 34
Window-painting basics 36
Staining windows 38
Staining trim 40
Painting kitchen and bath cabinets 42
Painting floors 44
Painting interior brick .47
Painting interior concrete 48
Painting garage floors 48
Helpful paint tips 49
Special finishes 50
Stippling 51
Sponging 52
Ragging on and ragging off 54
Creating textured effects 56
Painting exteriors 57
Painting exterior walls 61
Priming and painting trim 64
Painting windows 66
Paint cleanup and disposal 68
Wallpaper basics 69
The wallpapering tool kit 71
Measuring and estimating wallpaper 72
Wallpapering walls 73
Wallpapering around obstacles 82
Wallpapering ceilings .83
Hanging borders on painted walls 84
Repair and maintenance 87
Combining a border with wallpaper 88
Handling wallpaper transitions 90
Finishing touches 91

Chapter 2: Walls and Ceilings

Walls and ceilings basics 94
The walls and ceilings tool kit 95
Repairing drywall 96
Repairing corner damage 98
Repairing a plaster ceiling 99
Repairing plaster walls 100
Installing ceiling tile 102
Installing a tongue-and-groove ceiling 104
Installing a suspended ceiling 105
Removing a wall 109
Building a partition wall 113
Soundproofing a room 118
Installing drywall 119
Finishing drywall 124
Installing paneling 127
Installing no-miter moldings 130
Molding installation skills 131
Installing baseboards and chair rails 135
Installing crown molding 137
Installing polyurethane molding 140
Creating custom molding 141
Installing wainscoting 143
Wainscot choices 146
Hanging and arranging artwork 147
Tiling a wall 148

Chapter 3: Floors

Flooring materials . . . 154
The flooring tool kit . . . 155
Stopping squeaks . . . 156
Patching concrete floors . . . 158
Measuring for flooring . . . 160
Removing existing flooring . . . 161
Replacing underlayment . . . 165
Installing sheet vinyl . . . 167
Installing resilient vinyl tile . . . 172
Laying a tile floor . . . 174
Installing vinyl plank flooring . . . 180
Sanding and refinishing a floor . . . 182
Installing a strip-wood floor . . . 186
Installing a decorative border . . . 189
Installing wide-plank flooring . . . 190
Installing laminate and engineered floors . . . 191
Installing carpeting and carpet pad . . . 195
Installing baseboard . . . 199
Thresholds . . . 203

Chapter 4: Doors and Windows

Door basics . . . 206
The doors tool kit . . . 207
Locksets and latches . . . 208
Solving door-latch problems . . . 209
Freeing a sticking door . . . 210
Installing a door lock . . . 211
Making an opening for a door or window . . . 213
Making headers . . . 215
Installing a prehung interior door . . . 216
Installing molding for interior doors . . . 218
Installing a prehung entry door . . . 220
Installing a storm door . . . 224
Installing a hinged patio door . . . 226
Installing a garage door . . . 231
Adjusting an out-of-balance garage door . . . 234
Installing a garage door opener . . . 235
Maintaining a garage door opener . . . 237
Safety-testing a garage door opener . . . 238
Getting to know your windows . . . 239
Window basics and maintenance tips . . . 240
Replacing broken sash cords . . . 241
The windows tool kit . . . 242
Repairing a broken window pane . . . 243
Replacing a screen . . . 245
Window and glass door security . . . 246
Installing a window . . . 248
Installing a storm window . . . 252

Chapter 5: Cabinets, Countertops, and Storage

Cabinet and countertop basics . . . 256
The cabinetmaker's tool kit . . . 257
Replacing cabinet hardware . . . 258
Replacing cabinet doors and drawers . . . 260
Cabinet refacing . . . 261
Getting ready to install cabinets . . . 262
Installing kitchen cabinets . . . 265
Installing a kitchen island . . . 270
Countertop basics . . . 271
Installing countertops . . . 272
Tiling a countertop . . . 275
Adding a closet . . . 279
Installing a modular storage system . . . 283

Table of contents (continued)

Chapter 6: Plumbing

How the plumbing system works . . . 288
The plumbing tool kit . . . 290
Quick fixes for frozen or leaking pipes . . . 291
Planning for accessibilty . . . 292
Working with rigid plastic pipe . . . 293
Connecting PVC . . . 294
Connecting CPVC . . . 295
Connecting ABS . . . 296
Soldering copper pipe . . . 297
Running new supply lines . . . 299
Installing PEX supply lines . . . 301
Installing shut-off valves & supply tubes . . . 302
Repairing or replacing a sink strainer . . . 303
Installing a single-bowl PVC P-trap . . . 305
Unclogging the clogs . . . 307
Unclogging drains and waste lines . . . 308
Unclogging sink drains . . . 309
Unclogging jammed disposers . . . 309
Unclogging bathtub and shower drains . . . 310
Unclogging a toilet . . . 311
Repairing a compression faucet . . . 312
Replacing a worn valve seat . . . 313
Repairing a ceramic disk faucet . . . 314
Replacing a cartridge faucet . . . 315
Repairing a rotary ball faucet . . . 316
Repairing a tub and shower faucet . . . 317
Repairing a tub diverter valve . . . 318
Installing a tub spout . . . 319
Cleaning a showerhead . . . 319
Repairing toilets . . . 320
Adjusting the tank and water level . . . 321
Repairing a leaking tank . . . 322
Replacing a toilet fill valve . . . 323
Replacing a flapper . . . 325
Installing a countertop sink . . . 326
Installing a vanity and sink . . . 328
Installing a self-rimmming sink . . . 329
Removing an old sink . . . 329
Installing a wall-hung sink . . . 330
Installing a pedestal sink . . . 330
Installing a bowl-type sink . . . 331
Installing a farmer's/apron sink . . . 332
Installing a widespread faucet . . . 333
Installing a center-set faucet . . . 334
Installing a pop-up drain . . . 335
Removing an old tub . . . 337
Installing a bathtub in an alcove . . . 338
Installing a sliding glass door for a tub . . . 342
Installing a shower surround . . . 343
Removing an old toilet . . . 345
Installing a new toilet . . . 346
Installing a garbage disposer . . . 349
Replacing a dishwasher . . . 351
Connecting a refrigerator ice maker . . . 352
Installing a water softener . . . 353
Water heaters . . . 355
Water heater installation basics . . . 356
Installing an on-demand water heater . . . 359

Chapter 7: Electrical

How the electrical system works . . . 362
Electrical safety . . . 363
The electrical tool kit . . . 364
Wires and cables . . . 365
Wire nuts and tape . . . 366
Receptacles and switches . . . 367
How a circuit works . . . 368
Grounding and polarization . . . 369
Using testers . . . 370
Stripping and splicing wire . . . 371
Attaching wire to a terminal . . . 372
Wiring receptacles and switches . . . 374
Installing or replacing a receptacle . . . 375
Installing a GFCI receptacle . . . 376
Installing an outdoor receptacle . . . 377
Adding a wall switch for a ceiling fixture . . . 378
Controlling a single outlet with a switch . . . 379
Replacing a three-way switch . . . 380
Replacing a dimmer switch . . . 381
Choosing electrical boxes . . . 382
Installing electrical boxes . . . 382
Installing remodeling boxes . . . 383
Installing ceiling boxes . . . 385
Installing a junction box . . . 386
Installing NM cable in new walls . . . 387
Working with NM cable . . . 388
Fishing and running cable . . . 389
Working with armored cable . . . 391
Running conduit . . . 392
Installing surface-mounted wiring . . . 394
Adding a circuit . . . 396
Lighting a kitchen . . . 398

Lighting a bathroom 399
Lighting living areas 400
Planning for can lighting 401
Choosing ceiling fixtures 402
Seeing green: energy-efficient lighting 404
Installing or replacing wall lights 405
Installing a hanging light fixture 406
Installing recessed lighting 408
Installing halogen lighting. 411
Installing fluorescent lighting 412
Installing track lighting 413
Installing motion-sensor lights. 415
Hanging a ceiling fan 416
Installing an attic fan 420
Installing a whole-house fan 421
Installing a bathroom vent 423
Installing a range hood 426
Installing low-voltage landscape lighting 427
Installing telephone and CAT 5 wiring 429
Installing coaxial cable 431
Planning a structured wiring system 432
Installing structured cable 433
Troubleshooting a door chime. 435
Troubleshooting a thermostat 437
Adding surge protection 438

Chapter 8: Heating, Ventilation, & Air-Conditioning

Maintaining a forced-air furnace 442
Maintianing a gas burner 449
Maintaining an oil furnace 454
Maintaining a hot water heat system 458
Maintaining a heat pump 467
Installing an electric baseboard heater 471
Adding a hot water baseboard heater 473
Adding a forced-air heat run. 475
Installing auxiliary gas heaters. 477
Window air-conditioner maintenance 480
Installing a window air-conditioner 482
Maintaining a central-air system 484
Installing an evaporative cooler. 486
Installing underfloor radiant heat 488
Installing a furnace humidifier 490
Maintaining a furnace humidifier. 492
Installing soffit and roof vents 494

Chapter 9: Insulation and Weatherproofing

Insulation and weatherproofing basics 500
Choosing insulation 501
Insulation and weatherproofing tool kit 502
Improving energy efficiency 503
Evaluating home energy efficiency. 506
Weatherproofing your home 508
Insulating an attic 516
Insulating basements. 518

Chapter 10: Maintaining Exteriors

Exterior maintenance materials 524
The exterior maintenance tool kit 525
Preventing water-infiltration problems 526
Preventing ice dams 526
Working safely 528
Repairing gutters 530
Cleaning gutters. 533
Installing a vinyl gutter systems. 534
Repairing siding and trim 536
Repairing wood siding 538
Repairing vinyl and metal siding 542
Repairing masonry walls 544
Repairing fascia and soffits. 548
Roofing basics. 552
The roofer's tool kit 555
Inspecting a roof 556
Checking for leaks 557
Repairing roofs 558
Roof tear-off and repair 562
Installing underlayment 564
Installing flashing 566
Installing asphalt shingles. 570
Reroofing over an existing roof 575
Installing roll roofing 576
Repairing walks, drives, and setps. 578

Meeting Canadian code. 584
Tool glossary. 592
Index. 600

How to use this book

People work on their homes for many reasons: to save money; improve their quality of life; provide a safe and attractive place for their families to live; feel the satisfaction of a job well done; and maybe, simply because they like doing it. Whatever the reasons, there are four basic components of success:

- Mastering unfamiliar skills
- Using the right tools and materials
- Working safely
- Doing the job right the first time

Most homeowners need a little help balancing these components, so a home-improvement resource that's accessible, easy to use, and full of the right information can become one of the most valuable additions to a do-it-yourselfer's bookshelf. Here's how to get the most out of *Home Improvement 1-2-3*.

Trust the wisdom of the aisles

A genuine desire to help people say, "I can do that!" is what the associates at The Home Depot® are all about. And it's why these experts from around the country have contributed their years of on-the-job experience and wisdom of the aisles to this revision of *Home Improvement 1-2-3*. Their contributions have helped create a hardworking, accurate, and easy-to-follow guide for every aspect of home improvement, maintenance, and repair.

The organizing principle

Home Improvement 1-2-3 consists of twelve sections that provide detailed coverage of the most common projects and techniques.

Take a look inside!

- **Chapter 1:** Painting and Wallpapering
- **Chapter 2:** Walls and Ceilings
- **Chapter 3:** Floors
- **Chapter 4:** Doors and Windows
- **Chapter 5:** Cabinets, Countertops, and Storage
- **Chapter 6:** Plumbing
- **Chapter 7:** Electrical
- **Chapter 8:** Heating, Ventilation, and Air Conditioning
- **Chapter 9:** Insulation and Weatherproofing
- **Chapter 10:** Maintaining Exteriors
- **Meeting Canadian Code**
- **Tool Glossary**

Doing the job—step by step

All the projects include complete instructions along with detailed, step-by-step photographs to ensure successful completion. You have everything you need to do the job right the first time following standards set by manufacturers and the trades–just like the pros.

Tips, tricks, and time-savers

Each page includes more than just how to do the job. To help you plan your project and to schedule your time, you'll find expert advice: how hard a job is, how long it takes a pro, and how long it might take you.

At the beginning of each project you will find a materials list, along with commonly needed tools.

Additional features on the pages are filled with specific information. **Safety Alert, Buyer's Guide, Work Smart, Closer Look, Tool Tip, Oops,** and **Design Tip** are all there to help you work efficiently and economically. Whenever a project involves something special—whether it's safety or getting the right tool—you'll be prepared for whatever comes up. **Tool kits** at the beginning

Support your local building inspector

Building codes are often confusing to the do-it-yourselfer, but they exist to enforce consistent methods of installation and, more important, ensure the safety of your family. For example, the National Electrical Code, which is written by the National Fire Protection Association, says you can only put one wire under each screw on a receptacle or switch. It doesn't seem like two wires are more dangerous than one. But the code writers have seen one too many fires caused by the second wire popping out from under the screw.

The fire prevention code says that if you're going to put in foam insulation (say in your basement) and then cover it with wood paneling, you have to put drywall over the foam first. Why? Foam insulation produces thick black smoke in a fire and drywall delays the spread of fire, giving you time to get out safely.

Sometimes the reason for code rules is common sense. Ever wonder why the code requires outlets every six feet along walls, but every two feet along kitchen counters? It's because of the length of appliance cords—they're shorter on toasters than they are on lamps.

You must follow codes, so you should find out what's required and do it from the start. This book is written to meet the relevant national codes. But codes change, and local codes can sometimes be more stringent than national codes. Legally, it's up to you to make sure the job you're doing meets code. The consequences of not meeting code are serious: you've potentially exposed yourself and your family to danger, an inspector who happens across your work can make you tear it out and start over (which can get expensive), and you may not be able to sell your house until you fix the violation.

You want to do a job you can be proud of, so follow through. Check with your municipality's building inspector to find out what local standards you need to meet. Get some advice on how to best go about the job. Get a permit, do the job right, and sleep soundly at night. For more general information on inspections that is common to both the United States and Canada, see pages 584–591.

Meeting Canadian code

While most Canadian building codes are comparable with those in the United States, there are differences, and some are significant. Because this edition of *Home Improvement 1-2-3* generally reflects relevant U.S. national guidelines, a section called **Meeting Canadian Code** beginning on page 584 supplements the general information.

You'll also find the maple leaf symbol shown above appearing on pages and projects where there is a clear difference between code in the two countries. The symbol refers you to the **Meeting Canadian Code** section.

Remember, codes in both the United States and Canada can (and do) vary greatly from locale to locale, so it's impossible for any book to be comprehensive when it comes to code and code application. Always check with local authorities before you begin any projects that may require permits or inspections.

of each chapter show you the basic tools you'll need for the following projects.

Get the most out of your home-improvement experience

To make the best use of what's inside, read through each project carefully before you begin. Walk yourself mentally through the steps from beginning to end until you're comfortable with the process. Understanding the scope of the job will limit unnecessary mistakes and the need to spend the money to do things twice.

Take your time doing the job

If you're not a master plumber, don't expect to work like one. A little learning on the job will make it easier the next time. Expect problems, but also trust that you can solve them. If you can't, don't be afraid to ask the experts. There's no magic in home improvement: just a willingness to give it a try; a desire to learn how things work so you can fix them; and, finally, taking pride in what you can accomplish with a little elbow grease and good advice.

Tricks of the trade

Look for special icons, which signal detailed information on a specific topic.

SAFETY ALERT
Prevent unsafe situations

BUYER'S GUIDE
Select the best materials

WORK SMART
Make smart choices

CLOSER LOOK
Understand all the details

TOOL TIP
Use tools to their best advantage

OOPS
Fix or avoid common mistakes

DESIGN TIP
Design options to change your home

SAFETY ALERT

NINE TIPS FOR A SAFER JOB

Some aspects of home improvement can be dangerous, but it's hard to remember that when you're lying under the sink or bumping your head against a roof rafter. Being safe in potentially dangerous situations is not only a way of thinking, it's a way of working.

- Wear the proper safety gear, including recommended gloves and clothing; safety glasses; and ear protection when working with power tools. A piece of flying debris can blind you or distract you long enough to create a disaster. Regular eyeglasses can shatter when hit.
- Wear a respirator or particle mask that's rated for the job you're doing. Breathing toxic fumes or inhaling particles can have serious consequences.
- Wear safety glasses when driving nails or working with hammers. Nailheads are notorious for breaking off and flying off at odd angles.
- Always turn off the power at the circuit breaker when working with wiring. Also cut power when you're tearing down a wall or even drilling a hole in it. Live wires can cause serious injury.
- Choose the right tool for the job and know how to use it safely.
- Don't overreach. Move the ladder before you fall.
- Don't reach above your head to make a cut. Something is bound to fall on you. It may be the cutoff; it may be the saw.
- Ask questions. Store personnel can recommend the right tools and materials for the job; building inspectors can (and will) make sure you're doing the job right.
- Take your time. Read the directions carefully, look at the job at hand, and imagine what might go wrong. You don't do this kind of work every day, and short of having a pro in your house, the surest way to avoid trouble is to prepare properly.

CHAPTER 1

Painting and Wallpapering

Of all the home-improvement tasks, painting gives the most bang for the buck. Paint can drench a room with vibrant color, or tone it down—all for only a few dollars.

Wallpaper, though, offers a shortcut to pattern and texture and style. Some types have a vinyl coating that wipes clean, or are prepasted for easier application.

Paint chips and wallpapers are notorious for looking different once they are on the wall because light in the room plays a major role. Buy a quart of paint and test it before investing in more. Paint pieces of white poster board; see how they change under your lighting conditions.

Contents

Field guide to paint 12
The color wheel 14
Choosing a color scheme 15
The painting tool kit. 16
Brushes and rollers 17
Power rollers 18
Spraying paint. 19
Protection 20
Priming is essential 22
Preparing to paint. 24
Cleaning and deglossing 25
Treating stains, mold, and mildew 26
Painting over wallpaper. 27
Removing wallpaper. 28
Priming and painting walls 30
Using a brush 33
Painting doors and trim 34
Window-painting basics 36
Staining windows 38
Staining trim 40
Painting kitchen and bath cabinets. 42
Painting floors 44
Painting interior brick 47
Painting interior concrete 48
Painting garage floors. 48
Helpful paint tips 49
Special finishes 50
Stippling. 51
Sponging 52
Ragging on and ragging off. 54
Creating textured effects 56
Painting exteriors 57
Painting exterior walls 61
Priming and painting trim 64
Painting windows. 66
Paint cleanup and disposal 68
Wallpaper basics 69
The wallpapering tool kit 71
Measuring and estimating wallpaper. 72
Wallpapering walls 73
Wallpapering around obstacles 82
Wallpapering ceilings. 83
Hanging borders on painted walls 84
Repair and maintenance 87
Combining a border with wallpaper 88
Handling wallpaper transitions 90
Finishing touches 91

The right way to paint

Preparation takes longer than the actual painting. Taking the time to properly prepare the surface makes all the difference in the final results. Plan on spending at least as much time cleaning and repairing as you do painting.

Paint covers discolorations, but not surface flaws. It coats the bumps, nicks, dents, and cracks that are part of the wall, door, or trim, but it won't make the blemishes go away. That's your job.

Buy the best paint, rollers, and brushes you can get. Cheap paint, made with more filler than pigment, turns powdery after a couple of years. Cheap rollers and brushes mar the surface by leaving fuzz and bristles behind.

Protect all surfaces you are not painting, including floors, trim, woodwork, and furnishings. (See Protecting Surfaces on page 21.)

Clean the surface. Wipe down the walls or trim with trisodium phosphate (TSP) or a phosphate-free wall-cleaner substitute. Then rinse the wall with a sponge and clean water until the water runs clear.

Let the surface dry. Then look for and repair every imperfection you find. The staff in the paint department can advise you on the best products to use for your particular problems, but count on using some of these:

Caulk. Fill exterior cracks with caulk. Inside, caulk between walls and molding, and run caulk down the corners if they are cracked. Smooth the bead of caulk with a wet finger for a smooth transition between surfaces.

Surfacing compound is designed for repairing walls; use compund specifically designed for your walls, typically drywall or plaster. Fill very small holes or gouges with lightweight spackling compound, which has more body and won't shrink.

Glazier's compound. Glazier's compound is a putty that holds glass windowpanes in place from the outside. It sticks instantly and dries quickly so you can paint it. It's also perfect for filling exterior nail holes.

Prime surfaces before you paint. Primer forms a molecular bond between the paint and whatever you are painting. Applying a primer sealer to a stained wall or ceiling keeps any underlying stains from eventually bleeding through. (Water-base sealers may not be adequate for all jobs—read the label to make sure you get the right product.)

Sand between coats. This step is quick—just wipe the wall with 120-grit paper, brushing off the dust with a towel or an old paintbrush. A sanded wall, when finished, feels velvet-smooth to the touch. An unsanded wall feels slightly bumpy.

Practice decorative techniques on a sheet of base-coated poster board until you achieve the look you want. Variations in technique and the amount of glaze produce widely different effects, even if you are using the same colors.

Field guide to paint

Paint departments offer an array of choices: alkyd, latex, primer, stain-blocker, and enamel, gloss, semigloss, satin, eggshell, and flat paint. When you're only trying to redo the bathroom, it can seem complicated and confusing. But it's actually quite simple. There are two main types of paint: latex and alkyd. Everything else is just a variation.

In the United States, latex accounts for about 87 percent of the paint that is sold. Latex paint, in the past, contained natural rubber. These days it contains any number of manufactured resins, with acrylic being the best.

Much of latex's popularity comes from its convenience. Because it's a water-base paint, you can wipe up any drips or spills with a wet sponge. You can also clean brushes and rollers with soap and water, followed by a thorough rinse.

If you're applying two coats of latex paint on consecutive days, you don't need to clean the brush between days (although many people do). Wrap the brush in a plastic bag, and it will be ready for work the next day. Some people like to store the wrapped brush in the freezer for good measure.

The fumes from latex aren't nearly as strong as those from alkyd paints, but it's still not a good idea to inhale potentially toxic chemicals. Allow plenty of ventilation, and wear a mask if you are spraying paint. Once dry and thoroughly cured, the latex paint is durable and can be washed.

You can also choose low- or no-VOC (Volitile Organic Compound) paints which have virtually no odor and are ideal for those who are sensitive to paint fumes.

Alkyd paint was once known as oil paint because it had a linseed-oil base. New formulations led to its new name, but alkyd is often still called oil paint. It isn't water based, and it isn't water soluble. If you spill it or make a mistake, you'll need to clean it up with a rag dipped in mineral spirits (paint thinner). You'll need to clean the brushes with mineral spirits too, and rinse them afterward with soap and water.

Some professional painters still prefer alkyds, especially as primers. Alkyd paint is very effective at sealing in stains, and it provides a vapor barrier too. It is self-leveling and forms a smooth coating, which is especially important on doors and trim. Painters also like the fact that when they sand alkyd between coats, it leaves a powdery dust that wipes off easily with a tack cloth. (Latex can gum up the sandpaper.) Using a fine-grit sandpaper or steel wool to sand between coats creates a surface free of tiny imperfections.

Some states have regulations against using alkyd paints because of environmental concerns. Your paint store can advise you.

CLOSER LOOK

WHAT DOES SHEEN MEAN?

Sheen is a measure of how much light a paint reflects. Flat paint absorbs the most light, and tends to hide surface imperfections. Eggshell paint has a somewhat smoother surface that still has some hiding ability, but is easier to wash. Satin is even more washable, making it a good choice for high-traffic areas. Semigloss has a bit of a shine to it, and is often used on woodwork, trim, cabinets, and doors. Gloss paint has a high shine, but even minor surface imperfections will show through the paint film.

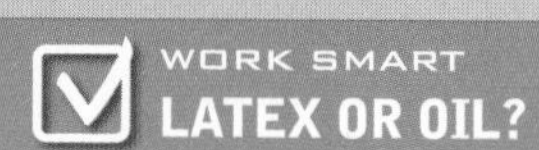

WORK SMART

LATEX OR OIL?

For most homeowners, the decision between using latex or oil (alkyd) comes down to drying time, odor, and ease of cleanup. See the chart on page 31 for other factors that may be equally important. Pay attention, too, to the fine print on the back of the can. Most manufacturers give specific recommendations about whether latex or oil will best cover your existing finish. There's usually a toll-free number if you need more help.

BUYER'S GUIDE

READ THE LABEL ON THE PAINT CAN

Generally speaking, the quality of paint can be judged by its price. Paint is one of those rare products for which you actually get what you pay for. Higher-quality paints are more expensive because they contain higher ratios of the more expensive ingredients. This results in better color, adhesion, and durability.

The Basics:

- A liquid carrier (water or mineral spirits) suspends the particles of paint so they can be applied. As the carrier evaporates, the paint dries.
- Pigments are the finely ground, naturally colored solids that, when mixed, produce the color. Expensive paints contain more complex mixtures of pigment. Higher percentages of TiO_2 (titanium dioxide) produce whiter and brighter paint.
- Additives are added chemicals that enhance the paint's mildew resistance, ability to stick, and ability to flow. Kaolin (clay) is added to control the gloss. Some additives are toxic. To avoid fumes or if you'll have trouble ventilating the room as the paint dries, purchase a brand that is labeled low in volatile organic chemicals (VOCs).
- Binders may be vinyl acrylic, 100 percent acrylic, or alkyd enhanced. The higher the percentage of acrylic resin, the harder and more durable the finish will be.
- The other ingredients listed are largely filler. If used in high amounts, filler dulls the colors, and the paint may later become powdery.

Primer basics

Whether you are working with alkyd or latex paint, always use a primer first. Keep in mind that primer is not just the first coat of paint applied. Primers are specifically formulated to adhere well to other surfaces; they form a strong bond between the paint and whatever is underneath the primer, including bare wood, bare wall, or paint. Without primer, paint tends to peel off. However, a stong connection is not the only function for primer. It can also help with the final color of the surface you are painting if you have it tinted. Have the primer tinted with about half as much color as in the top coat of paint. When the primer coat dries, apply a top coat of paint.

Latex primers work well in most situations. Faced with a difficult or chalky wall, however, professionals sometimes prefer an alkyd primer. You can usually apply latex over oil—profesionals do this frequently. Alkyd and latex have different drying properties; if more than five coats of alkyd paint are on an exterior wall, it may be safer to continue with alkyd primers and paint.

No matter how good the paint, some stains continue to bleed through a regular primer—so choose a stain-blocking primer in these situations. Water stains, for example, almost always reappear once paint has dried. If you're painting wood, resin from the knots bleeds through sooner or later. Smoke stains, oil stains, and any red chalk used in chalk lines are guaranteed to bleed through too—unless you have used a stain-blocking primer.

Stain-blocking primers come in alkyd and latex, in aerosol or liquid. Another alternative is shellac, which can be used alone to block stains and is also the base for other stain blockers. To seal in tough stains with a single coat, your best bet is to use only stain-blocking primers that are alkyd or shellac-base.

Selecting a sheen

Once you've chosen your color and decided between latex and oil, you still have five different sheens to choose from—flat, eggshell, satin, semigloss, and gloss. Each is a measure of how much light the paint reflects. A flat paint reflects perhaps 5 to 10 percent of the light that shines on it; a gloss reflects 50 percent of the light or more. This changes the appearance of both the surface and the color. A flat sheen looks duller and darker than the same color in a gloss, but glossy sheens show up more imperfections.

Flat paint absorbs light, thereby disguising many surface imperfections. Dents, dings, texture changes, and wavy walls all tend to disappear behind the matte finish of a flat paint. Because it hides blemishes so well, you can often get by with only a single coat. On the downside, flat paint tends to show dirt and usually doesn't stand up well to washing or scrubbing.

Eggshell hides many imperfections but is a bit smoother than flat paint, meaning it reflects more light. It's also easier to wash so you can go longer before repainting. Because of its washability, it has become a popular sheen for walls.

Satin. Think of washability when you think satin—this finish is ideal for kitchens, bathrooms, hallways, kids' rooms, woodwork, and trim. Silky satin paint looks good on walls in high-traffic rooms but is durable enough to stand up to dirt and repeated cleaning.

Semigloss. This finish offers both washability and shine. Semigloss reflects between 35 and 50 percent of the light that hits it, so most people find it too shiny to use on their walls. It is extremely durable, however. Semigloss is well-suited to surfaces that get a lot of handprints—woodwork, trim, cabinets, and doors. For the same reason, it's also popular for kitchens and baths.

Gloss. Choose glossy paint for utility rooms or playroom walls, or for trim that gets a lot of abuse. A high-gloss shine may be discomforting on walls, however. Against the mirror-smooth reflective finish, even minor surface imperfections can suddenly look like glaring errors.

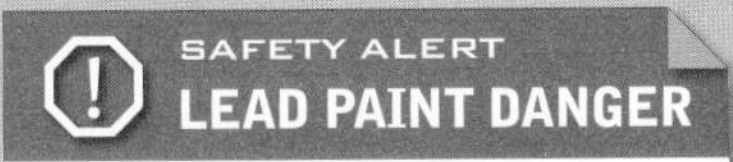

Paint made before 1978 may contain lead, which is very hazardous, especially to young children. If you remove or sand paint, first test it for lead with an inexpensive kit sold at home centers or paint stores. (The lead paint may be hidden beneath one or more top coats.) Ask local authorities or check with the EPA at www.epa.gov for advice on how to remove lead-base paint safely. Children who have lived or played in homes with lead paint should have a simple test (given by a doctor) for lead exposure.

The color wheel

The fun part of painting is choosing the color, even if doing so seems somewhat confusing at first.

White or off-white, of course, is always safe, but why be content with safe when you live in a world of color? Even the mention of the color wheel may make your eyes roll, but if you ever want to paint your walls and woodwork something other than another shade of white, it's worth a look. Selecting a color scheme is basically simple: you choose one color, and then choose other colors to use with it—based on their relative positions on the color wheel.

The *primary* colors—red, blue, and yellow—combine to form all other colors. Combine any two primary colors, and you'll get a *secondary* color—secondary colors always fall midway between two primary colors on the wheel. *Tertiary* colors are the combination of a secondary color and a primary color. You'll find them between the secondary and primary colors on the wheel. *Complementary* colors are directly opposite each other on the color wheel.

Remember a few guidelines, and you're on your way to making good choices:

- Color principles apply to pure colors and also to all of their darker shades or lighter tints.
- All colors look most vibrant when used with their complementary color.
- In a room, it's generally best to choose one main color and use accent colors in smaller amounts.
- A tried-and-true combination is to use one color, or even two colors, plus white.

▼ *The color wheel illustrates the relationship between primary, secondary, and tertiary colors. The colors in the band between the white rings are pure colors. Colors closer to the center of the wheel are tints. Those closer to the edge are shades.*

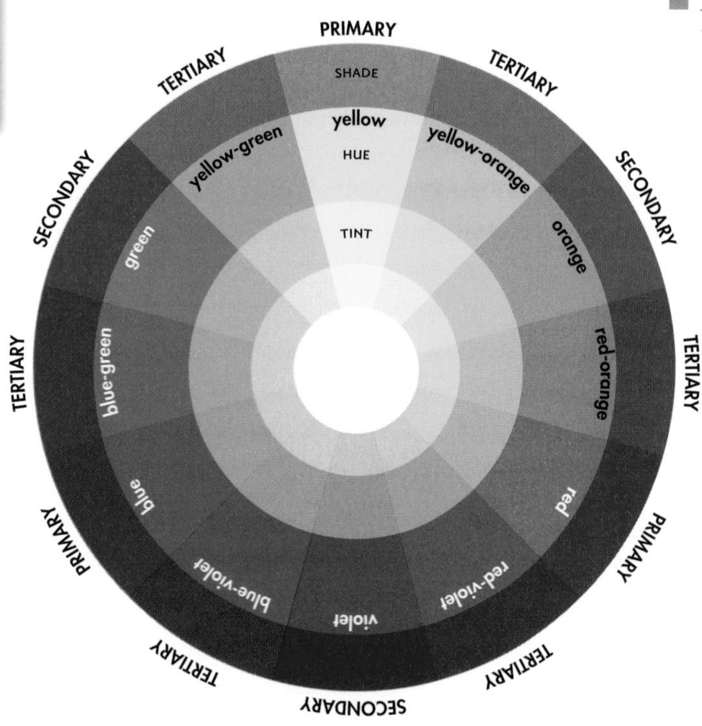

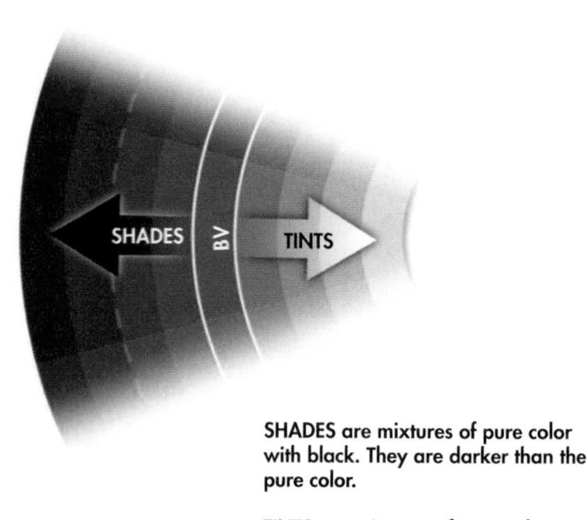

SHADES are mixtures of pure color with black. They are darker than the pure color.

TINTS are mixtures of pure color with white. They are lighter than the pure color.

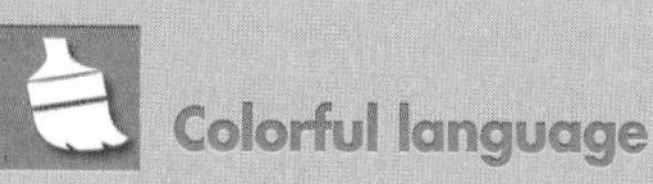

Colorful language

Color value: The lightness or darkness of a color.

Saturation: The purity of a color. Red is more saturated than pink.

Hue: Synonymous with color. Red, purple, blue, green, and yellow are all hues.

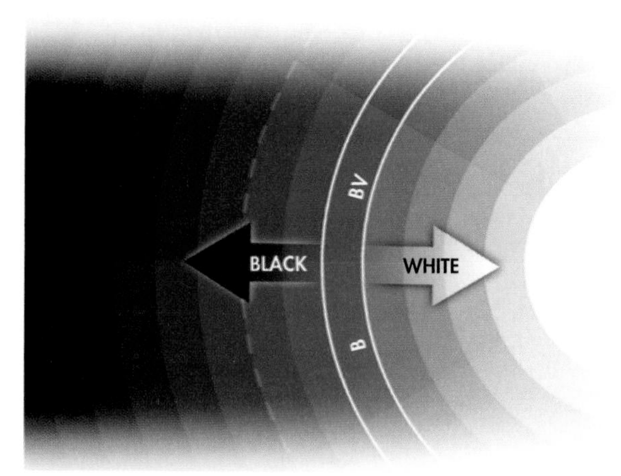

WHITE is equal parts of all colors.

BLACK is the absence of color or light.

Choosing a color scheme

All color schemes begin with a vision. You want a blue dining room. A red house. A yellow nursery. But after that, what?

Look at the blue dining room, for instance, and consider several approaches.

Monochromatic: Do the entire room in shades of blue. You might choose light-blue walls and deep-blue trim.

Analogous: Paint the walls that same light blue, but choose a trim color from one of blue's adjacent slices of the wheel.

Complementary: If blue-on-blue proves overpowering, add a touch of its complementary color, the one directly opposite on the color wheel. The complement of blue is orange; instead of painting the trim orange, you might add the color with a brass chandelier or terra-cotta upholstery on the furniture. Either way, the two colors work together to spark up the room.

Triadic: For more variety, choose triadic colors—those that are equidistant from each other on the wheel. Tints and shades of blue, red, and yellow are shown. Garish? Not if you choose an abstract painting or a neutral rug with small bits of these colors.

There are also other ways to simplify choosing a color scheme. Consider pulling colors from a favorite fabric or a rug. Or use a painting as inspiration for an entire room. Some perenially popular color combinations are classic: blue and white, blue and yellow, or red-white-and-blue, for instance.

Paint manufacturers have helped make your choices easier with brochures showing shades that go together. Some even offer sample-size containers or stick-on color patches so you can test a color on your walls. Photos in decorating magazines or books may give you ideas on up-to-date color combinations. When you see something you like, the paint department can scan the photo to match the colors shown.

Paint chips look different when they are in various lighting conditions. The same problem is true of photos in magazines and books. Often the text tells you what specific color the paint is, but it looks different when photographed. To ensure you get the color you want always buy a quart of each color you are considering, paint a small section of the wall, (or a piece of poster board that you tape up) and look at it under your own lights, both day and night. If the color you've selected doesn't work, try another shade.

Monochromatic colors
Shades and tints of a single color.

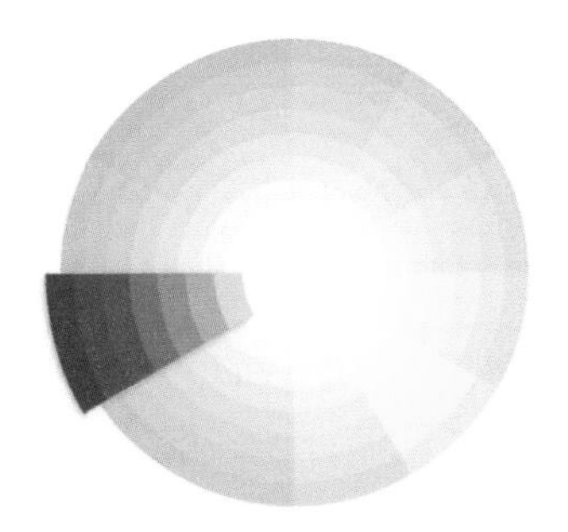

Analogous colors
Two colors adjacent to each other on the color wheel. One color dominates.

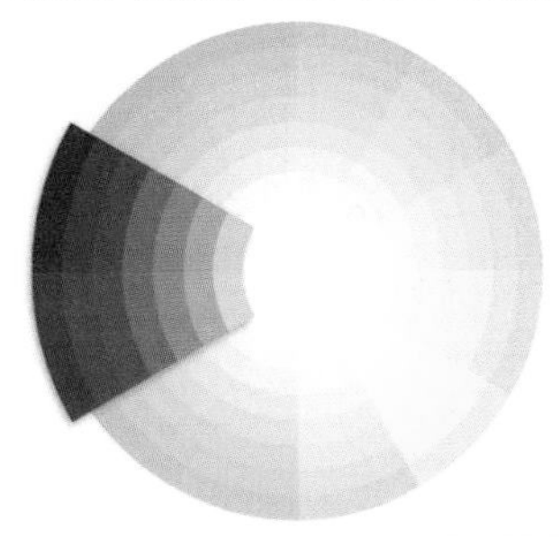

Complementary colors
Two colors opposite each other on the color wheel.

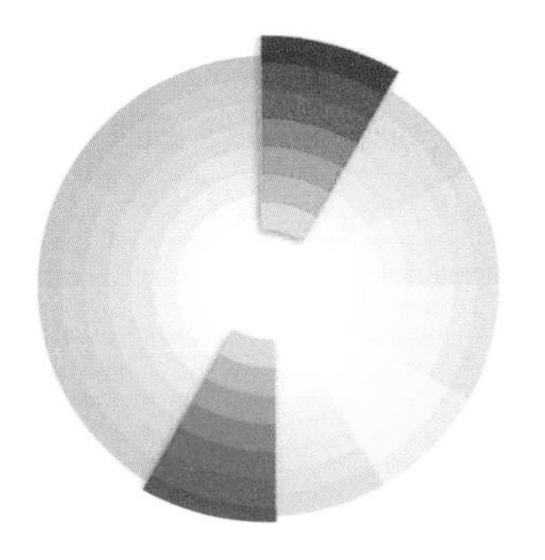

Triadic colors
Three colors equidistant from each other on the color wheel.

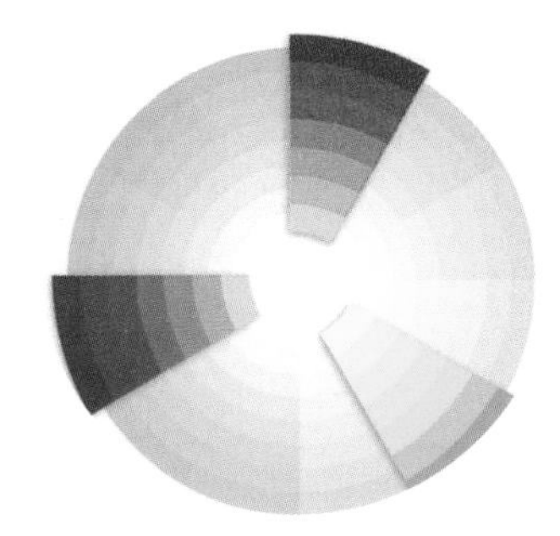

Analogous colors with complementary accents
Two adjacent colors combined with a third that is opposite either of the first two.

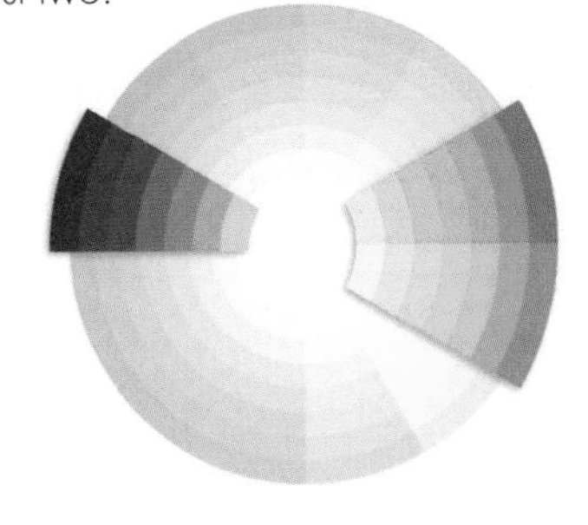

The painting tool kit

1-quart bucket

Brushes

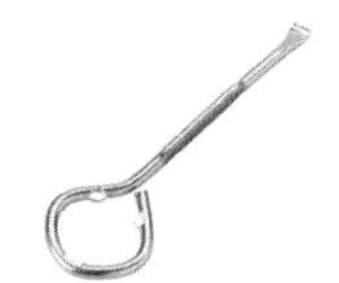
Paint can opener

Rags

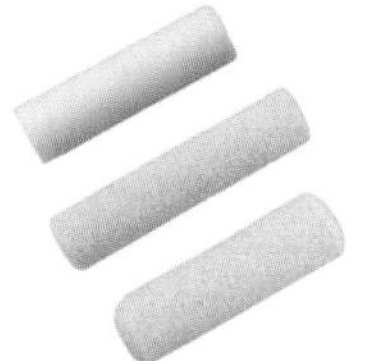
Rollers

Spray bottle

5-gallon bucket

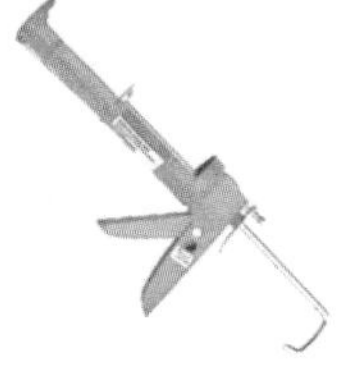
Caulking gun

Paint can pouring spout

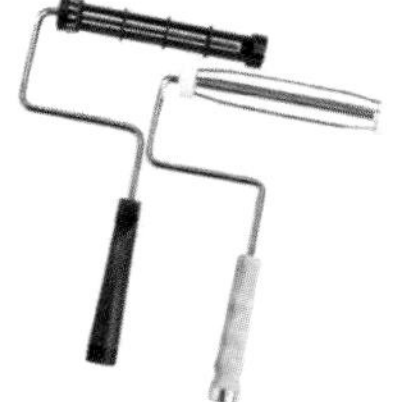
Roller cages

Round-cornered sponge

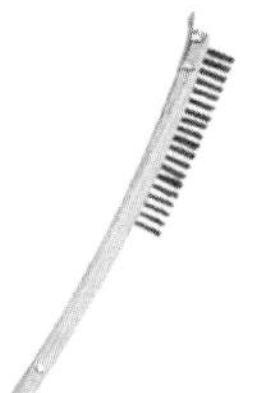
Stainless wire brush

5-in-1 tool

Drop cloths

Paint mixer

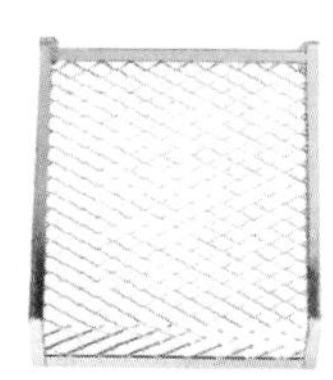
Roller grid for 5-gallon bucket

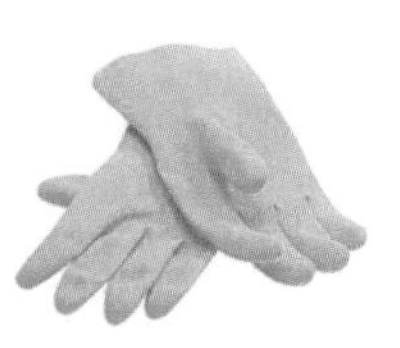
Rubber gloves

Stepladder

Brush and roller spinner

Extension pole

Painter's tape

Roller pan

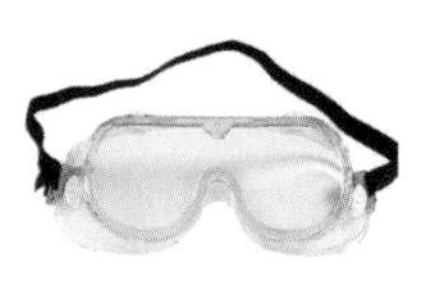
Safety goggles

Tape measure

Brush extender

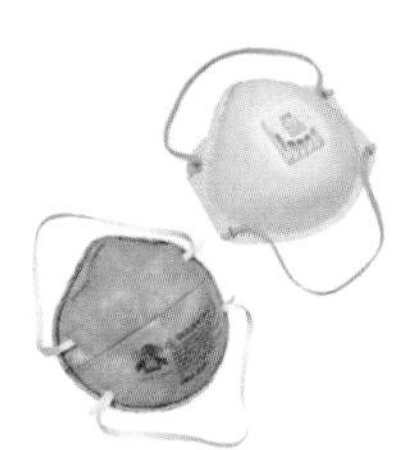
Masks

Putty knives

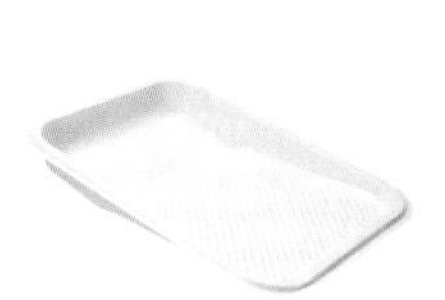
Roller pan liner

Sanding block

Utility knife

Brushes and rollers

You may wonder whether you'll need a roller or brush, but for most jobs you'll need both. The brush will handle narrow spaces or *cut in* (paint a sharp-edged line where the wall meets the molding, for instance). Use a brush for detailed work and also for the trim.

The roller can apply paint at least three times faster than even the widest brush, so you'll need it for speed. The beveled ends of the roller cover cannot lay down a sharp line of paint, but this prevents roller and overlap marks as well. Use a roller for large, flat areas, such as ceilings, walls, and floors. Special painting pads and other tools are available for corners, edges, and various faux finishes. These may be helpful, yet you'll still need the basic brush and roller.

Quality is the key to painting success: Don't economize on your brushes, rollers, or other painting tools. You may save money in the short term, but you'll leave a trail of loose bristles and roller fuzz on anything you paint.

▲ *A good quality brush, properly cared for, will last for years.*

There are two types of bristle brushes:

- Natural (usually hog bristles) for solvent-base finishes.
- Synthetic (nylon or polyester) for water-base finishes. (Some can also be used with alkyd-base finishes.)

Using the correct type of bristle brush is extremely important because natural bristles can swell in water-base paint, resulting in poor application. With proper care and cleaning, a paint brush will last for many years (see page 68).

In some situations, a disposable brush is best:

Disposable bristle brushes with unfinished-wood handles are the least expensive choice. They are fine for applying materials that are difficult to clean up, such as contact cement and fiberglass resin. Use them once and throw them away. Foam brushes are another low-cost alternative and should be considered disposable. They work well when applying smooth finishes to small areas.

Paint rollers

The basic paint roller is a handle with a wire cage and threaded base; a roller cover with a nap fits over the cage. You can buy an extender for the handle to reach higher.

Invest in the best roller you can afford because it lasts for years. Look for:

- A heavy frame with minimum flex under pressure

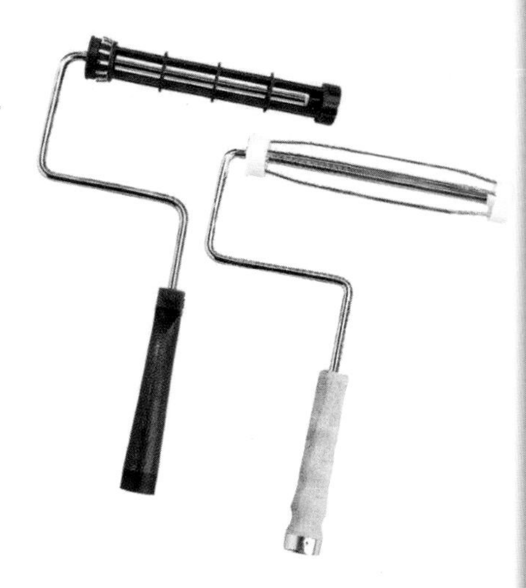

▲ *Quality roller cages with molded or wooden handles, used with high-quality roller covers, make every painting job easier.*

- Nylon bearings that spin easily
- A comfortable grip
- A cage with at least five wires and an antislip device to keep the roller in place

Roller covers

Buy a quality roller cover with the correct nap thickness. Most jobs require a roller with either a ⅜- or ½-inch nap. Bargain roller covers with paper cores (tubes) break down quickly and cannot be reused. Resin cores last longer; they can be cleaned and also reused. Look for:

- A durable resin core
- Beveled ends to avoid leaving beads of paint along the edges
- Seams that you cannot feel through the nap
- Heavy, uniform nap that sheds little lint

Why quality brushes cost more

QUALITY	VS.	DISPOSABLE
Flagged (split) bristle ends for a smoother finish	Bristles	Unflagged bristle ends
Multiple wood spacer plugs to create paint reservoirs between bristle rows	Dividers	Single wood spacer plug
Reinforced, rustproof ferrule to hold bristles securely	Ferrule	Weak ferrule that allows bristles to fall out more easily
Tapered end for better control	Handle	Blunt point

Power rollers

Regular rollers apply paint more quickly than brushes do. Every once in a while, you have to stop and reload the roller by dipping it into the bucket or paint tray, which takes up time. Now there are several systems designed to eliminate this step.

The disadvantage of power rollers is the slightly higher initial expense for the equipment and the need to carefully clean the equipment after use so that it is properly maintained. However, if you are facing a big job, those disadvantages are outweighed by the time you can save.

Special rollers have either a hollow handle that stores paint inside or a flexible plastic tube that leads from paint can to roller. The paint flows into the roller cover through small holes in the cylinder, enabling you to paint continuously as long as there's paint in the can.

These are somewhat more expensive than standard rollers, but they last longer save time. From the outside, the specialized roller covers look the same as regular covers. They are more expensive but they can be washed and reused. Don't try to use regular roller covers with a power roller—they won't work.

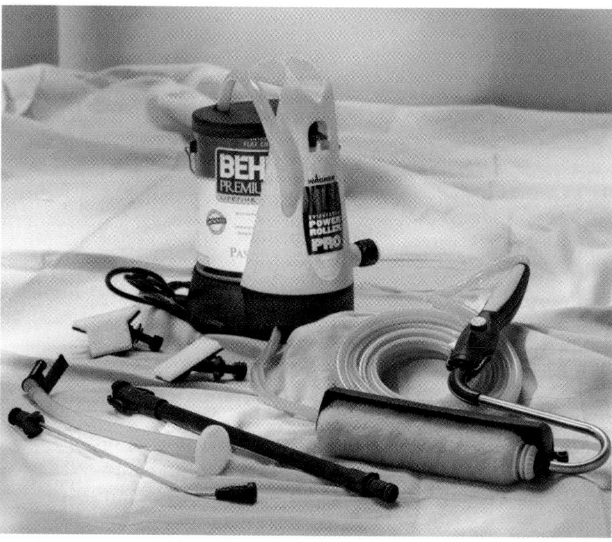

▲ *There are several different systems for continuous paint rolling. This one has a flexible tube that connects to the paint can; a pump pulls paint from the bottom of the can into the tube until the can is empty.*

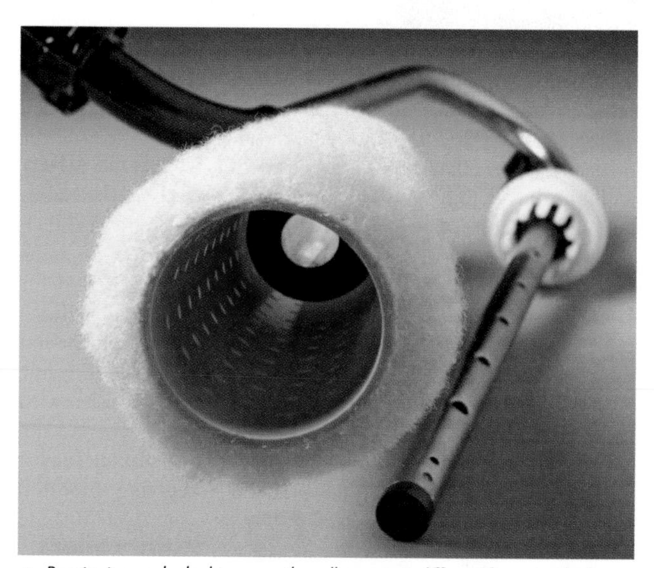

▲ *Despite its regular-looking nap, the roller cover is different from standard types. There are hundreds of small holes inside that let paint from the roller mechanism flow through to the nap for continuous painting.*

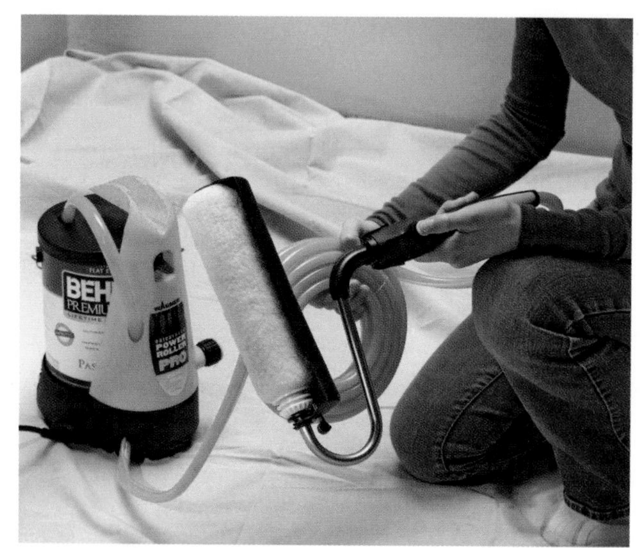

Connect the equipment. Place the paint can on the pump, and cover it with the special lid. A tube goes from the bottom of the can to the roller. The pump pulls paint through the tube and into the roller, where it enters the nap through holes on the underside. This continuous flow lets you paint without stopping to reload the roller.

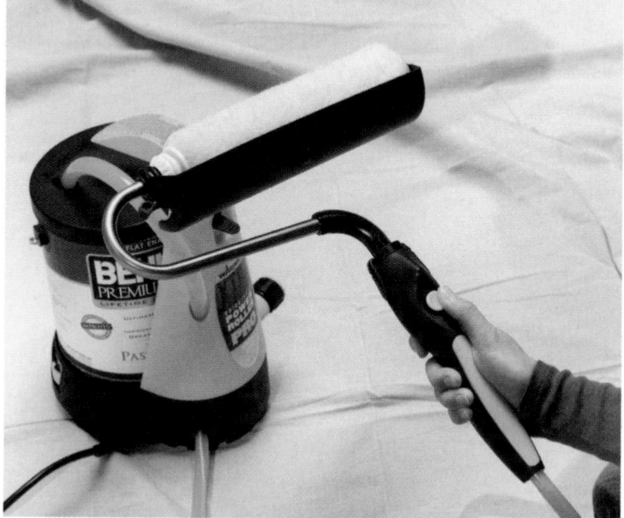

Start and stop the flow. You don't have to paint the whole room without stopping; the flow is controlled by a button on the handle. Whenever you press the button, more paint is released; when you're not pressing the button, you're simply painting with what is already in the roller. Note the spatter-guard that you can position to avoid spattering paint.

Spraying paint

At times you might have a really big painting job to do (an entire house) or a job in which surface details require getting paint into every nook and cranny (painting a fancy picket fence). This is the time to go airborne with your paint.

Spraying paint works better than either rolling or brushing in such cases. Sure, there are prefilled spray cans good for small jobs, but those come in a fairly limited array of colors, and each can holds only a little paint. You're talking equipment here—high-quality equipment that forces paint through tiny holes under pressure, transforming the liquid to a mist. By moving the nozzle at the desired speed and adjusting the spray pattern, you can aim paint toward the surface, covering it in a smooth layer. For best results, the paint may need to be thinned a little; follow the equipment guidelines to avoid clogging the nozzle.

Transfer the paint to the container. You may need to thin it first (latex paint with water, oil-base paint with paint thinner) so read the instructions that come with the paint sprayer. A nozzle on the sprayer can be adjusted to create different spray patterns; adjust it to suit the job by observing the pattern of the paint mist that comes out.

Prepare before you start painting. Spray painting goes fast once you start, so you should have prepped by taping off trim beforehand. It's very important to wear the right kind of respirator—here, a cartridge respirator—to avoid breathing in fine particles of paint that can damage your lungs. Wear long-sleeved clothing to keep paint off your skin.

Renting equipment

Buying tools is the way to go if you do a lot of projects or want to have a well-stocked workshop. But what if you're doing only one job, and it requires an expensive tool? Or your six-foot ladder looks laughable as you contemplate painting an 18-foot-high entry? Or you know you'd get better results with a high-end sprayer, but your present budget can't stretch? Don't worry.

Equipment rental stores exist for people like you. They stock the very best heavy-duty equipment even though it probably won't be shiny and pretty. They charge for using it by the day, the half-day, or even by the hour—so you'd better be ready for it by the time you go get it. Have your supplies and do all of your prep work beforehand to take maximum advantage of those precious minutes. Expect to haul the equipment yourself or pay an extra charge for delivery. The rental-store staff will show you how to use it; just bring it back clean and in good condition.

BUYER'S GUIDE

SPRAY PAINT CHOICES

Premixed spray paints offer not just basics, but also designer colors and special coatings. You'll find primers, clear finishes, metallics, and basic colors in flat, semigloss and gloss. You'll also find a wealth of designer colors, plus specialized coatings for painting plastic toys or outdoor furniture; heat-resistant paints for barbecue grills; paints that replicate the look of hammered metal; textured paints to simulate stone—even blackboard and magnetic paints.

TOOL TIP

CLEAN, NOT CLOGGED

Nozzles on spray equipment—or even spray cans—are finicky. The paint needs to be thin enough to push through the holes, yet thick enough to cover what you're painting. If it dries or gums up the nozzle, the paint won't spray as well, if at all. Whatever you do, don't poke a pin in the hole in an attempt to unclog it. Follow the instructions and take the time to clean the equipment when you're done. For spray paint, turn the can upside down and spray briefly. For power paint-spray equipment, this usually means running water or paint thinner through the spray-gun nozzle to clean out lingering traces of paint.

Protection

Protecting yourself

You are vulnerable to particles and fumes when you are sanding, painting, or working with solvents. Some ingredients in paints and varnishes are toxic, so it pays to take precautions, especially if you work with them repeatedly.

To protect your skin:

- Wear cotton gloves when using sharp or abrasive tools.
- Wear latex gloves when working with paint.
- Wear neoprene gloves when handling solvents, strippers, or other harsh chemicals.

Neoprene gloves

To protect your eyes:

- Wear safety glasses when working with tools.
- Wear goggles to protect against dust and aerosol droplets when sanding, spraying, or painting over your head.

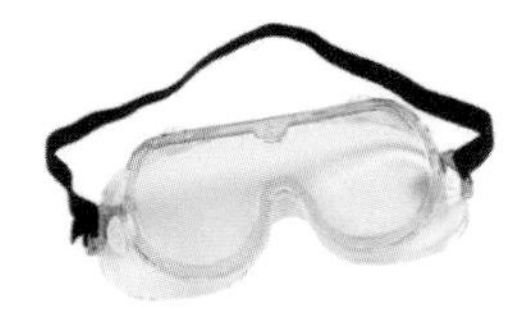

Safety goggles

To protect your lungs:

- Sand, paint, and strip outside if possible, or cross-ventilate with at least two open windows or doors.
- If there is a danger of breathing dust, aerosols, or solvent fumes, filter the air with a respirator. Use only the type recommended on the product label.

Respirators—There are two types:

Dust masks, also called particulate respirators, filter out dry particles and most non-oil-base liquid droplets. Use a dust mask when sanding bare or painted wood (except lead-base paint), drywall, and rusted surfaces. Special-purpose particulate respirators are available for spraying latex paint and sanding (but not burning off) lead-base paint.

Cartridge respirators contain both particulate filters and chemically active canisters for absorbing solvent vapors. Use a cartridge respirator when spraying solvent-base paints and working with solvents and strippers. See Choose the Right Respirator at lower left.

Fitting respirators:

A respirator must form an airtight seal around your nose and mouth. They don't work well with beards. If you have a beard and you're going to be working with hazardous chemicals, consider shaving beforehand to be safe.

To fit a dust mask:

- Position the mask under your chin.
- Pull the top and bottom straps over your head and position them just above and below your ears.
- Mold the soft metal tab to fit your nose.
- Test the fit by covering the mask with both hands and drawing a sharp breath; it should be difficult to breathe.

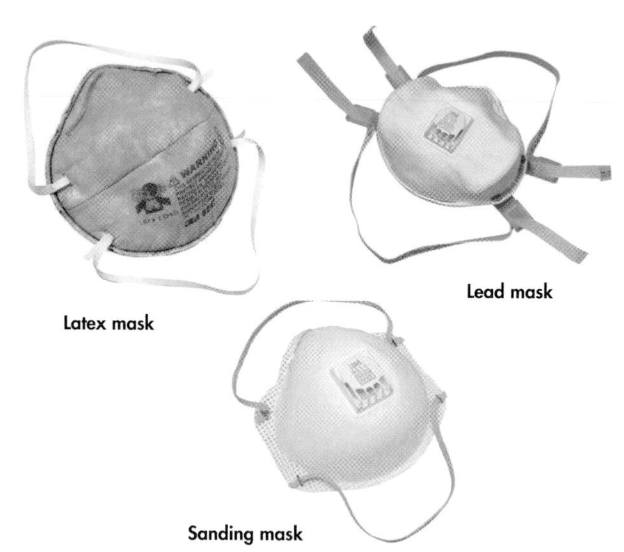

Latex mask

Lead mask

Sanding mask

To fit a cartridge respirator:

- Place the respirator loosely over your face, low on the bridge of your nose.
- Fasten the straps for a snug but comfortable fit.
- Test the fit by covering the air inlets and breathing out gently. The mask should bulge slightly, and you should neither hear nor feel any leakage. If you smell fumes or begin to feel dizzy, then the respirator doesn't fit, the canisters are the wrong type, or they are used up.

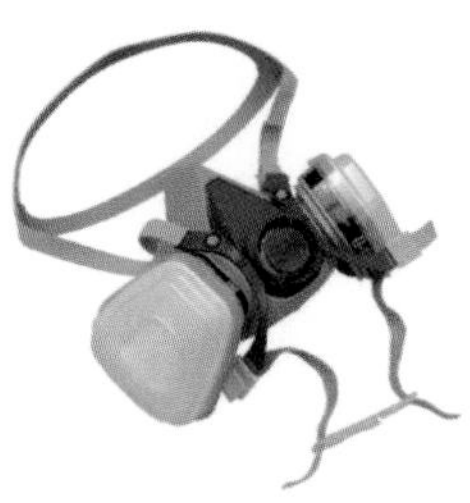

Cartridge respirator

Always read the warnings on paint, solvent, and stripper containers, and compare them to the listed capabilities of the respirator canister before you trust your life to it.

SAFETY ALERT

CHOOSE THE RIGHT RESPIRATOR

Protect yourself from toxic fumes by wearing the mask that the manufacturer recommends for the job. Unless specifically stated otherwise, no homeowner-type respirator offers absolute protection against lead fumes, asbestos fibers, or sandblasting. A regular dust mask may make you feel protected, but it does nothing to block fumes or very fine particles. Asbestos and lead are potentially deadly, causing lung and brain damage or even death. Even an organic respirator may not be sufficient. When dealing with either asbestos or lead, get advice from the Environmental Protection Agency or consider hiring a professional removal company. Children who have lived or played in homes with lead paint should be tested periodically by a doctor for lead exposure.

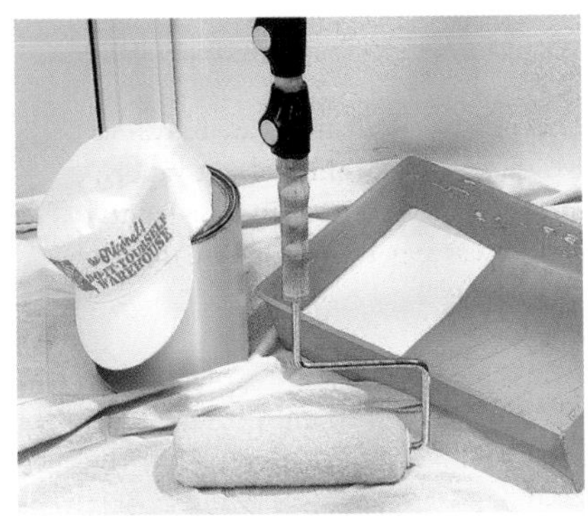

A painter's cap keeps the spatters out of your hair or off your glasses when you're painting overhead.

A coverall (or long pants and a long-sleeve shirt) offers neck-to-toe coverage and "breathes" to keep you cool.

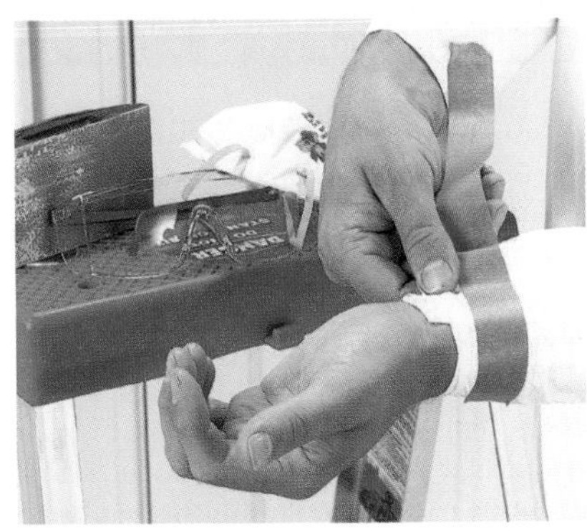

Cinch your sleeves and cuffs with masking tape when sanding or spray-painting.

Protecting surfaces

Paint always seems to spatter, no matter how careful you are. You'll save time in the long run by covering up vulnerable surfaces before you start. Remove the furniture, if possible, or move it to the center of the room. Next, spatter-proof the room: To protect large surfaces like floors and any remaining furnishings, invest in some drop cloths. To protect door and window trim, use painter's tape, a low-residue masking tape that won't damage finished surfaces when removed. Apply it to the edges, pressing firmly. Use paper masking and painter's tape along the baseboards, and cover lighting fixtures with plastic.

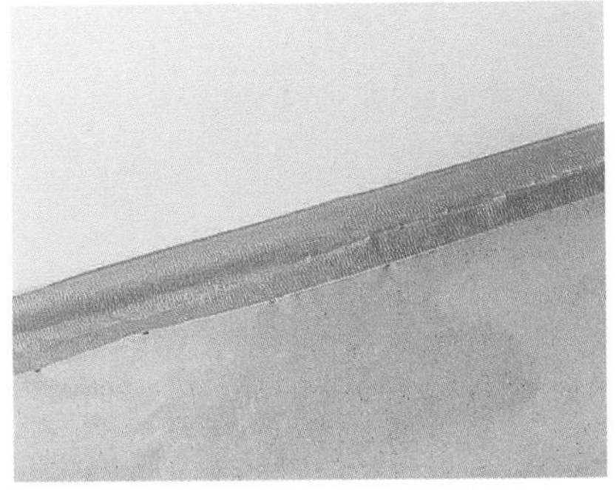

Painter's tape can remain for up to a week while prepping but must be removed immediately after painting and before the paint dries.

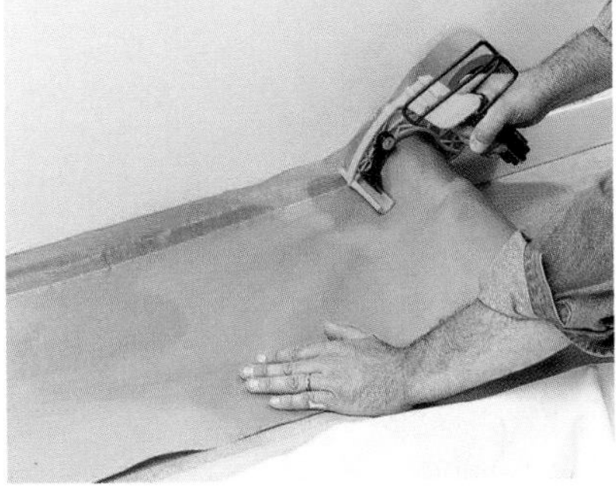

Paper masking comes in various widths. Unless it's self-adhesive, tape it to protect the baseboard. Slip the drop cloth beneath it to protect the floor.

Protect light fixtures by turning the lights off and draping or enclosing them in plastic. Loosen the ceiling canopy, if possible, to paint beneath it; reattach when paint dries.

$ BUYER'S GUIDE

THREE TYPES OF DROP CLOTHS

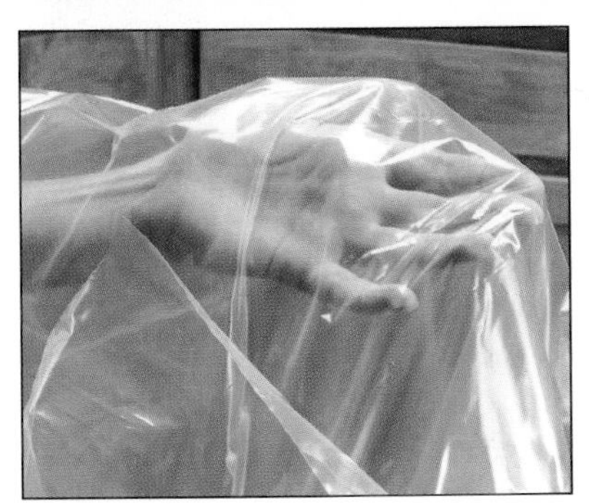

Poly sheeting, the least expensive, is waterproof. It's slippery underfoot but works well to cover furniture.

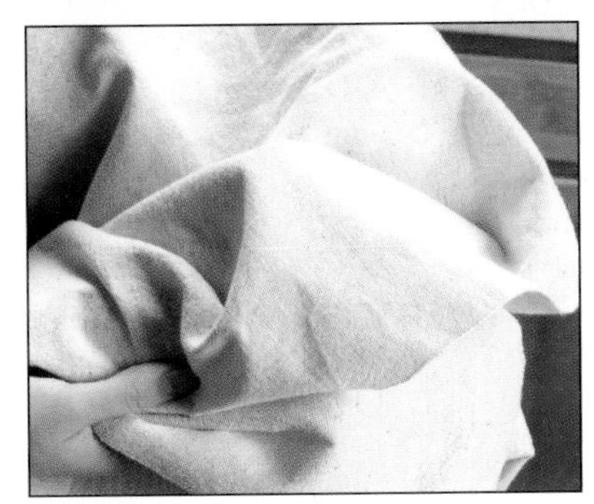

Canvas will last longest but is not waterproof; water-base (latex) paint will soak through it.

Paper/poly has paper lined with a waterproof poly backing. It costs less than canvas and is less slippery than pure poly.

Priming is essential

Priming is as important as painting for a professional-looking finish. This step can make the difference between a smooth, stain-free finish and one that looks blotchy or streaked—it's not just a way to sell you one more paint product. A specially formulated primer does several things:

- Increases adhesion.
- Prevents marks on an old surface from bleeding through the new coat of paint. These include stains from water, dirt, smoke, etc.; tannins from aromatic woods; or resins from knots and pitch pockets.
- Gives the finish coat a uniform appearance.
- Increases the finish coat coverage.
- Allows the finish coat to develop maximum sheen.
- Makes metal more corrosion-resistant.

Walls should be clean and smooth before you roll on a coat of high-adhesion primer. Make sure that old wallpaper is firmly attached to the wall. Repair any rips, gouges, nicks, indentations, bulges, and tears.

Prime new wood, old bare wood, and pressure-treated lumber with a stain-killing primer to block resins and tannins in the wood; otherwise, they will bleed through the paint. Let the primer dry thoroughly according to the manufacturer's instructions before applying the finish color.

Prime new drywall to conceal the difference between taped and untaped areas and screw patches. This step is critical, especially if you plan to install wallpaper; failure to prime beforehand will result in ripped drywall if wallpaper is later removed.

$ BUYER'S GUIDE

ENVIRONMENTALLY FRIENDLY PRODUCTS

Did you know that indoor air is about three times more polluted than outdoor air? Paints and primers with fumes cause a lot of the problem. The disposal of unused alkyd-base coatings has also become an important environmental issue, and some areas have outlawed them altogether. As a result, many products are changing as their levels of volatile organic compounds (VOCs) come down.

Oil-base primers and primer sealers are being replaced by urethane modified acrylics (UMAs) and water-base oil paints. Natural, Zero VOC, and Low VOC paints—safer for you and the environment—are replacing older latex paints. They may be slightly more expensive, but prices are likely to come down. If you can't find traditional oils, are sensitive to paint and primer fumes, have other health concerns, or want to lessen your environmental footprint, try newer paints and primers. At the very least, try to buy products with the highest percentages of solids (less room for volatile ingredients), the lowest percentages of *ethylene glycol* (a solvent in latex paints), and, if using paint strippers, little or no *methylene chloride* (MC), a caustic ingredient.

PAINTING & WALLPAPERING

Types of primer

Just as primer is different from finish paint, there are different primers for different problems and applications. Apply all primers with adequate ventilation in the room.

Polyvinyl acetate (PVA) latex primer seals new drywall for painting. If the joint compound and paper face on drywall are not primed, they absorb too much water from finish latex paint. PVA is not intended for trim or previously painted surfaces. Cleanup is with water.

High-adhesion primer (also called all-purpose primer) is a general term for any primer designed for maximum adhesion to nonporous surfaces, such as metal, glass, tile, and thermoplastics such as laminated plastic and melamine. It is slightly more difficult to work with than a conventional latex primer, but the results are well worth the effort. Cleanup is with soap and water.

Latex stain-blocking primer stops many stains from coming through the paint. For difficult stains, such as washable markers, use oil-base or alcohol-base primer instead.

Oil-base, stain-blocking primer effectively blocks crayon, permanent-marker inks, grease, and water stains. This is often the best primer to keep an unremovable stain from bleeding through paint. Clean-up is with paint thinner.

Alcohol-base, white-pigmented shellac is an excellent choice for hard-to-block stains. It has excellent adhesion, effectively blocks smoke and nicotine stains, water stains, and all of the tannins and resins in wood; it also inhibits pet odors. It is not weatherproof and can be damaged by UV rays, however, so it is recommended only for interior use. The exception is for spot-priming knots on pine trim and clapboards before painting them. Cleanup is with denatured alcohol.

Enamel undercoat contains a high percentage of solids and can be used under satin, semigloss, or gloss paints to enhance their gloss finishes. When it dries hard, you can sand it to produce the smoothest possible base for your finish coat. Cleanup is with soap and water.

Stains may still be visible, even after being coated with some primers because the primers absorb, rather than block, the stain. Use a stain blocker before you prime; allow it to dry thoroughly. This will help ensure that stubborn stains don't bleed through, ruining an otherwise perfect finish.

Tinting the primer helps ensure good coverage, especially when you make a dramatic color change. Ask a salesperson for advice. Remember that there are limitations on the amount of tint a primer can hold and still be effective. Follow the manufacturer's recommendations.

OOPS

PRIME MISTAKE

After applying four coats of expensive designer color, a homeowner wondered why it wasn't covering the stains on his wall. He insisted that he had primed first, and was proud that he had saved money by using leftover latex paint to do it. That was his problem: Regular latex paint isn't primer. Primer provides bonding and stain blocking; paint provides durability and color. You need the benefits of both to do a good job.

WORK SMART

PRIME INFO ON DARK COLORS

It seems logical that darker colors of paint hide underlying colors better, but it's not necessarily true. When changing to a dark, rich color, you'll need to use a tinted primer and at least two coats of paint to get good coverage. Otherwise, even a dark color looks streaky.

Preparing to paint

Skill level:	Time to complete:	Materials:	Tools:
★★★☆☆	Experienced Variable Handy Variable Novice Variable	12-inch baseboard-masking paper, TSP solution, bleach, water, lightweight crack filler, painter's masking tape, 220-grit sandpaper, latex- or oil-base stain-blocking primer	Bucket, rubber gloves, drop cloth, 4-foot stepladder, sponge, Phillips screwdriver, 3-inch putty knife, sanding block, 2-inch nylon brush, 9-inch roller with ⅜-inch nap, roller tray, brass-wire brush, tack cloth, mineral spirits

1 Move furniture away from walls and protect floor and baseboards with 12-inch masking paper and a paper/poly drop cloth.

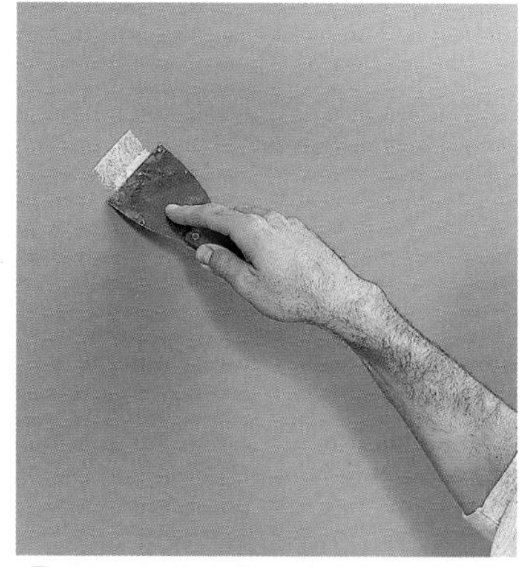

2 Set popped nails or screws (see page 98), repair cracks and holes (see pages 96 to 98), and fill dents with lightweight crack filler.

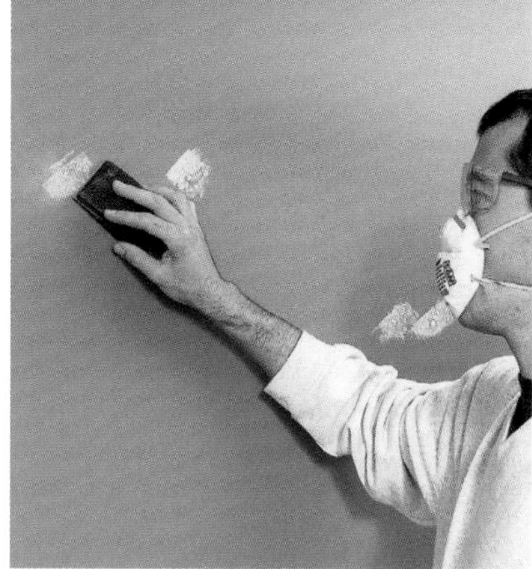

3 Let the crack filler dry according to the manufacturer's instructions; then sand the area using a sanding block with 220-grit sandpaper.

4 Treat any areas of mildew with a 3-to-1 water/bleach solution (see page 26), protecting your hands with rubber gloves. Rinse with water.

5 Rinse the entire wall surface with clean, fresh water and let it dry overnight before priming and painting. (If walls are dirty, first clean the entire wall with a TSP solution.)

6 Spot prime all of the repaired areas and stains with a latex, stain-blocking primer. If stains are still bleeding through, use an oil-base primer.

CLOSER LOOK

TSP=SQUEAKY-CLEAN WALLS

Trisodium phosphate (TSP) is a powerful cleaning product that many painters prefer because it cuts through grease and dirt easily. The phosphate also causes algae bloom in water bodies, however, so its use is restricted in some areas. Substitutes for TSP are available—ask your paint department. If you do use TSP or a similar product, rinse all residue from the walls with plenty of fresh water before it dries, because the residue will prevent the paint from bonding. Read the instructions.

7 Prime the entire wall with the same primer for uniformity, particularly if changing colors. The primer can be tinted to enhance the final coat.

Cleaning and deglossing

Glossy paints dry to a hard, nonporous surface, making it almost impossible for new paint to adhere effectively. The glossy surface lacks what painters call "tooth," a slight roughness that gives paint something to cling to. It doesn't take much effort to create tooth—just sand the surface lightly with either a fine-grit sandpaper or steel wool. Or you can use a chemical deglosser if you have a lot of area to cover or would prefer not to sand. When the entire surface looks dull and ceases to be reflective, it's ready to paint. To detect glossy areas, shine a flashlight across the surface and see if the light reflects.

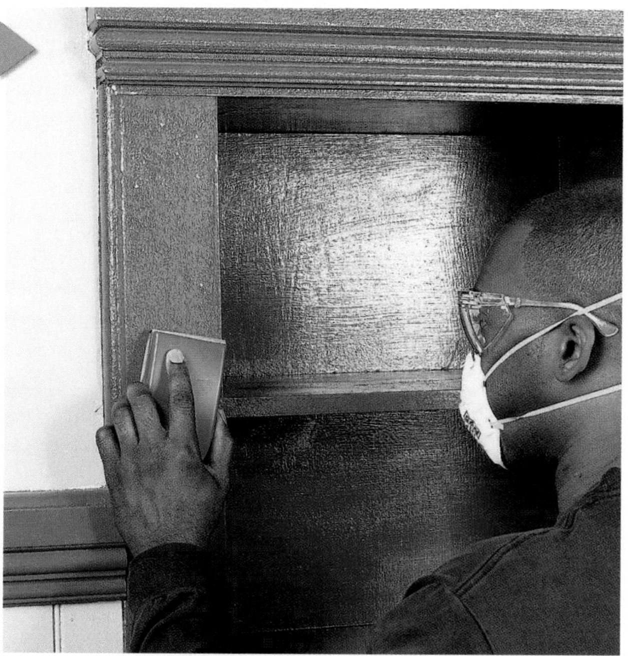

1 Fill gaps in trim and baseboard with paintable caulk. After drying, sand all glossy areas lightly with 220-grit sandpaper. Use a sanding block for even sanding on flat surfaces, a brass-wire brush for fluted surfaces.

2 Remove the sanding or brushing residue by wiping it with a damp rag or a tack cloth. You can also wipe down oil-base paint dust with a rag soaked in mineral spirits, which evaporates almost instantly.

High-volume deglossing

While roaming through the paint department, you may see something called liquid deglosser. It can save you some work by eliminating hand sanding, but it *won't* remove surface imperfections, which improve by sanding. What it *will* do is create a surface that the paint can cling to, as long as you apply the paint within the specified time (don't work too far ahead). It's also caustic, and the strong fumes are dangerous. If you use it, ventilate the area well, wear neoprene rubber gloves, goggles, and the respirator recommended by the deglosser manufacturer.

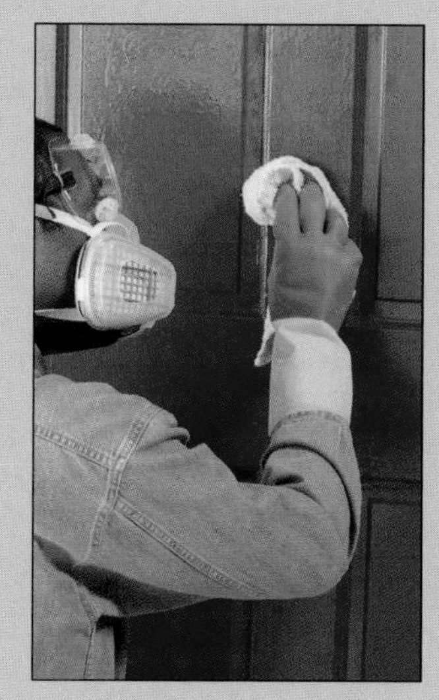

WORK SMART

PREP TIPS

Pros have developed tricks that make their jobs easier, and you can do the same things yourself:

- **Mark any areas that need special attention** by drawing around them or making an "X" with the edge of a quarter. The mark will remind you to fix those areas, and the faint marks cover up easily with primer.
- **Fine dust is a major annoyance** when sanding plaster, drywall, and joint compound. To minimize it, use a drywall wet-sander. This is a sponge with coarse abrasive on one side (to level ridges and high spots) and fine abrasive on the other side (to smooth).
- **Try sanding the walls with drywall screen** instead of using sandpaper. The durable open screen is coated with abrasive silicon carbide particles but resists clogging. Dust rinses out of the screen, which can then be used again.
- **If you're sanding a large area, close off the room** by taping plastic over the doors. Turn off the air-conditioning so dust won't be drawn into the return vent and travel to other rooms. Clean up dust promptly, using a shop-type vacuum fitted with a special filter for trapping fine particles.

Treating stains, mold, and mildew

Floods or even a leaking roof do a lot of damage on their own, but the worst part can be the aftermath, when walls or ceilings sprout a horrible coat of mold or mildew caused by dampness. Even if mold doesn't appear, the moisture wicks through plaster or drywall and leaves a stain.

First, fix the problem at its source to keep it from recurring. Then destroy any mold by treating it with household bleach. Severe damage may require complete replacement of plaster or drywall, but smaller damaged areas can be patched.

Painting isn't enough to cover a stain; sooner or later it rears its ugly head again. The only cure for a stain is to first apply a stain-blocking primer (see pages 22–23), and then put on that new coat of paint.

Water leaches chemicals from wood, drywall, and plaster. When it seeps through a wall or ceiling, unsightly stains are often left behind.

Mildew is a spore that grows in damp areas. Given enough moisture, mildew flourishes, particularly in closets or after water damage.

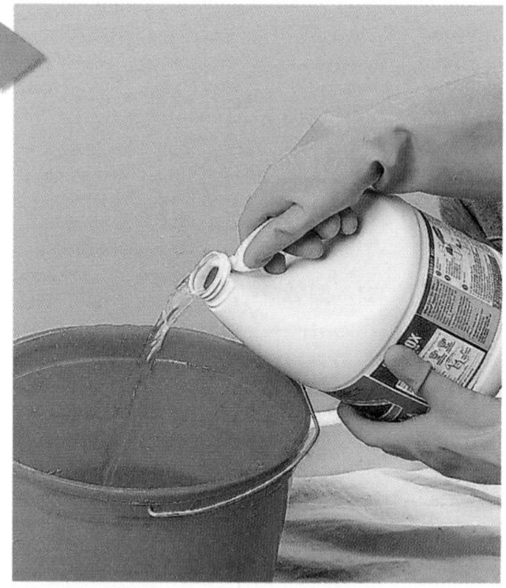

1 Use a mold remover product, or mix three parts water to one part laundry bleach in a bucket. Wear hand and eye protection.

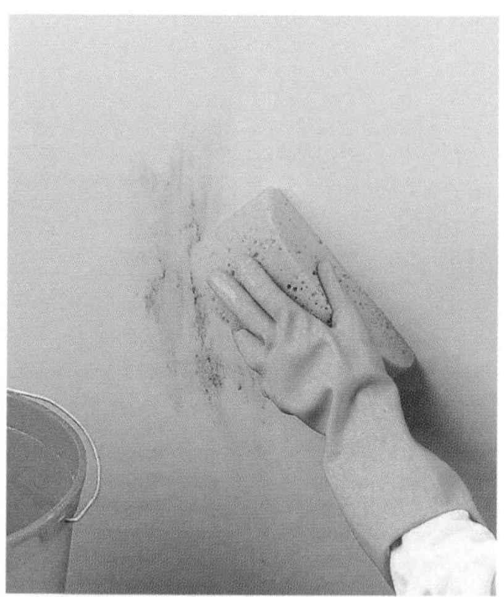

2 Apply the mixture liberally with a sponge. Apply again after 20 minutes even if the mold has disappeared, to be sure it is destroyed.

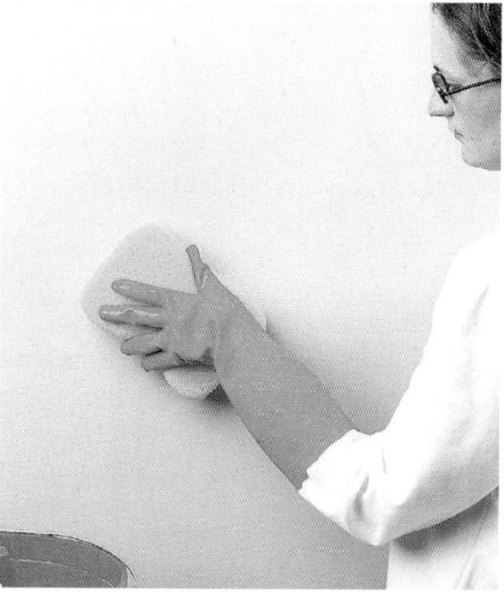

3 Rinse off the solution and dead mildew with clean, fresh water. Let it dry before cleaning with TSP or a TSP substitute (see page 24). Then apply a stain-blocking primer and, finally, paint.

SAFETY ALERT

BEWARE WHAT YOU BREATHE

Never mix bleach with ammonia or other household cleaners. Commonly used cleaners often contain ammonia, which reacts with bleach to produce toxic fumes. Inhaling these fumes can cause dizziness, nausea, cramps, or severe illness requiring hospitalization. If you breathe the fumes, go outside and breathe fresh air until your symptoms disappear.

Long-standing allergies, asthma, and illness can sometimes be traced to mold. Once established in a house, mold can be extremely difficult to eradicate. The job may require professional expertise. Mold-testing kits are available; look for help in the telephone directory or online.

WORK SMART

FIND THE REAL PROBLEM

Mildew or water stains are a sign of a larger problem. Find the source of the moisture and fix it before you try to make things look better.

Roof leaks are notoriously hard to locate because the water runs along rafters before dripping, causing damage far from the actual leak; you might need to consult a roofer.

In a seldom-used damp-smelling closet, leaving a light on is sometimes enough to solve the problem. Or keep an open container of desiccant on a shelf to absorb moisture.

You may need a dehumidifier to remove dampness from musty basements and below-grade areas of the house.

Painting over wallpaper

There are two schools of thought: One says you'll create a mess if you try to paint over wallpaper; the other says, "sure, you can paint it." It all depends on what you're starting with, and what you do.

Removing the paper might be your best course, but only if it comes off fairly easily (you'll know right away). If the paper was installed over unprimed drywall, or if there's very old paper on plaster walls, it can be almost impossible to remove without damaging the wall. If there are several layers, though, you may have to go ahead and remove it, and be prepared to repair the damage.

When the surface is smooth and in good condition, professional painters often prime and paint over existing paper unless its texture creates an odd-looking surface. However, they do make sure the seams are tight and that the paper is securely on the wall. They clean, prime, and paint a test area to make sure the paper will still hold.

There are a couple of reasons not to skip the priming step. A tinted stain-blocking primer keeps the wallpaper pattern and colors from faintly showing through the paint. It also helps paint bond with the wallpaper surface, which may have a vinyl coating that makes it difficult for any paint to adhere well.

1 Residual wallpaper paste is invisible, but it will interfere with paint adhesion. To remove it, wipe the wall thoroughly with a wet sponge, rinsing frequently. Reglue any loose wallpaper and repair tears or dents with fast-drying surfacing compound. Remove dust and debris before continuing.

2 Apply a stain-blocking primer on a test area. Wait 24 hours. Slit any minor blisters or bubbles with a utility knife and reglue them with wallpaper adhesive. Apply the finish coat. If the coverage looks good, continue priming and painting the rest of the room.

Glazing wallpaper—Compare two effects: aging and fading

Aging: Tone down overly bright wallpaper by antiquing it with glaze. Here, a coat of brown-tinted glaze is rubbed on the left side of black-and-white toile wallpaper to produce a muted, vintage effect. Control the amount of aging by wiping off the glaze until you are pleased with the effect. (Test first in an inconspicuous area.)

Fading: Simulate the fading effects of the sun, and make strong patterns less dominant, by applying white or light-tinted glaze. The left side of this paper was brushed with white glaze, which was then blended evenly with a rag. This process, like aging, can be done to any wallpaper that seems too bright or overly bold, even if the paper is already on the walls.

Removing wallpaper

Skill level:	Time to complete:	Materials:	Tools:
★★★☆☆	Experienced Variable Handy Variable Novice Variable	12-inch baseboard masking, blue painter's masking tape, wallpaper remover (white vinegar solution or chemical remover)	Screwdriver, wallpaper perforating tool, spray bottle or garden sprayer, vinyl gloves, plastic bucket, 3-inch plastic scraper, nonscratch plastic scrubber, sponge, moisture-proof drop cloth

Removing wallpaper is an inexact science—get the right tools, give yourself plenty of time, and try to develop a sense of humor about it. If you're lucky, someone will have prepared the wall properly and used a strippable paper. If they didn't do this, then good luck.

Removing layers of old wallpaper can be frustrating, but there are ways to make it easier. First, determine if you even need to remove it: If the surface is in good condition, professionals sometimes paper or paint right over it (see page 27). If you have any doubts about whether it needs to come off, remove the paper. In any case repair and priming are essential. You should usually soak and remove nonvinyl papers—cleaning does more damage than good. Clean vinyl and vinyl-coated papers the same way you clean painted walls—gently.

1 Turn off the power at the circuit breaker panel, then remove all switch and outlet covers on the walls you are stripping. Cover switches and outlets with blue painter's masking tape.

2 Cover the floor with a moisture-proof drop cloth, then apply baseboard masking paper and blue painter's masking tape to the baseboards. Let it overlap the drop cloth for complete coverage.

OOPS

THE VOICE OF EXPERIENCE

Someone should make a law against putting wallpaper over unprimed drywall. Why? Because if you later try to remove the paper, you're apt to take off the drywall's paper facing along with it, leaving ugly rips and gouges. (Of course, you won't even know you have a problem until you decide to redecorate.) Then, you have two choices: You can cover the damaged wall with a wallpaper liner so you can paint, or you might try testing a small section first and decide to paint over the wallpaper rather than remove it.

WORK SMART

DO THE CEILING FIRST

If you want to wallpaper the room but you're also freshening up paint on the ceiling and trim, leave the paper for last. Why take a chance on ruining pretty new paper with paint's inevitable drips and spatters? As a general rule, it's a good idea to start at the top of the room and work your way down.

3 Perforate the wallpaper so that water can penetrate beneath it. There are special tools, such as the one shown, that create shallow cuts to make the job go faster. Apply minimal pressure to perforate the wallpaper without damaging the underlying drywall.

4 Apply wallpaper remover generously with a spray bottle. Mix the remover with very hot water to speed up the removal. (Or make your own solution by mixing one cup of white vinegar per gallon of water. This is an effective alternative to commercial wallpaper removers.)

5 Let the wallpaper soak for 10 to 20 minutes or follow the manufacturer's instructions. Then peel off as much wallpaper as you can by hand. Before turning to the scraper, spray on a second application of remover, again letting it soak.

6 Peel off the remaining wallpaper with a 3-inch plastic scraper, wielding it lightly to keep from damaging the surface. Remove any lingering particles with a non-scratch plastic scrubber (the curly kind) made for washing dishes.

7 After removing all of the wallpaper wash the wall several times, using fresh water and a sponge to remove the residue of the paste. The residue keeps paint from bonding and will eventually cause it to peel.

Priming and painting walls

Skill level:	Time to complete:	Materials:	Tools:
★★★☆☆	Experienced 4 hrs. Handy 6 hrs. Novice 8 hrs.	Spackling compound or wall-repair materials, stain blocker and/or primer, high-quality latex paint, blue painter's tape, 120-grit sandpaper	Putty knife, brushes, rollers, spray bottle (for priming brushes and roller covers), extension pole, 5-gallon paint bucket with roller grid, small paint bucket, latex paint respirator (optional), safety glasses, drop cloth, ladder (if necessary), rags

Walls and ceilings are painted the same way. Priming both before painting is important to a good-looking finish, but there are also sound economic reasons. Not taking the time to prime and seal can ruin the paint job—when it dries you're apt to see stains or discoloration bleeding through the final coat. This wastes the $30 (or more) per gallon that you've spent for high-quality paint.

Primer, which is less expensive than paint, is different in other ways, too (see pages 22–23). It is formulated to adhere well to a variety of surfaces, and it also seals them to prevent stains from bleeding through the finish coat. Paint bonds more effectively to a primed surface than it does to plaster, wood, or even an earlier coat of paint. Priming adds durability, and it may prevent you from having to roll on a second (more expensive) top coat—especially if your primer is tinted to match the finish coat.

Follow a logical sequence for an efficient job: First stain and varnish new trim to protect the bare wood from paint. Next prime and paint the ceiling, proceed to the walls, and conclude with trim that needs repainting. (Some painters like to paint the trim before the walls, however.) Careful masking at each stage lets you work quickly, saving time in the long run.

If you buy multiple cans of the same paint there is the possibility they are not exactly the same color. If you are using more than one can of paint, mix the cans of paint together in a large bucket so you have the amount of paint required for the entire job. This is called "boxing" the paint and it ensures that all the paint is exactly the same color.

CLOSER LOOK

STAIN-BLOCKING PRIMERS

You may still see the blemishes you're trying to eliminate, even after applying a stain-blocking primer. Before you decide the primer is not doing its job, which is blocking the stain, test with your finish color to see if the stain shows after the final coat.

1 Fix the dings. Examine all the surfaces, then carefully repair and sand all cracks, holes, or dents before you apply the paint. For information on repairing walls, see pages 96 to 98.

2 Tint the primer. Only a limited percentage of the primer's volume can be made up of tint, so it may look lighter than the finish coat. Not all primers need tinting; let the paint salesperson follow the guidelines of the manufacturer.

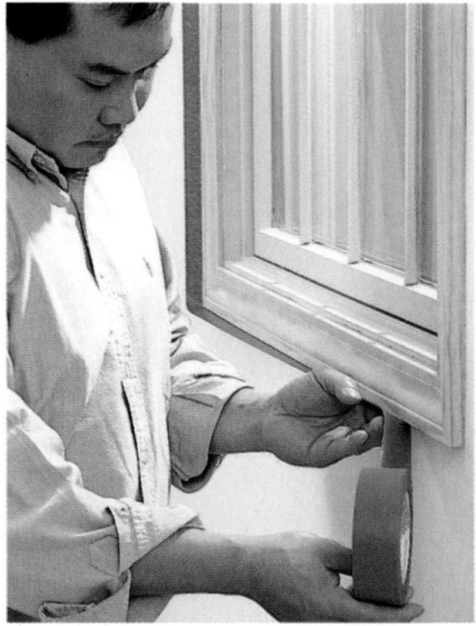

3 Mask the room. Determine the order for painting the room, working from top to bottom. Prime (and paint) the ceiling first, trim second, and walls last (wiping off wall drips from trim). Mask all areas being painted last from those that are painted first.

4 Spot prime. If using latex, dip the brush in water to help it absorb the primer. If using alkyd, dip the brush in mineral spirits. Brush out the liquid on a piece of cardboard to remove loose bristles. Prime all areas of walls and trim that need special attention: patches in drywall and plaster, areas of bare wood exposed by scraping or sanding, and any spots treated with stain blocker.

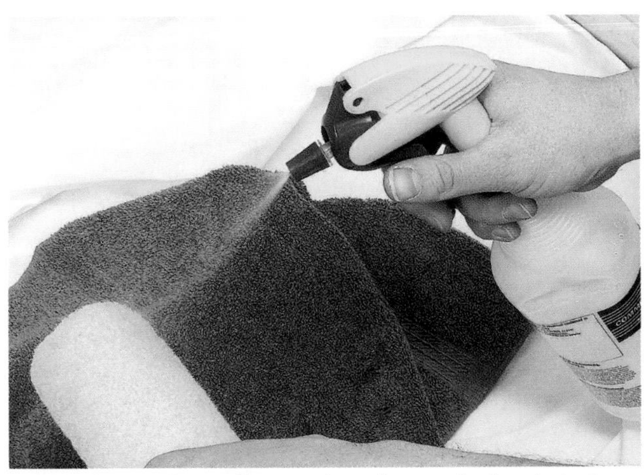

5 Moisten the roller. A dry roller won't absorb thick primer or paint well, so moisten the roller beforehand. For a latex primer, mist the roller with water and squeeze off the excess. Use mineral spirits for alkyd primer. Run the roller over the paint grid or roller tray several times to saturate the roller cover with primer.

6 Cut in the edges of the ceiling, brushing an area about 2 inches wide and 5 feet long at a time with primer. Then, wearing safety goggles and an old cap, roll primer onto the ceiling, overlapping the roller into the cut-in area. Roll with diagonal strokes, moving from the edge toward the middle of the room. Continue cutting in and rolling until you're finished.

7 Mask off the trim if you haven't already done so. Wait until the ceiling dries and mask it off with blue painter's masking tape. Cut in around the windows, doors, and corners. (Starting in a corner, brush primer along about 5 feet of trim, 5 feet of ceiling, and from top to bottom of the corner.)

8 Roll the walls, getting as close as possible to the masked trim, ceiling, or adjacent wall. This minimizes the area with a brush-stroke texture. Some professional painters reverse the rolling and cutting-in steps, rolling as close as they can to the masked trim; then, to save paint, they cut in only what's left.

Latex and alkyd (oil) paints compared

Paint type	General advantages	General limitations
Latex	• Cleans up with water • Excellent color and gloss retention • Good adhesion to many surfaces • Breathes (lets moisture vapor pass through)	• Most paint cannot be applied below 50% F • Freezing temperatures may ruin liquid paint
Alkyd	• Good hiding ability • High adhesion • Allows longer time to brush • Good leveling of brush marks • Flows easily; resistant to sticking (blocking)	• Flammability • Yellows, becomes brittle, cracks with age • Not for use on untreated galvanized metal or fresh masonry • High volatile organic compound (VOC) content, with the resulting odor

Priming and painting walls (continued)

9 Begin rolling at the top of the wall along the cut-in strip, working toward the bottom in a series of W-shape strokes, as shown above, to avoid creating a visible pattern. Move along the wall in 3- to 5-foot sections, cutting in and rolling until the job is done. Work in sections you can cover with a single load of the roller, and always roll up on the first stroke. The key is to overlap areas of wet paint.

10 Sand the walls if needed. When the primer is thoroughly dry, lightly sand any blemishes. If using a full sheet of 120-grit sandpaper, tear it in four pieces, folding each one in thirds. Lightly rub the wall to remove bumps and other high spots. When the paper fills with paint dust, refold it to reveal a fresh face and continue. As an alternative, use drywall screen or a 4- to 6-inch putty knife to knock down the bumps. Wipe the smoothed wall with a damp rag to remove dust and debris.

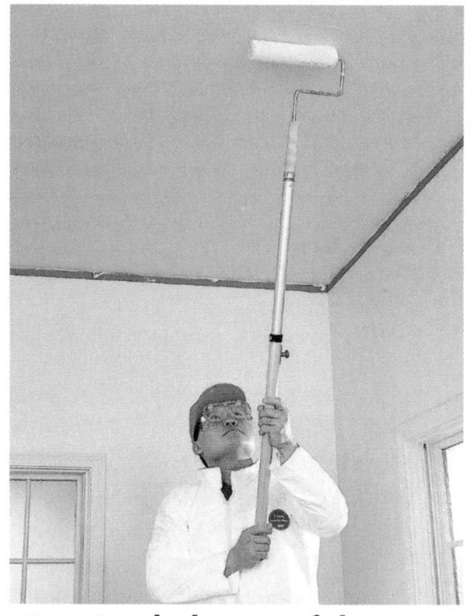

11 Mask the top of the walls, and roll the ceiling with paint. Cut in a section and roll, as in step 6. Protect your eyes with safety goggles and wear an old cap. Extension poles allow you to reach more areas safely, without leaning from a ladder. A 5-gallon bucket with a roller grid requires filling less often than a paint tray, and it is less likely to tip. Use a roller with a spatter guard to reduce spattering.

12 Cut in the walls. After you've painted the ceiling, remove the tape from the top of the walls and let the ceiling dry overnight. Then mask off the ceiling and trim to paint the walls. Starting in a corner, cut in a few feet along the ceiling, a few feet along the baseboard, and in the starting corner, as in Step 7.

13 Roll paint on the wall working from top to bottom in a series of W-shape strokes. The cut-in (brushed) areas have a different texture from the rolled areas. Paint into the freshly cut-in areas with a roller to minimize the difference; if you have masked properly, the roller can get very close to cover almost all of it.

14 Prime and paint the trim. Remove the masking tape from the walls, wait for the paint to dry thoroughly, and mask off for the trim. Control drips to minimize mistakes: pour the trim paint into a small bucket and dip the brush about halfway into the paint. Then tap the brush against the sides (instead of scraping it against the rim) to remove excess paint at the tip of the brush.

Using a brush

Learning to use a paintbrush properly is easy: just practice these basic techniques and use the right brush for the job. Wet the brush (using water for latex paint and mineral spirits for oil/alkyd) before you dip it into paint. Brush out the excess and load the brush with paint.

One step at a time

The most important thing to remember is this: Start at the wet edge, and paint toward the dry. Painting is a three-step process. Apply the first brush load, spreading it evenly. For the second load, start at the wet edge of that first stroke, moving toward dry areas. Then reverse and paint back toward the wet area, feathering the two edges together with light strokes. A generous coat flows and hides better than paint brushed out too thinly.

1 Tap each side of the loaded brush on the edge of the bucket. Dragging or pressing removes too much paint from the bristles.

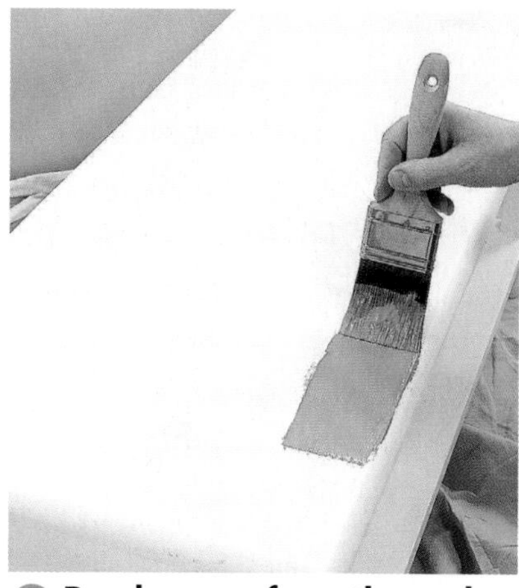

2 Brush away from the end. Starting your first brush stroke one brush width from the end, brush toward the other end.

3 Return the brush to the starting point by brushing back toward the end. Smooth the paint with a light touch.

4 Start again at the wet edge. To avoid overlap marks, start successive strokes at the wet edge of the previous stroke and paint toward the dry.

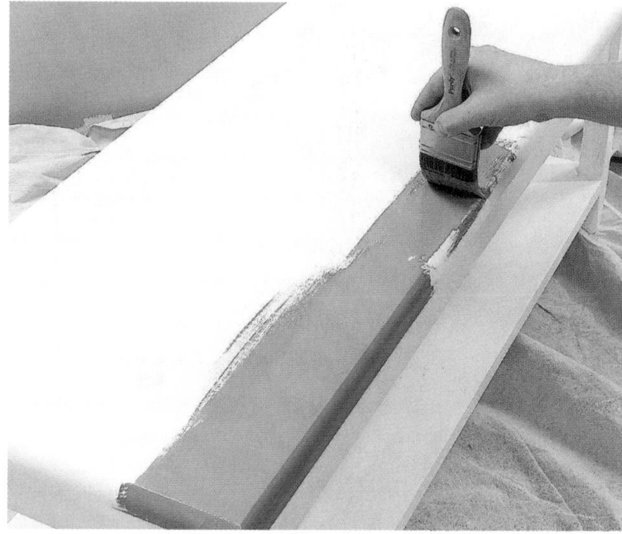

5 Blend areas together with feathered strokes. When painting back toward the wet area, decrease the pressure on the brush to leave a gradually thinner coat.

- **Don't overbrush.** Overbrushing results in what the pros call "roping." This term refers to the lines a brush makes when you pull it over paint that is partially dry. Let each coat of paint dry completely before trying to recoat it.
- **Don't hold the brush too tightly.** Too much gripping pressure tires your hand quickly and makes painting a chore.
- **Use your wrist and also your arm.** You'll have better control, and it's less tiring than using either one alone.

Painting doors and trim

Skill level:	Time to complete:	Materials:	Tools:
★★★☆☆	Experienced 1 hr. Handy 2 hrs. Novice 3 hrs.	Four 3-inch drywall screws, white-pigmented shellac (if door has knots), latex wood putty, acrylic-latex caulk, lightweight crack filler (optional), 80- and 220-grit sandpaper, stain-blocking primer, paint (probably enamel), TSP solution, denatured alcohol or chemical deglosser (optional), blue painter's masking tape	Screwdriver, two sawhorses, 2-handed paint scraper, pad sander or sanding block, 1½-inch sash brush, 2-inch trim brush, oval brush, plastic scrub pad, rubber gloves, lint-free rag, putty knife, caulking gun, sponge

Painting doors, windows, baseboards, and moldings successfully involves six key steps:

- Clean and prime to achieve maximum adhesion.
- Smooth the surface so that cracks, holes, dents, and chips don't show through the finish coat.
- Mask adjacent surfaces so you can paint quickly and confidently.
- Keep a wet edge to eliminate any lap marks.
- Avoid overworking paint; brush it on and let it flow to avoid brush marks.
- If closing a partially dry door is unavoidable, place plastic wrap between surfaces that touch.

Painting doors

Minimize brush marks by painting your door in the order shown at right. Moving from top to bottom, working in this order gives you time to feather the paint in adjacent sections before it dries. Paint all of the edges first; then work on sections 2 through 5 at the top of the door before moving to the bottom portion.

Professionals often paint a door without removing it from the jamb. Placing the door on sawhorses and painting in the order shown, though, will avoid the drips that inevitably occur when you're painting vertically.

If the door has knots or strong variations in grain or color, it's a good idea to spot-prime the offending areas with a stain-blocking primer to prevent problems with coverage in the final coat.

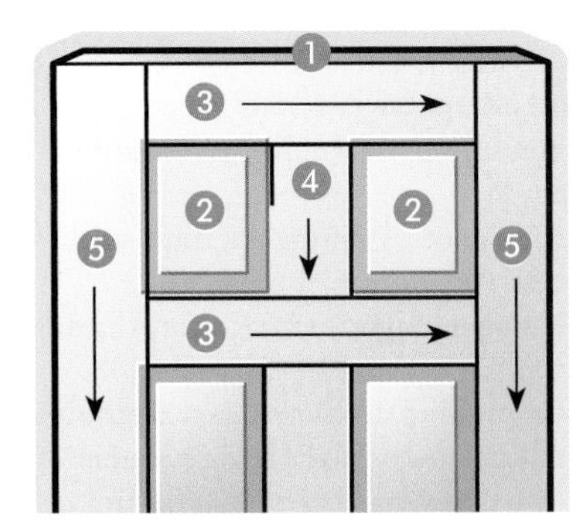

Painting order:
1 All edges
2 Panel bevels and flats
3 Rails
4 Stile middles
5 Stiles

Painting doors

1 Remove all hardware from the door. Insert long screws in the top and bottom edges and suspend the door on sawhorses. Fill holes and gouges, spot prime knots, and sand the door as necessary with 80-grit sandpaper. Follow up with 220-grit sandpaper so the sanding marks won't show under the finish coat.

2 Prime the door. Use a tinted, stain-blocking primer to prime the door, following the painting order above. When the primer dries, sand it lightly and remove the dust with a tack cloth. Apply the finish coat of paint in the same order.

Painting trim

When you are painting trim, the critical tools are the paintbrushes. Too wide, and you won't be able to paint neatly. Too narrow, and you'll have to rework the paint unnecessarily. Choose brushes with bristles appropriate for the kind of paint (latex or oil/alkyd) you are using, and don't skimp on the quality. For most trim jobs, a 1½- or 2-inch brush works well, but in some instances, you may need several brushes:

- An angled sash brush for laying down sharp edges.
- A square-edged trim brush for laying down flat areas of paint.
- An oval brush for getting paint into tight areas.

1 Clean the woodwork with a TSP solution (see page 24), using a plastic scrub pad to remove residue (wear rubber gloves). Rinse several times. Remove blistered or chipped paint with a paint scraper, trying not to gouge the wood. Sand with 80-grit then 220-grit sandpaper. Remove dust with a lint-free cloth.

2 Fill gaps and cracks with paintable caulk or glazing compound. Remove the excess and smooth the joint with your finger. Fill holes and gouges with lightweight spackling compound. Remove the excess material with the edge of a putty knife and let it dry.

WORK SMART

PROFESSIONAL TIPS

Don't overwork the paint. Flow it on, and then let it level itself to leave a surface free of brush marks. If you do get brush marks, let the paint dry, sand with 120-grit sandpaper, and repaint.

Professional painters may prefer a "cigar" or "hot dog" roller for painting doors. This 6-inch-wide dense foam roller leaves a smooth finish coat without brush marks. You will need to brush in the bevels in the door panels before rolling.

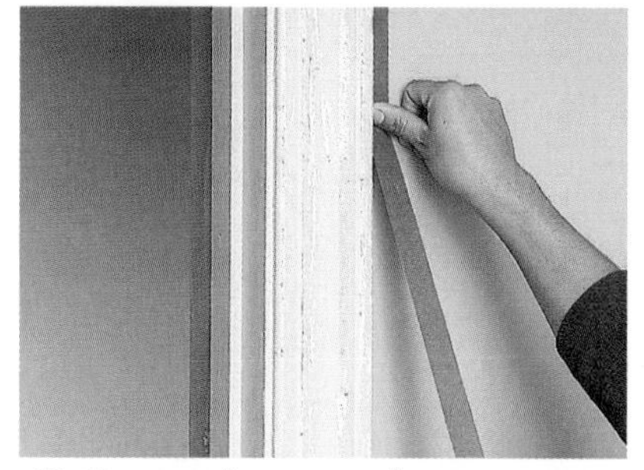

3 Spot prime any knots or resin pockets with white-pigmented shellac primer and let it dry. Mask all adjacent surfaces with blue painter's masking tape, sealing the edges firmly. Wipe down the surface with denatured alcohol or a paint deglosser immediately before priming.

4 Prime the entire surface with a stain-blocking primer. After 24 hours, sand with 220-grit sandpaper and wipe the sanded surface with a damp sponge or rag. Apply the finish coat of paint with a 2-inch trim brush. Remove the masking tape while the paint is still wet.

Window-painting basics

Skill level:	Time to complete:	Materials:	Tools:
★★★☆☆	Experienced 1 hr. Handy 1.5 hrs. Novice 2 hrs.	TSP solution, wood putty, paintable caulk, primer, paint, sandpaper, blue painter's masking tape	Paint scraper, sash knife, tack cloth, putty knife or pry bar (for removing trim), 2-inch sash brush, utility knife, window scraper or single-edge razor blades, bucket, sponge

Windows and sills work hard, taking a beating from sun, rain, and condensation, holding potted plants, and being opened and closed repeatedly. They deserve a high-quality, smooth, and durable finish, but it's not always an easy job. The sheer number of separate pieces is a challenge. The casing, the sill or *stool*, and the sashes with *muntins* (thin wooden strips that separate the *lights*, or panes, of glass) all need to be covered with paint, yet the panes must be completely paint-free.

Good prep work is essential when painting windows—the worse they are, the more it takes. Chips and blistering are common on windows, requiring a scraper and sandpaper. You'll also want to sand and degloss the existing finish—even if it's in good condition—so that the new finish will adhere. Mask off the glass and the surrounding wall to decrease cleanup time, but be prepared with new razor blades to clean off any paint that still adheres to the glass.

Finally, reduce frustration on this somewhat finicky job by purchasing a 1½-inch angled sash brush—it's a good choice for most situations.

1 Scrape and sand damaged areas. If either sash is painted shut, free it with a sash saw. Slip the blade into the crack, working the blade back and forth to break the paint bond. Wash greasy or dirty areas with TSP solution (see page 24). Being careful not to scratch the glass, remove loose paint with a scraper. Sand to remove the sheen from glossy paints and blend in scraped areas. Remove the dust with a tack cloth.

2 Fill holes and caulk any gaps. Use wood putty to fill holes or gouges, leveling it with a putty knife. Run a bead of paintable caulk along any gaps between the wall and the window frame; smooth the caulk with a wet finger.

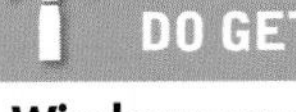

WORK SMART

DON'T PAINT THE CRACKS

Painting the crack between the frame and window sash is a no-no. Once the paint dries, you'll be unable to open the window (This may be helpful if you are trying to eliminate all air infiltration permanently). To avoid the problem, brush the sash and the frame in two separate strokes, using a minimum amount of paint. Move the sash up and down a few times as the paint dries.

TOOL TIP

DO GET THE WINDOW OPEN

Windows must be able to open for safety. Use a sash knife to open windows sealed shut by dried paint. Or try a utility knife or a hacksaw blade. Sometimes a good tap with a rubber mallet is enough to open it. Once the window opens, mask off the painted areas and spray the tracks with silicone spray for lubrication. Avoid getting the spray on finished areas because it will make it difficult for paint to adhere.

3 If possible, remove the sashes. If you paint them on sawhorses; it's easier to avoid runs. On many newer windows, the sashes pop out with little trouble. On older windows, you can paint the sashes in place or carefully pry off the side trim before removing the sashes. (Use a wide, stiff putty knife before graduating to a pry bar, which might leave marks.

4 Mask panes and the surrounding wall. If painting the sashes in place, as shown here, use painter's masking tape to avoid getting primer and paint on the glass and wall.

5 Apply tinted primer with a sash brush. If the window has snap-out grilles, remove them to paint. If it has muntins, paint them first. Next paint all horizontal parts of the sash, followed by the verticals, and finally the sill (painting in this order limits drips). To keep sashes from sticking, don't prime or paint the sides of the windows or the track in which they travel. If priming the sashes in place, raise and lower them to get to surfaces that are inaccessible when the window is closed; also move them as the primer dries to prevent sticking.

6 Apply one or more finish coats. Again using the sash brush, apply paint the same way you applied primer. If you used a tinted primer, one top coat may be enough. If the primer shows through or an edge didn't get painted, apply a second top coat.

7 Remove masking tape from the glass as soon as the paint skins over to prevent pulling up the paint later. Fix mistakes by drawing a sharp utility knife along the edges of each pane, leaving a thin margin of paint on the glass; push a window scraper or single-edge razor blade toward this cut line to remove the excess paint.

Use neutral colors for painted trim and save bolder colors for the walls. Later, if you change the color of the room, you won't have to repaint the trim, which is far more tedious to paint than walls.

Staining windows

Skill level:	Time to complete:	Materials:	Tools:
★★★☆☆	Experienced 1 hr. Handy 1.5 hrs. Novice 2 hrs.	Paint and varnish remover, stain (optional), clear finish, 120- and 180-grit sandpaper, wood putty, painter's masking tape	Rubber gloves, cartridge respirator, putty knife, utility knife, 2-inch sash brush, tack cloth or paper towel, window scraper or single-edge razor blade, drop cloth, #000 steel wool, denatured alcohol

Sun, moisture, and weather are hard on windows. Water might condense on the glass in winter and end up on the sill. Or you may forget to close the window when it rains. Sun streams in and causes the water-weakened finish to buckle, and the finish degrades over time. Eventually, it is necessary to sand and strip either the whole window, or parts of it.

Before the 1950s, the clear finish on most windows was shellac. Lacquers came after that, and now polyurethane coatings are almost standard. Fortunately, you don't need to know exactly what's on your windows because polyurethane will almost always do a good job of covering any surface. You have a choice of oil- or water-base poly; both work satisfactorily. Exterior spar varnish (made for boats) is especially durable and it can also be used inside.

Can you strip a painted window and then stain and varnish it? Yes, but it's hard to do well. You'll need to coax paint from the crevices of the trim, the window frame, and all the molding. It might be easier to remove the woodwork and send it out to a dip-and-strip shop than to do it yourself.

WORK SMART

FIX, THEN FINISH

Stain and varnish don't hide irregularities in the wood. It's essential that the underlying wood is smooth and defect-free. Fill any holes with wood putty, repair, sand, and stain the wood before putting on the final smooth coat of shiny finish. You'll be rewarded with windows that look good for many years.

1 Evaluate the present finish. If the window is in fairly good condition, you may only need to sand it enough to smooth it and dull the sheen. Begin with 120-grit sandpaper; then switch to 180-grit sandpaper for a smoother surface. If the finish is badly damaged or built up, it's best to remove it. On many newer windows the sashes pop out, but you may have to carefully pry off trim pieces to remove sashes on older windows. Cover the work surface with an inexpensive drop cloth. Brush paint and varnish remover onto the wood following the manufacturer's instructions. (Provide good ventilation, and wear rubber gloves and a vapor respirator.) Scrape off the finish with a putty knife. Rinse with the solvent recommended for the remover.

2 Fill holes and gouges. Buy a commercial wood putty that closely matches the stain you're using, or choose a stainable putty. Fill the flaws with wood putty, spot-sanding it when it dries. Remove the dust with a tack cloth (if you'll be using an oil-base finish) or damp paper towel (if using a water-base finish). If you stain the wood, either tinted or stainable putty comes close to a match, but it may not be perfect. If you're not going to stain, make your own putty: Collect a few pinches of fine sawdust from the type of wood you'll be patching, mix with five-minute epoxy, and fill in any holes. When the epoxy dries, trim off the excess with a utility knife or sharp chisel and then sand. For an extra-smooth finish do the final sanding with 000 steel wool.

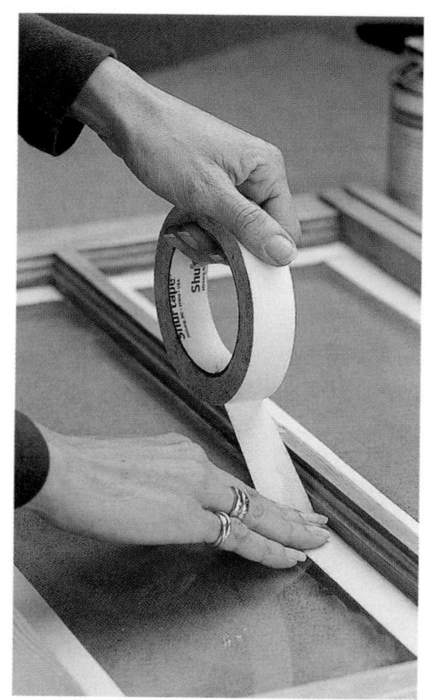

3 Mask the panes, and also the sides of the sash and the tracks. Masking with tape takes time, but it saves work later. Low-tack painter's tape is easy to remove and leaves little residue; it works well for masking off trim too. There are several types of low-tack tape so read the label carefully and choose the one that best meets your needs. Make sure you mask the two side edges of the sash and also the track; these parts are almost always left unfinished so the window opens and closes smoothly.

4 Apply the stain and finish. Staining the wood will darken or warm its color, but the color will look even only if you've been thorough in removing the old finish. Windows made of pine or another softwood often absorb stain unevenly, causing a blotchy effect. Avoid this by using a gel stain, which won't blotch because it doesn't soak deeply into the wood. Let the stain dry, and apply at least two finish coats (three coats on the sill, which takes the greatest beating). Sand lightly between coats, removing the dust with a rag dipped in denatured alcohol.

5 Remove the masking tape. Remove the tape from the glass as soon as the finish begins to dry. If you haven't taped off the glass (or if your masking job wasn't quite adequate), draw a sharp utility knife along the edges of each pane, leaving a narrow margin of finish on the glass. Push a window scraper or a single-edge razor blade toward this cut line to remove finish from the glass.

Sticking sashes

Is it hard to open and close your windows? Silicone makes the sashes glide more easily. Mask off the surrounding wood and use silicone spray along the channels in which the windows travel. (Failing to mask the overspray will keep any finish from adhering the next time you need to refinish the window.)

WORK SMART

TEST THE COLOR

Stain looks a lot different on your window than it does in the brochure. Test it on a scrap piece of wood—the same kind as your window.

Old, but clean, cotton T-shirts make the best applicators. Dip a bit of the shirt in stain, rub it on the wood, and wipe away the excess.

BUYER'S GUIDE

EXTERIOR-GRADE VARNISH

Marine spar varnish, originally designed for wooden masts on boats, is still made for exterior applications. Designed to withstand sun and moisture, it's also ideal for windows, especially the sills, and for exterior doors. Even though it says "for exterior use," it works well when used inside, too, if you provide ventilation.

Staining trim

Skill level:	Time to complete:	Materials:	Tools:
★★★☆☆	Experienced 1 hr. Handy 1.5 hrs. Novice 2 hrs.	Water- or oil-base varnish, t-shirts or rags, water- or oil-base stain to match varnish, denatured alcohol, stainable wood putty, wood conditioner or gel stain, 120-, 180-, and 220-grit sandpaper	Rubber gloves, cartridge respirator, putty knife, utility knife, 2-inch sash brush, tack cloth or paper towel, window scraper or single-edge razor blades, drop cloth, 000 steel wool

Stain and varnish are not the same. Compare the labels: you'll see that stain is made from dyes and pigments that change the color of wood; varnish is made of resins that protect it. Neither product does both jobs. Varnish can be used alone, but stain can't. Stain alone looks dull, and the dust and grime that settle on it are hard to remove. A top coat of varnish gives the stained wood some degree of shine, and it's far easier to clean.

There's a product called varnish stain that combines both color and protection, but it is not recommended for windows or trim. If a chip occurs, the color chips away too, and the entire finish is flawed.

Doors and trim are finished the same way. In both, the condition of the wood is highly important because stain emphasizes whatever is under it. If you put up new molding, make sure it's *stain grade* rather than *paint grade*. Paint grade is made up of short lengths glued together; when these are stained, the joints and different shades of wood show up glaringly.

Unless previously varnished trim is in poor condition, you don't have to remove the old finish. Modern varnishes adhere well to whatever is underneath. Sand and clean the finish well with a rag dipped in denatured alcohol. Let it dry thoroughly before applying the new finish.

Staining and varnishing trim that has previously been painted is more of a challenge. Even a soak-in stripper almost never removes all the paint, and the remaining traces will show. Plan to spend time with more stripper, a stiff brush, and assorted tools (try a nut pick) for removing paint from the crevasses before you stain and varnish.

1 Sand the trim and clean it with alcohol. Sand to lessen dents and imperfections and then to create a smooth surface on the trim. (Start with 120-grit sandpaper; follow with 180-grit to remove the marks left by the 120-grit, and finish with 220-grit.) Between sandings wipe up the dust with a rag dampened with denatured alcohol. (Tack cloths, popular with painters, often leave a waxy residue that may interfere with the finish, especially if it's a water-base finish.)

2 Repair anything you can't sand away. Patches may not match the rest of the wood perfectly, but damaged wood usually looks far worse. Fill dents and gouges with stainable putty, leveling it with a putty knife or your thumb. Let the patches dry; if any of them shrink while drying, add more putty to the patch. When dry, sand smooth and wipe with a rag dipped in denatured alcohol.

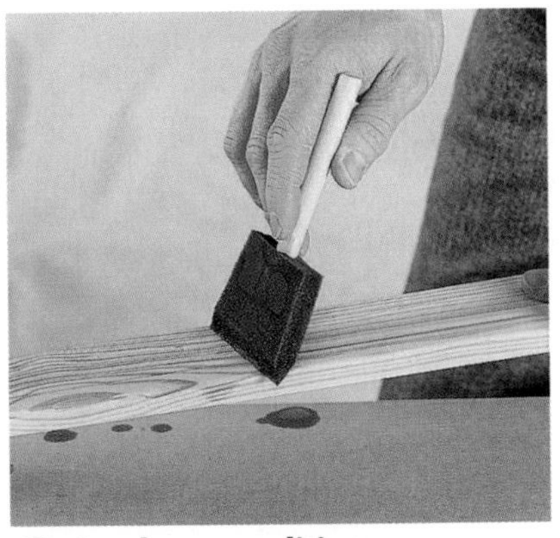

3 Apply a conditioner. To prevent the blotchiness that stained pine, fir, and other softwoods often develop, first brush on a thin finish sold as "wood conditioner." The instructions usually advise to let it dry 15 minutes to 2 hours. Some painters say it's better to wait only 10 minutes, and most agree that you should not wait longer than 2 hours. At that point, the resins in the conditioner have dried out, and you can barely stain the wood. If this happens, sand the surface, and reapply the conditioner. Or, avoid the need for conditioner entirely by using gel stains, which don't penetrate deeply and therefore don't blotch.

WORK SMART

SAND BY HAND

Moldings made of softwoods like pine or poplar can be damaged if you sand too heavily with a power sander. Hand sanding with a fine grit paper to prep for the finish is the safest way to go.

4 Brush or wipe on the stain. Apply the stain, let it soak in a bit (not long!), and then wipe it off, following the manufacturer's instructions. Have plenty of old T-shirts or lint-free rags on hand for wiping. If the color isn't dark enough, wait the recommended time and apply a second coat. If you use a gel stain, apply it with a sponge brush. Take off any excess very gently, using a brush instead of a rag.

5 Apply the varnish. Brush the varnish onto a short section of trim at a time, smoothing it quickly and lightly to cover completely and eliminate imperfections. Let the varnish dry the recommended time. Sand the trim with 220-grit sandpaper or very fine steel wool to level out any small dust bumps. Wipe down with a rag dipped in denatured alcohol, and apply another coat. Apply three coats of varnish for a durable and lasting finish.

CLOSER LOOK

VARNISH—STIR, DON'T SHAKE

You may find a layer of goo at the bottom of the can; this is a "flatting agent" designed to control the sheen, which may be matte, semigloss, or gloss. Mix the settled layer into the varnish before starting, otherwise you may not get the level of sheen promised on the label. Important: Stir the varnish—never shake it. Shaking creates tiny bubbles that show up in the finish coat.

WORK SMART

STRIPPING TRIM

Which type of stripper is best? It all depends on what you're stripping. An off-the-shelf liquid stripper will remove 90 percent of all clear finishes. Follow the instructions on the can and sand when the wood is dry. You may need to apply a new coat of stain to even out the color that the stripper leaves behind.

If you're stripping paint (particularly if you suspect it's lead paint) use a peel-and-strip paste that removes paint without fumes or chipping. Spread on the paste, cover with the plastic sheet that comes with it, and a few hours later you can peel off both paint and paste like a strip of putty. In a worst-case scenario involving a lot of paint that probably contains lead, gently remove the trim and have it stripped professionally at a dip-and-strip shop. Refinish the trim before reattaching it.

CLOSER LOOK

STAINING PINE

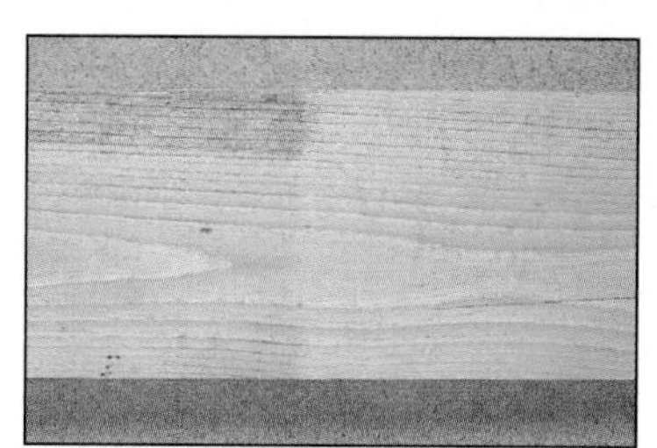

The density of softwood varies, even in a single board. Pine, fir, and other softwoods stain unevenly, as shown on the left side of this board. Test by staining a scrap or the back of your wood. If you don't like how it looks, even out the surface with a wood conditioner before staining, or else use a gel stain.

Painting kitchen and bath cabinets

Skill level:	Time to complete:	Materials:	Tools:
★★★☆☆	Experienced Variable Handy Variable Novice variable	TSP solution, 220-grit sandpaper, clean cotton cloth, denatured alcohol, liquid deglosser (optional), bonding primer, latex or alkyd enamel paint	Utility knife, screwdriver, large sponge, pad sander or sanding block, small paint pad or 2-inch trim brush, vinyl gloves

There's no need to live with kitchen or bath cabinets made from dark, dingy wood or outdated plastic laminate. Paint will adhere to practically any surface—even the metal front panel of a dishwasher—as long as it is clean and has enough *tooth* (surface roughness). Your job is to thoroughly clean the cabinets, add tooth to the surface, prime the cabinets, and paint them properly.

If you take the time to perform each critical step of the preparation, you can avoid the cost of buying new cabinets. The cabinets, though, will look like new, especially if you replace the old knobs. Look for replacement knobs in home stores or online. Save even more by buying knobs in bulk; "contractor packs" containing 10 or more cost less than individual knobs.

▲ *Stained and varnished cabinets can darken over time, and they often look dated as styles change. Refresh them with a coat of paint, especially if your home is decorated in a country French, Colonial, or cottage style, where painted cabinets are traditional.*

WORK SMART

NUMBER THE DOORS

Number the cabinet doors and openings as you remove them so you'll be able to rehang them easily, using the original screw holes.

No loose screws

Keep a container handy to hold the screws and other hardware from the cabinets. If a hole seems too big to hold the screw securely, take it out. Insert the wooden end of a match into the hole, breaking off the end with the head; put the screw back in, and it will now fit tightly. If you'll be reusing the same hinges or knobs, take the time to clean and degrease them with detergent and an old toothbrush before putting them back on.

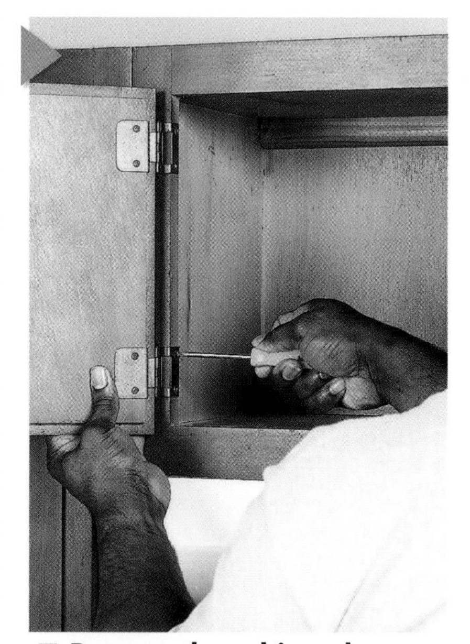

1 Remove the cabinet doors. Painting them horizontally eliminates unsightly drips that would be noticeable on cabinets.

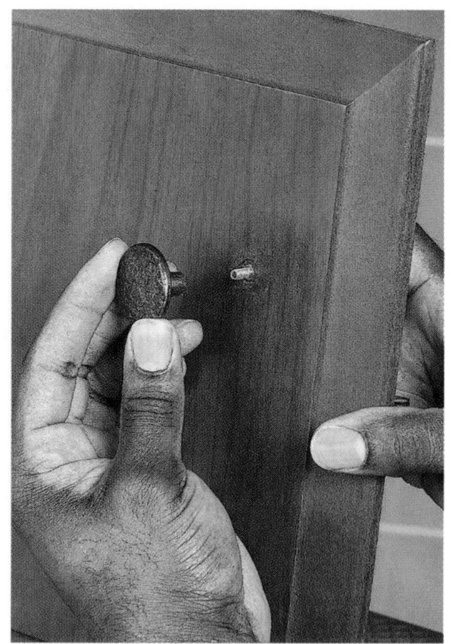

2 Remove all the hardware, including knobs, pulls, hinges, and catches. Paint on the hardware is the sign of a job done too fast—in which case your hard work is wasted.

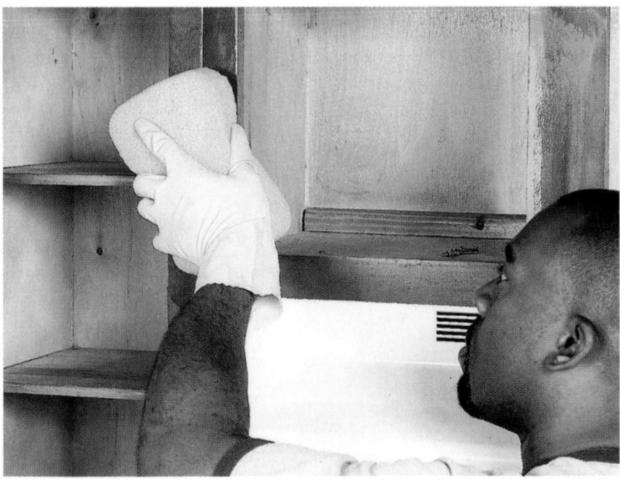

3 Cooking deposits a thin film of oil on kitchen surfaces, so scrub the cabinets and shelves with a TSP solution (see page 24). Rinse thoroughly with fresh water.

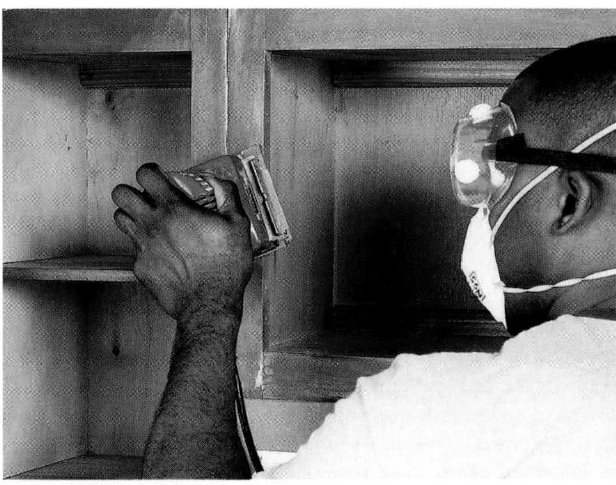

4 Roughen up the surface to create tooth by sanding with 220-grit sandpaper until the finish is completely dulled. Or, use a liquid deglosser (see page 25).

5 Wipe off the sanding dust with a clean cotton cloth dampened in denatured alcohol. Wear protective gloves.

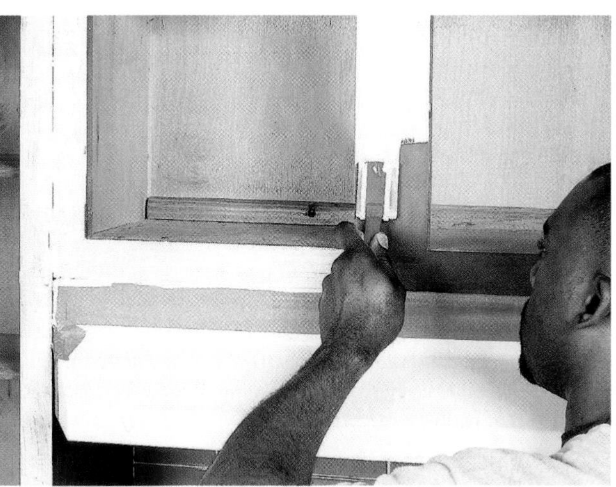

6 Apply white-pigmented shellac or a tinted enamel-undercoat primer with a brush, roller, or paint pad recommended by the manufacturer.

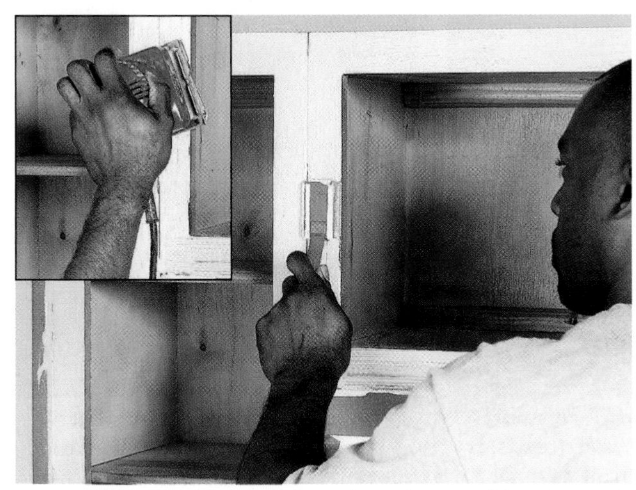

7 Lightly sand the primed surface with 220-grit sandpaper, and remove the dust with a damp rag. Using a brush or paint pad, apply a coat of enamel paint within 24 hours. A second finish coat may be necessary.

OOPS

CABINET KNOB MISHAPS

No matter how carefully you have prepped and painted the cabinets, there's still one last chance to mess up. Before you put the knobs back on, learn how to do it.

- **Wrong way:** Insert the screw from the back and turn the knob to tighten. This can gouge and even rip off paint on the front of the door or drawer.
- **Right way:** Lightly hold the knob in position against the front surface while using a screwdriver to tighten the screw from the back.

Painting floors

Skill level:	Time to complete:	Materials:	Tools:
★★★☆☆	Experienced Variable Handy Variable Novice Variable	1¼-inch drywall screws, wood glue, wood shims, latex wood filler, 80-grit sandpaper, blue painter's masking tape, floor paint	Hammer, nail set, drill, power screwdriver, putty knife, pad sander, dust-resistant mask, vacuum cleaner, sponge mop, 1-inch throwaway brush, 1½-inch polyester sash brush, 5-gallon bucket, 1-quart measure, 9-inch roller cover with ⅜-inch nap, roller cage with extension handle, paint tray

Owners of colonial-era homes often chose rich shades of paint to decorate their wooden floors, even applying stenciled patterns that looked like rugs. Today, with wear-resistant formulations and a much wider range of colors, paint is an even more appropriate choice.

Paint provides the best solution when you don't want wall-to-wall carpet (possibly because of allergies) and the existing floor isn't attractive. Plywood and wood floors that have been patched over time are among the best candidates.

Another option is to consider the floor a blank canvas and create a unique design. Consider painting a whimsical rug in a child's room. Or stencil or stamp a stylized border in the dining room or kitchen. Mask straight lines with painter's tape, then paint between the tape to make a simple border. It's up to you—have fun.

Whatever you do, move all of the furniture out of the room before starting. It makes the job easier, and your furniture will be out of harm's way.

▶ ***Painted wood floors*** *are a long-standing tradition, very popular in colonial-era homes and now used in any room where a fresh, uncluttered look is desired. Painted floors also look good with borders painted in contrasting colors.*

$ BUYER'S GUIDE
NO WALL PAINT ON FLOORS

Choose paints specifically made for use on floors and porches. Paints formulated for vertical surfaces won't wear as well on horizontal surfaces, which require a heavy-duty scuff-resistant finish. Floor paints come in a wide range of colors, in semigloss and gloss sheens. Follow the manufacturer's recommendations for best results.

Colorful cover-up

Painting a wood floor covers unsightly repair work and conceals unattractive, scuffed varnish. And a colorful, painted floor can be very attractive and is far less expensive than carpeting the room.

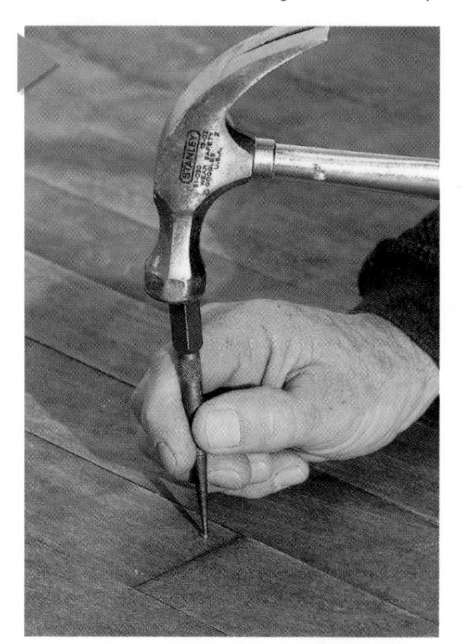

1 Drive protruding nailheads just below the surface using a hammer and a nail set. If the floor squeaks and you can't get at the subfloor from below, drive longer nails into the joists from the top.

2 If the floor squeaks and you can get to the subfloor, drill several pilot holes from below, and fasten the spot with drywall screws from beneath. (Make sure the screws aren't so long they stick up through the floor.)

3 If squeaks persist mark the exact location while someone walks across the floor, and drive glued wedges between the subfloor and the joist at that point.

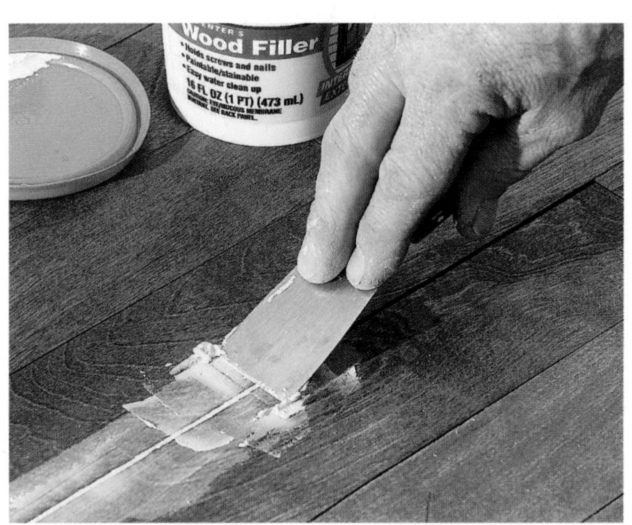

4 Fill any cracks more than ⅛-inch wide with latex wood filler. Check the label, making sure the product is formulated to accept paint and will also expand and contract with the wood.

5 If the wood is in rough shape, sand it with a floor sander. Otherwise sand lightly with a pad sander using 80- or 100-grit sandpaper (wear a dust mask while sanding).

6 Vacuum, and then damp-mop the floor. Remove any dust with clean water; it keeps paint from adhering. Mask the baseboards with painter's tape.

7 If new flooring is pine and contains knots, spot prime the knots with white-pigmented shellac to keep them from bleeding through the finished coat of paint.

8 If the floor is bare wood or a composition wood product, apply sanding sealer before priming. This keeps the grain from rising.

Painting floors (continued)

9 Use primer recommended by the manufacturer of the finish floor paint. If it requires thinning follow the manufacturer's directions.

10 Cut the primer around the baseboards, using either a 1½- or 2-inch angled sash brush.

11 Starting in the corner farthest from the door, apply the rest of the primer using a 9-inch roller cover with a ⅜-inch nap. Always roll in the direction of the flooring.

12 Don't paint yourself into a corner; plan ahead so you end at the door leading out of the room.

WORK SMART

PAINT UNDER THE RIGHT CONDITIONS

- Paint at the temperature and humidity recommended by the manufacturer.
- Provide ventilation, with airflow to promote drying. If dust or curious visitors may be a problem, just close the door and let the paint take longer to dry.
- Allow the paint to dry thoroughly between coats and cure fully before use. Even when a painted floor feels dry to the touch, it is usually best to wait several days before putting furniture back in the room.

13 After the primer dries (read the manufacturer's instructions), cut in the full-strength finish coat.

14 Apply the finish coat of paint in the same manner as the primer. You can even use the same roller cover, as long as it is stored properly (wrapped in airtight plastic) between coats. If possible, don't walk on the floor for several days, even if it feels dry to the touch.

Painting interior brick

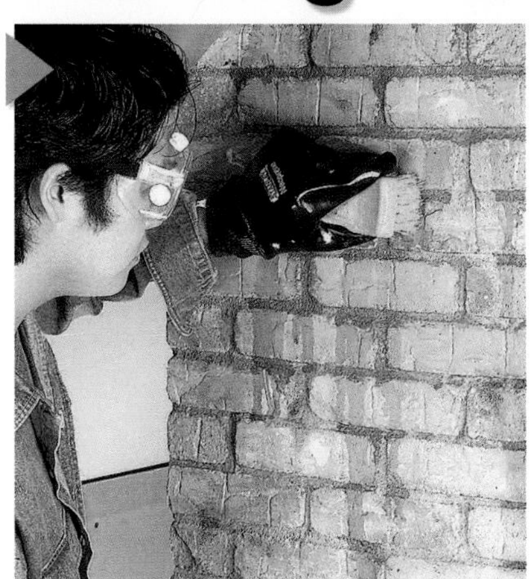

1 Scrub thoroughly with a TSP solution (see page 24) and a brush with firm, synthetic bristles while wearing goggles and protective gloves. Rinse at least twice. TSP is a suds-free cleanser; you may not see the residue, but it will interfere with paint adhesion. Allow the surface to dry thoroughly.

2 Repair the joints with thinset mortar and a small trowel, called a *tuck pointer*. Brush wet mortar off bricks with a stiff brush as you go. For a finished edge, smooth joints and corners with a tool called a *jointer* or with a short copper pipe, as shown above. Allow to dry completely. Mask adjacent surfaces with painter's tape and drop cloths to keep off paint spatters.

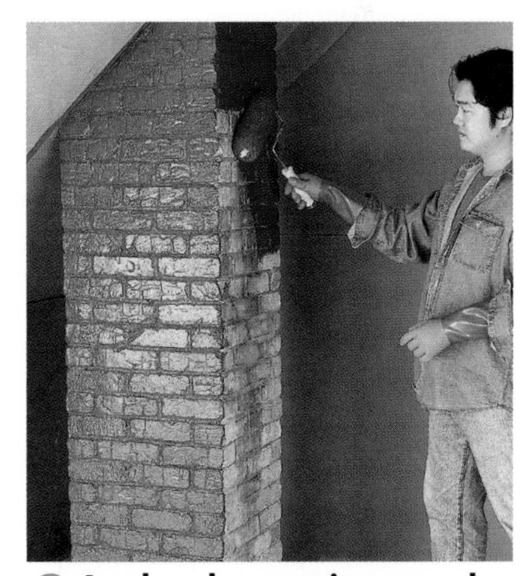

3 Apply a latex primer made for brick, masonry, and stucco, using a roller with a thick 1-inch nap. Let the primer dry, and roll on a semigloss or gloss latex paint. Use a 1-inch brush to touch up any cracks or crevices that are missing paint.

Painting interior concrete

1 Test for moisture in or under the concrete by taping a 4x4' poly sheet over the floor for at least 24 hours. If you see condensation or moisture under the sheet, there is too much moisture seeping through the concrete. Leave the surface unpainted; the moisture will make the paint blister. If the sheet is dry, proceed to Step 2.

2 Spray the concrete slab with water. If the water beads, scrub with a TSP solution (see page 24) to remove any grease; then rinse and test again. If the water still beads, then scrub with a degreaser/concrete cleaner.

When the concrete is clean, etch it with a solution recommended by the manufacturer of your chosen paint. Follow all safety recommendations carefully; the etching liquid is caustic.

Rinse each step thoroughly. Cleaners may react with the paint or interfere with paint adhesion.

3 Apply a concrete paint using a 9-inch roller with a 3/8-inch nap. Let the paint dry and apply the second coat. As with any floor painting project, don't paint yourself into a corner. Plan ahead so that you end painting the area right in front of the door, allowing you to step out of the room.

Painting garage floors

A garage floor, above all, must be practical—but it can also be pretty. New coatings can add color to your garage and function as well as or better than bare concrete. They also make it easier to clean the floor.

There are many different products on the market, each with slightly different instructions. There are clear coatings and colored epoxy coatings: Choose one specifically made for garages.

Good preparation is key to success: Vacuum and clean the existing floor to remove oil stains as recommended by the manufacturer. If there is already a coating or a previous coat of paint is peeling, follow instructions closely. Some concrete must be etched first for good adhesion.

Use only a paint made to withstand hot-tire pickup, such as one-part epoxy acrylic garage floor paint. Two-part epoxy is also available for particularly tough jobs. Don't use porch and floor enamel or ordinary epoxy in a garage. Hot car tires will stick to the coating and can even pull it off of the floor.

1 Use a roller to apply the coating to the garage floor. (Clean the floor as well as possible beforehand, vacuuming up every trace of dust.) Follow the manufacturer's instructions for cleaning and applying.

2 If desired, sprinkle small chips of an accent color in the wet coating. When cured, this finish will provide an attractive and practical surface that will last for many years, even with heavy use.

Helpful paint tips

Latex paint will store indefinitely, provided you meet two conditions: First, don't let it freeze. Second, seal it in an airtight container.

You can meet the first condition by storing the paint in a warm, dry location. To meet the second, either transfer the remaining paint to a new container or clean the rim of all hardened paint that might interfere with the seal.

Even in an airtight container, some air is left inside; the top layer of paint may dry, forming a "skin." Storing latex paint cans upside down keeps skinning to an absolute minimum and prevents rust from forming on the lip. When you're ready to open the can, turn it over, and the now-hardened skin will stay on the bottom of the can.

Storing paint

1 Transfer unused paint to a smaller can. If there is less than 1 quart of paint left, transfer it to a new quart-size can (sold in paint stores).

2 Remove paint from the rim. If you keep the original can, remove all paint inside the rim with a small screwdriver wrapped in cloth.

3 Tap the lid down until it's secure. Use a block of wood and a hammer to make sure it's down.

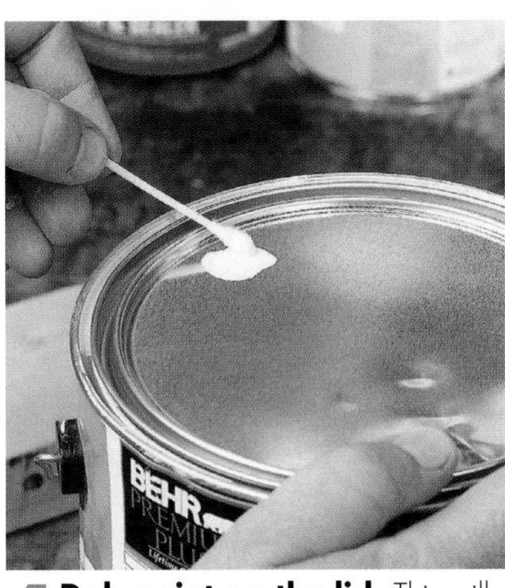

4 Dab paint on the lid. This will help you identify the color later.

5 Write on the lid, using a permanent marker. Include the color, type of paint, and perhaps the date and the room painted in that color.

Disposing of paint and solvents

It's against the law to toss out liquid paints and solvents with the trash. If you have a lot, donate it to a nonprofit organization, such as Habitat for Humanity. Otherwise you must let the paint evaporate and solidify and dispose of it in a manner recommended by your local waste management authority. (See page 68 for more information, or call 800-CLEANUP for information on disposal regulations.) Find a safe place to leave the open cans (not in the house or an enclosed space, and never in a room with a water heater or furnace); leave the lids off until the contents solidify. Speed up evaporation by adding paint hardener, vermiculite, or cat litter to the cans.

◀ ***To dispose of old latex paint,*** *mix it with paint hardener or vemiculite; let it solidify, and take it to the dump.*

◀ ***Place solvent rags in a can,*** *fill the can with water, seal it, and call your waste management authority to inquire about how to dispose of it.*

Jog your memory by taping the color chips used in your room under the cover plate of the main light switch.

Special finishes

Paint is such a versatile medium that it can be made to look like other materials: marble, stone, aged plaster, fabric, wood, wallpaper, or even precious metals. The word *faux* (as in *faux finish)* is French for "false," and it is often used to describe a paint finish that simulates something else.

The techniques aren't necessarily new— some of them have been around for hundreds, even thousands, of years. The Egyptians and Romans were masters of decorative painting. Then, as now, people wanted to create the luxurious effect of more expensive surfaces.

Materials, of course, are another story. Recently developed latex paints, glazes, special tools to create texture, and a wealth of instructional books have now made it easy to try your hand at creating these special effects.

Professional finishers often suggest starting with a semigloss latex base coat; its slightly slick surface lets you manipulate the glaze coat more freely. Also, you can vary the glaze formula, but don't just pour paint into glaze—always measure. Start with four parts glaze to one part paint; a little goes a long way, so don't mix too much. If you run out before completing the job, you'll get an exact match by using the same glaze/paint formula.

The key is to practice, but not on the wall. Instead, paint white poster board or a scrap of drywall with the base coat, and then work with the glaze until you've mastered the specific technique. A word of caution here: no matter how much you'd like to have help, everyone works with a slightly different arm pressure or technique, which will be readily apparent in the completed room. In most cases, it's best for one person to do the entire job.

▲ *The gentle mottling of two or three colors results in walls that appear to have more depth than a solid color. You can use tone-on-tone colors for subtle effects, or gain more contrast by varying the colors.*

▲ *Specialty rollers make mottling two colors of paint on the wall much easier than doing it by hand, but there's also somewhat less control.*

▲ *The bristle length and flexibility of specialized brushes help create striated or stippled finishes by manipulating the glaze on a base coat of paint.*

Stippling

Skill level:	Time to complete:	Materials:	Tools:
★★★☆☆	Experienced 30 min. Handy 45 min. Novice 1 hr.	Semigloss latex paint, latex glaze, blue painter's masking tape	Edging brush, roller, paint bucket and grid, stippling brush, edge stippler, lint-free rags, stepladder

Stippling is a subtractive finish. You apply glaze and then take some of it off—in this case by pouncing the ends of a finely bristled stippling brush up and down in the wet glaze. It's in the same family as sponging off and ragging off but creates a more finely textured surface. It also requires more effort—pouncing the brush over every square inch of the freshly glazed wall.

A stippling brush has long bristles that cover a larger area than the end of a regular brush with each pounce. The specialized brushes can be expensive, but to get the right effect there is really no substitute. An edge stippler, another special-purpose tool, has a narrow design that makes it easier to pounce along the edges of the wall.

Spattering is an additive finish that creates an effect similar to stippling. Dip a paintbrush into the glaze mix and lightly slap the bristles against the palm of your hand, splattering tiny droplets of glaze onto the base coat.

▲ *Stippling produces a finely textured wall that looks almost like leather.*

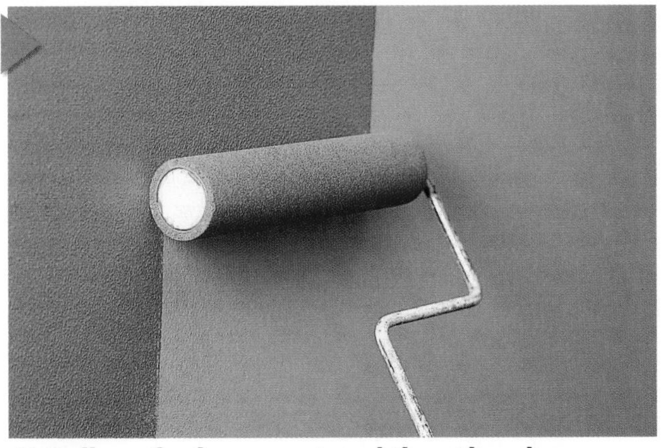

1 Roll on the base coat and then the glaze. Roll on a smooth semigloss base coat and let it dry. Mix a glaze solution in a 4:1 ratio (four parts glaze to one part paint). Cut in and roll a section of wall with the glaze mixture, covering only as much area as you can stipple before the surface starts drying.

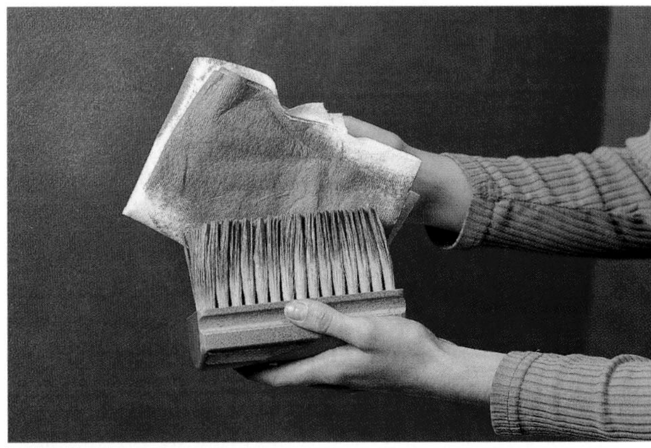

2 Stipple the glaze, working from top to bottom of the wall. Pounce the brush so that you feel a rebound from the bending bristles. The overall effect on the wall should be even, but turn your wrist between each pounce to avoid creating a pattern. Remove excess glaze from the brush as you go with a lint-free rag because a loaded brush won't leave a finely textured surface. Move along the wall, rolling and stippling, section by section.

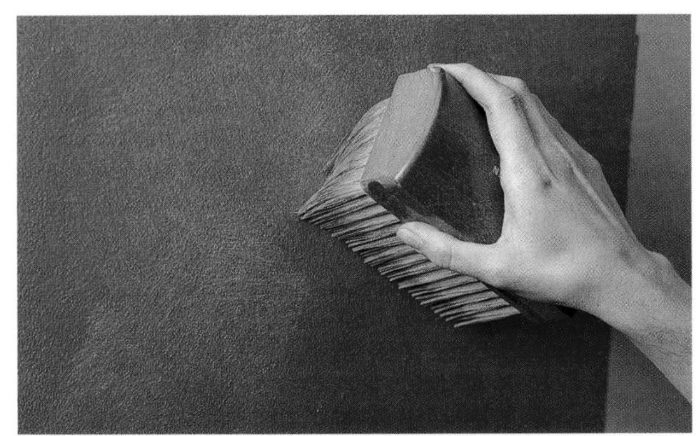

3 Pounce the ends of the stippling-brush bristles against the glazed surface, over and over, while gradually moving the brush. For a lighter finish, use less glaze and apply it in random swirls with a paintbrush before pouncing with the stippling brush.

4 Stipple the corners and edges of the wall with a small, stiff-bristled brush (tape where corners meet, letting the glaze dry before working on the adjacent wall).

Sponging

Skill level:	Time to complete:	Materials:	Tools:
★★★☆☆	Experienced 5 hrs. Handy 6 hrs. Novice 12 hrs.	Semigloss latex paint for base coat, second-color latex paint for glaze coat, latex glaze, disposable latex gloves, blue painter's masking tape	Natural sea sponge, lint-free rags, measuring cup or paint bucket with marked measurements, stepladder, roller and pan for base coat, small plate for glaze

Sponging is a popular way to apply a second color to a wall. After you apply a base coat in the first color, you either apply a glaze mixture in the second color with a sponge *(sponge on),* or roll it on and then *sponge off* the excess. Sponging on makes the base color more dominant; sponging off draws more attention to the second color.

Choose the right sponge

Natural sea sponges work best—random holes and varying textures create more varied patterns than factory-made synthetic sponges. Most paint departments carry sea sponges. You'll need a large one and also a small one (or a torn-off piece) for the edges and corners.

Glaze is the key

Glaze, sold in most paint departments, is a neutral finish with no added pigment—it comes in both latex and oil bases. Mixing paint with glaze slows the drying time and makes the paint translucent. Use latex paint and glaze for easy cleanup with water. A ratio of one part paint to four parts glaze works well, but you might experiment with different ratios or even add metallic or pearlized powders to the mix. Most painters prefer a semigloss base coat.

Practice makes perfect

Paint white poster board or a scrap of drywall with the base coat and let it dry. Mix the glaze and sponge on or off to see how it looks over the base coat—remember that paint changes color when it dries. When you're happy with your technique, it's time to begin on the actual walls.

Picking color combinations

It may be dramatic to use a high-contrast base coat and glaze coat (black against white, for instance). Most people, though, find it easier to live with more subtle gradations in color. When selecting from color chips, pick a base color and then choose a glaze color two or three gradients away from it, or use one of the combinations recommended by the paint company.

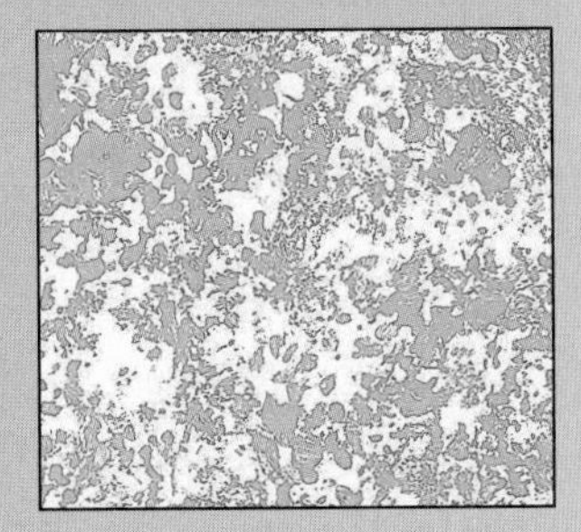

Sponging is easy, once you get the hang of it.
Follow some simple tips to make your finished results look even better.

- **Mask off:** It's almost impossible not to get paint on an adjacent wall when you're sponging an inside corner. Mask the wall with painter's masking tape, do the first wall, and let it dry. Then tape off that wall and sponge the other one.
- **Reach small areas:** Tear off a little piece of sponge and use it for tight spaces and inside corners.
- **Stand back:** Every few minutes, check to see how your job looks from a slight distance. Watch for blotchiness (sponge closer together), too-light or too-dark areas (reload the sponge with paint as necessary, but blot it each time), and missed areas (you can always go back).
- **Vary the pattern:** use different parts of the sponge, but don't twist the sponge while it's touching the wall. A light touch gives the best finish.
- **Don't overwork the paint:** Let each coat dry before doing another. Overworked sponging looks muddy.

Sponging on

1 Start sponging in an upper corner. Dip the sponge in water, squeezing out the excess, and dip it into a small dish of glaze (keep it in your other hand). Rotating the sponge or your wrist slightly each time varies the pattern.

2 Sponge diagonally from the top to the bottom of the wall in a swath as wide as your arm is long.

3 Blot the sponge on a clean rag after you dip it in the dish of glaze (otherwise, the sponge is likely to leave blotches).

4 Step back and look at the results occasionally. If you need to add more glaze, this is the time, but don't work the glaze too much.

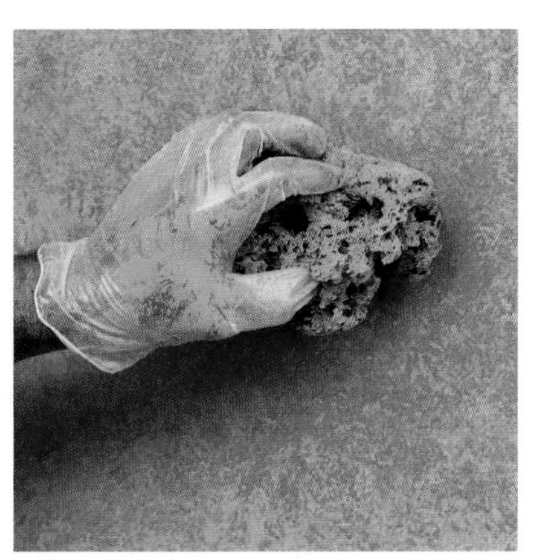

5 If some spots have too much glaze, go back after the glaze dries and sponge on more of the base coat.

6 After the previous glaze color dries, sponge on additional color(s), if you like, for more complexity.

Sponging on and off

The how-to shots on these pages show the *sponging on* technique, which lets the base coat color predominate. The sponging off technique puts more emphasis on the glaze color: roll the entire wall with glaze; then use a clean, damp sponge to remove some of it, rinsing the sponge with clean water as needed. Notice the difference between the samples below: Even using the same colors, results can vary widely.

▲ *Sponging on a diluted glaze shows more of the yellow base coat, which now looks dominant.*

▲ *Sponging off leaves a much denser layer of the greenish glaze, and the yellow base coat recedes.*

Ragging on and ragging off

Skill level:	Time to complete:	Materials:	Tools:
★★★☆☆	Experienced 5 hrs. Handy 8 hrs. Novice 10 hrs.	Semigloss latex paint, second color latex paint, latex glaze	Lint-free rags, roller, rubber bands, measuring cup and container for mixing paint, paint tray

Ragging helps disguise rough or uneven surfaces—though it won't hide bad prep work. Before you apply the base coat, scrape, sand, clean, and prime the walls as you would for any other paint job.

Ragging on adds paint, meaning that a paint-loaded rag rolls over (or is scrunched onto) the base coat, leaving an irregular pattern of paint behind. Roll the rag across a wall that has been base-coated, changing the rag when it becomes too saturated.

Ragging off takes away paint. This look is achieved by rolling a rag through wet glaze to reveal the color underneath. When the base coat is dry, roll the wall with glaze, and then begin the process of removing some of it. Change the rag when it no longer picks up enough glaze.

Painters have come up with various techniques for both ragging on and ragging off. These include:

- Using fabric: Any lint-free fabric works; old T-shirts and cheesecloth are favorites. You can make a roller from the fabric, or just scrunch it up and dab.
- Using a roller: Instead of holding the fabric in your hands, wrap it around a paint roller, fix it with rubber bands, and roll the rag and roller across the wall.
- Using paper: Try using crumpled-up newsprint instead of a rag. It leaves an interesting texture.
- Using special tools: Some paint departments sell ready-made roller covers already covered with wrinkled fabric.

Ragging off

Ragging off (top) leaves more yellow glaze on the wall. Ragging on (at right) shows more of the white base coat. Both create irregular marks.

WORK SMART

MOISTEN THE RAG FIRST

Rolling on: A slightly damp rag absorbs the glaze mix better than a dry rag. Dip the rag briefly in water and then blot it on a towel. Put the roller in the paint tray and load it with paint the same way you would load a regular paint roller. Or, if you're simply holding crumpled-up fabric, dip the fabric in a little dish of paint, scrunch it up as much as you like, and start dabbing it on the wall. Either process is fairly messy; wear gloves, long sleeves, and long pants.

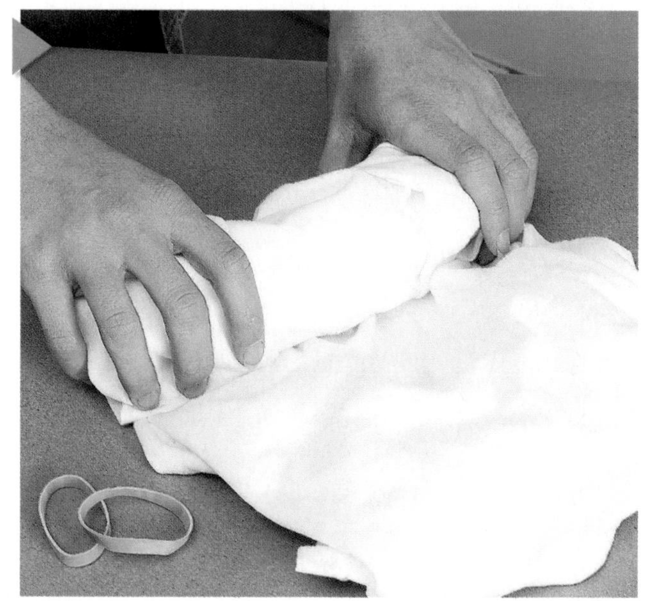

1 Loosely fold (with wrinkles) a 2x2-foot clean cotton cloth, and roll it into a tube 6 to 8 inches long. Slip rubber bands over the ends to maintain its shape.

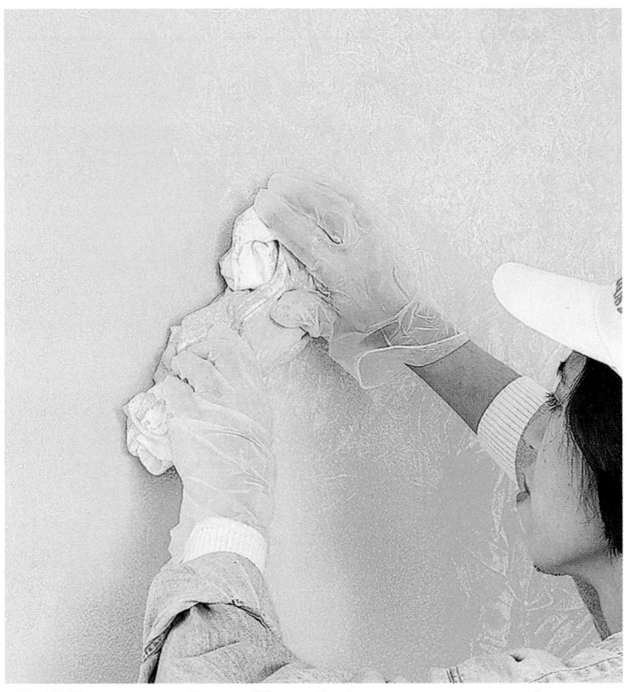

2 When ragging off, roll the rag across the wet glaze randomly until you finish the entire section. Either rinse or replace the rag as it fills up with paint, until you achieve the desired effect on that section.

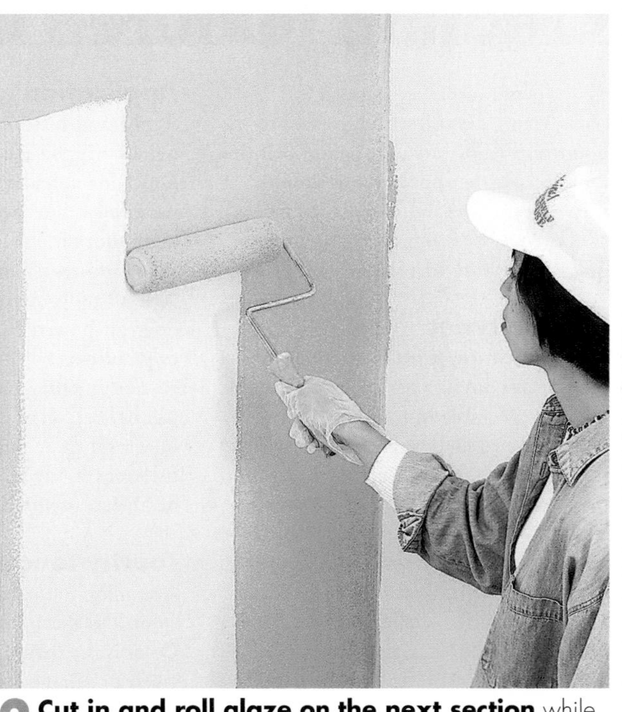

3 Cut in and roll glaze on the next section while the first is still wet so that the sections blend seamlessly. Rag off the glaze as before.

On or off—what's the difference?

Two coats—paint plus glaze—yet the results can look entirely different depending on whether you are taking the glaze off with a crumpled rag, or putting it on. It's hard to tell which you've done by looking at the wall; the only reason it's important is to help you control how the color appears.

If you want the base coat to predominate, you'll want to rag on: You can dab on as much or as little glaze as you like. If you're ragging off, you roll on solid coats of both the paint and the glaze—then it's hard to take off enough glaze for the base coat to be revealed as the main color. This variance is why it's so important to experiment on either the wall (before it's painted) or on pieces of posterboard prior to tackling the real job.

Ragging off leaves a much denser layer of the glaze color.

Ragging on leaves a lot of the base coat still exposed.

Ragging on

Ragging on is the exact opposite of ragging off because you're using the rag to apply, not remove, the glaze. Those who like to work quickly might prefer to use a roller fitted with a covering of wrinkled cloth (buy this, or make your own). Simply dip it in the glaze and start rolling, but be careful not to overwork the glaze enough to make it look solid. For more control, crumple up a rag, dip it in the glaze, and dab it on the wall with a delicate touch. You can obtain interesting effects by combining glazes in several colors, either letting one dry before using the other or just combining them as you go. That's the fun of working with glazes—the final look is up to you.

Creating textured effects

Textured finishes are popular for covering drywall without spending hours on a labor-intensive perfect painting job. Because the application is simple, it is less expensive, but repairs can be tricky. Textured finishes are also more difficult to clean than smooth ones.

Texture types

- Sand-texture paint is interior latex paint that contains perlite, a sandlike additive available in fine, medium, and coarse particle sizes. You can purchase the additive separately, or buy premixed paint in 1- and 5-gallon sizes.
- Orange peel is a slightly pebbly finish without the sharpness of sand. Apply it over primer with a spray gun, seal it with white-pigmented shellac primer, and paint it with a top coat that has a little gloss. It's a good choice for the bath or kitchen because it is durable and can also be scrubbed.
- Knockdown is a two-step process. A rough ⅛-inch coating is sprayed on, and a helper follows 10 to 15 minutes later "knocking down" the high points with a mason's trowel. The resulting finish looks like old-world hand-finished plaster. This look is popular in living rooms, bedrooms, and hallways, especially in the Southwest.
- Acoustic (also called popcorn) is used only on ceilings. It is either sprayed on or applied with a looped texture roller.

Application tools

Apply sand-texture paint with a thick-napped roller. For orange peel, knockdown, and acoustic finishes, you can use a roller, but these finishes are most often shot onto a primed surface from a spray gun with an attached hopper. (Use a hand-powered spray texture pump or an air-powered spray texture gun, rented or purchased.)

For touching up small areas (10 square feet or less), all of the texture types come in aerosol spray cans. When released, these textures get out of hand very easily; protect nearby areas with dropcloths.

Touchy touch-ups

A seamless job requires matching texture, color, and sheen of the original finish. Color is the main problem, especially when a ceiling has been exposed to cigarette smoke.

Apply a stain-blocking primer, followed by quality interior latex paint. The primer blocks smoke and water stains and provides maximum adhesion, while the top coat provides uniform color and sheen.

Acoustic (popcorn) texture is heavy and loses adhesion when wet by latex paint; it can slide or even fall off of the ceiling. The solution: prime the entire ceiling with white-pigmented shellac, then repair it with a spray can. When the repair dries, prime it too. The dried shellac provides a waterproof surface that is ready to paint.

Texture types

Sand

Orange Peel

Knockdown

Acoustic (popcorn)

BUYER'S GUIDE

USE THE RIGHT ROLLER FOR ACOUSTIC CEILINGS

Acoustic ceilings require special rollers that allow the paint to fill in properly. Depending on the thickness of the texture, you'll need to use a thick-napped or split-foam roller. Ask the experts at your home center or paint store for information.

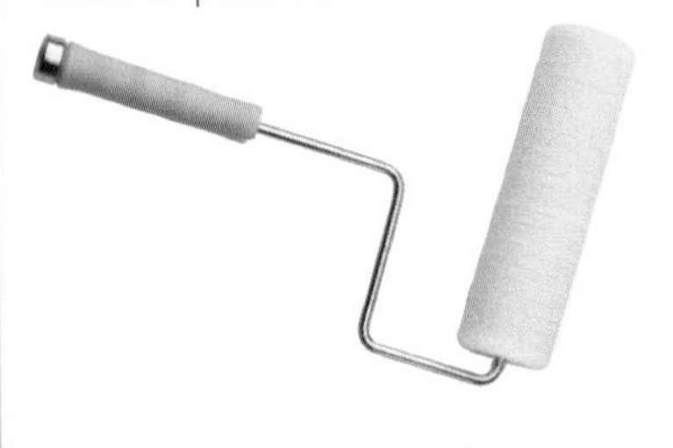

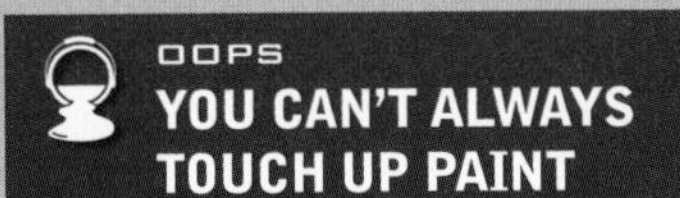

OOPS

YOU CAN'T ALWAYS TOUCH UP PAINT

Did you touch up the paint and the result is worse than the problem? Paint cures and changes color over time. When it has been on the wall a long time, it no longer matches paint left in the can. Smoke, grime, or general wear and tear may mean a wall-to-wall paint job is the only way to get a touch-up that actually works. In out-of-the-way spots not liable to be noticed, make small touch-ups with an artist's brush dipped in paint.

WORK SMART

PROBLEM POPCORN

Many people dislike acoustic (popcorn) ceilings. They can be removed, but it involves a bit of work. Basically, you take advantage of the fact that the texture loosens when moistened. Working with a spray bottle of water, moisten about a 3-foot-square area, let the water soak in, and carefully scrape away the offending texture with an 8- to 10-inch-wide drywall knife. Important: Many older acoustic ceilings contain asbestos, which was outlawed in 1978 but still showed up later if builders used old supplies. Take samples and send them to a lab that tests for asbestos (look in the phone directory). If you do have asbestos, either leave it in place or hire an abatement expert.

Painting exteriors

Skill level:	Time to complete:	Materials:	Tools:
★★★☆☆	Experienced Variable Handy Variable Novice Variable	TSP/bleach solution (or a phosphate-free cleaner), wood filler, glazing compound, caulk, tape, oil-base primer	Putty knife, broad knife, grinder, sander, wire brush, broom, caulking gun, hammer, screwdriver, garden hose, garbage bags or drop cloths or tarps, paintbrush

Good preparation—washing the surfaces, scraping off bad paint, and patching rot or damage—is undoubtedly the most important step in exterior painting.

Until recently there were only two ways to get paint off your siding: scrapers and disk sanders; both involved a lot of work. If paint on your siding is in relatively good condition, a scraper may still be the best bet.

If the paint is rough, though, new tools help solve the problem. One is a sander with a housing that fits around the disk. The housing rides on the surface you're sanding, allowing you to sand, but not deep enough to damage the surface.

The other tools mount on a power drill and also have carbide sandpaper, either on a drum or on flaps that spin at high speed to remove the paint.

Painting a house is a lot of work, so unless you're changing colors, break the job down into a series of smaller projects—one side every few months or a year, perhaps, then the trim, and then some time off before you start again.

Preparation

1 Cover exterior HVAC units and vents with plastic and tape, after first turning off the air-conditioning and exhaust fans. Trim or tie back limbs or bushes that touch the house, covering all plants in the work area with plastic garbage bags, drop cloths,or tarps.

2 Remove shutters and hardware and close storm windows. Repair the siding and trim as necessary and fill rotted or insect-damaged areas with exterior-grade wood filler or a two-part epoxy filler.

SAFETY ALERT

STARTLING DISCOVERY

Beware of hidden bee and animal nests when working at high elevations. Sudden surprises can cause serious injuries from falls. Many painters routinely keep a can of bee and hornet spray on hand when they paint outside; it can shoot a stream of spray into nests up to 20 feet away. One type of bee, called the carpenter bee, makes its nest in wood, entering through the ½-inch-wide round holes it drills. Be on the lookout for such holes, especially in soffits and the lip of fascia boards, and under decks.

Painting exteriors (continued)

3 Reglaze the windows as needed. If the old glazing is cracked and falling out, pry out the old putty with a chisel or putty knife and apply new glazing. When you remove the old putty, be careful not to exert so much pressure that you break the glass.

4 Clean the siding and trim by washing it with a TSP (trisodium phosphate) and bleach solution or a phosphate-free TSP substitute. Apply it with a scrub brush in 8×8' sections and let the solution work, without any more scrubbing on your part.

5 Rinse the entire house with a garden hose and water until the runoff water is clear and the solution is completely gone; residue will keep the paint from adhering. Let the siding and trim dry completely, usually about two days, before painting.

6 While cleaning, don't forget to clean the soffits and the area under the porch roof. These are nearly impossible to sand. Power wash them with TSP/bleach solution instead. Set the spray to remove the loose paint, but don't set it so hard that you cause damage to the wood.

7 Remove loose paint with a tool made for the job. Scrape off paint in areas a sander won't reach. If sanding, start with a coarse (16-, 24-, or 36-grit) disc. Sand the bottom edges of the siding even if the surface seems sound. A sander cuts through paint quickly—avoid damaging the siding. When you're done, resand with a 60-grit disc to remove swirl marks that may be visible under paint.

8 Remove dust from the sanded areas and also areas around them with a paintbrush. Prime all bare areas with an oil-base primer made by the manufacturer of the paint you'll use (so it will be compatible). Oil-base primer is the most durable, and contrary to prevailing wisdom, you can apply latex paint over it.

TOOL TIP
LADDER SAFETY

Working with tall ladders can be tricky and dangerous unless you follow a few guidelines. Whatever the height of the ladder, its feet should be placed on the ground at a distance one-fourth of that height (an 8-foot ladder should have its feet 2 feet away from the house, for instance).

Make sure the legs are on a level surface; on uneven surfaces, use wood shims or blocks to level them.

If the surface slopes away from the house, place a 2×4 across the base of the ladder and drive two 2×4 stakes into the ground to secure the ladder base.

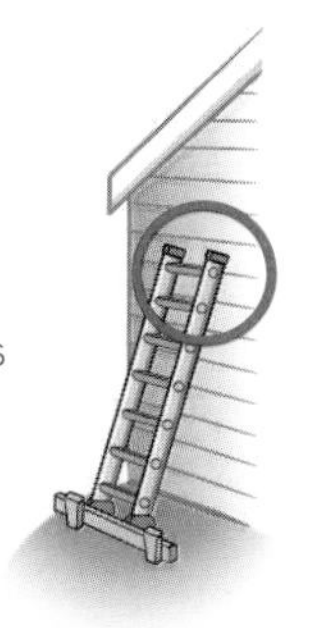

Use ladder boots (see Step 1, page 61) or wrap cloth around the tops of the ladder legs to keep them from slipping or making dents in the siding.

Don't take a chance on being injured—be careful and ask for help when you need it.

SAFETY ALERT
HANDLING A LADDER

Have a helper stand at the end of the ladder nearest the house, with a foot on each leg to brace it. Grab the other end, lift the ladder up over your head, and hold it by a rung.

Take a step forward, moving your hand to the next rung as you do. Continue walking toward your helper, moving your hands and body forward one rung at a time.

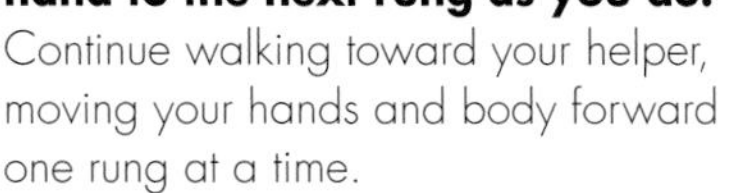

When you get close enough, have the helper grab a rung too so that you are both holding the ladder as it approaches vertical.

Once the ladder is vertical, trade roles with your helper. You become the anchor, placing your feet against the base of the ladder.

Have the helper hold the ladder and slowly back up, until it is leaning against the house. Make sure both feet are level and secure. Extend the ladder to the desired height by holding it just away from the house and using the rope to pull the extension ladder up.

Reverse the process to take the ladder down. Put your feet against the base of the ladder as an anchor. Have your helper walk the ladder back toward you. Once it is vertical, let your helper act as the anchor while you walk backward to lower the ladder.

Painting exteriors (continued)

Basic techniques

After washing, wait until the surface is dry and make sure there is no rain in the forecast. Apply primer to any bare siding. Wood contains resins that bleed through water-base paints, so use an oil-base primer. Let the primer dry as long as the manufacturer recommends.

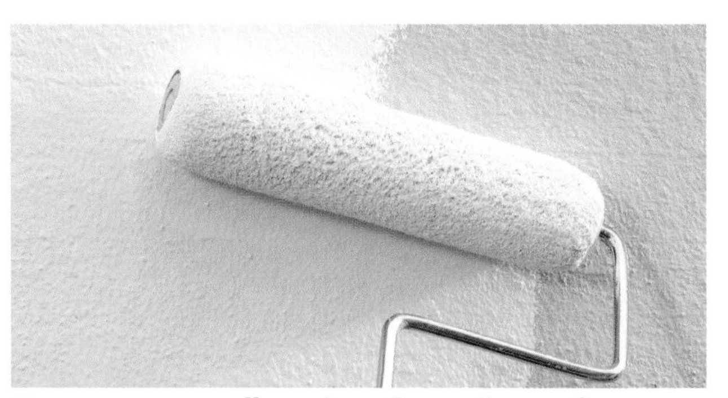

On masonry walls, prime the entire surface. Masonry surfaces can usually be painted with a roller. For brick walls, get one with a long nap—up to 1 inch thick—so paint can get into all the nooks and crannies.

Paint the roof trim and soffits first if they will be a different color from the walls. This keeps trim paint from dripping onto newly painted walls.

Mask the siding and paint the trim. Use a corner roller or trim brush to cut in these areas.

TOOL TIP
SPRAY GUNS

A spray gun speeds up a paint job immensely. When painting an entire house, price shouldn't be the deciding factor. You'll probably find that the gun the pros use is best—and expensive. Think about renting good equipment rather then buying inexpensive, mediocre equipment. A good spray gun is comfortable to hold, doesn't clog, and puts out enough paint for the job. The shape of the mist coming out of the gun, called the pattern, is important too—you need to be able to adjust it easily. Talk to your dealer about how to get the right pattern.

Select the right caulk

Caulk Type	General Advantages	General Limitations
Acrylic or siliconized acrylic	• Good for most exteriors • Fully paintable • Easy to use	• Buy the kind that lasts longest
Butyl rubber	• Not recommended	• Shrinks, cracks, breaks • Cleans up with solvent • Hard to use
Elastomeric	• Flexible • Fully paintable • Cleans up with water • Bridges gaps to ½-inch wide	• Buy the kind that lasts longest
Latex	• Inexpensive	• Hardens and cracks • Not recommended for exteriors
Polyurethane	• Paintable • Extremely flexible • Adheres to almost any surface	• Hard to apply neatly • Cleans up with mineral spirits • More expensive
Silicone	• Adheres best • Lasts longest	• Not paintable • Hard to correct mistakes

Painting exterior walls

Skill level:	Time to complete:	Materials:	Tools:
★★★☆☆	Experienced Variable Handy Variable Novice Variable	Exterior house paint, exterior trim paint, paintable caulk, disposable latex gloves	Paintbrush, trim brush, foam pad, extension ladder, stepladder, edge roller, wire brush, 2-inch putty knife, wide putty knife, soft-bristled brush

Painting exterior walls is more complex than painting interior walls in some respects. Various construction materials require different equipment and painting techniques. You're apt to be working higher from the ground as well. On the plus side, a slight mistake on the second floor isn't nearly as obvious as one inside at eye level.

Siding material ranges from board-and-batten, cedar lap, cement board, masonite, and wood shakes to stucco and masonry. But basics are basics and, whatever you're painting, you'll follow the principles discussed here.

Use quality ladders and scaffolds in proper working condition to ensure a smooth and safe job. You are quite literally trusting your life to this equipment, so buy or rent the best available.

1 Start at the peak of the roof with the ladder centered on the wall. Paint three or four pieces of siding, working from one eave across to the other. Notice the ladder boots that fit over the ladder tops to protect the siding and prevent the ladder from slipping. These cost only a few dollars and are available in most paint departments. (See the ladder precautions on page 59.)

2 Move the ladder down a couple of rungs, then work your way across the top of the wall again. Be very careful not to overreach—tipping the ladder over or falling off can cause serious injury.

3 Lower the ladder again, and move it over to one side of the house. Paint two or three boards, starting on the side, working across the top of the ladder, and painting as much as you can reach comfortably on the other side. Lefties generally like to start on the left; right-handed painters generally like to start on the right.

4 Move the ladder so you can reach the newly painted block of siding. Avoid lap marks by repainting the edges of the last area you painted as you start each stroke. Start at the side and paint across the top of the ladder to the other side.

Repeat the process, painting only those areas you can reach before moving or lowering the ladder. Repeat until you've painted the entire side.

Painting exterior walls (continued)

Painting stucco

1 Scrub around windows and doors with water and a wire brush, and then wash the rest of the surface with a garden hose. Clean away loose paint with a wire brush and a putty knife (if the surface is smooth enough to use one).

2 Roll on acrylic-latex masonry primer and check for cracks or rust marks on the stucco. When the primer is dry, patch the cracks with vinyl concrete patch or elastomeric (synthetic rubber) stucco patch, applying it with a flexible 2-inch putty knife. While the patch is still wet, dip a wider knife in some water and skim over the face of the stucco to remove excess patch material and smooth it. Caulk narrower cracks with concrete repair caulk.

3 After the patch dries, spot prime the repairs, and also any discoloration. Roll on a finish coat of acrylic-latex paint (read the label carefully and use only paint that is specifically formulated for stucco).

Painting board-and-batten

1 Pressure wash the walls, staying away from windows and doors so water won't leak through and stain the inside surfaces. Clean around doors and windows by scrubbing with a scrub brush. Once the wood is dry (up to 2 days), caulk along the space between the batten and board with a 20- or 30-year paintable caulk. Wet your finger and smooth the caulk, or put on disposable gloves before wetting your finger and smoothing it.

2 Prime with a latex or oil primer, tinted to match the finish coat. Prime the edges of the horizontal board above the siding (called the frieze) and the bottom kick board too, if you have these. Working from the top down, brush primer on the face and edges of the battens and also the sides of the boards.

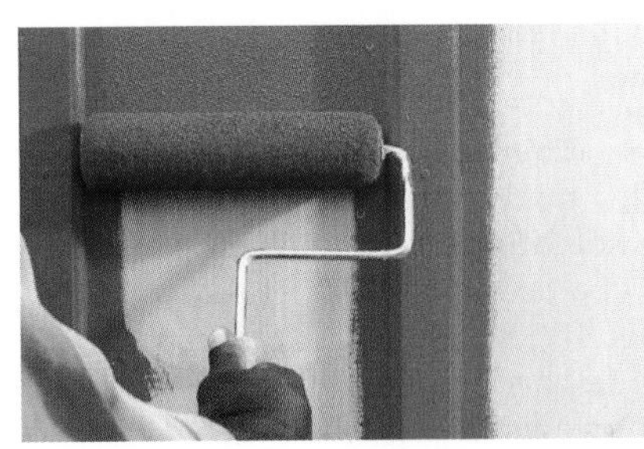

3 Roll primer onto the face of the first board, working from the top down and across the building. Let the primer dry, and apply a top coat of cover acrylic-latex in the same order.

WORK SMART

PAINT PADS

If you're painting clapboard siding, check into using handy painting pads. Easier to wield than a brush, a pad can cover the entire width of the siding in one pass. Some pads are even shaped to paint corners. They do require frequent reloading with paint.

Painting vinyl or aluminum siding

1 Examine the siding and replace any pieces that are damaged or cracked. Pressure-wash the siding, but stay away from windows and doors where water can leak through and stain the inside walls. Clean around doors and windows with a soft-bristled scrub brush.

2 Brush on an acrylic-latex stain-blocking primer. (Read the label before buying, and use only one that specifically states it is suitable for aluminum or vinyl—whichever surface you're painting.)

3 When the primer has dried, apply an acrylic-latex top coat—again, one designed for the surface you're painting. Don't select a color darker than the original; it will absorb more heat and may even cause the siding to warp.

Painting concrete

1 Pressure-wash the surface and scrape off any flaking paint or raised areas with a putty knife.

2 Painted concrete sometimes shows shiny and dull spots if the right primer isn't used. Prime the entire wall with an acrylic-latex stain-blocking primer specifically designed for masonry. (Some masonry paints double as primers, but these usually leave shiny spots. Stick with a stain-blocking primer.)

3 Repair any cracks with a specially formulated masonry repair caulk. Work the caulk in with a damp finger or rag, removing the excess with a damp sponge. When the caulk dries, roll on acrylic-latex masonry paint. This paint dries to the touch in 24 hours but may take up to 30 days to fully cure.

Priming and painting trim

Skill level:	Time to complete:	Materials:	Tools:
★★★☆☆	Experienced Variable. Handy Variable. Novice Variable.	Exterior trim paint, appropriate primer for the surface	4" brush, 2" tapered sash brush, corner roller, wire brush (optional)

House trim—roof trim, porches, railings, doors, and windows—must withstand temperature extremes and all types of moisture. For it to survive and still look attractive, the key is in preparation. When you've already repaired, scraped, and cleaned, and the trim is ready to paint, give it a final once-over by wiping off dust immediately before applying primer.

When the primer is thoroughly dry, paint the trim— as soon as possible, and no later than three days after priming. The longer you wait to paint, the greater the chance for dirt and airborne chemical deposits to affect the surface.

Trim paint is formulated to withstand exposure and is exceptionally durable. It is available in most popular finishes and can be custom blended to match your colors.

▲ ***Select the right primer.*** *Most all-purpose primers can be used on any surface. For best results on metal gutters or railings, use a metal primer with a rust inhibitor. Masonry primers are specially formulated to adhere to chalky surfaces.*

▲ ***Remove loose paint from metal railing and trim with a wire brush.*** *If you remove rust from iron or steel, you'll need to prime the surface right away to prevent further rusting. Finish with an enamel paint to ensure a long-lasting, protective coating.*

▲ ***Prime and paint wooden steps and porch floors after everything else has been painted.*** *This prevents having to touch up drips on the horizontal surfaces. Use only a specially formulated enamel floor paint (one suited to a high volume of traffic), and add an emulsifying bonder to the first coat to help the paint stick to chalky, powdery surfaces. You won't need the bonder in subsequent coats.*

▲ ***After painting the walls and trim, you may wish to prime and paint the foundation walls.*** *Use the same color as the siding or choose an accent color. Paint areas around the windows and doors first with a sash brush, then paint broader areas with a 4-inch brush, working paint into the mortar lines.*

Painting soffits and fascia

1 Paint soffits and fascia first; this keeps paint drips from ruining prior work on the siding. Paint the overhang (soffit) first and then work your way onto the edges facing the soffit. If the soffit is supported by brackets (corbels), paint them once you've painted all the panels (see inset).

2 After the soffit and trim have been painted, paint any moldings below the soffit.

3 Paint the surface above the soffit, called the fascia, next. If there is a cornice molding, paint both it and the fascia as you move along the wall.

Painting jambs, casings, and trim

1 Mask the siding where it runs into the casing; mask the floors underneath the doors. Wedge the doors and windows open so they'll stay put while you paint them; see painting instructions on page 34 for doors and pages 66–67 for windows.

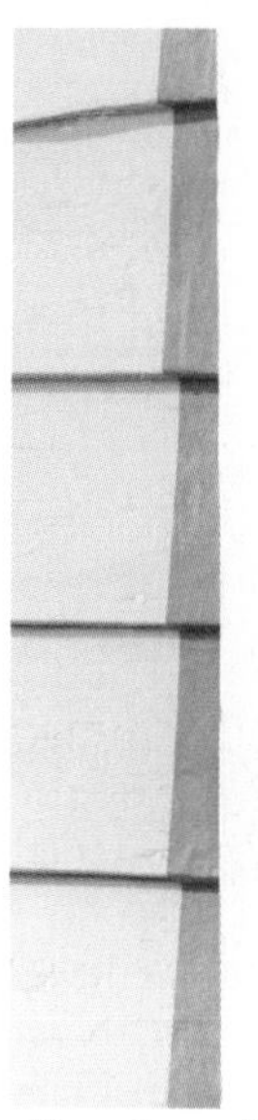

2 After the door or window is dry, paint the jamb. Start at the top on the inside, using a beveled sash brush. After the top, move to the inside edge (hinge side on doors and casement windows), saving the outside edge for last.

3 Paint the casings while the jambs are still wet. Feather the paint into the mitered joints; then angle your brush to match the miter line, and paint right up to it. Paint thresholds after the jambs and casings have dried.

Painting windows

Skill level:	Time to complete:	Materials:	Tools:
★★★☆☆	Experienced 20 min. Handy 35 min. Novice 1 hr.	TSP, primer, trim paint, glazing putty, linseed oil, painter's masking tape (optional)	Tapered sash brush, putty knife, window scraper or single-edge razor blade

Windows seem to get the worst of weather. They're expected to hold up in rain, wind, blinding sun, and hot humid weather followed in some parts of the country by snow and cold winters with sub-zero temperatures.

It's no wonder they often have flakes, chipping paint, broken putty, rotten wood, and dirt, dirt, dirt.

If it's time to repaint your windows, prep work is a must. Wash everything down with TSP (see page 24). Scrape off any loose paint, sand the rest, then prime any bare wood.

Should you use masking tape? Putting masking tape along the line between the frame and glass eliminates the need to be overly neat with the brush, but this may involve more time than it's worth. Many painters just try to be careful, then scrape off extra paint with a razor blade.

Open and close the window several times as the paint dries. This prevents the moving parts from forming a bond and keeps you from dealing with a window that won't open because it's painted shut.

It's a rare house that doesn't have at least one window painted shut, but there are several ways to free them. Sometimes a sharp rap on the frame with a rubber mallet or the heel of your hand is all it takes (don't hit the glass). If not, work around the seam between the sash and frame with either a utility knife or a special sash saw (see page 36). And before you get too frustrated, remember every window has two sides—yours could be painted shut on either side.

Parts of a basic double-hung window

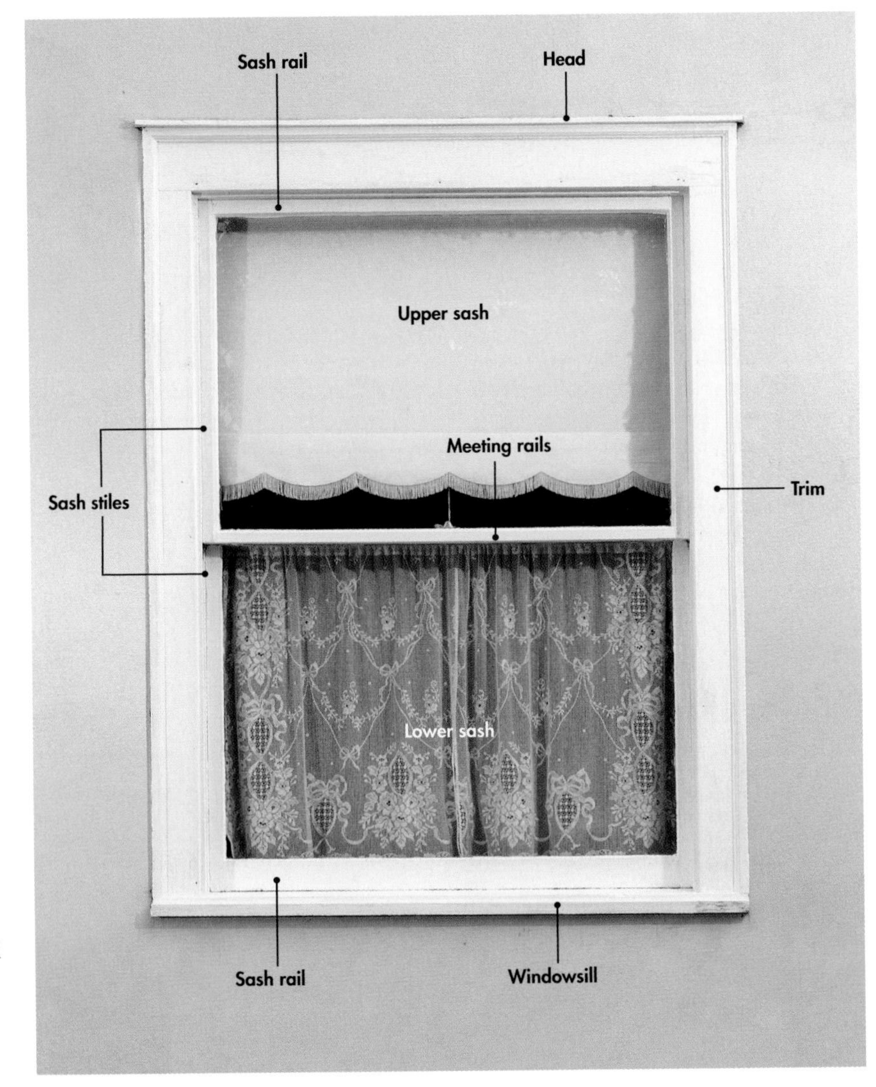

- **Upper sash:** upper frame of a double-hung window.
- **Lower sash:** lower frame of a double-hung window.
- **Sash rails:** horizontal pieces of the frame forming the sash.
- **Sash stiles:** vertical pieces of the frame forming the sash.
- **Meeting rails:** rails that overlap each other in the middle of the window.
- **Windowsill:** piece of wood, metal, or plastic at the bottom of the window. Usually slanted so water drains away from the house.
- **Trim:** wood, metal, or plastic that frames the outside of the window.
- **Head:** piece of wood, metal, or plastic at the top of the window.

1 Scrape any loose putty around the window panes, brushing the sash clean. To help new putty stick and last longer, brush the newly exposed wood with linseed oil, and let it soak in. Roll some putty between your hands, and press it into the bare spots. Smooth it with a putty knife to create an angled surface. Remove small imperfections by running a damp finger along the putty.

2 Let the putty dry for about a week. Then open the window and pull the top down until it's about 3 inches from the sill. Push the bottom sash up until it's about 3 inches from the top of the window frame.

3 Paint all the parts of the sash you can reach. Start with the pieces in the grid (called *muntins)* if there are any. Then paint horizontal pieces followed by vertical for the neatest job.

4 Put the sashes back into their regular positions but leave them slightly open, with about a 1-inch gap at the top and bottom. Paint the parts of the sash you were unable to reach in Step 2. Move the sashes occasionally as the paint dries to keep them from sticking.

5 Paint the stops and jambs. Don't paint the tracks where the windows travel—any paint buildup could cause the windows to jam.

6 Paint the window casing. Mask the siding unless you plan to paint it as well.

Paint cleanup and disposal

Paint ingredients may be good for the wall, but they're often bad for water, plants, and animals. Recent studies show paint's toxic effects, so clean-up methods have changed. The basic process is the same—clean up latex paint with water and alkyd paint with mineral spirits. The new goal is to use as little of either as possible, and to dispose of the used liquids wisely. Since requirements may vary, check with local authorities to find out which disposal methods are approved in your area.

Cleaning equipment

- Retrieve paint from rollers, brushes, and trays, and put it back into the paint can. Use a painter's 5-in-1 tool to scrape the other painting tools.
- Use as little water or mineral spirits as possible, and don't let them go down a drain. They pollute the water; even nontoxic solids can affect aquatic life.
- When cleaning more than one roller tray, reuse water or mineral spirits from the first tray in the other tray.
- Place the water or mineral spirits used for cleaning into a covered bucket, and let the solids settle. The next step depends on whether the paint is latex or alkyd.

Cleaning up latex

- Use a paint hardner to convert any unused liquid paint to a solid, or
- Place the paint solids in a can and let evaporate until hard (add kitty litter to speed up the process).
- Consult your local waste disposal regulations for disposal of the solids.

Cleaning up alkyd

- Once the solids settle, pour the liquids into a sealable container and cap it.
- You will be able to reuse the liquids the next time you need to clean up alkyd-covered brushes, rollers, and pans.
- Seal the solid wastes in a can and put the can out for a trash disposal service that will take it to a licensed landfill.
- If the liquids are too old or too paint-laden to use again, do *not* dump them on the ground or pour them down the drain. Do *not* let the solvents evaporate and throw out the remaining solids. Solvents are prime sources of volatile organic compounds and are strictly regulated in most areas. Instead take the solvents to a household hazardous waste disposal site for proper disposal.

1 Brush out as much of the paint as you can on a newspaper or other porous, disposable surface.

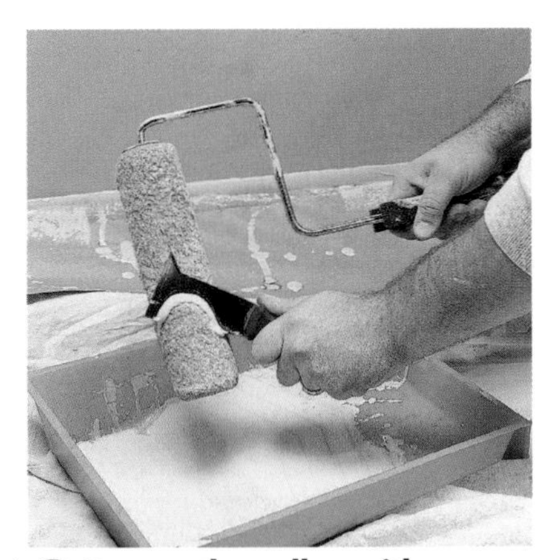

2 Scrape the roller with a 5-in-1 tool to remove as much excess paint as possible.

Safe cleaning of oil-base (alkyd) paint

Use this process to clean brushes; it's environmentally friendly and cuts down on the amount of solvent used.

Let the solids settle at the bottom of the cans. Pour the water or thinner into clean cans for reuse. When solids have dried, discard them; check with local authorities to see how to dispose of alkyd solids.

1 Fill three cans with a couple of inches of water (for latex paints) or paint thinner (for oil-base paints).

2 In the first can, clean the brush by swishing it around to remove most of the paint. Blot the brush on newspaper.

3 Repeat the process in can #2, and then again in can #3.

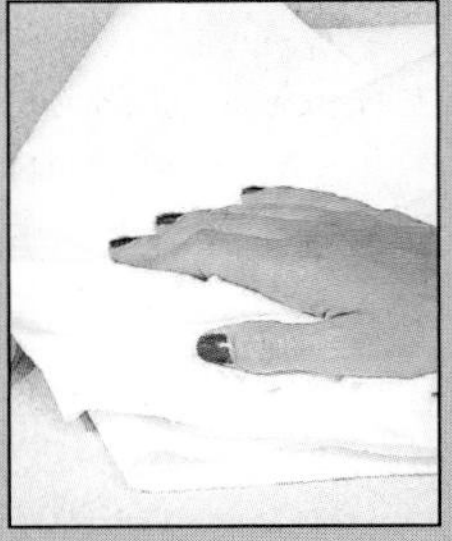

4 Dry the brush by slapping the ferrule on the heel of your hand, then blot the bristles with newspaper or paper towels. Hang the brush vertically to dry; store in the original cardboard holder to keep its shape.

Wallpaper basics

Wallpaper establishes the basic style of a room more than any other single element, including paint, even before you have furniture. Cottage-style—use one with tiny flowers or checks. Contemporary—choose a textured paper or a stylized geometric. If you're not sure what you want and you're looking for inspiration, just flip through some wallpaper sample books.

Wallpaper outlets have hundreds of books to select from, all organized by categories. After a few minutes of browsing, you may find that you gravitate toward a certain look. For more complex arrangements the books show various combinations that work well together, such as two papers divided by a chair-rail border, or maybe a border along the ceiling.

Fashions in wallpaper colors and textures change over the years, and one of the quickest ways to refresh your home is to replace the paper. A lot of the styles you'll find today are vinyl-coated to make the paper easier to clean and better able to resist scrapes and tears. It also lasts longer and is easier to install than the easily damaged paper available in the past.

Even historically accurate designs are available in vinyl-coated paper, although for complete accuracy, you can special order true paper. (This is more expensive and can be a challenge to hang.)

For more depth and texture on the walls, consider using embossed paper, grasscloth, or wallcovering in other natural fibers; installing them is almost the same as installing regular papers.

Stores have hundreds of wallpaper sample books. Most outlets will allow you to borrow several books at a time, taking them home to help you choose.

Collect paint and fabric samples and use them to help you select suitable wallpaper. Designers make sample books with all the colors and textures in each room to aid them in making decisions.

Tape samples of wallpaper to the wall and look at them under different lighting conditions. You'll probably live with the paper for many years, so take time now to be sure you're making the right choice.

BUYER'S GUIDE

SOME WALLS NEED A LINER

Extremely rough walls—concrete block or those made of grooved paneling, for instance—need to be lined before you paper them. The liner evens out the surface differences so they aren't visible on the finished wall. A liner might also take the place of extensive repairs on plaster walls—and be less expensive, too.

Wallpaper liner is made of a dense, non-woven material that goes on damp but shrinks as it dries, creating an extremely taut surface that serves as a firm base for a layer of regular wallpaper. Follow the manufacturer's instructions for installing it. In most cases, you should plan to install the liner horizontally across each wall; this keeps seams from occurring under the regular wallpaper seams. For more information, see page 74.

Fewer layers are better

Yes, you can paper over old wallpaper, but it's not always a good idea. A previously papered surface is not as firm as the wall itself, and new paper might even pull the old paper off. (You never know what kind of paste was used; very old paper may even have flour paste underneath it.) Old seams can look unsightly under the new paper, especially if they're crooked or lapped. For best results, remove the old paper before you spend time and money applying more. New liquid wallpaper removers work extremely well in most cases (see pages 28–29 for instructions).

Wallpaper basics (continued)

Preparation

Any wallpaper you put up will never look better than the wall it's covering. Every bump, dimple, ding, dent, and crack will still be there and will still be visible, even if only slightly. Paper shrinks as it dries, clinging to the wall as much as it covers it.

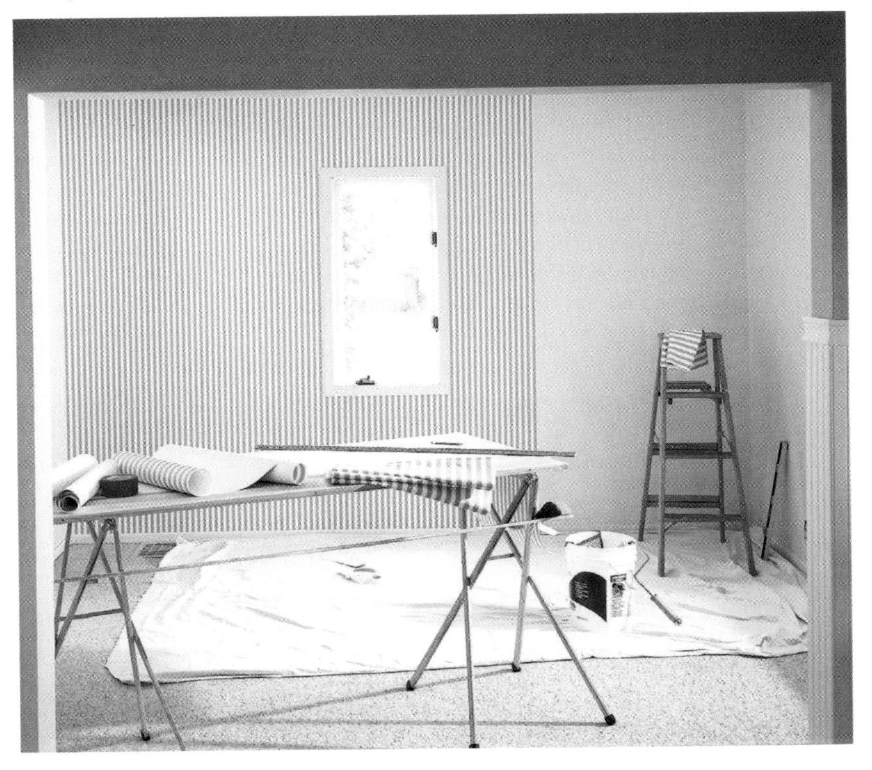

Clean and repair

After removing the old paper, clean the wall with TSP solution (see page 24). Dirt, grease, and grime keep paper from adhering. When you're done washing, rinse with clean water until the water runs clear.

Fill small cracks with lightweight spackling compound. Buy it premixed, push the compound in place with a putty knife, and then run the knife over it so that the repair is flush with the wall. If the patch shrinks as it dries, repeat until the crack disappears.

Fill larger cracks and holes with joint compound. Apply with a wide-blade putty knife, filling the hole entirely (it may take several layers; let each one dry before recoating with another layer).

For big holes or loose plaster, you'll need more extensive repairs. On drywall, cut away the damaged area and patch the hole as described on page 96. Plaster-patching compound works well for patching plaster over lath (see pages 100–101), but it will probably take a couple of applications. Patching large areas can be a nuisance, but it's not nearly as annoying as having the wall crumble behind your carefully hung wallpaper.

When patches are dry, lightly sand them so they are smooth and level with the wall. Wipe the surfaces down with a slightly damp sponge.

Seal, prime, and size

This used to be a three-step job until paint companies combined the three products into one. Sealer keeps water, smoke, and other stains from showing through the paper. Primer provides a smooth surface for the paper to cling to. Sizing is thin paste that seals the wall's pores to prevent moisture from soaking into the plaster; it provides extra adhesion. Primer/sealer can be clear or tinted to match the wallpaper backgound color.

When putting up the paper, select an appropriate paste. For a border, or if you're applying paper to paper, you'll need a heavy-duty paste. Even on prepasted paper, brush a paste activator on the back. It's neater than soaking, makes manipulating the paper easy, and provides a better bond.

Tips from the pros

For the best wallpapering results, follow these guidelines from experienced paperhangers.

- Ignore the advice about soaking prepasted papers in water; use a paste activator instead. If you don't, the wallpaper won't bond well and it could fall down later.
- Before beginning, mark the top of each strip (especially important to do when you're using grasscloth or another no-match pattern). Apply each strip from the top down.
- To save paper, select a pattern with either no repeat or a small repeat. The repeat, or drop, is listed in wallpaper books and on the roll. Papers with a large repeat require the adjacent strip to slide several inches to create a perfect match at the seams. The wasted paper adds up over the course of a whole room.
- For clean, straight cuts, use a sharp blade and replace it often. Some pros advocate changing to a new blade after every cut. Pros often use single-edge razor blades in special handles.
- Wallpaper colors vary slightly from one dye-lot batch to another. Buy only paper from the same batch, and if you special order it, check dye-lot numbers to confirm. Save the labels from every roll.
- Cut lengths of wallpaper in the order you'll use them, working from one corner of the room to the other. Do not cut all of the short pieces at one time, for instance; there may be a slight color differences between these and the adjacent strips.

The wallpapering tool kit

1-quart bucket

Extension pole

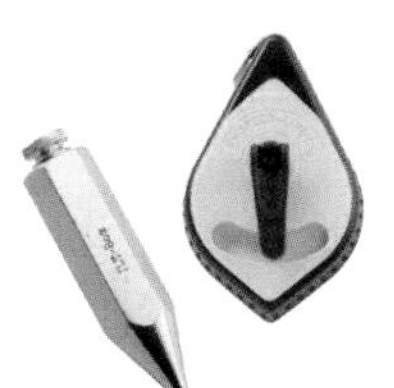
Plumb bob and chalkline

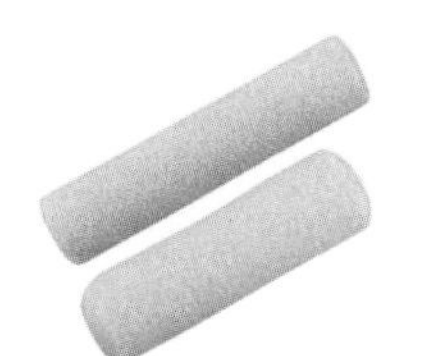
Rollers

Straightedge

Wallpaper scoring tool

3-inch putty knife

Garden sprayer

Rags

Sanding block

Tape measure

Wallpaper sponge

5-in-1 tool

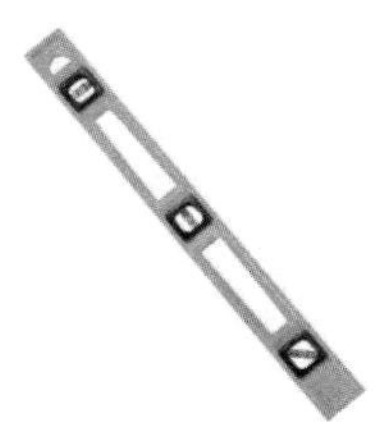
Level

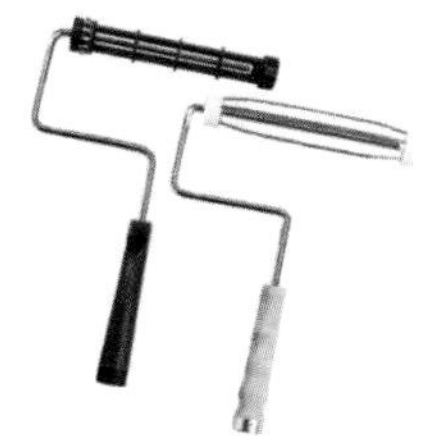
Roller cages

Seam roller

Utility knife

Water tray

Broad knife

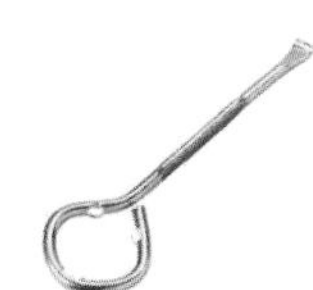
Paint can opener

Roller pan

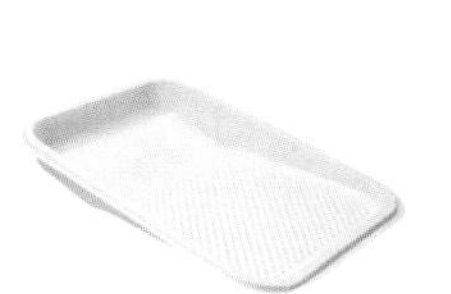
Roller pan liner

Smoothing brush

Wallpaper paste brush

Caulking gun

Painter's tape

Stepladder

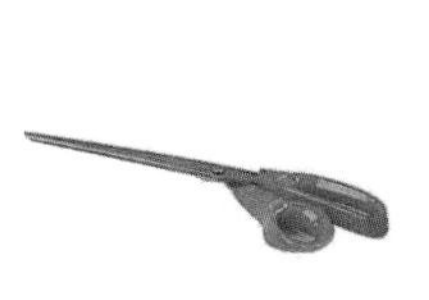
Wallpaper scissors

PAINTING & WALLPAPERING

Measuring and estimating wallpaper

You're only estimating, but it's easier to return unused wallpaper than to run out halfway through the job.

Quick and easy way: To estimate the number of double rolls you need for each wall, divide the square footage of the wall by 50. Round up to the nearest whole number, and add 1.

Now, the technical way: When you paper a room, you need to have enough paper to do the wall, plus about 10 percent extra for trimming, matching, and possibly fixing mistakes. Because papers quickly go out of print and you can no longer buy them, you may also want to buy an extra roll for subsequent repairs. At an average cost of $15 to $40 per double roll, it's good insurance.

Start by figuring out the square footage of your room: Measure the height times the length of each wall in feet, then add together. Don't subtract for doors, windows, or obstructions because you won't necessarily be able to use the pieces you cut out.

While a double roll covers 56 square feet, the formula pretends that it only covers 50 square feet, giving you the approximately 10 percent extra you need. Even 10 percent extra may not be enough if you have a large pattern repeat; ask your wallpaper dealer to advise you.

Consider a 9×12-foot room with 8-foot ceilings. Two 12-foot walls with 8-foot ceilings account for 192 square feet (2×12×8=192). The two 9-foot walls total 160 square feet (2×9×8=144). Altogether the room has 336 square feet of wall (192+144=336).

Dividing the square footage by 50 and rounding up to the next whole number means you need seven double rolls (336÷50= 6.7, which rounds up to 7). Add one more, and buy eight. Keep the extra roll for repairs. If you have an unused (and unwanted) extra roll when the job is finished, most stores will let you return it.

The language of wallpaper

Like any craft, wallpapering has a language of its own. Here are a few terms you'll need to know:

Double Roll: A double roll (sometimes called a bolt) is twice as long as a single roll, creating less waste. American rolls are 27 inches wide (European rolls are narrower), and each double roll covers 56 square feet of wall. Nearly all wallpaper sold now comes in double rolls.

Random-Match: If the pattern automatically aligns when you put one strip of paper next to the other, it is a random-match paper. Striped or solid-color papers, for instance, are random-match.

Straight-Match: The pattern is a horizontal match, with the same design element at the ceiling in every roll. When you hang a strip, make sure the pattern aligns with the previous strip. If not, the pattern will zigzag.

Drop-Match: The pattern runs diagonally and meets the right edge of the strip at a point lower than on the left edge. If the edge of a drop-match paper cuts a flower in half, you would have to align the edge of the next strip to get a complete flower. The amount of drop, called the pattern repeat, is printed on the back of the paper and is listed in wallpaper books.

Peelable: This paper is easy to remove. When you pull off peelable paper, however, some of the backing remains on the wall. This part can usually be removed fairly easily with water or a wallpaper-stripping solution.

Repeat: This is the amount of diagonal drop, or the distance between identical points on the pattern. The pattern repeat is listed in wallpaper books. The larger the repeat, the more paper that must be wasted in order to match the pattern. To save money, choose wallpaper with a minimal repeat.

Strippable: Lifting a corner and pulling it will remove the entire strip of paper, including its backing.

Vinyl: Vinyl refers to solid vinyl, possibly printed with a pattern and always backed by paper or fabric. It is durable and scrubbable but fairly expensive; for that reason it's generally used in commercial settings.

Vinyl-Coated: Paper is coated with vinyl to make it more durable. There are two kinds: washable (can be wiped occasionally with a sponge, mild soap, and water) and scrubbable (can hold up under more frequent washing). No paper can stand up to the rigors of a stiff scrub brush.

Professional worktables are about as wide as a roll of wallpaper, but you can make your own. Cut an 8-foot-long piece of plywood a little wider than your paper. Wrap the plywood in an old sheet to absorb activator and water and set it on two sawhorses or on an old table covered with newspapers. You can also use a card table covered with a plastic drop cloth. Clean it with a damp sponge after each length of paper to remove stray paste.

Finding the area when walls aren't rectangular

Stairs: Divide the wall into two triangles and a rectangle. To determine the area of a triangle, multiply its length by its height and divide by 2. On the stairway, repeat for the second triangle. To calculate the area of the rectangle, multiply the length by the height. Add the three areas together to get the total square footage.

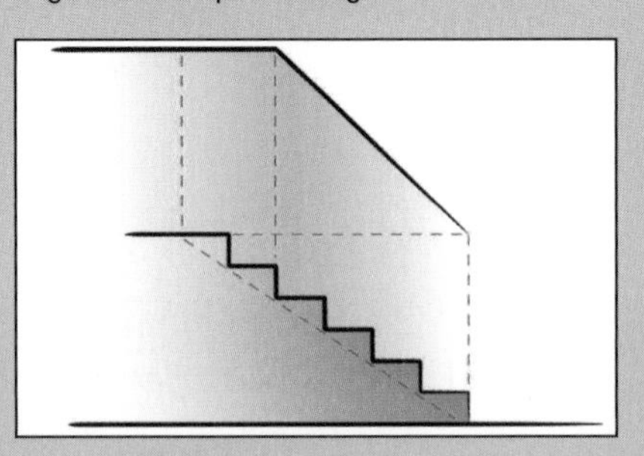

Gable walls: Measure as though the surface were a square or rectangle. Measure the length and the height; multiply the two numbers to find the area.

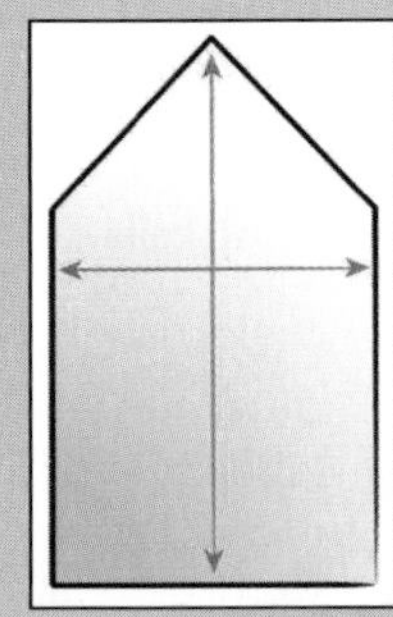

Wallpapering walls

Skill level:	Time to complete:	Materials:	Tools:
★★★☆☆	Experienced 6 hrs. Handy 7 hrs. Novice 8 hrs.	Wallpaper, paste (for unpasted papers), wallpaper paste activator, vinyl-to-vinyl adhesive (optional, only for edges of vinyl and vinyl-coated papers)	Tape measure, scissors, pencil, 2-foot level, paint roller or brush (for paste), smoothing brush, seam roller, utility knife, trimming tool (also called a broad knife), sponge, wallpaper table or plywood on sawhorses

Wallpapering the wall

Before beginning to paper, be sure that you have already done all of the preparation work needed to ensure a good finished job. To prepare, you'll need to wash, patch, prime, seal, and size (see page 70). Paper won't stick to a greasy surface, and underlying irregularities in the wall may remain visible beneath the paper.

Try to avoid the common temptation to paper above all the doors and windows first. And never cut all of the lengths at one time. In the first case, you'll see differences in the color if the rolls vary even slightly. In the second, if you make a mistake in cutting, there's no sense in multiplying it. Work around the room.

1 The pattern of your paper determines how strips are cut and glued on the wall. On straight-match and random-match papers, patterns along the left and right edges of the paper are the same, and installation is straightforward with minimal waste. On drop-match papers, such as the one above, the elements are staggered along both edges. Aligning the pattern results in an uneven top edge, which is trimmed off. This takes more time and wastes some paper, but complex patterns are usually more interesting. Cutting alternating strips from two rolls of wallpaper cuts down on some of the waste, but don't get too far ahead of yourself. If you do cut a couple of strips ahead, number the pieces.

2 Begin at an inconspicuous inside corner of the room. Plan to position the first strip so that all but about 1 to 2 inches of paper is on the first wall to be papered; the narrow part wraps around the corner onto the adjoining wall, hiding potential corner cracks. To lay out the strip, measure from the corner by the width of the paper minus the wrap. Guided by a level, snap a plumb line at this point.

WORK SMART

PRIMER/SEALER OPTIONS

Wallpaper primers come in clear and white. Use a clear primer where you're worried about drips and spills showing—papering above wooden wainscoting, for example. If you're putting up a dark paper, tint either white or clear primer before papering. Tinted primer makes inadvertent gaps less noticeable.

BUYER'S GUIDE

CHOOSE THE SAME DYE LOT

Wallpaper is printed in dye-lot batches, and colors may vary from lot to lot. Ask your retailer for rolls from the same lot, and then check to make sure you get them. Save a label or write down the lot number. If you need to order more wallpaper, you'll be able to give the manufacturer the exact lot number, which it will try to match.

Wallpapering walls (continued)

3 Cut the first strip of paper about 4 inches longer than needed so it can temporarily overlap the ceiling or crown molding and baseboard. Roll out the paper on a long work surface and cut the strip to length, using scissors with long blades.

4 Apply an activator or the recommended paste, even if you are using a prepasted paper (see Paste it anyway, below). Brush or roll on the activator or paste following the instructions.

5 Gently fold the ends toward the middle, glued sides together with the patterned sides out—this is called *booking* the strip. Try not to crease the paper. Wait several minutes before hanging, so moisture soaks in to relax the paper and the paste has a chance to activate. If you're interrupted, cover the booked paper with plastic so the paste stays wet.

WORK SMART

LASER LEVELS

This tool is one of the handiest when wallpapering. With it, you can shoot a beam of light around the room to make sure everything is lined up perfectly. Or, you can find a true vertical when lining up your strips—no more crooked wallpaper.

Paste it anyway

Prepasted papers may advise: Just dip in water and hang. But don't you believe it. Doing it that way is very messy, and the paper may not even stick to the wall. Wallpaper *paste activator* eliminates the mess and gives you a longer working time and more "slip," which means you can slide the paper around on the wall to position it. Activator also provides a better bond.

Covering paneling and cement block

It seems unlikely, but wallpaper can be installed over rough surfaces— even grooved paneling or cement-block walls. It simply takes good preparation and a product called wallpaper liner.

Wallpaper liner is a heavy-duty, unprinted wallcovering that you apply horizontally—before you put up the good stuff. It shrinks as it dries, leaving a very taut, smooth surface that wallpaper can grip. Because it is thick, it hides most unevenness. Good prep work is vital.

Paneling: Nail down any loose edges or panels. Pull out loose nails and replace them with drywall screws. Fill grooves and imperfections in the paneling with surfacing compound, scraping it flat with a putty knife. When the compound is dry, sand the panel with 200-grit paper to create tooth so the primer, sealer, and sizing will adhere.

Cement block: Check for signs of mildew or efflorescence, a powdery residue that appears on walls. Either is a sign of excessive moisture, making the wall an unlikely candidate for wallpaper. Basement walls are poor candidates for papering unless the moisture problem is fixed first. Fill any cracks or voids with surfacing compound. If the wall looks sound, sand it to remove cement or surface imperfections.

Wash down the wall, whatever the surface, with TSP (see page 24) or with a 50-50 mixture of ammonia and water to remove the sanding dust, grease, or wax buildup. Rinse with clean water and a sponge until the water runs clear. Let the surface dry for at least 24 hours.

Paint the wall with a combination primer/sealer/sizing product; let it dry as recommended by the manufacturer.

Now it's time to paper. Wallpaper liner contains no paste: Apply the recommended paste to the back, letting it soak in a few minutes before hanging it. Hang the strips horizontally, not vertically—this avoids having the seams of the liner and the paper fall in the same spot.

Let the paper dry, and inspect the wall for high and low spots. Hang the final paper as you normally would.

Wallpaper liner makes removing the top layer easier when you're ready for a change. Just peel up a corner of the strip, and pull off the paper.

6 Position the first strip along the plumb line with a gentle but firm hand. Starting at the middle of the strip, work your way up to the top, sliding the paper to align it. Align the bottom and work it gently against the wall. Go back to the top and smooth—but don't stretch—the paper onto the wall with a brush or a flexible plastic smoother. Coax any bubbles out to the edges.

7 Hang the second strip and then trim the first. Allow the paste to dry on the first strip while you hang the second strip, and then go back to trim the first. Trim as shown, placing a broad knife between the paper and the cutting knife to guide the cut. A plastic smoother can also be used as a straightedge. You can also use a single-edge razor blade to make clean cuts, changing to a new blade often.

$ BUYER'S GUIDE

DURABILITY

Select the type of wallpaper best suited for your specific area. Washability is a big consideration for certain rooms. All vinyl-coated wallpapers are washable, but fewer are scrubbable.

- **Washable wallpaper** can be cleaned with mild soap and water and a sponge. Use it for bathrooms or laundry rooms, where walls will probably be splashed with water or need an occasional light washing.
- **Scrubbable wallpaper** is the best choice for heavy-use areas or anywhere there are apt to be muddy boots, such as in mudrooms or service entries. This paper is durable enough to be scrubbed more often with a soft (never stiff) brush. Use a 100-percent-vinyl wallcovering for best results.

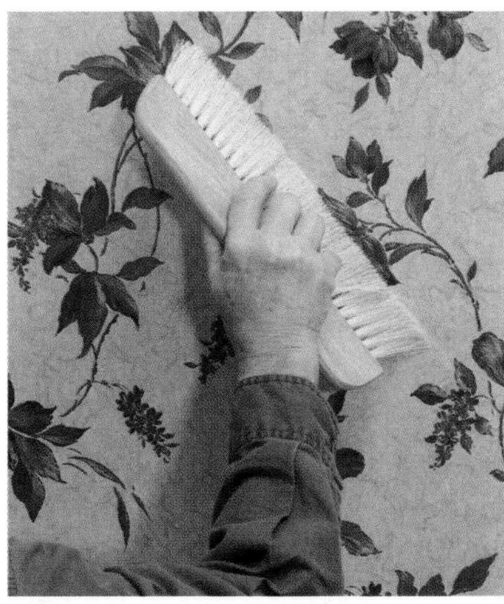

8 Butt, but don't overlap, subsequent strips. After you've hung a few strips, go over the seams with a seam roller to press the edges in place. (Don't press too hard—you'll force too much paste out and the seams will loosen.) Sponge off excess paste with clean, warm water. Note: Foils and flocked or embossed papers may be damaged by rolling; instead, smooth the seams with a smoothing brush.

9 Paper right over electric switches and outlets after the coverplate has been removed. Cut away excess paper later. Before cutting around an electrical box, shut off the power to the room. Cut an X across the box with scissors, working toward the corners (avoid cutting into the outlet or switch). Trim with a blade to make a rectangular opening, leaving enough paper for the cover plate to conceal the edges.

Wallpapering walls (continued)

Wallpapering inside corners

1 Measure in three places: from the edge of the previous strip to the corner at the top, middle, and bottom of the corner. These steps are designed to eliminate sloping paper caused by out-of-plumb corners (which, unfortunately, most are).

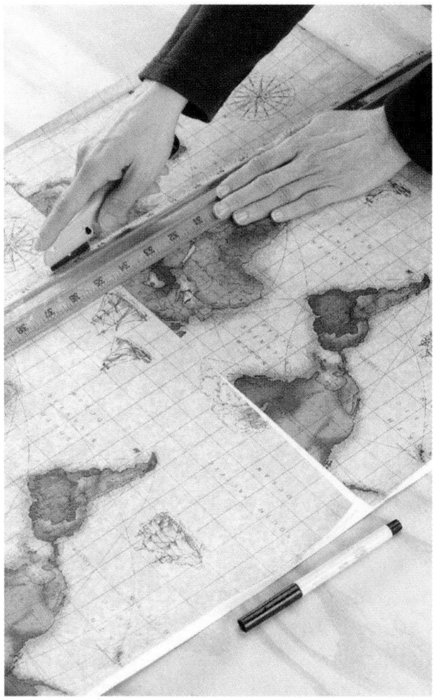

2 Align the edges of the booked strip. Add ½ to 1 inch to the widest distance measured in Step 1. Mark that measurement at both folds and several spots along the pasted, booked strip. Hold a straightedge against the marks, guiding a utility knife against it to cut the strip to width. Save the pasted cutoff, keeping it moist.

3 Position the strip on the wall, butting the edges and matching the pattern on the previous strip. Let any extra width go around the corner onto the next wall.

4 Gently smooth the paper onto the walls and into the corner with your hands (make sure they're clean and free of paste).

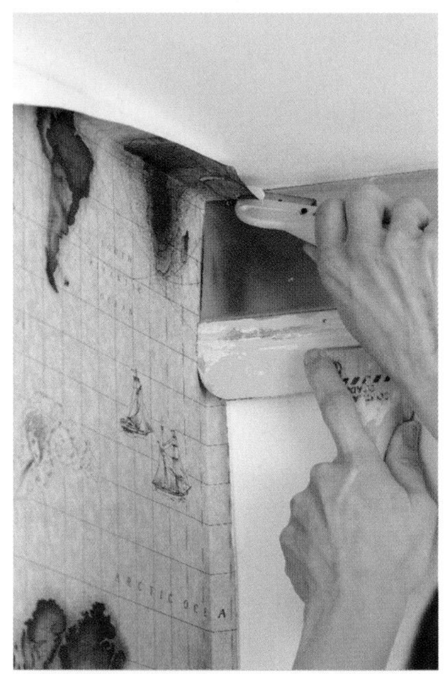

5 Make slits from the corner to the edge of the paper at the top and bottom of the strip so that you can wrap the overlap around the corner without any wrinkles.

6 Flatten the strip with a smoothing tool, pressing firmly but not so hard that you squeeze the paste out. Trim excess paper at the ceiling and baseboard.

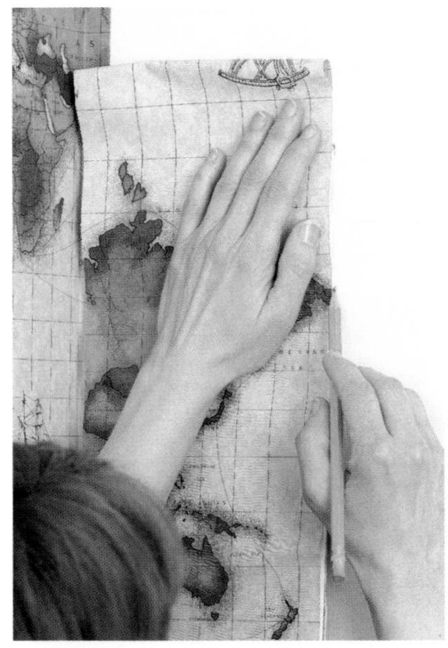

7 Measure the width of the cutoff from step 2. Measure this distance from the corner onto the unpapered wall and make a pencil mark. Guided by a level (or laser level) draw or pop a plumb line through this mark from ceiling to floor.

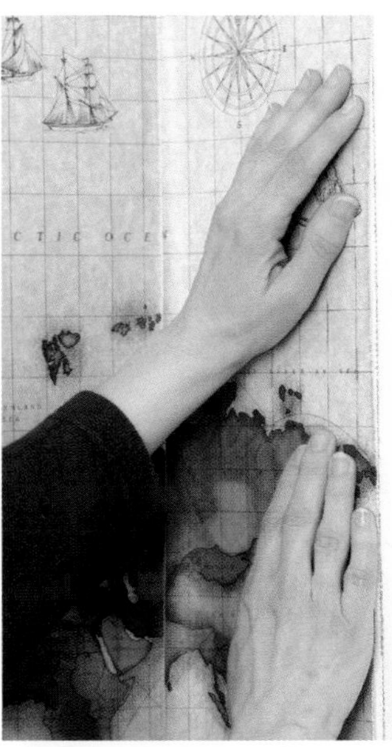

8 Hang the cutoff on the wall, with the cut edge toward the corner and the factory edge against the plumb line. Align the pattern, overlapping the two pieces as necessary. Smooth the strip with a smoothing brush. Trim at the ceiling and baseboard.

9 Press the seam area flat (if using vinyl wallpaper, peel back the top edge and apply vinyl-to-vinyl adhesive between the overlapping strips of paper before pressing them). After half an hour, or as directed on the package, roll the seams. Wipe excess paste off with a damp sponge.

Wallpapering outside corners

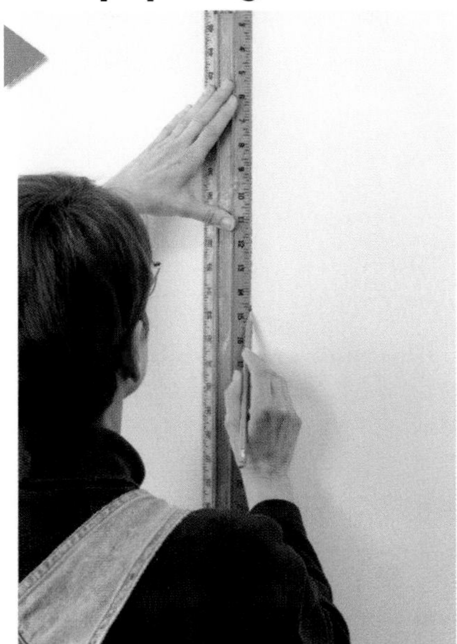

1 Most corners are out of plumb, so the edge you wrap around it will also be out of plumb. Measure from the existing strip to the outside corner at the top, bottom and middle of the wall. Add ½ inch to the longest distance. Subtract this from the width of the paper. Starting at the corner, measure and mark a distance equal to the remaining paper width; draw a plumb line on the wall around the corner.

2 Align the factory edge with the plumb line. Hang the strip of paper, and smooth it against the wall. Wrap the paper back around the corner, overlapping the previous strip if necessary.

3 Cut the paper at the top and bottom using scissors so it turns the corner smoothly. Smooth the paper against the wall, sliding it to match the pattern. If the edges don't butt exactly, use a straight edge to guide the blade and cut through both layers of paper at the same time; remove the top layer. Roll the edges of the seam.

Wallpapering walls (continued)

Wallpapering around windows and doors

Think of window and door openings as simply larger electrical outlets. Paper over them as you would over an outlet, at least in part, by hanging the strip right over the casing, and then cut off the waste. If you decide to precut the strips to "fit" the shape of the windows and doors, be sure to allow a few extra inches of paper to allow for trimming. Before trimming the edges, push a straightedge into the molding as a guide for your blade and also smooth the paper with a smoothing brush. Clean excess paste off of the casings with a damp sponge (you may not be able to see it when it dries, but it will keep any future paint from sticking).

1 Prime and seal the walls (See page 70). Position the strip on the wall, letting it cover the window or door casing. Butt the seam carefully against the edge of the previous strip. Smooth the flat areas as much as possible with a smoothing tool. Press the strip tightly against the ceiling.

2 Hold your finger at the corner of the trim and cut diagonally toward it with wallpaper scissors. If you're hanging the paper around a window, make a similar cut at the bottom corner.

3 Push the paper tight against the trim with a wide blade or flexible smoothing tool.

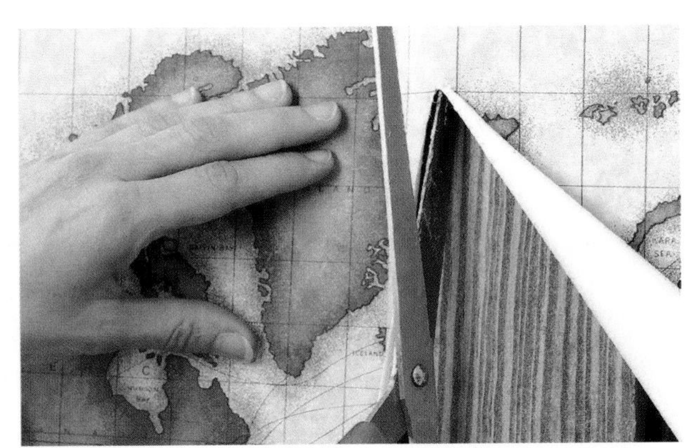

4 Using scissors, trim the excess wallpaper to within about 1 inch of the outside edge of the window frame. Smooth the wallpaper and any bubbles as you work.

WORK SMART

BE STRIP WISE

Just keep going when you come to a short strip above a window or door. Working your way around the room, make sure the leading edges are still plumb to ensure a good match with the next full strip. Wait to trim the short ones until the next full strip is aligned; then go back and trim. Short lengths can be cut from scrap pieces (at the end of a roll, for instance) to save paper, as long as the pattern matches. Never cut all of the short pieces at once; slight color variations between rolls can become very apparent.

OOPS

FIX THOSE GOOFS

Good paperhangers know a few tricks that will make their jobs look almost perfect:

- Club soda breaks down dried glue without harming the paper.
- Smooth wet bubbles toward the seams. Don't cut bubbles unless the glue is dry. (See Fixing a Bubble, page 87.)
- Wipe excess glue from ceilings and moldings before it dries, or it will cause the paint to lift off the surface.
- Use toothpicks to help you remember picture-hanging holes. Smooth the paper, find the hole with your fingers, and poke a toothpick into the hole to mark the spot.

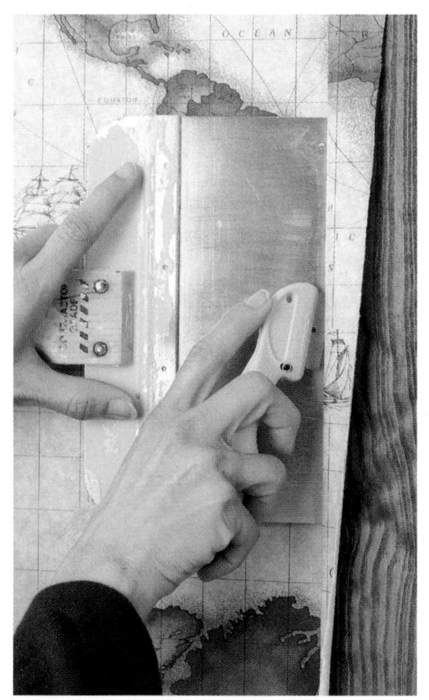

5 Trim excess paper with a razor knife, holding the wallpaper against the casing with a broad knife. Trim the overlaps at the ceiling and baseboard. Remove excess paste from the wallpaper and casings with a damp sponge.

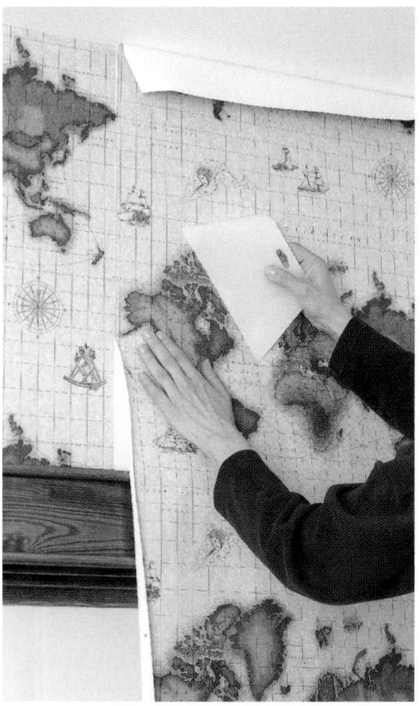

6 Cut short strips for the sections above and below the window. Hang each strip, and double-check to make sure it's plumb. Work your way across the opening. Repeat below the window.

7 Cut and prepare the next strip. No matter how careful you've been, the wallpaper will want to hang at an angle here. Snap a plumb line to guide placement of the outside edge. Hang the strip, aligning the edge with the line. If necessary, adjust the previous (short) strip for a better match.

8 Make diagonal cuts at the top and bottom corners as in Step 2. Trim excess wallpaper to about 1 inch inside the outer edge of the window or door frame.

9 Apply the short length below the windowsill. Use wallpaper scissors to trim any excess wallpaper to about 1 inch. Then flatten the strip with a smoothing tool.

10 Cut off excess paper with a razor knife, holding the paper against the casing with a broad knife. Trim off overlaps at the ceiling and baseboard. Wipe the excess paste with a damp sponge.

Wallpapering walls (continued)

Wallpapering a recessed window

1 Hang a strip over the opening for the window as if the opening weren't there. Make two horizontal cuts—one slightly above the top of the opening, the other slightly above the bottom. Fold the flap formed by the cuts against the side walls of the recess. Fold the remaining paper over to form a flap on the sill and on the recessed wall above the window. Measure 2 inches to the right of the left corner of the recess, and use a level to make a vertical cut from it to the ceiling. Remove paper at right of the cut.

2 Make all cuts with a clean, fresh blade. Cut a strip long enough to reach from the ceiling around the top edge of the recess, overlapping the window slightly. Starting at the ceiling, hang the strip so it overlaps the entire width of the first strip. Align your straightedge with the edge of the window and cut along it to the corner of the opening. Fold the paper around the top edge of the recess and smooth it in place. Repeat below the window, as shown.

3 You're about to make what paperhangers call a "double cut." Align a straightedge with the left-hand edge of the recess. Cut along the edge, cutting through both layers of paper at the top of the window. Pull off the scrap to the left of the cut. Peel back the right-hand strip, and remove any paper underneath it. Put the right-hand strip back in place, smooth it, and roll the seam. Repeat below the window.

4 If the remaining unpapered space above the recess is more than one strip wide, hang the next strip, wrapping the paper around the top edge of the recess and across the upper recessed wall, trimming it at the window. Repeat below the window.

5 Position the next strip so that it overlaps the previous strips completely and hangs from ceiling to floor. Cut vertically at the edge of the recess and fold the flap against the recess above the window and at the sill.

6 Align a straightedge with the edge of the recess and double-cut by guiding a knife along it. Peel back the top layer of paper as in Step 3 to remove any scrap paper underneath it. Smooth it back in place. Sponge away excess paste.

Wallpapering inside an archway

1 Apply wallpaper on one or both sides of the archway with strips hanging over the opening. Smooth the strips and trim the excess at the ceiling and baseboard.

2 Use scissors to trim the wallpaper about 1 inch below the arch, following its curve.

3 Make slits or notches in the wallpaper along the curved section of the arch, cutting as close as possible to the edge but avoiding snipping into the portion that will be on the wall. The tighter the arch, the more slits are necessary.

4 Press the cut edges against the inside of the arch. If the adjacent room is being wallpapered, wrap that wallpaper around the edge of the archway as well.

5 Measure the thickness of the arch. Cut two long strips of paper. Measure each strip ¼ inch less than the arch's thickness. Together they total the distance around the inside of the arch. Join the strips somewhere near the center for the best pattern match.

6 Coat the back of the strip with vinyl-to-vinyl adhesive. Position the strip along the inside of the arch with a ⅛-inch space left at each edge. Smooth the strip with a smoothing brush and clean off excess paste with a damp sponge.

Wallpapering around obstacles

Skill level:	Time to complete:	Materials:	Tools:
★★★☆☆	Experienced 30 min. Handy 45 min. Novice 1 hr.	Wallpaper strips, wallpaper paste or activator, tube or strip silicone caulk	Wallpaper brush, razor knife, yardstick, wallpaper table, smoothing tool, chalk line, putty knife

Hanging wallpaper around obstacles such as sinks, pipes, and other protrusions requires careful cutting, but it's not very hard. Position the already-pasted strips so the patterns match, and cut from the edge closest to the fixture or pipe.

If possible, cut along a pattern line to hide the slit, even if it means the cut isn't straight. Press the paper as close to the protrusion as possible, and mark the spot. At the end of the slit, cut an opening to fit around the fixture (cut small to begin with; you can always enlarge the opening if it's too small). Press the paper in place, continuing with the rest of the strip as usual.

Around wall-mounted sinks, tuck or push the small ends of the wallpaper overlaps behind the sink rather than cutting the wallpaper flush with the edge of the sink. This gives a professional appearance, and the inevitable water splashes won't curl the paper.

Wallpapering around a wall-mounted sink

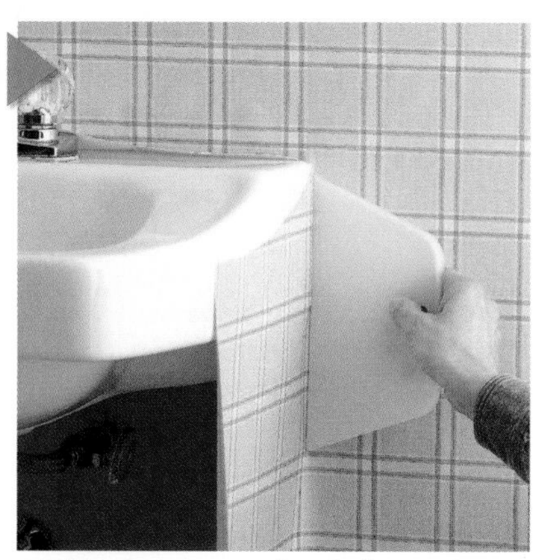

1 Hang as much of the strip as you can, then make a horizontal cut about 1 inch below the top of the sink, stopping about 1 inch short of the side. Notch the corner as necessary to make a smooth turn; trim the paper a little longer than the side. Continue smoothing the paper against the wall and into the edges of the sink, cutting as you go.

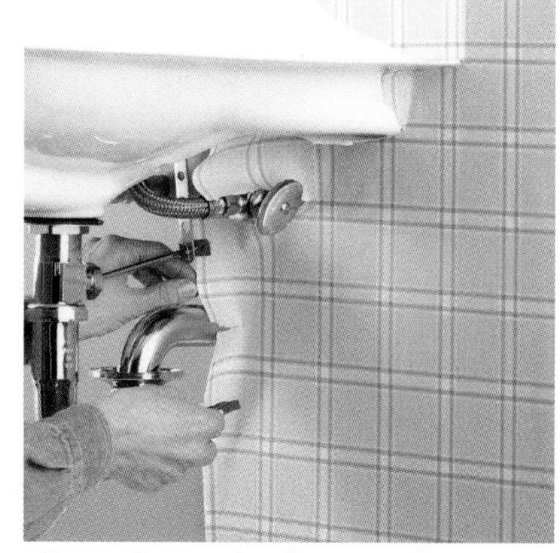

2 Make a single cut wherever the paper meets a pipe, cutting from the edge of the paper past the obstruction. Smooth the paper against the wall, trimming off the excess against each pipe with either a razor knife or scissors.

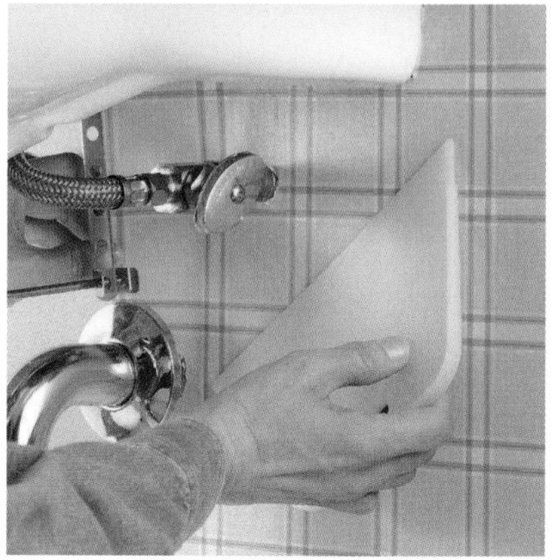

3 Smooth the wallpaper with a smoothing tool. Trim any excess paper off the side of the sink. Gently tuck the 1-inch-wide flaps of wallpaper along the top and sides behind the sink, if possible, using the smoothing tool or a thin putty knife. Otherwise, trim the overlap and caulk to cover the exposed paper edge.

Wallpapering behind a radiator

1 Smooth the paper onto the wall behind the radiator with a yardstick, and crease it at the baseboard.

2 Pull up the bottom of the paper; cut it along the creased line and then smooth it back down.

Electric baseboard heaters

Wallpaper around baseboard heaters the same as for other wall-mounted fixtures. Smooth the strip up to the edge of the heater. Then trim the wallpaper around the heater, leaving a slight overlap, which you can tuck behind it.

Wallpapering ceilings

Skill level:	Time to complete:	Materials:	Tools:
★★★★★	Experienced 8 hrs. Handy 12 hrs. Novice 16 hrs.	Wallpaper strips, wallpaper paste or activator	Wallpaper brush, razor knife, yardstick, wallpaper table, smoothing tool, chalk line, pencil, putty knife

Wallpapering a ceiling is always a two-person job, so you'll need to sweet-talk someone into helping you or collect a favor. Use a heavy-duty adhesive and allow plenty of time to complete the job. If you are using the same paper as on the walls, paper the ceiling first. Later line up the seams on the walls as closely as possible to those on the ceiling.

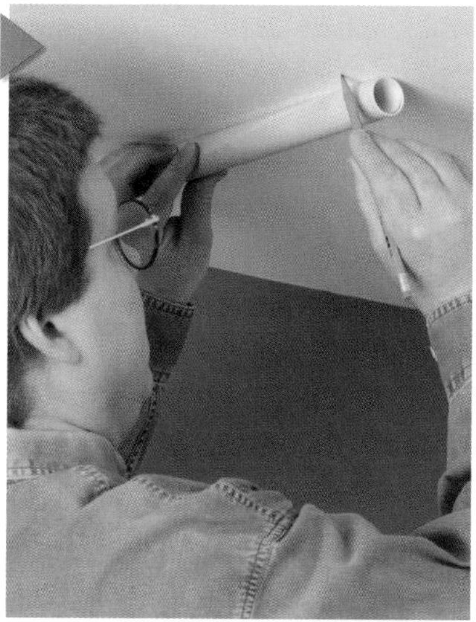

1 Prime and patch the ceiling. The wallpaper should overlap the wall on its long side by about ½ inch. To plan the layout, hold a roll of paper against the ceiling at one side of the room. Mark the ceiling ½ inch from the end of the roll. Go to the other side of the room and make a similar mark.

2 Snap a chalk line connecting the two marks. (Use blue chalk—red chalk will bleed through the paper.) Cut a strip of paper to the proper length (allow an extra 2 inches at each end) and then apply wallpaper paste or paste activator. Book the strip and let it rest the recommended time.

3 Starting at one end, position the strip along the chalk line. Work in small sections and flatten the strip with a smoothing brush as you go. If the walls will be papered, trim the ends of the ceiling paper to overlap the wall by only ½ inch.

4 To make wallpaper lie smooth in the corner, cut out a small wedge of paper as shown. Then press the wallpaper into the corner with a smoothing tool. If walls will not be papered, trim the excess all around by holding a broad knife against the corner and cutting with an extremely sharp razor knife. (Change the blade after cutting each side.)

WORK SMART
DEEP TEXTURES

Heavily embossed paper can imitate a lot of different materials, including pressed tin, tooled leather, and ornamental plaster. These effects are especially attractive on ceilings, stairways, or the wainscoting beneath a chair rail.

Available in whole rolls or decorative borders, embossed wallpaper comes only in white—it's up to you to add color. You can paint it, glaze it, or highlight details with an artist's brush to create the desired effect.

Highly textured embossed papers are able to hide cracks and unevenness in plaster ceilings. Use only the recommended adhesives, though; other kinds simply won't hold up the heavy paper.

Hanging borders on painted walls

Skill level:	Time to complete:	Materials:	Tools:
★☆☆☆☆	Experienced 1 hr. Handy 2 hrs. Novice 3 hrs.	Wallpaper border, wallpaper paste or activator, primer/sealer	Drafting triangle, 4-foot level, tape measure, scissors, razor knife, broad knife, wallpaper brush, sponge, smoothing tool, seam roller

Adding a wallpaper border is one of the easiest ways to dress up a room and even a novice can do it. No matter where you put the border—along the ceiling, around a door or window, on the wall as a chair rail—installation is basically the same.

When choosing a border, buy one that's in scale with your room. A dark-color one-foot-deep border pasted directly under an 8-foot ceiling looks too heavy, pulling the eye down and making the room seem much too short. A light-color border with less depth might be a better choice for that location.

First, decide where you'll put the border so you'll know how much to buy. A chair rail is usually one-third of the way up the wall, but you might change that. See how that height works in relation to your windows, for instance. If the bottom of the window trim would split the border in half, move the border up or down a couple of inches. Or, if the furniture is going to hide all your work, position the border a little higher on the wall.

Most borders come in rolls of only 15 feet. To figure out how much border you'll need, add up the distance around the walls. Add enough to go around doors and windows, if you're using it there, plus an extra foot for each corner you will turn. Plan ahead for waste. If the border is in 5-yard rolls, add about ½ yard extra for each 5 yards you measure.

Ceiling borders often show up slight differences in the wall height. Minimize perceptible flaws by painting the top ¼ inch of the wall the same color as the ceiling. Also, make sure the bottom edge of the border looks straight. If necessary, you can slide it down the wall in spots. The ceiling paint you put on the wall will camouflage the resulting gap.

Start by priming and sizing (see page 70) so stains or paint don't show through the border, and the paper will adhere well. Buy a combination wallpaper primer and sizing solution, and you can do everything to prepare in one step.

Hanging the border

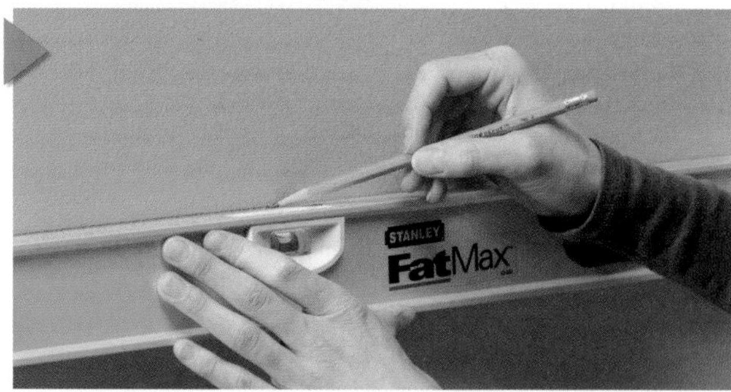

1 Measure and draw a faint line marking the top of the border, using a pencil and a level. Or, if you're satisfied the measurements are level, snap a blue (not red) chalk line.

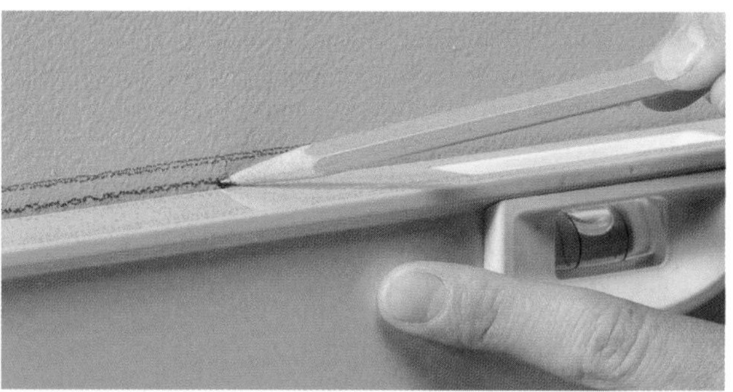

2 Prime an area slightly narrower than the border. To lay it out, draw a second line parallel to and ¼ inch below the first. To mark the bottom of the primed area, measure and draw a line ¼ inch above what will be the bottom of the border. You can also mark the borders with 2 rows of masking tape and prime between them.

DESIGN TIP
BORDER DISPUTE

Traditionally a chair rail border goes about one-third of the way up the wall, but this "rule" can be broken. If your room has windows, you may want to run the border so that it meets the bottom of the frame. If there's a sofa against the wall, you might want to position the border slightly above it for more visibility. In an Arts-and-Crafts-style room, the molding is usually two-thirds of the way up the wall, so a border should be about the same. Whatever you do, though, avoid placing the border exactly halfway—it looks awkward.

3 Brush a primer/sealer between the lines. Let the primer dry according to the instructions on the can.

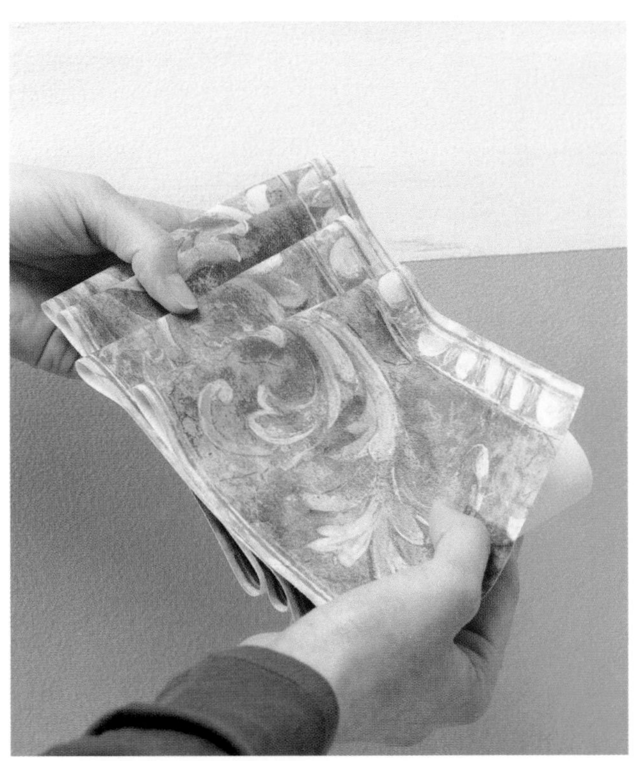

4 Brush paste activator onto the paper (or paste if the paper isn't prepasted). To make the paper easier to handle, "ribbon-fold" the strip as shown so that the pasted sides face each other. Let the strip rest for a few minutes, so that the paper relaxes and the glue can reach full strength.

5 Start the roll ½ inch from the corner on what will be the last wall. Push the paper into the corner with a broad knife and continue along the wall, smoothing with a smoothing tool as you work.

Painted borders

Create a harmonizing custom border for your room: Start with embossed, plain-paper border (sold by the roll in many paint and wallpaper departments). Apply a base coat of latex paint, perhaps to match your wall. When the paint dries, apply glaze to highlight the details. Another (one-step) process is to keep the paper its original white, while rolling paint or glaze on the embossed details, as shown below. Let dry and paste on as for any border.

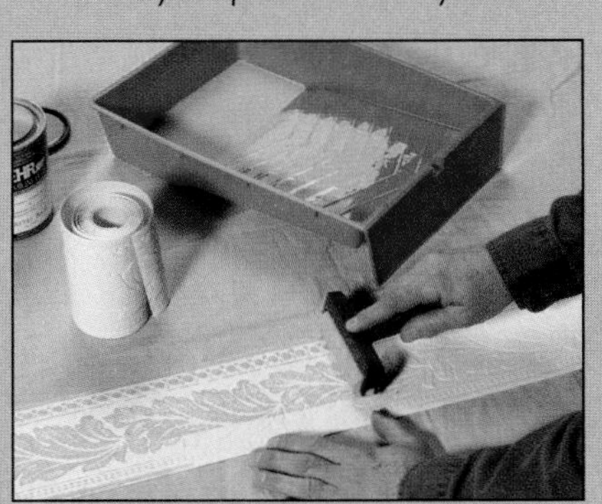

WORK SMART

PRIME THE SURFACE

For best results, prime even a painted wall underneath a border. Priming seals the wall better than regular paint, filling the pores and helping the border adhere better. To make quick work of painting the narrow strip, mark it off with two strips of masking tape and paint the area with a wide brush.

On the (almost) level

Some people won't take the time to use a level when drawing lines for a border. So they measure up from the floor at each end of a wall and snap a chalk line, assuming the floor is level. Well, the eye may accept a not-quite-level floor but an out-of-level border is very apparent. So, either use a level or tape your border in place first, and let your eyes judge.

6 When a roll runs out, join it to the next with a "double cut." Apply the end of the second roll so it overlaps the end of the first roll, sliding it until the patterns match. Cut through both strips, guiding the blade along a straightedge. Peel off the scraps and press the ends of the border together. Hang the remaining part of that strip. Roll the seams with a seam roller and sponge away excess paste.

Hanging borders on painted walls (continued)

7 When you reach an inside corner, cut the strip so that it runs ½ inch onto the next wall. Place a dry strip over the first, align the patterns and make a crisp fold in the dry strip at the corner. Cut along the fold with scissors and hang that end against the corner.

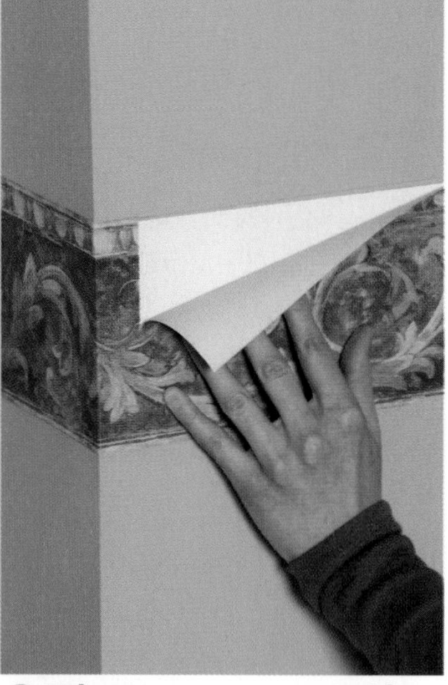

8 When you turn an outside corner, the border will go out of level unless the corner is perfectly plumb. To avoid this, cut the border so it's about 1 inch longer than the corner edge. Position the cutoff so it barely overlaps the cut end, align the new piece with the layout lines, and continue along the wall.

9 As you finish the last wall, you'll come to the small section of border that started the job. Push the final strip into the corner with the smoothing tool, creating a crease. Cut along the crease with scissors and smooth the paper in place, overlapping that first section.

Mitering border corners

1 Apply the horizontal and vertical strips so they both extend beyond the corner. The extra length should be equal to the width of the border, plus about 2 inches.

2 Check the border strips to see if important design elements remain intact at the diagonal cuts. Adjust the strips if necessary. Then make a diagonal double cut (through both layers) from the corner of the molding to where the borders intersect.

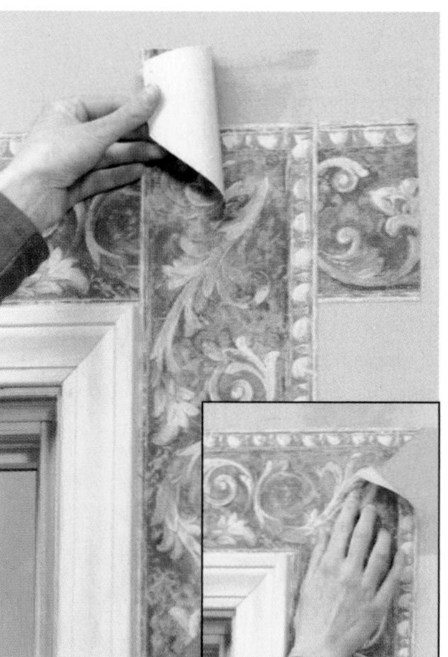

3 Remove the scrap pieces. Press the border back in place with a sponge (see inset) and let it stand for half an hour. Lightly roll the seams and sponge off any excess glue.

Repair and maintenance

Patching wallpaper

1 Place a matching scrap of wallpaper over the damaged portion, aligning the scrap so that the patterns match. Use blue painter's masking tape to hold it in place.

2 Cut through both layers of wallpaper, using a razor knife held at a 90-degree angle to the wall. If the wallpaper has strong pattern lines, cut along the lines to help hide the seams. With less definite patterns, you can cut irregular lines.

3 Remove both layers of paper. Peel away the damaged wallpaper. Apply adhesive to the back of the patch and, matching the pattern again, position it in the hole. Wipe the patched area with a damp sponge.

Fixing a bubble

1 Cut a slit through a dried bubble, using a razor knife and hiding the slit along a pattern line. (If the bubble is still wet, try to smooth it toward the seam line and release it.)

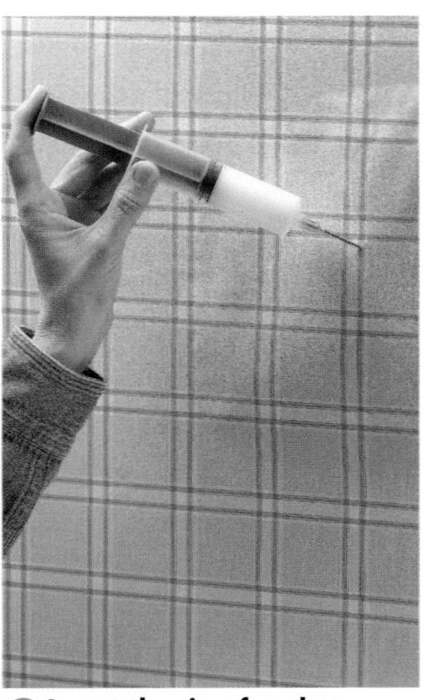

2 Insert the tip of a glue applicator through the slit and squirt adhesive sparingly onto the wall. Press down and sponge off any excess glue.

Fixing loose seams

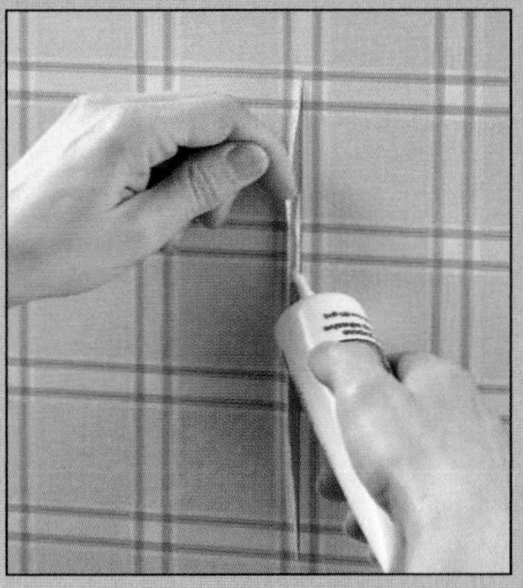

Dampen the wallpaper first to make it easier to put back in position. Lift one or both edges and insert the tip of the glue applicator. Squirt vinyl-to-vinyl adhesive onto the wall and gently press the seam flat. Let it stand for half an hour; then smooth the seam lightly with a roller and wipe off the glue with a damp sponge.

Combining a border with wallpaper

Skill level:	Time to complete:	Materials:	Tools:
★☆☆☆☆	Experienced 6 hrs. Handy 7 hrs. Novice 8 hrs.	Primer, wallpaper paste or paste activator, wallpaper, companion border	Tape measure, 4-foot level, scissors, wallpaper smoothing tool, seam roller, razor knife, sponge, chalk plumb tool

Wallpaper wainscoting—wallpaper topped by a border—can dress up a room in no time. You might also use a border to cover the bottom edge of wallpaper on the top part of the wall. A border, in styles ranging from cottage to Victorian, can bridge the transition between patterns and textures at any point.

It takes a little patience to install, but the job isn't difficult. You'll need a sharp razor knife with extra blades, a good straightedge level, and time to work.

The method shown gives the best results because it eliminates shadow lines or ridges where the wallpaper and the border meet. It also makes matching complex patterns easier but it does require a little practice and careful cutting. One advantage to this method is that you can change either the border or the paper without having to redo both sections.

If this is not a factor, two alternative (and even easier) methods are shown on page 89.

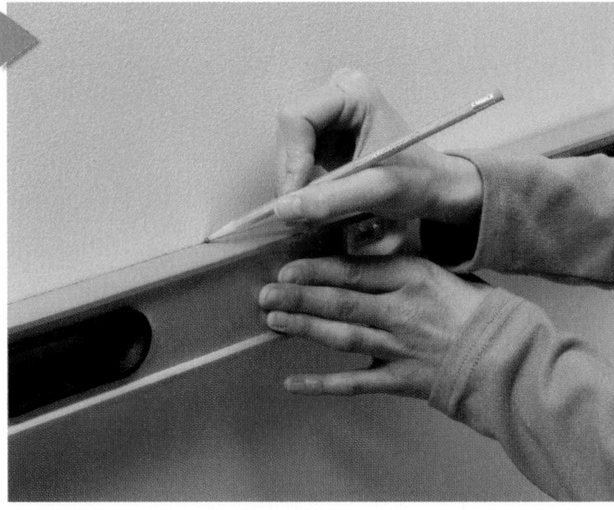

1 Draw a faint pencil line on the wall marking where the top and bottom of the border will be. (Use a level when drawing the line.) Apply a primer/sealer between the lines if you're putting border over paint.

2 Hang the border, following the instructions on pages 84 to 86. Smooth it with a smoothing tool and wipe it clean with a damp sponge.

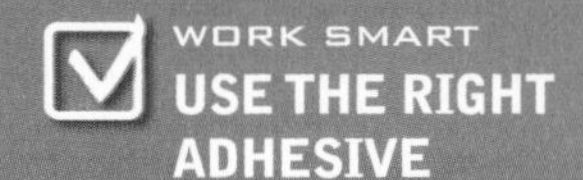

Using the right adhesive is critical when applying borders over papered walls. Don't prime or size, but do make sure you use vinyl-to-vinyl adhesives for vinyl papers and special border adhesives for most others. You'll be drawing a single faint line marking either the top or bottom of the border. Cover this line by about 1/16 inch when you hang the border.

3 Before cutting the bottom paper, decide how to position it. Slide a scrap of the border up and down to see how it looks on the paper—you don't want it to cut off an important part of the pattern. When you find the right spot, cut the wallpaper a few inches above it. Then cut the first strip to length, measuring from where the border will cross it and adding 3 inches for trimming.

4 Draw a plumb line to mark where the edge of the paper will be on the wall. (Use a level, and position the line so that about ½ inch of paper goes around the corner and onto the adjacent wall.) Hang the strip of paper along the line, positioning the top so it crosses the border as planned.

5 You will see a slight ridge in the paper where it crosses the border. Put a straightedge along the ridge and, with a new blade in your knife, cut lightly along the straightedge. Trim the bottom of the paper where it meets the baseboard.

6 Peel back the scrap paper, cleaning up any excess glue with a damp sponge. Continue along the wall, checking each piece for plumb and smoothing as you hang it. Then trim the top and bottom, and hang the next piece. Continue until you've hung paper below the entire border.

Two other (easier) options

Draw a line for the border, (see step 1, opposite, but draw the line at the *top* of the border instead). Hang the wallpaper, following the line. Activate and book the border strip; apply it over the wallpaper, using the top of the wallpaper as a guide.

Draw lines for the top and bottom of the border. Hang the wallpaper so it slightly overlaps the bottom border line. Hang the border following the top trim line once you've installed the wallpaper wainscoting.

OOPS

CHALK IT UP TO EXPERIENCE

Is it OK to use any color of chalk to make your chalkline?

No! If your store is out of blue chalk, don't make the mistake of buying red instead. Red chalk is considered permanent—it will bleed through paint and sometimes even wallpaper unless you apply a special sealer over it. Blue (or yellow) washes off easily and won't bleed. If you've already discovered the problem with red chalk on your own, you can prime and seal your walls to get rid of it.

Handling wallpaper transitions

Wallpaper doesn't always end conveniently. Sometimes it ends mid-wall, runs into and ends at ceramic tile, or reaches the corner but doesn't wrap around it. In these situations, it will probably start peeling after a while.

When you come to the point where the paper stops, you simply don't put up the next strip. If the stopping point doesn't fall at the factory edge of a strip, measure carefully and cut that strip before you hang it. Trying to cut it on the wall is a good way to 1) cut into the wall; 2) move the paper you've positioned so carefully; and 3) get a ragged seam. Instead, cut the paper on the table—the same way you would if cutting a corner strip. (See Wallpapering Inside Corners, page 76 and Wallpapering outside corners, page 77.)

An unprotected edge is vulnerable to ripping and loosening; once the glue dries, you'll need to protect it somehow.

If you've stopped the paper mid-wall, protect the edge with a decorative molding. Any molding you like will do—from simple half-round to fancy pressed moldings or door trim; just paint or stain it before installation. Bevel the molding an inch or two from the crown molding and the baseboard to avoid visual clutter where the profiles meet. Nail the molding on or attach it with construction adhesive, making sure that the molding covers the paper edge.

If the paper ends where it meets ceramic tile, cut it to width and caulk it by running a ⅛-inch-wide bead of caulk along the transition. (Or use the new peelable strip caulk for a neatly finished edge.) Select silicone caulk in a color that goes with both the tile and wallpaper. On a light paper, white may be your best choice—you want it to seem to disappear.

When paper ends at an outside corner it almost always starts to peel as people brush by. (In fact, you'll want to protect any outside corner in a high-traffic area, whether paper ends there or not.) The least expensive option is to use a clear plastic corner guard, either a nail-on or self-stick one. You can also use corner molding—an L-shape trim profile with unadorned flat surfaces—nailed on over the corner. The most elegant option is a lathe-turned corner molding, notched to fit over a corner. It is available in several profiles, at specialty molding suppliers and some home improvement stores.

▼ *A chair rail bridges the transition from wallpaper on the bottom to paint at the top of the wall. This creates an attractive division, but more important, it keeps the raw edge of the paper from peeling.*

Finishing touches

Papering cover plates

1 Remove the cover plate and reinsert the screw so you won't lose it. Place a piece of wallpaper over the outlet so the patterns match. Rub the surface of the wallpaper to emboss the outline of the outlet.

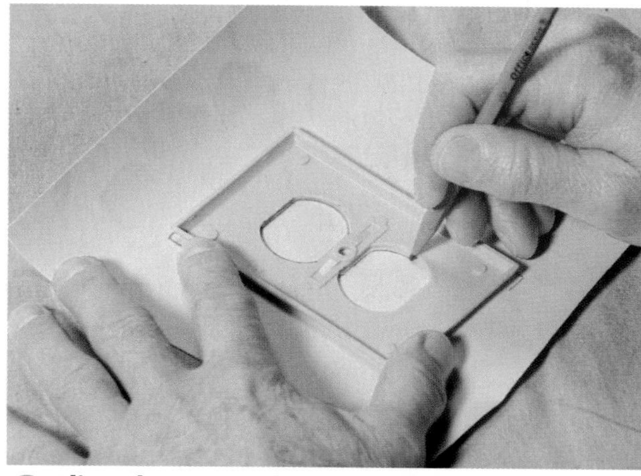

2 Align the cover plate with the embossed marks on the wallpaper. Trace around the corners and the openings of the cover plate with a pencil. Trim the wallpaper ½ inch wider than the cover plate. Cut across the corners diagonally, cutting just outside the corner marks.

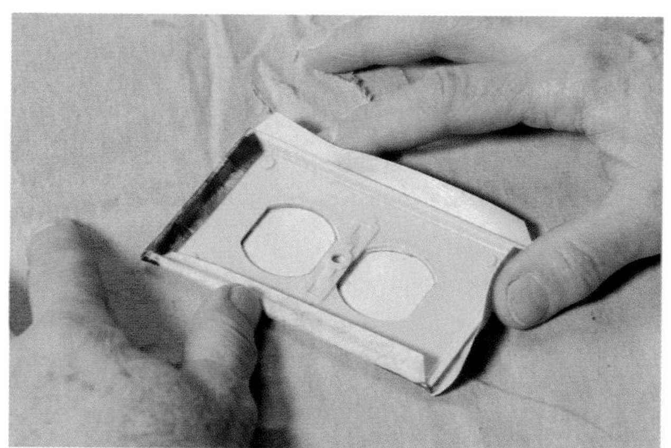

3 Apply vinyl-on-vinyl adhesive to the wallpaper. Press the cover plate onto the wallpaper, smoothing out any bubbles. Wrap the overlap around the cover plate and tape the edges in place.

4 Cut out the cover plate openings with a razor knife. Open up the screw hole by gently pushing a finishing nail through it from front to back. Attach the cover plate to the wall with the original screw.

$ BUYER'S GUIDE

CLEAR PLASTIC COVER PLATES–THERE IS ANOTHER WAY!

Covering switchplates and receptacle plates takes very little time. But if you're in a real hurry, there's also another quick fix. Look in the electrical-supply or wallpaper department for a clear plastic cover made for wallpaper. It has two pieces that snap together. Cut a piece of paper to fit, sandwich it between the two pieces, and then snap them together. Cut out holes for the switch or outlets and poke a smaller hole for each screw. Finally screw the plate in place. It wipes clean with a damp sponge and will last for years.

For professional results

When you finish wallpapering a room, check for minor problems while the job is still fresh and all of your tools are still out:

- Pay special attention to the seams: If you rolled them too hard or before the adhesive had set, you may have squeezed out too much adhesive. Edges may look tight while they are wet but they'll bubble when the paper dries.
- Stand close to the wall, looking down its length with a strong sidelight to check for imperfections or bubbles.
- If you see bubbles or loose spots in the paper, repair them now (see page 87 for easy fixes).

CHAPTER 2

Walls and Ceilings

Walls are the unsung heroes in a home. Few people walk into a room with smooth, well-finished walls and are moved to say, "Wow, look at the walls." If the walls bear the dents, scrapes, and gouges of a poorly done job, though, they will definitely be noticed.

When you're tackling the job of doing or redoing the walls yourself, you can ensure good results by learning a few techniques. It's also smart to become familiar with the tools you'll be using—think ahead to make sure you have everything you need.

- Most wall and ceiling projects, except for very minor repairs, require some general carpentry and drywalling skills.
- You'll need to be handy with a utility knife and a hammer.
- Know how to use power tools such as circular saws, jigsaws, and drills safely, so you'll feel comfortable with them.
- Good measuring and marking tools such as tape measures, levels, and combination and framing squares are essential.
- You'll be spending part of your time on a ladder or scaffolding; learn how to work safely off the ground.
- Wear a dust mask or respirator to keep airborne particles out of your lungs.
- Use proper safety goggles for eye protection when hammering, drilling, cutting, sanding, or working above your head—even if you wear glasses.
- To protect your hands, wear work gloves when handling lumber or materials with sharp edges.

Contents

Walls and ceilings basics . . . 94
The walls and ceilings tool kit . . . 95
Repairing drywall . . . 96
Repairing corner damage . . . 98
Repairing a plaster ceiling . . . 99
Repairing plaster walls . . . 100
Installing ceiling tile . . . 102
Installing a tongue-and-groove ceiling . . . 104
Installing a suspended ceiling . . . 105
Removing a wall . . . 109
Building a partition wall . . . 113
Soundproofing a room . . . 118
Installing drywall . . . 119
Finishing drywall . . . 124
Installing paneling . . . 127
Installing no-miter moldings . . . 130
Molding installation skills . . . 131
Installing baseboards and chair rails . . . 135
Installing crown molding . . . 137
Installing polyurethane molding . . . 140
Creating custom molding . . . 141
Installing wainscoting . . . 143
Wainscot choices . . . 146
Hanging and arranging artwork . . . 147
Tiling a wall . . . 148

What's behind that wall?

Walls may look smooth on the surface, but they're almost always hiding something. There may be other rooms on the far side of walls, but these thin partitions also contain the entire infrastructure of your home: framing, water pipes, drainpipes, electrical wires, gas lines, phone lines, and cable for television or computers—to name a few items. Then there's insulation, in regular, blown-in, or expandable-foam varieties. In other words, a wall is complex.

So before you start enthusiastically knocking into your walls, know what's behind them. Three tools will help: First a stud finder beeps whenever it passes over a stud inside the wall. Second a no-contact voltage detector lights up when it passes over an electrical line. Both are musts if you're going to do so much as drive a nail—have them on hand before you start.

The third tool is common sense. You know, for instance, that if there is a toilet upstairs, a drainpipe runs from it and a supply pipe runs to it. Plumbers like to run both pipes straight up and down; if you're working on a wall below and behind the toilet, you'll probably find them there. Lines for faucets, sinks, and bathtubs usually run down through the wall behind them too, though in some cases they'll run through the floor for a short distance in order to reach the wall.

If a gas line runs to a stove, heater, or fireplace, trace its route back to the gas meter. The line most likely runs into the wall and then straight down, or through the floor and straight down. Once the line reaches the basement or crawlspace, it runs horizontally to the gas meter.

If you have a hot-air register in the wall, there's also a heating duct there. Much of the horizontal travel occurs where the vents first come out of the heater. From there the vents run inside the walls with as little branching as possible. The same is true of pipes for hot-water heat.

You'll want to check and double-check thoroughly for electrical lines with the no-contact voltage detector. They may or may not run up the wall or over to the next outlet; electricians sometimes resort to very creative placement. Turn off the water and power if there is a faucet, tub, toilet, electrical outlet, or switch anywhere in the vicinity. Look for phone lines, cable TV lines, and anything else you can imagine. If you're doing major work on the wall, carefully remove part of it to get an idea of what's going on behind it. And if you're removing a wall, plan ahead. You still need all those wires and pipes it conceals, and each will need to find a new home once the old wall is gone.

Walls and ceilings basics

The vast majority of homes built since the 1950s have interior walls and ceilings framed with wood and finished with drywall. Sheets of drywall are nailed or screwed to wooden studs, and the seams are reinforced with tape and filled with a plasterlike joint compound. Repairs require troweling on more compound, though a hole may require piecing a drywall patch into the wall.

Older houses usually have thin, closely spaced wood lath strips nailed to the studs, with layers of plaster troweled over the lath. These walls tend to be thicker and also more brittle because of age. Repair cracks in these walls with surfacing compound (which, unlike joint compound, is formulated specifically for plaster).

Repairing holes usually involves removing the damaged plaster and troweling on a repair compound.

Wood paneling or wainscoting and tile are usually installed over existing drywall or plaster without repairing the existing wall. Suspended ceilings or a new layer of drywall can cover up damaged plaster or ceiling joists.

A new surface may be more pleasing than the old, but putting one up is seldom less work than repairing the original. When deciding on materials, check out recently developed options; one of these may suit your needs. Look online, in magazines, and at product literature for the latest in building materials.

Ceiling materials include drywall, plaster, and the following: Decorative 12-inch and 24-inch ceiling tiles are nailed or stapled to a wooden grid built on the ceiling. Insulated suspended ceiling panels and acoustical suspended ceiling panels hang from a metal grid. This grid is made up of wall angles, suspended ceiling main tees (sometimes called runners), and 2-foot and 4-foot cross-tees.

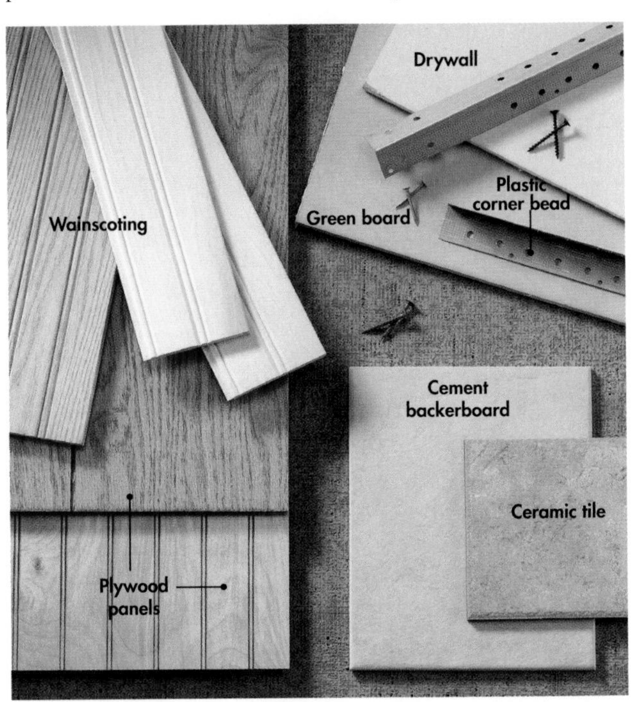

Using plywood panels is one of the quickest ways to cover a wall; they come grooved, in a variety of wood veneers and colors. Wainscoting is a tongue-and-groove solid wood paneling that you cut and piece together on the wall. Drywall is screwed in place directly over the studs, but in bathrooms, use moisture-resistant "green board" instead. Fill in seams between pieces of drywall with reinforcing tape and plasterlike joint compound. Protect the corners, which are used in basements to avoid rust stains, with preformed corner bead, which comes in metal or plastic. Ceramic tile is an extremely durable wall surface. Install it over cement backerboard, which comes in sheets.

$ BUYER'S GUIDE

WHAT IS THAT PRODUCT CALLED?

Names of products vary from region to region, store to store, and even contractor to contractor. If you're unsure of what something is called, take a sample or picture to the store when you go shopping, or be able to describe how you'll use it. Some manufacturers have proprietary names for their tools or products, but you'll need to know the "generic" version. The tool chart on the opposite page may help you identify what you need.

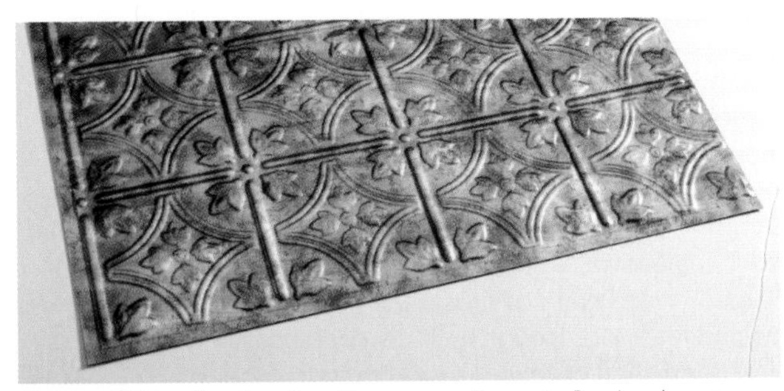

If you like the look of pressed metal, check out the new thermoplastic panels that look like embossed tin. Individual panels snap together to cover larger areas, such as ceilings, walls, or backsplashes.

The walls and ceilings tool kit

3-pound sledgehammer

Drywall bucket

Flat pry bar

Line clamp

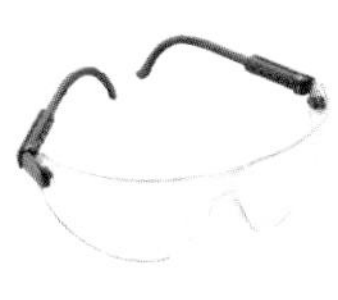
Safety glasses

Straightedge

Carpenter's square

Drywall knives

Foam paintbrushes

Line level

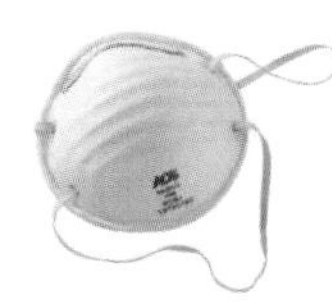
Sanding mask

Stud driver

Caulking gun

Drywall mud pan

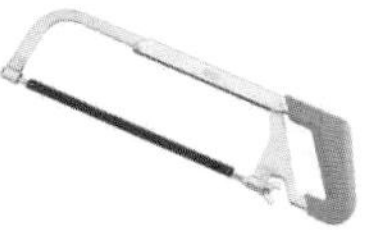
Hacksaw

Nail puller

Sanding pole

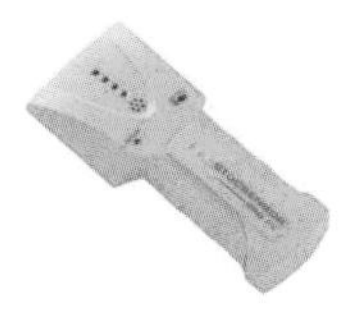
Stud finder

Chalkline and mason's string

Drywall sanding screen

Hammers

Pliers

Sanding sponge

Tape measure

Clamp

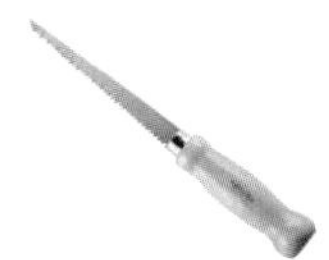
Drywall saw

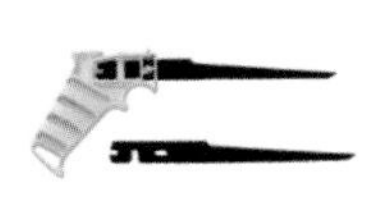
Keyhole saw

Putty knives

Sawhorse

Tin snips

Drill

Drywall square

Ladder

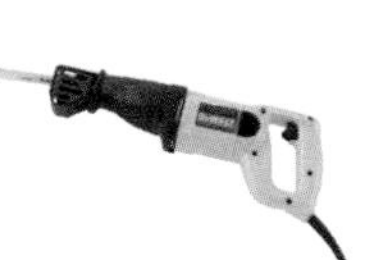
Reciprocating saw

Slotted & Phillips screwdrivers

Utility knife

Drill bits

Ear protection

Levels

Saber saw

Spiral cutting tool

Wire strippers

Repairing drywall

Skill level:	Time to complete:	Materials:	Tools:
★★☆☆☆	Experienced 30 min. Handy 45 min. Novice 1 hr.	1×3 scrap lumber or ¾-inch plywood, 3-inch drywall screws, drywall scrap, self-adhesive fiberglass drywall tape, lightweight drywall compound, fine-grit sandpaper	Framing square, drywall saw, utility knife, electric drill with clutch and phillips-head bit or drywall screw gun, 9-inch and 12-inch putty knives

Unlike traditional plastering, a messy, highly skilled job that takes weeks to complete, drywall can be done quickly. Drywall is a manufactured product: a sheet of gypsum sandwiched between two layers of paper. It comes in several thicknesses and is most commonly sold in 4×8- and 4×12-foot panels. The drywall sheets break and crumble easily until they're installed, but once you nail or screw them to studs and joists, they are largely out of harm's way. The chalky material can be dented by normal traffic. Fill small dents with lightweight surfacing compound, then sand before repainting. Repairing a larger area involves cutting and fitting a patch.

Repairing holes

1 Outline the damaged area with a carpenter's square. The top and bottom of the rectangle should be an inch or so outside the damaged area. Center the sides over the studs on both sides of the hole.

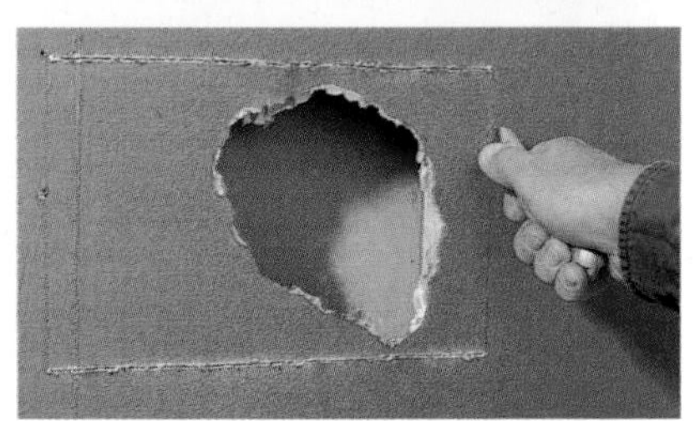

2 Cut along the horizontal outlines with a drywall saw. When the saw blade runs into the studs, make a mark and measure over the stud ¾ inch. This is the center of the stud; the edge of the patch should be directly over it so the existing drywall and also the patch will have support. Cut along the vertical lines with a utility knife using several cuts, each one slightly deeper than the previous one.

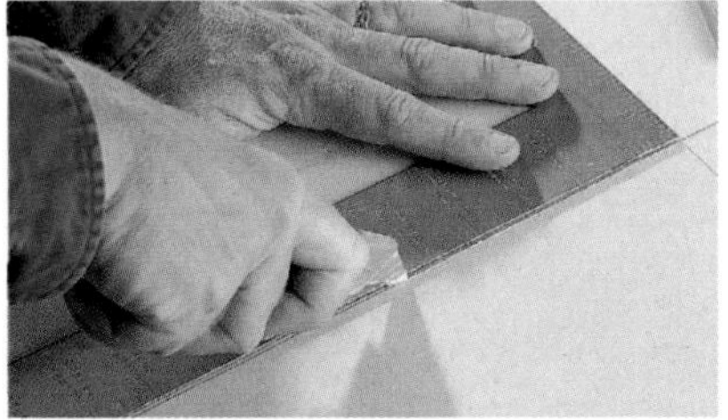

3 Cut the supports, then the patch. Cut one or two 1×3 or ¾-inch plywood scraps 2 to 4 inches longer than the patch is high. Insert a support in the hole; holding it in place with one hand, secure it with drywall screws. (Dent, but don't drive the screwhead through the drywall's paper covering.) Repeat for the other support, if needed. Make a patch the size of the opening using the framing square and a scrap piece of drywall; cut it out with a utility knife.

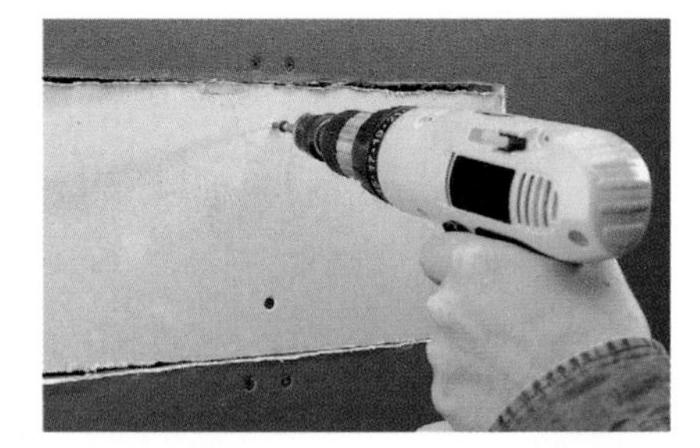

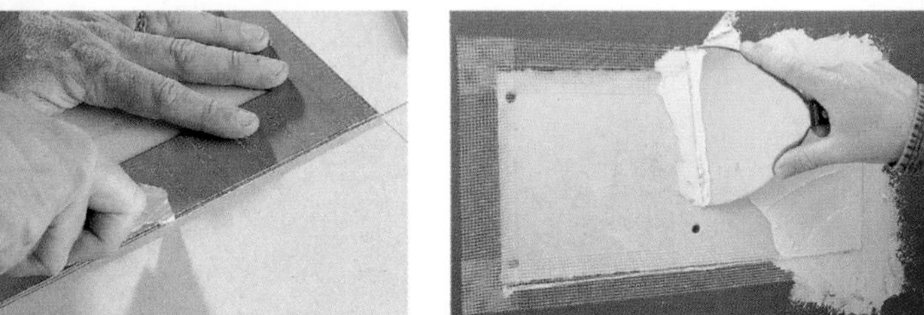

4 Place the patch in the opening. Attach it with 1¼-inch drywall screws as far as possible from the edges to avoid splitting or crumbling the drywall. Cut short strips of self-adhesive fiberglass drywall tape to fit on the seams around the patch. Using a 9-inch putty knife, spread drywall joint compound across the tape and patch to create a smooth, flat surface. Let it dry overnight, sand, and apply a second coat. For the smoothest patch, sand the surface to remove any irregularities; then spread a third coat—this time with a 12-inch putty knife.

Drywall crack repair

1 To fill a narrow drywall crack, widen it slightly. Brush off any loose pieces.

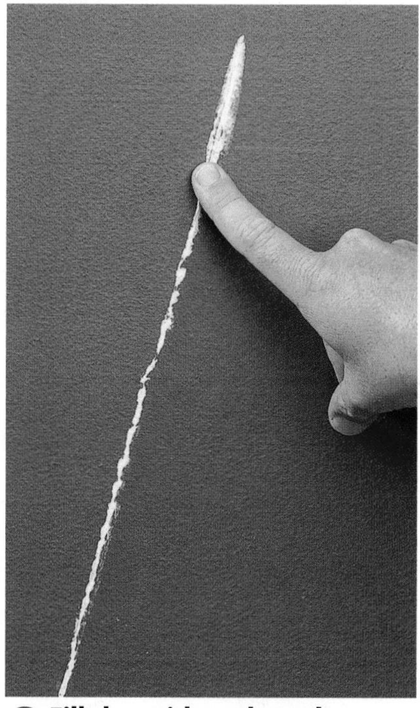

2 Fill the widened crack with lightweight surfacing compound, using a putty knife or your finger to apply it.

3 Smooth the area by applying more thin coats of the surfacing compound. When the patch is dry, sand and prime it.

WALLS AND CEILINGS

Using tape to repair a severe crack

When a crack is severe or is subject to pressures that may cause it to reopen, you may want to reinforce it with joint tape. Tape and finish the crack the same way you would tape a new drywall joint (see pages 124 to 126), smoothing it to match the existing wall. It's best to prime and paint the entire wall—corner to corner—rather than hoping for the best and painting only the repaired area, which will rarely match.

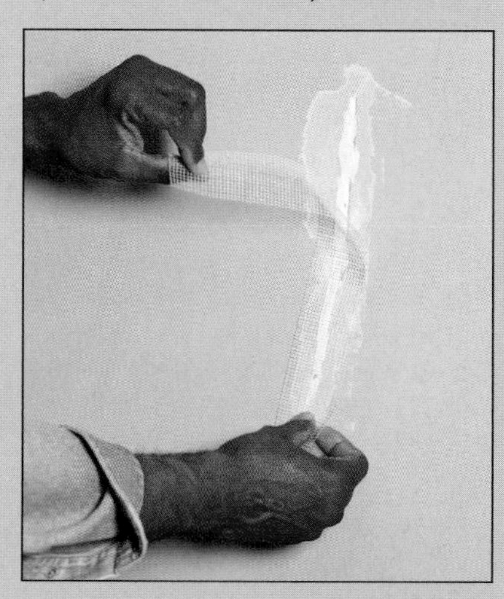

WORK SMART

NOT SO FAST

You'll get the best results from any drywall repair job by allowing the coats of joint compound to dry thoroughly before you proceed. Put up the mud and leave it for at least 24 hours. For a smoother finish, use water to thin the final coat of compound to the consistency of mayonnaise, or buy a product made specifically for the final coat.

Drywall patch kit

If the hole in your drywall is very small, you may be able to use a ready-made patch kit, with self-adhesive screen mesh that presses on, over the hole. Spread the joint compound over the mesh, which acts as a backing, and finish as for a seam.

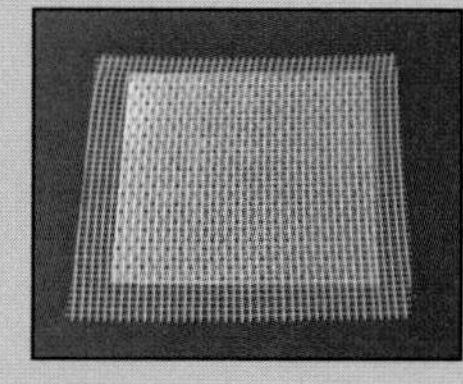

BUYER'S GUIDE

CHOOSE A FILLER

Lightweight spackling is used for shallow dents and nail holes. It sands easily and dries in 15 to 30 minutes.

Spackling paste is used to fill larger holes and dents. Build it up in ¼-inch-thick layers; each layer dries in 10 to 40 minutes and can then be sanded.

Wallboard joint compound is used only on taped wallboard joints and corner bead; apply it in layers no more than ¼-inch thick, sanding between each coat. Containers hold from 1 to 5 gallons.

Paintable latex caulk is the only filler that can handle unstable gaps and cracks on surfaces. On the downside, caulk cannot be sanded, so smooth it with a putty knife right after you apply it.

Repairing corner damage

Skill level:	Time to complete:	Materials:	Tools:
★★★☆☆	Experienced 30 min. Handy 45 min. Novice 1 hour	paper joint tape, corner bead, joint compound, drywall screws	hacksaw (optional), power drill, 6-inch drywall knife, hammer

Repairing outside corners

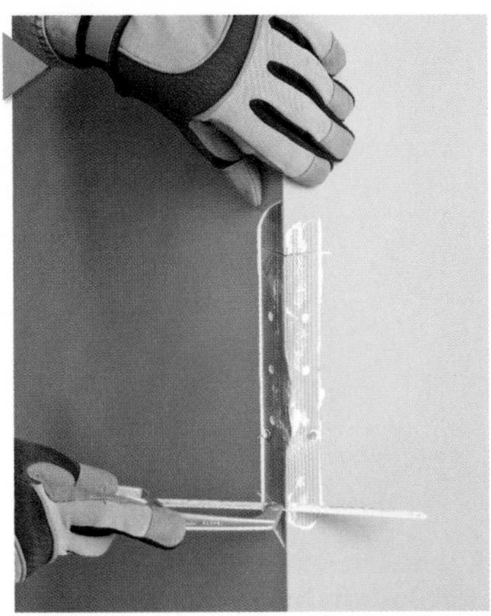

1 Remove the joint compound from the damaged portion of the corner bead. For very damaged areas, replace that section (cut it out with a hacksaw and fit in a new piece).

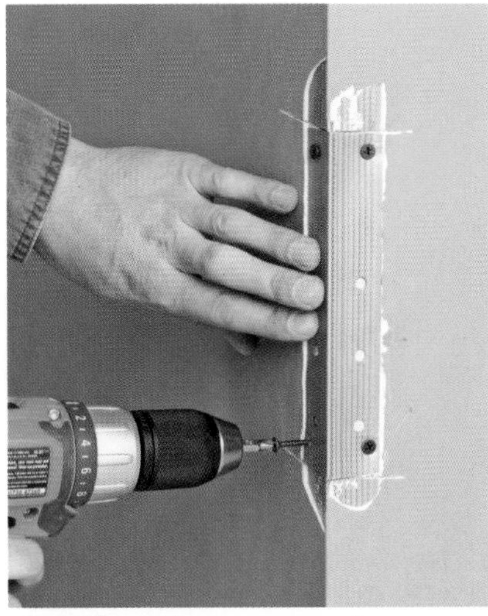

2 Otherwise, secure the corner bead with drywall nails or screws. Apply a thin coat of joint compound with a 6-inch knife. Smooth it out, feather the edges, and let it dry.

3 Add another coat of joint compound. Smooth and feather it as before; sand it well before priming and painting.

Repairing popped nails

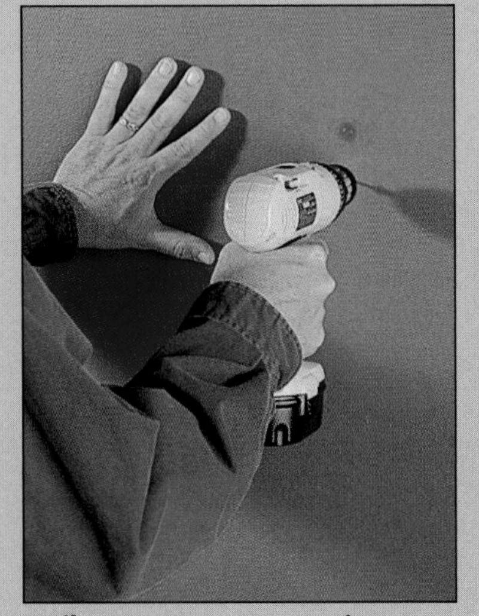

Nails may pop out over time as the stud holding them dries out. If this happens, the head of the nail shows, or it looks as if a small disk has been slipped under the drywall paper. You may be able to remove the nail without damage. Drive drywall screws an inch above and below the pop to secure the wall.

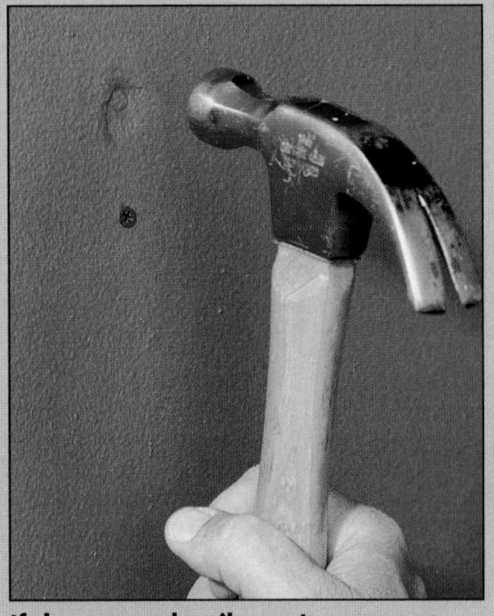

If the popped nail won't come out, drive it back in place, finishing with a slight dent in the drywall that doesn't tear the surface. Fill the dents or screw holes with surfacing compound. When dry, sand the patch, then prime and paint.

Repairing inside corners

For minor cracks in the corners cut out and remove any loose pieces. Run a very narrow bead of latex caulk along the crack, and smooth it with a wet finger. For wider cracks, apply a thin layer of joint compound. Crease a short length of paper tape down the middle (or use the pre-creased kind), press it into the joint compound and finish the corner as for new drywall (see pages125 and 126).

Repairing a plaster ceiling

Skill level:	Time to complete:	Materials:	Tools:
★★★☆☆	Experienced Variable Handy Variable Novice Variable	drywall, joint compound, joint tape, construction adhesive, drywall screws, finishing nails, wood or urethane corner molding, primer, paint	8- and 12-inch drywall knives, power drill or dimple drill, miter saw, hammer, caulking gun, roller, paintbrush

▲ **Covering up a cracked plaster sealing with a new layer of drywall is often a good solution.** If you leave a narrow border of the old ceiling and paint it an accent color, you'll create the decorative effect of a tray ceiling while solving a problem at the same time.

1 Attach drywall panels to the ceiling joists, directly under the cracked plaster, with long sheetrock screws and construction adhesive. Leave the last 3 to 8 inches from the crown molding uncovered, all around.

Good moldings, bad plaster

Age, in a house, is both a plus and a minus. On the plus side, an older house often has very attractive crown moldings. On the minus side, those moldings may surround a plaster ceiling that has cracked with age. Minor ceiling cracks can be repaired with patching plaster (not regular joint compound), but it may be easier to simply cover up major cracks.

If you take off the moldings to replace the ceiling with drywall, they'll never fit the right way again. A much better solution is to keep the molding in place and add a layer of drywall that stops just short (3 to 8 inches) of the moldings. Finish the new drywall as you would any new ceiling. Paint the ceiling and then the recessed space around it, perhaps using an accent color to create a decorative ceiling treatment. To hide the raw edges of the drywall, tack on narrow corner molding (either plain or a contoured profile (prime and paint the molding before installing it).

2 Cover the raw outside edges of the drywall with metal corner bead attached with drywall screws or nails. Or, for a more decorative appearance, use lengths of outside-corner molding made of wood. Prepaint the wood molding, miter it at the corners, and attach it with small finishing nails or construction adhesive.

3 Finish as for a new ceiling (see page 121). Prime and paint the ceiling. Paint the open space between the new drywall and the crown moldings. (If you use the wall color on the open space, your ceiling will appear higher.) Or paint it an accent color that harmonizes with the room for a more decorative ceiling.

Repairing plaster walls

Skill level:	Time to complete:	Materials:	Tools:
★★★☆☆	Experienced 30 min. Handy 45 min. Novice 1 hr.	Plaster patching compound, drywall scrap (optional), 150-grit sandpaper	Pocket can opener or paint can opener or plaster scraping tool, spray bottle, cup or pan, dust respirator, utility knife, 2-inch and 6-inch putty knives, 10-12 inch drywall knife, finishing nails

Older homes, particularly if they were built prior to World War II, are likely to have plaster walls. A plaster wall is actually three layers of plaster applied over narrow wooden strips called lath. Plastering an entire wall is highly skilled work, but repairing a plaster wall is well within most homeowners' abilities.

Having the right materials and tools on hand will make the job easier. A powdered material called plaster patch contains added adhesives that bond with the existing plaster—this will give you the best results. Surface and joint compounds are designed for other uses, and they make a good plaster repair job next to impossible.

Plaster repair requires patience because each layer needs to dry before the next can be added. Apply the compound in thin (1/8-inch to 1/4-inch) layers. This keeps the compound from cracking and makes the repair permanent.

1 Remove loose plaster from the damaged area; most of it can be pried away with your fingers. Check to see if the remaining plaster is attached to the lath by trying to slip a 1-inch putty knife between the lath and plaster. If the knife slips under the plaster, it's loose; pry gently to remove it. Undercut the hole: Using a pocket knife, paint can opener, or plaster-scraping tool, cut out beneath the edges of the hole so the side toward the lath is wider. This creates a void or notch under the good plaster, which anchors the plaster patch. Remove dust and debris.

WORK SMART
DON'T STOP SHORT

Small holes in plaster walls tend to get bigger. When you begin removing the loose plaster around a hole, you'll need to keep going until you get rid of all plaster no longer attached to the lath. The final repair may turn out to be much larger than the original hole.

$ BUYER'S GUIDE
PLASTER REPAIRS

Patching plaster mixed from powder fills larger holes and cracks up to 1/4 inch wide. Apply it in several layers, each no more than 1/4 inch thick. It dries in 90 minutes and can be sanded.

Plaster of Paris is mixed from powder and water. It is extremely durable but is difficult to sand. A 1/4-inch thickness hardens in 30 minutes.

Paintable latex caulk fills unstable gaps and cracks in walls and ceilings. It's paintable but not sandable, so smooth it immediately after you apply it.

2 Moisten the area with water. Plaster and lath will draw water out of the patching compound if you don't wet it beforehand, leaving you with a crumbling mass that won't stick. Spraying the area with water keeps the patching compound from drying too quickly. Mix the plaster patch while wearing safety glasses and a respirator (to avoid breathing the fine particles). Mix according to package instructions, using only enough water to form a paste. For a small hole, mix the compound in a cup; for larger holes, mix it in a larger pan. Stop stirring when the paste is free of lumps; overmixing causes the compound to set too quickly.

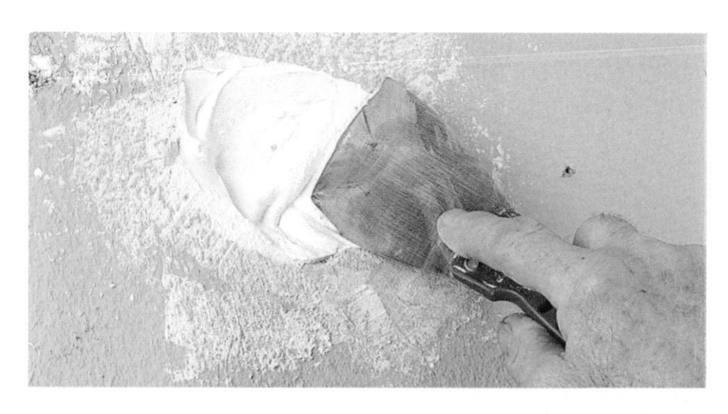

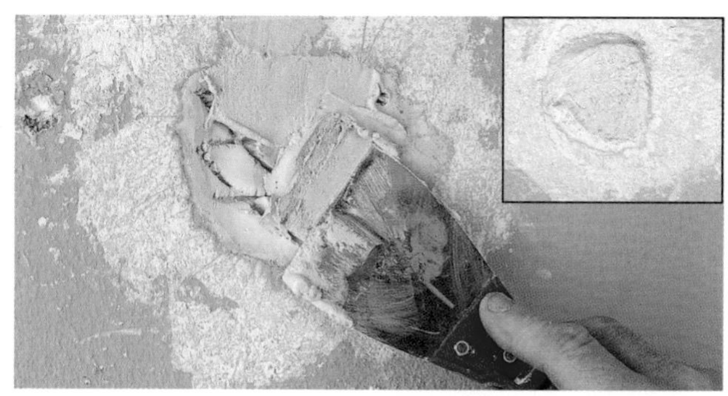

3 Work the compound into the damaged area with a broad knife or putty knife, pressing it through the spaces between the lath. (The first layer should be about half as thick as the plaster.) Cross score the surface of the wet compound with a nail—this lets the next coat lodge in the grooves, creating a mechanical bond in addition to the chemical bond that exists between coats. Let the patch dry thoroughly before applying the second coat.

4 When the first coat dries, mix another batch of compound. Apply a second coat, filling about half the space between the first coat and the wall surface, leaving no more than a ¼-inch recess. (See inset, above.) When the second coat dries, mix and apply a third coat, smoothing it with a 10- to 12-inch-wide drywalll knife. Feather the edges of the compound beyond the original hole, blending the edges flush with the wall. Sand lightly while wearing a dust mask; then prime and paint.

CLOSER LOOK

WHEN GOOD PLASTER GOES BAD

Cracks and broken plaster may be signs of other problems—usually a settling house. Some settling is normal over time. If the house continues settling after you patch the wall, the wall will crack again, often in the same place. If so, install one or two basement floor jacks underneath the wall with the recurring crack, being careful not to raise them *too* much. This may eliminate the problem; ask for advice from a pro.

Brown spots or crumbly plaster usually indicate water damage from the roof, a leaky window, or a leaky pipe. Find and correct the problem before repairing the plaster to avoid it happening again.

When repairing plaster, you'll need to remove all the loose material (you may be taking out more than you intended). If the hole is larger than 10 to 12 inches wide, fill it with a piece of drywall, as shown at right.

Patching plaster with drywall

Most small plaster repairs involve building up layers of plaster until the patch is thick enough to match the original wall. Layers are generally ⅛ inch to ¼ inch thick.

For larger holes, borrow a technique from drywall repairs: Square off the damaged area with a hammer and cold chisel. Tap gently to remove only the damaged area. In the example shown at right, the lath is missing because the patch is being put over an outlet opening that is no longer used. Unless the lath is already missing, leave it intact to provide extra support.

Cut out a piece from scrap drywall the same thickness as the plaster, making it larger than the opening in the wall by about 2 inches in each direction.

Find the center of the patch and draw another rectangle slightly smaller than the opening in the wall. Score along the line with a utility knife and pick away the gypsum, leaving a 2-inch paper flange around the edge of the patch.

Test-fit the drywall in the opening; make necessary adjustments. Trowel a layer of plaster patching compound on the wall, making it a little larger than the flange on the patch. Put the patch

in the hole and screw it in place with drywall screws. Trowel the flange tightly against the wall with patching compound. Feather the edges and sand smooth when the patching compound is dry. Prime and paint the wall.

Installing ceiling tile

Skill level:	Time to complete:	Materials:	Tools:
★★★☆☆	Experienced 4 hrs. Handy 6 hrs. Novice 8 hrs.	Ceiling tile, furring strips, drywall screws, shims	Chalkline, tape measure, hammer, utility knife, safety glasses, 4-foot level, drill and screwdriver bit, straightedge, stapler, keyhole saw

Putting up ceiling tiles is a big job, but the process isn't necessarily difficult. Basically, you'll screw a grid of 1×3s to the ceiling, shim it to create a flat surface, and then staple the tiles to the grid.

The order in which you apply materials is important if you want to end up with a balanced ceiling. Balanced means that the center seam of the ceiling runs down the center of the room. It also means that tiles on opposite sides of the room are equal in size. (Remember, some of these may have to be trimmed.) Order 10 percent more tile than the ceiling area to allow for trimming and later replacement.

You'll start the grid from the center of the room, but you'll start applying tiles at the wall edges.

The ceiling here is attached to exposed floor joists, as in an unfinished basement. If you're applying the tiles over a finished ceiling, locate the joists with a stud finder. Drive nails to make sure you're directly under the joist, and snap a chalkline to mark the location of each one.

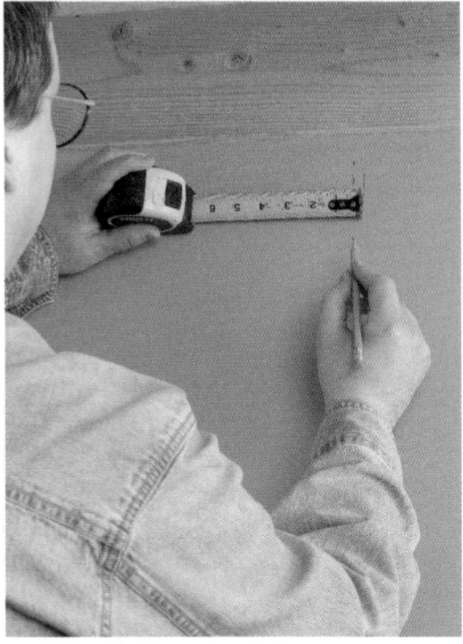

1 Mark the center of walls that run parallel to the joists. The visible edges (not including the tongues) of the tiles will be along this line. Measure over the width of the tile's tongue (usually about ½ inch) to indicate where the tongue will be. Repeat the centering process on the two walls that are perpendicular to the joists. Snap chalklines between the opposite tongue marks; you will have two chalklines crossing each other on the ceiling.

WORK SMART
PROFESSIONAL TIPS

Screw support blocks to the joists to help support the ends of the furring strips; this is optional, but it adds stability to the finished ceiling. This step is important in basements, where moisture may cause supports to warp or sag, or when the furring strips themselves may be warped.

Let ceiling tiles acclimate to the room for a full 24 hours before installing them.

Adhesive as alternative

If your ceiling is flat, level, and in good condition, save time by applying the tiles directly to the ceiling with construction adhesive. Remember that any unevenness in the ceiling will also show in the tiles.

2 Center a 1×3 furring strip on the chalkline, screwing it to the ceiling joist with 1⅝-inch-long #8 drywall screws. (Screws are easier to use than the nails usually recommended, and if you have to back one of the 1×3s away from the joist to level the ceiling later, it is easy to loosen the screws.) You may want to add support blocks to hold the edge of the furring strip against the joist. (See Work Smart, left.)

3 Screw 1×3s to the rest of the ceiling, spacing the centers so they are as far apart as the visible part of the tiles is wide, usually about 12 inches. On walls perpendicular to the joists, install 1×3s right against the wall so you'll have something behind the last tile edges.

4 The new ceiling will only be as level (flat) as the furring strips. Check by putting a level at various points against the furring strip grid. If you see gaps between the level and the furring strips, back a screw out and slip in a shim. Drive each shim in farther or slide it partway out as needed. Tighten the screw until it is just snug, and check again with the level before proceeding.

5 Most tiles are installed full size, but the border tiles are trimmed to fit. Before you install any tiles, lay out a grid for the full-size ones—start at the lines you snapped in the middle of the ceiling and snap a new line exactly every 12 inches (or the visible width of the tile).

6 Measure the distance between the last line and two adjacent walls. Cut individual tiles to fit, sizing them so that there is a ¼-inch gap between the tile and the wall—this leaves you room to maneuver the tile. It also prevents needing to cut tapered tiles as long as the wall isn't more than ¼ inch off at its two ends. Molding will cover the gaps later.

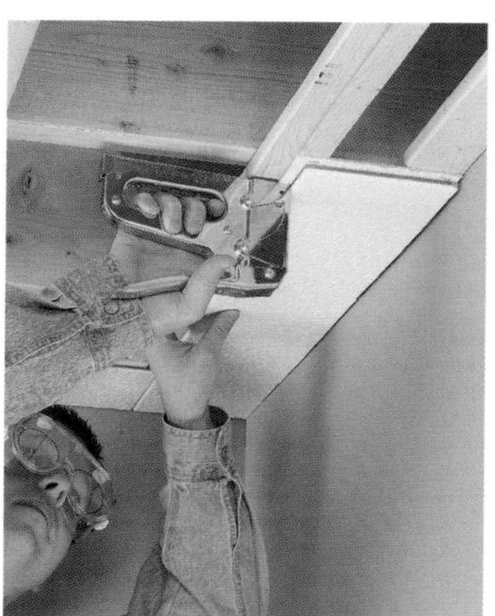

7 Staple the border tiles in place; drive the staples through the tongue of the tile so they won't show later. On two walls, you'll be able to staple the tiles to the 1×3 furring against the wall, as shown here. On the other walls, nail the edge of the tiles into the joists, if possible. If you can't, the molding you'll apply later will provide adequate support.

8 Begin stapling the full-size tiles once there are border tiles on two adjacent walls. Work your way across the room. Trim the border tiles against the remaining walls to the proper size and staple in place. If you need to make cutouts for lighting (see inset above), put the tile in place, marking each edge of the cut. Connect the lines on the back of the tile and cut the opening with a keyhole saw. (Or, use a hole-saw blade in the correct diameter if installing can lights.)

When all tiles are in place, cut molding to fit tightly against the ceiling and wall. Nail it in place, covering the gaps around the edges.

Installing a tongue-and-groove ceiling

Skill level:	Time to complete:	Materials:	Tools:
★★★☆☆	Experienced Varies Handy Varies Novice Varies	Tongue-and-groove lumber, recommended nails, quick-gripping building adhesive (optional), molding for edges	Hammer (or power hammer), saw, tape measure, carpenter's square, 4-foot level, ladder or scaffolding, caulking gun (optional)

Covering a ceiling with tongue-and-groove planks is a stylish way to add architectural character to any room, but it is particularly attractive on a cathedral ceiling, It can also cover up a multitude of ugly problems, including cracked plaster and water-stained drywall (fix whatever caused that problem before you begin). A power nailer makes the job go much faster, whatever the ceiling height.

Tongue-and-groove planks come in several different widths and grades (the higher the grade, the fewer knotholes the wood will have). Long, wide pieces of wood with few imperfections are naturally the most expensive.

It's ideal if you can buy lengths wide enough to span the room without the need to butt them. If you must butt them, there are two ways: you can randomly stagger the butted joints, or use long pieces in the center, cut both sides to match, and cover the rows of butted joints with lath strips.

For a similar look, you can also buy 4×8 plywood panels that are grooved to resemble individual planks; these are especially useful for the ceilings of porches and small rooms that are no wider than the panel is long.

If you plan to stain and varnish the ceiling, it's a good idea to finish the individual boards before you install them. You can also prime and paint them beforehand if you like (remember to seal or prime the back too, to avoid warping). Otherwise, be prepared to spend quite a while working on all of those overhead grooves—it's a lot easier to do just touch-ups.

1 Planks will run perpendicular to the joists or furring strips (use these if you need to level the ceiling or want planks to run in a different direction). Securely fasten the furring strips into the joists.

2 Cut the strips to length, allowing ¼ inch of space at each end. With the grooved side of the first plank next to the wall, nail the tongue of each successive plank wherever it crosses a furring strip, going in at an angle.

3 Work across the room until all planks have been nailed. Measure each side and cut inside-corner molding or wider crown molding to fit (see pages 137–138 for instructions on installing it). Prefinish the molding to match the planks, if desired.

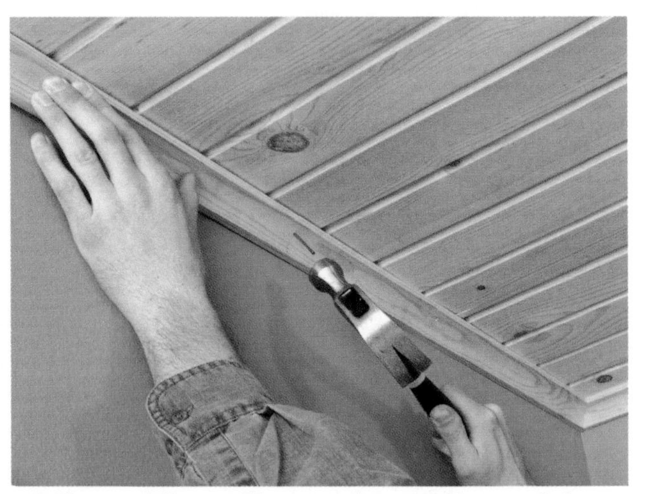

4 The molding will cover the small gaps left around the edges. Test fit the molding to make sure you've cut it correctly. Then attach it with small finishing nails. recessing the heads and filling the holes with putty.

Installing a suspended ceiling

Skill level:	Time to complete:	Materials:	Tools:
★★★☆☆	Experienced 3 hrs. Handy 5 hrs. Novice 7 hrs.	Nails, wall angles, hanger screws, hanger wire, cross tees, runners, suspended-ceiling tiles, common nails, lights, translucent plastic panels, wire nuts, electrician's tape	Hammer, tape measure, chalkline and mason's string, line level, tin snips or hacksaw, screwdriver, 4-foot level, utility knife, straightedge, pliers

Suspended ceilings are a good way to reduce the height of too-tall ceilings, saving heating costs in the process (heat always rises). There are two main parts to such ceilings: a metal grid that provides a structure and lightweight panels that slip into the grid. Installation, which varies in difficulty depending on what the ceiling is suspended from, requires only common tools.

When doing this project, leave at least 4 inches of space above the framework (or 6 inches if you're installing lighting) to provide maneuvering room for the panels. Install the grid first, starting by fastening the wall angles to the walls. Next, put up the runners (or main tees), which hang by wires from the ceiling and run perpendicular to the joists. Then come the short cross tees; these are installed between the runners and perpendicular to them.

The loose ceiling panels, which sit on the flanges of the installed grid, can be removed easily for access to the ductwork, plumbing, or electrical circuits. Damaged tiles can also be replaced easily.

A successful installation depends on two things, but the first is most important: measure, and then level. Unless you want a room with a sloping ceiling and a diagonal grid, make sure you do both.

Standard ceiling panels usually measure either 2×2 feet or 2×4 feet. It's likely that the ceiling will also require some partial panels. For a balanced look, plan on two equally sized partial panels, one on each side of the room. (See Balancing the Ceiling, below.)

You'll be stringing lots of layout lines as you begin the actual installation. Use mason's line because it won't sag as regular string will. Lines must be level; double-check the grid with a 4-foot level as you build it. Correcting problems is easy—it's usually just a matter of tightening a screw.

BUYER'S GUIDE

HANDY HANGERS

Using the correct hanger makes the job a lot easier. The simplest type of hanger is an eye hook, but there are other types that are easy to install and also easy to adjust. One company makes a flattened bolt to drive in with a socket that fits in a drill. Another company makes hanger wires with eyelets on one end: You attach the eyelet/hanger with a drywall screw and drive the screw in or out to level the grid. Check out other options too, such as the line clamps that simplify attaching leveling lines to the grid.

WORK SMART

FINDING CEILING JOISTS

It may be difficult to locate ceiling joists with a stud finder. If you have access, simply peek into the attic to see which direction the ceiling joists go and how far apart they are. If you don't have access you'll need to measure from below. Joists are usually spaced either 16 or 24 inches from center to center. Once you determine the direction, measure either 16 or 24 inches from the end wall; drive a nail through the ceiling. If it doesn't hit a joist, move in either direction in ½-inch increments until you hit it. Mark the joist position, and from that point, continue measuring across the ceiling.

Balancing the ceiling

To balance the ceiling make the border tiles (those next to the wall) the same size on opposite sides of the room. This example uses 2x2-foot tiles in a 11x14-foot room. First divide the width of the room by the width of the tiles. (11 divided by 2=5½ tiles.) Divide the fraction by two to determine the size of the border tiles. (½ divided by 2=¼ tile.) The border tiles would only be ¼ tile (or 6 inches) wide, which would appear out of proportion to the other tiles. Instead, add ½ tile to the size of the border tile, making it ¾ of a tile. Doing this means you use one less full tile. (4 full tiles and two border tiles of 18 inches each.) Repeat the process for the length of the room, if necessary.

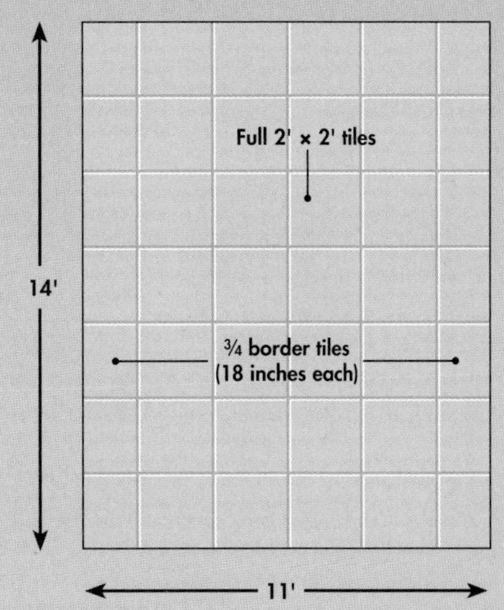

Installing a suspended ceiling (continued)

Hanging a suspended ceiling

To ensure a level ceiling, draw a level line around the top of the room, marking where you will install the wall angles. For the best results, rent a tripod laser. Most manufacturers advise you to put it in the center of the room and level the legs. When you turn on the laser, it begins to spin around, tracing a level line around the room. Hang the wall angles along this line.

If you'd rather not rent equipment, count on spending more time doing the layout. To start, drive a nail at one end of the wall to mark the height of the suspended ceiling. Tie mason's line to the nail—this type of line won't sag like regular chalklines do—and rub it with a piece of chalk. Hang a line level on the line and stretch the line to the far end of the wall. Raise or lower the line until it's level and snap a chalkline on the wall. Repeat on the remaining walls.

1 Lay out the bottom of the wall angle, either 4 inches below the joists or 6 inches if the ceiling will have a light in it. Cut the wall angle as necessary, using tin snips or a hacksaw. Nail or screw the wall angle along the line; butt the inside corners and miter the outside ones.

2 Snap a line along the joists; this marks the locations of the hangers (or the wires) that support the runners. Working at 4-foot intervals along the chalkline, screw the hangers into the joists.

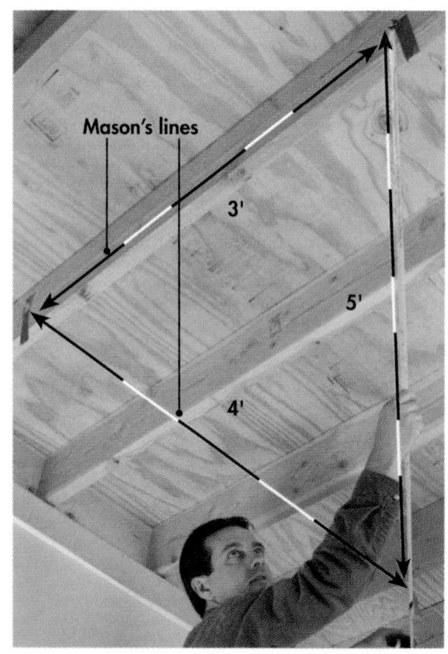

3 To lay out a square grid, first run mason's line from wall angle to wall angle along the path of the runner nearest the wall. Then stretch mason's line along the path of cross-tees nearest the wall. To square up, mark one line 3 feet from the intersection and another line 4 feet from the intersection. When the distance between these marks is exactly 5 feet, the lines are square. Slide the lines as necessary to square them.

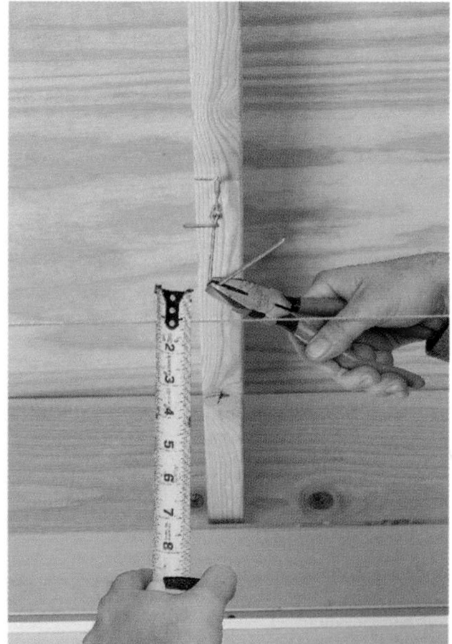

4 To make sure the grid will be level, measure up from the lines to the hanger wires, and bend them at the point where they will slip through the hanging holes in the runners. The exact distance varies from brand to brand, but it's equal to the distance from the bottom of the runner to the center of the hole.

5 Cut the runner to size. Make the cut so that when you place the runner on the wall angle, the hole into which the cross-tee fits is directly over the line marking the path of the cross-tee.

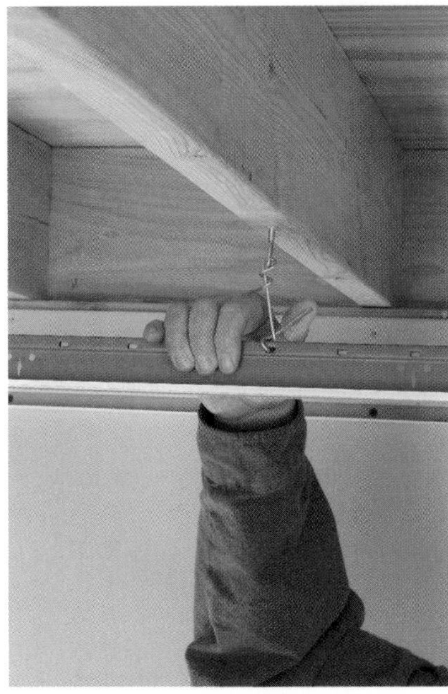

6 Rest one end of the runner on the wall angle, and slide the bent hanging wire through the hole. Snap sections of the runner together as needed to span the room, adding a hanger and wire to support the runner wherever joints occur. If necessary, trim the last section of runner to fit.

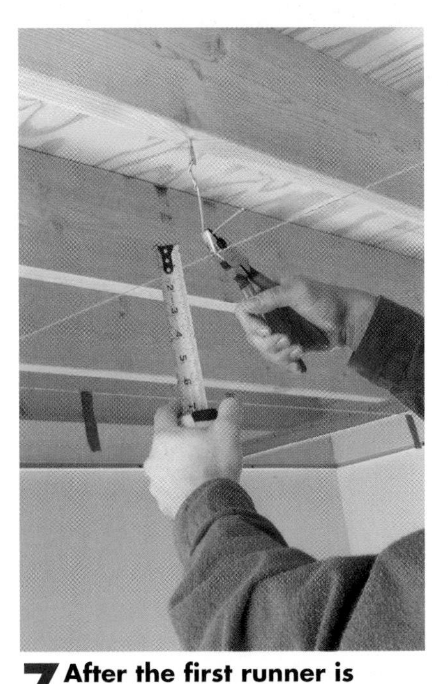

7 After the first runner is installed, run level lines to mark the paths of the others. Measure up, bend the hangers, and hang each runner as before. Check with a 4-foot level to make sure each runner is level. Make necessary adjustments by bending the hangers.

8 When the runners are all installed, hang the cross-tees. Starting in the middle of the room, put in a few cross-tees; then install some ceiling panels to square up the grid. Install the rest of the cross-tees.

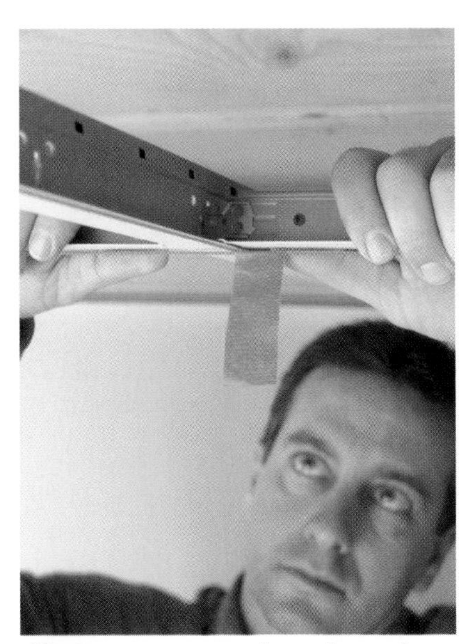

9 Cross-tees at the edge of the room may need to be cut to fit. Measure, cut, and install them one at a time. To keep the grid uniform, alternate sides: Put a tee on one side of the room, follow the line of tees to the other side of the room, and then install the next tee.

10 Install all of the full-size panels first. Save those around the edge of the room for last, because they will need to be cut to fit.

11 Cut tiles to fit around the edge of the room. Placing the tiles face-up on a flat surface, make repeated shallow cuts with a utility knife along a straightedge; then snap the panel in two. Place the trimmed panels in their openings. **Note:** If your tiles have a rabbeted (grooved) edge you will have to cut a similar rabbet into the edges of the border tiles with a utility knife so they will fit flush in the grid.

Installing a suspended ceiling (continued)

Lighting a suspended ceiling

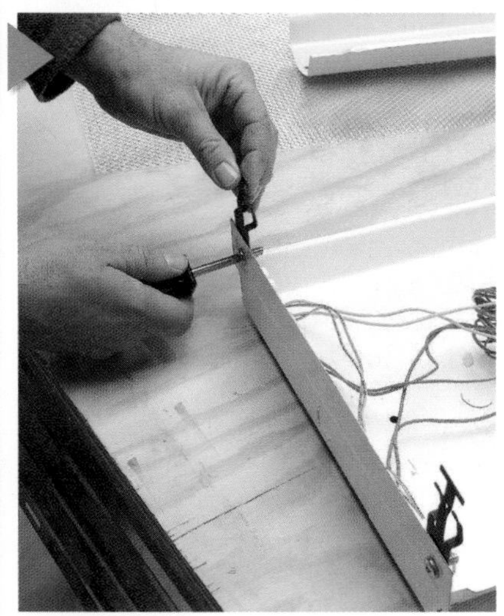

1 Most fluorescent lights for suspended ceilings require assembly; this varies from brand to brand. The fixture may come in several pieces: a reflector, which may be part of the main housing; two sockets per bulb; two end caps; and mounting brackets. Snap the sockets in place. Put the end caps on the housing and screw them in place.

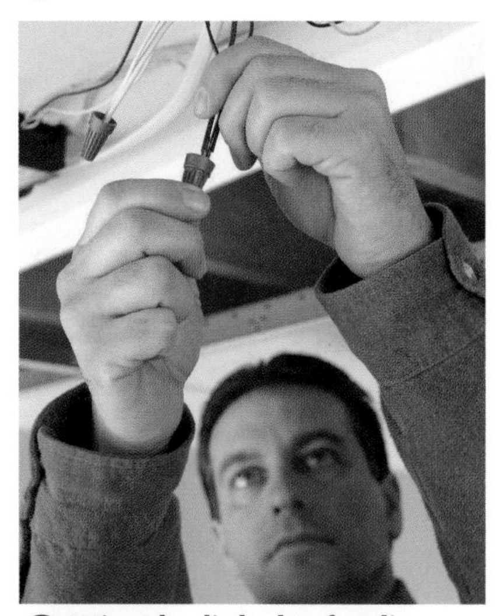

2 Wire the light by feeding cable through the opening in the top. Twist the light's black wire and the black cable wire together; then twist the white wire and cable together. Twist a wire nut over each one and wrap electrician's tape around each nut and its wires. Screw the ground wire to the green screw in the fixture.

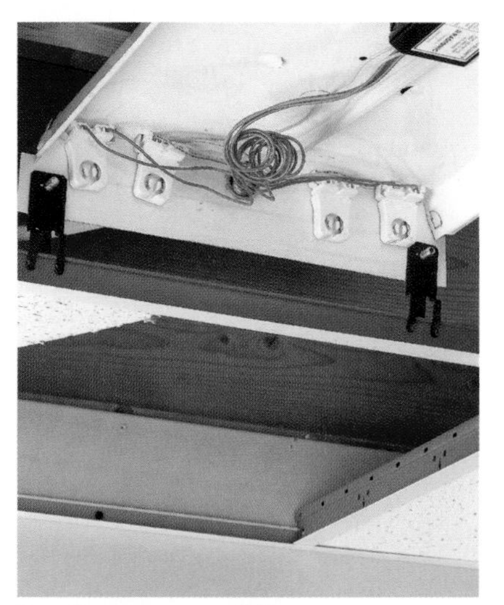

For long runs of fluorescent lighting, save time by connecting the fixtures end to end with special locknuts and connectors (available where you buy the fixtures). It's more efficient to wire them in sequence than to have individual rows of lights connected to a single junction box.

3 Fasten the reflector to the end caps, if necessary. The mounting bracket varies from brand to brand, but the light shown here has a tee-bracket that attaches to each end cap. Attach the bracket ends to the fixture, lift the fixture into place, and attach the brackets to the ceiling grid. Install the bulbs in the fixture.

4 Insert the cover. Slide a translucent plastic panel into place under the fixture. Angle the piece so you can position first one side and then the other on the grid. If the fit is tight, create temporary flexibility by removing a ceiling panel next to the fixture. Replace that panel when the light is done.

$ BUYER'S GUIDE: THE RIGHT LIGHT

Standard lighting for a suspended ceiling involves ceiling grid fixtures like those shown here. These are not the only kind available. Fixtures called "troffers" fit into the grid, covering the bulbs with a hinged door that may have dressy slats, translucent panels, or a combination.

Another option is to create a completely luminous ceiling with light fixtures and translucent panels running the width and breadth of the room.

The best choice for use in a luminous ceiling is a 4-foot long 40-watt rapid-start unit. To determine the number of lamps required for the entire area, sketch out the dimensions of the ceiling. Plan for the lamps to lie in parallel lines between 18 inches and 24 inches apart. Narrower spacing provides more light but is, naturally, more expensive. Allow about 8 inches between the ends of the lines and the wall.

Removing a wall

Skill level:	Time to complete:	Materials:	Tools:
★★★☆☆	Experienced Variable Handy Variable Novice Variable	None	Pry bar, hammer, end cutters, utility knife, circular saw, flat-backed garden spade, 3-lb. sledgehammer, reciprocating saw

Taking out a wall with pure muscle power is a great way to relieve some stress. It's fun too, because it's messy, it's not hard to do, and it reveals things that you might not otherwise see.

Before you start, take a good look at the wall. Besides dividing a large space into smaller spaces, some walls—called load-bearing walls—actually hold up the house. Removing them requires some knowledgeable carpentry, and the approval of your local building inspector. For the most part, removing a load-bearing wall or even enlarging a doorway in one is something most homeowners should not attempt to do. Unless you're pretty confident of your knowledge and skills, it's best to hire a pro in this situation.

Partition walls, however, provide no structural support. Removing them to create a more convenient traffic flow or open up a room is one of the easiest ways to improve on an existing floor plan. Fortunately the two types of walls are easy to tell apart.

All exterior walls are load-bearing walls. So are walls that sit on support beams, which are often visible in an unfinished basement. Walls that support lapped joists are also load-bearing; these are also easiest to see in an unfinished basement. Instead of running the entire width of the house, a joist starts at an exterior wall and runs to a middle, load-bearing wall. A separate joist runs from that wall to the second exterior wall. The surest way to know is to remove a little plaster or drywall. For strength, the top plate of a load-bearing wall is made of at least two stacked 2×4s, as shown at top left. The plate on a partition wall is made of a single 2×4 as shown at bottom left.

Before you swing a hammer, try to determine what is behind the wall. Outlets mean hidden wires; nearby plumbing means water pipes; stoves or furnaces may mean gas pipes. Make plans for relocating these, and turn off the utilities before you start.

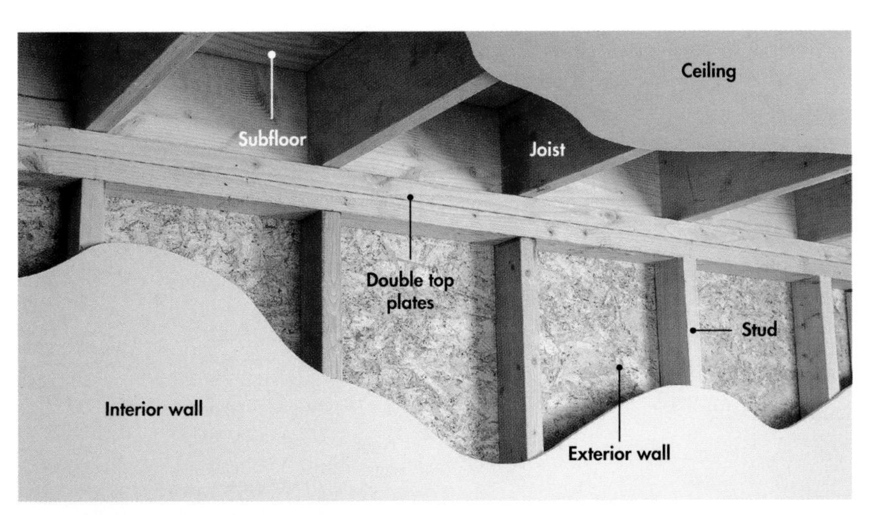

◀ Load-bearing walls carry the structural weight of your home. They can be identified by double top plates made from two layers of framing lumber. Load-bearing walls include all adjacent exterior walls and any interior walls that are aligned above support beams or that are positioned to support ceiling or floor joist lap joints.

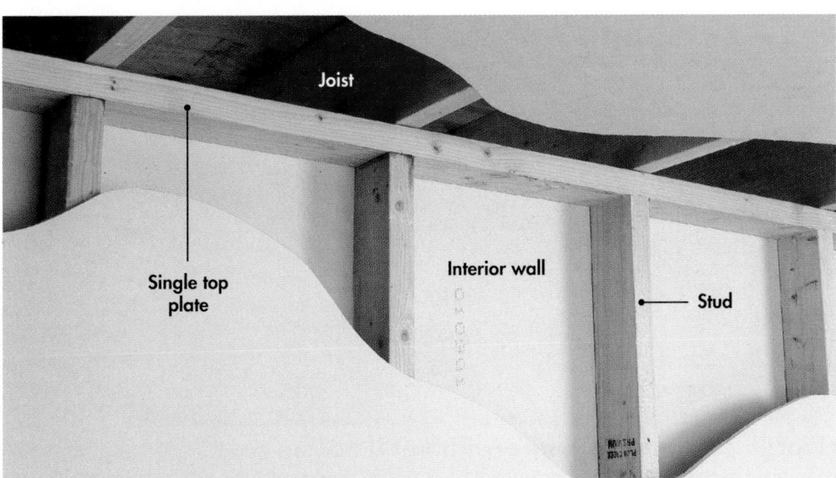

▲ Partition walls are interior walls that are not load-bearing. You can usually identify one by its single top plate. Any interior wall parallel to floor and ceiling joists is a partition wall, but a wall perpendicular to the joists might be either a partition or a load-bearing wall. The load-bearing wall will be aligned above a support beam; the partition wall probably won't be. If you're not sure, consider it a load-bearing wall until you have a professional take a look at it.

SAFETY ALERT

TURN OFF THE UTILITIES

Turn off the electricity, water, and gas at the main breaker or valves before removing wall surfaces. Work by daylight or use an independent lighting source.

WORK SMART

BLOCK THE DUST

Tearing out a wall can make some serious mess. Protect the rest of the house by sealing up doors to other rooms with plastic, at least until you've vacuumed. Always wear a respirator too.

Removing a wall (continued)

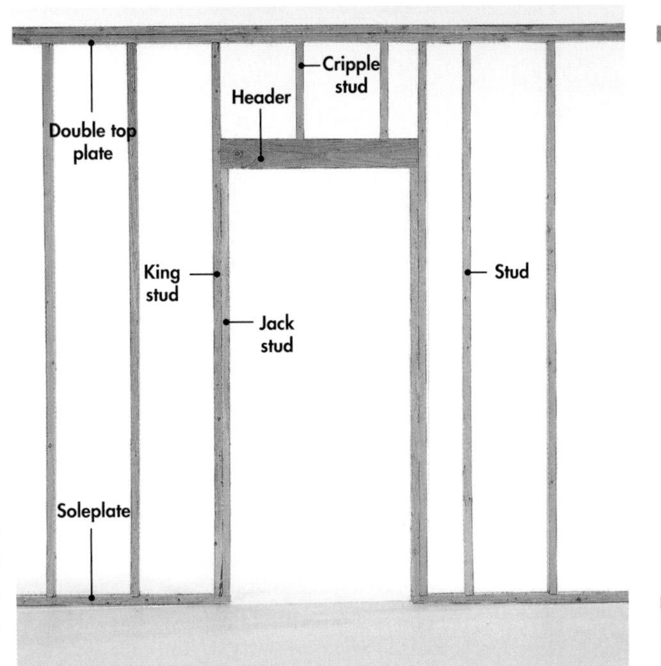

Each door opening in a load-bearing wall needs a header to provide adequate support. A header is like a sandwich with 2× stock on the outside and plywood inside; it is supported by jack studs running down to the floor. Short studs, called cripples, run between the header and the top plate of the wall. All exterior doors are in load-bearing walls, as are some interior doors. Non-load-bearing walls (see page 113) have headers made of single 2×4s mounted horizontally.

Cripple stud
Header
Double top plate
King stud
Stud
Jack stud
Rough sill
Soleplate
Cripple stud

Window openings also have headers. Because windows are in exterior walls, which are always load-bearing, they have built-up headers consisting of 2× lumber (a 2×4, a 2×6, or even wider) sandwiched around a piece of plywood. Using wider headers creates a solid-wood wall behind the drywall—very useful for installing heavy window treatments. The header is supported by jack studs; the rough sill below it is supported by cripple studs.

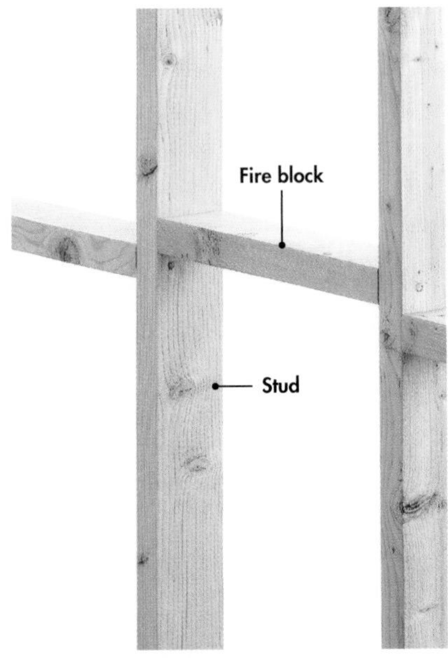

Install fire blocks on walls taller than 8 feet; some local codes also require them on shorter walls. Fire blocks prevent (or at least slow down) fire from traveling up the wall cavity. Cut 2×4s to fit between the studs and stagger them to make nailing easier.

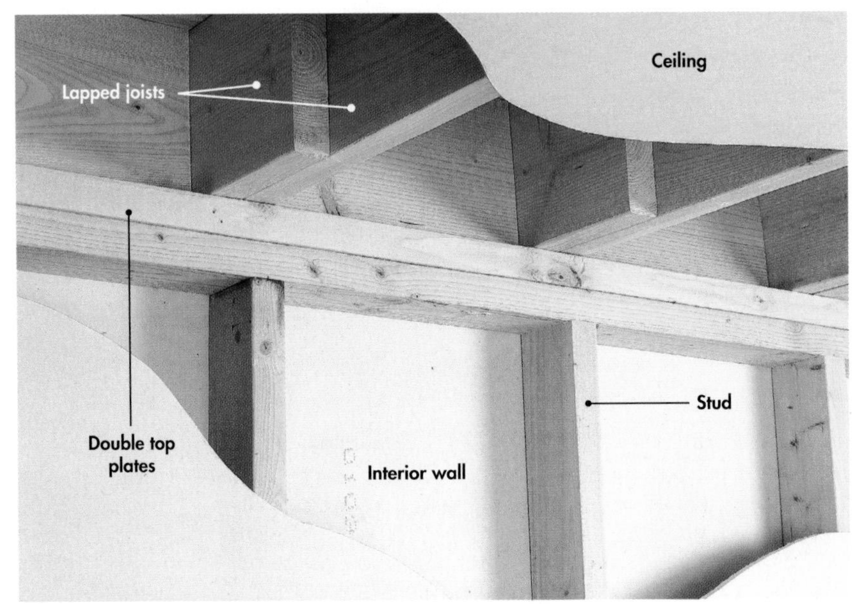

Floor joists span the entire width of a house, and it's often impractical or even impossible to make them out of a single length of wood. To solve the problem, they are often lapped, as shown here. The wall below the lap is always load-bearing, as is the wall above it.

1 Remove the trim gently. Baseboards are probably nailed into the studs and floor plate. Start at a doorway, driving a pry bar between a stud and the baseboard with a hammer. Working along the wall, pry at every stud, and then pull the board loose by hand. Door and window trim is nailed into studs, usually with a double row of nails. Pry at each nail until the trim has loosened; gently finish by hand.

2 If you will reuse the trim, remove the nails. To avoid splintering (especially on old wood), pull the nails out from the back or cut them off level—this is important. To pull them out, pinch the nail from the back of the board, rolling the cutter sideways to pull the nail partially out. Repeat to remove. If you're discarding the trim, bend the nails over so no one accidentally steps on one.

3 Open up the wall. If you're removing only part of a wall, start by drawing a line centered on the first stud that will remain on each side of the opening. On drywall cut along the line with a utility knife. On plaster cut the line with a circular saw, cutting through the lath but not into the stud. Break a hole in the wall with a 3-pound sledgehammer.

Behind the scenes

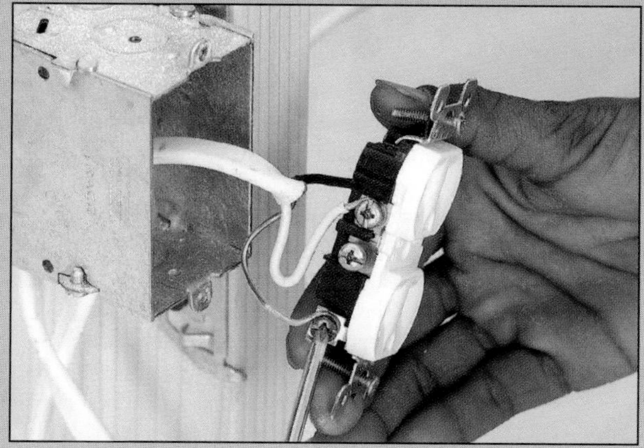

Removing a wall means removing the wiring and pipes in it too. Double-check to make sure the power is still off after the plaster or drywall is removed, before you unhook outlets or switches. (Someone may have turned it back on; hang a sign on the power box that says "leave power off.") Remove the cable as needed from the wall. Cables must end in an electrical box so you may have to remove cable beyond the area you are working and back to the next box in the circuit. You may even need to remove it back to the circuit breaker box.

You'll also need to cut and cap the pipes. Usually, copper and smaller plastic pipes carry water; black iron pipes carry gas; and larger-diameter pipe is drainpipe. Follow the pipe back toward the meter. Double-check to make sure gas and water are off. Cut copper or plastic and cap it where convenient. Disconnect and cap gas pipe or drainpipe at the nearest convenient fitting (it is definitely wise to call a professional for this).

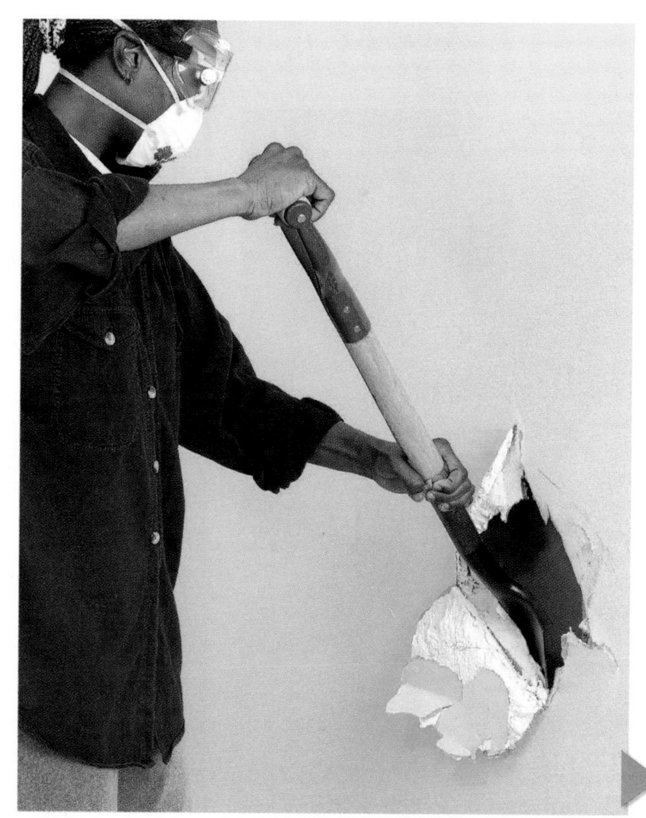

4 Remove the plaster or drywall. If you try to remove the entire wall surface with a hammer, it will break the wall into too-small pieces, and the work will go slowly. Once you've made an initial hole in the wall with the hammer, make quick work of the rest of the job with a flat-back garden spade.

Removing a wall (continued)

5 Remove studs by cutting through the middle using a handsaw or reciprocating saw. Wiggle them back and forth to pry them away from the soleplate and top plate. To remove the end studs, cut through them without cutting into studs on adjacent walls; then pry the studs loose.

6 To remove the top plate, first make two cuts through it, about 3 inches apart, using a reciprocating saw or handsaw. Knock the cut section out with a pry bar and hammer.

7 Pry off the remaining length of top plate, working slowly to avoid damaging the ceiling beneath the plate, which will be visible in the new room. (If you do damage it you can patch it later.)

8 Remove a 3-inch-wide section of soleplate using a reciprocating saw or a handsaw. Then pry out the entire soleplate with a pry bar.

Alternative method: Reuse the lumber

To reuse the full length of lumber, put a metal-cutting blade in the reciprocating saw. Instead of cutting through the middle of the stud, run the blade between the stud and the soleplate. Cut right through the nails, and then do the same on nails between the stud and the top plate. Pull the stud free by hand.

SAFETY ALERT

DUST MAY BE DANGEROUS

You never know what was used in an old house. Old plaster might contain anything from horsehair or straw to asbestos. Textured coatings, old vinyl floor tiles, backer board, roofing felt, and caulking might also be hazardous. It's not worth taking a chance, because asbestos can cause life-threatening illness that might not show up for years. Protect yourself with goggles and a proper mask—a simple sanding mask won't do. Choose a HEPA (high efficiency particulate arresting) mask.

Note: No mask that is generally available to homeowners is completely safe when it comes to asbestos; if you strongly suspect its presence, get advice from your local EPA office.

When you vacuum up the dust, use a shop vac with a HEPA filter. Replacement filters are available.

Building a partition wall

Skill level:	Time to complete:	Materials:	Tools:
★★★☆☆	Experienced 1.5 hrs. Handy 2 hrs. Novice 2.5 hrs.	Framing lumber, 16d nails, metal connectors, 4d nails, shims	Drill and bit, combination square, plumb bob and line, chalkline, hammer, stud driver, ear protection, safety glasses for concrete floors, circular saw, 4-foot level

Installing partition walls can change the way you live by defining new, more suitable, areas. They are often used to create new rooms in an unfinished basement or attic. You can build a partition wall two ways: Frame the wall in place, or build the frame on the floor and tilt it into position. If space permits, building the wall flat on the floor is easier.

Measure carefully, and use the same tape measure for everything on the wall. Slight differences in tapes could result in some studs being irregular. Check precut studs before you use them to make sure they're all exactly the same length.

Before finishing the walls with drywall (see page 119), the local building inspector will want to check the construction, making sure that required plumbing and wiring changes are complete. The electrical and plumbing sections of this book tell you how to make those changes, but check local building codes too.

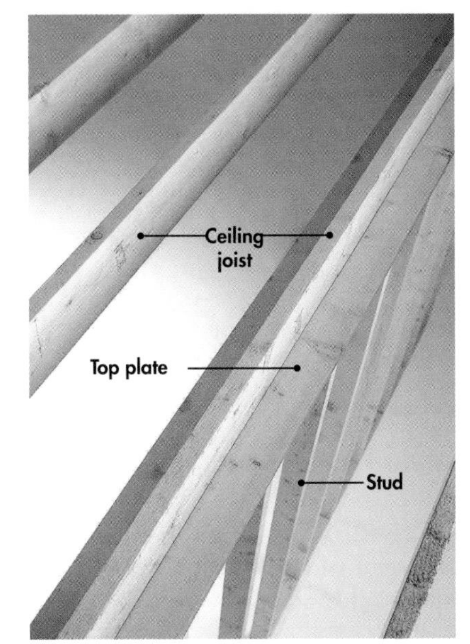

Fasten new walls that are parallel to the joists by attaching the top plate directly to the ceiling joist and the soleplate directly to the floor joists, using 16d nails. If the new wall won't be directly under a joist, consider moving it a few inches so that it is. Attaching the top plate to the ceiling will be much more difficult if you don't (see the next column for instructions).

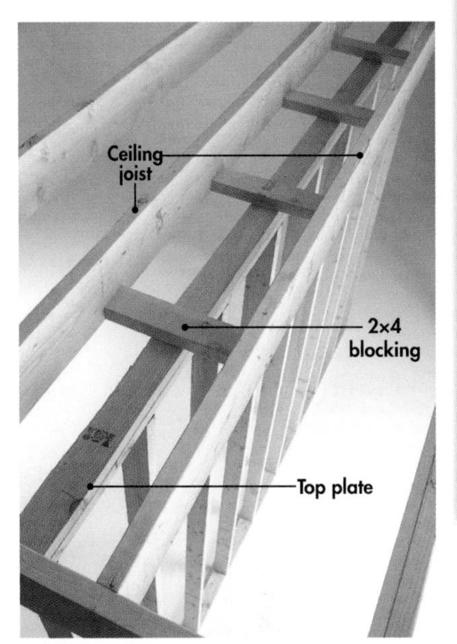

New walls that run parallel to the joists but aren't directly under one need additional blocking. Install 2×4 blocking every 2 feet between the joists, using 16d nails. The bottom of the blocking should be flush with the bottom edges of joists. Unless you can install the blocks from above, you'll need to cut—and repair—holes in the ceiling.

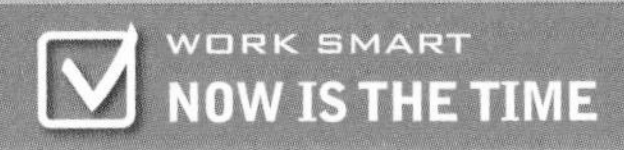

WORK SMART
NOW IS THE TIME

- **In some situations it is better to frame with 2×6 lumber** rather than use standard 2×4 framing. Use 2×6 lumber to frame walls that must hold large plumbing pipes, such as waste pipes or drainpipes. Wherever the wall plates must be cut in order to fit around pipes or other mechanical fixtures, use metal straps to join the framing members and tie them together structurally.
- **You may want to consider soundproofing the walls** if you'll use the new room as a bath where privacy is important, a home theater with surround-sound, or a practice room for your teenager's band. There are many ways to do it, but it can be as easy as filling the wall with fiberglass insulation (see page 118) before applying drywall.

New walls that run perpendicular to joists are attached by fastening the top plate directly to the ceiling joists. The soleplate at the bottom will be fastened to the floor joists with 16d nails.

Building a partition wall (continued)

Attaching new walls to existing joists

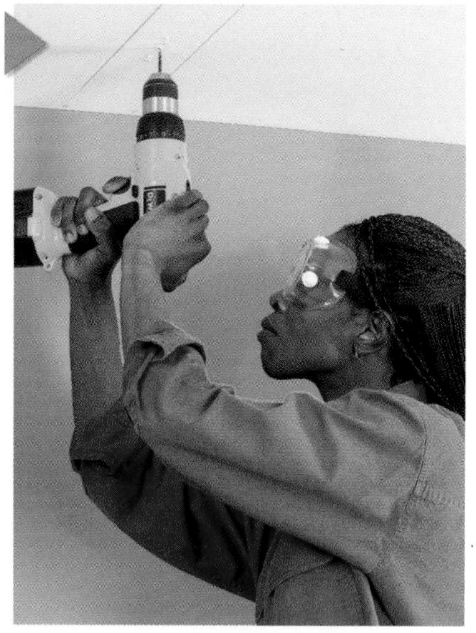

1 Mark the location of the new wall on the ceiling, and snap two chalklines to represent the edges of the new top plate. Locate the first ceiling joist by drilling into the ceiling between the lines, then measure to find and mark the remaining joists.

2 To make the top and bottom wall plates, cut two 2×4s to the wall length. Lay the plates side by side; using a combination square, make marks for studs every16-inches *on center* (meaning from the center of one stud to the center of the next).

3 Double-check that the lines you snapped are parallel to the wall. Make any necessary corrections, and nail the top plate in place with 16d nails. (It helps to start the nails when the plate is still on the floor instead of hammering overhead.)

4 Determine the position of the soleplate by hanging a plumb bob from the edge of the top plate so that the plumb bob tip nearly touches the floor. Mark the position on the floor. Repeat at the opposite end of the top plate, then snap a chalkline between the marks to indicate the location of the soleplate.

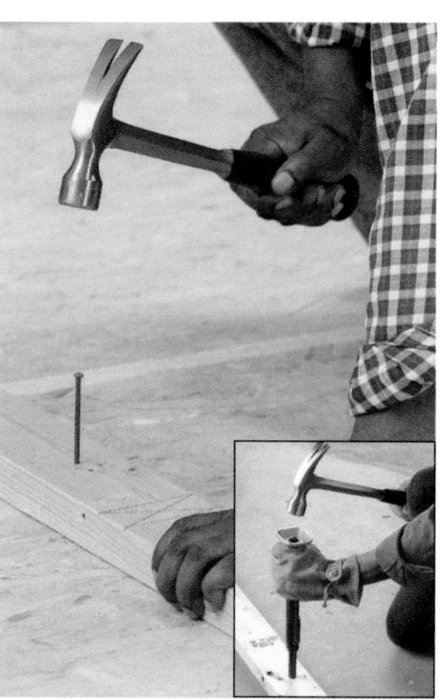

5 On wood floors anchor the soleplate by driving 16d nails into the floor joists. On concrete floors attach the soleplate with a stud driver (inset), available at rental centers. A stud driver fires a small gunpowder charge to drive a masonry nail through the framing member and into the concrete. Wear hearing and eye protection when using a stud driver.

6 Install the first stud tight against the wall. Measure the distance between the soleplate and the top plate at this point. Add ⅛ inch to ensure a snug fit and cut the stud to the correct length.

7 Position the stud against the wall, align it with the soleplate, and nail it in place with 16d nails. Double-check to make sure the stud is still aligned with the top plate, and then nail the top of the stud in place. Nail the rest of the stud to the wall every 2 feet. If there is no stud to nail to, attach the new stud to the old wall with construction adhesive.

8 Fasten the stud at the other end of the wall in place. Once it's attached, measure and cut the stud next to it. Position the stud between the top plate and the soleplate so the stud markings are covered.

9 Attach the studs to the soleplate and top plate with metal connectors and 4d nails. (Or toenail them in place as shown at bottom left.)

CLOSER LOOK

TOENAILING

Toenailing—once you get the hang of it—is faster and just as effective as using metal connectors. Begin with the stud 1/8 inch to 1/4 inch in front of the layout lines, as shown. Drive the nail at an angle a bit steeper than 45 degrees; at least half the nail should enter the plate. Support the 2×4 with your hand, foot, or body and drive the nail, knocking the stud into position with your final blows. Drive a second nail from the other side but not so that it's immediately opposite the first.

Framing partition wall corners

If you're adding more than one wall, you'll need a little extra framing to form and strengthen the corners.

Frame L-corners by nailing an extra stud **(A)** to the plates and nailing 2×4 spacers **(B)** to the inside of the end stud **(C)**. Nail the new wall to the studs and spacer.

Frame T-corners by nailing a stud **(D)** in one wall to a stud **(E)** behind it in the other. Add a 2×4 nailer **(F)** to each side to provide a nailing surface for the drywall.

Building a partition wall (continued)

Framing a partition wall on the floor

1 To lay out the bottom plate of the new wall, snap a line on the floor. (Locate the line by measuring from an existing wall.) This may not create perfectly square corners, but it's more important that the new wall and old wall be parallel, especially if you'll be installing tile or a suspended ceiling later.

2 Determine the length of the wall; cut a 2×4 top plate and soleplate to length. Place the 2×4s side by side and lay out the position of the studs, spacing them 16 inches on center. Lay out doors and windows as described on page 213. Mark the edge of the plates too, so that the marks will be easy to see while nailing.

3 Measure the distance between the floor and the ceiling, or the joists, at several locations along where the wall will be constructed. Take the shortest distance and subtract 3⅛ inches (1½ inches each for the top and soleplates and ⅛ inch for space to maneuver the wall into place). This will be the stud length. (For extra accuracy use a plumb bob.)

4 Count the layout marks to see how many studs you'll need, and cut them to length. Sight down the edge of each stud to see whether it's straight. If not, mark the edge to show which side has the high spot (called the *crown*).

5 Lay the soleplate on its edge along the floor line. Select the best two studs, and place them at each end of the wall with the crown up. Nail the soleplate and studs together with 16d nails.

6 Place the top plate on edge with the layout marks facing the soleplate; nail it to the end studs using 16d nails. Insert the remaining studs, crown up, and nail them in place with 16d nails.

7 When all studs have been attached to the top and soleplates, raise the wall and position the plates on the floor and ceiling lines. (It helps to have two people.)

8 If the wall fits too loosely, shim under the bottom plate to tighten the wall in the space. Nail the wall to the floor and ceiling joists, again with 16d nails.

WORK SMART

BUILDING FLOATING WALLS

In many areas of the country the soil expands and contracts with changes in the season or varying moisture levels. Extreme changes can play havoc with basement partition walls as the soil beneath the slab moves. Improperly installed basement wall systems can actually move houses off of their foundations. If your area has these conditions, you will have to build "floating" walls below grade in your basement to accommodate the changes. Floating walls are fixed to the ceiling joists but the wall is constructed to leave a gap at the bottom; it floats on pins in a plate anchored to the slab. This lets the slab move up and down without affecting the partition wall. So, what should you do? Check with your local building authority and local codes before you finish the basement.

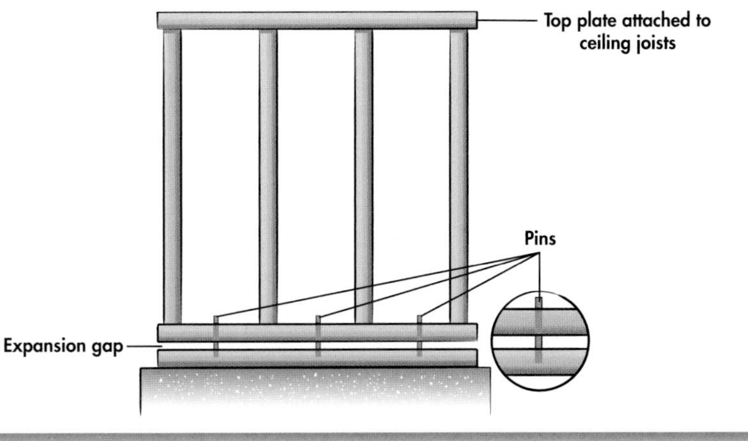

Soundproofing a room

With the advent of flat-screen televisions and advanced sound equipment, home theaters and mixed-media rooms are fast becoming popular projects, especially in finished basements. Basements and garages are also used for band practice and for workshops where someone might be using a saw. If you build regular walls around those spaces, you may end up with loud noise, whines, and reverberations in the rest of the house as well. It would be wise to consider soundproofing.

There's a lot of information available online to help you in planning, plus a lot of products (some expensive, some not). What you ultimately decide to use depends on your pocketbook and commitment to the project, but knowing basic principles will help.

To simplify, sound waves travel through the air and anything in their path until they break up and dissipate. When sound hits an object, it is either absorbed or reflected, and the object vibrates—that vibration changes the quality of the sound. Low-pitched or loud noise can literally shake the house unless you find ways to break up its path. The term that describes how a room handles sound is acoustics.

There are two places to consider acoustics: inside the room and in all other areas of your home.

Inside-the-room acoustics

In mixed-media rooms or home theaters, focus on eliminating echoes and distortions caused by sound bouncing from surface to surface. Hard surfaces are the worst. You can somewhat handle the problem by adding "soft" elements—upholstery, pillows, carpet, and draperies—the same elements needed for comfort. The fabric and padding absorb sound and keep it from traveling any farther. You might also attach acoustical panels to the walls or ceiling, staple pleated fabric to the walls (as in a movie theater), and use various other sound-absorbing products.

Keep sound from traveling

Sound that hits standard walls travels through them, moving right along through the studs, joists, and ductwork to cause a ruckus in nearby areas. To keep this from happening, you'll need to stop the sound in its tracks.

The low-tech way to do this is to make the wall thicker and weave insulation between offset studs (see below). Or you can attach clips (called resilient channels) to the studs during construction; these keep drywall from passing along its sound to the wood and thereby the rest of the house. Layer products to break up the sound.

Don't forget the ceiling or the floor if your media room is on the second story; principles that apply to walls also apply here. By using some combination of insulation, clips, staggered studs, sound-muffling products, and a double layer of drywall, you should end up with a snug little island of sound in a sea of silence. That is your aim at least.

Soundproofing a wall

You can soundproof a room—at least for most purposes—with regular unfaced fiberglass insulation. Start by using top plates and soleplates that are wider than the wall studs. Place the wall studs 8 inches on center, staggering them so they alternate as shown at right (adjacent studs should be on opposite edges of the plate). Weave unfaced fiberglass batt insulation between the studs along the entire wall, filling the full height of the studs. Apply a layer of soundproofing drywall to the wall studs, then cover that with regular drywall. This creates a thick, fairly sound-proof wall that is useful for home theaters, band-practice rooms, workshops, or baths where privacy is a concern. For a soundproof closure, your best choice is usually an exterior door with a high R-rating, indicating effective insulation.

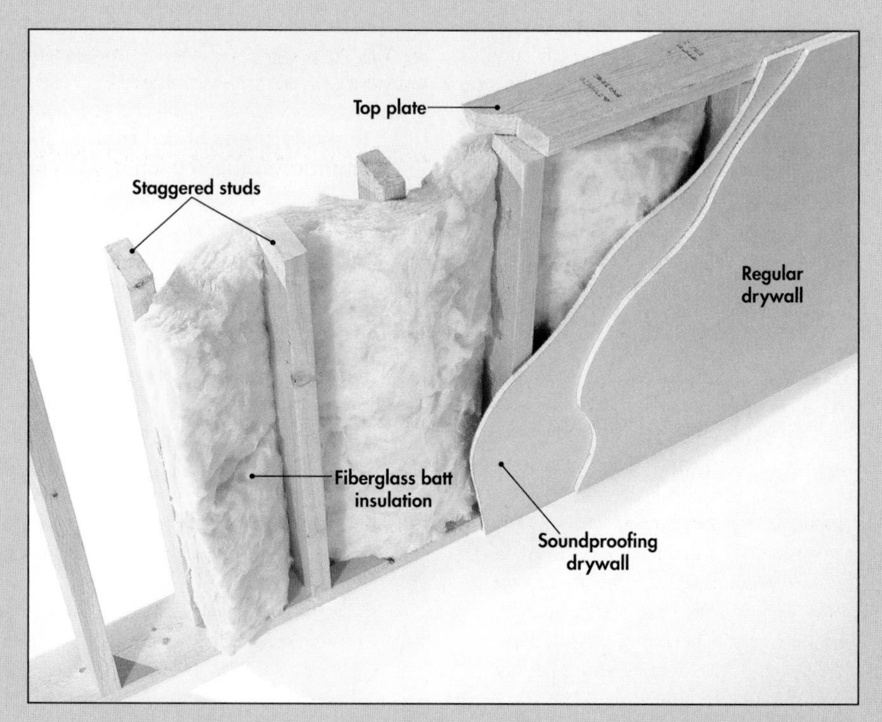

Installing drywall

Skill level:	Time to complete:	Materials:	Tools:
★★★☆☆	Experienced Variable Handy Variable Novice Variable	Drywall, drywall screws, joint compound, drywall tape	Sawhorses, drywall T-square, tape measure, utility knife, drywall saw, coarse rasp, screw gun, drywall router, panel lifter

Hanging drywall would seem to be fairly simple: You stand the heavy sheets up against the studs, and then you drive screws through them. Still, you can learn a few things that will help you work smarter instead of harder.

Start with how you buy it, for instance. If possible buy sheets the same length as the wall. (If necessary buy sheets a bit longer, then trim them to length.) These might be longer than the 4×8 sheets usually seen. They're heavier too, so you'll definitely need help carrying them; flexing the sheets too much will break them.

When you hang the sheets, hang them sideways, with the longest edge parallel to the floor. Start at the top of the wall. Then, if a sheet needs to be trimmed to height, it's at floor level and much easier to haul back to the sawhorses.

Plenty of good reasons exist for hanging the sheet parallel to the floor. To start with, it cuts down on the taping by as much as 25 percent. Applying tape and compound (often called mud) has to be done along the seams to fill them in and produce a smooth finish. It's also the most miserable part of the job because it takes so many steps and so much time. Anything you can do to lessen the task is a plus.

This installation is also stronger because each board ties more studs together and because the drywall's strongest dimension bridges irregularities like warped studs. The seam you'll tape is at a convenient height—you don't have to bend over to apply mud as you would for vertical seams.

Other hints: Center the short edges of the panels on studs or joists so that you'll have something firm on which to attach the next panel. Drywall screws hold much better than nails, which often pop out as the wood expands and contracts with seasonal changes in humidity.

Never force a panel into place. Even if it doesn't crack right away, something almost always goes wrong—a joint will pop open somewhere, or a section may break loose of its screws. For the best fit, trim drywall with a utility knife. You can take small amounts off the edges with a coarse rasp.

▲ *Hanging drywall with the seams horizontal instead of vertical cuts down on the amount of taping required; it also places the seam at a convenient height.*

BUYER'S GUIDE

DIFFERENT TYPES OF DRYWALL

Standard drywall panels have almost completely replaced plaster and lath as the preferred material for covering walls. It is more economical and easier to install, especially for novices.

- **Drywall panels** are made of gypsum sandwiched between paper layers on both sides. Screw the panels to the wall. Fill the cracks between them with paper drywall tape, and then level the seams with joint compound.
  Thickness: ½- and ⅝-inch are most common, but ¼- and ⅜-inch thicknesses are also made.
  Sheet size: 4×8 feet is most common; 4×10, 4×12, 4×14, and 4×16 feet are also made, as well as 54 inches wide by all these lengths (harder to find).
- **Soundproof drywall** is a layered panel that breaks up sound waves passing through it, thereby reducing noise. It is used in both old and new construction, where it is applied in the same manner as regular drywall.
- **Green board** is a water-resistant form of drywall and installs the same way. It is not meant for ceilings, however, because it is too heavy. It is often used for bathroom walls that will be exposed to moisture.
- **Backer board,** though not technically drywall, is a smaller, harder panel with a concrete core and fiberglass facing. It's used as a base underneath ceramic tile. Screw it to walls or floors with special backer-board screws.

Installing drywall (continued)

Drywall cutting and screwing

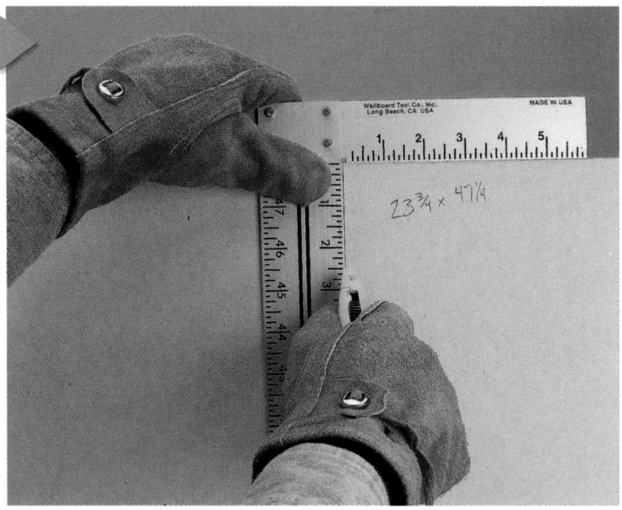

1 Make straight cuts by scoring the face paper with a sharp utility knife, using a drywall T-square as a guide. A series of shallow cuts is better than one deeper one. Always cut so the knife travels away from your other hand.

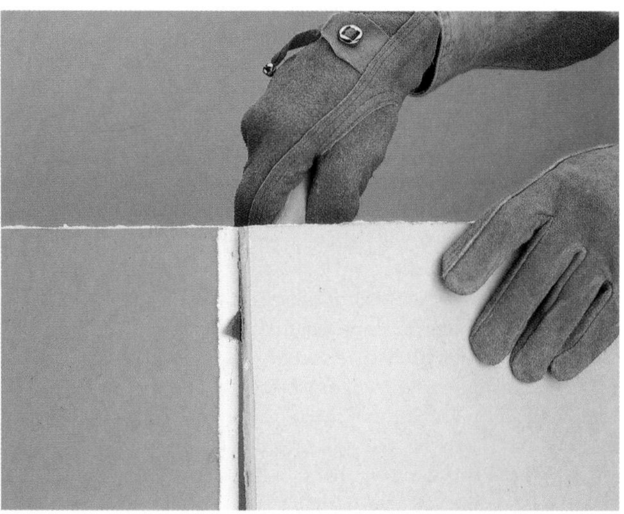

2 Bend the panel away from the scored line until it breaks. Cut through the back paper with a sharp utility knife to separate the pieces. Smooth the edges as needed with a coarse rasp.

$ BUYER'S GUIDE

CHOOSING SCREWS

Drywall Thickness	Framing	Screw length	Screw spacing Walls	Screw spacing Ceiling	Thread
3⁄8", 1⁄2", or 5⁄8"	Wood	1¼"	16"	16"	Coarse
1⁄2" or 5⁄8"	Steel	1"	16"	12"	Fine
5⁄8"	Steel	1⅛"	16"	12"	Fine
¾"	Steel	1¼"	16"	12"	Fine

WORK SMART

HEAD OFF THE DUST

Almost nothing creates as much dust in a house as the process of finishing drywall—as soon as you are about ready to sand it, start preparing. Hang plastic sheeting at each door leading to other rooms. Buy a dust mask, and commit to using it. Invest in a heavy-duty shop-type vacuum with a filter made to trap ultra-fine particles. When you're actually sanding, shut off the air-conditioning so it won't suck the sanding dust into the ductwork and spread it around the house.

TOOL TIP

NICE DIMPLES

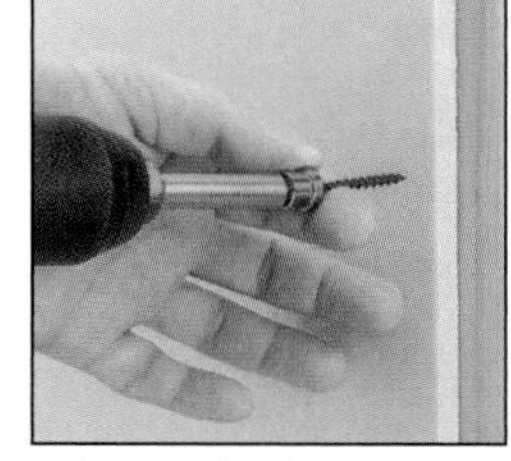

When hanging drywall, use drywall screws instead of nails. Nails often work their way back to the surface as the studs expand and contract with the weather. Drive the screw deep enough to create a dimple without breaking the face paper–a break significantly weakens the screw's holding power. Then fill the dimple with joint compund to cover the screw.

Professional drywallers use a special drywall gun to drive drywall screws. It looks like a drill with a screwdriver in the chuck. The one important difference is it has a clutch with an adjustable depth gauge. Professional drywallers set the clutch so that the drywall screw goes just below the surface of the sheet, dimpling–but not breaking–the paper. This is definitely the fastest route to go, but you may not need it.

Unless you're drywalling a whole house, you probably can get by with a regular cordless drill. Insert a "dimpler" bit (like the one shown), which will set the screws like a drywall gun, although not quite as fast. When buying screws, always check the screw heads to make sure they're compatible (some require Phillips-head bits, some square bits).

Drywalling a ceiling

When drywalling a room, always start with the ceiling, even though it's the most challenging part. You'll constantly reach over your head, and more than once you may find yourself holding something in place with the top of your head. Stand on a scaffold while you work—sawhorses and boards won't do.

Cut panels so they stop about ¼ inch short of the wall studs. They will be easier to hang, and the wall panels will give some support when you later install them. If you're installing a ceiling in a room that already has walls, leave a space of about 1/16 inch between the ceiling and walls so you don't have to force panels in place. If you're installing drywall over a cracked plaster ceiling and you don't want to disturb the existing moldings, leave several inches clear around the perimeter (see page 99).

Use the longest panels you can handle. If you must butt ends to span the room, stagger the panels so the butt joints don't align.

Before you cover the walls, mark the floor to show where the studs are. This makes it easier to drive screws into studs once you've covered them with drywall.

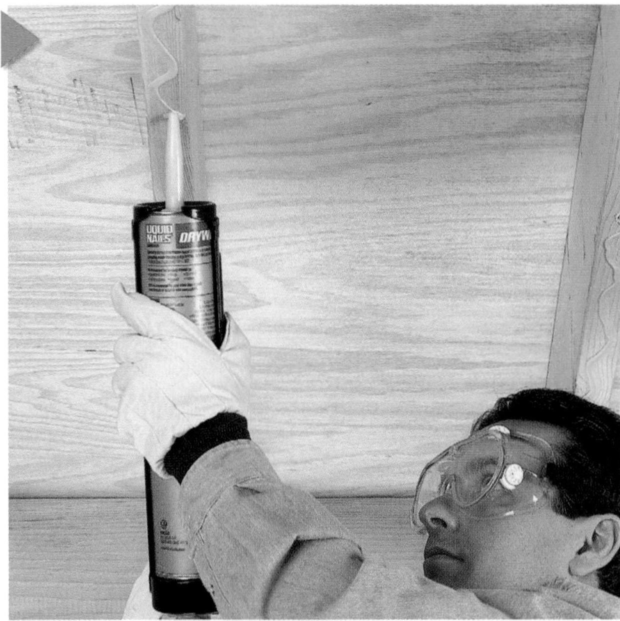

1 Cut a ⅜-inch-diameter hole in the tip of a tube of construction adhesive. Run a continuous bead of adhesive on the joists above the first panel you'll install. If you will be butting panels at the end, run the bead about ⅜ inch from the edge of the joist that supports the end. This leaves room to run a new bead for the next piece.

TOOL TIP

HELPING HAND

A cradle lift raises sheets into place quickly and safely. These are available at most rental centers. The lift lets you load the drywall and lift the panel as high as 11 feet. It is on casters so you can roll it where it's needed, set the caster brakes, and safely and securely maneuver the panel into position. Most lifts can hold up to a full 4-×16-foot sheet of drywall. They even have a tilting platform feature that lets you easily install drywall on steep, sloped ceilings.

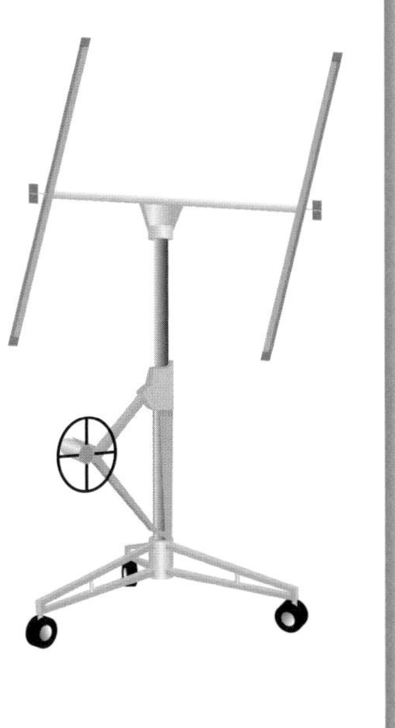

2 Work with a partner when installing a drywall ceiling. Build a 2×4 T-support for your helper to use when holding up the panel. Starting in a corner, work together to lift the sheet against the ceiling. Then support the sheet with your hand (or tuck a sponge inside your hat and use your head) while your helper supports it with the 2×4 T-support. Beginning at one end of the sheet and working at 16-inch intervals, drive 1¼-inch drywall screws through the drywall into the joists. For a more secure installation, press the sheet firmly along each joist to make sure it is full contact with the adhesive.

Installing drywall (continued)

Hanging drywall on walls

1 Measure the width of the wall and cut the sheet so it's about ¼ inch shorter. Have someone help you position the sheet tight against the ceiling; begin driving 1¼-inch drywall screws in the middle of the panel at a convenient height.

2 When the first screws are in place, put in the rest, working your way from the center of the panel toward the outside edges. Drive the screws 16 inches apart into all of the studs, stopping ½ inch short of the edges.

3 Leave a ½-inch-wide gap between the floor and the drywall. This keeps the drywall away from potential moisture on the floor; baseboard will cover the gap later. Position the lower sheet of drywall by slipping a panel lifter under the bottom edge; step on the lifter, then screw the panel in place.

Outlet options

There are two ways to cut a hole for an outlet. The high-tech way is to use a drywall router. The low-tech way is to use lipstick.

If using a router, note the height of the box, draw marks on the floor to show the edges of the box. Remove the wires, and push the drywall in place, covering the box. Hold the drywall in place with two screws partially driven into the framing. Plunge the router into the approximate center of the box and move it sideways until you find the edge. Guide the router counterclockwise to make the cutout.

For a low-tech solution, rub lipstick on the edges of the outlet box, and put the panel in place. Push it lightly against the box. Remove it; cut along the lipstick marks on the back of the panel with a drywall saw.

If the box extends beyond the framing you may need to expand your hole to fit around the box. Once you've cut the hole, pull the wires into the box and install the drywall.

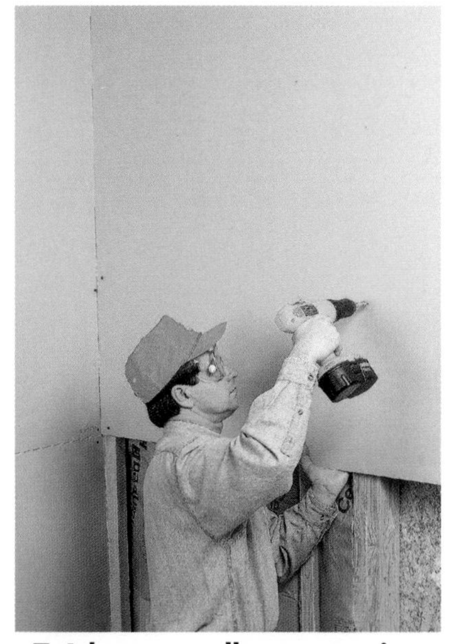

4 A longer wall may require more than one length of drywall. Start by hanging a full sheet as before. Tack it in place, and then drive screws into the studs every 16 inches. Cut additional panels for the top row to size.

5 Lay out a door cut as you would for a window (see the opposite page). Remove the trim, place the drywall panel against the opening, mark the location of the studs, and draw a line for the top of the door opening. Using a drywall saw, cut out for the door, then screw the panel in place.

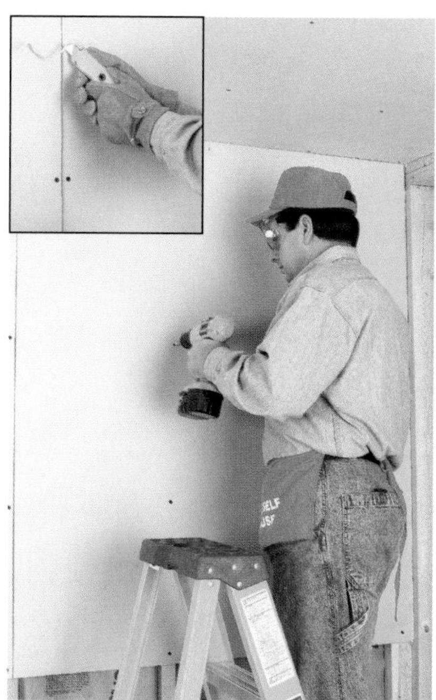

6 At a corner, cut drywall to fit next to the last piece hung; cut it slightly undersized to leave a ¼-inch gap in the corner. Screw the drywall in place. Where panels meet, cut a V-groove with your utility knife (see inset) or a special beveling tool; this makes it easier to hide taped joints.

7 Begin the bottom row with a shorter piece, if necessary, so that seams in the top row won't line up with seams in the bottom row. Position the piece, and screw it in place. When the short piece is in place, install the next piece.

8 When framing outside corners, cut the piece long so it will hang over the corner. Then trim it with a drywall router or saw after it's in place. Hang the abutting panel, leaving it long, and trim to create a tight, well-fitting corner.

9 Protect outside corners with a corner bead. Metal and plastic ones are available. A slightly too-long metal bead will kink when you fasten it; prevent this by cutting the bead about ½ inch short with tin snips. Hold the bead tight against the ceiling. Screws will distort the bead, so nail it in place, spacing the nails every 9 inches. Follow the manufacturers' instructions for installing plastic beads.

Installing around existing windows

If a window is in place, take off the trim. Position the sheet on the floor and mark where it meets the inside edges of the window framing. Measure from the ceiling to the window top to lay out the top of the cut. Cut with a drywall saw.

Installing around future windows

If a sheet covers a window that has yet to be installed, cover the window with drywall the same way you covered an outlet. Later, rout out the drywall and add drywall screws around the opening as necessary.

Finishing drywall

Skill level:	Time to complete:	Materials:	Tools:
★★★☆☆	Experienced 2 hrs. Handy 3 hrs. Novice 4 hrs.	Joint or drywall tape, joint compound, 200-grit sandpaper or sanding mesh	6-, 8-, and 10- or 12-inch drywall knives, pole sander

Finishing drywall refers to the process of taping and filling the seams between adjacent sheets with joint compound. It's a time-consuming, three-coat process. The first coat, called bedding, goes on about 6 inches wide. It holds a strip of joint tape (paper or fiberglass mesh) to cover the seams and help prevent cracks. The second coat, about 8 inches wide, fills slight imperfections in the first coat. The third finish coat is about 12 inches wide, and its feathered edges gradually taper out to the flat drywall. Each coat must dry overnight.

Inside corners, including those at the ceiling, are reinforced with tape too. Several types are available at home improvement stores. Outside corners, because they are often bumped, are reinforced with a metal or plastic right angle called a corner bead.

The finish coat is either sanded or smoothed with a damp sponge. Use the sponge, if you can, to cut down on dust. If you sand, be sure to wear a dust mask. Vacuum the dust right away, using a special dust filter that traps fine particles.

Applying the first coat

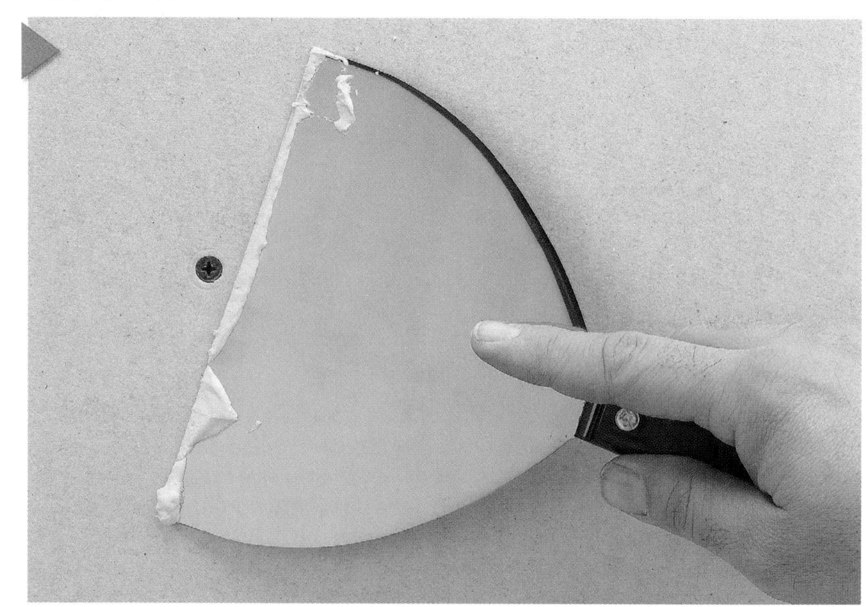

1 Cover screw dimples or nailheads with joint compound, troweling it on with a 6-inch drywall knife. Level the compound with the knife. If a screw missed the stud, it will eventually work its way out—take it out now, fill the hole, and put in a new screw.

TOOL TIP

DRYWALL KNIVES AND TAPE

Joint compound goes on in three coats, and you'll want a different knife for each. Use a 6-inch knife for the first coat, an 8-inch one for the second coat, and a 10- or 12-inch one for the final coat. This gradually feathers the compound toward the flat areas.

Before you start, round the corners of the knives with a file so they won't dig into the drywall. There are specialty knives made for inside and outside corners. Some people swear by them, some swear at them—but they're worth a look the next time you browse the drywall aisle.

Drywall tape comes in two main types: fiberglass mesh and paper. Fiberglass is self-stick and easy to handle, and it looks good. It has its issues though. Fiberglass mesh is designed to be used with a strong, fast-drying compound that is mixed from a powder. Pros love it, but it's a bit tricky for homeowner use. You may have better luck with a premixed joint compound that will give you plenty of time to work.

If used with a standard, ready-mix compound, fiberglass tape joints can crack at about half the stress it would take to crack a paper-tape joint. If that happens, you'll have to strip off everything, including the tape, and start from scratch. Recently developed tapes made for corners are pre-creased to make the job of initially taping or repairing corners easier (see the opposite page and page 98).

2 Put joint compound on the 6-inch knife. Starting at the top of the wall, rest one end of the blade on the raised part of the corner bead and the other end on one of the walls. Draw the knife along the wall, applying compound to the corner and reloading the knife as necessary. Repeat on the other side of the corner.

3 Working with the 6-inch knife, fill the trough created by the beveled edges with joint compound. Pull the knife along the trough to create a smooth, continuous bed of the joint compound.

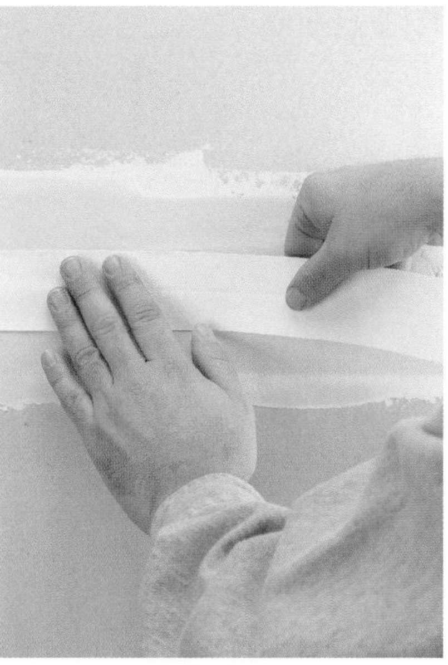

4 Cover the moist seam immediately with a single piece of tape. (Multiple short pieces are more likely to slip and wrinkle when you embed them.) Push the tape into the compound every foot or so to hold it in place while you work.

5 Starting in the center of the wall, hold the 6-inch knife so that it bridges the tape at a slight angle to the seam. Draw it along the seam, applying a bit of pressure to embed the tape and also remove excess joint compound. (Leave only enough compound under the tape edges to hold them in place—about 1⁄32 inch.) When you reach the corner, start again at the middle of the wall, working toward the other corner.

Applying the first coat in corners

1 Apply a thin layer of joint compound to both sides of the inside corner with the 6-inch knife.

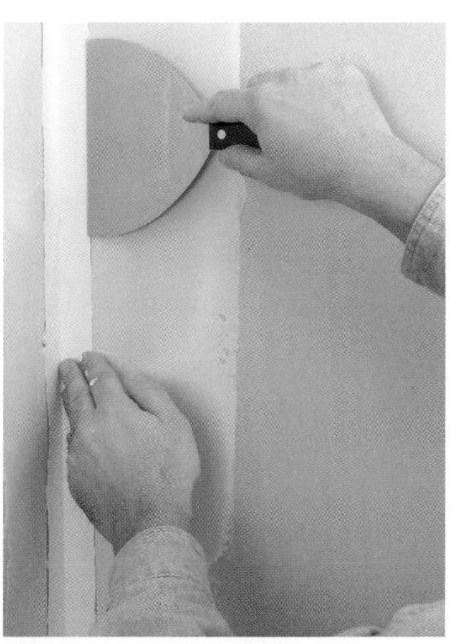

2 Fold a strip of drywall paper tape in half by pinching and pulling the strip between your thumb and forefinger. Position the end of the folded tape strip at the top of the corner joint. Press the tape into the wet compound about 12 inches.

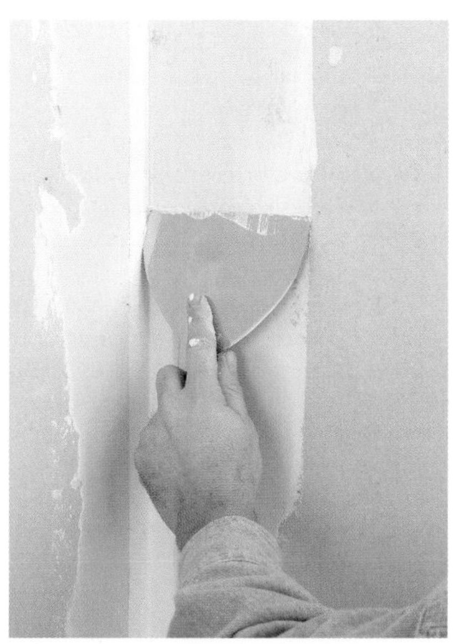

3 Draw the knife along one of the walls to smooth the tape, starting at the top. Repeat on the other wall. Move the knife a couple of inches away from the corner and pull again from ceiling to floor, removing the excess compound left by the first pass.

Finishing drywall (continued)

Applying the second coat

1 Let the first coat of compound dry overnight. Apply a second coat over the screws. Coat the outside corners and seams as before, this time using an 8-inch knife to feather the edges. Feather the edges of any butt seams in the same manner.

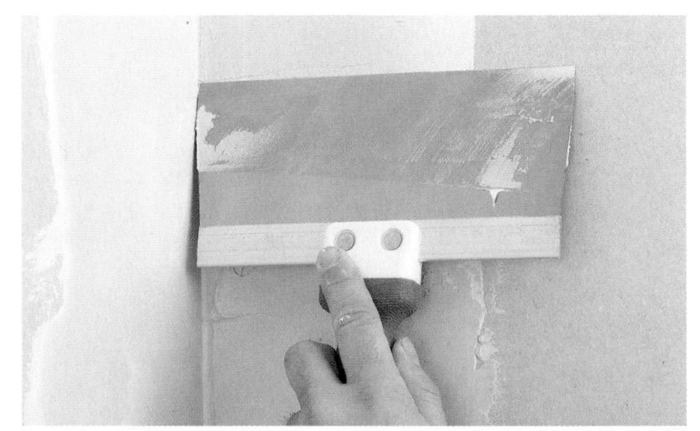

2 Finish the inside corners one wall at a time. Apply a coat of compound on one wall, feathering it out 2 inches beyond the first coat. Wait until the compound dries, then repeat on the adjacent wall (this prevents damaging the wall just done).

Finishing butt joints

Tape butt joints. Butt joints occur where two narrow ends of a sheet meet. Unlike the long side, these ends aren't beveled to make taping easier. Widen the joints by cutting 45-degree, ⅛-inch-deep bevels in the end of each panel with a utility knife. (Or, use a beveling tool made for the purpose.) Apply joint compound, leaving a bed ⅛ inch thick. Press the tape into the bed as with a tapered seam; draw a 6-inch knife along the tape to smooth it.

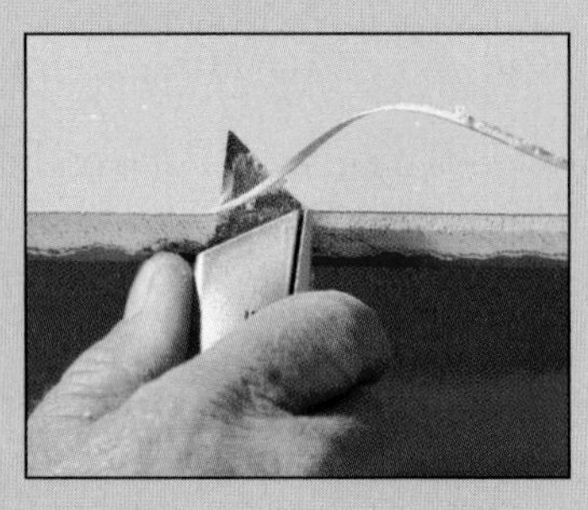

Sanding high areas

Ceilings and high areas are easier to reach with a pole sander. Its pad holds 200-grit sanding mesh—run it back and forth along the seams. Sanding mesh is a piece of screen coated with abrasives; it won't clog when you sand and can be rinsed and reused many times.

Applying and smoothing the third coat

1 Thin the compound with water to the consistency of mayonnaise (or use a specially made finish-coat compound). Apply a third coat to screw holes, seams, and outside corners with a 12-inch knife, again feathering the edges until they blend seamlessly with the flat drywall.

2 When the final coat has dried, smooth out any irregularities with a barely damp sponge. This works as well as sanding—without creating dust—but you'll need to rinse frequently. Or, use 220-grit sandpaper or sanding mesh if you're worried about water damaging the paper facing.

Installing paneling

Skill level:	Time to complete:	Materials:	Tools:
★★★☆☆	Experienced 4 hrs. Handy 6 hrs. Novice 8 hrs.	Paneling, ringshank nails, construction adhesive, 4-mil vapor barrier, foam insulation, 1×3 furring strips, shims, masonry nails, ½-inch drywall screws	Hammer, saber saw with blade for plastic laminates, fine-tooth file, scribing compass, circular saw, chalk line, level, electronic stud finder, tape measure

Aside from painting, paneling with 4×8 sheets is the quickest way to dress up a wall or provide a quick facelift for badly damaged drywall or plaster.

Panels expand and contract with changes in humidity: Give them time to reach your room's moisture content before you start nailing. Stack them on the floor with spacers between them. Wait 72 hours for the panels to acclimate; then you can start nailing.

In the meantime, remove the existing baseboard. Reapply it and add molding at the ceiling when you're done paneling.

As you unstack the panels, lean each one against the wall at the spot where you think it will go. Each panel varies slightly so position them as needed to produce a pleasing arrangement of grain and color.

There are many uses for paneling other than covering whole walls. Use it for kitchen backsplashes, make framed panels to face outdated cabinet doors, cover a kitchen island, make wainscoting, or even use it to cover a ceiling.

Yesterday's paneling left a lot to be desired, but today there are many attractive styles. Some look like beaded board (for cottage- or country-style homes) and some have veneers of exotic woods. Check them out at home improvement stores.

1 Find the studs, which are usually spaced 16 inches from center to center. Measure from the corner to find the first one. Use a stud finder or drive nails through the wall until you hit something solid, then mark it. Measure over to find the next stud; pinpoint and mark it too. When all studs have been located, snap vertical chalk lines along the center of each.

2 Put the first panel against the wall in the corner. Have a helper check with a level and help you hold the panel plumb. If any gaps greater than ¼ inch occur between the wall and panel, you'll have to cut the contour of the wall into the panel by scribing. (See Step 3, page 128.) Paneling on the adjacent wall can cover any smaller gaps.

The elements of a paneled basement wall

If you panel masonry walls, including basements, you'll have to put up a 4-mil plastic vapor barrier and foam insulation, unless you want to void the warranty. To meet fire code, you'll also have to cover the foam with drywall—foam smokes heavily if it catches fire.

Start by applying the vapor barrier, holding it in place with 1×3 boards nailed to the wall. Run the 1×3s horizontally to bridge any dips in the wall, spacing them so the insulation fits snugly between them. Nail shorter vertical pieces to the wall to support the edge of the paneling. Shim as necessary to keep the 1×3s aligned.

Once everything is in place, cover the entire surface with ⅛-inch drywall to bring the wall up to fire code (check your local codes). Leave the joints alone—there's no need to apply tape and joint compound because the drywall will not be seen.

Double-check the rating of any paneling you're putting in a basement: Not all paneling is designed for use below grade, where periodic moisture might be a problem.

Acclimate the panels for 72 hours before installation.

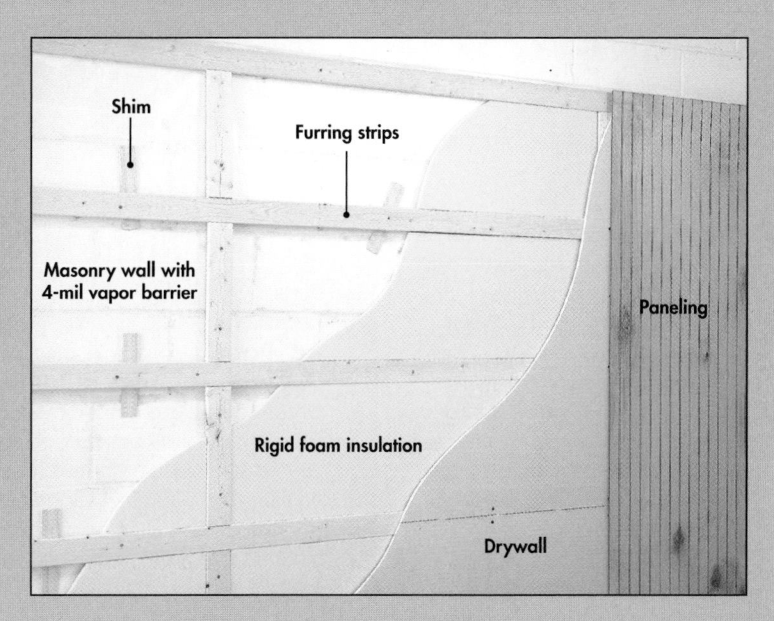

Installing paneling (continued)

3 To scribe a panel, set a compass at a distance equal to the largest gap. Trace along the wall with the pointed end of the compass while drawing a line on the panel with the compass pencil.

4 Cut face-up along the line with a saber saw. Most saber saw blades cut on the upstroke, which can easily splinter the panel; use a blade designed for plastic laminates—these cut on the downstroke. Put the panel back on the wall to see how it fits.Use a fine-tooth file to make any minor adjustments.

5 After checking the fit, see if the unscribed edge is centered over a stud to allow for nailing. If it's not, then cut it so it is. Measure and mark the cut on the back of the panel to minimize splintering. Make the cut along a straight edge with a circular saw equipped with a fine-tooth panel-cutting blade. Allow for expansion by leaving a ¼-inch gap at both the ceiling and floor. (You may have to cut the panel to allow for the gap.)

TOOL TIP

CUTTING PANELS

To get a good, straight cut, guide the saw against a jig. Make one by screwing a 3- or 4-inch-wide piece of ¾-inch-thick plywood to a wider piece. Before you trim the panel, trim the jig. Guide the saw against the narrow piece of plywood to cut off the wider piece. Align the cut edge of the jig with your layout line, clamp the jig to the panel, and make the cut.

6 Panels expand and contract with changes in humidity. Disguise any gaps that may appear by painting the wall behind each seam with a strip of color to match grooves in the panel. To allow for possible expansion, use quarters on edge as spacers between the panels when putting them up.

7 Hold panels in place with both nails and construction adhesive. Run adhesive in a zigzag pattern between the studs and around the perimeter on the back of the panels.

8 Double-check the position of the panel to make sure it's plumb. Nail it to the wall, using 1½-inch paneling nails in a color to match the paneling. Space the nails 6 inches apart along the panel edges. Space them 12 inches apart on the studs in between. Hang the remaining panels the same way, using quarters as spacers to create gaps between them.

9 If you come to an outlet, hold the panel next to it, and mark the panel at the upper and lower edges of the outlet box. Snap a line at each mark across the face of the board. Then measure the distance between the outlet and the last panel installed. Measure this distance along each chalkline and make a mark. Repeat for the other side of the outlet. Connect the marks to outline the outlet.

10 Drill a ½-inch-diameter hole at each corner of the outline. Slip a plastic laminate blade mounted on a saber saw through one of the holes. Cut along the lines to remove the waste and make the cutout needed for the outlet.

11 Turn off the power; unscrew the outlet from its box, but don't disconnect the wires. Feed the outlet through the opening in the panel, and glue and nail the panel to the wall. Reattach the outlet, but before you tighten the screws, slip an extension ring over the outlet. Required by the fire code, this keeps the outlet flush with the paneling.

12 At doors and windows trim the panel; the seam should lie midway over the opening. Then lay out the window cut the same way you laid out the outlet cuts. Make the cuts that begin at the edge of the panel first. Then clamp the cutoff jig along the interior cut.

13 Set the blade to cut about ⅜ inch deep. Put the nose of the saw on the panel; hold the heel up so the blade clears the wood. Keep the side of the saw against the jig. Pull the guard back, start the saw, and gently lower the back onto the panel. Stop the cut ½ inch short of your earlier cut and finish cutting by hand for a perfect corner.

Installing no-miter moldings

Skill level:	**Time to complete:**	**Materials:** Inside and outside corner blocks, base molding, 6d finishing nails, caulking, paint or wood stain and finish	**Tools:** Pry bar, wood shims, hammer, nail set, caulking gun, miter box
★★★☆☆	Experienced Variable Handy Variable Novice Variable		

Cutting miters and coping joints are two jobs that discourage homeowners from installing new molding and trim. If the walls are out of square, as they often are, there's a need to adjust the angle of the miter cut or the position of the molding. Usually it's both. If the angle of the cut is off, the joint won't fit—it's that simple and that frustrating.

If you're serious about carpentry, mitering and coping are essential skills to learn. However, if all you want is good-looking molding, there's a no miter/no cope alternative that eliminates mitering and coping joints altogether. Instead of running the molding around the corners, install precut corner blocks that fit the inside and outside corners. Nail the blocks in place and make square cuts at each end of the molding to fit between them. These cuts are easily made with a fixed-angle miter box or a power miter saw. The blocks come in several sizes and styles to fit the look of your room.

1 Cut the corner blocks, if needed. If the corner blocks are higher than the base molding you use, cut them down. Position a corner block and straight molding to judge how much to trim. Clamp a stop inside the miter box and, if possible, cut all the blocks to length at the same time.

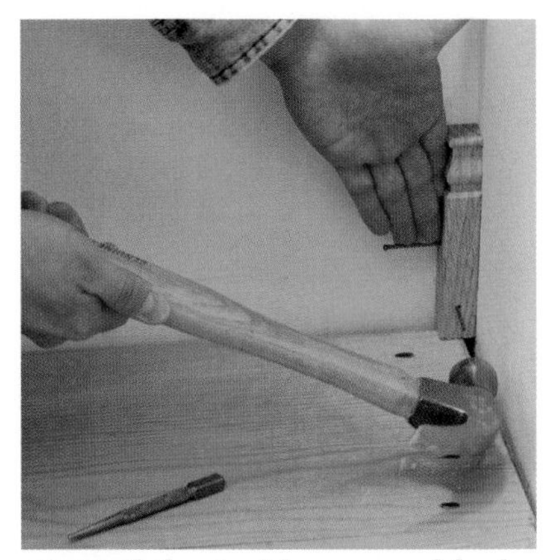

2 Nail the inside corner block. Predrill, and nail into one face of the inside corner blocks with 6d finishing nails, angling the nails toward the corners to draw it in. (Keep the nails at least 1 inch from the top and bottom of the blocks to prevent splitting.)

3 Nail the outside corner blocks. Drive nails through predrilled holes into the corner of the wall. Repeat for each of the corners.

4 Test each corner to see if it's square by holding up a squared-off scrap of wood. If it's not square, scribe the molding: Place a straight edge against the corner and mark the angle on the molding with a pencil. Cut along this line. It's more important to meet the corner well than it is to have a perfectly square cut.

5 Nail the molding to the wall between the corner blocks. Use 6d finishing nails. Locate the nails about 1 inch from the floor to catch the bottom plate of the wall. Nails higher than 1½ inches from the floor need to hit a stud or they won't hold. Drive all nails and countersink the heads below the surface with a nail set.

6 Fill gaps with caulk. Gaps are inevitable around the top of the corner blocks. Fill the gaps with wood-tone caulk before you stain the base molding. Use plain white latex caulk if you plan to paint.

Molding installation skills

Skill level: ★★★☆☆	**Time to complete:** Experienced Variable, Handy Variable, Novice Variable	**Materials:** Molding, 4d finishing nails, white or yellow glue, caulking	**Tools:** Tape measure, stepladder, chalkline, 4-foot level, power miter saw, stud finder, electric drill, hammer, glue brush, caulking gun, coping saw, clamps, nail set

Mitering outside corners

1 Lay out the joint. Start with a piece longer than needed. Hold it in place so that the extra length extends beyond the corner. Draw a line from the bottom of the molding up and away from the corner at about a 45-degree angle. The line shows you the general direction the saw should cut (so you won't get confused); it doesn't need to be straight or at a precise angle.

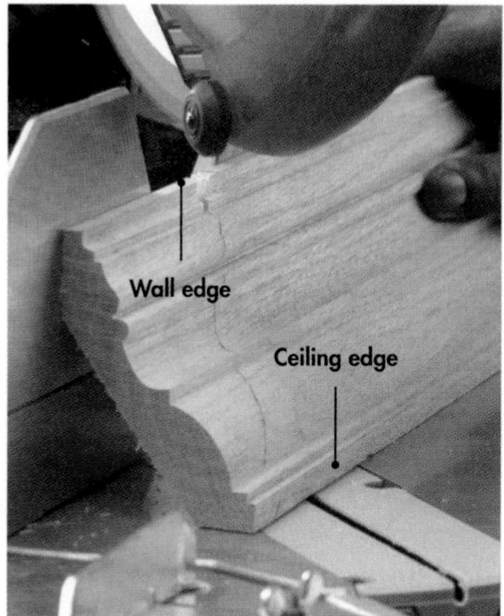

2 Put the molding on the saw bed with the ceiling edge down and the wall edge on the fence. Set the saw handle to 45 degrees in the direction indicated by the line. Position the molding so the piece will be longer than needed, and make the cut. Reset the saw to make a square cut. If the end is to butt up against a wall, measure and cut the piece to length by cutting the unmitered end square.

3 Put the other piece for the corner in place; repeat the process of marking it with a line from the bottom to the corner. Lean the molding back in the miter saw as in Step 2, and cut a 45-degree angle in the direction of the layout line. Cut the unmitered end to length by cutting it square, as in Step 2.

4 Test fit the moldings. If necessary, trim them to length by making a cut on the square end. Drill pilot holes and nail one piece in place with nails along the top and bottom at each stud. Repeat for the other piece, first brushing a little wood glue on the end grain of the mitered surfaces (to hold them together even if the wood later shrinks).

5 Drill pilot holes to avoid splitting the wood; then drive 4d finishing nails through the top and bottom of the joint. If gaps persist, run the edge of a screwdriver shaft along the joint to force fibers into the gap (inset). Countersink the nail heads by using a nail set when you hammer the final few blows. Putty the nail holes and caulk any gaps.

Molding installation skills (continued)

Coping inside corners

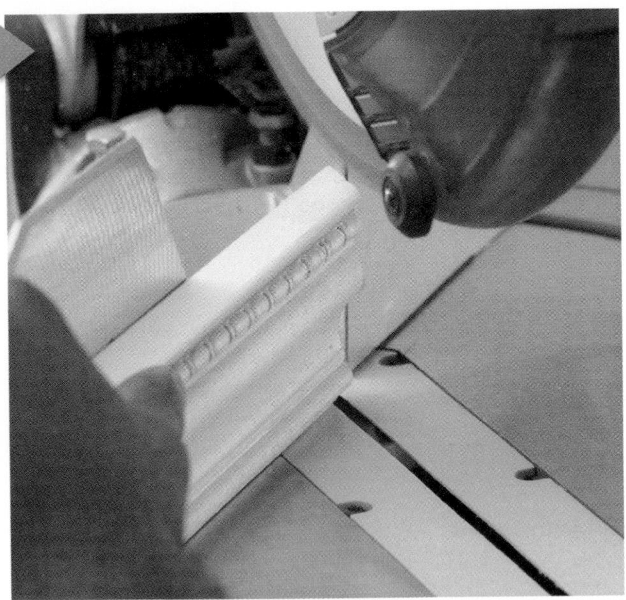

1 Position the saw to cut a 45-degree angle. Start with molding a few inches longer than you'll need; close to the end, cut a 45-degree miter (for an inside corner, the face of the molding is shorter than the back). Cut another piece of molding (for the other side of the corner) with a square cut.

2 You will cope the mitered piece. To do this, make an undercut along the profile with a coping saw. (Look at the face of the molding; the miter cut exposed the profile of the molding, outlined here in pencil.) Cutting away the excess wood beneath the profile creates an outline with curves that can nest against the adjacent molding. Tilt the coping saw back at a 45-degree angle to create a razor-thin edge where the two pieces of molding will meet.

Scarf joints

If a room is too big for one piece of molding to span it, you'll need to join two or more pieces of wood. To make this less noticeable, use angled scarf joints wherever the pieces meet. Plan the joints so they occur directly over a wall stud. Mark each piece, and bevel them at 45-degree angles (the feathered edge of one will overlap the other). Brush a little white or yellow glue on the cut ends; press together before nailing for the best bond.

WORK SMART

PLAN AHEAD

To keep molding from warping, prime all sides, including the back, before you cut it. If the molding will be stained and varnished instead of painted, do it before it's installed, and varnish the back. Touching up paint and stain on the molding is much easier than trying to do the whole job without getting paint on the walls.

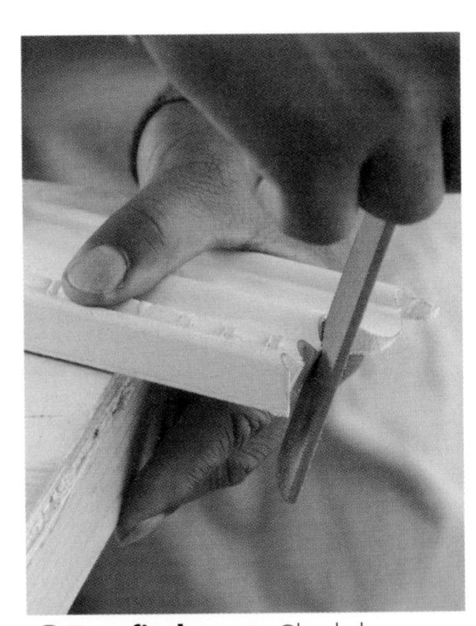

3 Test-fit the cut. Check the joint by fitting it against a cutoff. Be prepared for an imperfect fit; even experienced carpenters often have to fine-tune a joint until it fits. Sand or file any high spots to create a tight fit. Install the mitered molding first; then install the coped piece, pressing it tightly against the other piece before nailing it. The coped end can be manipulated slightly to compensate for corners that aren't quite square.

Nailing on molding

1 Determine the height and mark the wall, using a level to extend a horizontal line. Mark the locations of the wall studs in pencil. Cut the molding to length and miter or cope any corners (see pages 131–132). Make square cuts as needed.

2 Prevent splits by drilling pilot holes the diameter of the finishing nails. Mark the locations for pilot holes by holding the molding in place and transferring the wall stud marks onto the molding.

3 Nail the chair rail. Countersink the nails and putty the holes. Smooth the outside corners by sanding the exposed edges. Caulk any gaps along the edges.

Muscle power

As with most things, you get what you pay for with miter saws. If you don't want to invest in a power miter saw, there are two other choices:

Fixed-angle miter box and backsaw: The miter box is made from either hard maple or plastic, it has slots for 90-degree square cuts and 45-degree miters. It can be used with any saw, but a straight, backsaw with metal reinforcement at the top for strength works best. While inexpensive, it doesn't hold large moldings, and it loses accuracy over time.

Adjustable miter saw: This saw is mounted in a rigid metal frame that rotates on a stand. You can adjust it to lock at any angle from 45 to 90 degrees. There is no play in the saw, so the cuts are smooth and accurate. Unless you're trimming a lot of rooms, this is a good choice.

TOOL TIP

TUNING UP YOUR POWER MITER SAW

A power miter saw (or "chop" saw) is used to cut molding. It has a pivoting 10-inch blade that comes down to cut wood on a small table with a built-in fence. If you've just bought one, you may think it's ready to plug in and use—and maybe it is.

On the other hand, it might have been jostled around during shipping. The saw that was perfectly aligned back at the factory may now be slightly out of whack. If so, it's easy to fix. Unplug the saw and remove the guards so you can get to the blade.

Put a speed square between the fence and the body of the saw blade. (Speed squares are the triangular ones used by carpenters. Their lack of moving parts makes them more reliable than combination squares.) Turn the saw blade, or push the saw down slightly, so the square isn't resting against any saw teeth.

If you see a gap between the saw fence and the square anywhere along the length of the square, your saw is out of alignment and needs to be adjusted. Check your owner's manual for exact instructions; details vary from saw to saw, but it usually involves adjusting one or two screws.

If you have a compound miter saw, also check the relationship between the saw blade and the saw bed: Is the saw cutting straight up and down? Put the square on the bed of the saw and slide it gently against the saw blade, turning the blade so the square doesn't hit any teeth. If there are gaps between the saw and the square, you'll need to adjust the stop that holds the saw in position. Follow the instructions in your owner's manual. Once you've made the necessary adjustments, set the saw to 45 degrees and check against the sloping side of the square. Adjust the stops as needed.

Molding installation skills (continued)

Cutting molding returns

Moldings may go around the wall, but eventually many of them run into door or window trim. When they do, the transition from one to the other looks neat and clean. What do you do, though, if the molding must end where there is no trim? And what if the molding is thicker than the trim it meets, leaving the exposed end sticking out like a sore thumb?

You may be able to solve the problem by rounding the end with sandpaper or by slightly beveling the exposed end. Professional carpenters, however, handle this situation by cutting what's called a molding return.

A return is a small mitered piece that allows the profile to turn back (or return) to the wall, creating a tiny corner that looks like any other outside corner. This eliminates abrupt endings and exposed end grain. Best of all, even though it's easy to do, it adds an elegant, custom detail to your room.

1 Cut a 45-degree miter, as for an outside corner, at the end of the molding running along the wall—it should end a bit short of the door or window. Nail the molding in place (see page 133).

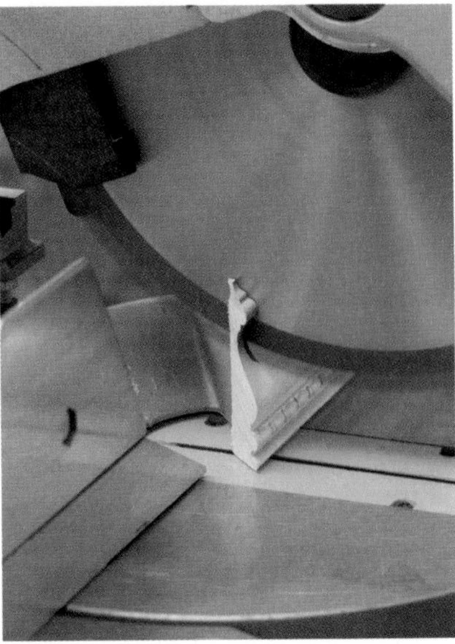

2 Cut a scrap piece of molding in another 45-degree angle that will mate with the one already cut. Together, they will form a 90-degree angle. Cut off a piece the width of the thickest part, making a square cut as shown above; this frees the mitered section of molding from the rest of the stock.

3 Dab white or yellow glue onto the mating surfaces and press the piece into place. Do not use a nail, or it will split. Hold it for a few seconds or wrap masking tape around it until the glue sets. Lightly sand as necessary to clean the joint.

Installing picture rails

A picture rail may seem like a quaint holdover from Victorian times, but think again. They are highly practical, because they let you hang numerous pictures and other objects without hammering nails into the wall. Better yet, when you change your pictures, you won't have to fill the holes, touch up the paint, and put in new nails. They also add architectural interest or authentic historical detail to a room, and can even change the visual perception of a room's height.

Picture rails usually run from 10 to 16 inches below the ceiling, depending on the height of the wall. The molding has a cove along the top edge to hold specialized hardware from which pairs of wires descend to support pictures. Instead of plain wires, you might choose decorative hangers with tassels for a period look, or even steel chain or clear fishing line in a contemporary room. If the trim is purely decorative you can nail it in place, as with any molding. If it will be used to hang pictures, however, it must be able to hold weight. Screw it to the studs, countersink the screws, cover them with putty, and paint or stain to match the rail.

Think about how your eyes work: If there's something interesting above eye level, your eye is drawn to it. If your ceiling is overly high, paint the wall above the picture rail the same color as the ceiling and it will appear as though the wall ends at the railing. To create the illusion of maximum height, don't let the railing stop your eye: Paint the picture rail the same color as the wall above and beneath it. To simply create interest, paint the picture rail and the wall above it in accent colors.

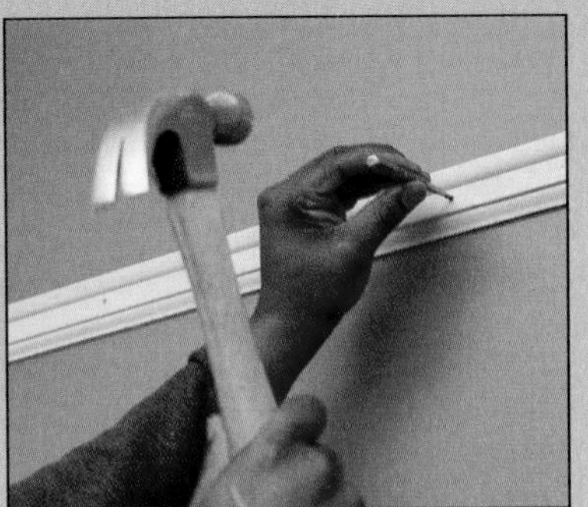

Installing baseboards and chair rails

Skill level:	Time to complete:	Materials:	Tools:
★★★☆☆	Experienced 3.5 hrs. Handy 6 hrs. Novice 8 hrs.	Chair or picture rail, primer or varnish, finish color, wood putty, caulk, finishing nails	Paintbrush, level, tape measure, power miter saw or handsaw and miter box, stud finder, electric drill, hammer, nail set, caulking gun

Chair rails, like baseboards, can dress up a room and help define its period and style. Both are installed the same way.

Originally chair rails came into use to protect plaster walls from being damaged when chairs were placed against the wall (hence the name). They also establish a border between two different wall treatments, such as a wallpapered lower section and a painted upper section. Chair rails also provide transition between paneling or paint below and paint or wallpaper above.

Whether it is purely functional or not, place your chair rail at a height that would protect the wall from damage by furniture. Most rails are between 32 and 36 inches from the floor. Adjust the height as necessary to avoid awkward meetings with the bottom of window frames.

Select base molding that fits the scale of your room. The depth of the baseboards lends weight and substance to a room—wider styles usually seem more elegant. By adding a cap above it, and shoe mold at its base, you can build up an impressive baseboard molding profile using off-the-shelf elements.

▲ *Chair rails protect wallpaper and paint from damage and create an attractive transition between different surfaces. Baseboards anchor the room and cover up the awkward gap between walls and flooring.*

WORK SMART

BUY FROM THE SAME BUNDLE

If possible, buy molding from the same bundle; this ensures that pieces will be nearly identical. The molding profile undergoes subtle changes as the cutting blades wear down. They aren't apparent until two different lengths are joined. Make finishing nails less conspicuous by driving them at an angle into a crevice in the profile.

How high? Your call

How high should a chair rail or wainscoting be? It's really up to you. Many builders have arrived at standardized heights for chair rails and wainscotting. They put the top of chair rails 32 to 36 inches above the floor, with 36 inches being most common. Wainscoting is either at that height or—in Craftsman- or cottage-style homes—at about 5 feet (see Installing Wainscoting on pages 143–144). By doing the work yourself, you can adjust the height slightly to avoid running into window sills or having most of your molding hidden by a high-back sofa.

You may have seen rooms where something was off, but you weren't sure what the problem was. Chances are, someone simply divided the height of the room in half and put a chair rail there. The proportion was all wrong.

The Greeks had it right. They came up with a design principle called the Golden Ratio. This ratio is supposed to produce the most pleasing proportions: The preferred ratio is 1:1.618.

Here's an ultra-simple way to figure it: Divide the height (in inches) of your room by 3; place the top of the chair rail that many inches above the floor.

To be more exact—and find the golden ratio of your wall—multiply the height of your wall (in inches) by 0.618. You can put the top of the molding at that height, or else subtract that measurement from the total and use the remainder as your height. (Either way, your wall is divided into two sections that relate well to each other.) For example: An 8-foot wall is 96 inches. 96 x 0.618 = 59.328. The top edge of wainscoting should be placed at 59.33 inches (or about 5 feet); a chair rail should be at 36.67 inches (or just over 3 feet). The ideal measurements come remarkably close to builders' standards.

Installing baseboards and chair rails (continued)

1 Prime the rail. To prevent warping, paint, stain, or varnish both sides of the rail before installing it. If the trim will be finished after it is already nailed on, go ahead and apply a coat of finish to the back now.

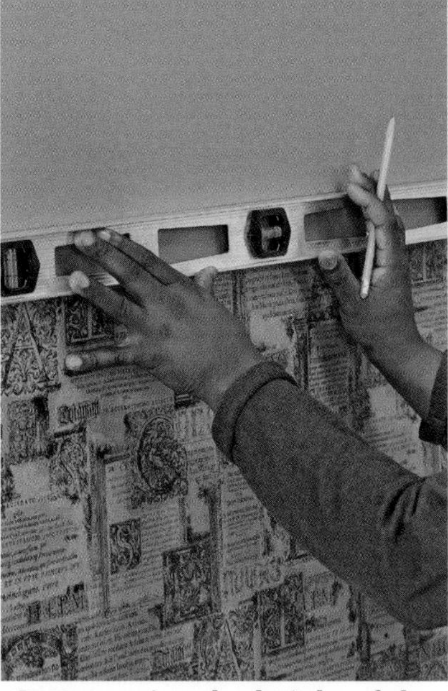

2 Determine the height of the rail. Mark the wall at that height, and use a level to extend a horizontal line for the top edge of the rail.

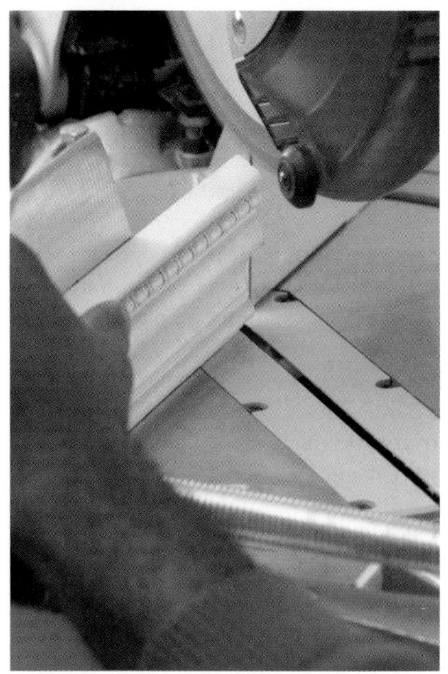

3 If they will be painted, and small gaps can be puttied, moldings with simple profiles can meet at 45-degree miter joints for both inside and outside corners. Complex moldings and stained moldings look better at inside corners if the joints are coped.

WORK SMART

LEARN AS YOU GO

When installing a chair rail or baseboard around a room, lay it out so that you start and end in the least conspicuous corner, such as next to the entrance door. Your technique will get better as you move around the room, and it will be easier to hide small errors.

Level around the whole room

Use your level: Check to see that the layout line on one wall is level with the layout line on the adjacent wall. Do not rely on simply measuring the same distance up from the floor. Starting a couple of feet from the corner, put one end of the level on the line. Put the other end of the level on the line on the other wall. It's OK if only the ends of the level touch the wall. If you get a level reading, the lines are level. If not, redraw one of the lines. Repeat this at every corner.

4 At door and window casings, end the molding with a square cut. If the molding is thicker than the casing, create a better transition by cutting a bevel on the portion that protrudes. Along walls too long to be spanned by a single length of rail, scarf two or more pieces (see page132).

5 Find the studs by using a stud finder or by tapping a nail through the wall at a level where holes will be concealed by the trim. Holding the chair rail in place, transfer the stud locations to the molding. Drill pilot holes at each mark and attach the molding with finishing nails. Countersink the nails, putty the holes, and sand the outside corners until smooth.

Installing crown molding

Skill level:	Time to complete:	Materials:	Tools:
★★★☆☆	Experienced Variable Handy Variable Novice Variable	Crown molding, finishing nails, wood putty, caulk	Tape measure, stepladder, 4-foot level, power miter saw, stud finder, electric drill, hammer, caulking gun, coping saw, clamps, nail set

Crown molding fits in the corner where the wall meets the ceiling. It might be simple, or very elaborate depending on the style of the house. In some instances, there are several moldings put together to create a more complex effect, but they are all put on in basically the same way. Study the basic molding skills on pages 131 to 134.

Outside corners are mitered, but inside corners should be coped. (A coped joint is one in which one molding is cut to nest against the profile of another.) This helps to disguise out-of-square corners, wall irregularities, and problems caused by wood expansion.

Crown molding slopes from wall to ceiling, complicating both mitered and coped joints somewhat. Once you've made the initial cut, though, the rest of it is no harder than working with baseboard or chair rail (see page 135).

▲ *In a coped inside-corner joint, you cut the profile of one molding into the end of another with a coping saw. The two pieces nest together, creating the look, without the potential problems, of a mitered joint.*

DESIGN TIP

BUILT-UP MOLDINGS

Crown moldings come in a few basic profiles (see page 141) but you can combine them many different ways for a fancier appearance.
A couple of ideas shown here use moldings that are widely available, including plain 1x2s.

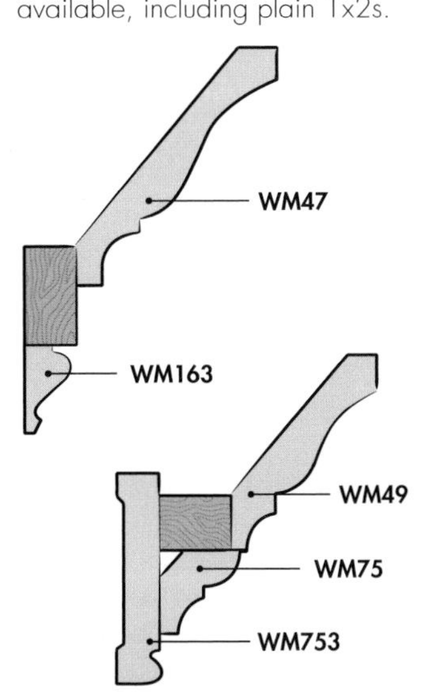

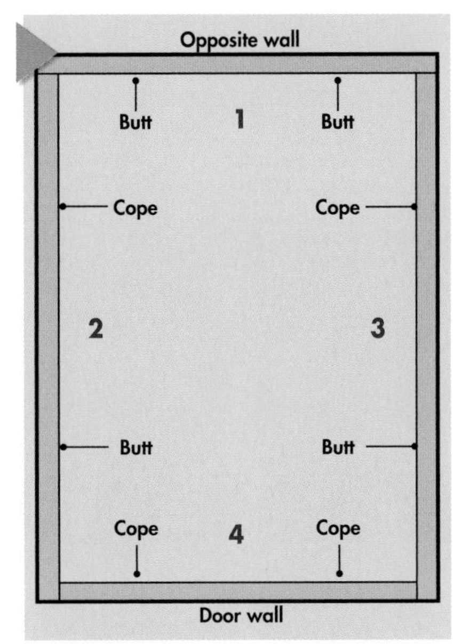

1 Plan your installation. Some joints are more visible than others, and these are the ones you want to look best. Experienced carpenters install crown molding in the order above for the easiest and best-looking job. Start on the wall opposite the door **(1)** and install a piece that's square at both ends. This presents the best (and easiest to cut) side of the joint to anyone entering the room. The molding on the second wall **(2)** is coped where it meets the installed molding, and square where it meets the other wall. The third wall **(3)** is treated the same way, and the fourth wall **(4)** is coped at both ends.

2 Measure the room and mark the stud locations. You'll nail the molding into the wall studs. Locate the studs with a stud finder and make faint pencil marks high on the wall (where they won't be covered by molding) to guide you as you nail.

Installing crown molding (continued)

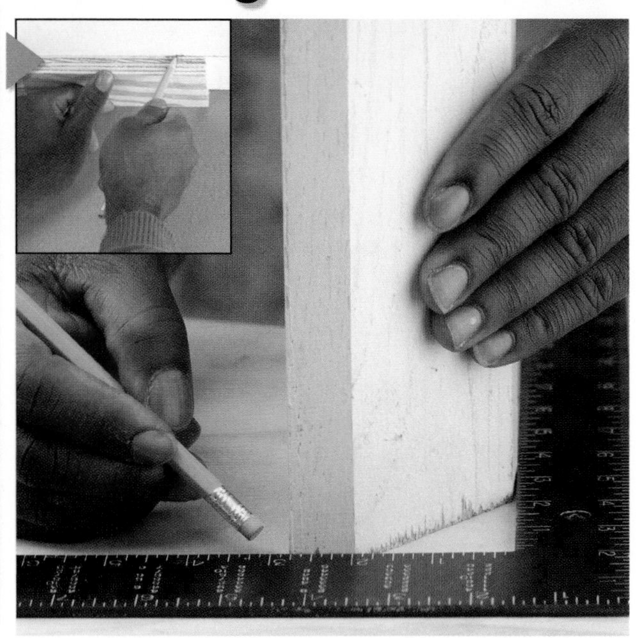

3 Put the molding against a framing square, noting the distance between the face of the molding edge and the corner. Cut a scrap of lumber to the correct dimension and draw layout lines on the wall and ceiling (see inset). When you install the molding, align it with the layout lines.

4 Begin at the wall opposite the door (see page 137), and cut molding to that length. Mark the locations of the studs by holding the molding in place and transferring the marks onto the molding. To prevent splitting drill pilot holes the diameter of the finishing nails (see inset); drill holes at each mark at the top and bottom of the molding. Nail in place.

Blocking: What to do if nails won't reach the ceiling joists

On the two walls perpendicular to the ceiling joists, you'll nail the bottom edge of the molding into the studs, and the top edge into the ceiling joists. On the other two walls, there are plenty of studs, but the first ceiling joist may be 16 inches from the wall.

The best way to solve this problem is to make infill blocks by beveling a 2x4 and cutting it into short lengths. Nail one of these to the corner at each stud. This gives you a solid surface on which to nail the molding.

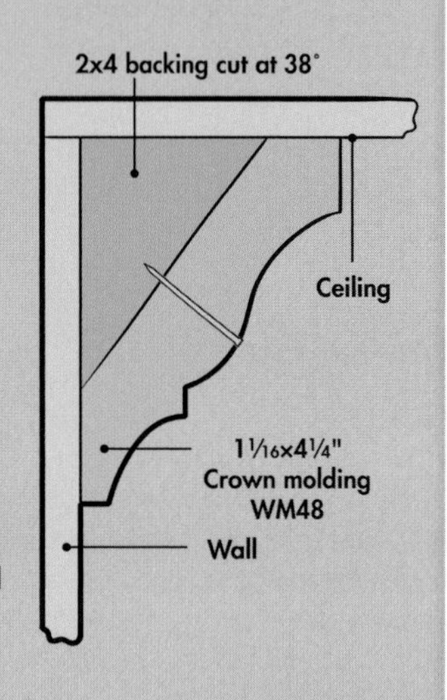

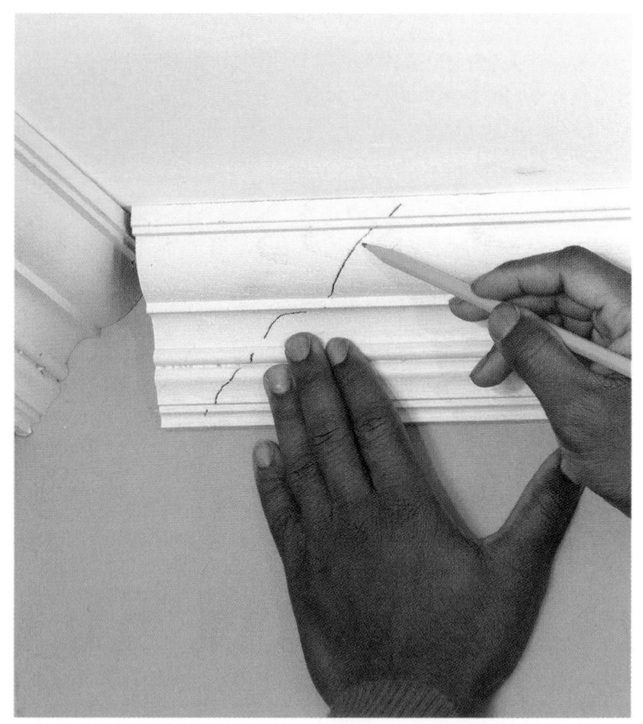

5 Lay out the cope joint on a second piece of molding; start with a piece a few inches longer than finished length and flex it in place. At the end you'll cope, draw a line in the general direction you'll cut at roughly a 45-degree angle (it's OK if the line isn't straight).

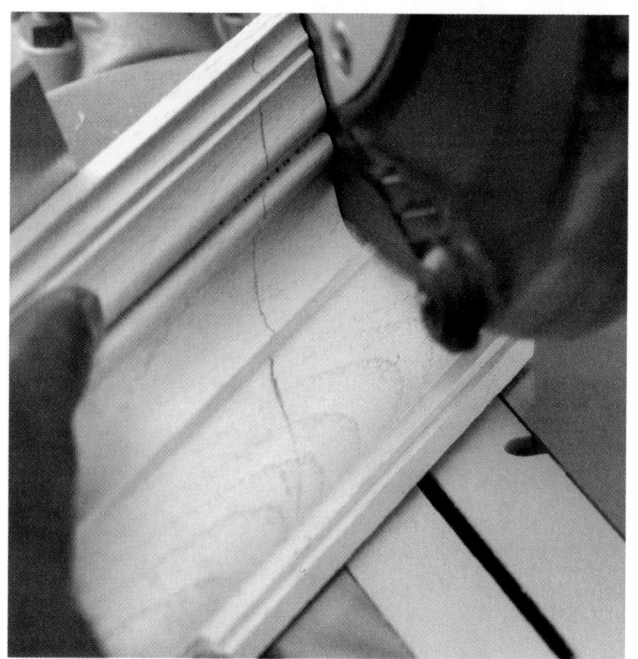

6 Set up the miter saw. Position the molding so that the ceiling edge is flat on the bottom of the miter box and the wall edge is tight against the fence. Set the saw to cut at 45 degrees in the general direction of the line you drew in Step 1. (If the blade and line won't even come close to aligning, turn the molding upside down and try again.) Cut a miter close to the end.

7 Undercut along the profile with a coping saw. Look at the face of the molding; the miter cut exposed the profile of the molding, outlined here in pencil. Cutting away the excess wood beneath the profile creates an outline that can nest against the adjacent molding. Tilt the coping saw back at a 45-degree angle to create a razor-thin edge where the two moldings will meet.

8 Test-fit the cut. Check the joint by fitting it against a cutoff. Be prepared for an imperfect fit; even experienced carpenters may have to fine-tune the joint until it fits.

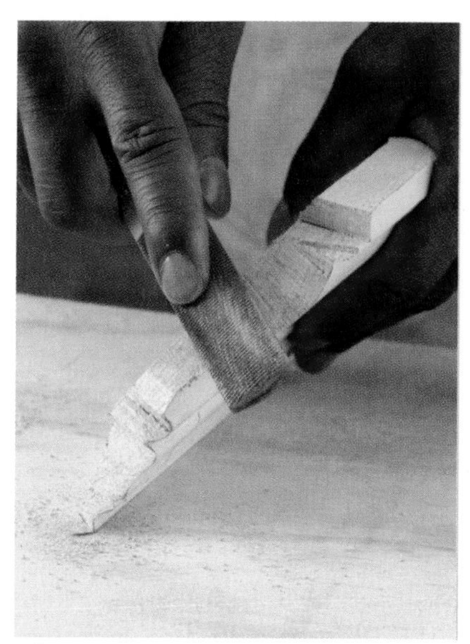

9 Sand and file any high spots to create a tight fit. When the joint fits, measure the wall. Cut the molding ⅛ inch longer than measured (usually by making a square cut on the uncoped end—see Step 1 on page 137). Flex the molding in place—the extra length will help push the cope joint closed.

10 Nail the molding in place. When the moldings fit together without any gaps, nail the molding to the wall and ceiling. Putty the nail holes. If you're painting the molding, run a bead of caulk in the seam and wipe it smooth with a wet finger.

Installing polyurethane molding

Skill level:	Time to complete:	Materials:	Tools:
★★★☆☆	Experienced Variable Handy Variable Novice Variable	Inside and outside corners, straight moldings, latex adhesive caulk, trim-head screws, glazing putty	Electric drill, power miter saw or miter box, tape measure, pencil, adjustable combination square, caulking gun

Those who are daunted by the thought of trying to miter crown moldings can breathe a deep sigh of relief. Polyurethane molding eliminates the need to make anything but straight cuts yet it's almost indistinguishable from solid wood once it's painted. Corners are made from small blocks that screw in place. Because the blocks have square outside edges, adjoining moldings can simply butt against them. You'll only need to cut the molding to length.

Polyurethane molding screws to the wall with trim-head screws—essentially drywall screws with a smaller head. Fill the holes by rolling some glazing putty into a ball and packing it into the hole. Then run your thumb over the putty to create a patch that follows the molding contour.

Although polyurethane won't take a stain, it paints very smoothly. You can paint it over the glazing putty almost immediately too.

1 Install the inside and outside corner blocks with latex adhesive caulk, making sure they fit squarely. Screw the blocks to the corner studs with trim-head screws, and putty the holes.

2 Measure the distance between two corner blocks. Mark the straight moldings across the face, using a pencil and adjustable combination square. Cut the molding by hand in a miter box or with a power miter saw.

DESIGN TIP
INSTANT ELEGANCE

Dress up formal rooms with polyurethane rosettes made to fit around light fixtures. The installation is quick and easy but you might want to finish or paint the rosette first. The rosette screws into ceiling joists; first position it on the ceiling and trace around it in pencil. Use a stud finder to locate where joists cross the pencil line, making light marks. Put some construction adhesive on the back of the rosette, put it back in place, and drive trim-head screws into the joists. Putty the holes and touch up the paint before installing the light fixture.

Wood vs. poly

If you're comparing polyurethane and real wood crown moldings, which one is the better choice? It depends upon who is judging.

Traditional wooden crown molding can be stained, varnished, painted, stripped, salvaged, and reused, and it can outlast the home's occupants. It also requires a fairly high level of skill to install well because of the mitered and perfectly coped joints, and it may shrink over the years. For the purist, though, wood is the only choice because various moldings can be built up to create an unlimited number of custom styles.

Polyurethane moldings are much easier to install, requiring only square cuts and, hopefully, a helper to hold up the other end. Latex adhesive caulk grabs instantly to hold the molding in place, and screws finish the job. These moldings come preprimed, and they must be painted, not stained. Styles are also limited to what you can buy. Those in the know can tell by the corners that they are a synthetic material. Still, they are an attractive, reasonably priced alternative to wood.

3 Run latex adhesive caulk along the edges of the molding. Position the molding to contact the wall and ceiling. Drive trim-head screws through the molding and into the wall studs and ceiling joists. Wipe away excess caulk. Fill any gaps along the wall and ceiling with latex caulk. Use glazing putty to fill the screw holes and then paint the molding.

Creating custom molding

Skill level:	Time to complete:	Materials:	Tools:
★★★☆☆	Experienced Variable Handy Variable Novice Variable	1×3 pine for twice room perimeter plus 8 feet, 11⁄16×2⅝-inch chair rail (WM390) for room perimeter plus 8 feet, 11⁄16×2½-inch chair rail (WM298) for room perimeter plus 8 feet, 11⁄16×11⁄16-inch cove molding (WM100) for twice room perimeter plus 16 feet, wood putty	Chalk line, 4-foot level, saw, hammer, finishing nails (#4, #6, and #8), nail set, blue painter's masking tape, paint or stain, miter box or power miter saw, wood form

Home centers and lumberyards carry large selections of wood moldings for various purposes. Look at them closely—some of them have the same profile but are different woods (usually pine and oak). Others are similar profiles in a choice of different widths. By combining various moldings and plain stock, you'll be able to make an attractive profile for any use.

The chair rail at right, also shown below, combines several stock profiles, each identified by a number assigned by the Wood Moulding and Millwork Association. The upper rail, for example, uses a 11⁄16×2⅝-inch chair rail—WM390. The lower rail uses WM298, a 11⁄16×2½-inch chair rail. The other stock can be a 1×3 or cove molding. If you're unsure of which molding or trim to use, ask an experienced associate at your home center or lumberyard to help you decide.

▲ *Multiple built-up moldings create a distinctive chair rail.*

Molding profiles

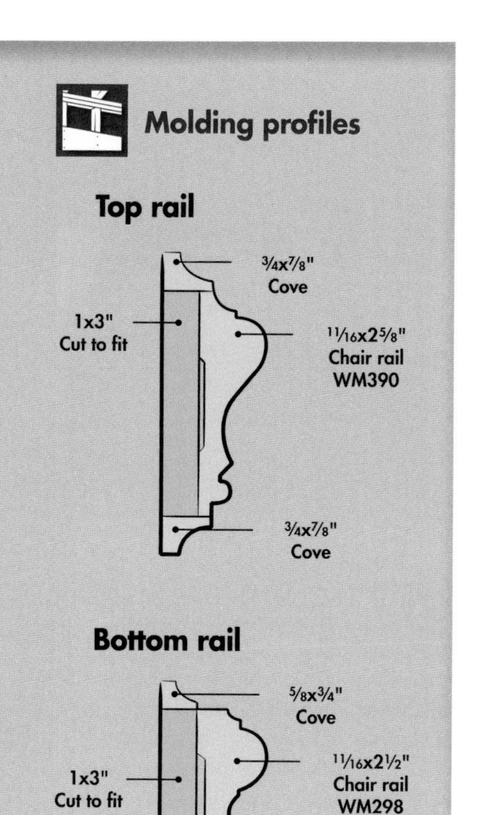

1 Design a profile: Look at molding profiles similar to the samples at left to get ideas for your own. Sketch the molding and make a full-size drawing to take to the store. You may be able to buy short lengths of the moldings to see how they fit together, or the store may have scraps. Before you purchase the molding you need, hold a sample in place in the room to get a sense of scale.

2 Draw layout lines on the wall. The double chair rail molding shown has a pair of 1×3s as its base. Determine the height of the chair rail; 36 inches above the floor is typical for the top edge. Also draw a level line where the bottom edge of the lower 1×3 will be.

Creating custom molding (continued)

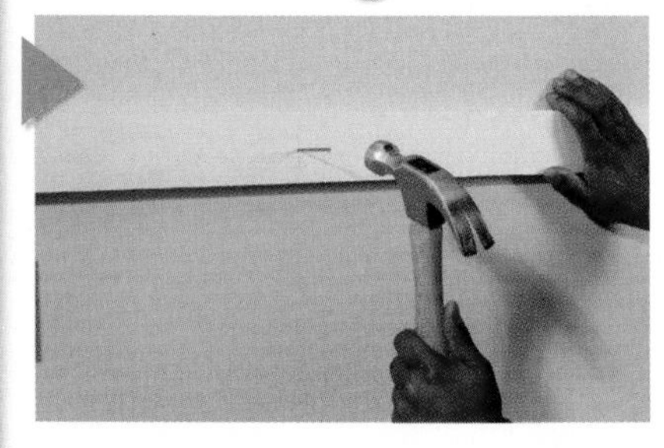

3 Cut the lower 1×3 to length. Butt the 1×3s at the inside corners, and miter the outside corners. Nail the 1×3s to the wall with #6 or #8 finishing nails or, better yet, screw them into the studs. (Rest a scrap of 1×3 on top of the piece already on the wall, using it as a spacer to keep the second 1×3 parallel to the first.)

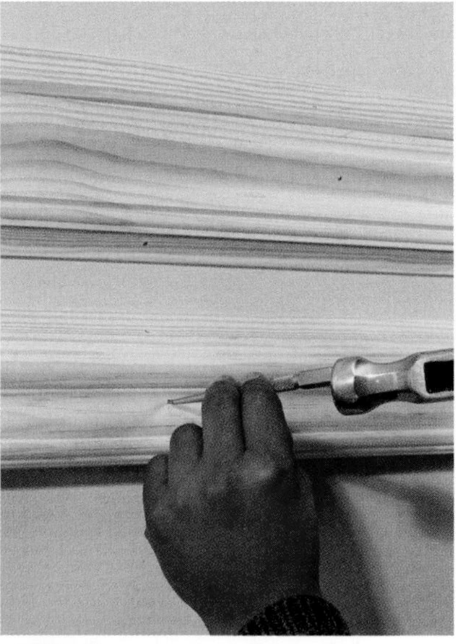

4 Before you nail on the molding, bevel the cut edge wherever it fits against window or door frames if the chair rail projects more than the frames (this provides a clean appearance).

5 Miter molding at outside corners and cope or miter the inside corners (see pages 131–132). Wherever possible miter the end of the first piece and nail it in place. Hold the second piece in place, mark it to meet the first piece, miter it, and put it in place (this is faster and more reliable than measuring). Cut long, and trim it to fit (see Work Smart, below left).

Your choice in chair rails

Chair rails come in all sorts of profiles. Some are flat, or almost flat, to the wall, such as the blue one below. Others are capped by a narrow piece of molding turned horizontally—this is called a cap rail. Extending this idea, cap rails can be even wider for display shelves, like the one on the opposite page used to hold plates. For one like this, consider routing a lengthwise groove to secure the plate edges.

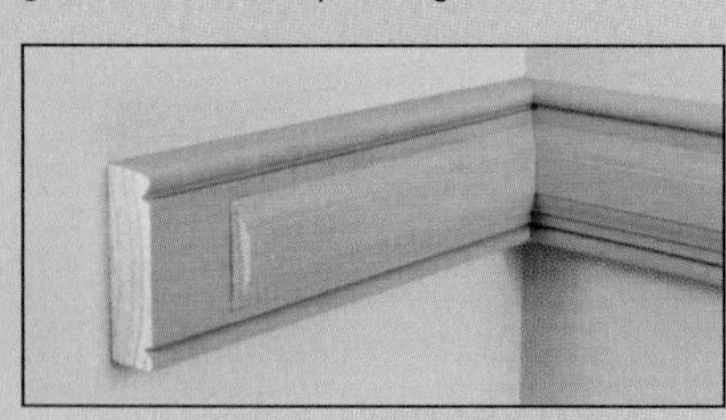

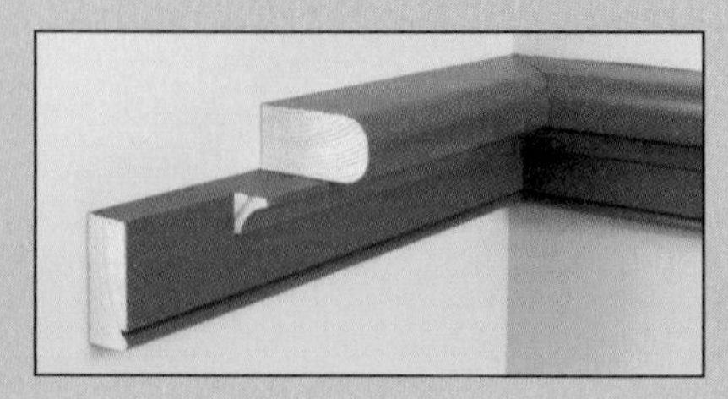

WORK SMART

CUT LONG

When you make a cut in a miter box, don't try to cut the piece to the exact length on the first try. By making a cut that leaves the piece a bit long, you have the opportunity to nudge it in and mark directly on the molding. Cut and nudge until the piece is the right length. If you want the piece to fit tightly between two walls, cut it 1⁄32 to 1⁄16 inch long, flex it into place, and nail it down.

6 Mask the wall at the top and bottom edges of the molding. Set all the nails and fill the holes with latex wood putty. Prime and paint the new molding. Either paint between the moldings or fill the space with a decorative treatment, perhaps another paint color or a strip of wallpaper that matches other elements in the room.

Installing wainscoting

Skill level:	Time to complete:	Materials:	Tools:
★★★☆☆	Experienced Variable Handy Variable Novice Variable	Tongue-and-groove beaded board, cap rail, baseboard (optional), varnish or paint, construction adhesive, #6 and #8 finishing nails, paintable caulk	Pry bar, 4-foot level, stud finder, saw and miter box or power miter saw, saber saw, tape measure, pencil, notched trowel, hammer, caulking gun, nail set, saber saw, combination square, paintbrush

Wainscoting adds architectural interest and texture to a room, making it seem more intimate and traditional. The style can be casual, as in beaded-board wainscoting in cottage- or country-style rooms. It can also look more formal, as in a Craftsman-style home with recessed-panel wainscoting and a horizontal display shelf, or a Colonial-style home with raised-panel wainscoting and a chair rail. Use it in bedrooms, baths, family rooms, kitchens, dining rooms, and entries.

Wainscoting is typically installed with its top 32 to 36 inches off the floor, or roughly one-third of the room height (see page 135). For real drama, reverse that proportion and install the wainscoting about two-thirds of the way up the wall. Whatever the height, adjust the top edge to avoid running directly into windowsills or other trim. Select wainscoting that is less deep (thinner) than the door and window casings if possible.

Tongue-and-groove beaded board, in which the edges between boards have a ridge or bead, is the most popular type. Or you can build a series of framed panels, similar to a row of traditional cabinet doors. Plywood wainscoting that comes in a sheet is a cost-effective, easy-to-install alternative to individual boards.

▶ *Beaded-board wainscoting is usually made of 2- or 3-inch-wide vertical strips that are nailed and glued over the existing wall. This one is capped by a display shelf with a plate groove on the top.*

1 Before you begin, prime (or stain and seal) the materials, including the back. Remove the outlet covers; install outlet box extension rings to bring the outlet to the wainscoting surface. If reusing the baseboard carefully pry it from the wall (new baseboards may have a rabbeted groove to hold the lower ends of the boards).

2 Draw a line for the top edge of the wainscoting. To determine the height for the wainscoting, measure up from the floor and, using a level, extend a line around the room (don't just measure up from the floor).

Installing wainscoting (continued)

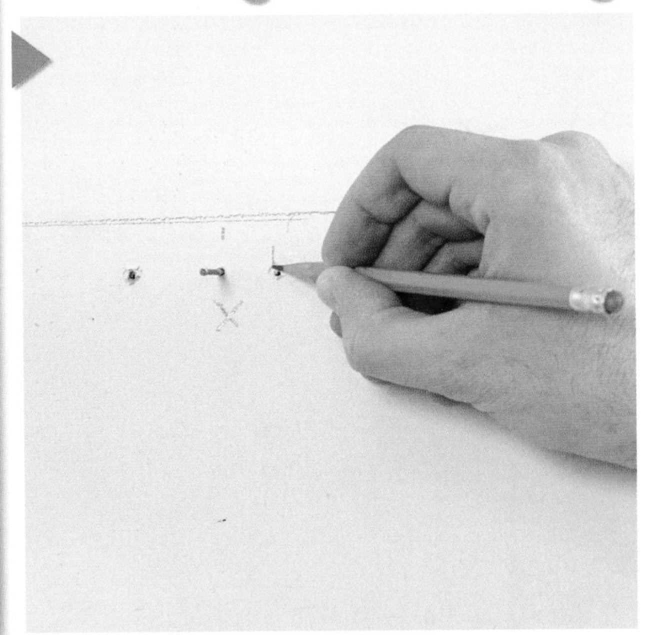

3 Locate the studs with a nail or stud finder, marking each of them at floor level and just above the level line. These marks show where the cap rail and baseboard should be nailed to hold the top and bottom of the wainscoting in place.

4 Measure and cut the wainscot boards to length. If you have a rabbeted baseboard, measure from the bottom of the rabbet to the line marking the top of the wainscoting. If the baseboard will be attached after the wainscoting is installed, measure between the line and the floor. Don't cut everything at once; the length of the boards may change as you move along because of uneven or unlevel floors.

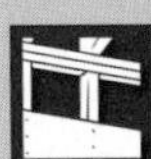

Scribing to fit an irregular corner

When you have one board left to go but it won't fit in the irregular corner, here's what to do: Hold the board in the corner so that its edge is against the problem wall. Plumb the board with a level so that it is perfectly vertical. Lay out the cut with the help of a simple compass. Set the distance between the pencil and point to the width of the widest part of the gap. Run the metal point along the wall and the pencil along the board to lay out the cut. (Make sure the compass setting doesn't change while you do this.) Cut along the pencil line with a saber saw.

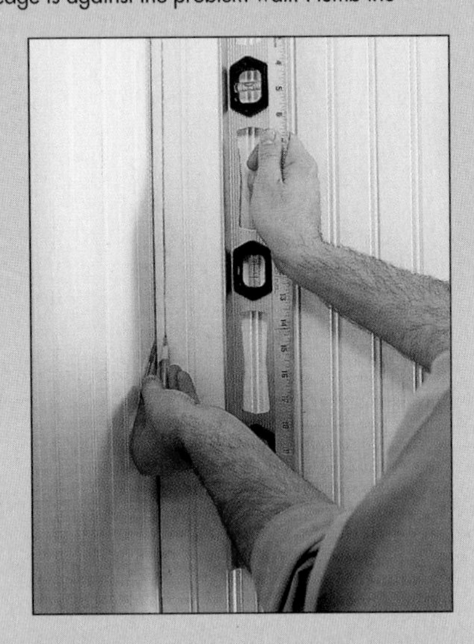

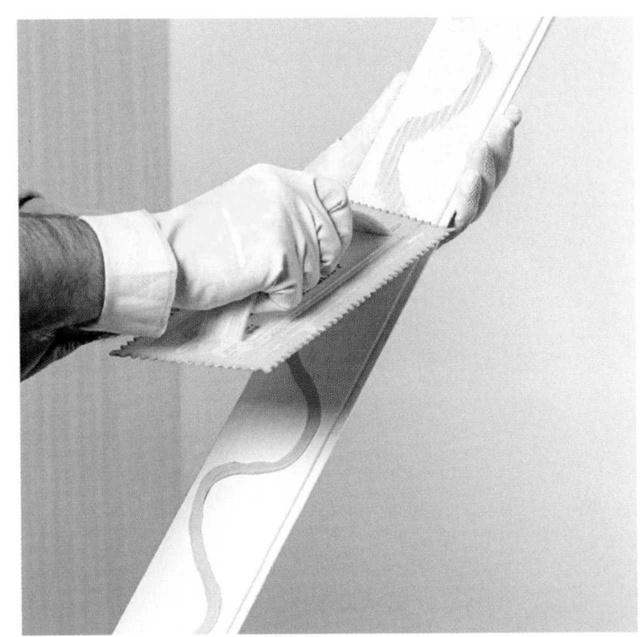

5 Glue the wainscoting in place: Butt the grooved end of a board into a corner and nail it. Run a wavy line of construction adhesive along the back of several boards, spreading it with a notched trowel as you slide each tongue into a groove. (Leave a 1⁄16-inch space between the visible edges to allow for expansion in humid weather.) Align the top edges with the level line; check the vertical edge with a level. Press the boards onto the wall with the heels of your hands.

6 Measure and cut several more boards and install them. Whenever a board is over a stud, nail it in place (drive the nail in the groove or through the tongue if possible). Cut or plane the last board as needed to make it fit. Install it by slipping it down from above (or saw off the last tongue if all else fails); nail it in place, catching the corner framing.

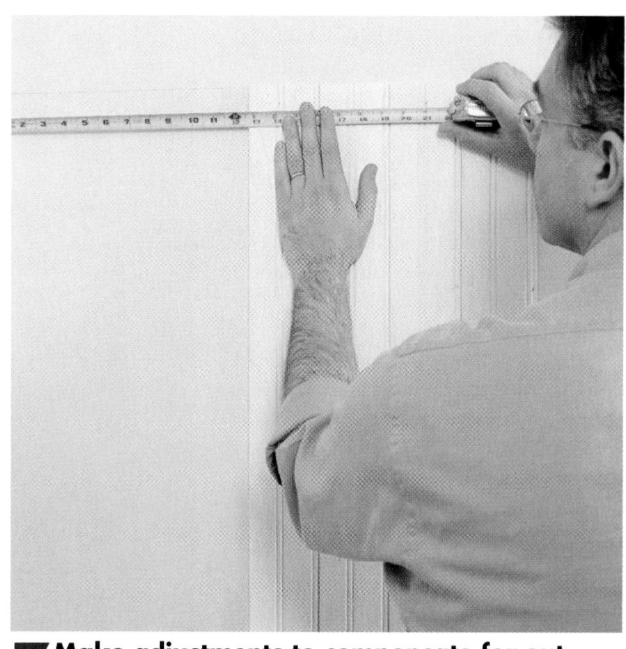

7 Make adjustments to compensate for out-of-plumb corners, starting several boards away. Measure between the corner and the last board installed, at both the top and bottom; divide the difference by the number of boards left to be installed on that wall. For very small differences, install the remaining boards slightly out of plumb so the last one will be flush with the adjoining wall. Or, scribe the last board to fit (see the opposite page).

8 Nail on the cap rail and baseboard with #6 or #8 finishing nails. (Avoid driving nails near electrical outlets or switches.) Miter inside and outside corners. If the rail is complex, cope the inside corners (see page132). If the baseboards go on top of the beaded boards, nail them on with #8 finishing nails. Countersink the heads and fill the holes with putty. If you are painting the wainscoting, seal any gaps beforehand with paintable caulk.

Cutting a hole for an outlet

Turn the power off and disconnect the screws holding the receptacle. Rub lipstick or chalk on the edges of the electrical box; position the board on the wall and press it against the box so that the color transfers. Screw on the plug and turn on the power. Put the board on a work surface and drill a ½-inch hole just inside each corner of the marks. Cut along the colored line with a saber saw to make the opening.

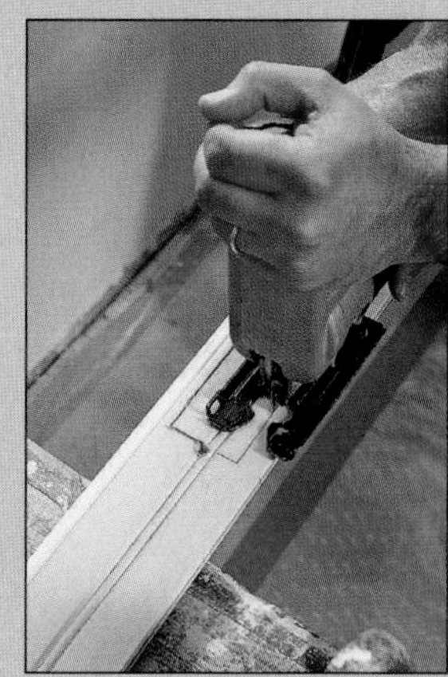

Wainscot choices

There may be times when you want to accent a wall. Perhaps you'd like a staircase treatment more decorative and durable than painted drywall. Or you may wish to dress up your kitchen with an attractive cottage-style backsplash. These and other specialized areas are as easy to work with as regular walls—although they do involve different-sized pieces—and they can dramatically alter the character of your home.

When installing paneling in specialized areas, measure carefully but plan on being able to cover rough edges and possible gaps with molding. Otherwise, attach the paneling with adhesive caulk and nails, filling the holes and finishing it as usual.

► *Paneling unifies this his-and-her bath, creating a cottage-style profile against bare walls. Applying flat boards to the drywall, and painting the resulting panels to match, makes the most of a room that formerly had little character.*

Today's wainscoting is easier than ever to install, and there are many possible choices that reflect the broad spectrum of decorating styles. Options even include prefabricated panels to which you add only the cap and baseboard. This wainscoting comes in several different types of wood, beaded board, or even thick sections of drywall molded to look like raised panels. See new choices at your home center or search online.

▲ *This frame-and-panel wainscoting has oak panels shaped to run along a stairway. It is more durable and easier to clean than a regular wall in a heavy-traffic area.*

▲ *Beaded board paneling can add interest to various nooks around the house. Here, a desk backs up to painted paneling that continues around the room at a different height.*

Hanging and arranging artwork

1 Plan the layout by tracing the outline of each frame on paper. Cut out the shapes, marking where the fully extended wire comes (in one or two places, depending on the number of hooks). Place masking-tape loops on the backs, and experiment with placement. Heavy pieces must be anchored in wall studs; locate studs with a stud finder. Common picture-hanging mistakes include: hanging too high (the very center of large pieces should be about 5 feet above the floor) and hanging small pieces too far apart (treat several as one unit, leaving only a couple of inches between them).

2 Choose a mechanism for hanging the art. Lightweight pieces can hang by a sawtooth hanger nailed into the back of the frame. Hang heavier art with screw eyes and braided wire made to handle the weight of that particular piece. Measure one-third of the way down the frame and drill two pilot holes for the eyes; avoid boring through the frame. Twist in the eyes. Cut a length of wire that equals the width of the frame, plus 50 percent. Wrap one end around each screw eye and twist it in place, first making sure the fully extended wire doesn't come above the frame.

3 Mark the wall when you find the best location for the picture, going in at the mark made for the fully extended wire. Select a picture hanger large enough for the weight of the artwork. Measure the distance from the nail to the hook on the hanger; raise the mark on the wall by this distance. To help prevent plaster from chipping, apply criss-crossed tape to the wall before driving in the hanger nail. Hang the picture, and check it with a level to make sure it's straight.

Picture-hanger hardware

Most hardware departments sell a variety of picture hangers that will accommodate various weights. One of these common hangers works in almost every situation, but you'll need to consider your wall as well as the weight of the picture. A hanger is only as strong as the wall it is in—chipped plaster can lead to disaster. Holes can also enlarge gradually, and then a prized piece suddenly falls. Check your walls periodically.

If walls are drywall, most hangers work fine, unless the artwork is very heavy. In such cases, you'll need to anchor the hanger in a stud or use a sleeve-type anchor, molly bolt, or toggle bolt.

In plaster walls, using hangers with plain nails might chip the plaster. "Professional" hangers with thin, sharp nails work better.

Read the packaging to see how much weight a particular hanger is designed to support. Always err toward using sturdier hangers, especially if hanging a mirror, for which you might even use an extra hanger or two.

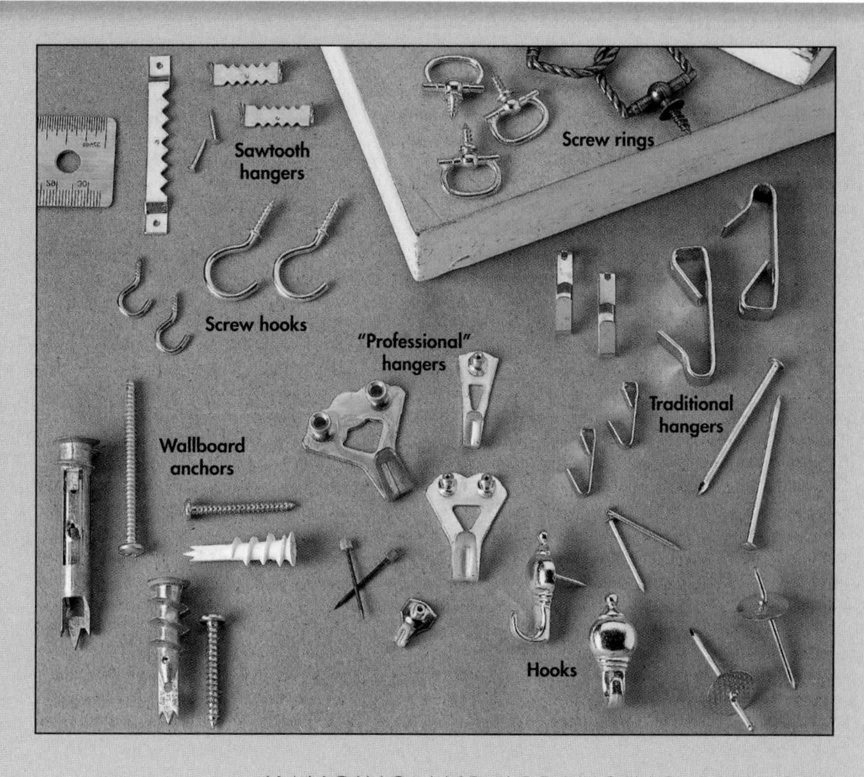

Tiling a wall

Skill level:	Time to complete:	Materials:	Tools:
★★★☆☆	Experienced 8 hrs. Handy 10 hrs. Novice 12 hrs.	Ceramic tile, thinset mortar, latex admix (if called for), wood spacers, plastic spacers, grout, grout sealant, silicone caulk, pencil, tile stick	Combination square, tape measure, 4-foot level, tile cutter, rod saw, file, notched trowel, electric drill, mixing blade, tile-cutting bit, clamp, rubber grout float, plastic spacer remover, grout sponge, foam brush

Tile may be on the surface, but the backerboard and thinset behind it hold it up and make it strong. Backerboard is often called "mason's drywall." It can be made of cement, fiber cement, gypsum, plywood, or plastic, but the critical factor is that it's sound and inflexible. Follow the manufacturers' instructions when screwing backerboard to the wall.

Mortar for tile is called thinset, and some types need to be mixed with a latex admix for strength and ease of working.

Grout is similar to thinset, but it fills the space between the tiles. Read the label to see if a latex admix is recommended to make the grout more resistant to water and staining. If the tiles are less than ⅛ inch apart or you're working with polished marble that scratches easily, use a sandless grout for a waterproof joint.

Joints between the tub and floor or adjacent walls will eventually crack; fill them with silicone caulk, not grout. Elastic caulk withstands settling without cracking and prevents wall damage from moisture behind the tiles.

1 Make a tile stick to help you when spacing the tiles. Line the tiles up on the floor, separated by commercially available plastic spacers the thickness of the grout line. With a square and pencil, mark a straight piece of wood showing the spacing between tiles.

2 Using a 4-foot level, draw a reference line around the room. In a bathroom, the line level is level with the top of the tub. In other rooms, draw a level line halfway between the floor and ceiling. Draw a second horizontal line to lay out border tiles, if any. Mark the location of any recessed fixtures, such as soap dishes.

Tile layout

Tile layout is always a compromise. In this room, there is a full tile immediately above the tub—something that wouldn't be possible if there was a full tile at the floor line. Notice, too, that the grout line that runs along the top of the knee wall aligns with the grout line on the wall.

As you'll see in step 9, aligning the grout lines results in a very narrow tile in one corner of the room. It's hard to put in, and some people object to how it looks. So, simply move the vertical reference line so that trimmed tiles of the same width are at both corners.

Likewise, if you are using cove tiles with an edge that curves to meet the floor, you'll start with a much lower horizontal reference line—one that marks the top edge of the cove tile.

In short, feel free to move the reference lines. Move the vertical line left or right to control the size of the tiles that meet the wall. Move the horizontal line to control how important elements—tub, floor, or chair rail—meet the tile.

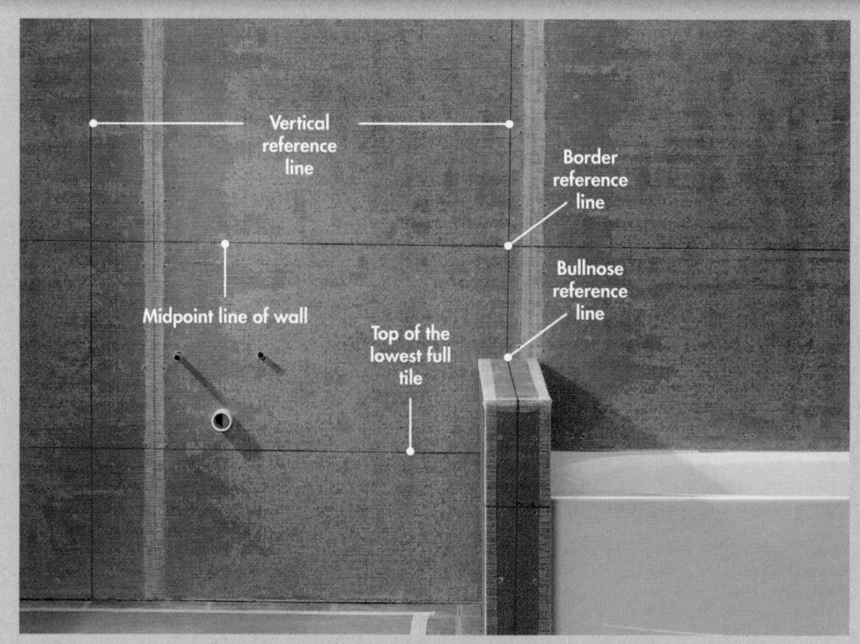

▲ *After you've drawn reference lines, the wall will look somewhat like this. The lower horizontal line denotes the top of the tub and also the bottom of a tile. The upper horizontal line marks a row of narrow border tiles that will run around the room. The vertical lines mark the center of the knee wall and a grout line on the wall. The edge of the divider will consist of rounded-edge bullnose tiles.*

3 If there's a short knee wall, draw a line down the middle of it; transfer the line to the main wall with a level. This vertical line will help center a grout line over the knee wall.

4 Place the tile stick where horizontal and vertical reference lines intersect. Mark the horizontal line, to show the tile edges and the grout lines between them.

5 Draw a level vertical line to show the outside edge of the last full tile before the corner. With the tile stick, mark the wall to show the location of the tiles and grout lines. When the time comes, you'll start tiling in this corner.

6 Mix a batch (or half-batch) of thinset mortar, following the label instructions. Latex strengthens the thinset and slows the drying time, giving you more time to work. Some thinset already contains latex; if yours doesn't, stir in a separate latex additive (sold in tile departments). Adding too much water weakens the mix—consider using a special mixing blade that goes on a drill; thinset can be very difficult to stir.

7 Spread thinset on a portion of the wall; score it with a notched trowel (with the recommended spacing between notches). Place a tile where your reference lines intersect.

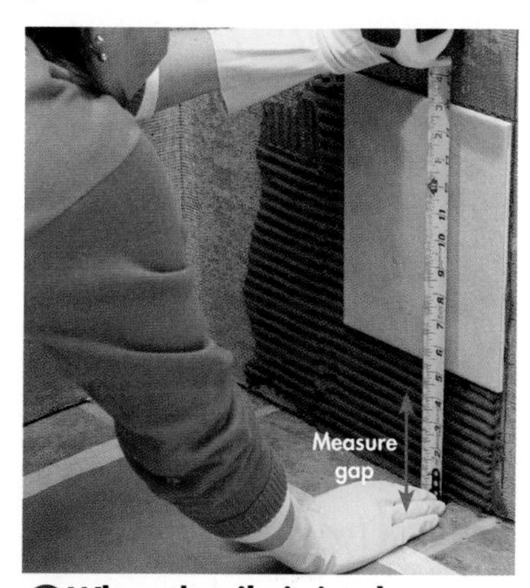

8 When the tile is in place, measure the gap below it. Subtract the width of a grout line from this measurement; use a combination square to mark a line on the face of a tile. Cut the tile to size.

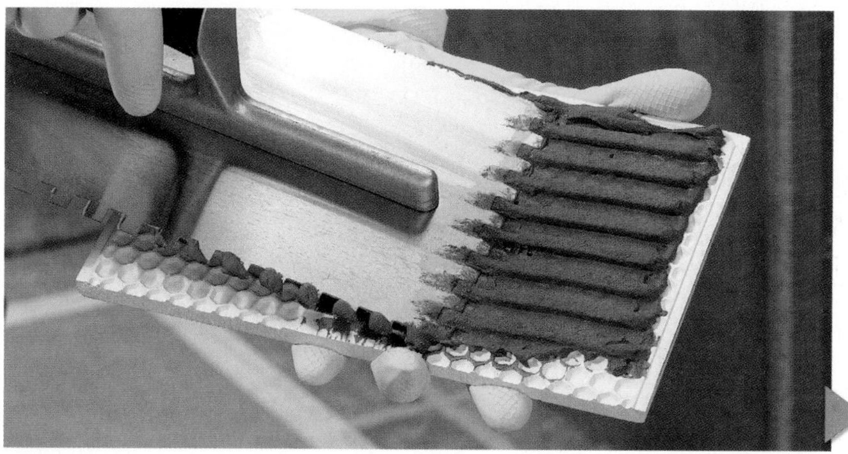

9 Butter tiles in hard-to-reach areas. It may be hard to put thinset directly on the wall in areas along the floor or near a corner. If so, apply about the same amount to the back of the tile, scoring it with the notched trowel.

Tiling a wall (continued)

10 Use tile spacers between tiles for perfect joints. (Place thinset on the wall first if you haven't buttered the tile.) Spacers are sold in tile departments and come in various widths—be sure to select the right size for your particular tiles because a lot of the strength comes from mortar joints.

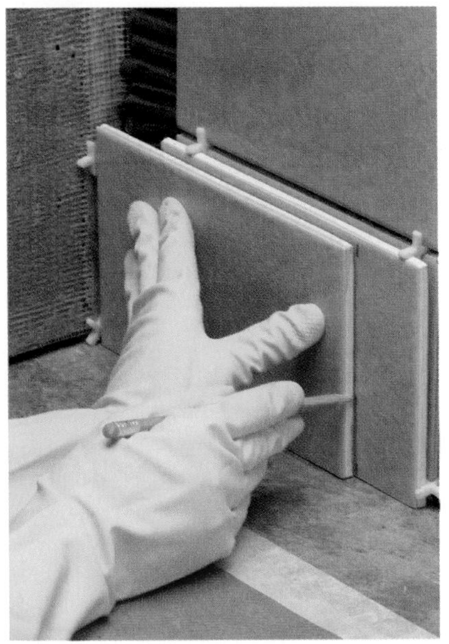

11 To plan corner-tile cuts, position a tile directly over the last full tile installed. Place another tile so its edge butts against spacers set against the wall. Trace along the edge of the top tile onto the middle tile to mark it for cutting. Cut the tile to size, butter it, and set it in the corner.

12 Continue setting tiles, aligning them with the reference lines and using spacers to keep them the proper distance apart. See Step 13 to cut tile around pipe or other obstacles, as shown here. See Step 14 for fitting tile edges against any obstacles.

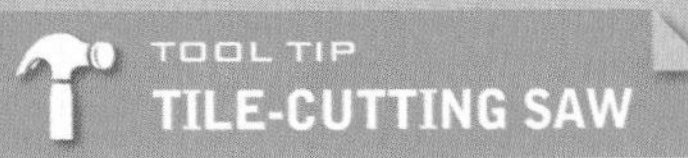

TOOL TIP

TILE-CUTTING SAW

For the best cuts use a wet saw with a diamond blade. This is the only way, in fact, to cut porcelain tiles or stone tiles. Follow the instructions exactly, using a good blade and plenty of water in the tank. Test cut a scrap to see if your glaze chips less face down or face up (they do vary). Then align the cutting mark on the tile with the blade and guide it gently as it moves forward. You can also use hand tools or a manual tile cutter to score a line on cermaic tile, then break the tile, but it's laborious and best confined to small jobs.

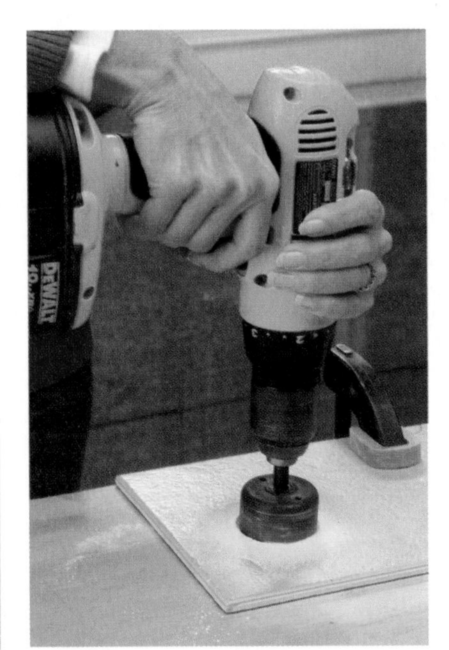

13 Fit a tile-cutting tool on an electric drill to cut holes for obstacles. Mark the center of the hole on the tile, then set the diameter of the cutter to the required size. Clamp the tile to a piece of scrap wood on a flat surface and cut the hole, using slow speed on a variable-speed drill.

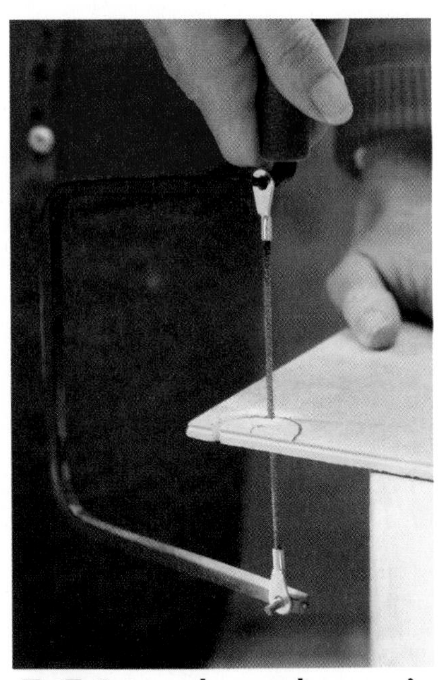

14 Cut notches and curves in tile by clamping the tile to a flat surface, then cutting it with a rod saw fitted with an abrasive blade designed for cutting tile. Smooth rough edges with a file (many obstacles such as plumbing pipes have a metal flange that will cover slight irregularities or mistakes).

15 Fit the tile over pipes (or other obstructions) as you go. Keep the grout lines uniform so that this particular tile doesn't create problems later. When the mortar and grout have dried and cured completely (several days later) go back and fill spaces around the pipes with a bead of silicone caulk.

16 Cut tiles to accommodate soap dishes or other accessories as you go. Apply thinset mortar to the wall and also to the back of the soap dish. Guide it into the saved space, supporting it with masking tape until the mortar dries. Grout around the edges as you grout the other tile joints.

17 Border tiles dress up a wall, yet they're no harder to install than regular tiles. When you reach the line marking their location, set the tiles in place with spacers between them and the tiles next to them. Follow the layout line to keep the border level.

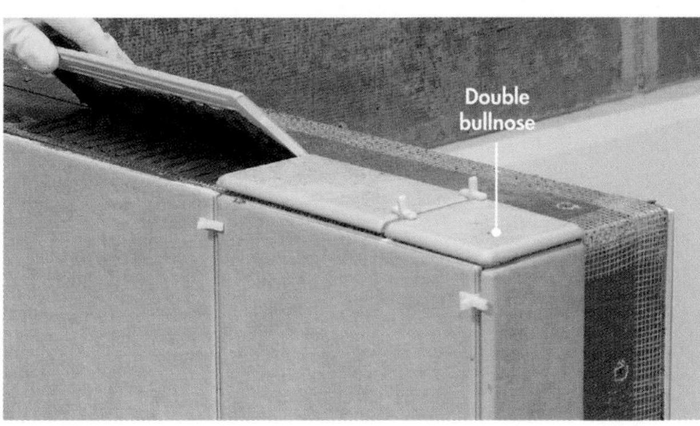

18 Use bullnose tiles that are half as wide as the wall is thick for the top and front edges of the knee wall. (Tile it as you come to it, keeping the grout lines aligned with those on the wall.) Start in the top front corner of the knee wall with a double bullnose, which has two rounded edges. Install it first; then use single bullnoses to work along the top and front of the knee wall.

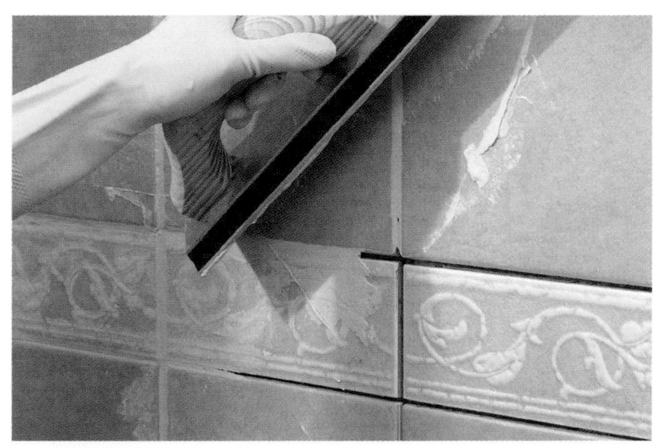

19 When the thinset mortar sets, remove the tile spacers. Mix grout, but not so much that it dries before you can use it. Fill the joints with grout in 3-foot-square sections, using a rubber grout float held at a 45-degree angle. Do not grout joints along the floor, the tub, or the corners.

Finish the job

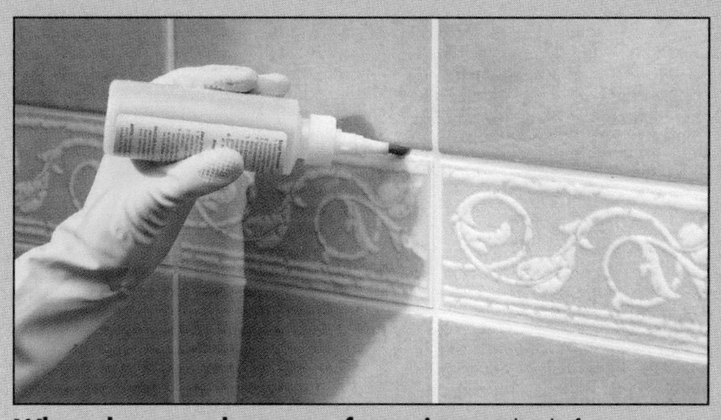

When the grout has set a few minutes (but before it cures), remove the excess by wiping the joints with a damp sponge, rinsing it frequently. When the grout cures, sponge off any remaining excess and polish the tiles with a soft dry towel. Apply a silicone tile sealer to the joints only, using a special applicator or a small brush.

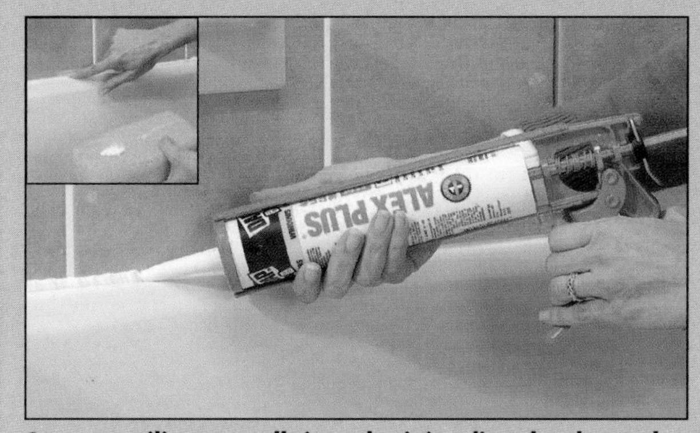

Squeeze silicone caulk into the joint directly above the tub, as well as all floor and corner joints, to seal out moisture. Smooth the caulk quickly with a wet finger because silicone dries very fast.

CHAPTER 3

Floors

Choosing a floor is a balancing act. You begin by balancing what you want with what you need. Carpet, for example, a common choice for a living room or bedroom. But avoid carpet in the kitchen unless the kids are gone and cooking is at a minimum.

Next balance the look of the floor against the appearance of the rest of the room. Is the floor the focal point? Think about ceramic tile. Or should it disappear into the wallpaper? Think of carpet. Do you want it to warm up a cool wall? (You're talking wood now.) Or is your goal to brighten up a plain room? (Consider tile or sheet vinyl.)

Finally you're balancing what you want with what you can afford. Budget, of course, is a real factor. But so is location: Vinyl or ceramic tile may be perfect for a bath, and wood great for the family room. Don't be let a room's current flooring material prevent you from considering other options: many flooring materials can often be installed right over old vinyl, wood—even concrete, with proper preparation. And just about anyone can remove old wall-to-wall carpeting, opening up worn or dated floor to new possibilities.

Fortunately no act is impossible to balance. Take a look at the opposite page to see what goes where, and look at individual projects to see how to make the floor work in a given situation.

Contents

Flooring materials . . . 154
The flooring tool kit . . . 155
Stopping squeaks . . . 156
Patching concrete floors . . . 158
Measuring for flooring . . . 160
Removing existing flooring . . . 161
Replacing underlayment . . . 165
Installing sheet vinyl . . . 167
Installing resilient vinyl tile . . . 172
Laying a tile floor . . . 174
Installing vinyl plank flooring . . . 180
Sanding and refinishing a floor . . . 182
Installing a strip-wood floor . . . 186
Installing a decorative border . . . 189
Installing wide-plank flooring . . . 190
Installing laminate and engineered floors . . . 191
Installing carpeting and carpet pad . . . 195
Installing baseboard . . . 199
Thresholds . . . 203

Put the right floor in the right place

If you properly install the right floor in the right place you will enjoy it for years. Check and double-check the manufacturer's instructions and recommendations before you begin. Following is a list of various types of floors and where you can install them.

- **Solid wood floors** can be installed above grade (ground level), but not below. The preferred subfloor is $\frac{3}{4}$-inch CD grade exterior (CDX) plywood. You can also use $\frac{3}{4}$-inch Oriented Strand Board (OSB) underlayment, $\frac{5}{8}$-inch CDX, or tongue-and-groove subflooring.

- **Laminate floors** can be installed above or below grade and over radiant heat. Recommendations on use in bathrooms vary by manufacturer. Laminate can go over almost any subfloor, including concrete slabs, ceramic tile, stone, vinyl sheet and tile, chipboard, particleboard, and terrazzo. If installed over a crawlspace, there must be at least 24 inches between the bottom of the joists and the ground.

- **Engineered wood** can be installed above or below grade. Recommendations on use in bathrooms vary by manufacturer. This cannot be installed on moist or damp floors. If applied over a crawlspace, there must be at least 24 inches between the bottom of the joists and the ground.

- **Sheet vinyl** can be installed above or below grade over existing sheet vinyl, linoleum, tile, new plywood, concrete, ceramic tile, or marble. Do not apply over lauan. Some plywoods are made especially to be used as underlayments for vinyl.

- **Vinyl plank** flooring can be installed over most reasonably smooth surfaces, including vinyl, wood, and smooth concrete. It does not require an underlayment.

- **Vinyl tile** is not recommended below grade. Install over smooth, single-layer vinyl floors that are firmly attached, dry concrete, and wood floors with a plywood overlay. Do not apply over lauan.

- **Ceramic, porcelain and stone** tile can be installed above or below grade and over radiant heat. Suitable subfloors include cement backerboard and concrete. They cannot be installed over moist or damp floors.

- **Carpeting** can go over almost any subfloor. If planning to use it below grade, make sure it is suitable for such use.

FLOORS

Flooring materials

Flooring materials are available in a great array of types, colors, styles, sizes, and prices. Whether you choose ceramic floor tile, hardwood strips, vinyl tiles, carpeting, or sheet vinyl, each has several grades and costs.

Professional flooring installers use a number of specialty tools, which will be introduced as they come up in various projects. For professional-grade results, use professional-grade tools. The work will go faster and easier, too. For one-time use, renting is the way to go, as you can rent professional-grade tools for far less than it costs to purchase them. But no matter whether you're doing a single floor or an entire house, spend a few extra bucks to help yourself do it right.

Common flooring materials

A - Sheet vinyl
B - Adhesive-backed vinyl floor tiles

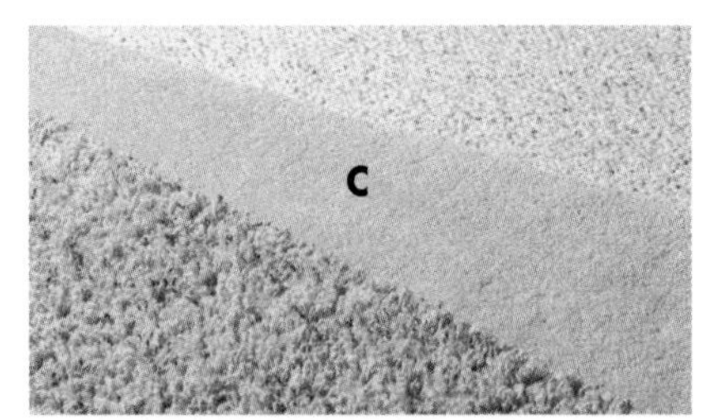

C - Carpeting

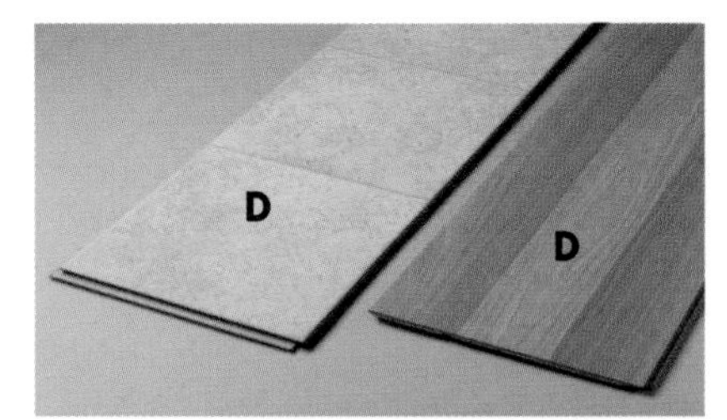

D - Snap-together laminate flooring

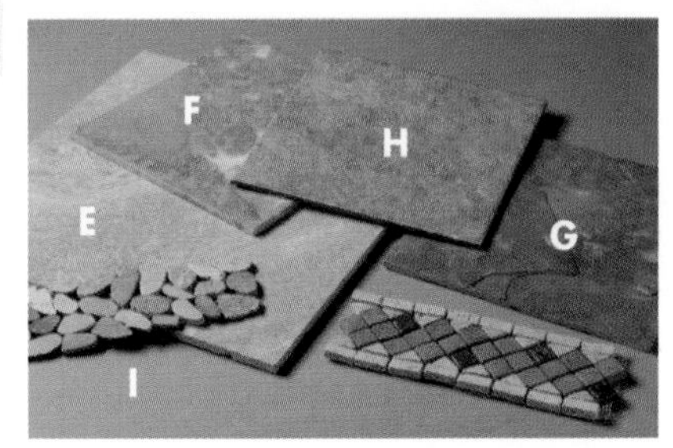

E - Travertine tile, **F** - Marble tile, **G**- Slate tile, **H** - Ceramic tile, **I** - Border tile

J- Wide planks **K** - Prefinished hardwood floor plank
L - Unfinished hardwood floor strip
M - Prefinished hardwood floor strip

N - Cork flooring
O - Bamboo flooring strip

Selecting the right materials

	Ceramic tile	Carpeting	Vinyl tiles	Sheet vinyl	Porcelain tiles	Hardwood	Stone	Laminate
Installation	Labor-intensive	Somewhat difficult to handle and install	Easy to handle and install	Somewhat difficult to install	Labor-intensive	Relatively easy to handle and install	Labor-intensive	Relatively easy to handle and install
Durability	Extremely durable	Durabillity depends on grade	Fairly durable	Durability depends on grade	Extremely durable	Fairly durable	Extremely durable	Extremely durable
Water-resistance	Yes	No	Yes	Yes	Yes	No	Yes	Yes
Cost	Moderate to high	Moderate to high	Low to moderate	Low to moderate	Moderate to high	Moderate to high	Moderate to high	Moderate to high
Maintenance	Easy; damp-mop	Easy; vacuum, steam cleaning	Easy; use manufacturer's recommended products	Easy; use manufacturer's recommended products	Easy; damp-mop	Moderate; sweep and damp-mop, refinish	Moderate to difficult; clean with damp-mop; use sealer	Easy; sweep, damp-mop

The flooring tool kit

5-Gallon bucket

Drill

Flooring drum sander

Nail puller

Saber saw

Tape measure

Caulking gun

Drill bits

Flooring edge sander

Paintbrushes

Safety glasses

Trowels

Chalk line

Files

Flooring vibrating sander

Power miter saw

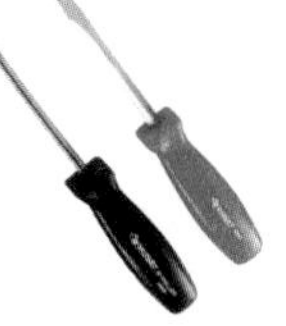
Screwdrivers

Utility knife

Circular saw

Flat pry bar

Hammer and nail sets

Putty knife

Shop vacuum

Wide-blade putty knife

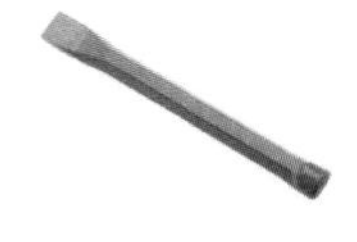
Cold chisel

Floor nailer

Handsaw

Rotary hammer

Sliding T-bevel

Wire brush

Compass

Floor roller

Lamb's wool varnish applicator

Router

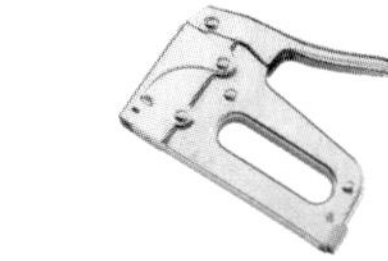
Stapler

Wood chisels

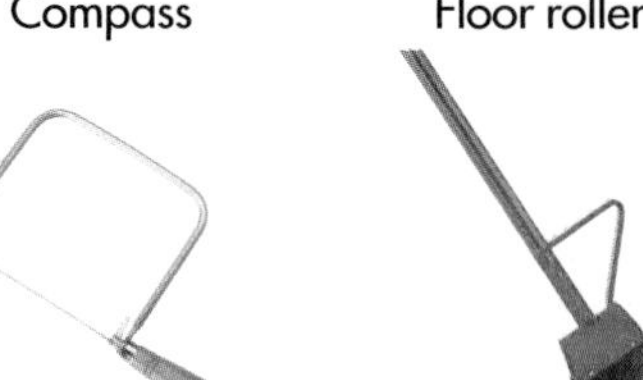
Coping saw

Floor scraper

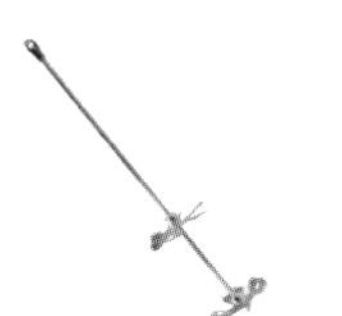
Mixing hoe

Rubber mallet

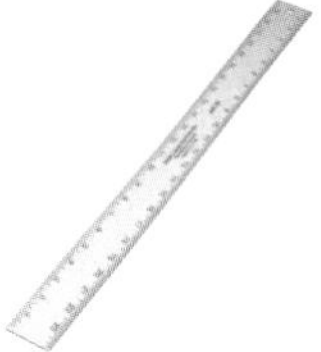
Straightedge

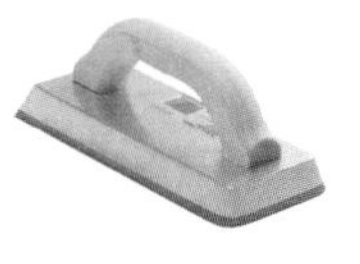
Grout float

FLOORS

Stopping squeaks

Skill level:	Time to complete:	Materials:	Tools:
★★★☆☆	Experienced 1 hr. Handy 1.5 hrs. Novice 2 hrs.	Wood shims, 16d finishing nails, wood screws, drywall screws	Hammer, screwdriver, drill

Flexing of the floor usually causes floor squeaks. They could come from floorboards rubbing against each other, bridging pieces rubbing against each other below the floor, or even water pipes or air ducts rubbing against floor joists.

Most often the root of the problem is a loose board, and the solution is a few well-placed ring shank nails or wood screws. When possible, fix squeaks from underneath the floor or staircase. If the bottom of the floor or staircase is covered by a finished ceiling, work on squeaks from the topside. On hardwood floors, drive finishing nails into the seams between planks to silence squeaking. Check pipe hangers, heating ducts, and bridging for rubbing and friction that can cause noise.

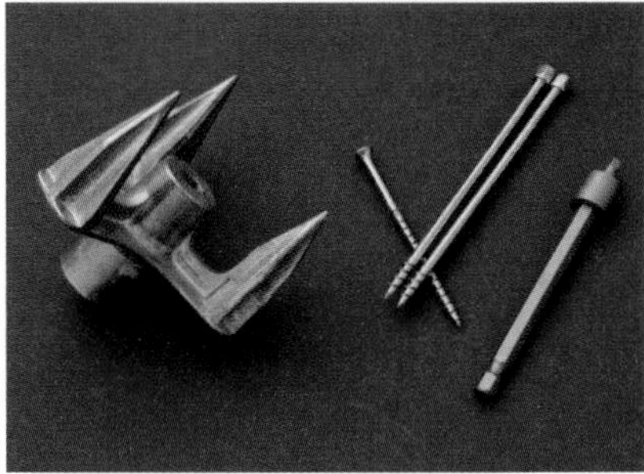

Silence squeaky floors covered with long-piled carpet by driving a shanked nail or drywall screw through both carpet and pad into the floor joist deep enough so that the carpet will lie flat. Kits with special fasteners and an alignment fixture (shown left) for silencing floor squeaks are also available to make the job much easier.

TOOL TIP

A TWO-BIT SOLUTION

If you're drilling pilot holes and driving screws with the same drill, changing back and forth between bits and drills can get old quickly. A multi-bit solves the problem. A magnetic socket that fits in your drill houses the screwdriver. The drills that come with the multi-bit also have an end that fits the socket. Changing from screwdriver to drill bit is a matter of popping one out and popping the other in.

Shimming the subfloor

If floor joists are not tight against the subfloor in the area that squeaks, shimming may solve it. Dip wood shims in woodworker's glue, then drive them into the gaps between the joist and subfloor, tapping them in place. Don't drive them more than needed to fill the gap or the floor will lift and only cause more squeaking.

Cleating the subfloor

Where neighboring boards above a joist are moving, a cleat is more effective than individually shimming the boards. A piece of 1×4, wedged against the subfloor and screwed or nailed to the joist and the flooring above, will keep the subfloor from moving and stop the squeak.

Reinforcing joists

Squeaking over a large area may indicate that the joists beneath the floor are slightly shifting and providing inadequate support for the subfloor. Steel bridging, attached between joists, keeps them from moving side to side. Or, nail in place lengths of 2x6 solid wood bridging as reinforcement.

Driving screws

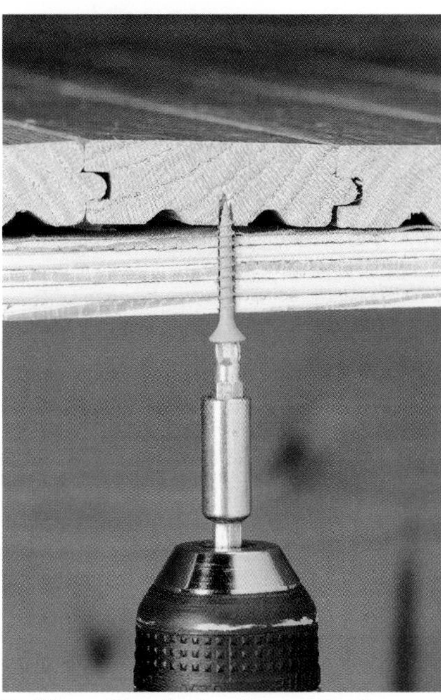

Drill a pilot hole through the subfloor and into the finished floor. Have someone stand on the raised boards while you drive a deck screw through the subfloor to pull the loose boards down.

Surface nailing

Nail down from the top with 16d finishing nails when you can't get access to the floor from below. Locate the floor joists and nail directly into them—nails will solve the problem only if they catch a joist.

FLOORS

Squeaky stairs

Anchor stair treads by driving nails into the risers at opposing angles. If the stairs will be covered by carpet, use flooring nails. If not, use finishing nails. On hardwood treads, drill pilot holes for the finishing nails and then drive the nails into the risers. Drive the nails below the surface using a nail set, fill the holes with wood putty, then smooth even with the tread.

Or drive wedges as shown from beneath the stairs. If the stairs aren't exposed from below, do the same from the topside, but drive shims at rear of treads against the risers.

Patching concrete floors

Skill level:	Time to complete:	Materials:	Tools:
★★★☆☆	Experienced 30 min. Handy 45 min. Novice 1 hr.	Concrete cleaner, sand, crack sealer, repair caulk, vinyl concrete patch or sand mix, bonding adhesive for deep cracks, self-leveling floor compound for uneven floors	Wire brush, caulking gun, putty knife, hammer drill and bit, trowel, wooden float, paintbrush, bucket, wheelbarrow or mixing bin, mixing hoe, goggles and rubber gloves (optional)

When a good floor goes bad, it can happen in many ways. The floor can develop small cracks, large cracks, or pitting, or it can become uneven. The causes vary and usually have something to do with either the original mixture of concrete or a shifting surface below the concrete. But it's the size of the crack, not the cause, that determines the cure.

Fix small cracks with a crack sealer, usually a ready-mix material that trowels in place. It comes both in a caulklike form and as a liquid. Use the liquid on floors and pads and the caulk on walls.

Larger cracks require more work. Chisel away any weak spots and widen the bottom of the groove. Repair with a cement-and-sand mixture known as sand mix. (It's stronger than concrete, which also contains gravel.) Use sand mix to fill pitted surfaces too.

If the crack resulted from shifting of the material under it, the floor may also have shifted, leaving one part higher than another. If you're covering the floor with vinyl or laminate flooring, the floor will wear through at the crack. Start by using a self-leveling resurfacer, a mixture thin enough that it forms a smooth, level surface when you pour it on. This can be a lot of work, so find several helpers.

If the patching compound requires mixing, add a little water and mix compound with a garden hoe (or a mason's hoe, which has a couple of extra holes in it to help with the job). Add more water as needed.

A big crack in a slab can mean that shifting and settling are going on below. Before you install a new floor over a big crack, find out what's causing it and make sure the shifting is no longer active, or the crack will reappear.

If you are planning on using an acid-base concrete cleaner, be sure to wear goggles and rubber gloves while you apply it.

Repairing small cracks

1 Clean out the crack with a wire brush to remove dirt and loose stones. Wash the crack with a concrete cleaner. Get a commercially available nonacid concrete cleaner made by the same company that makes your patching compound. It's more convenient and safer than the large bottles of muriatic acid masons use.

2 Let the surface dry. If the crack is deep and it's in a floor, fill it partially with sand, leaving an opening about 1/4 to 1/2 inch deep. Pour in the crack sealer until it forms a layer 1/4 inch deep. Let it dry overnight and then apply another layer. Repeat until the surface is flush with the floor. Don't overfill—apply just enough patch material to bring the surface flush with the floor. If using caulk, smooth with a putty knife.

Fixing large cracks

1 With a hammer drill reshape the crack so the bottom is wider than the top; this helps hold the patch in place. Chisel out any weak or crumbling spots too. If the crack is deeper than ½ inch, paint it with a bonding adhesive made by the company that manufactures the patch you're using. Let glue dry thoroughly before applying the patch.

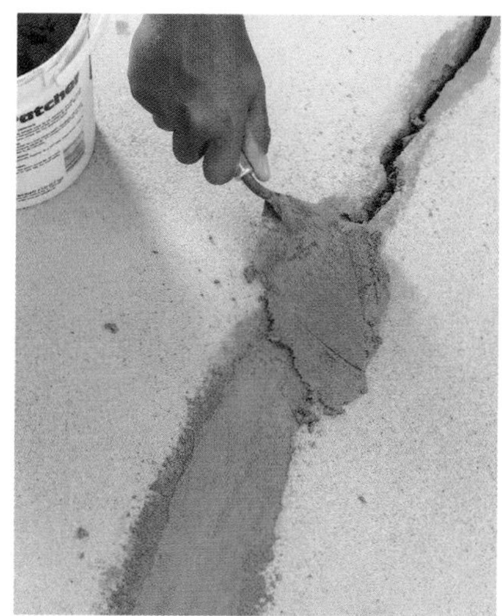

2 On cracks up to about ½ inch deep, trowel in a vinyl concrete patch. Mix according to the directions on the bag or pail and trowel a ¼-inch layer into the crack. If more layers are necessary, let the patch dry for several days before applying a new layer. Trowel the final layer flush with the surface and smooth.

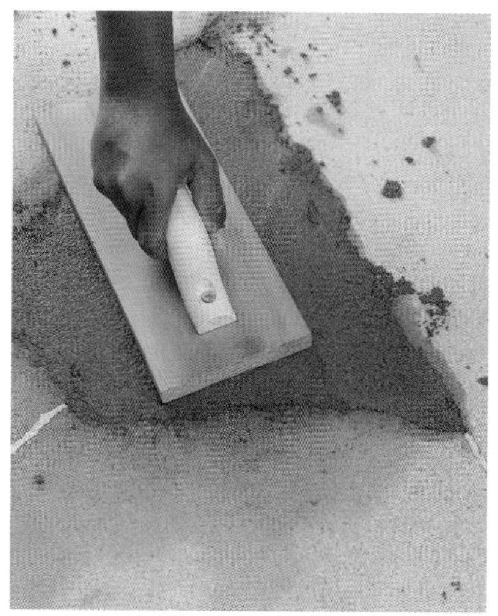

3 On deeper cracks mix some sand mix according to the directions on the bag. Trowel it into the crack, filling it flush with the surface. Initially the patch on both deep and shallow cracks will have a watery sheen. When the sheen dries off, use a wooden float to smooth the surface and give it a texture that matches the rest of the concrete. If the existing concrete is very smooth, then smooth the surface with a metal finishing trowel.

Leveling uneven floors

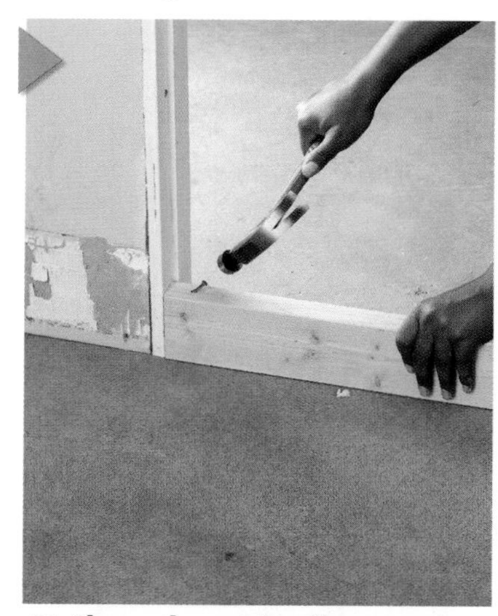

1 Clean the entire floor and patch any holes following the directions above. Nail a strip of wood across door openings to keep the patching material from pouring into the next room.

2 Mix the leveling compound and brush it on the floor as a primer. New concrete usually requires only one coat of primer; older concrete may require two coats. Follow the directions on the bag for both mixing and priming. Let the primer dry as specified by the manufacturer—usually for 1 to 2 hours.

3 Mix a thicker consistency of compound, following the proportions on the bag. Starting in a corner on the narrow end of the room, pour the mixture on the floor. Pour the second batch next to it along the narrow wall. Repeat along the entire wall, and then work your way back across the room, pouring a new row of compound next to the old. Let the compound flow to level itself.

Measuring for flooring

To calculate the amount of material you'll need for a rectangular room: Multiply the length by the width, and add 10 percent. For example, a 10-foot-wide by 15-foot-long room will need 150 square feet of flooring material. Add 10 percent for waste to ensure you have enough material for the job. Some stores will take back unused material, but you may want to keep some extra for later repairs.

If the room has counters, protruding closets, or other obstructions, subtract the square footage they occupy from the overall footage of the room. Begin by taking the overall dimensions: Multiply the longest dimension of the room by the widest dimension. Then measure the length of each obstruction, and multiply it by its width. Subtract these amounts from the overall square footage of the room, add 10 percent for waste, and head for the store.

Note that adding a tile floor could add ¾ inch to 1 inch to the overall height of the floor. This may make it impossible to remove objects like dishwashers when the time comes. And whether you're putting in carpet, tile, wood, vinyl, or laminate, plan on having to trim the bottom of doors once the job is done.

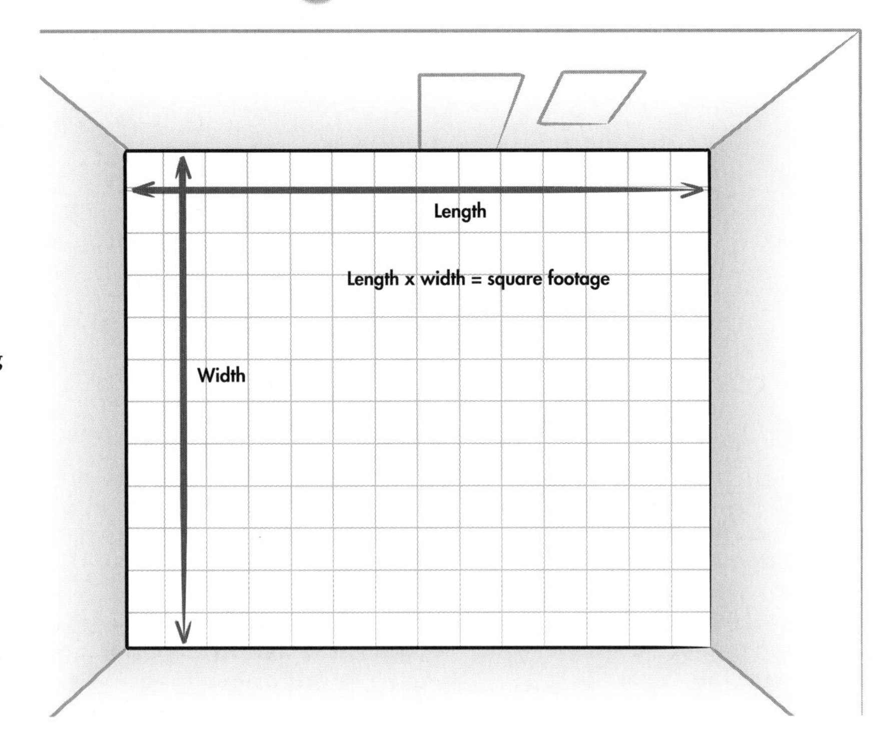

In a square or rectangular room, multiply the length by the width to get the total square footage. Add 10 percent for waste when you purchase the flooring.

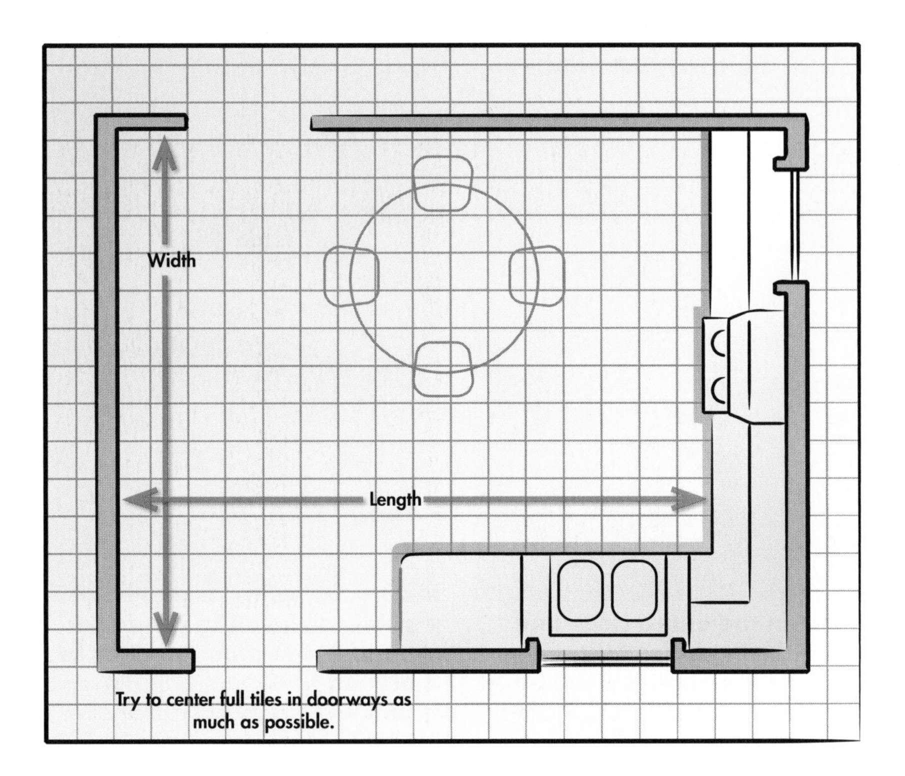

Make a floor plan. Draw the walls of the room as accurately as you can on a sheet of graph paper. Include doorways and floor obstructions such as cabinets and fixtures. Graph paper is available in ⅛-inch, ¼-inch, and ½-inch grid spacing.

Removing existing flooring

Skill level:	Time to complete:	Materials:	Tools:
★★★☆☆	Experienced 30 min. Handy 45 min. Novice 1 hr.	None	Pry bar, handsaw, utility knife, wide-blade putty knife, safety glasses, hammer, cold chisel, long-handled floor scraper, floor sander, circular saw, drill, bits, screwdriver

Before you install a new floor, you'll have to deal with the old one. In some cases, it's simple. Sheet vinyl can be installed right over old sheet vinyl unless the old vinyl is loose, more than one layer thick, or cushioned. New ceramic floors can go right on top of old ones. Products like laminated or engineered flooring often can go over the existing floor, no matter what material it is.

Old resilient floor coverings that are either cushioned or damaged are also straightforward: You must either remove them or cover them with a new layer of plywood underlayment. If the old flooring is embossed vinyl, you can either remove it or trowel on an embossing leveler, which fills the low spots in the surface.

Ceramic floor tile that is damaged or loose must be completely removed. It is easiest to break the tiles with a hammer and then pry up the pieces with a cold chisel and hammer. If the tile was set in mortar bed, you'll also have to replace the subfloor. Cut the old subfloor into small sections with a circular saw equipped with a diamond blade, and use a respirator, safety glasses, and hand protection. Remove the floor sections with a pry bar.

Sometimes it is easier to install new underlayment than it is to remove the existing flooring. Keep in mind that each layer of flooring and underlayment on a floor increases the height of the floor. Consequently, you'll have to undercut door jambs and door stops to make them fit properly. Also the kickboard on kitchen cabinets will be shorter if the flooring and underlayment is installed around the cabinets. Your biggest problem may come in later years when you try to remove a built-in dishwasher. To remove the machine you'll have to lift the front edge, perhaps higher than the counter will allow, because of the now-higher floor.

Give yourself extra time

Many jobs tend to take longer than you think they will. That's especially true if you've never done them before. That's because no two houses are exactly alike, and no matter how well informed you are about the specific steps, tools, and techniques involved, you never know exactly what you may find when you dig into hidden areas of your home such as beneath a floor surface. Some old tile may pop off easily with just a hammer and a cold chisel; other tile floors may require a rented jackhammer to remove. So don't let your schedule—or your pre-job expectations—box you in. It's better to take a bit longer and do the job right than to start taking shortcuts to meet an unrealistic deadline.

Preparing for removal

Remove thresholds by prying them up from the floor with a metal pry bar. If the floor jambs were undercut to house the threshold, saw the threshold into two pieces and remove each piece separately. Since you're removing the old flooring you don't have to worry about the saw scarring the wood when you cut the threshold.

Baseboard often sits on top of wood or sheet-vinyl floors. If you need to remove the baseboard, pry it gently away from the wall with a flat pry bar. Protect the wall by putting a piece of wood between the bar and the wall.

Removing existing flooring (continued)

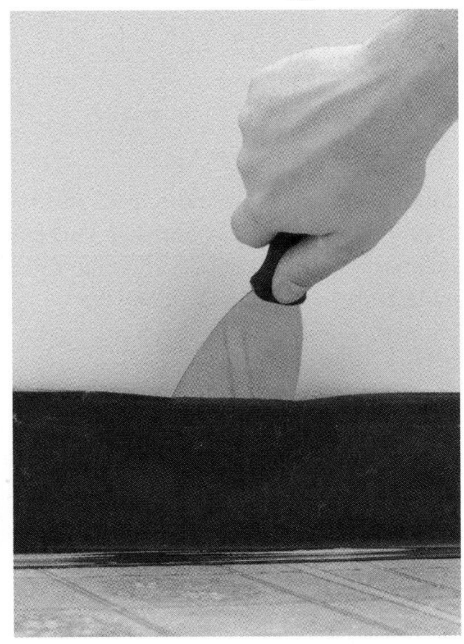

To remove cove base from the wall, first run along the top with a utility knife to cut through any paint that may be holding it to the wall. Then loosen the cove base with a wide-blade putty knife and strip it away. Scrape the wall with the putty knife to remove any remaining adhesive.

Cut along the top of wall tiles with a utility knife. Pop each tile loose from the wall with a metal pry bar. If you are concerned about scratching or damaging your wall, place a scrap piece of wood behind the pry bar. Scrape the wall free of any remaining grout or adhesive.

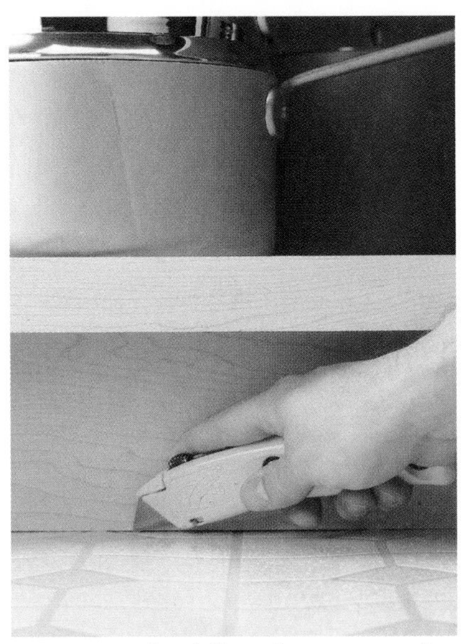

Remove vinyl flooring around cabinets by cutting with a sharp utility knife along the base of the cabinets. If you have ceramic or hardwood flooring underneath the cabinets, you will probably have to remove the cabinets to pry up the flooring.

Removing carpet

1 To remove carpet installed on a tackless strip, first remove all metal edgings, and the quarter round, if any, along the baseboard. Pry up the carpet corner and, working around the room, remove carpet from the strips along the walls. Then roll the carpet up and carry it out. If you're planning to install new carpet, leave the tackless strip in place.

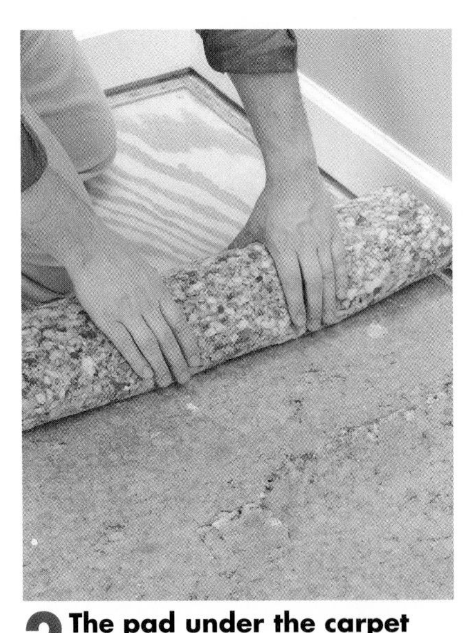

2 The pad under the carpet is usually stapled in place. To remove it, grab one end of the pad and pull on it as you cross the room. Roll up the padding and remove it. Check the floor for staples that didn't come up with the padding and remove them. If the padding is glued down, remove it with a long-handled floor scraper. Sand the floor smooth with a floor sander if necessary.

Prying up carpet tacks

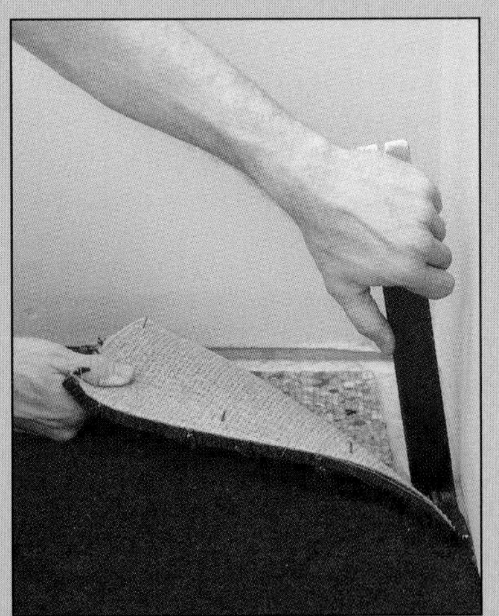

To remove carpet installed with carpet tacks, slide a flat pry bar under one edge of the carpet and pry up several tacks. Proceed until all tacks are removed.

Removing wood flooring

1 Before prying up plank flooring, bore out the screw plugs—if any—and remove the screws that hold the floor in place.

2 Set the blade on your circular saw to cut through the floor but not the subfloor. In most cases this will be 3/8 inch or 3/4 inch, but start with a shallow cut and adjust the blade until you just cut through the floor. When the setting is right, cut down the length of one of the floorboards.

3 Put a pry bar in the slot left by the saw cut and pry the board loose. Put the bar under the next board and pry it free. Work your way across the floor, board by board. If the flooring has been glued down, drive a chisel under the board to break it free before prying it loose.

FLOORS

SAFETY ALERT

BETTER SAFE THAN SORRY

Always wear safety glasses and hearing protection when running a saw. Also make sure the blade is tight to the arbor, and all the lockdown wing nuts and levers are tight before you start cutting. Be sure to keep the power cord well out of the saw's path.

SAFETY ALERT

ASBESTOS ALERT

Asbestos, which can cause cancer, can be found in linoleum, vinyl flooring, and mastics made before 1978. The long, thin fibers in asbestos were used to reinforce these materials. Enlarged under a microscope, however, the fibers resemble tiny swords. The shape of these fibers allows them to be breathed deep into the lungs, where they get trapped. Scar tissue develops around the fibers, causing irreversible damage that can lead to cancer. If you think your house has asbestos-containing materials, don't panic. Undamaged (not cracked, gouged, etc.) asbestos is generally safe, and covering it usually eliminates the risk. (Engineered and laminate floors may be the perfect cover.)

If you decide the asbestos has to go, do not attempt to remove it yourself. Paint masks and standard respirators will not protect you from fibers, and you're likely to track asbestos throughout the house, endangering your family too. Check with your state department of environmental affairs or your local health department for advice. They can tell you how to find a certified professional to test the flooring material and do whatever needs to be done.

In the meantime, make sure you leave the material alone. Don't sand it, don't break any of it away, and don't cut it. Until you get a professional opinion on your old flooring's makeup, leaving it undisturbed is the safest thing you can do.

Removing existing flooring (continued)

Removing ceramic tile

1 Put on your safety glasses, and chip out the grout between the tiles with a hammer and cold chisel. Once you've removed the grout, continue using the hammer and chisel to break the tiles free.

2 Option A: For ceramic tile set in mastic, use a long-handled floor scraper to scrape away tile fragments and any adhesive residue. Sand the floor smooth with a floor sander if necessary.

Option B: If the tile was set in a mortar bed, you will not be able to salvage the surface below. Cut the old subfloor into small sections using a circular saw with a diamond blade. Pry up the sections with a pry bar. If the tile was laid on underlayment, cut through the underlayment and mortar but not the subfloor.

WORK SMART
LOOK BEFORE YOU LEAP

You have several options when removing old flooring. Analyze the condition of the existing flooring and determine the course of action. If the flooring is mildly worn or damaged, use an embossing leveler to smooth out the flooring surface to provide a stable base for the new flooring material. Remove the existing flooring if it is too badly damaged to resurface with the embossing leveler and is relatively easy to remove. If the surface is too rough for the leveler and too difficult to remove, cover the existing flooring material with new underlayment.

Underlayment options

Pour embossing leveler over clean embossed or mildly rough flooring. Then trowel the entire surface to smooth it out. Leveler must be applied on a clean floor. It won't work on all surfaces, so be sure to read the label. Hold the trowel at a 60-degree angle and use light pressure. After the leveler dries, sand or scrape away any ridges.

Apply new underlayment over existing flooring if the flooring material is too difficult to remove and too badly damaged for an embossing leveler. This raises the floor, so make sure that when replacement time comes you'll have enough clearance to remove appliances such as dishwashers from under the counter.

Replacing underlayment

Skill level:	Time to complete:	Materials:	Tools:
★★★☆☆	Experienced 4 hrs. Handy 6 hrs. Novice 8 hrs.	Ready-mix latex underlayment, 6d ringshank nails, 80- or 100-grit sandpaper, underlayment	Hammer, pry bar, jigsaw, tape measure, handsaw, trowel, safety goggles

FLOORS

Most manufacturers require a properly installed underlayment in order to honor warranties on their products. The most commonly approved underlayments for sheet vinyl and vinyl tiles are exterior plywood products with a grade of BC or better, poplar or birch plywood with a fully sanded face and exterior glue, and lauan plywood, Type 1 (exterior), grade BB or CC. The minimum thickness for underlayment is ¼ inch.

Before you install underlayment, nail down any loose subflooring with 6d ringshank nails. Set all nailheads below the flooring surface. Check the seams between boards or sheets of plywood on the subfloor. If a board is higher than its neighbor, sand with a flooring edge sander to create a smooth surface. Look for high spots and sand them too. Fill any low spots with liquid underlayment—a latex gap filler that you trowel on.

And if you don't do all this? Count on soft spots and squeaks. On vinyl, high edges will show through and will wear out the top flooring prematurely.

1 If you need to remove the old underlayment, pry the edges loose with a pry bar. Underlayment is nailed in place every 6 inches and can be extremely stubborn. A 36-inch wrecking bar will give you extra leverage. In tough cases, you may want to pry with something longer, like an ice fisherman's spud.

2 Nail down any loose subfloor boards with 6d ringshank nails. Replace warped, bowed, or damaged boards. If one edge of a board is higher than its neighbor, sand it flush with a flooring edge sander.

$ BUYER'S GUIDE
CEMENT UNDERLAYMENT

If you're installing a floor in a bathroom, kitchen, or entry area and want the ultimate protection against moisture-related deterioration, choose cement board instead of plywood for an underlayment. Premium cement boards are available with mold-inhibiting technology and a no-mesh design that is lighter and easier to cut and handle than other varieties.

3 Make sure the finished height of the new floor will allow room for replacing appliances. The countertop may need to be shimmed up, or the old flooring removed, to allow appliances to fit. Also remove any heating vents that will interfere with the floor. If necessary, relocate the vent, as described on page 475.

4 Remove the base molding, then undercut the bottom edges of door casings to make room for the new underlayment and flooring. Use a piece of flooring and underlayment as a spacing guide. Rest a handsaw on the guide, and trim the casings. Use the same tile on each jamb as the saw may scratch the tile. If you have a lot of jambs, consider renting a power jamb saw.

Replacing underlayment (continued)

5 Inspect the subfloor for low spots. Fill any low areas with ready-mix latex underlayment. Trowel it on, let it dry, then sand it smooth with 80- or 100-grit sandpaper. Wrap the paper around a scrap of 2×4 when sanding to help ensure a flat surface.

6 Make a cardboard or paper template for irregular edges, then trace the template outline onto the underlayment. Cut the underlayment to fit, using a circular saw for long, straight cuts and a jigsaw for irregular-shaped cuts. (Top right.)

7 Put on your safety glasses and begin installation along the longest wall.

8 Drive 6d ringshank nails on a 6-inch grid along the entire face of the plywood and every 3 inches around the perimeter of the floor. Leave ⅛ inch between the underlayment sheets for expansion caused by changes in the temperature and humidity.

9 Cover the remaining areas, staggering the plywood seams. Fill the seams and any other irregularities in the subfloor with ready-mix latex underlayment. (Any irregularities will be visible through the finished floor.) Let the subfloor dry, then sand it smooth. Clean the surface thoroughly to remove debris and dust before installing the flooring material.

Installing sheet vinyl

Skill level:	Time to complete:	Materials:	Tools:
★★★☆☆	Experienced 2 hrs. Handy 6 hrs. Novice 8 hrs.	Ready-mix latex underlayment, 6d ringshank nails, primer, adhesive	Pry bar, handsaw, tape measure, compass, utility knife, flooring knife, hand roller or rolling pin, floor roller, trowel, safety goggles

Sheet vinyl is manufactured in 6- or 12-foot widths. Large areas may require that pieces of flooring be joined together. If you have to use two pieces of vinyl flooring, try to put the seams in inconspicuous areas.

To eliminate cutting errors, create a template of your room with heavy paper or with a template kit offered by some flooring manufacturers. A template allows you to trace an accurate outline of your room onto the new flooring.

You'll need to find a large, level area to lay the flooring completely flat to transfer the template markings. Sweep it well before you put your vinyl on it.

Some vinyls require a slightly different installation than the one described here. Follow the manufacturer's directions closely.

FLOORS

Making a flooring template

1 Remove the quarter-round molding that runs along the baseboard. Remove doors. Undercut the door trim by cutting into it while the saw rests on a scrap piece of flooring.

2 You can install vinyl over old vinyl flooring, plywood, ceramic floors, or concrete. Make sure old vinyl is firmly attached and wax-free. Fill embossed patterns with embossing leveler. For plywood, nail down loose boards, then fill gaps and knotholes. Patch and fill concrete or ceramic to create a smooth surface. Prime the floor as directed by the manufacturer.

BUYER'S GUIDE

INSTALLATION KITS

Many sheet vinyl flooring manufacturers make installation template kits, which normally include a roll of heavy paper, masking tape, a marking guide, a trimming knife, and a complete set of instructions. The kits make it relatively easy to lay out the flooring and can save on your material cost by reducing the mistake factor.

Some manufacturers actually guarantee do-it-yourself installations if you use their kits. Be sure to ask about the warranty and about installation specifics before purchasing your sheet vinyl.

WORK SMART

CUT AN ACCURATE TEMPLATE

An accurate template is the key to a tight and well-fitting installation. Paper is cheap but vinyl sheeting isn't, so make your mistakes on the paper and get everything right before you start cutting.

When working in a bathroom, remove the toilet and pedestal sink to make the template. Cut it so that it extends into areas normally hidden by these fixtures. It's easier than cutting around them.

Installing sheet vinyl (continued)

3 Make a pattern from sheets of butcher paper. Place the paper's edges against walls. (Some flooring requires a ¼-inch gap between the vinyl and the wall; follow the manufacturer's directions.) Cut triangles in the paper with a utility knife. Tape the template to the floor through the holes.

4 Work your way around the room, taping the paper in place as you go. At corners, overlap adjoining sheets of paper by 2 inches and tape them together. Continue taping pieces around obstacles that you couldn't remove. Mark the seams, as shown, so you can put the pieces back together if they come apart.

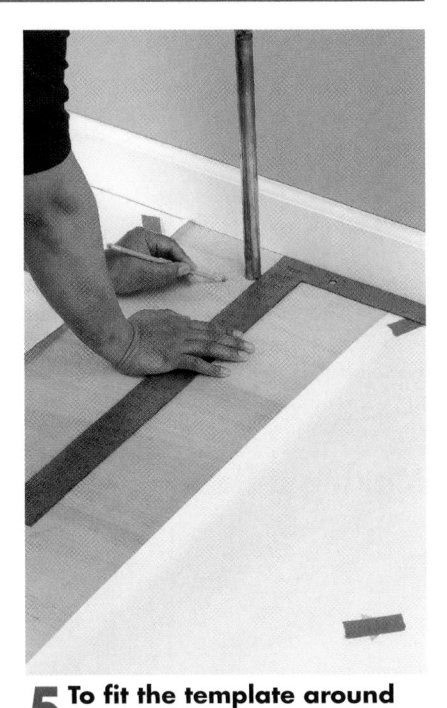

5 To fit the template around pipes, tape sheets of paper on each side of the pipe. Measure the distance from the wall to the center of the pipe, using a framing square or combination square.

6 Transfer the measurement to a separate piece of paper. Use a compass to draw the pipe diameter onto the paper and cut a hole with scissors or a utility knife. Cut a slit from the edge of the paper to the hole.

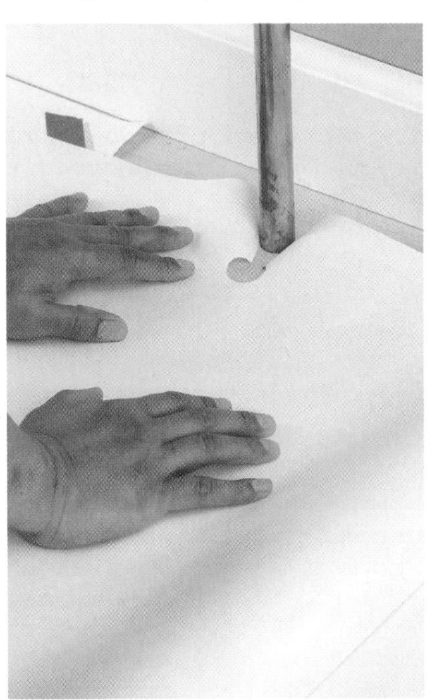

7 Fit the hole cutout around the pipe. Tape the hole template to adjoining sheets.

8 When you've finished making the template, roll or loosely fold it and set it aside until you've unrolled the sheet vinyl.

Cutting and installing sheet vinyl

1 Once you cut the vinyl, you'll need to install it within 3 or 4 hours, as directed by the manufacturer. If you wait longer, the vinyl will lose its flexibility. When you're ready, unroll the flooring on any large, flat, clean surface—even one in another room. As you unroll it, it will be pattern-side down. When you've unrolled the sheet, turn it pattern-side up for marking.

2 Position the paper template on the vinyl sheet and tape it in place. Trace the outline of the template onto the flooring with a ballpoint pen.

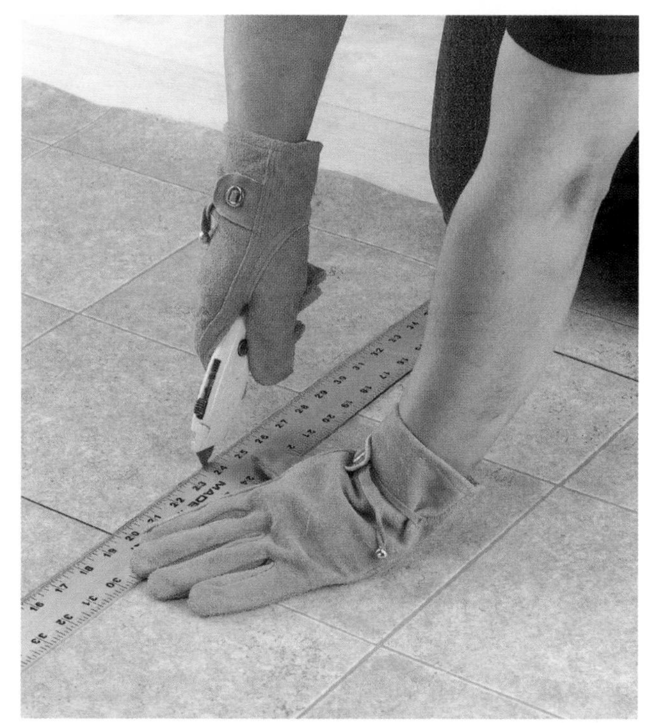

3 Remove the template. Cut along the template marks using a sharp flooring knife guided by a straightedge. If you're working in the room the vinyl will go in, don't cut on the underlayment, as the scratches may show through. Cut on a piece of scrap instead.

4 Cut holes for pipes or posts using a flooring knife. Then cut a slit from the hole to the nearest edge of the vinyl. Make the cut on a piece of scrap underlayment to protect the surface below.

Installing sheet vinyl (continued)

5 If you cut the vinyl somewhere other than its final location, roll it up loosely and take the roll to the room it will be in. Be careful not to fold the flooring. Unroll and position the vinyl carefully. Slide the edges beneath the undercut door casings.

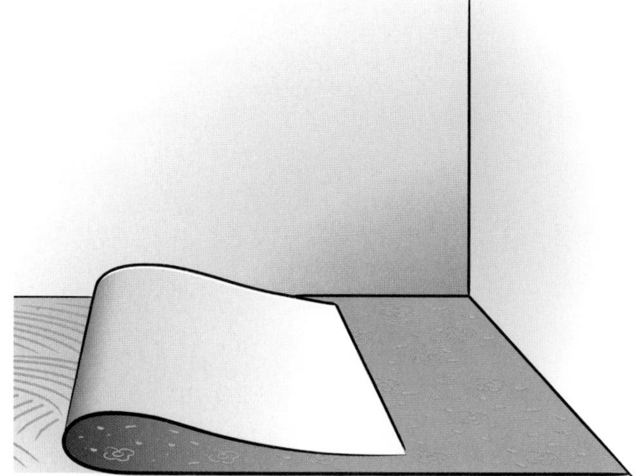

6 Fold the material back halfway across the room. Make sure the subfloor is clean, then apply adhesive with a notched trowel. The size of the notch depends both on the manufacturer and the application; follow manufacturer's directions carefully. Let the adhesive dry for 10 to 20 minutes. Then fold the floor down over it. Fold back the other half of the vinyl and repeat the process.

7 For a firm bond, roll the vinyl with a hand roller or an old rolling pin. Start in the middle of the floor and work your way to the edges.

Seam sealer

If your floor requires a seam, be sure to use a seam sealer. It joins the two sheets into one, making the flooring stronger. Sealer comes in a package with a cleaner, an applicator, and two small bottles that you mix together to form the sealant. Start by cleaning the vinyl; then pour about half of each bottle into the applicator. Apply as directed. Leave any extra sealer that gets on the surface of the vinyl; it will wear away with use, leaving a level seam. Be sure to get a high-gloss sealer for high-gloss floors, and a low-gloss sealer for low-gloss floors.

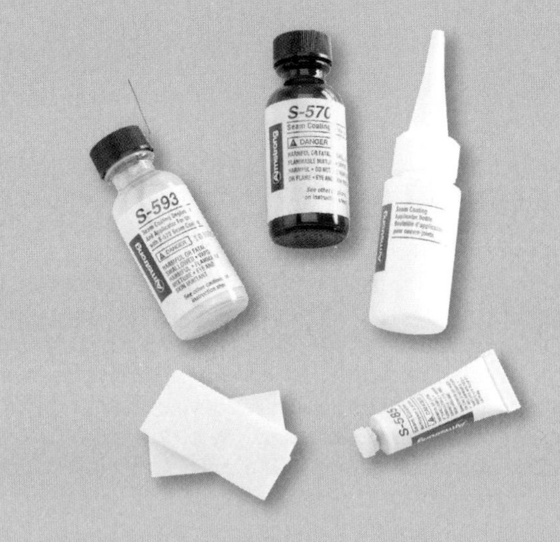

Laying vinyl floors with seams

1 If your floor is large enough to require a seam, tape the pieces together before you apply the template. Align the sheets so they overlap by at least 2 inches and so the patterns match. Tape the sheets together.

2 Cut the seams using a straightedge as a guide. Choose a line in the pattern and put a straightedge against it. Hold the straightedge tightly against the flooring and cut along the pattern lines through both pieces of vinyl flooring.

3 Remove both pieces of scrap flooring. The patterns on the two sheets now match.

4 Put the vinyl in place, roll back one side, and draw a line on the floor showing where the seam is. Draw two guidelines, each 12 inches from the one marking the seam. Put the vinyl back in place, match the patterns, and tape across the seam.

Fold the vinyl back the same way you would with a one-piece floor, but make the fold perpendicular to the seam.

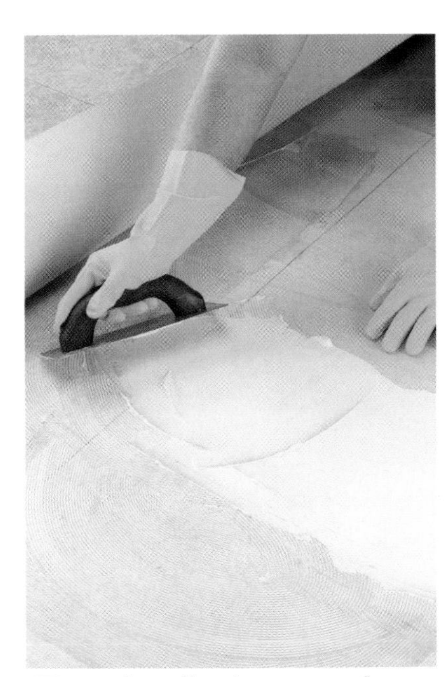

5 Apply adhesive up to the guidelines, and roll the vinyl back onto the floor. Fold back the second half of the vinyl and apply adhesive up to the guidelines. Put the vinyl in place and roll the floor with a heavy floor roller before you start work on the seam.

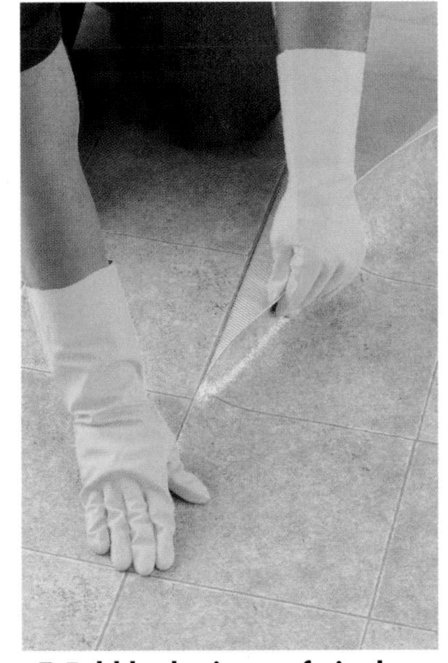

6 Fold both pieces of vinyl back from the seam. Apply adhesive, then fold the vinyl back onto the floor. Roll with a hand roller and seal the seam.

Installing resilient vinyl tile

Skill level:	Time to complete:	Materials:	Tools:
★★★☆☆	Experienced 4 hrs. Handy 6 hrs. Novice 8 hrs.	Vinyl floor tile, floor tile adhesive, primer	Chalkline, paintbrush, floor roller, notched trowel, tape measure, framing square, flooring knife

Resilient vinyl tiles are relatively easy to install. Many have self-sticking adhesive backs, perfect for do-it-yourself projects. Others require flooring adhesive but can still be installed by the homeowner.

You can lay tile over dry concrete, underlayment, or sheet vinyl (but not vinyl tile). Tiles will eventually sag into any gaps below them, so fill all cracks as recommended by the manufacturer. If you're laying tile over an embossed tile floor, fill the embossing with embossing leveler. Make sure the floor is spotlessly clean and free of wax and oil first.

Resilient vinyl tiles don't require an expansion gap where the floor meets the wall. Mount them flush to the vertical surface or the tiles will eventually slide and separate from each other, leaving an unsightly gap. If you have molding attached to the baseboard, remove it carefully first if you are pulling up the old flooring so that you can replace it later.

Let the tiles adjust to the room temperature by placing them in the room to be floored at least 24 hours before installation.

Establishing layout lines

1 Paint the floor with a primer meant for self-stick tiles, if you're using them. Then measure opposite sides of the room and mark the center of each wall. Snap a chalk line between the marks.

2 Measure and mark the center of the chalkline. From this point, use a framing square to lay out a second line perpendicular to the first. Snap the new line across the room.

3 Check for square by drawing a carpenter's triangle, also known as a 3-4-5 triangle. Measure and mark one layout line 3 feet from the center point, then measure and mark the perpendicular layout line 4 feet from the center point.

4 Measure the distance between the marks. If the layout lines are perpendicular, the distance will be exactly 5 feet. Adjust the lines, if necessary, until they are square with each other.

Installing vinyl tile

1 Lay tiles along the layout lines. Check on opposite sides of the room to see if all the tiles against the wall will be the same size. If not, snap new layout lines so that they are. Double-check by laying the tiles along the new lines.

2 Begin laying tiles where the layout lines cross. If the tiles have arrows on the back, make sure they all point the same direction. With self-stick tiles, remove the paper backing and apply the tiles to one quadrant of the floor. Lay the tiles in a stair-step pattern, as shown. Repeat for the remaining quadrants.

3 Trim the tiles that meet the walls. Mark the cut so that the tile is flush to the wall or cabinet—don't leave an expansion gap. To cut a tile to size, place a cutoff against the wall. Place a loose tile **A** directly over the last full tile. Place another tile **B** against the wall or cabinet, over tile **A**. Mark as shown. Cut tile **A** with a flooring knife.

4 At outside corners, mark the tile as in Step 3, and then use a square to draw a line at the mark, outlining the final shape of the tile. Cut with a flooring knife and a straightedge. At inside corners, mark as in Step 3, putting the loose tile first against one wall and then against the other.

5 Form a firm bond between the tile and the floor by rolling it in both directions with a hand roller or rolling pin. Then install baseboard, quarter-round molding, or both to give the edge a finished, stylish apearance.

Using adhesive

If using tiles that need adhesive (rather than self-stick tiles), apply the adhesive recommended by the manufacturer with a notched trowel. Start with a section about 4x4 feet. When the adhesive is dry enough to touch without sticking to your hands, lay tiles in the same stair-step pattern used for self-stick tile.

Laying a tile floor

Skill level: ★★★☆☆

Time to complete:
Experienced 11 hrs.
Handy 18 hrs.
Novice 25 hrs.

Materials: ¼-inch or ½-inch backerboard, backerboard screws, thinset mortar, latex primer, self-leveling mortar tiles, grout, grout sealer, fiberglass tape

Tools: Level, framing square, tape measure, straightedge, chalkline, carbide backerboard cutter, mortar mixing paddle, screw gun, ½" drill, tile cutter or tile saw, safety glasses, grout bag, grout float, margin trowel, notched trowel, sponge, soft cloth, nonabrasive scouring pad, rubber gloves, foam paintbrushes, tile nippers

Tile is a layered floor. Underneath those fancy tiles that you so carefully chose is a dull gray base that carries all the weight. Without it, the floor would flex, the tiles would crack, and the grout between them would pop out.

The base is backerboard, a rigid panel that, depending on the manufacturer, is composed of cement, fiber cement, gypsum, plywood, or plastic that provides a sound substrate for setting tile. It sits in a thin coat of wet mortar and is screwed to the floor or wall underneath. It is sometimes referred to as "mason's drywall."

Some companies make a mastic that you can use to stick tiles to a plywood subfloor, but most tilers are against using it. When you're tiling, using mortar over a recommended backerboard results in a far superior bond and a more rigid base. In short, the tiles stick better and won't crack.

Once the base is down, laying the tiles is a matter of spreading mortar and putting the tiles in place. The mortar is called "thinset" not because it's runny, but because you can use a thinner layer than with older products. Thinset mortar is plenty strong, but if you want the highest strength mortar available, use an epoxy mortar.

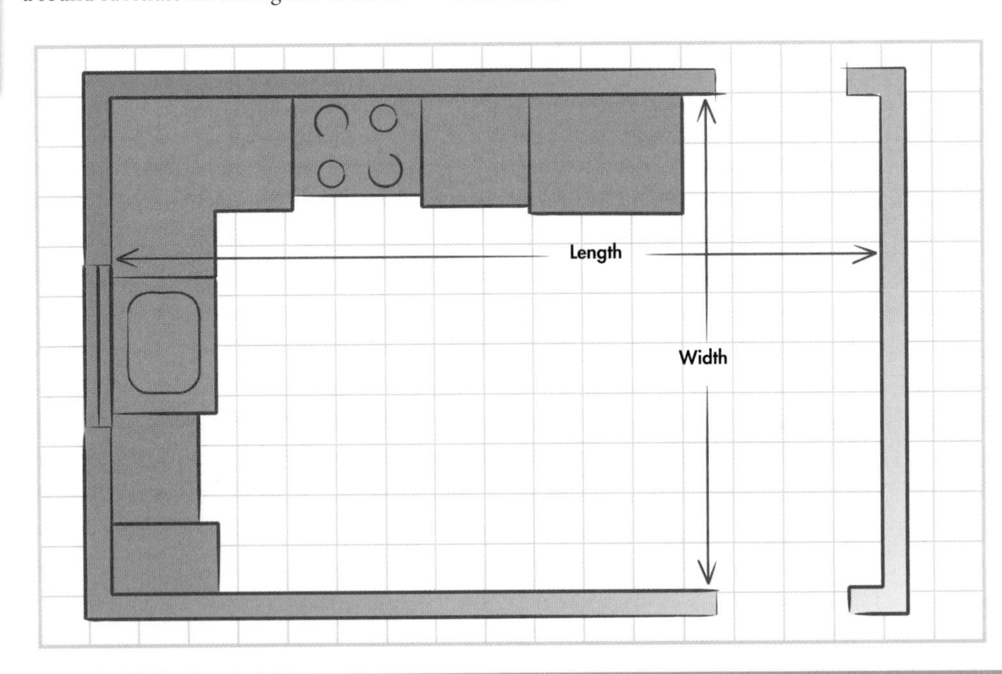

Make a floor plan
Draw the walls of the room as accurately as you can on a sheet of grid paper. Include doorways and floor obstructions such as cabinets and fixtures. Grid paper is available with ⅛-, ¼-, and ½-inch grid spacing. For greatest accuracy, draw your plan as large as possible on the page. Mark dimensions and your scale.

$ BUYER'S GUIDE

GET THE RIGHT ADHESIVE

Mortar is a combination of sand and cement, which dries hard and holds the tile in place. (Grout, which you apply between the tiles, is made of the same materials, but because the proportions are different, you can't substitute one for the other.)

The mortar used to set tile is called thinset—not because it's thin, but because you install a sheet of precast concrete as a subfloor, instead of laying a thick mortar base in advance of the mortar that holds the tile. Use a latex-modified thinset, which results in a stronger bond, especially with porous tiles. With light and translucent tiles, make sure you use white thinset, as gray may show through.

Both marble and granite stain easily so use a mortar especially designed for use with them.

Most mortars are made for both wall and floor use. Some (usually containing lime for extra strength) are specifically for walls. Buy a mortar designed for floor, or floor and wall, use.

WORK SMART

WHAT IT TAKES FOR TILE

To make sure your joists will support the tile floor, look at the nailing pattern. If the rows of nails are spaced 16 inches apart or less, you're fine; if not, you'll have to add support or put in another kind of floor.

Laying backerboard

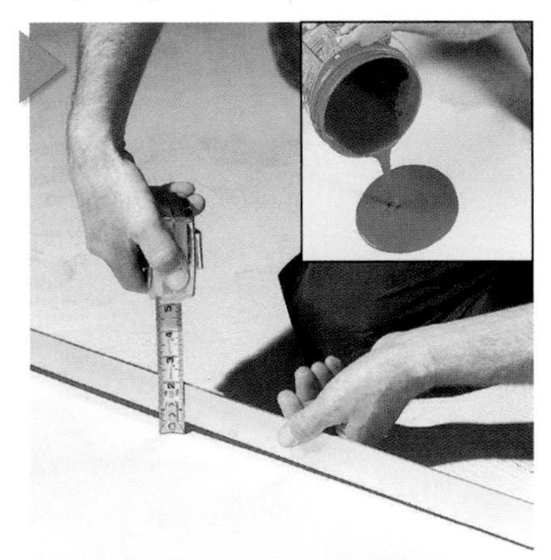

1 Check to see whether the floor on which the tile will go is flat. To do this, put a straightedge on the floor, and look for gaps between it and the floor. Mark gaps on the floor; clean the area and paint it with a latex primer. Pour self-leveling mortar over the area (see inset), then feather the edges with a straightedge.

2 Snap chalklines on the floor to show where the sheets of backerboard will go. Arrange the sheets so that the ends are staggered. If some sheets need to be cut to fit, lay out the cut on the backerboard. Score along the line with a carbide backerboard cutter guided by a straightedge. If recommended by the manufacturer, score both sides. Press down with your hand and knee on one side of the line, and lift the opposite edge to snap the panel.

3 A layer of mortar under the backerboard helps keep the board from flexing and is an important part of the installation. Mix mortar according to the directions on the bag. Spread mortar on the floor where your first sheet of backerboard will go. Once it's spread, comb it out with the notched edge of the trowel, holding the trowel at about a 45-degree angle to the floor.

4 Put the first sheet of backerboard in place and screw it down with backerboard screws placed every 4 inches. (Use 1 ½-inch screws for ½-inch board and 1 ¼-inch screws for ¼-inch board. Do not screw directly into joists.) Spread mortar for the next sheet; put the sheet on edge against the previous sheet and pivot it down into the mortar. Leave a ⅛-inch gap between sheets, and screw each board as you go. At the corners, keep the screws 2 inches from the edge to avoid cracking it. (If directed by the manufacturer, use a screw gun with a clutch.)

5 Lay the rest of the backerboard sheets. Fill the spaces between them with thinset mortar and a margin trowel. Reinforce by covering the gap with fiberglass tape, embedding it firmly in the wet thinset. Cover the tape with a second layer of thinset. Feather the edges with the trowel to create a flat surface.

Mosaic tiles can add some eye appeal

As an accent to a plain, monochrome tile floor, you might consider laying down occasional 12×12-inch squares of smaller 2×2 inch tiles. Today they're offered in a wide selection of colors, from multi-hued patterns to high-gloss solid colors. Setting them is the same as one-piece tile. You also can cut them into strips or pieces to make unique patterns. Use them on countertops and backsplashes too.

Laying a tile floor (continued)

Laying out the floor

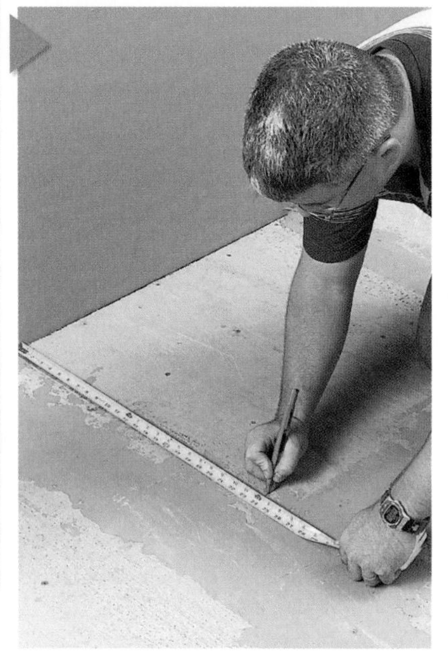

1 Measure from both ends of the longest wall out several tile spaces (allowing a ¼-inch gap at the wall) and mark with pencil.

2 Snap a chalkline between the two points just marked. This line should represent the center of one of the tile joints.

3 Repeat Step 1 for the next longest adjacent wall and snap a second chalkline. This line also will represent the center of a tile joint.

Thanks, Pythagoras

The ancient Greek mathematician Pythagoras provided a useful rule of carpentry: A triangle with sides in the proportions 3-4-5 always forms a 90-degree angle. For larger triangles, use multiples of 3-4-5 (6-8-10, 9-12-15, etc.).

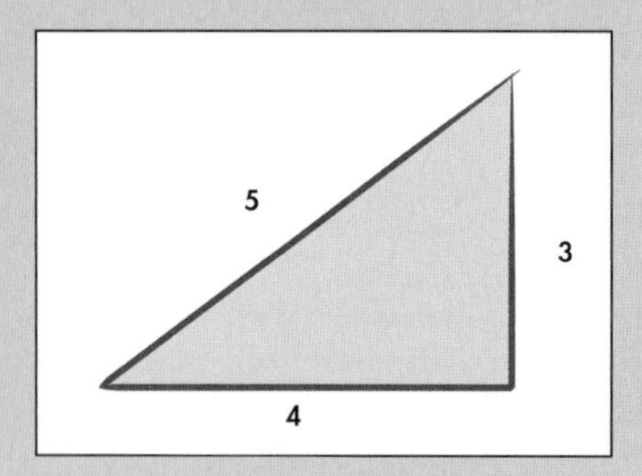

Ten times more accurate than measuring a single tile and spacer is measuring 10 tiles and 10 spacers. Simply line up 10 in a row, measure the span, and divide by 10. See next page for spacer installation instructions.

4 Check the angle by marking points 3 feet and 4 feet from the intersection. Measure the diagonal. If it is exactly 5 feet, your lines are square. If not, repeat the first three steps.

Setting the tile

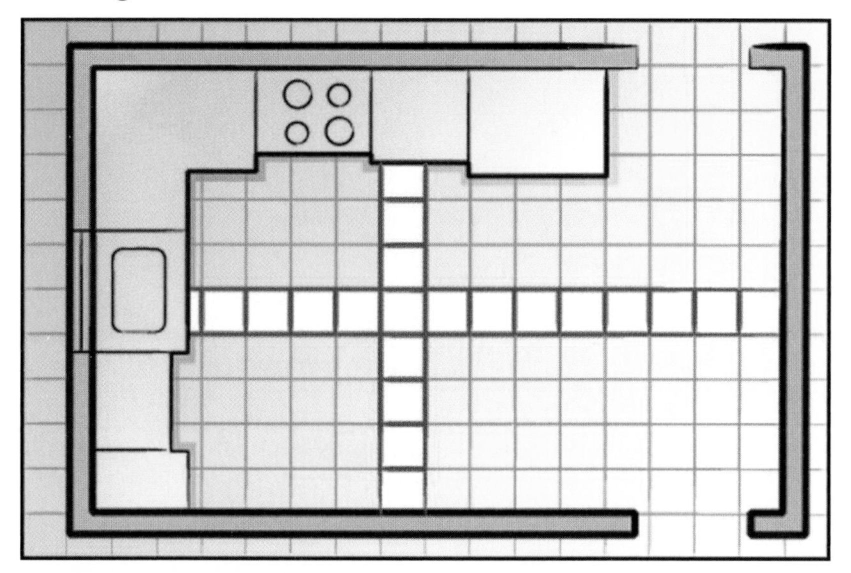

▲ ***Laying out the tiles.*** *Test-fit the tiles along the layout lines as shown below. The object is to make the most use of whole tiles and to cut as few as possible. Shift the layout lines as necessary to get maximum use of the tiles. Once you're satisfied with the look of the layout, you can begin installing the floor.* *(See Installing resilient vinyl tile on page 172 for more information.)*

1 Mix thinset mortar with a paddle designed for mortar, not paint. Make sure the drill has enough power for the job, and mix at slow speed. Mix only what you can use before it hardens. Start by mixing enough to fill a 3½-quart bucket, then adjust the amount as you become more experienced.

2 Spread adhesive. Press the mortar into the backerboard with the trowel at a shallow angle in order to make it fully adhere to the backerboard.

3 Comb the adhesive out into straight lines, holding the trowel at a 45-degree angle to the floor and pushing the trowel teeth to the floor. Set the first tile in place, pressing it firmly into the mortar.

4 Lift the first tile and check the mortar on its back. Dry areas (inset) mean the mortar is not thick enough. Scrape the morter off the back of the tile, reapply it with a thcker layer to the floor and test again.

5 Set remaining tiles by butting edge against edge, hinging down, twisting slightly back and forth, placing spacers, and sliding into the final position.

6 Place spacers on end so you can remove them easily. Although this requires more spacers, you can reuse them in another part of the project.

WORK SMART

PROPER USE OF SPACERS

Spacers may be used flat, requiring only one per four-way intersection. However, removal requires use of a special tool and risks disturbing the set tile. It is better to place four spacers on end, as shown in step 6. Placed on end, the spacers are easily removed before grouting, allowing for a better grout seal.

Laying a tile floor (continued)

Marking special cuts

Gaps at walls. Place the tile to be cut on the last tile set. Place a marker tile on top, against a spacer tile at the wall. Trace the edge of the marker tile onto the tile to be cut.

Around pipes. Mark the width of the notch on the edge of the tile, with the tile to be notched lined up with the tile beneath and butted against the pipe.

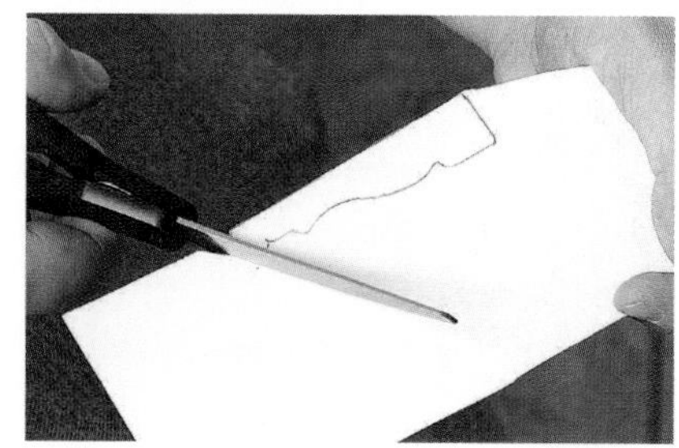

Other contours. Mark the outline of the cut on heavy paper stock or cardboard. Cut it out with scissors or a utility knife.

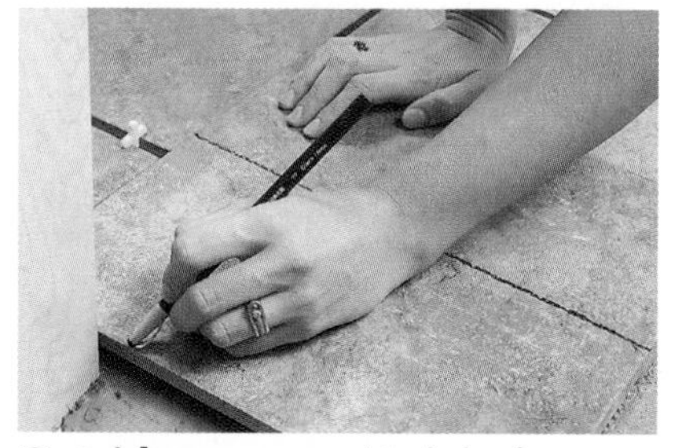

Outside corners. Mark the first cutting line as above. To mark the second cut, mark the corner on the marker tile, allowing a ¼-inch gap.

Measure the depth of the notch with a tape measure butted against a ¼-inch spacer held against the wall.

Trace the outline by applying masking tape to the edge of the tile. Mark the outline with a grease pencil. Cut with a saw or nippers.

Cutting tile

Using a tile cutter. Align the cutting wheel, raise the pressing bar, and then pull the wheel toward you with moderate pressure. Pull several times. Lift the cutting wheel, lower the pressing tee, and strike the handle to snap the tile.

Using a tile-cutting saw. Adjust the fence (guide) so the cut mark lines up with the blade. Hold the tile with both hands; wear safety glasses. Advance the tile into the blade, guided by the fence. Avoid chipping the tile by cutting slowly.

Curved cuts with a nipper. Start at one end of the cut line, using one-quarter of the jaw to make the bite. Work from both ends toward the middle, taking small bites.

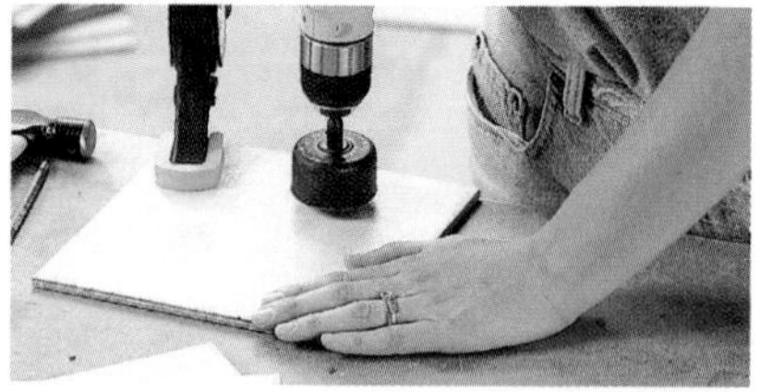

Hole cuts. Mark the center of the hole on the tile. Break through the glaze with a center punch to keep the drill bit from wandering. Clamp the tile firmly to a table or workbench. Drill slowly and lightly to avoid breaking the tile.

Grouting tile

1 Mix the grout per the manufacturer's instructions. Spread grout in sweeping arcs with a rubber grout float held at a shallow angle. Press the grout into the joints, filling them completely. For joints wider than 3⁄8 inch, use a grout bag.

2 Remove the excess with the grout float held at a steep angle. Sweep the float diagonally across the tiles to avoid dipping into the joints.

3 Wipe the tiles with a damp grout sponge (wring dripless) to remove grout residue. If the residue persists, use a scrub pad but avoid scrubbing the joints.

4 Remove the haze immediately; do not take a break. First wipe the haze with a damp cloth, then buff the tiles with a clean, dry cloth.

5 Damp-cure the grout by misting it twice a day for three days. Do not damp-cure tinted grout; it will discolor.

6 Apply tile and grout cleaner with a sponge once the grout is dry, then scrub the surface with a stiff brush. Rinse thoroughly and let the floor dry before applying a penetrating sealer.

Installing vinyl plank flooring

Skill level:	Time to complete:	Materials:	Tools:
★★☆☆☆	Experienced 3 hrs. Handy 4 hrs. Novice 6 hrs.	Vinyl plank flooring, double-face tape	Tape measure, tile cutter, utility knife, straightedge, framing square, saw, compass, pry bar, roller

Vinyl plank flooring is a relatively new product that's durable, attractive, and among the easiest flooring materials to apply. The "planks" are actually 6-inch-wide strips of heavy vinyl flooring material similar to, but thicker than sheet vinyl flooring or vinyl tiles. The surface looks and feels like wood, with a photographic replication of various wood species and an embossed grain pattern. The material is very stable and can be installed directly over almost any reasonably smooth hard-surface floor, including wood, vinyl, and concrete.
No pad or underlayment is required.

Vinyl plank flooring is a floating floor system: It is not attached to the surface beneath it except at the floor's edges. The planks are fastened to one another by adhesive strips that are factory-applied to each plank. These strips, called "underedges," project from one side of each plank and are used to fasten each plank to an "overedge" of the adjoining plank. Laying a vinyl plank floor is similar to installing laminate flooring.

1 Acclimate the flooring. Place the materials in the room you're flooring two days before you install them. Set the thermostat on its normal setting for the time of year.
Put the unopened boxes flat on the floor. After 48 hours, they will have come to the temperature and humidity of the room and will be ready to install.

2 Remove the baseboard, the quarter-round, or both. Undercut door trim by placing a saw on a vinyl plank and cutting through the trim. When it comes time to install the planking, slip it under the trim.

3 Start in a corner and proceed from the wall with the adhesive underedge of the planks facing toward the center of the room. Leave a ⅛-inch gap between the planks and the wall to allow for expansion.

4 If the wall is uneven and the gap between the wall and the planks is at any point wider than the molding that will cover it, trim the first course of planks to match the contour of the wall. Set a compass to the space of the largest gap plus ⅛ inch. Guide the compass along the wall so that the marker makes a line on the planks. Score along the line with a utility knife three or four times, then bend the plank along the line to snap it in two.

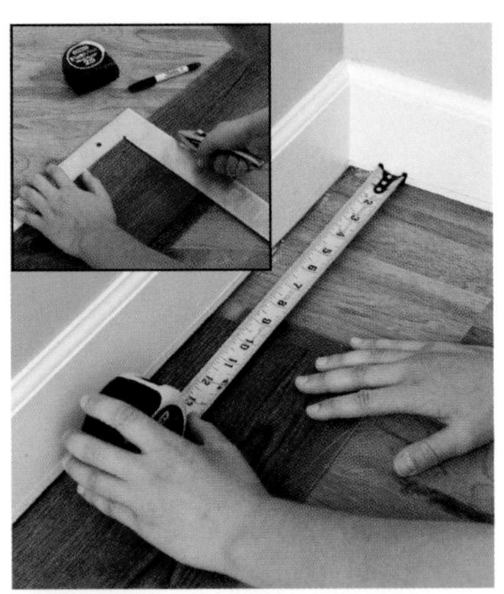

5 Test-lay the first course loose. If the final plank in the course will need to be cut shorter than 12 inches, cut the first plank in the course so that both the first and last plank are longer than 12 inches.
Cut the plank using a framing square as a straightedge to get a perfectly square cut. Score the plank with a utility knife and snap it at the score mark.
Or cut the plank with a tile cutter.

6 Apply double-face tape to the subfloor at about 3 inches from the wall. Start in the corner and work from left to right. Press the first plank firmly onto the tape and parallel with the wall, maintaining a ⅛-inch gap between the plank and the wall.

7 Apply the overedge of the end of the second plank to the underedge of the first plank. Push planks firmly together to create a tight seam. Continue until the first course is in place.

8 Lay the second course. When securing two planks together long-edge to long-edge, lower the overedge of the loose plank at a 45-degree angle to the underedge of the secured plank. Use one hand to hold the plank and the other to guide the plank's edge into place. Push the loose plank gently but firmly against the secured plank to create a tight seam. Avoid gaps in the seams. At the end of the course, score and snap the final plank to length before installing it.

9 Lay the remaining courses. Stagger the length of the starting plank in each course so that the short-edged seams fall at random points in the floor and not in a straight line.

10 Trim the final row to fit. Start by assembling a row directly on top of the row just laid. Use a scrap plank 6 to 10 inches long. Cut off the underedge. Hold the scrap against the wall, put a pen against the other edge, and drag the pen to mark the planks. As with the first row, use a utility knife to score the planks. Install the final row.

11 Roll the seams with a roller to ensure bonding of the adhesive edges. Replace moldings.

Sanding and refinishing a floor

Skill level:	Time to complete:	Materials:	Tools:
★★★★★	Experienced 2 days Handy 2 days Novice 3 days	#8 finishing nails, wood putty, wood stain, 220-grit sandpaper or 000 steel wool, varnish, blue painter's masking tape	Plastic sheeting, pry bar, hammer, nail set, putty knife, drum sander and sandpaper, vibrating sander and sandpaper, edge sander or random-orbit sander and sandpaper, dust respirator, shop vacuum, paint tray, lamb's-wool applicator pads (for varnish), clean rags, paintbrush or foam brush, ventilating respirator

Hardwood floors typically last for the life of a home, but eventually they will need refurbishing or refinishing.

Refinishing. If the floors are simply dirty from years of use but aren't worn through to bare wood, you can probably clean them with household detergent and elbow grease, or you can rent a floor-buffing machine with an abrasive pad. Remove all the dirt and wax from the floor but not the finish itself, then apply a new finish coat.

Refurbishing. If your floors are deeply stained, discolored, or damaged, you can often sand them back to their original state. Solid-wood-strip floors can be sanded and refinished several times. Some wood-strip floors, however, are made from laminated wood products and can be sanded only once and with great care. Examine an edge of the floor—under a threshold, for example—to determine the floor's thickness. If the floor is laminated wood, leave the job to professionals.

If the floor is reasonably flat and free of dips and gouges, all you need to do is remove the finish with a vibrating sander. Vibrating sanders work on the same principle as handheld finishing sanders: A flat pad or plate with sandpaper on it vibrates and oscillates to remove the old finish. Floor models are bigger and heavier, of course, but work gently enough to control easily.

If the floor is uneven or has scratches or deep gouges, you need to use a drum sander. If you're not comfortable running the machine, call a professional to do the sanding, then do the finishing and staining yourself.

▲ *Refinishing saves the character of an old floor while giving it the shine of a new one.*

Renting floor sanders

Drum and vibrating floor sanders and edgers are rental items. The drum and edging sanders are powerful, aggressive tools and take some practice to operate properly. Many rental companies offer a training demonstration, so take advantage of the opportunity. After class you're on your own. To minimize potential damage to your floor, start by using fine sandpaper on a small area to become familiar with the machine. Later switch to coarse paper and start the real sanding. Sandpaper comes with the sanders but you pay per piece. Get more than you think you'll need—unused paper can be returned when you return the sander.

WORK SMART

TO THIN TO SAND?

Wondering whether the floor is too thin to sand? Pull up the floor vents or take off the threshold or the baseboard to reveal the edge of a floorboard. How far can you sand? Down to the tongue and groove but no deeper.

1 Remove the base molding. A floor sander may bang against base molding, so remove it. Usually all it requires is removing the shoe molding—the quarter round that runs along the floor. Pry it off as shown, protecting the baseboard with a piece of scrap wood. If there is no shoe molding, either remove the base molding or take care not to damage it with the sanders.

2 Check for squeaks and nail loose floorboards. The best approach is to nail into a floor joist, not just the subfloor, with #8 finishing nails. Set the nails and fill the holes with latex wood putty. Set protruding nails that would tear the sandpaper.

3 Contain the dust. To prevent dust from sifting throughout the house, close off doorways with plastic sheeting. Stick strips of masking tape around the edges of closet doors. If possible, pull the dust toward a window or door with a box fan. Wear a dust mask when sanding.

4 Rough-sand with a drum or vibrating sander. If the floor itself is in bad shape, start with a drum sander. If refinishing is all that's necessary, use a vibrating sander (Step 6) instead. Get advice from the tool rental company. When drum sanding, start with the coarsest sandpaper grit—typically 36- or 40-grit—then switch to 60-grit. Finish with 80- or 100-grit. Move the sander so that it travels along the length of the boards, with the grain of the wood. Work the drum sander forward and back over 3-foot to 4-foot lengths of floor, overlapping the strokes by at least one-third of the belt.

Sanding and refinishing a floor (continued)

5 Sweep and vacuum between sandings. The sanding dust eventually gets in the way of the sanding process and has to be swept and vacuumed. Always sweep and vacuum before starting with the next grit of sandpaper. It not only makes the floor cleaner, it also picks up any grit that may have been left by the sandpaper—grit that would scratch the job of the finer-grit paper.

6 Fine-sand with a vibrating sander (optional). These sanders level minor unevenness left by drum sanders. If you use both tools, use the drum sander for the two coarse grits (36 and 60), then use the vibrating sander for the medium and fine grits (80 and 100). If you use only the vibrating sander, start with 60-grit, then sand with 80-grit, and finally with 100-grit.

TOOL TIP
A DIFFERENT DRUMMER

A sander drum is usually made of rubber wedged between two discs held in place by a nut. To lock a roll of sandpaper in place, tighten the nut, squeezing the sides of the drum together. This increases the diameter just enough to prevent the sandpaper from slipping off. Loosen the nut to remove the sandpaper.

7 Sand corners and edges with an edge sander. The edge sander usually comes as part of the rental. Use 80-grit paper to reach areas that the large sanders cannot reach: corners, under radiators, in small closets, etc. Edge sanders can be difficult to control; practice on a hidden area, such as the inside of a closet, until you get the hang of it.

8 A random-orbit sander is easier to control than the edger. Use it to finish tight places such as corners. Random-orbit sanders are less aggressive and less likely to gouge, and they do an excellent but slower job.

9 Apply a wood stain (optional). When the sanding is done, clean up all the dust with a vacuum and tack cloth. Apply wood stain with a foam applicator pad. Work one manageable area at a time—4 square feet, for example. Always stain in the direction of the wood grain.

10 Wipe off the excess stain as you go. Most manufacturers recommend removing excess stain as you go—usually after a few minutes. Use clean cotton cloths or paper towels. Try wiping the floor with a cloth wrapped around a dry applicator pad.

11 Apply a clear finish. Allow the stain to dry as recommended before applying the first coat of varnish. Polyurethane, either oil-base or water-base, is a reliable finish for floors. Apply the finish with a lamb's-wool applicator. You may need to sand between coats. Follow the directions of the manufacturer to the letter. Often the length of time between coats can be critical to the outcome.

Sanding parquet

Parquet floors require a special technique or a special machine. Unless you're a pro, use the machine. To create a parquet pattern the tile is made of several strips with the grain running in different directions. As a result, sanding across the grain is unavoidable, and the sandpaper leaves noticeable scratches.

Rent an orbital floor sander, which has a pad that moves in a random semi-circular pattern that doesn't scratch the grain. Use a 36-grit sandpaper to remove the finish. Change to a 60-grit paper for a first pass over the floor. Make a second pass with 80-grit, and a final pass with a 100-grit sandpaper. Sand around the edges of the floor with a hand sander, using the same progression of grits.

BUYER'S GUIDE

OIL-BASE VS. WATER-BASE POLYURETHANE

Oil-base polyurethane is reliable and has been around for years. It imparts warmth to most wood colors, darkening them slightly. Use a brand that is recommended for flooring and has a warranty. Some brands dry slowly, requiring a full day between coats. Others are fast-drying (4 hours is about the minimum), which allows you to get two, even three, coats on in a single day. Good ventilation is a must, and you should wear a ventilating respirator.

Water-base polyurethanes dry quickly and are nearly odorless. They're also virtually clear when dry—an advantage if you don't want the finish to darken the wood. Many professionals use commercial water-base polyurethane that holds up well, but reports are mixed on the water-base varnishes available to consumers. Quality seems to vary from brand to brand. Check warranties and discuss your choice with knowledgeable floor-finish experts.

SAFETY ALERT

OIL-SOAKED RAGS ARE A FIRE HAZARD

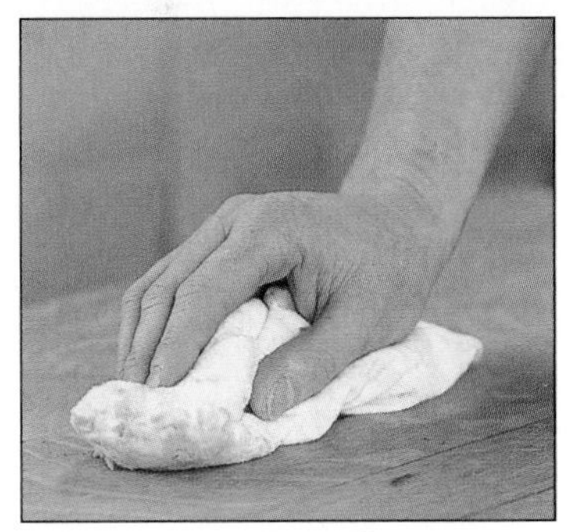

The heat from dry, oily rags can set the rags on fire, especially if they are bunched together. Hang the rags outside, away from any structures, and allow them to dry thoroughly before you throw them out.

Installing a strip-wood floor

Skill level:	Time to complete:	Materials:	Tools:
★★★☆☆	Experienced 8 hrs. Handy 10 hrs. Novice 14 hrs.	Wood flooring, building paper, floor finish, #6 finishing nails, #6 ringshank nails, latex wood putty	Pry bar, hammer stapler, tape measure, chalkline, hammer, nail set, drill, 3/32" drill bit, flooring nailer, miter saw, saber saw, table saw (optional)

All strip-wood floors require a stable subfloor. Materials such as ¾-inch plywood, tongue-and-groove pine, or oriented-strand board (OSB) are all typical and acceptable. Floorboards should be installed perpendicular to the floor joists. Parallel installation is acceptable in hallways if the subfloor is sturdy, but it may cause more spring in the floor and possibly more squeaks.

A strip-wood floor consists of solid strips of wood, typically ¾ inch thick and less than three inches wide, with tongue-and-groove joints along the edges. The tongue-and-groove joints keep the surface of each board flush and conceal the nails, which are driven through the tongue and covered by the groove of the next board.

Oak strip flooring is available as a stock item in most home centers. For a slightly higher cost, you can choose from maple, walnut, cherry, and hickory. All will probably last the life of the house and will withstand sanding and refinishing several times.

You can buy strip flooring in bundles of approximately 22 square feet. It's also sold in random widths to create less-formal floors. Buy it either unfinished or prefinished with a durable commercial finish. The higher cost of prefinished strip flooring is worth considering because you won't have to sand and finish after installation. Because prefinished boards can't be sanded flush the way unfinished flooring can, some prefinished strip flooring has a small V-groove along the length that conceals slight unevenness.

▲ *Solid-wood floors add warmth to a room.*

1 Remove shoe molding or base molding, if necessary. It's often easier to lay a floor if the trim isn't in the way. Removing it, however, can be tricky because it's easy to damage and can break. If necessary, remove the molding with a pry bar, wedging a scrap between the wall and the bar to avoid damage. Reinstall the molding after the new floor is installed.

2 Tack down building paper. Building paper makes it easier to slide the flooring into place and provides somewhat of a vapor barrier. Roll it out and staple every 8 to 10 inches. At the seams, overlap the pieces about 3 inches.

3 Determine the width of the starter strip. Figure how many strips it will take to complete the width. The first and last strip should be relatively equal in width. Lay out flooring, or use a calculator and divide the room width by the width of an individual strip of flooring. Allow a gap the thickness of the flooring for expansion along both walls; the shoe or base molding will cover the gap.

4 Rip-cut the starter-row strips. Use a table saw with a sharp rip blade to cut the starter strips of flooring. Because the tongue edge of the first strip must face into the room, you will cut off the groove edge.

5 Snap a chalkline for the starter row using the marks on the floor; this will show where the edge of the tongue will fall. This line must be straight because the straightness of the starter row affects the entire installation. Don't guide along the wall as it may not be perfectly straight.

Flooring installation tips

- **Acclimating the flooring.** Wood expands and contracts with changes in moisture, and even kiln-dried boards will warp. To acclimate the wood to the moisture content of your house, put the bundles in the room where they'll be installed. Unpackage them, cut any binding, and leave the flooring for 48 hours. The wood will gradually come to the same moisture content as the room, minimizing problems that might occur after installation.
- **Hallways.** In a large room, install the flooring perpendicular to the joists because it results in a stronger floor. In hallways, run the boards the length of the hall because it looks better.
- **Shuffling the deck.** As you unbundle the flooring, you'll see that all wood is not alike. Some boards will be dark; some will be light. Some will be highly figured; others won't. Professional floor installers don't try to group similar boards. Instead, they shuffle the boards, mixing them for a random-looking floor.

TOOL TIP

PREDRILLING FOR NAILS

Nails seem to bend and wood seems to split in the most visible places on a floor—it's almost guaranteed. For finish carpentry, it pays to drill a pilot hole in the visible surface to keep the wood from splitting and help prevent the nail from bending over and marring the wood. A 3⁄32-inch drill bit is about right for #6 finishing nails.

6 Face-nail the first one or two strips (a flooring nailer can't be used). Align the first piece with the tongue edge on the chalkline. Drill holes every 12 inches along the length of the strip, drive #6 ringshank flooring nails through the holes, and set the heads flush with the surface. Note the expansion gap between the first floorboard and the wall.

Installing a strip-wood floor (continued)

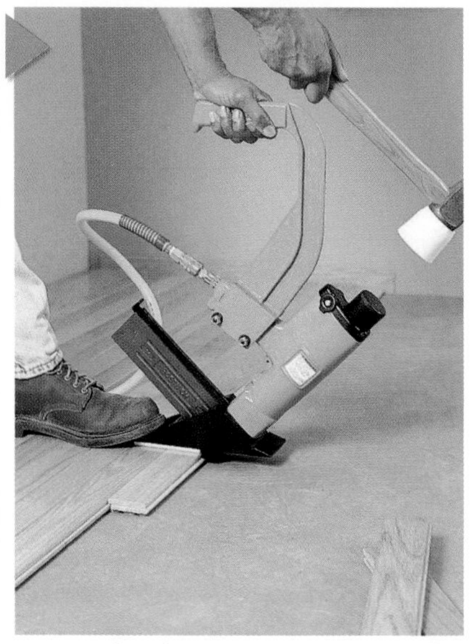

7 Nail subsequent strips with a flooring nailer. You can use a hammer, but nailers save a lot of time. (Both manual and air-powered models are available.) Position the nailer on the tongue edge of the board, and whack the plunger head with the heavy rubber mallet that's supplied with the nailer. After a little practice you'll nail down this skill.

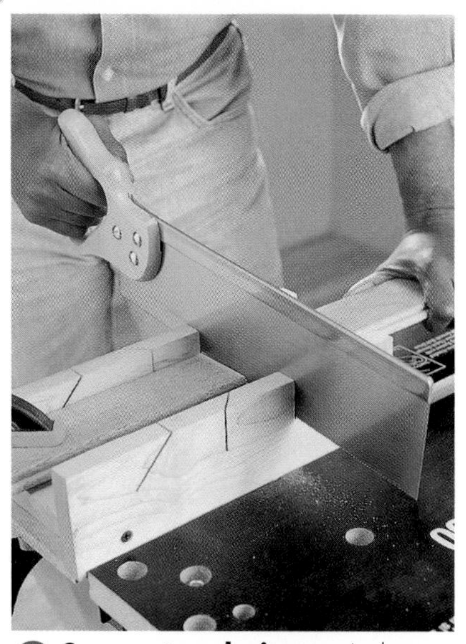

8 Crosscut end pieces. At the end of each row, the last piece needs to be crosscut to fit. Allow a small gap here to make getting the piece in place easier. Avoid using an end piece that's less than a foot long; instead, use two medium-length pieces to end the row.

9 Tighten seams. Some pieces will be bowed. If you have enough extra pieces, these may not be needed. If you have to use a piece that's bowed, screw a piece of scrap to the floor about an inch from the strip and tap a wood wedge into the gap, as shown. Also try wedging a pry bar edge into the subfloor and prying against the edge of the bowed strip. Then nail the strip in place.

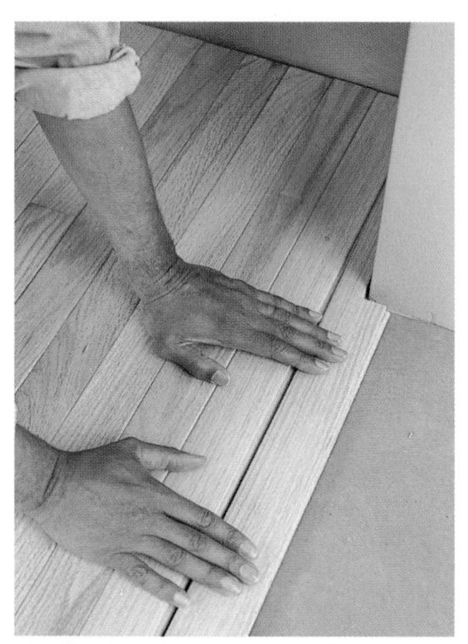

10 Fit pieces around obstacles. Where the flooring meets a jog in the wall or another obstruction, cut the pieces to fit. Position the piece of flooring as close to its destination as possible, then transfer the measurements for the cuts directly from the wall or obstruction to the flooring. Remember to allow a gap along the wall length.

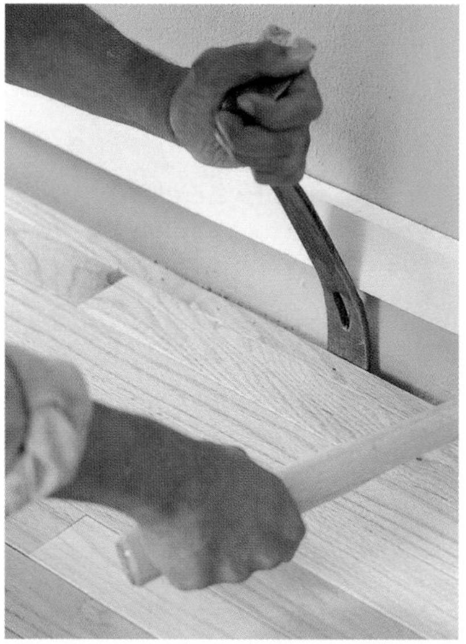

11 Cut and fit the last row. The last row, like the first, may have to be sawed to width. It also will have to be face-nailed. To tighten the joint between the final two pieces, use a pry bar between the wall and the edge of the last strip, with a scrap block of wood protecting the wall. Then nail the strip in place.

12 Apply base and shoe molding. If you use unfinished flooring, sand it and apply the finish before installing the base molding. (See Sanding and refinishing a floor, page 182.) If installing new baseboard, cut and fit it once the floor is completely finished. Rest the molding on a piece of paper when you nail it in place to allow the floor to expand and contract under it. Remove the paper when done.

Installing a decorative border

A simple decorative border of a contrasting band of wood frames the room and defines its shape. To make one, buy a small amount of flooring in a different wood species as the rest of the floor, but from the same manufacturer. This works whether you use finished or unfinished strip flooring. For example, if you use natural oak for the floor, use walnut for the border.

A border creates two distinct spaces: the perimeter area outside the border, and the main floor field inside the border. The floor strips outside the border as well as the border itself are either mitered at the corners or lapped one over the next for a "log cabin" effect. Either approach creates the framed look that visually distinguishes the border and perimeter from the floor field.

The space inside the border is treated the same as a regular strip-floor installation except that the end joints that meet the border have to be cut to fit precisely. Install the wood border first, then the perimeter area, and finally the main body of the floor.

▲ *A decorative border is usually just a strip of regular flooring in a contrasting color. Install the border first, making sure that the corners are square and the sides parallel. Once the border is in place, fit the flooring on both sides of it.*

1 Determine the location. A border can be located a few inches to a foot from the wall, depending on the size of the room. Lay out short lengths of the flooring across the whole width of the floor. Measure carefully, and then lay out a field composed entirely of full-width strips. Snap chalklines to mark the inside edge of the inlay. (See page 187, Step 5.)

2 Cut the inlay and nail it to the floor. If you use a piece of standard flooring for the inlay material, first cut off the tongue edge on a tablesaw. If desired rip the inlay piece to a narrower width at the same time. Miter the inlay at the corners (or lap it as in inset), using a miter box and handsaw or a power miter saw. Predrill holes through the inlay and nail it to the subfloor with #6 finishing nails. With a framing square, check that the inlay is square in the corners. Countersink the nails and fill the holes with a matching latex wood putty.

3 Install the perimeter flooring. Cut and fit mitered pieces of the regular flooring at the corners. Because they are close to the wall, you won't be able to use a flooring nailer; face-nail them instead. You may be able to use the tongue-and-groove joint for the perimeter pieces, but you will have to cut off the tongue to fit the last piece against the wall. Install the field as if the borders were walls surrounding a standard strip floor.

Installing wide-plank flooring

Skill level: ★★★☆☆

Time to complete:
Experienced 8 hrs.
Handy 10 hrs.
Novice 14 hrs.

Materials: Wide-plank flooring, cut nails.

Tools: Circular saw, quick square, hammer (Installation is similar to strip flooring; see page 186 for additional tools and materials necessary.)

Wide-plank flooring is typically more than five inches wide and provides an appealing country look. Installing wide-plank flooring has notable differences from installing regular wood flooring. You'll use from one-third to one-half as many pieces of wide-plank floor, which means the installation will go more quickly. Though the long edges in wide-plank floors are sometimes tongue and groove, the end joints are not. Wide-plank floorboards are face-nailed across the wide widths into the joists. Square-head cut nails (if they're really rectangular) hold well and mimic the look of older floors.

This flooring expands and contracts more than narrow boards, creating wider gaps or cracks along the seams, especially during heating season. Gaps and cracks are considered part of the look.

▶ *Wide-plank flooring adds a touch of warmth and a hint of country to any room.*

1 Mark the floor joists with a chalkline. Wide boards expand and contract, so they must be nailed into the floor joists. On plywood subfloors, the nailing pattern should reveal the joist locations. Typical spacing from center to center of joists is 16 inches. After you find one, move over and drive more nails to find the next joist.

Will cut nails cut it?

They look authentic in wide-plank flooring, perfect for a country or Colonial decorating theme. But they're relatively hard to find, expensive, and add greatly to installation time.

If you're set on using them, remember that they're brittle compared to other nails and hard to pull. Sink them by starting with short, tapping, hammer strokes until firmly in place, then drive them home. Carefully straighten bent ones if you can, and drive again.

2 Nail down the boards. A power nailer can be used to start tongue-and-groove boards, but face-nailing is necessary as well. Cut nails, with square heads, hold well and provide an old-time look. Keep the nails at least ¾ inch from the edge of the board to prevent splitting. Orient the nailheads so that the long side is parallel to the length of the board. Predrill pilot holes for best results.

3 Screw down the planks. Pegging is an alternative look. Some planks come predrilled; if they don't, use a counterbore bit to drill a hole that will match wooden dowel plugs. Screw down the planks, then apply glue to the holes and tap in the plugs.

Installing laminate and engineered floors

Skill level:	Time to complete:	Materials:	Tools:
★★★☆☆	Experienced 6 hrs. Handy 8 hrs. Novice 8-10 hrs.	Engineered flooring and adhesive or laminate flooring and foam underlayment	Tape measure, metric tape measure, chalkline and chalk, handsaw, circular saw, table saw or saber saw, hammer, trowel (for engineered flooring), ¼-inch spacers, taping block, pull bar (for laminate flooring)

Laminate and engineered floors have a top layer of flooring material that is bonded in the factory to a layer of high density fiberboard. On laminate floors, the top layer is a laminated plastic material. On engineered floors, the top layer is solid wood. The resulting planks are wider than strip-wood floors and thus go down more quickly. They are also more stable, and unlike solid wood, can be installed directly over almost any subfloor, including concrete and concrete below grade. Installing over concrete, however, requires a plastic moisture barrier.

On a floating floor, the strips against the wall will need to be at least 2 inches wide if they're going to stay put. (The width doesn't matter on a glue-down installation because the glue holds materials in place.) To make sure the planks in a floating floor will be wide enough, measure the room carefully and divide by the width of a plank. Unless you enjoy dividing fractions by fractions, make the measurements with a metric tape. (You don't have to understand metrics to do this. It just works.) If the remainder is less than 50 mm, the last plank will be less than 2 inches wide.

If you need to trim the first plank, add the calculated width of the final planks to the width of a full plank. Divide by two and cut the first plank to this width. You'll end up with equally sized planks on each side of the room. Once you have the answer, just lay out the cut using the metric tape.

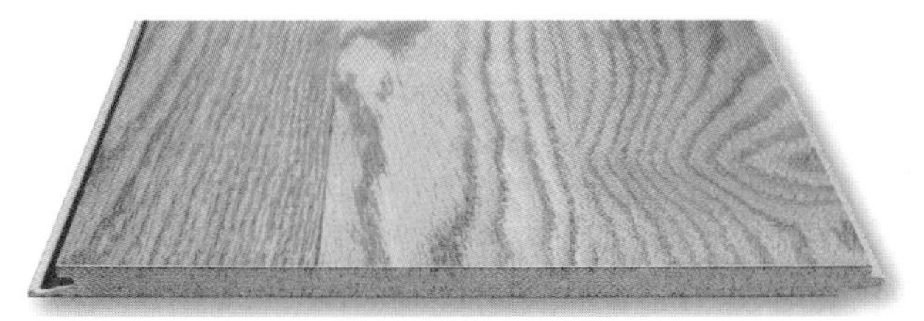

Snap-together laminate

Engineered wood

Some sound flooring advice

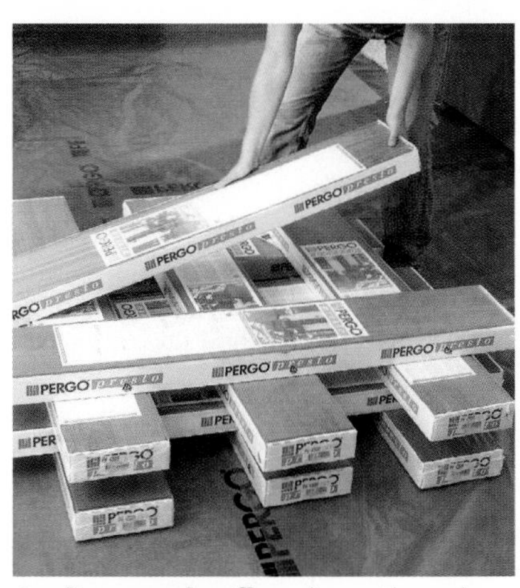

Acclimate the flooring. Place the materials in the room you're flooring two days before you install them. Set the thermostat on its normal setting for the time of year. Put the unopened boxes flat on the floor, or stack them three or four high, log cabin style. After 48 hours, they will have gradually come to the temperature and humidity of the room.

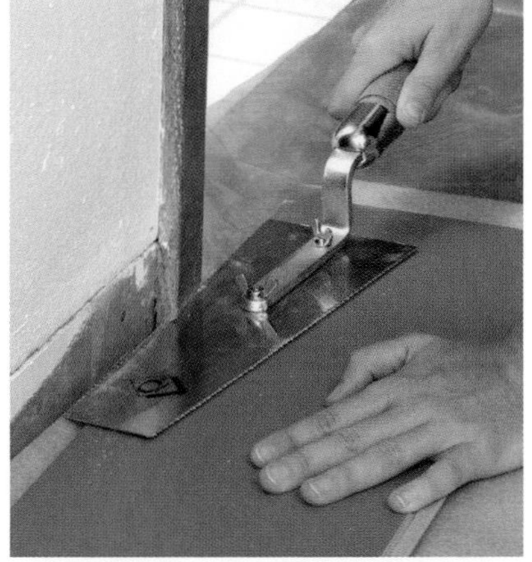

Instead of trying to cut flooring to fit around door moldings, installers cut away part of the jamb and slip the floor underneath. To do this, put a piece of flooring upside down next to the jamb; if it's a laminate floor, set it on a piece of foam underlayment. If it's engineered flooring, put it on the subfloor you're installing, if any. Put an undercutting saw on the plank and cut at least ½ inch into the jamb. Pop out the waste with a screwdriver or chisel. Also remove the quarter-round molding or shoe molding that's nailed to the baseboard, if any.

CLOSER LOOK

LAMINATE FLOORS ARE FLOATING FLOORS

Laminate floors are neither glued nor nailed to the subfloor. They're installed over a thin layer of foam cushioning (some laminate floors include attached underlayment) and are held in place by the walls. Engineered floors are usually glued to the subfloor with a mastic, but they can also be nailed down, and in some cases can be installed as a floating floor.

Installing laminate and engineered floors (continued)

Installing laminate flooring

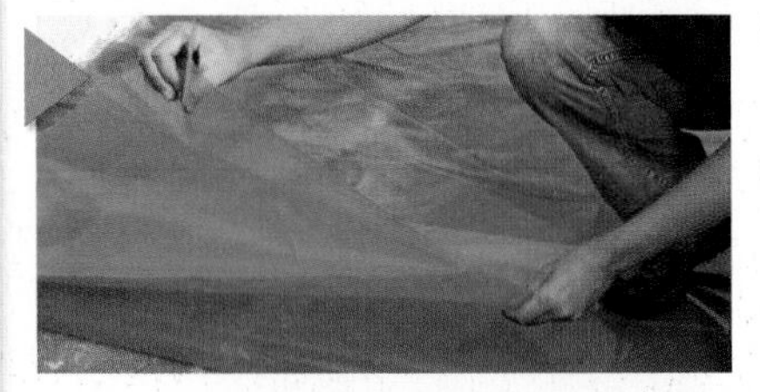

1 Install a 6 mil plastic moisture barrier over concrete. Overlap the seams as recommended by the manufacturer, then roll out the foam underlayment. Other subfloors need only foam underlayment. Some planks come with the underlayment already attached. If your planks do, you won't need to put more down. Choose the wall you'll start flooring against and roll a single strip of underlayment along it. Roll additional underlayment as you install the planks.

2 Trim the planks in the first row to width if necessary. If the last row will be less than 2 inches wide, you'll need to trim the first row to width to create a wider final row. Measure and calculate the width. If you need to trim the first row, add the calculated width of the final row to the width of a plank and divide by two. Cut the plank to this width. To minimize chipping on a table saw, cut the plank face-up with a sharp carbide blade. To minimize chipping on a circular saw, run the saw along the bottom of the plank.

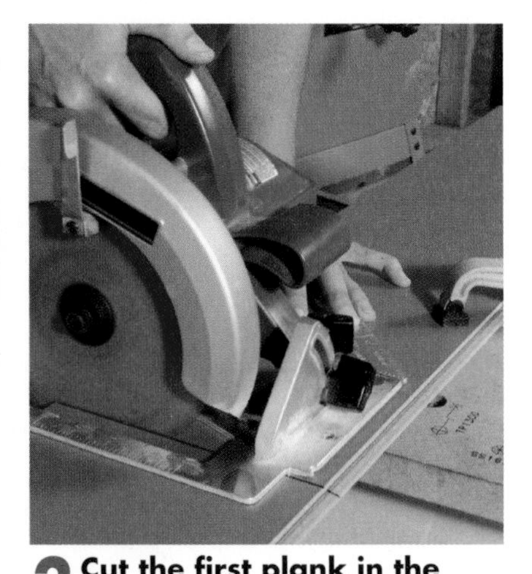

3 Cut the first plank in the second row to length. While you're at the saw, cut the first plank in the second row to the length called for by the manufacturer. Cutting the plank staggers the ends of neighboring boards and keeps them from aligning. Staggering creates a stronger and more attractive floor. In this case, the manufacturer recommends a plank 32 inches long for the first plank in the second row. Once you've made the cut, temporarily set the plank aside.

4 Put down the first plank. (If you didn't cut the tongue off the planks during earlier trimming, do so now.) It's easiest to assemble the first two rows when they're away from the wall. Start with a full-length plank, positioned with the groove facing into the room. Take the piece you cut to length earlier and put the tongue into the groove in the edge of the first plank.

5 Snap the pieces together. Different brands interlock differently, so follow the manufacturer's directions. For the brand shown here, lift one edge of the plank off the floor, and slide the tongue into the groove on the other plank. Press the plank flat to snap the pieces together.

6 Put down a third plank. Snap the end of the third plank into the end of the first plank, as shown. Put down a fourth plank, snapping the end into the end of plank two, and leaving a slight gap between it and plank three. To close the gap, kneel on plank one, reach over and lift the far edge of plank three slightly. Pull the plank toward you while pushing down along the groove of plank one. The planks will snap together. Put ¼-inch spacers against the wall and slide the assembled planks against them.

7 Continue laying the first two rows across the length of the room. When you get to the far wall, put a spacer against the wall and cut planks to fit in the opening. Put each plank in place, then snap it into the end groove as shown, using a hammer and a pull bar made by the flooring manufacturer.

8 Slide the assembled rows against spacers you've put along the starting wall. If the gap between the wall and the planks is at any point wider than the molding that will cover it, you will have to trim the board to match the contour of the wall. Set a compass to the space of the largest gap, plus ½ inch. Guide the compass along the wall so that the marker makes a line on the planks.

9 Unsnap the planks and cut along the scribe line with a saber saw using a laminate blade that is designed to minimize chipping. Reassemble the rows, put spacers against the walls and slide the plank assembly against them. Begin assembling the next rows.

10 Once the first two rows are in place, begin the third row. Cut a plank to length so that the end will fall at least 8 inches from the end of its neighbor in the second row. Put a spacer against the wall, put a plank against the spacer, and snap the plank into the edge of the second row. Work your way across the room, laying a single row. Snap the ends of the planks together first, and then join the sides.

11 If a gap appears anywhere along the edges, close it by tapping the edge with a block and hammer. When you reach the end of a row, cut the piece to fit and put it in place against a spacer as before. Work your way across the room, installing one row at a time. Unroll additional underlayment as needed. Butt underlayment seams, but don't overlap them. Continue across the width of the floor until the space is too narrow for a full plank.

12 Trim the final row to fit. Start by assembling a row directly on top of the row just laid. Find a piece of scrap 6 to 10 inches long. If the manufacturer makes the flooring with a bottom lip wider than the top lip, break off the bottom lip. Hold the scrap against the wall, put a pen against the other edge, and pull it along the wall to mark the planks. As before, use a saber saw to trim the planks. Nail quarter-round molding to the baseboard to cover the gap.

Installing laminate and engineered floors (continued)

Installing a glue-down engineered floor

1 Nail down a straightedge as a guide. Snap a line parallel to the wall—outside walls are usually the straightest and best to use. Add the width of several planks together plus the width of the recommended expansion gap between the flooring and wall. Snap a chalkline this distance from the wall. Nail a straight board on the wall side of the line to use as a guide.

2 Spread a row of adhesive about two planks wide along the straightedge, using the notched trowel recommended by the manufacturer. The size and spacing of the notches control the amount of adhesive you put down. Make sure you're putting down the proper amount by pulling up a board every now and then; about 80 percent of the glue should stick to the back of the flooring.

3 Put the tongue side of the first plank against the straightedge, keeping the end away from the wall by the width of the expansion gap. Put the end of the next plank snugly against the end of the installed plank and push the two together. Work your way down the straightedge. Cut the last plank to length accounting for the expansion gap on this end when you make the cut.

4 Begin the second row with the cutoff from the first row. (Offset the board from the end of the board in the first row as required by the manufacturer; cut a new board if necessary.) Work your way down the second row, putting the ends of the boards together, then sliding them into the planks of the first row. Cut the last board to fit, leaving the proper expansion gap.

5 Spread adhesive and work your way across the room, one row at a time. Clean off excess glue with the recommended cleaner. Trim the first plank in each row as needed to create the proper offset. Always leave the required expansion gap between the ends of the planks and the wall. If a board won't seat against its neighbor, place a piece of scrap against it and tap it into place with a hammer.

6 Remove the straightedge and install the last rows. Once the adhesive dries, remove the straightedge you nailed to the floor earlier. Spread adhesive in the remaining space, and lay flooring one row at a time. Measure and trim the last row as needed, leaving the proper size expansion gap.

Installing carpeting and carpet pad

Skill level:	Time to complete:	Materials:	Tools:
★★★☆☆	Experienced 8 hrs. Handy 10 hrs. Novice 14 hrs.	Staples, duct tape, tack strips, carpet padding, carpet, seaming tape, binder bar	Tape measure, stapler, carpet knife, straightedge, row cutter, seam iron, knee kicker, power stretcher, hammer, wall trimmer, plastic broad knife, carpet trimmer

Unlike vinyl tile or wood flooring, carpet is stretched across the floor like the head of a drum and held in place around the edges by tack strips. They're made of countless tacks, the points of which stick up through the top of the strip and hold the carpet in place.

You'll use two tools in carpet installation that you won't need in any other home improvement job. A knee kicker is a rod with teeth mounted in a head at one end and a pad mounted on the other. You put the teeth in the carpet and push—don't kick—the pad with your knee to stretch the carpet onto one of the tack strips. The carpet stretcher is a variation of the same tool and is a bit easier on the knee. One end butts against the wall on the side of the room already attached to the tack strip. The other end has teeth that grab the carpet on the other side of the room. By pushing on a lever, you stretch the unattached edge of the carpet over the tack strips. Consider renting these tools rather than buying.

1 Cut the tack strips to fit the perimeter of the room, including the door areas.

2 Position the strips with the points facing the wall. Keep a space equal to the thickness of the carpet between the walls and the strips. Nail the strips to the floor, using concrete nails if installing on a slab.

BUYER'S GUIDE

GET THE RIGHT PADDING

Carpet padding generally is overlooked because it's not visible below the carpeting, but the consequences of installing an inferior pad are definitely noticeable.

Many people try to save some money by installing a bargain pad under expensive carpet. There's no difference in the installation process, and the job will look great—for a while.

After a few months of use and abuse, though, you'll start to notice wear spots, unevenness, and lumps because the inexpensive pad isn't giving the carpet enough support. Avoid this expensive lesson by buying pad of the same quality as the carpet.

BUYER'S GUIDE

INDOOR/OUTDOOR CARPET

Indoor/outdoor carpeting, is now available in many colorful patterns, designs, and textures, which are easy on feet as well as the eyes.

Installation is similar to that of vinyl flooring except that the adhesive is designed specifically for indoor/outdoor applications. To install, follow the directions for installing vinyl sheet flooring on pages 167-169.

3 Lay the carpet padding over the entire floor. Tape the seams together with duct tape, and then staple along them every 10 to 12 inches. Work toward the tack strips, stretching the pad and stapling as you go. Staple the pad against the edge of the tack strip. Run a knife against the strip to trim the pad.

Installing carpeting and carpet pad (continued)

4 Measure the room. Snap chalklines across the back of the carpet to outline a piece 6 inches longer and wider than the room. Fold the carpet over a piece of scrap wood so that the layout lines face up. Put a straightedge along the lines, and guide a knife along it. Change blades frequently.

5 Center the carpet in the room. If there are outside corners, make relief cuts so that the carpet lies flat.

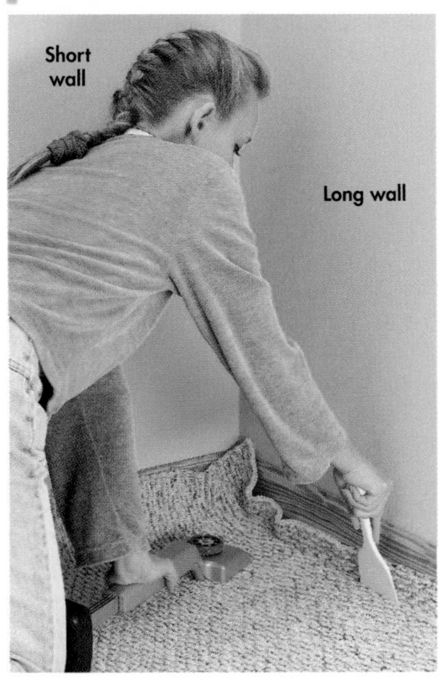

6 Face the long wall near a corner of the room. Put the toothed end of a knee kicker in the carpet about 1 to 3 inches from the wall. Push the padded end with your knee, hooking the back of the carpet over the tack strips in the process. Push down with a plastic broad knife to anchor the carpet. Push, hook, and anchor carpet along about 3 feet of the wall. Repeat on the short wall.

SAFETY ALERT

HERE'S THE KICKER

Be careful using the knee kicker—it can severely hurt you. Hit it with the part of your leg just above the knee and don't be overly aggressive.

7 Trim the carpet as you go. Set a carpet trimmer to the thickness of the carpet and guide it along the wall to trim the edges of the carpet. Tuck the cut edges into the space between the strips and the wall using a plastic broad knife. Trim and tuck every time you hook a length of carpet over the tack strips.

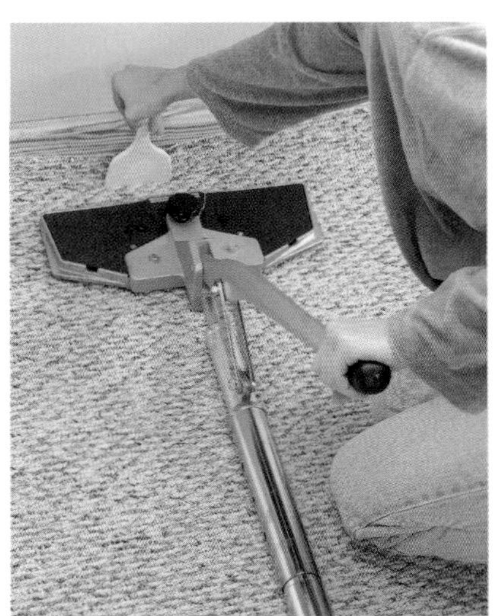

8 Put the foot of the stretcher against the short wall of the starting corner. Run the stretcher at about a 15-degree angle toward the opposite corner, as shown in "Closer Look" on the opposite page. Set the head of the stretcher about 6 inches from the wall. Push on the handle to stretch the carpet. Hook and anchor it to about 3 feet of tack strips along both walls of the corner.

9 With the knee kicker, push the carpet against the long wall between the two installed corners. Anchor with the broad knife. When you're finished, put the foot of the stretcher against the wall, and run it at about a 15-degree angle to the corner, as shown in "Closer Look" below. Stretch the carpet, and anchor about 3 feet along both corner walls.

10 Starting in a corner, use the knee kicker to push the carpet against the short wall, attaching it to the tack strips. Anchor, and then work your way along the short wall, pushing the carpet and attaching it as you go.

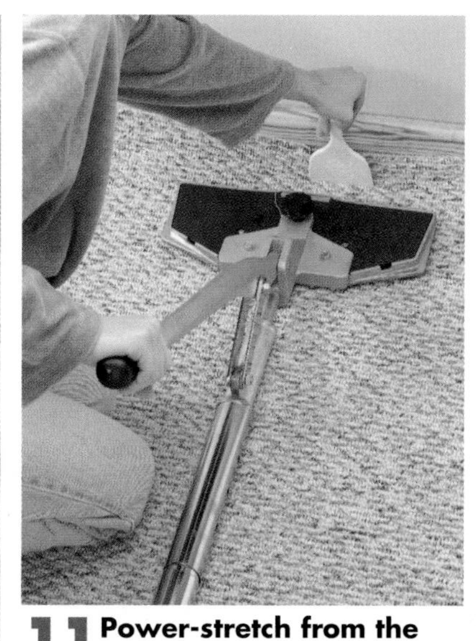

11 Power-stretch from the long wall of the starting corner to the opposite long wall, running the stretcher at about a 15-degree angle. Hook and anchor the carpet over the tack strips near the stretcher head. Move the stretcher along the wall, stretching, hooking, and anchoring the carpet section by section. Power-stretch from the short wall of the starting corner, running the stretcher straight across the room. Attach the carpet to the strips, and then work your way across the wall.

12 Install a binder bar wherever the carpet meets other flooring. Nail it to the floor, and push with the kicker to fit over the hooks in the binder bar. When the carpet's in place, put a block of wood over the bar to protect it, and hammer the flange closed.

CLOSER LOOK

TYPICAL ROOM INSTALLATION

Carpet layers begin by anchoring carpet first in one corner and then in the other corner of a long wall. The rest of the corners are anchored as the job progresses, but the overall picture looks like this: The installer anchors carpet on the long wall, followed by the adjoining short wall. The remaining long wall is next, followed by the remaining short wall.

The exact order of work is shown here. Short arrows indicate where you push the carpet with the knee kicker. Long arrows show the angle and starting point of the power stretcher. Once you've attached the carpet near either the kicker or the stretcher, reposition the tool, and work your way along the wall.

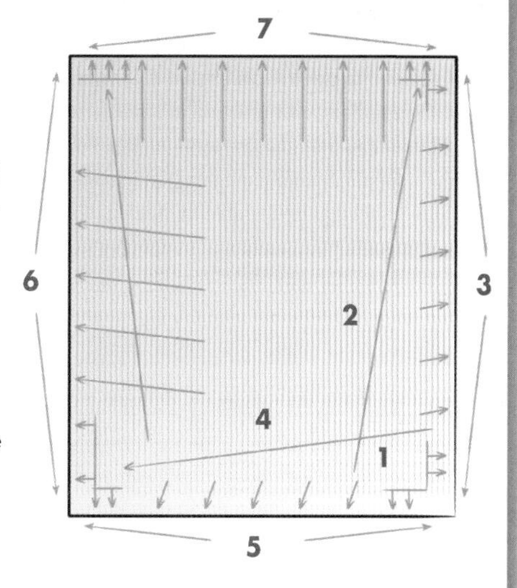

Installing carpeting and carpet pad (continued)

Choosing carpet and padding

You have a wide range of carpet styles, textures, and types to choose from, as well as a selection of pad materials.

Most carpet falls into one of four categories: twist, pattern, loop, and texture. All are available in a variety of grades and colors—including those with multicolored fibers. In general, the better the grade of carpet, the longer the product warrantee, the more durable and stain-resistant the carpet fibers, and the more luxurious the look and feel.

When choosing a carpet, ask to take returnable samples of the carpets you like best home with you before you make your final choice. That way, you can view each carpet option in the room where it will be installed. View the carpet samples in the context of the other decorative elements in the room and at different times of day under varying lighting conditions to determine which you like best.

Just as important as your choice of carpet is your choice of pad. In general, a better quality pad offers a more comfortable surface, longer carpet life, and better sound and energy insulation. In addition, some premium carpet pads have an antimicrobial treatment throughout the entire cushion to combat odors and mold growth, are made of hypoallergenic materials, and have a solid moisture barrier on the top surface of the pad that keeps spills from penetrating into the cushion.

▲ *Match the carpet color to other design elements in the room.*

Carpet cuts

Twist carpet (sometimes called "cut-pile" carpet) is dense and has twisted fibers that offer a firm surface. Some twist carpets, called plush, have longer, less-dense fibers that give the carpet an especially soft, luxurious feel. Both varieties are casual and comfortable, and provide an updated, contemporary look. They're often used in living rooms, dining rooms, and bedrooms.

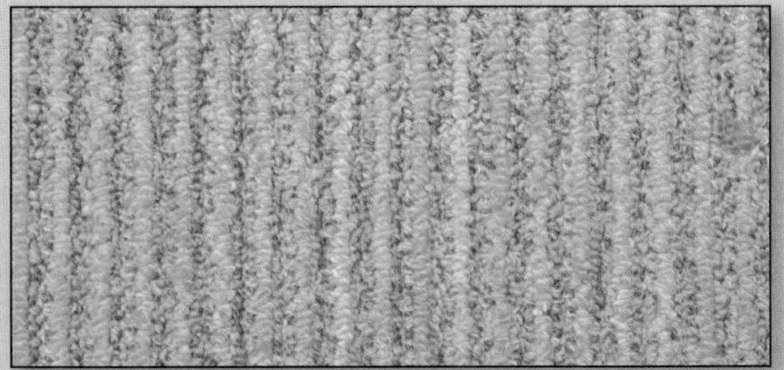

Pattern carpet has both long and short fibers combined to make a subtly patterned, textured design. Pattern carpet adds a bit of drama to a floor, and personalizes a room and sets it off from other spaces in the house.

Loop carpet has a smooth, dense surface that cleans easily and wears well. Its durable, yet resilient, and is great for active areas of you home that see a great deal of traffic or hard use.

Texture carpet is also a great choice for active areas. It has an inviting, casual-yet-traditional look that's both durable and appealing.

Installing baseboard

Skill level: ★★★☆☆

Time to complete:
Experienced Variable
Handy Variable
Novice Variable

Materials: Molding, finishing nails, caulk

Tools: Tape measure, hand or power miter saw, hammer, nail set, coping saw, chop saw, rat-tail file, sliding T-bevel

Installing baseboard requires only two things: a sharp saw and a sharp mind. The joint used to connect two pieces of baseboard is unlike any other joint in woodworking. It's called a cope joint because it's cut with a coping saw; one board is cut to nest into the profile of another.

A simple miter joint for molding work is inadequate. While the joint looks great when installed, changes in the weather cause the wood to expand and contract. Gaps develop and the joint looks sloppy and unfinished.

The cope joint solves this problem. With the two pieces fitting together like jigsaw puzzle pieces, they expand and contract in unison, leaving no gaps.

Installing coped baseboard usually begins on the wall opposite the door. The baseboard runs from wall to wall, with each end cut square. The pieces that meet the first piece are coped to fit it, and then cut square on the other end. On the wall with the door in it, the baseboard is coped in the corner and cut square where it meets the door trim.

Cut the molding a bit longer than the wall it goes against, and then nail it flat to the wall. The extra length ensures a tight joint and holds the molding in place.

If you're putting in a lot of baseboard, consider renting an air compressor and a nail gun that drives finishing nails. They will make the job easier and faster.

◀ *Baseboard molding comes in several basic profiles and varying heights.*

▲ *A cope joint hides wood expansion and contraction by nesting pieces of molding in the corner.*

FLOORS

$ BUYER'S GUIDE
BASEBOARD OPTIONS

Do your research when it comes to buying baseboard. You'll find three broad types to choose from, and making the wrong choice will either cost you money or cause you no end of problems.

- **Stainable baseboard** is the most expensive and best grade. It's allowed to have a few imperfections such as small pitch pockets or checks, for example, but the size and amount of defects are limited. However, most molding is made of pine and it turns blotchy when you apply liquid stains. Use a gel stain for a uniform color—it's also thicker and the wood absorbs it more evenly.

- **Paintable molding** is allowed to have a few more blemishes—the kind a coat of stain will show but a coat of good paint will hide. It can be made of several shorter pieces joined together by finger joints and is less expensive than stainable grade. You can buy preprimed molding, but it's best to prime it anyway. The factory-applied primer will have aged and lost some of its characteristics by the time you purchase the board.

- **Medium Density Fiberboard (MDF)** is a manufactured board made of ground wood fibers glued together. It has no grain; the surface is smooth and, as a result, it takes paint beautifully. It also comes pre-primed but benefits from a coat of primer. Sand with a fine-grit paper to smooth, but less aggressively than you would sand wood, as you can raise more grain than you knock down.

Installing baseboard (continued)

1 Lay out the cut in pencil, using a square to transfer the mark to the top of the molding. Put the molding in the chop saw, positioning it so that the cut will result in a board that is too long.

2 Start the cut but go no deeper than ⅛ inch into the molding. While holding the molding, slide it along the fence until the saw cut just touches the pencil line.

3 Ease the saw into the molding and finish the cut. The slower you lower the saw, the smoother it will cut and the better the joint will be.

4 Begin on the wall opposite the door. Cut a piece ¹⁄₁₆ inch longer than the wall. Put the ends into the corners. The piece will bow away from the wall slightly. Push on it to put it into place. Don't try to force the molding down into any irregular dips in the floor. Any floor irregularities will be hard to see after installation.

5 Nail the baseboard in place. Drive nails through the bottom of the baseboard into the 2×4 plate that runs along the floor inside the wall. Drive nails through the top into the studs. If the wood is difficult to nail, predrill for the nails. Clip the head off a finishing nail, put it in your drill, and use it like a regular bit.

6 Cope the baseboard that meets the board you've just installed. Begin with a piece longer than you'll need. Cut a miter on the end you'll be coping. Trace along the edge of the miter with a pencil to outline the profile.

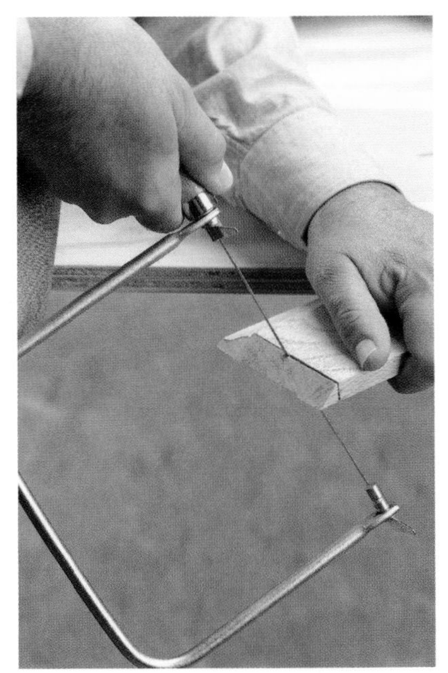

7 Cut along the pencil line with a coping saw. Angle the saw slightly to create a pointed edge that will fit the other side of the joint snugly. For a smooth cut, use the finest blade you can get and let the saw do the work. Trying to push the saw forward will cause it to jam in the wood.

8 Even the pros need to fine-tune a coped joint. Test-fit your joint and make any necessary corrections by filing with a rat-tail file. Fill in any small mistakes with caulk once the molding is in place. If you make a big mistake, cut off the joint and try again. Stain and finish the baseboard before installation.

9 Cut the molding for the remaining walls the same way: Cope, measure, cut, and nail. On the fourth wall—which has the door in it—cope the molding in the corners, and cut butt joints where the molding meets the door trim.

WORK SMART

GETTING A TIGHT FIT

Many carpenters, including the pros, wish there was a tool called a "board stretcher," which would magically add length to a piece that was mistakenly cut too short. Board stretchers don't exist, so experienced carpenters always add about 1⁄16 inch to the overall length of the wall. Cut the molding to this length by making a square cut at the end opposite the coped joint. Spring the molding in place and nail as before. For a neater job some carpenters cut off the tip of the coped piece where it overlaps the top of the mating piece.

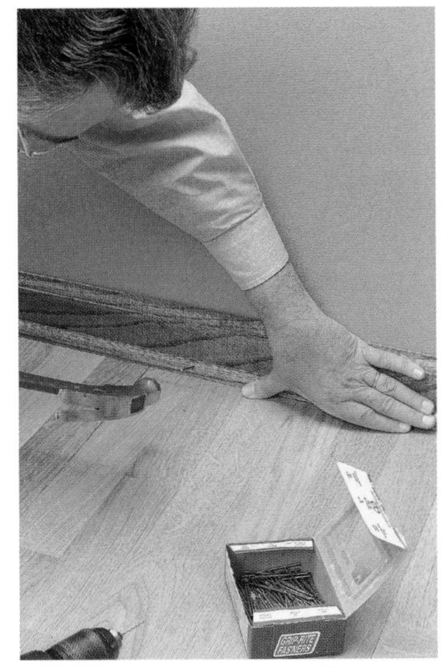

10 Cut quarter round (also called shoe mold) to fit along the baseboard on the wall opposite the door. Like the piece it sits against, it should be 1⁄16 inch longer than the wall, and both ends should be butt joints. Nail the quarter round to the floor so it won't lift up and down with the expansion and contraction of the baseboard.

11 Install the rest of the quarter round, following the pattern of the baseboard. Cope the ends that meet the first wall. Cut butt joints in the end of the molding that meets the wall with the door in it. Cut a butt joint where the molding meets the door trim; cope the other end.

Installing baseboard (continued)

12 Outside corners are mitered. Start by cutting a couple of sample miters to see how the corners meet. A gap means that the corner isn't a true 90 degrees. If the gap is wider at the wall, the corner is greater than 90 degrees; if it is wider at the point of the miter, the corner is less than 90 degrees.

13 Recut the samples to close the gaps. To lay out the cut, draw a line parallel to each wall by putting your framing square against the wall and tracing along it lightly with a pencil. Make sure the lines intersect.

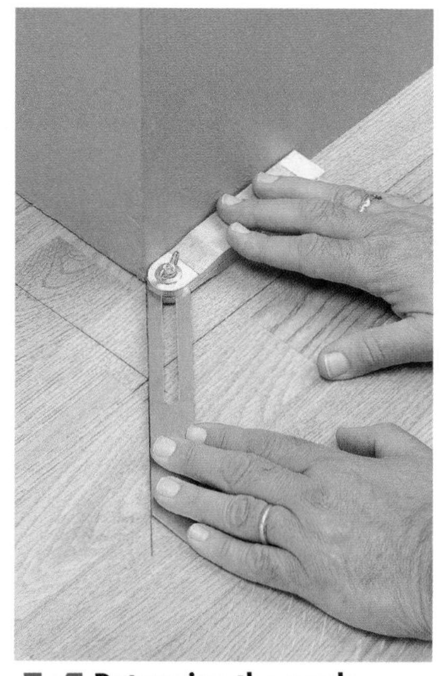

14 Determine the angle of the line with a sliding T-bevel; set the miter saw to this angle. Cut a trial joint, test the fit, and correct as necessary. Make small angle adjustments without moving the saw itself by slipping a playing card or a bit of sawdust between the molding and the fence of the miter saw.

Built-up moldings

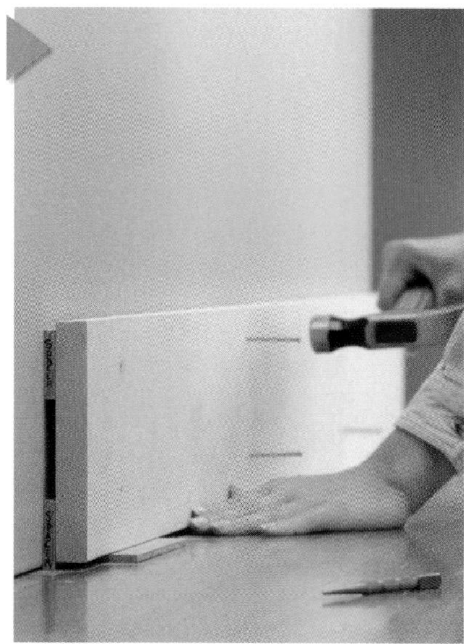

1 Some baseboards are made up of several moldings. A typical example begins by cutting and nailing a 1×4 or a 1×6 to the wall. All the joints are butt joints. Sometimes you'll need to nail thinner strips to the wall first so that the cap molding, installed in the next step, will seat properly.

2 Nail on a cap mold, cutting and coping the joints as you would for regular baseboard.

3 Install quarter-round molding. Cope, miter, and nail it to the wall as you would for any other baseboard. Drilling pilot holes will make nailing more accurate and easier to do. If you're installing a lot of molding, renting an air compressor and a nail gun will save you time and effort.

Thresholds

Skill level:	Time to complete:	Materials:	Tools:
★★★☆☆	Experienced 1 hr. Handy 1.5 hrs. Novice 2 hrs.	Threshold, 8d nails	Hammer, pry bar, handsaw, cat's paw (nail puller), circular saw or chop saw, tape measure, drill, nail set

FLOORS

When a floor meets a doorway, the edge is usually covered by a threshold. It not only provides a graceful edge to the floor, it often serves as a transition to other flooring such as carpet, vinyl, ceramics, or hardwood. An old threshold usually has to be removed to make way for new flooring. New flooring often requires a threshold as a transition to the old flooring in the next room. Home improvement centers stock ready-made thresholds. They're traditionally made of wood, although some are made of material similar to that in solid-surface countertops. Either can be worked with simple woodworking tools.

Removing a threshold

1 If the threshold isn't tucked under the door stop, pry it loose with a hammer and metal pry bar. Use the hammer to drive the pry bar underneath the threshold.

2 If the threshold is tucked under the stop, remove the nails with a cat's paw. Drive the threshold out from under the door stops with a hammer. If that doesn't work, saw the threshold into two pieces and remove them separately.

Installing a new threshold

1 Before installing a new threshold, undercut the door stops. Make the cut by resting a saw on a piece of wood the thickness of the threshold and cutting through the stops, but not into the jambs. Cut the threshold to length with a circular saw or chop saw and slide it under the stops.

2 Thresholds are usually made of hardwood, which can bend the nails you try to drive into them. Drill pilot holes by clipping the head off an 8d nail and using the nail as a drill bit. Once you've drilled the holes, drive and set 8d nails to hold the threshold in place.

Finishing—the *first* step

Just as with baseboard moldings, it's easier and cleaner to finish the threshold piece with paint or stain/varnish before it's installed. This way, you won't have to worry about cleaning up spills or brush strokes on the floor.

You will, though, have to fill the sunken nail holes with wood putty and coat them with finish. But even that's easier if you finish the threshold first because you're better able to match the color. That's how the pros do it.

CHAPTER 4

Doors & Windows

We count on doors to make a good impression and we can accomplish this three ways: Repair and paint or stain; attach new hardware; or replace them. Paint or stain is inexpensive and quick. New hardware offers an old door a new lease on life. Doors that are damaged, warped, or just out of style should be replaced.

If you want a professional-looking job, follow the advice of professional painters and finishers:

- Preparation work is the most important part of painting or staining. Prep may take 80 to 90 percent of the total time for a project.
- Keep your work area clean and free of dust.
- Mask surfaces you don't want to paint or stain. Work in well-ventilated spaces.
- Wear a respirator and rubber gloves as required by the manufacturer of the product you're using.
- Always prime the surface. Primer seals any stains in the surface below it and improves adhesion of the finish coat.
- The door will always reflect what's underneath. Scratches, gouges, and discoloration will show right through the most expensive products. Fill, sand, and seal (prime) before you apply the finish.
- Apply paint or stain generously to get complete, uniform coverage.
- Start with the edges. You can roll extra paint up onto the wider surface and work it into that paint.

Contents

Door basics . . . 206
The door tool kit . . . 207
Locksets and latches . . . 208
Solving door latch problems . . . 209
Freeing a sticking door . . . 210
Installing a door lock . . . 211
Making an opening for a door or window . . . 213
Making headers . . . 215
Installing a prehung interior door . . . 216
Installing split-jamb interior doors . . . 217
Installing molding for interior doors . . . 218
Installing a prehung entry door . . . 220
Installing a storm door . . . 224
Installing a hinged patio door . . . 226
Installing a garage door . . . 231
Adjusting an out-of-balance garage door . . . 234
Installing a garage door opener . . . 235
Maintaining a garage door opener . . . 237
Safety testing a garage door opener . . . 238
Getting to know your windows . . . 239
Window basics and maintenance tips . . . 240
Replacing broken sash cords . . . 241
The windows tool kit . . . 242
Repairing a broken windowpane . . . 243
Replacing a screen . . . 245
Window and glass door security . . . 246
Installing a window . . . 248
Installing a storm window . . . 252

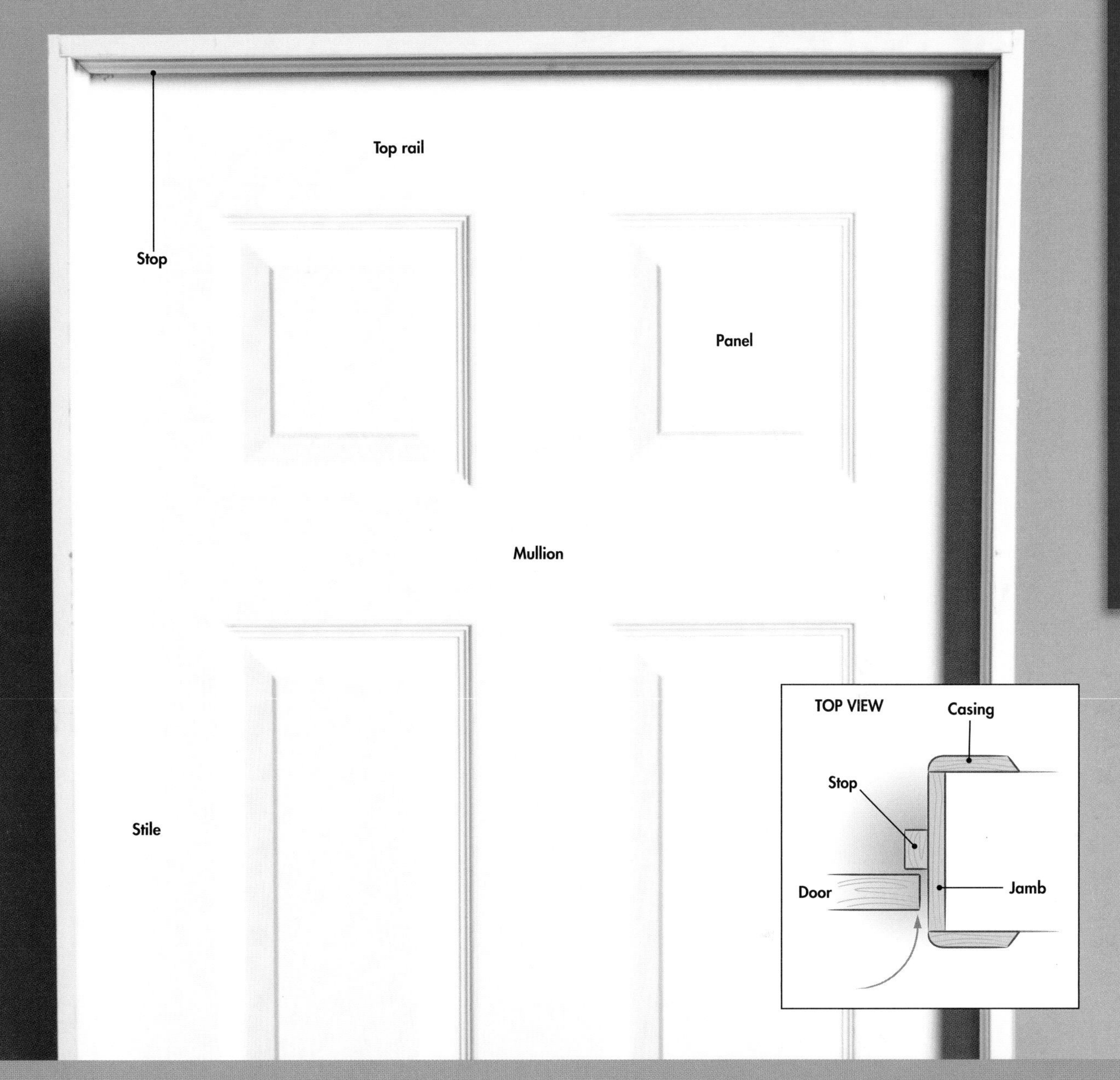

All doors—interior and exterior—have common components, although a flush door hides them under a "skin" of wood or other material. (Interior, hollow-core doors have only a framework covered by thin plywood.) Knowing the parts of a door and how they work—or should work—will go a long way in your repair of an old door or nstallation of a new one.

Stiles are a door's shoulders, the outer vertical framework that helps hold the construction together.

Rails, the horizontal crosspieces, are part of the framework too. There is the top rail, the bottom or kick rail, and the center lock rail.

A mullion is the center vertical piece in the frame of a paneled door that, along with the stiles and rails, holds the panels securely in place.

Panels make up the flesh of a door and can be of solid wood or other material. (A flush door has no visible panels.) Panels can also be made of glass inserts (called lights).

A French glass (glazed) door has both stiles and rails, but the space within them is equally divided by bars called muntins that hold the glass.

Framing is the opening in the wall that surrounds the door. Framing consists of a head jamb at the top, side jambs, a stop on three sides, and a threshold at the bottom.

Casing (or trim) provides weather protection for the framing and adds a finishing touch.

Standard exterior doors are normally 6 feet 8 inches high and vary in width from 18 to 36 inches and thickness from 1½ to 1¾ inches. Interior doors are usually thinner. Of course, custom-made or special-order doors can be taller and wider, and highly insulated entry doors may be 4 inches thick.

If you buy a prehung door, it's already mounted in the jamb, has its hinges, and has either a precut hole for the lockset or even a preinstalled lockset.

Door basics

When the time comes to replace an old door, you'll have a choice between a prehung door and what manufacturers call a "slab" door. A prehung door comes attached to hinges and a doorjamb; a slab comes with nothing. To install a prehung door, you'll take out the existing door and the trim and jamb, then nail the prehung jamb and door in place. Once everything's ready, add some new trim and you're finished.

Prehung doors sound like a bit of work, but then so is most home improvement. The fact is, hanging a slab door is about as fussy as it gets. Given the choice, most carpenters would prefer working with a prehung door, even though they're perfectly capable of hanging a slab. Follow their lead. The detail work has already been done at the factory.

Prehung and slab doors both come in a variety of styles, some of which are shown here.

Common door styles

▲ **Insulated exterior doors** keep out cold the way old-style wooden doors never could. This "oak" door is really a wood composite with foam insulation inside. The glass in both doors is double layered to reduce heat loss.

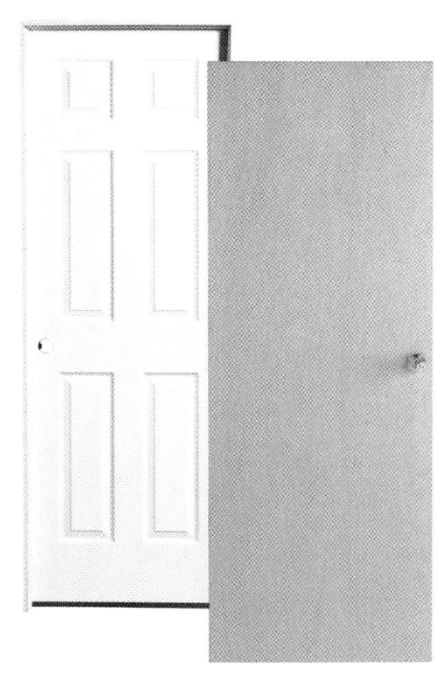

▲ **Interior hollow-core prehung doors** have a contemporary look and are available in many stock sizes. Hollow-core doors are lightweight and inexpensive. Paneled doors are heavier, cost more, and have a traditional look.

▲ **Sliding patio doors** offer good visibility and lighting. Because they slide on tracks and require no floor space for opening, sliding doors are ideal for cramped spaces where swinging doors do not fit.

▲ **Hinged patio or interior doors** have an elegant appearance. Weathertight models are used to join indoor and outdoor living areas, while indoor models are used to link two rooms. Because these doors open on hinges, your room design must allow space for them to swing.

▲ **Decorative storm doors** can improve the security, energy efficiency, and appearance of your entry. A storm door prolongs the life of an expensive entry door by protecting it from the elements.

The door tool kit

Locksets and latches

Locksets and latches fall into three basic types: passage locksets, which may include a lock but which principally serve as a mechanism to hold the door shut; entry locksets, which include a keyed security lock; and security or dead-bolt locks, which offer a more secure barrier to unauthorized entry but do not include a knob or latch mechanism.

While most modern locksets are more or less interchangeable within their basic types, older passage locksets used a mortise that may not accept a new lock. If you can't repair an older lockset, check the fit of a new one, and if necessary, look for a reproduction. If neither works, you may have to replace the whole door.

Backset is the distance from the center of the doorknob spindle to the edge of the door. The backset on some locksets is adjustable. Be sure to buy your replacement with the same backset as the previous unit.

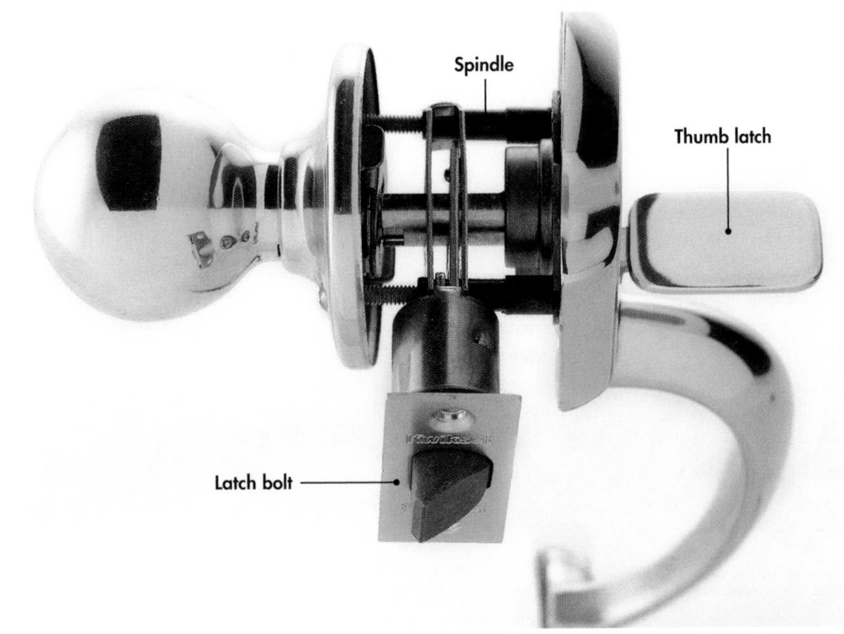

Locksets operate by extending the latch bolt into a strike plate (see opposite page) set in the door frame. The latch bolt is moved back and forth by a spindle or connecting rod operated by a thumb latch, handle, or keyed cylinder. If the doorknob or key binds when turned, the problem usually lies in the spindle and latch bolt mechanism. Cleaning and lubricating the moving parts will correct most problems.

A sliding latch bolt (shown above) allows the door to be pushed shut; it can lock automatically, depending on how you set the lock mechanism. A dead bolt, shown below on the security lock, must always be opened and closed with a key or handle.

Types of locksets

Older passage locksets are easily cleaned and lubricated by loosening the handle setscrew and removing the handles and spindle. Loosen the faceplate screws and pry the lockset from the door. Remove the lockset cover, lubricate the parts, and then reassemble the unit.

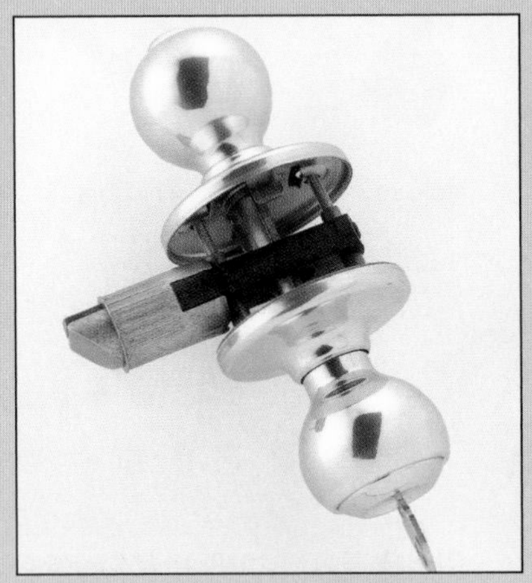

Modern passage locksets usually need little maintenance. If necessary clean and lubricate the lockset by releasing the spring catch and connecting screws, and removing the handles. Remove the faceplate and latch bolt, lubricate the parts, and reassemble.

Security locks, like passage locksets, should be relatively trouble-free. If they need maintenance, remove the connecting screws and cylinders. Remove the faceplate and latch bolt. Lubricate the components and reassemble.

Solving door latch problems

Skill level:	Time to complete:	Materials:	Tools:
★★★☆☆	Experienced 30 min. Handy 45 min. Novice 1 hr.	Penetrating oil, shims	File, combination square, screwdrivers

When a door fails to latch the problem is usually alignment. The latch bolt, for some reason, fails to drop smoothly into the center of the strike plate.

Determine the direction in which the latch bolt is off-center. If it meets the strike plate above or below center, correct the problem by shimming a hinge to change the angle at which the door hangs. The shim may solve the problem but it also may cause the door to bind with the jamb. If the alignment seems fine but the door won't latch or must be pushed firmly to latch, the door is probably warped. A warped door may indicate a moisture problem. Check the edges of the door to make sure they're properly sealed. Suspending the door between two sawhorses and weighting down the center may counteract the warp. As this method of straightening the door will likely be temporary, plan on replacing the door.

▲ *Misalignment with the strike plate will prevent the latch bolt from extending into the strike plate opening. If necessary, you can raise the position of the latch bolt by inserting a thin cardboard shim behind the bottom hinge. Lower it by putting the shim behind the top hinge. If this causes the door to jamb, explore the solutions below.*

Aligning the latch bolt and strike plate

1 Tighten any loose hinge screws and test the door. If the door continues to sag, replace the hinges. If the latch bolt still doesn't catch, fix minor alignment problems by filing the strike plate until the latch bolt fits.

2 Check the door for a square fit. If the size of the gap between the door and frame changes as it moves from top to bottom or side to side, the door is crooked in its opening. Remove the door and shim either the top or bottom hinge with an index card or playing card to correct the problem.

3 If the latch and strike plate are still misaligned, they may have been installed incorrectly. Remove the plate and mark where the latch meets the doorjamb. Move the strike plate to this point, chiseling away wood behind it if necessary. Fill in gaps around the plate with wood filler, and paint or stain to match.

Freeing a sticking door

Skill level:	Time to complete:	Materials:	Tools:
★★★☆☆	Experienced 30 min. Handy 45 min. Novice 1 hr.	Golf tee or dowel, epoxy	Hammer, slot-head screwdriver, utility knife, drill and bits

Doors stick when the hinges sag, when the door frame shifts, or when humidity causes the door to swell.

If the door seems to sag within the frame, make sure the hinge screws are tight. Once you have tightened the hinge screws, if a door continues to stick, sand or plane the door edge at the sticking point. Avoid doing this during a period of high humidity, as you may remove too much of the surface. Wait for dry weather, test to see whether the door is still sticking, then have at it. Varnish or paint the edges of the sanded or planed door to minimize the effects of humidity in the future.

1 If the door sags because one of the screws is loose and won't tighten, drive the lower hinge pin out with a screwdriver and hammer. Hold the door in place and drive out the upper hinge pin. Some hinges have a hole in the bottom. On these hinges, put a nail in the hole and tap on it with a hammer to drive the pin upward.

2 Once you remove the door from its hinges, check to see which screws won't tighten and then remove the hinges completely.

3 Coat wooden golf tees or dowels with epoxy and then drive them into the worn screw holes. Let the epoxy dry completely and cut off the excess wood.

4 Drill pilot holes in the new wood and reattach the hinge plate with the new wood as a base for the screws.

Installing a door lock

Skill level:	Time to complete:	Materials:	Tools:
★★★☆☆	Experienced 30 min. Handy 45 min. Novice 1.5 hrs.	Lock template, security lock	Screwdriver, drill and bits, hole saw, utility knife, wood chisel

If you're installing a new lock on your door, chances are it's a security (or dead-bolt) lock. Entrance door and passage locks are usually already in place. If you do find yourself replacing an entrance or passage lock, it's much like installing a dead bolt. Instead of putting in the key cylinders, however, you'll put in the doorknobs. If you're putting in a new door and lock, get a predrilled door—the hole for the knob and latch are already there. Just screw the lock in place.

When you buy a dead bolt you'll have a few choices. The biggest is how you want to open the door. Single-cylinder locks can be opened from the inside with a thumb latch. Double-cylinder locks require a key from either side.

In most applications, a single cylinder is fine. A key opens it from the outside; a twist of the thumbscrew opens it from the inside. But if you have a door with a window, a double cylinder provides more security. Someone breaking the window will still need a key to get in. However, someone needing to get out—in the case of a fire, for example—will also need a key. Most people solve the problem by leaving the key in the inside cylinder; this helps in the event of fire but won't prevent break-ins.

All door locks have what is called a "setback"—the distance from the edge of the door to the center of the knob or cylinder. The two standard setbacks are 2¾ and 2⅜ inches. If you're drilling the holes yourself, a lock with either setback is fine, and neither has an advantage over the other. If the hole is predrilled, measure the setback and get a lock that matches. If you arrive at the store only to discover you forgot the measurements, good news. Both locks and dead bolts are available with an adjustable setback.

1 Measure to find the lock location. Tape the cardboard template, supplied with the lockset, onto the door. Use a nail or awl to mark the center of the cylinder on the face and the latch bolt on the edge of the door.

2 Bore a hole for the lock cylinder with a hole saw and drill. To avoid splintering the door, drill through one side until the drill bit just starts to come out the other side. Remove the hole saw and then complete the hole from the opposite side of the door.

3 Using a spade bit, drill to bore the latch bolt hole from the edge of the door into the cylinder hole. Keep the drill perpendicular to the door edge while drilling. To keep from boring at an angle, slip a close-fitting metal washer over the bit. If the drill is level, the washer won't walk along the bit.

4 The plate on the bolt mechanism needs to be inset so that it's flush with the edge of the door. Lay out the recess by putting the bolt in its hole. Line up the plate and screw it into the door. Trace around the plate with a utility knife. Remove the plate from the door.

WORK SMART
INSTALL THE LOCKSET FIRST

If hanging a door from scratch, install the lockset while the door is on the sawhorses. That way you won't have a swinging door to contend with while you're drilling holes.

Installing a door lock (continued)

5 Cut the outline of the recess by holding a chisel with the bevel side facing the inside of the recess. Tap the butt end lightly with a mallet or hammer until the cut is as deep as the plate is thick. To help gauge the depth, measure back from the cutting edge of the chisel by the thickness of the plate, and draw a line on the chisel.

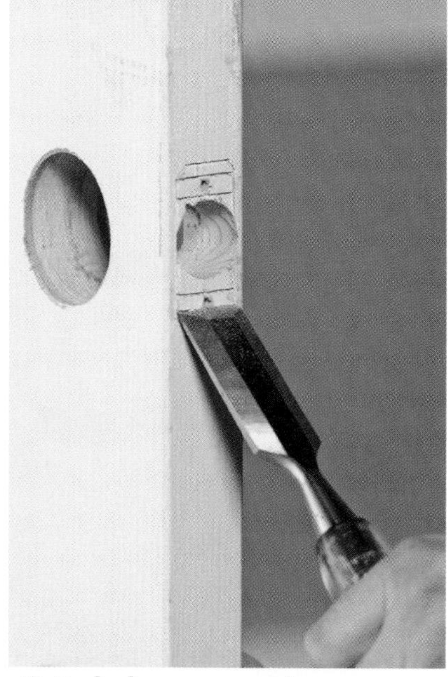

6 To help remove the waste, make a series of parallel depth cuts ¼ inch apart across the recess while holding the chisel at a 45-degree angle. Drive the chisel with light mallet blows to the butt end of the chisel.

7 Cut out the waste chips by holding the chisel at a low angle with the bevel side toward the work surface. Striking the chisel with a mallet will drive the chisel too deep; push the chisel by hand to make the cut.

Door lock parts

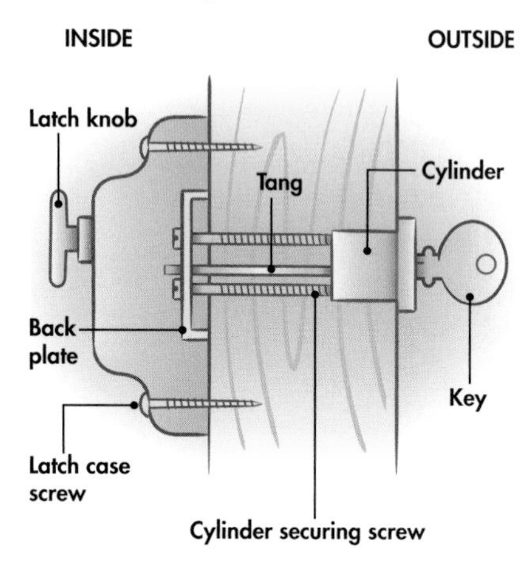

8 Insert the latch bolt in the edge hole. Insert the lock tailpiece (see illustration at left) through the latch bolt mechanism, and test-fit the cylinders. If the tang is too long, snap it at the indentations by bending it with one set of pliers while holding it with a second set.

9 Put the strike plate in place and trace around the hole. Mark the center. Drill the latch bolt hole with a spade bit. Install the strike plate using the retaining screws provided with the lockset. Trace around it with a knife, and cut a recess for it the same way you cut one for the bolt. Screw the plate in place.

Making an opening for a door or window

Skill level:	Time to complete:	Materials:	Tools:
★★★☆☆	Experienced Variable Handy Variable Novice Variable	2×6, ½" plywood for header; 8d nails; 16d nails	Hammer, pry bar, screwdriver, jack posts, short lengths of 2×6, utility knife, circular saw, stud finder, square, level, tape measure, reciprocating saw

The first step in cutting an opening for a door or window is to buy the door or window, then read the directions. What you're looking for is the size of the rough opening—the distance between the pieces of framing that support the door or window. It will be slightly larger than the size of the door or window.

The opening for doors, for example, is usually 2 inches larger than the door size (but follow the directions for your door). This leaves room for two ¾-inch doorjambs, plus ½ inch of wiggle room that you'll fill with shims.

See page 110 for full-size examples of how door and window openings are framed.

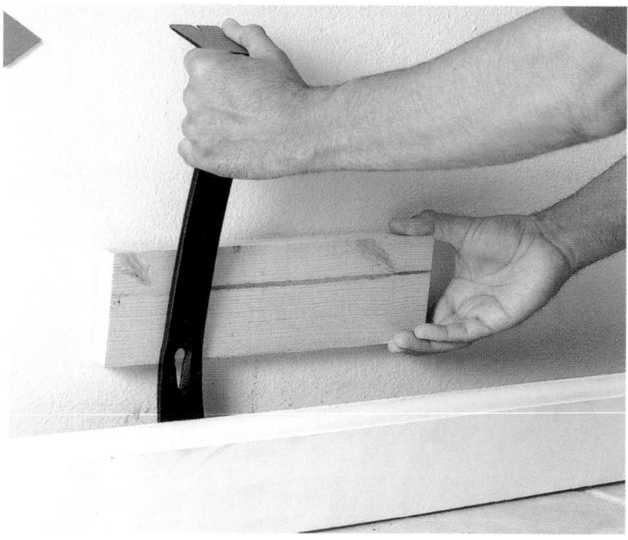

1 Remove the trim with a pry bar and hammer, then protect the floor with drop cloths. Cover interior doorways with plastic to confine dust. Shut off power and water that may run through the wall. Remove electrical cover plates and heating duct covers if they are located in the area to be removed.

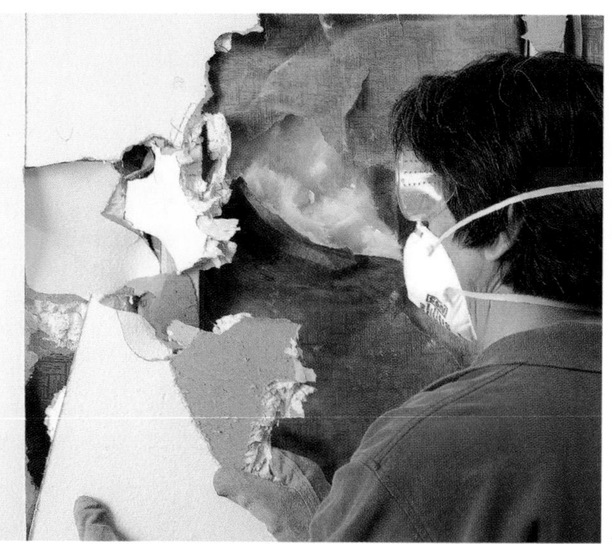

2 Mark the area of the wall you will remove. Put on safety glasses and a dust mask. On drywall, cut along the layout line with a utility knife. On plaster, cut the line with a circular saw, cutting through the lath but not into the studs. Remove the plaster or drywall surface with a hammer and pry bar.

3 All exterior walls are load-bearing, so you will need to provide support for the floor and roof above while you work. Begin by using a stud finder to locate the joists nearest the area you're opening. Brace them with jack posts and a 36-inch 2×6, which is long enough to span the joists. Interior walls that have a double top plate (see inset) are also load-bearing and will need the same support.

4 Remove the studs. (First relocate wires and pipes that are in the way.) Cut them at top and bottom with a reciprocating saw or push the studs from side to side and remove them with a pry bar. If possible reuse some of the material for jack or cripple studs when you frame the opening.

Making an opening for a door or window (continued)

5 Lay out the framing on the soleplate. Start by drawing lines marking the edges of the rough opening. Measure 3 inches outside the opening and draw a line marking the outside edge of the king stud you'll use to help frame the opening. See page 110 for what your finished opening will look like.

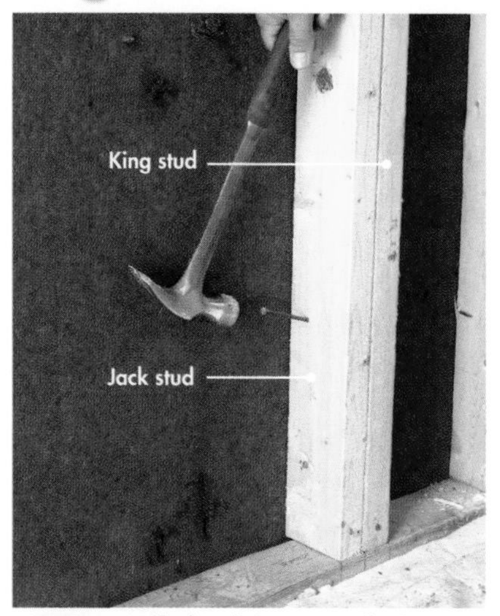

6 Toenail the king studs in place, with four 8d nails at each end. (Face-nail with 16d nails; toenail with 8d.) Then cut a jack stud long enough to reach from the soleplate to the top of the rough opening. Nail it to the king studs you just installed.

7 On non–load-bearing walls, nail a 2x4 header across the top of the trimmers. On load-bearing walls, nail a built-up header in place. (See Making headers on the opposite page) Cut short pieces of 2x4 to fit between the top of the header and the top plate. Nail pieces with 16d nails and toenail them in place with four 8d nails.

8 If framing a door, cut through and remove the soleplate.

If framing a window, mark the bottom of the rough opening on the jack studs. Cut a rough sill to fit snugly between the jack studs, and wedge it in place. Make sure it's level and toenail it in place. Cut cripple studs to fit between the sill and soleplate—one under each end every 16 inches.

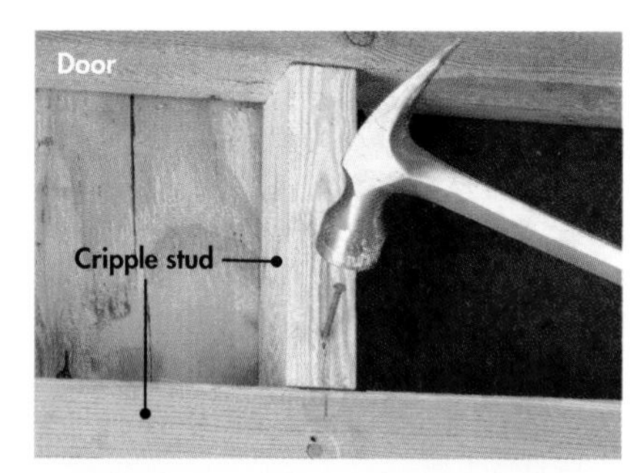

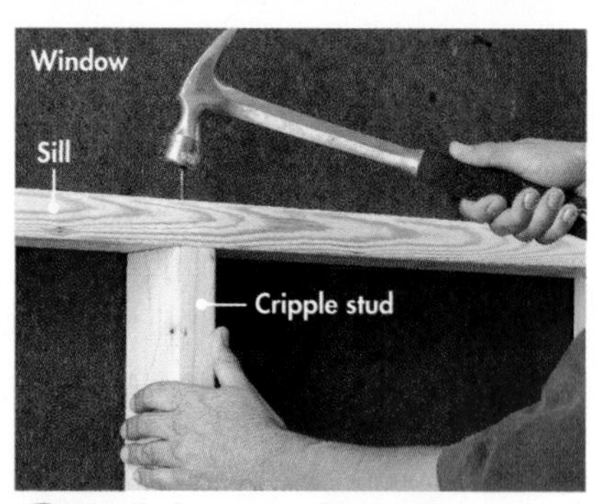

9 Nail the cripple studs in place. A. For doors toenail cripple studs between the header and the top plate every 16 inches. B. For windows install cripple studs every 16 inches between the sill and the soleplate and the header and the top plate.

10 When you're ready to install the door or window, remove the wall section behind it. Start by drilling through the wall at each corner of the rough opening. Put the blade of a reciprocating saw in one of the holes and cut along the trimmer until you reach the next hole. Continue until you've cut out the sheathing.

Making headers

A header is a wooden beam that provides support for the framing above it. It spans a doorway or window in a load-bearing wall—and all outside walls are load-bearing. On a non-load-bearing wall, you won't need a header over the doorway: A single 2×4 laid flat is enough. (Some interior walls are load-bearing; to determine, see page 109, Removing a Wall.)

Headers are built up to be as wide as the surrounding framing. In 2×4 framing, for example, the header is a sandwich of two 2×4s on edge, with ½-inch plywood in the middle. The "real" dimensions of 2×4s are 1½ inches by 3½ inches, so the built-up beam is 3½ inches thick and fits perfectly in place.

If the thickness of the header is determined by the surrounding framing, the width depends on the application. Codes vary, but generally speaking, the solid wood in a header for an opening up to 4 feet long should be 2×4s. From 4 to 6 feet, the lumber should be 2×6s. (Beyond that, you should call a carpenter.)

When you make a header, cut a piece of ½-inch plywood to the same width as the 2×, and then cut all three to length. Make a sandwich, and nail it together with 16d nails at 16-inch (or 24-inch if that is your stud span) centers along the edges.

The section of wall that supports a header is framed a bit differently from the rest of the wall. The header fits between two "king studs," which run floor to ceiling. The header sits on top of two "jack studs," which are nailed to and supported by the king studs. In practice, you'll install both the king and jack studs before you put the header in place. (See page 110 for a diagram of king and jack studs.)

Because codes vary, don't drive a nail until you've talked with your local building inspector. You must get a permit anyway. Ask a few questions and get some advice while you're at the permit office.

Load-bearing wall

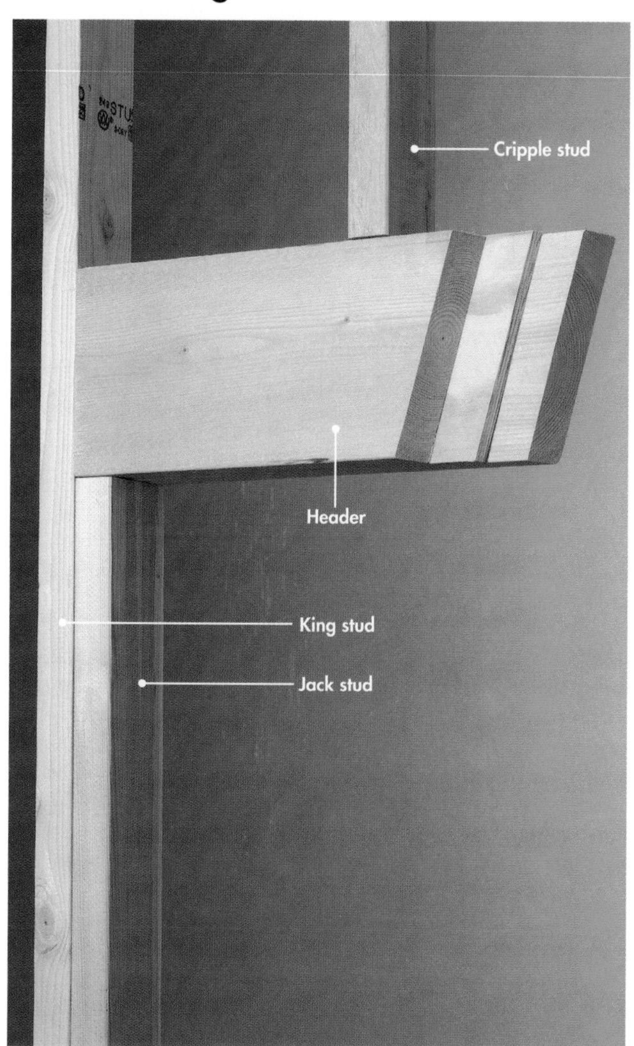

Non-load-bearing wall

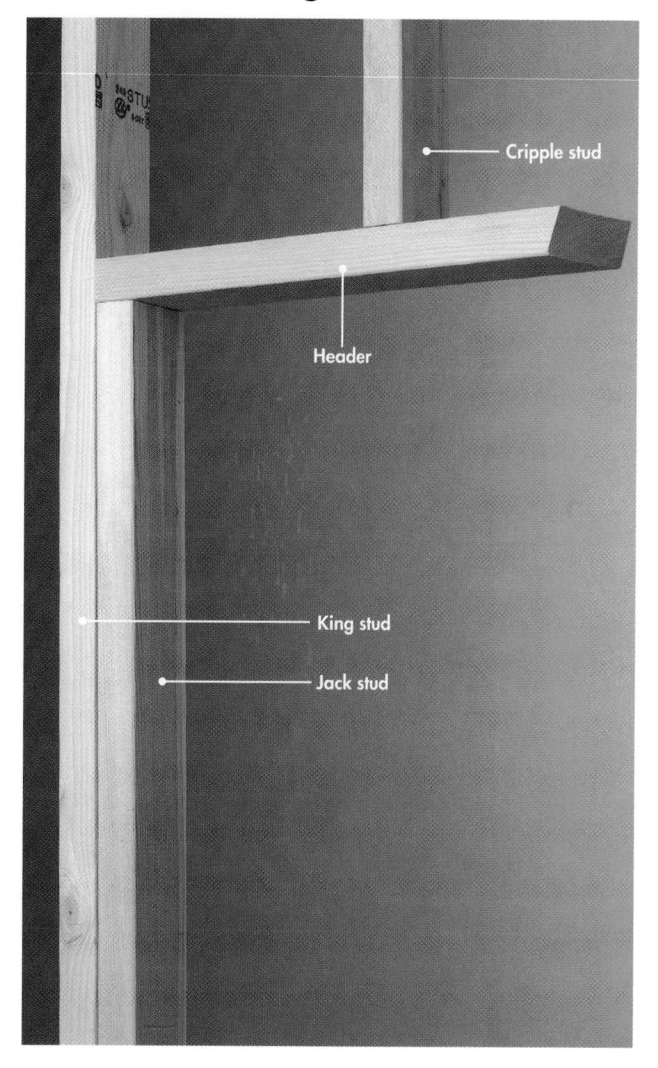

Installing a prehung interior door

Skill level:	Time to complete:	Materials:	Tools:
★★★☆☆	Experienced 45 min. Handy 1 hr. Novice 2.5 hrs.	Prehung door, shims, #6 and #8 finishing nails, 2¼-inch screws	Stiff putty knife, small pry bar, large pry bar or crowbar, level, hammer, nail set

Installing a prehung door is easier and faster than starting from scratch because most of the difficult operations have already been completed. All that's left is to pop off the trim from the existing opening and remove the jambs. This may sound and look like major work, but all it takes is time and muscle. Once the jamb is out, putting in the new door is a matter of shims and a few finishing nails.

1 Remove the existing door. Start by loosening the trim with a stiff putty knife, then use a pry bar and a block of wood to remove the trim without damaging the wall. The head and side jambs are usually nailed together. It's easier to remove them from the opening at the same time. Pry the side jambs away from the studs. Then pry down the head jamb.

Allowing for carpet

If you're installing over carpet, remember to account for its thickness before you hang the door. You may have to trim the bottom (and make sure it is the bottom) in order for the door to swing properly.

Stuff you won't need

Most prehung doors have packing that you should remove before you put up the door. Wrappers and plastic banding are obvious, but you also may find a plastic plug in the lock mortise. (This kept the door from swinging open during shipping.) The strip of wood across the bottom of the opening is there to keep the legs (vertical pieces) from coming loose during shipping. Pull it off before you hang the door.

2 Slide the prehung door unit into the rough opening. Put the door in the opening and slide it until the jamb is flush with the wall. Make sure that the door opens in the desired direction, and into the room you want it to swing into. Remove and reposition, if necessary.

3 Shim the jamb plumb, level, and straight. The door frame is slightly smaller than the opening it fits in to allow for adjustments. Slip shims under the side jamb until the head jamb is level. Then shim between the side jambs and the studs to fill in the spaces between them. On the hinge side, start with the bottom and top of the jamb. Then shim between the hinges and the studs, positioning the shims so that about half the shim is above the hinge. (This will help you later when nailing.) Make sure the jambs are plumb. On the latch side, shim at roughly the same places and at latch level.

4 Nail the door frame to the studs. Drive #8 finishing nails through the frame, through the shims, and into the studs. Drive two nails through each shim about an inch from each edge of the jamb, with one about ½ inch above the other. Before driving the nails home, open and close the door, and make any necessary adjustments. When you're happy with the way it works, drive and set the nails.

5 Nail the trim to the jamb and studs. Drive #6 finishing nails through the trim and into the studs behind the wall, spacing the nails about 16 inches apart. Trim any exposed shims by scoring them with a knife and then breaking along the line. Cut and install trim on the second side of the door.

Installing split-jamb interior doors

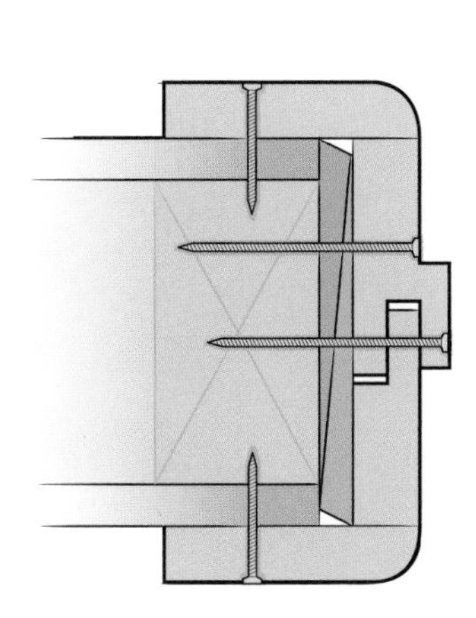

Split-jamb prehung doors work well in situations where the rough frame is wider than a standard opening. They have a two-piece jamb that sandwiches the wall. One added advantage of a split-jamb door is that the casing is already attached, so no mitering is necessary.

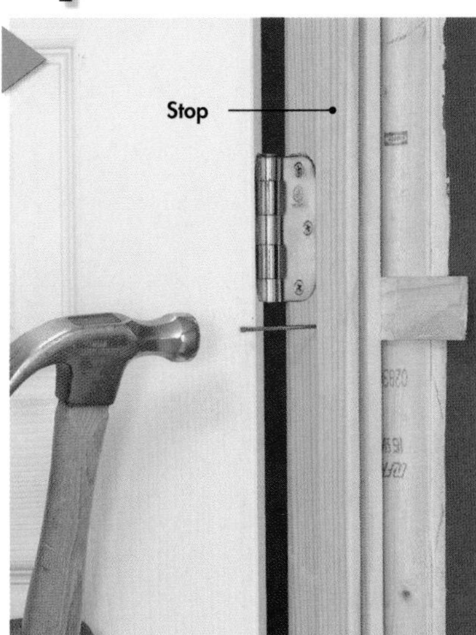

1 Separate the two halves of the jamb. Set the "slip" (or unhinged) side in the room where it will be installed. Put the hinge stop side in the opening. Tack through the casing near the top. Block and shim near the hinges on both jambs and above the jamb. Plumb and square the unit. Nail through the jamb (not the stop) into the frame with 6d finishing nails.

2 Cut the shims flush with the first half of the jamb. Inset the other slip of the door into the first half and gently push it into place until the casing reaches the wall. Use 6d finishing nails to nail through both halves of the jamb directly in the center of the stop. Nail the casing to the wall with 4d finishing nails.

Installing molding for interior doors

Skill level:	Time to complete:	Materials:	Tools:
★★★☆☆	Experienced 30 min. Handy 45 min. Novice 1 hr.	Molding, #6 and #8 finishing nails, glazing putty or wax stick for filling nail holes	Hammer, tape measure, marking pencil, combination square, miter box, nail set

When installing door trim, some carpenters begin with the legs (vertical pieces); others prefer to hang the top trim first. Installing the top first has the advantage of offering precise control over the most finicky part of the installation—the miters. Once the top trim is up, install the legs one at a time, positioning each so that the miter is perfect. If you install the legs first, you'll have to fit the top trim on both miters simultaneously. Unless both miters are perfect and the legs perfectly parallel, you're bound to get gaps you can't close.

Lay out the reveal—a space between the door and trim piece that allows room for the hinge barrel. The door trim is never flush with the edge of the jamb; typically it sits back from the edge by about ⅛ inch. The reveal also provides a margin of error if the jamb dips.

The frame on a prehung door is likely to have a layout line on it that marks the edge of the reveal. If you work on an unmarked door frame, set a combination square to ⅛ inch, and guide it and a pencil along the frame. Mark the reveal on both sides and above the door.

▲ *Getting the trim to fit is the last step in hanging a door. The molding around a door is one of the most visible finish elements in a room.*

1 Measure and miter the top trim. First cut a 45-degree miter on one end of the top trim piece; hold it in place to mark the inside point of the second miter cut. Lay out the cut with a combination square, and cut it with a miter box.

2 Nail the top trim in place. To help position the trim, miter two scrap pieces of molding and clamp them in place along the sides of the door frame. Cut and place the top trim and adjust as necessary to get a tight miter. Nail the top trim into the jamb. (Leave at least ⅛ inch of the nails exposed in case you need to adjust the piece later.) Use #6 finishing nails for the jambs and #8 finishing nails through the trim and into the studs.

3 Miter the legs. Mitering a piece to fit can be tricky. Make it easy on yourself by mitering the legs before you square them off. Then place the legs against the frame so they're upside down. This leaves the miter on the floor and the full length of the trim extending toward the ceiling. Mark where the top trim touches the leg and cut the leg square at the mark.

4 Nail the legs to the door frame. Start at the top, holding the leg so the miter closes tightly, and drive a #6 finishing nail through it and into the jamb. Work down the leg, flexing it if necessary so that it aligns with the line that marks the reveal. When you're satisfied, drive #8 finishing nails into the framing behind the wall. Repeat on the opposite leg, and then set all the nails. To keep the corners tight, predrill and drive a #6 finishing nail at an angle up through the edge of the leg, through the miter, and into the header molding.

WORK SMART

HIDE THE NAIL

Hide nails by driving them into one of the grooves in the molding. After you set the nail, fill the hole with glazing putty if you're going to paint the trim. If you're going to stain the trim, stain and varnish before you put up the molding, as shown. After the trim is up, fill the nail holes with colored wax sticks sold in paint departments. Pick a stick that matches the stain and rub it across the nail hole until it is filled.

TOOL TIP

LIPSTICK MAKES MEASURING EASY

On a door trim, rub lipstick against the point of the miter. When you put the leg against the miter, the lipstick makes a mark where you need to make the cut.

Use the same technique to install drywall. To lay out the hole for a switch or outlet, rub lipstick on the junction box. Put the drywall in place and push gently in the general area of the box. You'll get a bright mark on the back of the drywall, showing the location of the box.

The Victorian approach

Victorian molding took a more decorative—and simpler-to-install—approach toward doors. Plinth blocks were installed at the bottom trim and rosette blocks at the top corners. Molding was then cut square to fit between the blocks.

An advantage of this approach is that you have no miter joints to cut; another is that it adds Victorian style.

Plinth blocks, rosettes, and reversible pilaster trim are available in packaged kits. Install the end blocks first with construction adhesive; then crosscut lengths of trim to fit between blocks.

Installing a prehung entry door

Skill level:	Time to complete:	Materials:	Tools:
★★★☆☆	Experienced 1 hr. Handy 1.5 hrs. Novice 2 hrs.	Drip edge, wood shims, casing nails, silicone caulk	Tin snips, hammer, carpenter's level, pencil, pry bar, circular saw, wood chisel, nail set, caulking gun, handsaw, screwdriver

A new steel entry door—with energy-efficient insulation and weather stripping, easy-to-maintain baked enamel primer coat, and in one of many styles—can greatly enhance the comfort, security, and appearance of your home.

Because replacement steel entry doors are prehung with jambs, brick molding, and hardware (except locksets), installing them need not be difficult. Insulated steel entry doors can be heavy, though, so you may want to line up a helper before you begin.

Entry doors are also made of wood or fiberglass. Talk to your door supplier about the door most appropriate for your situation.

1 Prepare the rough opening, if necessary, and remove the new door and frame from their packing. Leave in place the retaining brackets that hold the door closed while you're working on it. Measure both the door and rough opening to make sure the door is the right size.

2 Test-fit the door and frame, centering them in the rough opening. Use a level to make sure the door is plumb. If necessary, shim under the lower side jamb until the door is plumb. Adjust as necessary to keep the doorjambs square with each other. Double-check to make sure the door is centered.

BUYER'S GUIDE

SELECTING A DOOR

When buying a door, you'll need to specify a left- or right-hand swing as well as an in-swing or out-swing door. To determine which version you need, imagine yourself standing in the doorway with the door opening toward you. In that position, a left-hand door would have the knob on the left and a right-hand door would have the knob on the right.

Another critical factor is the size of the door. If you're replacing an existing door, be sure to purchase a replacement with the same size requirements as the old one. Sidelights are not included in the door size but warrant consideration when determining the rough opening. Make sure of the rough measurements for the opening and check them with the measurements of the door you'll purchase.

TOOL TIP

SQUARE TALK ON LEVELS

Levels are a carpenter's best friend, especially if they're used properly. Here are some tips to keep your projects plumb.

- Always use the longest level that will fit into your work space. Low spots and high spots will be more apparent and you'll get a more accurate reading.
- Use a level that allows you to adjust the vials that hold the bubbles so you can keep the level true.
- Be precise. Make sure the bubble is centered between the lines on the vial when you're taking a reading. A little bit off can become a significant problem over two or three feet.

3 Trace the outline of the brick molding onto the siding. If you have vinyl or metal siding, be sure to enlarge the outline to make room for the extra trim required. Remove the door and frame after finishing the outline.

4 Put on your safety glasses and cut along the outline down to, but not into, the sheathing. Start the cut with the blade clear of the siding, and then lower the moving blade into it. Stop just short of the corners to prevent damaging the siding that will remain. Finish the corners with a sharp wood chisel.

5 To provide a moisture barrier, cut a piece of drip edge to fit the width of the rough opening, then slide it underneath the siding at the top of the opening. Do not nail the drip edge.

6 Check the fit of the door and enlarge the opening as necessary. Remove the door and apply several thick beads of silicone caulk to the bottom of the doorsill. Caulk underneath the spots where the bottom of the jamb and brick molding will be.

7 Center the door unit in the rough opening and push the molding tight against the sheathing.

8 Check that the doorjamb on the hinge side is plumb; shim underneath it as necessary to correct any problems. Temporarily screw the hinge jamb in place by driving two #8 3-inch drywall screws through it: one about 2 inches above the top hinge and the other about 2 inches from the center hinge. Loosen the screws if necessary to bring the jamb back into plumb.

Installing a prehung entry door (continued)

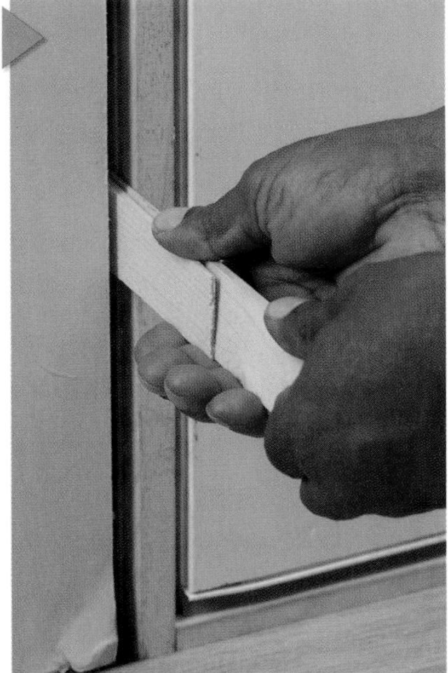

9 Go inside the house through another door and place pairs of wedge-shape cedar shims together to form flat shims. Insert them into the gaps behind the hinges and between the jamb and framing to stabilize the jamb. Cedar shims are preferable to pine because they are more weather-resistant.

10 Remove the retaining brackets installed by the manufacturer; open and close the door to make sure it works properly.

11 Remove two of the screws on the top hinge and replace them with long anchor screws (usually included with the unit). These anchor screws will penetrate the framing members to strengthen the installation. DO NOT use longer screws than the manufacturer calls for on doors with sidelights—the screws might break the glass.

12 Anchor the brick molding to the framing members with 10d galvanized casing nails driven every 12 inches. Use a nail set to drive the nailheads below the surface of the wood.

13 If your door has an adjustable threshold, adjust it for a tight seal as directed by the manufacturer.

Note: If you make the threshold too high, it will make the door difficult to open and eventually could damage either the door or the weatherstripping.

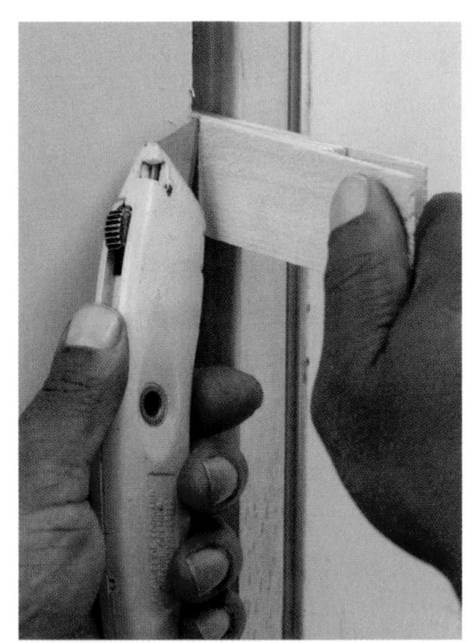

14 Cut the shims flush with the framing using a utility knife.

15 Apply paintable silicone caulk around the entire door unit. Fill all nail holes with caulk. Finish the door as directed by the manufacturer.

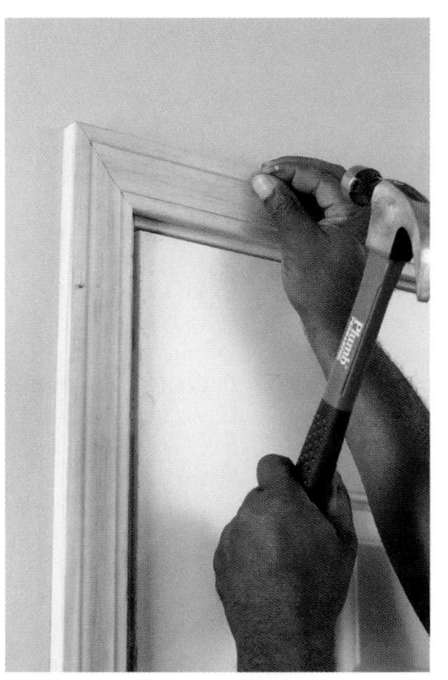

16 Replace the casing on the inside of the doorjamb. If the trim was damaged during removal, cut and install new casing.

17 Install a new door lock. Insert the latch through the hole provided in the door. Then insert the lockset tailpieces through the latch bolt, and screw the handles together by tightening the retaining screws.

18 Screw the strike plate to the doorjamb and adjust the plate position to fit the latch bolt. Avoid damage to the screw heads by using a hand screwdriver.

CLOSER LOOK

SIDELIGHTS

Some doorways have windows, called sidelights, immediately to one or both sides of the opening.

If you have sidelights, you can leave them in place as we did here, as long as they aren't part of a prefabricated frame. If you'd like to install sidelights where there aren't any, get a prefabricated door with attached sidelights. You'll have to enlarge the rough opening to make room for the sidelights, so look before you leap. Make sure you want to—and can—do the carpentry. Take a look at page 213, Making an opening for a door or window, to see what's involved. Start framing when you have the new door on site.

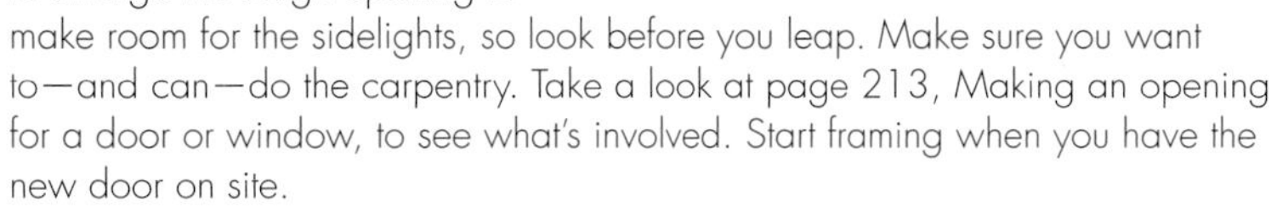

Installing a storm door

Skill level:	Time to complete:	Materials:	Tools:
★★★☆☆	Experienced 30 min. Handy 45 min. Novice 1 hr.	Storm door unit, wood spacer strips, casing nails	Hacksaw, hammer, level, tape measure, masking tape, marker, drill and bits, screwdrivers

A storm door, as simple as it is, provides many benefits to your home. It can add years to the outward finish and surface of your entry door, it helps to insulate and weatherproof your entry door, it provides additional security, and it improves the appearance of your house, all at the same time.

When you buy your storm door, look for a model that has a solid inner core, low-maintenance finish, and a seamless outer shell. You can find a storm door to complement just about any house style. Look closely at your current door, however. If it juts out beyond the trim by even the slightest amount, you'll have a bit of extra carpentry to do. Take off the trim and replace it with a new layer of wood thick enough so that the door no longer juts out. Nail the trim to the new layer of wood.

Storm door frames allow for a small degree of accommodation to your existing door opening, but it is important to measure the opening carefully. Find the dimensions from the inside edges of the entry door's brick molding. Subtract approximately ¼ inch from the width of the opening to arrive at a suitable storm door size. Any difference in opening size can easily be adjusted and compensated for when you install the storm door frame.

Most storm doors are made so that you can install the door with the hinge on either the left or right side. Some manufacturers require you to choose either a left- or right-handed door when you order. When you install your storm door, install it so the hinge is on the same side as for the entry door. It makes getting through the door a lot easier—especially if you have groceries in your arms.

Storm doors, because of the large amount of glass combined with weather stripping, can cause sunlight to produce considerable heat buildup in the space between the storm door and the entry door. In the winter, this additional heat can be beneficial. But not all storm doors have screens, and the summer heat buildup from a glass storm door can actually damage the plastic trim on entry doors. As a result, some manufacturers recommend avoiding certain types of storm doors. Check with the maker of your entry door to verify it is compatible with the storm door you have in mind. Ask the salesperson for advice when you buy your new storm door.

1 Installation varies slightly from one manufacturer to another. Some brands require installing the drip cap (the top part of the storm door frame) first; others install the cap later. Install the drip cap now if indicated by the directions that came with your door. If not, follow the manufacturer's directions.

2 Find the frame piece, called a Z-channel because it remotely resembles a "Z," that's marked for the hinges. Most doors are made so you can hang them with the hinges on either the left or right, using the same channel. Put the channel against the opening on the hinge side, and mark the top with tape.

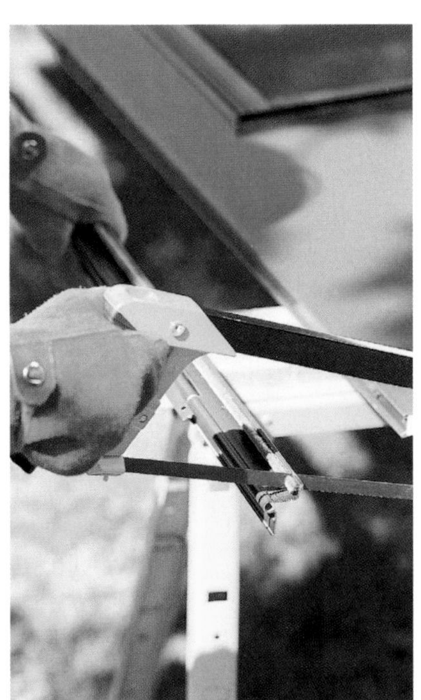

3 Subtract ⅛ inch from the distance between the doorsill and the top of the opening. Draw a cutoff line this distance from the top of the Z-channel. If the sill slants, follow the manufacturer's directions. Cut along the line with a hacksaw.

4 Position the channel against the hinge side of the door so that it extends about 1/8 inch above the top of the door. (This ensures that when closing, the top of the door will clear the drip cap.) Screw the Z-channel to the door hinges, which usually come installed on the door.

5 Set the door in the doorway with the Z-channel tight against the top. Use a level to make sure the channel is plumb. Have a helper drive a couple of screws to hold the channel; check to make sure that the door opens and closes freely. Adjust if necessary, and install the remaining screws.

6 Install the drip cap. Position it so there's an even 1/8-inch gap between the drip cap and the top of the door. If the door seats against the weather stripping and closes without hitting the drip cap, drive the remaining screws. If not, make the necessary adjustments before driving the screws.

7 Cut the latch-side Z-channel as in Step 3. Put it in the opening, tight against the drip cap. Adjust it so there's a gap between the channel and the door's edge; the amount varies between brands. Screw it in place. For a gap of more than 1/4 inch, the directions may require you to cut a filler strip to close it.

8 Attach the sweep to the bottom of the door. A sweep is either a wide strip or a U-channel with weatherstripping across the bottom. Read the directions carefully: Some installations require that you attach the strip before you hang the door. Position the sweep so its weather stripping touches the sill; screw it in place.

9 Mount the door handle following the manufacturer's directions. Depending on the model, the holes may be predrilled, or you may have to drill them yourself. Mount a hydraulic door closer on the door. Most are adjustable so that you can control how quickly the door closes. Follow the manufacturer's directions to make any adjustments.

Installing a hinged patio door

Skill level:	Time to complete:	Materials:	Tools:
★★★★★	Experienced 4 hrs. Handy 6 hrs. Novice 8 hrs.	Door assembly, drip edge, caulk, shims, 2-inch galvanized finishing nails, 10d casing nails, fiberglass insulation	Screwdriver, 4-foot level, circular saw, chisel, caulking gun, utility knife, gloves, dust mask, safety glasses, ear protection

Patio doors dramatically incorporate an outdoor deck or patio into your living space, creating an easy flow of traffic into and out of your house. If you're installing a door in a new location, the first step is to cut and frame a rough opening in the wall. (See Making an Opening for a Door or Window, page 213.) If you're replacing just a door, start with Step 1 below.

Installation tips:

- To simplify installation, buy a patio door already mounted in preassembled frames. Install the patio door so that it is level and plumb, and anchor the unit securely to the framing to prevent the possibility of bowing and warping.
- Yearly caulking and touch-up painting will help prevent moisture from warping the jambs.
- Remove the doors if you're installing the frame without help. Reinstall the doors after you have placed the frame in the rough opening and nailed at opposite corners. Adjust the bottom rollers on a sliding door after the installation is complete.
- To detached a hinged door, remove the hinge pins. On sliding doors, remove the stop rail found on the top jamb of the door unit.

1 Remove the old doors. Lift the doors out of their tracks and set them aside. Remove all framing down to the rough opening. If installing a door in a new location, remove the necessary interior wall surfaces, then frame the rough opening for the patio door. Finally, remove the exterior surfaces inside the framed opening. For more information, see page 213.

2 Test-fit the new door unit. Center the unit in the rough opening. Check to make sure that the door is plumb. If necessary, shim under the threshold to level the door. Have a helper hold the door in place while it is unattached.

BUYER'S GUIDE
RETROFIT DOORS

If you're replacing a patio door, you can also get what's called a retrofit door. You won't need to take the wood back to the rough opening to install a retrofit door. Just take out the old door and attach the hinges of the new one to the jambs. If you're considering a retrofit door, check with the store to see what measurements they'll need to order your replacement.

Keep it simple

If you are installing a door in an existing opening, see whether you can find a new door that will fit without having to reframe the rough opening. It'll save you time and money.

3 Trace the outline of the brick molding or nailing fin onto the siding. Remove the door unit.

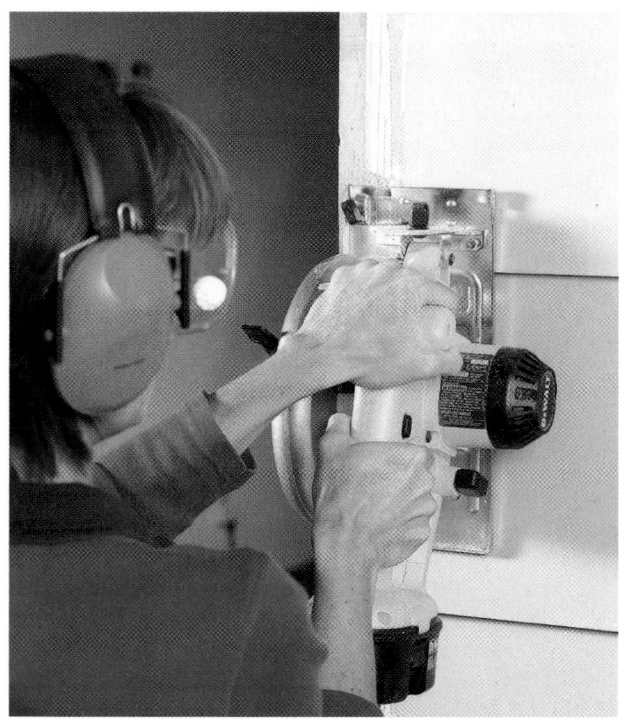

4 Cut the siding. Wear ear protection and safety glasses. Using a circular saw, cut the siding along the outline, just down to the sheathing. Stop just short of the corners to prevent damage to the siding that will remain. Finish the cuts at the corners with a sharp wood chisel. Be careful of kickback and of wiring inside the wall.

5 Check the opening for square. Measure diagonally from inside corner to inside corner. If the measurements on both diagonals are equal, the frame is square. If the diagonals differ by more than ¼ inch, the door will be too far out of alignment. Shim at the sides, directly under a jamb, to correct the problem.

6 Cut a drip edge. For extra protection from rain, cut a piece of drip edge to fit the width of the rough opening, and then slide it between the siding and the existing building paper at the top of the opening. Do not nail the drip edge.

7 Check the floor or subfloor. In some cases, removing an old door also removes part of the floor or subfloor. If so cut a piece of pressure-treated wood the same thickness as the interior floor to fit the opening. Put it in place and check to see whether it's level. If necessary level the surface with shims every 4 inches.

Installing a hinged patio door (continued)

8 Install the shims. Put the shims in place and apply two or three beads of caulk.

9 Nail the patch in place with galvanized roofing nails.

10 Caulk the threshold. Once you've prepared the subfloor, get ready to install the door. Apply beads of caulk along what will be the edges of the door threshold. Underneath on the threshold or deck, apply a bead of caulk positioned so that it will seal the end grain of the jambs and brick mold.

11 Caulk the fins. Some doors have metal fins that you nail through to hold the door against the house. Others have a piece of molding known as "brick mold" that extends beyond the door frame; nail the brick mold to the house. Caulk the back of the fins or molding before positioning. You'll nail them in Step 14.

12 Lift the door into place. Remove any packaging from the door and place it carefully in the opening so you don't accidentally smear the caulk onto an exposed part of the floor.

13 Check for square. Double-check the diagonals to make sure the door has remained square. If the diagonals differ by more than 1/8 inch, shim as necessary to bring the door back into square.

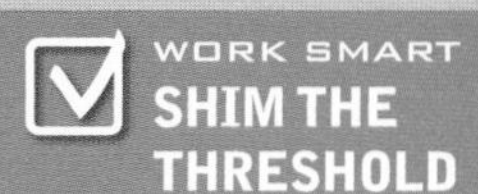

WORK SMART

SHIM THE THRESHOLD

Metal thresholds need a solid surface under them. Gaps or an out-of-level floor will cause the threshold to bend when you step on it. Many manufacturers specify that you support the bottom of the threshold with a solid surface that runs the entire length of the threshold. If you need to shim under such a threshold, you can still use individual shims as long as you don't leave spaces between them. Once you've installed the threshold, start any necessary shimming at one end. Install the first shims on each side of the threshold. Install the next two shims snugly against them. Work your way to the center, checking the threshold with a level as you go.

14 Nail the fins or brick mold to the sheathing near the top corners of the door. Use 2-inch galvanized roofing nails.

15 Shim the sides of the door. Drive the shims just far enough to make them snug. Double the shims, if necessary, or trim a few inches off the thin end in order to have a shim thick enough to do the job. Shim behind each hinge and behind the latch strike as well. Do not shim around the top of the door.

Installing a hinged patio door (continued)

16 Nail the door in place and trim the shims. Double-check for square and level, and make any necessary corrections. Then drive 2-inch galvanized finishing nails into the doorjamb, through the shims, and into the frame. Trim the shims by scoring them with a knife and then snapping off the excess.

17 Insulate around the door. To reduce drafts, use a shim to stuff scraps of fiberglass insulation into the voids around the frame. Wear safety glasses, gloves, and a dust mask when working with insulation. Wash work clothes separately from general laundry.

18 Attach the exterior molding. If your door is surrounded by brick mold, drive 10d casing nails through it every 12 inches, attaching the molding and door to the house. If your door has a nailing fin, drive the nails specified by the manufacturer through the holes in the fin; cover it with molding.

19 Caulk the sill. Caulk completely around the sill nosing and the brick mold or metal trim. Press the caulk into cracks with a damp finger or with an inexpensive caulking tool. As soon as the caulk is dry, paint the sill nosing. Finish the door and install the lockset as directed by the manufacturer.

Installing a garage door

Skill level:	Time to complete:	Materials:	Tools:
★★★☆☆	Experienced 5 hrs. Handy 8 hrs. Novice 12 hrs.	Garage door assembly, shims, rear track hangers, nails	Sawhorses, hammer, level, utility knife, drill, two wrenches, tape measure, locking pliers or C-clamps

Garage doors are made of wood, metal, or fiberglass. They can be highly decorative or plain. Whatever the style, they all depend on a good set of springs to make them work. The springs provide the lift that opens the door as well as the resistance that keeps it from crashing down on your head.

If the door has extension springs, like the door shown in the illustration bottom right, getting the proper tension on the springs is simple and safe for the homeowner. If the door has torsion springs, which are essentially huge window-shade rollers, leave the job to a pro. These springs need to be wound up, and losing control of them can be dangerous. (Fortunately most doors for residential use are on extension springs, and any style you do find on torsion springs is likely to be available with extension springs.)

Installation of garage doors varies both from brand to brand and situation to situation. The instructions here are typical, but pay close attention to the directions that come with your door. It's the largest moving part of your home, and safe installation requires attention to detail.

1 Put the door panels on a pair of sawhorses to make working on them easier. Slip the weather stripping into its channel, screw it in place if so directed, and trim off the excess with a knife.

SAFETY ALERT

TORSION SPRINGS ARE DANGEROUS

On some garage doors a tightly wound spring called a torsion spring runs over the top of the door and helps open and close it by counterbalancing the weight. These springs are always under tension and are extremely powerful. An unplanned release of the tension can cause serious injury if you don't know how to remove the spring safely. Instead of attempting to remove one yourself, get a garage door professional to do the removal or installation.

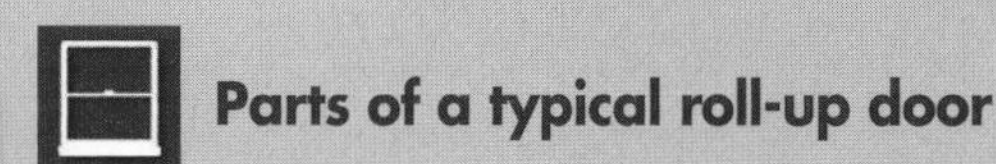

Parts of a typical roll-up door

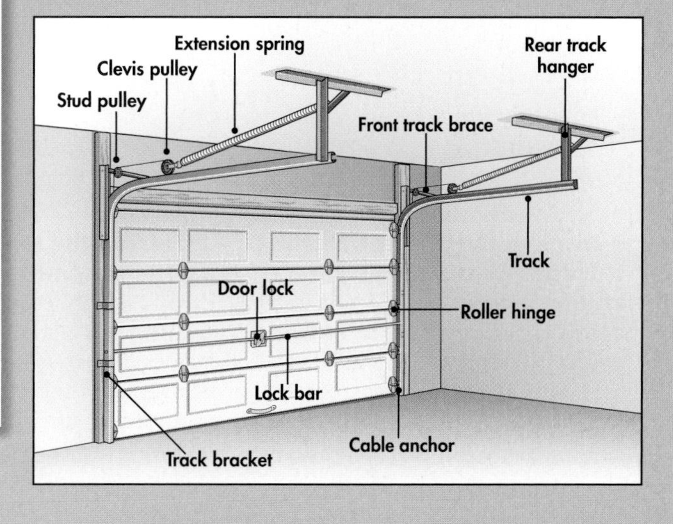

Installing a garage door (continued)

2 Set the first panel in the opening. Check for level and shim as necessary. Hold it in place by driving nails into the door framing at an angle so that the upper portion of the nail traps the door. Do not drive nails through the door.

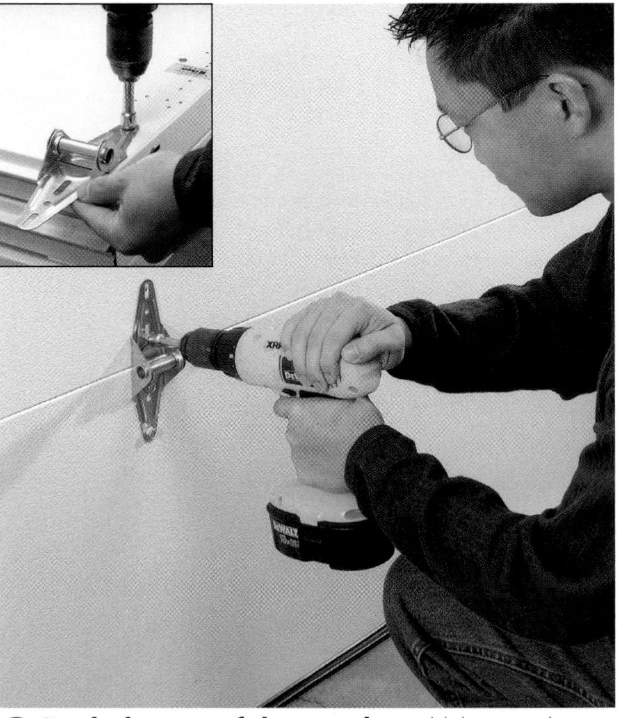

3 Stack the rest of the panels. Hold them in place with bent-over nails. Attach one side of the hinges along the edges and middle of the door before you stack them. (See inset.) Attach the top rollers to the top edges of the panel.

4 Insert roller shafts into the hinges as directed by the manufacturer. If any are held in place by special brackets, install them now too. If a separate bracket holds the rope you use to close the door, install it now.

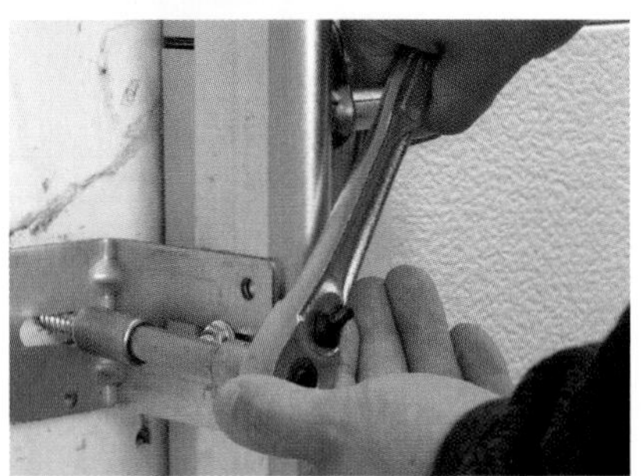

5 Install the tracks around the assembled door. Begin by slipping the straight tracks over the lower wheels in the door. Put the mounting brackets against the wood framing, positioning them to leave a ⅝- to ⅞-inch space between the door and track. Temporarily bolt the brackets in place. (You will need to adjust them later.)

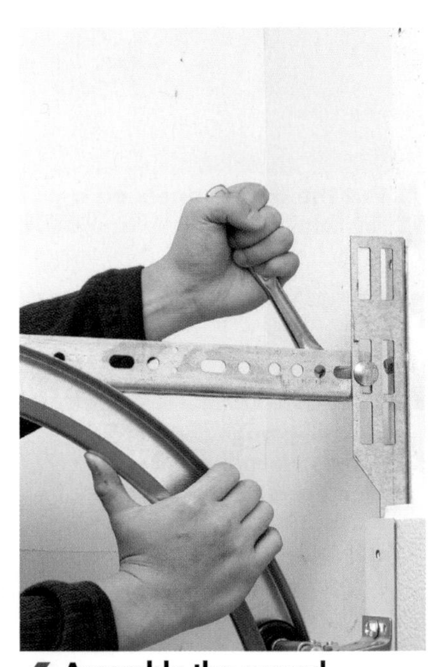

6 Assemble the curved, J-shape tracks next. Each side has a track that bolts to two angle irons, which are joined at 90 degrees. Assemble the pieces on the floor, then slip them over the door rollers. Temporarily support the back end with a ladder or board if necessary. Position the track so it's level and plumb, shimming from the ladder as necessary.

7 Install the rear track hangers. (You'll need to purchase these separately.) The track hangers must support the full weight of the door, so they must be attached securely to a rafter or joist. Measure the distance between the back end of the J-shape tracks and the nearest rafter. If necessary, cut the track hangers to length as directed by the manufacturer and attach them to the joist or rafter.

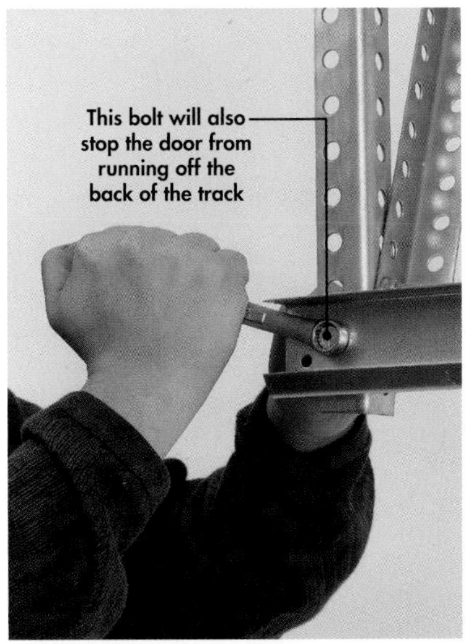

8 Attach the track to the hanger. The rear track hangers hold the track level and square to the door. Check by comparing two diagonal measurements: one from the top left-hand corner of the door to the rear right-hand horizontal track and the other from the right front to the left rear. Adjust the tracks until the measurements are within ½ inch; temporarily fasten the hangers.

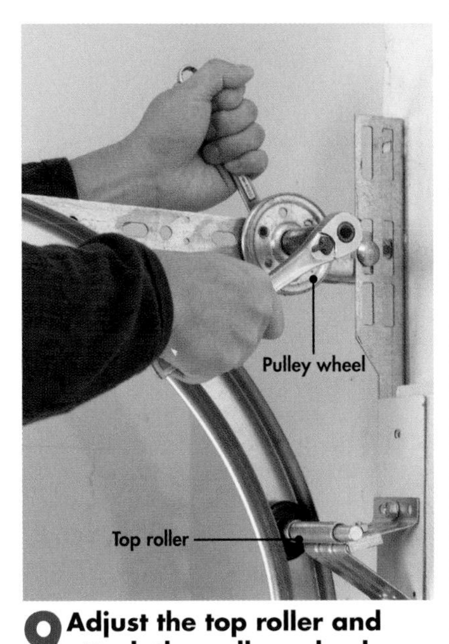

9 Adjust the top roller and attach the pulley wheel. Some doors will have a top roller that adjusts to keep the door tight against the jamb. Attach the front pulley wheels to the horizontal angles as directed by the manufacturer. Now you are ready to roll up the door for the first time. Remove the nails before you raise the door.

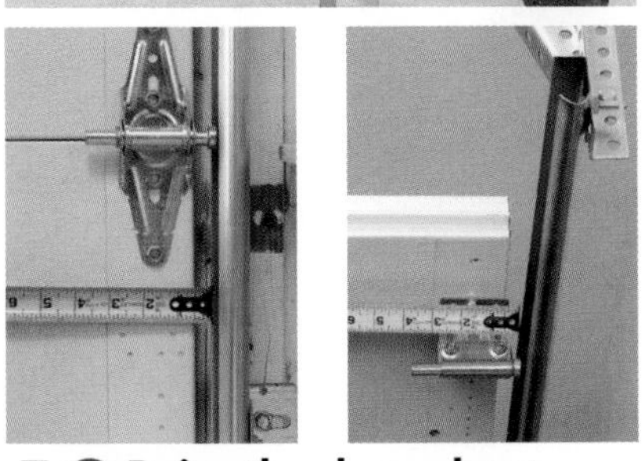

10 Raise the door about 4 feet, prop it open, and look to see whether the spacing between the door and track is between ⅝ inch and ⅞ inch along the entire track. If not, lower the door and correct the problem by repositioning the track hanger on the joist. Once the tracks are aligned and the door opens smoothly top to bottom, permanently fasten the tracks and hangers.

1 Lock pliers to track

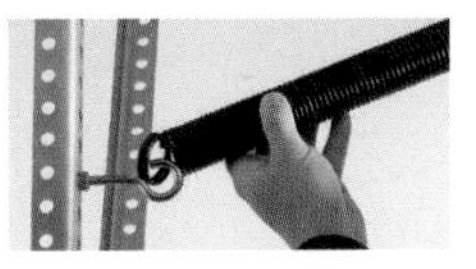
2 Attach spring

3 Attach S-hook

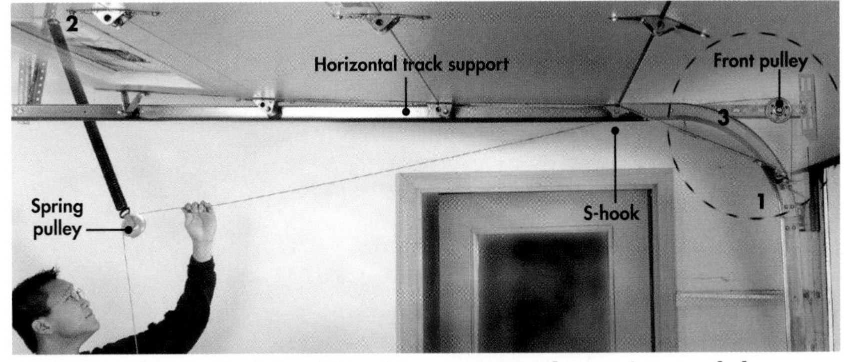

11 A cable called the lift cable connects the spring and doors. Carefully raise the door to the fully open position. **1** Attach locking pliers or C-clamps to the track to keep the door in place. **2** Attach the spring to a hook installed in the rear hanging bracket, then attach one end of the cable to the bottom of the door, as directed by the manufacturer. Thread the cable around the **front pulley** and around the **spring pulley**, and attach the end to an **S-hook**, using the hardware provided. **3** Attach the S-hook to the **horizontal track support**, leaving the same amount of slack in each cable, as directed by the manufacturer.

Release the door and test it to make sure it closes gently on the floor. If it comes down with a crash, increase the spring tension, either by moving the S-hook forward on the horizontal track support or by adjusting the cable where it attaches to the S-hook. If the door won't close all the way, decrease the spring tension.

Adjusting an out-of-balance garage door

With time, the cables and springs on a garage door stretch, and the door can become dangerously out-of-balance. The usual problem is a door that closes too quickly—endangering your feet, your children, or anything else in its path. The door can also open too quickly, which can damage the door or your shoulder. A properly balanced door remains stationary when it's opened 3 to 4 feet. When you open or close it, the door should come to a gentle stop. If it slams down, or closes and then reopens slightly, you'll need to adjust the spring tension.

Springs can cause injury if released suddenly. Prop the door open to relieve tension on the springs before you attempt to remove them.

1 Begin with the door about 3 feet above the ground. Move it up and down until you find the point where the door remains stationary when you release it. If that point is more than 4 feet or less than 3 feet above the ground, you need to balance the door.

2 Make all adjustments with the door open. This takes the pressure off the door springs. Prop the door open with a ladder to make sure the door won't close accidentally while you're working on it. If your ladder isn't tall enough, attach locking pliers or C-clamps in the door track to hold the door in place.

3 Make sure the spring is compressed completely, then remove it from the track hanger. If the door was closing too quickly, move the spring to the next higher hole on the bracket. If it was opening too quickly, move it to the next lower hole. Move both springs and retest the balance.

4 Close the door and check with a level to make sure the door comes down evenly on both sides. If it doesn't, adjust the spring tension on each side of the door until it does.

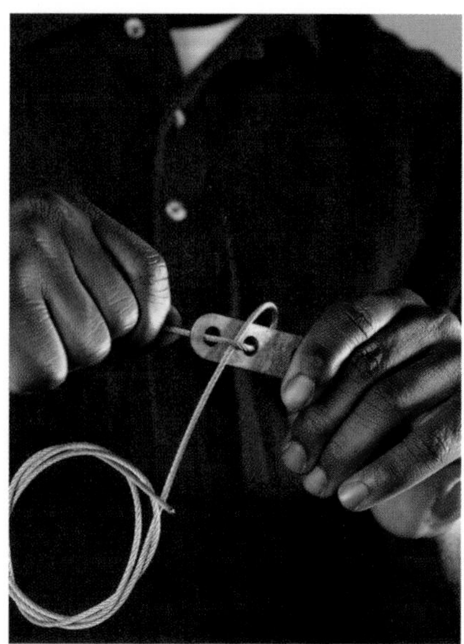

5 If you need to make fine adjustments, you can adjust the lifting cable instead of the spring. The cable is attached to the door and runs to an S-hook that attaches to the track support. With the door propped open, take the S-hook out of the support and tighten or loosen the cable as needed.

Installing a garage door opener

Skill level:	Time to complete:	Materials:	Tools:
★★★☆☆	Experienced 6 hrs. Handy 8 hrs. Novice 10 hrs.	Garage door opener kit	Tape mesure, level, screwdriver, drill, socket or wrench set

Almost any garage door opener you buy will open any garage door in America. The chain drive opener is the best-selling design on the market. A motor pulls a chain, the chain pulls a carriage, and the carriage pulls a cable that opens the door.

The direct drive opener (shown here) works basically the same way except that the carriage travels along a large, threaded rod (like a huge bolt) instead of the door being pulled by a chain. Direct drive openers are slightly more expensive but quieter. They work best in warmer climates and tend to bog down in freezing climates.

Garage-door opener components include:
The **power unit** is activated by a transmitter, key, or auxiliary switch.
The **rail guides** support the **traveler,** which connects the door-opener chain to the **support arm**, which is attached to the garage door. The manual **safety release** disengages the trolley from the garage-door arm and allows manual operation of the door in event of power failure. The **header bracket** secures the rail above the door and supports the idler assembly and pulley that guide the chain drive.
The **interior auxiliary switch** allows garage-door opener operation from inside the garage.

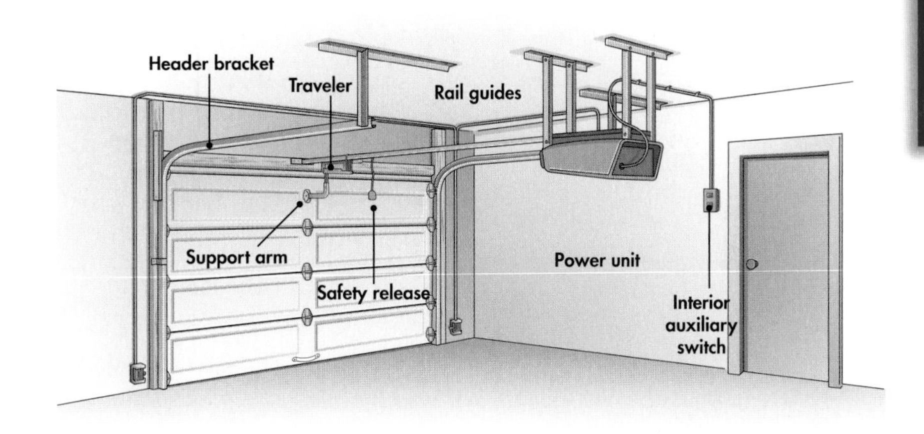

$ BUYER'S GUIDE
AN OPEN-AND-SHUT CASE

You can buy garage door openers with ¼-, ⅓-, or ½-horsepower motors; openers with chain drives; and openers with screw drives. They all open the door, and they're all viable options. Look for features you want, such as a rolling code (see "Buyer's Guide," page 237) or a keypad. But what you really care about is the warranty period. Given the choice between two doors, get the one with the longest warranty. A good manufacturer will stand behind a good product. Choose wisely.

1 Assemble the carriage tube. This tube runs from the power unit to the front wall of the garage. The carriage, which raises and lowers the door, travels along it. It's usually shipped in sections—assemble them as directed, making sure to seat the pieces securely. Measure to verify the assembled length matches the length required by the manufacturer. Make any necessary adjustments.

2 Mount the carriage on the front of the power unit, following the manufacturer's directions. Attach the rail clamps, which will later connect to a bracket on the wall above the door. On some doors you'll install switches and wiring at this point.

Installing a garage door opener (continued)

3 Slip the carriage over the tube. Different makes and models attach differently, so follow the manufacturer's directions.

4 Mount the header bracket, which holds the carriage tube to the wall above the door. The exact location depends on the type of door, so follow the directions supplied by the manufacturer. Lift the power unit and set it on top of a stepladder.

5 Hang the power unit from the ceiling. Most units hang from angle irons and metal straps that have holes drilled in them at regular intervals. Bolt the angle irons to a rafter (or rafters) with lag screws. Attach the straps to the irons with hex-head screws, and attach the straps to the power unit with the hardware provided. Open the door several times to make sure it doesn't hit the opener while moving.

Need to add an outlet?

A garage door opener power unit usually requires a grounded electrical outlet within three feet. If you don't have one within that distance, you'll have to add an end-of-run outlet from the nearest receptacle box or subpanel. According to most wiring codes, the wires to the new outlet must be housed in metal conduit if they're exposed. If you're new to wiring, call a licensed electrician to do the work.

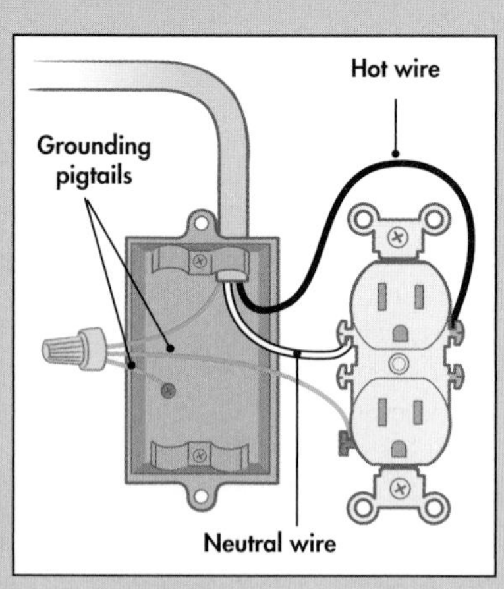

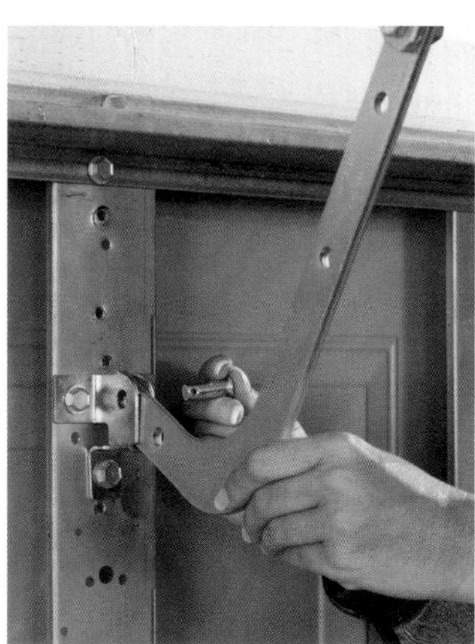

6 The door is opened by one arm that lifts it as the carriage travels along the tube. Before you can attach the arm, you must attach the bracket that connects it to the door. The exact location varies, depending on the door. Follow the manufacturer's instructions.

7 By law, all units have a safety device that shuts down the motor if something is in the path of a closing door. The safety device is usually a light beam and sensor. Mount one on each side of the door as directed. Plug the unit into its socket. Test the operation and make any necessary corrections. (See Safety Testing a Garage Door Opener, page 238.)

Maintaining a garage door opener

Adjust the chain tension to eliminate a sagging chain. If the chain sags more than ½ inch below the rail, it may bang against the rail and cause undue wear on the drive sprocket. Tighten the chain until it rests ½ inch above the base of the rail, but be careful not to overtighten.

Adjust the limit screws if the garage door opens more than 5 feet but fails to open completely. Unplug the opener and locate the open-force adjustment screw on the power unit. Turn the screw clockwise. Plug in the opener, run it through a cycle, and adjust as necessary to open the desired amount.

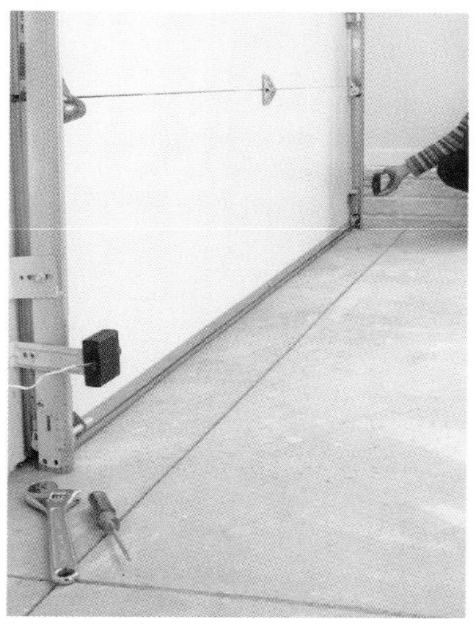

Check the alignment of the safety reversing sensors as recommended by the manufacturer and adjust as necessary to maintain proper operation. The sensors must face each other across the garage door opening in order to function properly.

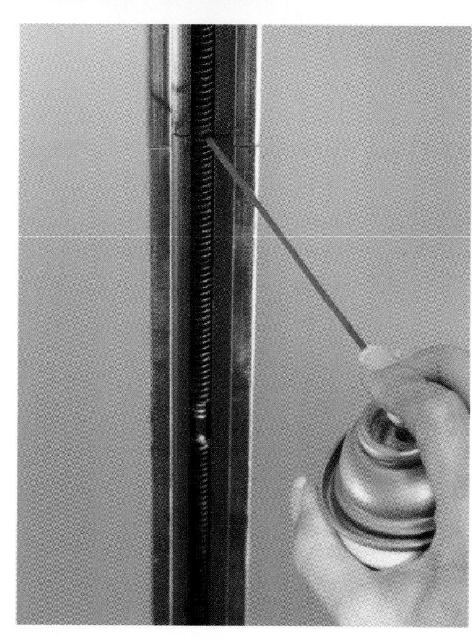

Lubricate the drive chain and track of the automatic door opener. Instead of grease, use a light penetrating oil which doesn't collect dirt and grit.

Always disconnect power to the garage door opener prior to making adjustments.

BUYER'S GUIDE

CHANGING FREQUENCIES

When you push the button on the opener's remote control, it transmits a frequency-coded message to the door. Send the right message and the door opens. Send the wrong one and the door stays put. Some remotes transmit the same message each time. Others transmit a randomly changing message, or "rolling code," making it harder for someone else's remote to open your door.

How much harder? Depending on the maker, a single-code opener may be preset to one of as many as 3.6 million codes. By listening in with a special decoder, however, a clever thief can record your code, reprogram an opener, and drive right into your garage.

A more secure option is a rolling-code opener, which may have as many as 16 billion codes to choose from, and the code changes randomly each time the door opens. A rolling code is virtually impossible to crack, and if you're at all worried about security, it's a feature you'll want in a new opener. If you have an existing single-code opener, ask about kits that will convert it to rolling code.

If you have a car with a built-in garage door remote control, it will probably work with a rolling-code door. Follow the directions for programming it carefully—you may have to press the button several times before the reprogramming takes effect.

Safety testing a garage door opener

Periodically test the close-force sensitivity setting of the garage door opener. Place a board 1 inch or thicker on the garage floor in the center of the doorway, then trigger the opener to close the door. When the door comes in contact with the board, the opener should strain slightly, then reverse and open the door. If the pressure is too great or too slight, you'll need to make adjustments.

Adjust the close-force sensitivity if the opener is either auto-reversing too easily or striking an obstacle too hard. Unplug the power unit and adjust the close-force screw according to which solution is required.

Test the close-force sensitivity by hand after you have used the board method mentioned above. This will allow you to physically determine the amount of pressure the opener is exerting in case the door comes in contact with people or pets. Stand in the center of the doorway and trigger the opener to close the door. As the door is closing, hold the bottom of the door in your hands and exert pressure to stop the door. Determine if the pressure to trigger the auto-reversing is too much or too little and make the necessary adjustments on the close-force sensitivity screws.

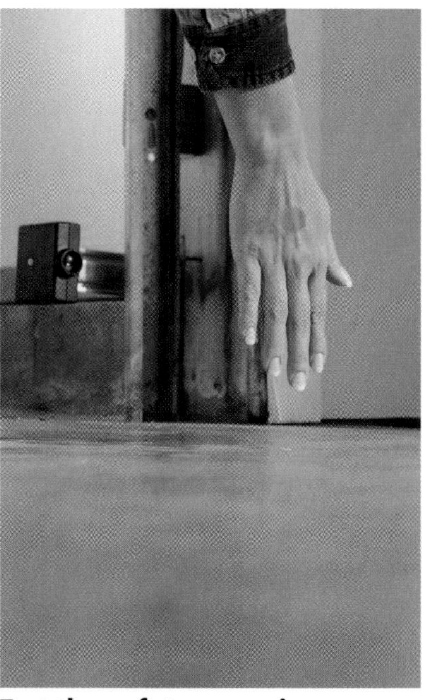

Test the safety reversing sensors by placing your hand in the sensor beam as the garage door is closing. The garage door mechanism should automatically reverse and open the door. If it doesn't, check the wire connections. Check the sensor alignment and clean the sensor lenses. Retest.

Getting to know your windows

When you deal with window installations or make repairs, it helps to be able to speak window to the retailer or installer. Knowing the parts will save you time and energy when you're in the store. The word "sash," as for the garment of the same name, has gone largely out of style. Most people would call the sash the window, or perhaps the window frame. But window installers need to be precise. Sash survives, as do several other words that the do-it-yourselfer should know.

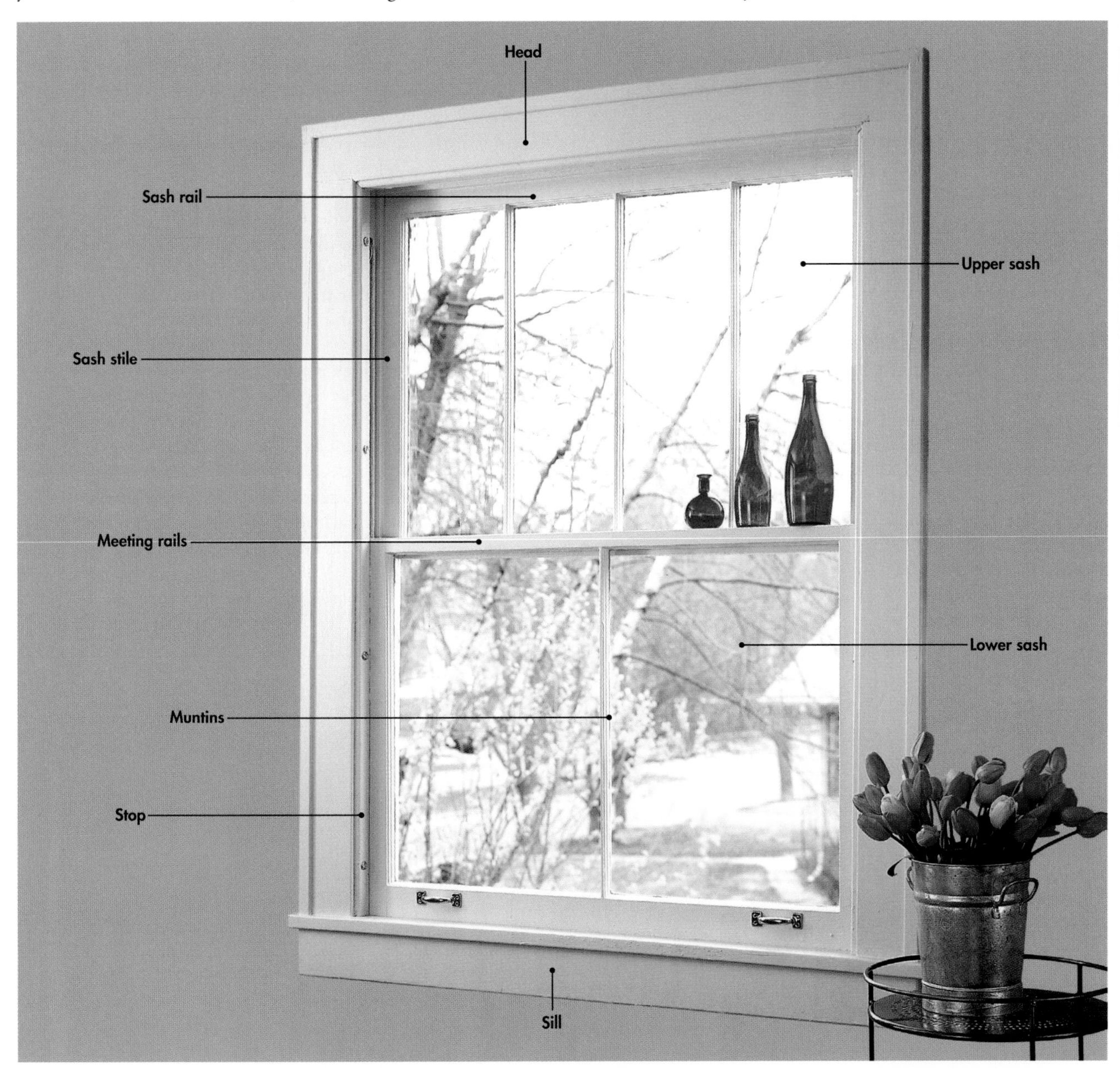

Head: The piece of wood, metal, or plastic at the top of the window frame.

Sash rail: The horizontal pieces of the frame that form the sash. If you have trouble distinguishing rails and stiles, think of a porch rail. Both rails are horizontal.

Sash stile: The vertical pieces of the frame that form the sash.

Upper sash: The upper window frame on a double-hung window.

Lower sash: The lower window frame.

Meeting rails: The rails that overlap each other in the middle of the window. Rather than describing them as the lower rail of the upper sash and the upper rail of the lower sash, both are called meeting rails.

Muntins: The dividers that form a grid in the window.

Stop: The piece of wood, metal, or plastic on the side of the window against which the windows slide up and down.

Sill: The piece of wood, metal, or plastic at the bottom of the window frame, usually slanted on the outside so that rain will run off.

Window basics

Choosing windows used to be a matter of deciding on double-hung, fixed, or casement windows. Now you're faced with U-factors (heat loss), SHGC (solar heat gain coefficient), VT (visible transmittance), argon, and krypton.

When buying windows, consider the following:

- **Without any bells and whistles,** the insulating value of a double-glazed window is about one-third greater than that of a single-glazed window.
- **A low-E coating is a microscopic layer of metal on the inside face of the glass** that reduces heat transmission. Because this coating also reflects incoming light and the resulting solar heat, manufacturers have developed low-E coatings for high, low, or moderate solar gain.
- **Sealing a gas between the layers reduces heat flow even more.** Argon is efficient and inexpensive. Krypton is a better insulator, but more expensive.
- **Frames can be made of wood, hardboard, aluminum, or vinyl.** Wood is strong and light but needs maintenance, as does hardboard. Aluminum is an ineffective insulator, but frames with added foam core board work well. Vinyl is maintenance-free and somewhat of an insulator.

Follow the energy star.

So now what? Look for an Energy Star sticker, which lists government performance standards for each of three climate zones: Northern, where heating is a primary energy concern; Central, where heating and cooling are both concerns; and Southern, where cooling is the major concern.

Energy Star labels rate windows for efficiency. Ratings are based on the following:

- **U-factor is the rate of heat loss.** The lower the U-factor, the better a window insulates.
- **SHGC stands for solar heat gain coefficient.** It's rated on a scale of 0 to 1 and the lower the number, the less solar heat the window transmits. People living at the equator would prefer a lower number.
- **VT stands for visible transmission**—the amount of light that gets through—and is rated on a scale of 0 to 1. The higher the number, the more light you'll have.
- **AL stands for air leakage, a measure of how much air slips past the weather stripping.** The lower the leakage, the better the window, but manufacturers say leakage is not as important a concern as U-factor or SHGC.

Once you understand the standards, look at the **Energy Performance** section of the label. Compare the factors you consider important with what the manufacturer says the window does.

Window maintenance tips

Freeing a stuck window

If a window is painted shut, you can often break the paint film by putting a block of wood against both the sash and the stop. Strike the block with a hammer in the direction of the stop to free the window.

If a hammer and block of wood won't break the paint film, cut the film with a tool known variously as a sash saw, window opener, or paint zipper. Put the teeth into the crack between the window stop and sash, and slide it along the sash to cut the paint.

Adjusting springs

Newer aluminum or vinyl windows have spiral counterbalances to keep them from crashing down when open. You can adjust the spring tension by turning screws in the track insert. Adjust until the window travels easily but won't slip down when put in place.

Cleaning and lubricating

Clean the tracks on windows and doors with a hand vacuum and a toothbrush to keep them operating smoothly. Dirt buildup is particularly a problem on storm window tracks. Aluminum and vinyl tracks can be washed with soap and water.

Once the window track is clean, coat it with wax or soap. Wax, being waterproof, will last longer. For windows with metal edges that run on metal tracks, you'll find a choice of lubricants: penetrating oils, silicone sprays, and powdered graphite. Vinyl-clad windows may be damaged by cleaners containing solvents; test them on a hidden part of the window first.

Clean weather stripping by spraying it with a household cleaner and wiping away the dirt. Soap will wash paint off vinyl weather stripping, metal, or plastic runners. If paint is causing the edge of a wooden window to bind, you will have to remove the window and sand it smooth.

Replacing broken sash cords

1 Older windows have sash weights as counterbalances. If the cord holding them breaks, pry off the window stops and remove the lower sash. Cut both cords, and then pry the cover off the weight pocket in the lower end of the window channels. Remove the weight and cut off the cord.

2 Tie a piece of string to a small nail and the other end to a new sash cord. Drop the nail over the pulley at the top of the window channel and into the weight pocket. Tie this end of the rope to the weight. Pull the cord to raise the weight against the pulley.

3 Rest the bottom sash on the sill. While holding the sash cord firmly against the side of the window, cut the cord 3 inches beyond the hole in the sash. Knot the sash cord and wedge the knot in the hole. Replace the pocket cover, put the sash back in place, and reattach the stops.

The windows tool kit

Repairing a broken windowpane

Skill level:	Time to complete:	Materials:	Tools:
★★★☆☆	Experienced 20 min. Handy 30 min. Novice 1 hr.	Glass, glazing points, glazing compound or caulk, paint	Framing square, glass cutter, heat gun, putty knife, glazing tool, marker or grease pencil, leather gloves

Repairing broken windows is messy but not hard. Chances are you'll have to repair at least one.

Put on a pair of stout leather gloves, remove the broken pane, and measure for a new one. Cut the glass yourself or have a home center or hardware store cut the glass to size. The replacement should be 1/16 inch to 1/8 inch smaller than the opening.

Glazing is the messy part. Traditional compound is a puttylike substance; a modern variation is caulklike. If you're adept with caulk, this is the route to go. Rest the nozzle (which is square) on the window frame and on the glass, and caulk away. By pulling the trigger gently and taking your time, you'll get a flat bead that slopes from muntin to windowsill. If your timing is a little off, you'll get some extra caulk here and there, which can be difficult to clean up.

Traditional putty has more body and takes direction better. Bed it firmly in the channel, and then create the slope by pulling a putty knife or glazing tool along it. A glazing tool is a bit easier to use. It has two short wings, mounted at an angle to each other, and a short center slot that you rest on the muntin as you work. About all you have to do is keep the angle constant. Whether you use a putty knife or a glazing tool, keep the angle high so that just the tip of the knife travels along the putty. Wipe the tool clean before you start the next side.

Paint the putty channel before you install the glass and apply the glaze or caulk. Dry wood will pull the moisture out of the putty and it won't stick.

The National Glazing Code requires that shatter-resistant panes be used in applications such as doors and sidelights. Let the salesperson know what the glass is for so that you purchase the right type. And if you're replacing glass in a factory-built window, you may not be able to do so by following the directions below—especially if the glass is double- or triple-paned. The major manufacturers recommend that you call your distributor to get the parts you'll need for repairs. In some cases you'll need to replace the entire sash.

Cutting glass

1 Although it's easiest to have the store cut glass to size, you can do it yourself. Make sure you have at least 1/2 inch or so between the edge and your cut. Smaller cuts are extremely difficult. Put the glass on a flat surface with several layers of newspaper.

2 Draw a line with a marker or a grease pencil, indicating where you want the cut. A framing square will help ensure a square cut.

3 Score the glass along the layout line with a glass cutter guided by a straightedge. Make the break by laying the glass scored-side-up over a board, holding the good side with one hand and quickly slapping down with the other. Wear leather gloves.

Repairing a broken windowpane (continued)

Installing new glass

1 Most windows can be repaired while they are still in the frame, but if you're removing the window for other repairs, it's a bit easier to work on a table or workbench.

Start by putting on heavy leather work gloves and removing the loose pieces of broken glass.

2 Soften the old putty with a heat gun, being careful not to scorch the wood. Scrape away the soft putty with a putty knife and remove the remaining glass. Small pieces of metal that hold the glass in place—called glazing points—probably remain in the frame. Pry them out with a putty knife or pull them out with pliers. Wire-brush the channel to completely remove the old putty, and sand the grooves to clean them.

3 Paint the bare wood with an oil-base paint, or coat it with linseed oil, so that the new putty will stick. (Bare wood pulls the moisture out of the putty, making it too dry to adhere.)

4 Put a thin bead of glazing compound in the channel that holds the glass. Press the replacement pane into the compound, bedding it. Press in new glazing points every 10 inches with the tip of a putty knife or glazing tool. Avoid pushing the glazing points toward the glass; the pressure may break the pane.

5 If using a puttylike glazing compound, roll a ball of it between your fingers to make a long thick noodle. Press the noodle against the glass and the side of the channel. Set it firmly with the tip of a putty knife or glazing tool. If using a caulklike glazing compound, put it in a caulking gun and poke a hole in the seal. (The nozzle is already shaped and need not be cut open.) Move the tip along the glass, applying even pressure to the trigger. (See inset.)

6 Smooth the glazing compound with a glazing tool or wet putty knife. Position the notched end of the glazing tool so that one edge rests on the glass and the other rests on the wood, and pull to the corners. Let the compound dry as directed on its container; clean away excess, then paint.

Replacing a screen

Replacing a screen in an aluminum frame

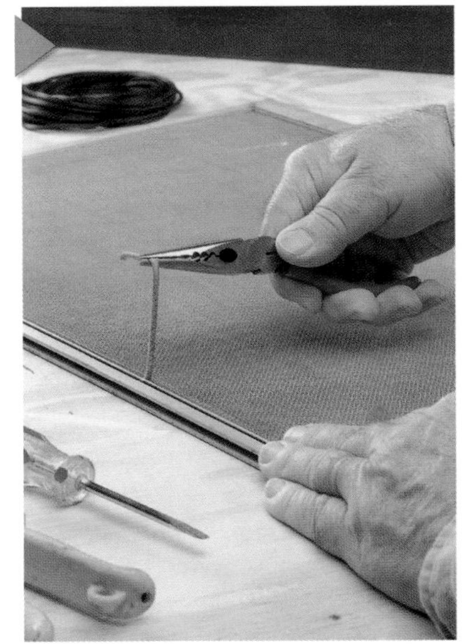

1 Pry and pull the vinyl spline from the grooves around the edge of the frame with a screwdriver and pliers. Keep the old spline if it's still flexible; if not, buy a new one.

2 Put the new screen fabric over the frame so that it overlaps the retaining grooves. Trim the corner as shown so that excess material won't interfere with installing the screen.

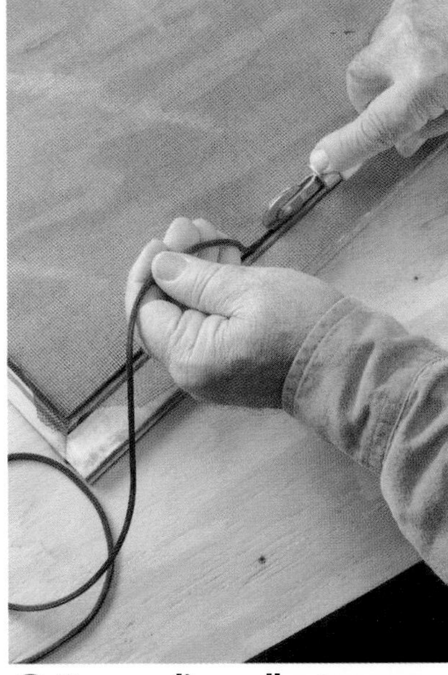

3 Use a spline roller to press the spline and screen into the grooves. Keep the screen tight as you advance the spline. Cut away the excess screen with a utility knife.

Replacing a screen in a wooden frame

1 On a wooden frame, pry up the screen molding with a scraper or putty knife. If the molding is sealed with paint, cut through the paint film with a putty knife to free the molding. Remove the old screen and put the new material in place, leaving it oversized so that you'll have excess to pull on to tighten the screen.

2 Staple the new screen in one corner and stretch the screen tight across to the nearest corner. Staple every few inches between the corners. Stretch screen tight to one remaining corner, staple, then work back with staples to previous corner. Repeat to last corner. Then nail the screen molding back in place and trim excess screen.

Patch small holes

For metal screens, cut a square piece of matching material ½ inch or so larger than the hole, bend the edges back to form a shallow box, then place it over the damage. Bend the protruding wire strands over the back of the screen. Press them flat with a board.

Repair holes in plastic screen by cutting a patch from the same screening material and adhere it in place with exterior glue. Spread glue on back of the patch and around the hole edge.

Window and glass door security

Skill level: ★☆☆☆☆

Time to complete:
Experienced 10 min.
Handy 15 min.
Novice 20 min.

Materials: Door or window lock

Tools: Screwdriver, drill and bits

Locks for sliding windows

To delay and, ideally, deter thieves, you need more than the standard window or patio door latch. Because you may need to exit through locked windows and doors in an emergency, keep the key near the lock but hidden from outside view. When possible buy all latches from the same manufacturer so that the keys will be interchangeable.

If local fire code permits this, ensure greater security by replacing single glazing with polycarbonate or wire-embedded glass. In some cases you may even want to install security shutters, a grill, or a security gate.

Casement windows can be closed with a door-bolt-like device that operates with a key. Screw the lock to the window and slide the bolt into a metal cup that mounts in the sill.

Drive a screw into the top of the upper track to keep thieves from lifting a sliding window out of its track (see inset). To keep the window from sliding, drive a screw horizontally through the track.

Double-check keyed locks

Doors and windows considered as fire or emergency exits may not be allowed by local law or fire codes to have locks requiring separate keys. Check with your local building office to see whether this applies to you before choosing locks.

Several companies make locks for sliding windows. On this one, a stop slips over the window track. Turn the lever one way to lock the window; turn it the other to allow it to slide. Other locks use a thumbscrew instead of a lever.

A key track stop is a locking stop that you can attach anywhere on the track. You can position it to lock the window shut or so that the window opens only a certain amount, allowing for ventilation and safety.

Double-hung window locks

On double-hung windows, you can install a locking pin that goes through one sash and into the next to keep intruders from lifting the sash. Some pins screw through a hole you drill, while others drive in and out with a special key that comes with them.

Ventilating locks screw to the side of the top sash an inch or so above the meeting rail. When the pin is positioned as shown, it allows you to open the window until the pin strikes a plate screwed to the other sash. Slide the pin around the corner and you can raise the window the full amount.

A hinged wedge lock nails in the window track of a double-hung window. Choose a position for the wedge that lets you open the window enough to get fresh air. When the wedge is in place, the window can't be raised beyond that point (see inset). When you swing the wedge out of the way, the window opens freely to any height.

A keyed turnbuckle replaces the normal latch, so you'll need a key to open the window. A child-safety latch also replaces the original latch. It's similar to the childproof caps on medicine containers, but easier to use. In order to open the window, a child has to be able to squeeze a lever while turning the latch.

Patio door locks

Reinforce the lock on a patio door with a security bar. Screw the hinged side to the doorjamb and the locking saddle to the other jamb. Swing the bar into the saddle to lock the door; lift it out to allow the door to open. You can also set the bar so the door will open partway.

A keyed patio door lock screws to the side of the door. When you want to lock the door, put the bolt into a hole you've drilled into the door frame. Unlock and lower the bolt to open the door.

Installing a window

Skill level:	Time to complete:	Materials:	Tools:
★★★☆☆	Experienced 30 min. Handy 45 min. Novice 1 hr.	Window, wood shims, drip edge, 16d casing nails, fiberglass insulation, silicone caulk	Hammer, 4-foot level, circular saw, drill and bit, nail set, utility knife, caulking gun, chisel

Replacement windows are available in various shapes, styles, colors, and construction types. They are commonly made of wood, aluminum, or vinyl. Each manufacturer's product has its own specific installation instructions, but on the whole all window units are installed in the same manner.

Prehung windows come complete with finish frames, and you can insert them in one piece into the rough opening left by the old window. Measure the rough opening and be sure to purchase a new window unit to fit.

You'll need to custom-order most windows, and delivery can take several weeks. It's risky to remove the existing windows before the replacements are on-site. Because of manufacturer's delays, bad weather, wrong orders, and shipping problems, it's difficult to guarantee an exact delivery date. If you're in a hurry, you could wind up with a big hole in the side of your house and no cover for it. The bottom line: Keep the old windows in place until the new ones have arrived and you have inspected them for damage and verified they are the correct sizes.

As important as windows are to the security, appearance, and energy efficiency of your home, you'll be pleasantly surprised by the simplicity of installing them. You'll need to rent scaffolding to safely install windows on upper levels of your home. Windows are awkward to handle so it's generally a good idea to find a helper when you're working above the first floor.

1 Remove the existing window or wall surface and then test-fit the window, centering it in the rough opening. Support the window with wood blocks and shims placed below the horizontal jambs. Make sure the window is plumb and level, and adjust the shims if necessary.

2 Clamp or hold the molding in place, then trace around it. If you have vinyl or aluminum siding, you may need to install something called a J-channel to hold the trim. This usually requires trimming away a bit more siding. If a J-channel is required it will be called for and explained in the manufacturer's instructions.

WORK SMART

MEASURE ALL WINDOWS

You might think it's safe to assume that all your windows are the same size and that if you've measured one you've measured them all. However, it's best to measure each rough opening to be sure that the window will fit properly and that you won't have a hole in your wall while you wait for the correct replacement. Mark the opening and the window to match correctly.

Removing a window: Don't rush the job

Taking out an old window isn't hard to do, but by hurrying the job you could do damage that will have to be repaired later.

Start with a utility knife and cut through the paint wherever trim meets the wall both inside and outside the house. This keeps paint from chipping or drywall from tearing when you remove the trim. Carefully remove the trim with a pry bar. To keep from damaging the wall surrounding the window, place a piece of scrap wood under the pry bar.

With the interior trim off, you may discover sash weights as part of vintage, double-hung windows. Remove them by cutting the cord. Hang onto the cord and raise the weights to remove them. Fill the voids with fiberglass insulation.

Pry off exterior trim and moldings with the pry bar, using scrap wood behind it to protect siding you may encounter. When that's done, cut through any framing nails with a reciprocating saw to loosen the window. If the window has nailing fins, pry loose the siding covering them and remove the nails that go into the sheathing. After removing any wooden shims in the frame, slide out the old window unit.

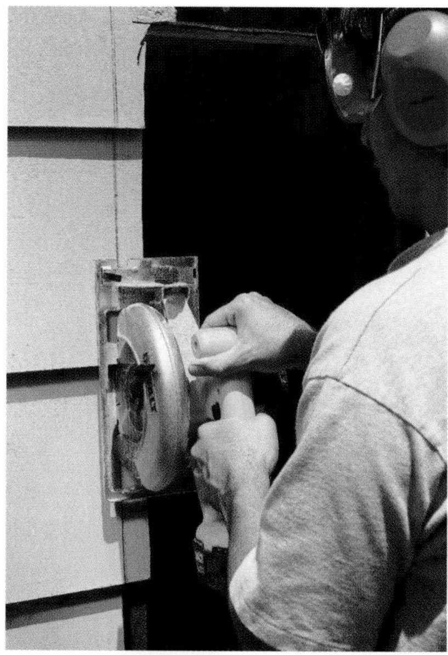

3 Cut the siding along the outline. Use a circular saw adjusted so the blade depth equals the thickness of the siding. Start the cut with the toe of the saw plate on the siding, but with the blade and heel of the plate above the surface. Slide the saw guard back, start the saw, and ease the blade into the wood. To avoid splintering, stop before the corner. Complete the corner cuts with a sharp chisel.

4 Cut a length of drip edge to fit over the top of the window and slide it between the siding and the building paper.

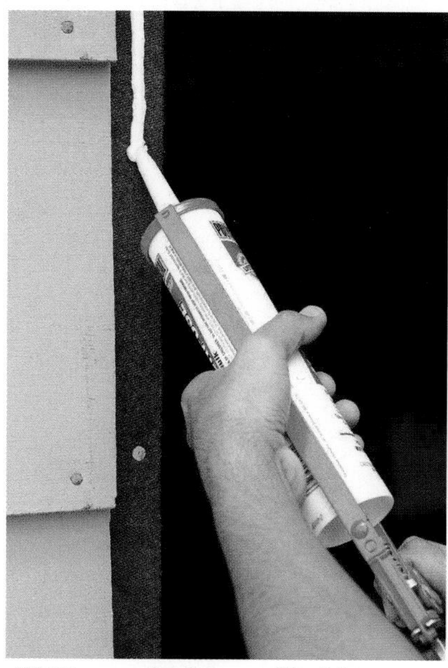

5 Your window will either have a piece of molding, called brick mold, around the outside, or a nailing fin. If it has brick mold, apply a continuous bead of caulk around the opening. If it has a nailing fin, apply the caulk to the back of the fin.

6 Insert the window into the opening and push the brick mold or nailing fin tight against the sheathing.

7 Check to see how much adjustment will be necessary to level and plumb the window unit.

8 If the window is uneven, correct it by shimming below the side jambs. Once the window is perfectly level, tack it in place. See "Nailing fins," page 250.

Installing a window (continued)

9 Place shims together so that their combined thickness will fill the opening between the jambs and framing. Despite the nails you just put in, the window will still move somewhat. Use the shims to center the window in the opening.

10 Measure the diagonals of the window for square. If they are equal, the window is square. If not, adjust the shims until the window is square. Always recheck for level and square after you adjust the shims.

11 If the window has a brick mold, predrill holes and drive 16d nails through the brick mold and into the framing. If the window has a nailing fin, nail through it into the framing. In either case, start at the corners and space the remaining nails as recommended by the manufacturer. Drive all nailheads below the wood surface with a nail set.

Nailing fins

On windows with nailing fins, drive 2-inch roofing nails into the holes at the upper corners and partway into the framing. Leave enough of the nail exposed so that you can remove it if you have problems later in the installation.

Vinyl replacement windows

Removing and replacing a window is a big carpentry job, even if it's not difficult. If you're unsure of your skills or you simply don't have time for the job, consider a vinyl replacement window.

A replacement window fits in the jamb that holds your existing window. To install one pull out the old window, moldings, and stops until you're left with just the sill and jambs. Some replacement windows sit in a frame that you slide between the jambs—window and all—and then screw in place. Others are designed so that you'll attach tracks to the jambs and then slip windows into the jambs. The first option is easier but reduces your view by the thickness of the frame holding the window. The second option involves a few more pieces, but they're thinner, improving your view.

Replacement windows are custom-built to your specifications. Building them can take a few weeks, so keep any old windows in place until the new ones arrive. Stop by the millwork department of your home center and ask what measurements they'll need to place the order. (They should have a form with clear directions.)

Because the window frames are vinyl, they're energy-efficient. Some windows are better insulated than others, however, and some have better glass than others. Read the brochures and make sure you get what you want. For definitions of terms, see "Window Basics," page 240.

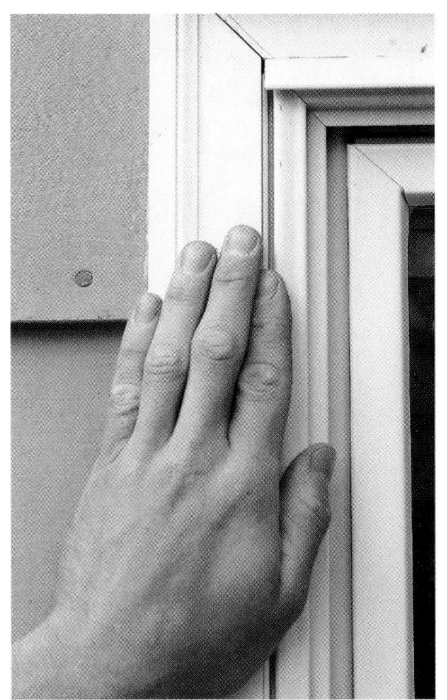

12 A window with a nailing fin often has a special-order molding that you apply over it. Install as directed by the manufacturer.

13 Fill the gaps between the window jambs and the framing members with loosely packed fiberglass insulation. Wear leather work gloves, safety glasses, and a dust mask when handling insulation.

14 Trim the shims flush with the framing by scoring them with a utility knife and then snapping off the excess.

Installation variation: masonry clips

Use metal masonry clips when a masonry or brick surface prevents you from nailing brick molding in place. The clips hook into grooves in the window jamb and attach with screws. After the new unit is placed in the rough opening, you bend the clips around the framing. These clips can also be used in normal lap siding installations to avoid nail holes in the surface of prefinished brick moldings.

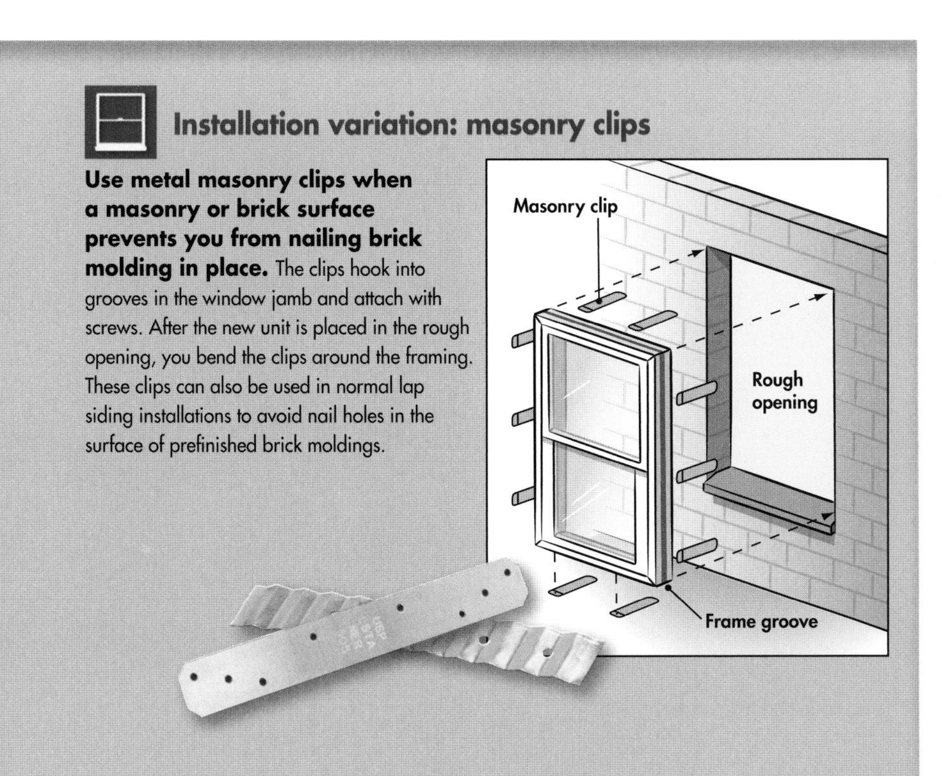

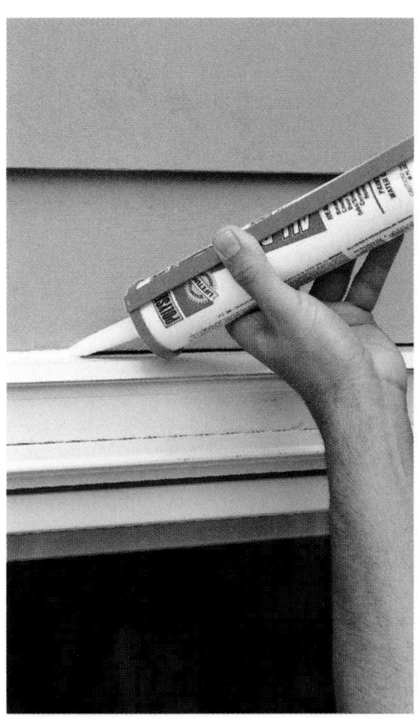

15 Apply paintable silicone caulk around the entire window unit and fill the nail holes with caulk. When the caulk dries, paint to match the trim on the rest of your house.

Installing a storm window

Skill level:	Time to complete:	Materials:	Tools:
★☆☆☆☆	Experienced 15 min. Handy 30 min. Novice 45 min.	Storm window, caulk, screws specified by the manufacturer	Tape measure, tin snips, caulking gun, drill with drill bits and screwdriver bits

Before you install storm windows, you'll have to buy them, and before you buy them, you'll have to know what size you need. Begin by measuring what's called the clear opening. When measuring the width, measure from jamb to jamb, as shown in the photo and inset, right. When measuring the height, measure from the sill to the top jamb. You'll also want to note the spot where the top and bottom sashes meet. Measure from the top jamb down to the bottom of either sash. When you select your storm windows, make sure the top and bottom sashes meet at the same point as those on the window they'll cover. Take all three measurements with you to the store.

Once you're there, you may discover that storms don't come in the exact size you need. Within reason, this is OK. The skirt or "fins" around the window are made to be easily trimmed. Depending on the window, you may have as much as 2 inches that you can trim. Owners of older homes, however, may find that their windows are a nonstandard size. For them the only alternative is to custom-order windows.

Each storm window has a small hole (called a weep hole) in the bottom fin that allows trapped moisture to escape. A little heat gets out too, but not enough to worry about. Trapped moisture causes the paint to flake and the wood to rot. Check periodically to make sure the hole isn't plugged.

Never underestimate the importance of accurate measurements when you're ordering windows of any kind. After you choose a window, carefully follow the manufacturer's recommendations for clearance to ensure the proper fit.

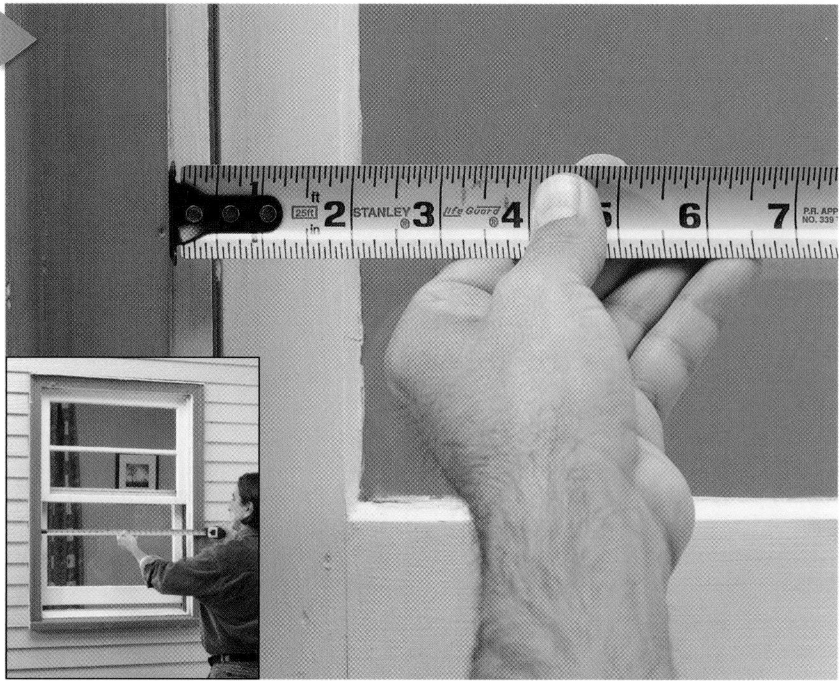

1 Looking at the window from the outside, find the narrow strips of wood near the edges. These are called blind stops, and the window slides up and down behind them. Measure the distance from the outside of one stop to the outside of the other (see inset). Then measure the distance from the top of the sill to the outside edge of the top stop. Get a window designed to fit this size opening.

2 Trim the storm window, if necessary, to fit the opening. Use tin snips to cut along the lines stamped in the fins of the window. Cut equal amounts off each side. If the window is too tall, trim the bottom only; the cut will be less visible.

3 Apply a bead of caulk along each of the blind stops. Leave the sill uncaulked, however, to allow moisture trapped between the windows to escape.

4 Put the window in the opening with the bottom resting on the sill. Tilt the window into place.

5 Have a helper hold the window while you drill holes for screws near the edge of the fins. The exact size and spacing depends on the manufacturer's instructions. Drive screws through the holes and into the wood behind them to hold the window in place. If the small weep hole at the bottom of the window is plugged by dirt, clean it out with a small finishing nail.

Do you really want to work up on the roof?

Before you decide to install a skylight on your own, take the gumption test that follows. For each of the nine tasks that follow, give yourself two gumption points for each task you're willing to do, one skill point for each task you know how to do, and another skill point for each task you've actually done. If you're unwilling to do any one of the tasks, or if your "yes" score is anything less than a tie, hire a pro.

- Any skylight wider than 13¾ inches requires a cut through a roof rafter. Once you make the cut, you'll have to reframe that section of the roof—doubling up rafters on both sides of the opening and framing in double headers above and below the opening.
- The hole you cut in the ceiling requires similar treatment.
- You'll need to lay out the opening on the ceiling, the attic floor (if any), and the roof, keeping all carefully aligned.
- To create the opening, you'll need to go up to the roof and cut through the shingles and plywood. The easiest way is to make a plunge cut with a circular saw: Rest the toe of the saw on the roof, start the saw, and lower the spinning blade into the roof.
- Once you've made the cuts, the plywood will still be nailed to a center rafter: You'll need to pry it loose while balancing yourself on the roof.
- Skylights weigh between 40 and 110 pounds and must be hauled up to and installed from the top of the roof.
- To prevent leaks you'll need to put in felt paper, flashing, and shingles. You'll also need to insulate to prevent condensation and heat loss.
- A skylight that isn't square in its opening may leak and probably won't open correctly. You'll need to shim from below, but measuring is most accurately done from above.
- The light shaft between the roof and the room below has to be framed, drywalled, taped, and finished. Most likely, at least one of the shaft walls will have to slope.

CHAPTER 5

Cabinets, Countertops & Storage

Efficient storage creates order in the home. Carefully placing everyday and rarely used items is important throughout the house, whether in the kitchen, garage, laundry room, or your closets. Whatever you need to store and wherever you need to store it, easy access and organization are keys to well-run working and living spaces. Certain areas of the house, such as the kitchen, bathroom, and closets, are constantly in use. In these spaces good organization and easy access are essential. Tennis rackets, seasonal clothing, golf clubs, and air hockey games may go through cycles of use. They need to be more accessible at some times than at others. Here's how to make storage decisions:

- Take an inventory of your belongings. What items do you need access to every day? Once a week? Once a month? What about items you never use, but for sentimental reasons just can't bear to see them go? Also take into account the needs of different family members.

- Review your lifestyle and the patterns of use and movement that make up your daily life. Do you have room to pursue ongoing projects and hobbies? Do all the cleaning supplies fall to the floor when you open the utility closet? Do you even have a utility closet?

- Tour your house and take a hard look at the existing storage areas. Are they big enough? Deep enough? Easy to access? Then look around for underused areas that could provide storage space through a little carpentry or a trip to a home center or store that specializes in storage solutions.

Contents

Cabinet and countertop basics . . . 256
The cabinets, counters & storage tool kit . . . 257
Replacing cabinet hardware . . . 258
Replacing cabinet doors and drawers . . . 260
Cabinet refacing . . . 261
Getting ready to install cabinets . . . 262
Installing kitchen cabinets . . . 265
Installing a kitchen island . . . 270
Countertop basics . . . 271
Installing countertops . . . 272
Tiling a countertop . . . 275
Adding a closet . . . 279
Installing a modular storage system . . . 283

Storage solutions are big business

Home centers, hardware stores, discount chains, and even antiques shops are into storage solutions in a big way. Other stores specialize in every conceivable type of off-the-shelf storage you can imagine. Of course, some types of storage can only be custom-made, such as built-to-order kitchen cabinetry or built-in bookshelves and closets, or even additions to your living space. But it's worth a shopping trip or two to see what's available ready-made before you decide to start swinging a hammer. Here's a room-by-room look at storage issues and solutions:

Kitchens. Cabinets are the storage unit of choice in kitchens. But while they're wide and deep, cabinets sacrifice a large volume of useful space in the back. By contrast, sliding and staggered shelving, door racks, lazy Susans, tilt-out bins, drawer dividers, and pullout trays with dividers make maximum use of space.

Bathrooms. Adequate storage in most bathrooms is nonexistent, partly because most bathrooms are too small to accommodate storage areas. One area of opportunity is the medicine cabinet. Consider installing the largest ready-made unit you can fit or have one custom-made to the room specifications. Install the largest vanity possible and add rolling trays as well as interior shelving. Home centers and discount chains offer a multitude of ready-made storage solutions for small bathrooms.

Closets. Custom shelving and rods with storage for folded and hanging clothes, as well as shoes, can be supplemented with flexible wire closet products that are easily customized and installed.

Living spaces. Foyers, hallways, and living, dining, and family rooms lend themselves to built-in closets, bookcases, and entertainment units. Also consider furniture to enclose televisions and stereo equipment.

Laundry rooms. Stackable washers and dryers maximize laundry room space, as do cabinets with pullout or pull-down ironing boards. Consider stacked recycling bins on sliders and wire containers for supplies. Open cubicles and cabinets work well for holding items that are in transition from one part of the house to another.

Garages and basements. Consider open shelving, hooks to suspend bicycles and tools, workbenches with pegboard wall attachments for tools and materials, rolling containers, and plastic storage boxes that stack. Ready-to-assemble wardrobes provide storage for seasonal clothing.

Cabinet and countertop basics

Cabinets come in various shapes, finishes, and styles. As for cars or appliances, quality and durability are about what you see and what you don't.

What you don't see. All cabinets are boxes made of either medium-density fiberboard (MDF), particleboard, or plywood. MDF and particleboard are made of ground wood pressed with glue into sheets. The ground wood content in particleboard is greater than in MDF, making it somewhat stronger. Plywood is made of thin sheets of wood glued together so that the grain in one layer is perpendicular to the grain in the next, making it the strongest of the three choices. It's also the most water-resistant and the most expensive.

What you do see. MDF is often covered with a smooth white or wood-grained resin called melamine. It's a cheap, cleanable finish, but it's not as durable as similar looking laminates—thicker sheets of plastic glued in place.

MDF, plywood, and particleboard can be veneered, and once they are, it's hard to tell them apart. You'll probably have to ask to find out, but don't take "solid wood" for an answer. Technically all three are "solid wood," as is a board that's one piece of solid wood.

You'll hear a lot of talk about framed versus frameless cabinets. (See right.) The difference is more important to the person building the cabinets than to the person buying them. Once installed, both are equally durable. Frameless cabinets are easier to build; thus, they cost somewhat less. Keeping frameless cabinets square during installation is fussier than it is with framed cabinets. The hardware on both types of cabinets typically lets you adjust the position of the doors, making it easier to align the tops of doors than with old-style fixed hinges.

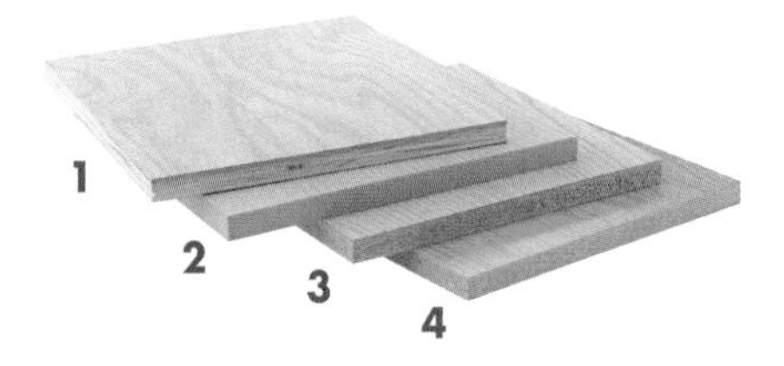

1 Bare plywood
2 Bare MDF
3 Bare particleboard
4 MDF with melamine

Frameless cabinets, sometimes called European-style, lack face frames. Contemporary-looking cabinets are almost guaranteed to be frameless, and more styles have become available as frameless cabinets have gained popularity. Most framed and frameless cabinets look virtually alike.

Framed cabinets have openings that are completely surrounded by face frames made of vertical stiles and horizontal rails. Door hinges are attached directly to these frames. This is the classic cabinetmaker's approach to construction, and most framed cabinets are traditional-looking.

Breaking the cabinet code

If you look through a catalog of kitchen cabinets, you'll find all sorts of codes, such as BBD1824D3, used for description. So once you know what you want, how do you crack the ordering code? First you need to know that two elements are standard and don't appear at all. Wall cabinets are always 12 inches deep. Base cabinets are always 34½ inches high. So this is how the code BBD1824D3 breaks down:

- The first character denotes the general type: W=wall; T=tall; B=base; V=vanity; D=desk. (B)
- The next one or two characters refer to the specific type of cabinet: BB=blind base; BC=blind corner; BD=base with drawers; C=corner. (BD)
- The next two digits are the unit's width in inches. (18)
- The next two digits are either the height of a wall cabinet or, in this case, the depth of a base cabinet. (24)
- The last one or two characters identify anything nonstandard about the unit. D=diagonal corner unit; GD=glass doors; D3=three drawers. (D3)
- An R or an L anywhere in the code would indicate the location of the door hinges.

So BBD1824D3 is a 3-drawer base cabinet measuring 18 inches wide, 34½ inches high, and 24 inches deep.

The cabinets, counters & storage tool kit

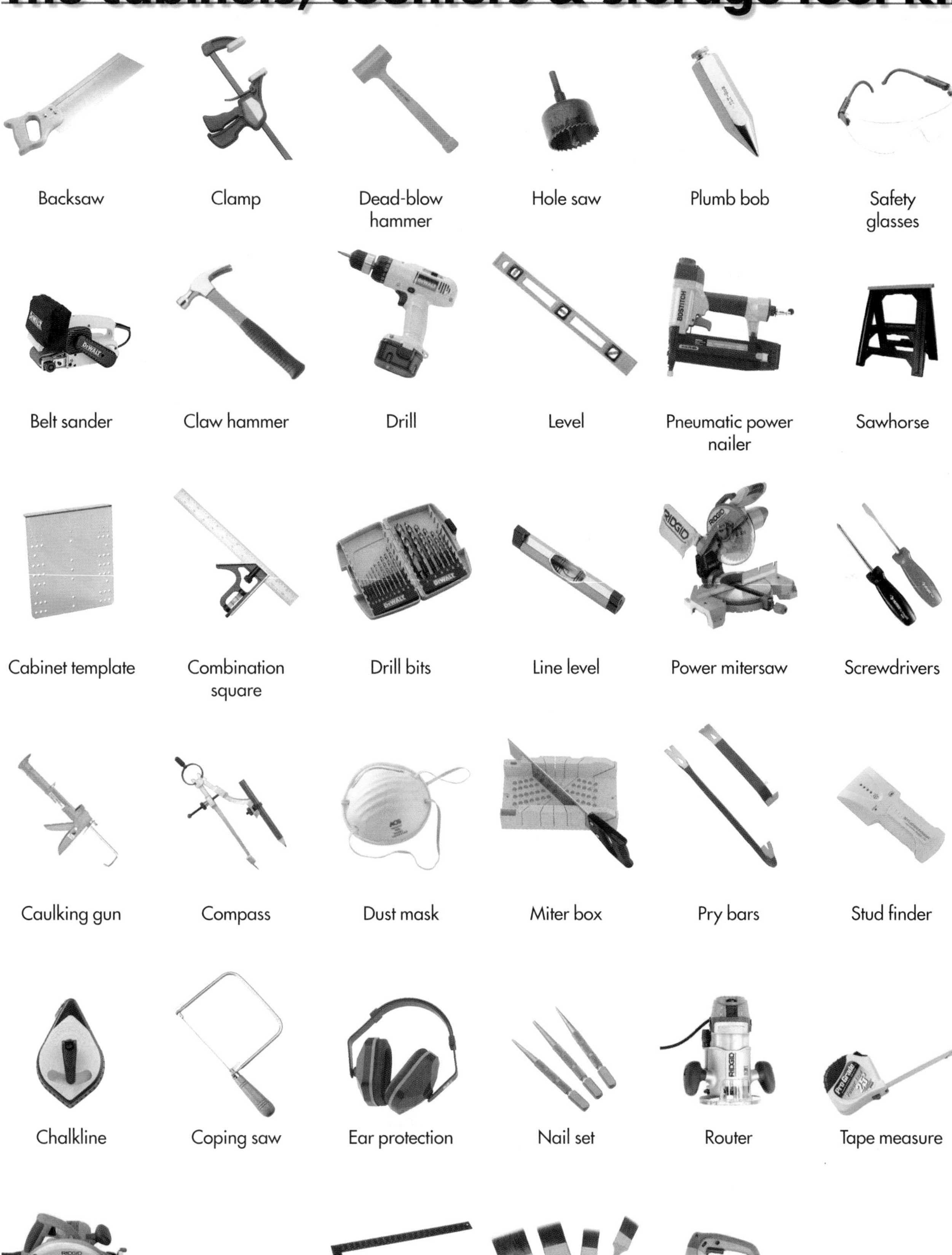

Backsaw

Clamp

Dead-blow hammer

Hole saw

Plumb bob

Safety glasses

Belt sander

Claw hammer

Drill

Level

Pneumatic power nailer

Sawhorse

Cabinet template

Combination square

Drill bits

Line level

Power mitersaw

Screwdrivers

Caulking gun

Compass

Dust mask

Miter box

Pry bars

Stud finder

Chalkline

Coping saw

Ear protection

Nail set

Router

Tape measure

Circular saw

Countersink bit

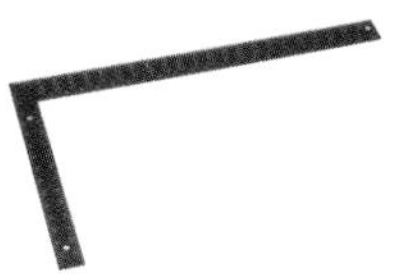

Framing square

Paintbrushes

Saber saw

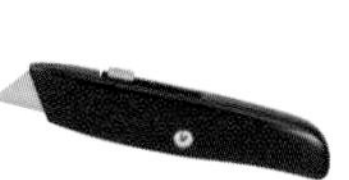

Utility knife

Replacing cabinet hardware

Skill level:	Time to complete:	Materials:	Tools:
★☆☆☆☆	Experienced 5 min. Handy 7 min. Novice 10 min.	Hardware, bolts	Screwdriver, brad puller, cabinet template, putty knife

Much of a cabinet's appearance depends on its hardware. Replacing a cabinet's Early American knobs with wooden ones gives it a Shaker look. Replacing them with bin pulls can give it a Victorian look. Putting on hammered metal pulls can steer a cabinet toward the Mission style.

Any of the above, done poorly, can make a mess out of the finest cabinet. To do the job right you must consider two things: fit and appearance. Fit is the simplest: When you remove a piece of hardware, you have to replace it with one that requires the same mounting holes, or one that is big enough to cover the old holes.

Look is a different issue. Mission furniture was almost always oak, and it can be hard to make maple, cherry, or walnut fit the bill. Shaker furniture was plain and unadorned. Most Victorian cabinets would have a hard time passing for Shaker no matter what hardware you put on them.

But it's your house, and who left the art critics in charge, anyway? If you like the way the hardware looks, it's the right hardware. First do a little reading about the look you're trying to create. Then check stores, mail-order catalogs, and old house magazines to see what's available. Try a knob on a door and a drawer, and live with it for a while. If it works, install the rest.

DESIGN TIP

IT'S LIKE CHOOSING JEWELRY

Cabinet knobs enhance drawers like the right jewelry dresses up an outfit. Replacing hardware can create a new look immediately and can help focus the overall design of the room. You'll find literally thousands of choices in home centers and hardware stores, online, and through mail order. You can also create your own pulls from found materials such as old silverware, alphabet blocks, yo-yos, or even copper plumbing fittings. Your choices are limited only by your imagination and interests.

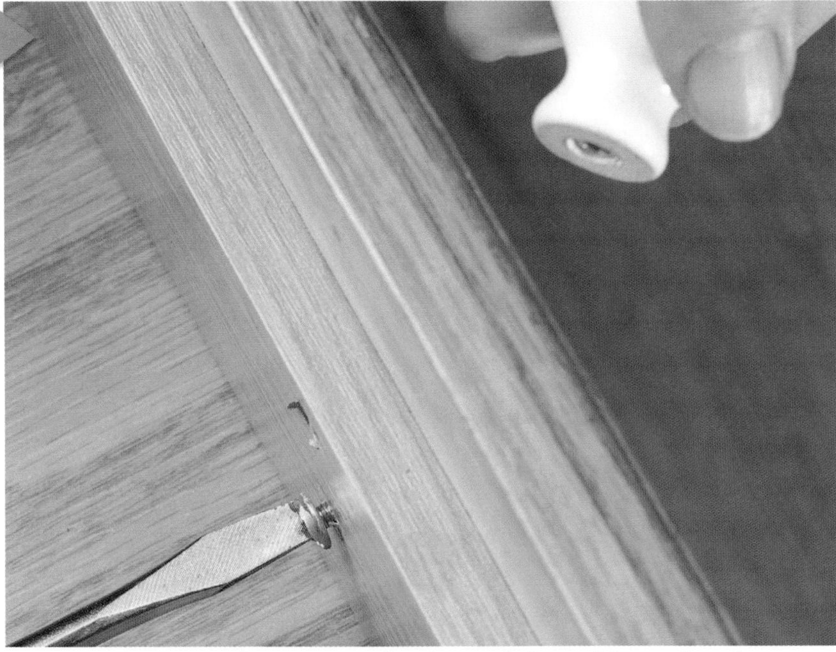

1 Begin by removing a sample piece of the cabinet's hardware. To remove a drawer handle, open the drawer and remove the bolt or bolts that go through the drawer front and into the handle. Then open a door and remove the bolt or bolts holding the handle.

2 Door or drawer handles may have plates, called escutcheons, behind them. They may be made of brass, porcelain, or contrasting wood, and are held in place with brads. Depending on the door, you may be able to pull the brads with a brad puller or small "cat's paw." If not, work a narrow putty knife under the center of the escutcheon and pry. When prying, always make sure the end of the knife is under the escutcheon. Putting it elsewhere will leave a mark.

3 If any of the hardware had two bolts holding it in place, you need to know the distance from the center of one bolt to the center of the other. Special templates, like the one shown here, help you measure the distance or lay out new holes. If you can't get a template, measure the distance between the center of the bolt holes. Accuracy to the nearest ⅛ inch is sufficient here.

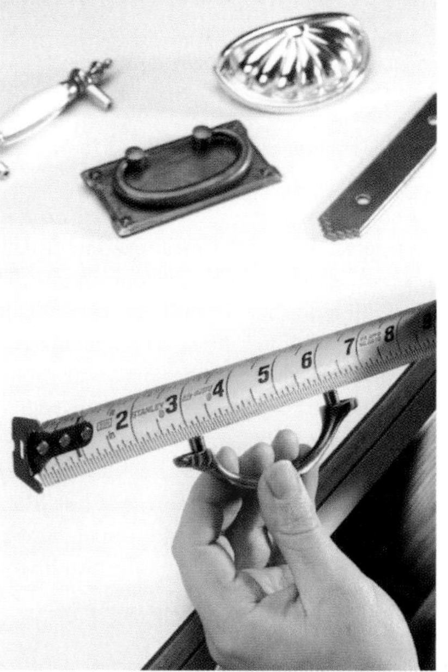

4 Take the hardware and the measurements to the store. Most hardware comes in a few different sizes. Find something you like, and then find the size that matches your center-to-center measurements. Double-check by measuring and holding the old hardware next to the new hardware to compare the spacing for the bolts.

5 Buy a sample piece of hardware and install it to make sure it fits properly. If the new bolts aren't the right length, you can usually substitute the old bolts or buy replacements in the store's hardware section. Live with and use the new hardware for a few days to make sure you really like it. When you're sure, buy and install the rest of the hardware.

Be cautious when buying thin handles such as these "wire" pulls. Their base is so narrow that they can actually slip through oversized or worn bolt holes. They also can expose much of the wood covered by the old pull. Even after refinishing the surface, you may see the silhouette of the old hardware.

Surface-mount pulls, such as this one, free you from having to worry about the distance between the old bolt holes. Its broad surface covers the bolt holes and often the silhouette of the old hardware.

Replacing cabinet doors and drawers

Skill level:	Time to complete:	Materials:	Tools:
★★★☆☆	Experienced Variable Handy Variable Novice Variable	New door and drawer fronts, double-sided tape	Screwdriver, utility knife

If a close look tells you that your doors and drawers are a wreck but the cabinets are in good shape, replacing or upgrading them may be smarter than putting $20,000 into a new set of cabinets. The trick is to find doors and drawer fronts in a matching finish, and to hang the doors. Begin by looking at the hinges: Traditional hinges look like small house-door hinges. Hanging doors on them requires some intermediate cabinetmaking skills. If they're European hinges, such as those shown below, hanging doors on them is much easier—as long as the holes are predrilled in the proper places.

The parts on ready-to-assemble cabinets—the ones that come in a box—are usually interchangeable. Hinge holes are uniform from unit to unit. However, replacement doors on custom cabinets, even if factory-built, may not be uniform.

Buy replacement doors and drawer fronts from the company that made the cabinets in the first place. Hang samples to see what problems you may run into.

Complete do-it-yourself cabinet refacing is another option. (The extra work comes in applying self-stick veneer over the face frames.) While it may cost more, you can save time by getting custom-made drawer and door fronts that come with fasteners guaranteed to fit your cabinets.

1 Remove an old door from the cabinet. European-style hinges have a big round or square piece, called a hinge cup, that fits in a matching hole in the door. The base that mounts on the cabinet is usually T-shape and often has sliding parts so you can move the door up or down to bring it into alignment with other doors. Remove the screws holding the cups in place and take the doors off the cups.

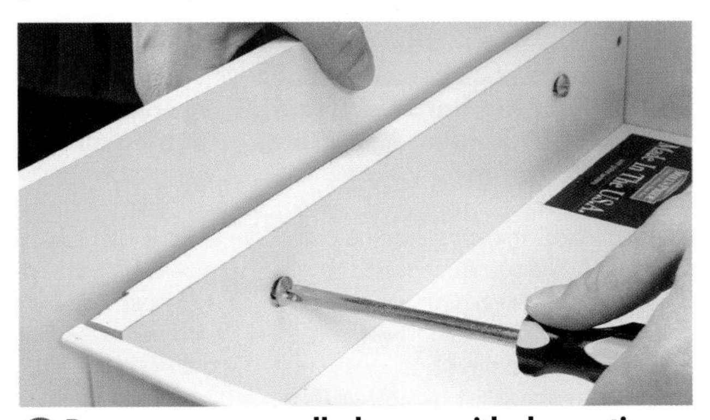

2 Drawers are usually boxes with decorative false fronts screwed over the front of the box. Remove the screws to remove the false front. If the front isn't removable, you'll have a hard time replacing it. Consider a complete refacing job, in which custom fronts and minor drawer alterations make the upgrade possible.

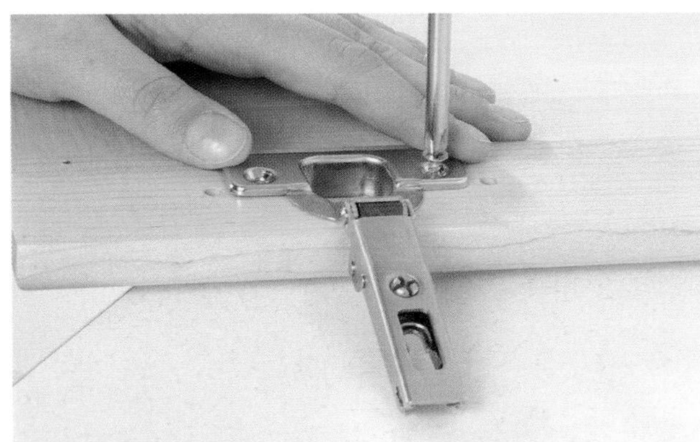

3 Put the hinge cup in the hole in the door and screw it in place. Slide the arm of the hinge over the base piece inside the cabinet and tighten the screw. Close the door and see how it sits on the cabinet. If the door juts out from the cabinet or binds when it closes, loosen the screw you just tightened, slide the arm along the base piece, and retighten. Slide the arm away from the back of the cabinet to help fix binding doors; push it toward the back of the cabinet to help fix doors that jut out when closed.

4 Put a couple of pieces of double-sided tape on the new drawer front to help you position it. Close the drawer and bring the new front up to it. Align the edges so that an equal overhang exists on each side and the gap between the drawer bottom and door top is constant, then push the drawer front against the tape. Open the drawer carefully, clamp the false front to the box as shown above, and then screw the new false front in place.

Cabinet refacing

Cabinet refacing involves replacing the doors and drawer fronts and refacing the cabinet exteriors. It's a real kitchen overhaul and, therefore, a notch up from simply replacing doors and drawer fronts. You have more choices of doors and drawers because you veneer over the frames as well, giving your kitchen an entirely new look. Generally, refacing is a good choice if you like your existing kitchen layout and do not want to put your kitchen out of comission for the weeks it make take to do a full remodel.

Many do-it-yourself refacing suppliers work with home improvement centers. They'll custom-build doors and drawer fronts in any style and finish you like, and provide you with matching self-stick veneer. All of the techniques are basic, allowing you to do your entire kitchen in a weekend or two.

The job starts with measuring—find out from the home center which measurements they need. Parts are custom-made to your specs, so expect to wait three or four weeks before they're ready.

The peel-and-stick veneer goes on the face frames first. It's easy to align because you apply it oversized and then trim it with a knife to fit. You can cover exposed cabinet sides with plywood to match or with a panel that matches your doors. Once you've dressed up the cabinets, hang the doors, which come with new adjustable hinges. The matching drawer fronts screw in place.

If you're unsure whether to reface or replace, look at it this way: If you're keeping the countertop, reface the cabinets. If you're replacing the countertop, also replace the cabinets. Your choice will result in a project that is either a little harder or a little more expensive.

▲ *Old doors or drawers can be dressed up with peel-and-stick veneer sold especially for cabinet refacing. The strips on the right are applied to the faces and trimmed to size.*

Wood veneer

Old cabinets can benefit from a facelift. Although paint is a standard-pick-me-up, wood veneer is a good alternative if you want to maintain a stained finish.

This project features thin strips of veneer typically used to finish thin edges of plywood. It's easier to work with than larger pieces of veneer.

This type of veneer is made to iron on, which means it is an easy technique for improving the look of the cabinet door.

When two types of veneer strips are alternated—white birch and red oak for this project—it results in an interesting texture with seams that become part of the design rather than something you'd rather disguise.

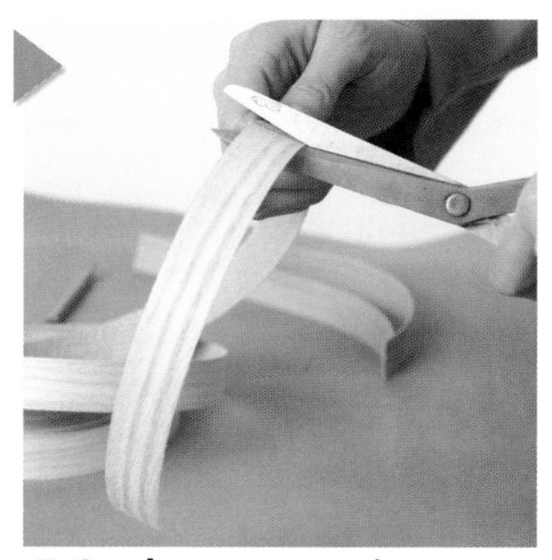

1 Cut the veneer to size. Remove the doors from cabinet. Remove any knobs or hardware. Clean and dry the cabinet. Measure the length and width of the inside door panel. Calculate how many strips will cover the panel. Transfer the measurement of the panel length to the veneer and mark with a pencil. Mark and cut enough strips to cover the door.

2 Iron veneer on the doors. Beginning with the center strips, position the strips on the face of the door. You may need to cut the outer strips to get a precise fit that is centered on the door. Heat an iron to a cotton setting but do NOT use water or steam with the iron. Start at the center and heat the veneer with the iron to make it adhere. Allow the strips to cool and set.

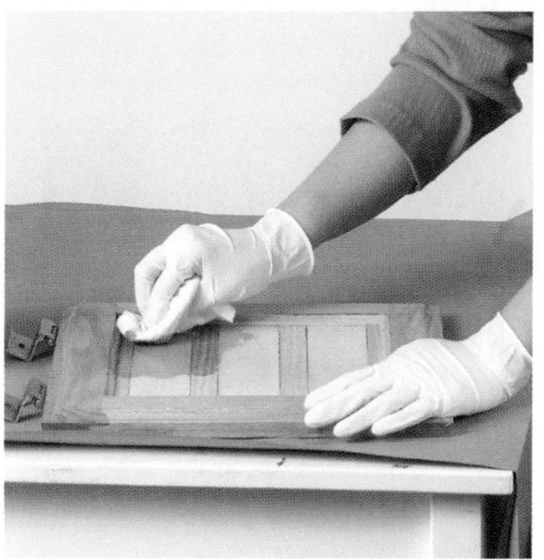

3 Apply stain. After the veneer cools, wear gloves to apply varnish with a rag. Wipe off any excess after the varnish has absorbed into the veneer for three minutes. Check manufacturer's directions for applying various types of varnish. Allow to dry and attach the doors and knobs.

Getting ready to install cabinets

Skill level:	**Time to complete:**	**Materials:**	**Tools:**
★★★★★	Experienced Variable Handy Variable Novice Variable	Cabinets, wood for ledgers, screws	Screwdriver, flat pry bar, hammer, tape measure, chalk line, line level, 4-foot level, stud finder

It's the little things that make a house a home and the little things can ruin a cabinet installation too. Doors that won't close, drawers that won't stay closed, countertops that run uphill—they're all signs of a hasty installation. Unless you want to spend the rest of your life looking at a bad job that saved you a little time, prepare properly.

First, avoid installing a kitchen the week before the holidays or any major events. This job will take time. Second, realize that the expected delivery date may change. Wait until the new cabinets arrive before tearing out the old ones.

Once your cabinets arrive, have a place where you can assemble them. Line them up as they'll go in the kitchen. Inspect the finish; look for dings, dents, and broken pieces. Be sure the color and patterns of adjacent cabinets look good together. If necessary, order replacements; you'll probably wait as long as you did for the first shipment. Once everything has arrived and is assembled, working, and damage-free, move everything out of the kitchen: appliances, tables, chairs, sinks, rugs, pots, pans, dishes, and pictures. Then, and only then, should you start to remove the old cabinets.

▶ *Installing cabinets involves making a proper plan, applying basic and intermediate carpentry skills, and being flexible about delivery schedules.*

WORK SMART

UPGRADE WIRING AND PLUMBING NOW

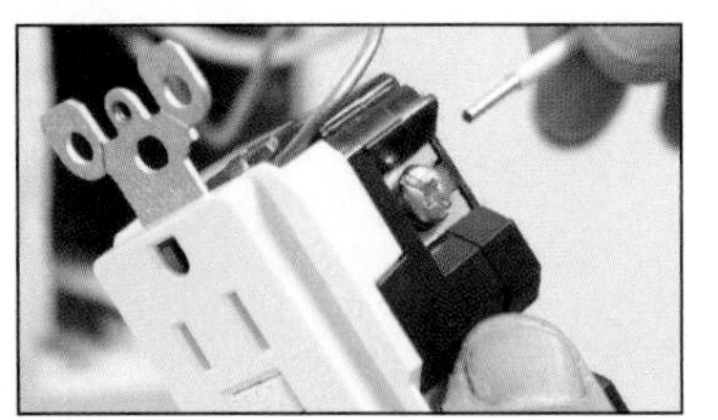

Like it or not, toasters, blenders, and coffeemakers come with fairly short cords. Put GFCI outlets every 8 feet along the counter, and you'll always be able to reach one. Replace any old or faulty plumbing. There'll never be a better time because you're making a mess anyway.

CLOSER LOOK

REMEMBER THE DISHWASHER

If you're putting in a new floor, build up the floor underneath the cabinets to the height of the finished floor. If you don't, you may discover that you need more room to slip the dishwasher underneath the counter. The thicker the new floor, of course, the greater the problem. Ask your flooring dealer how thick the finished floor will be. Include the thickness of the flooring material itself, plus any subfloor, mortar, underlayment, or other material that you'll put down. Once you have the answer, ask your cabinet dealer how far the cabinet toe-kick will be from the wall.

You'll probably need to apply a couple layers of plywood to get the right thickness. Combine various thicknesses to get what you need. Stack the sheets up and measure them—plywood is often a bit thinner than it claims to be.

Once you have the right thickness, cut the plywood to width on a table saw (or have the store do it for you). Give yourself a margin of error and cut each layer about ¼ inch narrower than the distance from toe-kick to wall. The floor will hide the gap. Nail the plywood to the floor so that you have a sturdy surface.

Resist the obvious shortcut of installing the floor first. Vinyl will compress under the weight of the cabinets. Ceramic tile grout lines will fall in the wrong place. Wood is guaranteed to get damaged, as is carpet.

Removing old cabinets

1 Prepare the space. Before you begin removing the old units, clear out the shelves, drawers, and underneath the sink. Start with the base cabinets. If you are saving the floor, protect it with ¼-inch plywood or kraft paper.

2 Remove the sink. Shut off the electricity and the water. Loosen the sink and remove it from the counter. Disconnect any electrical connections beneath the sink or in the cabinets.

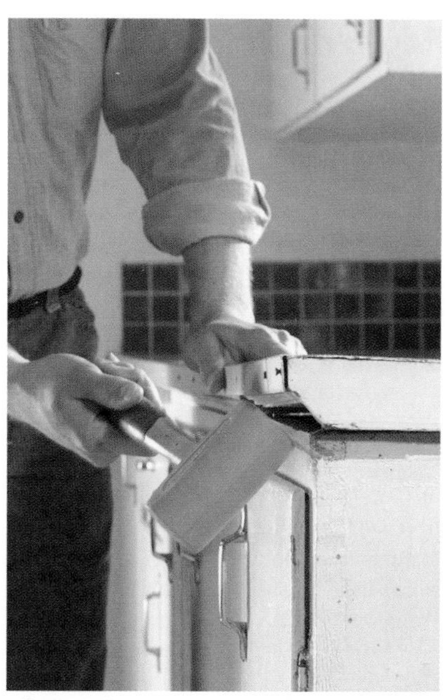

3 Begin removing the countertop. This is real demolition, but resist the impulse to just rip things out. Determine how the the countertop is attached; remove screws or nails you can reach. Use a heavy hammer to begin loosening the countertop.

4 Pry up the countertop using a flat pry bar. Start in a corner and work your way along the length until the top is free. Cut the top into manageable pieces and remove debris as you work. (For more information on removing different kinds of countertops, see page 264.)

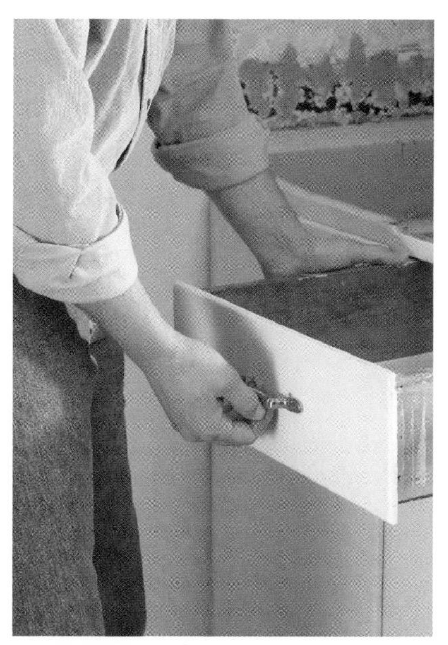

5 Remove doors and drawers. Pull the drawers out of their slots and remove the doors from the base frames. If you're going to reface, start at an open end and begin removing the base cabinets. First determine how they are attached to the wall and to each other. Remove debris as you work.

6 Remove the wall cabinets. Remove the cabinet doors, then strip the cabinets from the walls. Once the area is clear, perform any wiring or plumbing upgrades, such as adding outlets and switches, drains and supply risers, or dishwasher hookups. Repair wall or ceiling damage and paint before you begin installing new cabinetry and fixtures.

Getting ready to install cabinets (continued)

Removing countertops

Removing an old countertop is easiest if you're removing the cabinets too. It's usually a matter of taking out a couple of screws and perhaps doing some work with a pry bar.

If you want to keep the cabinets, however, work carefully. Cabinets that you've just destroyed while removing the counter will be unusable. The labor you'll have to do depends on what you find. And what you find depends on when the kitchen was put in and how inventive the installer was. Almost any cabinet could have anything holding it in place; but fortunately, a look at the surface tells you what's usually underneath.

Laminate countertops are made of a thin layer of material glued to a piece of plywood or chipboard. They're usually screwed to a corner block on the end cabinets. Remove the screws and try lifting. If the countertop doesn't budge, look for screws recessed into the bottom of the top front cabinet rail. If the cabinet has a top (most don't) or rails that run along the top (many do), look for screws that run through and into the counter. If the counter goes around a corner, a cleat spans the seam or, more likely, miter clamps. Unscrew and pry off any cleats. Loosen the heads of boltlike clamps until the clamps fall out. Once you've removed all the screws, the counter should lift easily off the cabinets.

"Solid surface" countertops are made of a single, thick layer of plastic resin. They're heavy and are usually supported by three top rails that run the length of the cabinets. The counter is usually attached to the rails with dabs of silicone caulk, and the backsplash is usually silicone-caulked to the wall. Miters are either chemically "welded" or held together by miter clamps, which you should remove. Run a utility knife along the top of the backsplash to score the wall and prevent it from tearing when you remove the counter. It's almost impossible to avoid damaging the cabinet when removing the counter by prying it off the rails. Pry gently—and if it looks, sounds, or feels like trouble, crawl inside the cabinet and cut through the support rails with a small backsaw.

SAFETY ALERT

LINOLEUM COUNTERTOPS

In the 1930s and 1940s, linoleum, which often contained asbestos, was used for countertops. Quite a few are still around, most of them in need of replacement. The countertops were usually built in place, a layer at a time. First the installer topped a cabinet by nailing (or perhaps screwing) on a plywood counter. The plywood was covered with linoleum and then trimmed with a metal edge. Taking the countertop off usually results in breaking it, thus releasing cancer-causing asbestos fibers into the air. If you have a linoleum countertop, contact your state health department for information on removing it.

Tile countertops sit on a cement backerboard, which is attached to a plywood substrate. If the cabinet is built to modern standards, 1×6 supports at the top of the cabinet run the length of the counter. The plywood is screwed to the 1×6 from below; remove the screws. Recruit as much help as you can to slide the countertop off—it will be heavy. If the countertop wasn't installed to modern standards, the nails or screws attaching it may be covered by the tiles. The only way to remove such a countertop is to break it. Nothing works well, but try a 3-pound sledgehammer with a short handle.

Butcher-block countertops work well on islands and as cutting blocks, but water will damage them elsewhere in the kitchen. If you have one you want to remove, it's probably bolted to the cabinet, usually into supports at the top of the cabinet. Some supports have slots in them for the bolts, allowing the bolt to travel back and forth as the countertop expands and contracts with changes in weather. Other supports have an oversized hole instead of a slot. In either case, you should find a bolt every couple of feet along the length and every foot across the width. Remove the bolts and lift or slide the countertop to remove it.

Installing kitchen cabinets

Skill level:	Time to complete:	Materials:	Tools:
★★★☆☆	Experienced 10 hrs. Handy 15 hrs. Novice 20 hrs.	Cabinets, 2×4, 1×4 ledger, shims, 1¼-inch drywall screws, 2½-inch drywall screws, trim molding, 4d finishing nails	4-foot level, stud finder, tape measure, electric drill with drill and screwdriver bits, saber saw, clamps, utility knife, spade bit or hole saw, hammer, nail set

Look in the average silverware drawer and you will understand the importance of planning. Stores that sell cabinets usually have a designer to help solve storage problems as well as create an efficient work flow around the sink, stove, and refrigerator.

Because cabinets are standard sizes, you can make a floor plan and then choose your cabinets. You'll have two broad choices: framed or frameless. Think of a picture frame glued to the front of a box, and you have a framed cabinet. The frame stiffens the box, and the doors are hung from it. Frameless cabinets, of course, lack the picture frame. The doors are hung directly on the side of the box, using special adjustable hinges. While they're just as strong as framed cabinets once installed, frameless cabinets do flex a little during installation. It's easier to put things in and take things out of a frameless cabinet because you don't have to work around that center post.

Once you've chosen between the two, choose from the countless styles—modern, traditional, country, French provincial, and more.

Even if your design requires help from the pros, installation can be a do-it-yourself job. The difficult part is keeping everything perfectly level and perfectly aligned while setting it on a floor that probably is neither. Start by removing all the cabinet doors and drawers: They only make the unit heavier and easier to damage. Get a good 4-foot level and use it constantly. Start with the wall cabinets—they're much easier to hang before the base cabinets are in place. Begin in a corner—about the only way to make sure the cabinet is properly positioned. Once the wall cabinets are up, install the base cabinets. Unlike the wall cabinets, which you installed one at a time, you'll put all of the base cabinets in place and double-check everything before screwing anything to the wall.

Two kinds of corner cabinets—blind and diagonal—are available. The following steps show how to install both.

TOOL TIP

NAIL GUNS VS. BRAD GUNS

A pneumatic brad gun, which shoots small nails, simplifies installing trim around cabinets. No slipping, no sliding. Hold the trim in one hand and pull the trigger with the other. A pneumatic nail gun uses larger nails, is more powerful, and is used for jobs such as nailing an island in place.

Think in detail

Don't forget about traffic patterns and electric and plumbing outlets before finalizing your cabinet plan. These are most important in a new kitchen if you want it to be all it can be. How far will you walk to put away fresh food in the refrigerator? Do you want under-cabinet lighting? Is the stove connection (gas or electric) in the right location? What about heating/cooling vents? Think, too, about details, such as how many shallow drawers and how many deep ones you'll want in a cabinet unit and exactly where you'll place it.

Installing wall cabinets

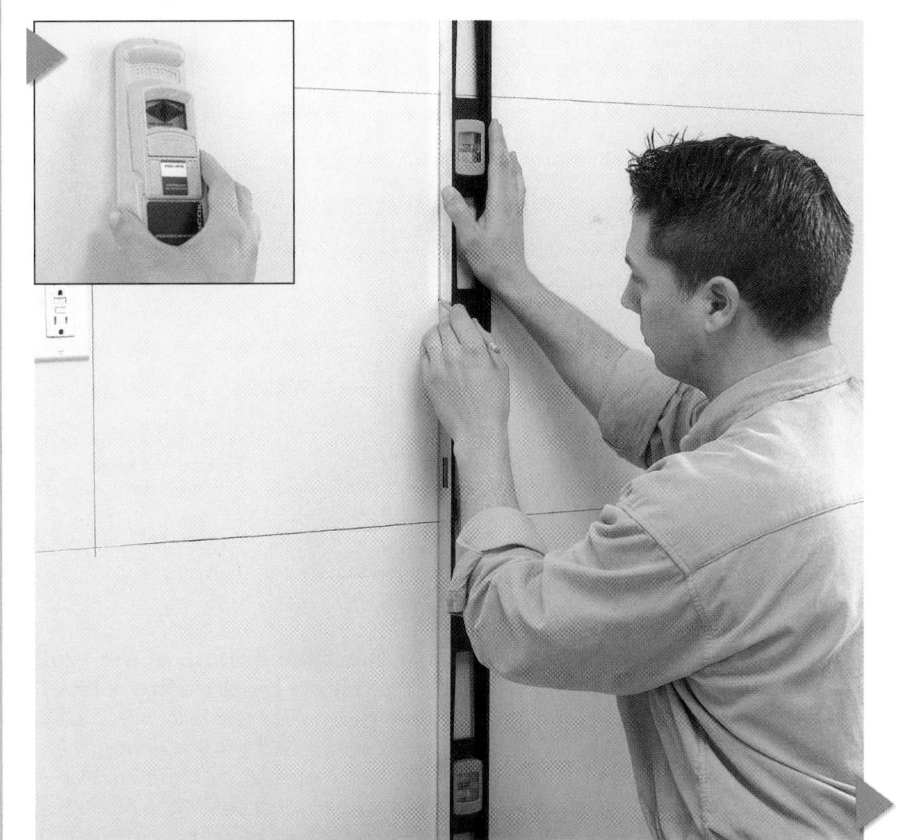

1 Use a stud finder to locate the studs in the wall. (See inset.) Mark the center of the studs with a pencil. Then extend the lines up and down the wall with a 4-foot level, making sure you keep the lines plumb.

Installing kitchen cabinets (continued)

2 Locate high spots in the floor. Begin by placing a straight 2×4 on the floor against the wall and placing a 4-foot level on top of it. Shim the low end of the 2×4 until you get a level reading. Transfer the top of the level line to the wall and extend it around the room. The point at which the distance between the line and floor is smallest is the high spot. This is the point from which you will begin laying out the cabinets. Mark it with an X.

3 Mark the top of the base cabinets on the wall. Begin at the high point on the floor and measure up 34½ inches, the standard height of a base cabinet before the counter is added. Extend a level line around the room at this height (see inset).

WORK SMART

LAY OUT THE COMPLETE JOB

Lay everything out on the wall with a pencil and level so that you know what goes where, and mark where each cabinet should be. A 15-inch cabinet looks much like an 18-inch cabinet—until you get to the end of the row and you notice a 3-inch gap you hadn't counted on. Drawing the cabinet outlines on the wall is one way to check your work as you go.

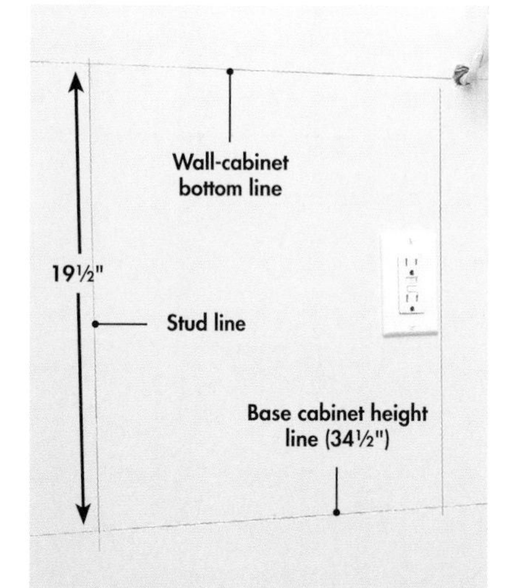

4 Mark the bottom of the wall cabinets by drawing a level line 19½ inches above the top line of the base cabinets that you drew in the last step. Then mark all of the cabinets on the wall with a pencil and level to double-check your layout. (See "Work Smart," left.)

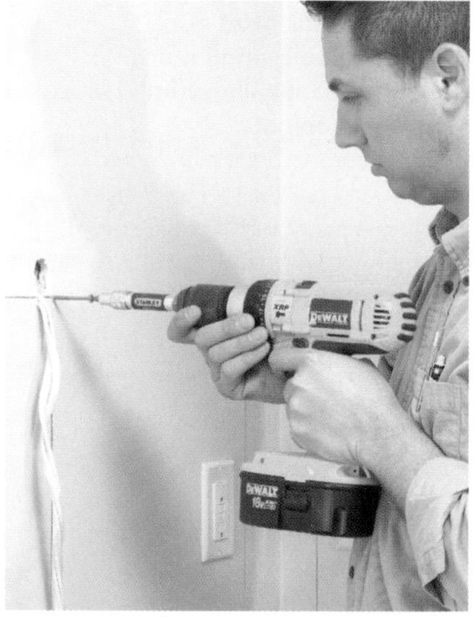

5 Install the upper cabinets first. It is easier to install them before the base cabinets are in place. Temporarily drive a couple of long screws into the studs along the line marking the bottom of the upper cabinets to help support them while you're installing. Some installers screw a board, called a ledger, along the entire length of the wall to hold the cabinets. The ledger works as long as the wall is flat and plumb. If it's not, you'll need to shim behind the cabinets to align them, and the ledger would get in the way.

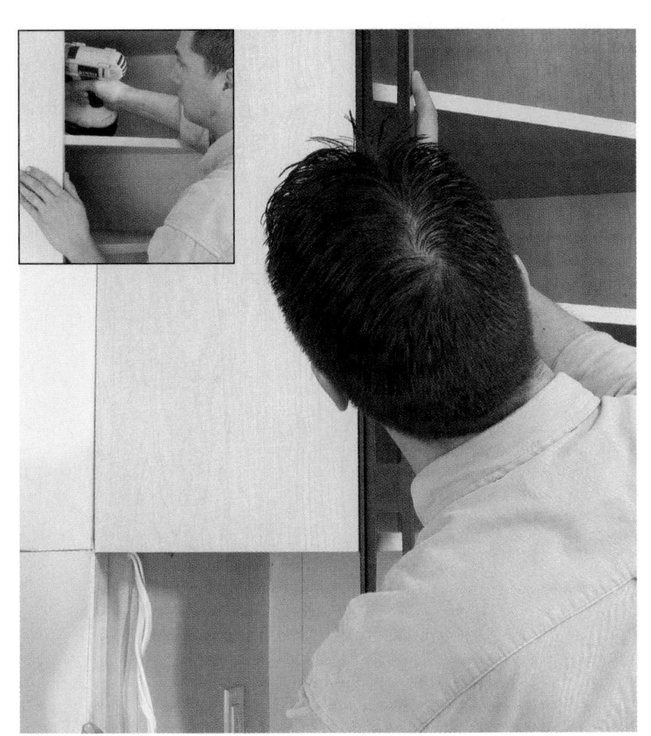

6 Start installation with a corner wall cabinet. Place the cabinet on the screws or ledger. If the cabinet isn't plumb, slip shims between the cabinet and wall at the stud lines and adjust as necessary. Drill and countersink two holes in each of the mounting rails inside the cabinet and drive 2½-inch drywall screws through the holes. (See inset.)

7 With a helper, rest the neighboring cabinet on the screw or ledger and line up the front with the cabinet you just installed. Clamp the two cabinets together. Check for level and plumb, and shim between the wall and cabinet as necessary.

TOOL TIP

EFFICIENT COUNTERSINKING

Screws you use to install the cabinet have to be countersunk so that their heads are below the surface of the wood. You'll also need to drill a pilot hole the same diameter as the screw so that the screw won't split the mounting rail. Get a combination bit, which bores both holes in one operation. Use a bit holder that allows you to change bits without having to open the chuck.

8 On frameless cabinets, such as the ones shown here, drill the holes for connectors (a screw-and-sleeve set found at most stores that sell cabinets). Screw the cabinets together. On framed cabinets, drill holes for 1¼-inch drywall screws in the recesses for the hinges to hide them.

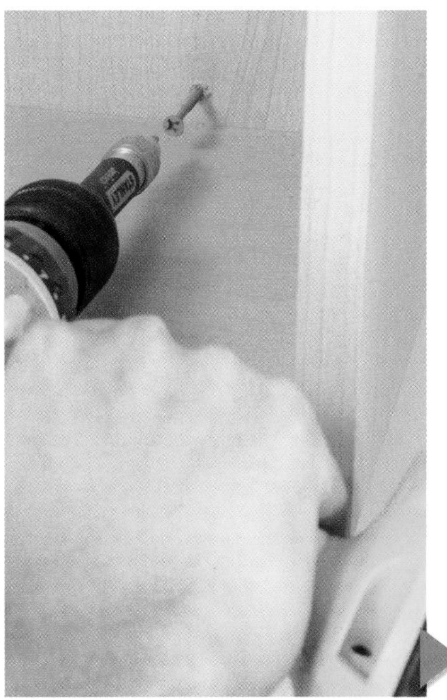

9 Drill and countersink two pilot holes through each of the mounting rails, centering the holes over the studs. (On some wall cabinets, the mounting rails are inside the cabinet. On others, they are hidden by the back.) Drive 2½-inch drywall screws through the holes and into the studs.

Installing kitchen cabinets (continued)

10 Hang the rest of the cabinets the way you hung the first ones, checking for level and plumb as you go. Once all the wall cabinets are in place, remove the ledger screws you installed in Step 5. Trim any visible shims flush with the cabinet using a utility knife.

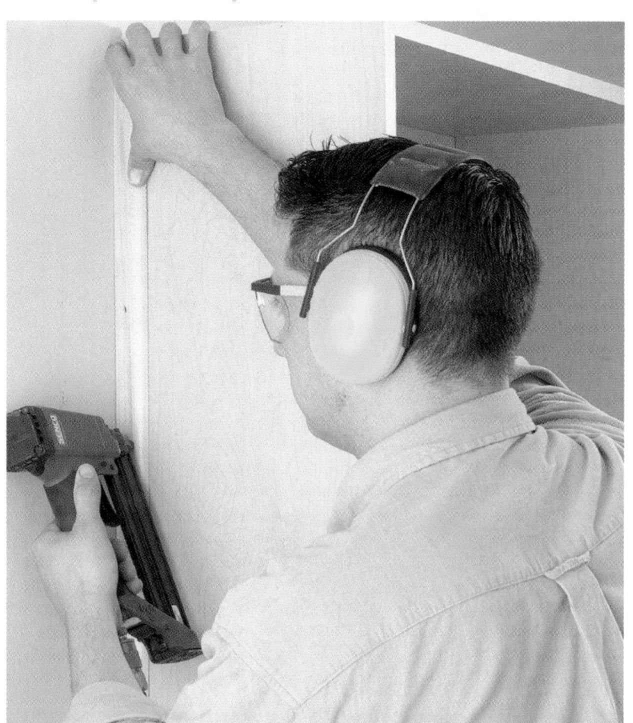

11 If you have a slight gap between the back of the last cabinet and the wall, cover it with a strip of molding. Cut a piece as long as the cabinet; stain and finish it to match. Nail it in place with a brad gun, and fill the holes with a putty made by the cabinet manufacturer to match the cabinet finish.

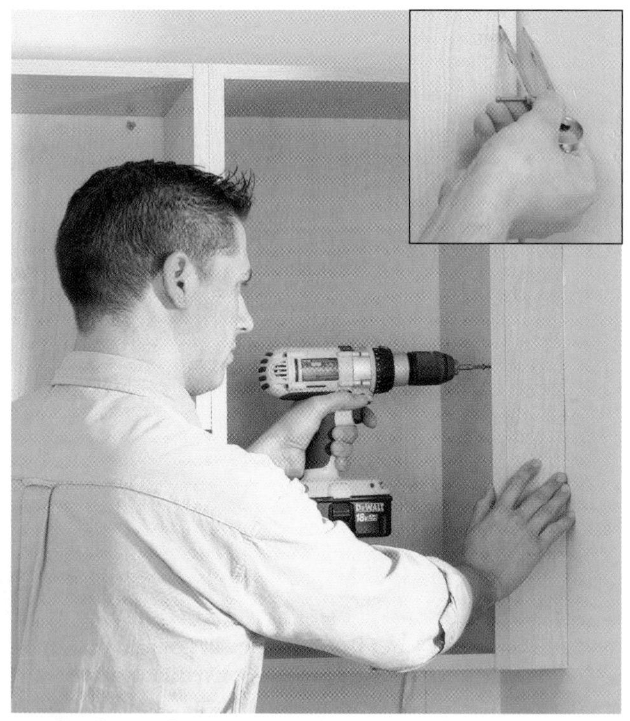

12 If you have a gap between the side of the cabinet and an end wall or appliance, cut a filler strip to close it. The cabinet distributor usually sells these strips. Scribe the strip with a compass (see inset) and cut along the line with a saber saw. Slip the strip in place and attach it with drywall screws.

13 A valance is a decorative piece that connects two wall cabinets above a sink. Have someone help you hold the valance in position; drill and countersink pilot holes into the side of the cabinets on each side, and attach the valance with drywall screws. (See the finished installation on page 255.)

Installing base cabinets

1 Put the corner cabinet—in this case, a blind corner cabinet—in place. (Leave a space between the cabinet and wall as required by the manufacturer.) Shim to align it with the top-of-cabinet line you drew on the wall. Check for level and plumb, and shim as necessary. You'll install a toe-kick later, which will cover the shims. The counter and cabinets will hide the other shims.

2 Drill and countersink pilot holes into the back of the corner cabinet. Using a combination bit, drill one hole at each stud, through any shims. Drive screws partway into the wall. Check for level again, shim as necessary, and drive the screws home.

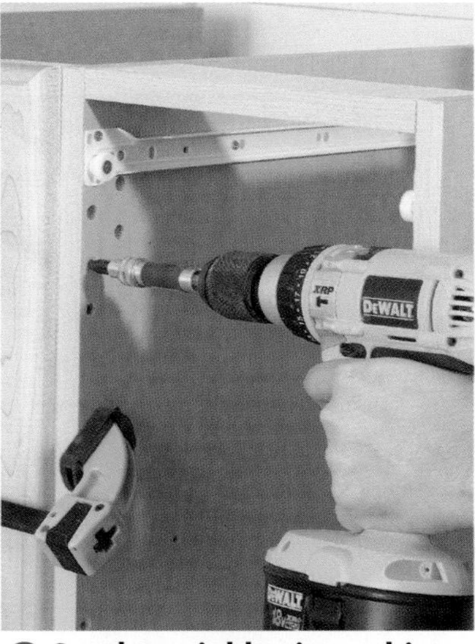

3 Set the neighboring cabinet in place, install doors or drawers, and verify that they'll open. If necessary, attach a filler strip between the cabinets. You can usually order the fillers at the same time as your cabinets. Clamp the filler flush with the front of the cabinet. Drill and countersink pilot holes into the edge of the filler and screw the filler to the cabinet.

Don't be blindsided by blind corner cabinets. All are designed to sit away from the wall in order to keep the doors and drawers from hitting neighboring doors and drawers. Most require mounting some kind of spacer on the side. Read the manufacturer's installation directions carefully. Because you removed the doors and drawers during installation, you usually don't realize you've made a mistake until you hang the doors. By then, you've usually installed the entire kitchen, and fixing the problem will require taking apart about half of it.

4 Check the second cabinet for level and plumb, and shim at the floor or wall if necessary. You will now begin assembling the row of base cabinets, making any cutouts for plumbing or wiring, as in Step 5.

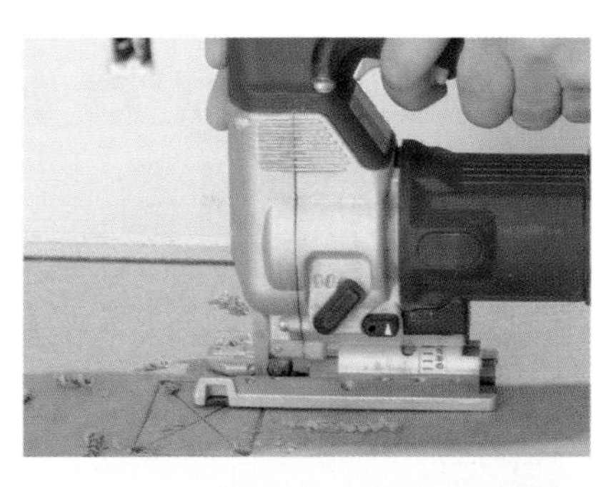

5 Before you install the sink cabinet, drill and cut holes for any wiring and the pipes. Measure how far they are from the adjoining cabinet. Subtract the thickness of the side of the sink cabinet, and mark the pipe locations on the cabinets. Drill at the marks with a spade bit or hole saw to cut holes for the pipes.

Installing kitchen cabinets (continued)

6 Install the rest of the cabinets, checking for level and plumb; shim as you go. When all the remaining cabinets are in position, step back and check for level and plumb before you screw any in place.

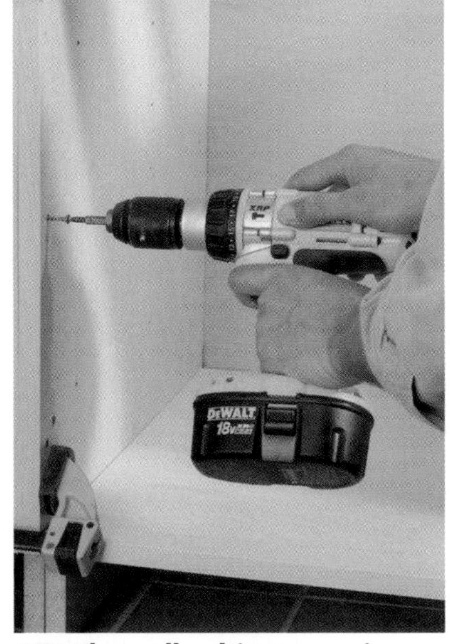

7 When all cabinets are in the proper place, drill and countersink pilot holes. Attach the cabinets to the studs with at least two screws in each mounting rail. Attach them to each other with at least four drywall screws.

8 Once all the cabinets are screwed in place, install a toe-kick to cover the gap along the bottom. This is often a two-step process: First nail a plain ¾-inch filler strip in place; then attach a thinner piece that is finished to match the cabinet. Drill pilot holes and drive 4d finishing nails through the toe-kick into the cabinets.

Installing a kitchen island

1 Begin by marking where the inside edges of the cabinet will be on the floor. To do this, put the island in position and trace around it, marking the outside corners on the floor. Remove the island. Measure in from the lines by the thickness of the island's sides, and draw lines marking the inside edges of the cabinet.

2 Cut short pieces of 2x4 to use as cleats. Screw these to the floor at the edge of each individual cabinet.

3 With a helper, lift the island over the cleats and set it in position. Check for level and shim as necessary. Nail it in place with a power nailer, or drill pilot holes and drive finishing nails through the base and into the cleats.

Countertop basics

▲ *Laminate*

▲ *Ceramic tile*

▲ *Marble*

▲ *Solid-surface*

Two types of countertops are available for the do-it-yourselfer: tile and prefabricated laminate. You'll learn how to install these countertops in this section.

Other choices—granite, solid-surface, metal, concrete, soapstone, and slate—should be installed by professionals. Some, such as granite, are difficult to install, and you probably lack the skills and equipment to complete the job. Others, such as solid-surface, can't be installed by the homeowner without voiding the warranty.

Despite these limitations, you can still consider some of the ritzier counters.

Here's a brief comparison of countertop materials:

■ **Laminate:** Generally the least expensive of the lot, it's low-maintenance and durable. Prefab counters called postform are made for do-it-yourself installation. Home centers, kitchen suppliers, and local cabinetmakers can supply countless custom variations.

■ **Ceramic:** As tough as they come, ceramic tile is easy to clean, although the grout can be a nuisance. Ceramic tile is moisture- and heat-resistant. You can do it yourself or hire a pro.

■ **Solid-surface:** Durable and available in many styles and colors, it can be special-ordered with a built-in sink. A solid-surface countertop looks as though it would make an ideal chopping board, but knife marks ruin its surface. Avoid sanding away dings, dents, and stains, unless you want a big divot in the middle of the counter.

■ **Stone:** Cost-competitive with solid-surface, stone is beautiful and durable, cleans easily, and stands up well to water. Marble, however, can stain and is not recommended in the kitchen or around sinks. Granite is the best all around but should be sealed to protect it from oil stains.

■ **Butcher block:** A wood counter is beautiful but hard to protect from scratches, water, and hot pans. Coat it occasionally with mineral oil. It's about the only finish that's considered "food safe," but it isn't as durable as other countertop options.

Installing countertops

Skill level:	Time to complete:	Materials:	Tools:
★★★☆☆	Experienced 4 hrs. Handy 8 hrs. Novice 10 hrs.	Postform countertop, miter-clamp kit with glue, end-cap kit, wood glue, drywall screws, masking tape, finishing nails, galvanized nails, silicone caulk	Tape measure, sawhorses, level, drill with ½- or ¾-inch bit, hole saw, saber saw with laminate blade, drafting compass, caulking gun, deadblow hammer, clothing iron, laminate trimmer

If your cabinets have lived on long after your countertop died, it's possible to fix the problem without ditching the cabinets.

As always, there's a catch: If you want solid stone—such as granite, or a wood solid surface, don't do it yourself. Let the pros come to the house, do the work, and give you a guarantee. (Some solid-surface manufacturers will void the warranty if the installation isn't done by a certified professional.) But if you like laminates and are adept using a saber saw, you can do the work yourself. Go to a home center and look at the "postform" counters. Postform counters come with pre-attached backsplashes, plus each has a sheet of laminate that starts on the top of the backsplash and continues around the counter's rounded front edge. You'll find several varieties and lengths, as well as counters with precut miters and those that are square on both ends. The ends come unfinished and are later covered by an iron-on piece of laminate.

If your cabinets require a nonstandard countertop length, you'll need to have one custom-made. The built-in backboard on postform counters makes them almost impossible to trim.

WORK SMART

WHEN TO HIRE A PRO

If two counters come together in a corner, verify that the corner is square. At the same height from the floor, start by marking 3 feet from the corner on one wall and 4 feet from the corner on the second wall. If the diagonal distance between the marks isn't 5 feet, your corner is out of square. Prefab counters are made to fit in square corners, and cutting a new miter is hard, even for a pro. Have the counter custom-made and professionally installed. The cabinetmaker will solve the problems right in the shop, and the installer knows how to solve the ones that crop up during installation.

If you're considering installing a prefab U-shape counter, you should know it's one of the most difficult installations. Both outside corners must be perfectly square, and any irregularity along the wall will affect how the counter sits against the other walls. Hire a pro.

1 Take accurate measurements of the cabinet layout and draw a plan on a piece of graph paper. Plan for a 1-inch overhang at any exposed end, and subtract 1/16 inch from pieces that will butt against an appliance, such as a range or refrigerator, to allow for easy installation and removal.

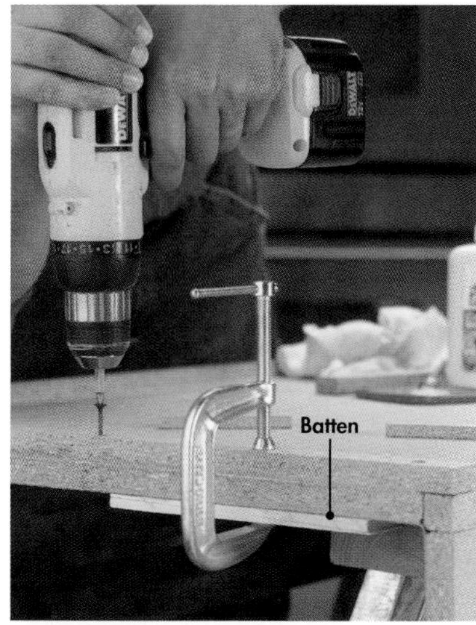

2 Put the countertop upside down on the sawhorses and clamp it in place. If either end of the counter will be exposed after installation, you'll need to put laminate on the end. End cap kits are available from home stores that sell countertops; the kits contain everything you'll need, including battens that you glue underneath the counter to build the ends up to the proper thickness. Begin by gluing the battens in place and fasten with finishing nails or screws.

3 The end cap is oversized—put it over the batten so that it covers the edge of the countertop. The end cap is backed with a heat-sensitive glue. Press the end cap against the end of the counter, using an iron set at medium heat, for the time suggested by the manufacturer. (If the iron is too hot, it will damage the laminate.) Wipe off excess adhesive while it's still hot.

4 Rout the end cap flush with the countertop using a small router called a laminate trimmer. Work carefully and hold the trimmer flat on the end cap—tipping the router will cut into the surface of the counter.

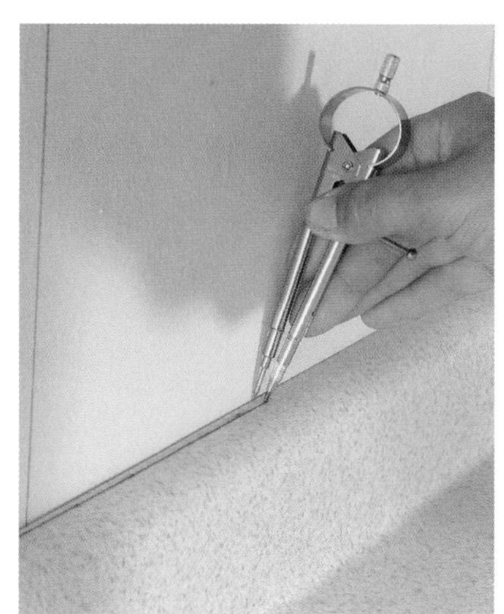

5 Set the countertop on the cabinets, clamp it in place, and check it for level. Shim it if necessary. Typically you'll have small gaps between the wall and backsplash; fill them later with caulk. If the gaps are large, however, you'll have to sand the countertop's edge so that it fits against the wall. Set the span of a compass to the size of the largest gap between the backsplash and the wall. Mark what you'll have to remove by pulling the compass along the wall.

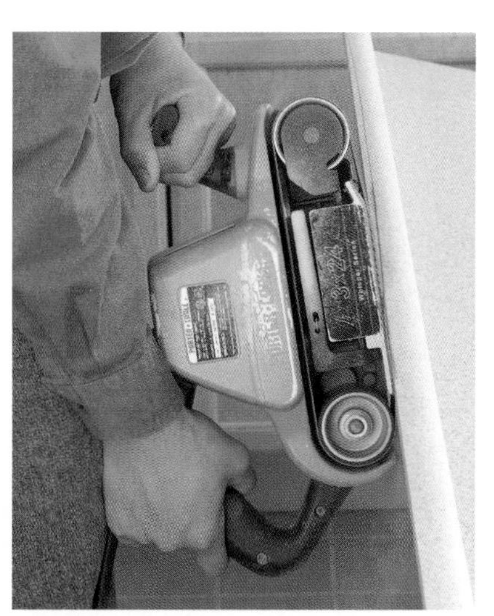

6 Remove the countertop and clamp and place it back on the sawhorses. Use a belt sander to sand the backsplash to the line you drew with the compass. This will eliminate any gaps between the countertop and the wall.

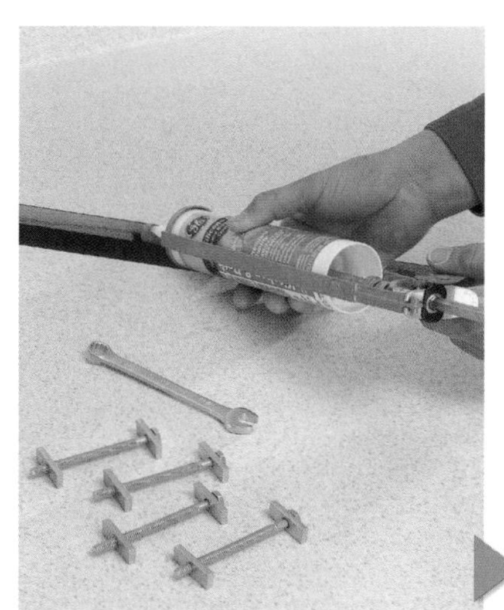

7 To hold pieces tightly together at the corners, most counters have grooves that hold joint-fastening bolts that span the seam. You'll get the best seam where two pieces of countertop meet if you join them before you put them on the cabinet. Start by gluing them together with the glue from a miter-clamp kit. If the kit has no glue, apply a thin bead of silicone caulk to the edge of both pieces and paint the rest of the edges heavily with wood glue. Then press the edges together.

Installing countertops (continued)

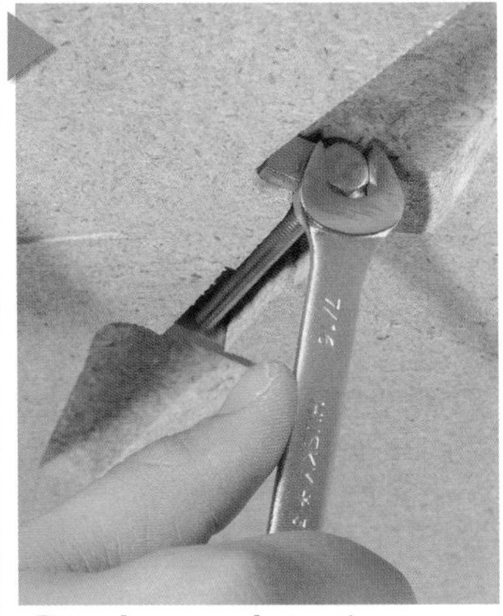

8 Make sure the entire surface is flush at the seam along the front edge of the counter. Adjust as necessary and tighten the nearest miter clamp. Wipe away any excess glue. Standing behind the backsplash, push the countertops up and down as necessary to make the seam flush along the back of the counter. Tighten the miter clamp nearest the backsplash.

9 Look at the rest of the seam. If one side is higher than the other, tap the countertop with a dead-blow hammer like the one shown here. If you use a regular hammer, protect the countertop with a piece of wood. Once the seam is level, tighten the remaining miter clamps.

10 Fasten the countertop to the cabinets by screwing up through the top of the cabinets. If your cabinets have no tops, screw through the front rail and through any blocks built into the cabinet for that purpose. Seal the seam between the backsplash and wall with a silicone caulk that matches the color of the countertop.

Don't screw up

Check, countercheck, cross-check, and double-check the length of every screw before you drive it through the cabinet and into the countertop. One lousy screw that's wrong spells disaster. A really good installer I know got a long screw in his pouch by mistake. He was in a hurry and not paying attention so he drove the screw right through the top of the laminate counter. An expensive mistake because all you can do at that point is ask the dealer to order some matching seam-fill and hope you can hide the damage. Seam-fill comes in a small, plastic tube. It's designed to help hide bad seams, but it can hide other mistakes too. Squeeze some on, work it flush using a small and flexible putty knife, and let it dry.

Sink cutout

All sink manufacturers supply a cutting template, or directions for making one, with their sinks. Set the countertop across a pair of sawhorses. Position the template on the countertop, following the manufacturer's instructions. Tape it in place and trace the outline with a pencil. Mark separate holes for the faucets, if necessary.

Clamp the countertop to the sawhorses and drill a ½-inch starter hole inside the outline with a spade bit. If other holes are necessary for faucets or other fixtures, drill them with a hole saw. Fit a saber saw with a laminate blade, which has special teeth to minimize chipping. Insert the blade into the starter hole to begin the cut.

Cut carefully along the outline. Once you've cut along part of the outline, screw a drywall screw into the gap left by the saw cut to keep the cutout from vibrating. If the backsplash interferes with the cut, change to a regular blade, turn the counter over, and continue the cut from the bottom to avoid chipping.

Tiling a countertop

Skill level:	**Time to complete:**	**Materials:**	**Tools:**
★★★☆☆	Experienced Variable Handy Variable Novice Variable	Ceramic tiles, edge tiles or edge bead, mortar, grout, grout sealer, scrap 2×4, ¾-inch exterior-grade plywood, 4-mil plastic sheeting, backerboard, backerboard screws, 1¼-inch drywall screws, 3-inch fiberglass tape, tile spacers	Drill with ⅛-inch masonry bit and phillips bit, tape measure, utility knife, notched trowel, drywall tape knife, tile cutter or wet saw, tile nippers, level, rubber grout float, burlap, saber saw, 2-foot level

Installing a ceramic-tile countertop creates a beautiful, long-lasting, and functional work surface. Like floor tile, countertop tile is permanently installed using mortar adhesive and grout. Most tiles are countertop material—glazed, quarry, mosaic, or even stone tiles, such as slate or granite. You have your choice of many sizes and shapes of tile, but be aware that different sizes affect the finished appearance. Smaller tiles require more grout lines that may stain or degrade with use. Larger tiles are more appropriate for floors. Midsize tiles (4 to 6 inches) are ideal for countertops.

The surface below the countertop tile may be more important than the surface beneath a tiled floor. Carefully follow the steps involved in preparing the substrate (the surface below the tile) to avoid problems.

DESIGN TIP

A BALANCED APPROACH

The tiles around your sink look best when they are the same width on all sides. The time to solve this problem is while you're laying them out. On a straight counter, lay out the tiles so the first one is centered over what will be the center of the sink, and work toward the ends. If the counter is L-shape, however, lay out the tiles with a full tile in the corner, as in Step 10 on page 277. If placing the tile there creates problems at the sink, reposition the sink opening before you cut it to make sure you have equal widths all around the sides.

1 Install a plywood substrate. The base cabinets form the structural support for the countertop. Install ¾-inch exterior-grade plywood cut to fit. Screw it in place with 1¼-inch drywall screws, shimming as necessary to ensure a flat surface.

2 Cut out plywood for the sink. New sinks often come with a template or measurements. (If you are reusing the old sink, measure the opening after you remove it.) Position the template. Make sure the new faucet will clear the wall behind the counter. Mark the cutout. Drill a ⅜-inch starter hole inside the cutout near one of the corners; then cut with a saber saw.

Tiling a countertop (continued)

3 Install backerboard. Cut it to fit by scoring and snapping. Cut sink curves freehand on both faces. Finish curves by snapping material away with pliers. Leave a ⅛-inch gap between pieces for mortar. Predrill screw holes every 6 to 8 inches. Remove the pieces and staple on a 4-mil plastic moisture barrier. Apply mortar on the plastic with a ¼-inch notch trowel. Reposition the pieces and install them with backerboard screws.

4 Tape and fill seams. Reinforce exposed edges of the backerboard with three layers of fiberglass tape. Then apply a 3-inch-wide layer of latex portland cement mortar to fill the gaps between sheets of backerboard. Lay a strip of fiberglass mesh tape across the gap. Press the tape firmly into the mortar with a 4-inch taping knife.

5 Apply an edge bead. Apply a stainless-steel decorative edge by bending it around the corners and nailing it into the backerboard with galvanized nails. An alternative is to use ceramic edge trim for a softer look. (See inset.)

BUYER'S GUIDE
TILING TERMS

- **Mortar** is a mixture of sand and portland cement.
- **Dry-set mortar** is a specially formulated mixture for application over backerboard.
- **Latex portland cement mortar** has a latex additive that makes the mortar more flexible, and is best suited for countertops. You'll find two types—one is a powder to which liquid latex is added; the other is a powder containing dry latex resin to which water is added. Both do the job equally well.
- **Backerboard** is a rigid panel that provides a sound substrate for setting tile. Depending on the manufacturer, backerboard can be made of cement, fiber cement, gypsum, plywood, or plastic. Fiber-cement panels do not require fiberglass mesh to bind the material into a panel. Although several thicknesses are available, ¼ and ½ inch are commonly used for walls and floors in residential construction. Follow the manufacturer's recommendations for installation.

6 Dry-fit the tiles. Tiles vary widely from the size they're supposed to be. To avoid surprises, lay out the entire countertop before applying mortar. Lay all the full tiles first, then cut the others to fit. In countertops with a sink, adjust the layout to ensure the tiles are even on each side of the sink. On an L-shape countertop, start with a full tile at the inside corner. Use tile spacers to maintain even spacing. Leave a ⅛-inch gap between perimeter tiles and the wall.

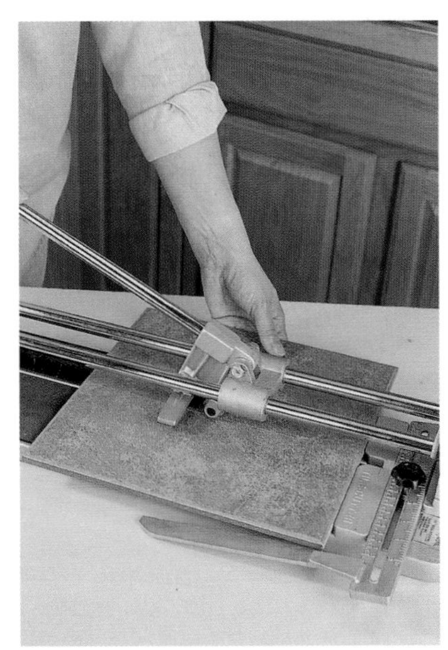

7 Cut the tiles to size. Use either a score-and-snap-type tile cutter or a wet saw to make straight cuts in the tile. Mark the tile with a felt-tip pen and position it against the fence on the tile cutter. Hold the tile firmly and slide the scoring wheel across the tile in a continuous motion. Reposition the tool with the pressure plate flat against the face of the tile and press down to snap the tile.

8 Cut the tiles around the sink. Cutting curves or notches is more challenging than straight cuts. (See inset.) Mark the cut with a felt-tip pen. Gradually nip off small pieces of tile with tile nippers to reach the mark. Smooth if necessary with sandpaper or a file.

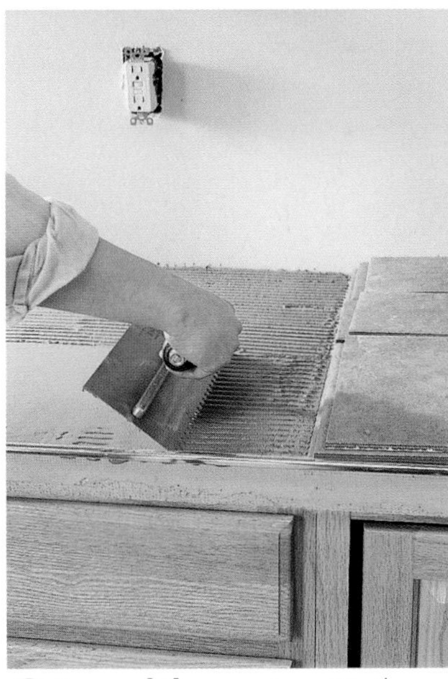

9 Spread the mortar. Mix the mortar according to the label directions. Spread an even coat of mortar with a notched trowel. The mortar instructions will specify the appropriate notch size, which is determined by the size of the tile. Hold the trowel at a consistent angle (about 45 degrees) and drag it against the backerboard surface.

Check tile sizes

Larger tiles (12"×12") can vary slightly in thickness and size even if they're from the same box, so be sure to compensate for differences when you lay out the tile.

Helping hand

Cutting tiles is fairly easy but if you're uncomfortable about it (or just don't want to spend money on the one-time use of a tool), mark all the tiles that need to be cut and take them to a tile supply company or a home center with a reputable tile department. They usually employ a tile cutter, who will make the cuts for a fee. Mark the tiles carefully with their locations in the layout.

10 Lay the tiles in the mortar. Start laying the full tiles at the more critical areas of the layout—around the sink or at an inside corner of an L-shape counter. Work from front to back, placing as many of the full tiles as possible. Press each tile into the mortar with a slight twisting motion. Use tile spacers to keep the tiles aligned. To level the set tiles, place a straight piece of 2×4 on its edge across the tile, then tap gently on it. Check for flatness with a 2-foot level.

11 Lay partial tiles at the perimeter and around the sink. When all the full tiles are in place, set the partial tiles and any tiles cut to fit around the sink. Use the spacers between cut tiles and full tiles. Let discrepancies in spacing end at the wall—the backsplash or trim will hide any flaws.

Tiling a countertop (continued)

12 Tile the backsplash, running the tiles from the counter up to the bottom of the wall cabinets, or stopping after a single row. If you're only applying a single row, use bullnose tile, which has a finished edge. If the backsplash wall contains electrical outlets, cut tiles around them and add box extension rings (available in the electrical department) to bring the outlets flush with the tiles.

13 Tile the edge. If using edge bead, cut the tiles so that they bridge the grout lines on the main countertop, as shown. Apply grout. Put the tiles tightly against the bead and tape them in place to hold them while the mortar dries. If using edge tiles, it's unnecessary to tape them because part of the tile sits on the countertop. Space edge tiles so the grout lines between them match those on the counter.

14 Grout the tile. After the tile has completely set (check the mortar instructions), pull out the spacers and apply the grout. Mix the grout following the manufacturer's directions. Spread grout across the counter with a rubber grout float. Work the grout into the joints by moving the float diagonally across the tile. Once all the joints are filled, remove excess grout by wiping diagonally with a wet sponge (see inset). Rinse the sponge frequently in clean water. Sponge off the excess grout from the surface of the tile and leave the grout slightly depressed in the joints. Let the grout dry, then rub the tiles with cheesecloth to remove the haze left by the grout.

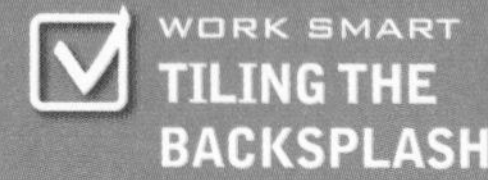

WORK SMART

TILING THE BACKSPLASH

The section of wall against the countertop covered with countertop material is called a backsplash because it protects the wall from splashes, bumps, and spills. You can make the backsplash a few inches high, or run it up to the cabinets above, as shown above. Whatever method you use, put up backerboard before you tile. Follow the same procedure as for the countertop: Put mortar directly on the wall, put backerboard over it, and screw it to the studs. Leave spaces between the edges, fill with mortar, and cover with fiberglass tape.

Tiling over plastic laminate

You can lay tile over a plastic laminate countertop as long as there are no loose areas, and as long as the edges are square. (Rounded-over edges, or "waterfalls," between the backsplash and counters can't be tiled.) Edges that have lifted should be glued down with construction adhesive and clamps. Then screw down cement backerboard and follow the steps on these pages. Tiling over an existing countertop will make counter edges thicker and may affect sink and faucet installation.

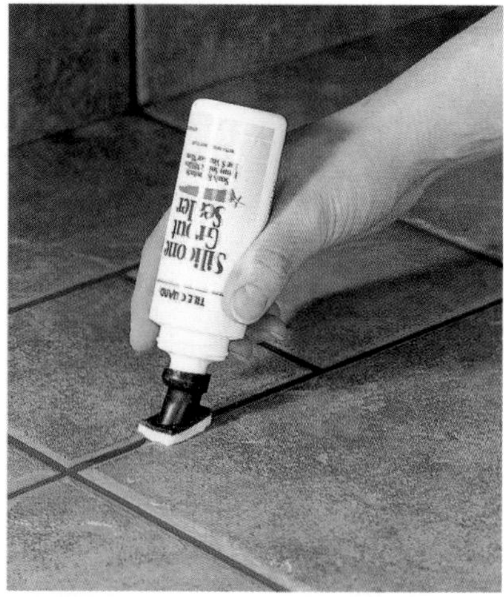

15 Seal the grout. Because grout is prone to staining, seal it with a silicone grout sealer after it has cured completely—about 30 days, or as recommended by the manufacturer. Apply the silicone grout sealer to the grout lines with a foam brush or applicator, let it soak in for a few minutes, and wipe away the excess.

Adding a closet

Skill level:	Time to complete:	Materials:	Tools:
★★★★★	Experienced 3 days Handy 4 days Novice 5 days	2×4 lumber, drywall, prehung door, 8d and 10d nails or 2½- and 3-inch drywall screws for framing, 6d and 8d nails for trim, toggle bolts, shims, metal corner bead, joint compound, drywall tape, paint, primer	Tape measure, framing square, combination square, chalkline, plumb bob and line, mitersaw, small backsaw, hammer, 4-foot level, drill with drill and screwdriver bits, screwdriver, clamps, utility knife, 6-, 8-, and 12-inch drywall knives, coping saw, paint roller or paintbrush

Before you start measuring hangers and making plans, the minimum depth you'll need for a closet is 24 inches. If you're hanging coats instead of suits and dresses, plan on a minimum of 28 inches. As for length, allow 48 inches per person.

This, of course, is the inside dimension. The outside dimension is an extra 4½ inches for each wall—3½ inches for the studs and another ½ inch on each side for the drywall. If you have the space, get out your tape measure and start making plans. Putting the closet in the middle of a long wall, for example, is sure to look like the afterthought that it is. Tucking it into an unused corner of a large room, or along the entire length of a windowless wall, on the other hand, will make the closet seem like part of the overall plan.

Building a closet in a room with a finished ceiling is a bit different from building one in an unfinished room. It's no longer possible to build the wall flat on the floor and then roll it up in place without wedging it at an angle between the floor and ceiling. Instead you'll have to nail a plate to the floor and one to the ceiling, then measure and cut the studs to fit between. (For more information on framing the door opening, see page 110.)

Note that when the time comes to draw layout lines, you should start on the ceiling. This simplifies aligning the floor and ceiling plates because you can transfer the lines to the floor with a plumb bob. If you find overhead layout confusing, by all means, start your layout on the floor. When you need to transfer lines to the ceiling, keep moving the string until the plumb bob is over the right spot on the floor.

On average you'll want the closet bar 63 inches off the floor for dresses or about 72 inches off the floor if you're storing a collection of ballroom gowns. Either of these heights works for suits, blouses, and skirts, but if you drop the bar down to 45 inches, you can install a lot of shelf space, or even another bar, above it. It's also an appropriate height for a kid's closet when they're from about 6 to 12 years old. Drop down to 30 inches for younger children.

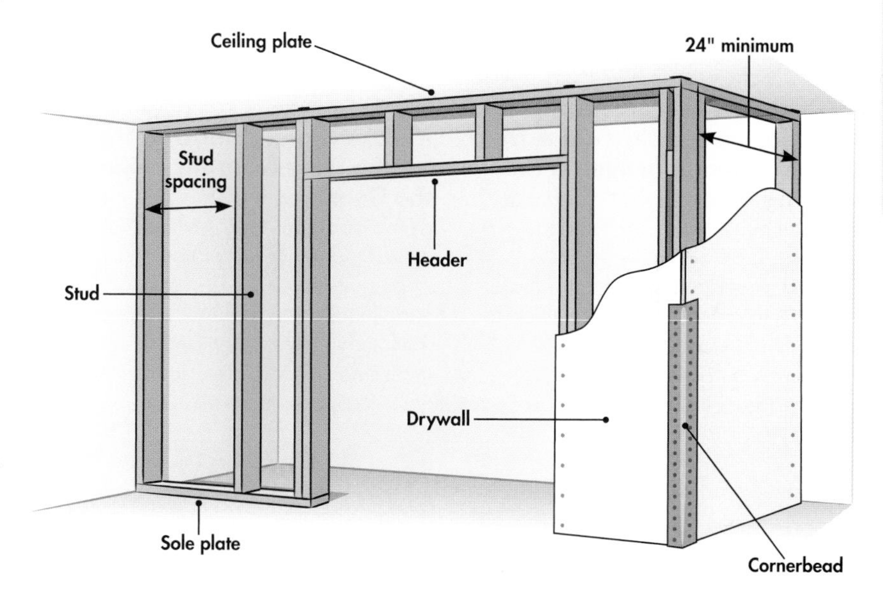

Up to code

In most municipalities, adding a closet is considered a major renovation. Check with your building officials to see whether you need to obtain a building permit.

1 Begin by laying out the shortest wall of the closet. Measure along what will become the back wall to what will be the outside edge of the new wall. Measure back the thickness of the drywall, ½ inch, and use a framing square to draw a line marking the outside edge of the ceiling plate. Draw a second line marking the inside edge of the ceiling plate.

Adding a closet (continued)

2 Measure and lay out a front closet wall parallel to the existing back wall. This assures that the closet depth won't change because of an out-of-kilter corner. Once you've located the front edge of the wall, measure back by the thickness of the drywall to lay out the plate. Draw a second line laying out the inside edge of the plate.

3 Use a plumb bob to transfer the lines from the ceiling to the floor. Begin by hanging the plumb bob from what will be the outside corner of the plates. When it stops swinging, mark the spot on the floor immediately below it. Repeat to mark the inside corner, and then mark the inside and outside edges of where the plates meet the wall.

4 Cut the plates to length. One ceiling plate and one soleplate will be the full length of the closet wall; the others will be shorter than their walls by 3½ inches—the width of the adjoining plates. Lay the long plates side by side, and lay out studs 16 inches apart, on center. Repeat on the shorter plates.

5 Buy a prehung door before doing this step. Find the rough opening required—it will be listed on the installation directions that come with the door. Lay out the opening on the plates. Each side of the opening requires two studs—one that runs floor to ceiling, and one that runs to the top of the rough opening. (See Step 15 photo on page 282.) For now, just lay out the edges of the rough opening.

6 The best way to match trim to the existing trim is to reuse as much of it as you can. Cut along the edge of any baseboard or other trim that you will have to remove—this breaks any paint seal between the trim and the wall. Pry the molding loose, protecting the wall with a piece of scrap wood as you pry, as shown. If the molding seems reluctant to come off, try driving the nails that are holding it all the way through the molding and into the wall.

7 Nail the plates to the floor, driving nails every 2 feet. Use common nails long enough to extend through the subfloor and into the framing; 10d nails are usually adequate.

8 Unless a joist just happens to fall in the right place, only the ceiling plate that runs perpendicular to the joists will have any framing above it. Nail or screw this plate into the joists that cross it. (If the ceiling is plaster and lath, attach the ceiling plate with screws to avoid cracking the plaster.)

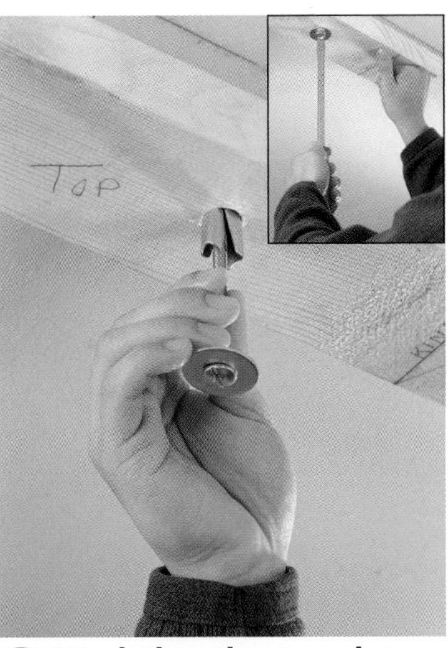

9 Attach the other top plate with toggle bolts. Begin by drilling holes in the top plate. Drill holes big enough to slip the folded toggle through. Put the plate in place and trace through the holes to mark the ceiling. Remove the plate and drill holes in the ceiling for the toggles. Secure the plate to the ceiling by tightening the toggles (see inset) and toenail it into the bottom plate.

10 Find the straightest studs for framing the door. Measure back 3 inches from the marks you made for the rough opening and make a second mark. This will be the outside edge of the king stud, the one that runs from ceiling to floor. Measure, cut to length, and nail it in place, leaving a 1½-inch space between the edge of the rough opening and the nearest face of the stud. The jack stud gets nailed into this space later. (See page 110.)

11 Because the distance between the plates may vary slightly, measure for length each of the remaining full-length studs one at a time. Cut them to length and toenail them to the plates with 8d nails. Nail the studs nearest the existing walls to the framing inside them. If there is no framing directly behind the new studs, attach them to the wall with toggle bolts, the same way you attached the plate to the ceiling.

12 Frame the corner to create a structure that looks like this. Begin by nailing a stud in place at the end of either of the walls that forms a corner. Nail spacers to it, and nail a full-length stud to the spacers. Once you've nailed in the spacers and both studs, begin work on the adjacent wall by nailing a full-length stud in place.

13 Now that all the full-length studs are in place, go back to the closet opening. Cut the jack studs to length—they will be as long as the rough opening is high. Clamp both jack studs to the king studs. Use a level to verify the top of one stud is level with the other. Adjust as necessary and nail in place. (See Step 15 on page 282.)

Adding a closet (continued)

14 Cut a 2x4 to fit across the opening. Put it in place and nail down through it to secure it.

15 To support the space above the door, you will need to place cripple studs at 16-inch centers between the top plate and the 2×4 across the opening. Lay out the locations and measure to see if the length varies. Cut the studs to length and nail in place. (See page 110 for general information on framing openings.)

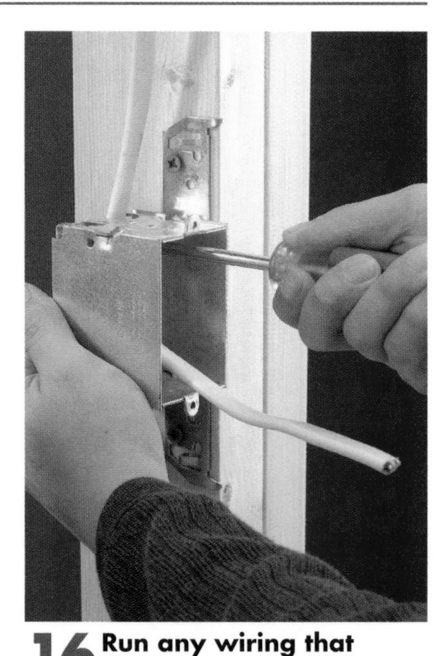

16 Run any wiring that you'll want for the closet. If you want a light, put the switch for it near the door and position it ½ inch beyond the framing to account for the thickness of the drywall. By law, closet lights must be recessed into the ceiling to prevent an accidental fire.

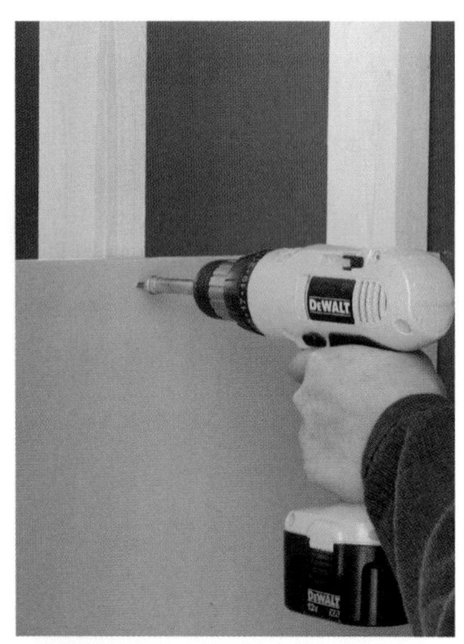

17 Cover the inside and outside of the closet with drywall. (It's easiest if you prime it first and then start hanging on the inside of the closet.) Cut any necessary openings for switches and receptacles, and screw the drywall in place. Put a metal corner bead on the outside corner and tape and finish the drywall with joint compound. For more on working with drywall, see "Installing Drywall," page 119.

18 Hang the door following the instructions that come with it. Start with the jamb on the hinge side, shimming as necessary until the jamb is straight and plumb. Shim the other side so that it is plumb and there's a gap about the thickness of a nickel between the door and the door jambs. Level and shim the top, leaving the same-size gap. For more on hanging doors, see "Installing a Prehung Interior Door," page 216.

19 Trim around the door and then install baseboard. If you saved the old baseboard, it will match up best with the baseboard already on the wall. For a tight fit, cope the joint—cut the piece going in so that it nests with the piece on the wall. Find the profile by mitering the closet molding and then cutting along the edge with a coping saw, as shown. Practice on a scrap first. See page 132 for more on coping.

Installing a modular storage system

Skill level:	Time to complete:	Materials:	Tools:
★★★☆☆	Experienced 2 hrs. Handy 3 hrs. Novice 6 hrs.	Hardboard panels, shelves, knockdown hardware, plastic brackets, metal rods, basket/drawer slides, shelf pins, wire baskets	Deadblow mallet, level, Phillips and slot-head screwdrivers, cordless drill/driver

Seem like you never have quite enough closet space? Short of renting a mini-storage unit for your out-of-season clothes and footwear, closet organization systems are one solution that won't cost a fortune.

Before now, your choices were mainly limited to coated wire organizers made in an array of styles and configurations. They were (and still are) basically systems of shelves, baskets, drawers, and supports that quickly go together to increase and organize available storage space. These systems aren't just for closets. You can buy them for the kitchen, garage, or any room in the house.

Manufacturers today have gone a step further by upscaling the appearance and versatility of these systems by adding handsome modular units of wood-look, laminated hardboard. The result (for a few more bucks) is customized storage that's quickly assembled and installed. Most companies offer design-it-yourself assistance so you'll be sure the end product is exactly what you wanted. And, after time, if it needs tweaking, the "knock-down" modules (no adhesives needed) can be readily reassembled and reconfigured.

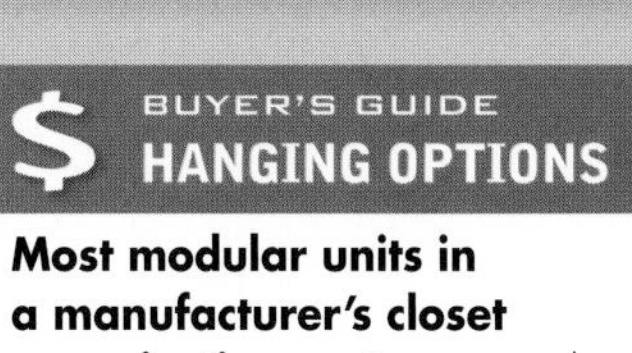

BUYER'S GUIDE: HANGING OPTIONS

Most modular units in a manufacturer's closet organization system can also be suspended from a ceiling-height or lower metal track and held in place by brackets supported by standards.

This option requires anchoring the track to the wall studs with screws. But once the track is in place, you'll have several types of storage options to choose from.

▲ ***Freestanding modular units have the advantage of not being attached to the walls.*** *Thus they can be easily rearranged later if the configuration isn't quite right. They're available in wood grains or plain white. Glass-fronted drawers and doors—so you can see what's inside—are also available.*

1 Familiarize yourself with all the parts and hardware before you start. Check what's in the package against the parts list. And then lay out all modular panels on the floor. Follow the manufacturer's directions and, where indicated, use a screwdriver to drive the threaded metal pins into the predrilled holes to the required depth.

2 Seat the locking cap nuts into the predrilled edges of the panels using a deadblow mallet as explained in the directions. Make sure that each cap nut is correctly oriented and completely seated in its designated hole. These nuts will interlock with the pins when you assemble the panels.

Installing a modular storage system (continued)

3 Assemble the modular units by aligning the pins in the panels with the holes in the respective mating panels, making sure there's a locking cap nut at each pin. Push or tap the panels together until the pins are seated in the holes. With a phillips head screwdriver, turn each cap nut until it engages its respective pin.

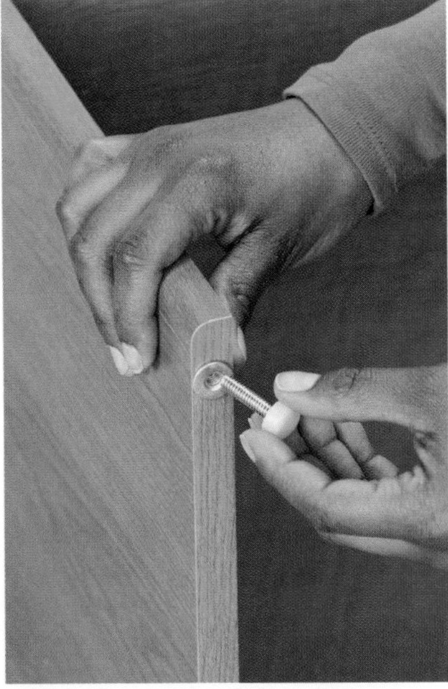

4 Push or tap the metal threaded inserts into the bottom of each corner of a modular base cabinet with a mallet. Carefully thread the cushioned leveling pins into the inserts.

5 Level freestanding base units before adding another on top. Turn the base unit right side up and set it in place. Check for level from front to back and side-to-side, raising or lowering the pins as necessary by turning them. (Uneven floors may require some shimming.)

6 Add an upper module by first inserting plastic joiner pins in the top of the base unit at each corner. Lift the upper unit, aligning the holes at the bottom corners with the joiner pins (you may need some help). When the holes align with the pins, the top unit will settle in place.

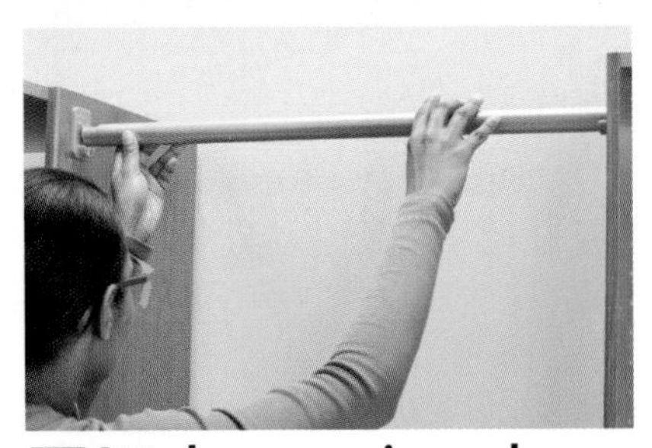

7 Attach accessories such as the clothes rod (or rods) by installing the appropriate hardware on the side of the modules as shown in the manufacturer's instructions. Normally the screw holes will have been predrilled. You can then slip the removable clothes rod(s) in place.

8 To add the doors to a unit, first lay them on a flat surface, inside up, and attach the largest part of each hinge with screws where indicated on the instructions. (Again, the holes will have been predrilled.)

Then attach the cabinet part of the hinges to the inside of the module in the locations shown in the instructions.

9 Raise the doors into place and interlock the hinge parts. Test for square by opening and closing the door. Adjust as necessary by loosening and retightening the hinge screws on the cabinet side.

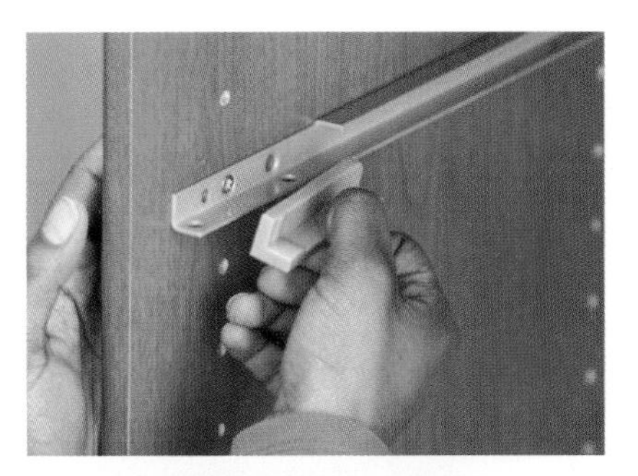

10 Add the drawer and basket slides to the insides of the cabinets. Check the instructions for the exact locations (they'll vary depending on drawer/basket height) and type of slide to be used. After determining their locations, fasten each set of slides to the cabinet sides with screws. Slip the plastic basket runner clips in place.

11 Clip the baskets into the plastic runners on the slides. Test to see that the baskets track smoothly on the slides. Add shelving to the unit with the shelf clips provided, pushed into the appropriate holes in the sides.

12 Assemble the drawer frames according to instructions. After sliding the drawer bottoms into the assemblies, fasten the other half of the drawer slides to each, again referring to the manufacturer's instructions. Fasten drawer pulls to drawer fronts. Finally, lift the drawers in place, engaging the slides.

13 Top off the space for hanging clothes by using screws to attach the lip hardware flush with the top of the adjacent modules.

PLUMBING

CHAPTER 6

Plumbing

Plumbing projects are often unpredictable. Failures and leaks can happen at any time and have to be dealt with quickly.

Become familiar with the materials and equipment needed for these jobs.

A working knowledge of your plumbing system will help you understand why something isn't functioning properly and where to address the problem.

Contents

How the plumbing system works 288
The plumbing tool kit. 290
Quick fixes for frozen or leaking pipes 291
Planning for accessibility 292
Working with rigid plastic pipe. 293
Connecting PVC 294
Connecting CPVC 295
Connecting ABS 296
Soldering copper pipe 297
Running new supply lines. 299
Installing PEX supply lines 301
Installing shutoff valves & supply tubes 302
Repairing or replacing a sink strainer 303
Installing a single-bowl PVC P-trap 305
Unclogging the clogs 307
Unclogging drains and waste lines 308
Unclogging sink drains 309
Unclogging jammed disposers 309
Unclogging bathtub and shower drains 310
Unclogging a toilet. 311
Repairing a compression faucet 312
Replacing a worn valve seat. 313
Repairing a ceramic disk faucet 314
Replacing a cartridge faucet. 315
Repairing a rotary ball faucet 316
Repairing a tub and shower faucet 317
Repairing a tub diverter valve 318
Installing a tub spout 319
Cleaning a showerhead 319
Repairing toilets 320
Adjusting the tank and water level 321
Repairing a leaking tank 322
Replacing a toilet fill valve 323
Replacing a flapper 325
Installing a countertop sink 326
Installing a vanity and sink 328
Installing a self-rimmming sink 329
Removing an old sink 329
Installing a wall-hung sink. 330
Installing a pedestal sink 330
Installing a bowl-type sink. 331
Installing a farmer's/apron sink 332
Installing a widespread faucet 333
Installing a center-set faucet 334
Installing a pop-up drain 335
Removing an old tub. 337
Installing a bathtub in an alcove 338
Installing a sliding glass door for a tub 342
Installing a shower surround 343
Removing an old toilet. 345
Installing a new toilet. 346
Installing a garbage disposer 349
Replacing a dishwasher 351
Connecting a refrigerator ice maker. 352
Installing a water softener. 353
Water heaters 355
Water heater installations. 356
Installing an on-demand water heater. 359

Mom, there's a swimming pool in the basement!

Plumbers will tell you two things about their trade: Water is tricky stuff, and there aren't any standard sizes. Here are some sure-fire plumbing tips from the professionals:

- **Leaks happen.** That's why plumbers have jobs. The first rule is that there are no easy fixes. Magic powders, pastes, and incantations won't solve the problem. Get some advice from a knowledgeable salesperson and do the job right the first time.
- **If you're working in plastic, clean and prime the joint before you cement it.** With copper, the only solid joint is a clean joint: Polish the surface with emery cloth, deburr the inside of the fitting with a wire brush, and brush on plenty of flux to further clean the surfaces. (You can never apply too much flux.)
- **If the joint has a compression fitting—a little metal sleeve that squishes tightly against the fitting to prevent leaks—you won't need solder.** But you can only use the sleeve once and will have to replace it every time you disconnect the fitting. You'll also have to cut off the compressed section of the pipe. Sleeves are cheap and the job is easy, but eventually the pipe will become too short to use.
- **Don't apply logic to plumbing sizes.** A faucet supply line and a toilet supply line are different diameters, for example. Kitchen faucets won't fit in a bathroom sink, and toilets are one of three different distances from the wall. There are at least a dozen kinds of toilet flappers and countless faucet washers. Fortunately a good salesperson can often look at a faucet stem and tell you the manufacturer and which part you need to fix it. While they can often recognize a part, they are seldom able to look across town and see inside your kitchen. Bring the piece in—or as much of it as you can. If it's too big, bring a photo. Call ahead to find out what else you need to know or bring. It's the best chance you'll get of walking out of the store with the right part.

How the plumbing system works

Understanding your home's plumbing system: Water enters your house through a main supply line. It passes through a water meter and a portion of the incoming water is then branched off to enter your water heater. The heated water and the remaining cold water are then piped to fixtures throughout the house. Toilets need only cold water. Waste water travels by gravity, but first it must pass through a trap located below each fixture. Traps allow water to flow through but prevent sewer gas from drifting up the drain. Vents on the roof let in air. This allows waste water to flow freely to the waste and vent stack and out the sewer line.

Multistory construction

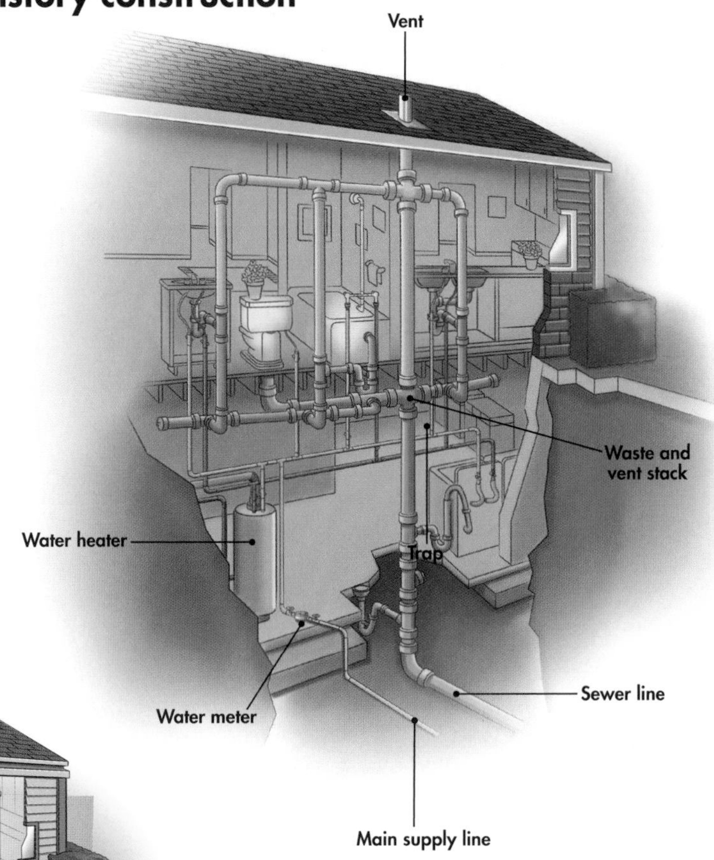

Vent
Waste and vent stack
Water heater
Trap
Sewer line
Water meter
Main supply line

Slab construction

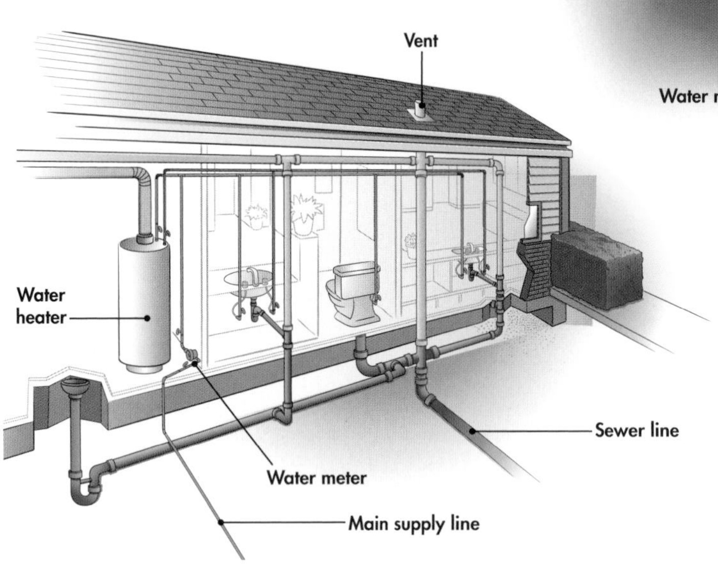

Vent
Water heater
Sewer line
Water meter
Main supply line

Confusing fittings

Fittings for drain and vent lines look alike and fit on the same pipe but are not interchangeable. The sanitary tee has a gentle sweep in one arm to keep it from clogging, and it is required on drain lines. The straighter vent tee is for use on vent pipe only. The clean-out plug is for drain line, but the threaded end is for a removable plug only. Use a long sweep 90 elbow for drain lines. The straighter vent 90 is for vent pipe only.

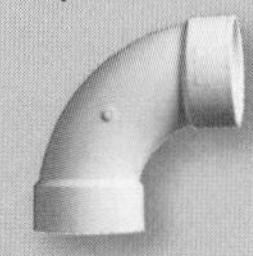

PVC long sweep elbow

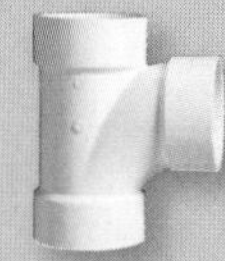

Sanitary tee

PVC cleanout and plug

Access panels can be a livesaver

If you need to get your hands on the plumbing in the wall adjacent to a bathtub or shower, consider adding access panels the next time you replace or work on a tub or shower. Cut out an adequately sized rectangle from the wall and use it as a template to cut a sheet of paint-grade plywood to the same shape. Ideally the vertical edges of the cutout will run along the centerline of studs in the wall. Glue and screw trim around the perimeter of the better side of the panel to provide a lip, mitering the corners as on a picture frame. Install the panel with screws through the trim and into studs, or into plastic anchors if its edges aren't backed up by studs.

Down in the basement: Tracing your home's plumbing

Most of us eventually get around to touring the valves and elbows of our home's plumbing, but usually that doesn't happen until there's a problem—a toilet or sink won't drain or a there's a big puddle of water from a mysterious source. A better way to go about it is to arm yourself with a good flashlight, a handful of manila strung tags, and a fine-tipped permanent marker, then take that tour before you have trouble. Use the tags to identify important valves—the things you'll want to shut off in a hurry if there is water spraying all over the place.

Most of your tour will take place in the basement, unless your construction is slab on grade, in which case much of the plumbing will be on the first floor, perhaps in a utility room or closet. There are going to be some components of the system that you can't see. Supply and drain lines snake out of sight within walls and between floors, and while these aren't apt to be a source of trouble, it's good to have a general idea of their location. You'll be less likely to puncture them when driving nails and screws when hanging pictures or installing shelving.

Master shut-off valve

While you don't have to be familiar with every twist and turn of your home's plumbing, be sure to know where to find the **master shut-off valve** for the household water supply. It typically will be located just inside an exterior wall. The handle may be in the form of a lever, as shown, or a wheel. If you have cold winters, this supply pipe may be prone to freezing where it enters the house; you can keep the water flowing and avoid a burst pipe by wrapping the line with insulating tape.

Main supply

The **main supply** divides into a cold-water line and a line running to the water heater. This appliance requires little attention, and there aren't any controls that you're likely to use. For a gas water heater, however, familiarize yourself with the shutoff valve; if you smell what might be a leak, close the valve and call the gas utility for help. If you have an electric water heater and your own well, turn off the circuit breaker for the heater at the service panel when a power outage interrupts the water supply. Otherwise, if you draw water from the water heater and empty it, the heating elements may be damaged when power is restored. Allow the heater to refill for a minimum of 30 minutes before turning on the breaker to that circuit.

Sewer stack cleanout

The down and dirtiest item in the home's plumbing system is the **sewer stack cleanout.** You can unscrew the cleanout plug with a heavy-duty adjustable wrench and use an auger (pages 307 and 308) to loosen clogs in the line. Before putting the plug back in place, spread pipe joint compound on the threads for a good seal.

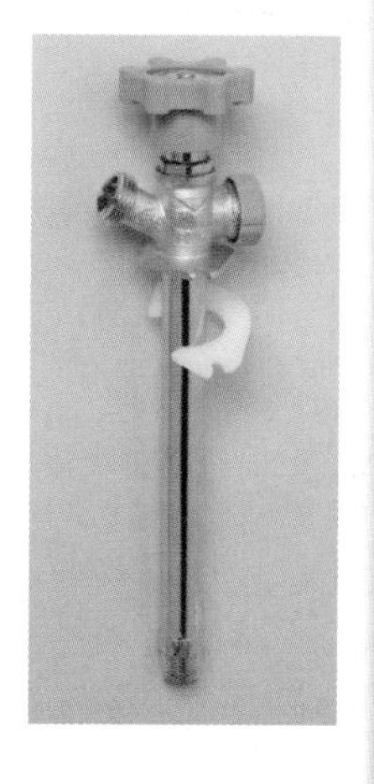

Hose bib

The shutoff valve to an exterior faucet **(or hose bib)** may have a small waste outlet that allows you to completely drain the line between the valve and faucet. To help ensure that freezing winter temperatures won't burst the pipe, close the valve, open the hose bib, and open the outlet. In spring, reverse the process to restore service to the faucet.

Shallow well (or sump)

An efficient way to deal with a chronically wet basement is to collect water in a **shallow well (or sump)** at the low point of the floor, then draw it out of the house with an automatically activated sump pump. There are submersible pumps, like the one shown here, and pedestal-style pumps that sit above the well on a stand.

Ball valve

Familiarize yourself with shutoff valves throughout the plumbing system. Newer **ball valves,** like the one shown here, are taking the place of gate valves with their round handles.

The plumbing tool kit

4-in-1 combination tool

Cordless reversible 3/8-inch drill

Hand auger

Plastic pipe primer

Self-adjusting pliers

Spud wrench

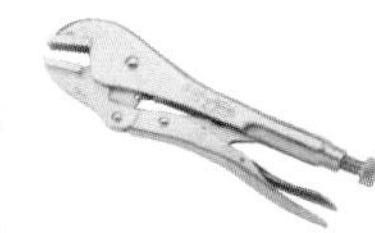
Adjustable locking pliers

Drain snake or drain auger

Hex key or allen wrench set

Plastic tubing cutter

Shower-stem socket

Strap wrench

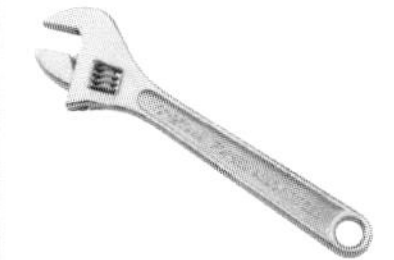
Adjustable wrench

Emery cloth

Lead-free flux and solder

Plumber's putty

Silicone grease

Tape measure

Basin wrenches

Faucet handle puller

MAPP torch

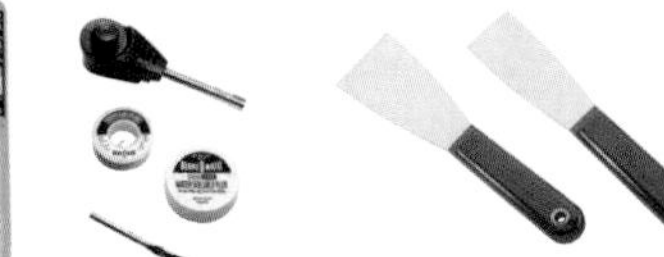
Putty knives

Slip pliers

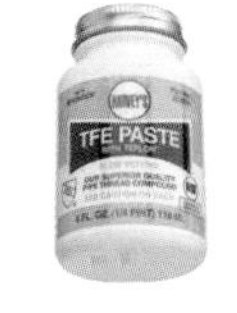

Teflon paste

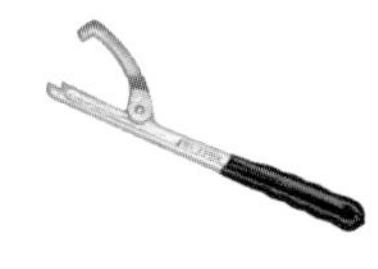
Basket strainer wrench

Flanged plunger

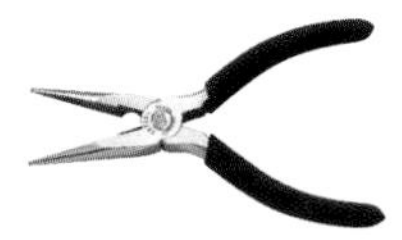
Needle-nose pliers

Ratchet-type PVC cutter

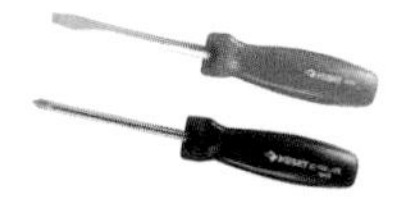
Slotted and phillips screwdrivers

Teflon tape

Caulking gun

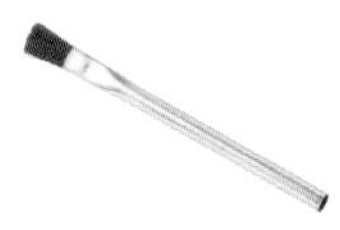
Flux brush

Pipe joint compound

Reamer (PVC)

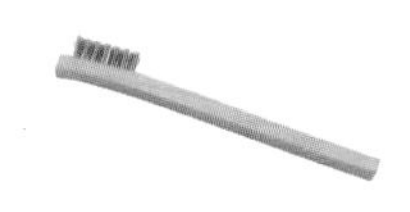
Small wire brush

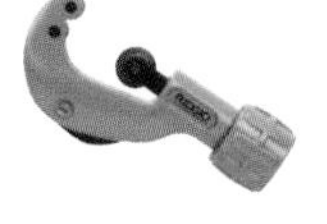
Tubing cutter

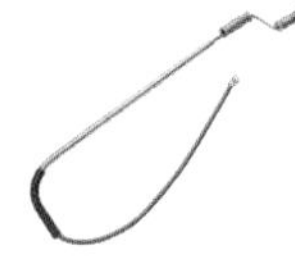
Closet auger

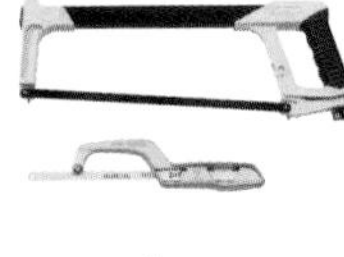
Hacksaws

Pipe wrench

Seat dressing tool

Spark lighter

Utility knife

Copper tubing deburrer

Hammers

Plastic pipe cement

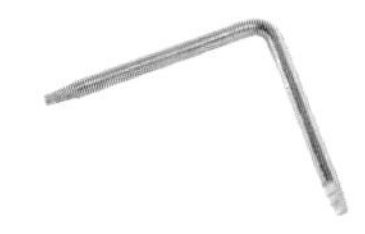
Seat wrench

Spiral cutting saw

Water-pump pliers

Quick fixes for frozen or leaking pipes

Finding a leak is only half the battle. Water can travel across joists and other surfaces long before reappearing to ruin a wall or ceiling. You may have to cut into walls and ceilings to find the source, but most leaks occur at pipe fittings. Temporary fixes are only that; permanent repairs should be made quickly. Never make a quick fix behind a wall.

Fractures, on the other hand, result from corrosion, dents, or freezing. Water expands when it freezes, fracturing pipes and valves. Bury pipe below the frost line outdoors. Prevent pipes from freezing by not running supply lines in exposed areas or against exterior walls, wrapping pipes with sleeve-type foam insulation, or protecting them with an insulation wrap such as heat tape. Be careful when using heat tape, however. It can deteriorate over time and pose a fire hazard. Inspect it occasionally and replace it if worn.

Quick fix for a leaky pipe

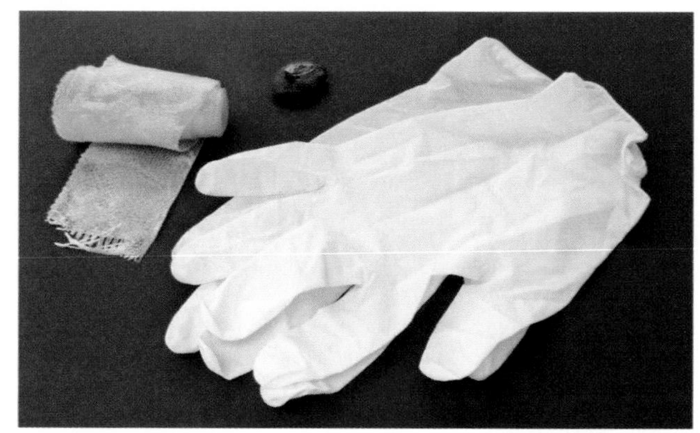

For fast, temporary fixes, keep a roll of water-activated fiberglass tape on hand—and a pair of gloves to protect yourself if it's a hot water line. The tape simply wraps around the pinhole or crack to make a seal.

Thawing frozen pipes

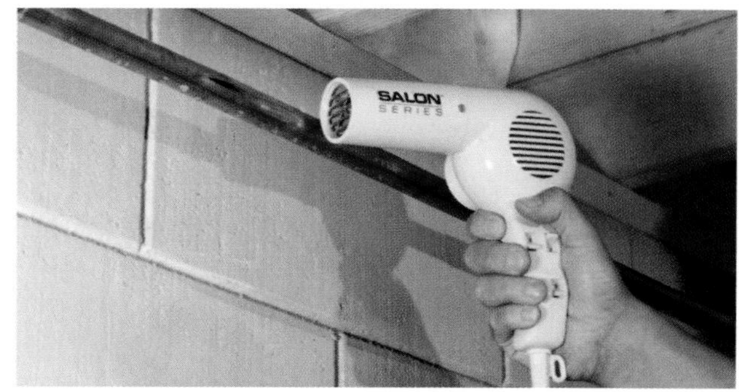

Turn off the water from the main shutoff valve. Inspect the pipe for damage. Look for ruptures that may have been caused by expansion of the freezing water. If the pipe does not appear to be fractured, drain the line by opening a downstream faucet. Then use a hair dryer or heat lamp to thaw the pipe.

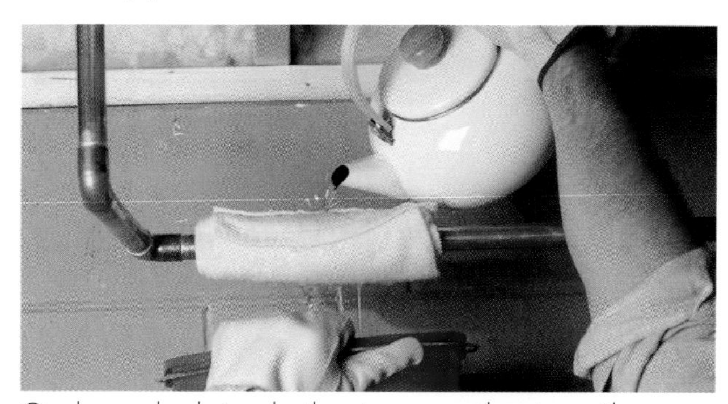

Or place a bucket under the pipe, wrap the pipe with an old towel, and pour hot water over the towel to thaw out the pipe. After thawing, turn on the water supply while you inspect the pipe for leaks and damage. Repair ruptures.

Pipe insulation

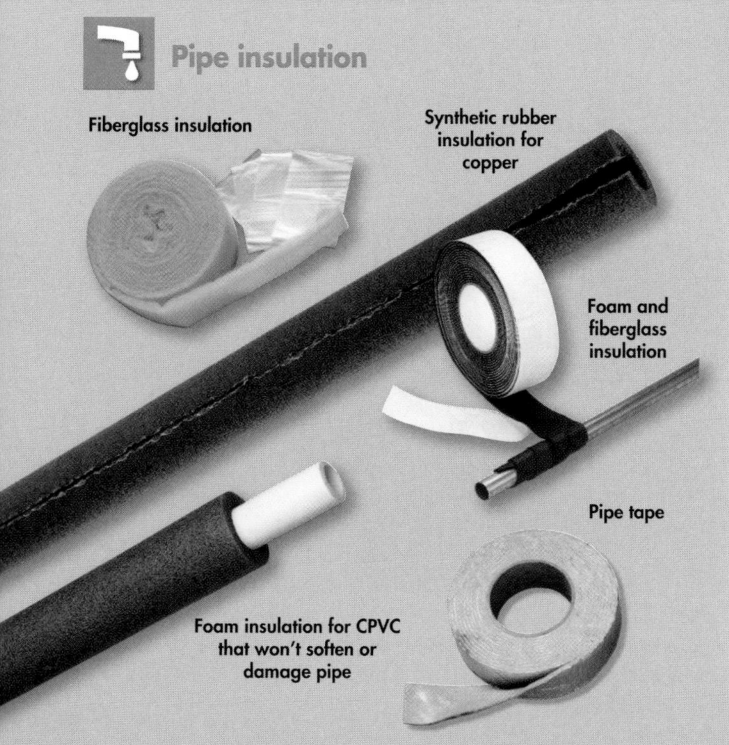

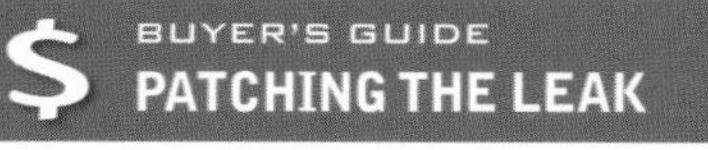

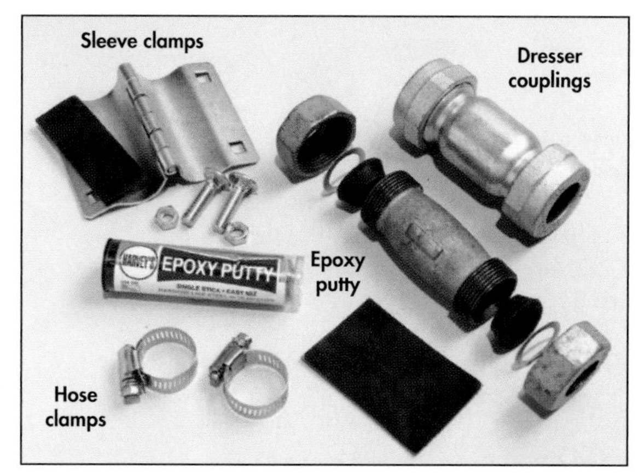

Small leaks and wet surfaces can be fixed quickly with plumber's **epoxy putty.** More serious leaks require more drastic measures, but solutions abound. Try 1⁄16-inch-thick neoprene rubber or a bicycle tube patch with **hose clamps, sleeve clamps,** or **dresser couplings.**

Planning for accessibility

Universal design helps make kitchens and baths convenient and comfortable for all people through all of life's stages and changes. If you're in the early planning stages of building or renovating a kitchen or bath, incorporating universal design can be a wise move.

In most cases, you won't need to make significant changes whatever the circumstances: a family member becoming permanently or temporarily disabled, an elderly parent in the home, a young child or shorter-than-average adult, or guests with disabilities. Free of obstacles, your home will be enjoyable for all. And if you're planning to live there many years, universal design features will accommodate your own needs in the future, whether you sprain a wrist, develop stiff joints, or need assistance to move about.

▲ *In the bathroom, sturdily-mounted grab bars and cabinet doors that swing open to reveal plenty of knee space make this bathroom wheelchair accessible.*

▲ *A few simple modifications make this tub and shower exceptionally flexible and easy to use: A sliding shower head accommodates seated as well as standing bathers; controls are mounted toward the outside of the tub so that anyone adjusting the temperature avoids putting hands under hot running water.*

Universal Design is:

Equitable and flexible—accommodating the preferences and abilities of many different people.

Simple and intuitive—easy to understand and use.

Tolerant of error—with minimal hazards and adverse consequences of accidents or unintended actions.

Easy and comfortable to operate—requires low physical effort to use.

Easy to approach—appropriately sized and shaped access for approach, reach, manipulation, and use, regardless of body size, posture, or mobility

▲ *Mounting the sink 34 inches off the floor and providing plenty of knee space underneath accommodates shorter people or a seated cook. The garbage disposer switch is mounted on the cabinet front for easy access, too.*

▲ *Raising the dishwasher reduces bending and stooping, providing better ergonomics for everyone.*

Working with rigid plastic pipe

Rigid plastic pipe was developed to replace cast iron and galvanized steel in plumbing supply and waste systems. Plastic pipe is cost-effective and easy to install. Use rigid plastic PVC (or ABS if codes allow) for drain, waste, and vent systems. Use CPVC or PEX for hot and cold water supplies. Plastic pipe is available with inside diameters (ID) of 1¼, 1½, 2, 3, and 4 inches.

- Use 1¼-, 1½-, and 2-inch ID PVC for sink drains and lavatories.
- Use 1½- and 2-inch ID pipe for tubs and showers.
- Use 3- or 4-inch ID pipe for toilets. New 1.6-gallon flush toilets work best with a 3-inch fitting.
- Drain lines and vent stacks can use 2-, 3-, or 4-inch ID pipe.

Assemble quickly

Plastic pipe is joined with fast-acting solvent cements. Once you glue a fitting in place, it can't be removed—you have to cut it apart and start over. You can't twist fittings apart, and fine-tuning is impossible. Cut sections to length and test-fit the entire run before cementing the lines in place.

Dry-fit all the connections before the final assembly. Dry-fit the connections before applying primer and cement—once you've cemented the pipe, it can't be changed. Check the fall with a level. There should be a ¼-inch fall, or slope, for each lineal foot of run.

BUYER'S GUIDE

USE THE RIGHT PRIMER

If you want your work to pass inspection—and not leak—use the right primer. Purple-tinted primer is required by code for drainage lines and will also work on supply lines. Clear primers are fine on supply lines but won't pass inspection when it comes to drain lines. Save yourself some grief—buy the purple primer and use it everywhere.

WORK SMART

TIPS FOR CONNECTING RIGID PLASTIC PIPE

- Use the correct pipe cleaners, primers, and cements for the pipe you're installing. CPVC, PVC, and ABS are not interchangeable without transition fittings or special glue.
- Cure time depends on the cement used, the size and tolerance of the pipe and fitting, and the air temperature. You will weaken the bond by trying to speed or retard the cure.
- Keep lids on cements and primers when not in use.
- Stir or shake cement before using.
- Do not mix primer with cement. Do not use thickened or lumpy cement. Cement should have the consistency of syrup or honey.
- The size of the adhesive and primer applicator, called a "dauber," depends on the size of its container. You'll want a ¼-inch dauber on small-diameter pipes; a 1½-inch dauber for pipes up to 3 inches; and a natural-bristle brush, swab, or roller half the pipe diameter for pipes 4 inches or more. Try to buy a can that has a dauber that matches the job at hand.
- Do not handle joints until they are fully cured.
- All colored cements and primers will leave a permanent and recognizable stain.

PLUMBING

Connecting PVC

Skill level:	Time to complete:	Materials:	Tools:
★☆☆☆☆	Experienced 10 min. Handy 20 min. Novice 25 min.	PVC pipe and fittings, cleaner, primer cement	Tubing cutter, hacksaw or miter saw and box, deburring tool, knife, emery cloth, rags

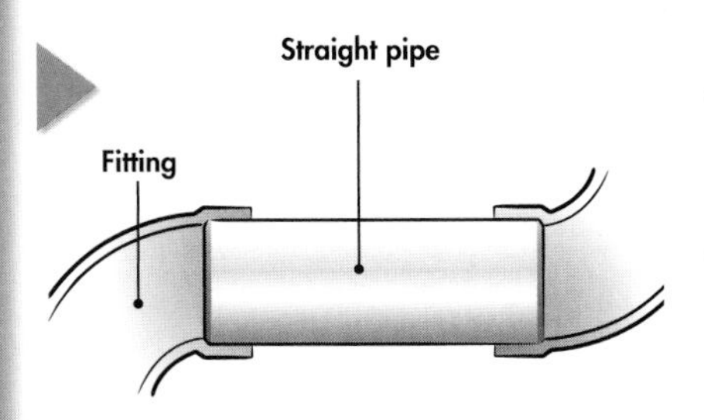

For a PVC joint to be effective the pipe must seat itself fully into the fitting. Without the adhesive as a lubricant, it's often hard to be sure that the pipe is seated properly.

1 A straight, square cut is necessary for a good connection. PVC tubing cutters are made for both small- and large-diameter pipes. If you don't have a cutter, you can cut the pipe with a mitersaw, hacksaw, or power mitersaw. Take your time and make sure you get a clean, square cut. Deburr the inside and outside edges of the pipe, and test-fit before final assembly. Clean the pipe with the manufacturer's recommended cleaner; then use the correct primer and adhesive to ensure a solid joint.

2 Deburr the cut. After each cut, deburr the pipe with a deburring tool, knife, or emery cloth to remove rough edges that could interfere with the flow of water or the fit of the joint. Sand the section of pipe that will be housed by the fitting too. If you don't, the pipe won't travel as far into the fitting as it will once you apply glue. The run will be slightly short as a result.

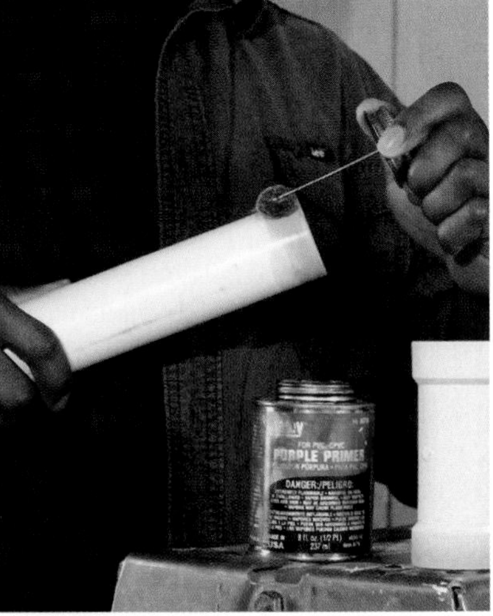

3 Apply primer to the connections. The primer softens the ends, preparing them for application of the cement. An inspector will often look for the permanent purple stain at the joint to make sure primer was used to help make the connection.

CLOSER LOOK

LOOKS CAN BE DECEIVING

Each type of plastic pipe is composed of different materials and requires its own blend of cleaners and cements to make a proper bond. If you have to join PVC to ABS, you'll need a special glue transition fitting to make the connection. Ask at the store, and check local codes.

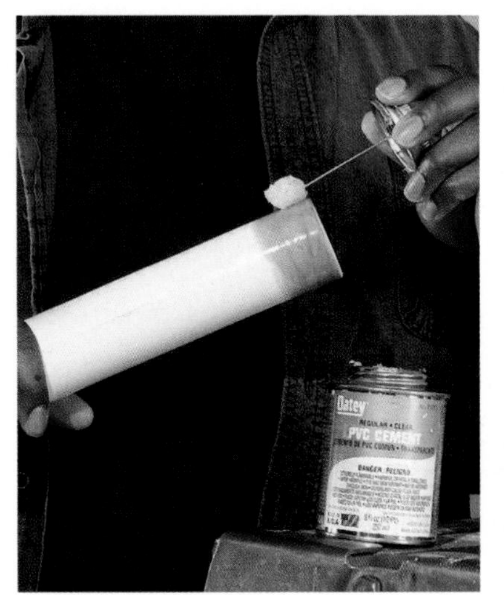

4 Coat the pipe and fitting with cement. While the primer is still damp, quickly apply a thin, even coat of cement to the surfaces. Too much cement can weaken the pipe and destroy the fitting.

5 Work quickly to connect the pieces. Insert the pipe into the fitting with a quick push and a quarter-turn to seat. Hold the connection for 30 seconds to prevent the heat produced by the cement from pushing the connection apart. The cement melts the surfaces and forms a secure bond. With a rag, wipe away excess cement, which can weaken the joint.

Connecting CPVC

Skill level:	Time to complete:	Materials:	Tools:
★☆☆☆☆	Experienced 10 min. Handy 20 min. Novice 25 min.	CPVC pipe and fittings, primer, dauber cement	Tubing cutter, hacksaw or mitersaw and box, deburring tool, knife, emery cloth, rags

CPVC is used for hot and cold water supply. It is less expensive than copper but just as durable, and it withstands high temperatures and pressure in the supply system. It cuts easily with a tubing cutter or hacksaw, connections are easy, and assembly is quick.

One-step cements are available for CPVC and eliminate the need to use purple primer. However one-step cements may not meet local code for many uses. Check local codes carefully to determine whether primer is required. In some localities you will fail inspection if you don't use it. Purple primer leaves a permanent and recognizable stain on the pipe, so inspectors will know whether you've used it. It's easier to do the job up to code the first time to avoid the hassle of redoing it when the inspector fails your installation.

1 Deburr the pipe. Removing burrs ensures even coverage with the primer and cement. Once you've deburred, sand lightly with emery cloth so that the pipe will seat in the bottom of the fitting.

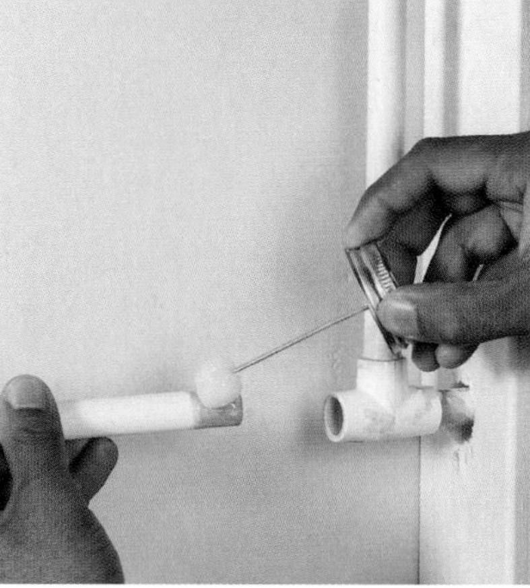

2 Coat the surfaces with primer if required. Apply an even coat of primer to the pipe and the fitting. Primer softens the pipe to help seat it and reacts with the cement to make a permanent bond. Using a purple primer is essential where priming is required by code. The resulting stain tells the inspector the joint has been properly treated prior to connection.

TOOL TIP

JOINING CVPC TO COPPER

You may run into a situation where copper pipe is in the walls and you don't want to remove it but you want to run CPVC for the hot and cold water supply for your new sink. No problem! A special transition fitting available at your home center or hardware store can join CPVC to brass or copper.

SAFETY ALERT

DANGEROUS FUMES

Fumes from primers and cements can lead to loss of consciousness. Work in a ventilated area. The fumes are also highly inflammable and explosive. DO NOT smoke or use torches or electric tools that spark (such as power drills) near areas where there may be fumes.

3 Apply cement and assemble the parts quickly but carefully. Use a dauber to apply an even coat of cement to the pipe and fitting. Insert the pipe all the way into the fitting until it stops. Twist a quarter of a turn to spread the cement evenly. Hold the pipe together for 30 seconds to prevent heat generated by the cement from pushing the connection apart. With a clean rag, wipe off excess cement on the fitting or pipe.

Connecting ABS

Skill level:	Time to complete:	Materials:	Tools:
★☆☆☆☆	Experienced 10 min. Handy 20 min. Novice 25 min.	ABS pipe and fittings, cleaner, primer cement, dauber	Tubing cutter, hacksaw or mitersaw and box, deburring tool, rags

PLUMBING

The first rigid plastic pipe approved for use in drain, waste, and vent systems was ABS. It is inexpensive, easy to cut, lightweight, and very rigid. However, it becomes brittle over time and therefore is susceptible to cracking and breaking.

Before purchasing ABS pipe, check your local plumbing codes. Some communities forbid the use of ABS.

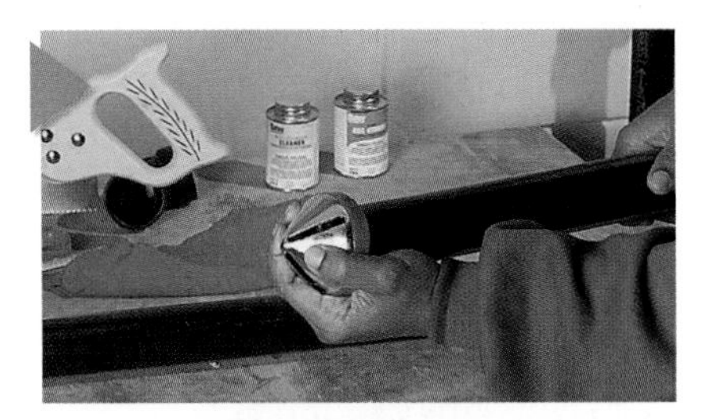

1 Cut and deburr the pipe. Removing burrs ensures even coverage with the primer and cement. Sanding can change the diameter and cause a poor fit. Test-fit the pipe to the fitting; it should seat snugly in the fitting.

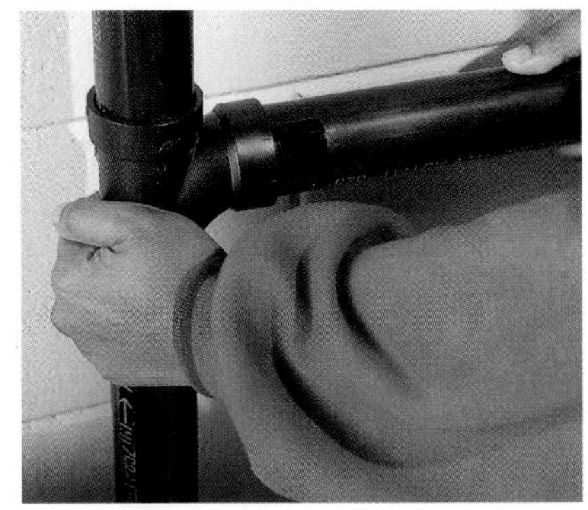

2 Apply cement and assemble the parts quickly but carefully. Don't puddle the cement on—too much cement can weaken the pipe wall. Push the connections together with a twisting motion until properly seated. Because the solvent produces heat that may cause the connection to push apart, hold the connection for 30 seconds. Wipe away excess cement with a rag to prevent weakening of the ABS pipe walls.

WORK SMART

LEARNING THE PLUMBER'S ABC'S: ATTACHING ABS TO PVC

When remodeling the kitchen or bath, you may find yourself needing to connect black ABS pipe with white PVC. The two are just about as different as their colors suggest, and plumbing codes typically don't permit gluing one to the other. Instead use a mechanical coupling–a neoprene sleeve rated as plastic-to-plastic. Install the coupling with the metal jacket and hose-type clamps that come with it. You tighten the clamps with a wrench or screwdriver for a tight fit.

BUYER'S GUIDE

SKIP THE TORCH AND GLUE WITH PUSH FITTINGS

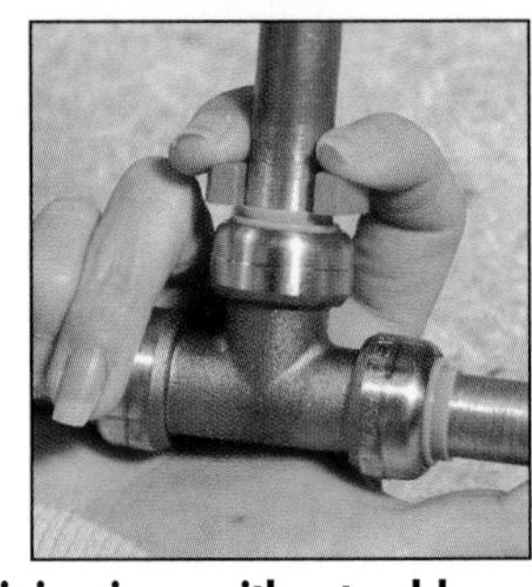

Push fittings allow you to join pipes without solder or solvents, and they are used for hot and cold water supply as well as heating lines. Connections can be made with some water still in the pipes, an advantage that's especially important when there's a plumbing emergency. These fittings cost more than those for other alternatives. But they take less time to use, and pipes of different materials—copper, CPVC, or PEX—can be joined because the connection is mechanical. Depending on the manufacturer, you may need to use a clip that comes with the fittings to release a connection.

Soldering copper pipe

Skill level:	Time to complete:	Materials:	Tools:
★★★☆☆	Experienced 10 min. Handy 20 min. Novice 30 min.	Type L copper pipe, plumber's pipe cutter, copper fitting, lead-free soldering paste (flux), water, lead-free solder, bread	Tubing cutter, MAPP torch, spark lighter, emery cloth, round wire brush or 4-in-1 combination tool, flux brush, fire extinguisher, fiberglass flame barrier, bucket, rags

Soldering copper pipe fittings isn't difficult, but you'll need to practice to make perfect. Gather some scraps of copper and solder a few joints until you get the hang of it. Once you've mastered the skill, you'll see why copper plumbing is appreciated for its professional look. Copper is a durable, clean, and functional connecting system.

Make sure you get type L pipe. (Type M pipe is for heating systems and has a thinner wall that may leak under the greater pressure of a water supply system.)

Cut and test-fit all the pieces of the puzzle before you begin soldering. Solder fittings with pipe already set in both ends. There's enough heat to make both joints at the same time.

In colder climates, run supply lines at a slight slope so they will drain easily. Add bleeder caps at the low points to get rid of excess water.

1 Cut pipe to length with either a plumber's pipe cutter for the tidiest results, or with a conventional hacksaw and miter box. The cutter clamps to the pipe and is rotated around it to incise the copper.

2 Prepare the inside of the fitting. Ream the inside of each fitting with a round wire brush and sand the end of the fitting with emery cloth. Clean connections ensure a good seal.

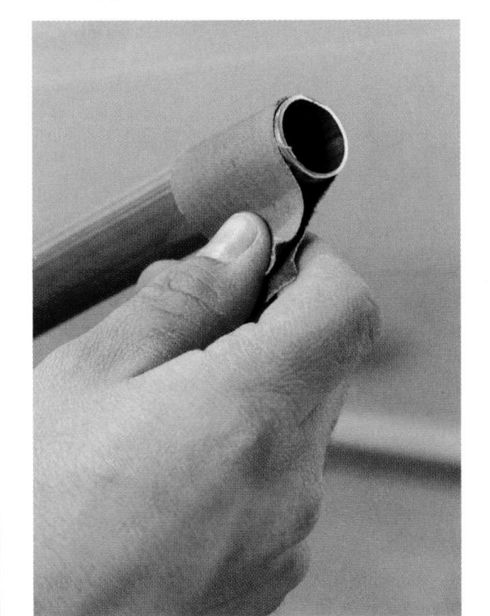

3 Clean the outside of the pipe with emery cloth or steel wool. Use a deburring tool or the handle of a pair of pliers to deburr the inside of the pipe. (A burr can cause an obnoxious hum once water starts running through the pipe.) Work carefully—the edges may be sharp!

4 Apply flux to the pipe. Apply a layer of lead-free soldering paste (flux) to the end of the pipe using a flux brush. The paste should cover about 1 inch of pipe. Insert the pipe into the fitting, making sure the pipe is tight against the bottom of the fitting. Twist the fitting slightly to spread the flux.

WORK SMART

REMOVE WORKING PARTS IN STOP VALVES BEFORE LIGHTING THE TORCH

The heat needed to melt solder can also damage the interior of a valve. It's best to remove the handle and stem of the valve to avoid damaging the stem's washers. You also can help protect a nearby fitting by wrapping the section of pipe between it and the heat source with a wet rag.

TOOL TIP

THE RIGHT COMBINATION

Wire brushes work well for cleaning fittings, but the 4-in-1 cleaning tool is a solderer's friend. It's a combination deburrer and cleaner for preparing ½- and ¾-inch copper pipe.

Soldering copper pipe (continued)

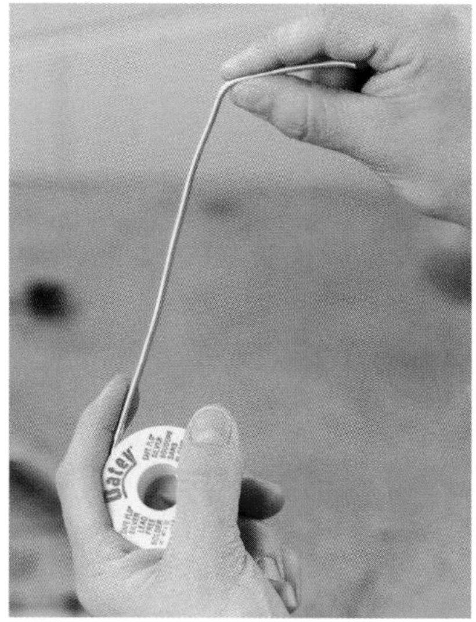

5 Unwind the solder wire. You will need 8 to 10 inches of the wire extended from the spool. Bend the first 2 inches to a 90-degree angle.

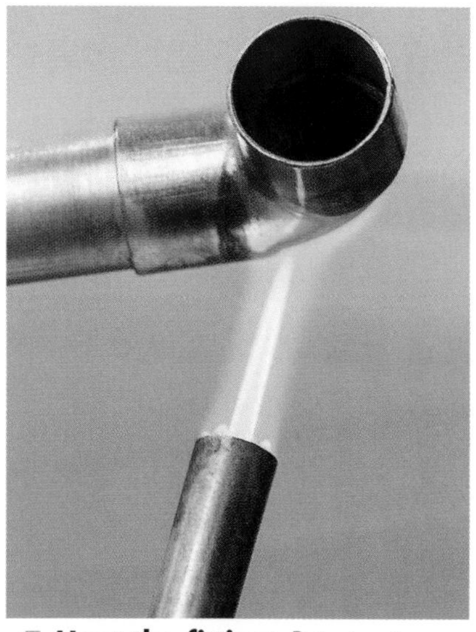

6 Heat the fitting. Put pipe in both sides of the fitting so that soot from the torch won't contaminate the joint. Light the torch. Hold the tip of the flame against the middle of the fitting for 4 to 5 seconds or until the soldering paste begins to sizzle.

7 Touch the solder to the pipe. Move the flame to the low end of the fitting. (Some of the heat you apply will migrate to the upper end, where you'll be working next.) Remove the flame and touch the solder against the pipe. If the solder melts, the pipe is ready to solder.

TOOL TIP

KEEPERS OF THE FLAME

Use MAPP gas cylinders for plumbing. MAPP comes in a yellow cylinder and is a combination of propane and methylacetylene-propadiene. It burns hotter and solders better than the pure propane that comes in the blue cylinders.

WORK SMART

KEEP YOUR COPPER DRY

Whether you're adding fittings to a system or starting from scratch, water in the line will keep the pipe from getting hot enough to make a secure solder joint.

- Drain the line and open a faucet down the run to release steam.
- Stuff bread into the pipe to absorb moisture; it will dissolve later when you run water.

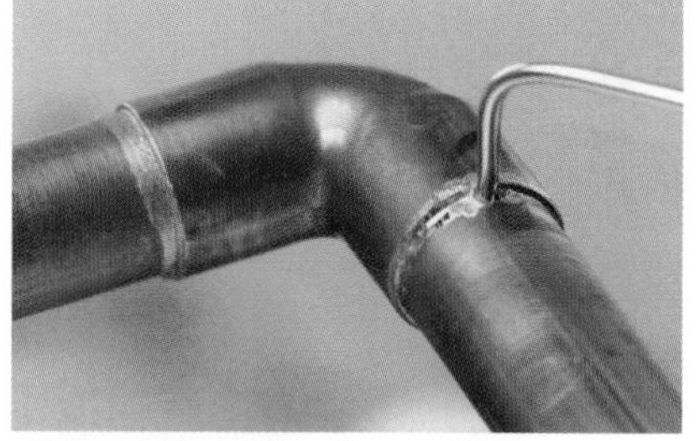

8 Apply more heat if it's necessary. Once the solder melts when touched against the pipe, remove the flame and quickly melt ½ to ¾ inch of solder into the joint. Capillary attraction will draw the liquid solder into the joint. A properly soldered joint should show a thin bead of solder around the fitting.

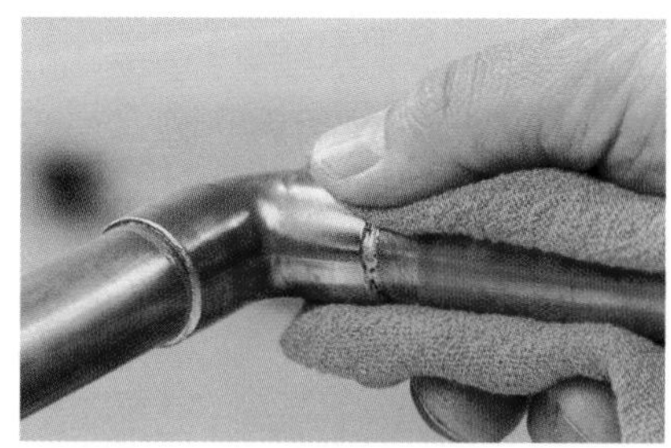

9 Clean the fitting. At this point, some plumbers reapply flux and briefly heat the pipe to clean it further. Always wipe away the excess solder with a rag. The pipe will be hot, so be careful while handling it. Cool the pipe and fitting with a damp rag, and then turn on the water and check for leaks.

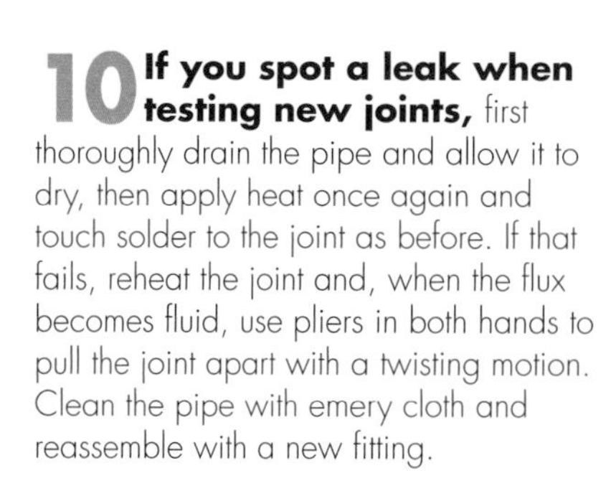

10 If you spot a leak when testing new joints, first thoroughly drain the pipe and allow it to dry, then apply heat once again and touch solder to the joint as before. If that fails, reheat the joint and, when the flux becomes fluid, use pliers in both hands to pull the joint apart with a twisting motion. Clean the pipe with emery cloth and reassemble with a new fitting.

Running new supply lines

Skill level: ★★★☆☆

Time to complete:
Experienced 6 hrs.
Handy 8 hrs.
Novice 12+ hrs.

Materials: Copper supply pipe, copper fittings, integral stops, copper tube straps and anti-vibration pads, brass screws, faucet assembly, shower tee, solder, flux, PVC P-trap, tub overflow and drain assembly, PVC primer and adhesive, bathtub, galvanized nails, 2×4 blocking, 1×3 ledger strips, silicone caulk

Tools: Electric drill, spade bits, tape measure, carpenter's level, pencil, hammer, MAPP torch and striker, tubing cutter, soldering kit, fiberglass flame barrier, hammer, screwdriver, saber saw, PVC cutter, gloves, safety glasses

Running new supply lines requires planning in order to choose the best route for the pipes and break the job down into manageable phases. Hot and cold supply lines can be either copper (as shown here), CPVC, or, if code allows, PEX.

You must decide the most convenient point to break into existing service and then track the pipe runs to the point of the new installation (in this case, a control riser for a new bathroom). The closest point may not be the best choice—remember pipe is cheap.

The idea is to plan a run that does the least damage to existing walls and installations and therefore requires the least patching and repair. (Once you've planned the run, you may find it easier to install the system in the bathroom first and then connect the supply lines downstairs.)

Order of work

- Plan ahead. Make a sketch of the installation.
- Create a tools and materials list.
- Purchase all materials and make everything you'll need accessible before you begin work.
- (NOTE: The diameter of the pipe you're installing must be the same as the existing supply line.)
- Turn off the water supply and drain the pipes you are cutting into so you can install the new lines.
- Mark the location of the new supply lines on the wall studs. Space the hot and cold water supply lines approximately 8 inches apart.
- Cut out sections of the existing supply lines and install T-fittings for connecting the new pipes.
- Cut and test-fit all the pipes and fittings before you solder the connections.
- Going through studs: Drill holes for the supply lines in the center of the studs, making the holes at least ¼ inch larger than the diameter of the pipe you are running. Code may require larger holes in earthquake zones.
- Attaching to floor joists: Prevent stress by securing the pipes to the joists with hangers as you go.

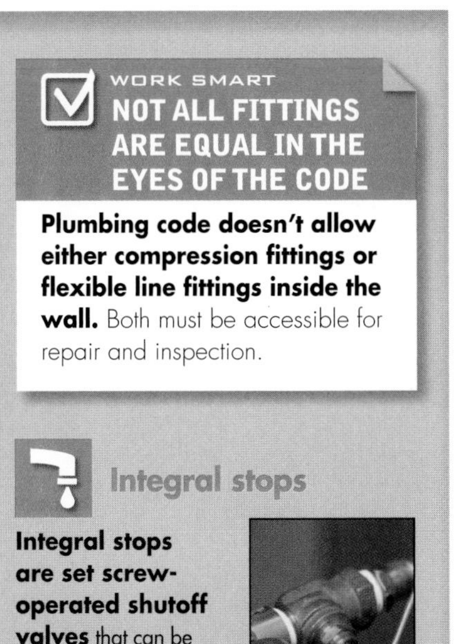

WORK SMART

NOT ALL FITTINGS ARE EQUAL IN THE EYES OF THE CODE

Plumbing code doesn't allow either compression fittings or flexible line fittings inside the wall. Both must be accessible for repair and inspection.

Integral stops

Integral stops are set screw-operated shutoff valves that can be installed as part of the valve body assembly. The advantage of using an integral stop is that you can access it by removing the escutcheon plate that covers the valve assembly.

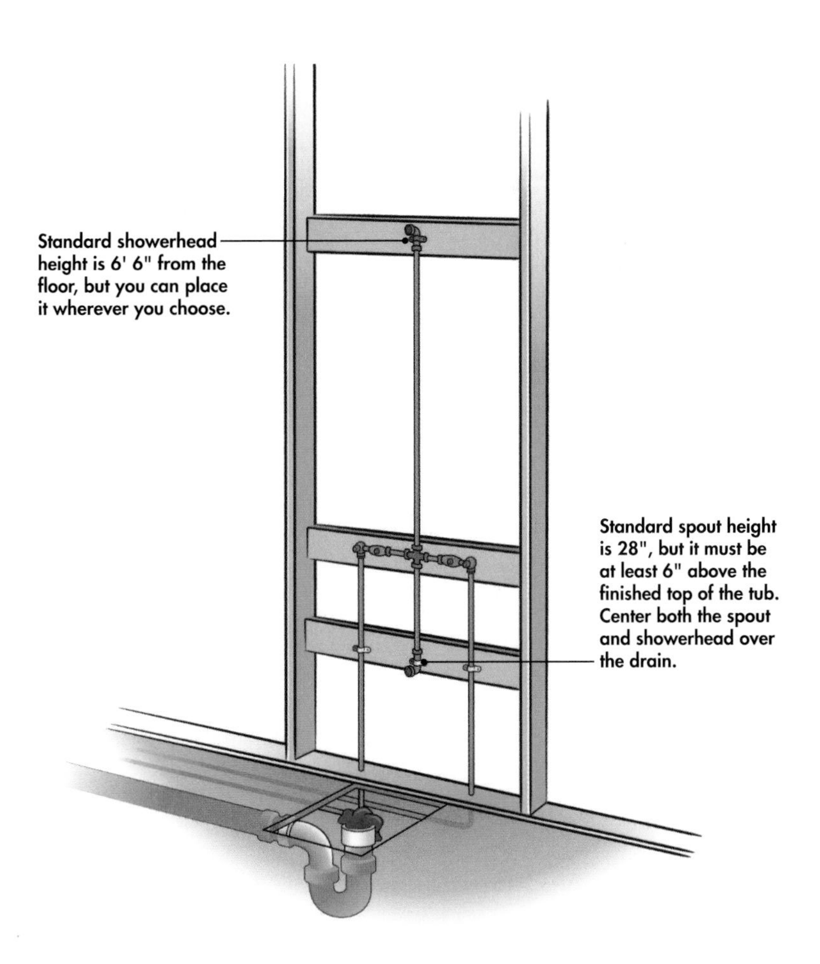

Running new supply lines (continued)

1 Drill holes for the risers. Drill riser holes through the stud wall into the basement. The diameter of the holes should be at least ¼ inch larger than the diameter of the riser to allow some flexibility when hooking up the supply lines. The type of faucet you're installing will determine the spread and placement of the riser holes.

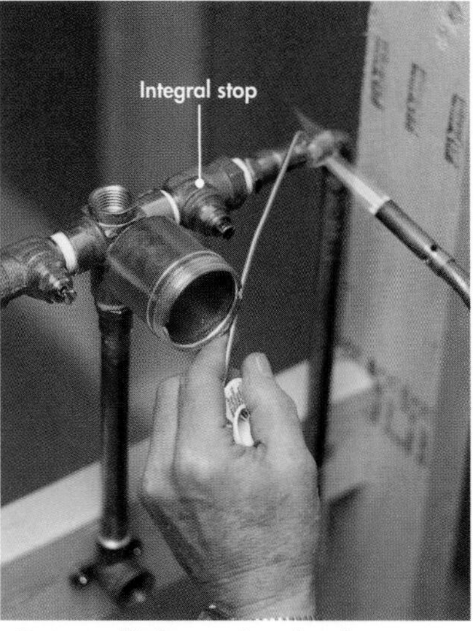

2 Install the valve body. Make sure the faucet controls are centered and level. Do a dry assembly to make sure everything fits. The heat of soldering may damage the internal parts of the valve or faucet. Remove them if possible. If the valve attaches to a screw-in fitting, solder the first piece of pipe to the fitting before screwing the fitting to the valve. (See "Soldering Copper Pipes," pages 297–298.)

3 Install the top blocking. Blocking for a tub spout should be centered 6 inches above the top of the tub. Faucets installed more than 6 inches above the spout need separate blocking. The blocking should be level, at the correct depth inside the wall, and toenailed firmly to the studs. Blocking for the showerhead is usually about 6½ feet above the floor, but you can adjust the height to suit your needs.

The banging caused by water pounding against a valve when you shut off the water is called water hammer. If it's a problem in your house, buy a commercial water hammer arrester, a small pipelike device that absorbs the shock.

Pipe down in there!

Believe it or not, water running through pipes can make a lot of noise. To isolate it, slide plastic or felt fittings around the pipes wherever you attach them to the framing.

4 Secure the spout and shower riser to the blocking. Connect all the pipes and fittings. Screw any brass fittings to the framing with brass screws to prevent the corrosion that occurs when dissimilar metals are in contact with each other. (See pages 297–298 for soldering copper pipe and page 295 for connecting CPVC pipe.)

5 Run supply lines to the risers. Cut pipe lengths. Test-fit each supply line, and mark adjustments on the piping. Take the runs apart and make the changes. Anchor the pipes securely to the joists as you make the runs, and solder in place.

Installing PEX supply lines

Skill level: ★☆☆☆☆

Time to complete:
Experienced 30 min.
Handy 45 min.
Novice 1.5 hrs.

Materials: PEX tubing, crimp rings, fittings

Tools: Crimp tool with gauge, tubing cutter, knife, water-pump pliers

Of the various types of supply pipes used in home plumbing, the newest and the most flexible is PEX (cross-linked polyethylene). This plastic pipe is easier to snake through a home's framing and can be connected readily with no-solder fittings. It isn't the perfect tubing for every application in every part of the country however, because it can be vulnerable to freezing and ultraviolet light. Check your local codes.

You'll pay more for PEX than other materials, but the added expense may be offset by the savings in time and trouble. Because of its flexibility, you may be able to run the pipe in the same way you would run electrical cable, fishing them through finished walls.

PEX systems are assembled in either of two methods. The easier way is to use plastic compression-type fittings that you tighten by hand and secure by turning with a pair of pliers. Although these junctions are reliable, they typically can be used only where there is ready access. The more durable choice is to make crimped connections, using a crimp tool with brass fittings and rings. The tool runs around $100 and takes a bit of getting used to, but the resulting connections are as dependable as those in traditional systems.

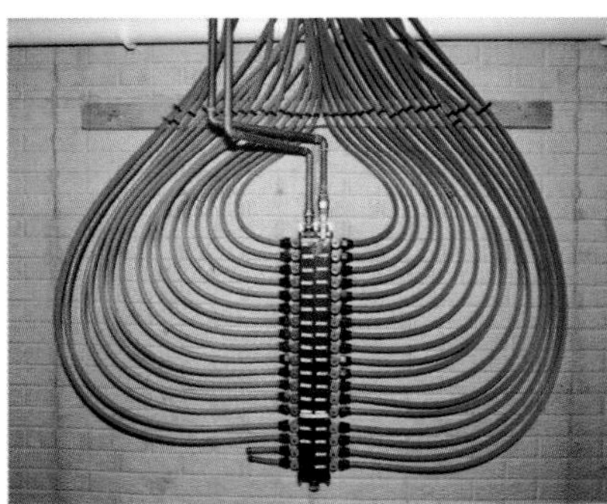

Run the tubing from a manifold. If you will be running new lines to a new addition or plan on replacing existing supply lines, install a manifold—a control center that's somewhat analogous to the service panel of the home electrical system. Instead of electrical circuits, dedicated hot and cold water lines run to individual fixtures. This so-called home run arrangement can cut down on water use and lower energy bills because less time is needed to purge standing water in the lines when delivering hot water where needed.

A typical PEX system

1 Assemble the necessary tools and fittings. With PEX tubing you can forget about propane torches and massive wrenches. But you'll need to be familiar with a crimping tool, crimp rings, and assorted metal fittings.

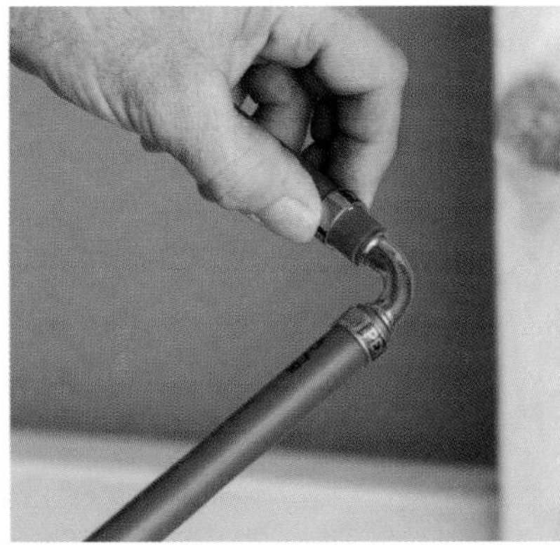

2 Slip on the crimp ring and insert the fitting. To connect PEX tubing, slip a crimp ring onto it, then slide the pipe onto the fitting until it reaches the fitting's shoulder.

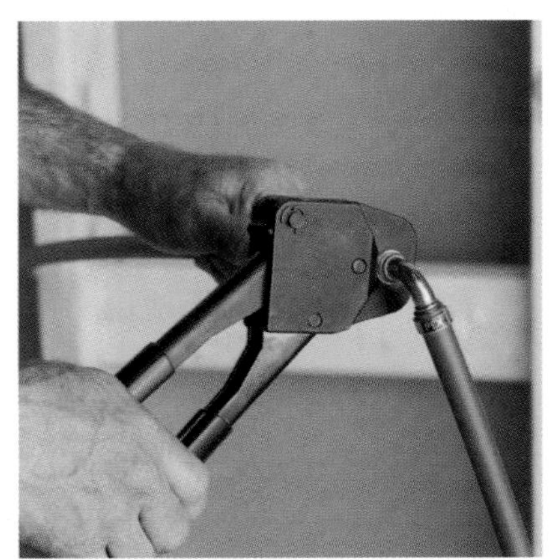

3 Crimp the ring. Adjust the ring so that it is from ⅛ to ¼ inch from the end. Secure the ring with the PEX crimping tool, closing the tool completely.

4 Check that the connection is secure. Use the gauge that comes with the crimp tool to make sure the connection will hold. It has test slots labeled GO and NO-GO for both of two tubing gauges. Try to slip the appropriate size GO over the crimped ring. If the slot fits snuggly, and if the NO-GO fitting is too tight, then the connection is good. Otherwise you'll have to cut the tubing and repeat the process with a new crimp ring.

Installing shutoff valves & supply tubes

Skill level:	Time to complete:	Materials:	Tools:
★★★☆☆	Experienced 25 min. Handy 45 min. Novice 1 hr.	Compression valve, compression fittings, flexible supply tubing	Minipipe tubing cutter or mini hacksaw, emery cloth, two adjustable wrenches

Shutoff valves let you turn off the water near your fixtures so you don't have to shut off water to the entire house every time you make a repair. They attach in different ways: by soldering, threading, or compression fittings. Compression fittings are easy to install and don't require pipe dope or compound—a metal sleeve makes the fitting watertight, as long as it's properly installed.

Turn off the water before you start. Open the faucet you're working on and another one somewhere below it in the house so that the water will drain from the line.

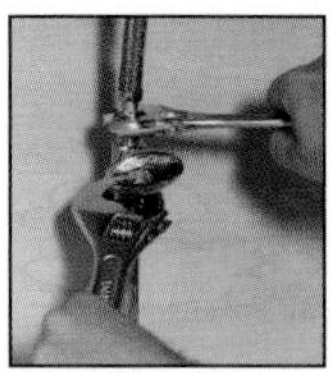

Braided flexible supply lines are stronger and last longer than straight chrome tubing. Some are actually made of stainless steel, but most are heavy-duty braided plastic. Use two adjustable wrenches to attach the compression fittings.

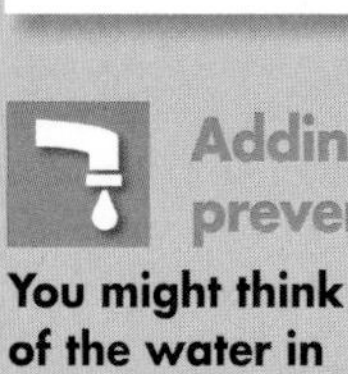

Adding a backflow preventor valve

You might think of the water in your plumbing as flowing only one way—the normal way. But a pressure fluctuation can cause it to reverse direction, contaminating your household supply by bringing water in from an irrigation system or a garden hose with an attachment for spraying fertilizer or herbicide. An easy solution is to buy an inexpensive hose bib backflow preventor and install it on any outside faucets that might be sources of contamination.

1 Disconnect the supply pipe. Turn off the main water supply. Unscrew the supply pipe at the wall. If it's soldered in place, cut it with a mini-pipe tubing cutter or, as a last resort, a minihacksaw. (Cut carefully. If the tube is out of round, the compression fitting will leak.) Leave enough room between the escutcheon plate and the cut to install the fitting. Deburr the pipe with emery cloth. Slide the compression nut over the supply pipe as far back as possible.

2 Place the compression ring over the end of the supply pipe. The ring should completely cover the end of the supply pipe.

Thread the compression valve into the compression nut. The valve should slide squarely and snugly over the ring. Hand-tighten. If the nut doesn't turn easily, add a tiny drop of oil to the threads. **Don't use pipe compound; the fitting doesn't require it, and it can actually make the fitting leak.**

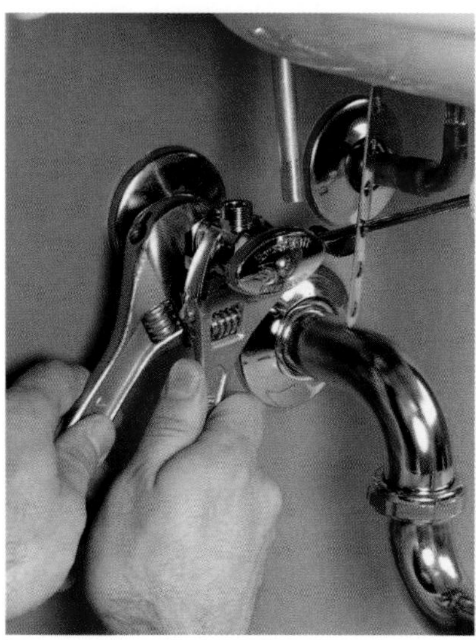

3 Tighten (but don't overtighten) the compression valve to the nut. Use one wrench to hold back the valve and keep it square and another to turn the nut. Follow the same procedure you used to install the valve to attach the supply lines. Turn the water on briefly (and let it flow into a bucket) to flush the lines before installing any new fixtures.

Repairing or replacing a sink strainer

Skill level:	Time to complete:	Materials:	Tools:
★★★☆☆	Experienced 20 min. Handy 40 min. Novice 1 hr.	Plumber's putty or silicone caulk, gaskets and washers	Water-pump pliers, hammer, basket strainer wrench, plastic putty knife, mini hacksaw, screwdriver

The sink strainer assembly connects the sink to the drain line. To fix a leak, you'll need to take it all apart. Remove and clean the sink strainer basket, then replace any worn washers and gaskets. If the seal where the strainer basket meets the lip of the drain line was not properly installed, it may leak.

Repairing does not mean replacing every part. If you don't mind reusing old parts, don't replace them. The sink drain body may be usable even though it may not shine like a new one; reuse it or any of its metal parts. The drain locknut can be reused because it is hidden below the sink. The only parts you should not reuse are washers and gaskets; they may not provide a proper seal. (They're also the least expensive parts to replace.)

If possible replace chrome drainpipe with plastic. Chrome pipes corrode on the inside. As a result they'll leak sooner and are more likely to break during minor repairs.

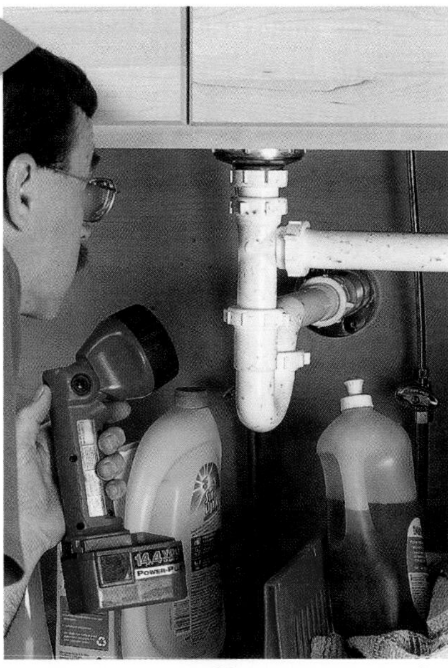

1 Give yourself room to work. Inspect the area below the sink and remove any obstacles.

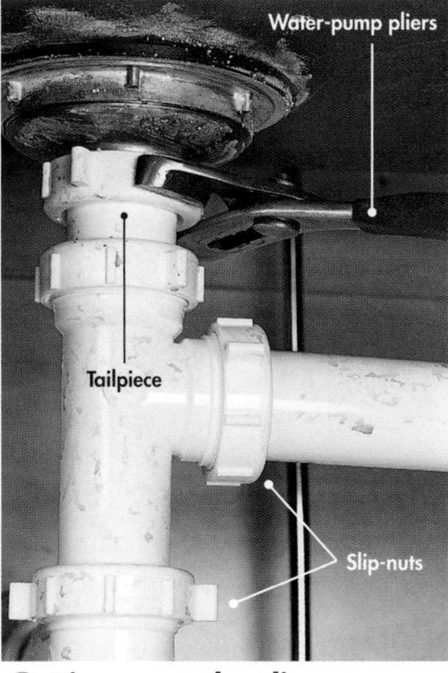

2 Disconnect the slip nuts. Use water-pump pliers to loosen the slip nuts and slide them out of the way. Remove the tailpiece.

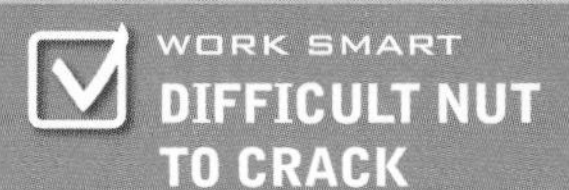

You may find the locking nut is difficult to loosen.
If all else fails, cut a groove in the nut at about a 30-degree angle with a minihacksaw. Insert a screwdriver into the groove and twist or tap with a hammer until the nut breaks off.

3 Unscrew the locking nut. Use a basket strainer wrench to remove the sink strainer assembly locknut. If the locknut won't budge, tap the lug with a hammer and screwdriver to loosen it. Remove the strainer assembly above and below the sink.

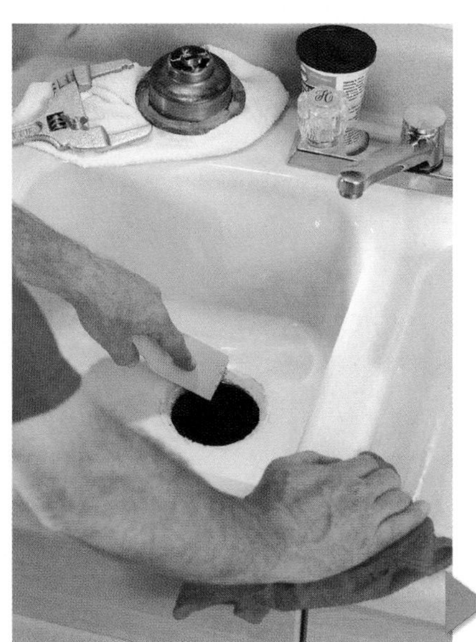

4 Scrape off the old putty with a plastic putty knife. If you reuse the old strainer, clean it as well. Always replace gaskets and washers.

PLUMBING

Repairing or replacing a sink strainer (continued)

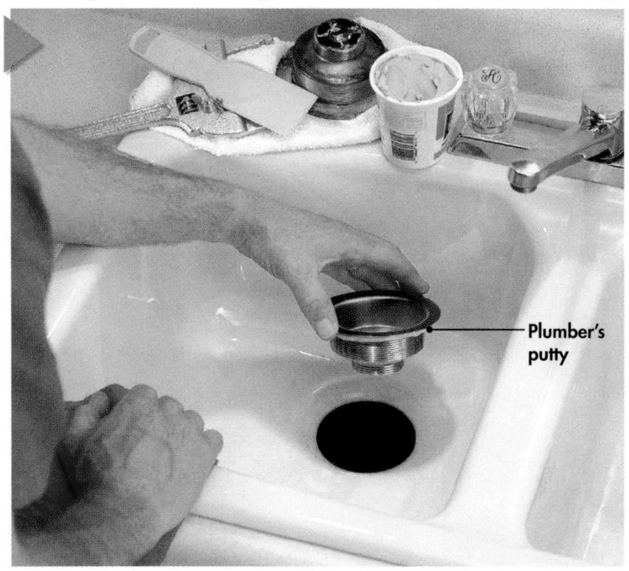

5 Coat the flange. If the sink is cultured marble or stainless steel, coat the bottom rim of the flange with silicone caulk. If the sink is enamel, use plumber's putty instead. Roll the putty between your hands to create a "rope" about 3⁄8 inch in diameter. Apply the putty to the underside of the flange rim. Insert the drain unit into the sink.

6 Reassemble the strainer. Install a new rubber gasket and friction ring. Hand-tighten the new locknut. Connect the tailpiece to the assembly body with slip nuts. Test by filling the sink with water and then draining. Tighten the nuts if you see any leaks.

Sink strainer assembly

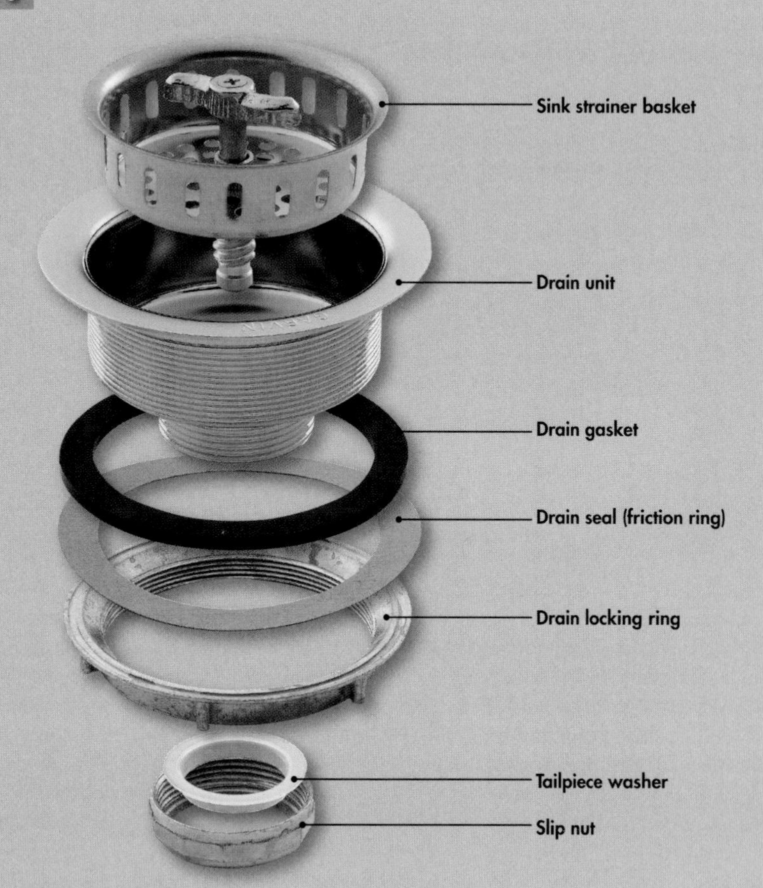

WORK SMART

TWIST AND SHOUT

If the drain unit turns every time you try to give the locking ring a final twist, you need a helper. Put a couple of screwdrivers between the crosspieces in the drain unit. Have a helper hold them firmly while you tighten the locking ring.

OOPS

EASY DOES IT!

Even experienced plumbers sometimes break plastic fittings. That final turn with the pliers may seem like a good idea, but it can result in a cracked fitting and a trip to the home center. Hand-tighten all fittings, then tighten a quarter-turn at a time with the pliers until the leaking stops.

Installing a single-bowl PVC P-trap

Skill level:	Time to complete:	Materials:	Tools:
★★★☆☆	Experienced 20 min. Handy 40 min. Novice 1 hr.	PVC P-trap (United States), ABS P-trap (Canada), slip-joint tailpiece	Felt marker, PVC pipe cutter, water-pump pliers

PLUMBING

Drains in the United States must have either a P-trap or an S-trap, depending on code requirements. (In Canada, you may only use a P-trap.) The trap serves as a safety device by preventing noxious gases from backing up the sewer pipe and entering the house. Sewer gases pose a health hazard and can also be explosive.

Here's how a P-trap works: The curved portion of the trap is filled with standing water, which prevents sewer gas from leaking into the room. Every time the drain is used, water is flushed through the trap and is replaced with fresh water. Over time, solids will adhere to the trap and may eventually clog the drain or possibly damage the trap—which means it's time to install a new one.

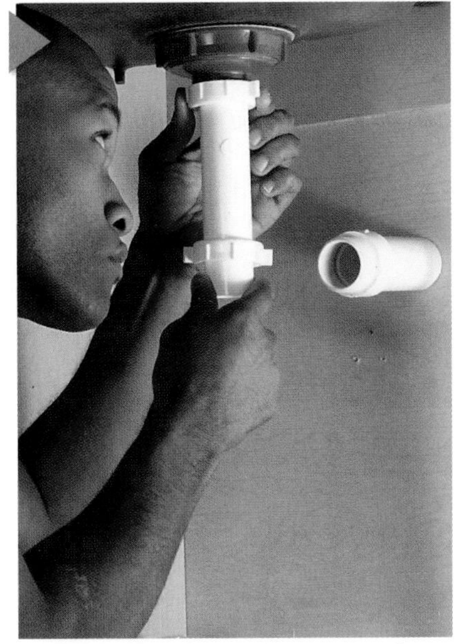

1 Connect the tailpiece to the sink drain. Hand-tighten the slip nut. Hand-tightening is usually sufficient for a pressure connection. Use pliers with gentle pressure to stop leaks only if necessary; too much stress on the fitting can crack or weaken it.

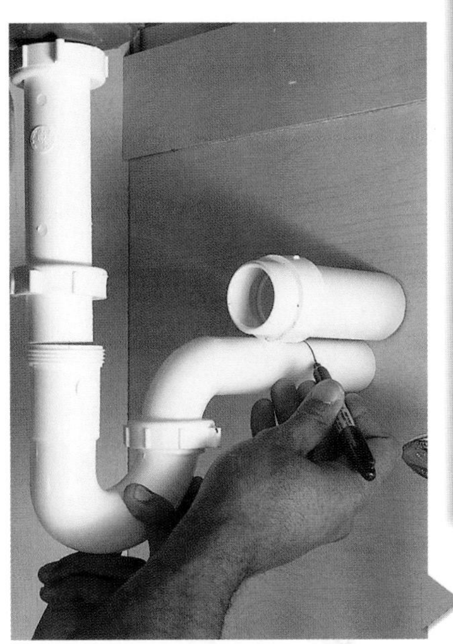

2 Measure the pipe. Test-fit the P-trap. Mark the P-trap inlet so it will seat inside the end of the drainpipe. Remove the P-trap. Cut the inlet of the trap to length using PVC pipe cutters. Insert the inlet into the pipe socket. Slide the slip nut over the end of the inlet and tighten by hand.

Canada watch

DWV systems in Canada use black ABS (acrylonitrile butadiene styrene) for running drain lines instead of white PVC. Techniques for cutting, connecting, and cementing ABS are similar to PVC. (See "Connecting ABS," page 296.)

Escutcheon plates help to fight bugs!

Escutcheon plates fit flush around the pipe where the drain line enters the wall or floor. They add a finishing touch where plumbing is visible, such as under a wall-hung lavatory. Escutcheon plates also seal the drainpipe hole and can prevent drafts or unwanted insects from entering your home.

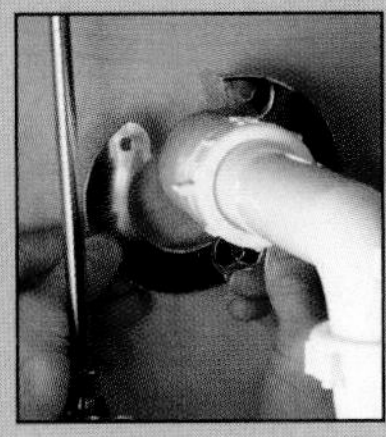

▲ *Split-ring escutcheon plates fit around a pipe that is already in place.*

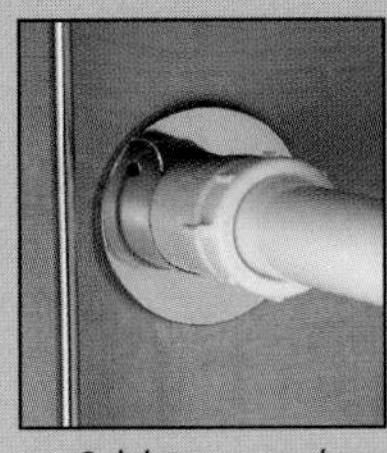

▲ *Solid-ring escutcheon plates slip onto the pipe before the drain is assembled.*

$ BUYER'S GUIDE
WHAT'S A SLIP JOINT ANYWAY?

Slip joints allow fixtures such as strainer baskets to be joined to drainpipes without making permanent connections. This means parts can be replaced easily. A smaller pipe with slip nuts at each end is inserted into a larger pipe, and the seal is made by the pressure that results from tightening the slip nuts to the threaded ends.

Installing a single-bowl PVC P-trap (continued)

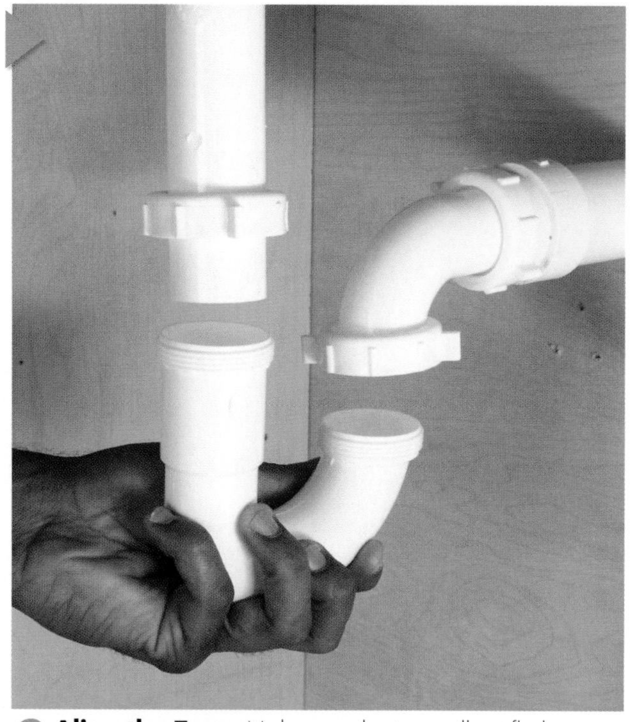

3 Align the Trap. Make sure the trap will set flush against the outlet and inlet pipes. Adjust the pipe if necessary.

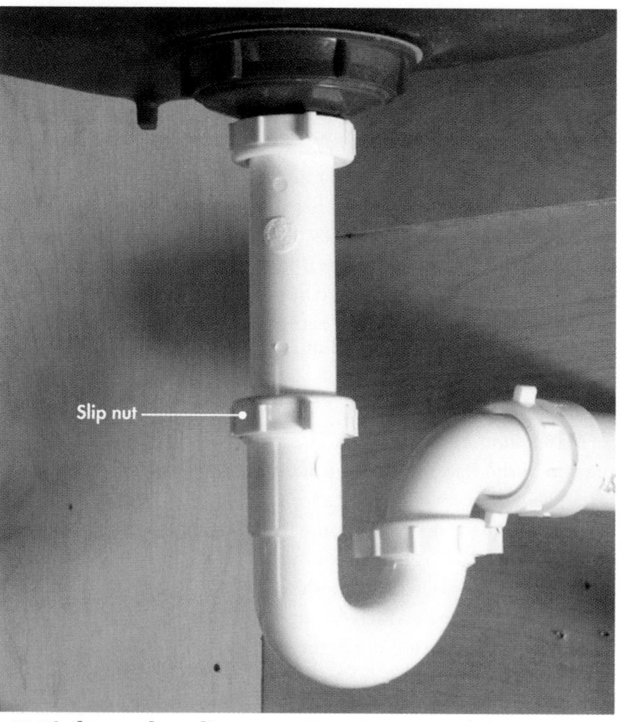

4 Tighten the slip nuts. Turn the nuts until they are hand-tight. Fill the sink with water and then drain it, inspecting for leaks as the sink drains. Tighten nuts if necessary.

CLOSER LOOK

CONNECTING OPTIONS FOR DOUBLE-BOWL SINKS

Two bowls can be served by one P-trap. Conversion kits are available at your local home center. One style has the P-trap centered between the bowls with a connecting tee and separate lengths running to the sink drains. Centering the P-trap does not meet code in Canada or California. Another style has the P-trap aligned beneath one of the drains with a vertical tee connecting to the second bowl, as shown at right.

Though the installation procedure is the same as for a single-bowl sink, make sure the horizontal run has a fall of ¼ inch per linear foot toward the tee connector. Otherwise solids will settle along the horizontal pipe and eventually stop or impede the flow of wastewater.

See page 586

Unclogging the clogs

Stopped or slow-moving drains are seldom the result of collapsed or defective pipes. Blockage in the lines caused by the accumulation of solid waste such as small objects, hair, or clumps of soap and grease is usually the culprit.

Isolating the problem

If one fixture seems to drain slowly or not at all, first check to see whether other fixtures have the same problem. If only one fixture is affected, fill the sink with water. If the water drains for two seconds or less before clogging, the problem is in the trap. If two or more fixtures are clogged, the clog may be in the branch line, the main line, or the vent stack. If more than one fixture is affected and all are on the second level of the house, the blockage may be high in the main line or in a vent stack. Isolating the affected area will help you decide how to clean out the line—and whether you need to hire a professional.

Drain lines are fragile—

more fragile than you might expect, especially because of all the fixtures attached to them. Be careful when using chemicals and augering—some chemicals can weaken the walls of the drain lines, and augers can shatter porcelain fixtures. Try using a plunger first. If that doesn't solve the problem, move on to snakes and augers, but work carefully and slowly.

The risks of using chemical cleaners

In general it's best to avoid using chemical cleaners, but if you do, follow the directions carefully and always let other people (like plumbers) know if you've put chemicals in a drain they may be working on. Never use a drain cleaner on a clogged drain or in a toilet. Never pour acid in standing water; it will probably make matters worse. Use cleaners only on sluggish drains, and be skeptical of cleaners that claim to be safe on pipes and gaskets.

▲ ***Maybe it's time for a heavy-duty solution.*** *Sometimes it's easier to get to a blockage in the main line through the vent system. If that's the case, you'll need to rent a commercial auger to remove the blockage. This might be the time to bring in a pro. But if you want to do it yourself, get some lessons from a rental center, take every precaution, and work carefully while on the roof.*

PLUMBING

Clog removers

For almost every clogged drain you'll encounter, a tool solution exists. Use the right auger for the right job. It's easy to damage pipes or scratch fixtures.

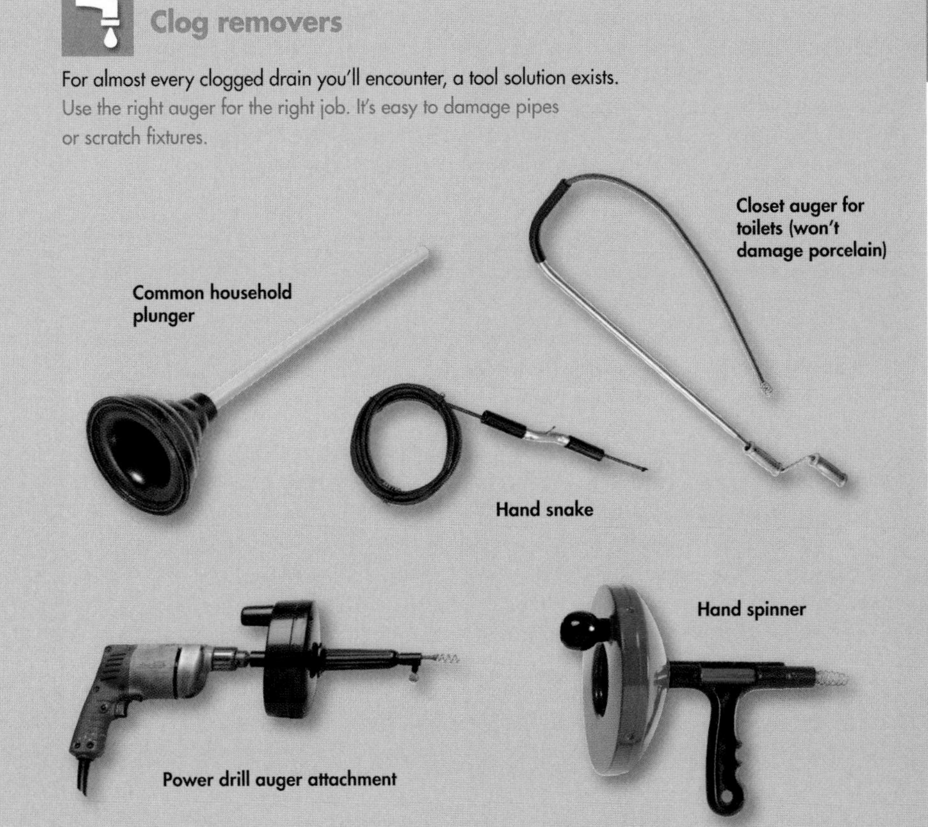

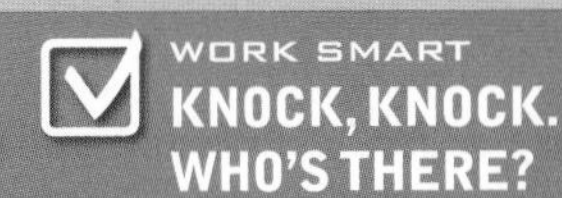

WORK SMART

KNOCK, KNOCK. WHO'S THERE?

If your pipes are exposed, as in a basement or crawlspace, here's a tip to speed up the clog search. From the clog to the drain, the pipe will be full of water. From the clog to the street, the pipe will be empty. Tap along the pipe from the side nearest the street using a broomstick or a piece of scrap lumber. (Don't use a hammer or piece of metal.) A ringing or hollow sound means a clear pipe. When you hear a thud, you've found the clog. Open up the nearest clean-out and put the auger to work!

Unclogging drains and waste lines

Most clogs that result from buildups of grease or hair can be removed by opening the drain line and using an auger to clear the blockage. Small objects such as toys or toothbrushes can be difficult to snag and remove. Sometimes the best solution is to remove the drain trap and push the blockage farther down the drain line system to a clean-out, or to flush the line with water once the blockage has been jarred loose.

Pushing an object farther down the system can cause a clog that's difficult to auger. You might have to call in a plumber or a drain service. If you don't have accessible clean-outs in your home and can get the blockage into the main drain line, it can sometimes be removed through the roof stack vent.

Using a hand auger

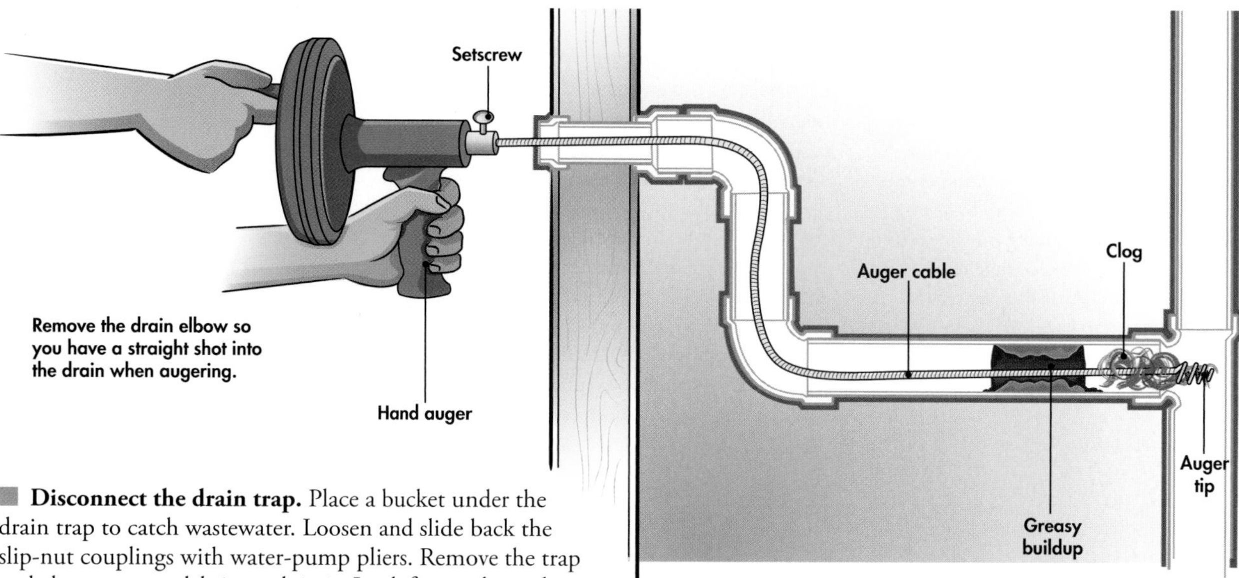

■ **Disconnect the drain trap.** Place a bucket under the drain trap to catch wastewater. Loosen and slide back the slip-nut couplings with water-pump pliers. Remove the trap and clean out any debris stuck in it. Look for cracks in the pipe or sediment buildup in the trap; in either case it means you'll have to replace the trap (see "Installing a Single-Bowl PVC P-Trap," page 305).

■ **Loosen the auger setscrew and pull out about a foot of cable.** Push the cable through until it meets resistance, which is probably a bend in the pipe. It's often difficult to tell the difference between a bend and the clog. Be patient. The auger will either push the blockage out of the pipe or snag it so you can pull it out.

■ **Tighten the setscrew and turn the handle clockwise until the cable moves forward again.** Loosen the set screw and feed cable until you meet resistance again. Repeat this process until you feel the obstruction is removed or that you've snagged the blockage. Remove the cable and clean the tip.

■ **Test by running water through the drain and waste line.** If the line is still blocked, the clog may be in the main drain. If that's the case call in a professional.

WORK SMART

PLUMBERS HAVE SPECIALTIES TOO

Don't be surprised if your plumber isn't interested in going after a tough clog. The plumber may suggest a drain cleaning service to handle the job instead.

WORK SMART

PREVENTIVE MEASURES TO AVOID CLOGS

The only fixture or appliance that is designed to handle solid waste is the toilet. Use preventive measures to avoid clogs and try to keep solid matter out of drain lines.

- Disposers grind food into a paste that can collect in the drain line and eventually form a clog. Avoid oily or dense matter and flush the lines thoroughly with cold water after each use.
- Hair and food clogs can be difficult to clear. Clean tubs and sinks regularly.
- Don't pour grease down the drain unless you have a grease trap.
- Don't put dental floss, sanitary napkins, or paper towels down the toilet.
- A capful of bleach in the drain lines once a week can help prevent odors.

Unclogging sink drains

Skill level:	Time to complete:	Materials:	Tools:
★★★☆☆	Experienced Variable Handy Variable Novice Variable	None	Flange plunger, bucket, water-pump pliers, sink auger, rags

Plunging is the best option for removing a clog because it's the easiest and least likely to damage pipes. Fill both basins with 4 inches of water. Have a helper hold a rag or a closed sink strainer over the opening of the disposer drain. Use a plunger to vigorously plunge the drain in the other sink. A dozen times should be enough for most clogs. If the drain is still clogged, switch positions with your helper and plunge the drain in the other basin.

While plunging is the best option, you may have to use a sink auger for stubborn clogs.

Unclogging jammed disposers

Skill level:	Time to complete:	Materials:	Tools:
★★★☆☆	Experienced Variable Handy Variable Novice Variable	None	Flashlight, ¼-inch allen wrench, a disposer wrench or adjustable wrench, broom handle

Turn off the power to the jammed disposer and unplug it. Look inside the opening with a flashlight to see what is jamming it. Remove the waste and restore power. If it's still jammed, try the following:

- Check the outside bottom of the unit; press the reset button. Turn on the power. The disposer should run freely. If it's still stuck, turn the power off.
- Insert a broom handle into the drain opening and try to free the impellers.
- If the broom handle doesn't do the job, insert a ¼-inch allen wrench into the hex socket on the outside bottom. The socket is connected to the impellers that crunch up the waste. Use the hex key to turn the impellers in both directions to free them.

Disposer wrench

Disposers without hex sockets have a special wrench that comes with the disposer. Keep it in a location you'll remember. If it's already lost or isn't working, buy a replacement in the plumbing department of your home center.

SAFETY ALERT

WORK SAFELY!

Before reaching into a disposer, disconnect the power. Unplug the unit from the outlet. If there is no outlet, turn off the circuit breaker. Never stick your hand into a connected disposer.

Unclogging bathtub and shower drains

Skill level:	Time to complete:	Materials: None	Tools: Screwdriver, flange plunger, hand auger
★★★☆☆	Experienced Variable Handy Variable Novice Variable		

PLUMBING

The drains in sinks and shower stalls work hard, and not just to drain away soap, grease and oil, hair, and the occasional hairpin or ring. We use these fixtures to wash the dog and the leaves of our plants. A shower is the perfect place to scrub miniblinds. When the weather is too cold to hose things down outside, we use the shower stall to clean dirty boots. It's no wonder the drain clogs.

Plunge the drain vigorously with a flange plunger to unclog it. For stubborn clogs, try a hand-driven auger. Try both options before calling a plumber or a drain cleaning specialist to do the job.

Waste and overflow drains

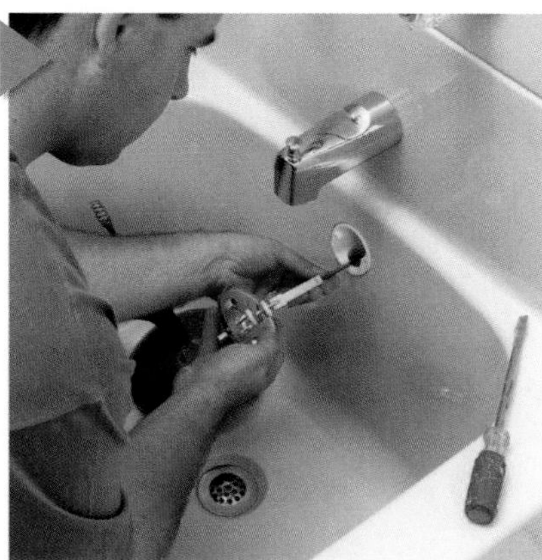

1 Remove the pop-up drain assembly. Flip the drain lever up and pull out the drain plunger. Remove the screws from the overflow cover plate with a screwdriver, then lift out the linkage.

2 Auger the drain. Insert the end of the hand auger into the overflow drain. Turn the handle clockwise, feeding out the cable until you meet resistance. Slowly withdraw the auger to dislodge or remove the blockage. Repeat until the tub drains normally. Insert the linkage back into the overflow drain and install the cover. Flip the lever up and insert the stopper.

Floor drains

1 Use a flange plunger. Remove the screws from and lift off the shower strainer. Fill the shower pan to a depth of 1 inch. Plunge forcefully about a dozen times. Remove the plunger and see whether the water drains freely. If not, repeat.

2 Auger the drain. Tougher clogs require a tougher approach. Feed a hand auger into the drain until it meets resistance. Turn the auger handle clockwise and slowly withdraw the auger. Repeat until the shower drains normally. If the blockage refuses to clear, call a plumber or a drain service.

TOOL TIP

PLASTIC TO THE RESCUE

If you don't have a plunger, try out a plastic drain tool, which has barbs along the edges. Slip it in the pipe; the barbs grab the clog and pull it out.

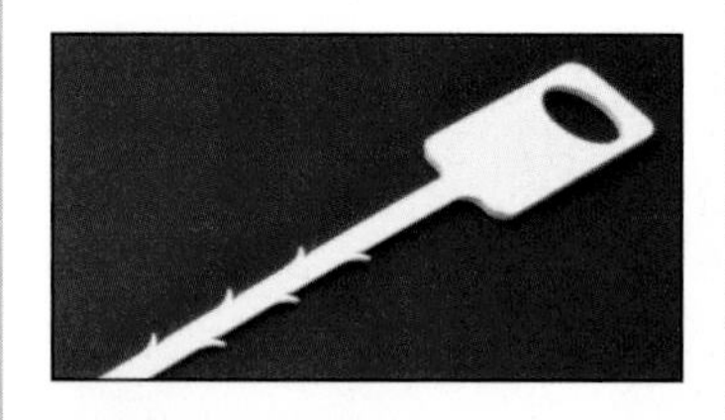

Auger with care

Don't use a power-driven auger in a bathtub drain; the assembly is too fragile and can be easily damaged.

Unclogging a toilet

Skill level:	Time to complete:	Materials:	Tools:
★★★☆☆	Experienced Variable Handy Variable Novice Variable	None	Flange plunger, closet auger, bucket, rags

PLUMBING

Toilets have built-in traps. Objects stuck in the trap cause slow draining or clogged toilets and usually can be dislodged by plunging.

Don't use a coat hanger to unclog a toilet—you will scratch the bowl. If the bowl is scratched, try removing the black marks with a heavy-duty powder-type cleanser containing bleach.

Never use chemical drain cleaners in a toilet. If there is no water in the bowl, pour some water into it. Water helps seal the plunger flange, creating a vacuum and allowing you to apply pressure to dislodge the blockage.

It's auger time. You may need a closet auger to remove stubborn objects such as small toys. Never use a hand auger on a toilet. The force of the auger when turning the crank may shatter the porcelain bowl. A closet auger is designed specifically to be used on toilets. It has a long handle with a crank, and the bend in the handle is covered with a protective sleeve to prevent scratching the porcelain.

Remove the toilet. When plunging or augering doesn't work, your only option will be to remove the toilet (see "Removing an Old Toilet," page 345) and try to fish out the object from the other end.

Household plunger

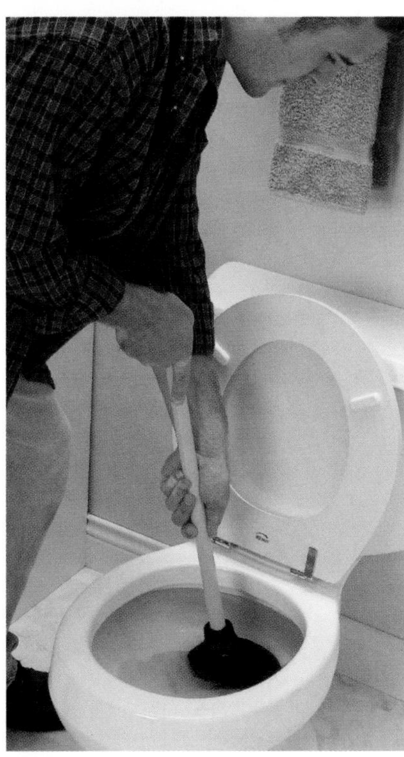

Plunge forcefully about a dozen times. Remove the plunger to allow the toilet to drain. If it doesn't drain, or drains slowly, repeat plunging.

Closet auger

Turn the crank clockwise and push. The auger can shove the blockage forward into the drain system. If the auger catches on the object, continue turning the crank as you pull out the cable until you can retrieve the object.

WORK SMART

KEEP IT PRETTY

Some augers, like the one shown above, have a protective rubber sleeve. Those that don't will leave noticeable scratches. Protect the surface by lining it with a towel.

TOOL TIP

AUGER MAINTENANCE

When you're done with the auger, rinse it in warm water. Then spray on an aerosol lubricant to keep rust from forming on the tool.

WORK SMART

HOW TO TAME A CLOG

This recipe for a clog buster really works. Add 3 tablespoons of dishwashing soap to the bowl. The soap will lubricate the interior of the drain and help to loosen the clog when you plunge. Wait a few minutes for the soap to do its work, then plunge vigorously.

Care and feeding of a septic tank

If you're hooked up to your own septic system, you should give extra thought to what goes down the drain. A septic tank isn't just a holding system but also a processor of wastes. Biological action breaks down solids so that the tank doesn't have to be pumped as often as otherwise would be the case. Don't bother with commercial "starters" that promise great benefits. Naturally occurring bacteria should do the job, so long as they aren't dealing with large quantities of cooking grease and coffee grounds, or non-compostables such as disposable diapers, facial tissues, and cigarette butts. If possible, process vegetable scraps in a compost pile rather than grinding them in a garbage disposer and washing them down the drain. Meat scraps should be put in the trash.

Repairing a compression faucet

Skill level:	Time to complete:	Materials:	Tools:
★★★☆☆	Experienced 20 min. Handy 40 min. Novice 1 hr.	Universal washer kit, O-ring, silicone grease	Screwdriver, water-pump pliers

PLUMBING

1 Turn off the water supply and unscrew the stem assembly. Pry off the handle cap. Remove the handle screw with a screwdriver. Lift it up and off the handle. To remove corroded handles, you may have to use a handle puller. (See "Closer Look," below.) Unscrew the packing nut from the faucet body with water-pump pliers.

2 Take off the washer. Use a screwdriver to remove the bib screw that holds the washer in place. If the screw is stuck, tap on it gently for about 30 seconds to loosen the rust. Remove the screw, pry out the worn washer, and discard it. While the valve is out, examine the valve seat by touch. If you feel any roughness, replace it. (See "Replacing a Worn Valve Seat," page 313.)

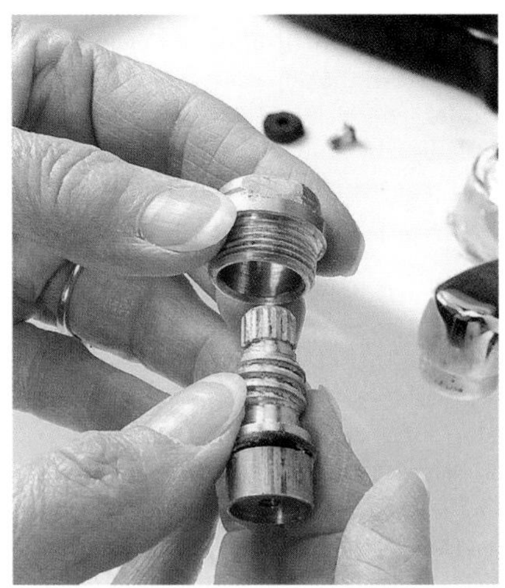

3 Remove the stem from the retaining nut. Inspect the threads for damage and replace the stem if necessary.

Compression faucet assembly

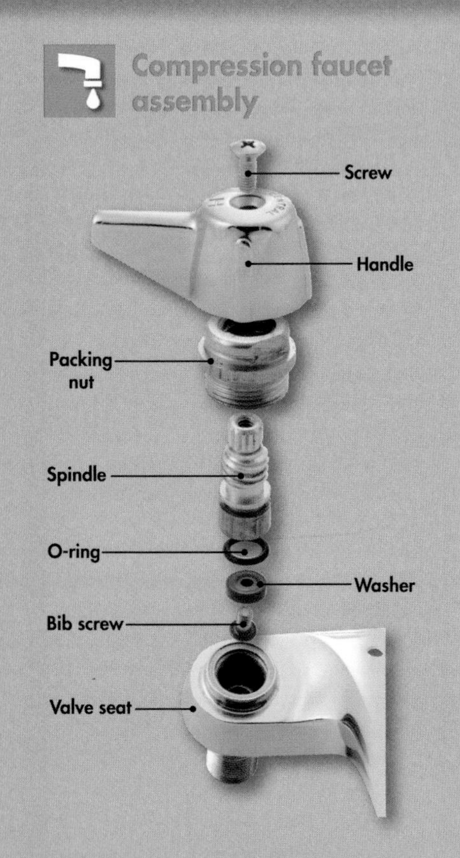

CLOSER LOOK

REMOVING A STUBBORN HANDLE

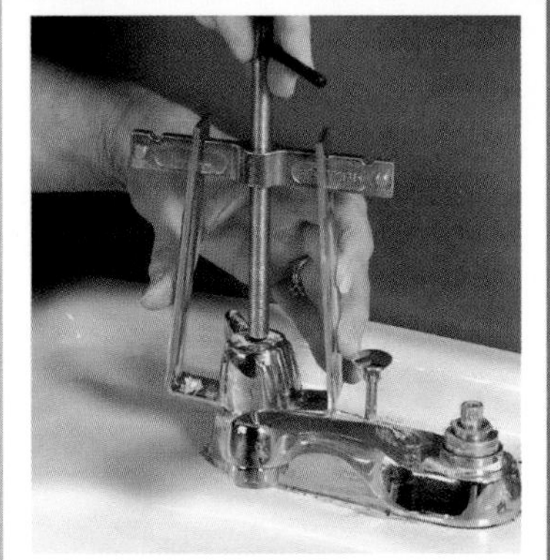

A handy tool to remove corroded handles is a handle puller. Clamp the side extensions of the handle puller beneath the handle. Thread the puller into the faucet stem. Continue to tighten the puller until the handle is free.

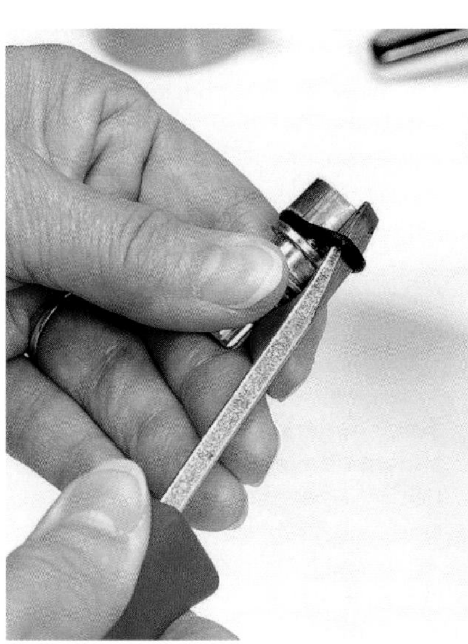

4 Peel off (don't cut) the O-ring. Slip the O-ring from its groove and peel it from the housing. It's important to keep the ring whole so you can find an exact replacement at the store. Use the tip of a screwdriver to help release it if necessary. If you can't peel it off, get an O-ring remover to help you with the job.

Replacing a worn valve seat

Skill level:	Time to complete:	Materials:	Tools:
★★★☆☆	Experienced 20 min. Handy 40 min. Novice 1 hr.	Valve seat, silicone grease, pipe dope	Screwdriver, water-pump pliers, seat wrench, valve seat dresser

Only compression valves have valve seats. When repairing a compression valve, check to see whether the valve seats need to be resurfaced. Poke your finger down into the faucet body to feel if the valve seat is rough. A rough seat will quickly damage a new washer. You should either replace or resurface the valve seat at the same time you are replacing the faucet washer. (See "Closer Look," below.)

Resurfacing the valve seat is actually an easy job but you've got to remember to clean the debris from inside the faucet body or it'll ruin that new washer you just put on. Flush the system before you reassemble the faucet. Cover the faucet hole with a rag and turn on the water gently to remove any debris or other gunk. You'll make a longer-lasting repair.

1 Turn off the water supply and disassemble the faucet valve. Lower the sink stopper and cover it with a cloth to prevent loose parts from falling into the drain. Pry off the handle cap and remove the handle with a screwdriver.

Remove the valve. Loosen the compression valve with water-pump pliers and remove it. Keep any washers or O-rings with the valve and set them aside.

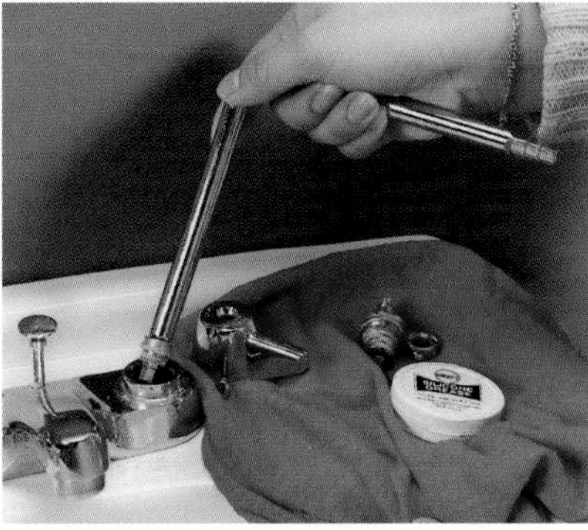

2 Back out the seat. Use a seat wrench to remove the valve seat. Select an end that fits snugly into the seat. Insert the end of the wrench into the seat and tap the top to seat it firmly. The valve seat may be stuck, so the first turn should be quick and firm to release it without stripping the threads. Once it's loose, turn the wrench counterclockwise and remove it. Take the old seat to your local home center to be sure you replace it with the correct part.

CLOSER LOOK

RESURFACING A WORN VALVE SEAT

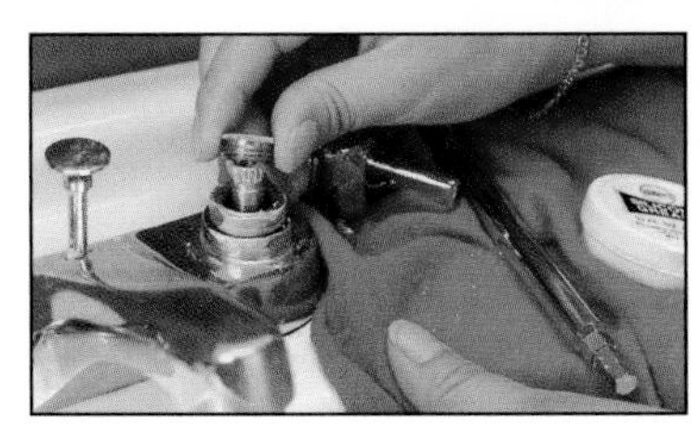

Worn valve seats can be resurfaced using a valve seat dresser, which can be purchased at a home center or hardware store. Select a seat cutter that will fit snugly inside the retaining nut. Slide the cutter and retaining nut over the threaded end of the valve seat dressing tool. Attach the locknut and cutter head to the shaft of the tool. Carefully screw the retaining nut into the faucet body. To resurface the seat, lightly press down on the handle while turning it clockwise two to three complete turns. Remove the tool and feel the seat to make sure it's smooth. If not, repeat the procedure. When smooth, reassemble the faucet.

WORK SMART

REPAIR OR REPLACE

Compression faucets can be repaired up to a point. When too much of the seat is ground away, the faucet will leak. If that happens, replace the assembly.

TOOL TIP

BUYING A VALVE-SEAT DRESSER

Valve seat dresser? It sounds like an oily tool you'd find lying around an auto repair shop. But the plumber's version, also known as a valve-seat grinder, is a simple and inexpensive device that can give a second life to compression faucets that leak even after you replace the washers.

3 Replace the seat. Install the new seat into the faucet. Apply pipe dope to the seat threads to seal them; insert the end of the seat wrench into the seat, and set the seat in place. Screw the valve into place. Assemble the compression valve, faucet handle, and handle cap. Turn on the water supply and check for leaks.

Repairing a ceramic disk faucet

Skill level:	Time to complete:	Materials:	Tools:
★★★☆☆	Experienced 20 min. Handy 40 min. Novice 1 hr.	Ceramic disk faucet replacement kit with seals, abrasive pad, silicone grease	Screwdriver or hex key set

1 Turn off the water at the supply or main shutoff. Loosen the setscrew with a hex key. Lift off the handle and dome housing. Unscrew the disk cartridge screws with a screwdriver. Lift the disk up and out. Inspect the disk for cracks—replace it if damaged.

2 Take out the seals. Take the disk and seals to your local home center to find the correct replacement parts.

3 Clean the seal seats with an abrasive pad.

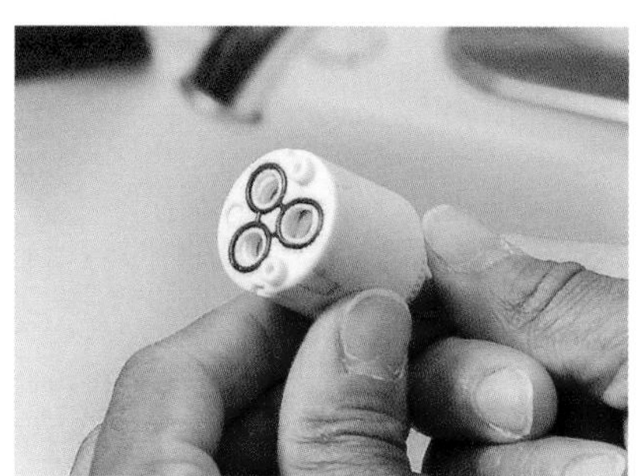

4 Install new seals. Coat them with silicone grease to prevent them from drying out, making them easier to remove.

5 Reassemble the faucet. Install the escutcheon cap and handle, and tighten the setscrew. Remove air from the line before fully opening the supply valves. (See "Work Smart," below.)

Ceramic disk faucet assembly

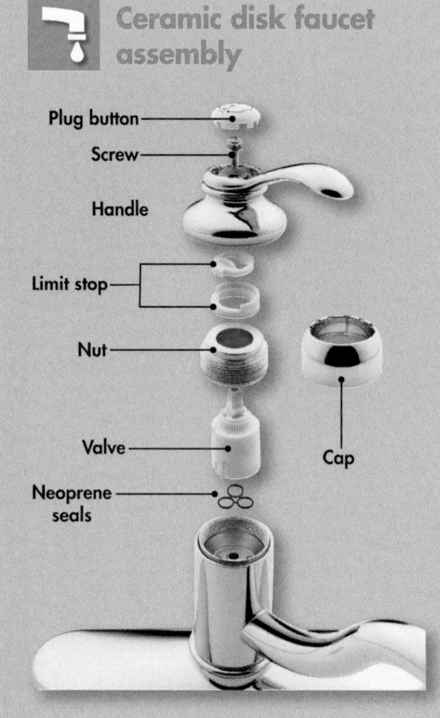

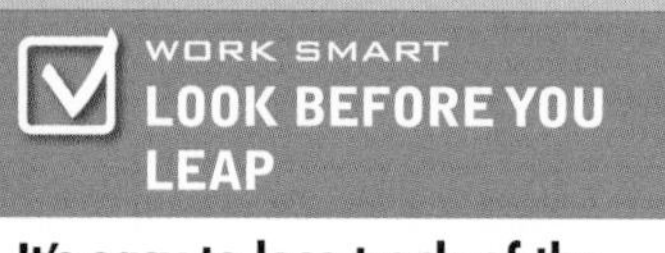

WORK SMART

LOOK BEFORE YOU LEAP

It's easy to lose track of the assembly order and even easier to lose faucet parts themselves. Read instructions carefully before you begin. Always cover the drain to keep pieces from falling into it and arrange the parts on a flat surface as you remove them.

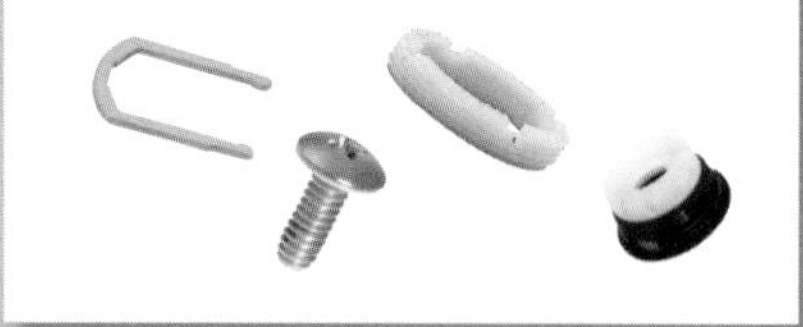

WORK SMART

DON'T CRACK THAT CERAMIC DISK!

Air rushing through a ceramic disk can crack it. First, open the faucet in the center position to balance the flow of water, then gradually open the shutoff valves to bleed out the air. Don't turn off the faucet until water flows freely and all the air is out.

Replacing a cartridge faucet

Skill level: ★★★☆☆

Time to complete:
Experienced 20 min.
Handy 40 min.
Novice 1 hr.

Materials: New cartridge, O-ring, silicone grease

Tools: Screwdriver, water-pump pliers, needle-nose pliers

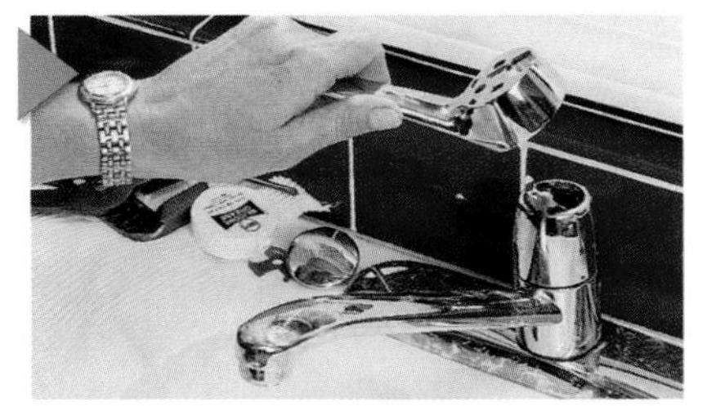

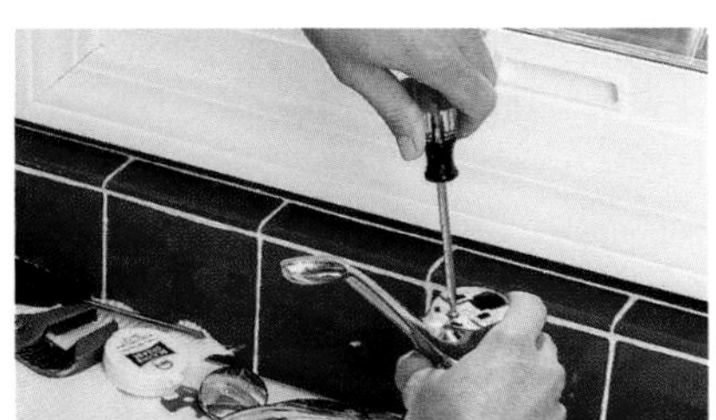

1 Turn off the water supply at the shutoff valve or the main valve. Pry off the handle cap. Unscrew the faucet handle screw using a screwdriver. Lift the handle from the faucet assembly.

2 Unscrew the retaining nut and remove the retaining clip. Spin the faucet out of the way and use water-pump pliers to remove the plastic retaining nut. Pull out the retaining clip that is just beneath it with needle-nose pliers. Lift the faucet spout straight up from the faucet body and remove.

3 Peel off (don't cut) the O-ring. Slip the O-ring from its groove and peel it from the housing. It's important to keep the ring whole so you can find an exact replacement at the store. Use the tip of a screwdriver to help release it if necessary. If you can't peel it off, pry it out with a screwdriver and cut it with a utility knife.

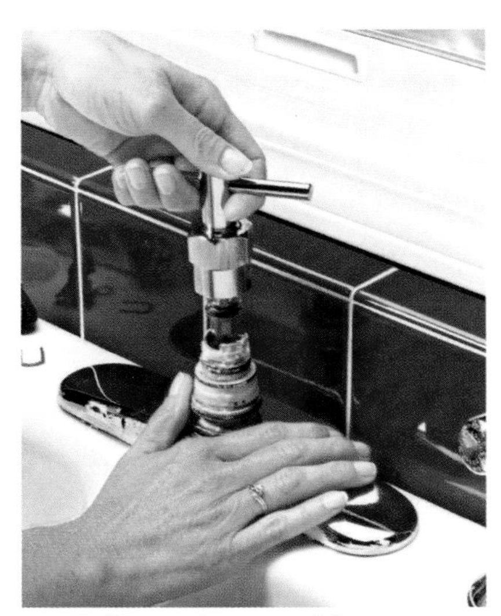

4 Pull out the cartridge stem. Grip the exposed end of the cartridge stem with a cartridge puller. Pull it straight up and out of the faucet body. Some replacement cartridges may come with a cartridge puller designed for the job. Others require a tool you'll have to buy separately. In any case, don't use pliers to remove the cartridge or you might damage or destroy it.

5 Clean and reassemble the faucet. Clean the faucet body with vinegar to remove debris. Coat the new O-ring with silicone grease to lubricate it, then seat it into the faucet body O-ring groove. Insert the new stem cartridge. Replace the faucet spout and reassemble. Turn on the water. Check the hot and cold water to make sure they are not reversed. If reversed, disassemble, turn the stem 180 degrees, then reassemble.

Cartridge faucet assembly

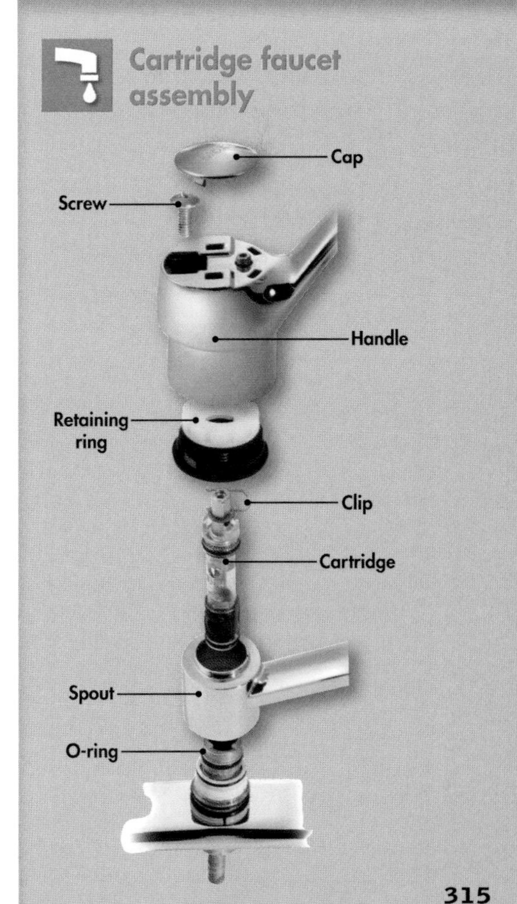

Repairing a rotary ball faucet

Skill level:	Time to complete:	Materials:	Tools:
★★★☆☆	Experienced 20 min. Handy 40 min. Novice 1 hr.	Silicone grease, rotary ball repair kit, rotary ball faucet replacement ball if necessary, masking tape	Hex set key wrench, water-pump pliers, tweezers, utility knife

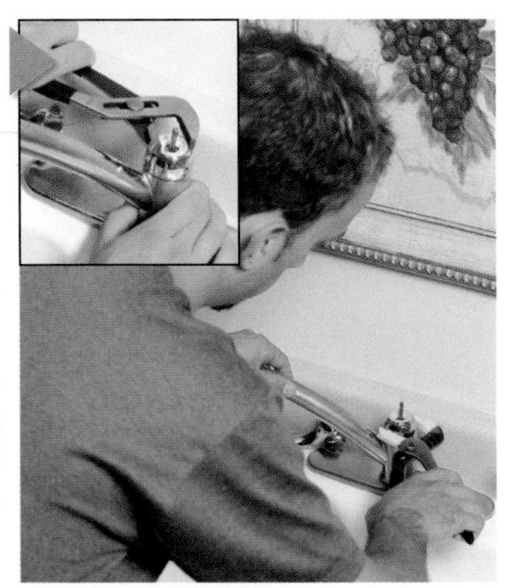

1 Shut off the water and unscrew the cap. Use a pair of water-pump pliers to remove the cap. Wrap the jaws of the pliers with masking tape to prevent damage to the cap.

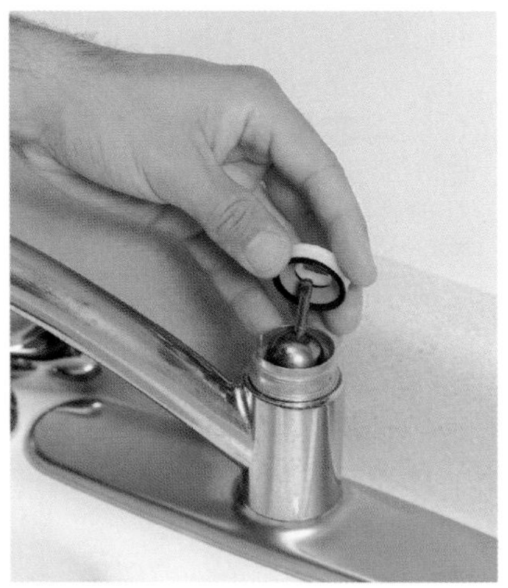

2 Remove the cam. Lift off the cam housing, seal, and ball. Inspect each part for damage and replace damaged parts.

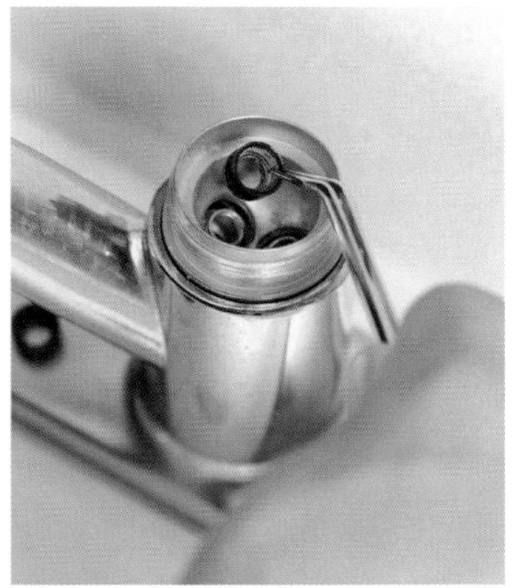

3 Lift out the seats. Use tweezers to remove the valve seats and springs. The springs are cone-shape, with one end larger than the other. Note how the springs are installed before you lift them out—you must install the replacement springs in exactly the same orientation you remove them or the faucet won't work properly. Remove the spout by twisting and lifting at the same time.

Rotary ball faucet assembly

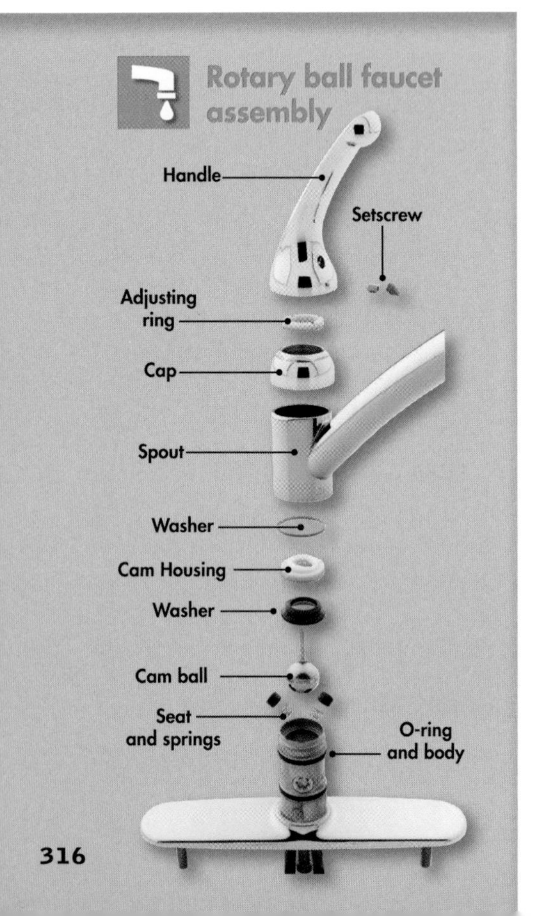

4 Peel off the O-ring. If possible, slip the O-ring from its groove and peel it from the housing. It's best if you can keep the ring whole so you can find an exact replacement at the store. If you can't peel it off, you may have to pry it out with a screwdriver or cut it with a utility knife.

5 Reassemble the faucet. Coat the new O-ring with silicone grease and seat it in the faucet housing groove. Push the spout over the O-ring and faucet housing. Install the new valve seats and springs, making sure they are installed correctly. Fit the cam ball into the notch in the body. Screw on the cam housing using the wrench included in the kit. Screw on the cap and install the handle. Turn the water on and check for leaks. Tighten the adjusting ring firmly to prevent leaks.

Repairing a tub and shower faucet

Skill level:	Time to complete:	Materials:	Tools:
★★★☆☆	Experienced 20 min. Handy 40 min. Novice 1 hr.	O-ring, cartridge replacement kit, silicone grease, white vinegar or lime-dissolving solution	Screwdriver, plastic putty knife, shower stem socket kit, pliers, utility knife

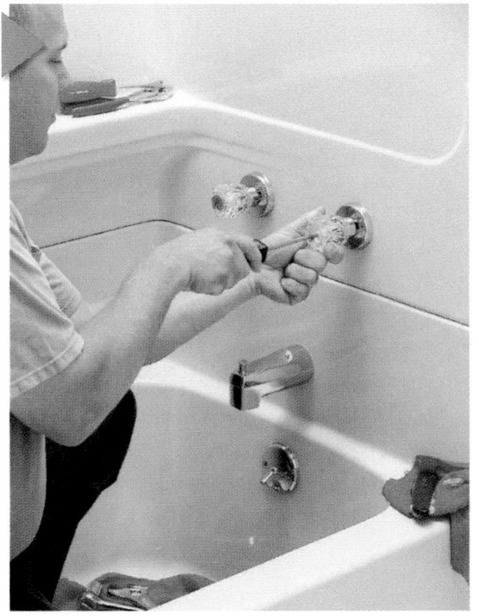

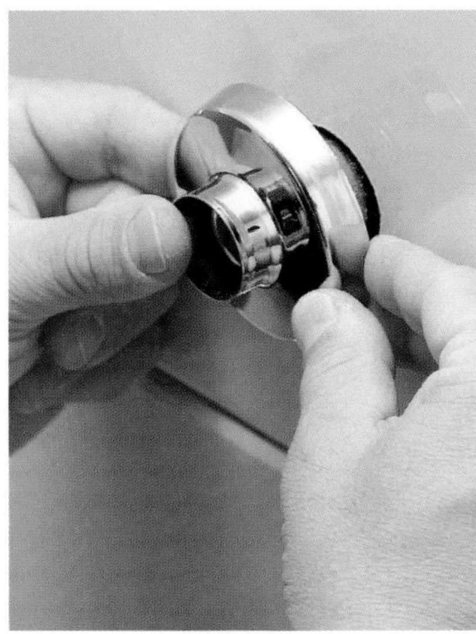

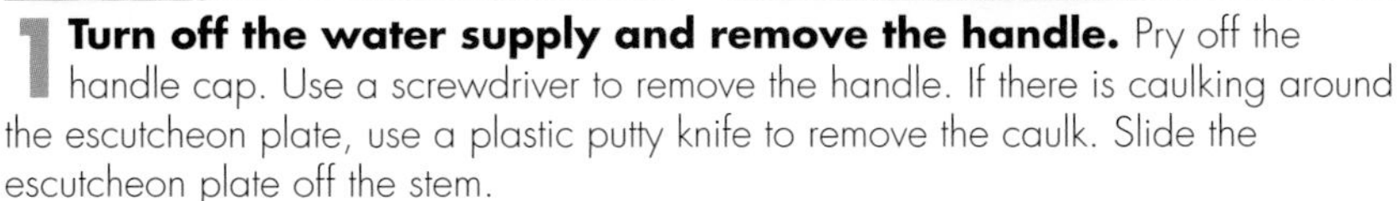

1 Turn off the water supply and remove the handle. Pry off the handle cap. Use a screwdriver to remove the handle. If there is caulking around the escutcheon plate, use a plastic putty knife to remove the caulk. Slide the escutcheon plate off the stem.

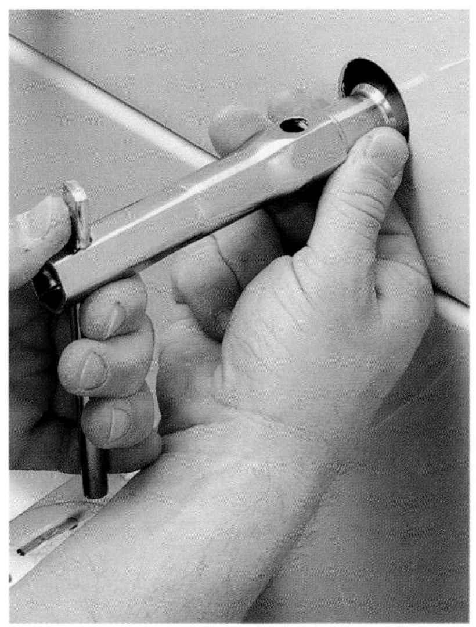

2 Unscrew the retaining nut. Use a shower stem socket (available at home centers and hardware stores) to remove the retaining nut.

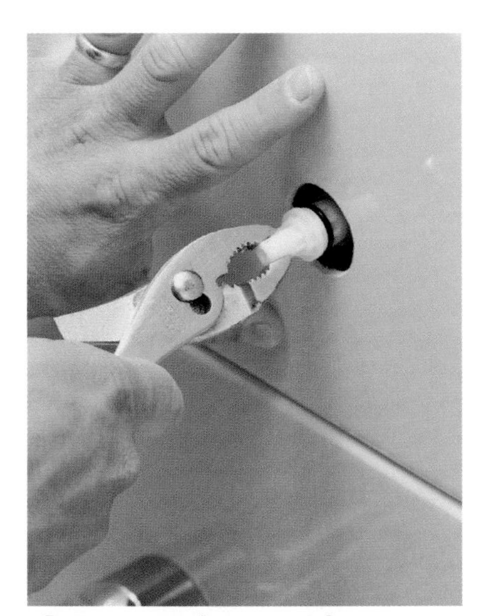

3 Remove the cartridge. Grasp the end of the cartridge with a pair of pliers and pull it straight out. If the hole in the tile is too small, enlarge it by chipping with a screwdriver and hammer.

4 Peel off (don't cut) the O-ring. Slip the O-ring from its groove and peel it from the housing. It's important to keep the ring whole so you can find an exact replacement at the store. Use the tip of a screwdriver to help release it if necessary. If you can't peel it off, pry it off with a screwdriver and cut it with a utility knife.

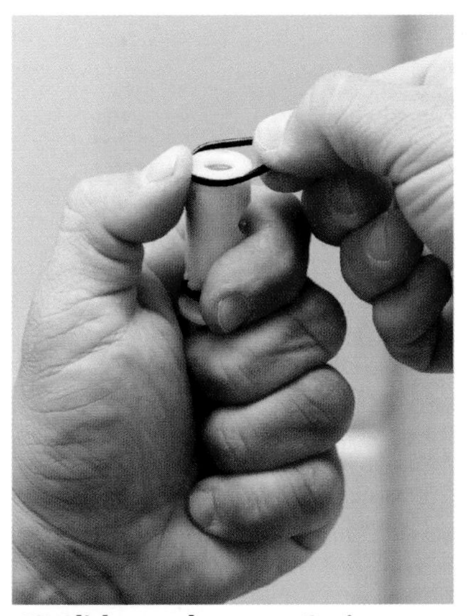

5 Slide on the new O-ring. Apply silicone grease to the new O-ring. Slide it over the cartridge, seating it into the O-ring groove. Reassemble the faucet. Turn on the water and test for leaks.

Repairing a tub diverter valve

Skill level:	Time to complete:	Materials:	Tools:
★★★☆☆	Experienced 20 min. Handy 40 min. Novice 1 hr.	Compression replacement kit, white vinegar solution, plumber's putty, silicone grease	Screwdriver, stem socket set, utility knife, water-pump pliers, toothbrush

PLUMBING

1 Remove the handle and escutcheon cap. Shut off the water supply. Pry the cap off the diverter handle. Remove the screw and slide off the handle. You may have to unscrew the escutcheon to remove it. If so, wrap the jaws of the pliers with masking tape to avoid scratching the surface.

2 Disconnect the bonnet nut. Use a shower stem socket set to remove the bonnet nut and stem. If the handle keeps hitting the tub or another faucet, put a stem socket over the one you're using as an extension.

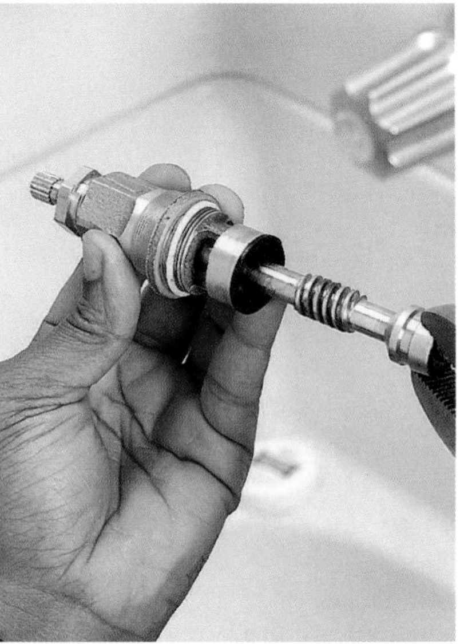

3 Unscrew the stem from the bonnet nut. Hold the bonnet nut with one hand. Use your other hand to remove the stem from the bonnet nut with water-pump pliers. Inspect the threads of the stem for damage. If there is evidence of damaged threads, replace the stem. Check the valve seat with a flashlight to make sure it's OK. It may need resurfacing or replacement. (See "Closer Look," page 313.)

WORK SMART

TEFLON TAPE

You probably are familiar with Teflon as the surface material on non-stick cookware. In the form of a thin tape, it also is a standard item in a plumber's tool kit. Teflon tape can be used as a tidier alternative to traditional pipe dope when lubricating and sealing threaded joints. The tape should be wrapped in the direction of the threads, beginning at the end of the pipe and working along its length. To make sure that the tape is drawn into the threads, keep it somewhat stretched and under tension while wrapping.

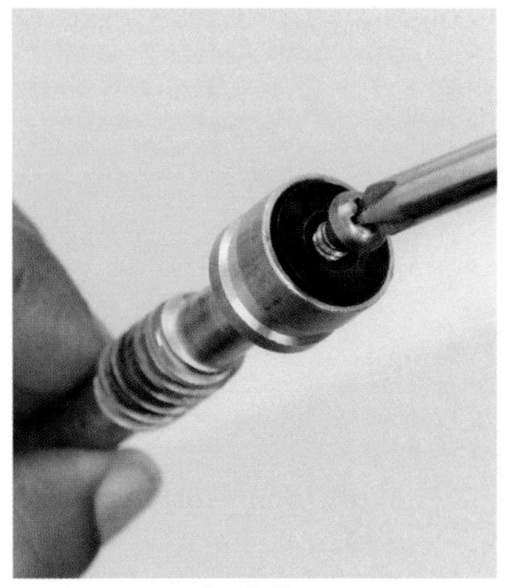

4 Remove the bib screw. Clean mineral deposits on the stem with a white vinegar solution, or buy a solution at your local home center to dissolve mineral deposits. A toothbrush easily removes deposits.

5 Replace the old washer. Seat the new washer in the stem. Apply silicone grease to the washer so it seats properly. Replace the bib screw with a new one. Reassemble the faucet, sealing the escutcheon in place with a bead of plumber's putty. Turn on the water supply and check for leaks and drips.

Installing a tub spout

Skill level:	Time to complete:	Materials:	Tools:
★★★☆☆	Experienced 20 min. Handy 40 min. Novice 1 hr.	New spout, pipe compound, silicone caulk	Small screwdriver or allen wrench, water-pump pliers, rags or towels

Tub spouts come in two basic types—screw-on and set-mounted. Examine the underside of the spout. If there is a hole in the bottom, it's mounted with a setscrew. Slide the fitting over the pipe until it's snug with the wall. Then tighten the setscrew with a small screwdriver or allen wrench. If there is no hole under the spout, screw it hand-tight. Spouts with setscrews are easier to install because they're easier to square up than the threaded variety.

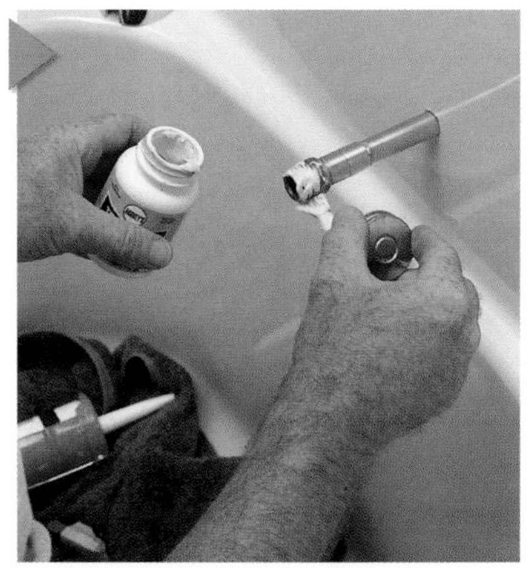

1 Disconnect the old spout. Check the underside of the spout to see whether there is a setscrew. If so, loosen the screw and slide off the spout. If there isn't a setscrew, use a pipe wrench to unscrew the spout from the threaded pipe. Twisting too hard can potentially bend the spout nipple, especially if it's copper. Apply joint compound to the nipple threads.

2 Install the new spout. Slide the new spout over the pipe and snug to the wall. If it has a setscrew, tighten it. If the pipe is threaded, screw on the spout hand-tight. If further tightening is required, put tape over the jaws of water-pump pliers to prevent scratching, and tighten until the spout is snug. Run silicone caulk around the spout or escutcheon plate if there is one.

Cleaning a showerhead

Showerheads, like faucet aerators, in areas with hard water will eventually become clogged with mineral deposits. Not all showerheads break down the same way, but what's shown here is a common example. Newer showerheads come with a water-conservation device, called a flow restrictor, that cannot be removed.

- Unscrew the swivel ball nut and remove the showerhead.
- Disassemble the internal parts.
- Soak overnight in white vinegar or a lime-dissolving solution.
- Reassemble the showerhead. Apply silicone grease to the shower arm threads and install the showerhead. Turn on the water and inspect for leaks.

▲ ***Use a small wire brush*** *to clean mineral deposits.*

▲ ***Use a paper clip*** *to remove mineral deposits from holes in the disk. Inspect for damage and replace components if necessary.*

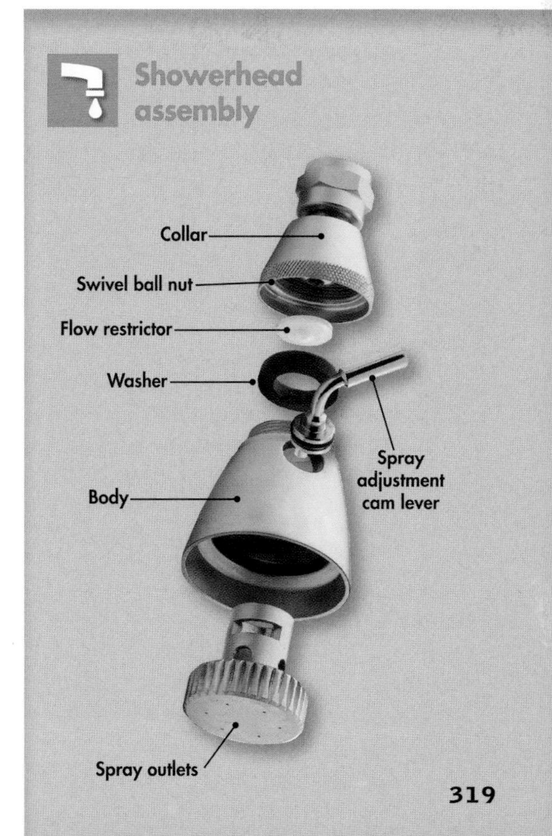

Repairing toilets

Fix a leaking toilet immediately. An unrepaired leak may become more than an annoyance. It can develop into structural damage to the floor and the ceiling below the toilet. Either may require hiring a contractor for a repair that can be extensive and expensive.

Troubleshooting

Troubleshooting a toilet to locate a leak is easy. No tools are required, just food coloring (red is recommended) and paper towels. The food coloring added to the tank or bowl will make the leak easily visible so you can see what repairs are needed (see "Troubleshooting a leaking toilet," below).

If the base is leaking see "Installing a New Toilet," page 346.

▶ ***Before you begin working on the toilet,*** *put on a pair of rubber gloves and clean the base thoroughly with a disinfectant. It will make the job a little more pleasant!*

Anatomy of a toilet

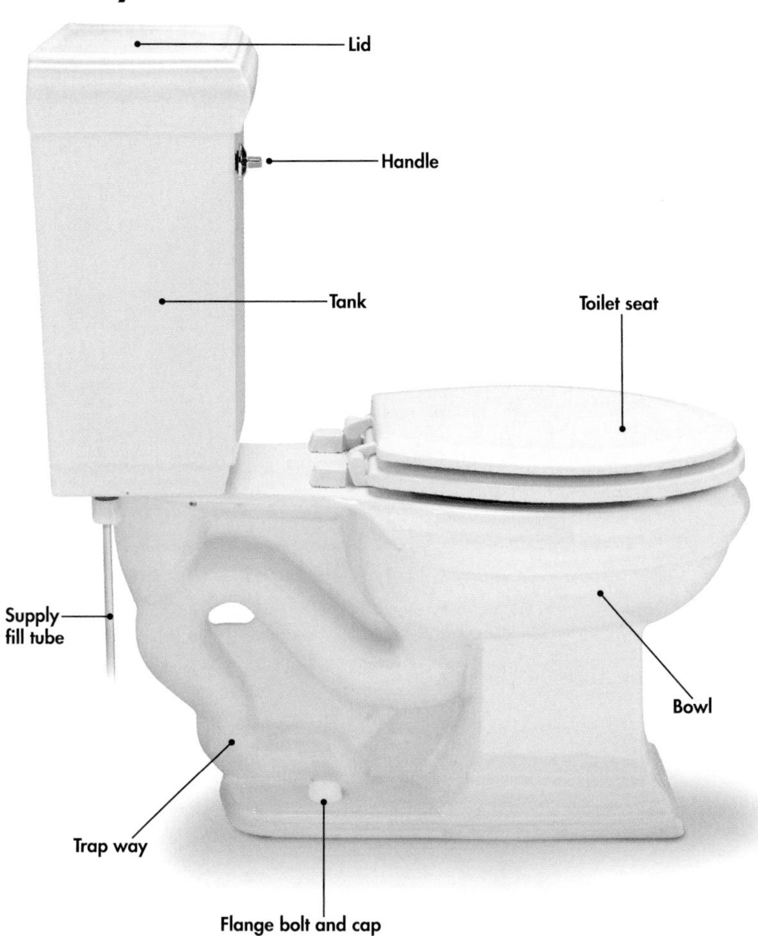

WORK SMART
DON'T OVERTIGHTEN

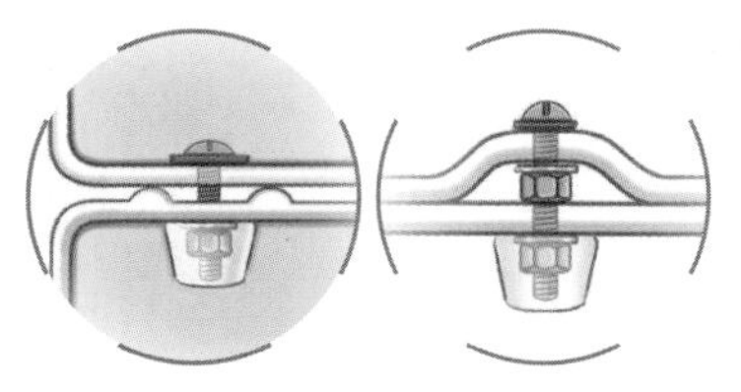

Overtightening the bolts that connect the tank to the toilet base can crack the base, the tank, or both. Tighten gently until snug and alternate from side to side to seat them evenly.

BUYER'S GUIDE
ENVIRONMENTAL ISSUES

Low-flow toilets using a maximum of 1.6 gallons of water per flush are required by federal regulations. Older models often needed an extra flush, but new toilet technology allows these environmental friends to do their job efficiently.

Get the right supply line

In earthquake zones, building code requires a flexible supply tube. Elsewhere you can use flex tube, rigid plastic, or rigid metal.

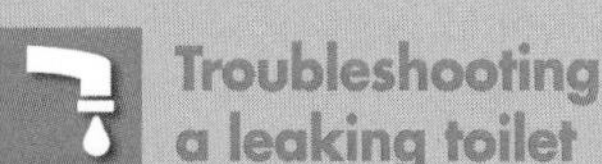

Troubleshooting a leaking toilet

- **Clean the outside of the toilet.** Flush the toilet. Thoroughly dry all exterior surfaces. This will help you spot a leak easily.
- **Pour about a teaspoon of red food coloring** into the water in the tank and a teaspoon into the bowl. Wait an hour.
- **Check for leaks.** Wipe a dry paper towel around the base and under the tank. Red coloring on the towel shows there's a leak. If the leak is around the base you will need to replace the wax ring (see "Removing an Old Toilet," page 345). Leaks under the tank could be either a leaking fill valve, bolt gasket, or spud washer.

Adjusting the tank and water level

Skill level: ★☆☆☆☆

Time to complete:
Experienced 10 min.
Handy 25 min.
Novice 30 min.

Materials: Existing

Tools: Adjustable wrench, screwdriver

PLUMBING

The sound of water bubbling from a fountain may be relaxing. But if it's coming from your toilet, it's just adding to the water bill. Quick fixes include shortening a chain, bending a wire, or adjusting a float clip. Each solution is easy and requires little time.

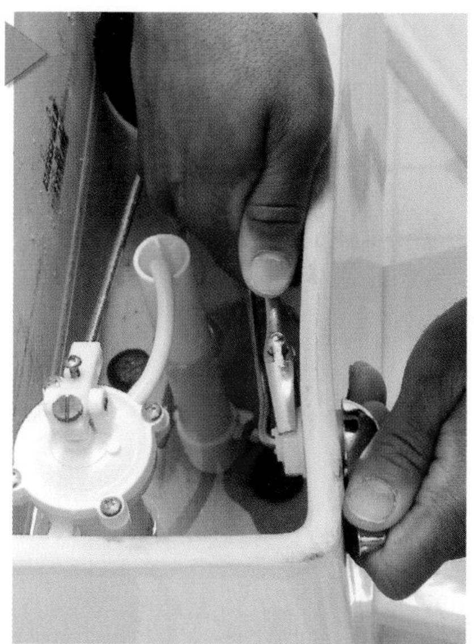

1 Adjust the tank handle. If the handle has too much play or binds, use an adjustable wrench to tighten the nut inside the toilet. Unlike other nuts and bolts, the threads on a tank handle are left-handed, so you'll tighten counterclockwise.

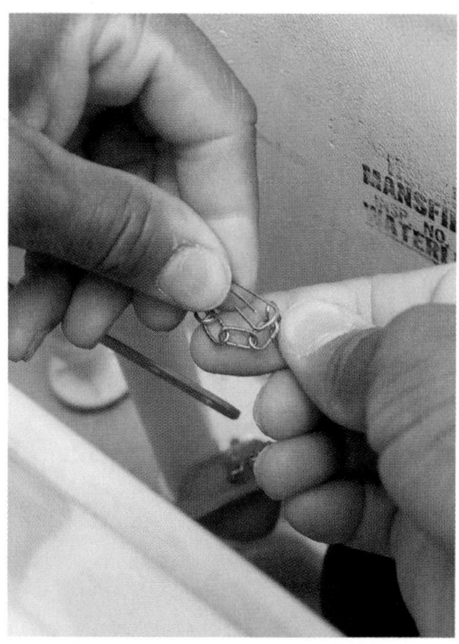

2 Shorten the chain. This will help if you have to hold the handle down to flush all the water from the toilet tank.

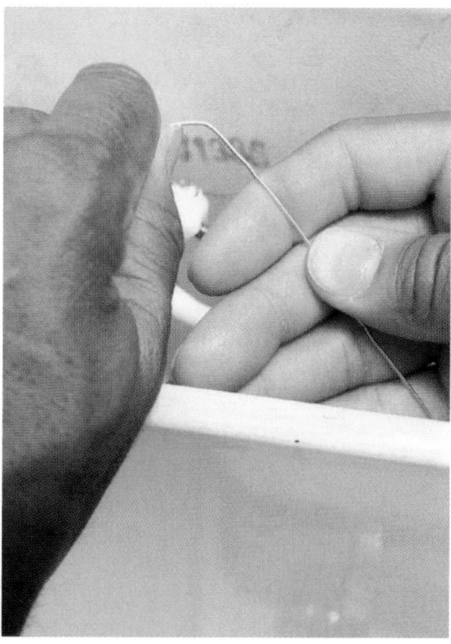

3 Bend the upper wire. If the tank doesn't have a chain, it has a wire you can bend.

WORK SMART
ADJUST THE FLOAT ARM

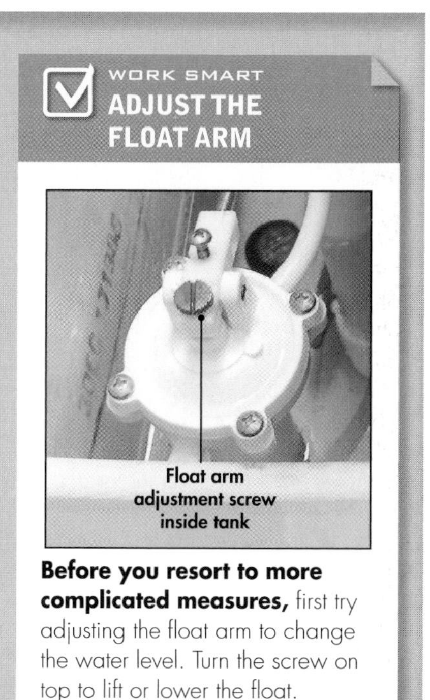

Before you resort to more complicated measures, first try adjusting the float arm to change the water level. Turn the screw on top to lift or lower the float.

4 Bend the float arm. The water level should be just below the overflow. To adjust the water level in the tank, bend it up for a higher water level or down to lower the water level.

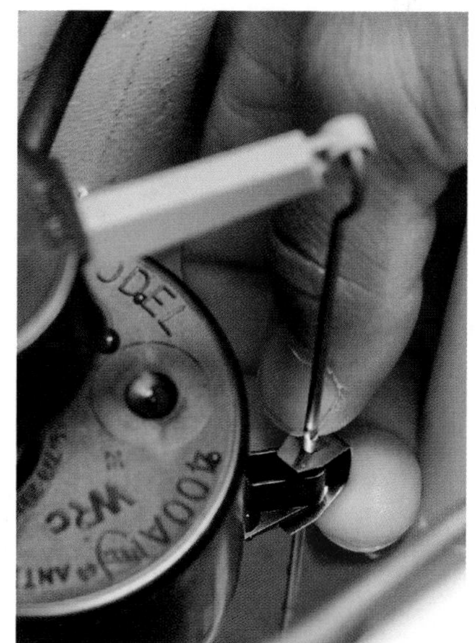

5 Slide the float cylinder. Squeeze the float clip to release the float cylinder, which can be raised or lowered to adjust the water level in float-style toilets.

Repairing a leaking tank

Skill level:	Time to complete:	Materials:	Tools:
★★★☆☆	Experienced 45 min. Handy 1.5 hrs. Novice 2 hrs.	Flush valve gasket, fill valve, gaskets, spud washer	Two adjustable wrenches, screwdriver, small wire brush, spud wrench

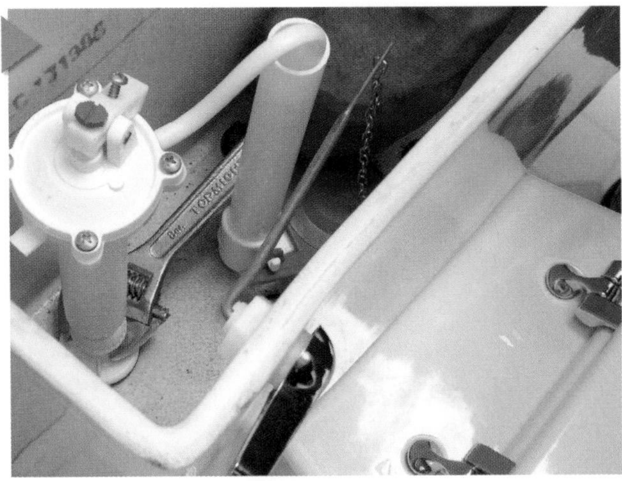

1 If the fill valve is leaking turn off the water supply valve. Flush the toilet. Disconnect the supply line from the tank and sponge the inside of the tank until it's dry. Use two adjustable wrenches to remove the fill valve assembly. If you're not replacing other parts, install the new fill valve assembly. Turn on the supply line and check for leaks. If necessary, tighten a quarter-turn. Otherwise proceed to Step 2.

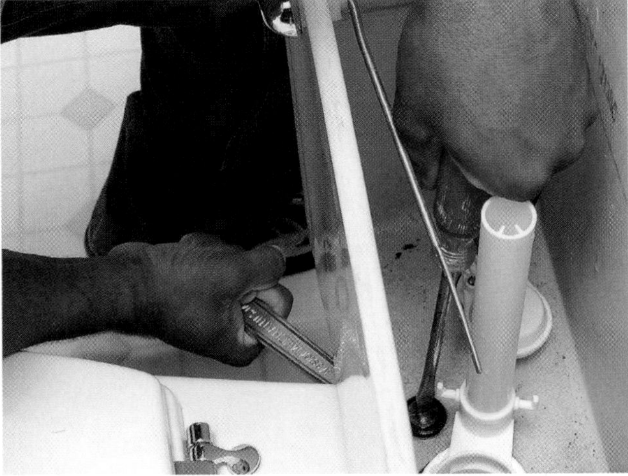

2 If the tank is leaking: A screwdriver and adjustable wrench will remove most tank bolts. Remove the tank bolt, nut, and gasket. Clean the bolt and nut with white vinegar and a small wire brush. If you aren't replacing the spud washer, reinstall bolts and nuts with new gaskets. Alternate the tightening of the nuts to evenly draw the tank tight. If you need to replace the spud washer, continue to Step 3.

WORK SMART
TRACING LEAKS

If there is a leak along the supply valve, tighten the fittings an additional quarter-turn. If the leak is around the base of the tank, check the washers in the tank to make sure they're seated properly. If the washers appear to be properly seated, tighten the tank nuts another quarter-turn.

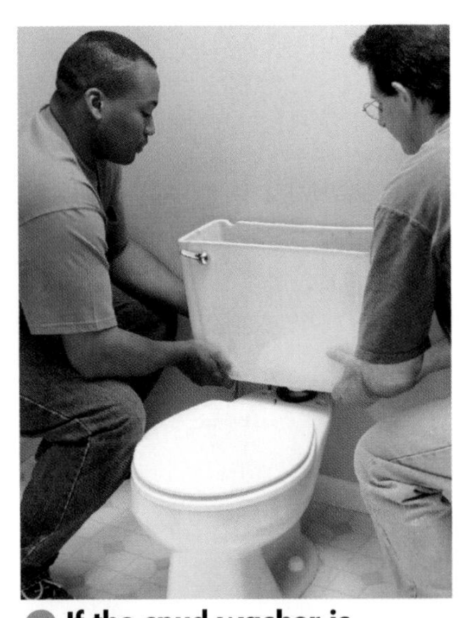

3 If the spud washer is leaking remove the bolts and lift the tank straight up and off the toilet base to remove it. Make sure you have a helper; toilet tanks are usually in an awkward place and are heavier than they appear to be. Set the tank upside down on the floor. It's best to set it on an old towel or rug because it may contain some water.

4 Replace the spud washer. Take the spud washer to your local home center to find the correct replacement. Place a new spud washer over the flush valve tailpiece. Lower the tank onto the base so the tank bolts go through the holes. Reinstall the tank bolts, gaskets, and nuts. Alternate tightening the nuts so they tighten evenly. Reinstall the supply tube coupling and fill valve. Turn on the water supply and check for leaks.

Replacing a toilet fill valve

Skill level:	Time to complete:	Materials:	Tools:
★★★☆☆	Experienced 20 min. Handy 40 min. Novice 1 hr.	Fill valve, fill valve gasket	Adjustable wrench

Old toilet fill valves can develop leaks. If water continues to run after you have made the adjustments on page 321, you may need to remove and replace the fill valve. You may also have to replace the supply line so that the new valve fits.

Know the locations of the main water shutoff valve or the supply valves for each fixture in your home.

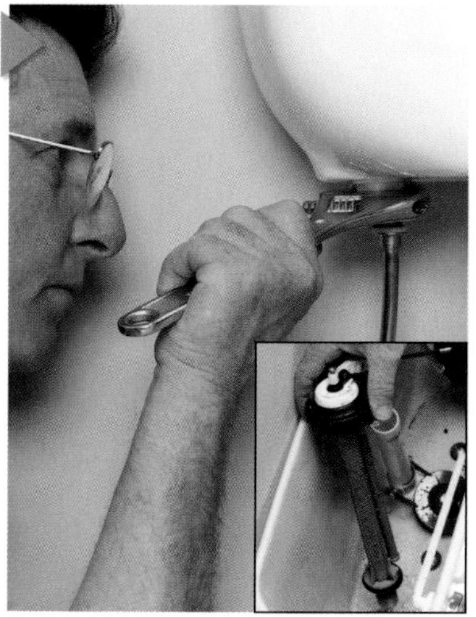

1 Shut off the water and drain the tank. Disconnect the fill valve nut and remove the old fill valve. (See inset.)

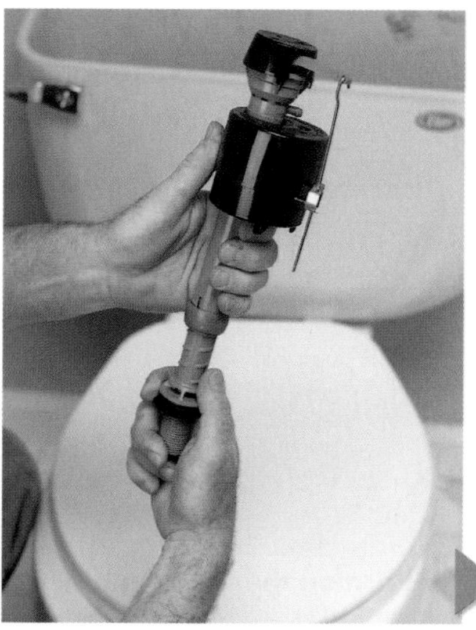

2 Adjust the height of the valve so that the marking on the top of the valve is at least 1 inch above the overflow tube.

Toilet fill valve components

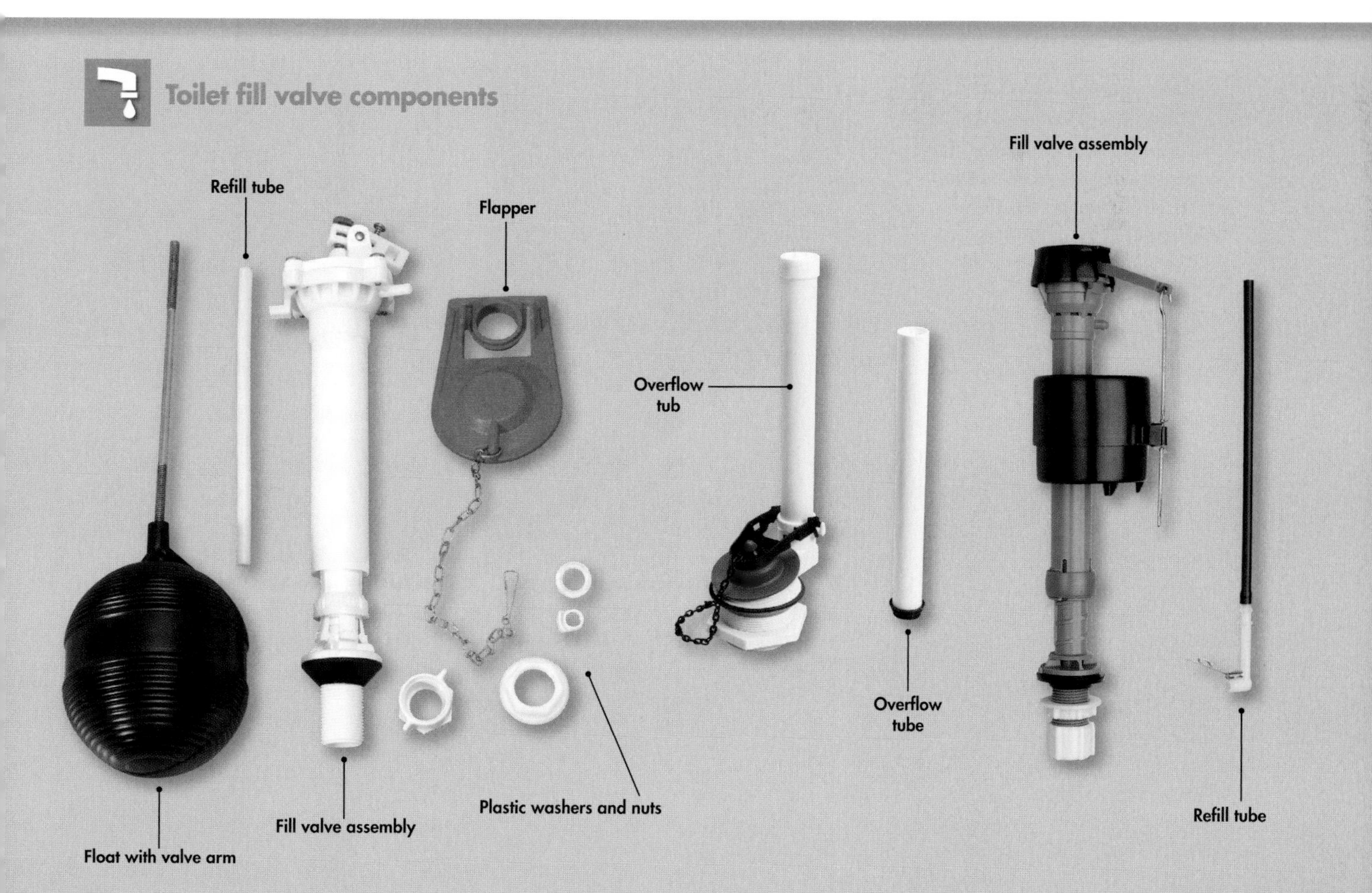

Replacing a toilet fill valve (continued)

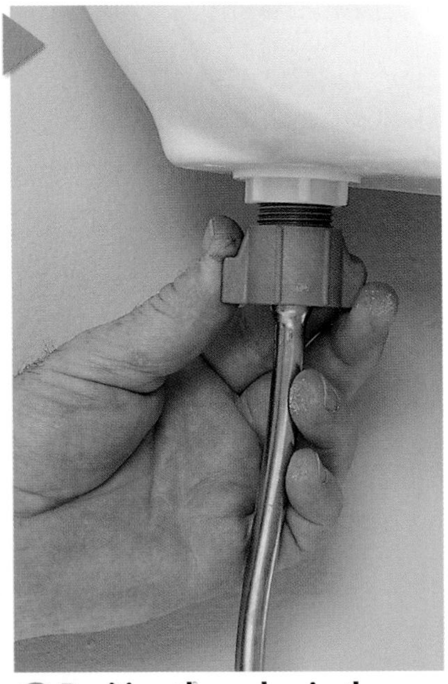

3 Position the valve in the tank. Push down on the valve shank and tighten the locknut a half-turn beyond hand-tight. Connect the supply.

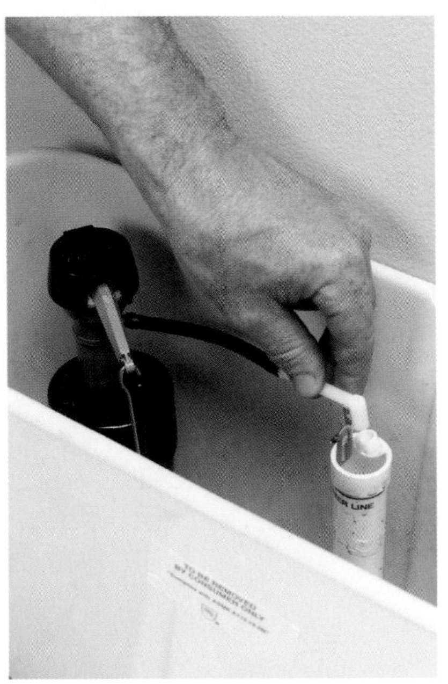

4 Attach the refill tube and angle the adapter to the overflow. Trim the tube if necessary to get rid of any kinks.

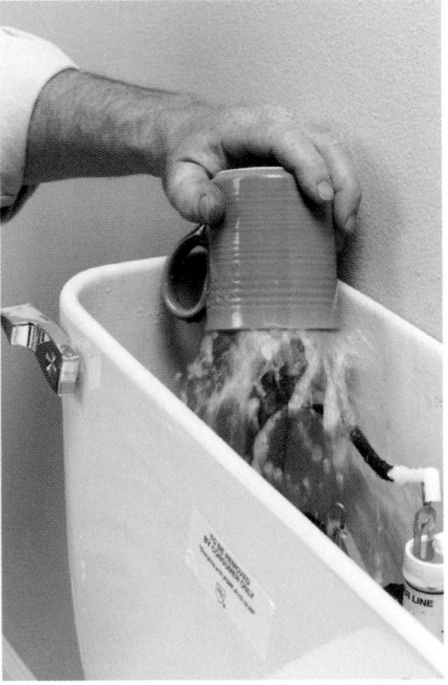

5 Flush the system. Remove the top valve. Hold a cup over the uncapped valve and turn on the water supply to flush the system of rust and debris. Turn off the water.

$ BUYER'S GUIDE

THREE VALVE TYPES—ONE WAY TO REPLACE

Three basic types of fill valves exist: the plunger valve, the diaphragm, and the float cup. Replace all three the same way. It may not be necessary to replace the fill valve with the exact same type that you remove, but it may be easier for you because the installation process is the opposite of the removal sequence.

6 Replace the top valve by engaging the lugs and rotating one-eighth turn clockwise. Make sure it's firmly locked into position.

7 Adjust the water level by squeezing the adjustment clip and moving the float cup up for more water or down for less water.

Replacing a flapper

Skill level:	Time to complete:	Materials:	Tools:
★★★☆☆	Experienced 5 min. Handy 10 min. Novice 15 min.	Flapper or tank ball	Bucket, sponge, scrub pad

If you have hard water, you will probably need to change the toilet flapper occasionally. Minerals in hard water build up around the base of the flapper and the opening of the toilet. The sediment will eventually destroy the flapper, causing the toilet to leak.

1 Turn off the water supply shutoff valve and flush the tank. If there isn't a shutoff valve, turn off the water at the main valve; this is also a good time to install a shutoff valve for future use. (See page 302.)

2 Remove the old flapper. Pull the flapper from the pivot arm. For ball-style toilets, grip a loop of lift wire and unscrew the old tank ball. Clean the surface area of the opening with a scrub pad to remove sediment.

WORK SMART

FLAPPER TIPS

Have about a half inch of slack in the chain that connects the flush lever to the flapper. Most replacements have side tabs or a ring that slides over the overflow tube so that they can work with any system. Make sure the flapper moves up and down freely.

BUYER'S GUIDE

SQUARE PEGS, ROUND HOLES

While universal replacement flappers are available, they still may not fit exactly. Take the old flapper with you to get an exact replacement.

Chemical reaction

If you are in the habit of placing chlorine-releasing tablets in a toilet tank to counteract the growth of mold, mildew, and bacteria, you should be aware that the chemical might shorten the useful life of the flapper and washers in the tank. You can buy replacement parts that are chlorine resistant, and keep on dropping those pellets. Or do without the chlorine and keep a clean bowl the old-fashioned way, by regularly going at it with a brush.

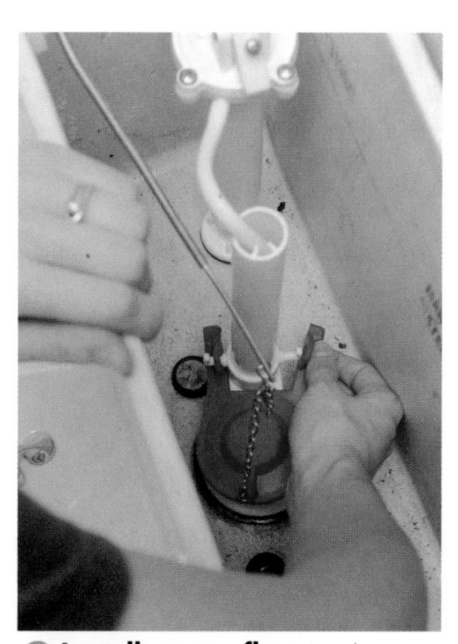

3 Install a new flapper. Line up the flap or ball with the valve seat by straightening the lift wire or adjusting the guide arm. This will provide a sufficient seat and keep the tank from leaking.

Installing a countertop sink

Skill level:	Time to complete:	Materials:	Tools:
★★★☆☆	Experienced 1 hr. Handy 1.5 hrs. Novice 2 hrs.	Countertop sink, fixtures, cardboard template, silicone caulk, masking tape	Tape measure, scissors, carpenter's pencil, power drill and bits, saber saw, caulking gun, putty knife, screwdriver, utility knife, rags

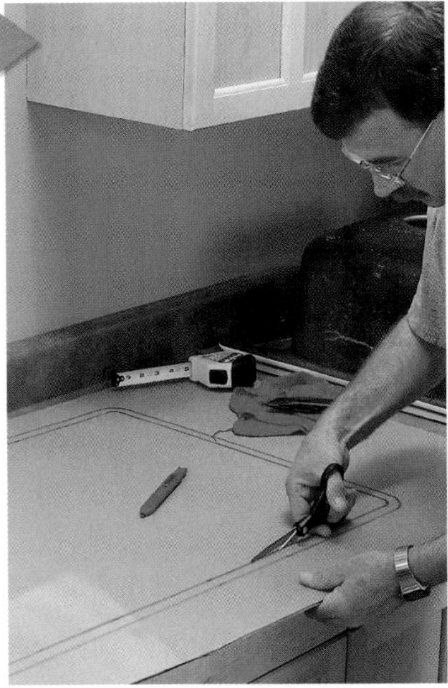

1 Create a template. If the sink doesn't come with a template, create one by laying the sink facedown on a sheet of cardboard and drawing a line around the edge. Lift off the sink and draw a second line ¾ inch inside the first line. Cut along the inside line with scissors.

2 Mark the center of the cabinet from below. Drill a hole large enough to fit a finishing nail.

3 Mark the center of the template. Push a nail through the center of the template into the hole. Center the template and square the edges so the sink rim will lie entirely on the cabinet surface.

4 Trace the outline on the countertop. Remove the template and place masking tape along the edge. Replace the template and draw the outline of the sink on the tape. Remove the template.

5 Drill a ¾-inch hole inside the cutout line. Use a power drill and spade bit to make a starter hole for the saber saw.

6 Install braces beneath the countertop. The braces will support the section to prevent it from binding while cutting.

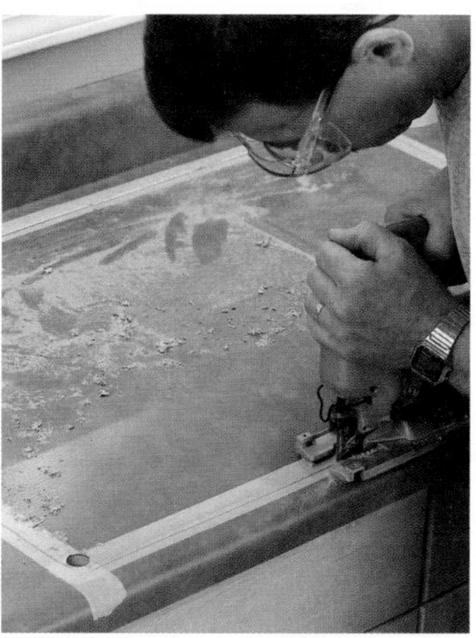

7 Cut out the opening. Use a saber saw with a blade designed to cut countertops without chipping the surface. Remove the masking tape. Test-fit the sink and trace the rim lightly on the countertop.

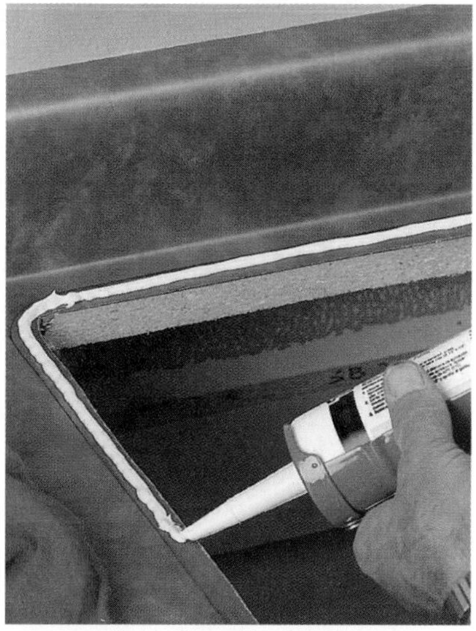

8 Apply a bead of silicone caulk inside the line. Apply a steady, continuous bead between the mark and the opening.

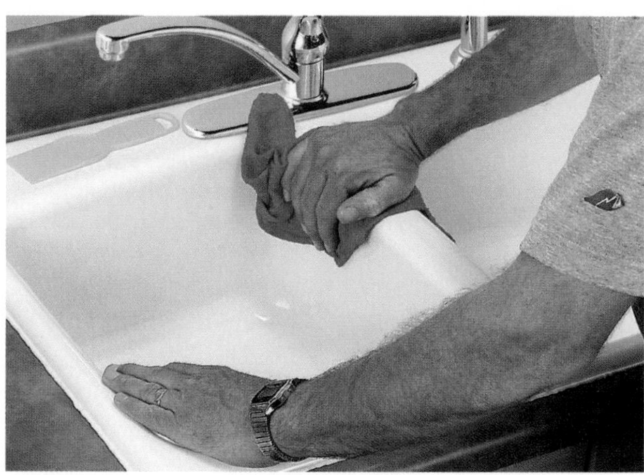

9 Place the sink in the opening. Press the sink firmly into the silicone caulking, then level and clean. Connect the faucets and the drains. Test for leaks.

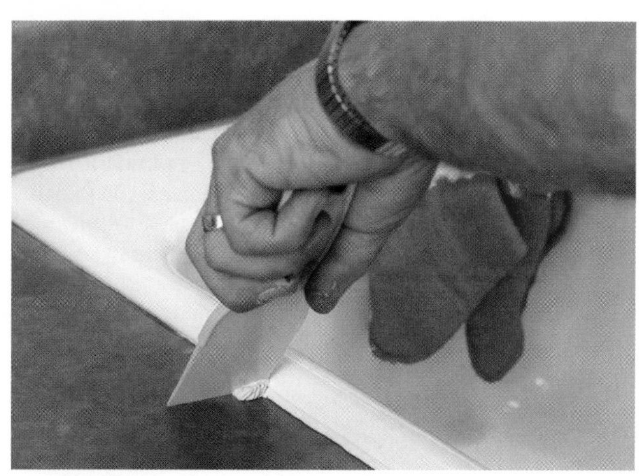

10 Clean away excess silicone. Trim silicone caulking with a plastic putty knife for a professional look.

TOOL TIP

CUT IT SHORT

High-speed cutting tools make short work of cutting holes in drywall. They are a perfect alternative to using a saber saw for cutting out a countertop.

WORK SMART

USING TEMPLATES

There are few DIY headaches worse than this one—cutting a hole in an expensive countertop for a sink, then finding that the hole is too big. A sure way to avoid trouble is to use a pattern, or template, when laying out the cut. The sink may come with a template, but if not, it won't take long to make your own. Place the sink face down on a sheet of thin cardboard or sturdy kraft paper, and trace a line around the edge. Then remove the sink and draw a second line ¾ inch inside the first line (or as directed in the manufacturer's directions). Cut along this second line with scissors or a utility knife. This template will ensure you've got the right size and shape, but you still need to position it. Find the center of the area where you want to place the sink and drill a hole at that point, just large enough to run a finishing nail through. Find the center of the template, measuring from top to bottom and left to right, and poke a nail through this spot. Place the template on the countertop and shift it until the nail finds the hole. Check the template for square, then tape it in place. Trace the outline of the template onto the countertop, and you're ready to cut that hole.

Installing a vanity and sink

Skill level:	Time to complete:	Materials:	Tools:
★★★☆☆	Experienced 2 hrs. Handy 4 hrs. Novice 6 hrs.	Vanity cabinet, sink, shims, faucet set, tailpiece, supply pipes, Teflon tape, silicone caulk, screws (to attach the cabinet to the wall).	Carpenter's level, stud finder, tape measure, adjustable wrench, caulking gun, electric drill.

A new bathroom vanity cabinet can give you more counter space and better storage options. Because vanities tend to get a lot of use and are exposed to moisture, pay particular attention to the quality of construction. Solid wood and plywood will hold up better than fiberboard. Note that the project will be somewhat more involved if you choose a larger vanity that's assembled from two or more units.

Begin by shutting off the water supply lines at the sink, or at the home's main supply if necessary. Disconnect the supply lines and the waste trap from the sink. Disassemble the sink and existing vanity. Once they are out of the way, it's time to patch up and paint or tile the wall where they stood.

1 Position the vanity. Temporarily put the vanity in place and use a level to position it, front to back and from one side to the other. You can slip wooden shims under the vanity to bring it to level as needed. Draw lines on the wall to mark the location of the vanity.

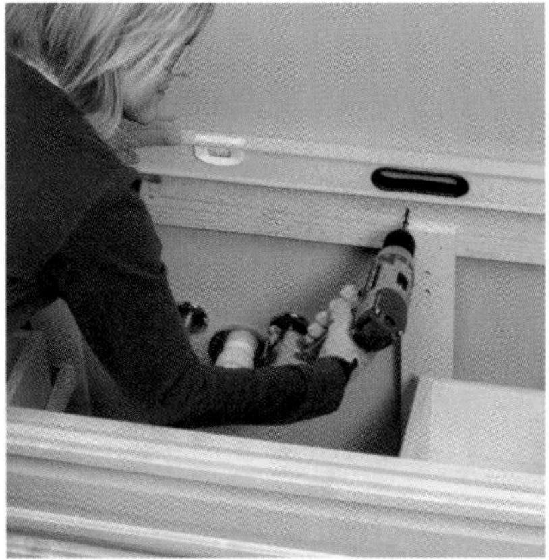

2 Install the vanity. Move the vanity to one side. Use a stud finder to locate where the vanity is to go. Put the vanity back in place and drill holes in its back rail to coincide with the framing. Drive screws through the rail and into the studs. If the walls are tiled, dimple the glazed surface with a nail punch and use a masonry or tile bit; secure the screws with plastic anchors.

3 Connect the faucets and the drain assembly. Before installing the top, connect the faucets and the drain assembly, following the manufacturer's instructions.

TOOL TIP

A DRILL WITH TEETH

If you need to drill holes in the back of the vanity for the supply and drain lines, consider using a hole saw and an electric drill. The saw makes quick work of drilling large-diameter holes, and it can be used with a ⅜-inch variable-speed drill—one you plug in, rather than a lighter duty battery-powered model. Keep a good hold on the drill and keep it level, or the saw may bind and cause the drill to twist out of your grip.

4 Put the top in place. Run a bead of silicone caulk around the top edge of the vanity cabinet. With a helper, lower the top onto the cabinet, then press down. Install any clips, screws, or other mechanical fasters that come with the sink to further secure it.

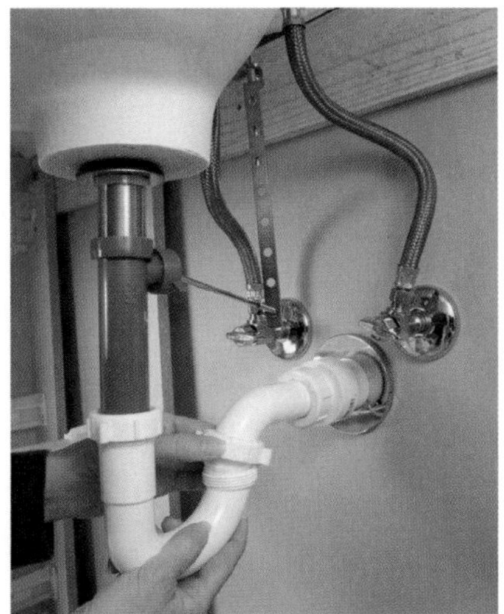

5 Connect the trap and supply pipes. Connect the trap, using a new tailpiece (the vertical section below the bowl) if necessary to make the hookup. Connect the supply pipes to the water supply; flexible plastic or braided stainless steel lines will make this job easier.

Installing a self-rimming sink

1 Install the sink. Follow the steps for installing a countertop sink through Step 7 on pages 326–327, check for fit, then caulk the rim and lower the undermount sink into place.

2 Tighten the clamps beneath the sink. Align the clamps over the countertop; stagger-tighten with a screwdriver as you would the lugs on a tire, alternating so that the clamps tighten evenly.

Removing an old sink

Out with the old. Like many plumbing projects, removing the old sink can be the toughest part of a replacement job. Fittings may be rusted or fused tight, and getting around under the counter can be tricky. If it's a cast-iron sink, it will be heavy, so get help for removal.

1. **Before you begin,** make sure the new fixture will fit properly into the old hole.
2. **Turn off the water supply valves to the hot and cold water faucets.** Place a bucket beneath the drain trap. Loosen the slip nuts and remove the trap. Support the bottom of the trap with your hand while loosening the nuts.
3. **Remove the bucket** and place a shallow tray or rags beneath the sink supply lines to catch remaining water.
4. **Remove the coupling nuts** connecting the supply tube to the faucet tailpiece.
5. **Disconnect additional plumbing for disposers** (see pages 349–350), dishwashers (see page 351), and sink sprayers.
6. **Slice through the caulking** around the rim using a utility knife.
7. **Lift the sink from the countertop** using the drain hole as a handhold.
8. **Look for water damage** to the countertop and clean any excess caulking from the rim before you install the new sink.

Call your local waste removal service for instructions on disposing of the old sink, or contact a used building supply outlet—they may be interested in taking it as a donation.

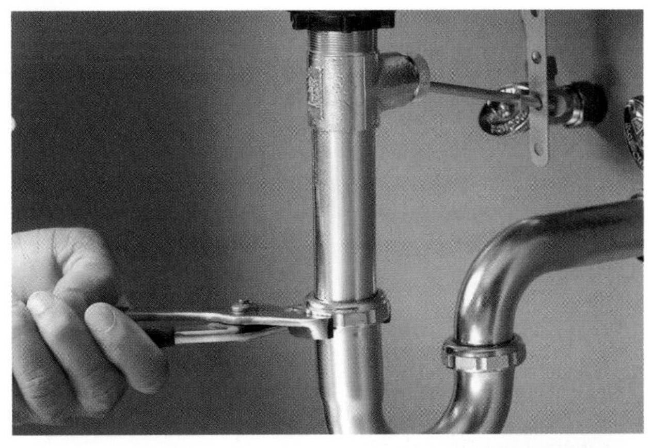

Installing a wall-hung sink

Skill level:	Time to complete:	Materials:	Tools:
★★☆☆☆	Experienced 2 hrs. Handy 4 hrs. Novice 6 hrs.	Wall-hung sink, mounting bracket, anchor bolts, 2×10 wood blocking, water-resistant drywall scrap, drywall tape and compound, paint, faucets and fittings, drainpipe and fitting, 2×4 brace, silicone caulk	Keyhole saw, hammer, tape measure, carpenter's pencil, power drill and bits, ratchet wrench and sockets, caulking gun, screwdriver, utility knife, rags

1 Cut away a 16×16-inch section of drywall and nail or screw the blocking into place. Use a keyhole saw to remove the drywall. Nail the 2×10 between the studs so that it's flush with the leading edge of the studs. Cut a piece of water-resistant drywall to cover the hole. You may be able to use the piece you cut away. Finish the drywall and paint it. Attach the mounting bracket after the paint has dried.

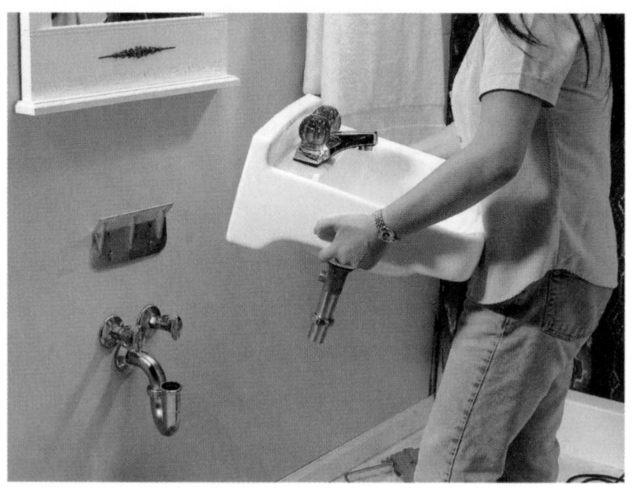

2 Prepare to set the sink. Attach the faucet and drain before mounting the sink. Run the supply line with stop valves. Install the drain line and P-trap. Set the sink on the bracket, securing it to the bracket with anchor bolts. Connect the supply line to the faucet, and the drain to the P-trap. Open the valves. Check for leaks. Tighten leaking fittings if necessary. Legs for most wall-mounted sinks are optional.

Installing a pedestal sink

1 Set the basin and pedestal in place. Install the fixtures and plumbing. Brace the basin with a 2×4. Outline the base of the pedestal on the floor with a pencil. Mark the floor with the location of the holes for the lag screws. Set the basin and pedestal aside. Drill holes in the floor for the lag screws.

2 Install the pedestal lag bolts, making sure they're snug. Don't overtighten; you could crack the base. Apply a bead of silicone caulk around the base. Install the faucet, then connect the supply lines and drain before you attach the basin to the wall so you'll have some play to make the hookup.

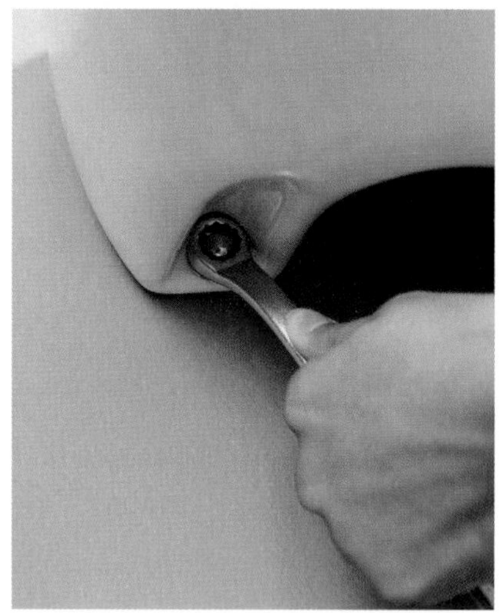

3 Connect the basin to the wall. Predrill a small hole through to the blocking, then insert and alternately tighten the lag screws until just snug—don't overtighten. Caulk the back of the basin with silicone caulk. Remove the brace and test the system for leaks.

Installing a bowl-type sink

Skill level:	Time to complete:	Materials:	Tools:
★★★☆☆	Experienced 1 hr. Handy 2 hrs. Novice 3 hrs.	Sink, vanity, masking tape, faucet set and drain assembly, Teflon tape, silicone caulk	Level, drill, saber saw, adjustable wrench

Even the lowly bathroom sink isn't immune to the tides of fashion. A hot item right now is the vessel or bowl-type sink, which hovers above (or sits lightly within) a vanity or counter top. Their unusual configurations require a bit of extra thought before going ahead with the installation.

- Some models aren't equipped with overflow valves, a consideration if you have forgetful kids. A way around that is to use a grid drain. It has little holes that allow you to fill the sink when washing your face while constantly dribbling a small amount of water, helping to avoid an overflow.
- A vessel sink may be 6 inches high, putting it at an uncomfortable height for shorter people if it sits atop a standard-size vanity. There are two possible fixes: recess the bowl rather than have it perched atop the countertop, or install a lower vanity.
- Most of these sinks come without holes for faucets. If you plan to use a countertop faucet set, make sure there will be enough room between the rim of the sink and the wall. Otherwise you'll be doing some extra work to install a wall-mounted set.
- Like the look (and the stability) of a recessed sink? Choose a bowl that isn't transparent (for aesthetic reasons) and that has a smooth, circular outline (for practical reasons, when making the cutout in the countertop).
- If you've chosen a stone countertop, have a shop specializing in them do the tricky work of drilling holes and making cutouts.

Cutouts without the clunk

When you cut a hole in a countertop for a sink, the cutout is apt to slump and cause the saw blade to bind. To prevent trouble, tap a couple of finishing nails from the underside of the nearly completed cut into the center of the cutout. This temporarily keeps the cutout in place and helps the saw kerf stay open.

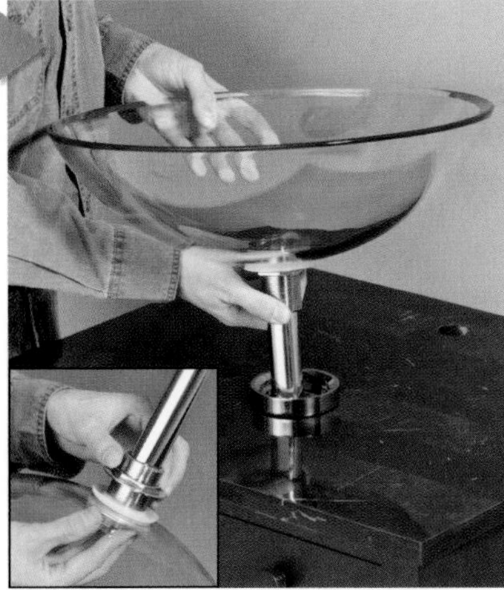

1 Position the bowl, measuring from either side to make sure there is sufficient room for the faucet set if it will be mounted on the countertop. Follow the manufacturer's instructions for using a mounting ring with the drain; the ring acts as a cushioning gasket. Apply silicone caulk as directed. Drill a drain hole for the sink and one for the faucet set if it installs on the countertop. Insert the drain body through the hole in the bottom and the drain flange from inside the bowl, screwing it into the drain body. Tighten the locknut under the bowl, first by hand and then gently with a wrench to avoid cracking the bowl.

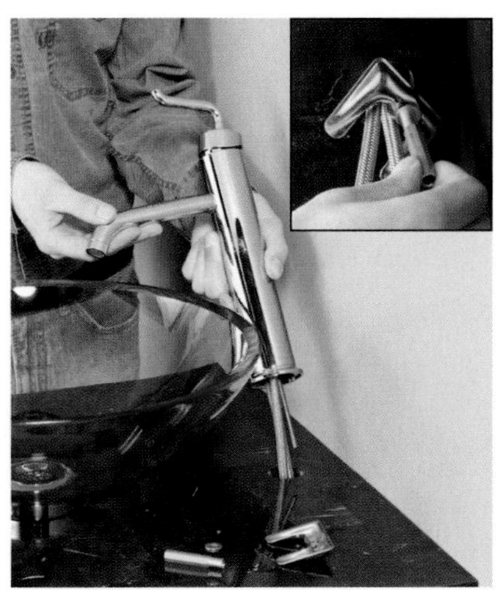

2 Install the faucet. Run the supply lines up through the hole for the faucet and screw them into the threaded holes in the bottom of the faucet body. Put the faucet in place and secure it as directed, using the provided parts—either a mounting bracket and screw as shown, or a locknut.

3 Attach the supply lines. Using Teflon tape to help seal the threads, screw the nuts on the supply lines to secure them to the supply valves.

4 Attach the P-trap. Turn the two slip nuts by hand to attach the trap to the drain and then tighten them with a wrench.

Installing a farmer's/apron sink

Skill level:	Time to complete:	Materials:	Tools:
★★★☆☆	Experienced 2 hrs. Handy 4 hrs. Novice 6 hrs.	Sink, template material and support system (if not included with sink), faucet set and drain, Teflon tape, silicone caulk	Level, saber saw, rasp

A farmer's sink, also known as an apron sink for its characteristic front panel, was a salvage yard item until recently. It's now a popular high-end accessory for traditional-style kitchens, and it can be had in fireclay, cast iron, and several types of stone. Most farmer's sinks have a single extra-deep basin that's suited for serious pot washing (as well as baby washing). Installation is somewhat involved. The doors on most standard cabinets are too high for the deep U-shape cutout required to seat the apron front. That means either adapting the cabinet or having one custom made. Also, the considerable weight of these heavy-duty sinks requires extra support. They can rest on a plywood panel or on a pair of ledgers or bars running front to back or from one side to the other.

1 Make a cutout in the face frame. Determine whether the sink will rest on the countertop or be an undermount installation. You'll need a template to make the cutout in the cabinet face frame. If one isn't supplied with the sink, place the sink face down on a sheet of thin cardboard and trace its outline. If the apron has a lip, draw a second line within the first to indicate where you'll need to cut for a tightly scribed fit. Cut out the template and test it with the sink. Adjust as necessary. Trace the outline onto the face frame and use a saber saw to make the cut.

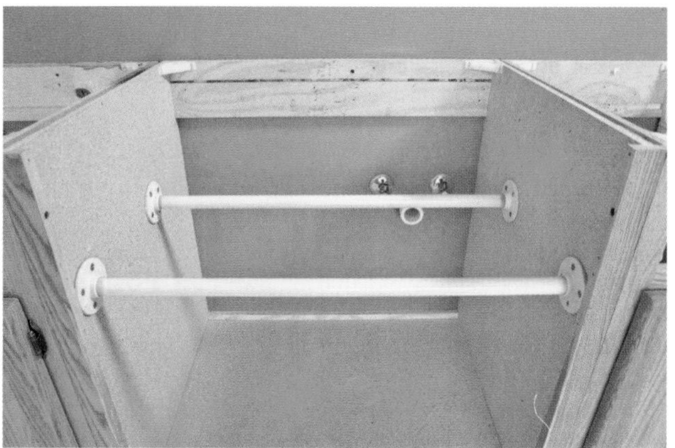

2 Support the sink. To handle the weight of the sink, either place a well-supported panel of ¾-inch plywood under it or run 2x ledgers on either side of the basin. The manufacturer may supply an installation kit like the horizontal rails shown here, and similar rails are marketed for heavy sinks.

$ BUYER'S GUIDE
WALL-MOUNTED FAUCETS

Traditionally, faucets were mounted on the wall above the sink, often with the supply pipes in plain view. A more refined adaptation, often used today with farmer's and vessel sinks, is to run supply pipes inside the wall. That requires cutting away a section of the wall, from the existing supply pipes to the height you've determined for the new faucets. Remove the stop valves and replace them with in-line shutoffs that you'll be able to reach through the open back of the base cabinet. Attach supply tubes that extend to the desired height and fit them with elbows and the horizontal extensions, or stubouts, for the faucets. Then patch up the wall, put the cabinet in place, and add the faucet set.

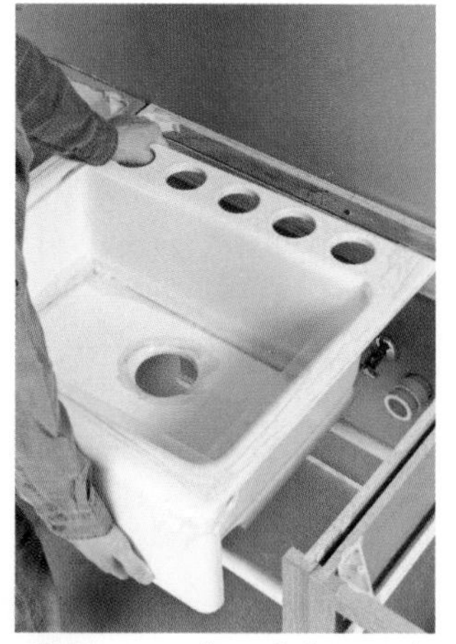

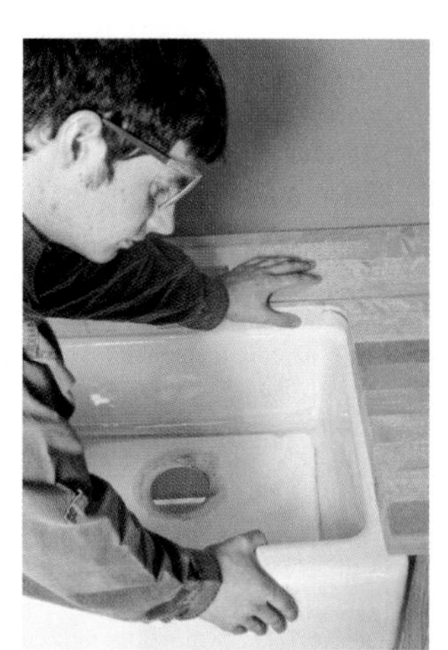

3 Insert the sink. Put the sink in place. Shim it as necessary to bring it level with the countertop. Check for the apron's fit. Use a rasp to remove just enough wood to allow the sink to seat properly. To conceal any gaps, you can run molding around the perimeter of the apron. Seal the sink as necessary with silicone caulk.

Connect the water supply and drain. Install the drain and the faucet as for other sinks.If you intend to connect a garbage disposer, make sure that the model can accommodate the thick sink bottom.

Installing a widespread faucet

Skill level:	Time to complete:	Materials:	Tools:
★★★☆☆	Experienced 40 min. Handy 1 hr. Novice 2 hrs.	Widespread faucet, gaskets, pipe compound, Teflon paste or Teflon tape, plumber's putty	Plastic putty knife, adjustable wrenches, basin wrench

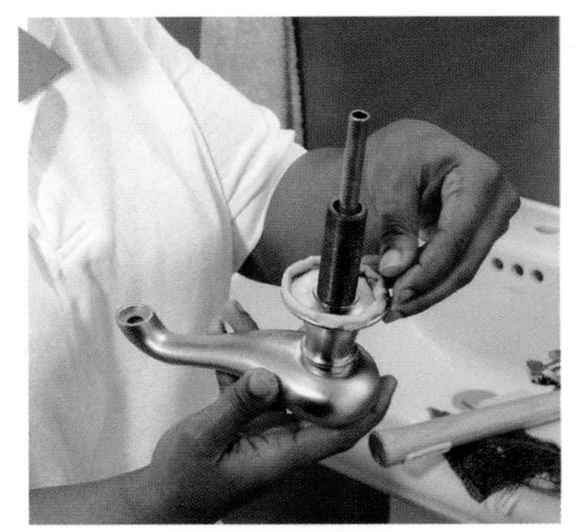

1 Seal the spout base. Form plumber's putty into a rope and place it on the base of the spout. Press the putty against the base, and set the spout in place.

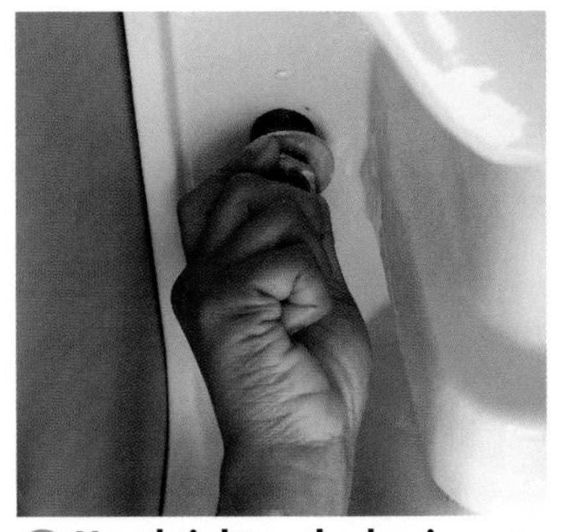

2 Hand-tighten the basin nut just enough to hold it in place. Don't overtighten because you will need to center the spout on the sink in Step 4.

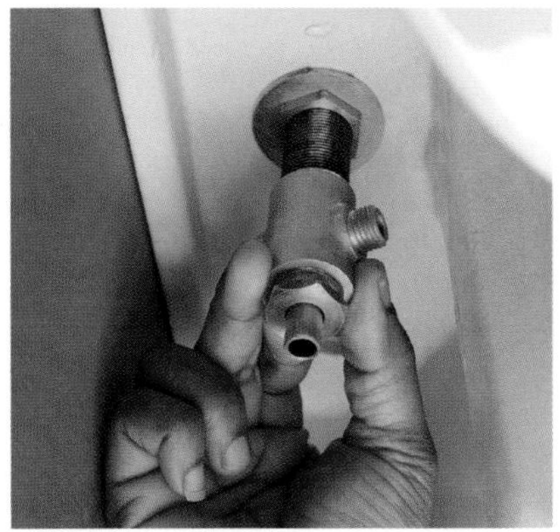

3 Thread the tee on the spout. Center the tee so that the outlets are approximately parallel to the back wall and line up with the faucets on either side. (See Step 7.)

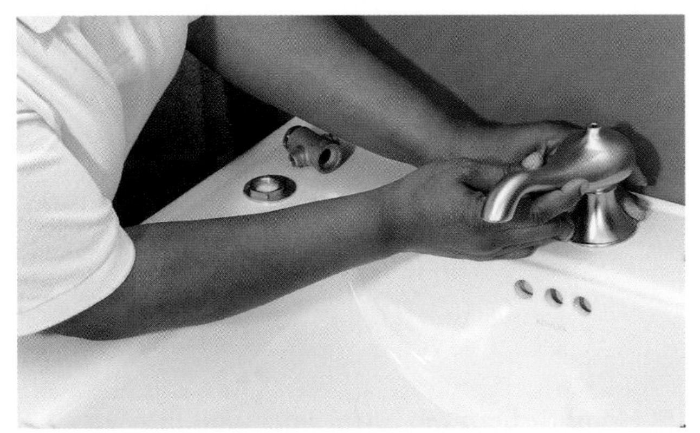

4 Center the spout and tighten it from beneath the sink using a basin wrench.

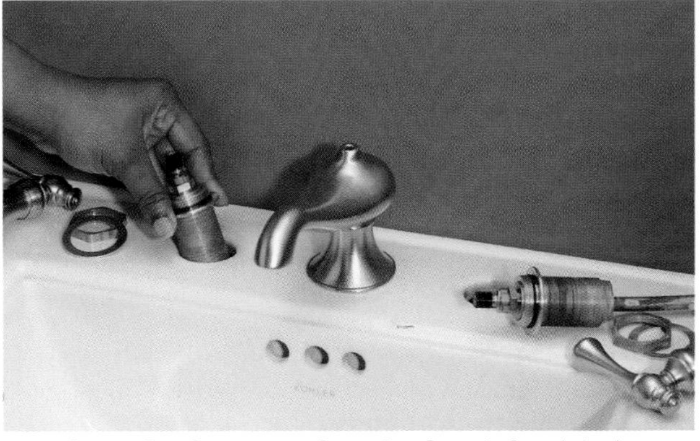

5 Place the faucet valves in the sink. Slide the washers over the threads from beneath the sink. Tighten the valve nuts until snug.

6 Connect the faucet valve lines to the faucet valves. Apply Teflon paste or Teflon tape to the threads of the valve lines, connect to the faucet valves, and hand-tighten. Apply pipe compound or Teflon tape to the other end of the valve lines and hand-tighten onto the spout tee.

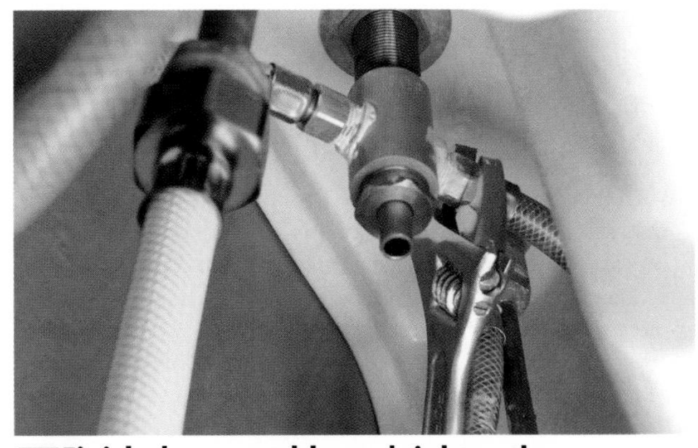

7 Finish the assembly and tighten the connections. Apply Teflon paste or tape to the threads of the water supply tailpieces and connect the hot and cold water supplies to the hot and cold supply valves.Tighten the connections with an adjustable wrench and connect the faucet handles to the valves. Turn on the water and test for leaks.

Installing a center-set faucet

Skill level:	Time to complete:	Materials:	Tools:
★★★☆☆	Experienced 40 min. Handy 1 hr. Novice 2 hrs.	Center-set faucet, gaskets, plumber's putty or silicone caulk	Putty knife, adjustable wrenches, basin wrench

1 Set the faucet. The tailpieces should fit into the hole spacing in the sink. Apply a bead of silicone caulk (or plumber's putty if the sink isn't cultured marble) around the faucet openings.

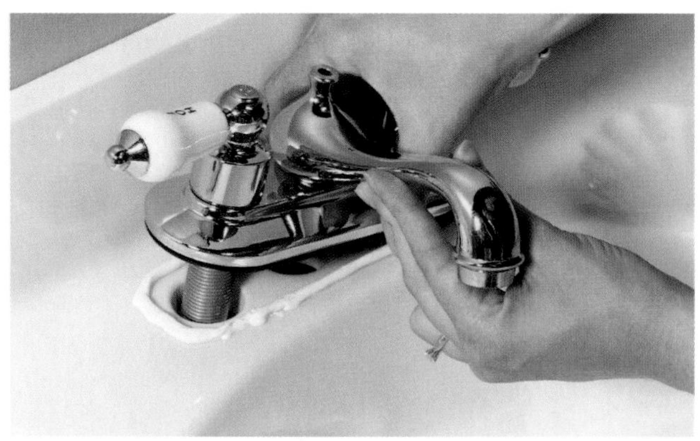

2 Place the faucet gasket. The gasket will set over the faucet tailpieces. Set the faucet in the holes.

3 Center the faucet body. Measure or visually center the faucet body on the lavatory.

4 Hand-tighten the basin nuts until they're snug. Install the pop-up drain. (See "Installing a Pop-Up Drain," opposite.) Connect the water supply lines, turn on the water, and test for leaks.

WORK SMART

CULTURE IS IMPORTANT

Use silicone caulk instead of plumber's putty on cultured marble or other composite sinks. Putty will discolor the sink.

Out with the old is the hardest part

As opposed to other home improvement jobs, such as installing cabinets or hanging doors, the hardest part of almost any plumbing job is usually removing the old stuff. Corrosion and inaccessibility can make taking out an old faucet a real pain in the neck. Give yourself extra time to remove old fixtures—it will save you from frustration and bruised knuckles.

WORK SMART

AVOIDING CLOGGED FAUCETS

Working on old pipes can dislodge grime or rust. If this gets in the lines, it can plug the faucet and actually stop water from flowing. To prevent this, unscrew the aerator at the tip of the faucet. Turn on the water and let it run for a minute or so to remove any dirt. Once you turn off the water and replace the aerator, the faucet should work well without clogging.

Installing a pop-up drain

Skill level:	Time to complete:	Materials:	Tools:
★★★☆☆	Experienced 20 min. Handy 40 min. Novice 45 min.	Pop-up drain kit, plumber's putty, Teflon tape, silicone caulk, 2×4 support	Water-pump pliers, plastic putty knife, rag

A pop-up drain requires a special faucet fixture. If your current faucet doesn't accept a pop-up, you'll have to replace it with one that does. Installing a pop-up is a little like solving a jigsaw puzzle—a lot of little parts have to come together in the right order for it to work. Use plumber's putty with cast-iron sinks, or silicone caulk on composites or cultured marble, to hold the flange in place. Before you begin carefully read the installation instructions for your particular pop-up.

As with any plumbing job, visualize the steps from start to finish and anticipate the parts of the installation that may cause problems. Clear out a work space in the bathroom and lay out all the tools and materials you'll need for the job before you begin. Heading for your home center late on a Friday night because you forgot something important isn't the best way to start the weekend.

1 Apply plumber's putty. (Use a 2×4 to support a wall-hung sink while you're working.) Cover the bottom of the flange with a rope of putty.

2 Thread the locknut onto the drain body. Then add the friction washer and beveled gasket.

3 Install the drain body. Push the drain body up through the lavatory hole from underneath.

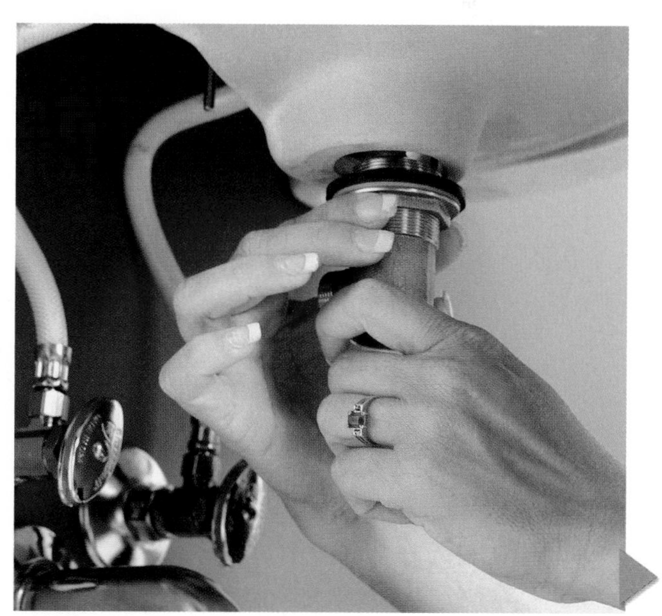

4 Hand-tighten the drain body to the flange. Turn the drain body and the flange to tighten the connection and line up with the linkage.

Installing a pop-up drain (continued)

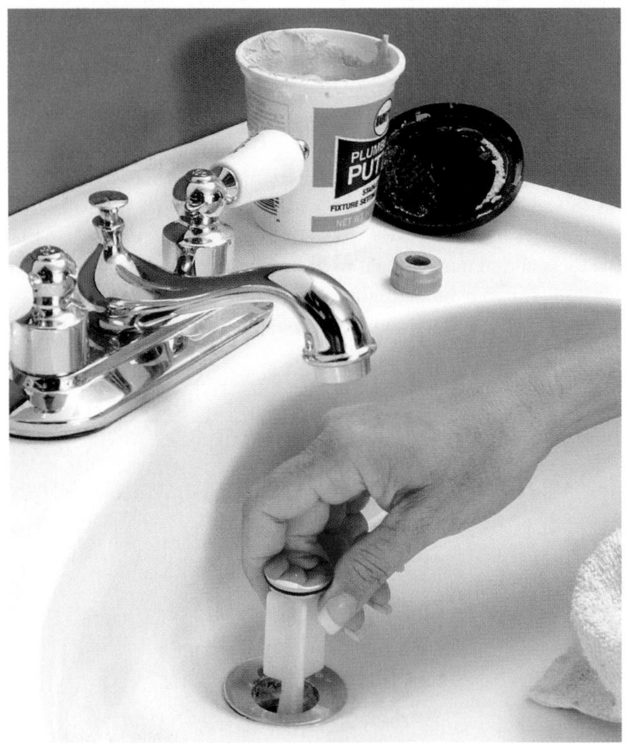

5 Install the drain plunger. Slide the plunger into the drain opening.

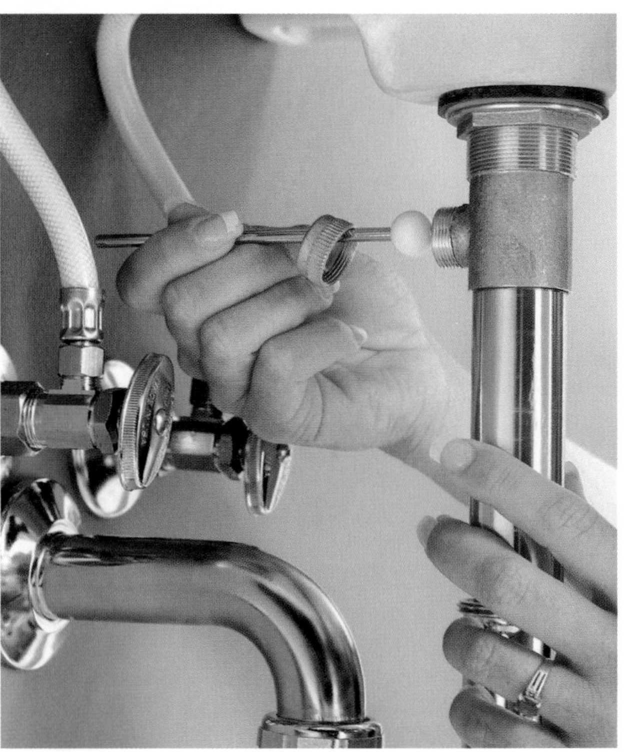

6 Under the counter insert the ball into the opening. The ball should fit snugly into the opening in the drain tailpiece.

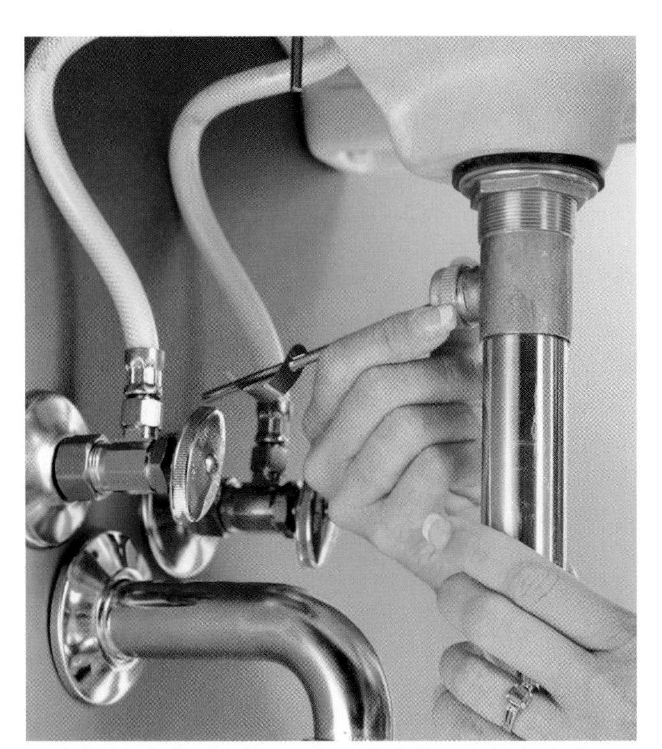

7 Thread the ball nut hand-tight. Slide the ball nut over the arm and screw it onto the threads of the drain tailpiece. Set the pop-up arm. Slide the arm through the nearest hole in the lever strap and fasten it with a clip. Connect the P-trap and adjust the arm if necessary.

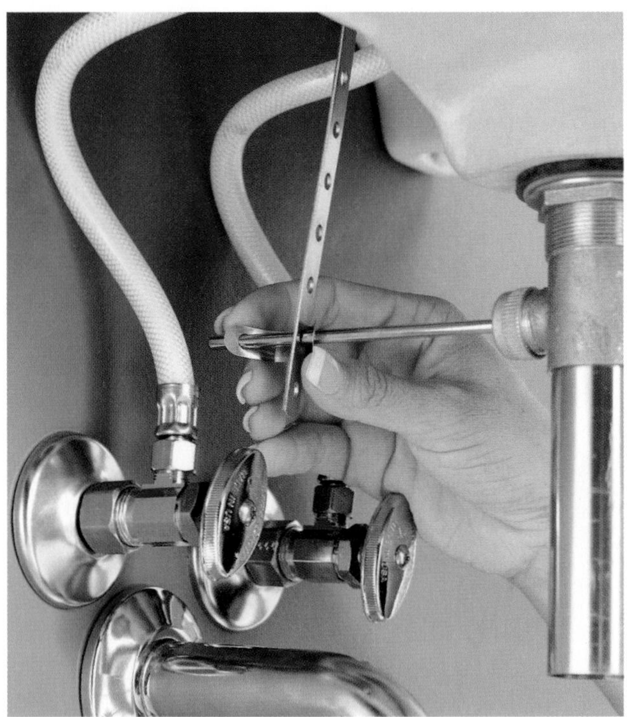

8 Set the pop-up arm. Slide the arm through the nearest hole in the lever strap and fasten it with a clip. Connect the P-trap and adjust the arm if necessary.

Removing an old tub

Skill level:	Time to complete:	Materials:	Tools:
★★★☆☆	Experienced 1 hr. Handy 1.5 hrs. Novice 2 hrs.	1×4 boards	Safety glasses, leather gloves, hammer, tarp, sledgehammer, reciprocating saw, pry bar

Make sure you have plenty of room to work before you tackle tub removal. You'll need a clear space at least 3 feet deep when pulling the tub straight out from the wall. You need to be able to work around the tub when it's away from the wall. It's a good idea to remove other fixtures such as the sink or vanity and toilet.

Map your route. Measure the width of all door openings and the hallway along the path for removing the tub. This is important for removing the old tub and is essential for bringing in the new one. Tearing up your bathroom to remove the old tub then discovering that the new one won't fit through the halls or doorway is not a pleasant way to spend the weekend.

The order of battle:

- **Turn off the water at the main shutoff.** Drain the water supply lines by opening a faucet below the tub level.
- **Remove the faucet handles, spout, and drain.**
- **Cut away at least 6 inches of drywall above the tub on all sides.** Remove the screws or nails holding the tub flange to the studs. If you find a galvanized strip along the tub flange, use a flat bar or pry bar to remove it.
- **Lift up on the front edge of the tub** with a pry bar and slide a pair of 1×4s beneath it.
- **Pull the tub away from the wall using the 1×4s as a skid.** You'll need help carrying the tub, especially if it's cast iron. If you're not saving or reusing a cast-iron tub, cover it with a tarp and break it into pieces with a sledgehammer. Wear safety glasses when hammering, and put on gloves when you're picking up pieces of the tub: they're sharp—very sharp. Cut fiberglass and polymer tubs into pieces with a reciprocating saw.

Give yourself plenty of room to work when you're removing a tub. Cut away at least 6 inches of drywall above the tub.

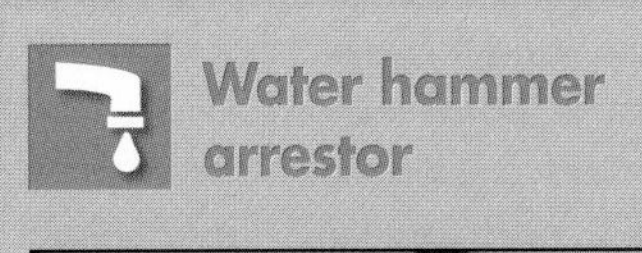

Water hammer arrestor

Though not generally required by code, it's a good idea to install a water hammer arrester when plumbing a bath. Pipes often make a loud bang, called water hammer, when you turn off a faucet. Water hammer arresters absorb the increase in pressure caused by turning off the water, keeping everything quiet in the walls.

Installing a bathtub in an alcove

Skill level: ★★★☆☆

Time to complete:
Experienced 3 hrs.
Handy 4 hrs.
Novice 8 hrs.

Materials: Copper supply pipe, copper fittings, integral stops, copper tube straps, faucet assembly, shower tee, solder, flux, soldering kit, PVC drainpipe, PVC fittings, PVC P-trap, tub overflow and drain assembly, PVC primer and adhesive, bathtub, galvanized nails, 2×4 blocking, 1×3 ledger strips, silicone caulk

Tools: Propane torch and striker, tubing cutter, fiberglass flame barrier, hammer, electric drill, spade bits, screwdriver, saber saw, PVC cutter, tape measure, carpenter's level, pencil, work gloves, safety glasses

Installing a tub isn't rocket science, but it does require solid plumbing, carpentry, and sometimes, tiling skills. Before installing a tub, review everything that affects the project. Bathtubs are heavy. Have someone help with the installation. Make sure you've qualified yourself for the job and are comfortable attempting it. Measure the width of doors, passages, and corners you must turn. Make sure you can get the old tub out and that the new one fits into the bathroom. Rather than having a halfway-completed project for which you must hire a contractor, it's better to consider hiring one before you begin.

Install an access panel behind the faucets and supply pipes so you won't have to remove the wall to work on them. Include shutoff valves or integral stops on the supply plumbing run. They isolate the plumbing from the rest of the house. Check whether local codes require installation of scald guards. These prevent someone from being scalded in the shower when cold water pressure changes, such as when a toilet is flushed.

1 Frame the walls and run the supply control riser. Frame the walls so that the alcove opening is just large enough to slide the tub into place. Leave a gap of ⅛ inch or less at the head and foot of the tub. Install plumbing for the risers, faucet, and showerhead (see page 299). Place 2x4 blocking as needed to secure the faucets, spout, and showerhead.

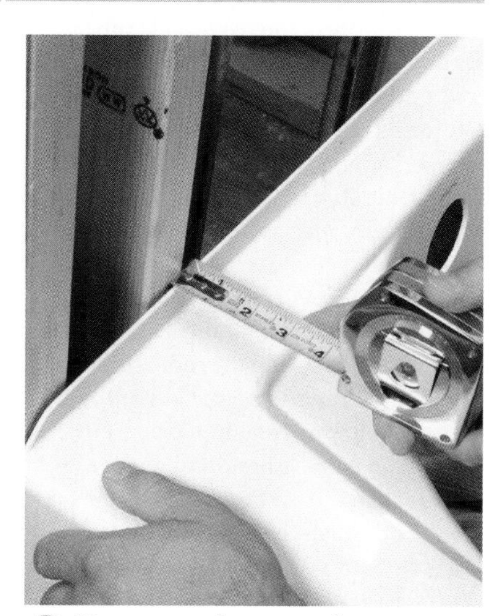

2 Measure the opening. Before you buy a tub, measure the alcove's width and length, and buy a tub to fit. Once you've run the supply lines and cut the access hole, slide the tub into the alcove for a test fit. (See "Work Smart," below.)

SAFETY ALERT

MAKE SURE YOUR HOUSEHOLD WON'T BE IN HOT WATER

In many homes, the thermostat on the water heater is set needlessly and dangerously high. It should be no higher than 120°F, a maximum that's legally mandated in some areas. Temperature settings above that level are potentially unsafe. They also increase mineral buildup in the heater and plumbing, and for every 10 degrees you lower the temperature you'll cut your water heating expenses by 3 to 5 percent. Follow the manufacturer's directions on adjusting the temperature. Because the heater's thermostat may be inaccurate, use a thermometer to check the temperature at hot water faucets after letting the water run at least two minutes, and make a further adjustment if necessary.

WORK SMART

MAKE A BED FOR MODERN TUBS

A cast-iron tub is plenty strong on its own, but tubs made of enameled steel, acrylics, fiberglass, and similar materials flex when you fill them with water. Give them some extra support with a bed of sand mix. (Check the warranty to make sure the mix and the tub are compatible.) Sand mix is similar to concrete mix without the stones. Mix according to directions, and pour on the floor directly beneath the tub before you position it. Cover the wet mix with 6 mil. plastic sheeting to prevent any possible reaction with the tub.

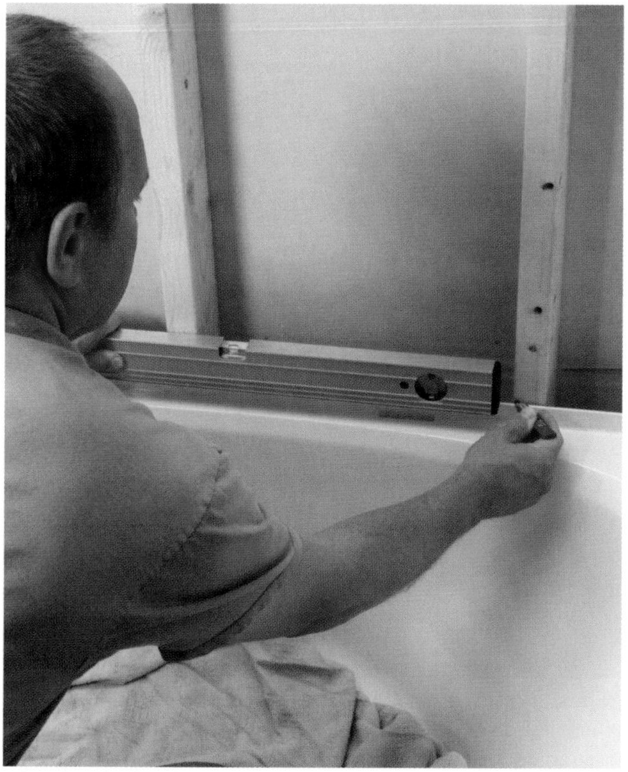

3 Check for level. Lay a carpenter's level on the tub to check for level. If you are not setting the tub in a sand bed (see "Work Smart," opposite), you will need to shim the tub to level it. Because wood shims will rot when exposed to moisture, use flattened copper tubing or plastic shims. Once level, mark the top of the nailing flange at each stud.

4 Determine the ledger board mounting height. Ledger boards are required for fiberglass and polymer/acrylic tubs. Measure the distance from the top of the nailing flange to the underside of the tub rim inset. Subtract that figure—about 1 inch—from the marks on the wall studs and mark the ledger board mounting height.

Installing a freestanding tub

The traditional claw-foot tub is making a comeback, both for its vintage look and because it offers a good, deep soak. Because it is freestanding and doesn't tie into the surrounding walls, a claw-foot tub installation doesn't involve dealing with tiled walls. But getting water into and out of the tub can be a challenge, because the tub likely will be some distance from existing plumbing lines in the walls. These tubs typically are installed with decorative floor-mounted drains and supply tubes, and you have to make sure there is room in the floor to accommodate the pitch required for the drain line. If you want to be able to shower in the tub, that means suspending a curtain rod around its perimeter and adding a shower riser pipe. Another consideration is weight. Make sure that the floor can safely support the load of both bather and brim-full tub.

5 Connect the P-trap. Install the drainpipe and P-trap if they have not already been roughed in (see pages 305–306). Cut an access hole into the subfloor. Make it 4 to 9 inches wide and extending 12 inches from the center of the end wall. Connect the 1½-inch P-trap below the floor level so that the slip-nut fitting is centered directly under the overflow and drainpipe on the tub.

Installing a bathtub in an alcove (continued)

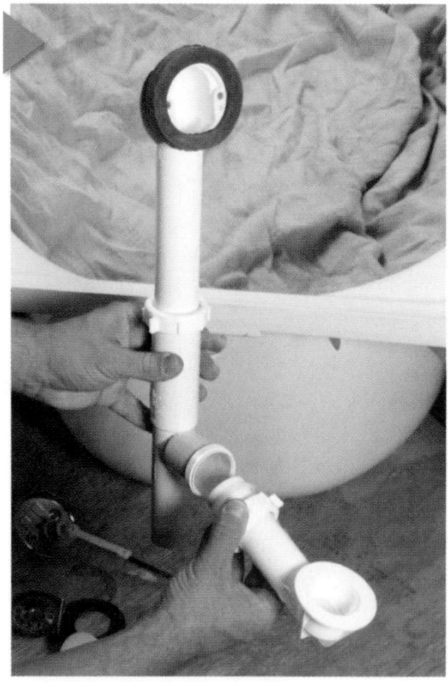

6 Dry-fit the tub drain and overflow. Following the manufacturer's instructions, assemble the drain system so that you can measure and trim the drain tailpiece to connect with the P-trap. (See "Tub Drain Assembly," below.)

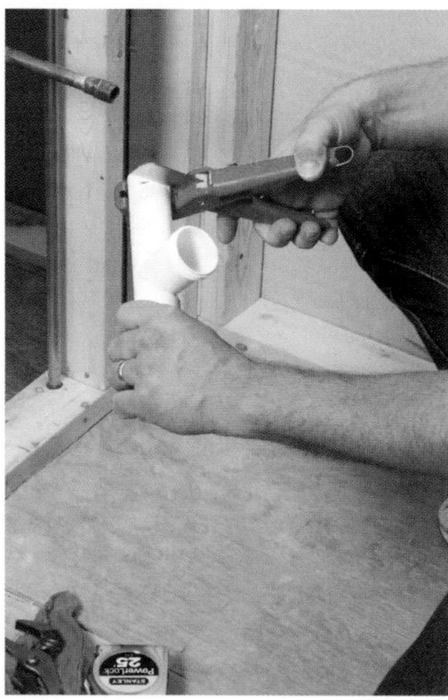

7 Trim the drainpipe. The tub drainpipe will slide into the pressure fitting on the P-trap. It may be necessary to trim the pipe to fit smoothly. Check the manufacturer's instructions for installation.

8 Connect the overflow and drain to the tub and set the tub in place.

Tub drain assembly

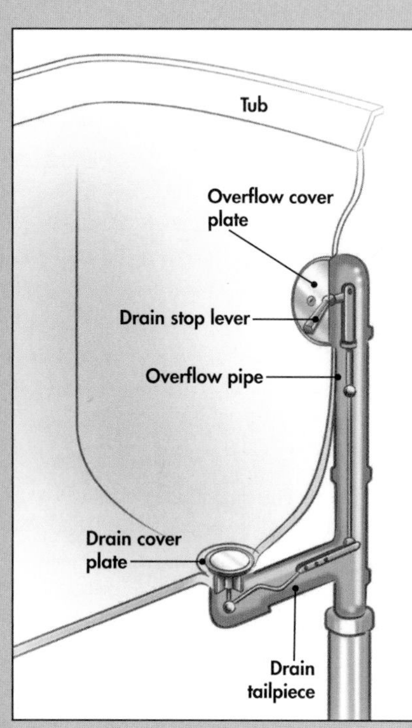

Spa tubs

The square footage of new homes is on the increase, and accommodating amenities like a spa tub is part of the reason. If you're planning on adding one, begin by making sure that the tub will fit through stairways and halls on its way to the bathroom, and that the framing can handle the load. In an older home, you may have to reinforce the joists in the floor below. Installation isn't much different than for a standard tub, but you have to add a dedicated ground fault circuit interrupter (GFCI) line (see right) to operate the whirlpool pump. Decide on whether to go with the existing wall-mounted faucet set or to order a tub with the faucet on its deck. Another consideration is whether to rest the tub on a mortar bed. This is a good idea for thin plastic tubs, which may flex and feel unsound without support, and some manufacturers require a mortar footing. You also have the choice

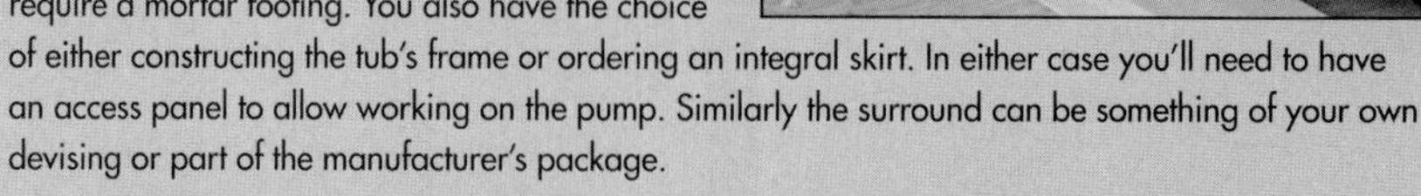

of either constructing the tub's frame or ordering an integral skirt. In either case you'll need to have an access panel to allow working on the pump. Similarly the surround can be something of your own devising or part of the manufacturer's package.

9 Install ledger boards. Cut the ledger boards to fit the alcove. Then use wood screws or galvanized nails to attach them to the studs following the marks you made in Step 4 (page 339). Install the boards in sections if necessary to make room for any structural braces at the ends of the tub. Double-check for level.

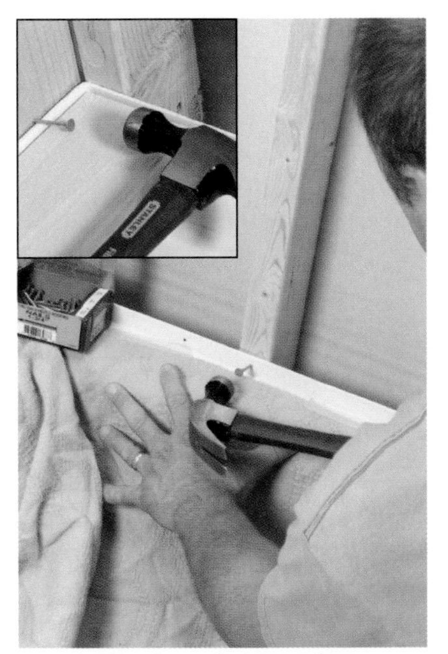

10 Set the tub into place. Seat the tub on the ledgers. The tub must sit firmly on the ledger strips and the drain must fit smoothly into the P-trap. Nail through the predrilled holes using galvanized nails. (If there are no holes, drive the nails so that the nailhead anchors the tub to the studs; see above inset.) To avoid scratches from the hammer, protect the tub with cardboard placed underneath a towel or rag.

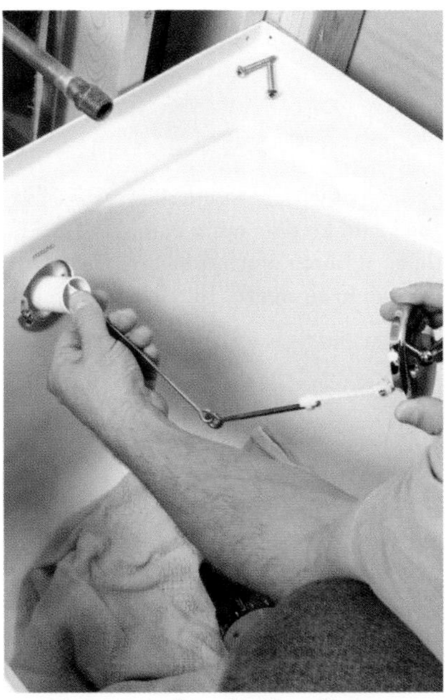

11 Insert the drain plug linkage. Install the drain linkage through the overflow opening. Attach the overflow cover plate to the mounting flange with screws. Test the system for leaks and schedule a city inspection, if necessary, before you finish the walls and tile.

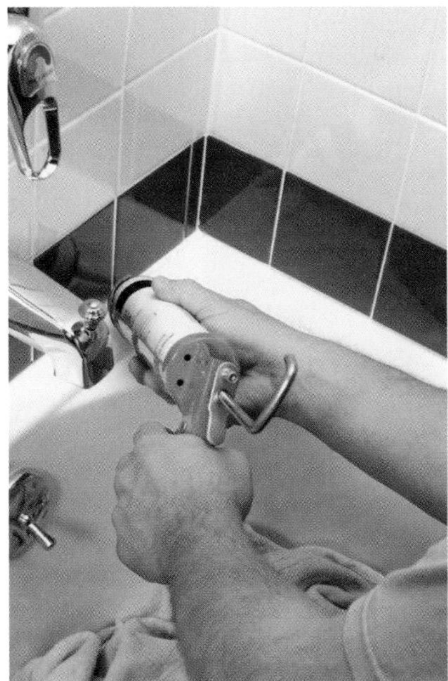

12 Connect the faucet handles and tub spout. Use tub-and-tile caulk to seal around the faucet handles and tub spout. Apply a bead of caulk around the edge of the tub. Turn the water on and check for leaks.

BUYER'S GUIDE

$ TILING THE WALLS

Planning to tile the walls? Tiles need a solid surface that can support their weight. Also, moisture may get behind the tiles, so the surface needs to withstand moisture damage. Use cement backerboard for the substrate; it's typically required by code.

Supplemental water heater

A whirlpool bath ceases to be an indulgent pleasure if the water becomes chilly. Your household heater may not be up to the task of filling the tub with warm water and then keeping the temperature in the comfort zone for a long soak. Consider upgrading to a larger heater if your existing one soon may be due for replacement. Or add an in-line heater just for the whirlpool, which will require running a second GFCI line.

BUYER'S GUIDE

$ ANTI-SCALD SHOWER FAUCETS

There's nothing more relaxing than soaking in the tub or taking a steamy shower. But hot water can be scaldingly hot, and children and the elderly are especially vulnerable to life-threatening burns. After setting the thermostat on your water heater to a safe level, install anti-scald faucets for showers and tubs. There are two basic types. The simplest and least expensive is pressure sensitive. When the cold-water pressure suddenly drops (as when someone flushes a toilet), a valve compensates by lowering the hot water pressure. The more sophisticated faucets monitor both pressure and temperature and are considered to be safer. Check your plumbing code for requirements concerning anti-scald faucets.

Installing a sliding glass door for a tub

Skill level:	Time to complete:	Materials:	Tools:
★★☆☆☆	Experienced 2 hrs. Handy 3 hrs. Novice 4 hrs.	Sliding door kit, masking tape, silicone caulk	Level, tape measure, hacksaw, miter box, hammer, electric drill, caulking gun, screwdriver

Tired of wrestling with shower curtains? They don't do a great job of keeping water in the tub, and mildew loves to grow on them. Without much trouble, you can add sliding shower doors to a tub in an alcove. They'll keep the floor drier and give you a bit of added support if you happen to slip while in the tub. And you can find models with ribbed or frosted glass that look as though they were built in from the start rather than added.

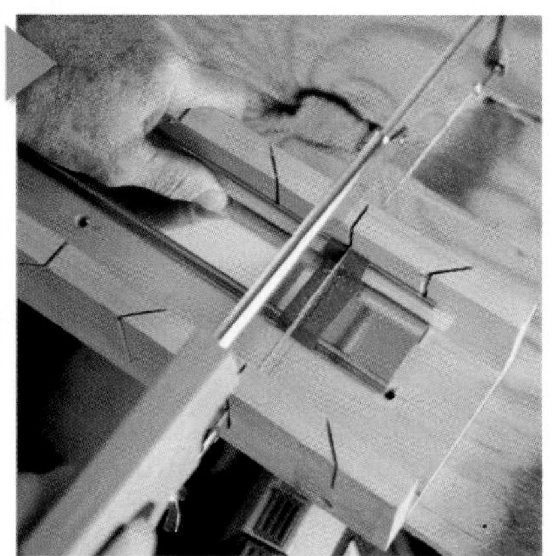

1 Cut the tub track to length. Carefully measure from wall to wall just above the tub rim. As specified by the manufacturer, subtract enough from this distance to allow for the vertical frame members, or jambs. Support the track in a miter box and cut it to length with a hacksaw. Temporarily place the track on the tub rim, keeping it there with a few pieces of masking tape. Mark its location on the rim.

2 Position the jambs. Hold each jamb in place in turn, fitting the lower end into the tub track and using a carpenter's level to plumb it. Mark the wall at the installation holes in the jamb with a pencil or by tapping lightly with a nail set for a tiled wall.

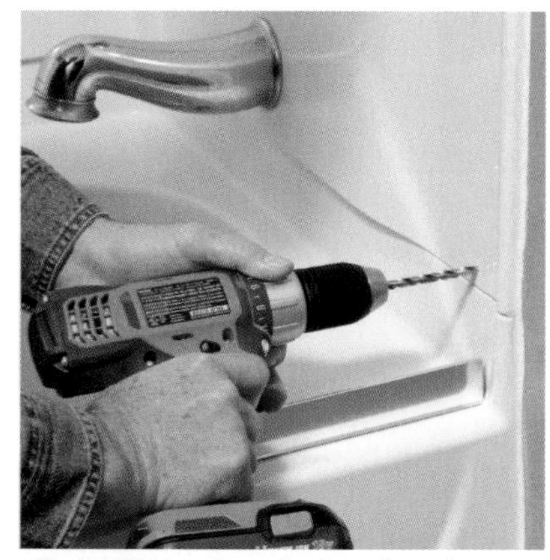

3 Drill anchor holes for the jambs. Drill holes at each mark, being sure to hold the drill level. Use a standard bit, or a masonry bit if the wall is tiled, choosing a diameter appropriate for the plastic anchors provided with the door kit. Clean out the holes and insert the plastic anchors, tapping as necessary to drive them in fully.

4 Install the tub track and jambs. Remove the track from the tub rim, turn it upside down, and run one or two beads of silicone caulk along its underside as described in the manufacturer's directions. Place the track on the rim, guided by the marks you've made, and press down to set it. Holding the jambs in place, drive screws into the anchors. Also consider installing bumpers along the jambs to cushion the closing doors.

5 Install the top track. Measure for the length of the top track as you did for the tub track, and cut it to size. Following the manufacturer's directions, place it atop the jambs and attach it.

6 Hang the doors. Install rollers on the top of the doors as directed. Lift the doors in place, suspending them by the rollers, and lower them into the tub track. You may need to adjust the rollers so that the door at the shower end of the tub meets the wall without a gap. Run a bead of caulk along the inside of the tub track and jambs.

Installing a shower surround

Skill level:	Time to complete:	Materials:	Tools:
★★★☆☆	Experienced 3 hrs. Handy 5 hrs. Novice 8 hrs.	Tub enclosure, detergent, cardboard for template, double-stick tape, tub surround adhesive, silicone caulk, expanding foam	Tape measure, pipe wrench, screwdriver or hex wrench set, bucket, sponge, hole saw, utility knife, carpenter's pencil, caulking gun, rags

Shower surrounds are relatively easy to install and have built-in soap and shampoo caddies. Surrounds can be installed directly over securely fastened ceramic tile. Loose ceramic tiles—and any plastic tiles—must be removed and the walls sanded smooth before installation. In new installations the enclosure should be applied over waterproof backerboard.

BUYER'S GUIDE

PROVIDING VENTILATIOIN

Bathrooms are the wettest places in the house and, therefore, need adequate ventilation to keep the buildup of moisture at a level that won't make the paint peel and the floor warp. A new shower surround will often cover a window that is the primary source of ventilation for the bathroom. If that's the case, you'll need to install a vent fan or make a cutout in the surround to allow access to the window.

Kits contain all the materials you'll need to do the framing job, or you can trim the surround with a primed, painted, and sealed wooden frame.

A neo-angle shower for tight corners

By sticking a shower in a corner, you can get away with not having to construct support walls. Trouble is, a conventional enclosure with a square footprint will jut out into the room, which can be an inconvenience if space is tight. Instead consider a neo-angle model, with its door mounted between two glass side panels.

1 Prepare the enclosure. Shut off the main water supply. Remove all fittings. Clean film and dirt from the wall surface and dry thoroughly. Prep cement backerboard with a stain-blocking primer to create good bonding. Allow the surface to dry completely before installing the surround.

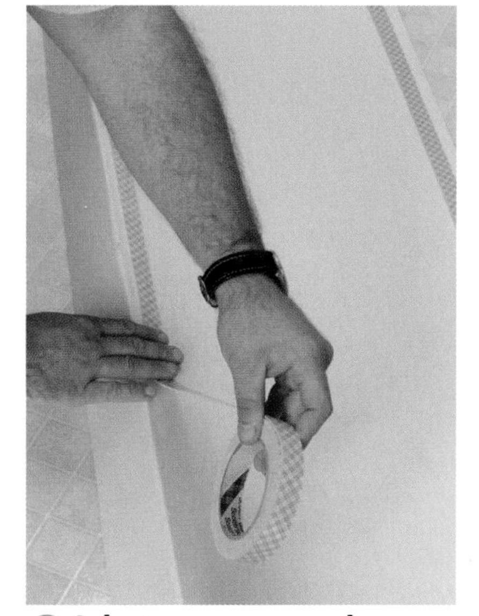

2 Select a corner panel. It doesn't matter which corner you start in. Select a corner panel and test-fit it. Remove the panel and lay it on the floor with the surface that goes next to the wall facing up. Apply a pressure-sensitive, double-sided, 1-inch tape along the vertical edges of the panel.

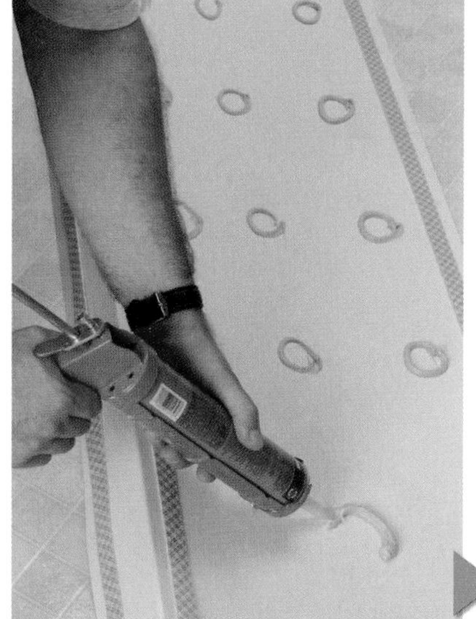

3 Apply adhesive to the panel using a caulking gun. Apply circles of the adhesive at intervals of no more than 12 inches along the vertical length of the panel. Rows of adhesive tape along edges should be set back from the adhesive by 3 inches.

Installing a shower surround (continued)

4 Install the first corner panel. Position the panel. Press it firmly onto the wall, then pull it back about 6 inches for a few minutes (or per the manufacturer's instructions) to let the adhesive set up. Push the panel back in place. Firmly apply pressure, up and down and side to side, making firm contact with the wall. Repeat in the opposite corner.

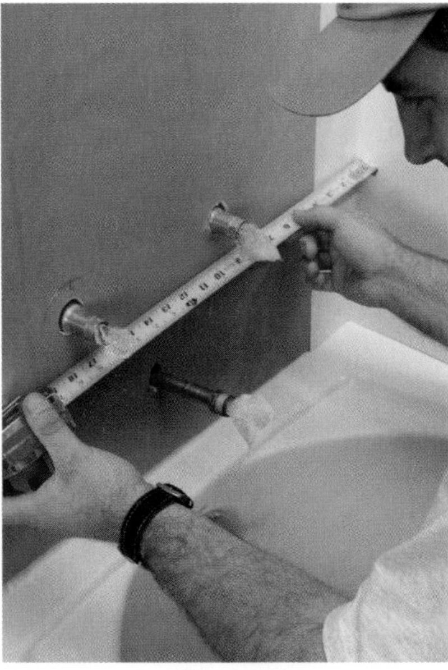

5 Measure the outlets. Create a cardboard template for the openings into one end panel for the faucet and spout piping. Determine the height from the bottom of the panel and the distance of each fitting from the inside edge of the panel.

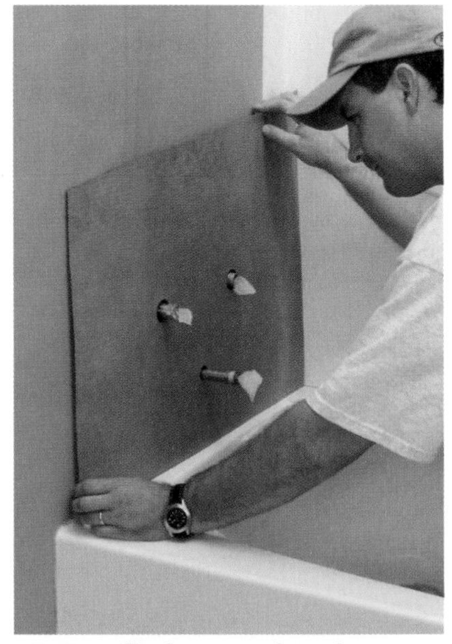

6 Test-fit the template by laying it against the wall, making sure the template openings line up with the pipe outlets. If they don't, remeasure them and make a new template.

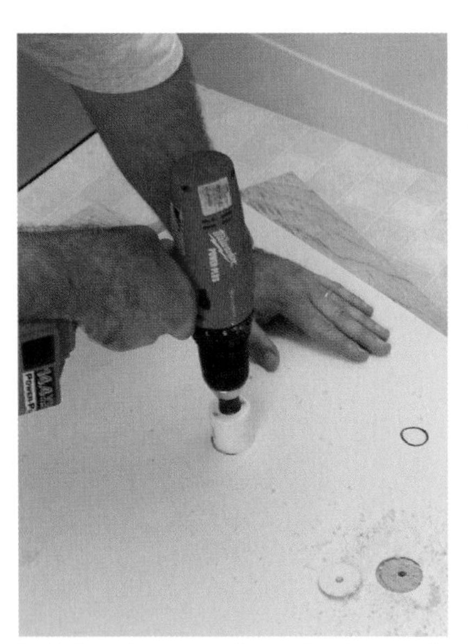

7 Cut the openings in the end panel. Mark the positions of the openings on the back (wall side) of the panel with the template—drilling from the back will minimize chipping. Placing a piece of scrap wood beneath the panel will produce a cleaner cut. Test-fit a final time and use a hole saw to cut the openings.

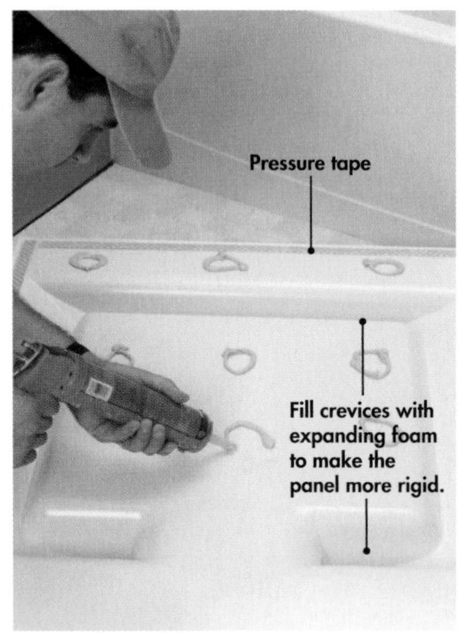

8 Apply pressure tape and adhesive. You can fill the crevices in the panel with expanding foam to make them more rigid. Apply carefully; too much foam can expand and crack the panel. Position the panel onto the wall. Apply pressure by hand—side to side—to mount. Install the remaining panels.

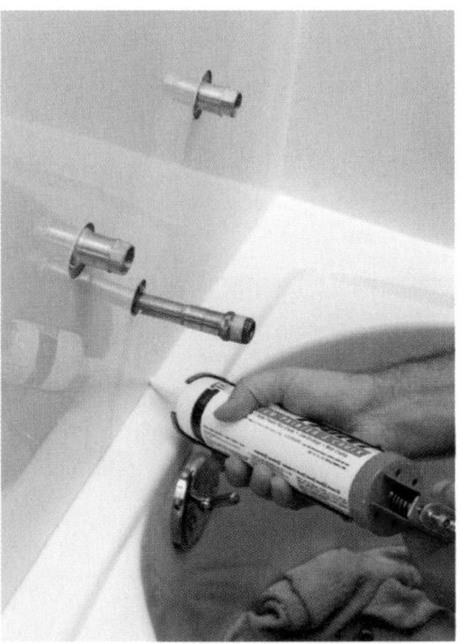

9 Seal with a bead of caulk. Use a caulking gun to apply a quality tub-and-tile sealant. Seal along the outside edges of the panel and around the fixtures. To get a "perfect bead," use a small spoon dipped in soapy water to smooth the caulk line. Avoid using the shower for at least 24 hours, or follow the manufacturer's instructions.

Removing an old toilet

The biggest challenges in removing a toilet are getting the job done without creating a watery mess and without filling the house with sewer gases.

1 **Turn off the water supply at the shutoff valve.** Flush the toilet until the tank is empty. Wipe up excess water with rags and a sponge. Disconnect the supply tube.

2 **Remove the tank bolts** with a ratcheting socket wrench.

3 **Lift the tank off the bowl.** Be careful—most toilets are made of porcelain, which is heavy and easily damaged.

4 **Remove the toilet base.** Remove the floor bolt caps and then the nuts from the floor bolts. Rock the toilet from side to side to break the wax seal; lift it off the bolts and set it on an old towel. Plug the drain opening with a rag to keep sewer gases in the pipes.

5 **Scrape the old wax from the toilet flange** with a putty knife as shown at left.

WORK SMART

CONNECTING OLD DRAINS TO NEW TOILETS

Before buying a new toilet, make sure it matches the location of the drain ("rough-in") on the bathroom floor. Measure from the wall to the toilet floor bolts, which are centered on the floor drain. In newer bathrooms, the distance is 12 inches from the wall. Most new toilets are designed to fit these specifications. If you live in a house built before the mid-1940s, however, the outlet may be 10 or 14 inches from the wall. You can get some toilets with a 10- or 14-inch rough-in, but not in all models, styles, and colors.

If you have your heart set on a toilet with a 12-inch rough-in, but your rough-in is 10 or 14 inches, it can be fixed. It's a big job, but you can install what's called an offset flange (shown here), then connect the drain for the new toilet to the floor outlet.

SAFETY ALERT

POTENTIAL BIOHAZARD!

The water in the toilet bowl contains harmful bacteria. Wear rubber gloves when cleaning or removing the bowl. Avoid splashes. Wash your hands thoroughly with an antibacterial soap afterward.

CLOSER LOOK

GOT SOME TOUGH NUTS TO CRACK?

Nuts and bolts on toilet bowls can become so corroded that an adjustable wrench won't budge them, or the wrench will round the corners of the nut, making removal next to impossible. You may expand your vocabulary, but you won't budge the nut without applying some special techniques.

- Before you attack the nut in the first place, assume it may be seized; squirt on some penetrating oil. Let the oil soak in thoroughly before you try removing the nut.
- Try a minihacksaw. Protect the toilet base with masking tape and cut the nut at a slight angle (about 30 degrees) until you have a deep groove. Insert a screwdriver into the groove and twist to break the nut.
- As a last resort (or first resort if you have one in your toolbox), you can use a nut splitter, which is a tool often found in the automotive section of your hardware store. The splitter fits over the nut. Hold it in position with an adjustable wrench and tighten it with a socket wrench. This closes the jaws of the nut splitter against the nut and cuts it in half.

Installing a new toilet

Skill level: ★★★☆☆	Time to complete: Experienced 45 min. Handy 1 hr. Novice 1.5 hrs.	Materials: Toilet, toilet seat, "no-seep" wax ring, plastic toilet shims, plumber's putty, felt marker, pipe compound, 3½-inch closet bolts or concrete screws	Tools: Two adjustable wrenches, ratchet wrench and sockets, screwdriver, hacksaw, tubing cutter

PLUMBING

If you're installing a new toilet in a new location, you'll need to run (or have someone run) a water supply line and a drainpipe, which must be connected to the drain/vent system in compliance with building code. If the toilet is in the basement, you'll need an upflush toilet (see page 348). Talk with your plumbing supplier to see what's involved.

Some parts are extra

Most of the parts you need to install the new toilet will come with it—except the toilet seat, which is a separate item on almost every model. The wax ring—which comes in several sizes—is a separate purchase too. The manual that comes with the new toilet will tell you the correct size of wax ring to buy.

1 Set the mounting bolts. If you're reusing the old flange, replace the 3½-inch flange bolts. Purchase two 3½-inch-long closet bolts at your local home center. If you're replacing the flange, it must be screwed into a wooden floor. Use self-tapping concrete screws for concrete. Closet bolts often tip over when you're trying to place the toilet. Put an extra nut on each bolt, and tighten it against the flange to hold the bolts in place.

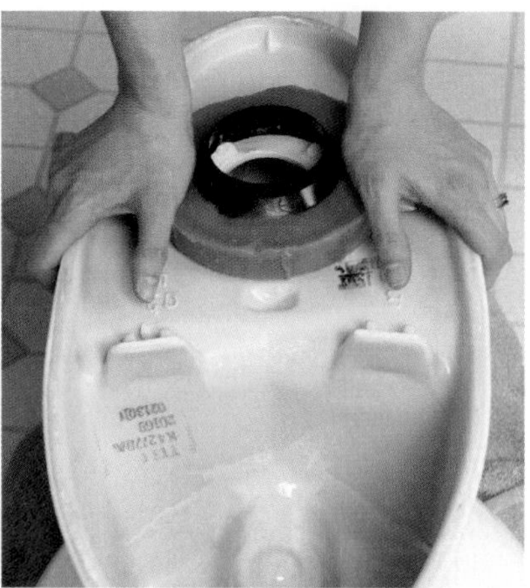

2 Place the wax ring on the toilet. The "no-seep" wax ring size will vary with the size of the flange. Be sure to purchase the proper size. A 3-inch neck will fit a 3-inch closet elbow, and a 4-inch neck will fit a 4-inch closet elbow. If the closet elbow is 4 inches and the neck is 3 inches in diameter, purchase a 4×3 reducer. If the flange is positioned below floor level, buy a double-thick ring.

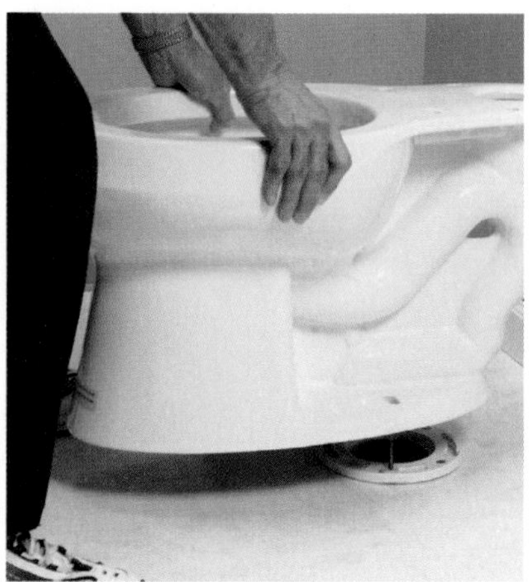

3 Set the toilet bowl. Straddle the toilet bowl and lift using your legs—not your back. Toilets are heavy, so get some help. Set the toilet over the anchor bolts and sit on the toilet, rocking it back and forth to seat the wax ring. Slip a washer over the closet bolt.

Get the right size toilet

Years ago I was browsing the plumbing aisle and saw the toilet of my dreams on clearance.
Well, just because something's on sale doesn't mean it'll work. After I lugged it home I discovered the toilet didn't fit over the closet flange. Back then I didn't know that the distance of the drain from the wall will determine the size of your toilet. Ninety percent of toilets are made for a drain opening 11 to 12 inches from the wall. The rest are either 9 to 10 or 13 to 14 inches away. On the plus side, I was lucky to pick a store that takes returns, and I took home a valuable lesson about being an informed shopper.

BUYER'S GUIDE

FIX THAT FLANGE

Closet flanges take a lot of abuse and can crack or break. If you don't want to pull out the old closet flange and connect a new one, use an adapter sometimes called a super flange that fits over the old model and makes a secure connection for the toilet. Other adapters are available as well. Check them out at your local home center.

WORK SMART

TOILET FACELIFT

You'll get a cleaner, neater flooring installation in your bathroom if you remove the toilet so you can avoid trimming around it. But the new floor will lift the toilet by its finished thickness, and you may need an extension flange (available at home centers) to reconnect the toilet to the soil pipe.

4 Tighten the nuts against the washer by hand. With a wrench, tighten each nut a half-turn. Alternate tightening each side a half-turn until the toilet fits snugly. Tightening either side too much will cause the toilet to crack. If the toilet rocks or isn't level, shim it with plastic toilet shims and cut the ends off so they won't be seen.

5 Cut the flange bolt to size. Use a minihacksaw to cut the flange bolt so only ¼ to ½ inch extends above the bolt. This will allow the cap to fit snugly. Most bolts have snap-offs every ½ inch or so, but you should still cut through so you don't bend the bolt.

6 Install the bolt cap. Some types of caps will snap over the bolt. Others have to be filled with plumber's putty and seated over the anchor bolt.

PLUMBING

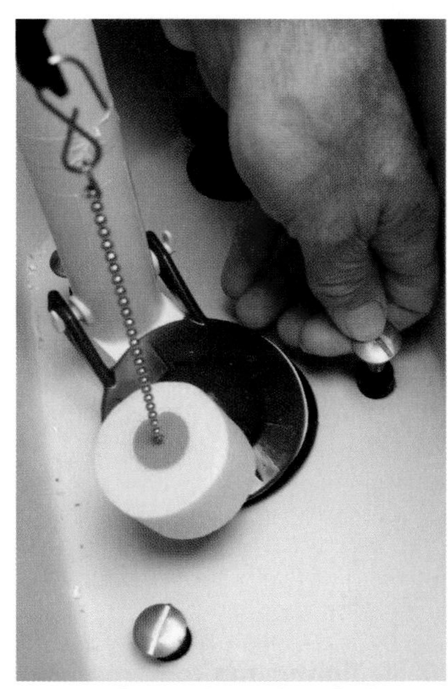

7 Set the tank anchor bolts. Place the tank anchor bolts in the holes of the tank to help guide the tank onto the bowl.

8 Place the tank on the bowl. Lift the tank and place it over the bowl. You may need some help with this. Guide the tank bolts into the corresponding holes on the toilet bowl.

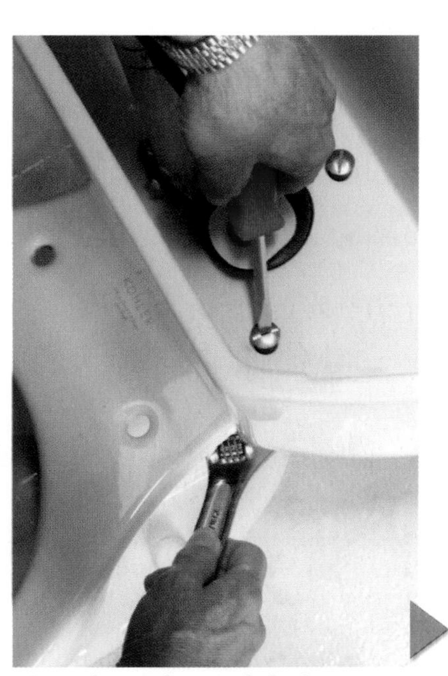

9 Tighten the tank bolts. Hold an adjustable wrench over the tank bolt nut while you tighten the bolt with a screwdriver. Don't overtighten; you can crack the tank or the bowl.

Installing a new toilet (continued)

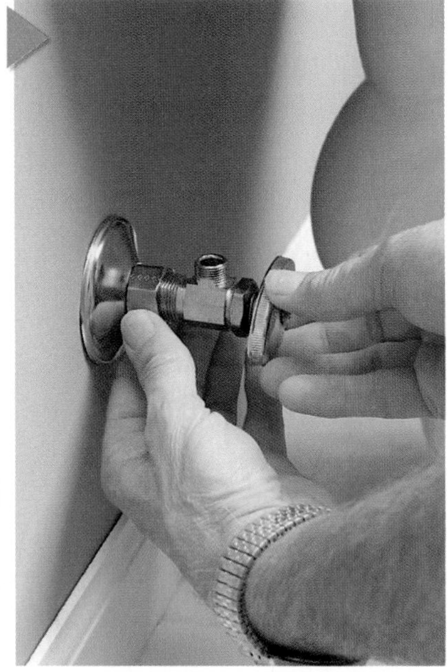

10 Install the shutoff valve. Set the valve over the compression ring and draw the nut to it. Tighten the nut until hand-tight. Use two adjustable wrenches to tighten until snug—one to hold back the valve and the other to tighten the compression nut.

11 Always replace the supply tube to help prevent leaks. Screw flex tube in place. If you're installing chrome tubing, hold it in place with the extra pipe extending past the shutoff. Mark the pipe for cutting. Leave enough pipe so it will fit inside the shutoff valve outlet. Cut with a tubing cutter.

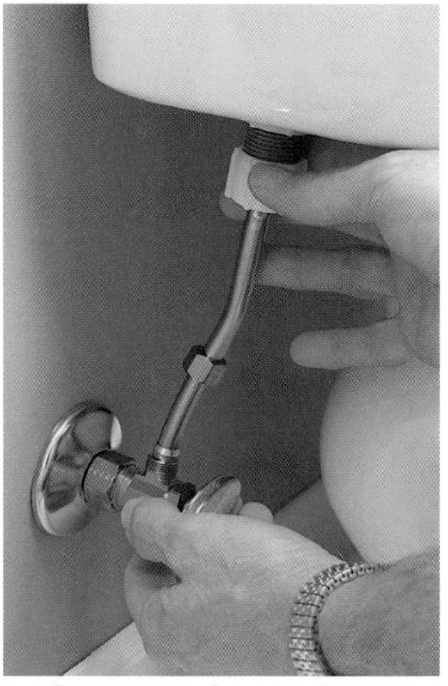

12 Connect the supply pipe to the tank. Seat the end of the pipe against the tank. Draw up the tank nut and hand-tighten until snug. Slide the compression nut over the other end, then place the compression ring over the end. Seat the end in the outlet of the shutoff valve.

Installing an upflush toilet

Yes, there are special-purpose toilets that defy gravity and flush up. An upflushing unit has an electric pump that discharges the waste up and away instead of using gravity to drain. A GFCI receptacle is required nearby to operate the pump. (See page 376 on installing a GFCI receptacle.)

An upflush toilet can also handle waste water from a nearby sink or shower.

The unit shown here is designed to fit between 2×6 joists. It must rest on a stable, fairly level surface.

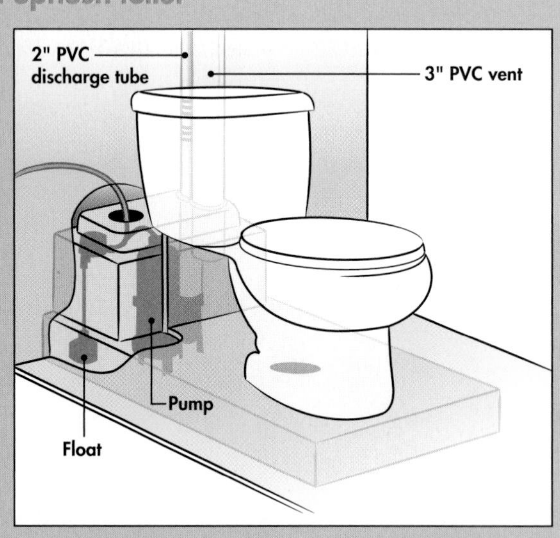

Other options include macerating toilets with a rear outlet. They are secured to the floor with metal or plastic anchors; drill holes in the floor with a masonry bit. These units have a rotating blade that liquifies the waste and sends it up and out of the home.

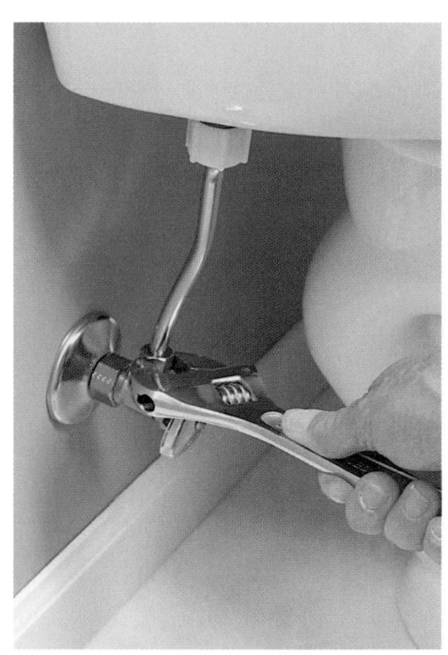

13 Tighten the compression nut. Use an adjustable wrench to carefully tighten the compression nut. Don't overtighten. Turn on the water supply and check for leaks along the supply line—visually and by feel. Flush the toilet and check for leaks around the base of the tank. If there is a leak, tighten the connections a half-turn.

Installing a garbage disposer

Skill level:	Time to complete:	Materials:	Tools:
★★★☆☆	Experienced 30 min. Handy 45 min. Novice 1.5 hrs.	Garbage disposer, electrical cord, plumber's putty or silicone caulk	Screwdriver or disposer wrench, hacksaw or tubing cutter, water-pump pliers

A garbage disposer requires an electrical source for power. If you don't have an electrical outlet under the sink, you'll need to install one. Check with local codes before installation. Some communities have codes that don't allow disposers because of limits on sewer capacity. They may also require an air gap for a disposer and a dishwasher.

If you have a septic system, install a disposer specifically designed for use with a septic tank. Too much food waste can interfere with the normal decomposition of septic waste.

How much horsepower?

In-home disposers with motors less than ½ horsepower are not recommended for households with more than two people. A 1-horsepower disposer is better. Not only is it more powerful, it has better sound insulation and may run more quietly than an underpowered unit.

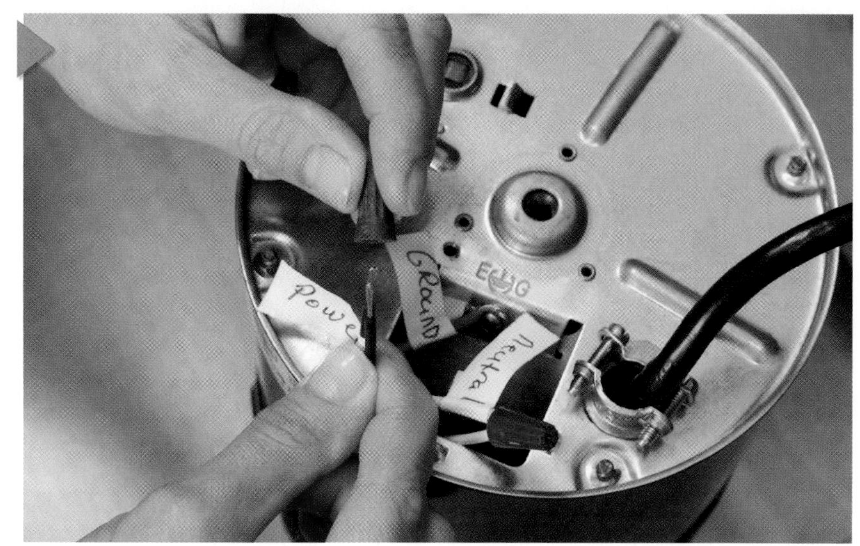

1 Wire the disposer. The disposer may come with the appliance cord attached. If not, you will have to connect one. Remove the cover plate beneath the disposer. Most cords and disposers have the same colored wires. Connect white to white, black to black, and the green wire to the disposer's ground screw. If the colors are different, read the manufacturer's instructions for wiring.

$ BUYER'S GUIDE

CHOOSING A GARBAGE DISPOSER

Garbage disposers are one of those out-of-sight, out-of-mind appliances that we don't give much thought. But they aren't all created equal. If you're concerned with safety, look into batch-feed models. You operate them by turning a special stopper, which guarantees that young hands won't find their way into the moving parts—and that bits of food won't come flying back out. Continuous feed models allow you the convenience of sending a steady flow of scraps into the unit rather than processing a batch at a time. They are operated with a wall switch located some distance away from the unit so you won't be reaching into the drain when the motor turns on. Generally you'll have less trouble with a disposer that has at least ¾ horsepower and with models that include an auto-reverse feature to clear jams.

2 Apply plumber's putty. Press a rope of plumber's putty onto the underside of the drain flange. Insert the flange into the drain hole and press down evenly. Install the backup ring, fiber gasket, and mounting ring from beneath the sink.

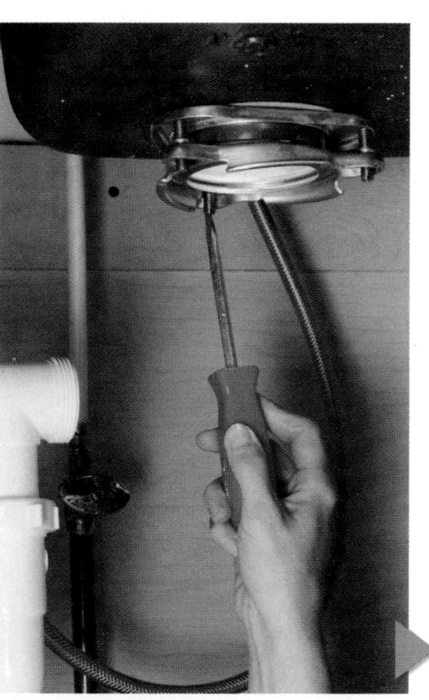

3 Install the mounting ring. Tighten the mounting screws for the upper mounting ring. Alternate the tightening of the screws to pull the ring up evenly against the sink.

Installing a garbage disposer (continued)

4 Mount the disposer. Place the disposer into the mounting ring, making sure the outlet of the disposer is facing the drainpipe connection. Turn the lower ring clockwise until the disposer is supported by the mounting assembly.

5 Connect the outlet to the P-trap. Measure and then use a hacksaw or tubing cutter to cut the discharge pipe to length. Install the discharge pipe to the outlet of the disposer. Attach to the drain line with slip nuts.

6 Tighten the mounting lug. Insert a screwdriver or disposer wrench into the mounting lug on the lower mounting ring. Turn clockwise until the disposer is locked into place. Tighten all slip nuts snug using water-pump pliers. Run water into the sink. Turn on the disposer and check for leaks. Tighten fittings if necessary.

Connect a dishwasher

Be sure the disposer you purchase has a knockout for a dishwasher. Remove the knockout for the dishwasher connection on the disposer. Connect the dishwasher discharge line to the disposer using hose clamps. If local codes require an air gap between the dishwasher and the disposer, see page 351 for instructions on installing one.

WORK SMART

GETTING SOME LEVERAGE

Sometimes the trickiest part of mounting the garbage disposer is the moment when you lift it up and lock it into the mounting rings. The pros will stack a couple of thick telephone books under the unit so they won't have so far to lift. You can do the same thing or use scrap lumber, a toolbox, or the box the unit came in.

TOOL TIP

DISPOSER WRENCH

Some disposers come with a special wrench that turns the impeller if the disposer gets jammed. Keep the wrench and manual together in a location you'll remember.

WORK SMART

SAVE THAT BRACKET

Are you replacing an existing garbage disposer with the same brand? You may be able to use the existing mounting bracket to make the job easier and quicker.

Replacing a dishwasher

Skill level:	Time to complete:	Materials:	Tools:
★★★☆☆	Experienced 1 hr. Handy 1.5 hrs. Novice 3 hrs.	Air gap, drain hose, hose clamps, wire nuts, flexible copper tubing and compression fittings, drain tailpiece with inlet	Level, power drill, hole saw, screwdriver, adjustable wrench, tubing cutter

A dishwasher will clean your plates and glasses, and your countertop as well—by eliminating stacks of dirty dishes on display. Measure your space to find out what size you need. Most dishwashers are 18 or 24 inches wide.

Many dishwashers are designed to drain directly into the garbage disposer while others drain through an air gap that prevents a clogged drain from backing up into the dishwasher.

Take a look at the yellow Energy Guide label for the efficiency rating of any model. The lower the number, the less energy the dishwasher will use over a one-year period.

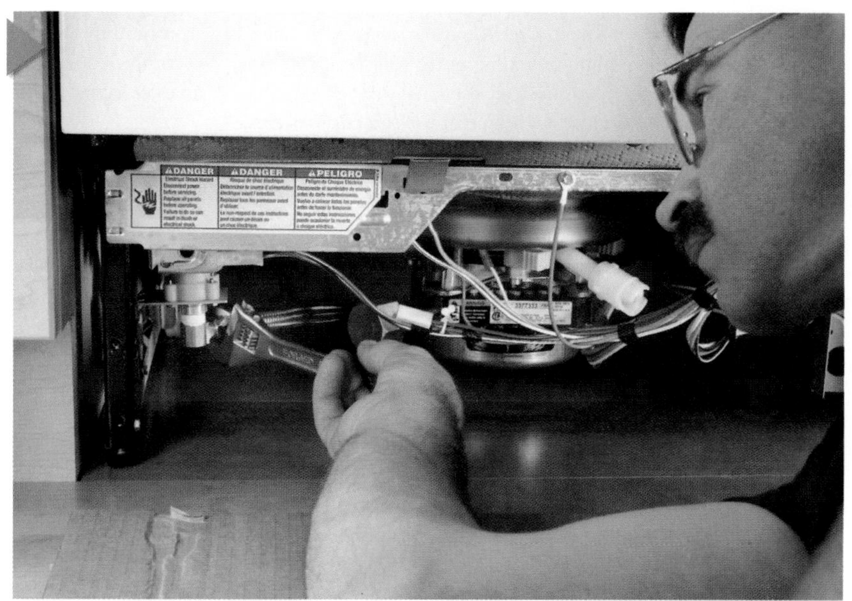

1 Connect the lines. Slide the dishwasher into place. Level it by adjusting the threaded feet. (Check the door. When level, it will open and close smoothly.) When the unit is level, tighten the locknuts. Align the mounting brackets with the counter. Follow the manufacturer's directions to connect the supply tubing to the dishwasher solenoid. Simplify the job by using braided, flexible tubing made for dishwasher supply.

Some local codes require an air gap between the dishwasher and the disposer. Mount the air gap in the countertop; if there is an extra hole available in the sink, mount it there. Connect a ⅝-inch drain hose to the ½-inch leg of the air gap with a hose clamp. Attach a ⅞-inch hose to the ¾-inch leg of the air gap. Make sure there are no low spots or kinks in either hose.

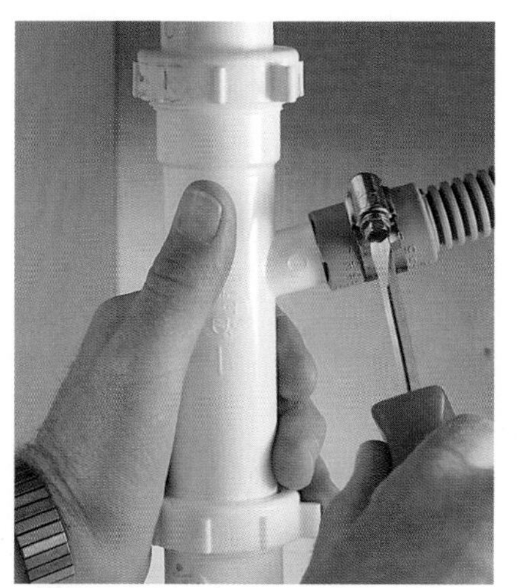

2 Install the drain line. Connect the drain line to the dishwasher outlet using hose clamps. Measure the hose and cut it to length so that it connects to the tailpiece inlet under the sink. Connect the hose to the inlet with another hose clamp. If local codes require an air gap, install one using the manufacturer's instructions.

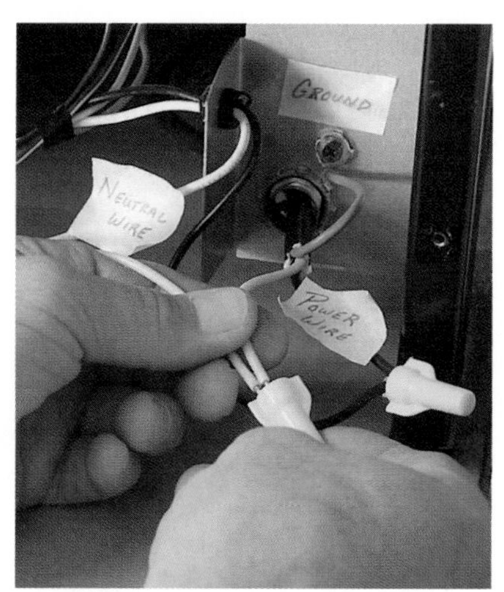

3 Hook up the power. Match the wires: white to white, black to black, and connect the green to the ground screw. If the colors are different, read the manufacturer's instructions for connecting the wires. Connect the wires with wire nuts. Plug the power supply cord into an electrical outlet installed under the sink cabinet. Run the dishwasher through a test cycle to make sure it works properly.

Connecting a refrigerator ice maker

Skill level:	Time to complete:	Materials:	Tools:
★★☆☆☆	Experienced 1 hr. Handy 2 hrs. Novice 3 hrs.	Self-piercing saddle valve, plastic or copper tubing, steel wool, paintable silicone caulk	Adjustable wrench, screwdriver, electric drill

Running a cold-water line to a refrigerator's icemaker is one of the easiest home plumbing jobs, and it will spare you the bother of filling (and spilling) those ice trays. With a self-tapping saddle valve, there's no need to cut a pipe or use solder or solvent. You can buy the necessary parts individually or shop for a complete kit. Note that some manufacturers also offer after-market icemaker kits that fit into the freezer compartment.

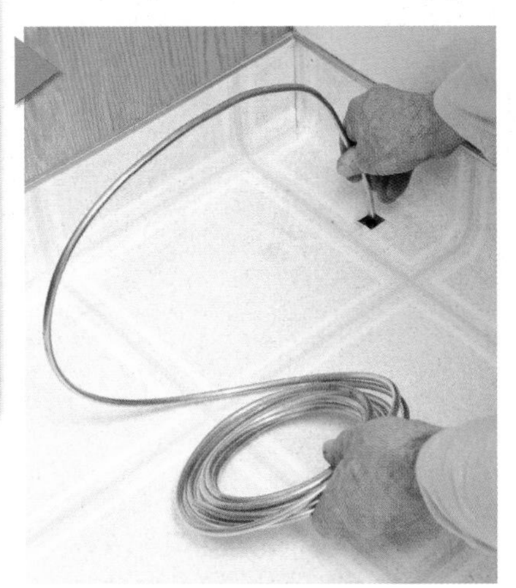

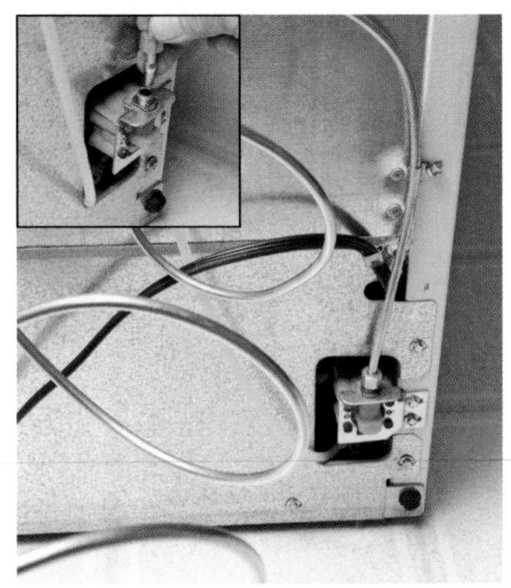

1 Provide a cold-water source. Locate a copper cold-water pipe relatively close to the refrigerator—in the basement or under the kitchen sink. Run a supply line from this pipe to the refrigerator's location. Drill access holes as necessary and seal them with paintable caulk.

2 Attach the supply line to the pipe. Turn off the water to the cold-water pipe. Clean an accessible section of the pipe by rubbing it lightly with steel wool followed with soap and water. Place the valve of the kit over the pipe and tighten the bolts connecting the top and bottom parts of the frame. This will cause the valve's needle to pierce the pipe. Restore water to the line, then flush any debris out of the valve by turning the handle at the top for a moment.

3 Connect the supply line. Attach the supply line to the valve and to the icemaker inlet on the back of the refrigerator. Open the valve and check for leaks.

CLOSER LOOK

WHAT IF YOUR PIPES AREN'T COPPER?

It is possible to attach a saddle valve to plastic or galvanized pipe, but you will have to drill a hole to allow the valve's needle to enter the pipe. Drain the pipe as thoroughly as you can, and use a battery-powered drill to prevent a serious electric shock. Make the hole as high on the pipe as possible to minimize the amount of remaining water that may pour out and to help ensure that the valve remains free of sediment.

For better-tasting ice

Ice not only cools down beverages but also can impart an unwanted flavor. If the household water is from a chlorinated public supply, you can leave the chlorine behind by installing an inexpensive filter, available at home centers, in the line running to the icemaker. Locate the filter in a spot that's relatively accessible so you can change it at recommended intervals.

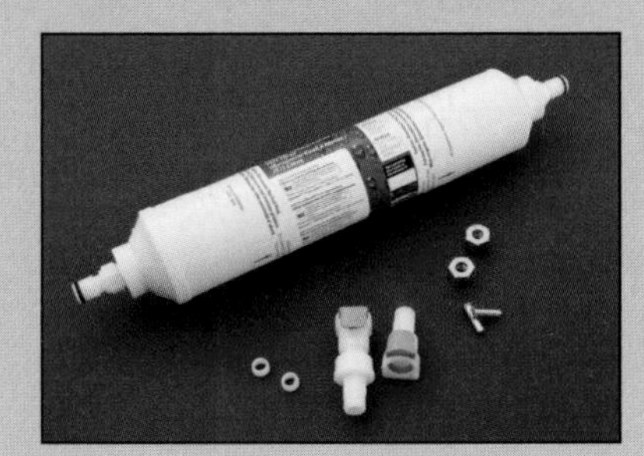

Installing a water softener

Skill level:	Time to complete:	Materials:	Tools:
★★★★☆	Experienced 2 hrs. Handy 4 hrs. Novice 6 hrs.	Water softener, copper pipe and fittings, soldering shield, Teflon tape, plastic tubing for drain and overflow lines, softener salt	Pipe cutter, propane torch

PLUMBING

Water is essential to life, of course, and reasonably soft water is essential if you are to keep yourself, your clothing, and your dishes and glassware satisfactorily clean. A water softener runs water through a salt solution to remove the minerals that make it difficult for soaps and detergents to do their job. The process adds sodium to the water, so you may want to bypass the unit and add a cold water line to the kitchen for drinking and cooking.

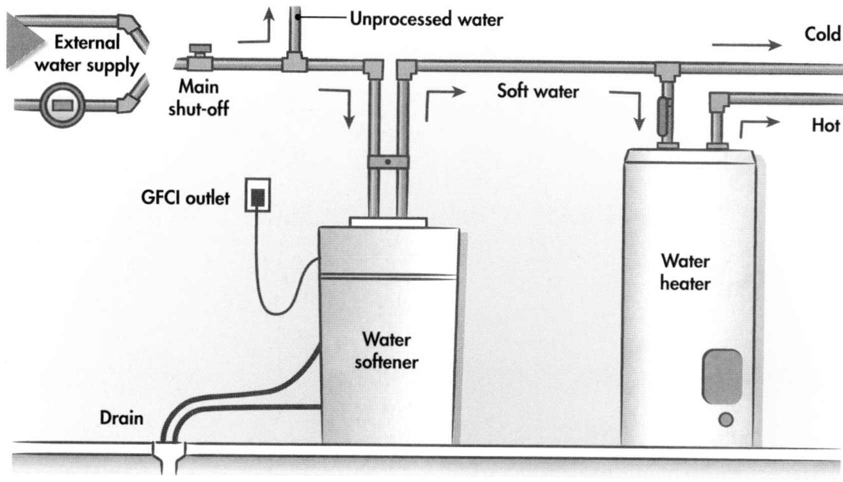

1 Plan the installation layout. When deciding where the softener should go, keep in mind that you will need access to the water supply, a 120-volt GFCI outlet, and a drain. To make it easier to add salt to the softener, make sure the unit is relatively accessible. If you want a separate line for unprocessed water for drinking and cooking, be sure to allow room to attach a fitting for it between the main shutoff valve and the connections for the water softener.

$ BUYER'S GUIDE

TWIN TANKS?

The most obvious difference between water softeners is that some have two tanks while others do their job with a single unit. Is two better than one? Not necessarily. A twin system is slightly more efficient because one tank can regenerate while the other is in use; the tanks are run to their full capacity. A single-tank unit like the one shown above right costs considerably less and takes less room. But the down side is that it can't generate a constant supply of soft water. Basic systems use a timer to initiate the regeneration cycle at night when demand is apt to be lowest and the temporary lack of soft water is less likely to be an inconvenience. A portion of the salt likely will go unused because the cycles aren't influenced by how much water has been processed.

For greater efficiency, choose a metered softener that regenerates only when a certain amount of water has gone through the system, ensuring that the salt is nearly used up.

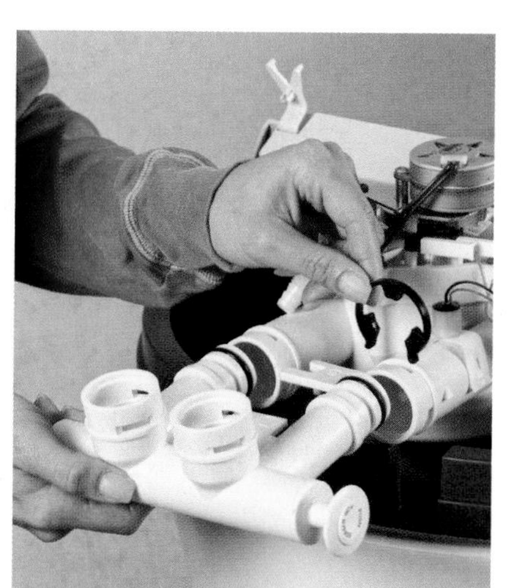

2 Install the bypass valve. Most systems now come with a bypass valve, which allows you to maintain the household supply while shutting off water to the softener to make repairs. Attach the bypass to the inlet and outlet of the control valve using either threaded connections or the U-shape clips shown here.

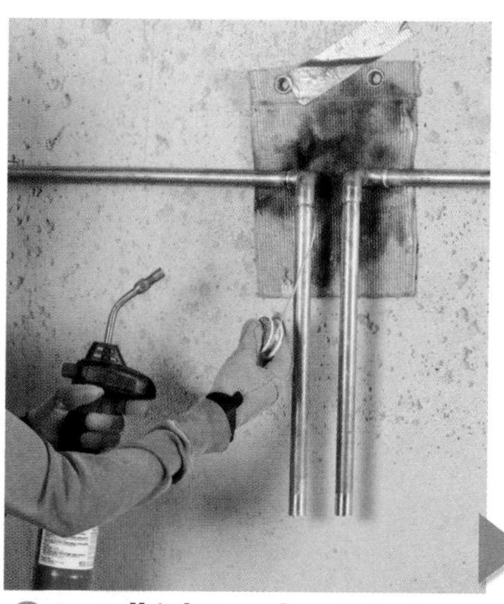

3 Install inlet and outlet pipes in the cold-water supply line. Turn off the power to the water heater. Shut off the water supply and open taps around the house to drain the system. Use a pipe cutter to remove a section from the cold-water supply line, making it as long as the bypass valve ports are apart. Use elbows at the cut ends to connect risers that will meet the short stub lines you will install coming from the bypass. Temporarily place a soldering heat shield on adjacent surfaces to keep from damaging them.

Installing a water softener (continued)

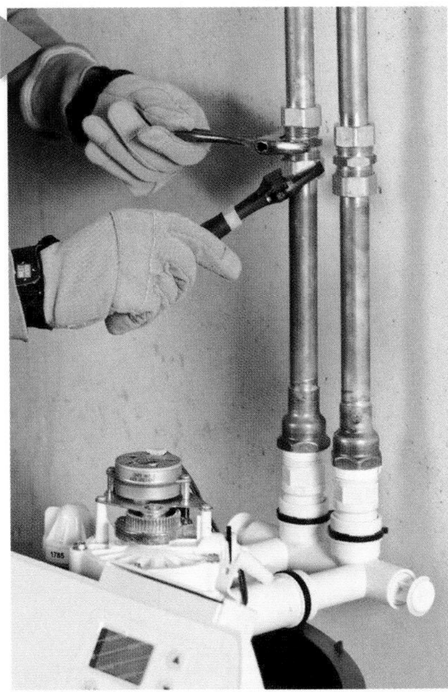

4 Connect the softener to the inlet and outlet pipes. Attach the risers to the stub lines with compression fittings using one wrench on the body of the fitting and another to turn the nut. Solderless connections avoid the possibility that the heat from the torch might damage the plastic bypass unit.

5 Install the drain and overflow lines. Attach the thin, flexible drain line to the drain outlet of the control valve and run it to a suitable drain—in the floor, a sink, or a sump. There must be an air gap at all times to prevent a backflow into the home water supply. Also attach a tube to the elbow for the salt storage tank overflow and run it to the drain.

6 Maintain the grounding function. If the electrical system is grounded via the plumbing supply lines, install a metal grounding strap between the inlet and outlet lines to maintain continuity.

SAFETY ALERT

ARE YOU STILL GROUNDED?

In many homes a metal cold water pipe is used to ground the electrical system. If you are using a plastic bypass valve, you can maintain electrical continuity by bridging the valve with a length of #4 copper wire clamped to both ends of the interrupted pipe.

7 Turn on the water supply and start up the system. Turn the water back on and keep the faucets around the home open until the flow is steady. Restore power to the water heater after it has had time to refill. Fill the softener with water, pulling out the bypass valve as shown. Add salt, plug in the unit, and set the timer.

Water heaters

Even with proper maintenance, your water heater will eventually need to be replaced. Either a gas or electric water heater will supply your hot water needs efficiently. Choosing one over the other is a matter of what kind of service is available to your home and what makes the most economic sense.

Pay attention to the warranty

Warranties vary in length. Six to 12 years on the tank is the usual lifespan. Check the limitations of different manufacturers' warranties. The life of the water heater will depend on environmental factors; hard water shortens its life.

The energy factor

Water heaters bear a yellow Energy Guide sticker that shows yearly usage for electricity and natural gas. Rate of recovery is not listed on the tag, but ask about it. It reports how quickly the unit heats the water.

Size matters—electricity

A family of up to four in a home with two full bathrooms, a washing machine, and a dishwasher should have a 50- to 80-gallon tank with a 5,500-watt heating element. A family of five with the same appliances should have a 65- to 80-gallon tank and a 5,500-watt model.

Size matters—gas

A family of up to four in a home with two full bathrooms, a washing machine, and a dishwasher needs a 50-gallon tank with a 40,000-Btu burner unit. A family of six with the same appliances needs a 50- to 75-gallon tank and a 40,000-Btu model. A family of up to seven needs a 50- to 75-gallon, high-input 52,500-Btu unit.

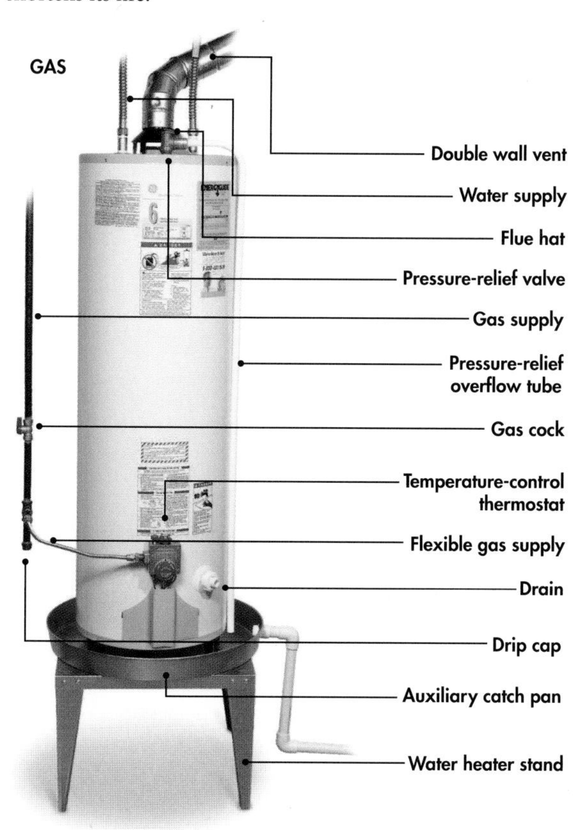

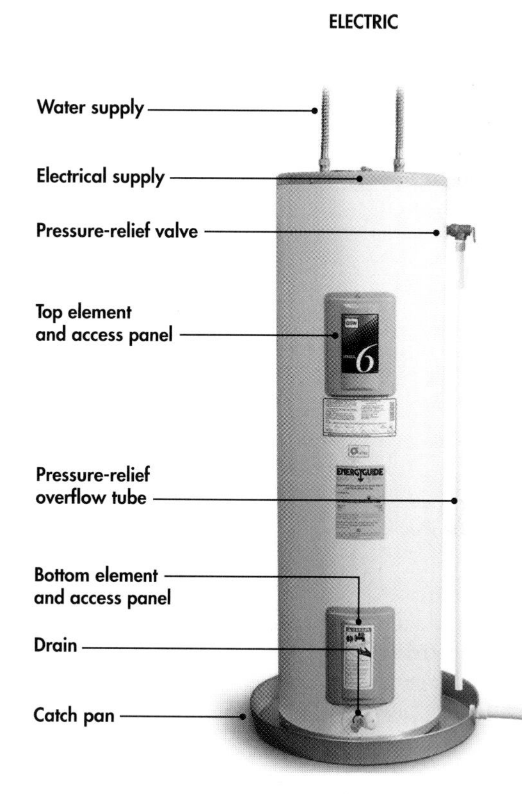

The tankless story

Electric or gas tankless "on demand" water heaters have recently been introduced in North America. While more expensive, they are more efficient than conventional water heaters. The savings in energy and maintenance could make up the difference in cost.

Tankless heaters save money because they don't need to heat a tank full of water. When you turn on the faucet, cold water flows through heating coils and is instantly heated to 105 to 115 degrees. When the faucet is turned off, the heating coils turn off as well.

Check details with your local home center. Large tankless heaters may require professional installation. Smaller "on demand" heaters can be installed in remote locations. (See page 359.)

SAFETY ALERT
CARBON MONOXIDE IS DANGEROUS

Colorless and odorless, carbon monoxide causes about 10,000 injuries a year. Symptoms of gas poisoning include headaches, fatigue, and nausea. Install a carbon monoxide detector and have gas appliances inspected once a year.

Water heater installations

Skill level:	Time to complete:	Materials:	Tools:
★★★☆☆	Experienced 30 min. Handy 45 min. Novice 1 hrs.	Electric water heater, acid-free flux, Teflon tape or pipe compound, wire nuts, water heater heat trap fittings, 2×4 support, plastic shims, matches or grill igniter, masking tape	Hacksaw or tubing cutter, wire brush, carpenter's level, two adjustable wrenches, MAPP torch, screwdriver, rags

Installing a new water heater begins with the old heater. If you've got an electric heater, replace it with an electric heater, unless you're willing and able to run gas line and exhaust vents. If you've got a gas heater, stick with gas, unless your breaker box has room for (and you're willing to install) a new 240-volt circuit.

Whether the heat source is gas or electricity, make sure you shut it off before beginning work. Electric heaters can be cut off at the breaker box and may have an additional breaker closer to the heater. Gas heaters will have a cut off valve, usually with a red handle, along the line leading to the hot water heater.

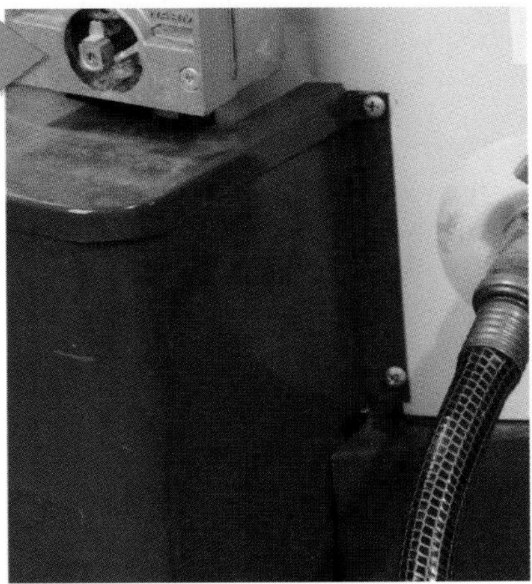

1 Remove the old water heater. Turn off the water and gas supply valves and the power. Remove the electrical supply access plate at the top of the water heater. Check the connections with a continuity tester to make sure the power is off. Attach a garden hose to the drain valve and empty the tank. Using two pipe wrenches, disconnect the gas line at the union fitting if the pipe is galvanized, or at the flare fitting if the gas supply line is copper.

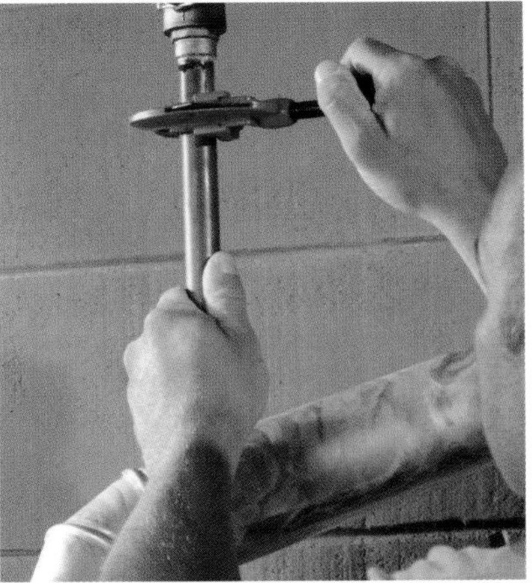

2 Disconnect the water lines. Using two adjustable wrenches or pipe wrenches, disconnect the piping above the tank. If the piping has been soldered into place, use a tubing cutter to cut it.

SAFETY ALERT

SHUT OFF THE POWER AS WELL AS THE GAS

Water and electricity are a dangerous mix. The power should be the first thing turned off and the last thing turned on during the installation process.

WORK SMART

DON'T BLOW OUT THOSE HEATING ELEMENTS

Heating elements for electric heaters are extremely fragile. You'll burn them out in an instant if you power up the heater before it is full of water. To prevent this:

- Open the heater's cold water supply valve so that water can flow into the heater.
- Open the hot water faucet in the bathtub.
- When water starts flowing into the bathtub, the heater is full. Close the faucet and turn on the electricity.

3 Set the new water heater. Install the water heater in an area where it won't be cramped. Leave at least 6 inches of clearance around it for ventilation. Don't set it next to flammables. Turn the water heater so that access to the burner and controls is unobstructed. Place a level on the side of the water heater and plumb it with plastic shims.

4 Wrap the heat trap fitting threads. Use Teflon tape on the pipe threads. These fittings are directional and must be installed properly. Both have arrows showing the correct direction for installation. Attach the blue-coded fitting to the cold water inlet with the arrow facing into the water heater. Attach the red fitting to the hot water outlet with the arrow pointing away from the water heater. Tighten using two pipe wrenches or adjustable pliers.

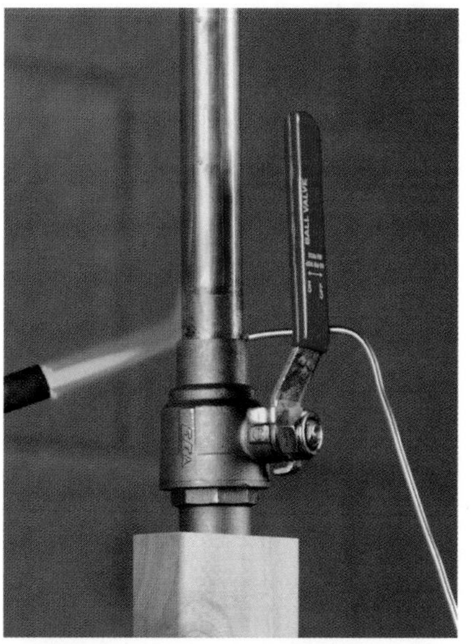

5 If you removed the shutoff valve, replace it. Sweat solder the shutoff valve to the end of the cold water supply pipe. Use a MAPP torch and lead-free solder to connect the valve to the supply line. Solder with the valve in the open position to avoid overheating the parts.

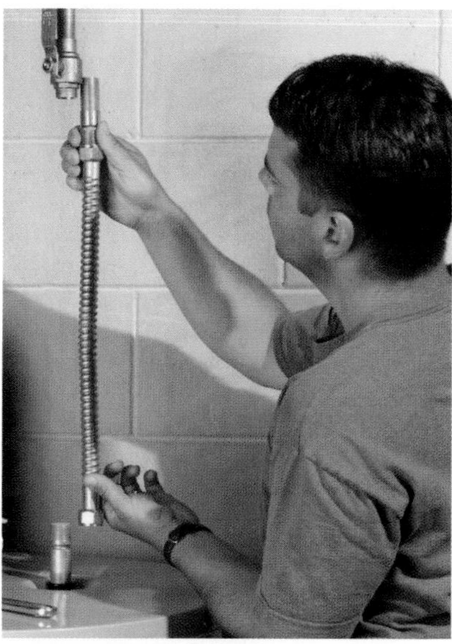

6 Install the water lines and pressure relief line. Use two adjustable wrenches to connect the pipe from the pipe run to the water heater. Turn the main shutoff on and open all line valves. Open all the faucets in the house and run the water until it flows steadily from them. Close the faucets.

Wiring an electric water heater

1 Remove the electrical access plate. Always turn off the power to the unit before you do any electrical work. Connect the electrical supply according to the manufacturer's instructions using wire nuts. Connect the bare copper or ground wire to the ground screw. Replace the electrical access plate. Remove the thermostat access plate.

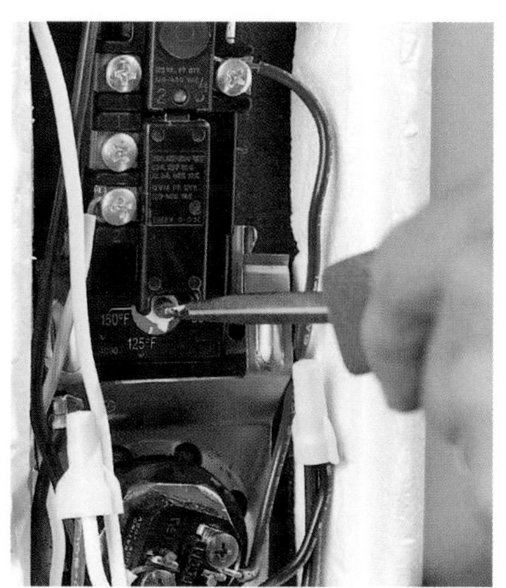

2 Adjust the thermostat. Recommended settings are 120 to 125 degrees. Now open a faucet near the heater, turn on the water supply, and fill the tank until the faucet is flowing. The tank must be full before you restore power. When the tank is full, restore power and press the reset button on the panel.

WORK SMART

HEAVY WATER

Even empty water heaters are heavy and clumsy. Get the old heater out of the way first. If possible, leave the new heater in its box and slide it gently down the stairs. Stand it up and slide it to where it belongs before you cut off the box.

Water heater installations (continued)

Installing a gas water heater

1 install the flue hat vent line. Measure, cut, and assemble the vent pipe that runs from the flue hat to the roof vent stack. Make sure horizontal sections have a slope of ¼ inch of rise for every foot of length to efficiently carry fumes away from the house.

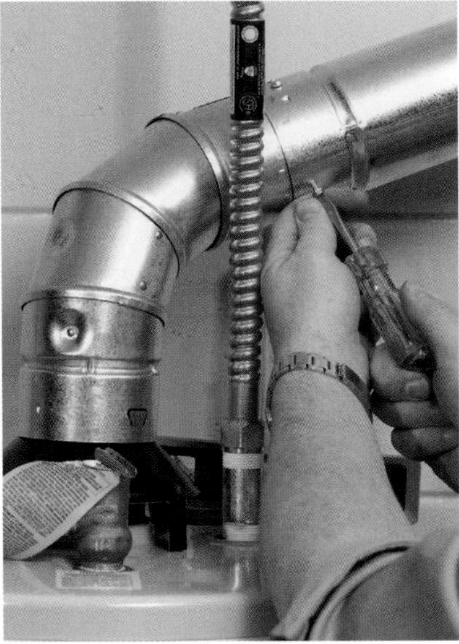

2 Attach the ductwork. Connect the ductwork by driving ⅜-inch sheet metal screws into the vent every 3 to 4 inches around the duct. You will need at least three screws per joint.

3 Connect the gas supply line. Clean all threads with a wire brush and rag. Apply pipe compound to the threads of the galvanized pipes as you connect them. Assemble and tighten each fitting with two pipe wrenches. Install the union fitting last because it connects the new line to the existing line. Once finished, open the gas supply valve.

WORK SMART

CHECKING FOR GAS LEAKS

Make sure the connections in your gas line are tight and that they don't leak any gas. Start by using plenty of pipe dope during assembly—it's cheap, and you can always wipe off the excess. When you turn the gas back on, check for leaks by brushing a 50-50 mixture of dishwashing soap and water on the joints. Leaks will show up quickly in the form of bubbles. Never test for leaks with a burning match. A small leak is enough to start a fire. A medium-size leak can put enough gas into the air to cause a small explosion. And you never know—the leak you discover could be a large one.

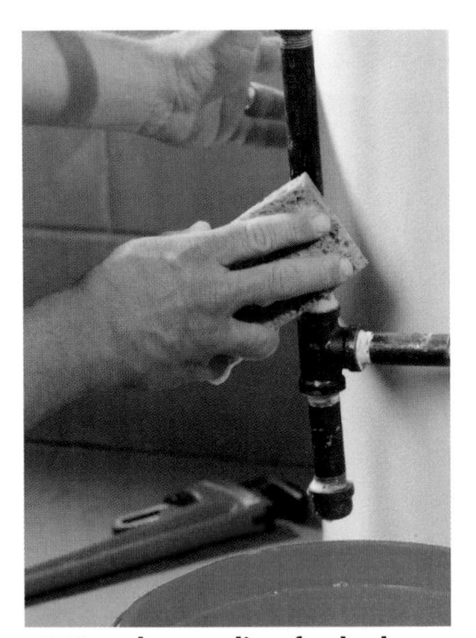

4 Test the gas line for leaks. Fill a sponge with liquid dishwashing soap and water. Apply it to the new fitting and look for bubbles. (The same process is used for finding a leak in a car tire.) If a leak is present, bubbles will form on the surface and you'll have to refit the joint. Test all connections.

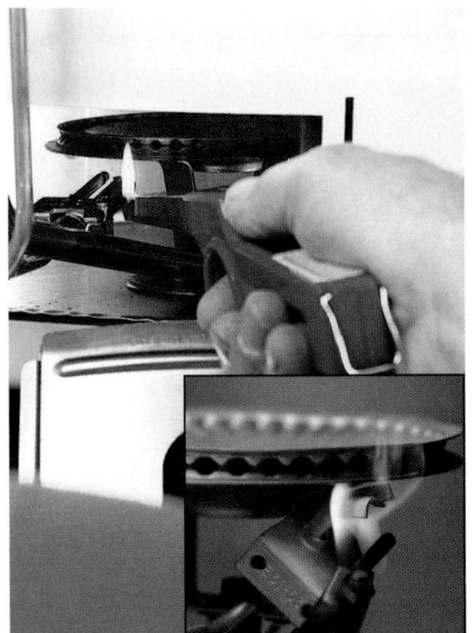

5 Light the pilot. Use a fireplace match or a grill igniter to light the pilot. Replace the burner access panel and set the control at 120 to 125 degrees.

Installing an on-demand water heater

Skill level:	Time to complete:	Materials:	Tools:
★★★★★	Experienced 2 hrs. Handy 4 hrs. Novice 6 hrs.	On-demand water heater, cutoff valves, solder, flux, Teflon tape, high-pressure flexible hose, cable, armored cable, junction box, cover and clamps, wire nuts, wire caps, electrician's tape	Pipe cutter, propane torch, wrench, drill and bits, screwdriver, wire cutter, needle-nose pliers

PLUMBING

An on-demand water heater can easily be mounted under a kitchen sink or off to the side in places where looks don't matter. When you turn on the hot water tap, the flow turns on an element that heats the water as it runs through copper tubes. When the faucet goes off, so does the heat. Because 20 percent of a home's energy use goes into heating water, an on-demand unit can save a lot of money.

To meet code you will need a cutoff switch within sight of the unit, and cable must be flexible or housed in conduit.

Before starting make sure your breaker or fuse box has an extra circuit. You'll need one free breaker for 120-volt heaters or two free breakers for 240-volt units. Time needed to run wire or pipe is not included in the estimate.

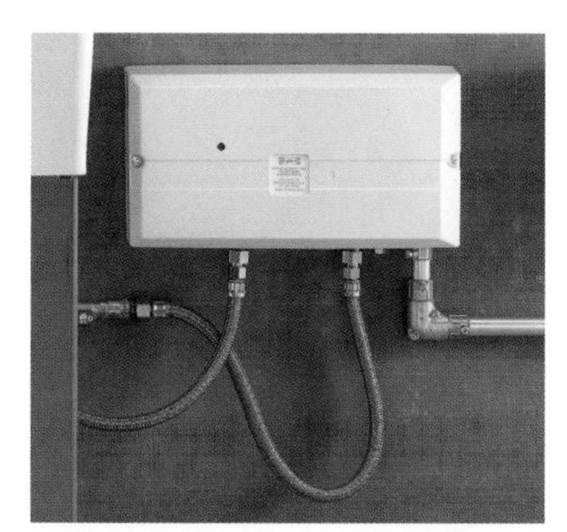

▲ ***Because they don't involve a bulky storage tank,*** *on-demand water heaters are compact enough to be wall mounted—a real boon if space is tight.*

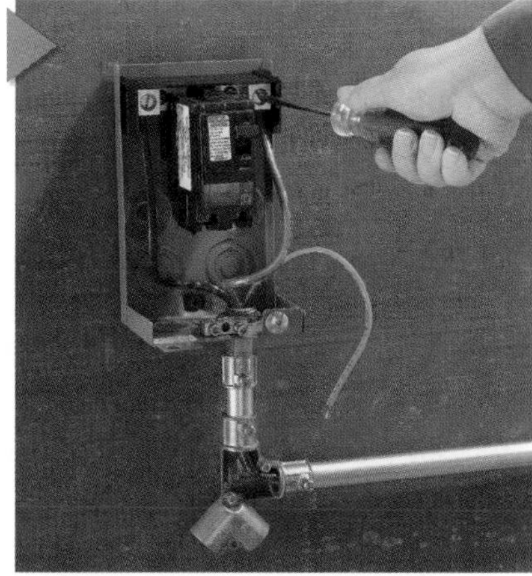

1 Run power for the unit. Turn off the power before you begin. It will be either a 120- or a 240-volt circuit, and it must be a circuit wholly devoted to the heater. Either voltage requires 8-gauge wire, and the section exposed to the area under the sink must be armored cable. If the manufacturer's instructions call for a larger cable, the National Electrical Code says you must comply.

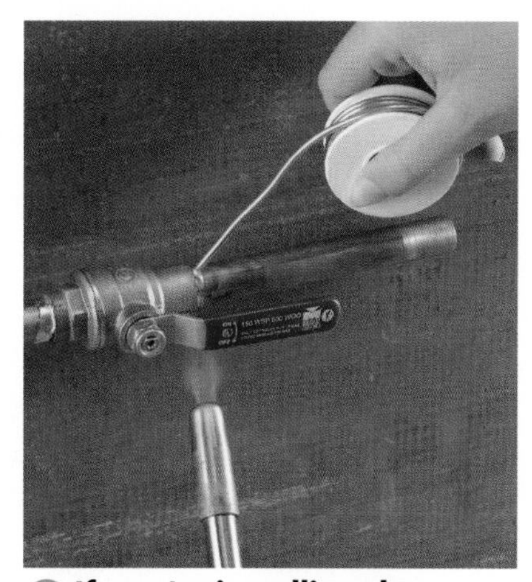

2 If you're installing the heater under an existing sink, turn off the water and cut through the water line. Drain the line by opening a faucet at a lower point somewhere in the house. Solder a cutoff valve onto the pipe stub that comes from the floor or wall. Solder a second valve onto what's left of the line that runs to the faucet, cutting the line as necessary to allow room for the heater. (For more on soldering, see page 297.)

3 Screw the unit to the wall following the manufacturer's directions. Connect the water supply line to the cold in-feed fitting with soldered copper pipe or high-pressure flex connections, above. Wrap Teflon tape around the threads before you make the connection and hand-tighen. Finish tightening with a wrench. Connect the line going to the faucet to the hot water outlet using the same materials.

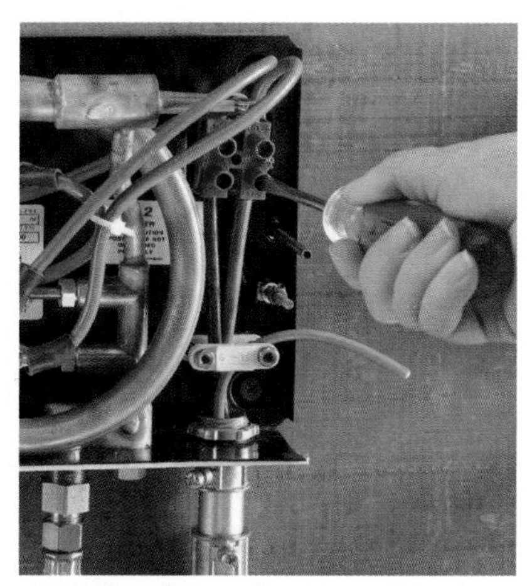

4 Wire the unit. On a 240-volt circuit, the white wire will attach to one of the hot terminals and the black to the other hot terminal—they're often labeled L1 and L2. The ground will go to the grounding screw on the unit. On a 120-volt unit, twist the white supply wire to the white wire in the unit, and twist the black wire to the black wire. Cover with wire caps, and tape the caps in place.

CHAPTER 7

Electrical

Many of the most popular home-improvement projects involve electrical wiring. On the face of it, electrical work may not seem that challenging, and the components are readily available. But those wires have the power to injure you during installation, start a fire, or administer a shock months or years later. Call an electrician if you are unsure of your skills; you still may be able to do other aspects of the job.

Contents

How the electrical system works 362
Electrical safety 363
The electrical tool kit 364
Wires and cables 365
Wire nuts and tape. 366
Receptacles and switches 367
How a circuit works 368
Grounding and polarization. 369
Using testers 370
Stripping and splicing wire. 371
Attaching wire to a terminal 372
Wiring receptacles and switches. 374
Installing or replacing a receptacle 375
Installing a GFCI receptacle 376
Installing an outdoor receptacle. 377
Adding a wall switch for a ceiling fixture. 378
Controlling a single outlet with a switch 379
Replacing a three-way switch 380
Replacing a dimmer switch 381
Choosing electrical boxes 382
Installing electrical boxes 382
Installing remodeling boxes 383
Installing ceiling boxes 385
Installing a junction box 386
Installing NM cable in new walls 387
Working with NM cable 388
Fishing and running cable 389
Working with armored cable 391
Running conduit 392
Installing surface-mounted wiring 394
Adding a circuit 396
Lighting a kitchen 398
Lighting a bathroom 399
Lighting living areas 400
Planning for can lighting 401
Choosing ceiling fixtures 402
Seeing green: energy-efficient lighting 404
Installing or replacing wall lights 405
Installing a hanging light fixture 406
Installing recessed lighting 408
Installing halogen lighting. 411
Installing fluorescent lighting 412
Installing track lighting 413
Installing motion-sensor lights. 415
Hanging a ceiling fan 416
Installing an attic fan 420
Installing a whole-house fan 421
Installing a bathroom vent 423
Installing a range hood 426
Installing low-voltage landscape lighting 427
Installing telephone and CAT 5 wiring 429
Installing coaxial cable 431
Planning a structured wiring system 432
Installing structured cable 433
Troubleshooting a door chime. 435
Troubleshooting a thermostat 437
Adding surge protection 439

Electrical codes must be followed!

Electrical codes are enforced to make sure electrical installations are safe and work properly, and inspectors don't kid around.

- When applying at your local building office for permits to do electrical work, present precise, easy-to-read drawings and include a complete list of materials for the project.
- Installations need to be seen to be inspected. Don't put up drywall or cover new wiring until the inspectors have signed off. If they don't approve the job, you'll do it over, and that can be expensive.

IMPORTANT NOTE: The projects in this section follow common national guidelines. Local codes may be stricter than national standards. Check local requirements carefully before you begin.

See page 588

How the electrical system works

See page 588

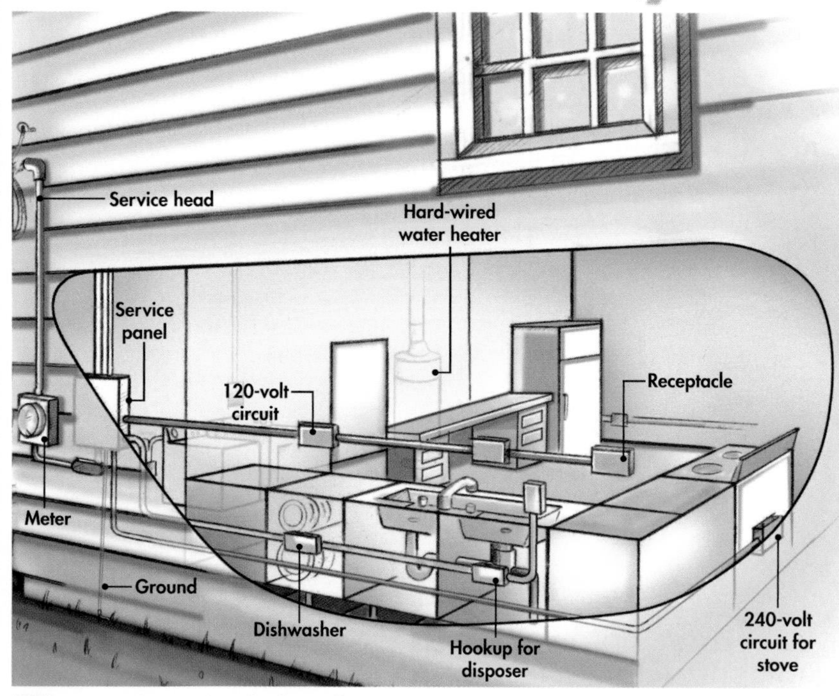

Circuit breaker box

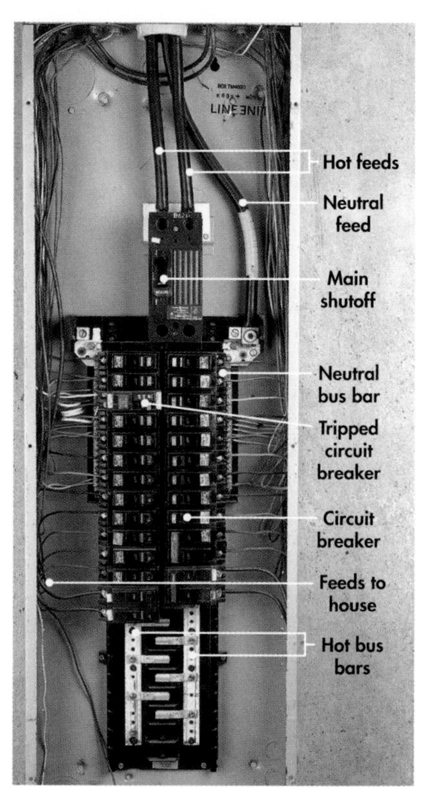

Electricity (current) is the flow of electrons through a conductor (usually copper or aluminum wire). The current travels in a loop, called a circuit, through a "hot" wire (usually black or red) to a fixture and returns through a "neutral" wire (usually white), completing the circuit. When the circuit is broken, the current ceases.

The system is grounded to the earth to prevent a user from being shocked from damaged or defective wiring.

Voltage and amps. Voltage is electrical pressure exerted by the power source. Most household fixtures use 120 or 240 volts. Wires, appliances, and fixtures have different resistances to the voltage—the thicker the wire, the less resistance. Amperes and watts refer to the amount of electrical current used by devices in the system (such as a lightbulb).

Powering your home. Electricity flows from the utility provider through high-voltage wires to transformers that reduce the amount of power to 120 volts per wire. The wires enter your home through a service head, which attaches to a meter that records your power use. The wires then enter the service panel, which divides the power into circuits and distributes power to outlets throughout your home.

Service to most homes is three-wire—two "hot" wires carrying power inside and one "neutral" wire completing the circuit. Two hot wires means that a home can run 120-volt and 240-volt circuits. Older homes with only one hot and a neutral are limited to 120-volt service.

Know your limits. Most repairs and installations can be performed safely inside the home. For any outdoor repairs or installations, including the service head and wires that feed the main shutoff in the service panel, call your local utility for service; that is its responsibility.

CLOSER LOOK

TECHNICAL ELECTRICAL

An **electrical outlet** is any place where electricity leaves the wires to perform a service—such as at a light fixture. A **receptacle** is an outlet where electricity exits the system through a plug. A **device** is something that carries but does not use electricity, such as a receptacle or switch. A **fixture** is an electrical outlet that is permanently fixed in place, and an **appliance** is a movable user of electricity. An overhead light is a fixture while a toaster is an appliance.

SAFETY ALERT

RESPECT YOUR BREAKER BOX

- Always know what's hot. Assume the wires entering from the outside are always hot.
- Never touch a bus bar; it remains hot even when a breaker has been shut off.
- Keep the cover on and closed (preferably locked) at all times.
- Post a circuit map on the inside of the door.
- Keep the area around the box clear. Always have a charged flashlight handy.
- Always wear rubber-soled shoes.
- Never clip temporary lines into the panel. (Welders and sanders will often want to clip temporary extension lines to the hot and neutral bars. Don't let them.)

Electrical safety

Electricity deserves your attention and respect. The wiring in a modern home should have safety features, such as grounding and ground fault circuit interruption. While both greatly reduce the possibility of dangerous shock, they fail to offer complete protection to a person working on exposed wires and devices. This danger is why professional electricians work very carefully; so should you.

Shut off the power. If there is no electrical current, you cannot receive a shock. **Always shut off power to the circuit on which you are working.** Do this by flipping a circuit breaker or completely unscrewing a fuse. Then make sure you chose the right circuit by using an outlet tester to test the line.

Test for power. Be aware that more than one circuit may be running in a box. **Test all the wires in an open box for power, not just the wires on which you will be working. Test everything twice.**

Stay focused. Most electrical mishaps occur because of small mental mistakes. Stories abound of someone turning off the power, only to have a family member or coworker turn it back on while work is in progress. **Post a sign telling others not to restore power;** lock the service panel if possible. Remove all distractions. Keep others, especially children, well out of the way. **Even after turning off the power, work as if the wires are live.** Work methodically and double-check all connections before restoring power.

Use protective tools and clothing. **Always use rubber-gripped tools.** Grab tools by the handle, not the metal shaft. Don't touch any metal while working.

Wear rubber-soled shoes and perhaps rubber gloves. Never work with wet feet or while standing on a wet surface. **Do not wear jewelry or a watch**—anything that could possibly get snagged on wires. **Use a fiberglass or wooden ladder**; an aluminum ladder conducts electricity.

Ask questions. **Never proceed with an installation or repair unless you are completely sure of what you are doing.** Don't hesitate to ask "stupid" questions of electrical experts; they know there aren't any.

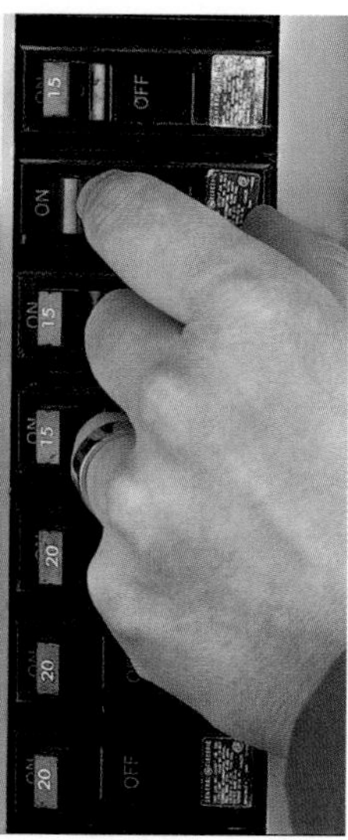

▲ *Shut off the power.*

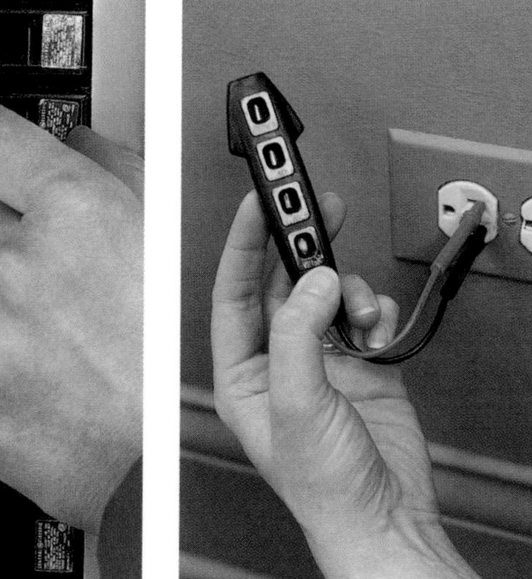

▲ *Test for power.*

▲ *Post a warning sign on the service panel.*

▲ *Use rubber gripped tools.*

▲ *Wear nonconductive clothing from the ground up.*

Shockproofing

A crucial first step in any home wiring task is to turn off the power to the circuit you will be working on. That should go without saying, although any book that covers wiring will say it loud and clear.
The second step should be to tape a note to the service panel telling other members of the household what you're up to. Locking the box is even better. Otherwise you run the chance that someone who discovers the lights won't go on restores power while you're at work. And you shouldn't feel foolish about posting your own reminder, in the form of a day-glo sticky note that inquires whether the power is off. Place the note on the wall next to the fixture you're working on, and thank yourself for your thoughtfulness.

The electrical tool kit

2-part circuit finder

Conduit reamer

Fishing bit

Levels

Rubber-grip screwdrivers

Tool belt

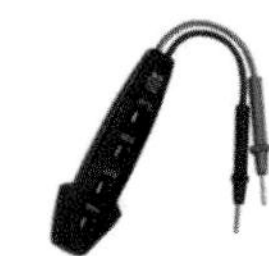
4-level voltage tester

Continuity tester

Flashlight

Lineman's pliers

Saber saw

Trenching spade

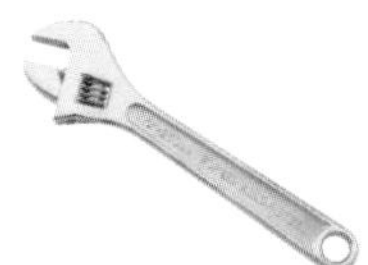
Adjustable wrench

Digital multitester

Flat pry bar

Long-nose pliers

Side-cutting pliers

Utility knife

Armored cable cutter

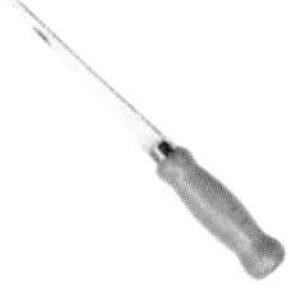
Drywall saw

GFCI receptacle analyzer

Magnetic sleeve and Bit

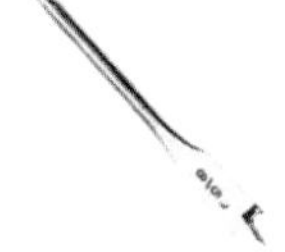
Spade bit

Voltage detector

Coaxial crimper

Electrical tape

Hacksaw

Nut driver

Spiral cutting saw

Water-pump pliers

Coaxial stripper

Fiberglass ladder

Hammer

Power drill with ⅜" chuck

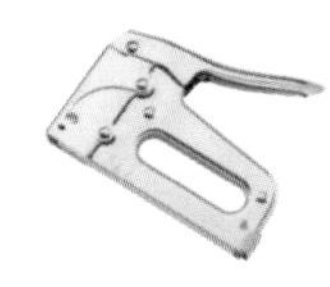
Stapler

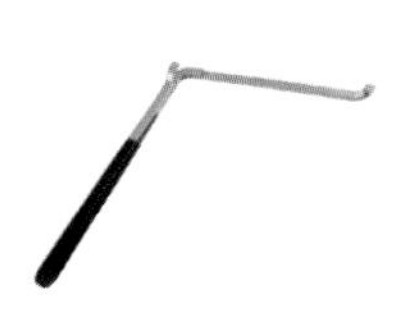
Wire-bending screwdriver

Combination stripper

Fish tape

Hole saw

Rotary screwdriver

Tape measure

Wire stripper/cutter

Wires and cables

See page 588

Use the right wire and cable to avoid creating a dangerous installation that you'll have to tear out and redo. Here are the basics:

Wires

Wire is usually made of a single, solid strand of metal encased in insulation. For flexibility and ease of pulling, some wire is stranded (below right). Wire is sized according to American Wire Gauge (AWG) categories. Size determines how much amperage the wire will carry, and as of 2002, the color of the outer jacket tells you what gauge the wire is. Common household wires and their ratings and colors are:

- **#14 wire** (also called 14-gauge) carries 15 amps and is white.
- **#12 wire** carries 20 amps and is yellow.
- **#10 wire** carries 30 amps and is orange.
- **#8 wire** carries 30 amps and is black (as are all the gauges with numbers less than 8).

A wire that is overloaded to carry more amperage than it is rated for will dangerously overheat. Older wires have rubber insulation, which deteriorates after about 30 years. New wires have longer-lasting polyvinyl insulation. Insulation color often tells the function of wire: **Black, red,** or other colors indicate hot wire. **White** or **off-white** wire generally is neutral. Green or bare wire is ground.

Types of electrical cable

Cable is two or more wires wrapped together and sheathed in plastic or metal. **Nonmetallic (NM) cable** is permitted inside wall, ceiling, and floor cavities. Special nailing plates must be added to the framing to protect the cable from puncture (see page 387). Printing on **NM cable** tells you what is inside: 12/3 means there are three #12 wires plus a ground wire. "G" means that there is a ground wire. For **underground installations and in damp areas use underground-feed (UF) cable.** UF cable encases the wires in solid plastic. **Telephone cable** is being supplanted by **CAT 5E cable,** suitable for telephones, modems, and computer networking. **Coaxial cable** carries television signals. **Armored cable** (see page 391) has a flexible, metal sheathing. One type of armored cable is **BX** (also called **AC**), which has no ground wire—the sheathing is used for grounding (the thin metal bonding strip cannot be used as a ground wire). The other armored cable is **metal-clad (MC) cable,** which has an insulated green grounding wire. (A similar material, Greenfield, or flexible conduit, is armored sheathing without wires. Install it, then pull wires through it.) **Conduit** is a pipe through which individual wires are run (see page 392). Metal conduit is often required in commercial installations. Most building departments require it only where the wiring is exposed (not behind plaster or drywall).

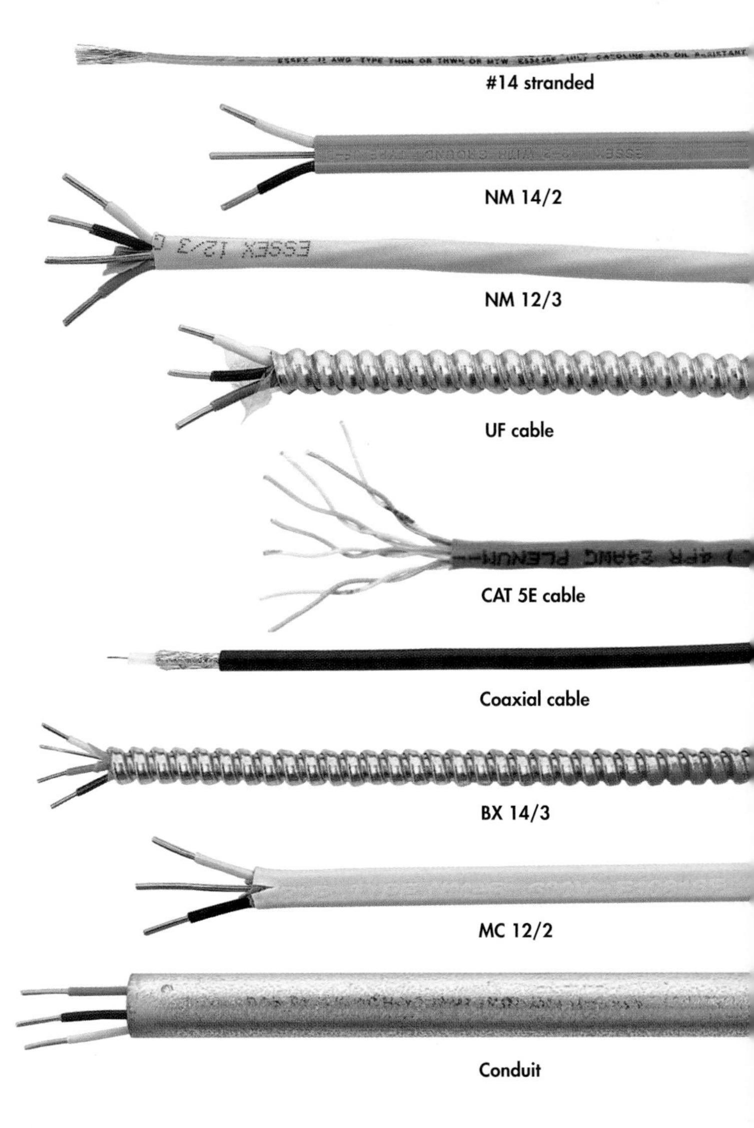

#14 stranded

NM 14/2

NM 12/3

UF cable

CAT 5E cable

Coaxial cable

BX 14/3

MC 12/2

Conduit

TOOL TIP

CIRCUIT FINDER

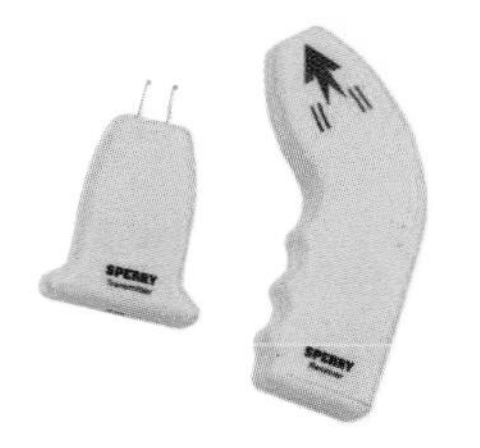

The wiring system in most homes is complex. It's also mostly hidden, slithering through the dark spaces behind walls and between floors. To carry out even basic electrical jobs safely and efficiently, you need to know where those wires are lurking. The tester shown here has two parts, a transmitter and a receiver. After making sure the power is off, connect the transmitter to the wiring and then explore the wall and floor surfaces with the receiver, noting the audible tone indicator or light as it grows weaker or stronger. The circuit finder can be used on coaxial cables and telephone lines as well as on home wiring.

Upgrade cable whenever you can

Remodeling makes a mess of your home, but it also gives you a relatively painless opportunity to bring aging systems up to date. If your work reveals antique wiring and fixtures, here's your chance to familiarize yourself with the current electrical code and new and improved hardware on the market. Replace old cable, ungrounded receptacles, and tired wall lights for the sake of safety and aesthetics.

Wire nuts and tape

Wire nuts are required for all splices. The color of the wire nut indicates how many wires of a given size it can handle. Use yellow connectors for splices as small as two #14s or as large as three #12s. Orange nuts handle combinations ranging from two #16 wires up to two #14s. Use green wire nuts for ground wires only. The hole in the top allows you to make an instant pigtail (see page 372), with one wire poking out. Red wire nuts will grab splices as small as two #12s and as large as four #12s. Black or blue silicone wire nuts are waterproof once connected, though they should be protected by waterproof junction boxes.

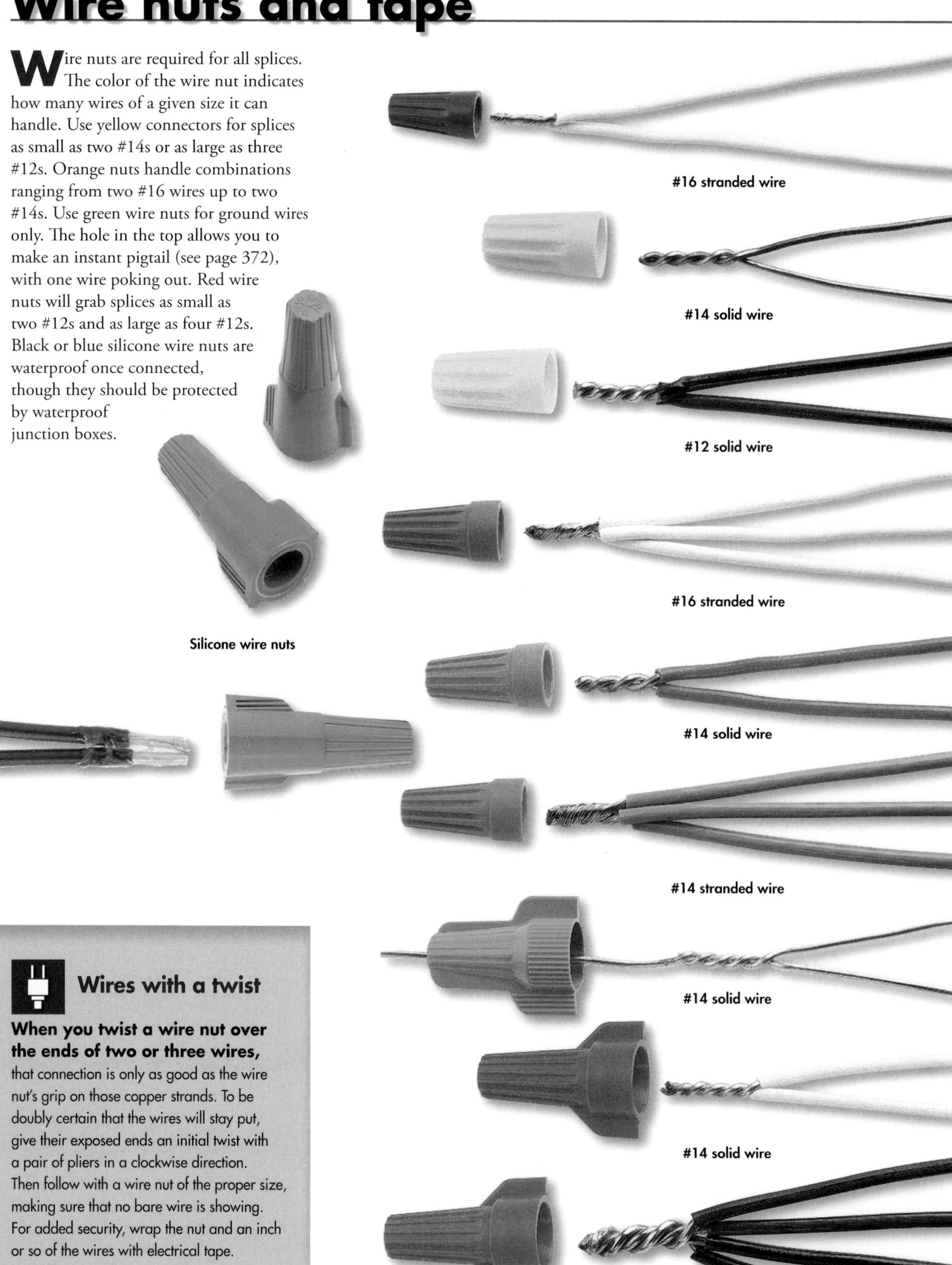

Wires with a twist

When you twist a wire nut over the ends of two or three wires, that connection is only as good as the wire nut's grip on those copper strands. To be doubly certain that the wires will stay put, give their exposed ends an initial twist with a pair of pliers in a clockwise direction. Then follow with a wire nut of the proper size, making sure that no bare wire is showing. For added security, wrap the nut and an inch or so of the wires with electrical tape.

Receptacles and switches

Most switches and receptacles in a home are designed to carry 15 amps. Look on the metal plate for the amperage rating. Any 15-amp device should be connected to #14 wire (see opposite page), which would lead to a 15-amp fuse or circuit breaker in the service panel.

Be sure that the amperage of a 240-volt receptacle is rated no lower than that of the appliance. If you are unsure as to which receptacle to use, check with your building department or ask an electrician.

Switches

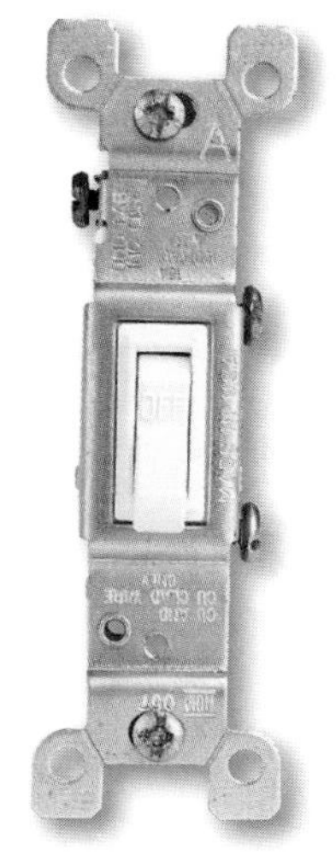

Single-pole. This switch has two terminals for hot wires and a green terminal for ground. It is the most common household switch.

Three-way. Three-ways are installed in pairs—both switches control the same light(s) in either direction. There are no ON and OFF markings.

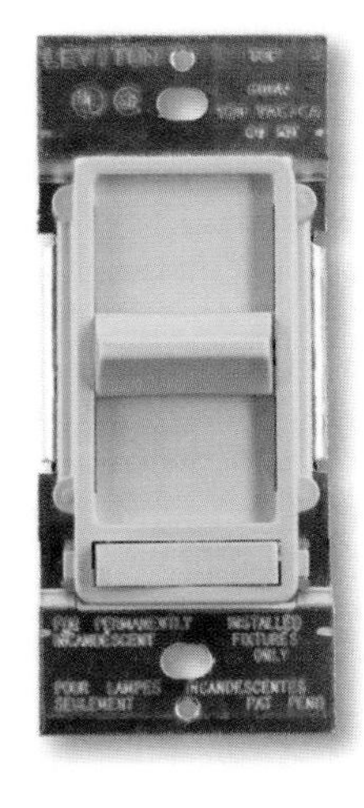

Designer switch. These have built-in illumination and large easy-to-find toggles. They are available in single-pole and three-way.

240-volt receptacles

Wall-mounted 240-volt receptacle. Appliances using 240-volts have different plug designs to ensure that they are plugged into the correct receptacle. To be safe, check the information plate on the appliance to confirm that the amperage also matches that of the receptacle.

Surface-mounted 120/240-volt receptacle. Some heavy-duty appliances require receptacles with both standard voltage and high voltage. For example, a range commonly uses 240 volts for its burners and 120 volts for the light and the clock. A 120/240-volt receptacle provides both levels of power.

Wall-mounted 120/240-volt receptacle. This receptacle is typically used with a stove. Install it in a standard electrical box.

120-volt receptacles

Ungrounded 120-grounded 15-amp, 120-volt. This is the most common household receptacle. It will overload if you plug in two items drawing more than 15 amps.

20-amp, 120-volt. This receptacle has a neutral slot shaped like a sideways T so that you can plug in large appliances or heavy-use tools. It should connect to #12 wires that lead to a 20-amp circuit or fuse in the service panel.

How a circuit works

See page 588

Service panels, whether they have breakers or fuses, divide household current into several circuits. Each circuit carries power from the service panel via hot (usually black or red) wires to various outlets in the house, and then back to the service panel via a neutral (usually white) wire.

Types of circuits. Most household circuits carry 120 volts; some may be 240-volt circuits. Circuits are rated according to amps. If the outlets on a circuit draw too many amps, the circuit overloads. When this happens, a fuse will blow or a breaker will trip (see pages 362–363), preventing an unsafe condition.

A 120-volt circuit usually serves a number of outlets. For instance, it may supply power to a series of lights, a series of receptacles, or some of each. A heavy-use item, such as a dishwasher or refrigerator, may have its own dedicated circuit. A 240-volt circuit is always dedicated to one outlet. A standard 120-volt 15-amp circuit uses #14 wire; a 20-amp circuit uses thicker #12 wire. Older 240-volt circuits use three wires; two hot and one neutral. Recent codes require four wires, as shown below; the added wire is for grounding.

Circuits provide convenience as well as safety. If you are making a repair or new installation, you can shut off power to an individual circuit rather than having to shut down power to the entire house.

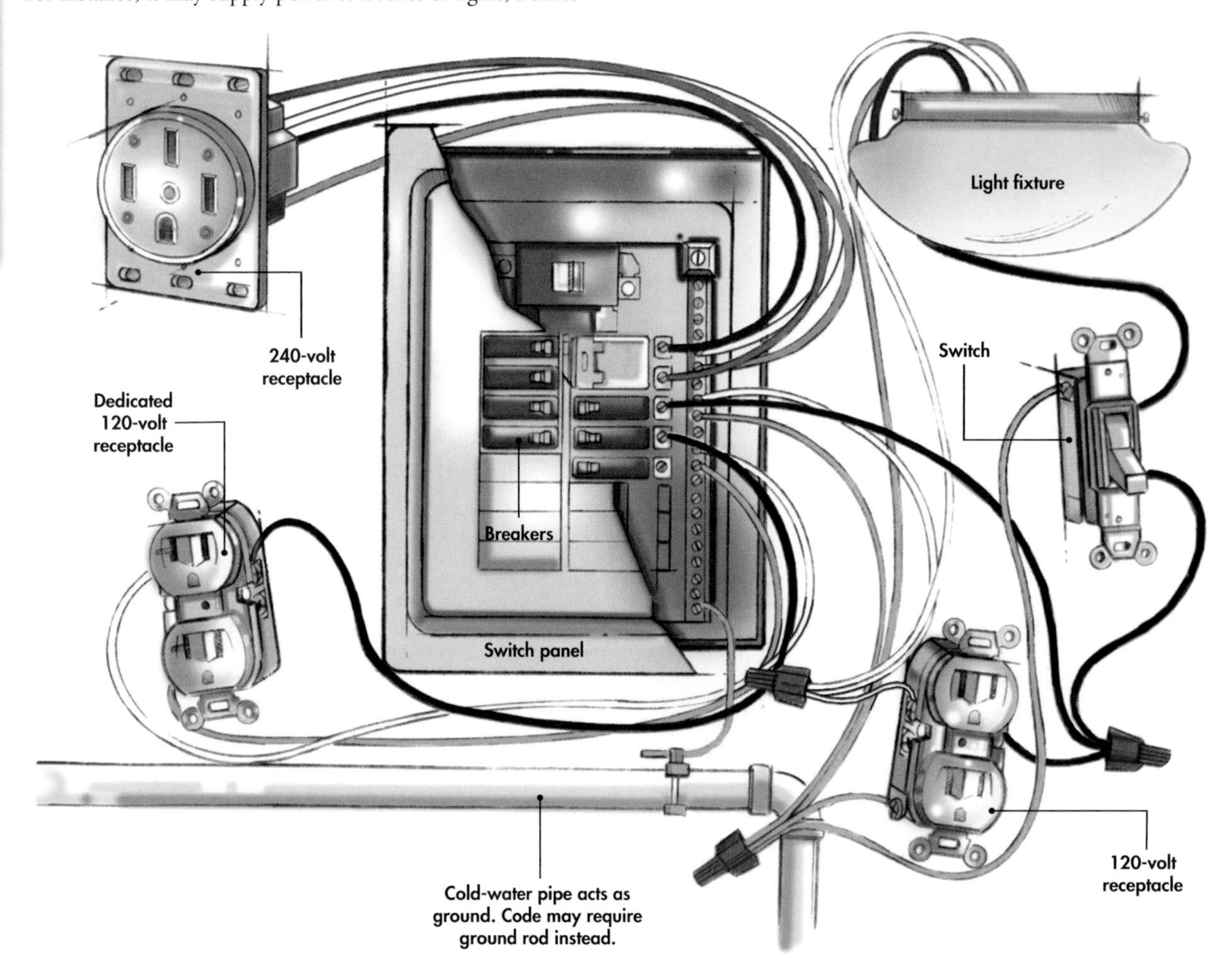

A service panel has 120- and 240-volt circuits. Your service panel distributes power according to the needs of a circuit. For example, a 240-volt circuit is designed to supply electricity to a heavy-duty user of power, such as an electric range or a clothes dryer. The single receptacle on a dedicated 120-volt circuit might feed a refrigerator or a large microwave oven while another 120-volt circuit feeds a series of receptacles and overhead light fixture switches.

Adding 220-volt and low-voltage circuits

Most household electrical needs are met with 120-volt circuits, but there are certain applications that call for either more or less juice. A 220-volt line is typically needed for such power-hungry items as a clothes dryer, electric range, and some stationary shop tools. The line is powered by a double-wide breaker in the service panel, taking up two adjacent slots. The cable carrying the power may be either two- or three-wire, depending on the configuration of the item's plug and outlet (see page 397).

Low-voltage lines once were largely restricted to such humble tasks as serving door bells and telephones, but households increasingly rely on a complex network of dedicated coax cables and light-gauge wire for audio, video, intercom, computer, and home security. These lines typically radiate out from their own control center and terminate in special-purpose wall outlets throughout the home. These so-called structured systems can be installed with fiber-optic lines as well, anticipating their wider use for data transmission (see page 432).

Grounding and polarization

See page 590

Normally electricity travels through insulated wires and exits through a fixture such as a lightbulb. If a wire comes loose or if a device cracks, a short circuit (ground fault) results, releasing electricity where you don't want it. A short can occur, for example, if a loose wire inside a dryer touches the dryer's frame or if cracked insulation allows bare wire to touch a metal electrical box. If you touch electrified metal, you'll get a dangerous shock. Grounding and polarization protect against this. Here's how they work:

Grounding minimizes the possibility that a short circuit will cause a shock. A grounded device, fixture, or appliance is usually connected to a grounding wire—either bare or green—that leads to the neutral bus bar in the service panel. This bar is connected to the earth by a heavy-gauge copper grounding wire running to one or a combination of the following:

- cold-water pipe (If the water meter is installed on the cold-water pipe, the ground must be connected on the street side of the meter or the water meter must be jumped with a grounding wire tightly clamped to both sides.)
- grounding rods driven at least 10 feet in the ground
- metal plate sunk in a footing

Another method uses the metal sheathing of armored cable or conduit (see page 365) instead of a ground wire as the ground path to the service panel.

When a ground fault occurs, the ground path carries the power to the service panel. This extra path lowers resistance, causing a great deal of power to flow back to the panel. This in turn trips a circuit breaker or blows a fuse. At the same time, power is directed harmlessly into the earth.

Whether your system uses grounding wires or sheathing as the ground path, it must be unbroken. A single disconnected ground wire or a loose connection in the sheathing or conduit can make the grounding system useless. To check whether a receptacle is grounded, plug in a receptacle analyzer (see page 370).

Polarization ensures that electricity goes where you want it to go. Because a polarized plug has one prong wider than the other, it can be inserted into a polarized receptacle only one way. If the receptacle is wired correctly and an appliance plug is polarized, the hot wire, not the neutral wire, will always be controlled by the appliance switch. If the receptacle or plug isn't polarized, the neutral wire might be connected to the appliance switch instead, and power would be present in the appliance even when it is switched off. For extra protection against shock, install GFCI protection (see page 376).

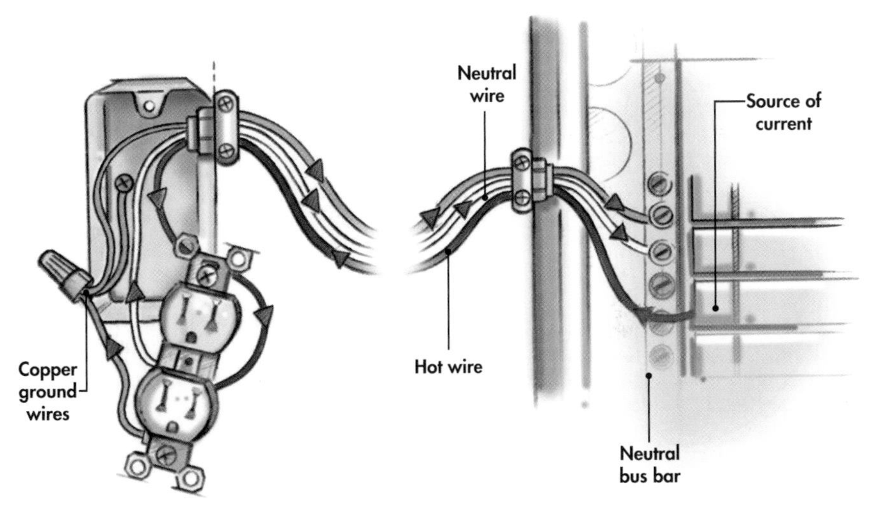

How a grounded receptacle works. To ground a receptacle, a ground wire (either **bare copper** or **green-clad copper**) is attached to the receptacle (and to the box, if it is metal) and leads to the neutral bus bar in the service panel. The panel itself is grounded. This receptacle is also polarized.

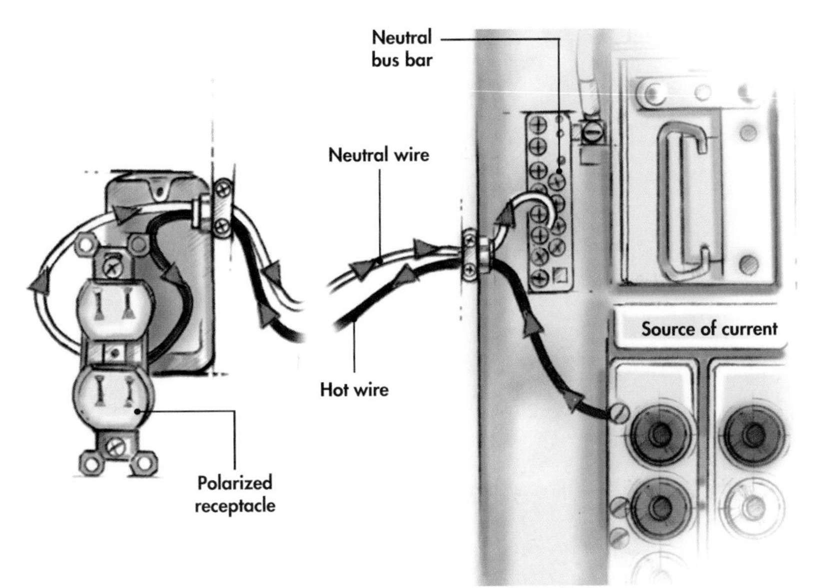

How a polarized receptacle works. The black wire is connected to the receptacle's brass terminal at one end and to the circuit breaker or fuse at the other end. The white wire runs from the silver terminal screw to the service panel's neutral bus bar.

Using testers

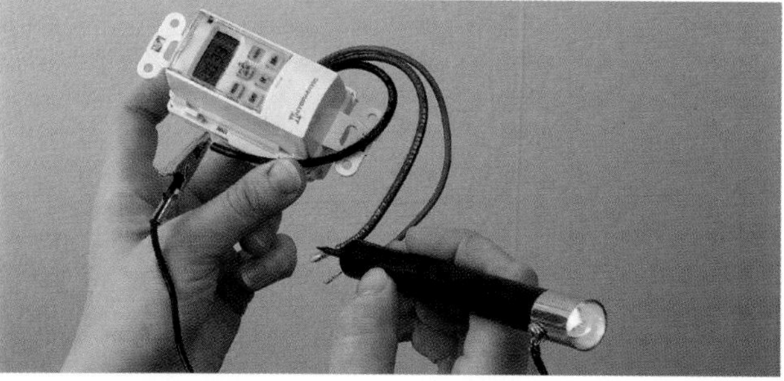

A continuity tester tells you whether a device is defective. Disconnect the device from all household wires. Attach the tester's alligator clip to one terminal and touch the probe to the other terminal. If the device switch is working, the tester light will glow when the switch is turned on and go out when the switch is turned off. To test the wiring in an appliance or lamp, touch both ends of each wire. The tester light will glow if the wire is unbroken.

A voltage detector senses power even through wire and cable insulation. This handy tester lets you check whether wires are live before you work on them. The probe doesn't need to touch a bare wire or terminal. Press the detector button and hold it on or near an insulated wire or cable to see whether power is present. If it is, a light comes on.

A voltage tester indicates the presence of power. A four-level voltage tester is safer and more reliable than one-level versions. **Always confirm that a voltage tester is working by trying it on a circuit you know to be live.** Touch the tester's probes to a hot wire and a grounded box or to a hot wire and a neutral wire, or insert them into the slots of a receptacle. If the tester light doesn't come on, the circuit is shut off.

A receptacle analyzer tells you whether your receptacles are safe. When you plug this analyzer into a receptacle, one or more of three lights will glow, telling you whether the receptacle is working, grounded, and polarized (see page 369). Several styles are available, including some that vibrate or make noise to indicate which slot is hot. Red analyzers test ground fault circuit interrupter (GFCI) receptacles as well as standard receptacles.

TOOL TIP

TEST FOR VOLTAGE AND CONTINUITY

Multitesters have negative and positive probes. Test for voltage by touching each probe to a wire, terminal, or receptacle slot. You also can touch one probe to the black wire and the other to a ground, such as a metal box. The display should show between 108 and 132 volts for a 120-volt circuit and between 216 and 264 volts for a 240-volt circuit. Low-voltage circuitry can register as low as 4 volts.

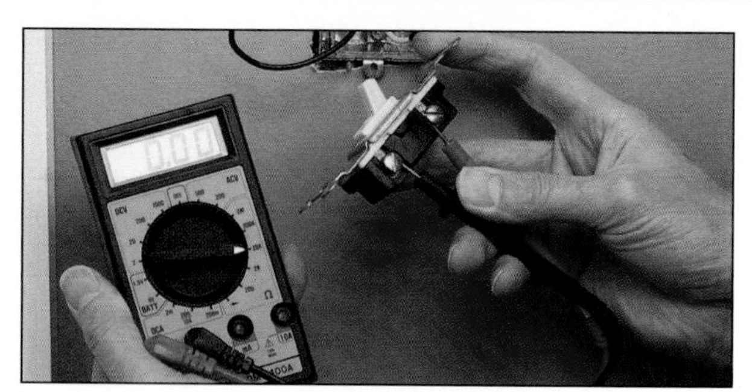

To test a switch with a multitester, shut off the power and disconnect the wires from the switch. Set the dial on the multitester to any ohms setting and touch a test probe to each terminal.Turn the switch on. Zero resistance shows the switch works; infinity means it is defective. The tester should indicate infinity when you turn the switch off.

Stripping and splicing wire

Skill level:	Time to complete:	Materials:	Tools:
★★★☆☆	Experienced 1 min. Handy 3 min. Novice 5 min.	Wire, wire nuts, electrician's tape	Combination stripper, lineman's pliers or side-cutting pliers

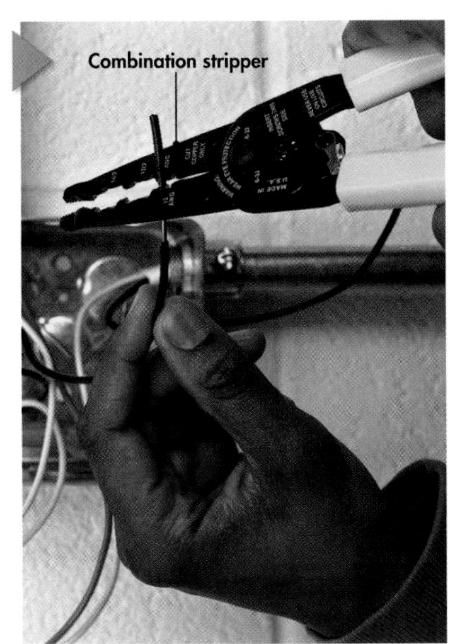

1 Strip wires with a combination stripper. To use a combination stripper, slip the wire into the correct-size hole, squeeze, twist, and pull off the insulation. Yellow-handled strippers are for solid wire. Red-handled strippers are for stranded wire such as that found in lamp cords.

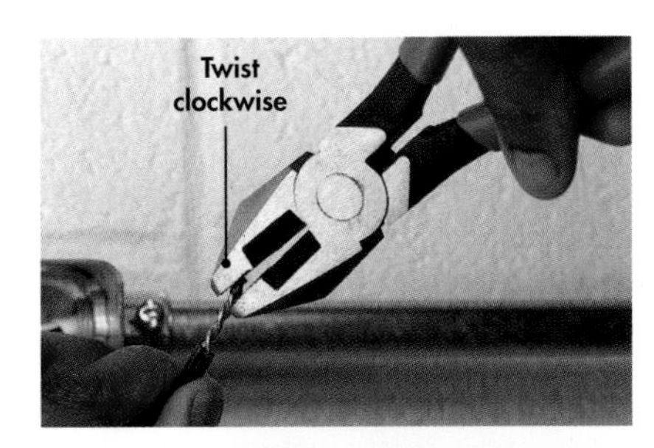

2 Twist wires together. Hold the stripped wires side by side. Grab both with lineman's pliers. Twist clockwise, making sure that both wires turn. Twist them together like a candy cane to form a neat-looking spiral. Don't overtwist; the wires may break.

Splicing three or four wires. When twisting three or four wires together, hold them parallel and twist them all at once with lineman's pliers.

3 Cut the end. Using the lineman's pliers or side-cutting pliers, snip off the end of the twist. Leave enough exposed metal so that the wire nut will just cover it—about ½ inch usually does it.

SAFETY ALERT
ALUMINUM WIRE

Connecting copper to aluminum wires causes corrosion and is both dangerous and against code unless you use special connectors.

4 Cap with a wire nut. Select a wire nut designed for the number and size of wires you have spliced (see page 366). Slip the nut on as far as it will go, then twist clockwise until tight. Test the connection by tugging on the nut; it should hold securely for dependable protection. Wrap electrician's tape around the bottom of the cap.

Attaching wire to a terminal

See page 588

Skill level:	Time to complete:	Materials:	Tools:
★★★☆☆	Experienced 1 min. Handy 3 min. Novice 7 min.	Wire, device with terminals	Long-nose pliers, side-cutting pliers, wire-bending screwdriver

Joining wire to a terminal is an important skill and a key step in most electrical projects. Do this step properly to ensure the device works and doesn't develop a short.

Making the right connection

Electricians wrap the wire nearly all the way around the screw to make a connection that is completely reliable; with some practice, you can make joints just as strong. Bend a wire in a quarter circle, slip it under the screw head, and tighten the screw.

Many devices come with terminal screws unscrewed. Screw in any unused terminal screws so they won't stick out dangerously, creating a shock hazard should the terminal touch a metal box.

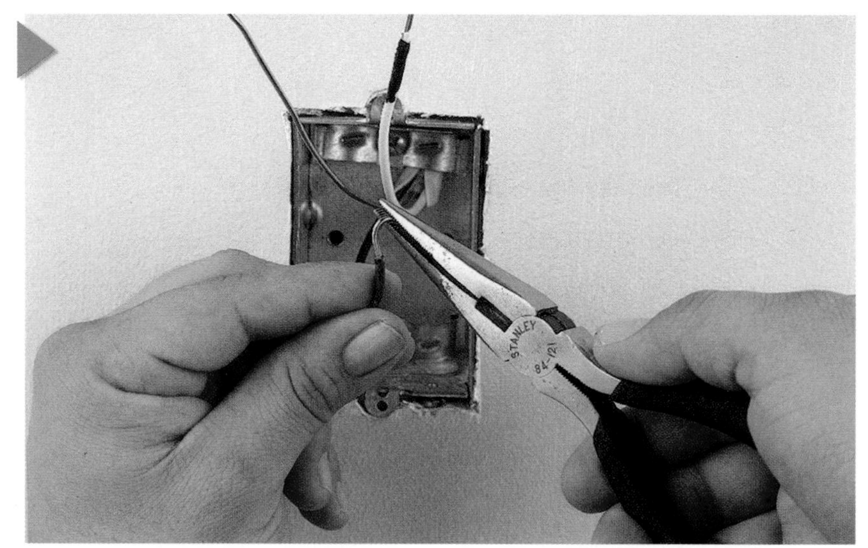

1 Start a loop. Check that the power is shut off. Strip about ¾ inch of insulation from a wire end. Using long-nose pliers or the tip of a combination stripper, grab the bare wire just above the insulation and bend it back at about a 45-degree angle. Move the pliers up about ¼ inch beyond the insulation and bend again in the opposite direction, about 90 degrees.

WORK SMART

USING PIGTAILS

Codes prohibit attaching two wires to one terminal on a switch or receptacle. If you need to attach two wires to one terminal, use a pigtail splice. Cut a wire 6 inches long and strip both ends. Splice the two original wires to one end of the pigtail and join the pigtail to the terminal.

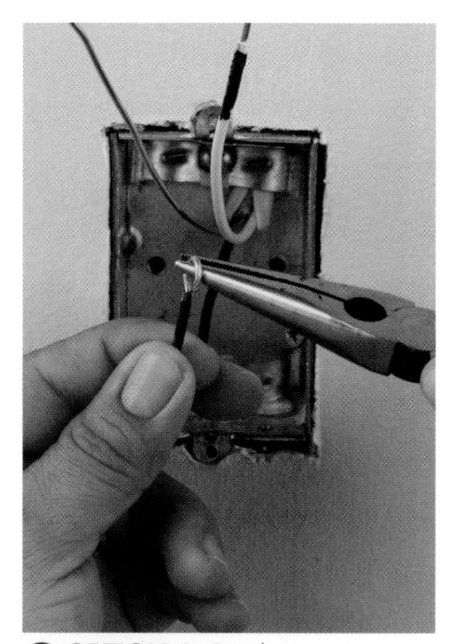

2 OPTION A: Bend a question mark. Use long-nose pliers to form a near loop with an opening just wide enough to slip over the threads of a terminal screw. Move the pliers another ¼ inch away from the insulation and bend the wire again to form a shape that looks like a question mark.

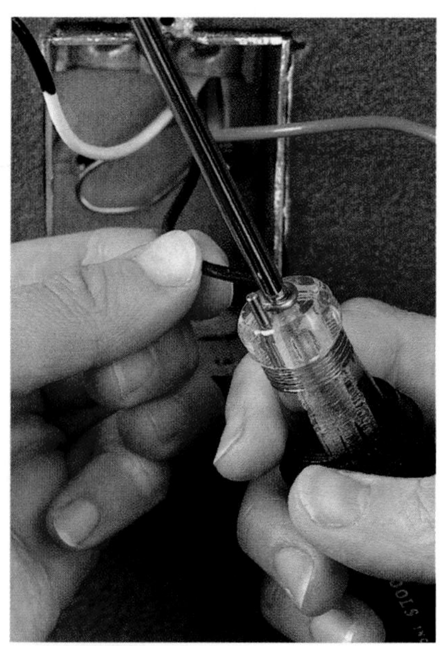

OPTION B: Use a wire-bending screwdriver. This tool makes perfect hooks every time. Just push the stripped wire between the screwdriver shaft and the stud at the base of the handle. Twist the screwdriver handle to make a perfect loop.

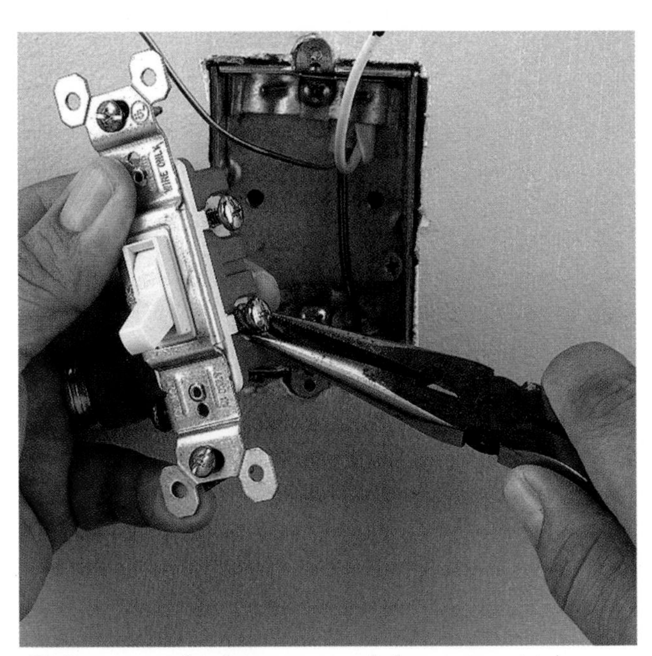

3 Squeeze the loop around the screw. Make sure the terminal screw is unscrewed enough to become hard to turn. Slip the loop over the screw threads, with the loop running clockwise. Use long-nose pliers or a combination stripper to squeeze the loop around the terminal, then tighten the screw.

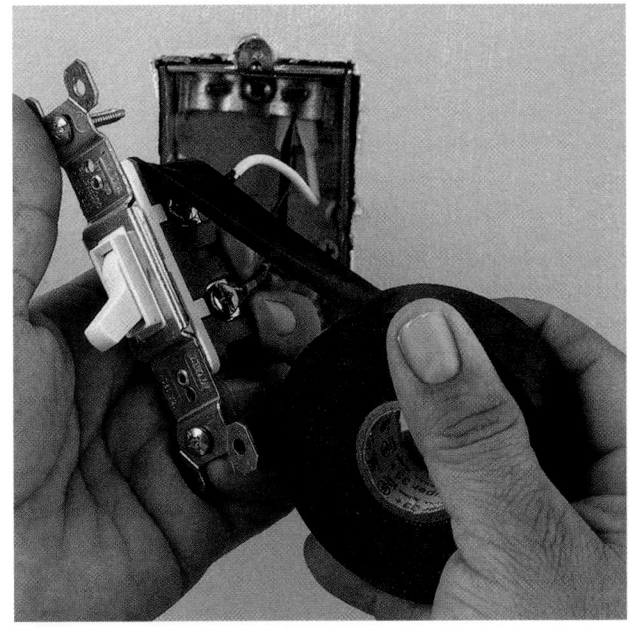

4 Wrap with tape. After all the wires are connected to a switch or receptacle, wrap electrician's tape around the body of the device to cover the screw heads and any exposed wires. The tape ensures that the wires stay attached and keeps the terminals from touching the box and risking a short circuit.

SAFETY ALERT

SKIP THE PUSH-IN OPTION

Many receptacles and switches have holes in the back for easy connection of wires. Once you've stripped the insulation (a strip gauge shows you how much), you poke the wire in. To remove a wire, insert a small screwdriver into a nearby slot. The wire releases.

The system works, but the resulting electrical connection is not as secure as a connection made using a terminal screw. Most professionals don't trust this method even though it saves time. Take the extra minute to do it right.

BUYER'S GUIDE

GET THE GOOD ELECTRICIAN'S TAPE

The inexpensive electrician's tape often found in large bins at a home center will do the job, but many electricians prefer to use professional-quality tape. It's thicker and has a better adhesive, which allows for a more secure and longer-lasting wrap.

Connecting to a 240-volt receptacle

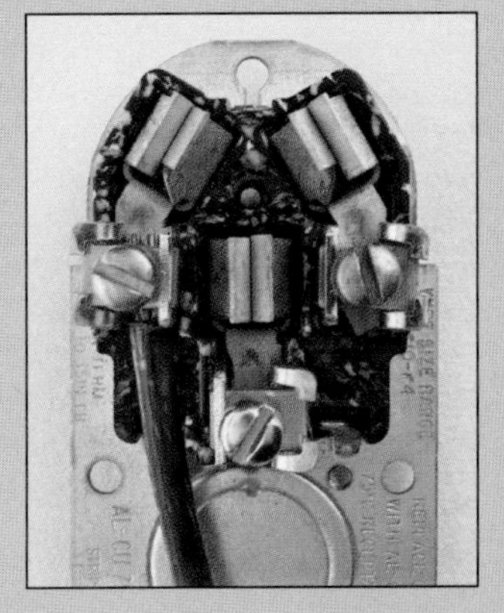

Be certain that power is shut off—there is a dangerous level of power here. Strip about ½ inch of insulation from the wire end. The wire should be straight, not looped. Loosen the setscrew, poke the wire into the hole beneath the screw, and tighten the screw.

Wiring receptacles and switches

See page 589

When you remove an electrical cover plate and pull out a switch or receptacle, you may find an arrangement involving a few wires going directly to the device. Or you may find a multicolored tangle of wires, some related to the switch or receptacle and some not. Here are some of the most common wiring configurations you'll find behind electrical cover plates.

Switches sharing a hot wire

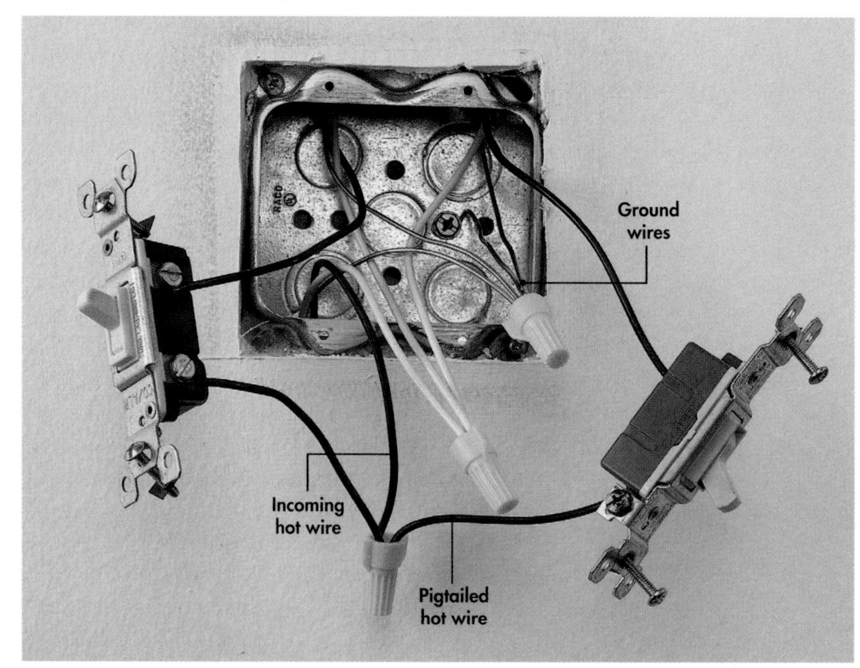

Switches that share a hot wire are on the same circuit. Two pigtails (see page 372) branch off from the incoming hot wire and connect to each switch. Another hot wire runs from each switch to a light. White wires are spliced.

A split receptacle

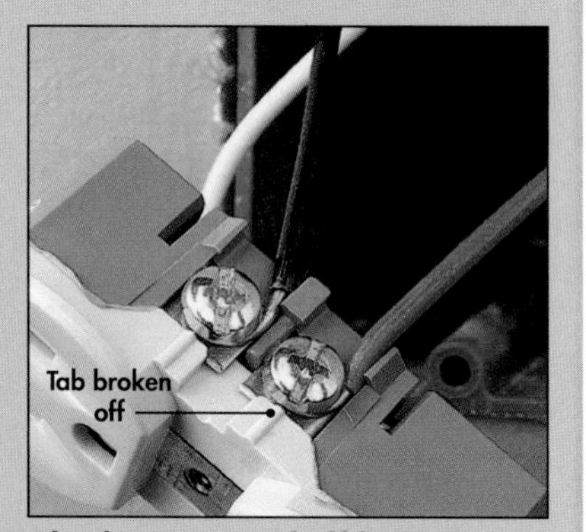

Also known as a half-hot receptacle, this is connected to two hot wires. The brass tab joining the brass terminals has been broken off. With the tab broken, each hot wire energizes one plug. Some split-circuit receptacles have each plug energized by a different circuit so that you can plug in two high-amperage appliances without the danger of tripping a breaker. Other circuits are wired so that half the receptacle is controlled by a wall switch while the other half is hot all the time.

Middle-of-the-run receptacle

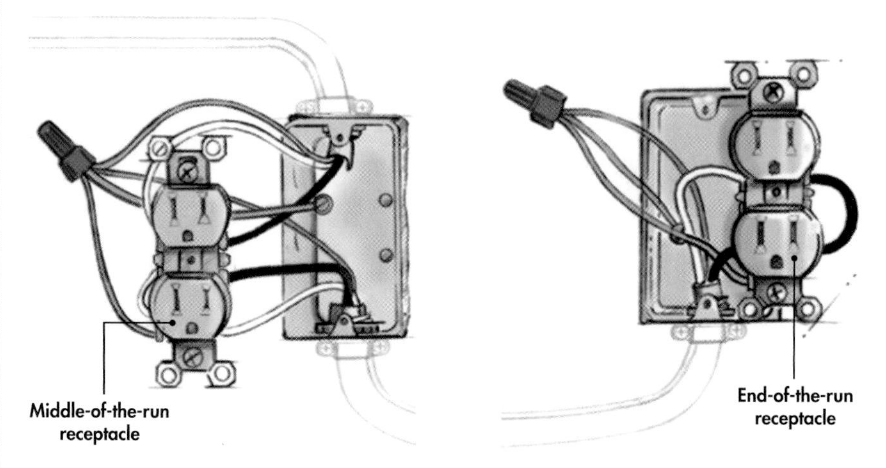

A receptacle with one cable that carries power into the receptacle and one that carries it to another device is called a middle-of-the-run receptacle.

Usually two black wires are connected to the brass terminals and two white wires to the silver terminals. Sometimes the blacks and the whites may be joined, with a pigtail at each splice.

Each pigtail is attached to the receptacle. If only one cable enters the box, the receptacle is at the end of the run. The black wire is attached to the brass terminal, the white wire is attached to the silver terminal, and the ground wire is attached to the receptacle.

Installing or replacing a receptacle

Skill level:	Time to complete:	Materials:	Tools:
★☆☆☆☆	Experienced 15 min. Handy 20 min. Novice 40 min.	New receptacle, wire nuts, electrician's tape	Screwdriver, lineman's pliers, long-nose pliers, side-cutting pliers, receptacle analyzer, combination stripper, level

ELECTRICAL

If a receptacle doesn't seem to work, first check that whatever is plugged into it works properly. Replace any receptacle that is cracked. Before buying a replacement receptacle, check the wiring. Usually the wires leading to a receptacle will be #14 and the circuit breaker or fuse will be 15 amps. In that case install a 15-amp receptacle. Install a 20-amp receptacle only if the wires are #12 and the circuit breaker or fuse is 20 amps or greater.

See page 588–589

1 Check that the power is off. Turn off power to the circuit. Test to confirm. If the tester shows current, check your service panel and turn off another likely circuit. Test again and proceed only if power is off. Remove the cover plate and unscrew the mounting screws. Being careful not to touch wires or terminals, pull out the receptacle.

2 Double check wires for power. In a damaged receptacle, wires may be hot even though testing shows no power. Touch tester probes to the top pair of terminals, then to the bottom pair (see page 370). If you have old wiring and both wires are black, use a receptacle analyzer to check that the neutral wire is connected to the silver terminal and the hot wire to the brass.

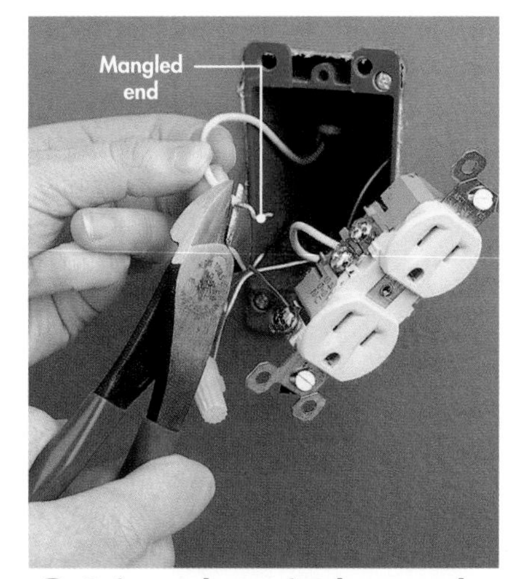

3 Snip and restrip damaged wire ends. Once you're sure the power is off, unscrew the terminals and pull away the wires, taking care not to twist them too much. If a wire end appears nicked or damaged or if it looks as though it has been twisted several times, snip off the end and restrip it (see page 371).

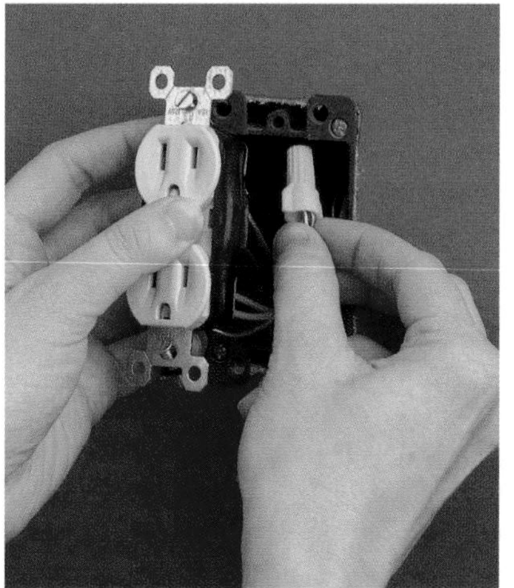

4 Install the receptacle. Wire the new receptacle as the old one was (each white wire connected to a silver terminal and each black or colored wire connected to a brass terminal). Wrap with electrician's tape to cover all terminals and bare wires (see page 373). Gently push the outlet into the box. Tighten the mounting screws and check that the receptacle is straight. Replace the cover plate, restore power, and test with a receptacle analyzer.

TOOL TIP

WIRE NUT TWISTERS

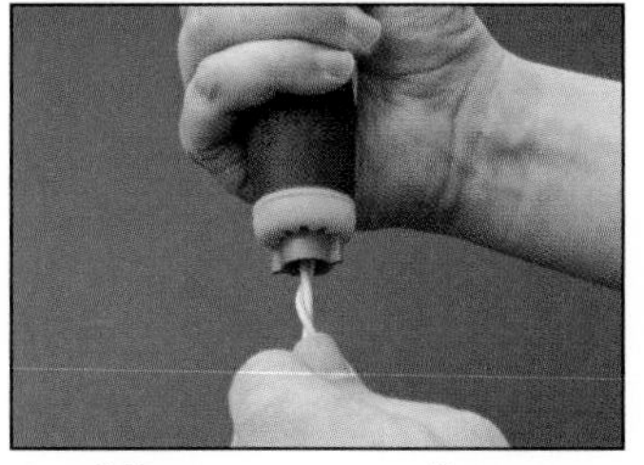

Got blisters on your fingers? That's apt to be a casualty of home electrical tasks, given all of the small and sharp objects involved in running wire and installing fixtures. For a bit of relief, try using a wire nut wrench to avoid having to twirl those knurled knobs over the ends of wires. You can buy a simple cone-shaped wrench that slips over the nut, or an electrician's screwdriver that has a wrench inset in the base of its handle.

Installing a GFCI receptacle

See page 588

Skill level:	**Time to complete:**	**Materials:** GFCI receptacle, wire nuts, electrician's tape	**Tools:** Screwdriver, lineman's pliers, side-cutting pliers, combination stripper
★☆☆☆☆	Experienced 20 min. Handy 35 min. Novice 45 min.		

A ground fault circuit interrupter (GFCI) protects you against the kind of shocks that occur around water. It compares the current coming into a circuit with the current leaving it. If the GFCI detects a difference between the two—as would be the case if power were traveling through your arm into the water in the sink—it immediately cuts off the power. GFCIs are required in bathrooms, along kitchen countertops, and for outdoor outlets. A GFCI outlet can protect up to four receptacles, switches, or lights on the same circuit. A GFCI circuit breaker can protect an entire circuit. If your home has ungrounded receptacles (see page 369), installing GFCIs will provide protection but won't ground your circuits.

Check your GFCIs at least once a month by pushing in the test button while the power is on. (The reset button should pop out. Push it back in.) A GFCI may provide power even though it has lost its ability to protect.

Don't use a GFCI as a receptacle for a refrigerator, freezer, or any other appliance that must stay on all the time; the device may trip off without your knowing. Also do not attempt to control a GFCI with a switch.

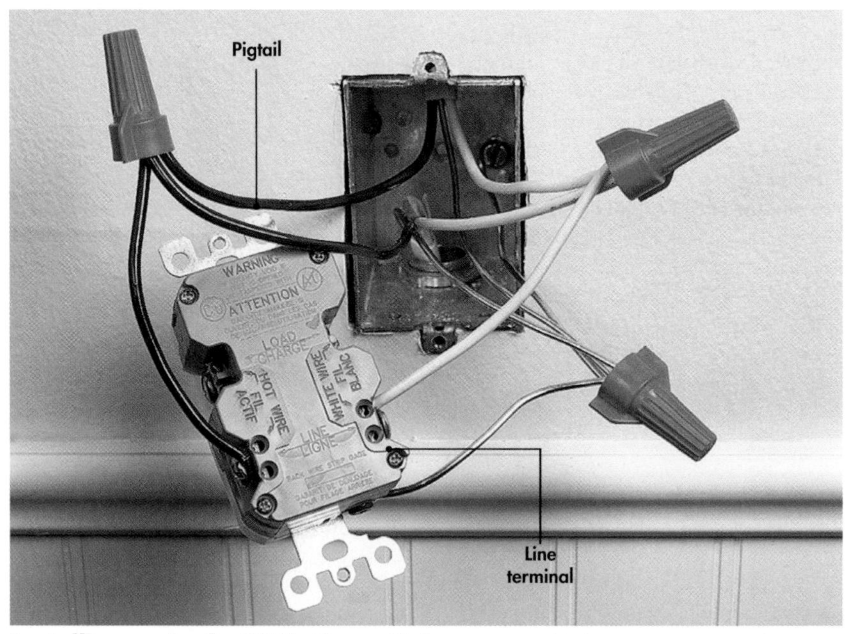

Installing a single GFCI. Shut off the power. Make connections only to the line terminals. For an end-of-the-run box, connect the wires to the terminals. If the box is middle-of-the-run (shown), for each connection, make a pigtail by stripping either end of a 6-inch-long wire. Splice each pigtail to the wire(s) with a wire nut, then connect it to the GFCI terminals. Put the white wire on the silver terminal and the black or colored wire on the brass terminal.

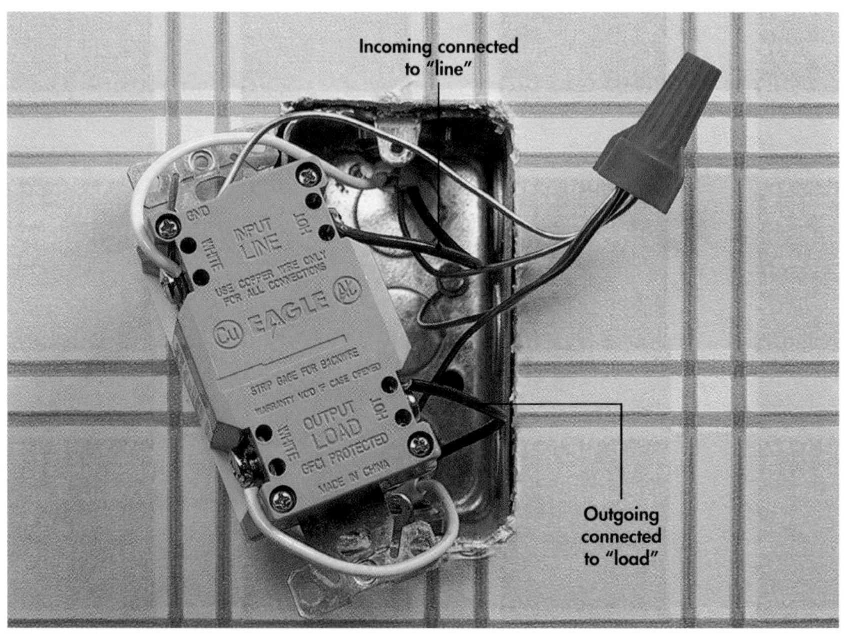

Protecting other outlets. Shut off the power. Connect the wires carrying power into the box to the line terminals marked on the outlet. Then connect the wires leading out of the box (to other receptacles or lights) to the load terminals marked on the outlet. If you're unsure which wires come from the service panel, pull the wires out of the box and position them so they will not touch each other, restore power, and use a tester to see which pair of wires is hot; connect these to the line terminals.

$ BUYER'S GUIDE

EXTEND A GFCI BOX

A bulky GFCI can dangerously crowd a box. Buy a box designed for raceway wiring and two 2-inch-long 6/32 screws. Fasten the screws through the GFCI and raceway box and into the box.

Installing an outdoor receptacle

Skill level:	Time to complete:	Materials:	Tools:
★★★☆☆	Experienced 3 hrs. Handy 5 hrs. Novice 8 hrs.	Rectangular metal watertight box, matching conduit nipple, conduit bushing, cover gasket, cover, GFCI, 12-2 NM cable, cable staples, silicone caulk	Drill, screwdriver, caulking gun, hammer

These days houses are built with at least two outdoor outlets. If your house doesn't have them, you may want to add some.

The sturdiest and simplest way to add an outlet is to screw a box built for outdoor exposure to the side of your house, put a receptacle in it, and put on a waterproof cover built to match the box.

You will, of course, need to install an outlet and run cable. To meet code, the outlet must be a GFCI outlet, which will keep any accidental shorts from running through the nearest human and into the ground. The best and easiest way to get cable to the GFCI is to drill through the rim joist, as shown. Power for the cable can either come from an existing circuit (see page 362), or by adding a new one to the breaker box, as shown on page 396.

To keep things watertight, make sure you caulk thoroughly, as described below, and install a gasket between the lid and the box. You also need to install a conduit bushing wherever cable leaves the conduit to protect the cable from fraying on rough edges.

1 Choose the spot for the outlet from outside the house, and measure how far it is from a basement window, exterior cellar entrance, spigot, or other feature visible from inside the basement. Inside the house, measure and mark the spot on the rim joist, moving as necessary to avoid obstructions. Drill a hole slightly larger than the conduit nipple through the rim joist and through the siding. If the exterior of the house is brick, change to a carbide masonry bit once you hit brick. If it's siding, drill through the entire hole with a spade bit. (See Step 2.)

2 Begin installing the box. On wood siding, you'll need to make the surface behind the box flat by building it up. Do this by cutting a short piece of siding and putting it upside down over the existing siding as shown. Screw the buildup to the siding (see inset). Attach the nipple into the receptacle box and slide it through the hole. Caulk around the nipple just before you push the box all the way in.

3 Screw the box to the wall. From inside the house, put a conduit bushing on the nipple. Run cable from the fuse or breaker box, or from an existing outlet or junction box. Strip off about a hand's length of the outer jacket, and feed the wires through the nipple. Use cable staples designed for electrical work to secure the cable to the framing every 4 feet and within 1 foot of the nipple. (These staples are driven with a hammer, not a staple gun.) Install a GFCI following the directions on the box. Put a gasket over the box, and screw the cover in place (see inset).

Adding a wall switch for a ceiling fixture

Skill level:	Time to complete:	Materials:	Tools:
★★★☆☆	Experienced 2 hrs. Handy 4 hrs. Novice 6 hrs.	Cable and clamps, remodeling box, staples, receptacle, wire nuts, nailing plates, electrician's tape	Drill, drywall saw or saber saw, fish tape, screwdriver, lineman's pliers, strippers

You can easily add a wall switch to a ceiling fixture currently controlled by a pull chain. The biggest challenge is planning the route and running cable from the fixture to the position for the new switch on the wall. If the wall is heavily insulated, push conduit through the insulation, and then feed wires or cable through the conduit.

See page 588

1 Run cable. Shut off power to the circuit supplying the fixture. Plan a cable pathway that crosses as few studs or joists as possible. You may have to cut an access hole to run cable through framing (see page 383).

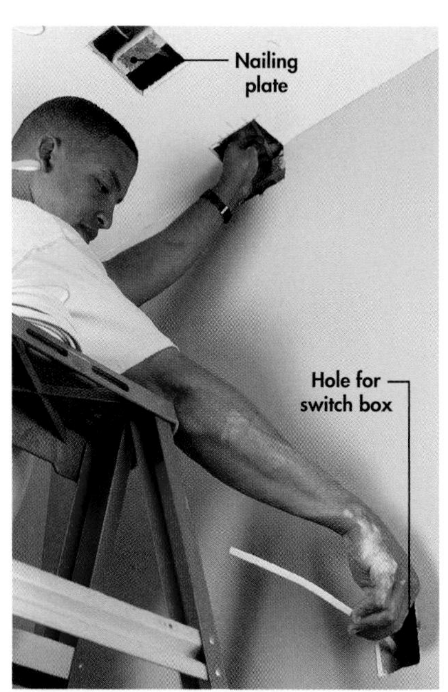

2 Run cable to the switch box. Add nailing plates where you bore holes in framing. Cut a hole for a remodel switch box and pull the cable through. Strip the wires.

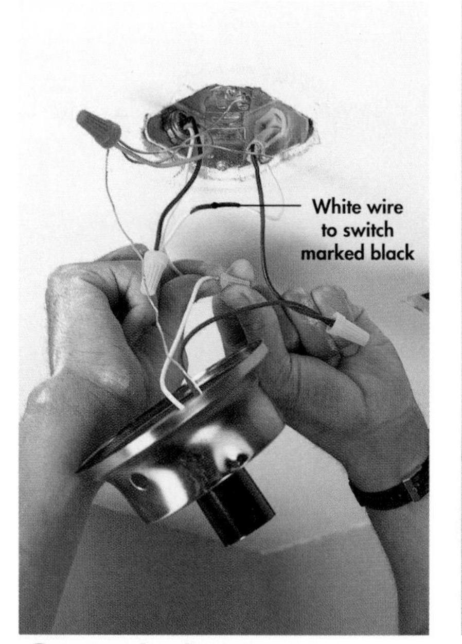

3 Wire the fixture. Connect the ground (see page 369). Remove the black wire from the fixture lead, splice it to the new white wire to the switch, and mark it black. Splice the new black wire to the fixture's black lead.

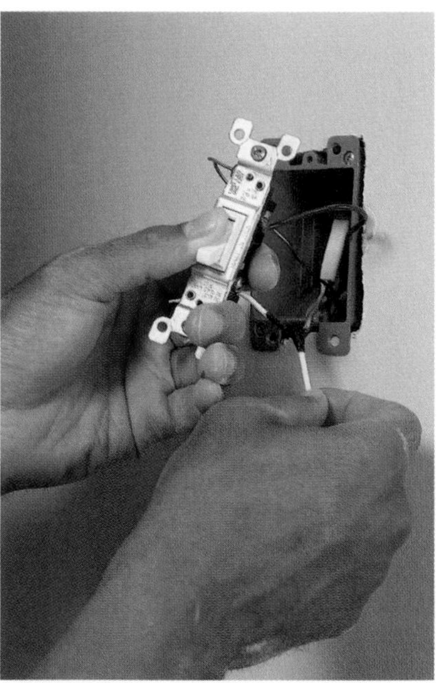

4 Connect the ground at the switch. Attach both wires to the terminals and mark the white wire black. Restore power to the circuit and test. Repair the access hole in the drywall.

Controlling a single outlet with a switch

Skill level:	Time to complete:	Materials:	Tools:
★★★☆☆	Experienced 1.5 hrs. Handy 2.5 hrs. Novice 4 hrs.	Cable and clamps, remodeling box, staples, switch, wire nuts, electrician's tape	Drill, saw, fish tape, screwdriver, long-nose pliers, combination stripper

ELECTRICAL

When you assign one outlet of a duplex receptacle to a wall switch, you can control a floor or table lamp from a doorway. The second outlet will remain hot at all times and be available for general use.

See page 589

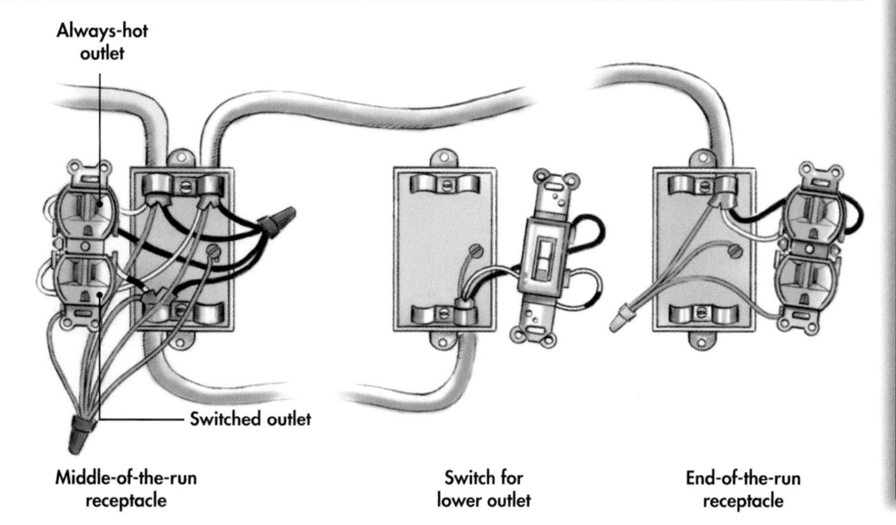

Working with a receptacle in the middle of a run. **Shut off power.** This project will be complicated if the receptacle you want to switch has wires attached to all four terminals. At the receptacle to be switched, remove both old black wires. Splice them with the new white wire and a black pigtail. Connect the pigtail to the always-hot outlet and the new black wire to the switched outlet. Wire the switch and connect the grounds.

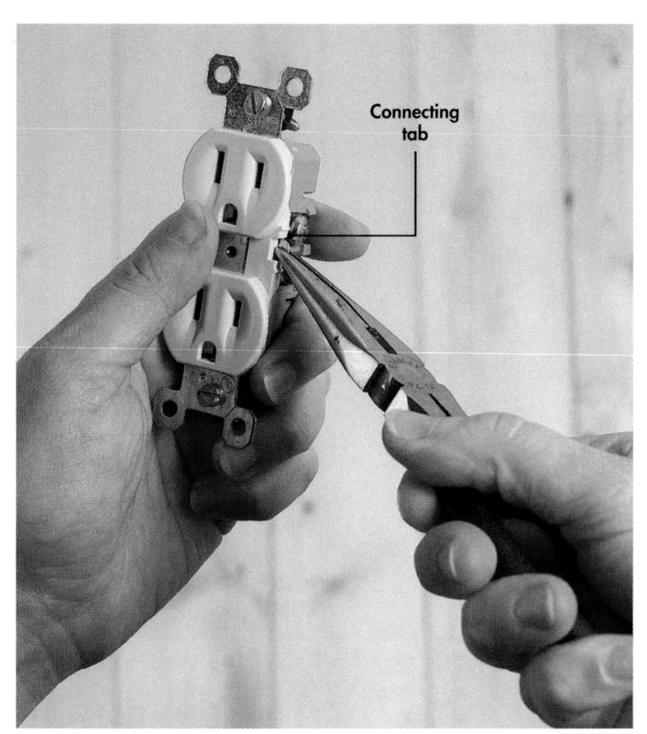

Making outlets operate separately. **Shut off power.** In order to make the two outlets of a receptacle operate separately, grasp the connecting tab between the two brass terminals with a pair of long-nose pliers. Bend the tab back and forth until it breaks off.

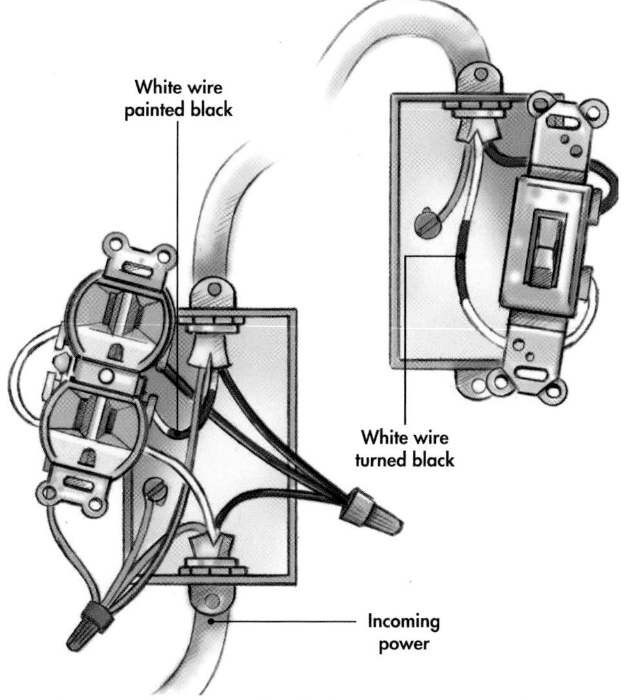

Working with an end-of-the-run receptacle. **Shut off power.** Run two-wire cable from the switch to the receptacle. Paint both ends of the white wires black. Connect the grounds. At the receptacle, remove the old black wire and splice it to the new white wire (marked black) and a black pigtail. Connect the pigtail to the always-hot terminal and the other black wire to the other terminal. Attach both wires to the switch.

Replacing a three-way switch

See page 589

Skill level:	Time to complete:	Materials:	Tools:
★☆☆☆☆	Experienced 10 min. Handy 20 min. Novice 30 min.	Three-way switch, electrician's tape, masking tape	Tester, screwdriver, combination strippers, long-nose pliers, lineman's pliers

Three-way switches work in pairs to control a light from two locations—handy for controlling a light from the top and the bottom of a stairway or from either end of a hallway. The toggle isn't marked OFF and ON. Either up or down can be ON depending on the position of the toggle of the other three-way.

Before you begin, shut off power to the circuit. Use pieces of tape to label each wire as you detach it from the old switch. At each switch, one of the wires goes to the common terminal, which is darker than the other terminals. The other two wires, called travelers, go to the lighter terminals. Restrip any damaged wires (see page 371). Most of the steps for replacing a three-way switch are the same as for a single-pole switch, but with three-ways you must know which wire is which.

You can also control a circuit with three switches, but the wiring can be confusing. Consider hiring a professional electrician.

1 Tag the common wire. Shut off power, remove the cover plate, and **test to make sure there is no power in the box.** Label the common wire with a piece of masking tape. The common terminal (see "Switches," page 367) is colored differently from the others (it's not the green ground screw) and may be marked "common" on the switch body.

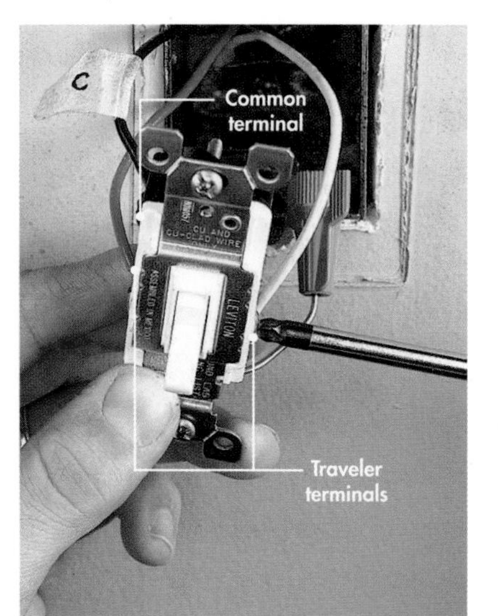

2 Option A: Wiring one cable. When only one cable enters the box, it will have three wires plus a ground. Identify the hot wire using a voltage detector (see page 370) or by touching one prong of a voltage tester to a ground and the other to each wire in turn. Attach the hot wire to the common terminal, which is a different color. Attach the other two wires to the traveler terminals. Connect the grounds.

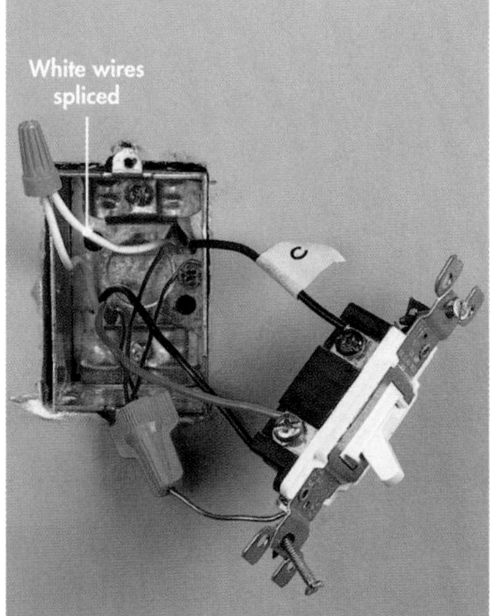

Option B: Wiring two cables. If two cables enter the box, one cable will have two wires plus ground and the other will have three wires plus ground. Despite all the extra wires, you'll find only three wire ends. Proceed just as you would for a one-cable installation (left).

$ BUYER'S GUIDE

THREE-WAY DIMMER

If you want two dimmers on a three- way circuit, make sure you get special multilocation dimmers. Standard three-way dimmers can replace one but not both of the switches in a three-way circuit. (Fluorescent fixtures also require special dimmers.)

Replacing a dimmer switch

See page 588

Skill level:	Time to complete:	Materials:	Tools:
★☆☆☆☆	Experienced 15 min. Handy 25 min. Novice 45 min.	Dimmer switch, wire nuts, electrician's tape	Screwdriver, side-cutting pliers, strippers

ELECTRICAL

Make sure the new dimmer switch is rated for the total wattage of the fixture. A chandelier with eight 100-watt bulbs is too much for a 600-watt dimmer to handle. Don't use a standard dimmer for a fan or you will burn out the motor. Install no more than one three-way dimmer per receptacle; the other switch must be a three-way toggle. You can buy rotary dimmers (the least expensive), dimmers that look like standard switches (the toggle can be placed anywhere between on and off position), or rotary models with their own included ON-OFF switch so the dimmer will turn on at the level of your choice.

1 Remove the dimmer knob. Shut off power at the service panel. Pull off the rotary knob with firm outward pressure. Underneath is a standard switchplate. Remove it. Remove the mounting screws and carefully pull out the switch body.

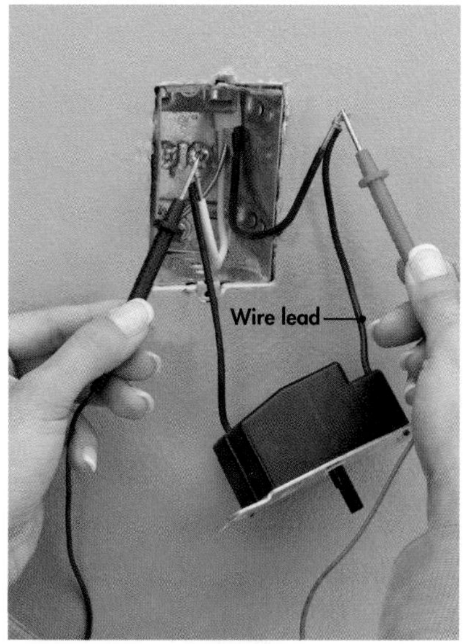

2 Test for power. A dimmer has wire leads instead of terminals. **Test for power** by slipping the probes of the tester against the base of the wire nuts. **If power is detected, shut off the correct circuit in the service panel.** (To test for continuity, see page 370.)

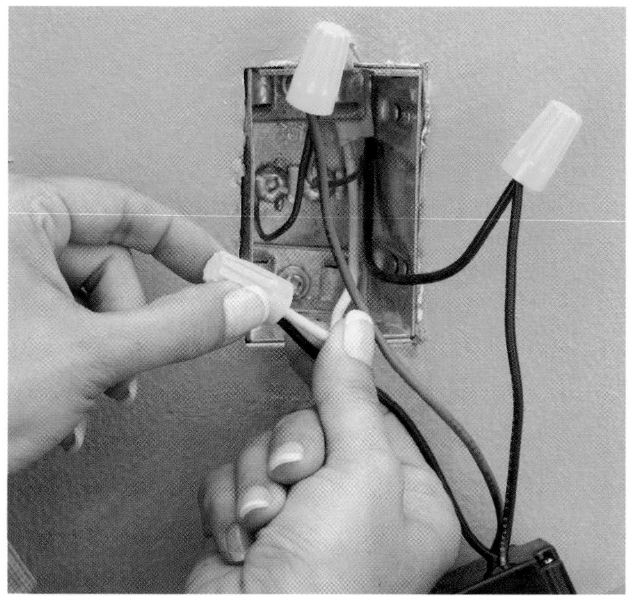

3 Option A: Installing a standard dimmer. Attach the ground wire if there is one. Strip ¾ inch of insulation from each solid house wire and 1 inch from each stranded dimmer lead. Wrap a lead around a wire with your fingers so that the lead protrudes past the wire about ⅛ inch. Slip on a wire nut and twist until tight. Test the strength of the connection by gently tugging on both wires.

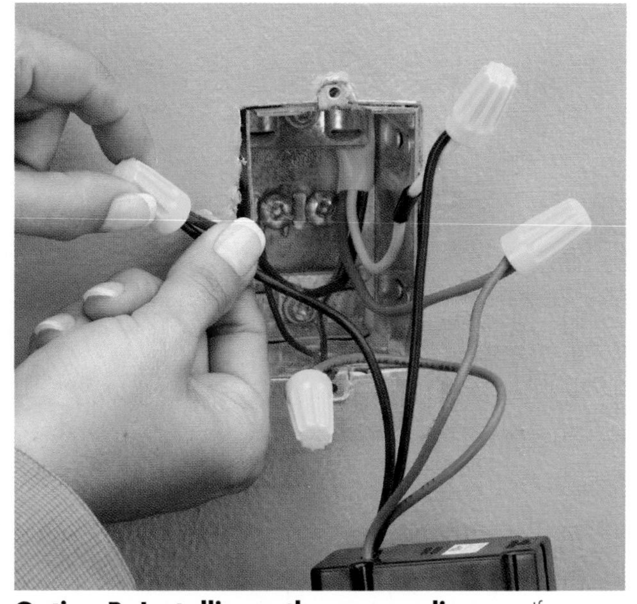

Option B: Installing a three-way dimmer. If you replace a three-way dimmer, tag the existing lead wires to connect the new dimmer in the same way as the old one. If only one cable enters the box, attach the black wire to the common terminal and the other two wires to the traveler terminals. If you replace a three-way toggle switch with a dimmer, tag the wire that leads to the common terminal. The other two wires are interchangeable.

Choosing electrical boxes

See page 588-590

All electrical connections must be contained inside a metal or plastic box that complies with local codes. And all boxes, including junction boxes, must be accessible. Never cover a box with drywall or paneling.

Electrical codes specify the number and size of wires that each box can accommodate because crowding wires in a box is a potential hazard. Check codes carefully and, to be safe, install larger boxes than you need now so you have the option to upgrade. Compared to metal boxes, plastic boxes are easily damaged and should only be installed in a wall. Use metal boxes in exposed locations. Inspectors generally expect to see ¼-inch or more of wire sheathing inside the box.

Metal boxes

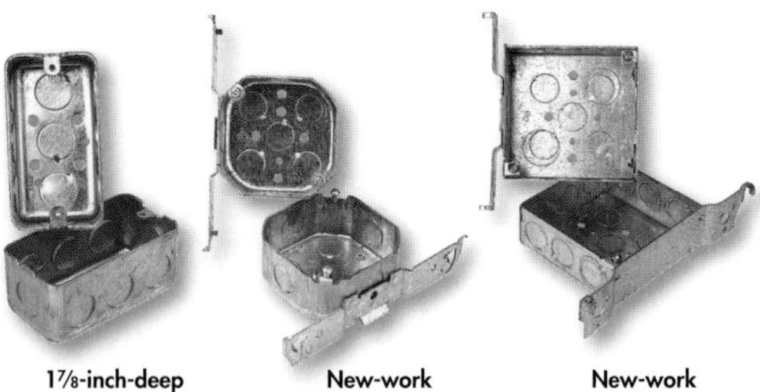

1⅞-inch-deep handy box

New-work octagonal box

New-work switch box

Tile mud ring

3½-inch gangable switch box

Plastic boxes

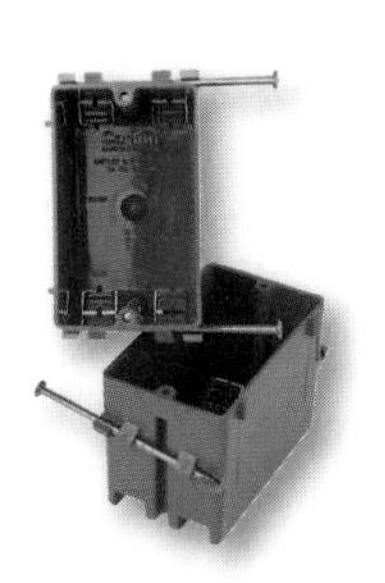

1-gang box

2- and 3-gang boxes

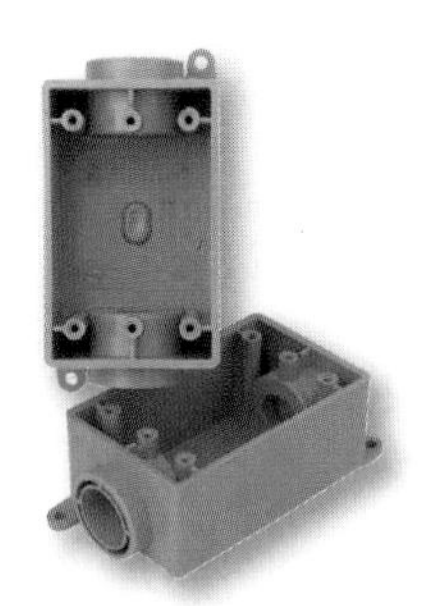

PVC outdoor box

Remodel box with ears

Ceiling remodel box

Installing electrical boxes

Installing electrical boxes is easy in new construction because the walls aren't in the way. You have more variables when working with existing walls. Self-attaching remodeling boxes make the job easier. All you have to do is cut a hole, run the cable, clamp the cable to the box, and install it in the wall.

Use a stud finder to make sure you won't hit a stud, joist, wiring, or anything else hiding in the wall.

Lay out the hole by tracing around the box, or ask the store for the layout template. (The templates are shipped with the electrical boxes but usually get separated from them by the time they reach the store shelf.)

Cut the hole carefully. The box should fit into the hole snugly, but not so tightly that you have to force it. If the hole is too wide, the box may not effectively attach to the drywall or plaster.

▲ *In new construction attach all the boxes to the studs before running cable. Receptacle boxes are usually placed 12 inches above the floor, and switch boxes 45 inches above the floor. Hold a nail-on box with its front edge positioned out from the stud the thickness of the drywall, and nail it in place.*

$ BUYERS GUIDE

SIZING ELECTRICAL BOXES

It's unsafe and violates code to cram too many wires into an electrical box. You can find the proper box size with a bit of math. Add the following:

1 for each hot and neutral wire
1 for all ground wires (not for ea.)
1 for all cable clamps (not for ea.)
2 for each switch or outlet

To get the minimum box size in cubic inches, multiply the total for 14-gauge wire by 2 and for 12-gauge wire by 2.25. Add these two numbers together. Plastic boxes are labeled with their volume, and you can look up the volume for steel boxes in the electrical code.

Installing remodeling boxes

Skill level:	Time to complete:	Materials:	Tools:
★☆☆☆☆	Experienced 20 min. Handy 45 min. Novice 1 hr.	Remodeling (old-work) box, screws	Electronic stud finder, utility knife, drywall saw, saber saw or rotary cutter, screwdriver, drill

Remodeling (or cut-in) boxes are made to be installed in a finished wall. The first step is to cut a hole in the wall for the box. You have three options, depending on whether the wall is drywall or plaster. Installation for different types of remodeling boxes follows on page 384.

When making a hole in the wall for a remodeling box, you need a fairly snug fit so that the mounting flanges on the box will overlap the wall. You can hold the box up to the wall and trace its outline, but if your weekend project involves installing a few boxes, take the time to make a template out of lightweight cardboard or tagboard. Trace around a box and cut out the shape.

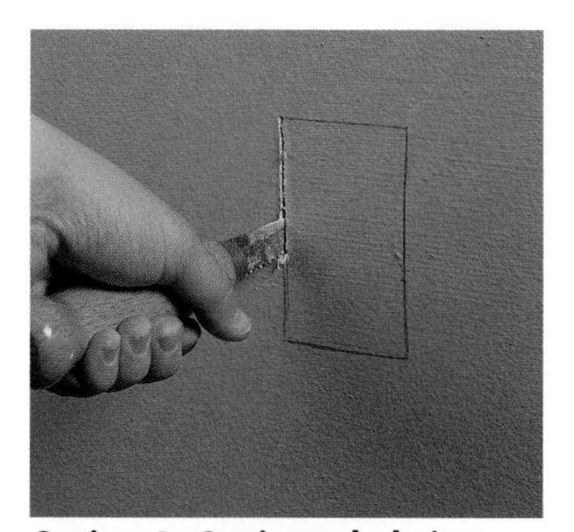

Option A. Cutting a hole in drywall. Use a pencil to mark the location of the hole (check for studs) and score the paper surface with a utility knife. Cut along the inside of the knife-cut with a drywall saw. The resulting hole will be free of ragged edges. You also can cut drywall with a spiral cutting tool or a saber saw.

Option B. Cutting a hole in plaster with a spiral cutting tool. Because of the high RPMs, this tool won't rattle lath or loosen plaster. Set the base on the wall and tip the blade away from the surface while you let it come to full speed. Then tilt the blade gently into the wall. Have extra blades on hand; they dull quickly on plaster.

Option C. Cutting a hole in plaster with a saber saw. Cutting through a lath and plaster wall is difficult and often results in cracked plaster. Drill holes at each corner and score the face of the plaster with a utility knife. Cut with a saber saw equipped with a fine-tooth blade. Press hard against the wall to reduce lath vibration.

CLOSER LOOK

FOUR WAYS TO ANCHOR NM CABLE TO A BOX

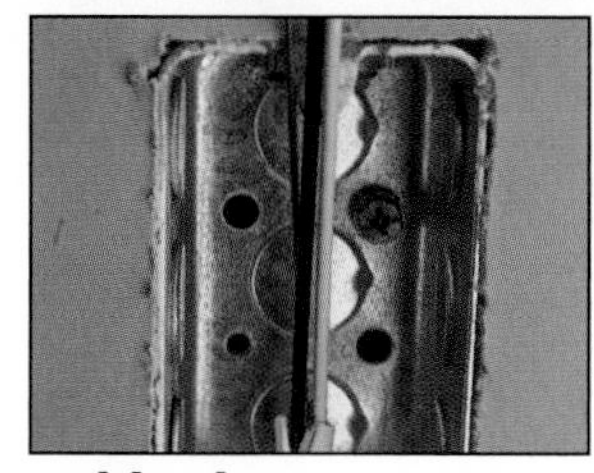

Cable clamp. Buy clamps made for NM cable. Remove the knockout. Screw the clamp to the cable, then slip it through the hole and screw on the locknut. Pinch the locknut by using a hammer to tap a screwdriver on it. Or attach it to the box first, slide the cable through the clamp, then tighten the screws.

Poke and staple. For many plastic boxes, to run cable you may need to push the cable past a plastic flap or knock out a plastic tab. Once you've inserted the cable into the box, staple the cable on a framing member within 8 inches of the box.

Built-in clamp. Plastic boxes large enough to hold more than one device have internal clamps, as do most remodel boxes. Tighten the clamp screw to firmly secure the cable.

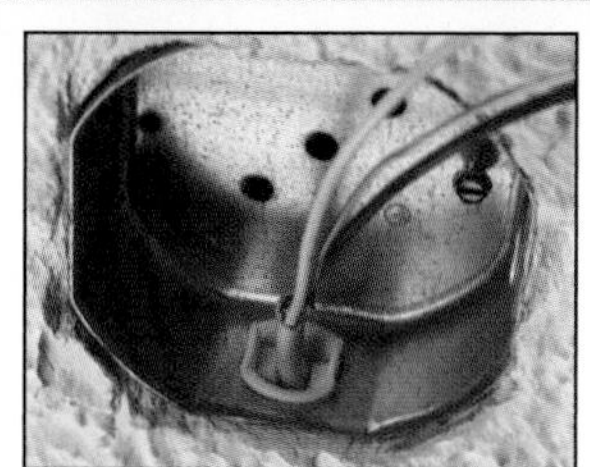

Pop-in plastic connector. Remove the knockout and push this connector in place. Then push the cable through; if accessible, staple the cable within 8 inches of the box.

Installing remodeling boxes (continued)

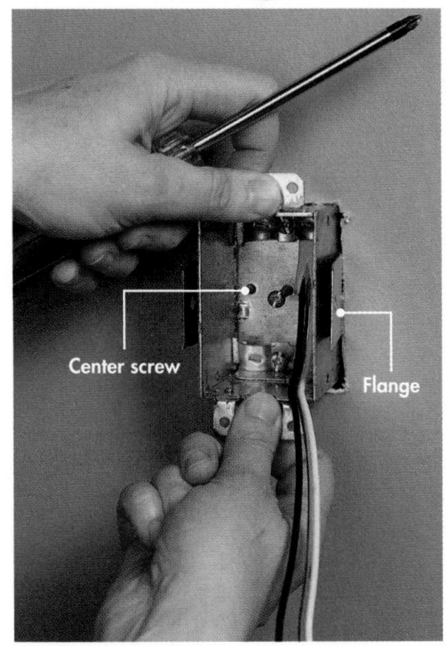

Installing a box with spring flanges. If you buy this kind of box, make sure both flanges spring out firmly from the box. Push the box into the hole until the flanges are free to spring outward. As you tighten the center screw, the flanges should move toward you until they fit snugly against the back of the drywall or plaster.

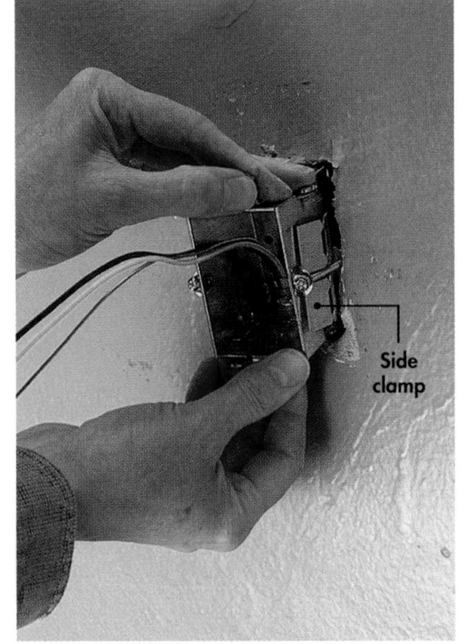

Installing a box with side clamps. After pushing the box into the hole, tighten the screw on each side. Each clamp extends behind the wall to hold the box in place.

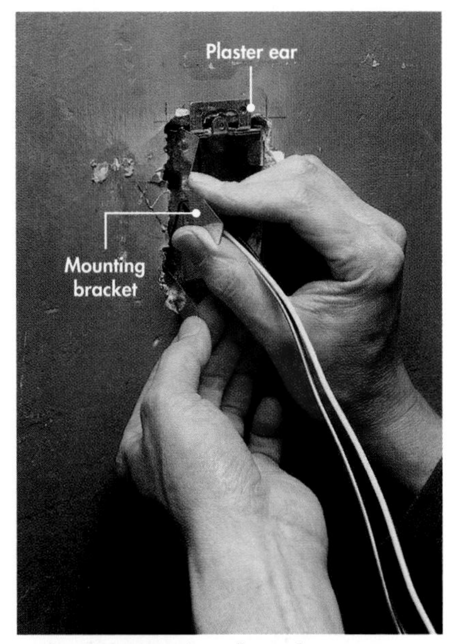

Using mounting brackets. Push a metal box with plaster ears into the hole. Slip a bracket in on each side, pushing it behind the wall's surface. Pull the bracket toward you until it's tight, push the box tightly against the wall, then fold the tabs into the box with your thumbs. Tighten the tabs with pliers.

CLOSER LOOK

INSTALLING METAL REMODELING BOXES

1 Adjust the plaster ears. Many metal boxes have adjustable ears. Cut the hole and chip out the plaster above and below so the ears will fit. Loosen the two screws and adjust each ear so the face of the box becomes flush with the wall surface. Tighten the screws.

2 Anchor the box to the lath. Lath cracks easily, so work carefully. Drill pilot holes, and drive short screws to anchor the ears to the lath. Expect to do some wall patching after using this method.

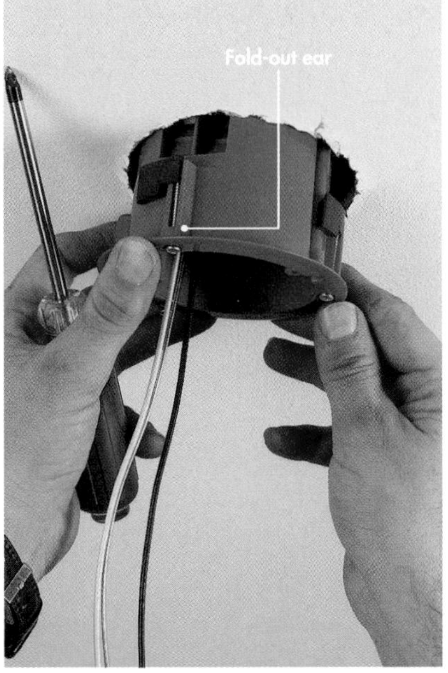

Installing a box with fold-out ears. These plastic remodeling boxes have ears that swing out behind the drywall or plaster. Push the box into the hole, then turn the screws clockwise until the ears clamp onto the back of the drywall or plaster. Switch boxes are also available with this same wall-grabbing mechanism.

Installing ceiling boxes

Skill level:	Time to complete:	Materials:	Tools:
★★★☆☆	Experienced 2 hrs. Handy 4 hrs. Novice 8 hrs.	Ceiling box, brace, 1¼-inch wood screws	Drywall saw, hammer, drill, screwdriver, reciprocating saw or metal-cutting keyhole saw, adjustable wrench

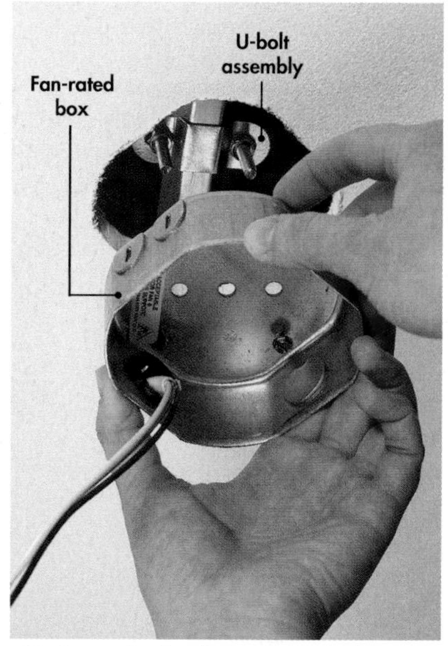

1 Slip in the brace. Assemble the box on the brace to understand how it goes together, then take it apart. Push the brace in through the hole and spread it apart until it touches the joists on both sides. The legs of the brace at each end should rest on top of the drywall or plaster.

2 Tighten the brace. Measure to make sure that the brace is centered in the hole. Position it on the joists at the correct height so that the box will be flush with the surface of the ceiling. Use an adjustable wrench or channel-type pliers to tighten the brace only until it is firm. Tightening beyond this point can cause the ceiling to crack.

3 Attach the box. Attach the U-bolt assembly to the brace so that the assembly is centered in the hole and the bolts face down. Thread cable through the cable connector and into the fan-rated box. Slip the box up so the bolts slide through it and tighten the nuts to secure the box.

WORK SMART

CEILING BOX HANGING OPTIONS

When framing is accessible, attach a ceiling box to a joist. Install this type of box in unfinished ceilings or ceilings with a large hole. Drill pilot holes and drive in 1¼-inch wood screws to attach it to joist.

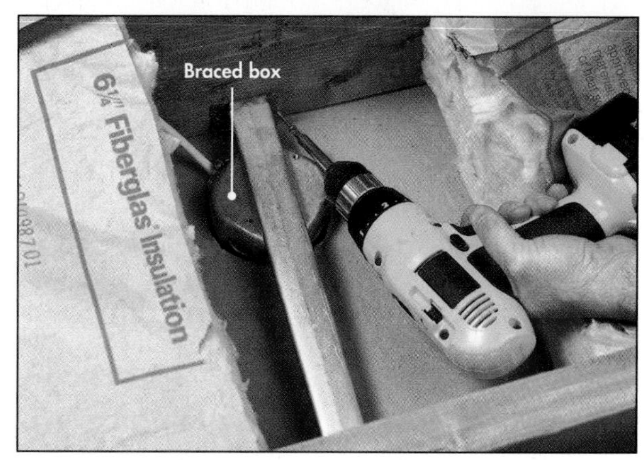

Install a braced box from above. Buy a new-work box with a brace. Slide the box along the brace to position it. Tighten the clamp. Attach the brace to the joist by driving in 1¼-inch wood screws.

Installing a junction box

See page 588

Skill level:	Time to complete:	Materials:	Tools:
★☆☆☆☆	Experienced 1 hr. Handy 2 hrs. Novice 3 hrs.	Junction box with cover, wire nuts, screws	Combination tool, lineman's pliers, screwdriver, drill, voltage tester

Install a junction box wherever wires must be spliced. Keep the box accessible—never bury it in a wall or ceiling. Junction boxes are usually flush-mounted to walls or attached to attic, basement, or crawlspace framing. But you can set one inside a wall as you would a switch box. Cover the junction box with a blank cover plate.

1 Attach the box. Shut off power to the wires that you will be splicing. Anchor the box with screws. To attach the box to a masonry surface, drill holes with a masonry bit. Drive masonry screws.

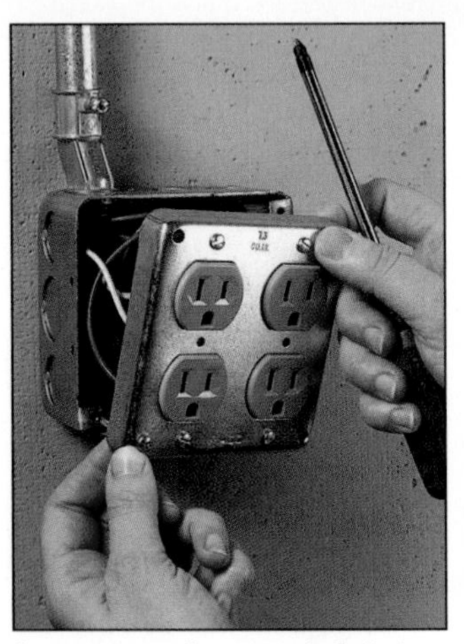

If a receptacle or switch is in an exposed box, use a metal rather than a plastic cover plate. You may need to break off the device's metal ears. Attach the device to the cover plate first and then attach the cover plate to the box.

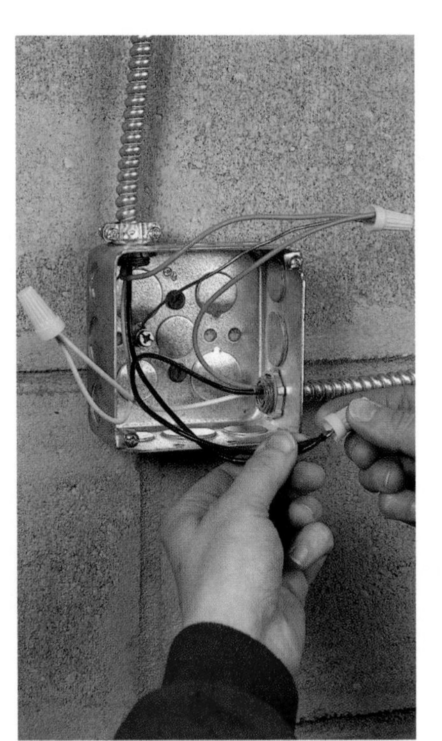

2 Wire the box. Strip cable sheathing and clamp the cable, or connect conduit. Strip wires and splice them with wire nuts. If the box is metal, make a grounding pigtail (see page 372) and connect it to the green grounding screw.

3 Cover the box. Fold the wires into the box and attach the cover plate. To do so, loosen the screws at two opposite corners of the box, hook the cover plate on one screw first and then the other; tighten the screws.

Installing NM cable in new walls

Skill level:	Time to complete:	Materials:	Tools:
★★★☆☆	Experienced 6 hrs. Handy 8 hrs. Novice 10 hrs.	NM or armored cable, electrical boxes, protective nailing plates, cable staples	Drill with ⅝-inch or ¾-inch bit, hammer, tape measure, level, long-nose pliers, utility knife, safety goggles

Nonmetallic (NM) cable is easy to cut and quick to install. Just be careful when you remove the sheathing so you don't accidentally slit the wire insulation. If you do, cut off the damaged wire and start again; otherwise you will get a short or a shock. Whenever possible, strip sheathing before cutting the cable to length. That way, if you make a mistake you can try again.

A typical cable rough-in
Run cable in a straight horizontal line, 1 foot above the receptacles (areas under windows are an exception) or according to local code. To keep cable out of the reach of nails, drill all holes in the center of studs and at least 1¼ inches up from the bottom of joists. Nail on protective nailing plates for extra safety. Even if you will only hang a light, install a ceiling fan box in case you choose to add a ceiling fan later.

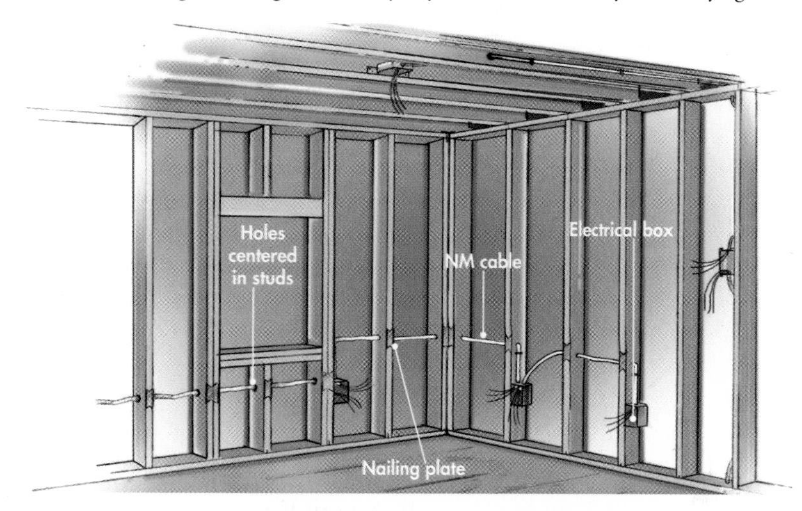

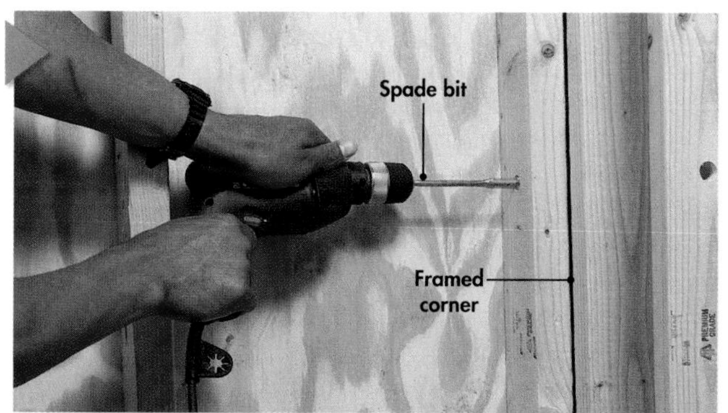

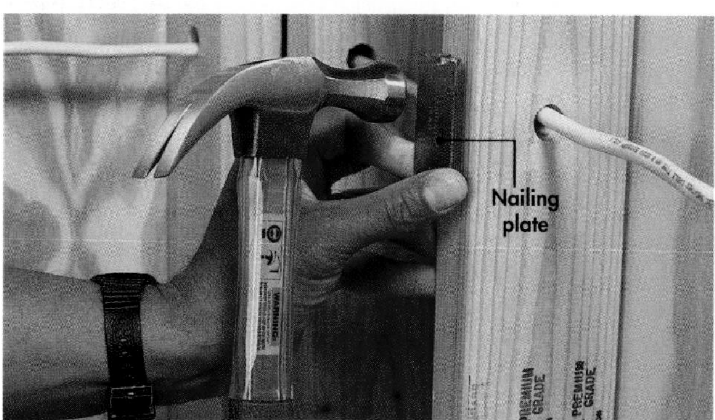

1 Drill the holes. Wherever possible, use a tape measure and level to mark studs and joists. Mark so holes will be in a straight horizontal line. Drill ⅝-inch holes for most NM cable and ¾-inch holes for three-wire cable or armored cable. A ⅜-inch drill works fine for small jobs, but give it a rest if it overheats.

Pull the cable. To avoid kinks, keep the cable straight and untwisted as you work. When possible pull the cable first and then cut it to length. If you must cut it first, allow plenty of extra length. Pull the cable fairly tight, but loose enough to have an inch or so of play between studs.

2 Protect the cable with nailing plates, which are inexpensive and quick to install. Be sure to nail one wherever the cable is within 1¼ inches of the front edge of a framing member. For added safety (and to satisfy some local codes), install nailing plates over every hole.

Staple the cable and run it into the boxes. Staple cable tightly wherever it runs along a joist so it is out of the reach of nails. Staple within 8 inches of a plastic box and within 12 inches of a metal box. See page 383 for clamping methods.

Working with NM cable

Skill level: ★☆☆☆☆

Time to complete: Experienced 5 min. Handy 10 min. Novice 15 min.

Materials: Nonmetallic (NM) cable

Tools: Knife, lineman's pliers, side-cutting pliers, cable ripper

ELECTRICAL

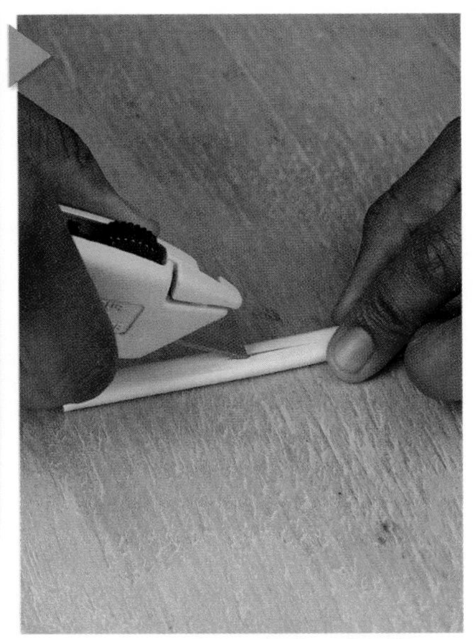

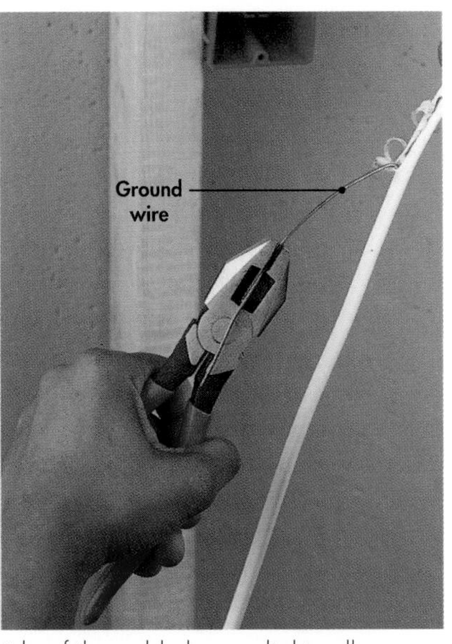

1 Slit the cable with a knife. One side of the cable has a slight valley. Insert the blade into the middle of the valley about 3 inches from the end so the blade just pierces the sheathing. Slit to the end of the cable. Be careful not to damage the ground or pierce the sheathing on the hot and neutral wires.

Pull the ground wire. Cut or pull back the sheathing so you can grab the green or bare ground wire with lineman's pliers. Hold the cable end in the other hand and pull back the ground wire until you have a 12-inch slit in the sheathing. Pull carefully so you don't break the ground wire.

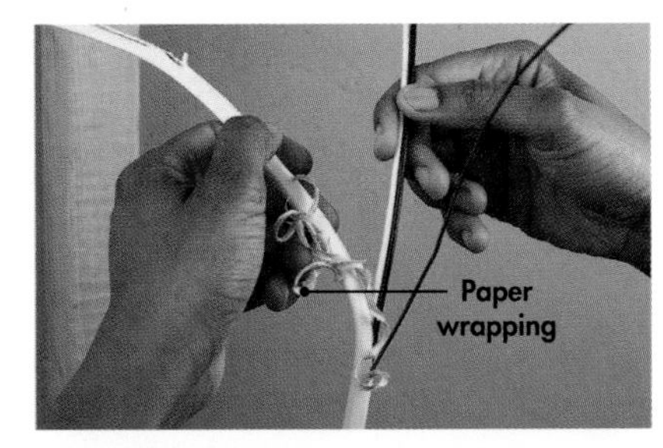

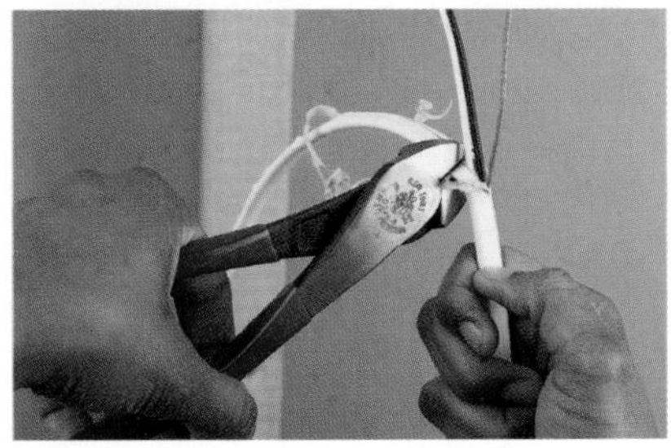

2 Remove the wrapping. Pull back the plastic sheathing. Peel back any protective paper wrapping or thin strips of plastic, and cut them off.

Snip the sheathing. Use side-cutting pliers, a combination stripper, or the cutting portion of lineman's pliers to cut the sheathing.

SAFETY ALERT

NEVER NOTCH

In a tight spot like this, you may be tempted to whip out the hammer and chisel and chop notches in the face of the studs so the cable runs easier. But the cable would then be dangerously exposed and severely bent at the corner. Instead drill slightly larger holes, bend the cable before poking it in, and grab it with long-nose pliers.

TOOL TIP

USING A CABLE RIPPER

Use this tool to strip cable that is already installed in a box. Practice on scrap cable first so you know how to make sure the ripper doesn't cut too deeply and damage wire insulation.

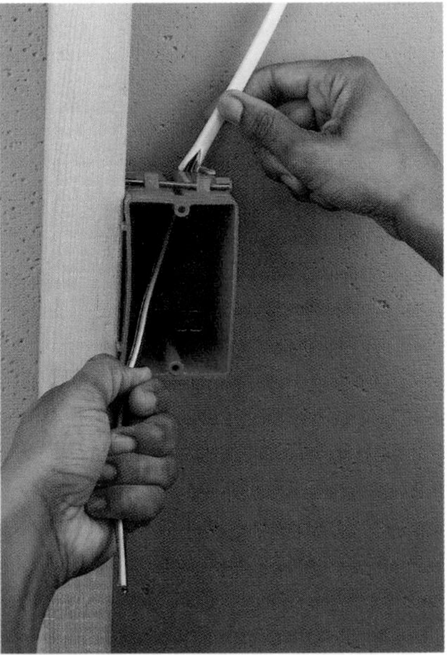

3 Pull the cable into the box. Push the wires through the clip or clamp on the box. Pull the cable into the box so at least ¼ inch of sheathing is inside. Clamp the cable to the box (see "Closer Look," page 383).

Fishing and running cable

Skill level:	Time to complete:	Materials:	Tools:
★★★☆☆	Experienced 6 hrs. Handy 10 hrs. Novice 14 hrs.	Cable, remodeling boxes	Electronic stud finder, drywall saw, saber saw, drill, hammer, screwdriver, fish tape, flat pry bar, safety goggles

You need the patience of a surgeon to run wiring through walls that are finished with drywall or plaster. At times you'll feel like grabbing a hammer and knocking big holes in the wall to get at that darned cable. But remember that wiring is more fun than patching and plastering, so any steps you can take to minimize wall or ceiling damage will pay off in the end.

Follow the easiest path

If you have an unfinished attic or a basement, run as much of the cable there as possible. If a basement or attic is finished, run armored cable instead of NM.

Use an electronic stud finder to locate joists and studs that may be in the way. You may be able to move a box a few inches to avoid an obstruction. Wherever possible, run cable parallel to studs or joists.

First cut holes for the boxes (see page 383), then run the cable. If you're running cable horizontally, guide it with a fish tape. If you're feeding it up or down, drop a small chain from the upper opening to the lower and use the chain as a fish tape.

If you plan to use power from an existing receptacle for your new service, make sure the circuit can handle the new load.

It may be easier to guide the snake if you drill a small inspection hole in the plate, next to the one you've made for the cable, then stick a flashlight into the wall opening for the receptacle you're aiming for. Use duct tape to keep the flashlight in place, if necessary. Another way to shed a little light on this darkest of home remodeling tasks is to use a set of luminescent fiberglass rods instead of traditional tape. The rods aren't inexpensive, but they can be easier to manipulate as well as allowing you to see where you're fishing.

Be sure to turn off power to circuits in the wall before using metal fish tape to avoid getting an electrical shock.

Running cable up, over, and down. If the attic is accessible, drill a hole through the top plate above the outlet you'll tap into and another above the new outlet. Drop a chain down through the hole above the new box and grab it through the opening you've cut for the box. Tape the cable to the chain and pull both up into the attic. Feed the cable over to the hole above the existing outlet. Drop a chain again and grab it through a small opening you've cut above the box. Install cable clamps, tape cable to the chain, and use the chain to pull cable from the attic into the box.

TOOL TIP

FISH TAPE

Flexible wire fish tape comes on reels and is essential for running cable in existing walls. Feed the tape through the wall from the junction box to the receptacle box. Then attach the wire to the tape and pull the wire through.

Fishing and running cable (continued)

Running cable through a floor

1 Work where the ceiling and wall meet. When there is no access from above or below, cut corner notches in the drywall or plaster, as shown. Drill a 1-inch hole up through the center of the top plate. Bend the cable, poke it up through the hole, and grab it from the other side.

2 Drill a locator hole. Remove the shoe molding below the box that you will be taking power from. Drill a ¼-inch hole through the floor directly below the box and tight up against the wall. Poke a scrap wire down through the hole. Using the wire as a reference point, measure over to the middle of the bottom plate of the wall above (approximately 1¾ inches) and drill a 1-inch hole up into the wall.

3 Feed the cable. Drop a chain through the hole you cut for the box and jiggle it until it falls through the hole you drilled. Tape the cable to the chain and pull the cable through the wall. Put a cable clamp in the box, feed the cable through it, and mount the box in the opening.

Running cable in finished walls

Running cable through a wall. Cut the hole for the remodel box (see page 382). Remove an existing receptacle and punch out a knockout in the back or bottom of its box. Run one fish tape through the existing box and one through the new hole. Hook them together. Pull tape back through the hole. Tape fish tape to cable, then pull cable from the hole to the box.

Running cable around a door. If you have a slab floor and no access to the ceiling, this may be your only option, but check to see if this is OK with local codes. Remove casing from around a door opening and run cable around the door. You may be able to slip the cable between the jamb and the stud. Or drill a hole and run the cable in the cavity on the side of the stud.

Running cable behind a baseboard. Use a flat pry bar to remove baseboard molding. With a drywall saw, cut a channel in the drywall at least 1 inch below the top of the baseboard. Drill holes through the centers of the studs and run cable through the holes. Protect all holes with nail plates.

Working with armored cable

Skill level:	Time to complete:	Materials:	Tools:
★☆☆☆☆	Experienced 5 min. Handy 10 min. Novice 15 min.	BX or MC cable, protective bushings	Side-cutting pliers, screwdriver, hammer, slip-joint pliers, armored cable cutter

Armored cable is the middle ground between NM and conduit. It is easier to install than conduit and less flexible than NM. It protects wires better than NM but not as well as conduit. There are two types of armored cable. BX cable has no ground wire; the sheathing itself providing the ground. MC cable has a green-insulated grounding wire and is often required by code. Some codes call for armored cable instead of NM. Others require NM or conduit where the cable is exposed. Run armored cable inside walls, and protect it from nails as you would NM cable.

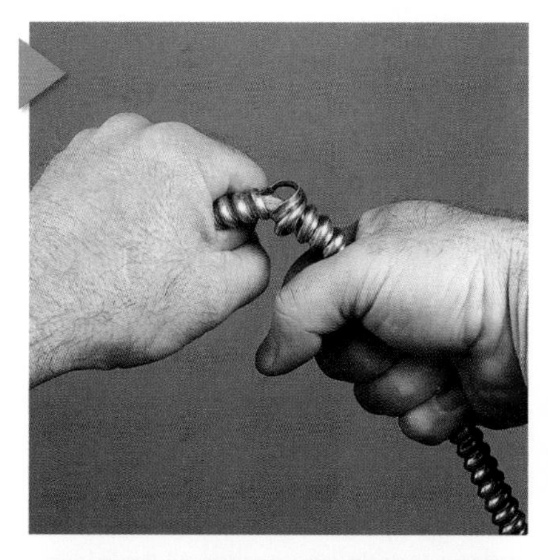

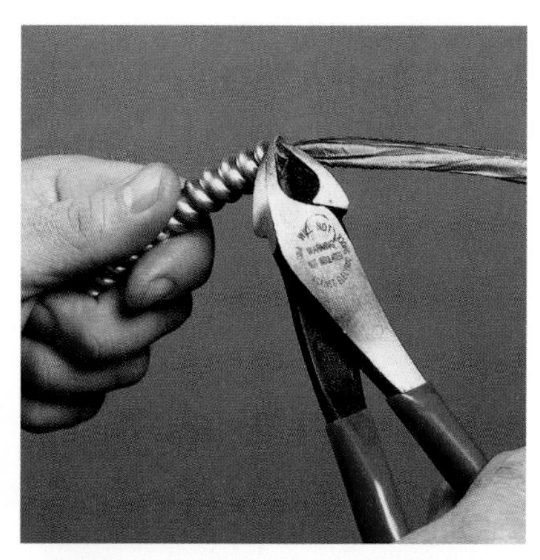

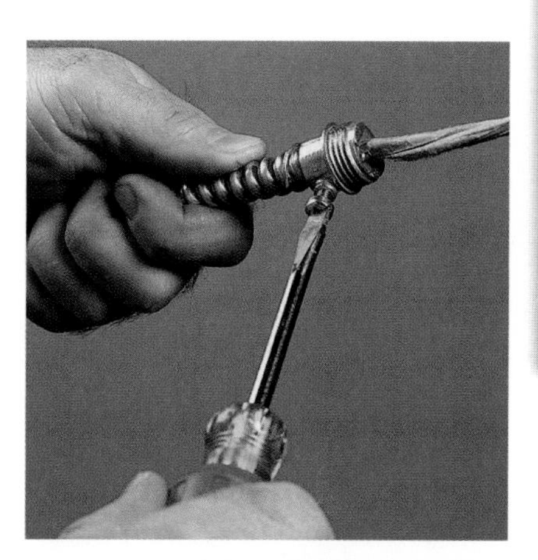

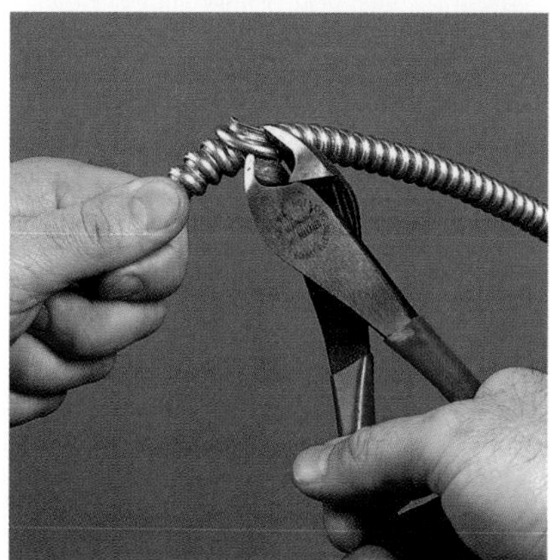

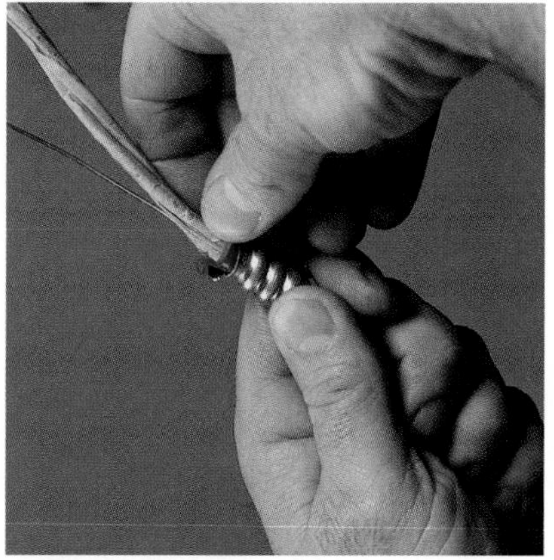

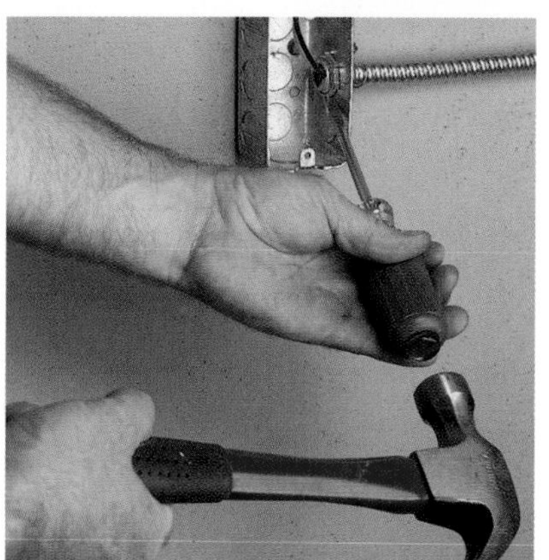

1 Twist the cable. Grasp the cable firmly on each side of the spot you want to cut. Twist the waste end clockwise until the armor comes apart far enough for you to slip in cutters. If you have trouble doing this with your bare hands, use two pliers.

Snip and remove the armor. Cut through one rib of the armor with a pair of side-cutting pliers. Slide the waste armor off the wires, keeping your hands clear of sharp edges.

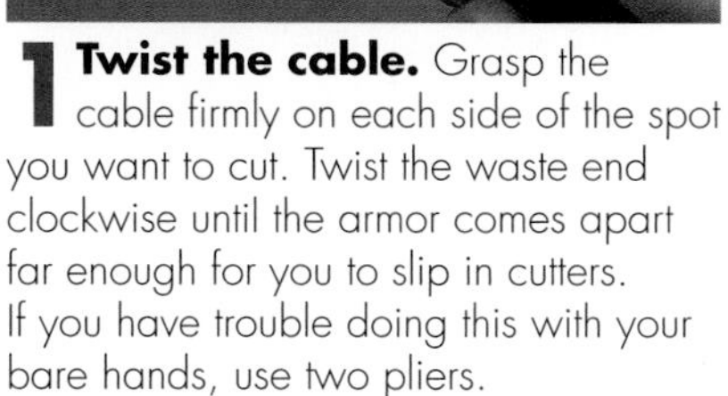

2 Trim sharp ends. Remove paper wrapping and plastic strips. Leave the thin metal bonding strip alone. Use side-cutting pliers to snip away pointed ends of sheathing that could nick wire insulation.

Slip on the bushing. Slip a bushing over the wires. Slide it down into the armor so the bushing protects the wires from the sharp edges of the armor. If there is a bonding strip, ask your inspector what to do with it. Most inspectors want you to cut it to about 2 inches and wrap it over the bushing and around the armor, helping to ensure conductive contact between the armor and the box.

3 Attach the clamp. Remove the locknut from an armored cable clamp. Slide the clamp down over the bushing as far as it will go, and tighten the setscrew. Double-check to make sure none of the wires are in danger of being nicked by the armor.

Connect to the box. Remove a knockout slug from a metal box and poke the connector into the hole. Slide the locknut over the wires and tighten it onto the cable clamp. Use a hammer and screwdriver to tap the locknut tight. On BX cable, this connection serves as the ground.

Running conduit

Skill level:	Time to complete:	Materials:	Tools:
★★★☆☆	Experienced 3 hrs. Handy 5 hrs. Novice 8 hrs.	Conduit and fittings, wire, PVC cement, lubricant	Screwdriver, lineman's pliers, hacksaw, conduit reamer, fish tape

ELECTRICAL

Conduit is the most durable product for running wire. It's more expensive and time-consuming to install than cable, but it is no longer necessary to learn how to bend conduit. Ready-made parts make installation easier than ever. Use conduit on unfinished walls and ceilings where wiring will be exposed. Use electrical metallic tubing (EMT), or thinwall conduit, for most indoor installations. Use thicker intermediate metal conduit (IMC) above ground outdoors. Use plastic rigid nonmetallic conduit (PVC) for underground applications.

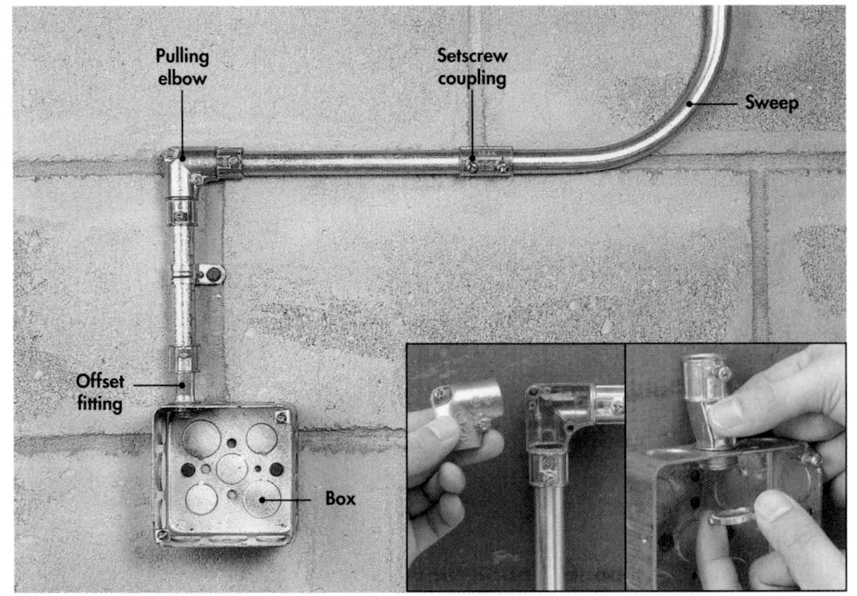

Assembling the parts. Take a rough drawing of your installation to a home center or electrical supply store. Ask a salesperson to help you gather all the pieces you need. Generally use ½-inch conduit for up to five #12 wires or six #14 wires, and ¾-inch conduit for more wires. (Larger conduit will make pulling easier, so consider buying ¾ inch in every case.) Use a sweep to turn most corners. Use setscrew couplings and elbows for indoor installations (you'll have to use compression fittings outdoors). At every four bends install a box or a pulling elbow (see inset above and "Closer Look," opposite). If the conduit and the box are installed flush against a wall, you'll need an offset fitting.

Greenfield conduit

Greenfield. Also called flexible metal conduit, Greenfield is essentially armored cable without the wires. It is expensive, so use it sparingly for places where rigid conduit would be difficult to install.

PVC conduit

PVC conduit. In many areas PVC is acceptable for indoor and outdoor installations. Cut it with a backsaw or hacksaw and a miter box. Glue the pieces together using PVC cement approved by an inspector.

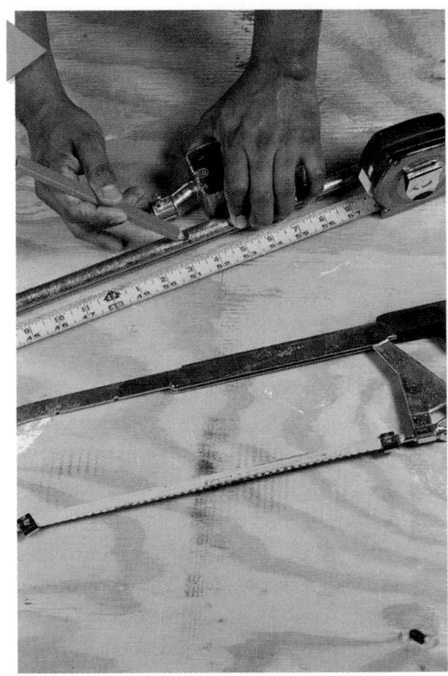

1 Measure and cut. Install the boxes first, then cut conduit to fit between them. At a corner have a helper hold a sweep in place while you mark the conduit for cutting. Use a hacksaw with a fine-tooth blade to cut.

2 Remove burrs. Ream out all burrs with a conduit reamer so the wires can slide smoothly past joints without damaging the sheathing.

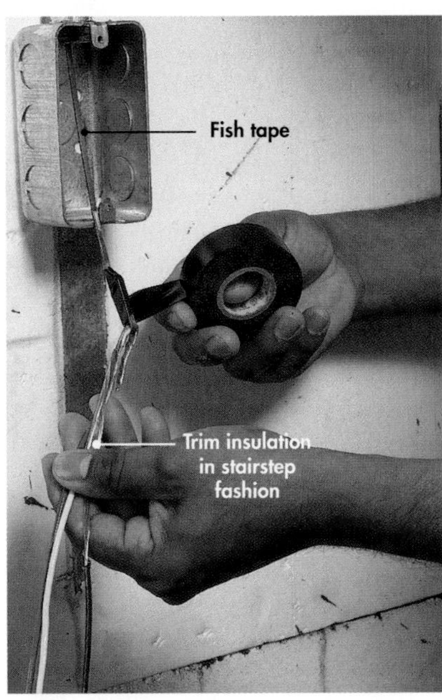

3 Run fish tape and attach the wires. Feed the fish tape through the conduit in the opposite direction from which you will pull the wires. Trim the insulation in a stair-step fashion (staggered exposure of wire) to make the wire easier to pull. Poke the wire ends through the fish tape's loop and bend them over. Wrap firmly and neatly with electrician's tape so the joint will not bind when it goes through a sweep.

4 Squirt lubricant. To make pulling easier on long runs, pour a bit of pulling lubricant on the wires. (Avoid using substitute lubricants such as dishwashing liquid or hand soap. Some can dangerously degrade wire insulation over time.)

5 Pull the wires. Have someone feed the wires through one end while you pull the fish tape on the other end. Pull with steady pressure and keep the wires parallel to avoid twists that will jam in the conduit. Try to keep the wires moving rather than starting and stopping. If they get stuck, back up a few inches to gain a running start.

CLOSER LOOK

INSTALL PULLING ELBOWS

If the conduit will make more than three turns between boxes, install a pulling elbow to make fishing easier. Don't splice wires here; just use the opening to pull the wires through.

Installing surface-mounted wiring

Skill level: ★★★☆☆

Time to complete:
Experienced 1 hr.
Handy 2 hrs.
Novice 3 hrs.

Materials: Surface-mount boxes, bushings, and face plates; receptacle; raceway and mounting clips; electrical cable; wire nuts, screws, plastic anchors

Tools: Screwdriver, hacksaw, lineman's pliers, metal file

The big challenge in adding electrical circuits to the home is fishing wires through the dark spaces between walls. You can get around that obstacle by using a surface-mount system, in which boxes and runs of cable (or raceways) are attached to the walls and ceiling. Raceways can be run around corners and from wall to ceiling with inside and outside elbows. In the project shown here, a circuit is extended by running cable in a raceway from an existing receptacle to a new receptacle on the same wall.

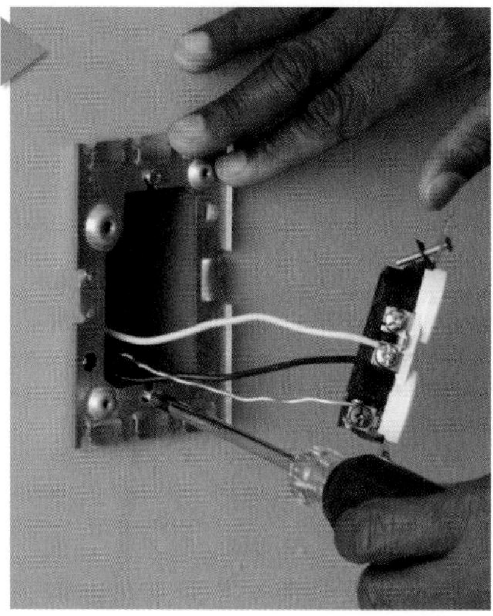

1 Install the starter box base. Remove the screws for the faceplate on an existing receptacle, then gently pull the receptacle through the opening in the starter box base. Attach the base to the existing box with the provided mounting screws.

2 Cut the raceway to length. Locate the second box. Attach its base to the wall, either driving screws into a stud or into hollow wall anchors. To find the length of the raceway, measure between the bases and add enough to allow inserting the raceway into the base at either end. Cut the raceway to length with a hacksaw, then use a metal file to remove the sharp burrs from the end. For longer runs, lengths of raceway can be connected with the manufacturer's couplings.

With a surface-mount system, all the parts are in plain view. Electrical cable runs through plastic or metal channels linked with elbows, tees, and other connectors. Boxes are mounted on a base plate attached to the wall with screws driven into studs or wall anchors.

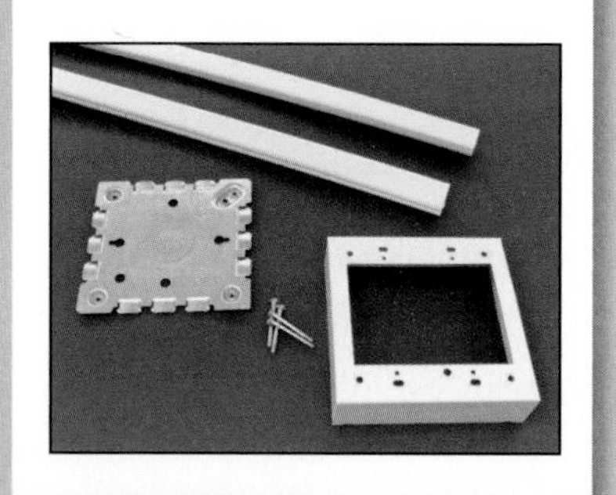

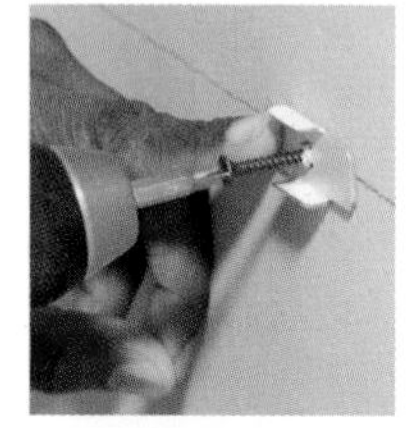

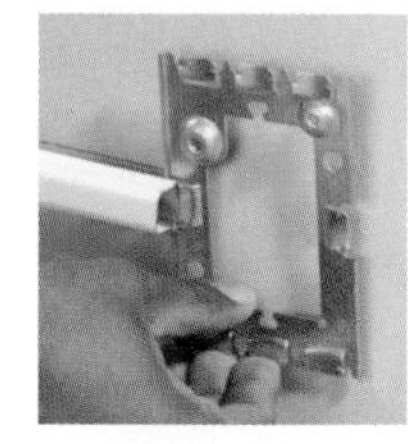

3 Assemble the raceway. Attach mounting clips along the line you've laid out, driving screws into studs or into hollow wall anchors. Slip the raceway onto a tongue of the starter box base, then slide the base of the second box onto the other end of the raceway.

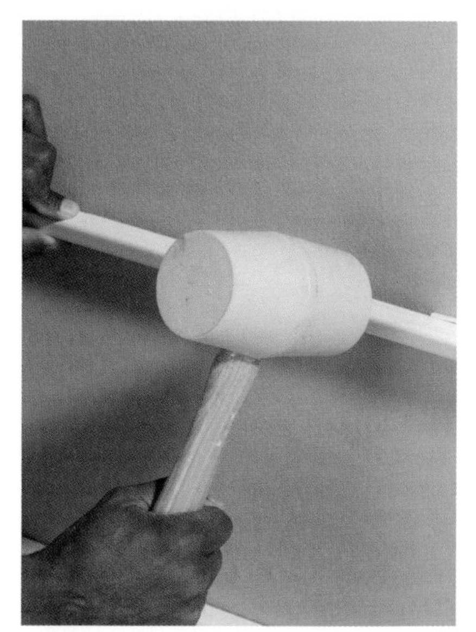

4 Attach the raceway. Snap the raceway into the mounting clips by tapping with either the heel of your hand or with a rubber mallet that will cushion the blow. Then attach the second base to the wall.

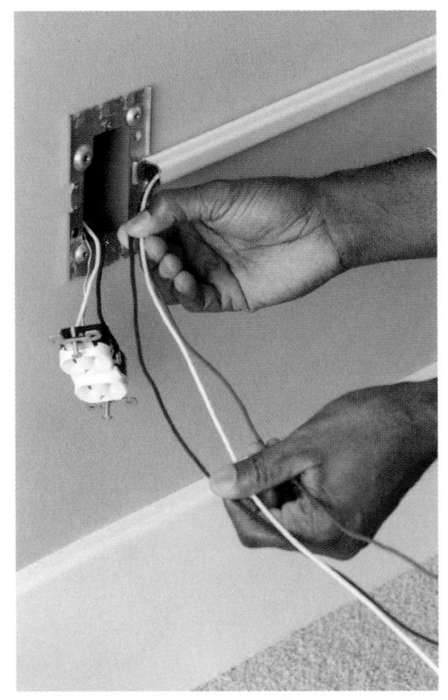

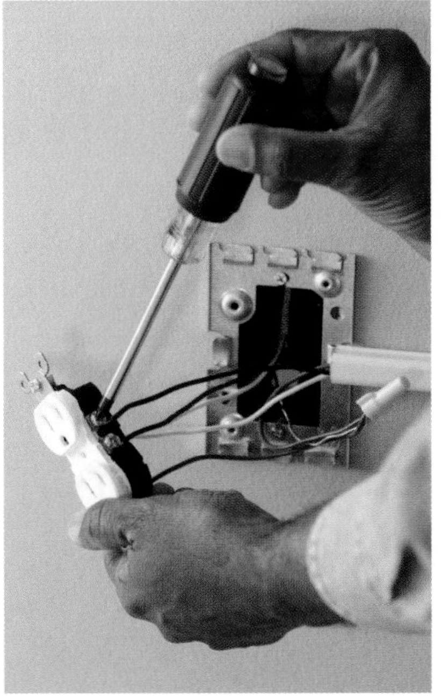

5 Feed wires into the raceway. Slide bushings supplied by the manufacturer into the ends of the raceway to avoid damaging the insulation on the wires, then slide the wires through the raceway.

6 Make the electrical connections. Loosen the grounding screw on the existing receptacle and remove the grounding wire. Make a pigtail with a wire nut by twisting together the stripped ends of two new 6-inch pieces of grounding wire and the grounding wire from the receptacle. Connect one of the free ends to the receptacle ground screw and the other to the green grounding screw on the starter box base. Attach the white and black wires of the raceway to the appropriate places on the receptacle: white goes with white, and black with black.

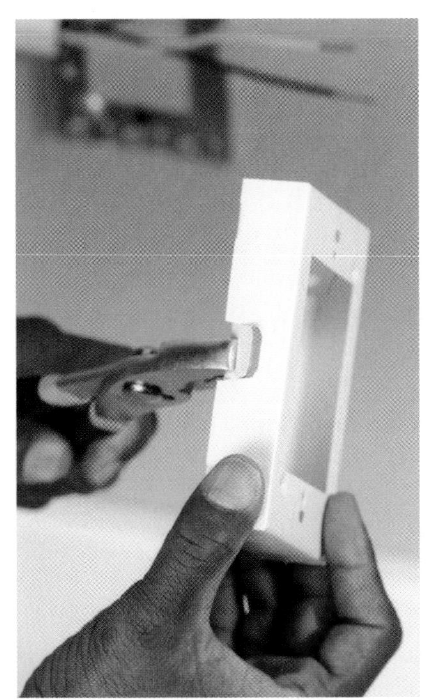

7 Attach the box. Attach the base with screws into a stud or into hollow wall anchors. Use pliers to remove the appropriate knockout in the side of the box for the raceway. Attach the box to the base with the screws provided.

8 Finish the installation. Attach the receptacle to the box, then attach the receptacle faceplate. Follow the same steps for the box at the other end of the raceway.

CLOSER LOOK

PLASTIC OR METAL?

You can buy surface-mount systems in either plastic or metal. Which is best? There's a tradeoff involved, as you might expect. Metal components will hold up better over time, and they're the better choice for surfaces that can be expected to take a beating—in high-traffic areas, and along lower walls where you notice a lot of scuffing. Plastic is easier to cut, and you don't have to deburr cut ends as with metal. Plastic also has the advantage of conforming more easily to curves in the wall. Either material can be painted along with the surrounding wall or ceiling so that the surface-mount system becomes less visible.

ELECTRICAL

Adding a circuit

See page 588

Skill level:	Time to complete:	Materials:	Tools:
★★★☆☆	Experienced 30 min. Handy 1 hr. Novice 2 hrs.	Cable and clamp, new circuit breaker	Hammer, screwdriver, lineman's pliers, combination stripper, flashlight

The physical work of installing a new electrical circuit is simple and calls for no special skills. Most of the work is completed outside the service panel. To get a breaker that will fit in your panel, jot down the brand and model number or bring a sample breaker to the store.

First determine whether your service panel can accommodate a new breaker, and then plan a circuit that will not be overloaded (see page 368). If the circuit will be in a bath or along a kitchen countertop, consider installing a GFCI breaker so you won't have to install individual GFCI outlets (see page 376). Install the new boxes. Run cable from the boxes back to the service panel. Electricians call this practice a "home run." Hook up the devices and fixtures. Now you're ready to energize the new circuit by installing a new breaker and connecting the wires to it.

Always buy breakers made by the same company that made the boxes they'll go in.

1 Shut off main power. Work during the daytime and have a reliable flashlight on hand. Turn off the main circuit breaker. All the wires and circuit breakers in the panel are now de-energized except for the thick wires that come from the outside and connect to the main breaker: Do not touch them.

2 Remove a knockout. Remove the service panel cover. Remove a knockout slug from the side of the service panel and install a cable clamp. Also remove a knockout tab from the panel cover. (For a double-pole breaker, remove two knockouts.)

SAFETY ALERT

A SMARTER CIRCUIT BREAKER

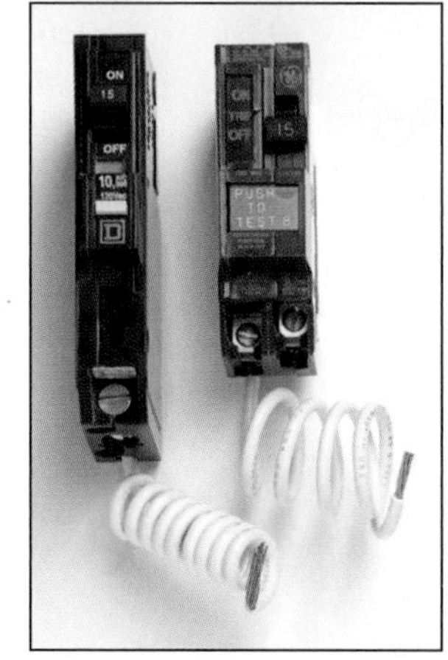

Decades have passed since the fuse box was replaced by a service panel with circuit breakers. The breakers serve as on-off switches for each circuit and also provide some protection from short circuits. And now circuit breakers are giving way to arc fault circuit interrupters, or AFCIs, which are sensitive enough to detect an electrical arc (caused by anything from a loose wire to a nibbling mouse) before it can generate temperatures high enough to cause a fire. AFCIs are significantly safer, and the National Electrical Code now requires them for new homes and large-scale renovations. They also are widely recommended for circuits to existing bedrooms. Note that an AFCI does not do the job of a ground fault circuit interrupter (GFCI), which is intended to protect from electrical shock rather than to prevent household fires. AFCIs are installed the same way as circuit breakers.

CLOSER LOOK

BREAKER OPTIONS

If the service panel has room, install full-size, single-pole breakers. If you're out of space, see whether your panel can accommodate half-size or skinny breakers, or tandem breakers. In some panels, these breakers only fit in slots near the bottom.

You'll need double-pole breakers or a wafer breaker for 240-volt circuits. A quad breaker can supply two 240-volt circuits.

Your building code limits the number of breakers that can be installed. If you add too many, an inspector will require you to put in a new panel or a subpanel.

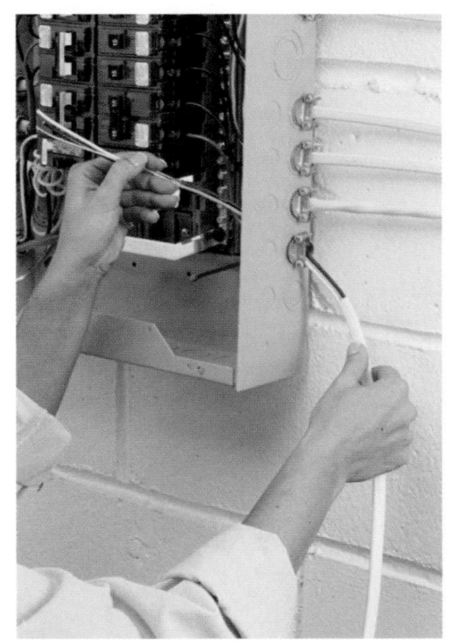

3 Clamp the cable. Determine how far the wires must travel to reach the breaker and the neutral bus bar. To avoid tangles, plan a path around the perimeter of the box. Strip about a foot more sheathing than you think you will need. Thread the wires through the clamp and secure the cable. Don't overtighten.

4 Connect the neutral wire. Run the neutral wire toward an open terminal in the neutral bus bar, bending the wire carefully so it will easily fit behind the panel cover. Cut the wire to length and strip off about ½ inch of insulation. Poke the end into the terminal and tighten the setscrew. Connect the ground wire to the ground bar (or neutral bus bar if there is no ground bar).

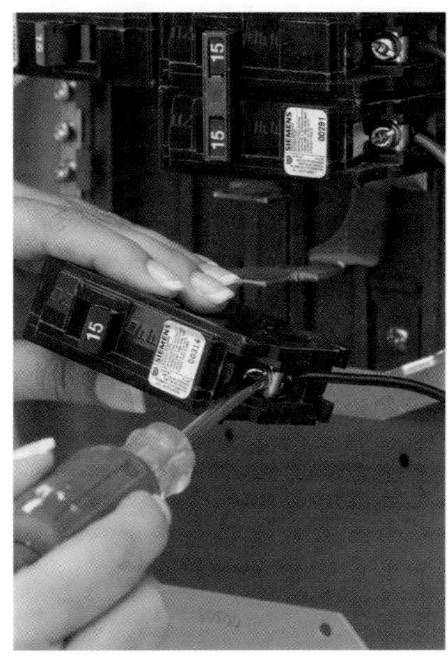

5 Wire the new breaker. Run the hot wire, bending it carefully so it will easily fit behind the panel cover. Cut the wire to length. Strip off ½ inch of insulation. Poke the wire into the new breaker terminal. If bare wire is visible, remove the wire, snip it a little shorter, and reinsert it. Tighten the setscrew.

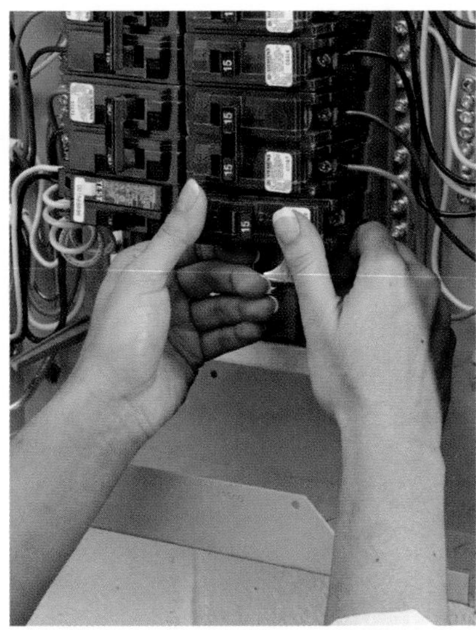

6 Snap the breaker into place. Make sure the breaker is in the off position, and then slip one side of the breaker under a tab to the right or left of the hot bus bar. Push the other side onto the bus bar until the new breaker is flush with the other breakers. (Some brands of breakers may require a slightly different installation method; check the instructions.) Restore power, turn on the breaker, and try the switches or receptacles to see whether they're getting power.

7 Installing double-pole breakers. Check to see whether you have the two free spots you'll need for a 240-volt breaker. (A tandem breaker takes up only one spot and can be substituted as long as there are two lugs for it.) Be sure the main power is shut off. Connect the black and red wires to the breaker terminals. Connect the white wire to the neutral bus bar and the ground wire to the ground bar (or neutral bus bar if there is no ground bar).

The familiar wall receptacle can be a serious hazard for young children if they probe the slots with a metal object. Outlet caps aren't a satisfactory answer because they may not be on hand when needed and can be pried off by older kids. A better answer is a tamper-resistant receptacle, required since 2008 by the National Electrical Code for new domestic construction and renovation—even if there isn't a curious young child living in the home. The slots have spring-loaded shutters that will open only when both prongs of a plug are inserted.

Lighting a kitchen

See page 588-590

Well-planned kitchen lighting will create cheerful and inviting spaces, increase the safety of food preparation, and highlight cabinetry and design features. Lighting serves three basic functions in the kitchen:

- **Ambient lighting produces a daylight effect.** Flush ceiling fixtures or track lights spread light more evenly than recessed can lights or pendants. (Ask for a kitchen/bath tube if using fluorescent lights in either of those rooms.) Windows and skylights are great sources of light during daylight hours, but they need help in the evening or during gloomy weather. A dimming system will make it easier to get the right amount of light.
- **Task lights under kitchen cabinets or in other strategic areas illuminate common kitchen tasks** such as food preparation and dish washing. Can lights and track lights may both be aimed and provide good task lighting.
- **In-between lights illuminate kitchen work spaces** while providing generous amounts of ambient light. These lights include recessed can lights over a sink, pendent fixtures above an eating area, and track lights in a semicircle near cabinetry.

Shaping up with track lighting

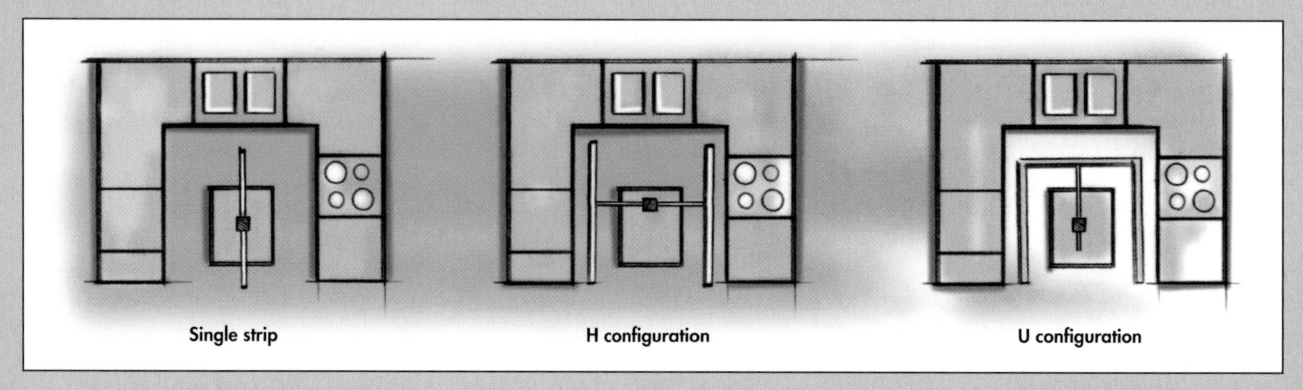

Many kitchens feature a single strip of track lighting running through the center of the ceiling. This kind of light provides adequate illumination but can sometimes bounce off wall cabinets and produce an uncomfortable glare—especially if the cabinets are shiny or light in color. The lights can cast a shadow from a person over a food preparation area at the countertop, contributing to poor visibility. Instead of installing a single strip of track lighting along the ceiling, wrap the tracks around the room in an H or a U pattern. Install the tracks about 3 feet out from the wall and 2 feet out from the wall cabinets. The lamps will then shine down over the shoulders of people working at counters, or toward the center of the room—providing both task lighting and ambient light.

Lighting a bathroom

See page 588-590

An average-size bathroom needs a ceiling fan/light in the center of the main room, a moisture-proof ceiling light over the shower/bath, and lights over the sink.

■ **Ambient lighting is typically provided by an overhead light combined with a vent fan.** Make sure the fan's blower is powerful enough to adequately vent your bathroom (see page 423). Spend a little more money to include a low-watt night-light or a forced-air heating unit. Some people prefer a heat lamp near the tub or shower for additional comfort while drying off after bathing.

■ **Bathroom mirror lighting deserves careful thought.** A horizontal strip of decorative lightbulbs above the mirror provides lots of light but may shine in your eyes. A fluorescent fixture with a lens provides more even light, but make sure you choose a kitchen and bath tube with a warm tone similar to incandescent light. Sconce lights placed on either side of the mirror are the best source for lighting your face for shaving or applying makeup. When planning circuits, remember to install a ground fault circuit interrupter (GFCI) receptacle near the sink.

■ **Shower lighting supplements what little light comes through the shower curtain or shower door.** Consider installing a moisture-proof recessed canister light with a watertight lens in the shower ceiling.

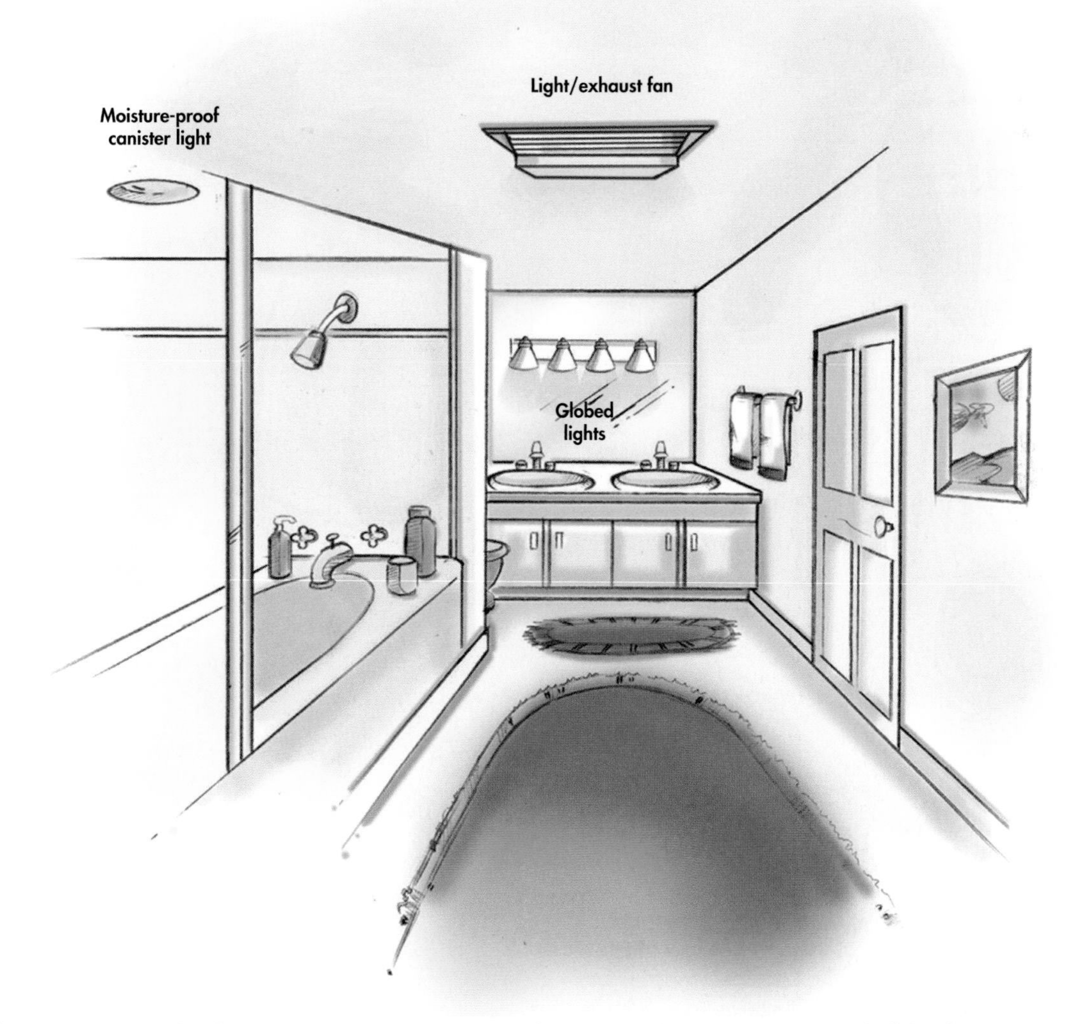

Lighting up your bathroom. The darker the color of your bathroom walls and fixtures, the more light you need. Sunlight from a window may be sufficient for daytime use. At night or in early morning, however, the shower in particular might need one or two moisture-proof canister lights. (Codes limit them to 60 watts each if the shower is enclosed.) Above the sink, install moisture-resistant globed lights that won't shine in your eyes. Overhead install a single fixture that efficiently and stylishly combines a light and exhaust fan, with perhaps a night-light and/or a heater.

See page 588-590

Lighting living areas

Living rooms, dining rooms, great-rooms, and large bedrooms all benefit from both ambient and task lighting. Rather than installing a single lighting component, think in terms of the total use of the room. Layering several types of lights makes a room more comforting and inviting by avoiding glare and dark shadows. Your goal is flexibility so you can set a variety of moods by brightening or dimming all or part of a room.

- Highlight a piece of art or cabinetry, or accentuate wall texture with can lights to give the room warmth and interest. (If you don't want to install can lights, you can accent paintings with picture lights that attach to the frames.)
- Put at least one of the components on a dimmer switch. Install several lights that are optional but not necessary. Don't be afraid to install too many lights; you don't have to use all of them at the same time.
- Install an in-between light such as a dining area chandelier to brighten the dinner table and provide some ambient light.
- Rope lights are strands of clear, flexible plastic that you can drape around the inside of cabinets or behind fascia to provide accent lighting.

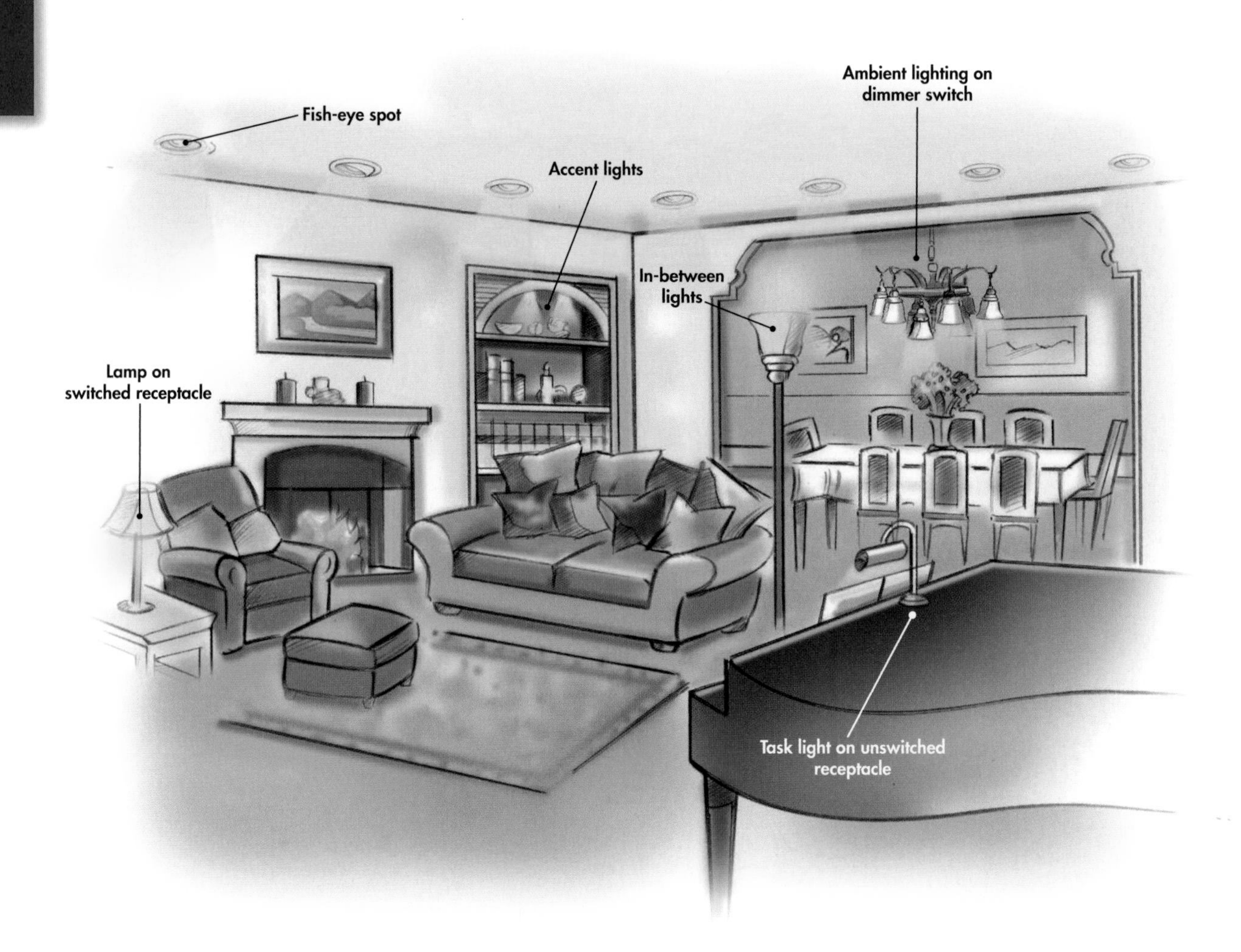

▲ ***Showing off a great-room with great lighting.*** *The lighting plan for this large family room includes a grid of recessed canister lights for general lighting and a centrally located chandelier over the dining table. A recessed light with fish-eye trim spotlights a wall painting. The chandelier in the dining room creates ambient lighting when controlled by a dimmer switch. The task light on the piano offers movable light for specific needs. The table lamp and floor lamp are controlled by wall switches. Accent lights brighten shelves.*

Planning for recessed lighting

See page 588-590

ELECTRICAL

Recessed canister lights vary in intensity and angle. The higher your ceiling, the more floor space a light will illuminate. In general, recessed cans should be positioned 6 feet from each other. Of course most rooms are not sized to accommodate this, so you'll have to adjust your calculations. In the example below, most of the lights are 5 feet apart. Make a similar plan for your own installation, experimenting with several configurations. Take your plans with you to your home center for advice.

Lay out can lights using the templates that come with them, and mark the center point with a nail. You may have to move some lights a few inches one way or another in order to avoid hitting the ceiling framing. Fortunately, this will not make a big difference in the overall effect.

Special techniques. In addition to providing general lighting, recessed can lights can enhance decorating strategies with:

- Wall washing. To light up a large wall area, install cans with wall-wash trims that are 24 to 30 inches apart and the same distance from the wall.
- Accent lighting. Spotlight a painting, fireplace mantel, or other feature with a can that has a fish-eye style trim. Place it 18 to 24 inches from the wall, centered on the object.
- Grazing. To dramatize an unusual vertical surface, such as a fireplace or a textured wall, place cans 6 to 12 inches from the wall and 12 to 18 inches apart. Wire them with a shared dimmer switch.

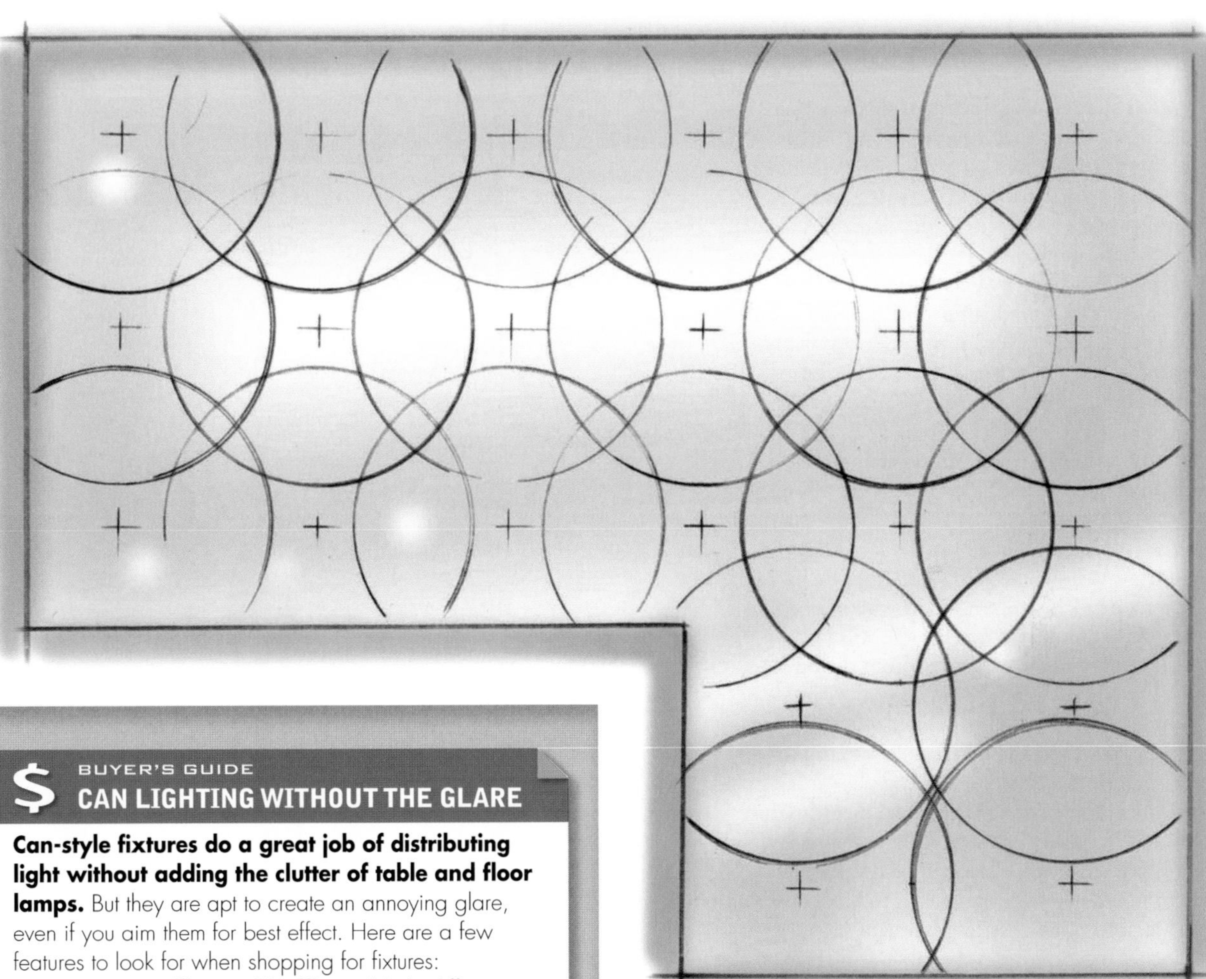

▲ ***Concentric circles of light.*** *On graph paper, make a scale drawing of your room and place dots in a fairly consistent pattern. To get a general idea of the distribution of light, use a compass to draw circles that are scaled to about 5 feet in radius (10 feet in diameter). In this example, the center of the room will get more light than the perimeter—which is usually desirable. Generally figure that a 65-watt floodlight in a room with an 8-foot ceiling will light up a circle that is 8 feet in diameter on the floor; if the ceiling is 10 feet high, it will illuminate a 10-foot circle.*

$ BUYER'S GUIDE

CAN LIGHTING WITHOUT THE GLARE

Can-style fixtures do a great job of distributing light without adding the clutter of table and floor lamps. But they are apt to create an annoying glare, even if you aim them for best effect. Here are a few features to look for when shopping for fixtures:

- **Egg crate grilles and baffles** will help diffuse the light.
- **Black liners** won't reflect light outside of the bulb's focus area.
- **Reflector trims** are simply extended lips that act as shades around the fixture's rim.
- **Lensed trims** use a plastic or glass lens to diffuse light, and they also serve to protect recessed fixtures from water in bathrooms.

Choosing ceiling fixtures

The broad range of overhead fixtures can be roughly divided into those with eye-catching decorative features (like the ones shown on this page) and those that are hardly noticeable but provide general illumination (like the flush ceiling fixtures shown opposite below). Track lights (opposite) fall in between. All come in many styles. Here are the basic types and features to choose from.

Pendant lights

Lights that hang down from the ceiling are called pendants. Use them for general lighting, to illuminate a dining room table, or to light up a work surface.

A chandelier or other type of pendant usually can't illuminate a large room on its own. A chandelier often hangs at eye level and would produce an unpleasant glare if it were bright enough to light an entire room.

- **Pendant shades.** Use a pendant shade to focus light on a specific space, such as a small table, a countertop, or a narrow work area. A pendant light with a glass shade will provide general lighting as well as directed light. A metal shade focuses light more directly. Older styles of pendant lights hang by decorative brass chains, with a neutral-colored lamp cord running through the chain. Newer fixtures use a plain chrome-colored wire for support, with the cord running alongside.

- **Pendant lanterns.** These lights resemble the old glass lanterns that protected candles from wind. Use them in narrow areas like foyers and stairways. Hang these at least 6½ feet from the ground so that people can walk under them. Center a pendant lantern width-wise in a narrow room. If it is near a large window, place it so it will look centered from the outside.

- **Chandeliers.** Originally designed as candleholders, chandeliers usually have five or more lightbulbs. Look for a model that is easy to clean; complex designs can be difficult to dust or wash. Keep the fixture in scale; a chandelier that is too small will appear to be dwarfed by the room. When choosing a unit to hang over a dining room table, select one that is about 12 inches narrower than the table. If it is any wider, people may bump their heads on it when they stand up from the table. In an entryway, maintain proportion by installing a chandelier that is 2 inches wide for every foot of room width (for example, use a 20-inch-wide light in a 10-foot-wide room).

Get the height right. A common mistake is to hang a chandelier too low. A chandelier should hang about 30 inches above a tabletop. The length of the chain will depend on your ceiling height.

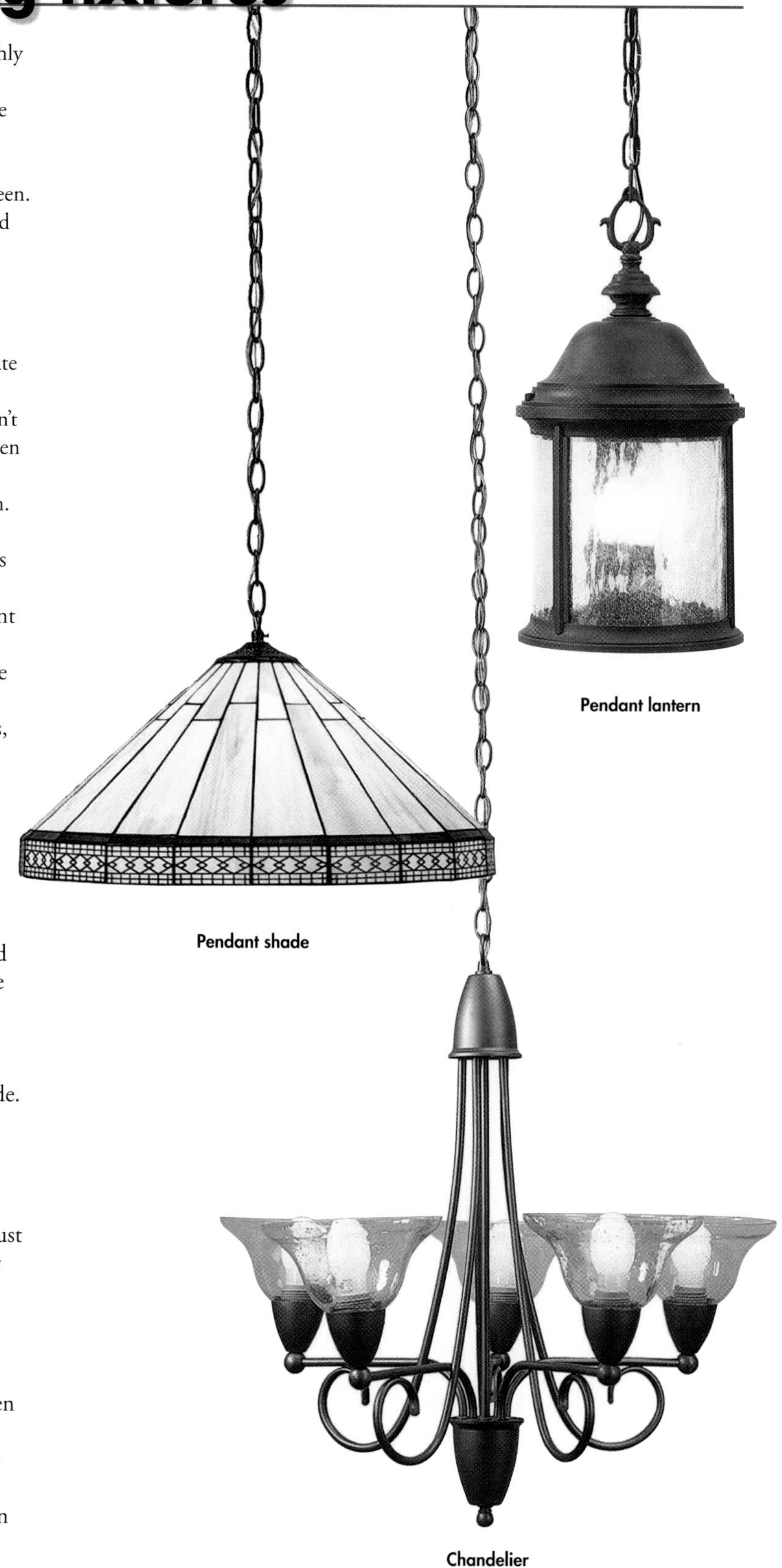

Pendant lantern

Pendant shade

Chandelier

Track ceiling fixtures

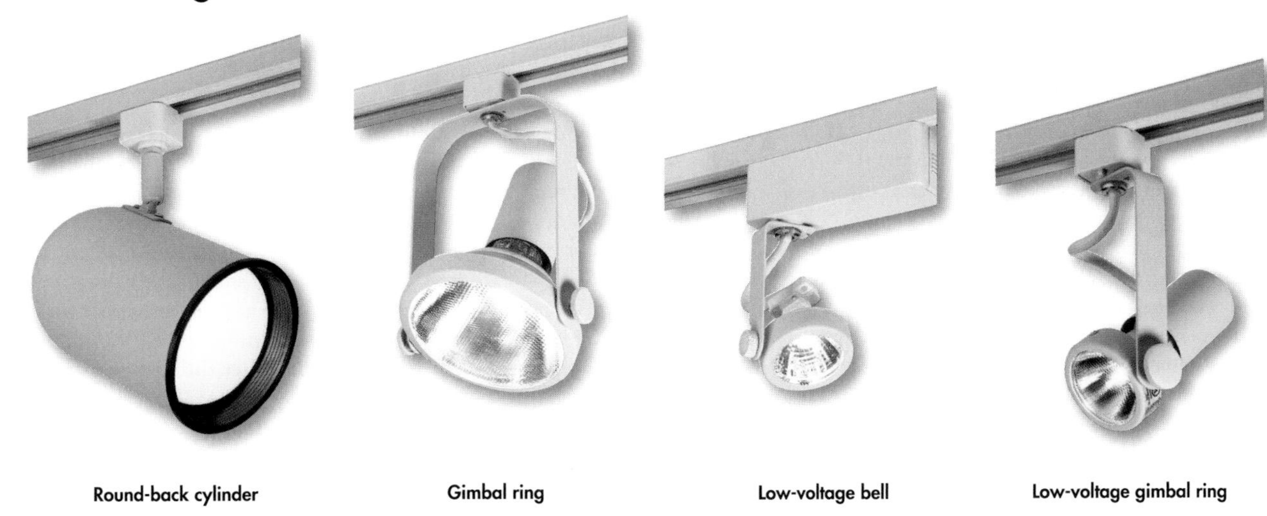

Choosing track lights. A single track lighting system can combine general lighting and accent lighting. When choosing a lamp, make sure it can handle the lightbulb of your choice and that it will fit onto your track. Incandescent lamps such as a **round-back cylinder** or a **gimbal ring** produce a broad, intense beam. Low-voltage halogen track lights such as a **low-voltage bell** or **low-voltage gimbal ring** produce a more intense, narrower beam of light. Each has its own transformer, so it can attach to a standard-voltage track. (However, these low-voltage lights require a special electronic dimmer; a standard magnetic dimmer will damage the lamps.) A track that partially encircles a room at a distance of 6 feet or so from the walls will disperse light more effectively than a single track running through the middle of the room.

Flush ceiling fixtures

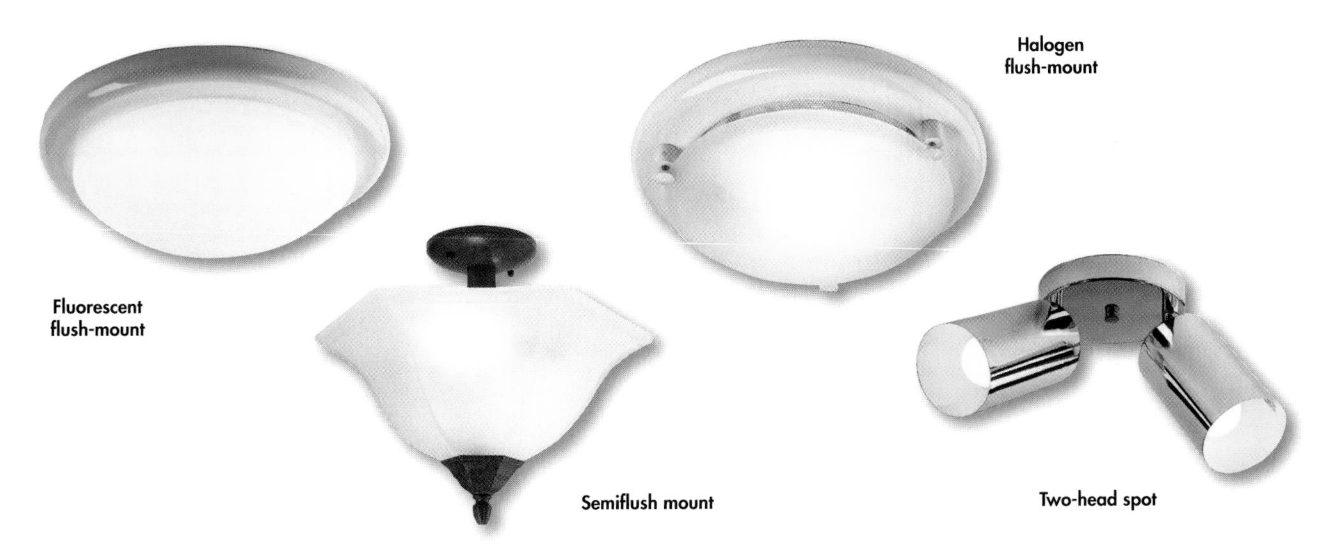

Choosing flush fixtures. A single flush fixture in the middle of the ceiling is the most common way to light a room. These fixtures usually produce enough light to adequately illuminate a 12'x12' room with an 8-foot ceiling or a 16'x16' room with a 10-foot ceiling (the higher the fixture, the broader the spread of its light). They hug the ceiling, consistently distributing light. Newer **fluorescent ceiling fixtures** with electronic ballasts look like incandescents, save energy, and have tubes that rarely burn out. A **semiflush fixture** hangs down a foot or so from the ceiling. It diffuses light through the globe as well as upward, evenly illuminating a room. **Halogens** offer more intense light. **Two- or three-head spotlights** provide some of track lighting's versatility. Point the lights horizontally for general lighting, or angle them downward to highlight certain areas of the room.

Seeing green: energy-efficient lighting

The familiar incandescent bulb may soon become an electrical dinosaur, given the advantages of compact fluorescent bulbs, or CFLs. They cost less to operate for a given level of illumination, they last far longer (up to 10,000 hours), and their reduced energy needs will appeal to your environmental sensibilities. If every household switched just a single bulb from incandescent to CFL, the reduction in greenhouse gas emissions would equal that of taking more than 800,000 cars off the road. A final inducement to make the switch: you can expect governments at various levels to mandate the use of CFLs.

Compact fluorescents

Compact fluorescents have come a long way from the familiar long tubes, with their cold light and persistent hum:

- The most popular configuration is a spiral bulb with a twist base that works with conventional sockets. The products now on the market are a big improvement over earlier CFLs, with a more pleasing light, silent operation, and a lower price. You can use them almost anywhere you would a standard incandescent. They may not be the best choice for stairways, because they can take from several seconds to more than a minute to reach full illumination. And you'll significantly decrease their life if they're turned on for only short periods, as in a closet or pantry.
- Only special-purpose CFLs can be used with standard dimmers; look for bulbs labeled as compatible with dimmers, or buy bulbs with three different light levels so that a dimmer isn't required.
- For recessed fixtures, choose a reflector or flood CFL to better project the light.

▶ ***CFLs come in all sorts of shapes and sizes.*** *Shown here from the left are globe, spiral, and bulbs.*

$ BUYER'S GUIDE
MISERLY LED BULBS

A promising gleam on the horizon is the LED (or light-emitting diode) lightbulb, offering a long life and pleasing color, while drawing a small fraction of the wattage of incandescents and about half of that used by CFLs. The drawbacks? Their economy comes at a considerable purchase price, and only relatively small-wattage bulbs are currently available. But expect to see LED bulbs winning more shelf space in the next several years, as scale of production lowers their cost.

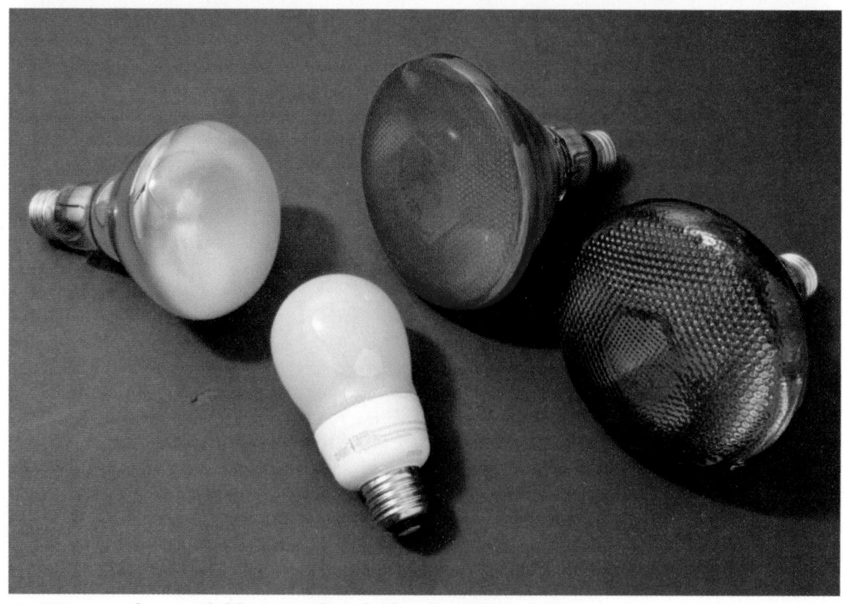

▲ ***CFLs are also available in outdoor bulbs of various types.***

Installing or replacing wall lights

See pages 588–590

Skill level:	**Time to complete:**	**Materials:** Wall sconces or bathroom wall fixture, boxes, cable with clamps, staples, wire nuts, electrician's tape	**Tools:** Drill, saw, screwdriver, lineman's pliers, combination stripper, level
★★★☆☆	Experienced 3 hrs. Handy 6 hrs. Novice 8 hrs.		

Wall sconces and vanity lights are lighting sources mounted on vertical surfaces. They are primarily used for ambient and task lighting. Most wall fixtures attach to a ceiling box with a swivel strap so you can easily adjust the fixture. A fluorescent fixture installed above a bathroom mirror may not require installing a box; read fixture instructions.

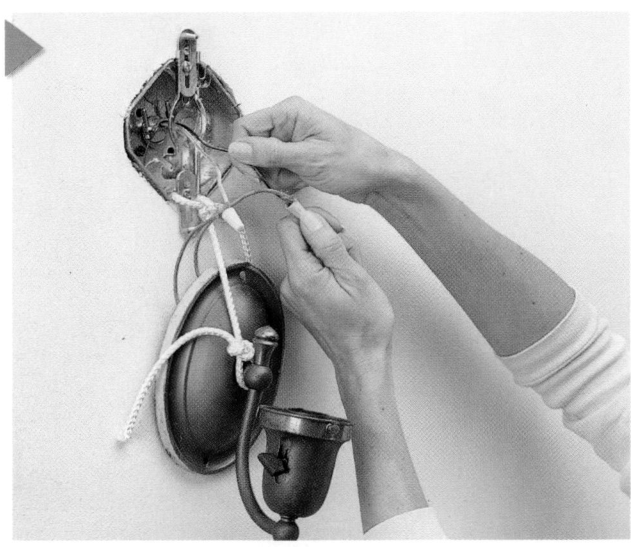

1 Remove the existing fixture. Turn off the power to the fixture. Test with a voltage meter (see page 370). Remove the glass globe, shade, and bulb. Remove any nuts or screws holding the fixture in place. Carefully pull the fixture from the wall (pry if it has been painted in place); avoid yanking on the wires. After you remove the fixture, twist off the wire nuts that connect the wires.

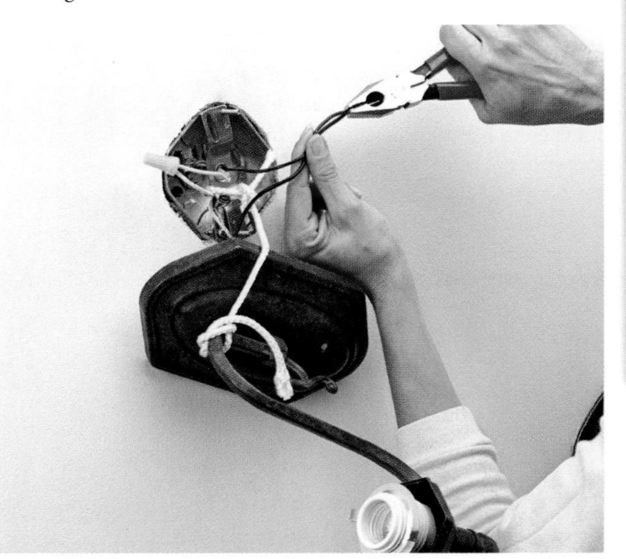

2 Install the new fixture. Strip ¼ inch of insulation from wire tips. Twist and connect wires—white to white, and black to black. Twist on a plastic wire cap. If the cap doesn't cover all the bare wire, remove the cap, trim the wire a bit shorter, and reattach the cap. Fold the wires into the junction box, place the fixture over the studs or nipple, then attach with the ornamental nuts provided.

Installing a sconce

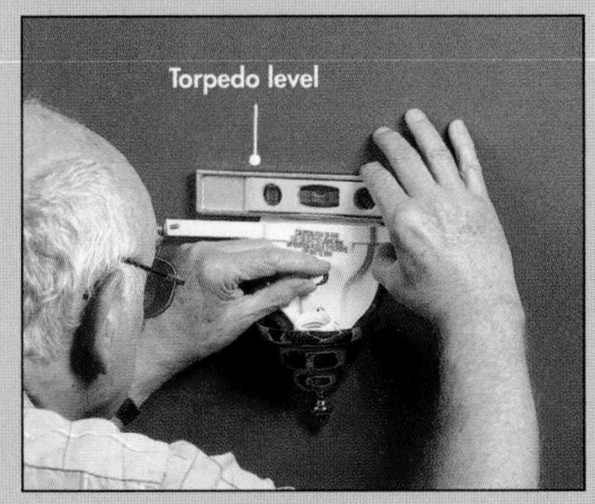

Run cable from a nearby receptacle or other power source into a switch box and then to a box mounted on the wall. Get a box with a swivel strap to let you adjust the base until it is level. Depending on the sconce, use either a round or octagonal box. Wire as you would for a ceiling fixture (see page 385).

Wiring a vanity light

Installing a light over a mirror or medicine cabinet calls for no special wiring techniques. Some fixtures require a box, while others can be wired and then attached directly to the wall. If you will be installing a mirror that reaches to the ceiling, give the glass company exact dimensions for cutting a hole in the mirror to attach the fixture to a box mounted in the wall behind the mirror.

$ BUYER'S GUIDE: TRY A SWIVEL BOX

Swivel boxes are junction boxes that have adjustable mounting straps that turn so you can level the lighting fixtures on the walls. They're available in the electrical department at your home center.

Installing a hanging light fixture

See pages 588–590

Skill level: ★★★☆☆

Time to complete:
Experienced 1 hr.
Handy 2 hrs.
Novice 3 hrs.

Materials: Light fixture, support bracket, wire nuts

Tools: Adjustable wrench, screwdriver, lineman's pliers, combination stripper

Hanging fixtures distribute light in the center of a room without the clutter of one or more floor lamps and their foot-snagging wires. But installing them can be somewhat of a challenge. This is a "high-wire" act, after all, requiring you to balance atop a ladder while doing delicate work. It's good to have a helper standing by to steady the ladder and to share some of the weight of a large fixture.

Hanging a fixture securely

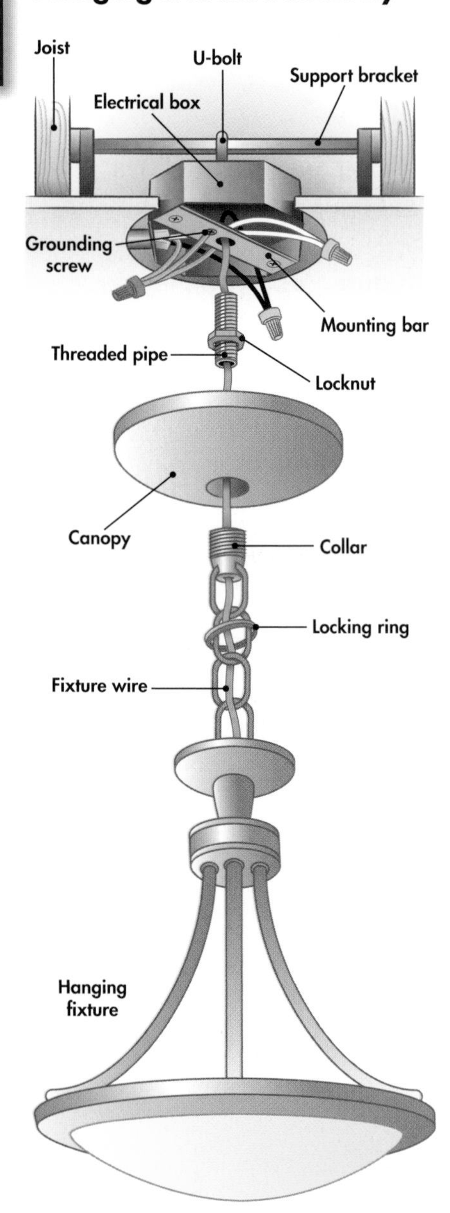

1 Remove the existing fixture. **Turn off power to the fixture's circuit at the service panel.** Working from a sturdy wooden stepladder, remove the fixture and hand it to a helper on the ground.

2 Use a support bracket. Hang heavier fixtures from a support bracket that fits between a pair of ceiling joists. If you have access to this space from the attic, you can use a sliding bracket with flanges that are screwed into the joists. It's a little trickier to install a telescoping bracket through the hole for the electrical box. Insert the bracket as shown.

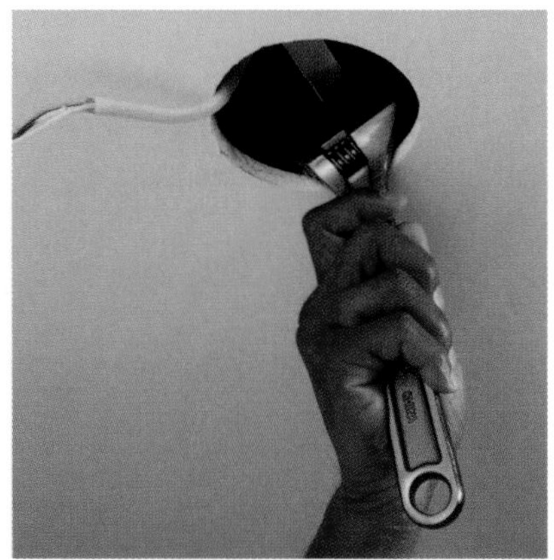

3 Rotate the bracket to secure it in place. Place the bracket perpendicular to the joists on either side. Using an adjustable wrench rotate the bracket to extend its ends and imbed their points in the joists.

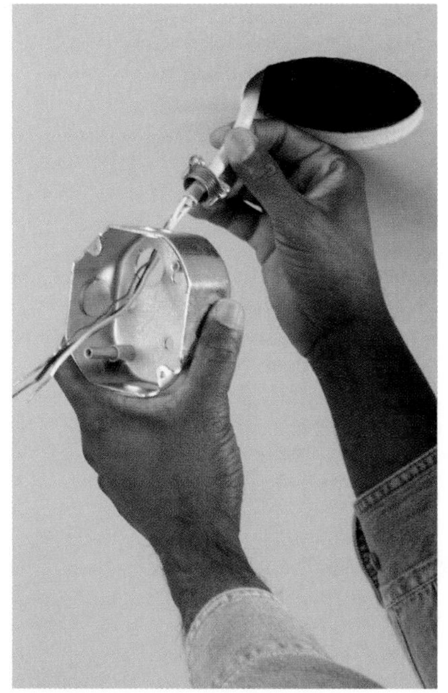

4 Draw wires through the electrical box. Attach an internal cable clamp. Remove a knockout plug from a side of the electrical box. Run the cable through the box as shown, far enough to allow making connections. Tighten the screw of the clamp to secure the cable without damaging its sheathing.

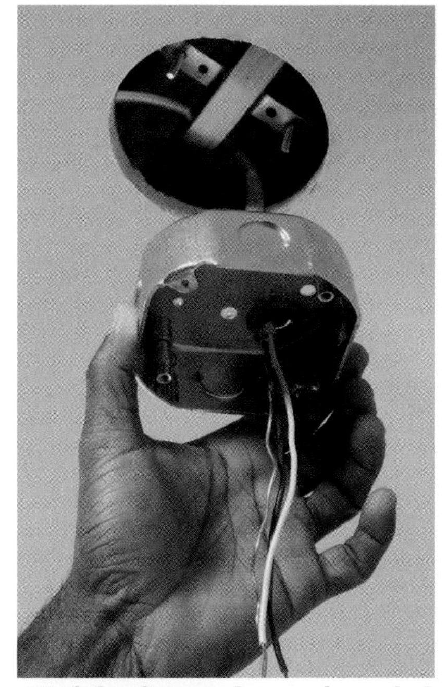

5 If the fixture has a threaded mounting stem from which the chain is suspended, thread it into the box's mounting bar. Or if there is a separate threaded nipple, thread one end into the fixture's chain holder and the other into the mounting bar.

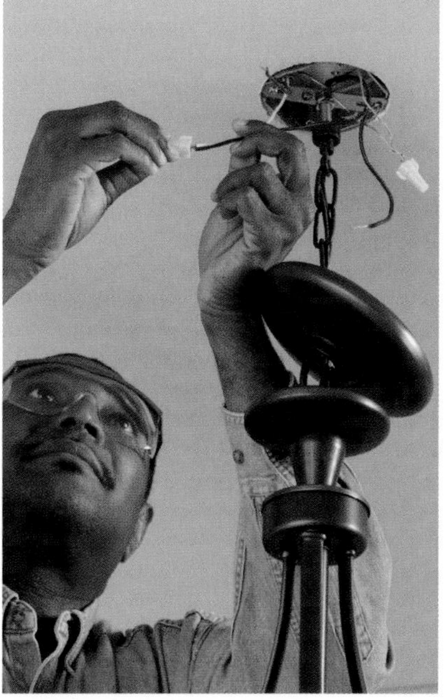

6 Drive screws to attach the mounting bar to the electrical box. Use wire nuts to connect the ground wires from the box, the fan, and the home's circuit; then connect the black and white wires between the circuit and the fixture.

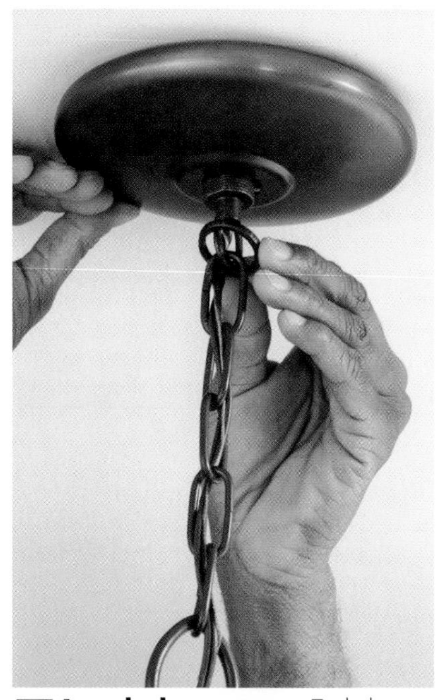

7 Attach the canopy. Tuck the wiring into the box and slide the canopy into place. Attach the canopy by hand-tightening the retaining locknut.

CLOSER LOOK

HANGING WITHOUT A THREADED PIPE

It would make life a little simpler if there were a standardized way to suspend a ceiling fixture. But your light may be held in place by attaching its canopy to a crossbar with screws instead of a threaded pipe. In that case drive the screws for the canopy through the crossbar far enough so you'll be able to spin on the cap nuts when the canopy is held in place at the end of the procedure. Immobilize the screws with the locknuts, then attach the crossbar to the box and continue with the installation.

WORK SMART

FINDING NEUTRAL ON A LIGHT FIXTURE CORD

Light fixture cords don't always have black and white cables, but it's still important to connect the neutral wire of the light with the neutral wire in the circuit. Look closely at the lamp cord—the plastic sleeve with the rib is the neutral wire. Connect it to the white cable coming into the junction box.

Do your groundwork

Before climbing a stepladder do as much of a procedure as possible. Review the steps of the project to determine what you can accomplish without leaving the ground. When hanging a light fixture, for example, you can do part of the assembly on terra firma.

Installing recessed lighting

See pages 588–590

ELECTRICAL

Skill level:	Time to complete:	Materials:	Tools:
★★★☆☆	Experienced 8 hrs. Handy 12 hrs. Novice 16 hrs.	Can lights and trims, switch box and switch, cable, cable clamps (if they're not built into the fixture), wire nuts, electrician's tape	Stud finder, drill with long bit, safety glasses, drywall saw or hole-cutting drill attachment, voltage tester or multitester, combination stripper, lineman's pliers, screwdriver, utility knife

Canister lights, also called "pot lights," are recessed lights that use 30- to 150-watt floodlight bulbs. They're ideal for task lighting, for highlighting artwork, or grouped to illuminate whole rooms. (See page 401 for tips on placement.) Cans get hot. Position them at least 1 inch away from wood and other flammables. Always follow the manufacturer's instructions.

If the joists are exposed, use a new-work can light (see page 410). For ceilings already covered by drywall or plaster and lath, buy a remodel can (opposite) that clips into a hole cut in the ceiling. (It's also called an old-work, or retrofit, can.) To install a remodel can, follow the steps beginning on the opposite page.

Choosing canister lights

Can lights are designed to suit specific situations. Here's how to choose the right one:

- If insulation is in the ceiling, buy IC (insulation compatible) lights. Standard recessed lights will dangerously overheat when surrounded by insulation.
- Tiny low-voltage can lights add sparkle. They're stylish but expensive and are wired the same way as standard can lights.
- Use bulbs of the recommended wattage or lower. Bulbs with too-high wattage will dangerously overheat. When putting a number of cans on a dimmer, add up all the wattage and make sure your dimmer is rated to handle the load.
- If you have fewer than 8 inches of vertical space above the ceiling, purchase a low-clearance canister.

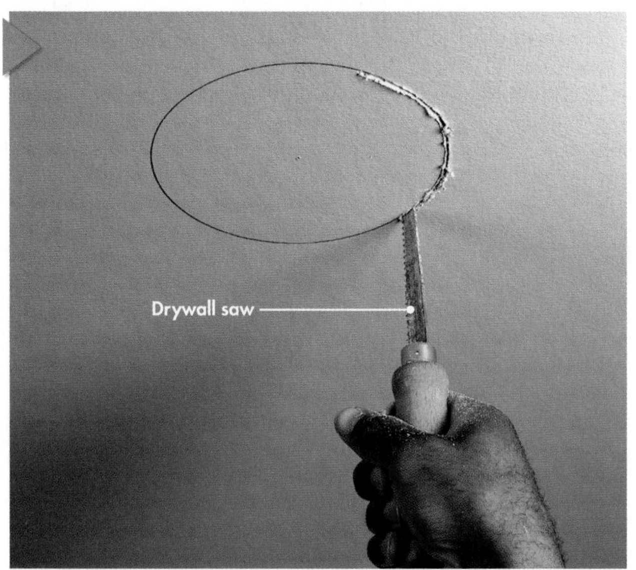

1 Option A: Cut the hole. Lay out and mark all light locations with the help of the mounting template that comes with the light. Use a stud finder to make sure the lights will not overlap a joist, or drill a hole and poke a bent wire up into it to make sure the hole is entirely between joists. Draw and cut each hole precisely. If it is even a little too big, the can may not clamp tightly. Wearing safety glasses cut the line lightly with a utility knife, then cut along the inside of the knife line with a drywall saw. Take care not to snag any wires that may be in the ceiling cavity.

DESIGN TIP

CHOOSING CANISTER LIGHTS

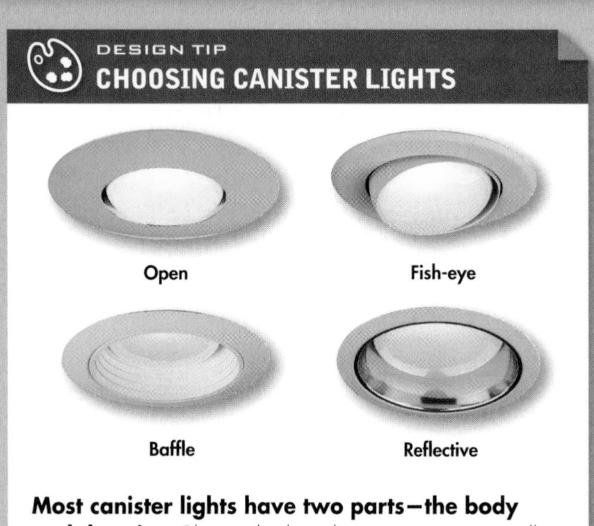

Most canister lights have two parts—the body and the trim. Choose both at the same time or install bodies with many trim options and choose later. Open trim is the simplest and least expensive option. Baffle trim diffuses light so it is more evenly distributed. Fish-eye (also called eyeball) trim swivels to highlight a decorative feature. Reflective trim offers maximum brightness.

Option B: Use a hole-cutting saw. This tool saves time and cuts holes precisely. Instead of drawing the outline of the hole on the ceiling, just mark the center point shown on the mounting template. Check to see that you will not run into a joist. Check that the lights fit snugly without having to be forced into place.

Note: This tool is costly (the saw and the arbor are sold separately), but it's worth the price if you have more than six holes to cut through plaster. A less-expensive hole-cutting tool (see inset) is available for cutting through drywall only.

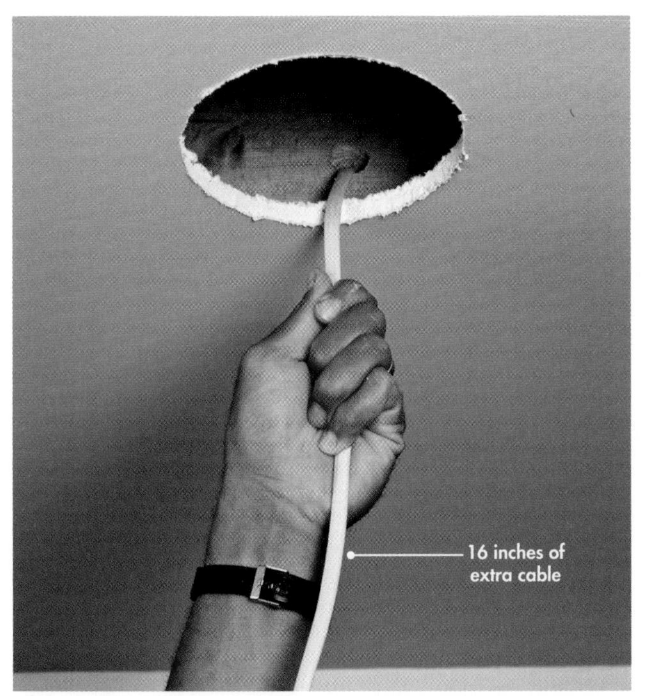

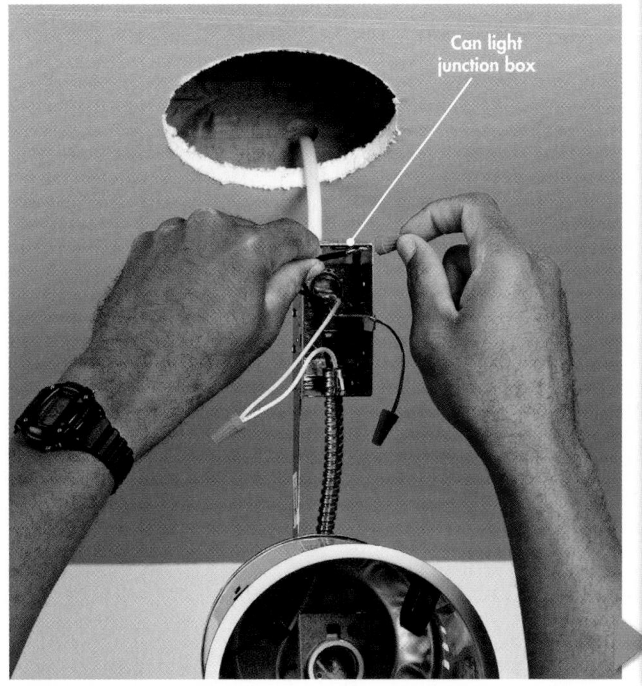

ELECTRICAL

2 Rough-in the wiring. Run cable from a power source to a switch box and then to the first hole, allowing at least 16 inches of extra cable to make wiring easy. (See page 389 for how to run cable.) Work carefully and use a drill with a long bit to avoid cutting additional access holes that will need patching later.

3 Wire the light. Open the light's junction box. Usually a plate will pop off. Run cable into the box and clamp it. Strip insulation and make wire splices—black to black, white to white, and ground to ground (see page 371). Fold the wires into the box and replace the cover.

Anatomy of a remodel canister light

A standard remodel canister fixture has an approved electrical box, suspended far enough from the light so it will not overheat. A thermal protector shuts the light off if it becomes too hot (for example if you use a bulb of too-high voltage). If you have fewer than 8 inches of vertical space above your ceiling, purchase special cans designed to fit into this smaller space. Be sure the special cans are IC (insulation compatible) rated so there will be no danger of overheating.

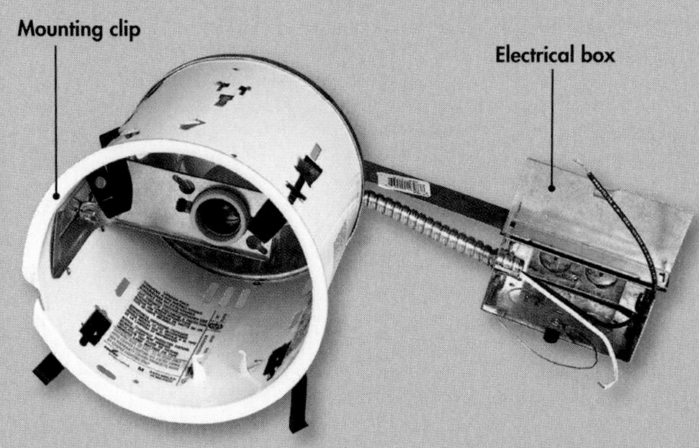

WORK SMART

POSITIONING LIGHTS

Canister lights come with mounting templates that show you what size hole to cut. Tape templates to the ceiling to get an idea of where your lights should go and how they will look.

TOOL TIP

USING AN ELONGATED FLEXIBLE BIT

This extra-long twist drill bit can spare you a lot of hassle when fishing wire through walls. The flexible bit allows you to drill through the wall at roughly a 45-degree angle, in the direction you want to thread the cable, and then continue until you reach what feels like a framing member. When the drill breaks through that plate or stud, have a look to see if you've come out roughly where you'd planned. To make it easier to run the cable, you can attach one end of the cable to the bit and pull them through together.

Installing recessed lighting (continued)

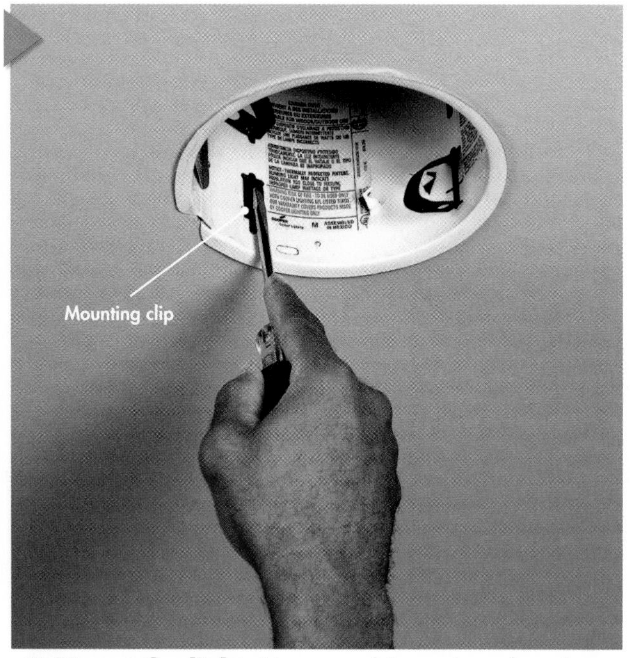

4 Mount the light. Most remodel cans have four clips that clamp the can to the ceiling by pushing down on the top of the drywall or plaster. Pull the clips in so they do not protrude outside the can. Slip the can's box into the hole, then push the can body up into the hole until its flange is tight to the ceiling. With your thumb or a screwdriver, push each clip up and outward until it clicks and clamps the fixture.

5 Add the trim. Most trims are mounted with coil springs or squeezable rod springs (as shown). If you have coil springs, hook each spring to its assigned hole inside the can (if it is not already there). Pull out each spring and hook it to the trim, then carefully guide the trim into position. If you have rod springs, squeeze and insert both ends of each spring into their assigned holes, then push the trim up. Different trims require different bulbs: The ones you'll need are marked on the inside of the trim.

CLOSER LOOK

MOUNTING A NEW-WORK CAN LIGHT

If ceiling joists are exposed, installation is easy.

On a workbench attach the plaster ring to the fixture. Adjust it to compensate for the thickness of the ceiling drywall that will be installed later. At the ceiling slide the mounting bars outward so they reach joists on each side. Hammer the four tabs into the joists. Strengthen with 1¼-inch wood screws.

Installing halogen lighting

See pages 588–590

Skill level:	Time to complete:	Materials:	Tools:
★☆☆☆☆	Experienced 30 min. Handy 1 hr. Novice 2 hrs.	Halogen kit (wire, lights, terminal block, transformer, cord switch), insulated staples	Drill with screwdriver bit, ¼-inch bit, and ½-inch bit; combination stripper; hammer

To light counters or display shelves, consider a halogen puck light kit that plugs into a receptacle. A typical kit includes a transformer, cord, cord switch, several hockey-puck-shape lights that attach to the underside of shelves or cabinets, and detailed instructions. If you don't like using a cord switch, plug the kit into a receptacle controlled by a switch or alter a receptacle and run cable so one outlet can be switched off and on (see page 167).

Halogen safety tips

Halogens provide intense, almost glittering light, and they get hot. Position them where people won't brush against them. Don't attach them to particleboard that may scorch. Use halogens in a closet only if you are sure they will always be 18 inches or more away from clothing or boxes. If you use them in small, enclosed spaces, such as above shelves enclosed with glass doors, reduce the heat by replacing a 20-watt bulb with a 10-watt bulb. Drill ¼-inch air vent holes in the cabinet above the puck lights.

- Halogens are very bright. Position them so they will be out of sight.
- Never use a halogen without the lens, which filters UV rays.
- Do not touch a bulb with your skin: Natural oils will cause the bulb to burn out. Always handle halogen bulbs with a soft cloth.

Installing puck lighting. Drill ½-inch holes to run wires or plan to staple wires to the surface. Remove the covers from the lights and mount the light bodies with screws. Most halogens are 120 volts, though some still run off low-voltage transformers. Wire the lights as directed.

To install rope lights simply staple a rope into place and plug it in. It's bright enough to use as undercabinet lighting for the countertop and doesn't get as hot as puck lighting. Install rope lights in a straight line or drape them in soft loops.

Installing fluorescent lighting

See pages 588–590

Skill level:	**Time to complete:**	**Materials:**	**Tools:**
★☆☆☆☆	Experienced 30 min. Handy 1 hr. Novice 2 hrs.	Fluorescent fixture, wire nuts, screws	Combination tool, lineman's pliers, drill with screwdriver bit

Fluorescent lights often are installed without a ceiling box: Cable is clamped to the fixture, which substitutes for a box. Some codes, however, require that fluorescent lights be attached to ceiling boxes. Suspend the fixture or set it in a suspended ceiling grid and make the connections. Square or rectangular fixtures with long tubes are the most common. Other fluorescent fixtures are shaped like incandescents and use circular or U-shape tubes.

▲ ***Installing a fluorescent.*** ***Shut off power at the service panel.*** *Remove the old fixture. Clamp the cable to a knockout in the new fixture and attach the fixture directly to the ceiling by driving screws into joists. Splice the fixture's wires to the incoming wires. Attach the cover plate.*

$ BUYER'S GUIDE

CONSIDER FLUORESCENT LIGHTING OPTIONS

- If an old fluorescent light needs a new ballast, consider replacing the fixture. Newer fluorescents with electronic ballasts will be trouble-free for decades.
- Save money by buying fixtures for 4-foot tubes. Smaller tubes are more expensive.
- Fluorescent tubes offer a greater variety of light than ever.
- A diffusing lens further softens the light.

▲ ***Installing fluorescents in a suspended ceiling.*** *Fluorescent fixtures fit into the ceiling grid, taking up the space of a 2'×2' (shown) or 2'×4' ceiling tile. For smaller fixtures install additional metal grid pieces and cut ceiling tiles to fit on either side.* ***Shut off power at the service panel;*** *run a cable with ground wire for the lights (see pages 389–390 for how to extend the incoming line), screw the light to the grid, and then attach the cable to the fixture. Leave more than enough cable to reach the power source. Connect the wires to the power source before installing the tiles.*

Installing track lighting

See pages 588–590

Skill level:	Time to complete:	Materials:	Tools:
★★★☆☆	Experienced 2 hrs. Handy 4 hrs. Novice 6 hrs.	Track system with lights, wire nuts, screws, plastic anchors	Combination tool, lineman's pliers, drill with screwdriver bit, tape measure, hacksaw or saber saw

A track system is the most versatile of all ceiling fixtures. You can configure it in many ways (see page 398), choose from several lamp styles (see page 403), and position the lamps to suit your needs. To begin installation remove the existing ceiling fixture to locate the track. If you don't have an existing ceiling fixture that is switched, see pages 378 and 385 for how to install one. Be sure to get a fixture with a floating canopy—this lets you move the track back and forth a few inches in case you need to make adjustments.

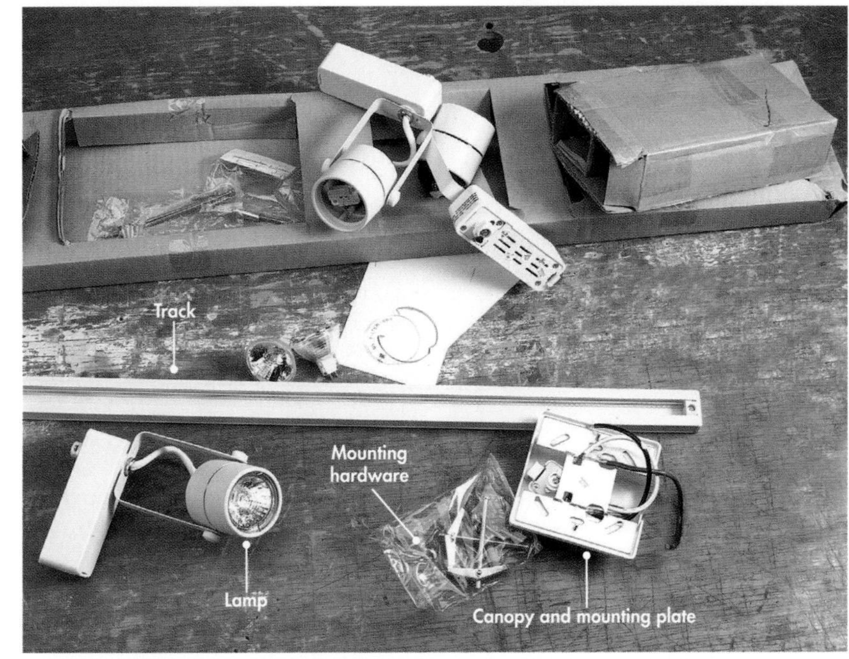

▲ ***Purchasing a track system.*** *Work with a salesperson; explain the size and configuration you want. Buy a kit that includes track, floating canopy mounting plate, end cap, and canopy. You also may have to buy additional track and end caps, as well as L- or T-fittings for the corners.*

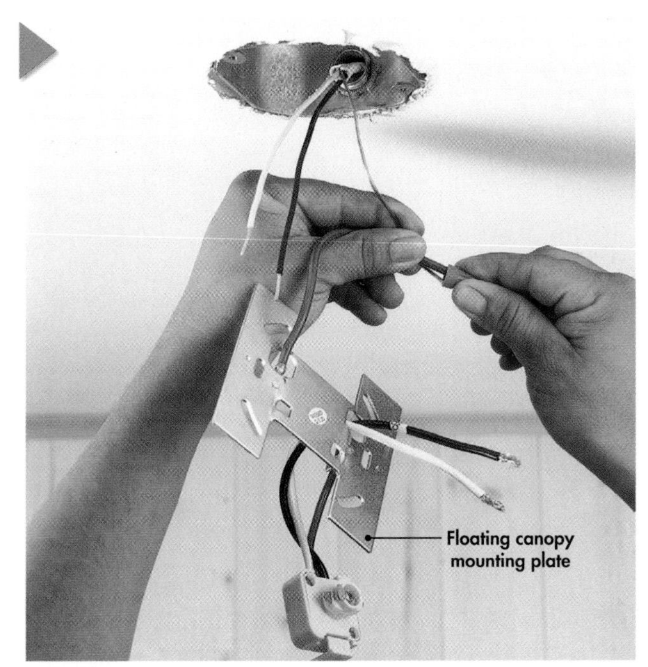

1 Install the mounting plate. Shut off power at the service panel. Use wire nuts to splice the house wires to the plate leads. Connect the ground wire to the plate and to the box if it is metal (see page 369). Push the wires into the box and screw the plate to the box so it is snug against the ceiling.

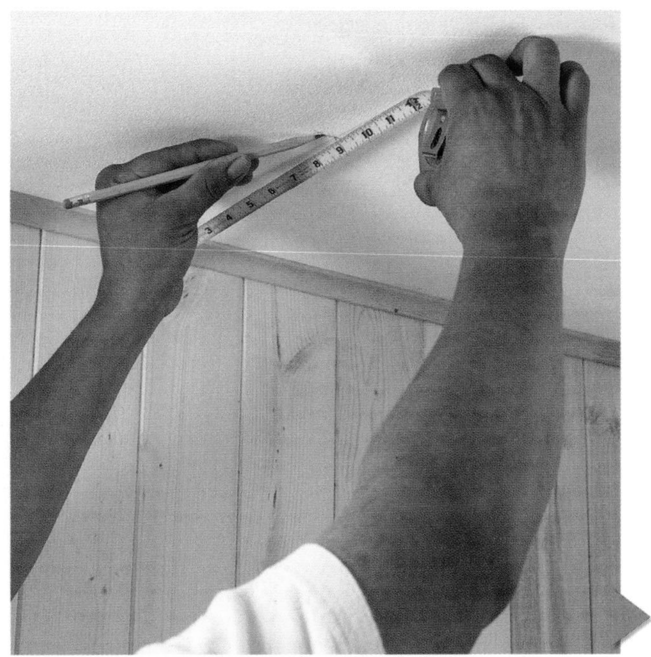

2 Measure and mark for the track. At the mounting plate measure to see how far the side of the track will be from the nearest wall. Mark the ceiling so the track will be parallel to the wall. Use a framing square to draw lines if the track turns a corner.

Installing track lighting (continued)

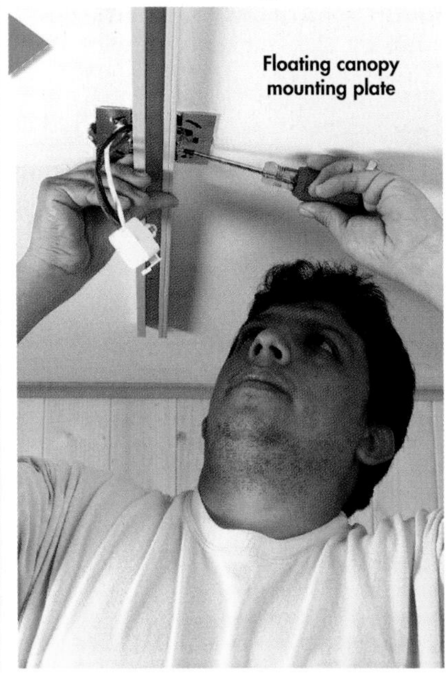

3 Attach the track to the mounting plate. Have a helper hold the track in place against the ceiling with it centered on the mounting plate. Drive the setscrews to anchor the track to the plate.

4 To locate joists if the track is more than 4 feet long, have a helper hold one end while you use a stud finder. Snap the track onto the plate and drive a screw into every available joist. If there are no joists, drill holes every foot or so, insert plastic anchors, and drive screws into the anchors.

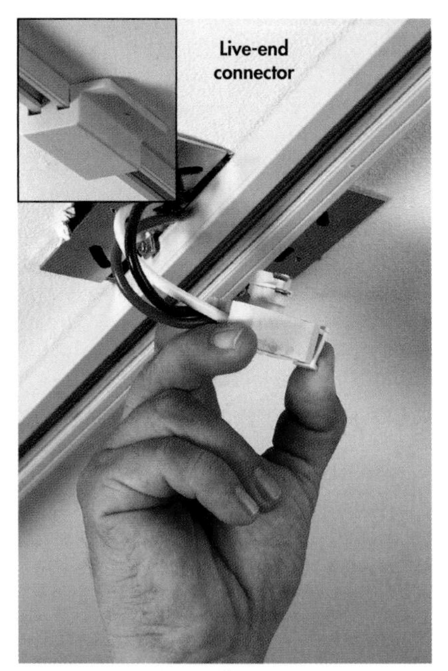

5 Twist on the live-end connector. Insert the live-end connector and turn it 90 degrees until it snaps into place. Align the connector's two copper tabs with the two copper bars inside the track. Snap the plastic canopy over the track and mounting plate. (See inset.)

CLOSER LOOK

CUTTING TRACK

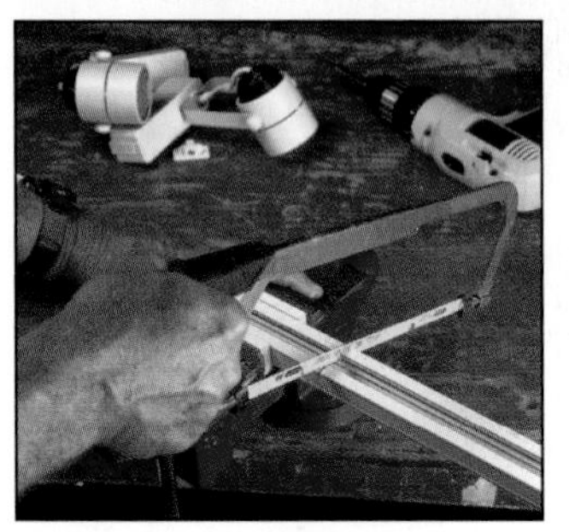

Tracks are available in standard lengths of 2, 4, 6, and 8 feet. If these sizes do not fit your needs, you can cut a track with a hacksaw or a saber saw equipped with a fine-tooth metal-cutting blade. Put some electrician's tape around the track first to protect it, then clamp the track in a vise. Cut slowly and take care not to bend the track while cutting. Attach the plastic end cap as necessary.

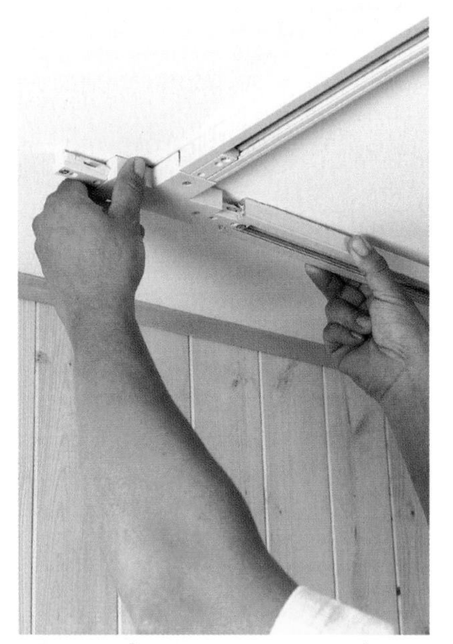

6 Attach a corner. You can buy connectors to make 90-degree turns, T-shapes, or odd-angled turns. Slide the connector into the track that is already installed, slide the next track onto the connector, and attach that track to the ceiling. Cover all open track ends with end caps.

7 Twist on a light. This type of light twists into place in the same way as the live-end connector (see Step 5). Another type has a metal arm that is twisted to tighten. Restore power, turn on the switch, and swivel the lights to position them to meet your needs.

Installing motion-sensor lights

See pages 588-590

Skill level:	Time to complete:	Materials:	Tools:
★★☆☆☆	Experienced 1 hr. Handy 1.5 hrs. Novice 2 hrs.	Motion-sensor light, wire nuts, perhaps a swivel strap	Combination tool, screwdriver

ELECTRICAL

Motion-sensor lights greet you when you come home at night, and they discourage potential burglars. If you have an existing floodlight, sensors are easy to install. (To install an exterior box for a new light, see page 377.)

Choose a fixture that lets you control the time and the sensitivity to motion. If the light is connected to a switch inside the house, you can override the motion sensor so the light stays on or off.

If you are using motion-sensor lights primarily to discourage intruders, position them at heights that will make it difficult to disable or knock them out. A safe height is usually above arm's reach, approximately 9 feet above the highest standing point.

1 Connect the light. Shut off power at the service panel. Remove the old light. If necessary install a swivel strap (also called an offset crossbar) so you can level the fixture after installation. Run the wires through the rubber gasket and splice them with wire nuts. While mounting the light to the box, position the gasket so it will keep the box dry.

2 Position the light. Restore power. Loosen the locknuts and twist the light until it is directed where you want it. Tighten the locknuts. At night switch the light on by flipping the wall switch off, then on again.

Ward off prowlers, not your neighbors

Neighbors may find it annoying if a floodlight is triggered to go on whenever they step out of their houses. Adjust the sensitivity of floods to ensure that they won't come on unless there is movement on your own property.

Locations for motion-sensor lights

Motion sensors should be installed in areas around your home where intruders are most likely to enter, such as near the front and back doors, above garage doors, and at the gate of a backyard fence.

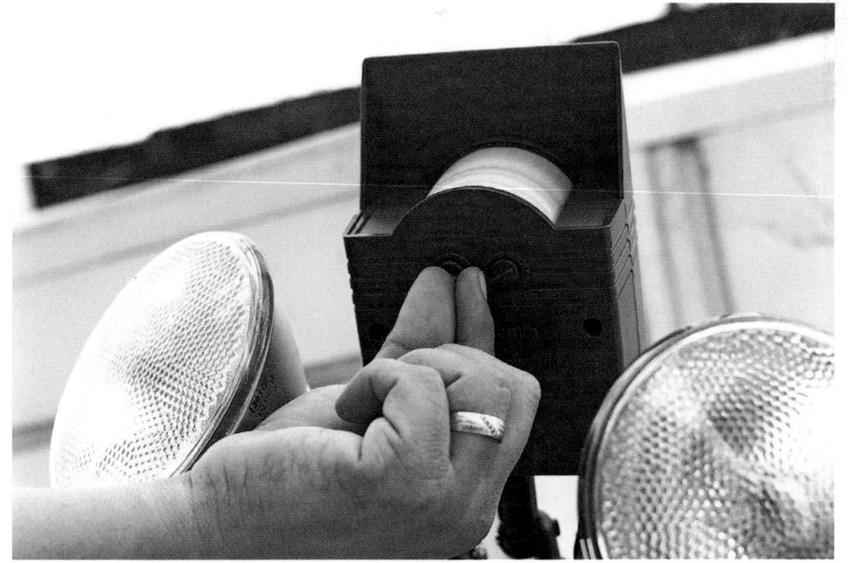

3 Make adjustments. To activate the motion sensor, manufacturer's instructions will probably tell you to turn off the wall switch, wait a few seconds, then turn it back on. Choose how long you want the light to stay on (set ON TIME). There may be a control that keeps the light less bright for the amount of time you choose (set DUAL BRIGHT). Set the RANGE to the middle position and test how sensitive the motion sensor is by walking around near it. Adjust as necessary.

Hanging a ceiling fan

See pages 588–590

Skill level: ★★★★★

Time to complete:
Experienced 2 hrs.
Handy 4 hrs.
Novice 8 hrs.

Materials: Fan, fan-rated box, downrod extender, light kit, fan/light switch (can be remote controlled), wire nuts, electrician's tape, wood screws

Tools: Drywall saw, hammer, adjustable wrench, screwdriver, voltage tester or multitester, combination stripper, lineman's pliers, long-nose pliers, side-cutting pliers, reciprocating saw or metal-cutting keyhole saw, drill

Ceiling fans circulate air downward to cool rooms in the summer and upward to evenly disperse heat in the winter. This is done be reversing the direction the fan turns, usually by a directional switch on the fan itself. Observe the following guidelines to install a fan, and it will effectively circulate the air in your home without hissing, wobbling, or pulling away from the ceiling.

Planning for a fan

Before installing a fan consider these issues:

- Decide whether to wire the switch to control the fan and the light separately. (See "Switching the Fan and Light" and ""Wireless Remote Switch" on page 419).
- Most fans include light kits. You can buy a separate light kit if your unit doesn't include one.
- Plan how you'll cover the hole once you remove the old ceiling box. Buy a light with a canopy that's wide enough to cover the hole or get a medallion to hide ceiling imperfections.
- Measure the length and width of the room you want to cool and talk to salespeople at your local home improvement center to find out what size fan(s) you need.
- Fans should have downrods long enough to position fan blades at least 10 inches from the ceiling and at least 7 feet from the floor.
- If you install a control use only a fan-rated speed control; a standard dimmer switch will burn out the fan motor.

WORK SMART

DOWNRODS

There are two broad options for hanging fans: close to the ceiling, or hung from a "downrod," an extension pipe that lets you drop the fan down lower. Get a downrod that puts the fan where you want it, but put it at least 10 inches from the ceiling and no fewer than 7 feet from the floor.

SAFETY ALERT

USE A FAN-RATED BOX

A ceiling fan box differs from an ordinary ceiling box in two ways: First it is designed to attach very firmly, either directly to a joist or with a support bar. Second it is equipped with deep-threaded holes or strong bolts so you can tightly clamp the fan to it. An ordinary ceiling box won't have the strength to hold the weight of a ceiling fan.

Removing and replacing the box

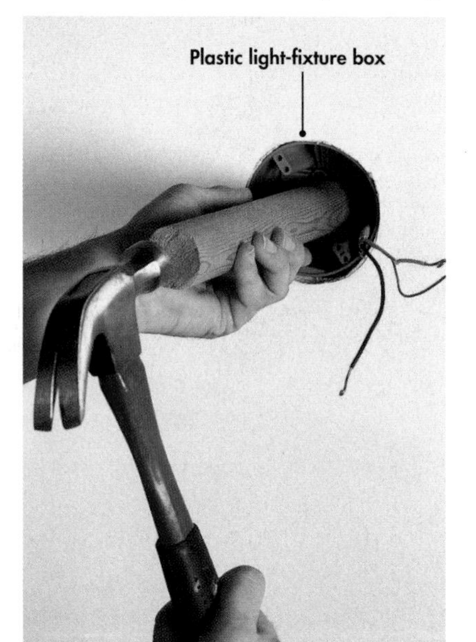

Remove the ceiling box. Shut off power at the service panel. Sometimes you can remove screws or nails and pry out the box. You may have to carefully cut away drywall or plaster to get to fasteners. If the box is nailed to a joist, cut around the box to enlarge the hole and tap the box loose using a piece of wood and a hammer. You may be able to cut through fasteners or nails with a reciprocating saw or a metal-cutting keyhole saw. Take great care not to slice through any cable.

Screw a fan box to a joist from below. If you have a joist in the middle of the hole (as may be the case if you removed a thin pancake ceiling box), attaching a fan box from below will be easy. Buy a thin fan-rated box and clamp the cable to it. Hold it in place and drill pilot holes, then drive in 2-inch wood screws. (Avoid using drywall screws or all-purpose screws; they break too easily.)

Adding a new ceiling box

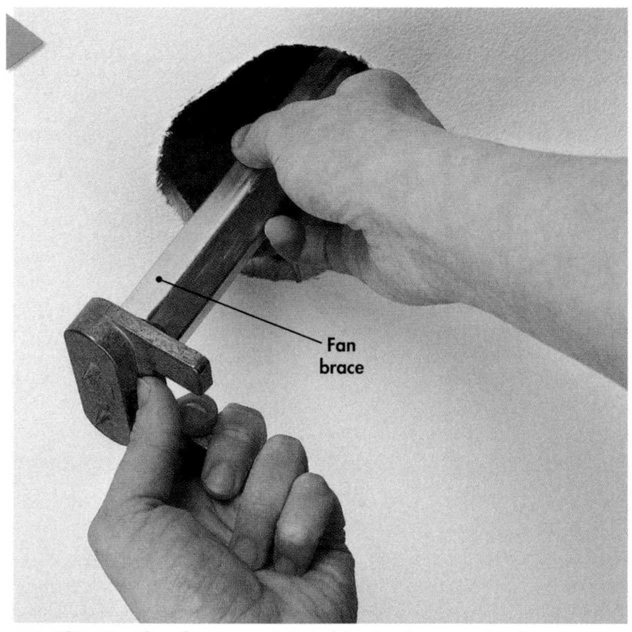

1 Slip in the brace. Assemble the box on the brace to understand how it goes together, then take it apart. Push the brace in through the hole and spread it apart until it touches the joists on both sides. The legs of the brace at each end should rest on top of the drywall or plaster.

2 Tighten the brace. Measure to make sure that the brace is centered in the hole. Position it on the joists at the correct height so that the box will be flush with the surface of the ceiling. Use an adjustable wrench or channel-type pliers to tighten the brace until it is firm. Tightening beyond this point can cause the ceiling to crack.

WORK SMART

CEILING BOX OPTIONS

When framing is accessible attach a ceiling box to a joist. Install this type of box in unfinished ceilings or ceilings with a large hole. Drill pilot holes and drive in 1 ¼-inch wood screws to attach it to a joist.

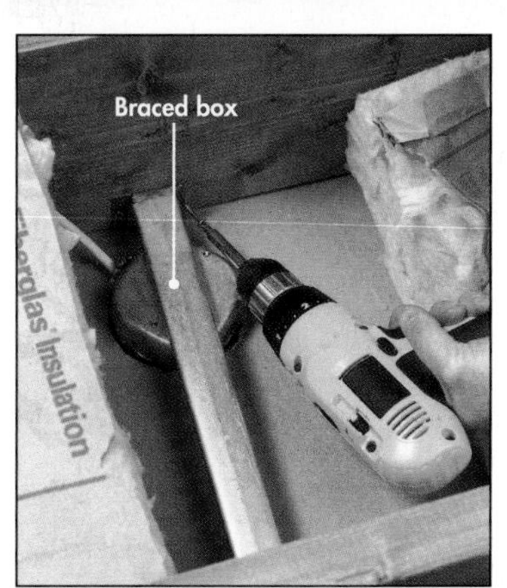

Or install a braced box from above. Buy a new-work box with a brace. Slide the box along the brace into position. Tighten the clamp. Attach the brace by driving in 1 ¼-inch wood screws.

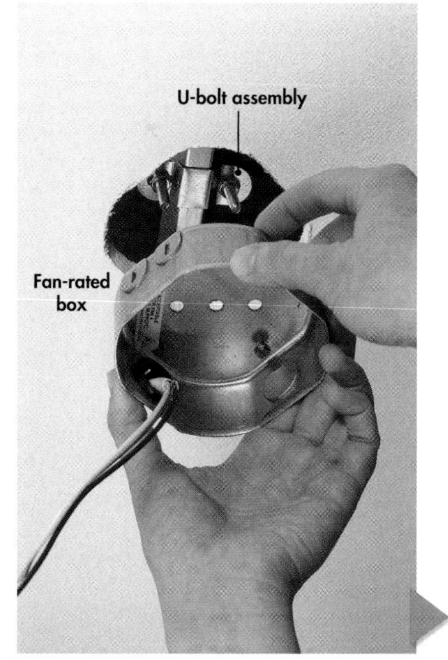

3 Attach the box. Attach the U-bolt assembly to the brace so that the assembly is centered in the hole and the bolts face down. Thread cable through the cable connector and into the fan-rated box. Slip the box up so the bolts slide through it and tighten the nuts to secure the box.

Hanging a ceiling fan (continued)

See pages 588–590

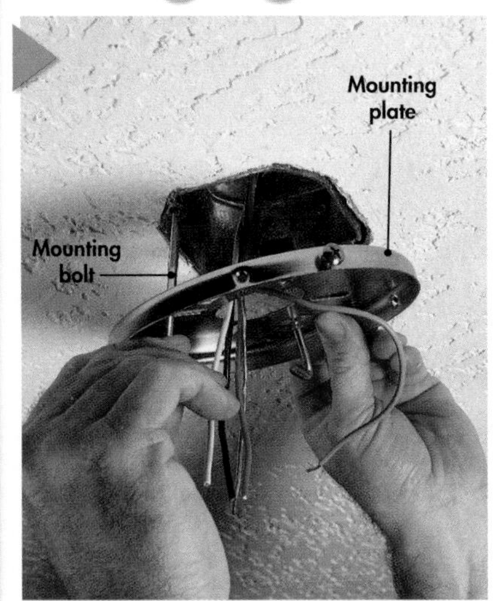

4 Install the mounting plate. Thread the wires through the center of the mounting plate. If the box has mounting bolts that poke through the plate, fit the mounting plate over the bolts and fasten it with nuts provided. If separate bolts are provided, push each one through the mounting plate as shown. When both bolts are in place, tighten the plate onto the ceiling. It is extremely important to attach the mounting plate securely to the ceilng and ensure that all rubber feet touch drywall to prevent fan wobbling. Plate and bracket designs vary.

5 Assemble the downrod and canopy. On a worktable ready the fan for installation, following manufacturer's instructions. Run the fan leads through the trim ring, canopy, and downrod and screw on the downrod tightly. Tighten the setscrews. The bulb-shape fitting at the top of the downrod will rest in the canopy when the canopy is attached to the ceiling. Do not to mangle the wires. Wait to attach the fan blades.

6 Wire the fan. Hang the fan from the temporary mounting system that comes with the fan (designs vary). Connect the copper ground wire to the green wire attached to the fan base. If you have only two wires, connect both the black lead (for the fan motor) and the blue or striped lead (for the light) to the black house wire, and the white lead to the white house wire. If you have three-wire cable, connect black to black, white to white, and red to the blue or striped light lead. Check the manufacturer's directions. You may choose to install a remote control unit (see Buyer's Guide, opposite).

Fanning your way to lower energy bills

A ceiling fan can do more than add atmosphere and generate a pleasant breeze. Used knowledgeably it also can reduce your energy bills for both heating and air-conditioning. In summer run the fan counter-clockwise to promote evaporative cooling. You may feel comfortable enough to adjust the thermostat upward, resulting in an energy saving of up to 47 percent on your cooling costs. In winter you can realize a saving of up to 10% by reversing the fan's rotation to distribute the warm air that tends to layer up at the ceiling.

CLOSER LOOK

SWITCHING THE FAN AND LIGHT

You probably have two-wire cable (not counting the ground wire) running into the ceiling fixture. If so you have three options to control the fan and the light:

- Hook the both the fan and light wires to the black lead coming out of the ceiling and use the wall switch to turn the fan and the light on or off at the same time. Use the pull chains on the fixture to control the speeds.
- Install a radio frequency remote remote-control to install the fan and the light, as shown on the opposite page. The receiver should be located inside the fan canopy, and the transmitter can be either wall-mounted or hand-held.
- Run three-wire cable from the fixture to the switch and hook it up. You can conveniently control the fan and light separately by using a special wall switch. If in addition you buy a hard-wired fan control, you can dim the light and adjust the fan speed from the switch. Such an installation is fairly labor-intensive, however.

7 Attach the canopy to the mounting plate. Use a helper to support the fan motor while you drive the screws. Most ceiling fans provide a system that allows for easy attachment of the canopy to the mounting plate without having to manually support the weight of the fan for a long period of time. Push the wires and wire nuts up into the box to keep them from getting pinched. against the canopy when the fan is running. Secure the canopy to the mounting plate by tighting all fasteners. Snap the trim ring in place to hide the mounting hardware.

8 Attach the blades and lights. Following the manufacturer's directions attach the fan blades to their brackets, then attach the brackets to the motor. If there are light fixtures, install them as specified.

9 Balance the blades. If the fan wobbles first check that the unit is mounted securely and the screws holding the blades are tight. If so, find the balancing kit included in the packaging for your fan. After turning off the fan, stick or clip a weight to any blade. Do a test run at various speeds. Repeat the procedure for each blade until the fan operates more smoothly. Then shift the weight along the blade's length in either direction, testing until the blades are rotating with little noise or vibration.

$ BUYER'S GUIDE

WIRELESS REMOTE SWITCH

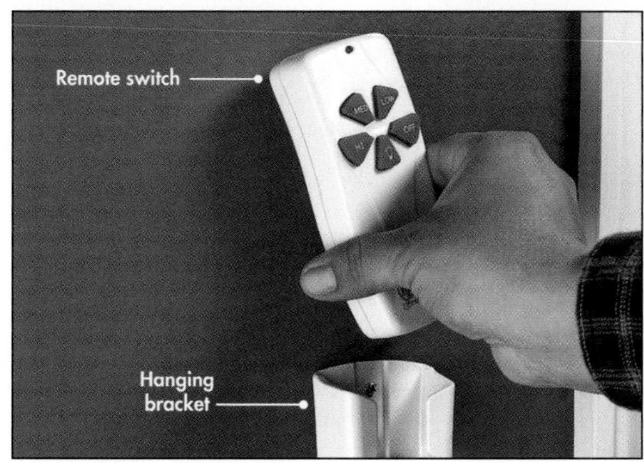

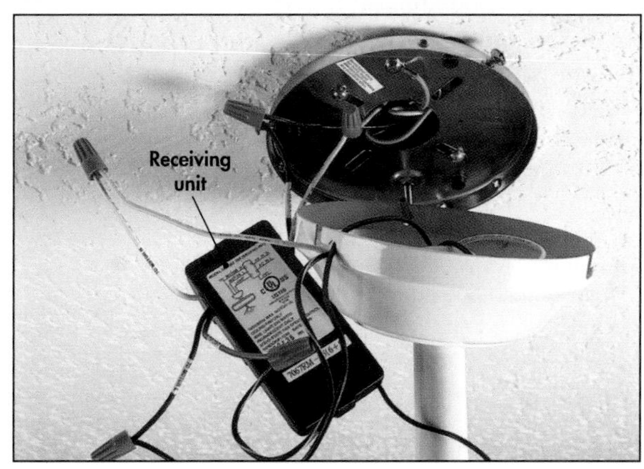

If you have only two wires running from the switch to the fan box, a remote control will let you control the fan and light separately. Before you install the canopy, hook up the receiving unit with both fan (black) and light (blue or striped) leads spliced to the remote's black lead, and the receiver's white wire spliced to the white lead. Make sure the little dip switches are set the same on the remote switch unit and the receiving unit. Install the canopy as in Step 7 above. Put a battery in the sending unit and attach a hanging bracket on a wall. If the ceiling fixture was originally switched, the two wires sending power to the fan are still controlled by that switch. The sending unit controls the fan or light, or both, only when the wall switch is on.

Installing an attic fan

See pages 588-590

Skill level:	Time to complete:	Materials:	Tools:
★★★☆☆	Experienced 4 hrs. Handy 6 hrs. Novice 9 hrs.	Attic fan, cable with clamps, wire nuts, electrician's tape	Drill, fish tape, screwdriver, lineman's pliers, combination stripper

ELECTRICAL

Temperatures in an attic can reach 150 degrees in the summer, making it difficult (and expensive) to keep a home cool. An attic fan, a whole-house fan, or a roof fan slashes energy costs and reduces temperatures.

The manufacturer should provide a chart detailing how powerful a fan you need based on the size of your attic. Depending on the size of your house, you may require more than one fan.

1 Bring power into the attic. Before tapping into a receptacle or junction box for power, check the amperage on your attic fan and make sure you will not overload the circuit. **Shut off power to the circuit.** See pages 389–390 for tips on running cable into the attic. Check with local codes to see whether you need to use armored cable instead of NM cable.

CLOSER LOOK

AN ATTIC MUST BREATHE

An attic fan, whole-house fan, or roof fan moves air efficiently only if the attic is properly ventilated. Usually a house needs vents near the bottom of the attic (usually under the eaves) and vents near the roof peak, such as turbine vents, gable vents, or a continuous vent running along the ridge. Check that eave vents are not clogged with insulation. If you are not sure that your attic is properly vented, have it inspected by a professional roofer.

2 Mount the fan. At a louvered opening in the attic, secure the fan by driving screws through its mounting brackets and into studs. If the studs do not allow you to center the fan in the opening, attach horizontal 2×4s that span between the studs. Attach the fan to the studs. You may choose to install louvers that close when the fan is not operating.

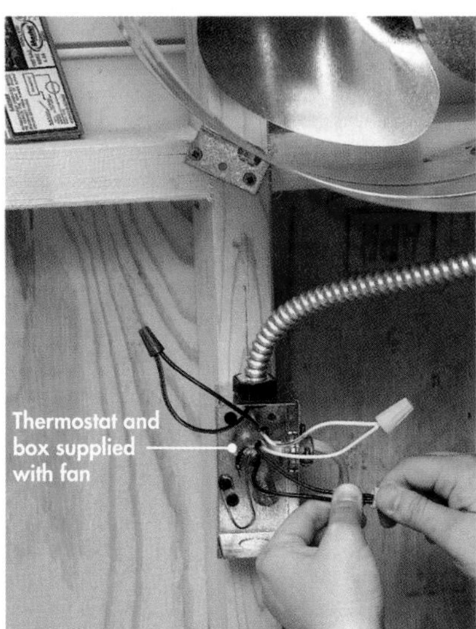

3 Make the electrical connections. The fan has its own thermostat switch. Mount the thermostat box to a framing member. Follow the manufacturer's instructions for connecting wires. Restore power and adjust the temperature control. Or you can control the fan with a switch located downstairs.

Installing a whole-house fan

See pages 588-590

Skill level:	Time to complete:	Materials:	Tools:
★★★★★	Experienced 6 hrs. Handy 8 hrs. Novice 12 hrs.	Whole-house fan, screws, junction box, switch box, cable with clamps, wire nuts, electrician's tape	Stud finder, drill, ladder, saw, combination stripper, lineman's pliers, screwdriver

ELECTRICAL

Find a powerful yet quiet whole-house fan to pull up air through the house and into your attic. A whole-house fan is ideal for spring and fall cooling in hot climates; it may be the only method of cooling you need in moderate climates. For the fan to work, the attic must have adequate ventilation (see opposite page), and windows on the first floor must be open. Measure your home's square footage to choose the right size fan. It takes as much time and effort to put in wiring for an undersize fan that will not cool your house as it does to put in the right fan to be comfortable.

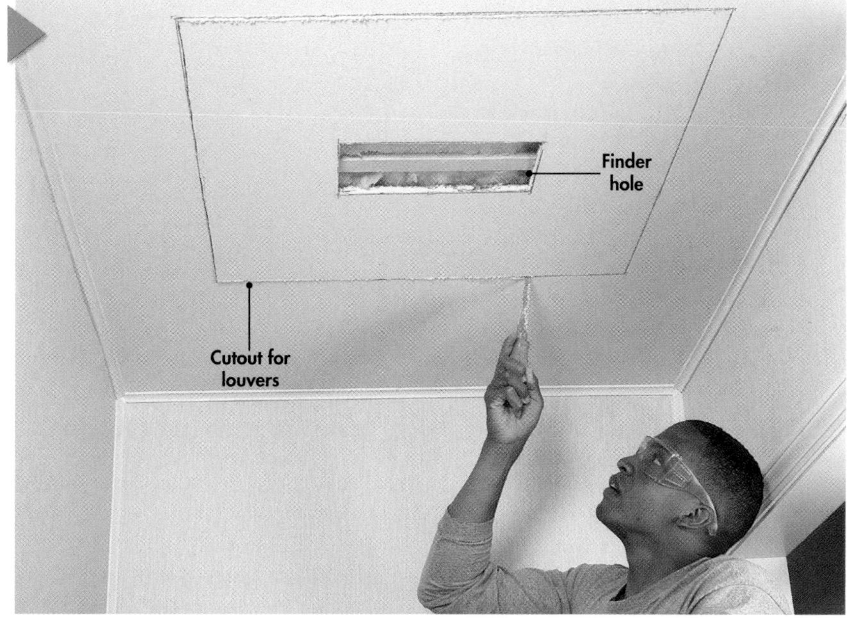

1 Cut a hole. Fans are designed to be positioned over one joist so you don't have to compromise ceiling framing. Use a stud finder, then cut a 1'×2' finder hole to confirm that the fan will center on a joist. Mark the cutout for the louvers and cut through the drywall or lath and plaster. The fan manufacturer will specify dimensions for the hole.

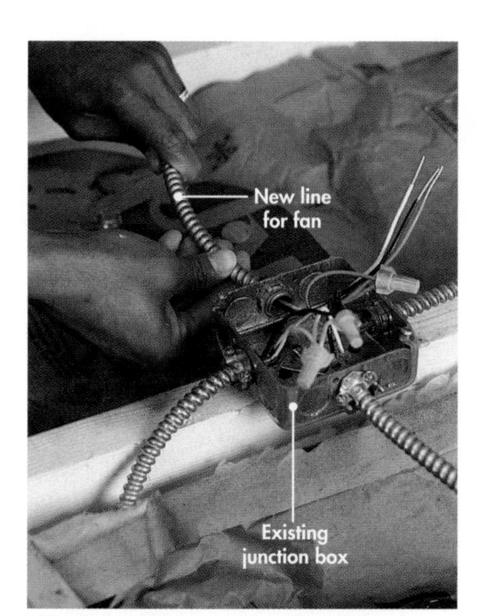

2 Bring power to the fan. After making sure that you will not overload a circuit (see page 368), **shut off power to the circuit.** Tap into a junction box or run cable up into the attic (see pages 389–390). Local codes may require you to use armored cable instead of NM cable (see page 391).

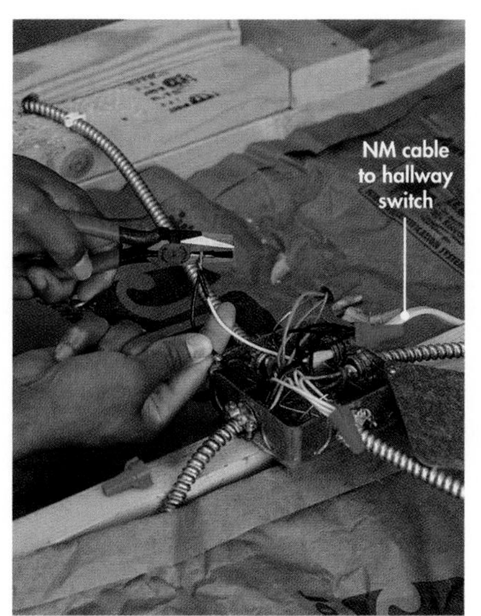

3 Wire for the switch. A fan-rated rheostat switch lets you vary the fan speed. Bring the two-wire switch cable to the box, marking the white wire black at both ends. Splice it to the black wires in the box. Splice the other switch wire to the fan's black wire and the fan's white to the white wires in the box. Connect the ground.

4 Mount the fan. With a helper lift the fan up through the opening and into the attic. Add 2×4 framing as needed so that the fan is securely centered over a joist. Attach brackets to the fan frame and position them so they will slip over the exposed joist. Center the fan over the opening and secure the brackets with bolts.

Installing a whole-house fan (continued)

5 Enclose the fan. Pull back the insulation and cut pieces of 2×4 blocking to fill gaps at either side of the fan. At each side cut two pieces to fit between the joists (shown) or one notched piece that fits over the joist. (Some manufacturers supply blocking.) Attach the wood to the joists by drilling pilot holes and driving 3-inch screws or 16D nails.

6 Wire the rheostat switch. Install a fan-rated rheostat switch in the hallway, connecting it to the cable you have run through the wall from the attic junction box. Wire as shown or use the manufacturer's directions.

7 Attach the louvers. Hold the louver panel against the ceiling so it covers the hole. Attach the panel by driving screws into the joists and blocking. Restore power and test the fan.

CLOSER LOOK

A ROOF FAN WILL PULL THE AIR OUT OF YOUR ATTIC

If your attic does not have a vertical wall to accommodate an attic fan (see page 420), this is the next most efficient way to pull air out of an attic. The most difficult part of this installation is not the electrical work but cutting the hole and properly sealing the roofing around the fan. The shingles must be laid correctly over the fan flashing or the roof will leak. Call a roofer if you aren't sure how to seal the fan. If you are uncomfortable working on the roof, hire a professional.

1 Cut the hole. Follow the manufacturer's directions for cutting a hole through the roof and for cutting back shingles from around the hole. Carefully fold back the shingles.

2 Install the fan. Slide the fan under the shingles and apply roofing cement as directed. Wire the fan as you would an attic fan (see page 420).

Installing a bathroom vent

Skill level:	Time to complete:	Materials:	Tools:
★★★★★	Experienced 8 hrs. Handy 12 hrs. Novice 15 hrs.	Bathroom vent fan, ducts, end cap or roof cap, straps and screws, roofing cement, shingles, roofing nails, caulk, wire nuts, cable with clamps, duct tape, electrician's tape	Drill, fish tape, keyhole saw or reciprocating saw or saber saw, hammer, combination stripper, lineman's pliers, screwdriver

A vent fan considerably improves the atmosphere in a bathroom by pulling out moisture, odors, and heat. Codes require bathrooms to have vent fans if there is no natural ventilation, such as a window. When choosing a fan use these guidelines:

- Make sure the fan will move the air. Unfortunately many bathroom fans do little more than make noise. This happens when either the fan is not strong enough or the path through the ductwork is not free and clear. Measure your room and determine how far the ductwork has to travel. Then ask a home center salesperson to help you choose a fan and the ductwork to do the job. Keep in mind that air travels more freely through solid ducts than through flexible hoses.
- Consider a fan equipped with a light. Some units have a fan only, while others include one or more added features: a ceiling light, a low-wattage nightlight, or a forced-air heating unit.
- Consider the wiring options. In some locations local codes require that the fan activates whenever the overhead light is turned on. Given the choice some people prefer separate switches for the fan and light.
- Check local practices. In hot, sunny climates venting through the roof may be asking for leaks. If so vent through the wall, as shown in "Installing a Range Hood," page 426.

Ductwork and vent fan installation

Running duct through a wall

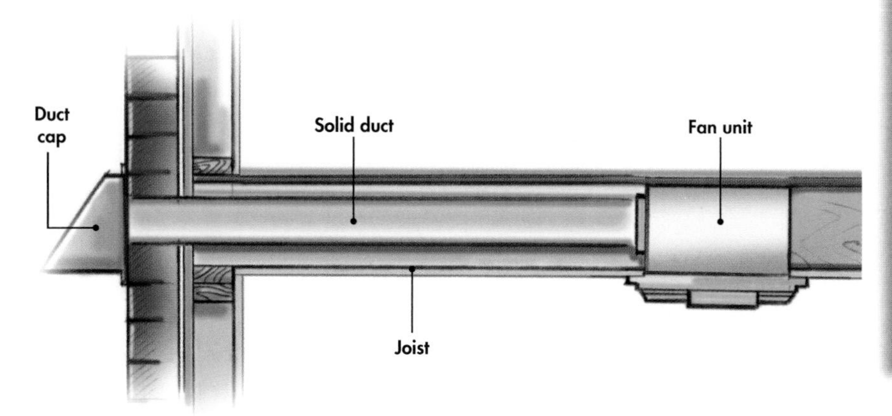

Choose the shortest and straightest route. A wall vent is the easiest to install because no roofing is involved. However it may be difficult to run ductwork between joists.

Duct through the roof

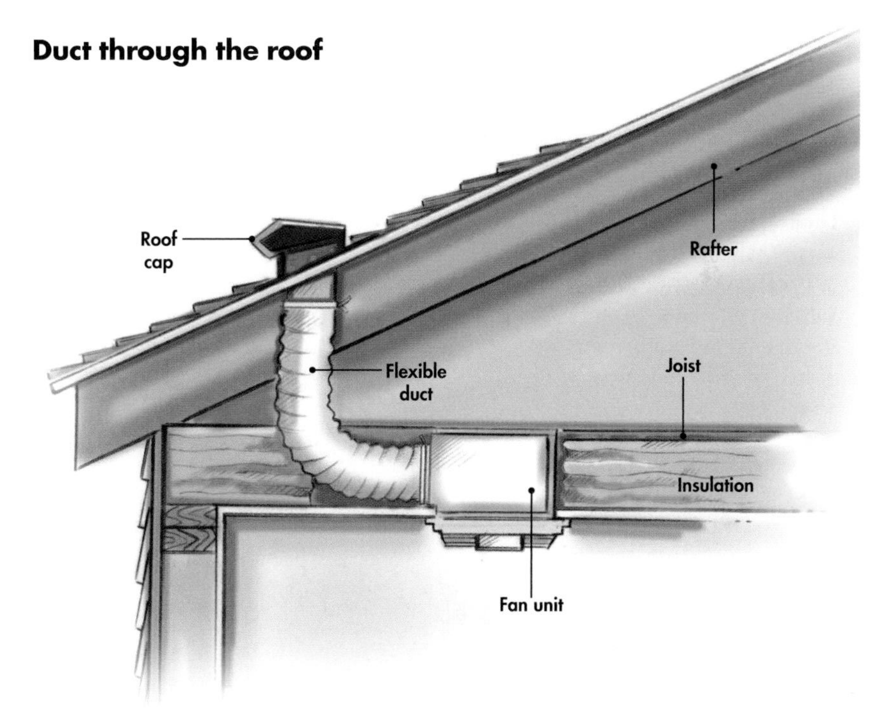

You may have no choice but to run ductwork through an attic and out the roof. Choose a short, straight path and cut the roof and shingles correctly to avoid leaks. Moist air inside can condense on the ducts and drip onto insulation; you may want to wrap the duct with pipe insulation.

Installing a bathroom vent (continued)

1 Cut the hole. From the attic hold the fan against a joist and mark its outline with a pencil. Cut out the opening. If there is no attic, from the bathroom use a stud sensor to locate a joist and cut the opening from below. Shut off power to the circuit and provide power if none is present (see pages 389–391).

2 Attach the fan and dam off insulation. Attach the fan to the joist with screws. Some models require a 6-inch gap between the unit and insulation. Cut or push back the insulation, then cut pieces of 2×4 lumber to fit between the joists and attach the lumber with screws or nails.

3 Cut a hole in the roof. On the underside of the roof, trace a circle just large enough for the roof cap tailpiece. Drill a hole large enough for the saw blade, then cut with a reciprocating saw, saber saw, or keyhole saw. (See Work Smart, page 425, for how to run the ductwork out the wall.)

A label on the fan packaging will indicate how many square feet of bathroom space the fan can successfully clear. If there's any doubt or if your ductwork will be more than 5 feet long, get a slightly more powerful fan than you need. (However don't overdo it. Keep the power of the fan appropriate to the size of the room.) Fans are rated by sones. The higher the sone rating, the more noise the fan will make.

4 Cut away shingles. Remove shingles from around the cutout without damaging the underlying roofing paper. The lower part of the roof cap flange will rest on top of the shingles, and the top part will slip under the shingles.

5 Install the roof cap. Smear roofing cement on the underside of the cap flange. Slip the upper flange under the shingles as you insert the cap into the hole. Install the shingles on the side, smearing the undersides with roofing cement. Attach the flange with roofing nails; cover the nailheads with roofing cement.

See pages 588–590

ELECTRICAL

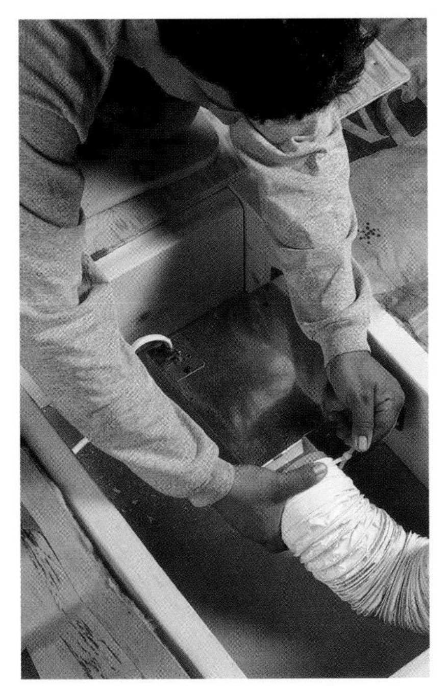

6 Connect the ductwork. At both the roof cap and the fan, slide a clamp over the flexible duct and slip the duct over the tailpiece. Slide the clamp back over the tailpiece and tighten the clamp. Wrap the joint with duct tape.

7 Wire the fan. If wiring does not exist, run cable to the fan and to a switch. If you are installing a fan/light, run three-wire cable from the switch to the fan. Connect the wiring according to the manufacturer's directions. Plug the motor into the built-in receptacle.

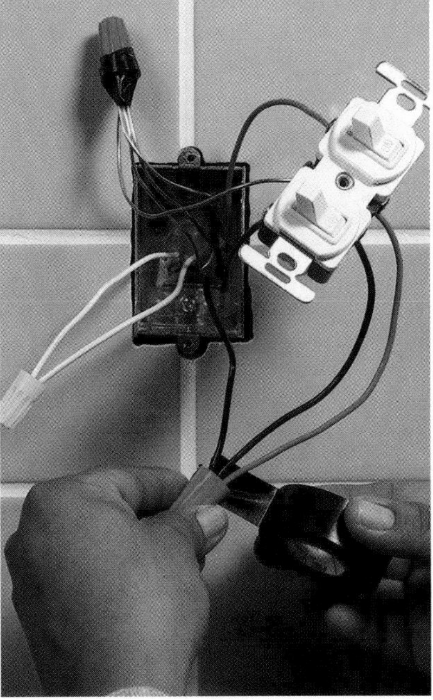

8 Wire the switch. For a fan/light switch that has power entering the switch box, splice the white wires and connect the grounds. Connect power to both switches through two pigtails (see page 372) spliced to the feed wire. Connect the red wire to one switch terminal and the black wire to the other terminal.

WORK SMART

INSTALLING A WALL VENT

If a bathroom is not located directly beneath an attic, you must vent air out through a wall. Even if there is an attic above, it may be easier to run the vent out through a gable wall rather than through the roof. When running ductwork through a ceiling cavity, it is sometimes easier to shove a piece of solid ductwork through rather than snaking flexible ducting. From inside the attic drill a locator hole through to the outside, then cut out the siding with a reciprocating saw, saber saw, or keyhole saw.

1 Make a tailpiece. Press the duct pipe into the cap. Use sheet metal screws to attach a piece of solid duct to the cap, then caulk the joint or wrap it with duct tape. Apply a bead of caulk to the back of the flange so that it will seal against the siding.

2 Attach the vent. Caulk around the hole and push in the tailpiece. Secure it with four screws. Caulk around the edge of the vent. Complete the connection to the fan indoors using solid or flexible ductwork.

Installing a range hood

See pages 588–590

Skill level: ★★★☆☆

Time to complete:
Experienced 6 hrs.
Handy 10 hrs.
Novice 14 hrs.

Materials: Range hood, solid duct, wall cap, masonry screws, cable and clamps, wire nuts, caulk, electrician's tape

Tools: Drill, fish tape, saber saw or reciprocating saw, safety goggles, hammer and cold chisel, screwdriver, combination stripper, lineman's pliers

For the best range hood efficiency, run the duct through the wall directly behind the range hood, in as straight a line as possible. You can run the vents of most hoods out the back or the top of the unit.

If a wall stud is in the way of the ductwork, you could do carpentry work to change the framing. An easier solution is to purchase a hood with an extra-strong motor and run the duct around the stud.

Before you purchase a fan, check its CFM rating, which indicates the number of cubic feet of air it pulls per minute. Choose a fan with a CFM rating that is double the square footage of your kitchen.

If the location of your stove makes it impossible to run a vent outside, ask about a ductless vent. A ductless vent pulls the air through a filter that removes odors and grease. It won't work as efficiently as a fully ducted unit, but it will help remove odors, smoke, and grease. You will have to change filters frequently for best results.

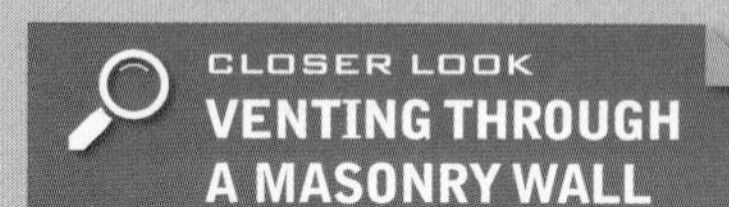

CLOSER LOOK
VENTING THROUGH A MASONRY WALL

Use a long masonry bit to drill the locator holes. Draw the outline and drill holes about every inch along the outline. Use a hammer and cold chisel to chip out the brick. To attach the duct cap, drill holes and drive masonry screws.

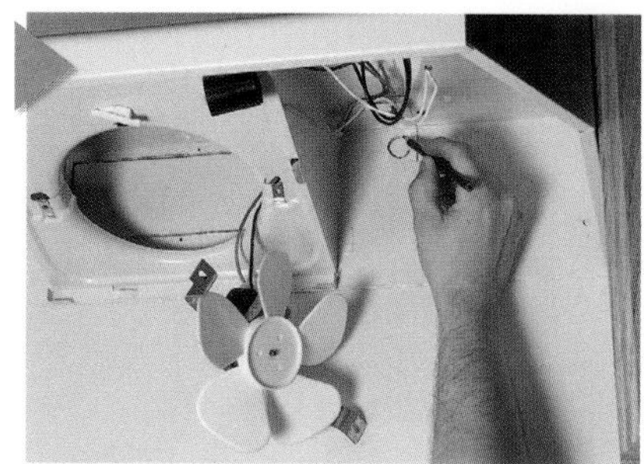

1 Mark the holes. Remove the filter, fan, and electrical housing cover from the range hood. Remove the knockouts for the electrical cable and the duct. Hold the hood in place and mark the holes for the duct and the cable.

2 Cut out the vent hole and drill a locator hole. Cut holes through the drywall or plaster. Drill holes at each corner all the way through the outside wall.

3 Cut the siding. Connect the dots between the holes on the outside to mark the outline of the hole. Cut out the opening. Remove any insulation or debris.

4 Attach the duct cap. Push the wall cap into the wall to see if the duct is long enough to reach the range hood. If not purchase an extension and attach it with sheet metal screws and duct tape. Apply caulk to the siding where the cap flange will rest. Push the cap into place and fasten with screws. Caulk the perimeter of the flange.

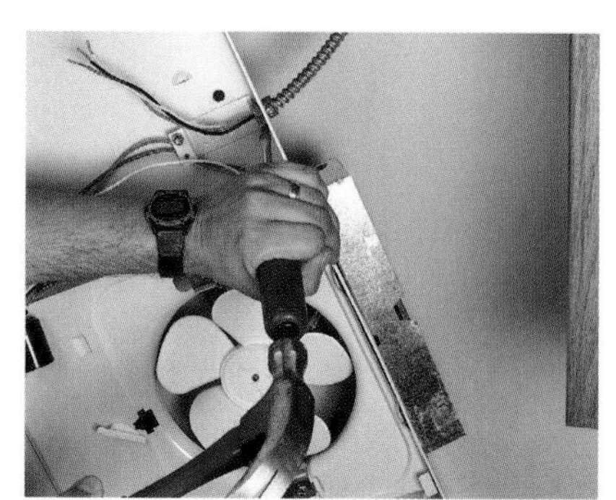

5 Run power to the hood. Shut off power to the circuit. Run cable from a nearby receptacle or junction box through the hole in the wall. Strip the sheathing and clamp the cable to the range hood electrical knockout. Mount the hood securely by driving screws into studs or adjacent cabinets.

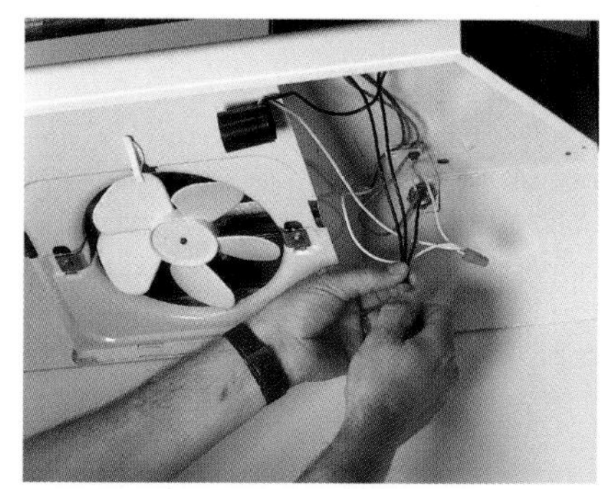

6 Connect the wires. Splice the white wire to the white fixture lead, the black wire to the black lead, and the ground wire to the green lead. Fold the wires into place and replace the electrical cover. Reattach the fan and filter. Restore power and test.

Installing low-voltage landscape lighting

Skill level:	Time to complete:	Materials:	Tools:
★★☆☆☆	Experienced 1 hr. Handy 2 hrs. Novice 3 hrs.	Set of low-voltage outdoor landscaping lights with a transformer/timer	Screwdriver, drill, tool for trenching, lineman's pliers

Low-voltage landscape lights—those that are 12-volt AC—literally are a snap to install. The lighting parts snap together, and the connectors snap into place. The cable looks like a lamp cord.

Landscape lights are available in a package that contains the transformer, the lights, and the connectors that you'll need. You also can buy the system piece by piece so you get exactly what you want. Talk with the sales staff to make sure you get the right transformer.

If necessary splice low-voltage wires. Strip the wires, put in a silicone-filled cap (sold as a grease cap), and attach the new wire. Some caps are brand-specific, so make sure you buy a cap designed for your wire.

Most low-voltage lighting systems include a transformer that is plugged into a regular outdoor receptacle.

The size of the transformer varies; most are rated to handle a load of 100 to 300 watts. The higher the rating, the more cable and light fixtures you can connect to the system. A timer in the transformer turns the system on at dusk and off at dawn. One end of the cable connects to the transformer; you can attach lights to the cable anywhere you want.

1 Wire the transformer. A transformer steps the voltage down from 120 volts to 12 volts. Attaching the cable for the lights is an easy task of screwing the wires in place. Details vary by manufacturer, so follow the directions that come with the transformer.

2 Hang the transformer. Mount the transformer on the wall next to a GFCI outlet. For most types of siding, you can make the attachment with a wood screw. Drive it into the plywood of the sheathing underneath the siding. For masonry drill a hole and drive a masonry screw.

The solar alternative

As simple as installing low-voltage lighting may be, you can have it simpler still by going with a solar-powered system. There are two basic approaches. Each lighting fixture can have its own collector, meaning that there's no need for running cable between them. Or place several lights along a circuit that's energized by a remote collector. This second alternative is a good idea if the lights run through a shady area and wouldn't be able to generate much juice. You can place the collector in a sunny patch—even on the side of an outbuilding. Keep in mind that solar lights typically aren't as bright as those with a transformer. That's why these fixtures are best used to delineate a walk or driveway, rather than to flood an area with light.

WORK SMART

GET ENOUGH POWER

If you want to light a long path with low-voltage lighting, it's not enough to just buy a kit and a few extra lights. Your transformer might not be able to supply enough power for a long cable with so many lights, resulting in lighting that is extremely dim. Ask the salesperson if the transformer you're buying will do the job you want it to do.

Installing low-voltage landscape lighting (continued)

3 Assemble the lights. Light fixtures usually require assembly. You'll need to snap the socket in place at the very least, and you may need to do some simple wiring. Follow the manufacturer's directions.

4 Place the lights. Lay the light fixtures in the approximate spots they will be installed and run the cable across the ground from light to light.

5 Connect the lights. Attach the cable connectors. For this light put half the connector on each side of the cable and snap it together to connect the lights.

WORK SMART

SHOVELPROOF THE WIRING

After a while you'll tend to forget just where you buried the wires for the landscape lighting, and one poke with a shovel can make big trouble. To protect those thin wires, run them through rigid but flexible PVC hose, available at plumbing supply stores. This will take a bit more work during installation because you'll have to dig a wider trench. But if the wiring passes through beds where you plan to do some gardening, the time will be well spent.

6 Dig for the cable. Dig a shallow trench alongside the cable and place the cable in the trench, but do not bury it yet.

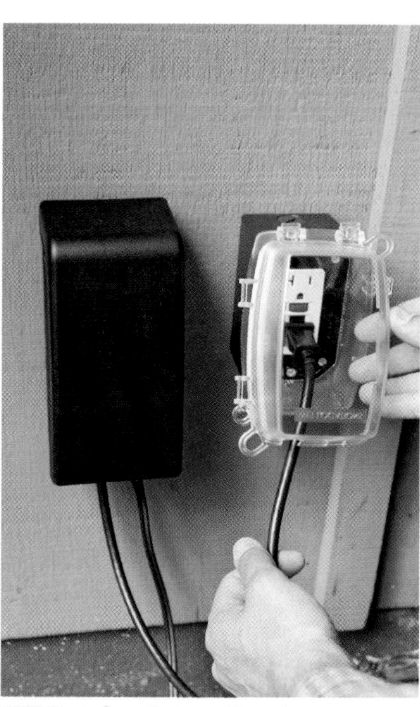

7 Set the timer. Plug the transformer into the outdoor receptacle and set the timer. Cover the GFCI outlet with a plastic cover, usually sold separately. Test the lights; if they work correctly bury the cable.

Installing telephone and CAT 5 wiring

Skill level:	Time to complete:	Materials:	Tools:
★★★☆☆	Experienced 2 hrs. Handy 4 hrs. Novice 6 hrs.	Solid-core telephone cable, phone jacks, staples	Screwdriver, combination stripper, lineman's pliers, drill, round-top stapler

ELECTRICAL

Adding a new telephone jack is straightforward work. Just run cable and connect wires to terminals labeled with their colors. The most difficult part is running, and then hiding, the cable.

Depending on your service contract, it may be cost-effective to have the phone company install new service for you. The lines they install will be under warranty—all future repairs will be free. Be aware that they may charge you a usage fee for the lines they run and maintain; this will appear on your monthly telephone bill.

Category 5 (CAT 5) cable and telephone wires are fragile. Don't bend, flatten, stretch, or otherwise compromise these wires. A damaged wire can result in a distorted connection, especially for computers.

Make all connections in a jack or junction box. Plan cable paths so as little of the cable as possible can be seen. For instance going through a wall (see page 430) saves you from running unsightly cable around door moldings. Use these same techniques to run speaker wire.

1 Option A: Tap into a phone jack. Unscrew the cover from a phone jack or a phone junction box. Strip about 2 inches of sheathing and ½ inch of insulation from each wire. (Standard phones use only two of the wires, but it doesn't hurt to connect all the wires.) Loosen each terminal screw. Bend the wire end in a clockwise loop, slip it under the screw head, and tighten the screw.

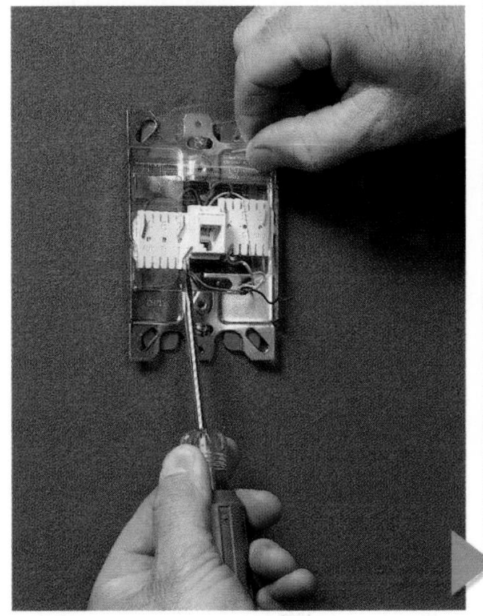

Option B: Use push-on connectors. Some jacks have terminals that clamp onto the wire so you don't have to strip it. Just push the wire down into the slot until it snaps into place.

$ BUYER'S GUIDE: WHICH CAT TO BUY?

Category 5 (CAT 5) cable consists of 4 pairs of cable and is used for computer networks, phone, audio, and video. CAT 5e has 4 twisted pairs of cable and is less subject to interference. CAT 6 is made of slightly heavier gauge wire for even better performance. All three types are excellent for wiring your house for entertainment/media systems and come in several colors to help you identify which cable came from where.

$ BUYER'S GUIDE: GET CONNECTED

You can now buy faceplates that hold several interchangeable jacks along with distribution boxes that let you customize the phone, computer network, and cable services that go to each room in the house. Here's how it works: Run all of the incoming wires—such as phone, cable or satellite, and Internet—to the distribution box. Run cables to each room and snap in and connect the jacks that match the services you want there. One room might have Internet, phone, and television, while another might have a different phone line and outlets for two computers. Connect the cables to the distribution box so the appropriate service is going to the jack in the correct room (it's easier done than said), and the job is finished.

Installing telephone and CAT 5 wiring (continued)

2 Option A: Hide cable. Use any trick you can think of to tuck away unsightly cable. Pry moldings away from the wall, slip the cable in behind, and renail the molding. Or pull carpeting back one short section at a time, run cable along the floor behind the tack strip, and push the carpet back into place.

Option B: Run cable through a wall. To go through a wall, drill a hole using a long ¼-inch drill bit. Insert a large drinking straw through the hole. Fish the cable through the straw. When you're finished split and remove the straw.

Option C: Staple exposed cable. When you have no choice but to leave cable exposed, staple it in place every foot or so along the top of the baseboard. Use a round-top stapler or plastic-shielded staples that hammer into place. (Square-cornered staples damage the cable sheathing.)

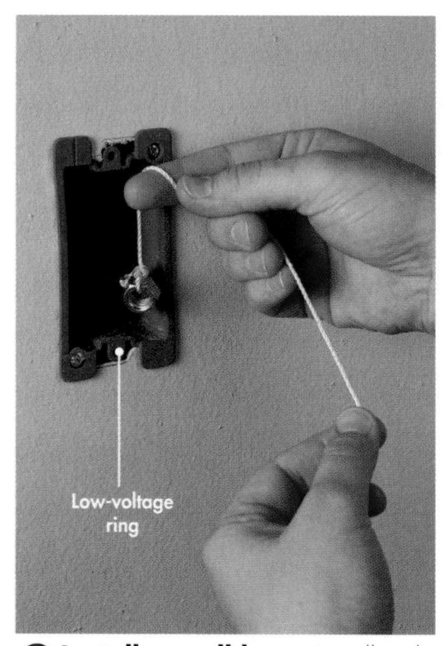

3 Install a wall box. A wall jack can attach to a low-voltage ring (as shown) or to an electrical remodel box. Cut a hole in the wall and install the ring. Tie a small weight to a string and lower it through the hole until you feel it hit the floor.

4 Pull the cable. Drill a ⅜-inch hole just above the baseboard of the wall where you want the wire to go. Bend a piece of wire into a hook, slip it into the hole, and pull out a loop of the string. Tape the string to the cable and pull the cable up through the remodel box.

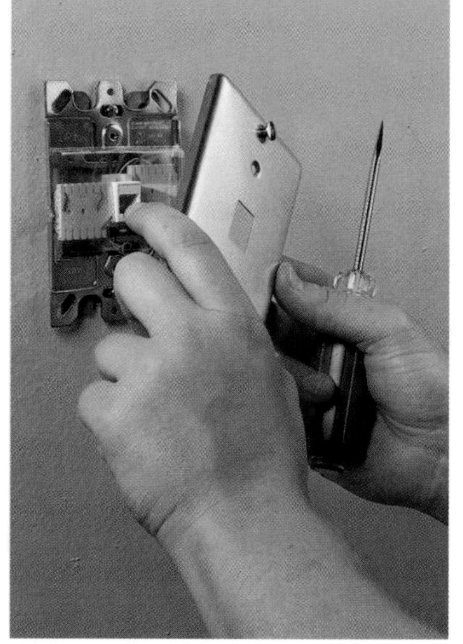

5 Install a wall jack. Attach the base of the jack and make the connections. Install the cover plate.

Installing coaxial cable

Skill level:	Time to complete:	Materials:	Tools:
★★★☆☆	Experienced 2 hrs. Handy 4 hrs. Novice 6 hrs.	RG6 coaxial cable, splitter, male connectors, wall jack, staples, screws	Drill, screwdriver, knife, combination stripper, pliers or wrench

Cable TV companies will run new lines and install jacks. Some do simple installations for free; for longer runs they may charge and may not hide as much of the cable as you'd like. They also may increase your monthly fee after installing a second or third jack. Still it's worth checking out the service options before deciding whether to do your own installations.

Purchase RG6 coaxial cable for all runs through the house. Don't use RG59; it has less-substantial wire wrapping. Coaxial cable is thick and ugly, so fish it through walls when possible.

If your cable signal is weak after adding new lines, install a signal booster to solve the problem. The booster attaches to the coaxial cable and plugs into a receptacle.

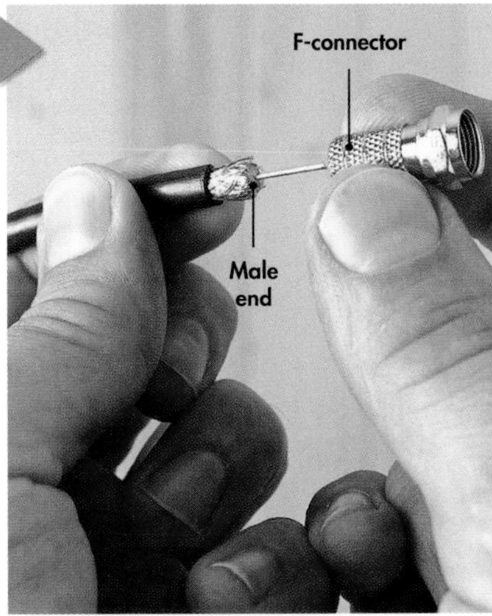

1 Make a male end. Use a combination stripper to remove ¾ inch of insulation from the end. Do not bend the exposed wire. With a knife carefully strip ⅜ inch of the thin outer sheathing only—do not cut through the metal mesh wrapping. Firmly attach a screw-on F-connector. You also can purchase a coaxial crimping tool and attach a crimp-on F-connector.

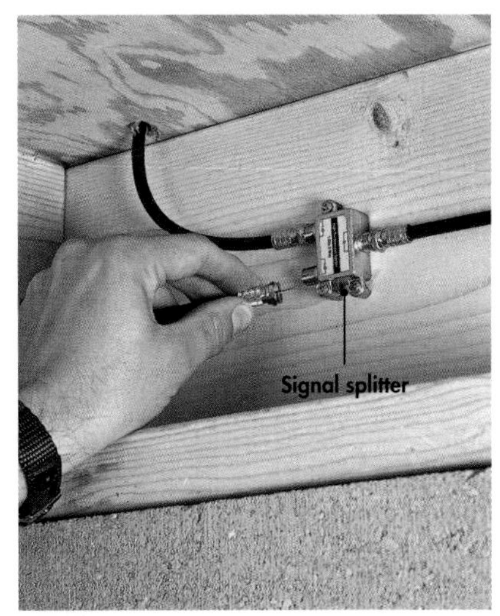

2 Split a line. Cut the line you want to tap into. Install male ends on both ends of the cut line and the end of the new line. Insert and twist all three male connectors onto a signal splitter. Anchor the splitter with screws.

ELECTRICAL

$ BUYER'S GUIDE

INSIDE COAX

Coax cable is designed to carry radio and television frequencies with a minimum of interference and maximum efficiency. The signal runs down a copper wire in the center of the cable. The wire is surrounded by an insulator; then by a grounded, braided wire jacket; and finally by another insulator. Because they all have the same center, or axis, the cable is known as coaxial, or coax. The braided jacket prevents radio interference from other sources. Coax cables have a given impedance, usually 50 or 75 ohms. It's the alternating current version of resistance, and for the stronger signal transmission the impedance of the cable should match that of the television. Use 50 ohms unless otherwise specified.

3 Install a jack. Cut a hole in the wall and run cable to it using the technique shown on page 389. (A regular electrical box can be used, though a low-voltage ring is preferable. See opposite page.) Strip the insulation to make a male end in the cable. Clamp the mounting brackets in the hole. Connect the cable end to the back of the jack by attaching the F-connector. Tighten the connection with pliers or a wrench. Attach the jack to the wall by driving screws into the mounting brackets.

Planning a structured wiring system

Wiring a house isn't what it used to be. Our homes have become entertainment complexes and workplaces, linked to the outside world via phone lines, cable, and satellite. The low-voltage lines that carry all that data have the potential to create tangles of electronic spaghetti in your walls and crawlspaces. Instead you can impose order with a structured wiring system that routes tidy bundles of various wires and cables to multipurpose wall plates throughout the house.

Panel

The nerve center of this system is a structured wiring panel. It somewhat resembles the familiar service panel for 120- and 240-volt power, but its functions are more varied. The panel controls the distribution of lines for phone, computer, video, audio, and security, as well as networking within the home. And you can expect wiring panels to become increasingly elaborate as information technologies evolve and become more commonplace in the home.

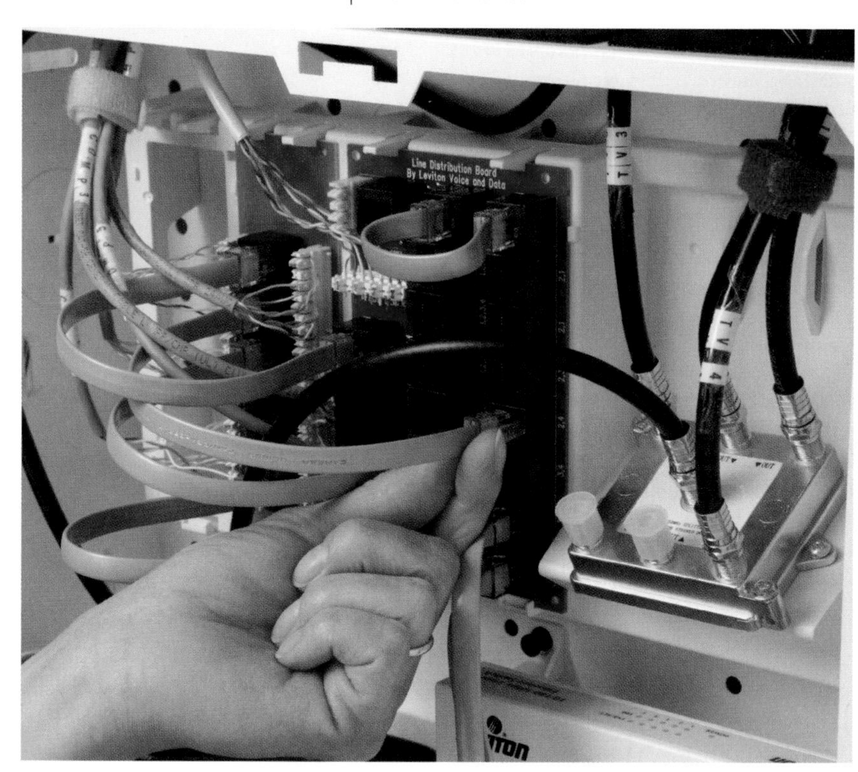

Cable

The system conducts its business though beefy structured cables, with several cables within its plastic sheathing.

You don't have to commit yourself to a system with all the trimmings. Incorporate only the features that you want now, leaving space for expansion. Panels are available preconfigured for only telephone and video, or only home networking if that is your preference.

CLOSER LOOK
THE FUTURE OF FIBER OPTICS

For a time it seemed as though the near-miraculous speed of fiber-optic data transmission would remain an unrealized dream, along with monorail travel and free electricity from nuclear plants. But those strands of glass are making inroads around the country. Hundreds of communities have installed FTTH (fiber to the home) lines, and many utilities now offer it as an option. How does it work? A conventional electrical signal is converted to pulses of light, which travel far faster than a DSL (digital subscriber line) signal poking along through strands of copper. In the home the pulses are converted back to an electrical signal by means of a terminal. From there the signals travel conventionally through the home's copper wiring—unless, that is, you've had the foresight to install fiber-optic lines as part of a structured wiring system. Expect FTTH to become more popular as computer users demand greater speed for CD-quality audio, streaming video, online gaming, and Internet use. The considerable price should come down, too, as the technology becomes more widespread.

Installing structured cable

Skill level:	Time to complete:	Materials:	Tools:
★★★★☆	Experienced Variable Handy Variable Novice Variable	Structured cable, with RG6 coax cable and connectors, and CAT 5 or CAT 5e cable and connectors; J-hooks or tie wraps and cable staples; modular wall plates and jacks	Electric drill, screwdriver, hammer, linesman's pliers, wire cutter, cable stripper, punch-down tool, coax crimper, multitester

It's hard to keep track of the various wiring systems that now seem indispensable in the home—for telephone, cable TV, computer networking, audio, home security, and so on. Things really get complex if nearly every room is to be served by multiple functions.

Instead of threading each line separately, you can do it once with a structured cable that bundles several individual lines. Typically a structured bundle has two CAT 5 cables for telecommunications and networking and two RG6 coax cables for distributing video from outside the home and running feeds within the home from a DVD player or security cameras. The resulting configuration is known as 2+2 cable. You also may want to anticipate advances in technology by adding two fiber-optic lines, for a 2+2+2 structure.

Structured cables are usually installed as home-run systems, with each line running from the panel to a wall plate. Although you'll use more wire than with a so-called daisy chain or series layout, there are no splitters to cause a drop in signal strength or splices that might come loose.

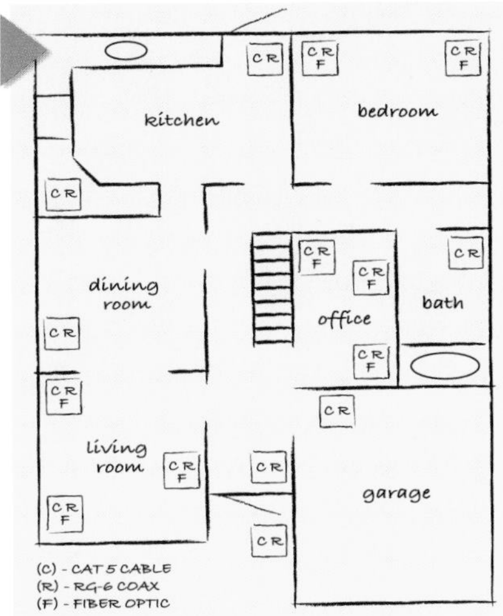

1 Plan the number and location of zones. Decide which areas of the home should be served by runs of structured wiring. Try to anticipate your needs, and perhaps those of the people to whom you may one day sell the house. Determine where in each room you'll put one or more modular wall plates. Choose a central location for the structured wiring panel that will both minimize the length of runs and allow easy access when you need to reconfigure the system.

2 Install the wall plates and structured wiring panel. You may want to have two or more wall plates in certain rooms. They typically are placed at the same height from the floor as power outlets but at least one stud cavity away from them to avoid electrical interference. Install them as for standard receptacle boxes. Place the structured wiring panel, shown here, in an easily accessible location and preferably close to incoming lines for phone, DSL, and TV cable, as well as audio and home security lines.

BUYER'S GUIDE

KNOW YOUR CABLE RATINGS

When assembling a structured wiring system, you may notice that there are good-quality wires and also better cables. While CAT 5 cable is now often the standard, some installers prefer to spend a bit more for CAT 5e with its improved performance, and CAT 6 is better still, offering a higher bandwidth. As you assemble the parts of a structured system, note which type is recommended for each of the various components.

The other type of wire you'll become familiar with is RG coaxial cable. Again pay attention to the numbers. Older RG59 cable has fallen from favor because of problems with signal leakage. Instead use cable labeled as RG6.

BUYER'S GUIDE

CHOOSING PLUG-IN MODULES FOR PANELS

A structured wiring panel is just a box. Its functions are dependent on the modules that come with it or that you elect to install.

- A **phone module** brings in one or more lines from outside the home, then routes these lines to jacks along the structured pathways. This allows you to decide which line serves which phone and to change this routing as needed. If you are hooked up to the Internet by a phone line, you can configure this connection as well, choosing the wall outlets that will have service. If you add a PBX (private branch exchange) or KSU (key service unit) module, you can link phones in the home, using them as an intercom and transferring calls.
- A **TV module** brings in the signal and splits it to four or more lines running to televisions. Consider adding a module that will allow you to route the signal from DVD players or security cameras to screens throughout the home.
- For whole-house stereo include an **audio module** when configuring the panel. These add-ons can be had with volume controls. There's even a model that automatically mutes the music so you can hear the chimes of the system's electronic doorbell.

Installing structured cable (continued)

3 Run the structured cable. In new construction the cable usually is run through stud walls. If you are adding a system to an existing home, make runs through the basement or attic, supporting the cable with J-hooks or tie wraps attached to joists or rafters. Allow enough extra cable to make gradual loops, avoiding tight bends. Make sure that cable staples don't pinch the line. To minimize electrical interference place cable runs a minimum of 16 inches (the distance between studs) from power lines.

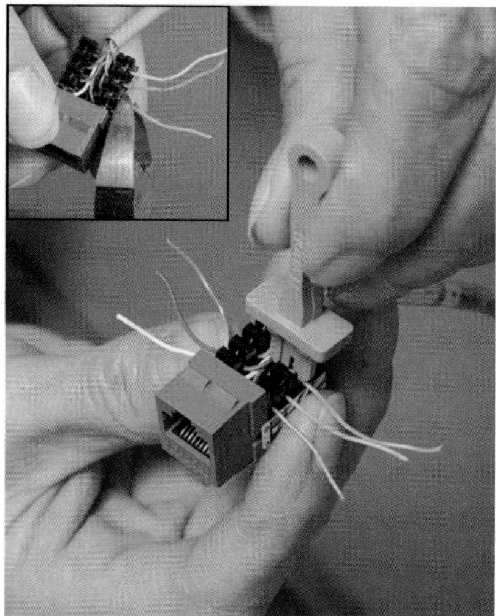

4 Connect the CAT 5 or CAT 5e cables. Use a punch-down tool to insert the cables into RJ 45 connectors. Connect the cables to the wall plates. Make connections at the panel as described in the manufacturer's directions. Use a pair of wire nippers to trim the wires even with the sides of the connector (inset).

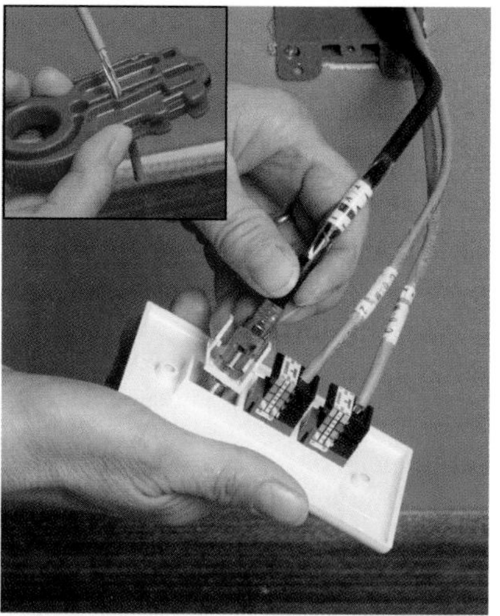

5 Connect the coax cables. Strip the ends of the cables (inset) and use a crimping tool to attach the appropriate connectors. Connect the cables to the wall plates. Make connections at the panel as described in the manufacturer's directions.

CLOSER LOOK

NETWORKING IN THE HOME

As homes take on some of the functions of the workplace and library, it becomes important to be able to route data between the household's computers and printers. In one configuration a modem with an ethernet port is connected to the Internet; a CAT 5 cable runs from the modem to a router; and CAT 5 lines in structured cables tie in the home's computers and printers. The computers should be equipped with network adapters to function within this setup. Another option is to use a wireless router rather than making physical connections.

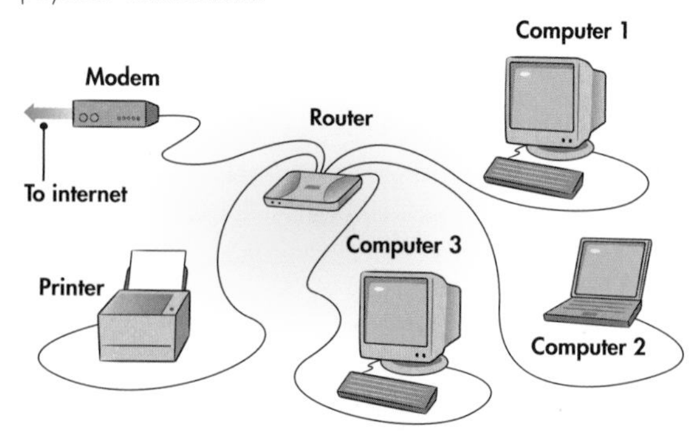

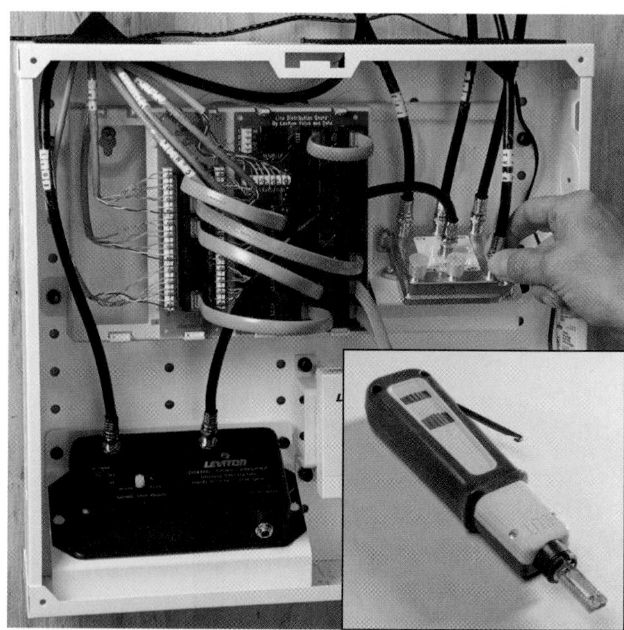

6 Plug in the various cables and modules and test the system. Give the system a trial run. To make sure that the connections are tight, check for continuity with a basic multitester (inset).

Troubleshooting a door chime

Skill level:	Time to complete:	Materials:	Tools:
★★★☆☆	Experienced 2 hrs. Handy 4 hrs. Novice 5 hrs.	Replacement button, chime, transformer or bell wire, electrician's tape	Screwdriver, multitester, combination stripper

ELECTRICAL

A doorbell or chime system is supplied with low-voltage power, between 8 and 24 volts, by a transformer. When the button is pressed, the circuit closes and sends power to the chime or bell.

Fixing common problems. Because the voltage needed by doorbells and chimes is low, there is no need to shut off power unless you are working on the transformer. Here's how to troubleshoot most problems:

- **If a bell or chime develops a fuzzy sound,** remove the chime cover and vacuum out any dust and debris and brush off the bell or chimes.
- **If you get only one tone when the front (or only) button is pushed, check the wiring in the chime** to see that the button is connected to the "front" terminal. On many two-button systems, the chime is supposed to "dingdong" when the front button is pushed and only "ding" when the rear button is pushed.
- **If the chime suddenly stops working at the same time you blow a fuse or trip a breaker,** restore power to the circuit supplying the transformer.
- **If the chime stops working altogether,** conduct a systematic investigation, moving from the simplest to the most complex repairs. First check out the button(s), then the chime, and then the transformer. If none of these reveals a problem, the wiring may be damaged.

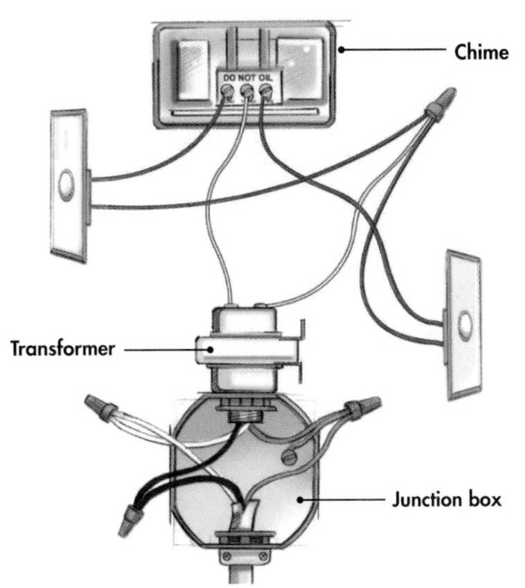

A typical two-button setup. The transformer—usually located in an out-of-the-way spot such as the basement, crawlspace, or cabinet interior—sends low-voltage power to the chime, where one wire is connected to the chime. Another wire is spliced to two different wires, each of which travels through a button and back to the chime. When either button is pressed, the circuit is completed, power travels to the chime, and the chime rings.

$ BUYER'S GUIDE

REPLACING A CHIME

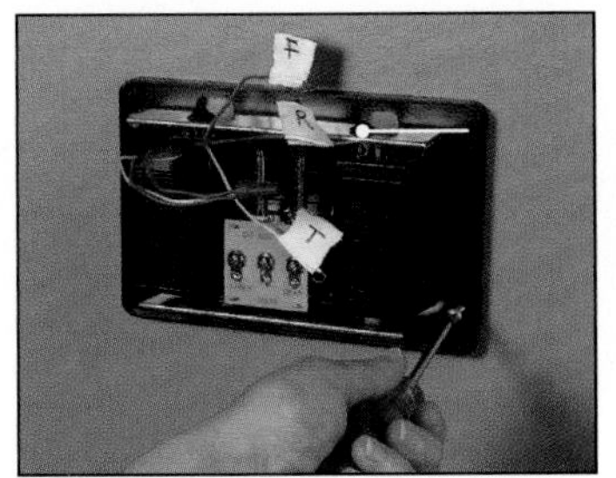

Purchase a chime with the same voltage rating as your transformer. It should be at least as large as the old chime so you don't have to paint the wall around it. Label the wires with pieces of tape. Unscrew and remove the terminal screws. Remove the screws holding the chime to the wall and pull the chime away. Thread the wires through the new chime, then fasten the chime to the wall. Connect the wires to the terminals.

1 Examine the button. Remove the screws while holding the button in place and gently pull out the button. (Make sure the wires do not slide back into the hole.) Use a toothbrush to clean away any debris, cocoons, or corrosion, and tighten the screws. If either wire is broken, restrip and reconnect it. Retest the button.

2 Touch wires together. If the button still doesn't work, loosen the terminal screws and remove the wires. Holding each wire by its insulation, touch the bare ends together. If the chime sounds the button is faulty and needs to be replaced. If you see or hear a tiny spark but the chime does not sound, the chime may be faulty (see page 436, Step 3). If there is no sound and no spark, check the transformer (see Step 4, page 436).

Troubleshooting a door chime (continued)

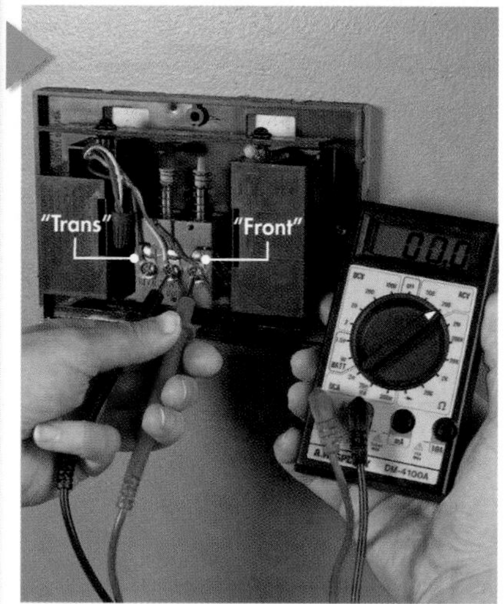

3 Test the chime. Remove the chime cover and ensure that all the wires are securely connected to terminals. Vacuum out any dust and scrape away any corrosion near the terminals. When you pull back a plunger and release it, the chime should sound. If not clean any greasy buildup that may be gumming up the springs. If the chime still does not work, touch the probes of a multitester to the "front" and "trans" terminals, then to the "rear" and "trans" terminals. If power present is below 2 volts of the chime's printed voltage rating, then the chime is faulty and should be replaced.

4 Test the transformer. Look for an exposed electrical box with the transformer attached. Tighten loose connections. Touch the probes of a multitester to both transformer terminals. If you get a reading of more than 2 volts below the transformer rating, the transformer is faulty and should be replaced.

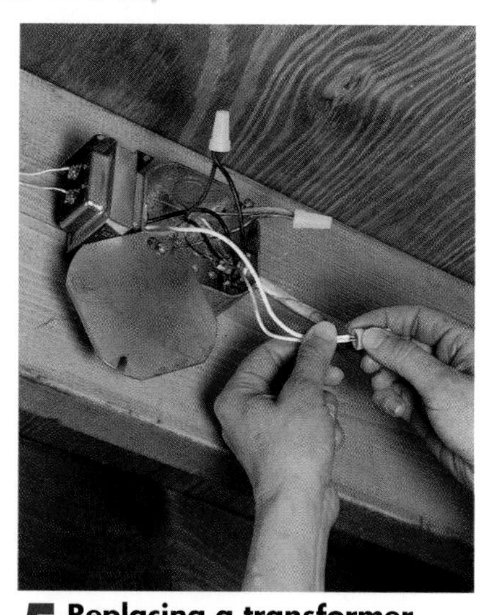

5 Replacing a transformer. Purchase a transformer with the same voltage rating as the old one. **Shut off power to the circuit and open the adjacent junction box.** Label the bell wires and disconnect them. Disconnect the transformer leads inside the junction box and disconnect the transformer. Thread the new transformer leads into the junction box, fasten the transformer to the box, and splice the leads to the wires. Connect the bell wires, turn the power back on, and test.

Installing wireless chimes

Installing the chime. Rather than going through the trouble of replacing defective bell wire, buy a wireless chime system. Installation is simple: Plug the chime into a standard receptacle, power the button with a battery, and attach the button to the house.

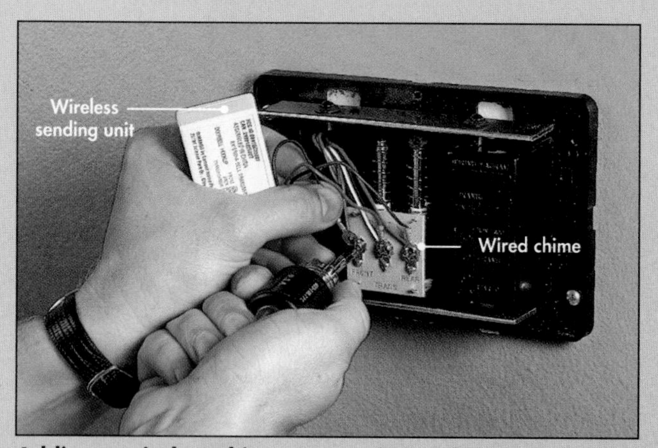

Adding a wireless chime to an existing chime system. If you can't hear your door chime everywhere in your home, add a wireless chime to your wired system. Remove the cover from the existing chime and loosen the terminal screws. Take the leads of the wireless chime's sending unit and insert them under the screws. Tighten the screws. Using its double-sided tape, stick the sending unit to the chime housing. Plug the wireless chime into a receptacle. Depending on the model, it will have a distance limitation of 75 to 150 feet.

Troubleshooting a thermostat

Skill level:	Time to complete:	Materials:	Tools:
★☆☆☆☆	Experienced 1 hr. Handy 2 hrs. Novice 3 hrs.	Scrap of bond paper, short length of wire, replacement thermostat	Small brush, screwdriver, combination stripper

The round, low-voltage unit featured in most of these pictures is the most common type of thermostat in use. Yours may be rectangular but its functions are the same.

If your furnace or air-conditioner fails to operate, check the thermostat for simple mechanical problems. The cover may be jammed in too far, disrupting the mechanism. A wire may have broken or come loose. Or the parts may be covered with dust, inhibiting electrical contact.

If cleaning and adjusting do not solve the problem, replacing a thermostat is a simple job. Consider installing a programmable unit for more control options and to save money. Remember that a thermostat contains mercury, so dispose of old units properly.

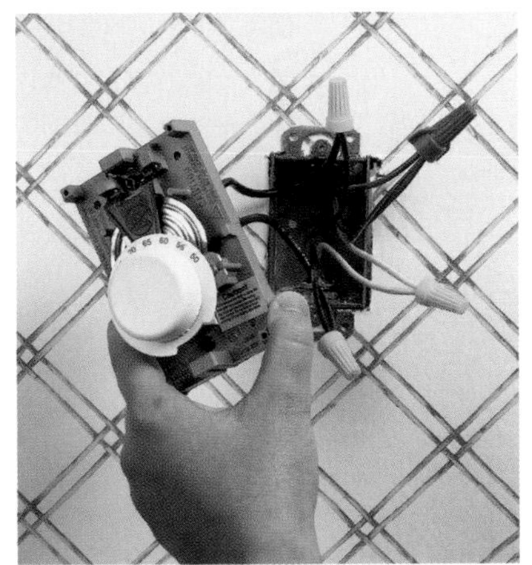

Checking a line-voltage thermostat. If your thermostat uses household current, always shut off power to the circuit before pulling it out. If it fails disconnect it and take it to a dealer for service or replacement.

Check the anatomy of a low-voltage thermostat. Thin wires come from a transformer and connect to the thermostat base. You'll probably find one wire for the transformer, one for heat, one for air-conditioning, and one for a fan. (A heat pump uses six or more wires and has a special thermostat. Contact a dealer for repairs.) To protect circuitry shut off power before you start to work.

WORK SMART

SEAL OFF DRAFTS

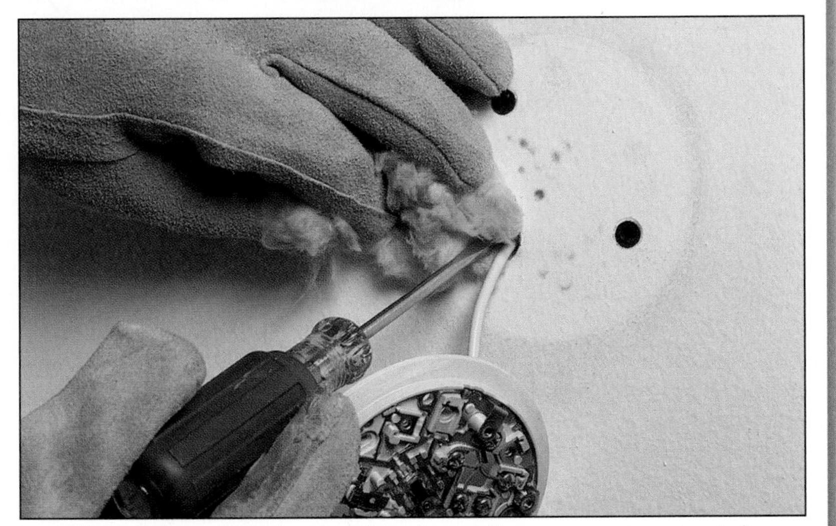

Even if your thermostat is on an interior wall, air coming through a hole behind it may throw its temperature readings out of whack, resulting in erratic heating. Remove the thermostat base from the wall and fill the hole with insulation or caulk.

BUYER'S GUIDE

A TERMINAL PROBLEM

In the simplest of cases, only two wires run from the furnace to the thermostat. Ever wonder why some thermostats have so many terminals inside? Some of the terminals are there to control central air-conditioning. Controlling a heat pump is even more complicated. There are terminals for heat, terminals for cooling, and terminals that send signals to keep the unit from freezing during cold weather. Don't worry if you don't know which terminal is which. Cable and terminal colors are standardized—as long as the color of the wire matches the label on the terminal, everything should be fine.

ELECTRICAL

Troubleshooting a thermostat (continued)

Clean the contacts with a brush. Pull off the outer cover and use a soft, clean, dry brush to remove dust from the bimetal coil. Turn the dial to clean all the nooks and crannies.

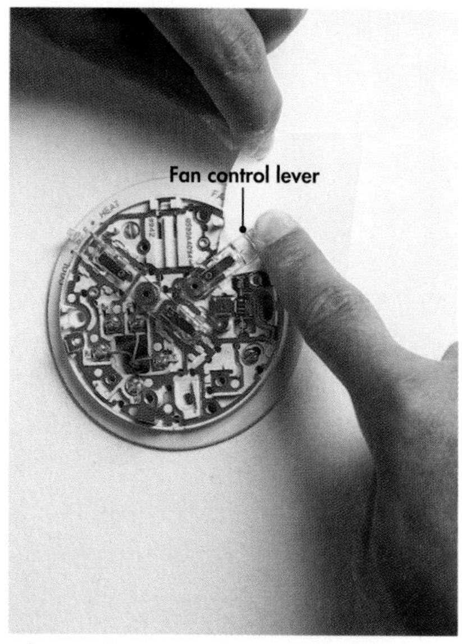

Clean the switch contacts. Remove the screws holding the thermostat body and pull out the body. Gently pull back on the fan control lever, then slip a piece of white bond paper behind it and slide the paper back and forth to clean the contact behind the lever. Do the same for the mode control lever, if there is one.

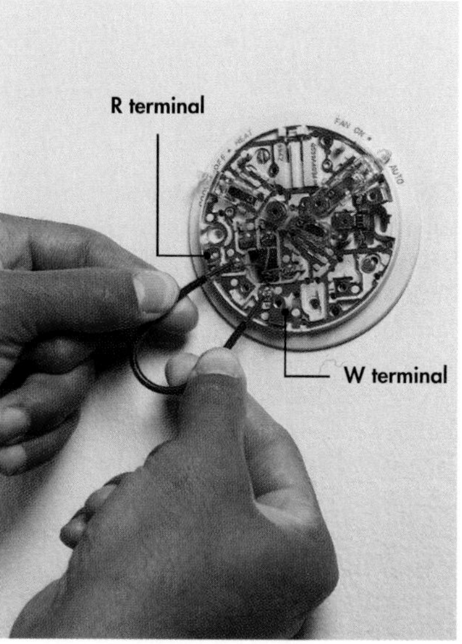

Conduct a hot-wire test. If heat does not come on, test to see if power is getting to the thermostat. Cut a short length of wire and strip both ends. Holding only the insulated portion, touch the bare ends to the terminals marked R and W. If the heating system starts to run, replace the thermostat. If nothing happens troubleshoot or replace the thermostat (as shown below).

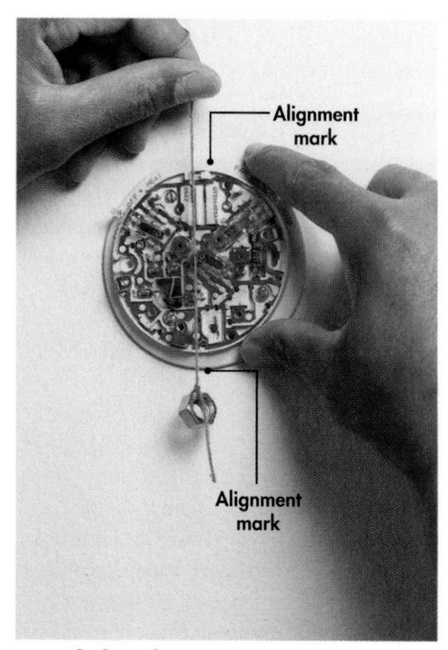

Level the thermostat. If the temperature is always warmer or cooler than the thermostat setting, the thermostat may be out of level. Hold a level or a weighted string in front of the thermostat to see if the two alignment marks line up. If they do not, remove the mounting screws, realign the thermostat, and drive new screws.

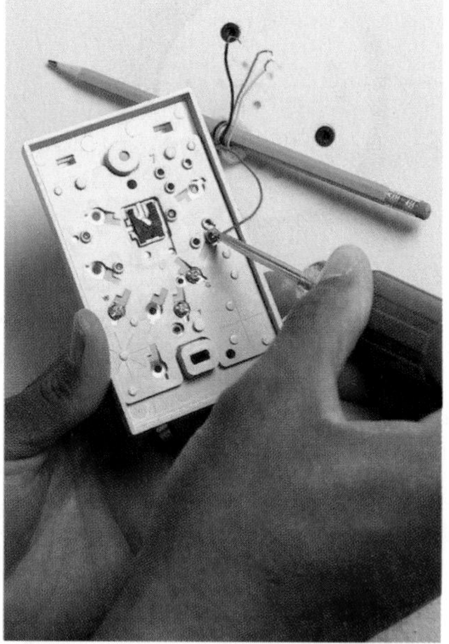

Replace a low-voltage thermostat. Loosen the terminal screws and pull out the wires. Remove the mounting screws and pull out the plate. Clip the wires so they cannot slide back through the hole. Thread the wires through the new thermostat and hook the wires to the terminals. Level and attach the base to the wall with screws.

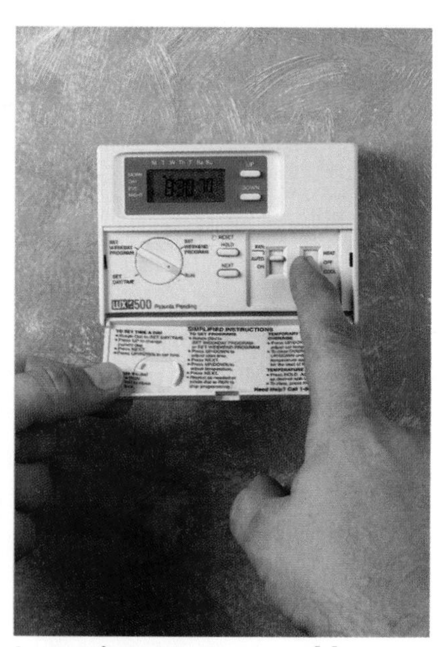

Invest in a programmable thermostat. Spend a little more and save money in the long run with a thermostat that adjusts heating or cooling several times a day.

Adding surge protection

If your household is like most, you've got a lot of electrical appliances, tools, and expensive toys that are vulnerable to power surges. These unwanted bursts of electricity can come from outside the house, when the utility experiences a spike. Less well known is that surges from within the home can be at least as troublesome. Household fluctuations in current are apt to be triggered when larger appliances—air-conditioners, dryers, and ovens in particular—draw more power as they start up. Products that use microprocessors in their circuitry are especially vulnerable.

There's no single solution to protecting your home. It's best to employ the following three lines of defense:

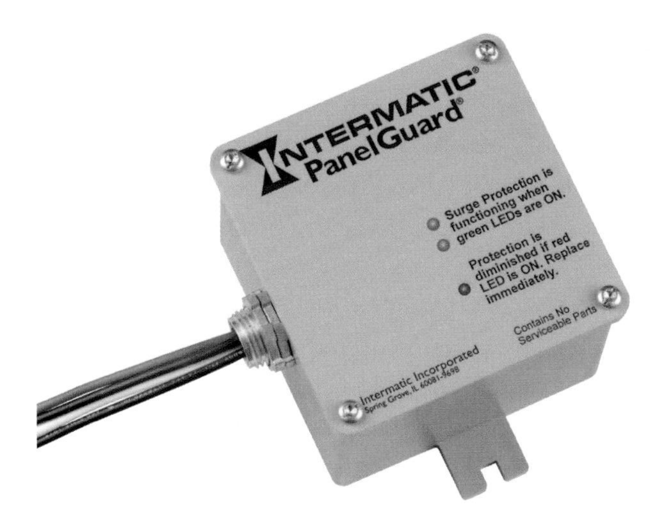

1. Have an electrician or the power utility company install a whole-house surge protector. This heavy-duty protector is installed either next to the meter or to one side of the service panel. It can monitor the power line, telephone line, and cable, shutting down your power as soon as a surge is detected. Installation isn't a homeowner project. It requires going inside the service panel and working with wires that remain hot even when the main breaker is turned off. Some utilities will charge a monthly fee rather than a one-time installation fee.

2. Use individual power strip surge protectors. Whole-house protectors suppress a spike of power but may still allow a smaller surge to enter the home's wiring. It's a good idea to plug appliances, computers, and audio and video systems into their own surge protectors for another line of defense. Check the packaging for the Underwriters Laboratories (UL) seal and note whether the manufacturer offers insurance to cover damage if the device doesn't protect up to a stated level.

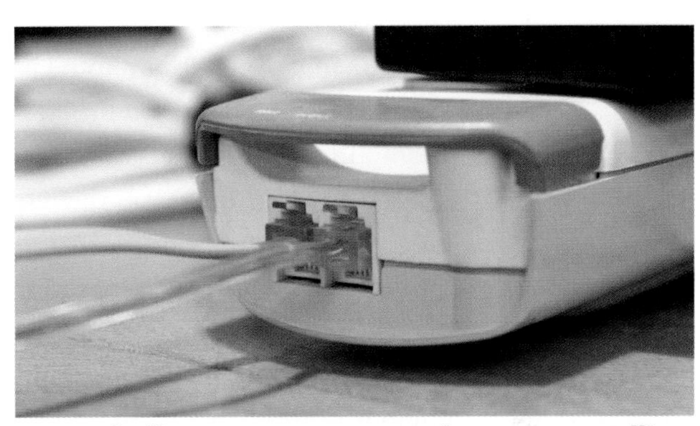

3. Use in-line surge protectors for coax, satellite, and phone lines. Damaging surges don't enter the home only through power lines. Add small, unobtrusive in-line devices to protect TVs, telephones, and desktop and laptop computers.

BUYER'S GUIDE

DON'T MISTAKE A POWER STRIP FOR A SURGE PROTECTOR

Unless you have a good look at the packaging, you might leave the home center with a simple power strip in your shopping cart rather than a strip that looks similar but has the ability to protect the devices plugged into it. Both have a row of outlets and likely some sort of indicator light as well.

A fourth line of defense...

If your house takes a hit from a lightning bolt, no device can fully protect everything with a wire running to it. To be on the safe side, get into the habit of pulling the plugs of valuable and vulnerable appliances and electronic equipment whenever you hear thunder. Disconnect phone and cable lines as well.

CLOSER LOOK

SURGE PROTECTORS DON'T LAST FOREVER

Surge protectors work by absorbing power fluctuations, and this capacity my be used up over time. A series of small surges or just one big jolt can render them worthless, leaving you without protection. How do you know when a protector's time is up? Some models have an indicator light that blinks or goes off when it has outlived its usefulness, while others alert you with an audible alarm. Better still are protectors that shut off their power, ensuring that you won't continue to rely on a device that no longer can do the job.

CHAPTER 8

Heating, Ventilation, & Air-Conditioning

See page 591

Gas, oil, or electric: Which way to go? Each type of heat has its pros and cons. Gas heat proponents point out that gas burns more cleanly and that it has historically been less expensive than oil or electricity. The oil heat fan club replies that oil burns 400 degrees hotter than gas, giving you more heat faster, and that new high-tech oil furnaces burn as cleanly and efficiently as gas.

Radiant electrical heat is the most expensive of the three to run, but it installs quickly in additions and renovations and doesn't require the large initial investment of a gas or oil furnace. An air-source heat pump is relatively inefficient at heating compared with other systems but is a good source of summer air-conditioning. Ground-source heat pumps take their heat from well or lake water that is generally warmer than the outdoor air. Such pumps are extremely efficient but more expensive to install.

If your furnace is functioning, the cost of changing to another fuel source wipes out any savings. If you need a new furnace, the most economical and best heat source varies from region to region. Talk to your gas, oil, and electric companies. Ask about cost, maintenance, and reliability of fuel delivery. Also ask about the cost of getting oil tanks, running new gas lines, or similar needs. And make sure you inquire about the cost of getting rid of the old furnace and ducting.

Contents

Maintaining a forced-air furnace 442
Maintaining a gas burner 449
Maintaining an oil furnace 454
Maintaining a hot-water heat system 458
Maintaining a heat pump 467
Installing an electric baseboard heater 471
Adding a hot-water baseboard heater 473
Adding a forced-air heat run 475
Installing auxiliary gas heaters 477
Window air-conditioner maintenance 480
Installing a window air-conditioner 482
Maintaining a central air system 484
Installing an evaporative cooler 486
Installing underfloor radiant heat 488
Installing a furnace humidifier 490
Maintaining a furnace humidifier 492
Installing soffit and roof vents 494

Running hot and cold

When making heating and cooling decisions, there are two considerations: first the source—oil, gas, or electric; second the delivery system—forced-air or radiant (including radiators and baseboard heaters). Because either delivery system can have any source, we'll look at factors one at a time: first forced air, then gas, followed by oil, hot water, and, finally, a heat pump.

Once you've read about furnaces, you'll learn how to do routine furnace maintenance. Most people avoid maintenance, but cleaning alone will prevent many problems.

On oil furnaces maintenance is often covered by a service contract you have with the supplier. Do the jobs you're comfortable with but keep the contract. Some of the services it provides for are less routine, and some of them create a huge mess if you lack the proper equipment. Although gas suppliers usually don't offer service contracts, the routine work is simple and clean enough that you should be comfortable giving it a try.

In addition to learning about furnace repair and maintenance, you'll learn how to install a window air-conditioner, an evaporative cooler, a new heat vent, auxillary gas and electric heaters, and a hot-water baseboard heater.

Putting in a furnace or replacing an existing one requires experience in determining the right-size unit, matching the existing venting, putting in new vents, and troubleshooting the air flow. Hire a professional.

Maintaining a forced-air furnace

Skill level:	Time to complete:	Materials:	Tools:
★★★☆☆	Experienced Variable Handy Variable Novice Variable	Filters, household oil, masking tape	Vacuum cleaner, wrenches, framing square, multimeter, needle-nose pliers

If you know anything about fans, you know most of what there is to know about forced-air heat: When the furnace is ready, the fan turns on. If the fan doesn't turn on, you're going to get cold.

If you see a fire in the firebox but the fan doesn't kick on, the next few pages should help you diagnose and repair the problem. (If there's no fire in the firebox, see Maintaining a Gas Burner, page 449, or Maintaining an Oil Furnace, page 454.) On older furnaces the problem may be a broken fan belt. Newer furnaces have direct-drive fans, so the problem is going to be in one of the controls or in the motor itself. All you'll need to find the problem is a relatively inexpensive multimeter (a meter that tests AC and DC voltage, as well as resistance—see page 452) and someone willing to run back and forth to turn up the thermostat.

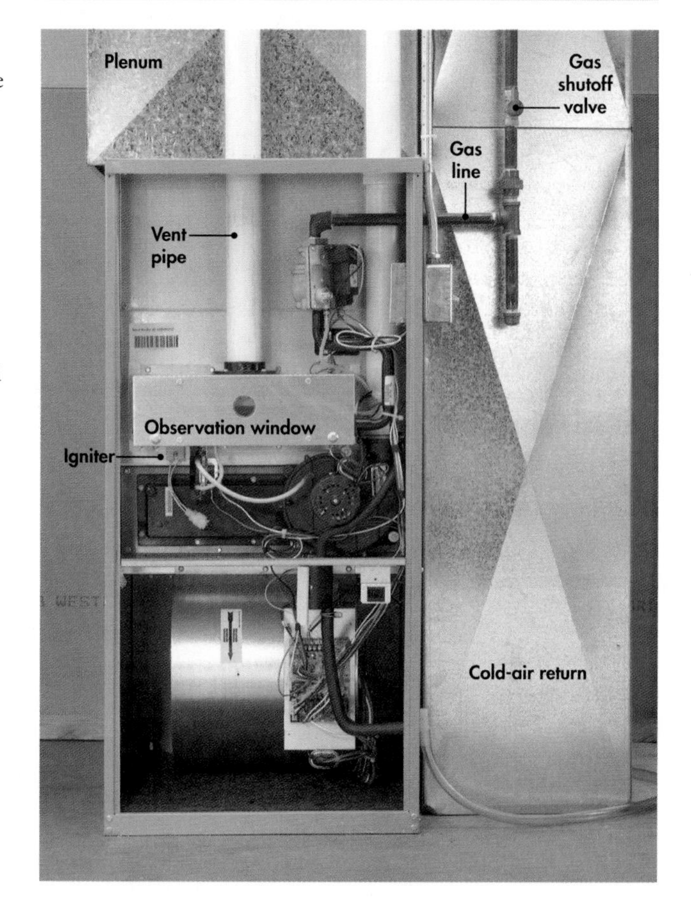

How a gas furnace works

On a modern gas furnace, when the temperature falls below the desired temperature, a call for heat goes to the furnace, which turns on the igniter. The igniter is usually what's called a hot-surface igniter: a piece of metal that glows bright red when electricity is fed to it. After about 20 seconds the igniter is warm enough to open a valve, letting gas flow into the furnace. The gas flows through a pipe called a manifold and then into tubelike burners attached to it. Each burner has an adjustable opening, called an air port, that mixes air with the gas to control how efficiently the gas burns. The burner ends inside a firebox, which heats up to provide heat for the house. The heat is distributed through either a forced-air or hot-water system (discussed later in the chapter). When the house reaches its set temperature, the thermostat cuts off the gas. The fire goes out until the thermostat calls for more heat. An older furnace has a constantly burning pilot light instead of a hot-surface igniter. On these a thermocouple monitors the heat created by the pilot. If the pilot goes out, the thermocouple notices a drop in temperature and shuts off the flow of gas.

If natural gas isn't piped to your home, you can use propane, or bottled gas, instead, though you'll need to change the orifice in the burner to do so. Talk to your propane dealer to see what's involved in having a bottled-gas system installed.

Add water for better breathing—Installing online humidifiers

Furnaces dry out the air in your home, causing dry skin, scratchy throats, and respiratory irritation. Dry air also causes wood to shrink, warping boards and ruining furniture joints.

Installing an online humidifier can help solve the problem. Humidifiers come in three basic types: spray, drum, and flow-through.

- Spray humidifiers spray water into the airstream of your furnace. They're the least expensive but produce less humidity.
- Drum humidifiers have large, water-absorbent rotating drums partially submerged in pools of water. Air blowing across the top adds moisture to the heated air.
- Flow-through humidifiers work on the same principle as drum humidifiers, but water drips across a pad through which air is blown. They're more efficient, and the amount of moisture added to the air can be precisely controlled. They have a drain line, which connects to a drain for the house plumbing system.

Each of the three types needs a water source, usually a simple plumbing job. A valve is attached to an existing pipe. PVC or flexible copper tubing supplies water to the humidifier.

Each humidifier mounts on one of the furnace's main ducts. A spray humidifier mounts on the plenum and sprays water into the warm airstream. Using a template supplied with the unit, you'll cut a hole into the plenum with a pair of tin snips. The humidifier bolts or screws in place.

Drum and flow-through humidifiers generally mount on the cold-air return duct using a vent that pipes humid air to the plenum. Once again use a template and tin snips.

Each type is controlled by a humidistat—a device that measures humidity in the air. You can mount the humidistat directly in the air vent or as a separate wallmounted control in the room of your choice. The humidistat, motors, and other controls all require electricity. This requires minimal wiring—usually just tapping into one of the connections in the furnace. (See pages 490–491 for installation instructions.)

How a forced-air system works

If air vents deliver heat to the rooms in your house, you have a forced-air system. Oil or gas is heating up inside the furnace, and a small fan is sending the air throughout the house. In addition to the fan, you'll want to understand a few important controls.

Once the thermostat hanging on your wall tells the furnace to send heat, the furnace starts a fire in the firebox. Before the heat reaches you, two more controls must do their jobs.

The first is the blower relay, which turns the fan off and on. The thermostat, operating at 24 volts, is connected to one side of the relay. The fan, connected to the other side, operates at 110 volts. With the help of the relay, the 24-volt thermostat starts (and later stops) the 110-volt blower.

Meanwhile the fan-and-limit control monitors the heat of the air as produced by the flame. The fan-and-limit control prevents the fan from starting until the firebox reaches a prescribed temperature, usually around 115°F (46°C). When the air does start flowing, the fan pumps it into a large central vent, called a plenum, to which all other vents are attached. The air flows through the house and then returns to the furnace through the cold-air return. Without the return vents the furnace would heat dank basement air and send it through the house. With no cold-air vent pulling air back out of the rooms, they would become slightly pressurized and resist the new hot air coming out of the vents. So the return vents allow the flow of air that maintains comfort.

When the house warms up and the thermostat turns off the heat, the fan-and-limit control still monitors the firebox. When most of the residual heat has been pumped into the house, the control lets the fan turn off. When the thermostat calls for heat again, the cycle starts over.

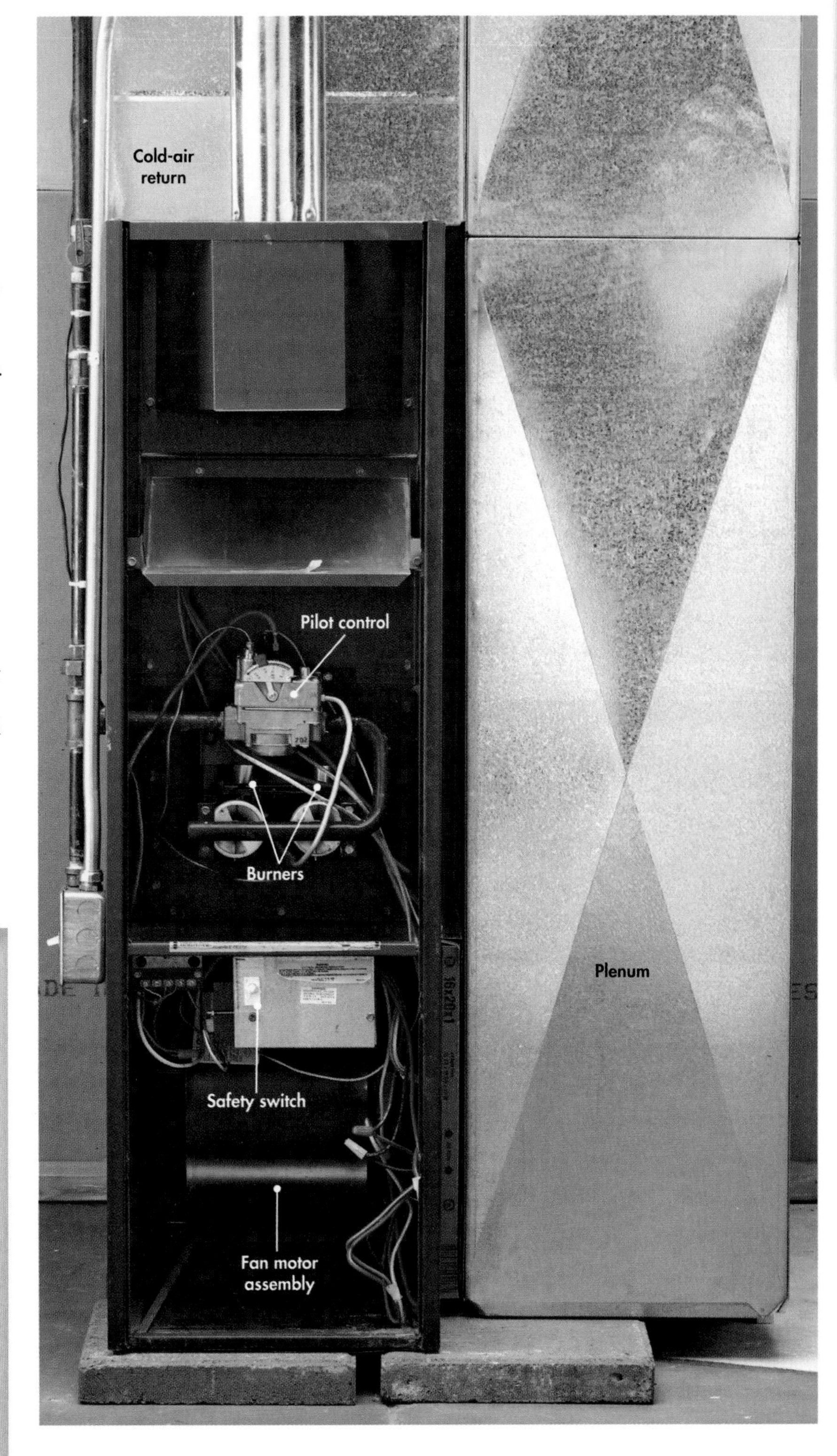

On and off

When you leave for vacation, it's wise to turn down the thermostat to 55 degrees to save energy. When you get back and turn the thermostat back up, however, you may notice that the furnace starts turning on and off and the house isn't getting warm. Unless this problem continues into the next day, you can rest assured that your furnace is probably fine. Turning on and off is its way of catching up and expelling all the cold air from the system.

Maintaining a forced-air furnace (continued)

Understanding furnace filters

The sole purpose of a dust filter is to pull dust out of the air. How thorough you want it to be is largely a matter of preference and budget. Whichever filter you settle on, however, replace or clean it as the manufacturer directs. A dirty filter won't damage your furnace in the short run. Trying to force air through a clogged filter, however, is like trying to force water through a brick. It's inefficient and will quickly wipe out all the savings your high-tech furnace is supposed to deliver.

The simplest filter is the oldest, most economical, and least efficient: spun glass. When it gets dirty you toss it out.

Fiber filters are essentially spun plastic. They're as efficient as glass but washable.

If you want to remove the most dust from the air, get a media filter or an electrostatic filter. The former is disposable, the latter recyclable, and both are efficient at pulling dust out of the air.

Last and most expensive is the electrostatic precipitator—the electrical version of the electrostatic filter. It removes just about everything but requires professional installation.

Spun glass. These are the least expensive filters, common on furnaces through the 1970s. They remove 10 to 15 percent of the dust in the air, enough to protect the fan but not much more. Replace these filters monthly. Of all the filter types, they allow the most dust to get through.

Fiber. This is a washable version of the spun-glass filter. It is no more effective; the benefit is that you can wash it instead of replacing it.

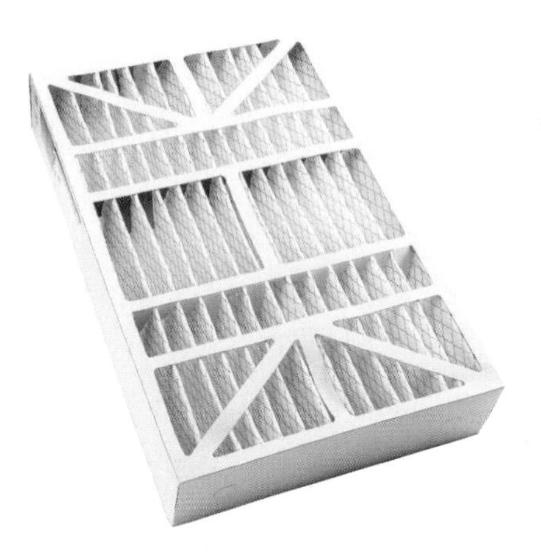

Media. These are spun-glass filters with pleated fiber cores. They remove from 45 to 90 percent of the dust in the air. Like spun-glass filters they are disposable—though some are good for as long as three months. If your furnace accepts two filters at once, you can extend the life of a media filter by putting a spun-glass filter in front of it.

Electrostatic. An electrostatic filter is layered to form an electrostatic charge that pulls dust out of the air and into a foam filter. Because the charge is permanent and the filter is plastic, you can clean it instead of throwing it out. Electrostatic HEPA (High-Efficiency Particulate Air) filters remove 99 percent of the pollutants in the air. Clean these filters every three months.

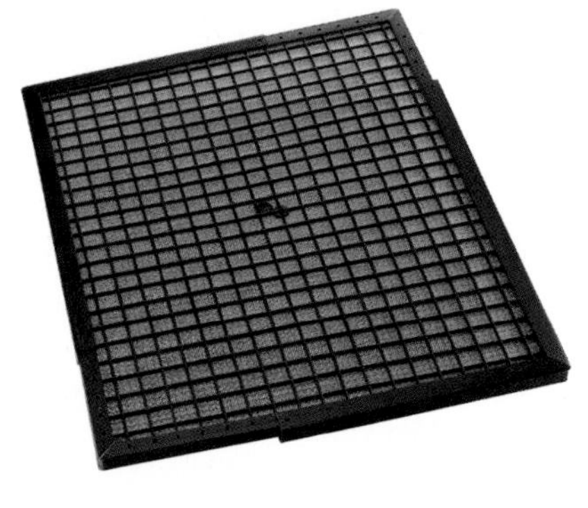

Electrostatic precipitators. These are similar to electrostatic filters except that a power source supplies the charge. Precipitators restrict airflow, so they usually include a small booster fan. Installation is complicated and best left to a pro. These filters extract down to 0.001 micron, which makes them efficient enough to remove smoke and similar pollutants from the air. They use about as much power as a small lightbulb. Clean these filters every three months.

Removing and cleaning a filter

Part of maintaining your furnace and its efficiency is keeping the filter clean. With some disposable filters you'll simply remove the old one and put in the new one. With other filters you'll vacuum and wash the filter and then reuse it. In either event removal is the same. Take off the furnace access panel and set it aside. In older furnaces the filter lifts in and out of a groove. In newer furnaces a flexible metal arm jams in place to hold the filter. The arm usually tucks behind a flange near the access panel. To remove the filter lift up on the arm and swing it forward once it clears the flange.

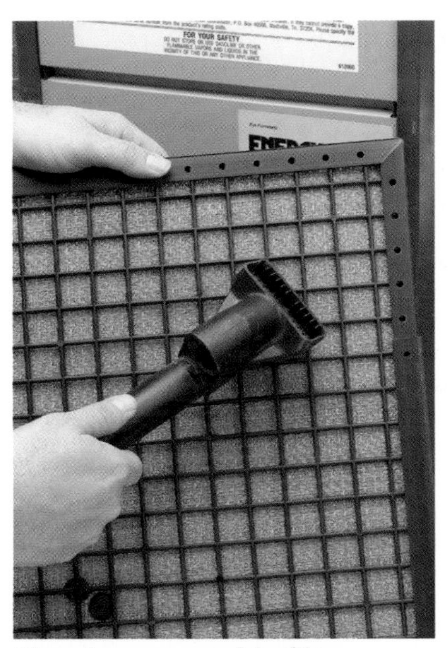

Cleaning a reusable filter. Remove the filter, vacuum it, then rinse thoroughly with water from a hose or in a bathtub. You can reinstall the filter while it's still wet.

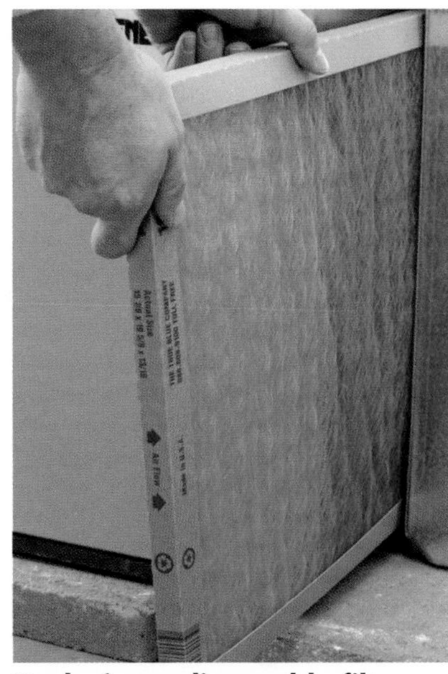

Replacing a disposable filter. Remove the filter and replace it with one that is the exact size and shape of the one you are replacing.

Maintaining a fan motor

Oiling the motor. Not all furnaces need to be oiled; many have permanent bearings that are sealed at the factory. To find out whether your blower needs oiling, remove the access panel and look at the blower motor. Those that need oiling will have small holes at either end of the motor. Put a couple of drops of household oil (usually 10W, nondetergent) through the holes.

Tightening the fan belt. If the fan runs off a belt (not all of them do), push down on the belt midway between the motor and the fan. The belt should flex about 1 inch. If it doesn't, loosen the locknut on the bracket that holds the motor and turn the second nut to tighten or loosen the belt. Retighten the locknut once the belt is properly tensioned. If the adjustment bolt is frozen, apply penetrating oil until it turns easily. Replace cracked or stretched belts and apply belt dressing for longer belt life.

Aligning the motor and fan pulleys. For the quietest and most efficient operation, the pulleys on the motor and on the fan should be in line with each other. **To check the alignment** put a straightedge, such as a level or framing square, against the sides of both pulleys. A triangular space between one of the pulleys and the straightedge means they aren't aligned. To correct this loosen the nuts or bolts that hold the motor bracket to the mounting bar. Once loosened the motor should slide along the bar. **Position the motor** so the pulleys are aligned and retighten the nuts or bolts.

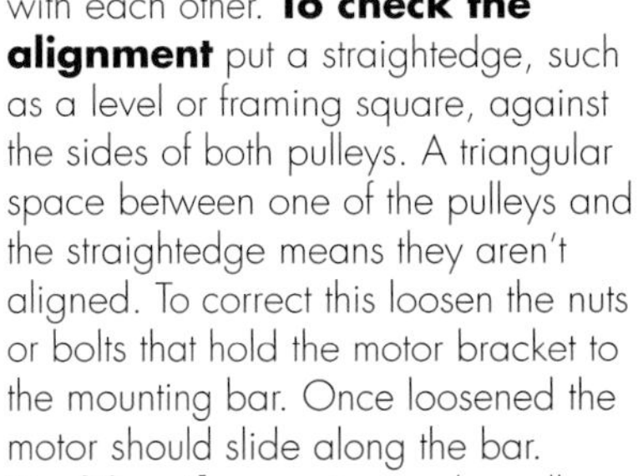

Maintaining a forced-air furnace (continued)

Tracking fan or motor problems

If the blower fan pumps no air into the vents, you have at least two problems. The first is that you're cold. The second is a bit harder to track down. To figure out where the problem is, trace the circuit from the thermostat through the other controls to the motor. Do what the pros do—check the obvious first.

The thermostat. The thermostat hanging on your wall is nothing more than a big switch. When the temperature falls below the point at which you've set the thermostat, its switch flips and the furnace comes on. When the temperature rises to the set point, the switch flips the other way and the furnace turns off. Verify that the thermostat is set to On and is turned up and that the wires are properly connected. If the thermostat has batteries, check them as well.

The blower relay. With the help of the blower relay, the 24-volt thermostat can start and stop the 110-volt blower.

The fan-and-limit control. The fan-and-limit control senses when the firebox is hot enough to send air through the ducts and into the house. Even if the thermostat and blower relay say it's time for the blower to kick on, nothing happens until the fan-and-limit control says the furnace is hot enough. When the thermostat and blower relay are ready to turn off the blower, the fan-and-limit control lets that happen only when most of the residual heat has been pumped into the house. If the fan were to turn on at the same moment the thermostat started the flame in the box, the air it blew would still be reasonably cold. And if the fan shut off the minute the flame stopped, a lot of hot air would remain in the furnace, doing no one any good.

Diagnosing fan or motor problems

Check the safety switch at the furnace. After you've checked the thermostat upstairs, head for the furnace. Make sure the access panels are in place and that they have depressed the push-button safety switch. Remove the panels and push the safety button down. If the furnace fires but the fan doesn't, test the thermostat. If the furnace doesn't fire, see the sections on oil furnaces and gas burners for more information.

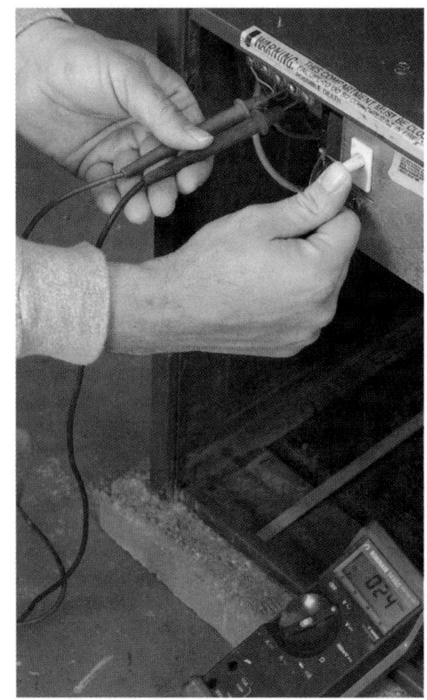

Test the thermostat. Find the blower relay, one side of which is connected to the thermostat. Set a multimeter to the 50 volts AC range. Put one of the leads onto the terminal labeled G—this is one of the blower wires. Put the other on C, which is one of the transformer terminals. Set the thermostat as high as it will go. The furnace should light, the meter should read about 24 volts, and the blower should start up in a few seconds. If not replace the thermostat.

Test the relay. Turn off the power to the furnace at the circuit breaker box. Set a multimeter to the ohmmeter setting. Put the leads on the relay's G and C terminals again. The readout should be 0 when you touch them and 1 when you separate them. If not the relay is faulty. Label the wires so that you'll know where each goes. Then remove and replace the relay.

Testing the fan-and-limit control

1 Test the blower. Look to see whether the fan-and-limit control (see Step 2) has a button or switch on it labeled something like "summer/winter" or "auto/manual." Push or flip the switch to the "summer" or "manual" position. Restore power to the furnace. If the blower is working, it will turn on immediately, indicating that the fan-and-limit control needs to be replaced. If the motor starts the problem is with the motor or its capacitor.

2 Test the fan-and-limit control. The fan-and-limit control is often enclosed in a small metal box. Turn the power off at the circuit breaker or fuse box and remove the fan-and-limit control cover.

3 Test the motor. If there is no switch, test by changing the control's settings. As you look at the dial, you'll notice either two or three sliding tabs and a numbered scale. Hold the dial firmly and move the two tabs at the lowest setting as far clockwise as you can. Restore power to the furnace. If the motor is functioning, it will turn on immediately, indicating that the fan-and-limit control needs to be replaced. You'll also need to replace the fan-and-limit switch.

Replacing the fan-and-limit control

1 If your tests have shown that the fan-and-limit control is bad, you will need to replace it. Label the wiring. Put a piece of tape next to each terminal, identifying it. Put a piece of tape on each wire identifying where it came from. Then remove the wires from their terminals.

2 With a pair of pliers, grab one of the grommets surrounding the wiring that comes into the control. Squeeze the grommet and slide it out of the bottom of the control. If there is a second set of wires, remove it in the same way.

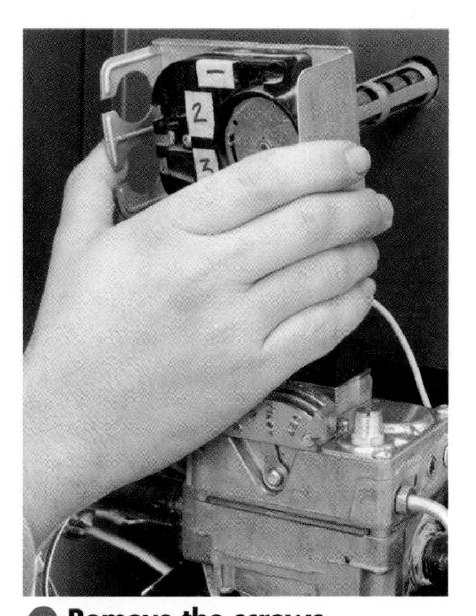

3 Remove the screws attaching the control to the furnace. A sensor tube extends into the firebox. Pull the control out until the tube clears. Take the control with you and get an identical replacement. You may have to reset the sliding tabs to match the settings on the old control. Don't move the dial. If there is a third tab on the dial, do not reset it.

Maintaining a forced-air furnace (continued)

Replacing the fan motor

1 If your thermostat, relay, and fan-and-limit control have all passed their tests, the problem is the motor. You can replace the motor, but if your motor has a capacitor in the circuit, call a pro. The capacitor is dangerous because it stores voltage even when the power is off. With no capacitor turn the power off, then mark the wires.

2 Unbolt the brackets holding the motor inside the fan. Pull the motor out and undo the collar bolts holding the front of the motor to the bracket. Put all the removed hardware in one place so you can locate it easily when installing the replacement motor.

3 If the blower is direct-drive, it will come off with the motor. Loosen the setscrew on the blower to free the blower shaft. Then turn the fan so it is motor-side up and disconnect the green ground wire if there is one.

4 Replace the unit. Slide the motor assembly into its slot and reattach the necessary wiring. Turn on the power at the breaker box and test the unit.

Maintaining a gas burner

Skill level:	Time to complete:	Materials:	Tools:
★★★★★	Experienced Variable Handy Variable Novice Variable	Dish soap, thermocouple, igniter, long lighter or match	Wrench, screwdriver, brass brush, fine-grit sandpaper, multimeter, shop vacuum

In a gas furnace burning fuel heats air or water, which is then distributed throughout the house. Because gas burns more cleanly than oil, the yearly service is less demanding. Problems could be as simple as relighting the pilot on some models. On others it might be replacing the igniter, a piece of high-resistance metal that lights the furnace without the use of a pilot.

Although homeowners can easily maintain gas furnaces, repair or installation of gas lines is best left to professionals.

Dirt that builds up in the burners can result in a yellow flame or in delayed ignition. Avoid a service call by cleaning the burners once a year.

In addition to a vacuum, you'll need either the owner's manual or an inquisitive mind: No two furnaces are built exactly alike. You can attach the burners any number of ways, so the directions here have to be general.

- If you must figure out the system on your own, trace the gas line to the burners and carefully examine the fittings and brackets along the way. Take particular note of the burners—how they are aligned and how they are held in—so that once you get them out, you'll get them back in correctly, with no extra pieces.
- If the pilot fails to stay lit when you release the control knob, relight it and look at the color of the flame. If it's mostly yellow the pilot's not getting enough oxygen and probably not producing enough heat to trigger the thermocouple. The nozzle may be clogged and needs to be cleaned. If the flame is mostly blue, check the thermocouple.
- The hole in the pilot's nozzle is sized to produce a flame of the right size, height, and temperature to activate the thermocouple. If it is too big, it can cause the thermocouple to fail or it can burn other components. When cleaning the nozzle first try blowing through it. If that doesn't work use a wire brush or replace the nozzle.

Begin any maintenance or repair by turning off the gas at the manual valve and the power at the circuit breaker box.

WORK SMART

THE ORDER OF BATTLE

When tracking a problem, always try the easiest and most obvious solution first. With a gas furnace:

- First make sure the pilot is lit.
- Second clean the nozzle.
- Third check the thermocouple. If you find ash buildup on the tip of the thermocouple, it needs to be cleaned or replaced.
- Ash buildup is also an indication that the burners are in need of cleaning. Cleaning and reassembling the thermocouple is easier with the burners out of the furnace, so you might as well clean them at the same time.

SAFETY ALERT

SHUT OFF THE GAS VALVE

Always turn off the gas before working on your furnace. To do this follow the gas line from the furnace back to a red-handled valve. This is the manual cutoff valve. To shut off the gas, turn the handle so it's perpendicular to the pipe (shown). Wait five minutes before doing any work.

Maintaining a gas burner (continued)

Checking for leaks

Gas leaks usually occur where two pipes meet. If you suspect a leak, test the joint with slightly diluted dish soap. Brush the soap on at all the joints. Bubbles indicate a leak. If you discover one immediately turn off the gas at the meter.

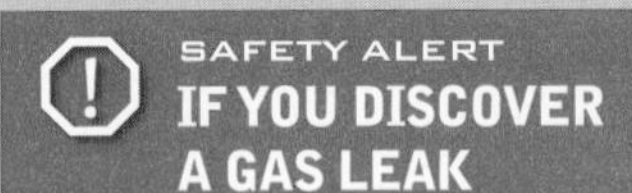

Gas leaks are rare but they do occur and can cause serious damage and personal injury. Always turn off the gas at the cutoff valve before working on your furnace or water heater. If you smell gas (it stinks like rotten eggs), you must act quickly to protect yourself and your family. There's no such thing as a false alarm in this kind of a situation.

- Gather any family members or pets and leave the house immediately. Go to a neighbor's home and call the fire department or your gas company's emergency number.
- Stay out of the house until the utility company has inspected the site and repaired any leaks or damage.
- Don't turn any electrical devices or power tools on or off; sparks could cause an explosion.
- Beware of static electricity; it sparks too.

Adjusting the air shutter

Most furnaces allow you to adjust the burner flame to make sure it is burning at the correct temperature. Turn the thermostat up to start the furnace, then remove the burner access cover so you can look at the flame.

Loosen the lock screw, turn the shutter, and watch the flame. It will change color and size. To achieve the correct setting, turn the shutter until the flame turns blue with a green core. (A yellow flame like the one shown here is starved for air. A blue flame with a dark blue center is getting too much air.) Once the flame is the right color, turn the shutter until the flame lifts away from the burner. Then turn the shutter back the other way until the flame reseats itself on the burner. Tighten the lock screw and repeat the process on the remaining burners.

Lighting the pilot

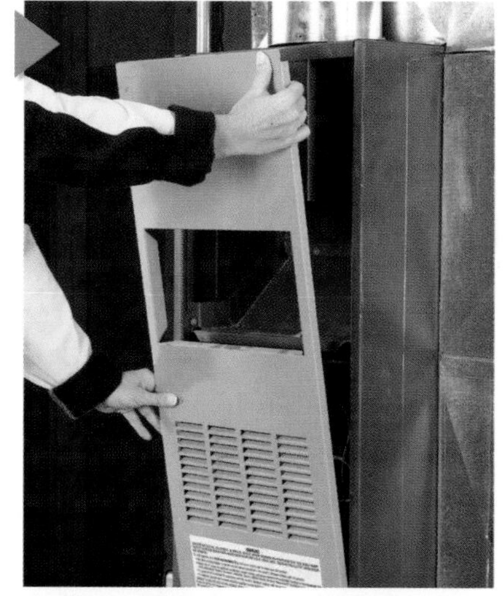

1 An older furnace has a constantly burning pilot light that ignites the furnace when you need heat. The furnace won't function if the pilot goes out. To check it take the access cover off the furnace and look for the gas control knob. If your furnace has a pilot, the knob will turn to three positions: Off, On, and Pilot.

2 Turn the knob until the arrow points at the word "Pilot." Push the knob (or the button next to it) down to start the flow of gas.

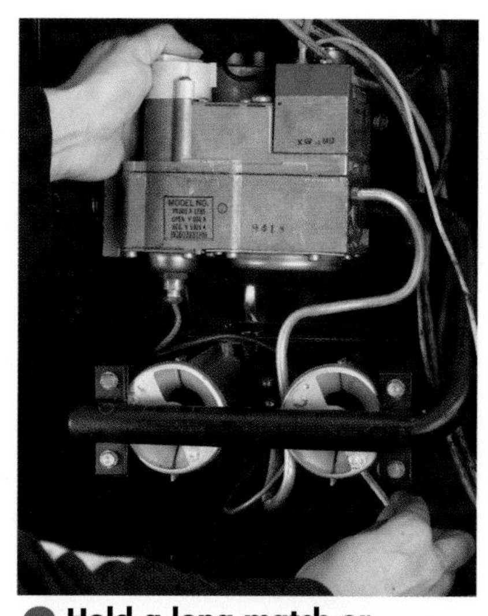

3 Hold a long match or a long-nose butane lighter designed for the fireplace up to the pilot nozzle to light the pilot. Once the flame is lit, hold the knob down for about a minute; then release it. If the pilot stays lit, turn the knob back to the On position. If it goes out try again, holding the button for a longer time. If the flame still goes out, the nozzle may be dirty. Clean it as explained below.

Cleaning the pilot

1 Check the flame. If it's burning mostly yellow, it needs more oxygen to produce enough heat to trigger the thermocouple (see page 452). The nozzle may have become clogged with debris and may need to be cleaned.

2 Turn off the gas and disconnect the pilot line from the bracket housing the burner. The pilot line feeds gas to the burners. Once the line is disconnected, remove and clean the nozzle.

3 The nozzle is usually housed in a barrel-shaped part of the pilot bracket. It's either a threaded piece that twists out of the bracket or a loose piece that you can shake out. Remove the nozzle and gently blow through it to remove debris. Clean it gently with a small brass brush or replace it with a new nozzle.

Maintaining a gas burner (continued)

Checking the thermocouple

1 The thermocouple is the thinner of the two tubes running toward the pilot light. If the flame is mostly blue, the thermocouple could be the problem; clean or replace it. Remove the nut at the end nearest the pilot and pull the thermocouple out of the bracket.

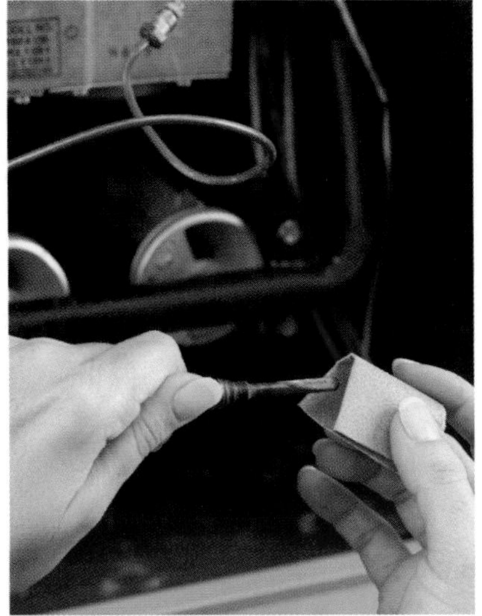

2 Gently clean the end of the thermocouple. Ash and other debris can build up on the end of the thermocouple, inhibiting its ability to fire the furnace. Before replacing it try cleaning it gently with fine-grit sandpaper. Replace it and retest the flame. If it fails to light or is the wrong color, replace the thermocouple.

3 If the thermocouple is bad, turn off the pilot and cut off the gas at the manual shutoff valve. Turn off the power at the circuit breaker or fuse box. Let the thermocouple cool; remove it by loosening the nut with a wrench (see inset). Remove the thermocouple and take it to a dealer for a replacement. Install the new thermocouple and relight the pilot.

Checking and replacing the igniter

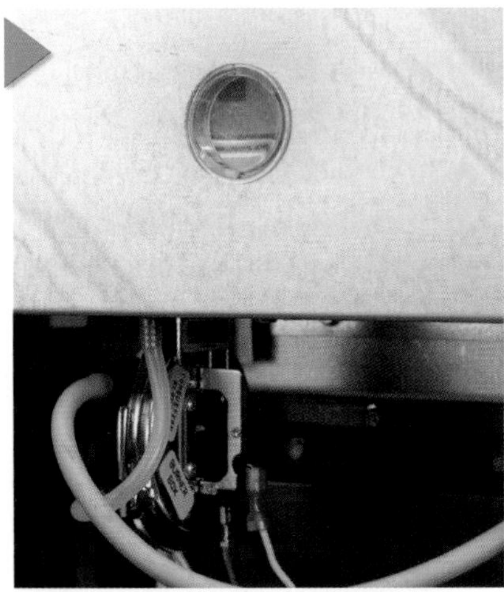

1 The igniter has replaced the pilot light on newer furnaces. If your furnace has an igniter but won't fire up, watch the igniter as someone turns up the thermostat. If you can't see the igniter glowing like this through the observation window, you may need to replace it.

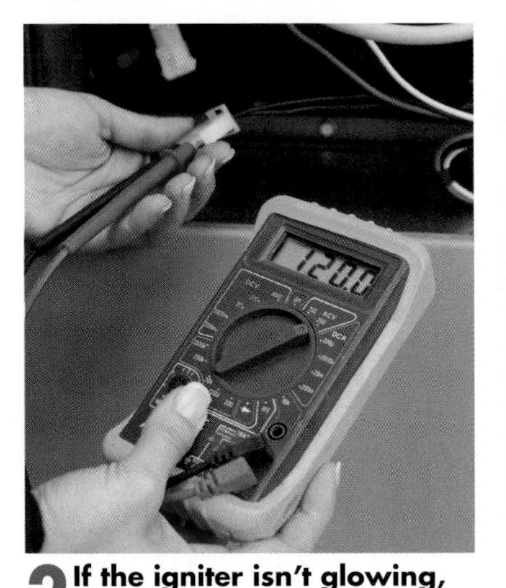

2 If the igniter isn't glowing, remove the cover that houses the observation window. Unplug the wires going into the igniter. Put a lead in each of the igniter wires that lead back into the furnace. Set a multimeter to read AC volts and turn the thermostat up enough to start the furnace. If the meter reads around 120 volts, the igniter is faulty. If there is no power, the control box may be bad; call a service person.

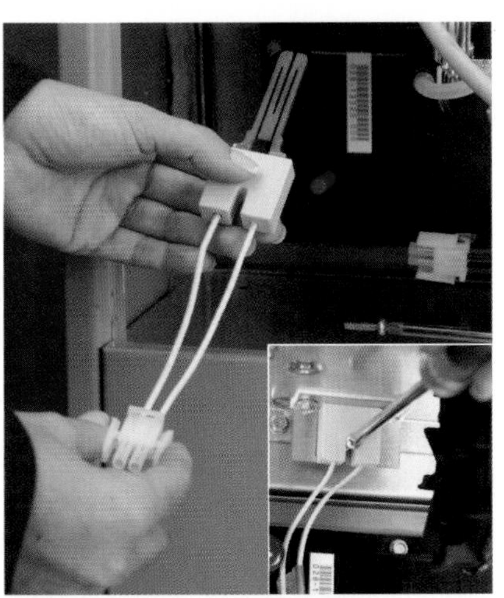

3 To replace the igniter, loosen the screw in the bracket that attaches it to the furnace. Replace it with an identical igniter and reattach it to the furnace. When you handle the igniter, hold it by the porcelain part or by the bracket—touching the surface that heats up may shorten its life. Reattach the wires, then screw the igniter in place (see inset). Turn up the thermostat to test it before reattaching the cover.

Cleaning the burner

1 Turn off the electricity at the breaker box and shut off the gas at the manual valve. Wait five minutes and remove the furnace access panel; then remove the access panel that covers the burners. The burners are tubes with openings along the side to let in air. Remove the tubes as recommended by the manufacturer.

2 In most cases you'll have to remove a gas pipe, called the manifold, that runs along the back of the burners. Look to see whether this is necessary; if so loosen the union where the pipe enters the gas control box until the line is free of the union. Lift the manifold to remove it, being careful not to hit the igniter.

3 Remove one of the round, tubelike burners. Clean it with a brush attached to a shop vacuum, then put it back in place. Look to see how it locks in place—some burners have locking tabs—then position it as necessary. Clean the other tubes one at a time; on some furnaces each tube is designed for a specific location.

4 When you've finished vacuuming all the burners, replace the manifold. Check the alignment, then screw the bracket holding the manifold back in place. If you've disconnected the gas line feeding the burners, reattach it.

5 Reconnect the gas line to the manifold. After the burners are fully seated in their channels (or channel), use a screwdriver to reconnect the gas line.

6 Reattach the pilot line to the control box. Once the gas line is reattached to the control box, turn the gas back on and test the furnace. You may have to readjust the air shutter to get the proper flame on the pilot.

Maintaining an oil furnace

Skill level: ★★★☆☆

Time to complete: Experienced 3 hrs. Handy 5 hrs. Novice 7 hrs.

Materials: Electric-motor oil, pie pan filled with sand or cat litter, paint thinner or kerosene, oil filter, nozzle (depending on furnace), electrodes (if damaged)

Tools: Screwdriver, shop vacuum with brush, open-ended wrenches, metal file, toothbrush, tape measure, caliper

In numerous cases your oil supplier includes a yearly oil burner tune-up in the price you pay for oil. If you don't have a service contract, you should nevertheless leave most of the maintenance chores associated with an oil-burning furnace to the pros. You can safely replace the filter and clean and oil the fan, as shown on the next page. But that should be about the limit of your DIY oil burner maintenance.

An oil-burning furnace is essentially a large campfire. Like a campfire a furnace is relatively easy to take apart. Getting everything back in exactly the same place, shape, and order, however, requires both skill and caution. The electrodes—which spark to start the fire that warms you—need to be filed to a point. They also need to be spaced the proper distance from each other and from the nozzle that shoots the oil into the furnace.

Calling in a certified maintenance person isn't just a case of letting someone else do the dirty work. It's a matter of your immediate and future safety. So before you pick up the screwdriver, pick up the phone.

Having said that, however, you should be familiar with the steps a pro will take during a routine maintenance call so you know the job is done correctly. The photos on the following pages will acquaint you with those steps.

Routine maintenance not only improves the efficiency of your furnace, it may also correct some problems. Cleaning or replacing the nozzle may cure a pulsating, thumping, or rumbling furnace. A smoky furnace may be caused by a dirty nozzle or a dirty fan. Smoke, in particular, may indicate a cracked firebox and the presence of deadly carbon monoxide in your home.

How an oil furnace works

On a modern oil furnace, when the furnace starts, a pump draws oil through a filter and forces it inside the firing assembly. There the oil is pumped through a nozzle, creating an oil spray. A transformer on top of the assembly provides power to an electrode that sparks and ignites the oil spray. One of two systems ensures that the oil has ignited—an electric eye senses the flame, or a sensor in the chimney notes a rise in temperature. If the sensors detect nothing, the furnace shuts down.

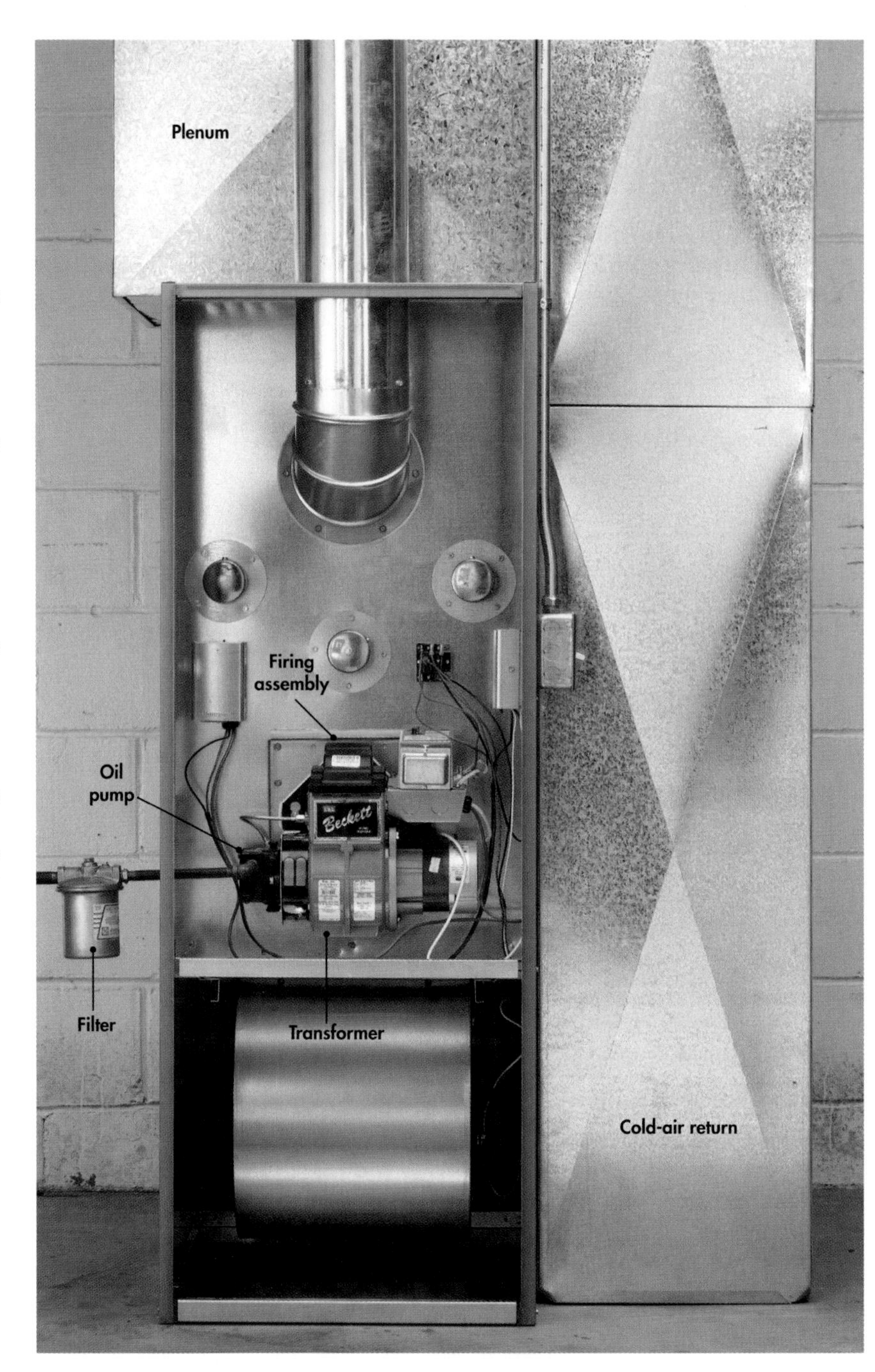

Replacing the oil filter

1 The oil filter keeps dirt from entering the fuel line. It should be replaced once a year as part of a routine furnace tune-up. Start by closing the oil supply valve, which is usually at the bottom of the oil tank. Fill a pie pan about halfway with cat litter, then set it under the filter. Unscrew the bolt on the top of the filter, remove the canister, and let the oil drain into the pan.

2 Inside the canister is a disposable filter cartridge. Loosen the bolt on top of the canister and disassemble it. Remove and replace the filter, then remove and replace the gasket on the lip of the filter canister or lid. Reattach the canister.

3 Replacing the filter allowed air to enter the fuel line—air that you must get back out. Loosen the bleeder valve on the filter top by turning it counterclockwise. Reopen the oil supply valve. Air will rush out the bleeder valve as oil begins to flow into the canister. When the air has been purged, oil will begin to come out the bleeder valve. Close it at this point.

Cleaning and oiling the fan

1 Locate the firing assembly by following the oil line into the furnace. Nearby you'll find a motor for the firing assembly fan. If it has oil ports, drop in two to five drops of SAE 10 nondetergent electric-motor oil. If no ports exist the motor is sealed and needs no oil.

2 Clean the firing assembly fan. This fan forces air into the combustion chamber. Dirt on it can keep the burner from getting enough air, resulting in a smoky furnace. To clean the fan remove the transformer on the top of the firing assembly, usually a matter of loosening a few screws. Put the brush attachment onto a shop vacuum and vacuum the fins on the fan to clean them.

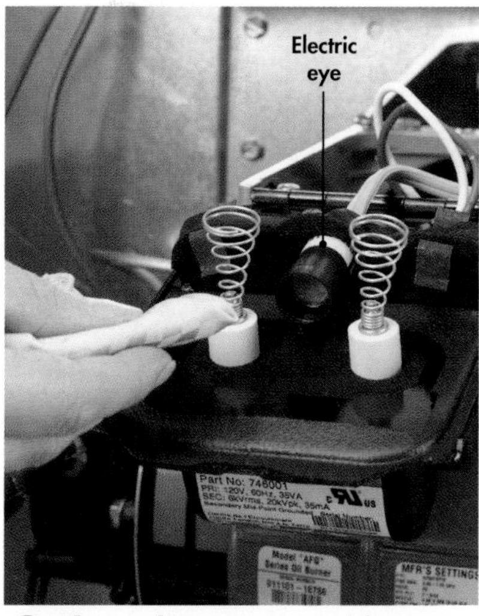

3 Clean the sensor. Oil furnaces have an electric eye (above) that senses whether the flame is lit and shuts down the motor if it isn't. If the glass over the sensor is dirty, clean it by wiping it with a clean, dry cloth.

Maintaining an oil furnace (continued)

Removing the firing assembly

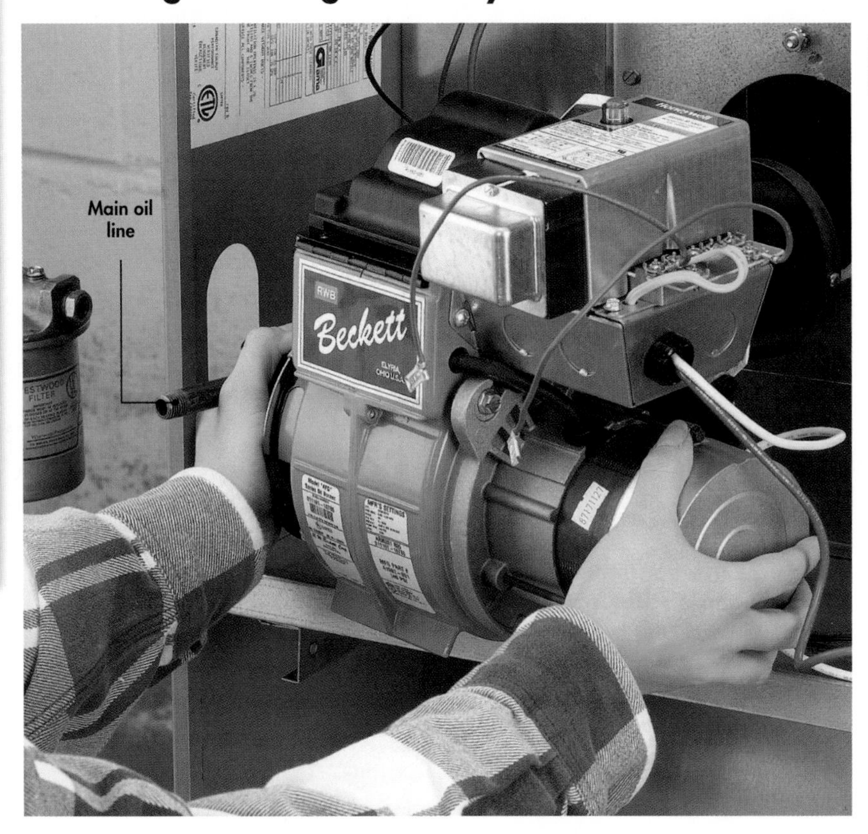

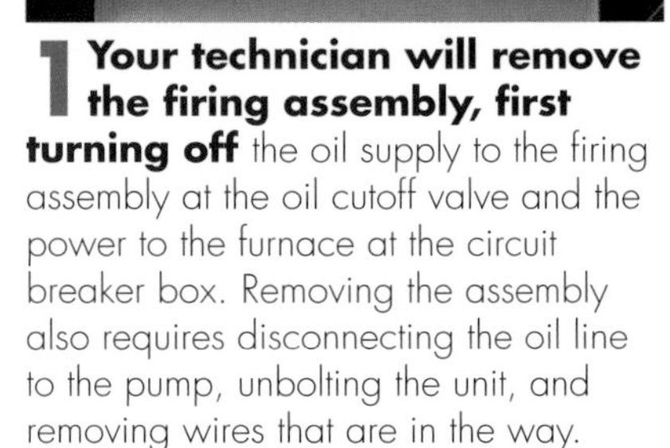

1 Your technician will remove the firing assembly, first turning off the oil supply to the firing assembly at the oil cutoff valve and the power to the furnace at the circuit breaker box. Removing the assembly also requires disconnecting the oil line to the pump, unbolting the unit, and removing wires that are in the way.

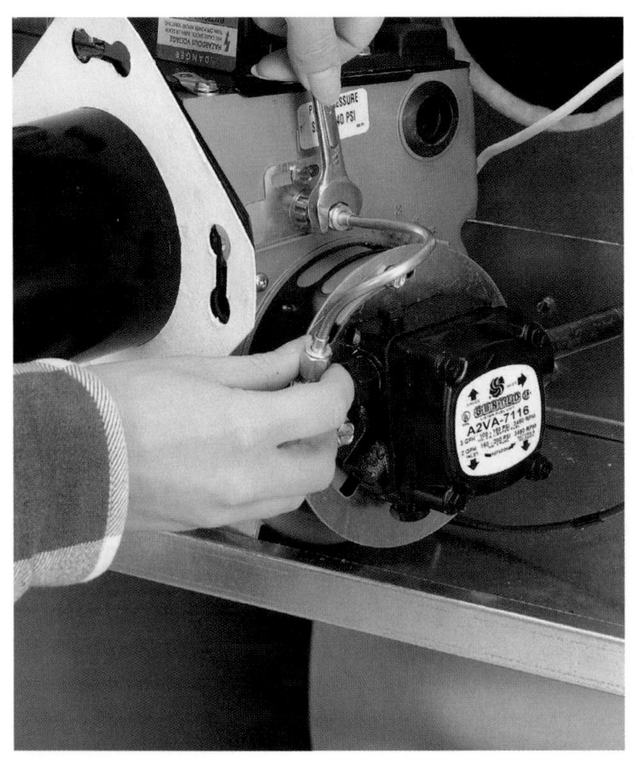

2 Disconnecting the copper oil line from the pump and body will allow the pump to be removed.

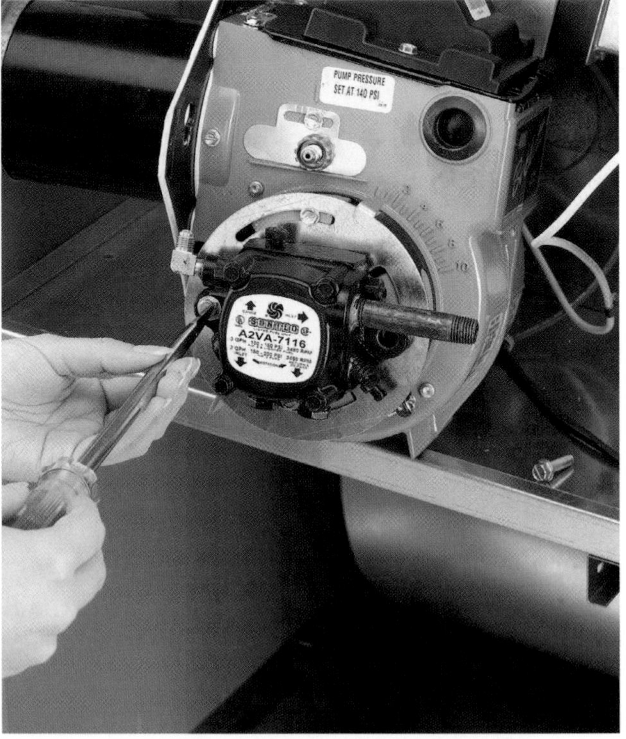

3 Removing the pump from the unit will require removing the screws that hold it. This will allow the technician to slide the pump out of the assembly.

Maintaining the firing assembly

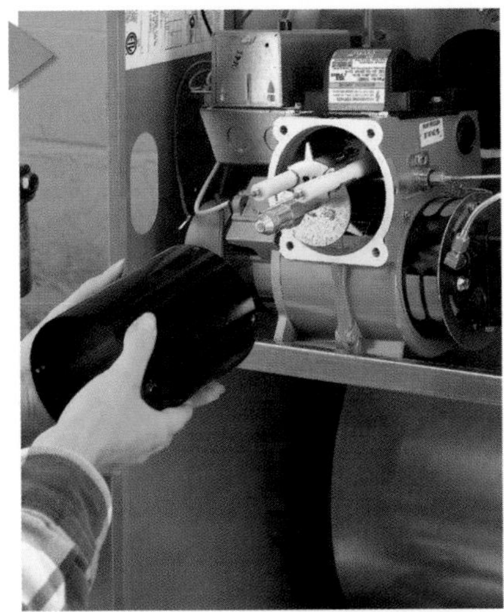

1 The firing assembly is the heart of the furnace. A nozzle shoots a fine mist of oil into the combustion chamber, a fan blows air into the chamber, and electrodes produce a spark to start the flame. Your technician will remove the oil line that runs from the firing assembly to the pump, loosen the bolts that hold the assembly in place, and pull the assembly out, twisting it as necessary to avoid bumping the electrodes against the rest of the furnace.

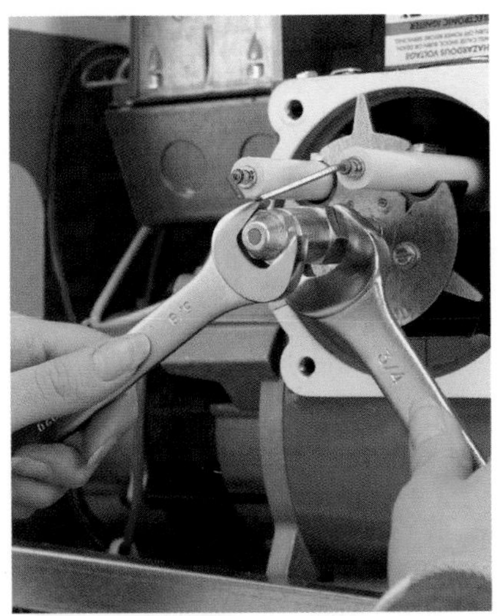

2 Remove the nozzle. Nozzles are designed to shoot a certain volume of oil per hour in a particular spray pattern. The volume and pattern vary from furnace to furnace. A clogged nozzle can seriously affect furnace performance. Removing the nozzle will take two wrenches, one on the hex nut on the oil line and another on the nozzle.

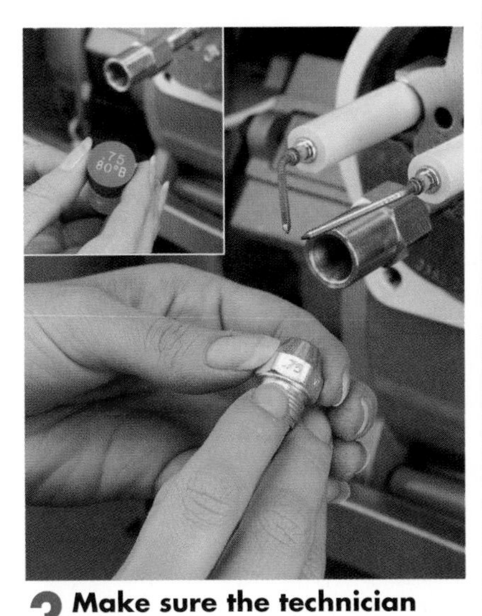

3 Make sure the technician inspects the nozzle to find out the size and spray angle, which are usually stamped on the hex end of the nozzle. If the nozzle is rated lower than 1.5 gallons per hour (gph), it should be replaced. The new nozzle container will also indicate the size of the nozzle (see inset). If the nozzle is rated higher than 1.5 gph, the technician will disassemble it and clean it in paint thinner.

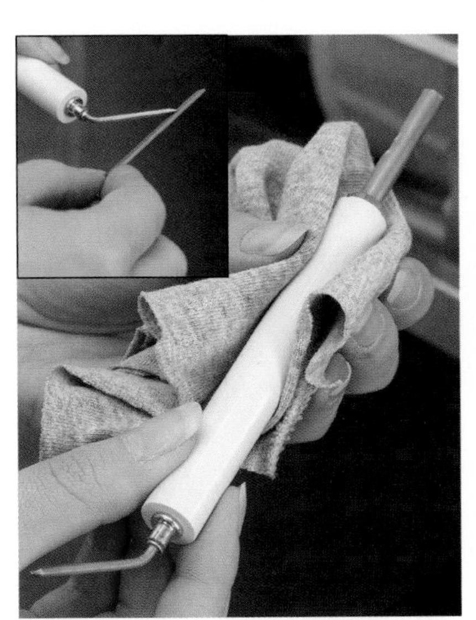

4 Make sure your technician cleans the electrodes, wiping the porcelain with a rag and paint thinner. If the sleeves are OK, he or she will file the ends of the electrodes into sharp points (see inset).

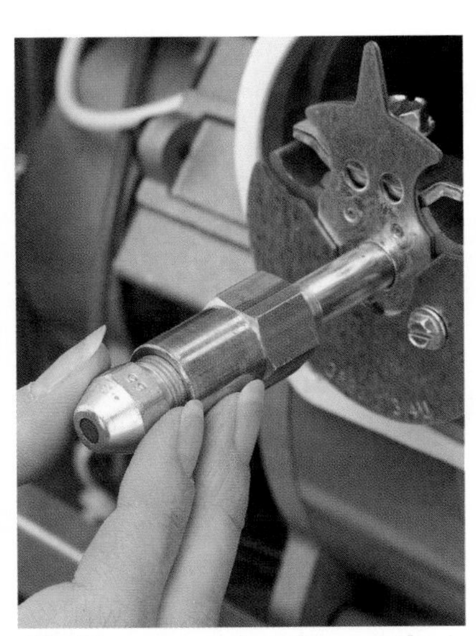

5 After removing the nozzle parts from the paint thinner, the technician will reassemble the nozzle. Reassembly requires threading the nozzle finger-tight and tightening a quarter-turn with the wrenches.

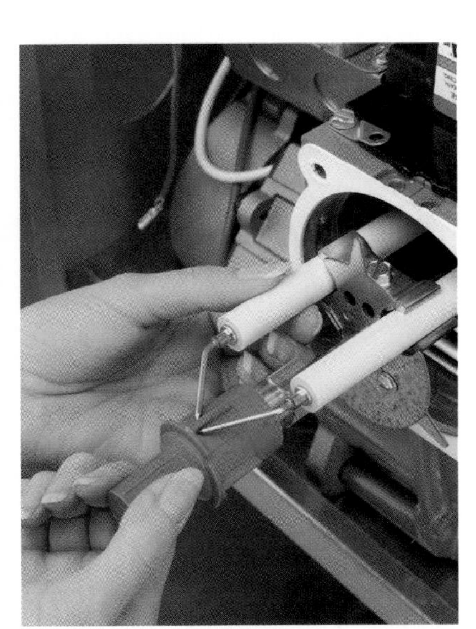

6 Electric alignment is critical in the maintenance process, and you'll see the technician using a caliper to adjust the electrodes to a gap that is specific to the model of your furnace.

Maintaining a hot-water heat system

Skill level: ★☆☆☆☆

Time to complete: Experienced 1 hr. Handy 1 hr. Novice 1 hr.

Materials: Household oil

Tools: Vacuum cleaner with soft brush attachment, screwdriver, radiator key, pipe wrench, water pump pliers, multimeter

Even if you'd rather not think about working on furnaces, you can do a few simple jobs to keep a hot-water system running well. Oiling the pump, a simple matter of dropping a bit of oil into the right places, can keep the motor from failing. Letting trapped air out of the system, or "bleeding" it, removes large air bubbles that keep warm water from running throughout the entire system. It's not usually part of a furnace tune-up, but it's simple, makes a big difference, and is more fun than something this important should be.

A good dusting should be part of your maintenance program. Dust buildup on the pump motor keeps it from running efficiently. Dust buildup on the fins inside the baseboard keeps heat from leaving the system and getting into the room.

Air is both a friend and an enemy in a hot-water system. The expansion tank, located near the furnace, needs air. As the boiler heats the water, the water expands and needs a place to go. The expansion tank contains a cushion of air that compresses as the water comes in and expands as the water cools.

Put the same air into a pipe, radiator, or baseboard heater and you've got trouble: The water can't get by it. Every radiator or baseboard downstream of the bubble goes cold. Since it's almost impossible to keep air out of the lines, hot-water systems have what are called bleeder valves. In essence they are tiny faucets attached to the radiator or baseboard. When you turn the faucet when the heat is on, trapped air is forced out through the valve. Once it's gone water flows out the valve, and you turn it off. Bleed the system at the beginning of the heating season, starting at the top of the house and working your way down.

▲ *Hot-water systems combine the worlds of plumbing, electrical, and HVAC.*

Twice a year oil the motor that runs the circulator. On most furnaces the motor is a separate unit attached to the side of the circulator. Look for three oil ports: one on the front of the funnel-shaped bearing housing and one each at the front and back of the motor. The port on the bearing housing will probably be an oil cup. Those on the motor may have plastic feeder tubes that help you get oil inside the port. Lubricate with a few drops of household oil. If you can't find oil ports, don't worry. Some motors are permanently sealed and don't need oil.

Clean the casing with a soft brush attached to a vacuum. Run the brush over the holes in the motor casing and in the bearing housing to remove dust that reduces efficiency.

How a hot-water heat system works

When the thermostat calls for heat, the furnace starts a fire in the boiler of a hot-water system. While the boiler heats, a thermometer called an aquastat measures water temperature. When the temperature reaches a set point, the aquastat activates a switch and the circulator starts pumping water through the convectors—baseboard units that have largely replaced radiators.

The circulator is really a three-part device. First is the electrical motor, which provides power once the aquastat turns it on. Second comes the coupling, a clutch that connects the motor to the last element, the pump. If any of the three fails, water won't flow, no matter how hot the boiler gets.

Fortunately the aquastat watches the system for this very situation. If the water in the boiler gets too hot, it shuts down the furnace before too much pressure can build up in the boiler.

Because water expands as it warms, some pressure buildup is inevitable. During routine operation—when the pump is functioning and the water temperature is neither too high nor too low—expanding water flows into an expansion tank. As the water flows into the tank, it compresses the air inside and creates the pressure that the system needs to run once the water has reached its final density.

▲ *Although boilers for hot-water systems can take many forms (some even appearing to be hot-water tanks for potable water and showers), most will look something like this. Many combine the tasks of home heating with domestic hot-water heating in one unit.*

▲ *Before starting even the most routine maintenance tasks, familiarize yourself with the major components of your system. It's best to perform any routine maintenance that requires you to shut off the power during the summer months, when you're not using the system to heat your home.*

Maintaining a hot-water heat system (continued)

Bleeding baseboards and radiators

Baseboard hot-water heaters, called convectors, have a bleeder located under the cover that shields the fins. As you look at the baseboard, you'll see a door at each end. Open the doors and look for the bleeder.

On some units the bleeder will be near or on top of the cutoff valve. On other units it will be at the opposite end. The valve has a small spout on one side that releases the air. Looking for the spout is an easy way to find the valve. Once you find the spout, you'll see a screw or knob on top that operates the valve. Open the valve until water runs out; then close the valve.

Radiators are usually relics of a steam-heat system that has been converted to hot water. Steam traveled through the pipes under its own pressure. Hot water needs to be pumped but can be produced with considerably less energy. Steam radiators need bleeding too. The valve is on the side near the top of the radiator and operates with a removable key, available from most HVAC retailers. Be careful: If your system is still steam, it will be hot enough to scald you when it comes out of the valve.

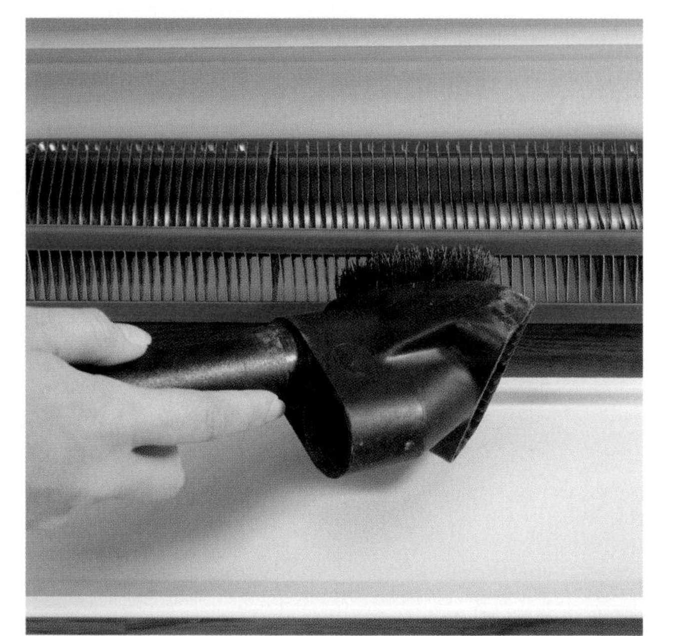

Baseboard fins collect dust quickly, compromising the efficiency of the system. Once a year slide or snap the cover off the front of the baseboard. Clean the fins by wiping them with a soft brush attachment on your vacuum.

Repairing a waterlogged expansion tank

When the boiler heats water in the system, the water expands. Unless it has a place to go, you've got trouble. Fortunately the expansion tank is there. Located near the furnace the expansion tank is basically a tank partially filled with air. The expanding water flows into the tank, relieving pressure on the system. As the water flows into the tank, it compresses the air inside and creates the pressure that the system needs to run once the water has reached its final density. Sometimes an older tank gets waterlogged—the air inside leaks out and the tank fills entirely with water. This probably won't happen if you have a newer tank. In new tanks the air is sealed into one side of the tank by a diaphragm. As the pressure in the system increases, it pushes against the diaphragm to compress the air. As the pressure drops the air expands, pushing the diaphragm back into its original position.

Your expansion tank is probably located a few feet away from the furnace and may be hung from the ceiling. To find it just follow the warm pipes coming out of the furnace.

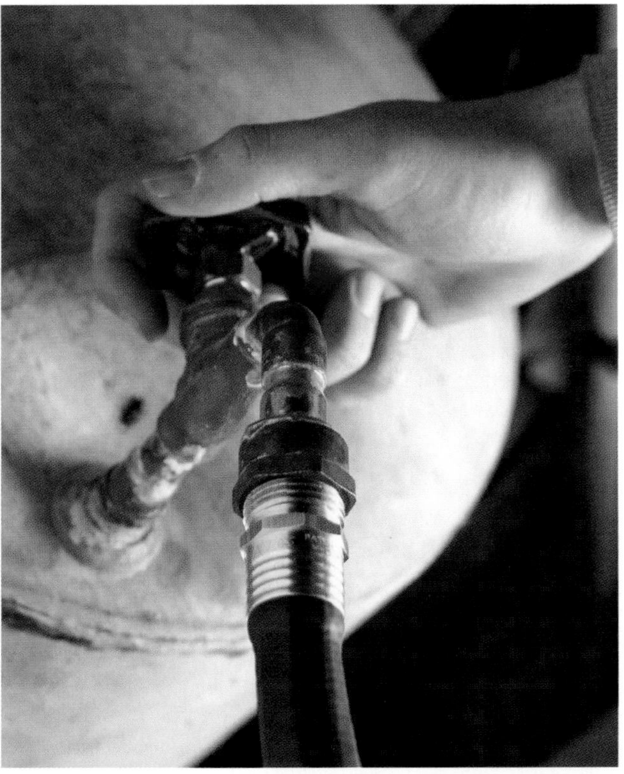

Older tanks have a drain valve you should open once a year to prevent waterlogging. Start by tracing the pipe that runs from the furnace to the tank and then close the valve between the two. Put a hose on the tank's drain valve and open the valve.

When the water starts draining, open the air valve. This may be located on the side of the tank or on the drain valve or it may be a small cap on the valve between the furnace and the tank. Open the valve or unscrew the cap to let air into the tank as it drains. Close the drain and air valve once water stops running and reopen the valve between the furnace and the tank. The tank will automatically refill to the proper level.

Make draining maintenance routine

Draining your expansion tank should be part of your yearly maintenance schedule. Sediment is the chief enemy of a hot-water heating system and it's an inevitable consequence of anything that carries water. Although it's natural, sediment impedes the flow of water, reduces the efficiency of your system, and can cause damage to internal parts.

Draining a system is not something you can accomplish in a flash. It takes time, and the water may smell a bit unpleasant. Don't perform this operation in the winter. You'll get cold in the time it takes and you'll want to open a few windows if the water smell becomes unbearable.

First shut off the boiler and let the water cool for an hour or two. Then drain the system as shown above. Be sure to open the bleed valve on the tank to let air in as the water goes out. To fill the system, close the drain valve on the boiler. Add rust inhibitor if recommended by the manufacturer, then close all the bleed valves in the system. Open the input valves and fill the system. Let the pressure come to the level recommended by the manufacturer, then turn the power on. Run the system for 24 hours, then bleed the air out again.

Maintaining a hot-water heat system (continued)

A newer tank has a diaphragm that seals the air in one part of the tank, separating it from the water. When the pressure in the heating system increases, it pushes against the diaphragm, compressing the air and letting more water into the tank. Because the air is sealed in, diaphragm tanks are less likely to become waterlogged. If the tank does become waterlogged, your heating technician can pump more air into the tank, which usually fixes the problem (and is often part of the yearly furnace maintenance). If the problem remains it's likely that the diaphragm is broken. (You can't repair a broken diaphragm; consequently some service people prefer nondiaphragm tanks.) If you need a new tank, look at the one you have and write down the brand and model number. Talk over the issue of diaphragm versus nondiaphragm with your supplier and have a replacement on hand before you start the repair. You'd hate to be standing by the furnace in midwinter with no heat and a replacement tank on back order.

Replacing an expansion tank

1 Shut off power to the furnace and let it cool down for several hours. Close the valve between the furnace and the expansion tank and drain it as described on page 461. Once the tank is empty, put a pipe wrench onto the fitting between the expansion tank and the valve and disconnect the fitting by turning the pipe with water pump pliers. If the pipe suspends the tank, get a helper to hold it while you work.

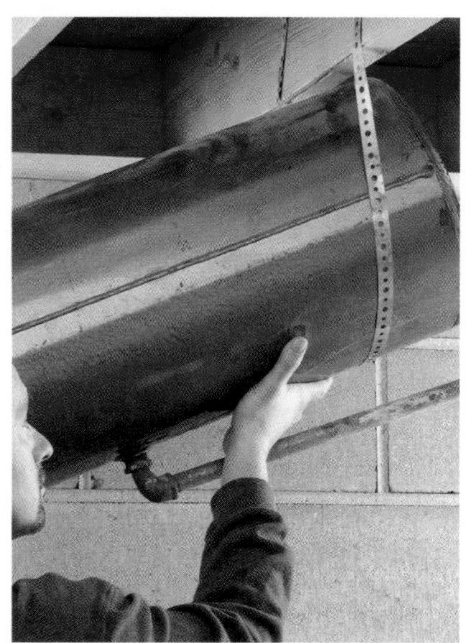

2 Once the tank is disconnected, remove it. The tank may be heavy—another reason for a helper.

3 Install your replacement tank. Reconnect the pipes and fittings you disconnected in Step 1 to the valve using plumber's tape. Support the pipe with pipe straps, adjusting as necessary. Wrap plumber's tape around the threads of the pipe that leads into the tank and screw the tank onto the fitting to install it. Turn on the valve to restore the water flow. Check the fittings for leaks.

Testing and fixing an aquastat

An aquastat is simply a thermostat (not to be confused with the thermostat upstairs) that measures water temperature in the boiler and activates a switch when the temperature reaches a certain point. A hot-water heat system has at least two aquastats. One turns the burner off to keep the boiler temperature from getting too hot. The other keeps the circulator from pumping water through the radiator unless it's hot enough to do some good. On some furnaces the aquastats are individual units. On others the aquastats are housed in the same box and share a sensor that passes through the furnace wall and into the boiler. What an aquastat looks like inside the box depends on the make and model.

If there are two dials, one controls the boiler temperature while the other controls the circulator temperature. Both temperatures are allowed to vary below the setting by a preset amount. If there are three dials, one controls the boiler temperature, the second controls the circulator, and the third sets the amount the two are allowed to vary.

Aquastats are usually mounted on the furnace but are sometimes found on a pipe leading from the circulator.

Testing an aquastat

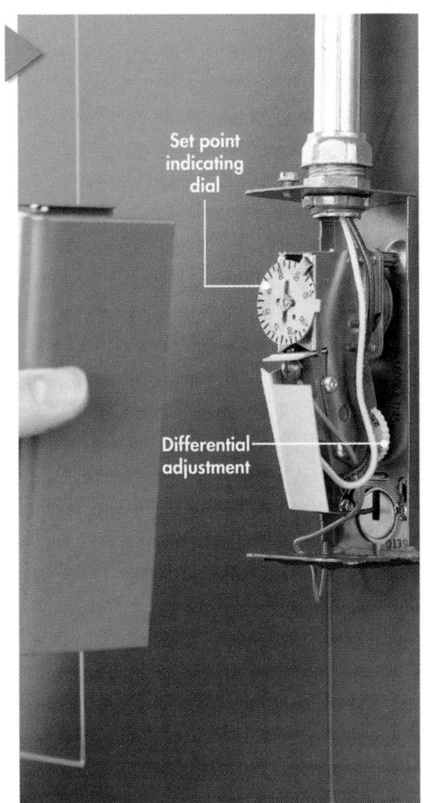

1 Remove the cover on the aquastat. Testing an aquastat is a matter of resetting the dials and watching what happens. On this furnace there are two aquastats (one for the burner and one for the circulator) mounted in different locations. On other furnaces both aquastats may be housed in the same box. The larger aquastat dial controls the set point—the temperature at which it will turn off the burner or pump. The smaller dial controls the differential, or number of degrees below the set point at which the burner or circulator will come on.

2 Turn the wall thermostat upstairs to its highest setting. If the furnace is functioning correctly it should turn on. If not test the burner (set point) aquastat on the furnace—the one set to the highest temperature—by lowering the setting to less than 100°F (38°C). If the aquastat is functioning the burner should go off. Return the burner aquastat to its original setting. If the aquastat is functioning the burner should go back on within 10 minutes. If the aquastat fails at either setting, replace it.

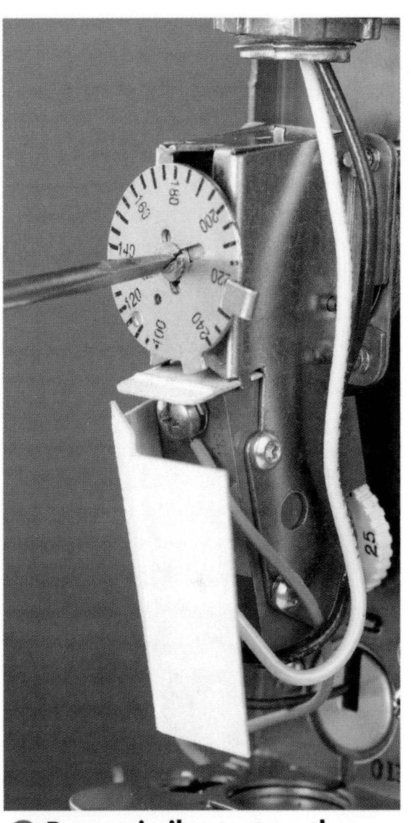

3 Run a similar test on the circulator aquastat. First raise the temperature setting to higher than 100°F (38°C). If the aquastat and circulator are both functioning the circulator will go on. If not find the source of the problem by putting a multimeter set to 120-volt AC across the aquastat terminals labeled C1 and C2, which lead to the circulator. If you get no reading the aquastat is defective. Once you've tested the setting, reset the aquastat to lower than 100°F (38°C). The circulator should go off. If not replace it.

Maintaining a hot-water heat system (continued)

Replacing an aquastat

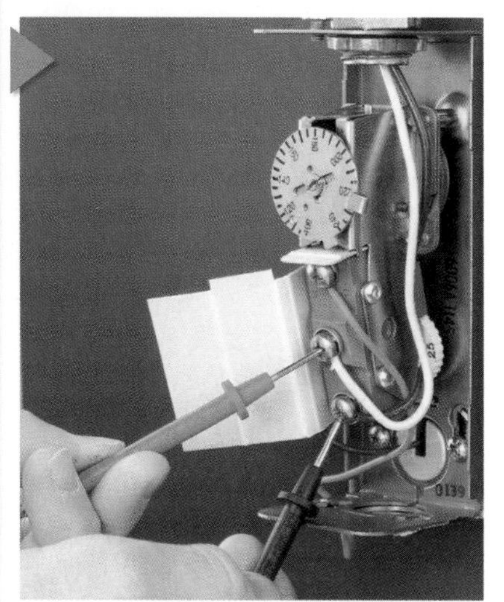

1 Turn off the power at the circuit breaker box and at the emergency cutoff switch. Make sure the power is off by applying a meter or voltage tester across the two terminals labeled Line. Double-check by putting one lead on a piece of bare metal inside the box and the other lead on first one line terminal and then the other. If the light comes on or the meter gives you a reading other than zero, you've turned off the wrong breaker. Do not work on the furnace until your meter or voltage tester tells you that you've turned off the correct breaker.

2 Disconnect the wires leading to the aquastat one at a time. Mark each wire with a piece of tape showing which terminal the wire came from.

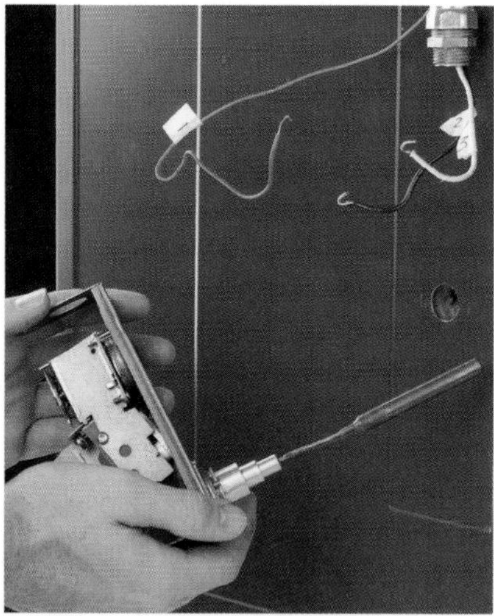

3 Remove the aquastat. In most cases, including this one, the aquastat fits on the surface of the furnace and has a sensor that fits into a well inside the boiler. Remove the screws holding the aquastat in place and remove it from the furnace. On rare occasions the aquastat is mounted on a pipe leading to a baseboard or radiator. If so remove the screws holding it in place. Take the aquastat to a dealer and buy a replacement that matches.

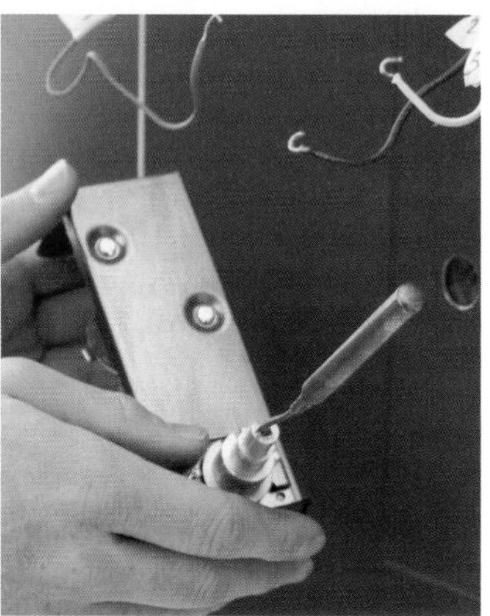

4 Remount and rewire the aquastat. Follow the manufacturer's directions when reinstalling an immersion aquastat. Among other things they will tell you how to properly position the sensor in the well. Reattach a pipe aquastat following the directions that come with it.

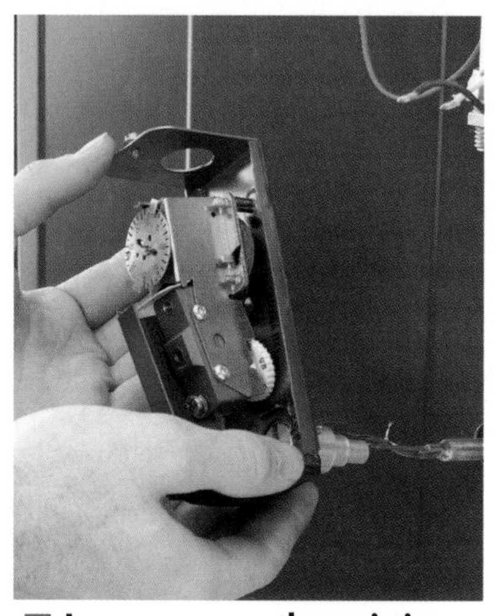

5 In some cases the existing well may not match the replacement aquastat. Make sure you have the correct aquastat and replace the well. Drain the boiler using the pressure-relief valve, then follow the manufacturer's directions for installing a new well. Insert the sensor into the well as directed and reattach the aquastat.

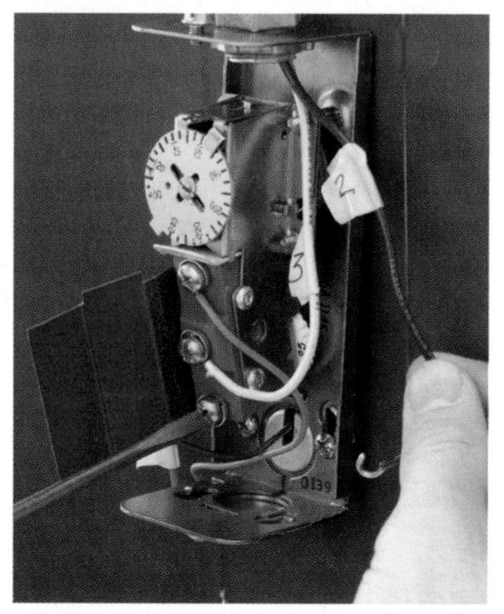

6 Reattach the wires using the labels to make sure each one is attached to the correct terminal. Set the dials on the new aquastat to match the pretesting settings on the old one.

Testing and replacing a pump motor

If you're reading these pages, you're either extremely curious or extremely cold. If curiosity brought you here, you're just interested in the way things work. If a failed motor brought you here, it means that no matter how hard the furnace is working, the heat isn't reaching the rest of the house.

You should have already tested the aquastat, which controls when the pump motor turns on. (If you haven't see page 463.) If you have, the problem is probably in your motor or very close to it. Traditionally the pump (known technically as a circulator) is a three-part assembly: motor, bearing housing, and pump. Inside the bearing housing a safety device called the coupler acts as a one-and-done clutch. If the pump jams, the coupler breaks the connection between the motor and pump so the motor won't burn itself out. Once the coupler goes into action, it's broken. You'll have to replace it.

Have someone turn the heat way up while you're standing next to the pump. If the motor comes on but the pump doesn't run, the problem is most likely the coupler. Replacing the coupler is a simple matter, but usually only a temporary cure. Whatever caused the coupler to break in the first place is likely to act up again. Unless you fix the core problem, sooner or later the new coupler will break.

If the coupler is intact and further tests indicate the motor or pump is broken, talk to your HVAC supplier about a combination pump, motor, and coupler sold as a single unit. Service people love them, and they're considerably less expensive than the traditional assemblies. Installing one is a matter of loosening a few bolts, putting the assembly in place, then retightening the bolts.

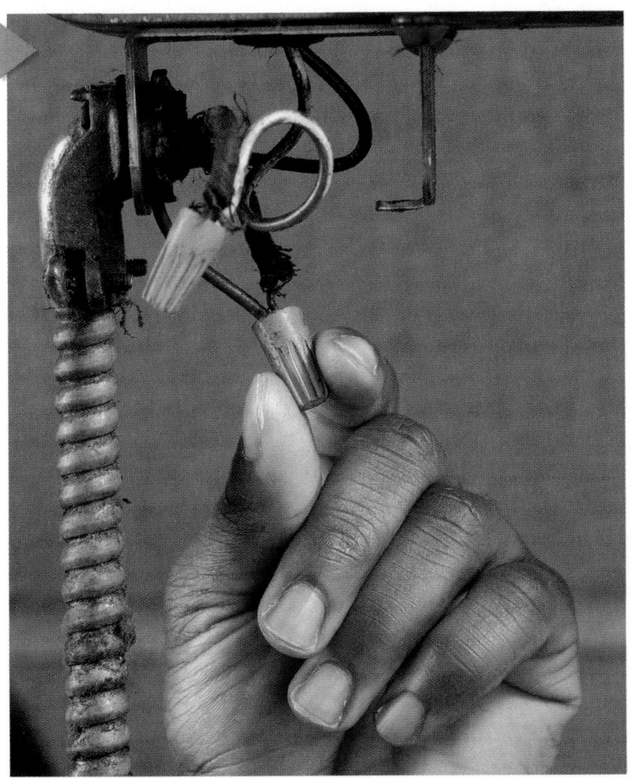

1 Turn off the power at the breaker box and emergency cutoff switch. Make sure the power is off by applying a meter across the line terminals of the aquastat. Remove the cover from the junction box on the pump motor. Gently remove the wire caps on the wires and double-check to make sure no power is going to them. Label the wires with pieces of tape so you'll know how to put them back together.

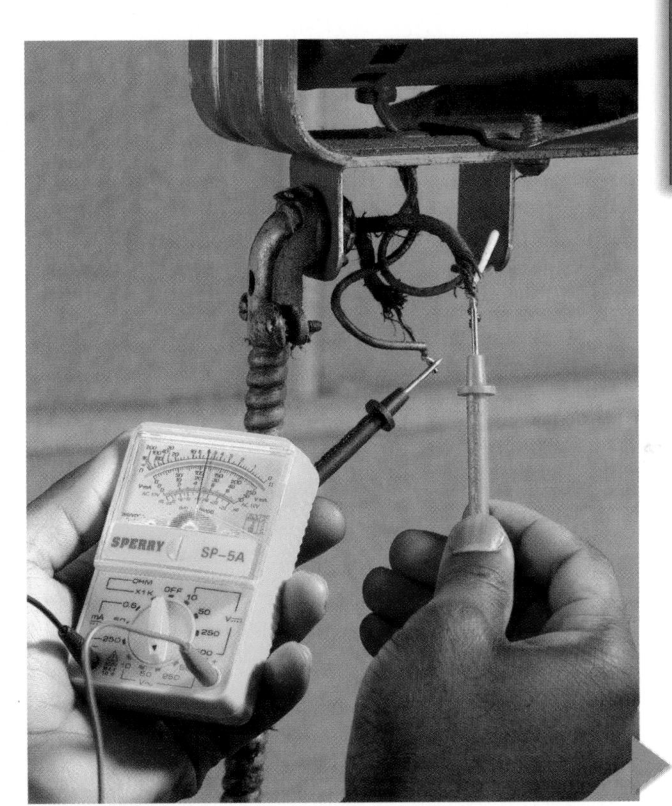

2 Test the motor by setting a multimeter to RX1 and putting a lead on each of the motor wires. The meter needle should swing or the readout change to indicate continuity. If you get no reading, replace or repair the motor. Talk to your supplier about replacing the motor and bearing assembly with a less expensive (but reliable) unit that combines the two.

A short-term solution if the pump fails

If the pump motor fails at 2:30 a.m. and the baby's crying and the pipes are freezing as you try to figure out what to do—you're having a bad night. But as long as the boiler is firing, there may be a short-term solution. You still must repair the pump but in the meantime try turning up the thermostat all the way. Hot water will still move slowly through the system of pipes and radiators without the pump by natural convection, and cold water will return to the boiler. The thermostat won't control the temperature until you've repaired the pump. But the house will be warmer and the pipes less likely to freeze.

Maintaining a hot-water heat system (continued)

3 If there is continuity the motor is probably usable. The problem may be the coupler, the spring-loaded device between the motor and pump that protects the motor if the pump jams. The coupler is located inside the bearing housing, the funnel-shaped piece between the motor and pump. Look inside for the setscrew on the pump end of the assembly and loosen it.

4 Remove the bolts holding the motor to the bearing assembly. Slide the motor and coupler off the pump shaft.

5 Look at the coupler and springs to check for broken parts. If there are and, remove the setscrew holding the coupler to the motor and replace the coupler. If the coupler appears to be intact and you are still not getting heat, call a service technician.

6 Slide the motor and coupler back onto the pump shaft. The motor is heavy and it can be difficult to get the spring assembly back over the shaft. Enlist a helper to support the motor while you wrestle the assembly into place.

7 Reattach the motor to the bearing housing. Tighten the setscrew attaching the coupler to the pump shaft and rewire the motor. Turn on the furnace. If the motor doesn't come on by the time the thermometer on the side of the furnace reaches the temperature on the aquastat, call a service technician.

Maintaining a heat pump

Skill level:	Time to complete:	Materials:	Tools:
★★★★★	Experienced Variable Handy Variable Novice Variable	Household oil, disposable air filter (if applicable), germicidal cleaner for coils, bleach, necessary replacement parts	Screwdriver, wrenches, or both; shop vacuum with brush attachment; 20,000-ohm, 5-watt resistor; two wire leads with alligator fin comb; clips at each end; multimeter

If you've ever stood outside a window air-conditioner, you've noticed the air coming out is hot. If you turned the air-conditioner around, it would take the heat out of the outdoor air and pump it inside. Simply stated a window air-conditioner is a heat pump: It takes heat from inside and pumps it outside.

The heat-pump systems that heat your house in the winter and cool it in the summer have a reversing valve in them. They comprise two units, one inside the house and one outside. When you call for heat, liquid refrigerant is pumped outdoors, where it absorbs whatever heat is there, turning the refrigerant into a gas in the process. The refrigerant flows through a compressor, which turns it into a liquid again, and the heat that is released by this process is released through coils inside the house and distributed by the fan and duct system.

When you call for air-conditioning, the process is reversed. The refrigerant absorbs heat inside the house and releases it outside. Depending on where you live, a heat pump can be based on an air source, ground source, or water source. In an air-source unit, the outdoor coils are exposed to the air. In a ground-source model the coils are underground. In a water-source pump the coils are cooled by water from a lake, well, or stream.

Each type has its advantages. Although air source is the least expensive, it is prone to frosting over and requires a small defrosting unit on the outside coils. Ground-source technology is more efficient because the ground is warmer than the air during the winter. The compressor works less, so it's likely to last longer; however the installation is considerably more expensive. A water-source pump can have coils on the bottom of a body of water, or it can get water from a well. Once the water has done its job, the pump sends it back to its source or into the sewer.

▶ ***Heat pumps are sophisticated and efficient.*** *They can require a higher initial investment, depending on their heat source, but are an efficient way of using natural resources to make your home comfortable.*

Maintaining a heat pump (continued)

Most heat pump manufacturers delight in telling you that a heat pump is not a household appliance, implying strongly that you ought to keep your hands off. They're probably right, but then a heating system that cost you several thousand dollars probably shouldn't break down at the first frost.

Where's the middle ground? There's no question that routine maintenance is up to you. At the very least it's your job to change or clean the filters once a month. In winter shovel snow or ice away from the outdoor unit. In summer wash it down with soap and water.

Beyond that, talk with your repair person. Find out what maintenance costs and check your warranty to see whether you can do the sorts of things described in this section without voiding the warranty. You'll be surprised at what you can do and how much money you can save.

Outdoor maintenance

1 Before you can do any maintenance you'll need to turn off the power at the circuit breaker or fuse panel and at the cutoff switch outside the home.

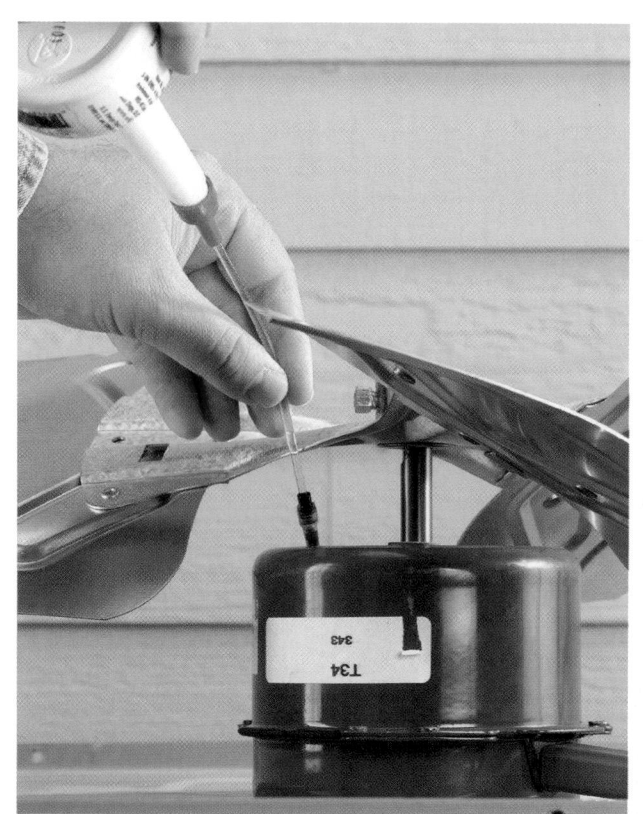

2 Take out the screws or bolts that hold the fan cover in place. Remove the screws or bolts holding the casing around the unit and take off the casing.

Oil the fan motor. Look for oil ports on the fan motor. If they exist squeeze in a couple drops of household oil.

3 Dirt in the coils can lower a heat pump's efficiency by as much as one-third. Most manufacturers recommend flushing out the dirt with a garden hose, spraying as best you can from the inside toward the outside. Scrub the fan, taking care not to bend the blades. Check to see whether any of the fins are bent. Straighten them with a fin comb.

Indoor maintenance

The indoor end of the heat pump looks much like any forced-air furnace but with no flame. Instead of fire the furnace has a series of coils that appear similar to those on the outside.

The purpose of the coils is different: The outdoor coils either absorb or give off heat, depending on whether the pump is heating or cooling; the indoor coils bring the air blown across them to the desired temperature. The coils and the filters that clean the air that goes across them need regular maintenance.

Maintenance is largely a matter of keeping things clean. Like the air filters on any other forced-air furnace, those on a heat pump must be cleaned regularly. Dirty filters drastically reduce the efficiency of a furnace. Having spent the money for an efficient furnace, it would be a shame to send all that heat up the stack.

Despite the filters dust and dirt are likely to build up on the inside coils. This will be less than what you find in the outside coils, so don't even think of hosing it down. Do the job with a vacuum cleaner. The best time is at the beginning and end of the heating season. During cooling season dust may stick to condensation on the coils.

Heat pumps can develop that classic smell you get when you first turn on the air-conditioner in a motel room. A germicidal cleaner for coils, applied according to manufacturer's recommendations, will help clear the air.

Underneath the coils you'll find a drain pan that collects water that drips from the air-conditioner coils. A clogged drain hole spells trouble, so as long as the unit is open, take a look and clean it out as necessary.

Once you're done with the furnace, walk around the house to make sure the vents are open and aren't blocked by rugs or furniture. Blocked vents mean that the compressor has to run longer to bring a room to the desired temperature. Excessive use costs money and shortens the life of the compressor and valves.

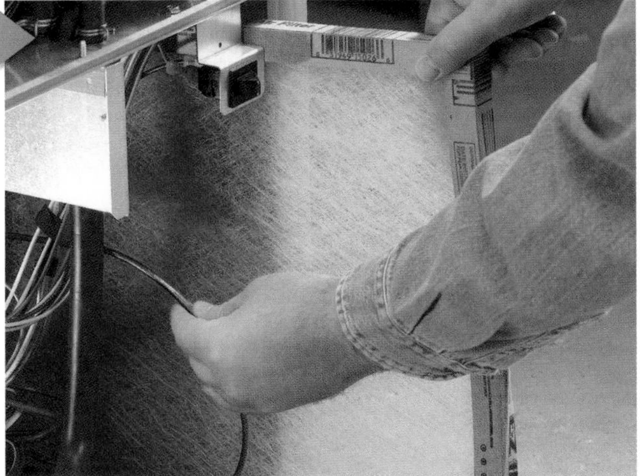

1 Double-check that the power is still off, remove the access panel, and look for the filter or filters. You'll find them near the coils. Pull out the springlike retaining arm and remove the filter. Vacuum and wash reusable filters with the hose; replace disposable filters.

2 Dirt on the coils not only reduces efficiency but can also be the source of dirt, spores, and odors that are blown through the house. Turn off the power, put a soft brush onto a shop vacuum, and thoroughly vacuum and brush the coils. Wash the coils with a germicidal cleaner designed for indoor coils. Vacuum the blower wheel on the fan.

3 Standing water in the drain pan is a sign that the drain hole is plugged. Mop up the water and unplug the drain hole. Rinse with a mixture of one part household bleach to four parts water. Put the filters back in and put the access panel in place. Clean the base pan at the bottom of the unit and make sure none of the drain holes are plugged. Replace the cover.

Get professional help

Heat pumps are extremely sophisticated furnaces. Simple maintenance is a matter of having the time. But the best way to guarantee the system won't crash when you need it most is to check and maintain the refrigerant system. This requires a pro.

A pro will check everything, one of the most important being the refrigerant level. The technician will visually check for leaks, monitor temperature in different parts of the system, and perhaps take a couple of readings with a gauge. If the test shows that the coolant level is low, recharging the system is in order, a task that only a licensed technician can do. Have a local HVAC company make a yearly inspection for refrigerant and other problems. You'll save yourself a cold and sleepless night.

Maintaining a heat pump (continued)

Diagnosing ice buildup on outside coils

Some ice buildup on the outside coils is normal—so normal that the system actually has a defrost cycle. The problem usually occurs when the outdoor temperature drops below the boiling point of the coolant—around 15°F (-9.4°C). The temperature drop causes the coolant to liquefy and act as a refrigerant on the outdoor coils. To prevent this a defrost cycle kicks in at about 28°F (-2°C). The heat pump temporarily runs backward, melting the ice. The auxiliary heat source in the house kicks on, and both you and the outdoor coils are warm.

Sometimes however things go wrong. This may be something like a faulty valve, which requires a trained technician who can work with refrigerants. But just as often it's a problem you can solve yourself.

1 If icing occurs first check the thermostat. Make sure it's set to heating, not cooling, and that the room temperature is above 55°F (13°C). If not reset the controls as needed and the problem will likely go away. Then go outside and make sure the outdoor coil isn't blocked by snow or leaves.

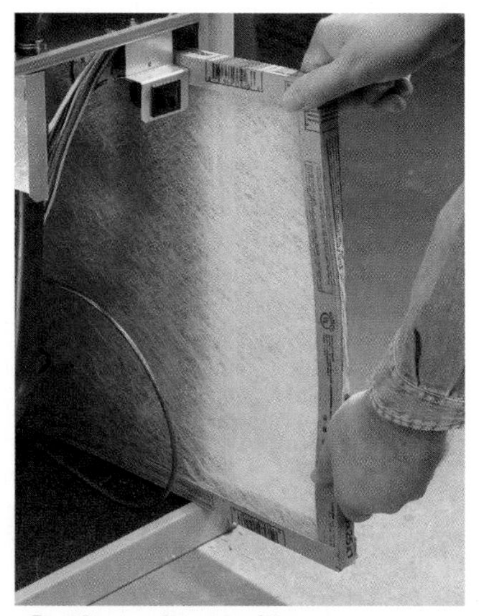

2 Clean the air filter. A dirty or clogged filter will keep the fan from blowing enough air over the indoor coils to warm them adequately. When the refrigerant makes the trip back outside, it can't give off enough heat to defrost the coils. No matter how clean you think the filter is, take it out and vacuum and wash it (or replace a disposable filter). Put parts back in place and if nothing else, you've eliminated the filter as a problem.

3 The reversing valve, found in the outside unit, is responsible for running the system in defrost mode and must be replaced professionally. You can however diagnose and fix the solenoid and the needle valve that controls it. To check the solenoid turn off the power, remove the cover, and look for a valve that has six tubes going into it. The solenoid coil is attached. Remove the wires going into it and put the ohmmeter leads where the wires were. If the reading isn't between zero and infinity, you'll need to replace the coil.

4 To replace the coil remove the nut holding it in place and slide it off its stem. Slide an identical replacement coil over the stem and tighten the nut over it. Reattach the wires.

Installing an electric baseboard heater

Skill level:	Time to complete:	Materials:	Tools:
★★★☆☆	Experienced 6 hrs. Handy 8 hrs. Novice 12 hrs.	240-volt electric heater, 10/2 cable, wire caps, electrical tape, thermostat and junction box, cable clamps, breaker or breakers	Drill and bits, drywall saw, utility knife, fish tape, screwdriver, wire stripper, needle-nose pliers, stud finder

An electric baseboard heater can distribute heat into a cold part of the house. But head for the breaker box first because a new heater requires a new circuit, and you want to make sure you have room for it. You will need at least one empty spot on the panel. Two are better. If there's no room for an extra circuit, find another way to heat the cold spot. Code requires an electric heater to have its own circuit. Even if you don't need to do that, combining it with an existing circuit would overload the breakers every time the heat came on.

Two open slots will let you put in a 240-volt heater, which, because it draws less current, wastes less electricity. Always go with a 240-volt heater if possible. If you only have space for a 120-volt circuit, make sure you buy a 120-volt heater. Putting a 240-volt heater on a 120-volt circuit is dangerous and won't give you enough heat anyway.

You can hang electric heaters against drywall, wallpaper, wood paneling, particleboard, chipboard, and tongue-and-groove panel. Putting a baseboard heater against soundproofing board, pegboard, or ceiling tile is a fire hazard.

The directions here are for a 240-volt heater, which is both the most efficient and the most common. Wiring for a 120-volt heater is slightly different. Follow the directions that come with the heater.

1 Choose a spot under a window for the heater— that's where the air in the room is the coolest. If you're using a heater with a built-in thermometer, run 10/2 cable from the heater to the breaker panel. The wires need to run through the wall—you can't leave them exposed, and you can't tuck them between the heater and the baseboard. Remove materials and drill holes for the cable through studs along the path. Fish the cable (see page 389), leaving about 2 feet extra at the heater. Run the cable to the panel, leaving the cable long enough to drape to the floor once it reaches the panel. Wait to connect it.

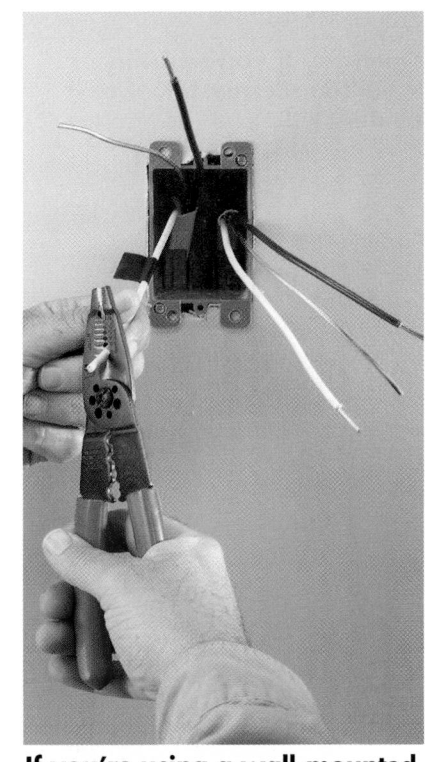

If you're using a wall-mounted thermostat, the cable from the breaker panel won't run directly to the heater. Instead run the cable to where the thermostat will be and run a second length of cable from there to the heater. Feed both through a junction box and install it, marking the wires so that you know which is which.

2 It's easiest to wire the heater before you mount it to the wall. Remove the knockout in the back of the heater by giving it a sharp blow with the blade of a screwdriver. Put in a connector—a type of clamp required by code to prevent the edge of the box from accidentally shorting out the cable. Strip about a hand's length of the outer insulation off the cable. Fish it through the connector and tighten the clamp around the end of the outer insulation.

Installing an electric baseboard heater (continued)

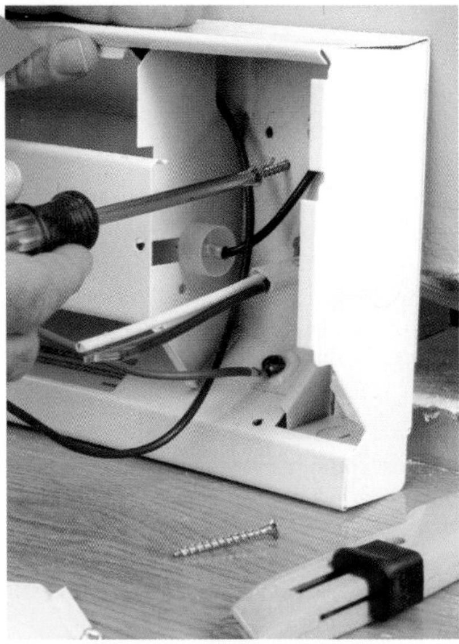

3 Find and mark the studs behind the heater. Line up the holes in the back of the heater with the studs. Push any extra cable inside the wall, then screw the heater in place as directed by the manufacturer. (Accessing the screw holes sometimes involves removing a part or two.) What you do next depends on what type of thermostat is being used. (See Options A and B at right.)

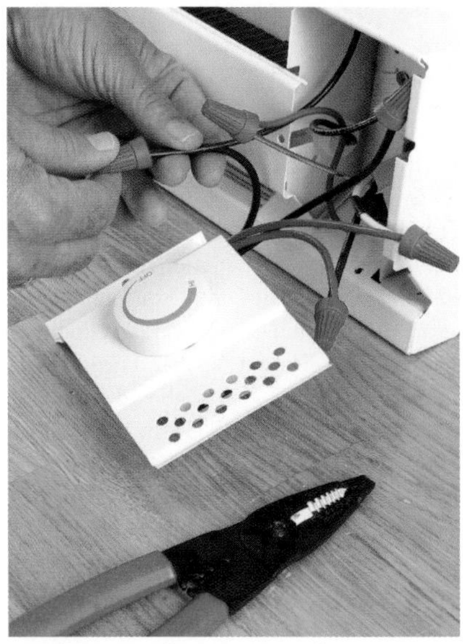

Option A: If you're using a built-in thermostat, wire it as directed. Usually the incoming black and white supply wires connect to two red wires on the thermostat. The two black wires on the thermostat connect to the two black heater wires that were twisted together.

On a 240-volt circuit like the one shown here, the white wire is hot, and code requires you to mark it with a piece of black tape as a reminder.

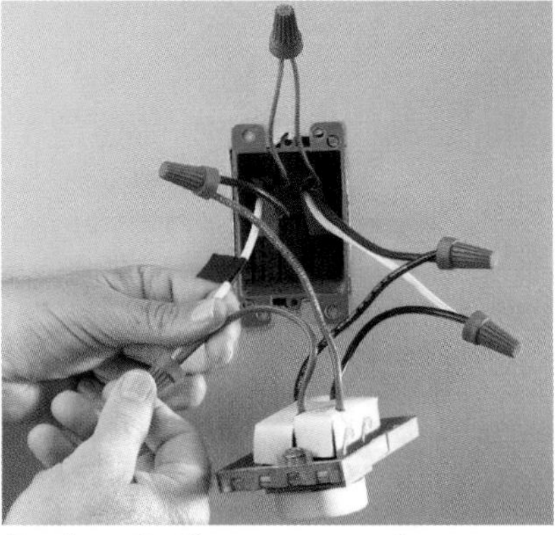

Option B: If you are using a wall-mounted thermostat, it must be a 240-volt, double-pole thermostat. A regular thermostat, designed to run at 24 volts, will burn up if connected to 240 volts. Necessary to meet code a double-pole switch shuts off power to both 120-volt lines that make up the 240 volts going to the heater. Wire the thermostat as directed. The black and white wires coming from the panel are usually connected to the two red thermostat wires. The black wires coming out of the thermostat are connected to the white and black wires that run to the heater. Connect the bare ground wires to each other and to the thermostat ground wire if there is one.

4 At the heater the incoming black and white wires are connected to the black heater wires. The bare wire coming into the heater is connected to a green ground screw in the heater. Mark the white wire with black tape to show anyone working on it in the future that the wire is hot.

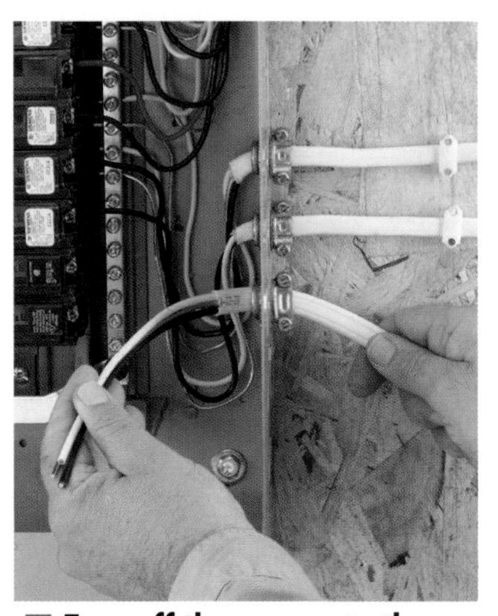

5 Turn off the power to the entire house. Punch out a new knockout in the side of the breaker box. Install a connector for the cable. Feed the cable through the connector to the slots for the new breakers. Mark the cable at the connector. Remove and strip the outer insulation back to the mark, put it back through the connector, and tighten it. Wrap a piece of black tape around the insulation of the white wire to show that it's hot.

6 A 240-volt circuit requires two breakers. To install put the tab on one end of the breakers under the notch for it. Bring the other end down onto the other tab and press until it snaps into place. Screw the black wire into one of the breakers; screw the white wire into the other and mark it with a piece of black tape. Screw the bare ground wire to the ground bus bar (see page 397, Step 7).

Adding a hot-water baseboard heater

Skill level:	Time to complete:	Materials:	Tools:
★★★★★	Experienced 5 hrs. Handy 8 hrs. Novice 12 hrs.	Hot-water baseboard heater, Type M pipe, reducer elbows or tees, other fittings as needed, pipe supports, plumbing solder, flux	Drill and bit, pipe cutter, tape measure, propane torch

Getting hot-water baseboard heat into an addition or a cold room is an issue of real estate as much as it is a plumbing issue. As always the three things you need to worry about are location, location, and location. First plan to put the new baseboard heater where you'll find the coldest air—on an outside wall, preferably under a window. Second decide where the couch is going to go before you pick your spot. Hiding the baseboard heater with furniture blocks off much of the heat. Third look at the floor framing underneath the intended location and adjust the position as necessary to avoid hitting the joists. If the finished floor has yet to be installed, make sure there will be a minimum of 1 inch between the bottom of the heater and the finished floor so air can flow through the heater.

As for plumbing baseboard pipe is either ½- or ¾-inch-diameter copper. Check what you have in the house and buy a baseboard heater to match. (Many are convertible and will fit either size pipe, but don't count on it without checking.) Instead of using regular plumbing pipe (Type L), use Type M copper pipe, the standard in heating. It's a low-pressure pipe with a thinner wall and costs less than Type L. When you buy the baseboard heater, get one that says it's complete, meaning that the pipe and heating fins are inside the case. You'll have to purchase the cutoff valve, bleeder, and end panels separately; get panels with doors so you can access the bleeder and cutoff valves when necessary.

Leaks are a problem and a real possibility. Even the pros test for them, though they usually test with pressurized air before turning on the water. You probably don't have a pressure tester on hand so you'll have to test with the furnace on and water running through the pipes. Know in advance where all the cutoff valves are.

Pipe layout depends on the size of the baseboard heater, so buy the heater before you start. Take the measurements of the room with you and talk to a salesperson about getting the proper size baseboard heater. Finally when you have the system installed, open the inlet valves and the outlet valve and bleed the system.

1 Avoid floor joists when choosing the location for the new heater. Slip a cutoff valve onto the infeed side of the baseboard. Slip a bleeder valve onto the other end and position the baseboard against the wall. Screw the heater in place, mark the floor underneath the center of each fitting, and remove the heater. Drill holes through the marks that are at least ⅜ inch larger in diameter than the pipe you'll be using to ensure easy assembly.

2 Reassemble the heater and test-fit all the pipes before soldering. Attach the elbow to the riser. (Make it a few inches longer than you will need.) Drop the riser down the hole. Attach the elbow to the valve. Friction-fit the pipes in the fittings while you are installing the run below. Now turn the furnace off and open the valve to drain the boiler. What you do next depends on how the existing plumbing is run. (See Options A and B, page 474.)

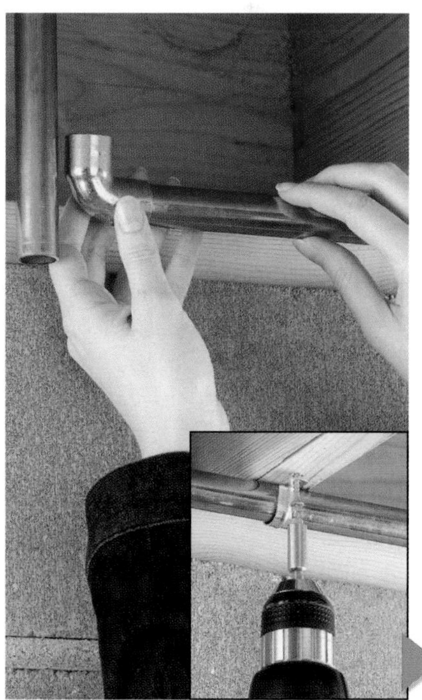

3 Run pipe from the fitting to the riser. If the pipe will run through joists, drill holes ⅜ inch larger than the pipe diameter. If the pipes run parallel to the joists, support them with pipe hangers spaced every 4 feet (see inset). Make sure the pipe is level, adjusting the supports as necessary.

Adding a hot-water baseboard heater (continued)

4 Mark each riser to length. You can measure the length of the riser, but it's as effective to do it by eye. Slip an elbow onto the run to the riser to help determine where you will make the cut.

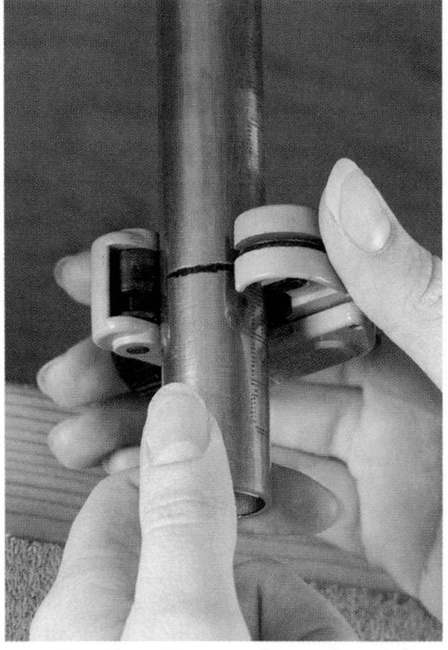

5 Cut the riser to length with a pipe cutter. Connect the riser to the run with the elbow and you're ready to solder the entire system together.

6 Double-check that all the pipes are the correct lengths. You don't want to solder a joint that's under pressure because the pipe's too long. Clean and solder the joints one by one. Once you've soldered the pipe and elbow going into the baseboard heater, install the end caps on the baseboard.

Option A: If the water flows in a large loop through all the baseboard heaters, you'll see risers going up through the floor at each end of the baseboard heater with no main supply pipe in between. In this kind of system cut through the main supply pipe opposite the new supply riser. Put on a reducer elbow that steps down from the size of the main to the size of the riser. Cut through the line opposite the return riser and add a reducer elbow.

Option B: If there are two parallel pipes with a pipe running from each into each of the baseboards, one pipe is supplying water and the other is returning it to the furnace. (The return line goes into the boiler at a lower point than the supply line.) Cut the supply line opposite what will be the new supply riser; cut the return pipe opposite the new return riser. On one end of the cut install a reducer tee that steps down from the pipe diameter to the riser diameter. Then cut each pipe again so it will fit into the other end of the tee.

Adding a forced-air heat run

Skill level:	Time to complete:	Materials:	Tools:
★★★☆☆	Experienced 1 hr. Handy 2 hrs. Novice 2.5 hrs.	Starting collar or side takeoff, register boot, roofing nails, round duct, damper fitting, flex duct, duct supports, plumber's tape, duct mastic, sheet metal screws, compression straps	Tin snips, jigsaw, hammer, flex duct tool, electric screw gun or drill, brush

When it comes to adding a run of ducting and register to a cold room, there's very little a pro can do that you can't. The first thing you need to know is that you should use rigid duct as much as possible. You'll find several different diameters of rigid duct; measure the room you're heating and install the recommended size. Flex duct—flexible plastic duct lined with a metal coil—may be easy to install and works well in certain situations, but sags and turns can severely restrict airflow and sometimes deliver no heat at all.

Elbows also restrict airflow but are absolutely necessary. An adjustable, round metal elbow is built like a piece of lightweight armor and adjusts from straight to 90 degrees. Rotate the ends to get the desired angle.

Ductwork is held together with sheet metal screws and sealed to prevent loss of air through joints and seams. Sealing the joints and seams properly can result in significant savings on heating and air-conditioning bills. Even though it's called duct tape, this is not an efficient or long-lasting solution and should not be used as a sealing agent.

Duct mastic, which is a water-base, flexible sealant that can be applied by brush or with gloved hand, is the sealant of choice of the U.S. Department of Energy for efficiency and durability.

Foil-backed tape with a rubber-base adhesive is also acceptable but somewhat less durable and versatile in application.

Support rigid ductwork with metal plumber's tape that nails to the framing. If you need to use short lengths of flex duct, support it with supports sold for that purpose.

1 Begin as close to the plenum as you can. Ideally you would install the vent on the top of the plenum next to the furnace, but that isn't always possible and you may need to come off an existing duct. Install a starting collar on the duct and trace a cutout line around it.

Cutting your losses

Maintain your duct system: Improperly sealed seams and joints in ductwork cause a significant loss of heat that will be reflected in your energy bills. Sealing seams and joints with duct mastic is an inexpensive way to save on heating and air-conditioning bills.

- Regular duct tape at seams and joints deteriorates quickly and should be replaced with duct mastic.
- Check for cracks in the seals where ductwork passes from conditioned areas to unconditioned ones such as attics and basements.
- Repair holes with duct mastic and fiber mesh tape.
- Apply duct mastic to the seams in swivel joints.

2 Cut a hole along the layout lines. If the duct is sheet metal, make the cut with tin snips. If it's a flat, rigid fiberglass panel with a metal facing, cut it with a jigsaw. Apply duct mastic and place the fitting in the hole. Bend back the fingers to hold the fitting in place and insert sheet metal screws through the lips of the collar.

Adding a forced-air heat run (continued)

3 Install the register boot next, tracing around it on the floor to lay out the hole you'll cut. Start the cutout by drilling a ½-inch or ¾-inch hole. Insert the blade of your jigsaw into the hole and then cut along the lines to create the opening (see inset). Put the boot inside the opening and nail it in place with a couple of roofing nails. Screw a register over the boot and into the floor.

4 Cut, test fit, and temporarily assemble the run of duct to connect the starter collar to the register boot. Use as much rigid duct and as few elbows and as little flex duct as possible. Cut rigid duct with tin snips. Cut flex duct with a flex duct tool. Support duct with plumber's tape nailed to the rafters every 4 feet and within 6 inches of any connection. Make sure flex duct doesn't sag more than ½ inch per foot.

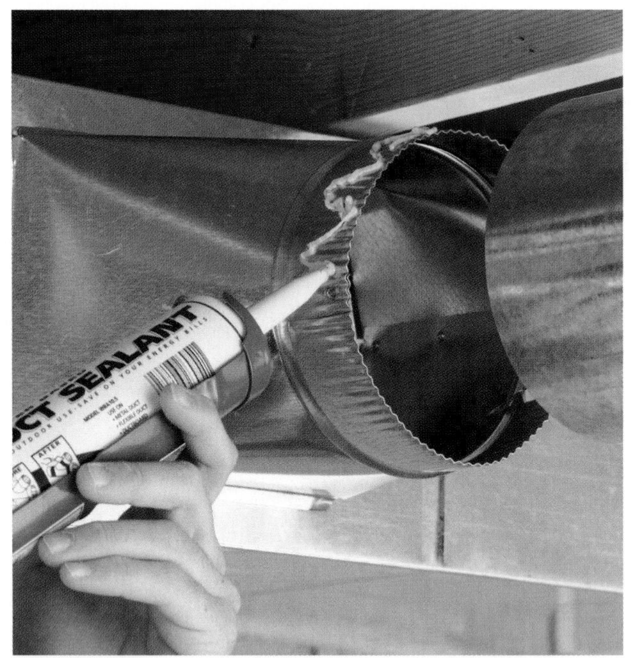

5 Seal the joints between sections with duct sealant. Begin on the metal ductwork by sliding the joint partially apart and covering the exposed surface with duct sealant. Reseat the joint and screw it together with two sheet metal screws.

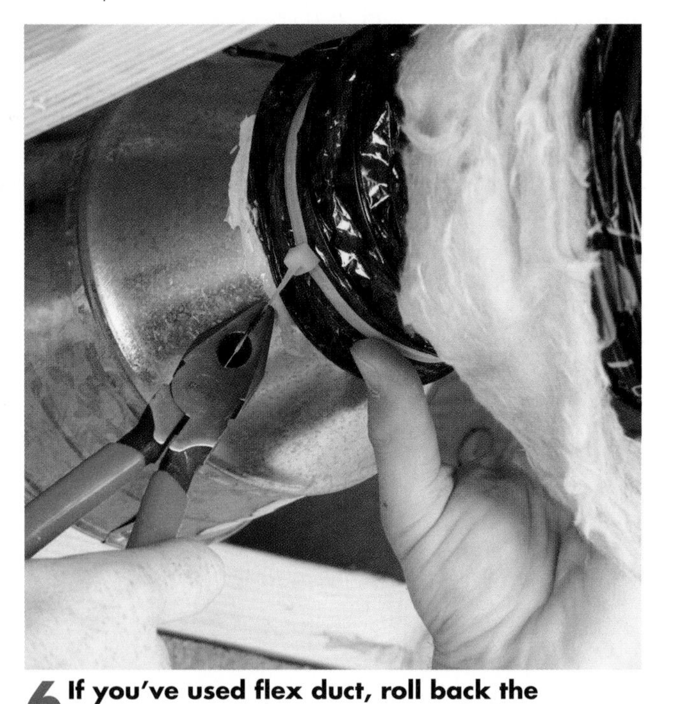

6 If you've used flex duct, roll back the insulation and the outer liner of plastic. Use mastic to coat the metal that the flex duct fits over. Slide the inner plastic over the sealant and attach it with a compression strap. Put the insulation and outer layer over the takeoff and attach it with a second compression strap. Stretch the duct to full length so it's as smooth as possible. Attach the other end using mastic and compression straps.

Installing auxiliary gas heaters

Skill level:	Time to complete:	Materials:	Tools:
★★★★★	Experienced 4 hrs. Handy 8 hrs. Novice 12 hrs.	Heater and masking tape, iron gas line and Type-B vent to be supplied by heating technician	Tape measure, level, stud finder, noncontact voltage tester, drill with bits and screwdriver, saber saw

Through-the-wall gas heaters reach places your main system can't. The three basic types are vent-free, vented, and direct-vent. Check local codes for the kinds of auxiliary gas heaters approved for use in your area.

A vent-free heater is the simplest to install and the most efficient. It actually hangs on the wall. Because its high-efficiency burner produces almost no fumes and doesn't require a chimney or vent, it's a perfect choice for an area that's used occasionally. The U.S. Department of Energy warns against operating a vent-free heater for more than two hours a day. It also recommends leaving the window open about 1⁄2 inch to provide a constant source of fresh air.

A vented heater has an exhaust vent that directs the fumes outside. As long as you use the appropriate vent pipe, the vent can go through the wall or roof, but it must go nearly to the roof peak. Like a vent-free heater it needs a constant source of fresh air. Most frame construction allows plenty of outside air to get into the house, but you may need to install registers to get fresh air into the room. The unit must also stand at least 6 inches from the wall because air flows to the flame from the back.

The vent on a direct-vent heater is a pipe within a pipe. The core pipe acts like a chimney; the outer section pulls fresh air in from outside. Because the fumes go outdoors, and because a direct-vent heater has an external air supply, it is a smart choice for a part of the house that gets more than a few hours' use a day.

All three types have optional fans that help to better distribute the heat.

Whichever heater you install you must leave installation of the gas pipe and vent to a trained professional. You can do much of the other work yourself however.

Vented through-the-wall gas heater

SAFETY ALERT
DANGEROUS FUMES

Never install any of these heaters in a bedroom, bathroom, or mobile home.

Remote controls

Many modern vent-free designs come with handheld or wall-mounted remote controls for lighting the unit and selecting the temperature. Most manufacturers offer thermostatically controlled models that automatically maintain the selected comfort level. Some units are equipped with a timer that automatically starts the appliance early in the morning, shuts it off when the house is unoccupied, and turns it on again later in the day.

Installing a vent-free gas heater

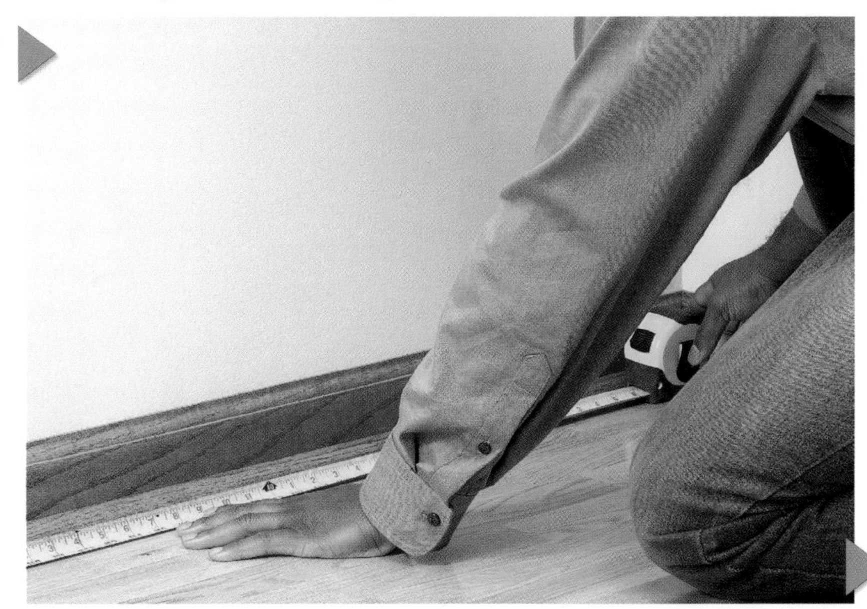

1 Measure the room to determine the proper size for the heater. A small room may not contain enough air for a large heater, so begin by figuring out the volume of the room. Multiply its length by its width by its height (all measured in feet). Multiply by 20 to see how large a heater (measured in British thermal units, or Btus) it can support. A 7'×10' room with an 8-foot ceiling would need an 11,200-Btu heater (7×10×8×20 = 11,200 Btus). The Btu rating of a heater is listed on its box. A heater producing 10,000 Btus/hour will probably work well in this space, but one producing 20,000 Btus/hour would require additional venting—usually just a register that passes through to another room. Follow the directions in the owner's manual.

Installing auxiliary gas heaters (continued)

2 Choose a spot on the wall for the heater. It's best to put the heater in the coldest spot, usually under a window. Heaters also require certain clearances between the objects in the room and the heater's top, bottom, and sides. Check the owner's manual and choose the spot with clearances in mind. If the unit has a fan, make sure you put the heater near an outlet. This type of heater usually hangs from a wall bracket that comes with it. Draw a level line on the wall indicating its position. The owner's manual will tell you how far from the floor it should be.

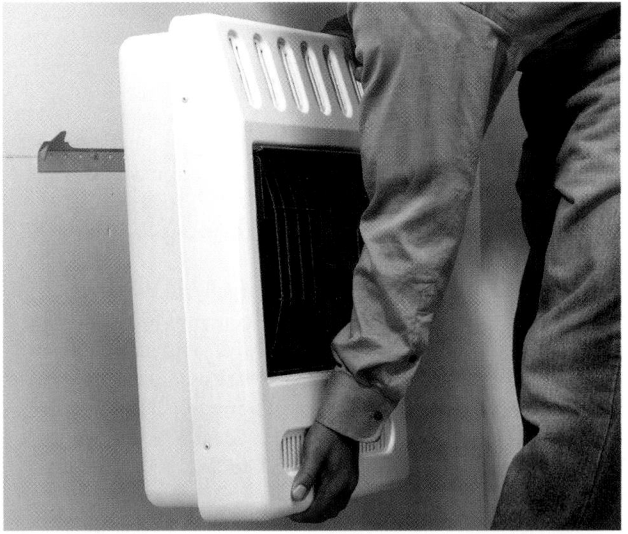

3 Find the studs in the wall with a stud finder. Line up the mounting bracket with the level line, moving it if possible so it will be screwed into a stud. Temporarily tape it in place. Trace around the screw holes to mark their locations on the wall. If the screws will miss the studs, drill for anchors—they're usually included with the heater—and put them into the wall. Screw the bracket in place. If there is a thermostat bulb, position it as directed in the owner's manual and hang the heater on the wall. Drive additional screws as directed. Have your gas company or a plumber connect the gas line.

Installing a vented heater

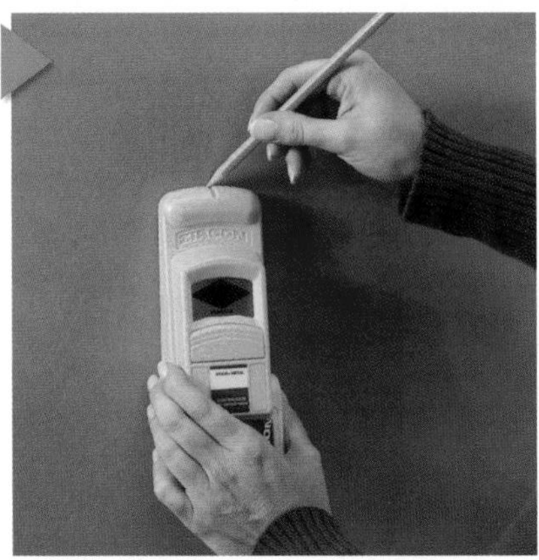

1 Choose a spot along an outside wall for the heater. Allow for manufacturer's clearances and the vent that will run through the wall. Find the studs near where the heater will be located. Position the heater in relation to the studs as directed. You'll want the heater to be near an outlet if it has a fan. If there is an outlet or switch in the wall cavity through which the vent will pass, choose a new spot to avoid cutting through any wires. With a noncontact voltage tester, double-check that there are no wires near where you'll be cutting.

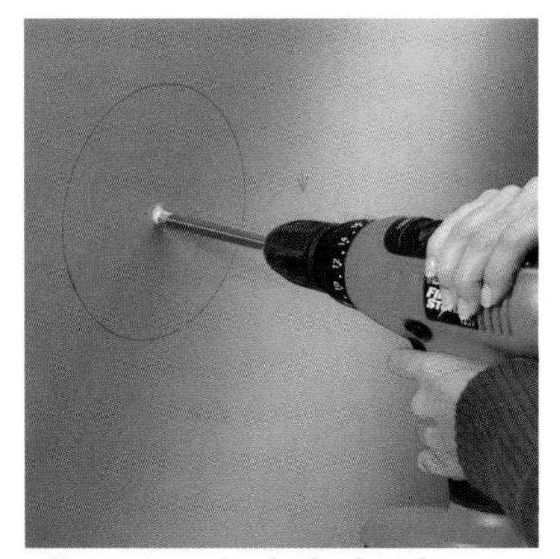

2 Lay out the hole for the vent with either the template or the dimensions supplied by the manufacturer. To make sure the hole you cut through the outside of the house aligns with the hole on the inside, drill a ⅜-inch-diameter locator hole through the center of what will be the vent hole and out through the siding of the house. Lay out the outside hole by centering the template over the locator hole.

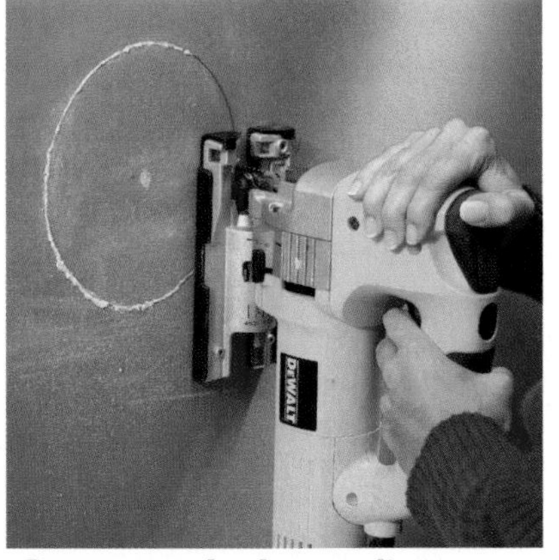

3 Cut out the layout line. Follow the line as closely as possible. The wall plates are large enough to cover almost any mistake. Once you've cut the inside opening, cut the outside opening. Have a qualified heating technician install the vent and gas line using Type-B double-walled vent pipe and allowing the proper clearance. The pipe must extend at least 3 feet beyond the roof and 2 feet above anything within 10 feet, including higher sections of the roof. The top of the pipe must have a cap to prevent back drafts.

Installing a direct-vent heater

The heart of a direct-vent heater is a sealed combustion box. Air for the fire comes in from an outside vent; any fumes go directly back out. In a properly operating system room air never mixes with the fire. This not only eliminates fumes but also eliminates a problem common to other heaters: room air that has already been heated at least partially. If room air feeds the fire, some of it will go up the chimney, taking heat with it.

The vent that takes air to and from the combustion chamber is a pipe within a pipe. Although you can place the heater yourself, have a pro install the vent to make sure no fumes work their way into the house.

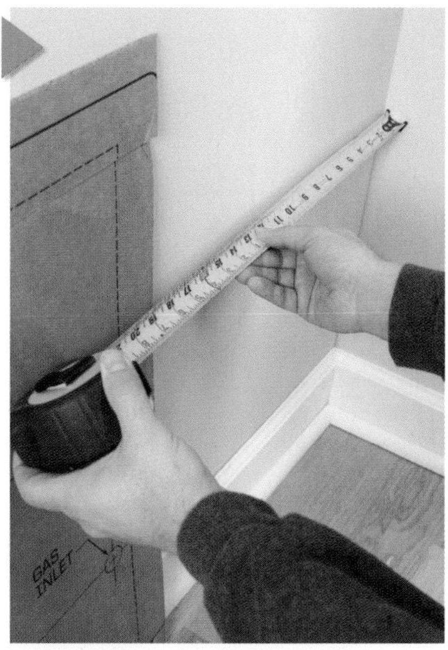

1 Position the heater as directed in the owner's manual. As with vented heaters choose the location based on wiring that may be in the way, a nearby power source for the fan (if necessary), and location of the studs.

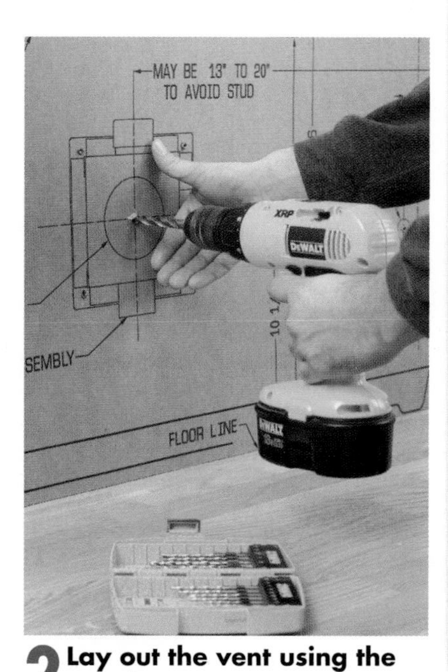

2 Lay out the vent using the template or measurements in your owner's manual. Make sure the inside and outside holes align by drilling a locator hole first. Center the template on the locator hole to lay out the inside and outside holes.

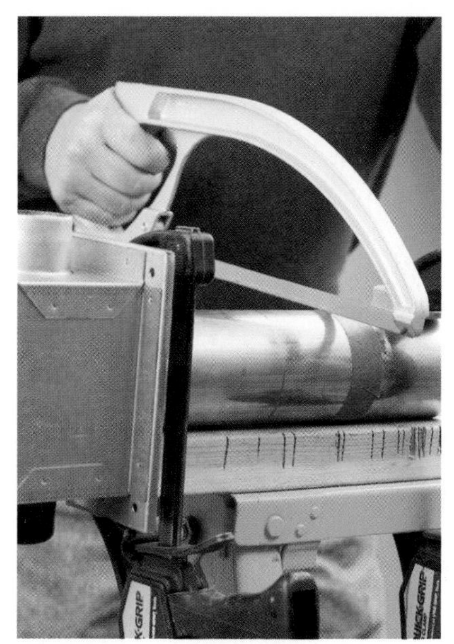

3 Unlike vented heaters direct-vent heaters can go through the wall without having to run up to the roof. Some manufacturers make a telescoping vent that adjusts to the thickness of the wall. Other types of vent must be cut to length, with the inner pipe being cut slightly longer than the outer pipe. Although you can cut the vent pipe, have your heating technician install it and the cap that goes over it.

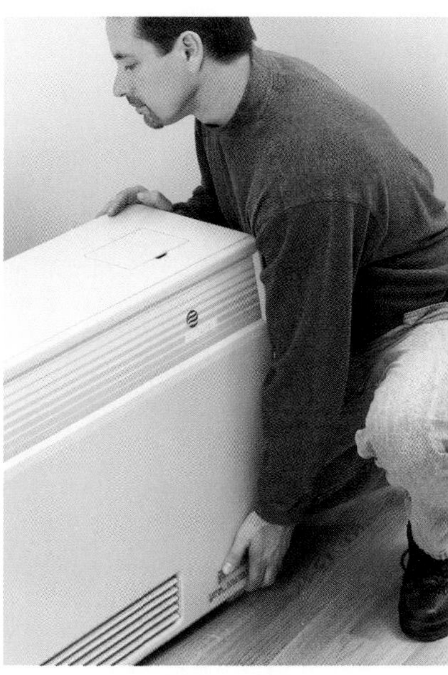

4 Direct-vent heaters vary depending on the manufacturer: Some screw directly to the wall, some have mounting brackets, and others sit on the floor. Install the heater as directed.

5 Have a heating technician install the vent and the gas line, using black iron or steel gas line, Type-B vent, and the appropriate cap to prevent back drafts.

Window air-conditioner maintenance

Skill level:	Time to complete:	Materials:	Tools:
★☆☆☆☆	Experienced 30 min. Handy 45 min. Novice 1 hr.	Soap, water, oil, bleach, cotton swabs	Screwdriver, wrench, soft brush or vacuum, fin comb

Air-conditioners are basically plug and play: You buy them, put them into the window, plug them in, and turn them on. There's not much more to it than that.

But neatness counts, and when it comes to air-conditioners, cleanliness is next to efficiency. Dirty coils or filters can increase the cost of cooling a room. In some cases the dirt can keep you from getting the room as cool as you want it. In the worst case dirt causes ice to form on the coils, reducing efficiency to the point where you'll be paying good money to keep the room just as hot as it was.

As you might suspect cleaning involves little more than soap and water. Begin by removing the air-conditioner from the window. Check the owner's manual to see how much disassembly you'll have to do to get to the filter, the front coils, and the rear coils. If you don't have the manual, remove the front of the unit to get started and unscrew or unsnap other parts as necessary.

Once you have access to the guts, vacuum, brush, or wash as directed below. If the motor requires it, squirt in a little oil.

Proper maintenance, even if it's just cleaning, can prolong the life of your air-conditioner. No matter what you do, however, it eventually may break down. The problem can be as simple as a faulty thermostat or as complicated as a broken compressor. Diagnosis can be difficult, and many repairs require someone licensed to recycle ozone-damaging refrigerant. If a problem crops up that maintenance won't solve, check the Yellow Pages for a reputable repair person.

1 Clean the air filter. This is a removable sponge sheet about ⅛ inch thick. On some air-conditioners you can remove a panel to get to it. On others you'll have to remove the entire front of the air-conditioner. Remove the filter; wash it in soap and water. Let it dry and then reinstall it.

2 Clean the exterior fins once a year. The fins are on the back side of the air-conditioner and may be covered by a protective grill. Dirt can plug the openings enough to seriously affect the ability of the fins to dissipate the heat the air-conditioner expels from inside the house. Remove the protective grill and either brush the fins gently with a soft brush—a clean paintbrush works well—or vacuum to remove the dirt.

3 Straighten the fins. If the fins are bent they restrict airflow and fail to dissipate heat properly. Straighten them with a fin comb, available at home centers or from heating and air-conditioning suppliers. Insert the comb between an undamaged section of fins and comb gently through damaged fins to straighten them.

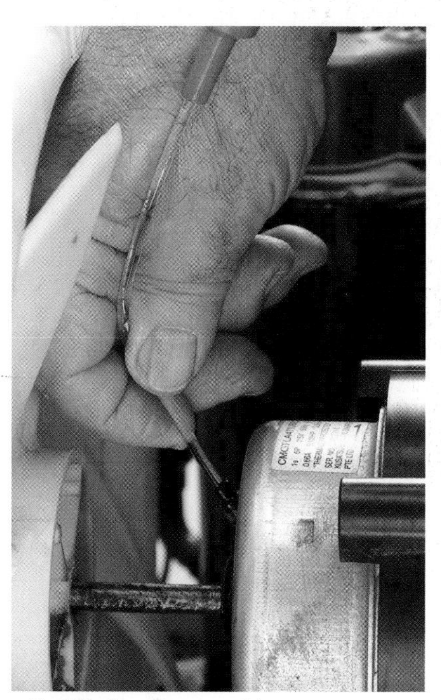

4 Oil the motor. Many air-conditioner fan motors contain oil ports. If yours does oil the motor twice a year: once before the season starts and once when it ends. Some motors are sealed at the factory and need no oil.

5 Vacuum the parts and clean the tray. A shallow tray at the bottom of the unit collects water that condenses on the coils. Remove the tray and wash it thoroughly in a solution of half water and half bleach.

6 Clean the drain hole. The water in the tray drains through a hole in the tray and out a hose somewhere in the back of the unit. Use a cotton swab or a piece of dowel to clean both the hole and the stem.

BUYER'S GUIDE

BE COOL

When you buy an air-conditioner, get the right size. A bigger air-conditioner isn't necessarily better: It costs more to buy, costs more to run, and cools the room unevenly.

The output of an air-conditioner is measured in British thermal units, or Btus. Your air-conditioner needs to produce about 20 to 30 Btus per square foot of a room. The Department of Energy says you'd need a 5,000-Btu air-conditioner for a room with 150 square feet of living space. If the room were a sunny kitchen you might need 9,500 Btus.

Once you've settled on the size of an air-conditioner, look at its efficiency. Look for an EER—energy efficiency ratio, which is the ratio between cooling power and energy draw—of 10 or higher. New air-conditioners are up to 70 percent more efficient than previously manufactured ones. Start by looking for the Energy Star label, an indication that the unit is eco-friendly. Then check the yellow Energy Guide label for the EER (see page 504 for more information).

Powering up

If you replace or add a window air-conditioner, make sure the electrical circuit has the proper amperage and voltage to handle the unit. Bigger units often require 220-volt service, a separate circuit, and a special receptacle.

Installing a window air-conditioner

Skill level:	Time to complete:	Materials:	Tools:
★☆☆☆☆	Experienced 20 min. Handy 30 min. Novice 45 min.	Window air-conditioner, mounting brackets, angle brackets, foam weatherstripping	Screwdriver or power drill with drill and screwdriver bits, torpedo level

Not long ago installing an air-conditioner was a hard, sweaty, two-person job. Newer units are easier to install.

Whether you're installing a brand-new unit, a hand-me-down, or old faithful, start with the window. Most air-conditioners are designed for double-hung windows. If you have another kind of window you have two choices, neither of which is desirable: Replace the window or install a through-the-wall air-conditioner. (Replacing windows is covered in Section 8 on page 377. Follow the directions that come with a through-the-wall unit. Pages 340–342 provide more information about creating a rough opening.)

Before installing the air-conditioner, make sure the window is sound. Repair any rot and damage. If the paint is peeling, repaint. Ideally the window you choose should be near the center of the room and shaded from the afternoon sun. If you must choose between one or the other, choose shade.

Install the air-conditioner in a window near an outlet or install a new outlet. You want it close to the power source because power drops and the temperature rises as electricity runs through an extension cord. Given the power that an air-conditioner draws, using an extension cord can result in a dangerously hot cord driving a sadly underpowered unit.

Older units have a mounting frame supported perhaps by a mounting bracket that holds the air-conditioner in the window. Newer air-conditioners are lighter and more efficient. The mounting frame is built-in and, except on heavier units, the mounting bracket has disappeared altogether.

Make sure to measure the dimensions of your window before purchasing a unit. Although modern units are designed with fins to accommodate windows of different widths, large models might fit too tightly to open the fins and provide the proper support.

1 Install the mounting brackets, if any. A heavy or older air-conditioner may have a bracket that screws to the windowsill. Screw it in place using sheet metal screws on a metal frame and wood screws on a wood or vinyl frame. Place a level across the bracket and sill and adjust the bracket as needed to level it.

Choosing a unit

Choosing a window air-conditioner for your home might require a few calculations and decisions about the features you want. Before you buy multiply the length by the width of the room you want to cool. Compare that square footage with prospective units. You'll need a 5,000-Btu unit for spaces 100–150 square feet and 1,000 Btus more for each additional 100 square feet. You'll have choices between units that come with timers, remote controls, and digital temperature readouts. Filters are another issue—look for models with filters you can easily clean. And make sure you get louvers so you can direct the airflow where you most want it.

SAFETY ALERT

SECOND STORY

Air-conditioners can be heavy, and their shape makes them awkward to handle. Be especially careful when installing them on upper stories. Have a watcher on the ground below and a helper to hold the unit in the window.

2 Insert the air-conditioner into the frame or window. If there is a frame, move the accordion panels aside and slide the air-conditioner in. If the frame is built-in, open the window a bit wider than necessary to make it easier to put the air-conditioner in place. Close the window to hold it in place.

3 Slide the accordion panels back in place so that they are tight against the air-conditioner. Secure the mounting frame and panels as directed by the manufacturer. If you're driving screws into a new location, drill pilot holes first, using a bit slightly smaller than the diameter of the screw.

4 If the installation kit that came with your unit contains angle brackets, screw them to the upper sash as directed. The brackets keep the weight of the air-conditioner from forcing the window open. If there aren't any brackets, buy and install ones that are similar to that shown here.

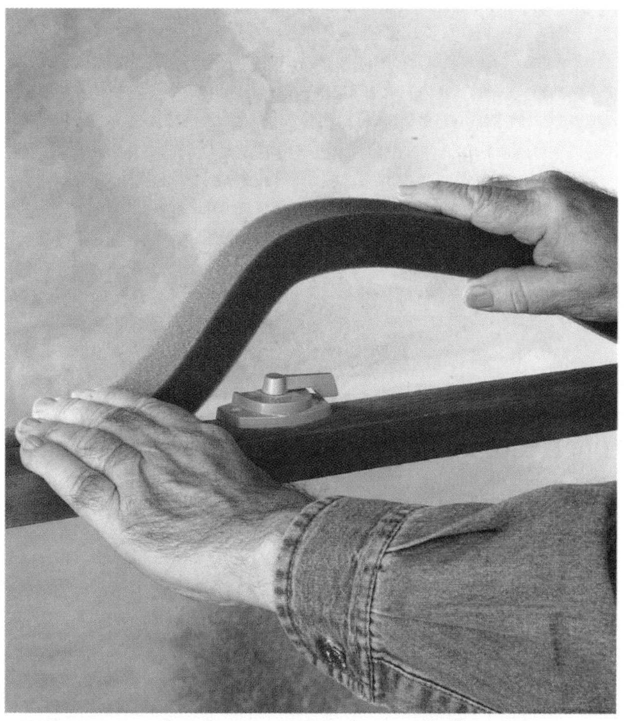

5 Because the lower sash is partially open, there is a large gap between it and the window. Fill the gap with the foam weatherstripping that came with the unit or buy some at a home improvement center.

Maintaining a central air system

Skill level:	Time to complete:	Materials:	Tools:
★★☆☆☆	Experienced 1 hr. Handy 1.5 hrs. Novice 2 hrs.	Rags, gloves, replacement fan if necessary, wood shims, all-purpose or machine oil	Screwdrivers, allen wrench set, 4-foot level, open-end wrench, fin comb, blower, trash bags

Even though the outdoor unit of a central air-conditioning system has to stand up to year-round weather conditions, it can last for years without requiring much attention, and that characteristic is often the cause of problems that regular maintenance can avoid. Simple tasks such as checking for bent fan blades, adjusting the level of the unit, and lubricating the fan motor don't take much time and can extend the life of your unit greatly. Cleaning the unit is the simplest of jobs, and if you use your air-conditioner only a few weeks out of every year, you can reserve this job for the spring. In fact it's a good idea to perform all these regular maintenance tasks in the spring so you don't have any downtime when you need it to cool your home. Some of the maintenance tasks require removing the external case, and that can leave you exposed to the capacitor that charges the motor. As a safety precaution turn off the main power to the unit before you start working on it and wait 10 more minutes to let the capacitor discharge. Better yet make sure you stay clear of the capacitor terminals completely when performing routine maintenance tasks.

If the air-conditioner fan seems to run noisily, inspect it for a bent blade. If a blade is bent, replace the fan. Often a blade will get caught and bend on debris that settles into the outside cage. A bent blade changes the equilibrium of the motor, damaging it, making it work harder, and reducing your cooling efficiency.

Dirt and debris will readily accumulate in front of the coil. Remove it with a brush and garden hose. Debris that clings to the intake fins of the compressor interferes with the airflow, making the motor work harder to deliver the cooling air your house needs.

Always shut off the main power to the air-conditioner unit before working on any interior parts. There's enough power in the unit and its capacitor to cause serious injury, even death.

Lift out the fan assembly and motor and clean out debris inside the unit. On many units you can gain the easiest access to the interior by removing the fan assembly.

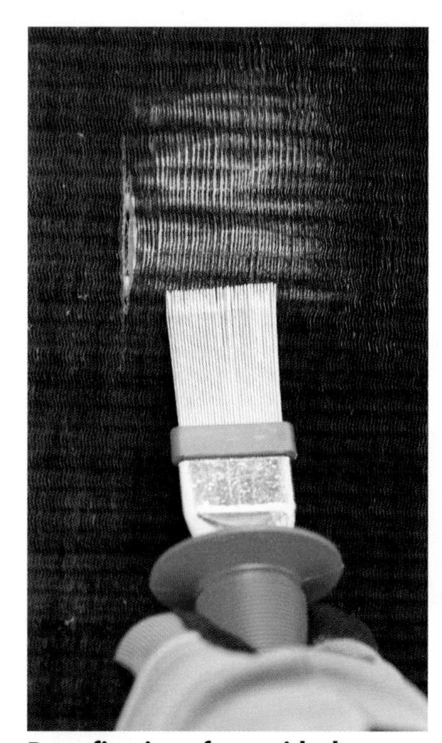

Bent fins interfere with the airflow, causing the unit to work inefficiently. Straighten the fins with a fin comb. If the outside cover of the unit is in the way, remove it by loosening the assembly screws. Put the screws in one place so you don't lose them.

Check to make sure the unit sits level. Use a 4-foot level and adjust the mounting if necessary. Over time the vibration of the unit and general erosion of the ground can cause it or its concrete pad to shift and go out of level. Adjust the feet if possible or shim the bottom of the unit to bring it level.

Lubricating the fan motor

Loosen the setscrew that holds the fan and collar to the motor shaft. Many models require removing the fan to access the oil ports. After oiling be sure to mount the fan in the same vertical location on its shaft—about 1 inch above the motor body.

Using household oil or a product for electrical motors, add three drops to each oil port on the motor. Pry out any rubber stoppers to open the oil ports. Use two hands when removing the plugs so they don't get away from you and fall down in the cover or fly out into the yard.

Installing an evaporative cooler

Skill level:	Time to complete:	Materials:	Tools:
★★★☆☆	Experienced Variable Handy Variable Novice Variable	Evaporative cooler, hanger kit, water pipe and fittings, hose	Power drill and bits, wrenches, level, general plumbing tools

Evaporative coolers, also known as swamp coolers, use water, air, and a fan to cool houses in areas with low or no humidity. They work on the same principle as a wet towel: Wrap a wet towel around yourself, and as the water evaporates it takes with it the heat of your body. Before you know it you get cool.

An evaporative cooler blows air through a water-soaked pad, cooling it with the wet-towel principle and then blowing it into your house. The drier the surrounding air, the greater the evaporation and the cooler the final product. Swamp coolers are more popular in drier climates such as Arizona, where manufacturers say the conditioned air may be as much as 30 degrees cooler than the outside air. On the East Coast, where the air is much more humid, the air produced may be only 10 degrees cooler than the outside air.

Whatever the results the evaporative cooler has a significant advantage over the refrigerant-powered air-conditioner: It's economical to run. A swamp cooler uses about one-quarter of the electricity an air-conditioner uses.

Whole-house units are often mounted on the roof, a fairly involved job (see "Installing a roof-mounted cooler," below). Installing a window-mounted unit, however, is simple. The actual cooler is a box-shaped unit that hangs outside the window. A cool-air vent extends through the window. From inside the house it looks much like a refrigerant air-conditioner.

Installing a roof-mounted cooler

A typical evaporative cooler is mounted on the roof and uses a blower to move the air from the cooling unit into the home. Rooftop installations are generally cheaper than wall-mounted units but come with additional maintenance problems. Because coolers tend to leak over time, they also tend to increase the deterioration of the roof on which they're mounted.

Before you purchase a cooler, find the unit that will adequately cool the cubic footage of your home. Then determine the rooftop location and mark the holes for mounting. Follow the manufacturer's instructions for the size of the outlet hole for the ductwork the cooler needs and any illustrations provided for framing and support. Some coolers are mounted in wood frames. Others are supported by commercial (or home-brew) angle-iron racks. Whatever support method you use, be sure to seal the fastener holes in the roof.

Connect the water line and run your electrical power lines to a dedicated-circuit junction box or through conduit into an interior box if codes allow. Then tie the switch into the unit as prescribed by the manufacturer. Most swamp coolers are made for 120-volt power. Turn on the power and water and adjust the float until the water is 2 to 3 inches deep. Check the float mechanism often if you have hard water. Sediment can build up quickly in the outside air and rapidly interfere with the operation of the float.

1 Install the hangers and support assembly. Following manufacturer's instructions mount the hangers, then assemble and install the support brackets. Build up the outside windowsill as directed to support the cool-air vent that goes through the window. If the cooler hangs from the top by chains, follow the manufacturer's instructions for assembly and installation.

2 Set the cooler on the support assembly. Put the cooler in the window, resting the vent on the sill. Attach the cooler to the brackets as directed by the manufacturer.

3 Run a water line to the cooler. Put in a cutoff valve that you can drain in the winter. On slab construction run the pipe from the cutoff up through the attic and then down the outside wall. If you have a basement, run the pipe through the rim joist and then outside the house to the cooler. The cooler has an overflow drain line that you attach to a hose. Run the hose on the ground, well away from the foundation.

4 Install the cool-air vent that directs air from the unit into the house. Plug in the cord attached to the vent that runs through the window. Use any grounded 120-volt circuit inside the house.

Maintaining an evaporative cooler

Manufacturers recommend routine maintenance three times a year: at the start of the cooling season, at the end of the season, and midway through the season. Maintenance includes oiling the blower shaft and other bearings, checking the belt tension, and checking the water supply lines for leaks. Also clean the water pump by removing and washing it with a mild detergent. (Most pumps are easy to remove.)

In addition replace the cooling pads at the beginning of and midway through the season. Drain the unit at the end of the season.

Installing underfloor radiant heat

Skill level:	Time to complete:	Materials:	Tools:
★★★☆☆	Experienced Variable Handy Variable Novice Variable	Electric mats, tinned copper sleeve, electrician's tape, insulation, thinset or self-leveling compound; PEX tubing, aluminum dissipation plates	Scissors, combination stripper, stapler, crimper, trowels, PEX tools, right-angle drill, Forstner bit

There are two basic electric radiant-heat systems: low-voltage mats and high-voltage cables. Cables are usually embedded in concrete and require some electrical skills to install. Mats, however, are easy to install and wire. Some have wires that double as thermostats: As the floor temperature rises, the ability of the wire to produce heat drops.

Mats made for above-the-floor installation need a layer of mortar for protection. Underfloor installations have to be insulated but otherwise need no protection.

Before starting an installation check with an electrician to be sure your electrical system can handle the new circuit if it needs one. In general you will need from 8 to 12 watts per square foot of heated floor. Make sure the floor you're installing under is suitable for radiant heat and make sure the system is designed to account for climate and building insulation.

The system shown here is one of many available. Installation procedures vary from manufacturer to manufacturer. The system shown here is low voltage and uses a wire that acts as its own thermostat. Other systems require either a wall thermostat or one mounted directly in the floor. Always follow the manufacturer's recommendations.

Installing underfloor mats

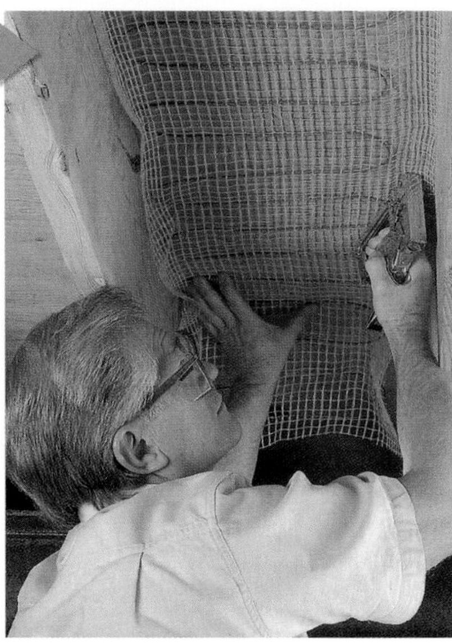

1 Unroll the mat material and cut it to length with scissors. Strip the insulation off an end of each of the two wires that run the length of the mat. Turn the mat so those ends are facing the wires that will bring it power. Have a helper hold the mats against the bottom of the subfloor while you staple them in place. Don't install the 2 feet or so of mat to which you'll be attaching wire.

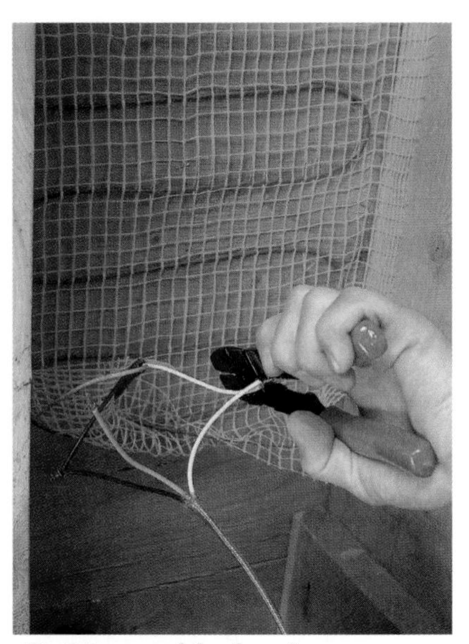

2 Crimp a black wire on one mat wire and a white wire on the other. You'll need a tinned copper sleeve for the job and a tool called a crimper. Slip the crimping sleeve over the wire at the end of the mat and put a 14-gauge stranded, tinned copper wire inside. Squeeze the crimping tool to crush the sleeve tightly over the wires. Cover the connection with electrician's tape.

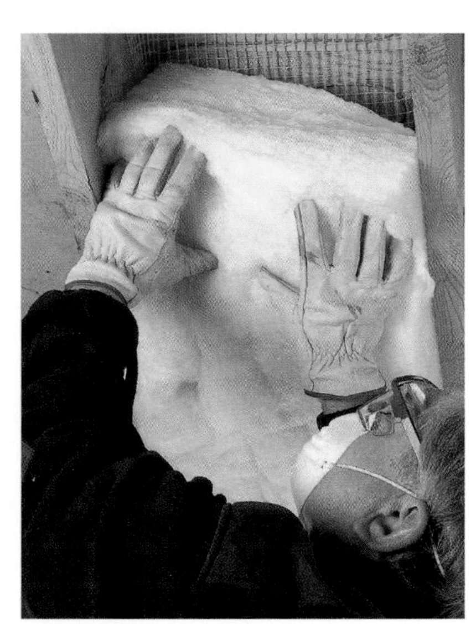

3 Install insulation. Once all the mats are in place, install insulation between the joists, keeping it the recommended distance from the heating mats.

Installing above the subfloor

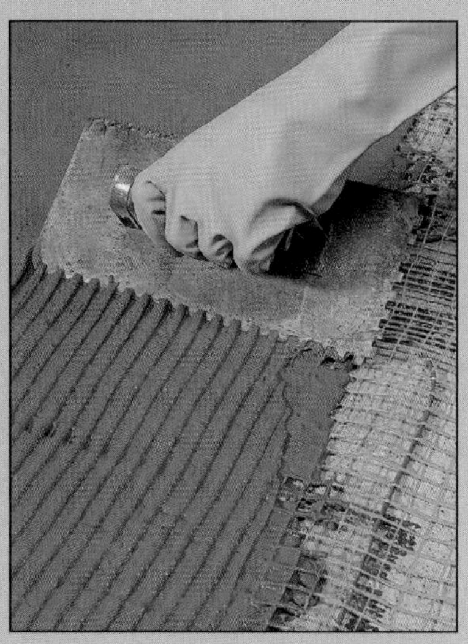

If you can't get to the underside of a floor, install electric mats above the floor. Keep in mind that they will have to be covered by a protective layer of gypsum or concrete. Staple the mats on top of the subfloor and wire as directed.

While some manufacturers advise spreading thinset over their mats, it can be difficult to keep the floor flat and level. Have the work done by a company that pumps a self-leveling gypsum mixture over the mats. Let the mixture dry the appropriate length of time, then cover it with flooring as if you were installing it over a concrete base. In bathrooms and kitchens you'll need to install a moisture barrier to protect the gypsum.

Installing an underfloor hydronic system

PEX tubing, the heart of a hydronic heating system, carries the hot water along the length and width of the floor. PEX is short for cross-linked polyethylene, a plastic that has been manufactured specifically to remain flexible and withstand heated water.

Unlike electric mats hydronic systems aren't prepackaged. Installation, however, is fairly simple. Work in the room below the floor you're going to heat. Start at a corner of the room and run tubing to the other side between the joists. Feed the tubing into the bay between the neighboring joists through predrilled holes. When you've snaked tubing from one side of the room to the other, hold it in place with aluminum plates stapled to the subfloor. Some companies prefabricate the plates; others require you to bend your own. It's not all that difficult, but prefab is definitely quicker.

Have a professional design the layout: PEX comes in various diameters, and you want to make sure your system is properly sized. In addition large areas or those with small spaces between the joists may require two sets of loops under the floor.

1 Drill a hole at one end of each bay so you can feed the tubing into the neighboring bay. Plan the location of each hole and drill them all before installation. Drill an oversize hole, as directed by the manufacturer, using a Forstner bit. Spade bits aren't durable enough for this job. Use a ½-inch right-angle drill.

2 Lay a coil of PEX on the floor at one end of the first bay while a helper stands on the other end. Carry one end of the pipe to your helper. Insert the tubing through the hole in the joist and pull it back to the other side of the room while your helper feeds it. When you reach the other side, feed the tubing through the hole. Have your helper walk the tubing back to the other side and feed it through the next joist hole. Continue until you've run tubing under the entire floor.

3 Once the tubing is in place, go back to the beginning. Hold the tubing to the subfloor and staple an aluminum plate to the subfloor. Space the plates as directed by the manufacturer. If you have multiple loops, tape the ends of the tubing, labeling which end goes to the heat source and which returns. Have an installer connect the valves, manifolds, and pipes.

Above-the-floor installation

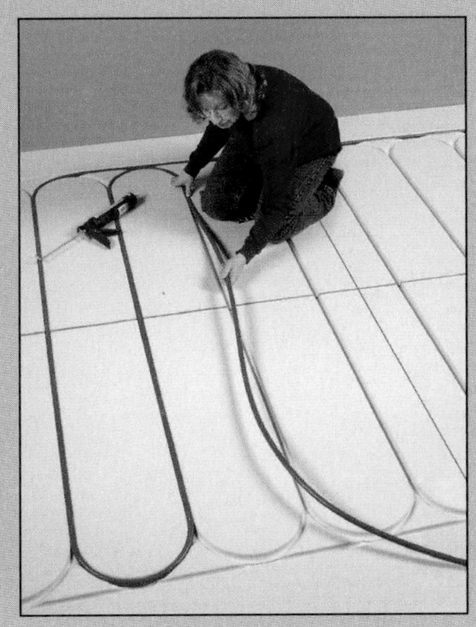

Like electric systems you can install hydronic systems in a concrete, mortar, or gypsum bed. It's easier to install the tubing in specially made plywood with precut channels. Nail the plywood in place as you would a subfloor or underlayment. At the wall install pieces with curved grooves that make a U-turn; send the tubing back across the room in another groove.

You can install carpeting and wood flooring directly over the plywood. Vinyl requires underlayment, and ceramic and stone floors should be set in a mortar bed or on cement backerboard.

Installing a furnace humidifier

Skill level:	Time to complete:	Materials:	Tools:
★★★☆☆	Experienced 2 hrs. Handy 2.5 hrs. Novice 3 hrs.	Humidifier unit, sheet metal screws, wire nuts, saddle valve/T-fitting, vent pipe	Felt marker, cordless drill and bit, aviator's snips, screwdriver, utility knife, combination stripper, wrenches

To get humidity evenly distributed throughout the entire house, what better way than introducing moisture into the heating supply? Forced-air furnace design, with its ductwork rising to feed the whole house with heat, provides the perfect location to install a whole-house humidifier.

Different manufacturers use different media for collecting water. Two of the most common are a rotating foam pad and fiber evaporative plates. The hot air travels over the medium and evaporates the water, sending the moisture into the living spaces. To monitor and regulate the humidity level these units use a humidistat, usually mounted on the cold-air return, and a float to shut the water off when the system is full.

Some models are installed in the return-air duct; others employ a bypass duct to reintroduce humidified air going to the house. Each system requires you to cut a hole in the venting.

▲ *Although a new furnace likely comes with a built-in whole-house humidifier, some may not. Installing a new humidifier can improve the comfort level throughout your home and increase the efficiency of your furnace.*

1 Set the manufacturer's template on the ductwork at the location of the humidifier and outline its cutout with a felt marker. Drill a starter hole in the center of the cutout and work an aviator's snips toward the outline. Cut out the hole on the outline. Drill holes for mounting screws and mount the plate.

2 Using the manufacturer's instructions mark the location of the humidistat and cut the humidistat hole as you did for the humidifier unit.

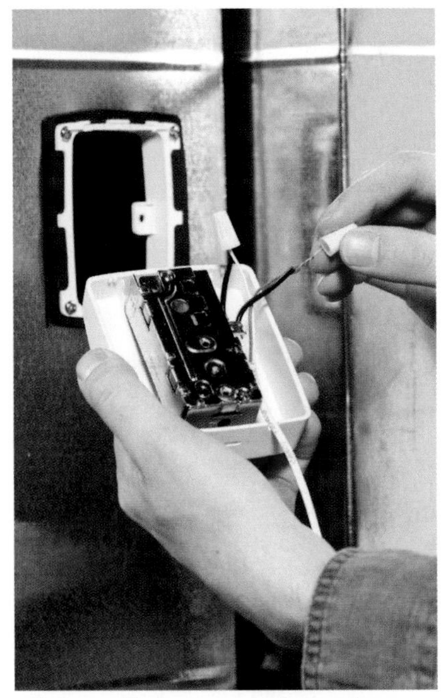

3 Install the mounting plate for the humidistat, then connect the humidistat to the furnace controls. If the unit requires a step-down transformer, shut the power off, install the transformer, and wire the humidistat.

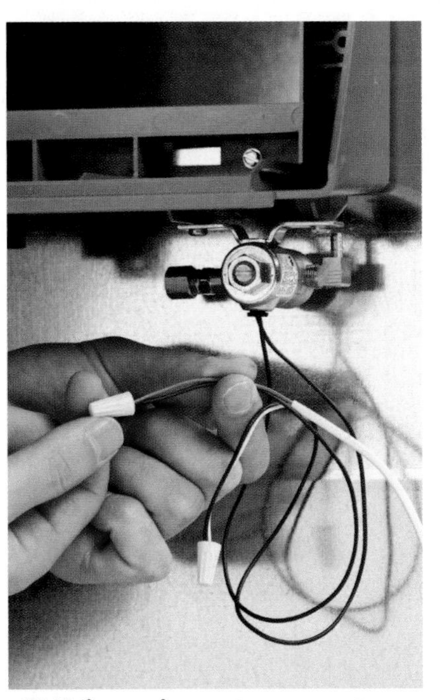

4 Using wire nuts connect the humidistat leads to the solenoid valve on the humidifier. Insert the wire ends into the nuts and turn the nuts until they're tight.

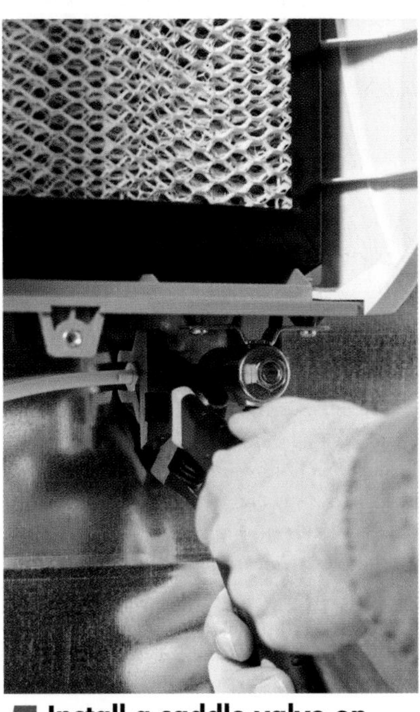

5 Install a saddle valve on the hot-water line and run the water line to the humidifier. If local codes do not allow saddle valves, turn the water off, cut the water line, and install a T-fitting.

Cutting a bypass vent

1 If your humidifier instructions stipulate the installation of a bypass vent, use the template to mark a 6-inch hole for the bypass pipe. As you did when cutting the other holes in the ductwork, drill a starter hole and cut the vent hole with an aviator's snips.

2 Push a round collar into the hole and fasten it with sheet metal screws. Cut the vent pipe to fit between the humidifier air inlet and the collar. Push elbows on both ends of the vent pipe and fasten the pipe assembly to the collar and humidifier air intake.

Connecting the water

Turn off the water to the supply pipe. Place the rubber gasket over the self-piercing tip and back the tip off about 1⁄16 inch from the gasket. Assemble the straps on the pipe and tighten the nuts. Turn the self-piercing valve full clockwise and install the water line to the humidifier. Turn the water on.

Maintaining a furnace humidifier

Skill level:	Time to complete:	Materials:	Tools:
★★★☆☆	Experienced 15 mins. Handy 20 mins. Novice 30 mins.	Replacement evaporator units	Wrenches, screwdriver, old kitchen knife, pipe cleaners

No whole-house humidifier will be immune from the inevitable effects of mineral deposits in the water and constant exposure to the effects of heated air in cold months. The chief consequence will be a gradual accumulation of sediment on the foam cylinder or fiber evaporative plates and a gradual diminishing of their capacity to hold water. Thus as any unit ages, it will put less humidity into the air.

Drip-style humidifiers will have a tendency to clean themselves somewhat as the water flows over the plates. Drum styles will need more maintenance and more frequent replacement of the foam cylinder.

These elements are actually picking up standing water and are more likely to develop mold growth, which will then be sent along with the moisture into the rest of the house. You can forestall replacing both cylinder and plate elements for a short time by washing them and manually removing sediment deposits. But in the long run you will have to replace any kind of element periodically.

Replacing a humidifier drum

1 Loosen the fasteners that hold the cover and remove it. Lift the drum out by grasping it on both sides. You may have to jockey it a bit to remove it.

2 Inspect the foam pad. If it's still somewhat pliable and not too clogged with hard bits of sediment, you can clean it. If it's hard and crusted, replace it. To clean it remove the pad from its cage by loosening any clips and pulling the two sides apart. Wash it in a mild detergent and wring it out gently.

3 Slip the pad back onto its frame, taking care not to tear it. Reassemble the frame and slide the axles into their recesses in the humidifier body. Make sure the gear on the drum is engaged within the drive gear on the humidifier. Turn the water on and wait for the tray to fill to the proper level.

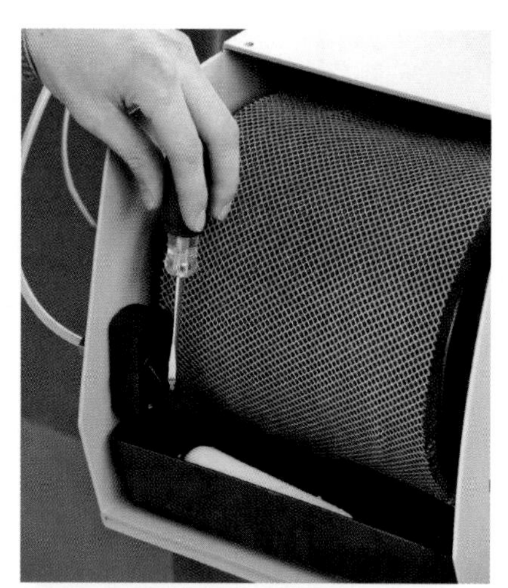

4 To adjust the water level to the manufacturer's specifications, loosen the screws on the float. To raise the water level, raise the float and tighten the screw. To lower the level lower the float and tighten the screw.

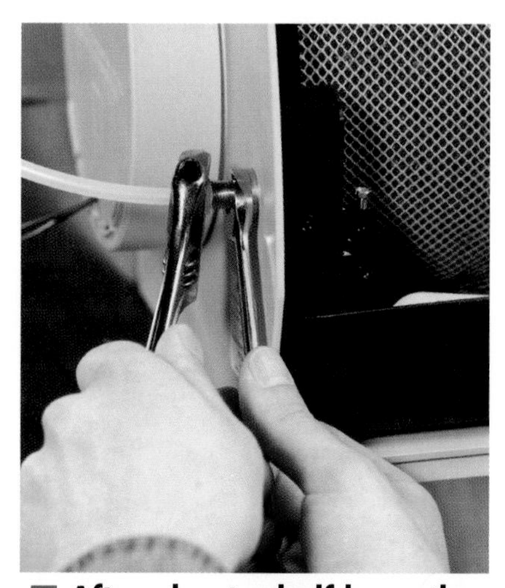

5 After about a half hour, the water should have reached its proper operating level. Readjust the float if necessary so there's sufficient water coming into the tray as the drum turns and removes it.

Maintaining a humidifier with evaporator elements or plates

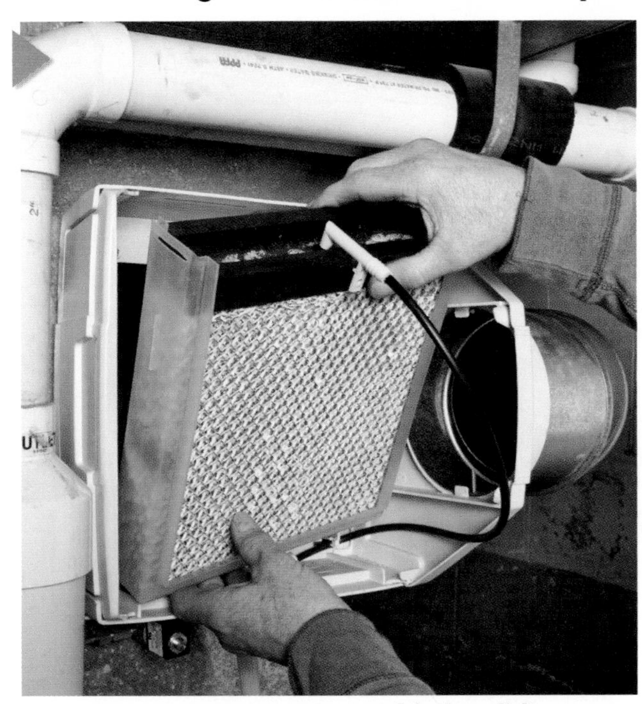

1 Remove evaporator assembly by sliding your fingers under the unit and lifting it out. If the assembly is especially heavily scaled, wear gloves—hardened mineral scales can be sharp. Pry the unit out gently with an old kitchen knife. Remove the distribution tray.

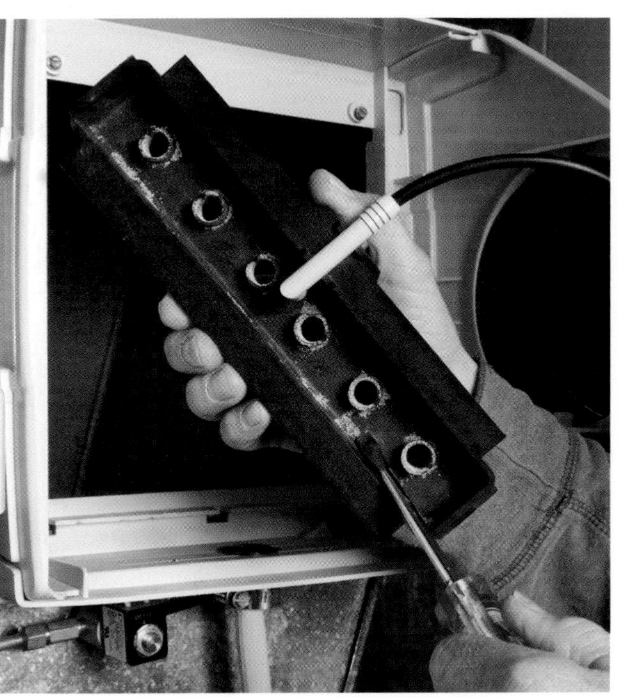

2 Clean mineral deposits from the distribution tray with an old kitchen knife or flat screwdriver.

3 Remove the evaporator element from its frame. Twist the corners of the element gently to pop off any mineral scales and wash it to remove loose particles. If the element begins to disintegrate, replace it.

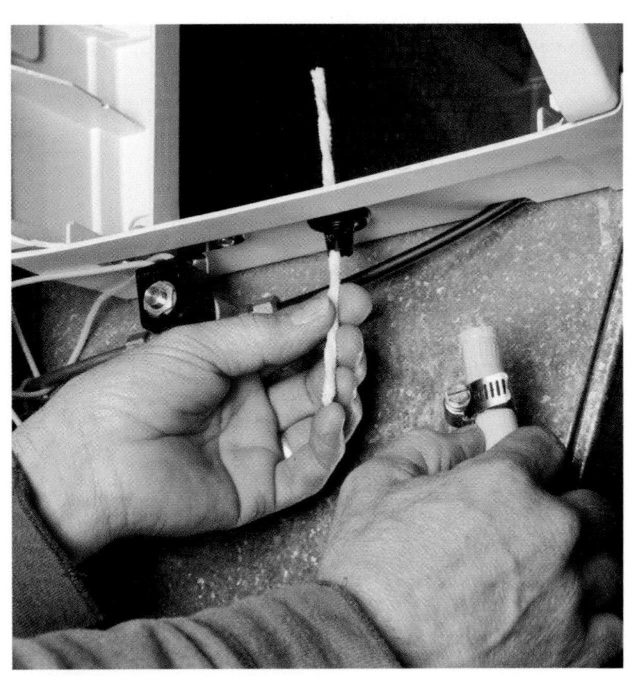

4 Disconnect the drain hose and run a pipe cleaner up and down the distribution orifice. Flush the drain hose with water and push it back on the plastic nipples that hold it.

Installing soffit and roof vents

Skill level:	Time to complete:	Materials:	Tools:
★★★☆☆	Experienced 1 hr. Handy 1.5 hrs. Novice 2 hrs.	Soffit vents, roof vents, screws, roofing cement, roofing nails	Ladder (or scaffolding), straightedge, hammer, reciprocating saw, drill with bits, screwdriver, roofing knife, saber saw

Proper air circulation is essential for effective insulation. If you have inadequate venting, warm, moist air that escapes through the insulation condenses in the cold attic air. This trapped moisture can cause wood rot, mildew, and water damage. You can also have exterior roofing problems, along with higher cooling costs in the summer.

A balanced circulation system will have 1 square foot of venting for every 150 square feet of attic. (Change this to 1 square foot for every 300 square feet if the insulation has a vapor barrier.)

You should have an equal amount of soffit intake and roof exhaust vents. Check for blockages of airflow in your attic vents, baffles, and roof vents. Also verify that attic insulation doesn't block any vents.

Vents range from static open units to thermostatically controlled electric fan units. The type of vent you purchase will depend on the amount of air you need to move, the size of your attic, the scope of the project you wish to undertake, and of course your budget!

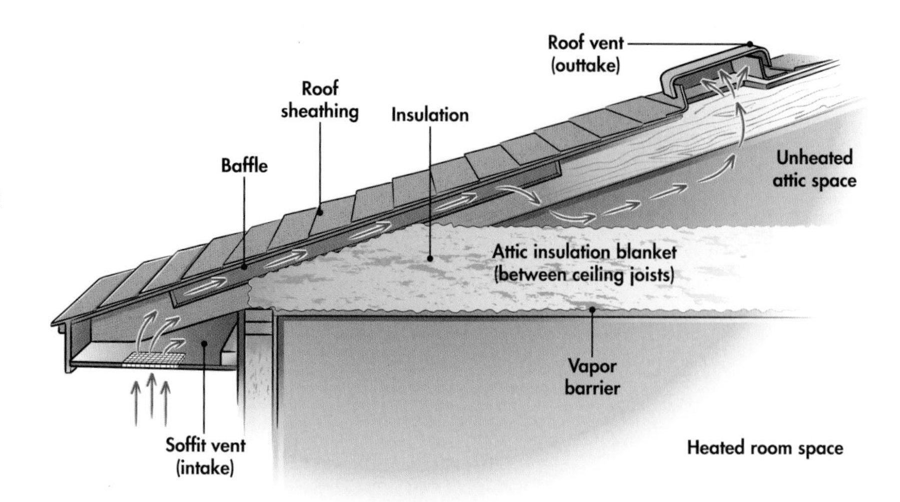

Effective insulation requires ventilation

Sufficient airflow is critical to proper roof-system ventilation. Airflow prevents heat buildup in your attic and helps protect your roof from damage caused by condensation and ice. A typical ventilation system has vents in the soffits to admit fresh air that flows upward through the baffle beneath the roof sheathing and exits through roof vents. You'll need several vents for adequate circulation. Distribute them evenly throughout your attic to ensure that the entire attic is ventilated.

Soffit blues

Insulation saves money but can cause rot if attic spaces are not properly vented. If you're having trouble with mildew and wood rot, you probably need some soffit vents to promote airflow. They're quite easy to install and can work wonders for keeping attics dry and soffits in good condition. If you already have soffit vents, take care not to block them when adding additional attic insulation. Use baffles such as those in the illustration above to prevent such blocking of airflow.

Venting the ridge

Ridge vents present an aesthetic alternative to roof vents and with a little advance planning can equal or exceed the venting capacity of roof vents. Besides a roof-vent system requires the installation of several units, while the installation of a ridge vent is accomplished as a single job. For maximum efficiency you want a balanced system—equal ventilation capacity at both the soffits and the ridge. Proper distribution of ridge and soffit vents is critical. If you can't achieve a balanced system, provide more than 50 percent of the total required ventilation at the soffit and the remainder at the ridge.

Soffit-vent options

Add soffit vents to increase airflow into attics. Make sure there is an unobstructed air passage from the soffit area to the roof before you install new soffit vents. Do not cover the vents with insulation. Vents should face toward the house.

Continuous soffit vents provide even airflow into attics. They are usually installed during new construction but can be added as retrofits to unvented soffit panels.

Roof-vent options

Roof vents are one way to get air out of the attic, and installation is fairly simple.

A powered roof vent (inset) has a thermostat-controlled fan that will increase air circulation; one of these may be all the venting your house needs.

Continuous ridge vents increase air circulation dramatically and are much less noticeable than traditional roof vents. Because these span the entire length of the ridge, they provide more consistent air circulation than other vents. Ridge vents are best installed during roof construction but can be retrofitted.

Gable vents, like roof vents, increase circulation without calling attention to themselves. Because you don't need to climb onto the roof to install them, they're ideal when the roof is too steep for comfort.

Installing soffit and roof vents (continued)

Installing a soffit vent

1 From inside the attic choose and mark a place for the soffit vent that allows the air to flow freely. Drill through the soffit to enable you to spot the location from outside. If you're unable to get near enough to the wall because of the roof slope, locate the joists with a stud finder, as shown here, and position the vent between them.

2 Trace around the vent on the soffit. Be sure the vent will fall between rafter ends or nailer strips.

SAFETY ALERT
SECURE YOUR LADDER

Use a secure platform (ladder or scaffolding) when working at aboveground elevations.

3 Cut the vent openings ¼ inch inside the marked layout lines (or as directed) to leave room for fastening the vent covers. Use a saber saw.

4 Install the soffit vents and fasten them with stainless-steel screws or galvanized wood screws.

Installing a roof vent

1 Drive a nail through the roof from inside to mark the position of the vent hole. Locate roof vents as high as possible on the roof but below the ridgeline and on the least visible slope of the house. Place the vent between rafters to avoid cutting through a rafter. Locate turbine vents close to the ridge with a minimum clearance of 8 inches to the ridgeline. Using the nail as a center point, draw a circle with a diameter equal to the vent's opening.

2 Remove the shingles just above and to the side of the cutout area that will be covered by the flange at the base of the vent. Do not remove shingles below the vent cutout—they will be covered by the flange. Hammer the centering nail back through the roof. Drill a pilot hole with a spade bit at each corner of the cutout area; then use a reciprocating saw to cut the vent hole.

3 Apply roofing cement to the underside of the flange. Slide the top edge of the flange under the shingles immediately above the hole you cut. Center the vent over the hole.

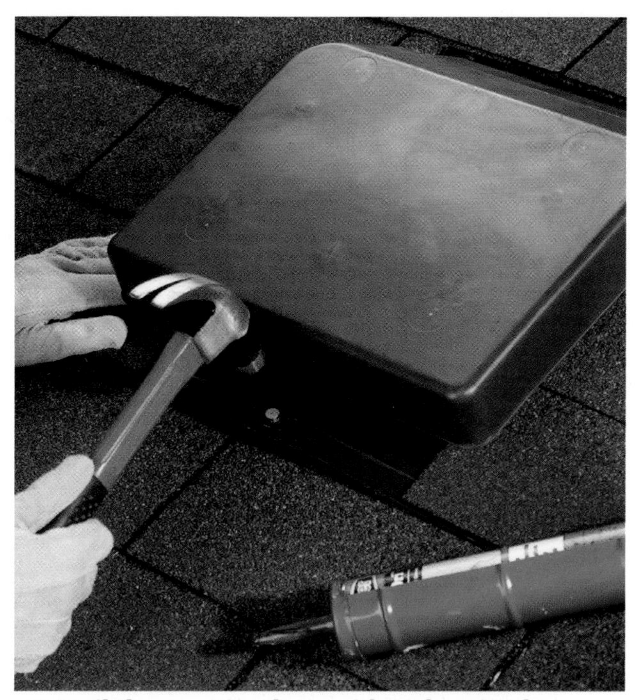

4 Nail the vent in place with galvanized roofing nails. Nail the base at the top, sides, and bottom. Cover the nail holes and the seam between the base and the roof with roofing cement. Leave the bottom edge exposed.

CHAPTER 9

Insulation & Weatherproofing

Insulation has come a long way since the days of stuffing mud and straw wattle between beams. And heat has come a long way from the open fireplace and a Franklin stove. But the central truth remains: You need both heat and insulation to stay warm.

The furnace gets most homeowners' attention. When it's not happy it groans, bangs, whines, and sometimes even goes on strike. Insulation, meanwhile, sits quietly in the attic. We ignore it, tending to the moans and whistles of the monster in the basement. If we understood the sounds, however, we might pay more attention—the furnace is telling us that it can't keep up; the job is more than it can handle.

More likely than not the long-term solution will be found in its silent partner, insulation. Older homes, built in the days of low-cost energy, lack the insulation they need to keep heat in the house. If you're cold, or if your heating bill soars through the roof, that's where you should start—at the roof. An uninsulated attic accounts for 40 percent of lost heat. Unrolling insulation in an unfinished attic is a simple enough task for any homeowner. In an attic with a floor you might want to consider blown-in insulation. In this chapter you'll learn the ins and outs of insulation and its cousin, weatherstripping. Installing these materials is among the simplest jobs a homeowner can do. Do them—you'll thank yourself, and your furnace will thank you too.

Contents

Insulation and weatherproofing basics 500
Choosing insulation 501
Insulation and weatherproofing tool kit 502
Improving home energy efficiency 503
Evaluating home energy efficiency 506
Weatherproofing your home 508
Insulating an attic 516
Insulating basements 518

Energy loss is expensive

Unless your house has proper weatherstripping, caulking, and storm windows, 20 to 50 percent of the money you spend is going to heat the great outdoors. Solutions are generally simple, low-tech, and with the possible exception of storm doors and windows, fairly inexpensive. A house should never be completely airtight however. Even with extensive weatherproofing, that's not a problem in older homes but newer homes need to "breathe" to avoid health and structural problems. If you want to know how your house rates, do a quick inventory:

- Verify that the seams between the house and window or door moldings are sealed with caulk.

- Check windows for weatherstripping. Windows should have weatherstripping on the tops, bottoms, and sides. Double-hung windows should have weatherstripping between the two sashes.

- Look for broken or loose windowpanes. If the putty around the windows is cracked or missing, replace it.

- Check the storm windows. If you have none get them. If you do have them, make sure the weep holes on the bottoms of the frames are open. A clogged hole traps moisture, causing fogged windows, paint failure, and rot.

- Check all exterior doors. They should be weatherstripped on both sides and at the tops. There should be a sweep across the bottom to prevent air leakage at the threshold.

- Look for leaks around openings in the foundation or siding. Typical suspects include plumbing and gas pipes, wiring, telephone lines, and TV antenna wires or cable. Caulk and seal any openings you find.

- Verify that you have foam gaskets behind electric switch and receptacle plates on exterior walls. Switches and outlets are notorious for leaking air. Gaskets solve the problem for the most part and are easy to install.

- Keep the fireplace flue closed when not in use.

- Check the amount of insulation in your attic and compare it to the chart on page 501. Get more insulation if you need it. Check the insulation under crawlspaces too. It can fall down, leaving you with an extremely cold floor. Wall insulation is harder to check. Contract with a pro for a full energy audit, which will include inspecting of the wall insulation and more. Check the Yellow Pages or with your power company to find someone who does audits.

Insulation and weatherproofing basics

Whether you live in a warm or a cold climate, adequately weatherizing and insulating your house has many benefits. Most important you save money. Even in homes with average insulation, heating and cooling costs account for more than half of the total energy bill. And because most insulating and weatherstripping products are relatively inexpensive, an investment in them can be recovered through energy savings in a short period of time.

A well-insulated house not only saves money but it's also easier on the environment because it uses less energy. By reducing energy use you help reduce pollution from carbon emissions and other greenhouse gases—you also slow the depletion of natural resources. In an average home in a cold climate, it is estimated that reducing energy usage by only 15 percent can save the equivalent of 500 pounds of coal each year. And finally a tightly sealed, well-insulated house eliminates drafts and cold spots, creating a more comfortable home for you to enjoy.

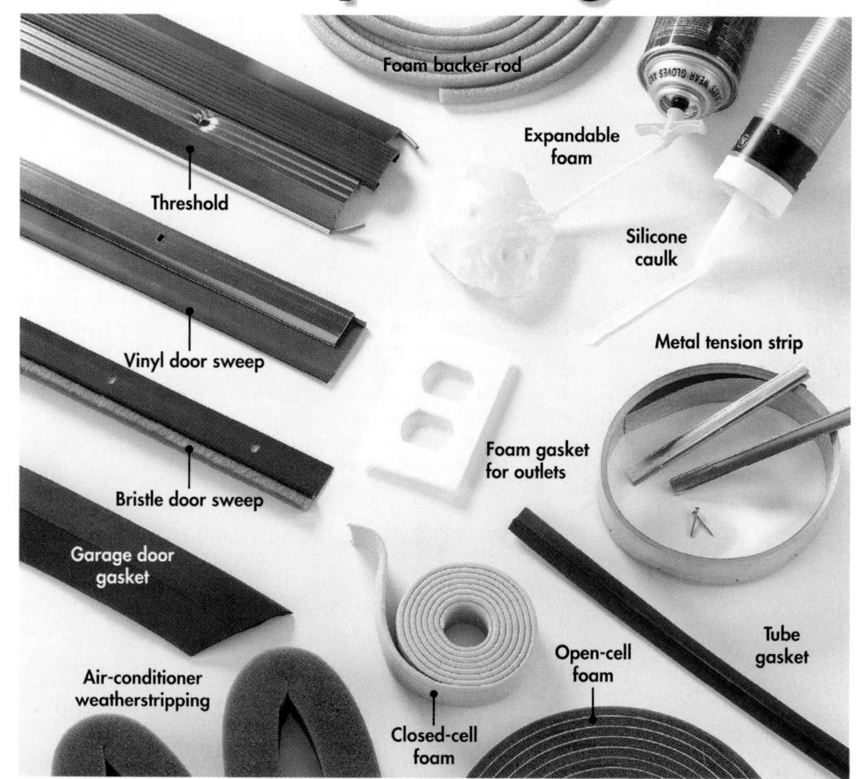

Tighten up the house with a variety of products (above): Foam backer rod, expandable foam, silicone caulk, metal tension strips for doors and windows, vinyl tube gaskets, open-cell foam, closed-cell foam, air-conditioner weatherstripping, garage door gasket, bristle door sweep, vinyl door sweep, threshold, and foam gasket for outlets.

The three types of insulation you'll commonly encounter are fiberglass, cellulose, and rigid foam. Fiberglass comes in rolls and bats that you stuff between the framing of walls and ceilings. Insulation stays support fiberglass in overhead ceilings and crawlspaces. Cellulose is blown into place and works well when you need to fit a lot of insulation into narrow spaces such as between the joists of attics. Rigid foam comes in three types—polyisocyanurate, molded expanded polystyrene (MEPS), and extruded polystyrene (EXPS).

MEPS is the foam from which coffee cups and coolers are made. It has an R-value of R-4 per inch. (See "How Much insulation is Enough?" on page 501.) EXPS is more common in commercial buildings; has a hard, flat surface; and an R-value of R-5 per inch. Polyisocyanurate is a closed-cell foam with an insulating gas trapped in the cells. Its R-value is between R-7 and R-8 per inch but drops slightly as the gas escapes naturally. The indoor surfaces of all foam boards must be covered with drywall to meet fire code.

Choosing insulation

Choosing the right kind of insulation to meet your needs can prove daunting because there are so many forms and types of materials. Ultimately your choice will hinge on the R-value you need in your geographic area and the part of the house in which you will install the insulation. Budget figures importantly also. The guiding rule here is: Buy as much R-value as you can afford. Sometimes your choice will be eased by where you'll put the new insulation. If you're remodeling a basement with 2× furring strips to support the finished wall, the easiest solution is one of the foam-board materials (with the highest R-value you can afford) covered with your finished drywall. In attics fiberglass batts go up quickly, both between the rafters and between the floor joists. Blown-in cellulose is also an easy-to-install material for attic floors. Its tendency to compact also impedes airflow through the cavity. Reflective insulation (see page 502) is also an effective material that installs quickly and won't leave you covered with fibers, as will some other materials.

Take an inventory of the amount and kind of insulation that exists in various parts of your home. Determine the R-value of each area and if you come up short of the recommendations shown in the table below, find the most practical way of increasing the R-value. Then add insulation where space allows. If one of your deficit areas is in your exterior walls, consider hiring a contractor to blow in loose-fill insulation. You can also add rigid insulation to the exterior of your home before installing new siding.

If you're building a new home and computing R-values needed, consider energy-engineered framing, structural insulated panels, and insulated concrete forms for their high R-values. Check with your local building code officials, however, before you start construction. With increasing emphasis placed on energy savings, many localities are raising their requirements for insulating new homes. And don't forget to ask about rebates for energy improvements for existing homes and new construction. Many states and localities offer tax rebates (and in some cases cash rebates on purchases) for a variety of energy-saving measures.

How much insulation is enough?

Insulation is measured in R-values—the ability to withstand heat transfer. The map at right will help you identify your needs. Here's a look at the R-values of common insulation:

Fiberglass

3½"	R-13
5¼"	R-21
7¼"	R-25
10"	R-30
12"	R-38

Molded Expanded Polystyrene

1"	R-4
1½"	R-6
2"	R-8

Extruded Polystyrene

1"	R-5
2"	R-10

Polyurethane and Polyisocyanurate

1"	R-7 to R-8

Cellulose

1"	R-3.4 to R-3.8

Reflective

Reflects up to 97% of radiated heat: R-values of 1.1 to 18, depending on installation location and method.

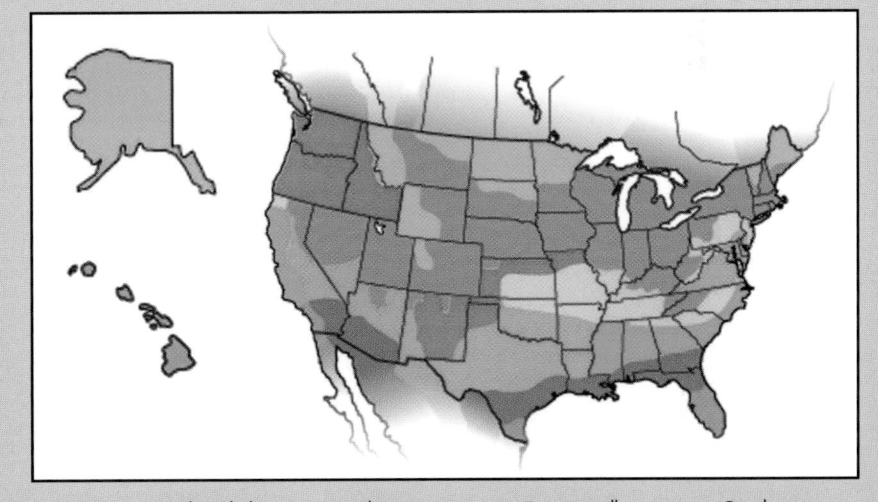

	Ceilings below ventilated attics		Floors over unheated crawl		Exterior walls(a) (wood frame)		Crawlspace walls(b)	
Insulation zone	Gas, oil, or heat pump	Electric resistance	Gas, oil, or heat pump	Electric resistance	Gas, oil, or heat pump	Electric resistance	Gas, oil, or heat pump	Electric resistance
1	R-49	R-49	R-19	R-19	R-11	R-11	R-19	R-19
2	R-38	R-49	R-19	R-19	R-11	R-11	R-19	R-19
3	R-38	R-38	R-19	R-19	R-11	R-11	R-19	R-19
4	R-38	R-38	R-19	R-19	R-11	R-11	R-19	R-19
5	R-30	R-38	R-19	R-19	R-11	R-11	R-19	R-19
6	R-30	R-38	(c)	R-19	R-11	R-11	R-19	R-19
7	R-30	R-30	(c)	(c)	R-11	R-11	R-19	R-19
8	R-19	R-30	(c)	(c)	(c)	R-11	R-11	R-11

(a) For new construction R-19 is recommended for exterior walls. Jamming an R-19 batt into a 3½-inch cavity will not yield R-19 because compression reduces the R-value.

(b) Insulate crawlspace walls only if the crawlspace is dry all year, the floor above is not insulated, and all ventilation to the crawlspace is blocked.

(c) Thermal response of existing space for cooling benefits does not suggest additional insulation.

Choosing insulation (continued)

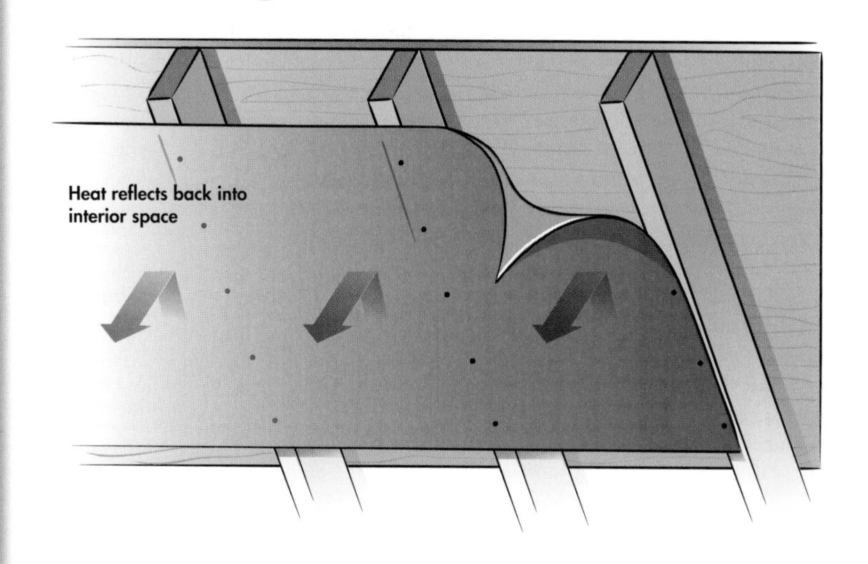

Reflective insulation

All surfaces transfer heat through convection. R-value, the common energy efficiency measurement, determines how well certain materials impede convective heat loss. Reflective insulation, consisting of flexible layers of aluminum foil, cardboard, or plastic bubbles encased in a metal (typically aluminum) skin, is designed to block radiant heat transfer as well. In many ways reflective insulation works like the interior of a thermos bottle, which helps keep liquids warm not only by means of its vacuum enclosure but also the mirrored surface of its interior glass. Reflective insulation easily staples to stud and joist faces.

Insulation & weatherproofing tool kit

Caulking gun, Drill, Gloves, Mask, Safety glasses, Stud finder

Circular saw, Drill bits, Handsaw, Putty knife, Scissors, Tack hammer

Claw hammer, Flat pry bar, Insulation blower, Reciprocating saw, Screwdrivers, Tape measure

Combination square, Framing square, Ladder and stabilizer bar, Saber saw, Stapler, Utility knife

Improving home energy efficiency

Insulating your home is of course one of your first-line defenses in containing your home-energy expenditures—but it's not the only one. Low-cost measures such as caulking around windows and doors to seal air leaks, weatherstripping windows and doors, and wrapping heating and cooling ducts, cost little time and money and can help save a bundle. So can energy-efficient appliances and fixtures.

One of the fist things you should do is conduct an energy audit of your home. The audit will tell you how much energy you consume and what you can do to make your home more energy efficient. You start by making a list of potential air leaks, then you take a look at everything in your home that uses energy—from the lightbulbs to the heating and air-conditioning system. Sometimes simple routine appliance maintenance will get you by, but upgrading appliances may prove to be your best bet in the long run. If you're not up to conducting the audit yourself, plenty of competent professionals can do it for you. It's money well spent in helping you develop a plan tailored to your needs and lifestyle.

Inspect your heating and cooling equipment each year—more frequently if your manufacturer suggests it. Clean or replace furnace filters, clean the heat exchanger and burners, look for dust streaks at joints in ductwork. (They mean air is leaking.) And if the system is more than 15 years old, strongly consider replacing it. Examine the wattage of all your lightbulbs and reduce the wattage if it won't impair the lighting in the room. Lighting accounts for almost 10 percent of your total energy use. Often a 60- or 75-watt bulb will provide ample light where you now have 100-watt bulbs. Especially where lights are on for long periods of time, consider compact fluorescent lamps. And don't forget the possibility of adding windows and skylights to rooms. Sunlight is free and can dramatically improve the usability and ambience of a room. It can also help reduce your heating costs.

Appliances in a typical U.S. home rack up almost 20 percent of the monthly energy bill. You can compute the cost of running each appliance by using formulas found at the U.S. Department of Energy's website (www.eere.energy.gov/consumer/your_home/appliances/index.cfm/mytopic). Then look at the energy guide sticker on any new appliances you're considering. Higher numbers on the sticker indicate higher efficiency and lower energy costs. Energy Star labels appear on appliances that meet strict government requirements for energy use.

▲ *A programmable thermostat lets you set the heating system to automatically lower temperatures when you're sleeping or away from home. Get one that allows a manual override of its automatic features.*

Energy-efficient window construction

New technologies make the old single-pane exterior window a thing of the past. Gone are the days of mysterious drafts, rattling panes, and the ambient chill that once seemed to issue from glazed windows, no matter what their style.

When energy costs were cheap, a window had merely to knock the wind down and let the light in. Energy-efficient designs do all that, but they also help keep heat in, protect you from the winter cold, reduce glare and condensation, and keep your furnishings from fading. They make you more comfortable in both summer and winter while imparting elements of style into your room decor.

Windows qualifying for an Energy Star rating meet or exceed the highest government standards for quality and energy efficiency. Their construction is tailored to four primary climate zones in the U.S. To help you make a purchase specific to your area, visit www.energystar.gov/index.cfm?c=windows_doors.pr_crit_windows.

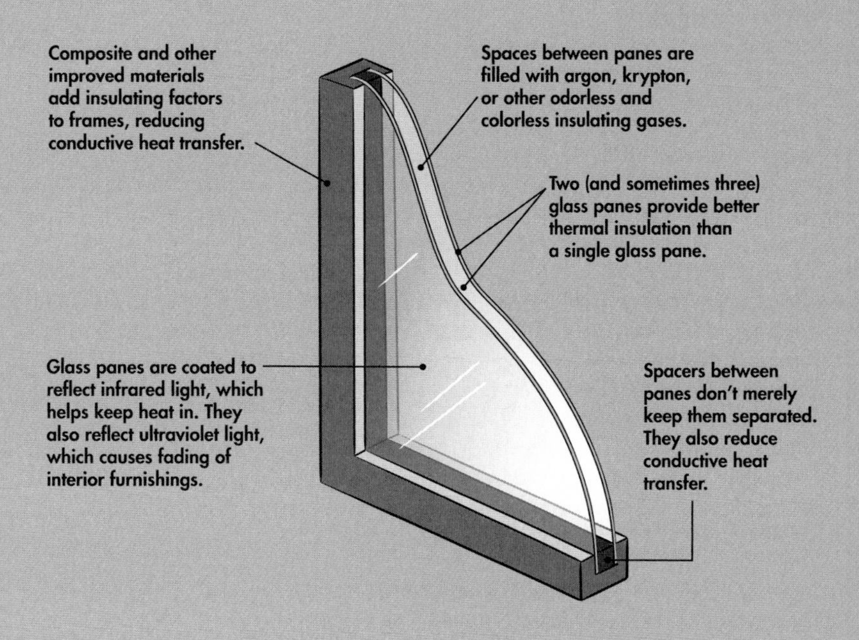

Improving home energy efficiency (continued)

Replacing an old dishwasher with an energy-efficient model can save you more than $40 a year in reduced energy costs. Look for the Energy Guide sticker on models you're considering and buy the one with the highest rating, preferably one that has merited an Energy Star rating.

If the walls of your home are not insulated, have them filled with blown-in cellulose. Cellulose can have a slightly higher R-value than fiberglass, and studies have shown it can be 20 to 40 percent more effective than fiberglass because cellulose stops air infiltration and convective air currents in the walls.

BUYER'S GUIDE

ENERGY STAR RATINGS

Energy Star ratings are granted to appliances and materials whose high-efficiency performance has met or exceeded stringent government standards for energy consumption and savings to consumers.

Although Energy Guide labels are placed on appliances to indicate the levels of effective power consumption, an "Energy Star" rating designates such an appliance as superior. This designation indicates that the consumer can save as much as 30 percent on energy costs associated with its use, or roughly $600 of the $1,900 the average consumer spends on energy costs each year. The rating also assumes that these savings occur without the loss of features, style, or comfort.

Energy Star ratings are applied to major appliances (except clothes dryers), office equipment, lighting, and home electronics.

Smart heating and cooling

In most homes the costs of heating and cooling can account for as much as half of your monthly power bill. Taking care of problems in your HVAC system can make a major impact on your finances and comfort. Here's where to start:

- Clean or replace your furnace filter monthly or at least as frequently as the manufacturer recommends. A dirty filter impedes airflow, makes the blower motor work harder, shortening its life, and causes the burners to stay lit longer. A clean filter reduces ambient dust in your home, making it a healthier place to live.
- Call in the pros for scheduled maintenance. The blower system and heat exchanger should be cleaned at least yearly, making your system perform more efficiently.
- Set your thermostat at 68 degrees for heating and 78 degrees for cooling. Better yet install a programmable thermostat, which makes the settings for you. Each degree can save you 3 to 5 percent in energy costs.
- Seal the joints in your heat runs. That can increase the efficiency of your system by as much as 20 percent.
- Set your water temperature to 120°F (140°F with a dishwasher unless manufacturer's instructions indicate 120°F is OK).
- Consider replacing any major appliance over 10 years old (including the furnace and air-conditioning unit) with an Energy Star model.

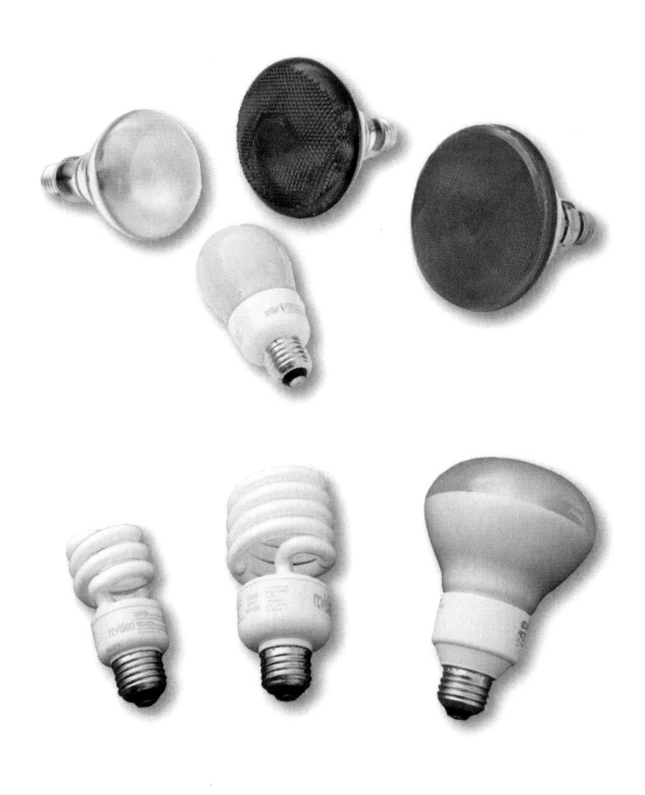

New fluorescent lightbulbs consume 75 percent less energy, produce less heat, and last 10 times longer than incandescent bulbs. They come in stylish, mood-setting colors too, and some newer models are dimmable.

A storm door decreases entry-door heat loss by about 50 percent. For directions on installation see "Installing a Storm Door," page 224.

Because motion sensors turn lights on only when you need them, they produce a dramatic savings over outdoor floods and spotlights left on continuously. Motion-detecting sockets are also available for indoor lightbulbs, turning them off when you leave the room.

Evaluating home energy efficiency

Skill level:	Time to complete:	Materials:	Tools:
★★★☆☆	Experienced 45 min. Handy 45 min. Novice 45 min.	None	Paper, incense sticks, thermometer

Leaks through small cracks around windows and doors are responsible for 30 to 40 percent of the heat that leaks out of your house. Before you tackle more extensive—and more expensive—insulating jobs, track down and fix these smaller problems. Companies will do this for you using infrared detectors and other sophisticated equipment. But although they may do a slightly more dramatic job, you'll be able to figure out on your own where the problems are.

Start outside by looking at places where two different materials meet: walls meeting windows, water spigots, pipes, or phone lines. These are the areas where leaks occur. Try slipping a sheet of paper between the two surfaces or look for light leaking through. Either indicates a space. Check for rattling—a window or door that rattles in its frame is loose, and loose equals leakage. Finally do what's called a depressurization test. Wait for a cool, windy day and close up the house as tightly as you can. Turn on any fans, such as bath or kitchen vents, that move air outdoors. Check for leaks with a smoking match or burning incense stick as described below.

Once you've checked 10 or 20 windows, it can be difficult to remember which of them needed to be fixed. Mark any leaks as soon as you find them, using a piece of red tape. It's guaranteed to nag you into fixing the problem.

Check for leaks around windows and doors on a cool, windy day. Close and lock all the windows and doors and turn off the furnace. To help encourage leaks turn on all the fans such as those in bathrooms or cooking hoods. Move a smoking incense stick around the doors and windows. If the smoke flutters you have a leak.

To locate the likely source of a leak, look at existing weatherstripping and caulking. Look for signs of deterioration such as crumbling foam or rubber, hardening of flexible products such as felt or foam rubber, or damaged or torn metal stripping. Replace the products as needed. Most weatherstripping products will last only a few years, so expect this to be a seasonal chore. When caulking, instead of filling the gap apply the caulk so it spans the gap and grabs onto the adjoining surfaces.

An infrared photo of your house is an invaluable tool for identifying heat loss from your home. Cool colors (shades of blue) indicate a cool exterior and no or little heat loss. Hot colors (red, orange, and yellow) indicate heat loss and areas that need attention. Generally, you'll see most hot colors around doors and windows, meaning that you need to caulk edges and/or replace the windows with energy-efficient models.

Look for condensation, frost, or ice buildup on the inside surfaces of interior window sashes. Such conditions indicate that you need storm windows or that air is leaking around the ones you have. Also check for condensation, frost, or ice buildup on storm windows. This indicates that warm, moist air is escaping and the seal between the interior window and the storm window needs attention.

Measure the temperature in different parts of a room. Differences of more than 1 or 2 degrees indicate the room is poorly sealed or that air movement inside the house is poor. Update weatherstripping around doors and windows, then measure temperatures again. If the differences still exist, you may have an airflow problem with your heating system. Often your public utility company will provide information about airflow problems and how to correct them.

Although you can conduct an air leakage test yourself, you'll get a much more complete analysis of air infiltration from a specialist using a blower door. The door seals an entrance to the house and draws out air with a powerful fan. The reduced air pressure inside the home brings air inside through leaks around areas such as windows and doors.

Weatherproofing your home

Skill level:	Time to complete:	Materials:	Tools:
★★★☆☆	Experienced 25 min. Handy 45 min. Novice 1 hr.	Silicone caulk, expandable insulating foam, weatherstripping, wood filler, foam gaskets, plastic sheeting	caulking gun, utility knive, screwdriver, hammer, putty knives, chisel, tin snips, pry bar, plane, handsaw, tape measure, squeegee, wood chisel, handsaw

Weatherproofing is the process of fixing unwanted leaks. Although your doors and windows are designed to keep the cold out and the heat in, they cannot be airtight. To open and close they need room to move—small gaps around the edges though which air quite easily seeps. In an average house these cracks account for as much air as you'd lose through a 2-foot-diameter hole. Given the low cost of weatherstripping and the ease of installation, you'll get a quick return on your investment. Of the many types available, the metal, foam-filled vinyl tubes, plastic V, and closed-cell vinyl foam have been the most effective and easiest to install. Metal is the most durable, lasting 10 to 20 years. Plastic V weatherstripping lasts 2 to 10 years. Foam-filled vinyl has a life expectancy of 5 to 10 years.

Caulk around the dryer vent, windows, exhaust fan vents, and any other fittings mounted to the sides of your house. Fill any cracks larger than ½ inch with expandable foam or foam backer rods before caulking.

Insulate around spigots, television cable jacks, telephone lines, and other entry points to your house with expandable insulating foam. Trim off the excess with a utility knife but avoid cutting into wires when trimming around electrical lines.

WORK SMART
MINIMIZE HEAT LOSS

Saving money on energy consumption doesn't have to cost you a fortune. This quick list of low- or no-cost solutions will cut your energy costs.

- Caulk windows and doors. Seal all openings to the outside on exterior walls.
- Replace your incandescent lightbulbs with low-wattage compact fluorescents. They emit less heat and consume less power.
- Fix drips. A dripping faucet can waste more than 200 gallons of water a month. That raises your water bill and your energy costs if it's the hot water tap that's dripping.
- Keep the sun out—install awnings or sunscreens on south- or west-facing windows. Motorized awnings can be switched with a timer that takes care of extending and retracting them on schedule.

Clear window-well covers let light in and keep the heat in your basement too. Measure the width and length of the window well and pick up a cover from your home center. Slide the flange under the siding and fasten it with wood screws or into block walls with screws and masonry anchors. Caulk around the edges to make your installation tight.

Even if the window is well-sealed, air can leak around and through an air-conditioner. Install foam air-conditioner weatherstripping around the edges of the air-conditioner and add a vinyl fabric cover over the outside of the air-conditioner at the first sign of cold weather.

A surprising amount of cold air seeps in around outlets and switches. Seal the leaks by slipping an inexpensive foam gasket between the faceplate and the electrical connection.

Seal between baseboards and floorboards. Remove the base molding and spray in expandable insulating foam. This not only prevents drafts but also helps stop insects from entering your living areas. A little foam goes a long way—it will expand too much if you overuse it.

Interior plastic sheeting is a clear shrink-wrap product that is also available in kits. It's even easier to install than polyethylene. Tape the plastic to the inside of the window with double-stick tape, then warm it with a hair dryer to remove the wrinkles. Once installed it's virtually invisible and easy to remove.

Weatherproofing your home (continued)

Which weatherstripping to use?

Sealing drafty windows and doors with weatherstripping can save you $10 or more per window each year in energy costs, plus eliminate uncomfortable drafts. But before you embark on a weatherstripping crusade, fix the major things first. Replace broken windowpanes, remove and replace worn glazing, and install or fix the window lock so it seals the frame tight. Then seal the gap around the window frame with caulk. Now you're ready.

If you've never purchased weatherstripping you may be in for a surprise when you visit your home center. Manufacturers turn out an amazing variety of styles and materials, many of which do the same job. (Some of course do them better and last longer.) Take measurements of your doors and windows with you and study the way the doors and windows close to make sure you're getting the style that will fit your installation. Read the package instructions carefully before you make your purchase.

Spring strips. Spring strips come in V-shape and S-shape configurations and are made to mount in the frame where the door closes or the window slides. They're reasonably priced and moderately effective in stopping drafts around the perimeters. Some styles fasten with small nails. Others rely on self-stick adhesives. The nail-on styles will last longer.

Foam strips. Adhesive-backed foam strips are your lowest-cost alternative. They're also the least durable. To install them you peel back a protective plastic film and press them into place. They have a habit of "worming," or rising up off the surface as you press them down, so take your time. Get these only if you can't afford something better.

Magnetic. Magnetic weatherstripping is an excellent but expensive option for steel doors and windows. One side fits into a kerf in the frame, and the other attaches to the door or window. When you close the door or window the magnetic strip creates a tight seal. This weatherstripping is not made for double-hung windows.

Vinyl bulbs. Vinyl bulbs encased in a metal or plastic nail-on track compress slightly on the edge of a door or window to seal out drafts. They're made in a flexible and rigid form, cost about the same as spring strips, and flexible and rigid styles seal doors better than windows. The rigid styles are more durable. Most manufacturers market them in different colors to make their appearance minimally obtrusive.

Door sweeps. Sweeps create a weatherproof seal at the bottom of a door by compressing a felt composition or vinyl material against the threshold when you close the door. They're not made for windows. You can adjust the height of the seal to compensate for uneven gaps created by sagging or improperly planed doors.

Door shoes. A door shoe consists of a vinyl bulb fit into a track attached to the bottom of the door. The bulb compresses against the threshold when you close the door, creating a very effective seal. These models are moderately expensive and very durable but require you to remove the door and possibly plane it to accommodate the track and bulb.

Bulb thresholds. A bulb threshold employs a compressible vinyl bulb in a track in an aluminum threshold. They are expensive but very effective and long-lasting solutions to blocking drafts at the bottom of the door. Installing them will require removing your threshold and possibly replaning the bottom of the door.

Interlocking thresholds. An interlocking threshold is a two-piece solution to blocking drafts at the bottom of the door. One piece fastens to the bottom of the door, and its flanges lock into recesses in the threshold that accompanies it. Installing this model will require removal of your threshold and possibly replaning the bottom of the door.

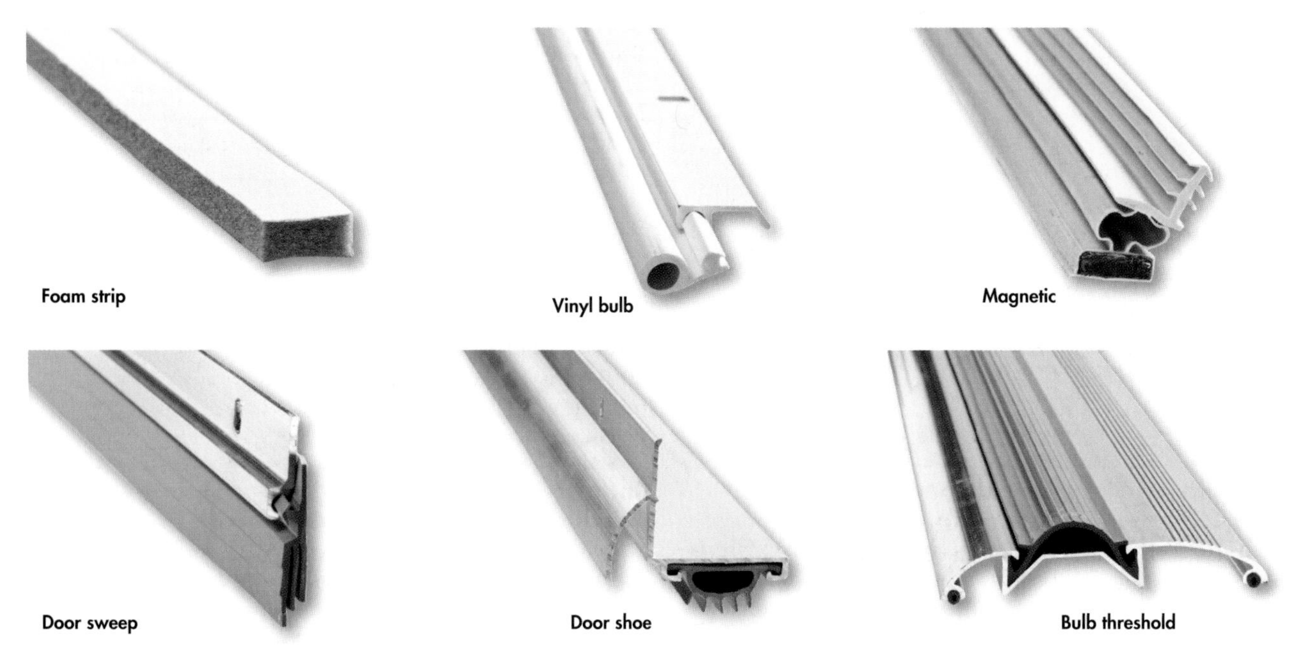
Foam strip

Vinyl bulb

Magnetic

Door sweep

Door shoe

Bulb threshold

Caulks and foams

When sealing up your home against drafts, use the simplest methods first. Caulks and foam sealants are two of them. But beware of buying just any old product. There's no "one-size-fits-all" caulk or sealant. Most are designed for specific purposes, and if you don't match the product to the problem you're wasting time and money.

Caulks and sealants require some preparation before you apply them. Surfaces must be dust free and dry for most caulks. Brush out the gap or blow it out (with canned compressed air). Be especially mindful of the corners. Most caulks will fill gaps up to about ⅜ inch wide and ½ inch deep. If you're faced with a deeper crack, fill it with foam backer rod. If the gap is too wide, use an expanding foam. Read the directions on the container before you start. You'll find information important to your installation—working temperatures, shrinkage rates, coverage, and paintability. Cut the tube at a 45-degree angle with a utility knife, puncture the seal with a nail or the pin attached to the caulking gun, and insert the tube into the gun. Make sure you apply enough caulk to the joint to fill it. Here's a list of common materials and some of their characteristics.

Oil-base painter's caulk is the least expensive, has a short lifespan of not more than 3 years, is minimally elastic (it will pull away in cold weather), and is paintable when cured.

Latex caulk is designed primarily for indoor use, doesn't cost much, and sticks only to porous surfaces. It goes on and cleans up easily, is not very elastic, but can last up to 10 years.

Butyl-rubber caulk has a 3- to 10-year lifespan and is very elastic and highly water resistant. It sticks to most surfaces, but that same property also makes it very difficult to work with.

Silicone caulk can last up to 50 years but has a few limitations. Some brands are not paintable, but others come in an array of colors. You'll need solvent to clean it up. Though it will stick to most woods or metal (some requiring a primer), it won't adhere to concrete block and bricks.

Acrylic latex will last up to 10 years, sticks to most surfaces including those that are damp, and exhibits good resistance to moisture. It's paintable—a good product for caulking around windows and doors—and it cleans up with water.

Urethane caulks stick well to most surfaces, including masonry, but may require a primer on some surfaces and won't stick to damp places. It's very durable and doesn't shrink, is paintable, and comes in various colors. Very long lasting—from 20 to 50 years.

Elastomeric copolymers exhibit excellent elasticity and long lifespans, up to 50 years. You can apply them to damp surfaces, and they will stick to most materials. Clean up with lacquer thinner. They come with one characteristic not shared by other caulks—you can apply them in freezing weather.

Styrene-butadiene rubber (SBR) will stick to damp surfaces and treated lumber and comes in various colors. It works easily, but indoors its fumes will require plenty of ventilation. You can paint it with latex paints but you'll need paint thinner to clean it up.

Kraton-base caulk will stick to most anything, is paintable, and comes in colors. It shrinks to fit, so you won't need to tool it. You'll need mineral spirits to clean it up.

Foam sealants come in different formulations. Some urethane foams expand by as much as 200 percent. Others, chiefly latex products, expand hardly at all. Some foams are made specifically for gaps up to 1⁄2 inch and others for gaps wider than this. Although manufacturer's terms such as "low expanding" and "low pressure" don't necessarily have standardized meanings, you can get guidance on what to purchase by carefully reading the label. One of the chief problems is that a high-pressure foam applied around a window frame can bend the frame as it cures. In any case applying any expandable foam requires practice to see how much a given product expands when cured.

Weatherproofing your home (continued)

Weatherproofing an entry door

Adjust the door if it has fallen out of alignment. Reset and shim the hinges to even out the gaps around the door, making the door easier to weatherstrip. Adjust the strike plates and latches to keep doors snug in their frames.

Fasten vinyl bulb weatherstripping to the exterior jambs against the edges of the door. Cut them to length with tin snips and screw or tack them in place so they are snug against the door.

With tin snips cut metal spring strips to fit in the door jamb. Tack the strips in place and open them slightly to create a tight seal. If using vinyl Vs cut them with scissors and fold them lengthwise along the seam. Remove the adhesive backing and stick the weatherstripping in place.

Fix any cracks in door panels with wood filler or caulk. Match the color of the finished door with a tinted wood filler.

Option A: Screw a bristle sweep to the bottom of the door. Sweeps help keep air from leaking under the door, and you can attach one without trimming the door. Sweeps also are available on rollers to compensate for an uneven floor.

Option B: Attach a new door bottom with an integral sweep on the inside and a drip edge on the outside. This may require you to adjust your threshold height or plane the bottom of the door slightly. If you plane the door, seal the wood by painting it before you attach the sweep.

Weatherproofing an entryway threshold

1 Older thresholds lack the built-in weatherstripping of newer doors. To replace an old threshold, protect the floor, cut through the threshold with a handsaw, then pry out the pieces. Clean out the area beneath it.

2 Measure the opening for the new threshold and cut it to fit. Make sure the threshold will slope away from the house when installed, shimming it if necessary. Lay a bead of caulk along the bottom of the threshold, then screw it in place through the area that will be underneath the gasket.

3 Cut and install the gasket. Test to see how the door closes over the new threshold. If the fit is too tight, cut or plane the door as necessary.

Weatherproofing other door types

Seal the jamb channels with closed-cell vinyl foam (not to be confused with foam rubber, which is less effective). If the door doesn't have thermal glass, buy clear plastic sheeting made to fit over the inside of windows and use a hair dryer to shrink it until tight.

Attach a new rubber gasket to the bottom of a garage door if the old one has deteriorated. Weatherstripping for the top and sides of the door is sold separately.

Adjust door-closer tension to close the door securely. The tension on most closers is adjustable so you can set the door to close without slamming. Most closers also lock in place to hold doors open when necessary.

Weatherproofing your home (continued)

Weatherproofing windows

1 Cut vinyl V-strips to fit in the sash channels. Using a scissors cut them long enough to extend at least 1 inch beyond the sash ends when the window is closed.

2 Remove the adhesive backing and stick the vinyl in place. Pull just the end of the protective backing away from the adhesive. Stick the end into the channel and pull the remainder of the backing away as you work your way down the window.

3 Wipe down the underside of the bottom sash with a damp rag and wait for it to dry. Then attach self-adhesive closed-cell vinyl foam to the edges of the underside. The temperature must be at least 50°F (10°C) for self-adhesive strips to stick.

Check the weep hole

The weep hole at the bottom of the window lets moisture out so it doesn't condense on the window. Check to see that the hole isn't plugged. If it is, clean it out with a small nail. If there is no weep hole, create one by poking a nail through the caulk at the bottom of the window.

Installing window film

1 Clean the outside and inside of the windowpane, removing any paint or stubborn debris with a razor blade. Anything left on the surface will cause the film to bubble. Respray the window and wipe it down with a squeegee, making sure to clean the corners out. Let the window dry. Measure the dimensions of the windowpane and unroll the film on a clean, dry, flat surface. Cut the film an inch larger than the pane in both dimensions (You'll trim the excess later.)

2 Spray the window with the manufacturer's wetting solution. Do not let any areas become dry. Position the cut film on the pane with the adhesive side to the glass. Line up a factory edge along the inside edge of the sash and smooth the film toward the opposite side with your hands. This will leave excess on the remaining three sides.

3 Spray the entire surface of the film with the manufacturer's wetting solution. Then following the manufacturer's instructions, lightly squeegee the center of the film from top to bottom. That will keep it anchored while you smooth the remaining film. Smooth out the remaining sections of the film as the instructions specify, leaving a 2" unsmoothed perimeter around the edges. To remove large air pockets rewet the film and squeegee it to the nearest edge.

4 Using a sharp utility knife and edging tool (a credit card will do if no tool is supplied), trim the film, leaving a $\frac{1}{16}$-inch gap around the perimeter. The gap allows for expansion of the film and for complete removal of water and air from under the film. Rewet the film and re-squeegee it from center to the right side, then repeat on the left side. Make sure you move all air bubbles to the side and out from under the edges of the film.

Insulating an attic

Skill level:	Time to complete:	Materials:	Tools:
★★★☆☆	Experienced 5 hrs. Handy 8 hrs. Novice 10 hrs.	Baffles, insulation	Tape measure, staple gun, utility knife and extra blades, straightedge, particle-resistant dust mask, safety glasses, gloves

Older homes in particular can be poorly insulated and when they are, heat and heating bills go through the roof. Even homes in the mildest climates should have about 9 inches of fiberglass insulation. Homes in northern areas—Buffalo, Des Moines, and Duluth, for example—should have more than 12 inches of fiberglass, according to the United States Department of Energy.

Insulating an attic is relatively easy if it has no floor: Simply roll the insulation between the joists. If your attic has a floor, you may want to blow in loose-fill insulation or remove the floor and replace it after insulating. Loose-fill comes as either fiberglass or cellulose. The manufacturers of each type trumpet the advantages of their products, but the tune goes like this: Cellulose provides more insulation than fiberglass. Fiberglass however is less prone to settling, which reduces the efficiency of the insulation over time. Cellulose turns into a gooey mess when wet; wet fiberglass temporarily loses its insulating ability but recovers when dry. Although research supports the contention that fiberglass is not a carcinogen, if you're concerned about potential health hazards you might be more comfortable using cellulose.

The amount of insulation you need may determine which kind you get. Find your location on the map on page 501 to determine which zone you're in. The chart tells you the R-value your insulation should have. The R-value is printed on insulation packages—the higher the R-value, the greater the insulation.

When warm, moist air hits cold, outdoor air, water vapor condenses and collects in the wall or ceiling, where it causes all sorts of problems. Because of this, roll or batt insulation comes with a facing that acts as a vapor barrier. In most parts of the country, install the facing toward the occupied part of the house. In some areas of the South, however, install the barrier facing the home's exterior. Check local codes. Two vapor barriers are actually worse than one, as condensation can be trapped between the two, so if you're adding insulation on top of insulation that already has a barrier, use insulation without a facing.

Insulating with fiberglass

1 Inspect your existing insulation by measuring its depth. Measure the distance between the joists so you can buy insulation that is the right width—standard widths are 15 or 23 inches for 16- or 24-inch stud spacing.

2 Adequate insulation requires proper venting, which is usually supplied by vents in the soffit. Blocking vents allows moist air to collect in the attic, causing wood rot and mildew. To avoid this install rigid plastic foam vents, called baffles or rafter vents. Put one end over the soffit vent and staple the baffle in place.

3 Measure and cut to length the pieces of insulation you'll need. Work in a well-ventilated area to minimize the amount of fiberglass dust raised. Cut the insulation with a sharp utility knife guided by a straightedge. Have a solid work surface beneath the insulation and apply lots of pressure.

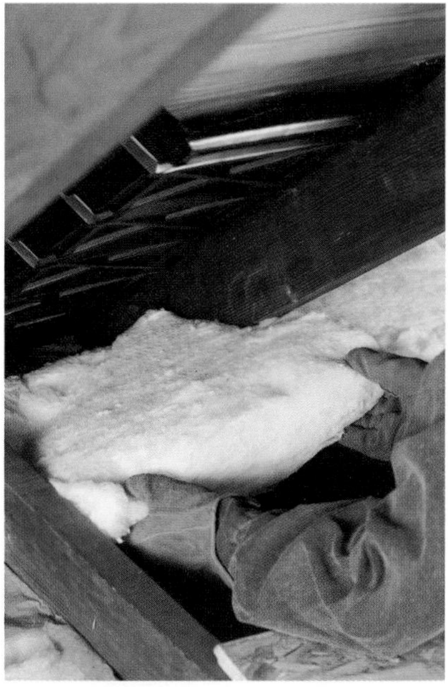

4 Once the baffles are in, block off each vent to prevent it from filling with insulation and causing moisture problems. Cut sections of fiberglass insulation and stuff them between the joists directly in front of the soffit.

5 Roll out the insulation between the joists, starting at an exterior wall and working toward the entry to the attic. If working in an uninsulated attic, get insulation with a vapor barrier and install the barrier face down. (See "Vapor Barrier Savvy," page 516.) If you're applying insulation over existing insulation, get insulation without a facing.

6 For non-insulation-contact electrical fixtures, the national electrical code requires a 3-inch gap between insulation and the fixture. Check to see whether your local code is stricter. Nail wooden barriers around the light to keep the insulation away from it, then cut the insulation to fit. As an alternative install fixtures rated for insulation contact (IC) as shown in the inset (above).

When working with loose-fill insulation, pour and spread it by hand, especially near electrical fixtures. The same electrical codes that apply to batt insulation apply to loose-fill—a separation of at least 3 inches from a non-insulation-contact fixture or the installation of a fixture rated "IC"—insulation contact.

Insulating basements

Skill level:	Time to complete:	Materials:	Tools:
★★★☆☆	Experienced 2 hrs. Handy 2.5 hrs. Novice 3 hrs.	Fiberglass insulation, 1×3 furring strips, construction adhesive, 6-mil poly, insulation stays or chicken wire, rigid insulation, tape, 3d nails, drywall, 1-inch drywall screws, water-heater blanket, pipe foam tubes	Particle-resistant dust mask, utility knife, caulking gun, hammer, circular saw, straightedge, drill and screwdriver bits, level

Because they house heating and cooling equipment, basements are prime targets for improved insulation. Even if you're not going to remodel the area into a usable living space, there are places in basements where a little additional insulation will go a long way toward reducing your heating and cooling costs.

For example an insulated basement makes the space more comfortable and helps keep upper floors warmer too. Rigid foam is available in urethane and polystyrene (plastic foam) in thicknesses from ½ inch to 2 inches. Urethane is more expensive but is easier to work with and is the better insulator. Both are flammable and must be covered by ½-inch drywall. If you don't want to install rigid foam insulation you can build a regular 2×4 stud wall and insulate it with fiberglass between the studs. Follow the same procedures shown here. Just change the orientation and size of the materials.

Water heaters and heat ducts are often overlooked when it comes to taking an energy inventory, but insulating both will make fewer demands on your hot water and room heating and cooling power, allowing you to lower the thermostats on both.

Insulating walls

1 Option A: If the wall will run perpendicular to the ceiling joists, fasten a 2×2 top plate along the entire length of the joists. Mark the location of the vertical strips on the top plate, centering them at 16-inch intervals. Use treated screws to fasten the top plate to the joists.

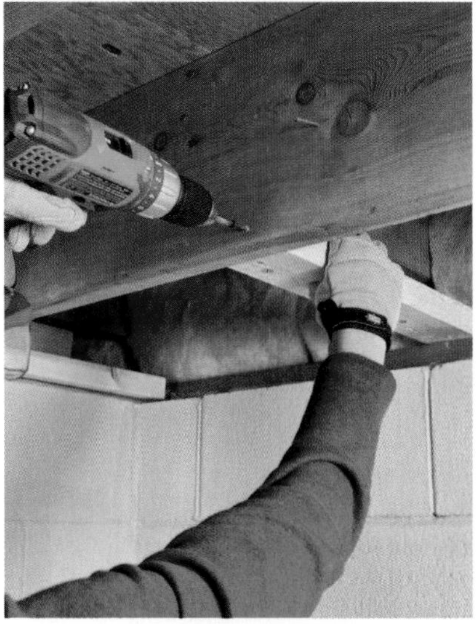

Option B: If the wall will run parallel to the ceiling joists, make footed cleats from 2×4 and 2×2 stock and install them between the joists and the sill plates as shown above. The cleats will give you a nailing surface for your finished ceiling material.

2 Install a 2×2 bottom plate along the entire length of the wall, first applying construction adhesive to its rear and bottom faces then using masonry screws to fasten it. From each stud location mark you made on the top plate, drop a plumb bob to the bottom plate and mark the stud location there also.

3 Cut the vertical furring strips to fit between the top and bottom plates, measuring and cutting each one separately to account for any variations in the floor. Apply construction adhesive to the rear face of the strips, set them on the marks you made on the top and bottom plates, and fasten them with masonry screws. Drive the screws into the webs—the solid parts of the blocks, not the hollows—whenever possible.

4 Option A: Using the same procedures continue to measure, cut, and install the vertical strips one at a time, using construction adhesive and masonry screws.

Option B: Wherever the wall will need to house an electrical run, cut the furring strips to leave a 2-inch gap for the conduit or NM cable, whichever local codes require.

5 Before you cut the rigid foam panels to fit between the furring strips, tack protective plates to the furring strips over any wiring you have installed. Then cut the foam boards to fit, including cutouts for electrical boxes. Secure the foam panels with construction adhesive and add a vapor barrier if required by local codes.

Dealing with wet walls

Before you build a basement wall, you have to fix any moisture problems or your new wall will quickly rot and deteriorate. To remove lime and efflorescence wash the walls (and floor) with muriatic acid, diluted 50/50 in water. Paint the block walls with a high-quality oil-base basement paint. Attach a sheet of ordinary 4 mil polyethylene plastic to the wall, adhering it with spray adhesive. If the walls run wet you may need a drainage system and/or a sump pump. This requires breaking the floor along the wall for a drainage trench and sump pump. Be sure to leave a 1/4-inch gap at the bottom of the drywall to keep it from wicking up moisture from the floor.

Insulating basements (continued)

Insulating a crawlspace

1 Cut insulation to fit between the joists above the foundation walls. Pack the insulation just tightly enough to prevent it from falling out.

2 Install fiberglass insulation between floor joists over crawlspaces or unheated basements. Make sure the vapor barrier faces up and install insulation stays (shown here) or staple chicken wire to the joists to hold the insulation in place.

3 Cut pieces of insulation long enough to drape from the mudsill, down the wall, and a couple of feet onto the floor. Hold each piece in place by laying a 1×3 over it and tacking both to the mudsill. Drive the nails enough to anchor the insulation while compressing it only slightly. Lay a 6-mil vapor barrier on the dirt floor, anchoring it with a few bricks.

Insulating a water heater

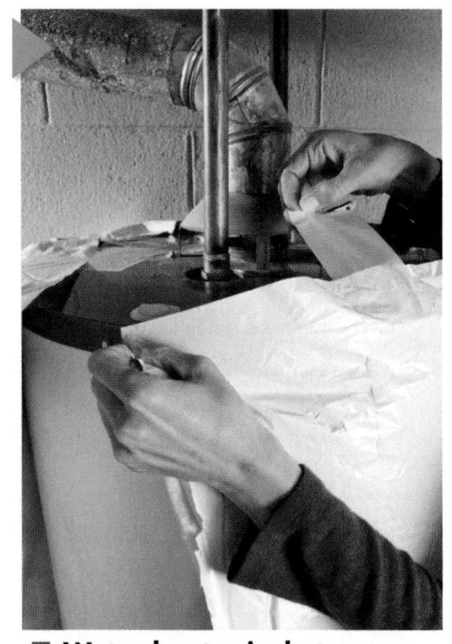

1 Water heater jackets come in kits at most home centers. If your kit doesn't include belts, use tape. Cut and slit the top to conform to the circumference of the heater. Cut circles for piping and tape the section to the top sides of the tank.

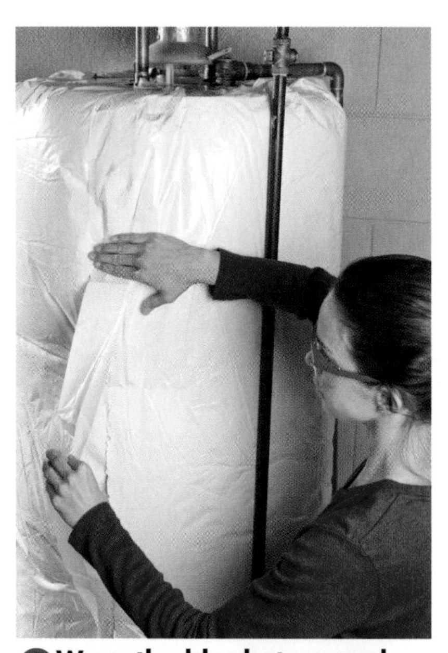

2 Wrap the blanket around the tank so the ends don't meet at the access door. Draw the belts around the blanket or tape the top and bottom circumferences of the blanket. Then tape the vertical edges of the blanket.

3 Locate the corners of the access panel and cut a small incision at each one. Cut out a rectangle between the incisions so you have access to the control panel and burner door.

Insulating heat runs and water pipes

Water pipes and heat runs carry their contents to needed parts of your home. But if not properly insulated, they also disperse heat into the surrounding areas, reducing the efficiency of your water heater and furnace or boiler. You can raise the temperature in a hot water pipe by insulating it. That will allow you to lower your water temperature in the heater and conserve energy. It will also reduce the waiting time for the hot water to reach the faucet. Use insulating sleeves for water pipes and fiberglass batts for heat runs.

Heat runs

1 To insulate your heat ducts, seal off all the junctures or joints in the system. Sealing keeps the air inside the duct and protects it from air loss and velocity. You can apply a mastic made for this purpose or use tape rated for it. Do not use duct tape. It will quickly degrade.

2 Wrap insulating jackets (fiberglass batts, foil-faced if available) around the duct with the fiberglass facing the duct. Butt the edges of the jackets together and seal them with foil tape. As an alternative staple the edges or use reflective insulation. This material achieves a greater R-value with less bulk and is not prone to deterioration from condensation or water vapor.

Water pipes

Use polyethylene or neoprene foam tubes with diameters that match the pipe. Cut the tube to length, open it at its split side, and slide it onto the pipe. Pull off the protective adhesive cover and pinch the edges of the tube together gently to seal the adhesive.

Specifications for insulating water pipes

Insulate all the pipe you find accessible, especially within 3 feet of the water heater. You should also insulate the cold water pipes within 3 feet of the water heater. In hard-to-get-at spots try starting the tube at an accessible end and pushing it down the length of the pipe. Within 8 inches of a flue use fiberglass wrap and fasten it with wire or aluminum tape.

If your closed-cell pipe insulation doesn't come with a self-adhesive strip, duct tape the seam at periodic intervals.

CHAPTER 10

Maintaining Exteriors

Maintaining the exterior of your home is equally as important as keeping the interior systems in prime working order. After all the exterior shell protects your family and your most valuable possessions. Whether you're repairing the siding, the gutters, or the roof, you need to apply the same pride and determination that goes along with improving and maintaining the interior.

As you make decisions about an exterior project, whether it's fixing the gutters, repairing siding, or redoing your roof, it's important that you evaluate yourself carefully in terms of what you feel confident about accomplishing.

Take into consideration that working outside is harder and potentially more dangerous than working inside. In some cases you'll be working on ladders or scaffolding, and no safety shortcuts are allowed. Nothing is wrong with hiring a pro to do work you're not comfortable doing. And if that's the route you choose, by studying these pages you'll be far more qualified to get the job done right.

That being said the skills required to do a lot of exterior work are, for the most part, basic and within the grasp of most handy homeowners. If you take your time, plan well, and get advice and professional help as necessary, you can have the satisfaction of a job well done. You'll save money that otherwise would go toward paying a contractor's labor bills, plus you'll have control of the job from beginning to end.

Contents

Exterior maintenance materials . . . 524
The exterior maintenance tool kit . . . 525
Preventing water infiltration . . . 526
Preventing ice dams . . . 526
Working safely . . . 528
Repairing gutters . . . 530
Cleaning gutters . . . 533
Installing a vinyl gutter system . . . 534
Repairing siding and trim . . . 536
Repairing wood siding . . . 538
Repairing vinyl and metal siding . . . 542
Repairing masonry walls . . . 544
Repairing fascia and soffits . . . 548
Roofing basics . . . 552
The roofer's tool kit . . . 555
Inspecting a roof . . . 556
Checking for leaks . . . 557
Repairing roofs . . . 558
Roof tear-off and repair . . . 562
Installing underlayment . . . 564
Installing flashing . . . 566
Installing asphalt shingles . . . 570
Reroofing over an existing roof . . . 575
Installing roll roofing . . . 576
Repairing walks, drives, and steps . . . 578

Working outside

The scale of exterior jobs requires careful planning and even more careful execution. Do your research and estimate materials carefully. Understand the project thoroughly before you start and make sure all the tools and materials are in place when you begin. Big exterior projects are almost always easier with some extra hands. If you can't round up volunteers, consider hiring day labor to help out as necessary.

- Addressing safety issues goes along with working on scaffolding, roofs, and ladders. Know how to set up and use ladders and scaffolding properly. Work safely in the air; if you get tired stop. Rent a safety harness and wear protective gear as necessary. Always have someone else at the worksite when you're working high above ground. If you're at all uncomfortable with heights, hire a pro.

- The weather is always a factor. Although you can't predict what's coming with 100 percent accuracy, it's common sense to consider it. Unexpected rain can delay completion and damage projects in progress. Several days of blistering heat can be dangerous to your health, too, especially if you're working on a roof. Work early in the morning and late in the afternoon if possible. Always drink plenty of liquids and protect yourself from the sun as much as possible.

- You're often dealing with heavy materials and sometimes unfamiliar tools. Stretch your legs and back on a break. Read the instructions and practice with tools you're not familiar with before you climb ladders or scaffolding. Nail guns and air compressors, for instance, are real timesavers but they take some getting used to. If you're renting tools the clerk can show you the ropes.

- You're dealing with disposal of substantial quantities of materials. Rent a large trash receptacle for removing old shingles or siding. A messy worksite invites accidents, and there's no point in ruining your lawn to make the roof pretty and leakproof.

Exterior maintenance materials

Every hour of every day, paint is peeling, shingles are curling, gutters are sagging, and decks are rotting all over America. It's called entropy—the natural tendency of things to break down over time—and it's hard at work on the exterior of your house.

When entropy visits its effects are right there for all to see. Without regular maintenance your house will quickly begin to deteriorate and soon take on a shabby appearance.

Although the demands of exterior maintenance are persistent, the skills required are basic. When the exterior of your house is well-maintained, it's safe, it functions properly, and it's right out there for everyone to see and admire.

► ***Fasteners you'll use for exterior maintenance include*** *nails, screws, and construction adhesive. Premix stucco and a caulklike stucco patch for cracks simplify stucco repairs.*

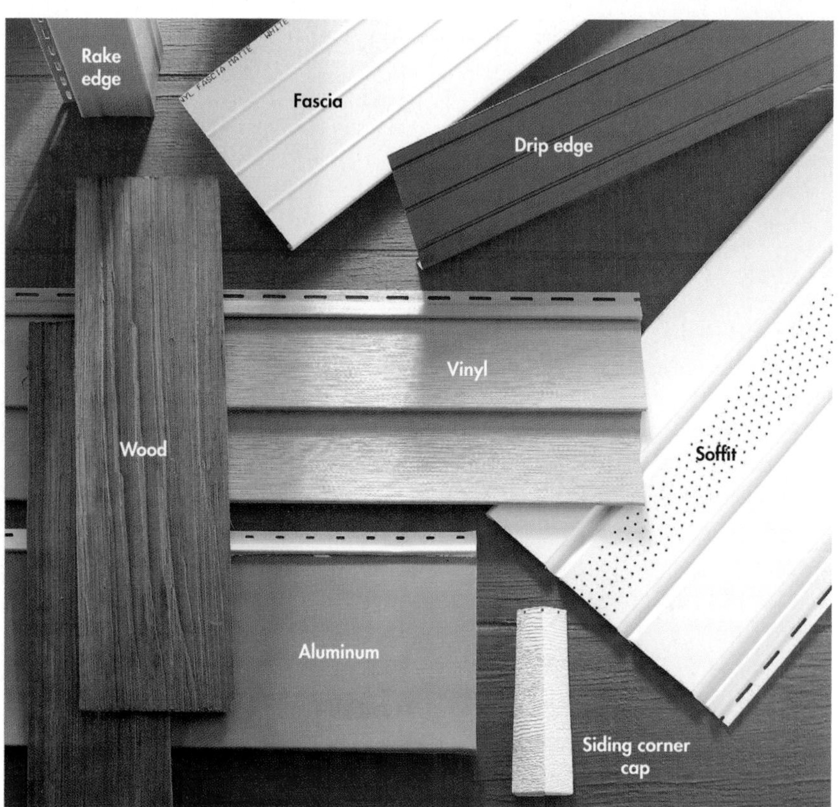

◄ ***Siding comes in a lot of materials, shapes, and sizes,*** *including wood, vinyl, and aluminum. All the options mean you may have more choices than you might think when you're considering updating your exterior. Soffits, fascia, and siding corner caps made of plastic or aluminum minimize painting. If you have structural problems under the eaves or behind the siding, however, you'll have to fix them before you do minor repairs or apply new materials. Also pictured are edging for roofing: rake edge and drip edge.*

The exterior maintenance tool kit

Hang on to the extras

Store leftover gutters, roofing, hardware, and other materials in a safe place. Being prepared to replace or repair items by having materials on hand will save you a trip to the store.

Make a maintenance routine

What most of us forget in the phrase "routine maintenance" is the word "routine." To keep that from happening, put the following tasks on a maintenance calendar. Spring and fall are good times for these tasks:

- Check your gutters, downspouts, and roof for leaks
- Fill cracks in the foundation and repair siding
- Wash house exterior
- Clean gaps between deck boards
- Clean air-conditioner compressor
- Trim any trees or vegetation touching the house
- Inspect and replace weatherstripping if needed
- Clean storm-window weep holes
- Inspect and repair window glazing compound
- Clean out window wells

TOOL TIP

RENTING SAFETY

Many tools make exterior home repair easier; many others make the work safer and the job go more smoothly.

If you're working from a ladder, rent one that will reach where you need to reach. Add ladder stabilizers for more stability and to distance the ladder from the gutter system, preventing damage to the gutters.

Ladder jacks, used with two or more extension ladders, allow you to work from a plank without having to use scaffolding. You can use wood or aluminum planks with ladder jacks.

Big projects may require the use of scaffolding. This takes a little longer to set up but makes a much more secure and stable platform. You may want to use aluminum planking to provide a work platform that is less bouncy than conventional wood planks.

If you're working just a few feet off the ground, a standard ladder is fine. Use a fiberglass or wood ladder if working around power lines or performing electrical repairs.

Preventing water infiltration

Proper grading will help keep water away from the foundation and out of the basement. If water is building up in the basement, haul in dirt and slope the ground around the foundation away from the house. If the basement still collects water, talk to a contractor about interior or exterior foundation drains.

Improperly maintained gutters will fail to direct water where you want it to go. Backups and clogs in gutters may cause roof leaks. Water on the ground below the gutters can seep into the basement or damage paint and wood below.

Downspout extensions direct gutter water away from the foundation and help to dissipate runoff along the grade.

Preventing ice dams

Icicles may make picturesque additions to the winter adornment of your home, but if they originate in an ice dam on your roof they're also causing hidden damage. The ice on the bottom of the snow layer melts from the interior heat of the house and works under the roof shingles. When it freezes it opens up the space under the shingles, where it then melts again and leaks through the roof sheathing. You may notice it first when rust spots appear on the nailheads in the ceiling drywall. Damp spots or peeling paint around windows and doors is also a sign of ice-dam damage.

Preventing the formation of ice dams means keeping the heat out of the attic so it doesn't warm the roof. You can accomplish this with the addition of insulation, proper soffit and roof ventilation, and by installing heat tapes along the edges of the roof.

Observe conditions on your roof after a snowfall. If the blanket of snow begins to develop holes from melting, the resulting downward flowing water freezes again, producing icicles. If a thicker layer of ice forms behind the icicles you have an ice dam, and it will continue working its way up the roof and under the shingles.

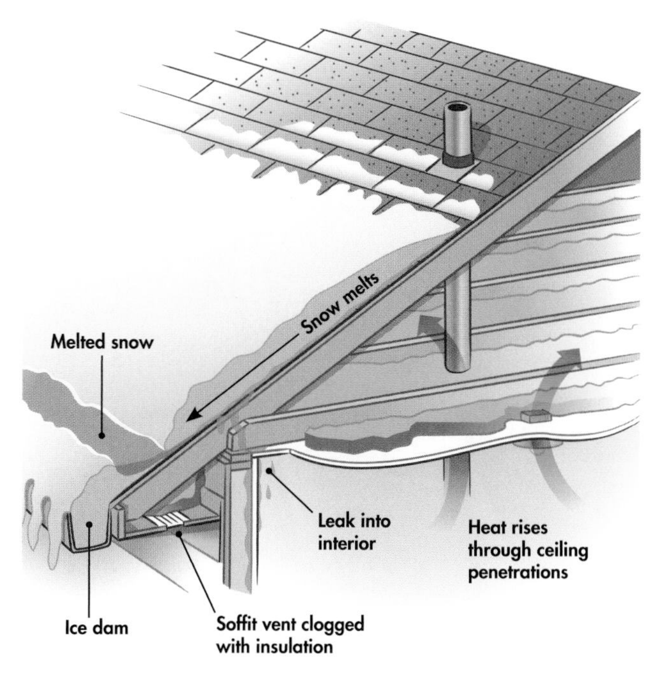

Ice dams form when heat rises from the interior of the house into the attic. The heat melts the ice on the roof, and the melt flows toward the eaves. Because the eaves are unheated by the interior warm air, the water refreezes. What starts as a small ice dam increases because the continuing melted water has no place to go—except to grow up the roof and into the shingles.

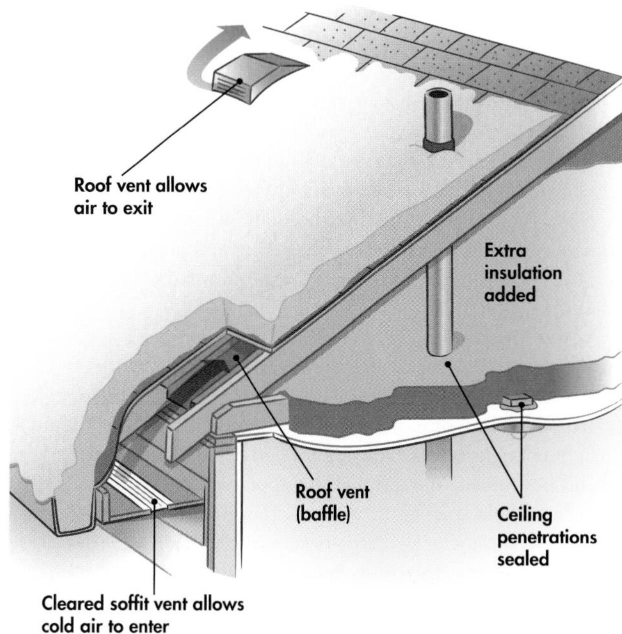

To control the formation of ice dams, insulate all roof penetrations to keep interior heat from expanding into the attic. Add extra insulation on the attic floor and make sure your soffits and roof are vented to allow cold air to enter the soffit vent and exit the roof vent. This maintains the roof at a temperature cold enough to keep the snow from melting.

Preventing ice-dam damage

In areas of the country with rough winters, roofers often install an ice-dam barrier. (This heavy-duty self-adhesive, waterproof sheet of underlayment prevents melting snow from getting under the shingles when it runs into ice at the bottom of the roof.) To be effective the ice dam barrier has to extend at least 24 inches up the outside of the roof, measuring from the interior attic wall. (The eaves must be covered but exclude them when you measure.) Measure up the roof from inside the attic to determine how many courses of ice-dam barrier to lay down.

Apply the ice-dam barrier along the bottom edge of the roof. Ideally the strip should run the length of the roof with no cuts. For longer runs cut the barrier into manageable lengths. Peel off about 2 feet of the backing on the underside to expose a contact adhesive. Put the sticky side face down on the roof, overhanging the drip edge by about 3/8 inch. Press the barrier onto the roof with your hands, nail across the top every 18 inches, and roll the edges with a hand roller. Work your way across the roof, peeling off the paper, pressing, nailing, and rolling as you go.

Overlap seams by 6 inches, nail every 6 or 8 inches, and roll the seam with the hand roller.

(The manufacturer may also recommend applying the barrier along the rake edges of the roof; if so follow the directions for installation.)

Electric heat tape. A low-cost, effective, but somewhat time-consuming solution is an electric heat tape installed on the roof and in the guttering. Run the power cord through a downspout to a GFCI outlet. Follow the manufacturer's instructions when fastening the tape.

See page 591

Working safely

Exterior repairs require an extra measure of safety precautions because the work is often far more dangerous than interior maintenance. The first rule of exterior safety is: Don't get into a rush. It's often difficult to gauge exactly how much time a task will take, and whatever your project entails, it's sure to take longer than your original estimate. So analyze the details and steps of a task carefully to stave off as many unforeseen difficulties as possible. Factor in weather conditions and dress for the day's climate and for safety. Boots, gloves, safety glasses, and work clothing are a must. Take frequent breaks in weather extremes and don't work alone.

Invest in a high-quality extension ladder, preferably made with an aluminum or fiberglass frame (fiberglass if you're working around electrical power lines). The ladder should be stiff enough not to bow, bend, or shake when your weight is on it but should be light enough to make moving it relatively easy. The locks should not impede the travel of the upper section as you raise it and they should snap on the rungs without requiring any extra maneuvering on your part to get them into place.

When you raise the ladder, adjust it so it extends about 3 feet above the edge of the roof. When you have to reach out from one side or the other, keep your hips within the rails. Overreaching can cause the ladder to lose its footing, risking a dangerous fall.

Equip your extension ladder with accessories that protect you and your home. An adjustable stabilizer will keep the edge of the ladder from denting gutters and keep your ladder from rocking or tipping to one side. Ladder boots (inset) will keep the tops of the ladder frame from gouging siding.

Once you get your ladder raised, adjust it to a safe angle and keep it there with stakes and blocking. Set the ladder on pieces of 2x stock to level it, then drive pointed 2×2 stakes at least a foot into the ground.

Tie your ladder to screw eyes driven into the fascia. Use a heavy-gauge nylon rope (it won't stretch) and cinch the ladder so it won't move. Stabilizing a ladder is an especially wise choice when you're carrying tools and heavy materials to the roof. When you're done remove the screw eyes and caulk the holes.

When your maintenance project keeps you in one area for a lengthy period, work on scaffolds. Scaffolding will save you time and physical wear and tear expended in climbing up and down a ladder and moving it back and forth. Set the scaffold on solid ground and level it with blocking and the adjustable legs.

Scaffolding will come from the rental outlet with steel plates that slip into the bottoms of the legs. Fasten these plates to wide 2× stock with duplex nails (they remove easily). Before erecting the upper sections, level the bottom sections by turning the adjustable leg collars. Tie the scaffold to the building whenever possible.

Use roof jacks

1 Nail two roof jacks on a steep roof after shingling the first four courses. Drive two 12d or 16d common nails into each jack and nail the jack firmly into a rafter. Nail into the section of a shingle that will be covered so the nail doesn't show and so the jack doesn't interfere with the nailing pattern. Run another set of jacks along the bottom of the roof to catch falling tools—or falling workers.

2 Shingle normally over the tops of the roof jacks, then insert a board across the two jacks to form a safe support for yourself and your tools. Continue your work at the new level.

3 Detach a roof jack by hitting the bottom of the jack toward the ridge and sliding it upward off the nails. Slip a pry bar under a shingle and use it to finish driving in the hidden nails left from the roof jack.

Repairing gutters

Skill level:	Time to complete:	Materials:	Tools:
★★★☆☆	Experienced 1 hr. Handy 1.5 hrs. Novice 2 hrs.	Gutter mesh cover, silicone gutter adhesive/caulk, sheet metal screws, rivets, rubber gaskets, plastic roofing cement	Pliers, wire brush, paintbrush, rivet gun, pry bar, hacksaw, hammer, putty knife, scissors, caulking gun, screwdriver

Gutters prevent the water that falls on your roof from collecting near your foundation. Houses without gutters usually have a distinct "drip line" where the water that has fallen from the roof edge has eroded the soil below. Where entrances or walkways pass under a roof edge, gutters prevent water from sheeting off the roof directly onto people below.

Because gutters are subject to some of the harshest natural elements—wind, water, ice, and sunlight—damage from corrosion and physical stress is almost inevitable. When that happens leaks and water damage can quickly follow.

Corrosion in a gutter system typically occurs from the inside out. If your gutters are beginning to leak as a result of corrosion, the prognosis is not good. Patching may provide a temporary solution, but now would be an excellent time to start shopping for a new gutter system.

Sometimes even when the gutter system is sound, the gutter supports have broken or pulled away from the house. If the gutters are sagging, water that would normally flow toward one of the downspouts will pool at the low spot and then spill over the side of the gutter.

If leaves are a problem, install plastic mesh gutter guards over the gutter. The mesh comes in a roll. Trim it to width if necessary and then slip it into the top of the gutter. Clean your gutters twice a year to avoid blockages.

Fixing sagging gutters

If your gutters are held in place with brackets, bend the brackets slightly with a pair of pliers to correct the sag. Pour a bucket of water into the gutter to check whether you've fixed the problem. If the water collects in a puddle, rebend and retest until it runs into the downspout.

If your gutters are held in place by spikes and ferrules, a loose spike is causing the sag. Find the spike and remove it. Replace it by running a 7-inch galvanized screw through the ferrule. (You can buy screws made specifically for the job, but any galvanized screw will do.)

BUYER'S GUIDE

EVALUATING GUTTERS

Since their invention gutters have been made of nearly everything—wood, copper, aluminum, vinyl, and galvanized steel.

Because of their cost wood and copper are seldom used today. Until recently most new gutters were aluminum. Enameled aluminum gutters are available in several colors and are lightweight and corrosion-resistant.

Vinyl gutters are becoming more popular because they are durable, available in several colors, and easy to install. Sections and fittings are precolored and come in standard sizes that basically snap together.

Galvanized-steel gutters are often the lowest priced of all systems and usually have an enameled finish. Unless they're painted frequently however, galvanized gutters have shorter lives than the alternatives.

Repairing leaky metal gutters

1 Patches won't stick to rusty or dirty metal. Clean the area around the leak with a wire brush and water. Once the area has dried, scrub it with an abrasive pad. Wash off all grit; let the gutter dry.

2 Patch small holes by applying plastic roofing cement over the hole. Feather the cement out onto the surrounding area and flatten out any steep edges created by the cement that would interfere with the water flow.

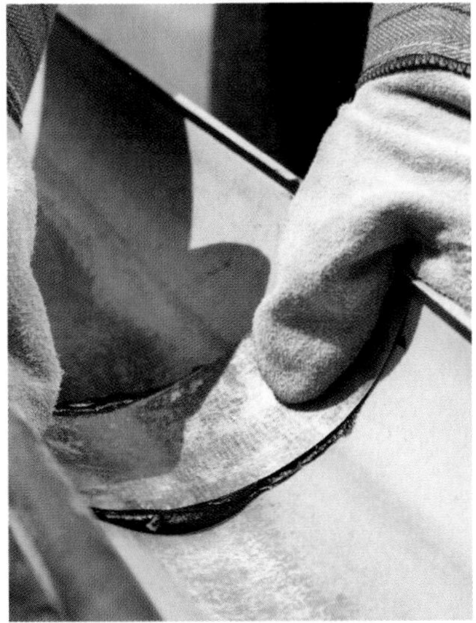

If the leaks are larger than nail holes, use tin snips to cut a strip of flashing. The flashing should be the same material as the gutter. If the gutter is made of galvanized steel, use galvanized steel; if aluminum use aluminum—mixing metals can cause corrosion. The flashing strip should be big enough to cover the hole and the area around it. Bend the strip to match the shape of the gutter and embed the flashing in the cement. Feather out the cement around the edges of the repair.

Repairing leaky joints

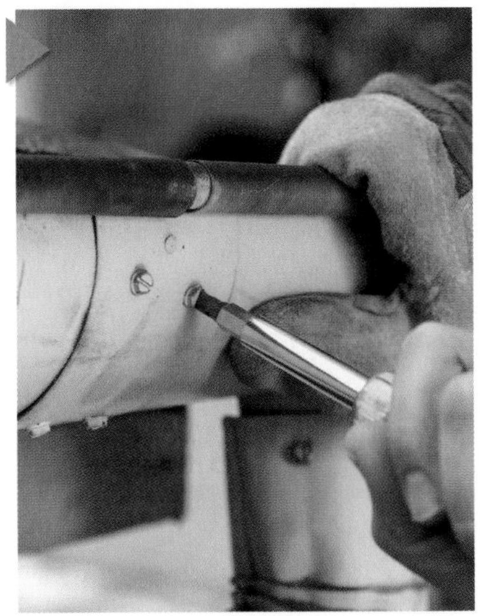

1 Pieces of metal downspout are screwed to each other and to the gutter. Remove the screws (or other connecting hardware) at the joint and disassemble it. You may need to remove other gutter or downspout sections near the leaky joint before inserting new sections.

2 Clean any caulk or adhesive from both parts of the joint using a stiff wire brush. Replace rubber gaskets on vinyl or PVC (polyvinyl chloride) gutters.

3 Apply silicone caulk to one of the parts that forms the joint. Then reassemble the gutter system by pressing the two parts together. Verify that the uphill section is always on top of the downhill section. Resecure fasteners or connectors.

Repairing gutters (continued)

Replacing a section of metal gutter

1 Remove the screws and connectors from the damaged area of the gutter. If you are prying out nails or spike-and-ferrule fasteners, temporarily put a piece of scrap wood across the opening to keep from crushing the gutter. Pull gently so you maintain your balance when the spike comes out.

2 Leave the scrap wood spacer in place to keep the gutter from bending. Cut out the damaged area by cutting through the gutter on each side of the damage.

3 Cut the replacement section of the gutter so it is 4 inches longer than the removed section.

4 Apply plastic roof cement or gutter repair compound on the 2 inches of gutter nearest the cuts. Set the new section in place so the uphill section of gutter is on top of the downhill section at each joint.

5 Drill pilot holes for rivets. Connect the two sections with rivets driven by a rivet gun.

6 Drill pilot holes for spike-and-ferrule fasteners through gutters, leaving the spacer blocks in place. Insert spikes into the front of the gutter, slip in the ferrules, and then drive the spikes into the fascia until the heads are flush with the gutter. Remove the spacers once you've hung the gutters.

Cleaning gutters

Skill level:	Time to complete:	Materials:	Tools:
★☆☆☆☆	Experienced 1 hr. Handy 1.5 hrs. Novice 2 hrs.	Gutter guards	Ladder, trowel, narrow broom, garden hose, 2-foot level

Cleaning gutters is a job that doesn't come with a lot of inspiration, but if done routinely it can keep you from having to make expensive and time-consuming repairs later. In fact when you consider that the majority of foundation water problems can often be traced to plugged gutters, it's easy to see why cleaning them is worthwhile.

Your gutters will generally tell you when they need cleaning. If you notice that no water is coming from the downspouts during a rain but is instead flowing over the front edge of the guttering, that's a sure sign. Leaves or other debris plastered to the house siding under the guttering is another, and debris extending visibly over the top of the gutters signals a system that needs immediate attention. Wear gloves and old clothes—gutter edges and sticks can cut your hands, and the job is generally a messy one. Always clean up debris on the ground before you flush the gutters with a hose. Otherwise you'll end up soaking the debris, making cleanup more difficult.

1 Use a trowel or similar tool to scoop out debris along the length of a section of guttering. Pull the debris up and out and let it fall to the ground. Dragging debris from a far end toward you with a narrow broom can help minimize the number of times you have to reposition the ladder.

2 Once you remove the majority of the debris, rake it into a bag. Then run water through the downspout. Spray out the inside of a gutter section and if leaks appear, fix them.

3 Lay a 2-foot level into the gutter and check to make sure the gutter slopes toward the downspout. Adjust any sections that slope improperly.

4 Install metal or plastic gutter guards to minimize further debris collection. Slide the top end of the guard under the shingles and slip the bottom edge into the recess in the top of the gutter.

Installing a vinyl gutter system

Skill level:	Time to complete:	Materials:	Tools:
★★★☆☆	Experienced 1.5 hrs. Handy 2 hrs. Novice 3 hrs.	End cap, hangers, gutter, connectors, screws, drop outlets, corners, elbows, downspout, splash block	Ladder, tape measure, chalkline, drill with screwdriver bit, hacksaw or chop saw

Vinyl is a bit easier to use than metal: You won't cut your fingers on the edges or have to try to squeeze a piece just right to get it to slip into another one.

Like metal gutters vinyl gutters must slope from one end or the other so that water will flow down them. Unlike metal gutters a fair amount of expansion and contraction occurs with changes in temperature.

Each manufacturer approaches slope and expansion differently, so follow your product's instructions carefully.

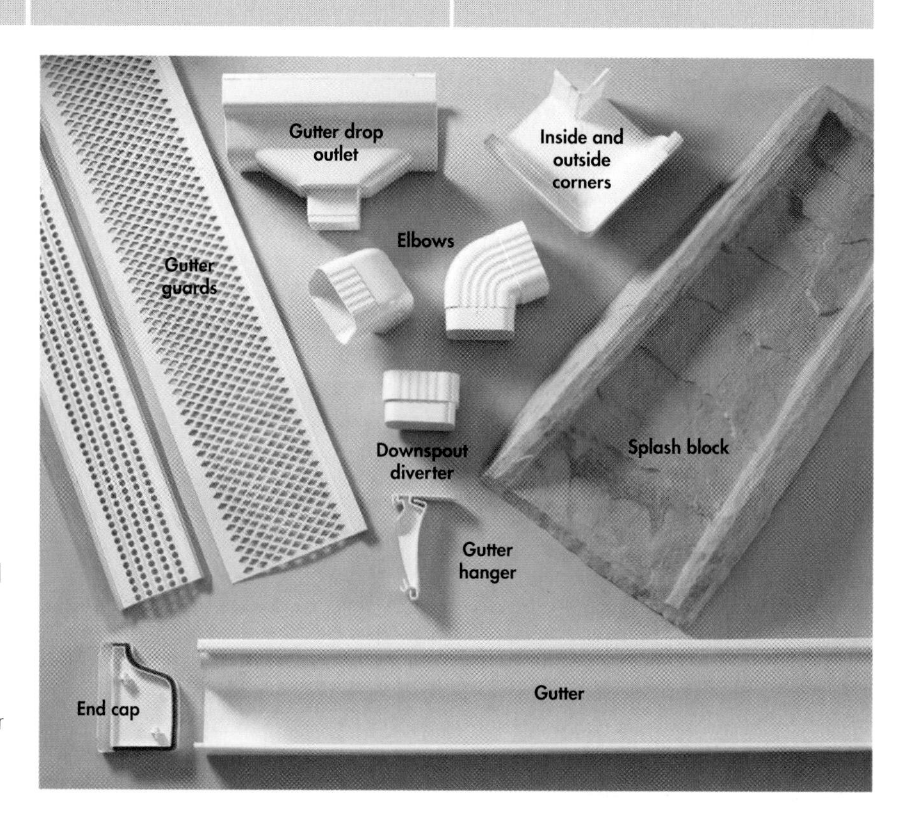

Snap-together gutter systems are assembled from preformed parts. Typical parts include gutter hangers, gutters, end caps, gutter drop outlets, elbows, downspout diverters, gutter guards, inside and outside corners, and splash blocks that sit under the downspouts and help divert water away from the foundation.

Assembling and hanging vinyl gutters

1 At the end of the gutter run farthest from the downspout, measure down ½ inch (or as directed by the manufacturer) from the eaves and make a mark. At the other end measure down at least ½ inch plus ⅛ inch for every 10 feet of gutter in the run. Snap a chalkline between these two points.

2 While the gutter is still on the ground, assemble as much as you can. Install the end cap, corners, and outlets. Apply hanging hooks onto the gutters, spacing them every 2 feet.

3 With a helper hold the gutter in place. Starting at the middle, screw the hanging hooks into the chalkline on the fascia. Vinyl expands and contracts, so after screwing each hook in place, make sure the gutter will move in its brackets. If not the hook is too high or low. Reposition it as needed.

If the gutter goes around a corner start at the corner. Put a corner piece instead of an end cap onto the first piece of gutter you install. Hang the rest as described on this page.

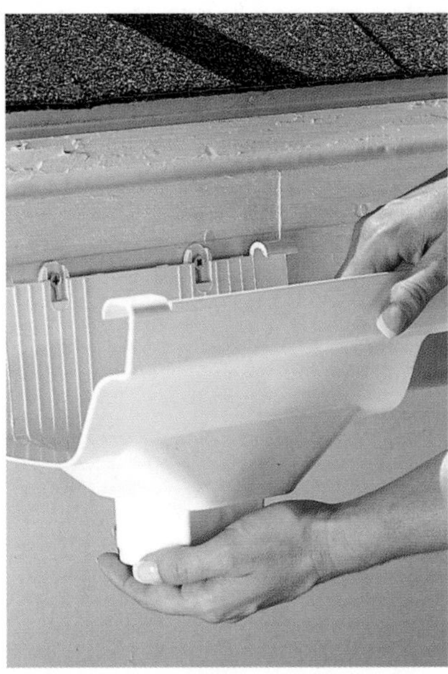

4 Attach the drop outlet to the last section of gutter before hanging. Then measure for the piece that extends to the corner. Cut a piece to length and put it in the drop outlet. Attach the hangers and hang the drop outlet on them.

5 Join the sections using the appropriate connectors and adjust for expansion according to the manufacturer's directions.

6 Install elbows as needed. Sometimes an elbow directs the flow to the side and into another elbow, as shown here. If the roof overhangs the wall, the elbow will direct the flow toward an elbow against the wall. Assemble the elbows and the piece between them. Measure from the lower elbow to a point 6–8 inches above the ground and cut a downspout to this length. Test-fit the entire assembly.

7 Attach the downspout to the house. Mark a spot a few inches above the end of the downspout and move the spout out of the way. Screw a hanger to the house at the mark. Attach the downspout to the hanger and attach an elbow and a section of downspout to direct the flow away from the foundation.

Repairing siding and trim

Although a large number of siding materials are available today, repair choices are simple and basic. Fortunately you can make most repairs yourself. Before you do this however, repair the problem that caused the damage—it's usually water. Check behind the siding for dampness and water damage. If you find any look for the leak that caused it. If the problem isn't behind the wall, the damage could be caused by a leaking gutter or a dripping faucet among other things. If the source isn't obvious wait until it rains and then look for the source.

Replacing sheathing

1 Using a framing square mark the corners of the damaged sheathing you need to remove. Snap chalklines between your marks and cut the sheathing out using a circular saw with a cutting depth set to the thickness of the sheathing.

2 If your damaged cutout falls between the studs, build the studs out by cutting 2×4 cleats to fit the height of the opening and attach the cleats with 3-inch screws. Make sure the front edge of the cleats is flush with the house wall studs.

Imminent repair

Fix damaged siding immediately. The longer you wait the more extensive the damage, and the more difficult the repair. Although seeping water will first damage the area of its most immediate contact, it will quickly spread to a larger area. Once mold growth starts, the spores can get into insulation and surrounding materials, making it necessary to remove more material than appears physically damaged.

SAFETY ALERT

ASBESTOS SIDING

Asbestos can be found in some older types of siding. If you have or think you have asbestos siding, check with your state's department of environmental affairs or your local health department. They can tell you how to find a certified professional to test the siding material and, if necessary, remove and dispose of it.

You can also contact the EPA (Environmental Protection Agency) at www.epa.gov/lead or at 800/424-LEAD (800/424-5323) for more information.

3 Cut a replacement sheathing panel of the same thickness as the original and fasten it to the studs or the 2×4 cleats. You don't have to use the same sheathing material as the original, but whatever the replacement it has to be the same thickness.

Patching exterior trim

Many times you'll run into damaged areas on exterior trim that seem so beyond repair they require replacement. Such areas are common at the corners of window frames and doors that have suffered water damage. Often however you can avoid replacing the trim by using one of several new epoxy repair products.

Epoxy is usually a two-part polymer mixture that hardens to a surface stronger than the wood itself. The new repair formulations are designed to fill gaps and when cured are workable with common tools.

Make sure you find and fix the problem that caused the deterioration in the first place. And do some sleuthing behind the repair before you start to verify there is no hidden structural damage beneath the trim. If structural damage exists it is likely you'll have to tear off the trim and repair the hidden damage and replace the trim. If the damage hasn't gone beyond the trim itself, however, epoxy is the way to go.

Follow the steps illustrated below before you mix the epoxy. Don't be afraid to chip away loose material but leave any soft wood that's still attached to good wood. Many products come with a consolidating chemical formulation that will increase the hardness of rotted wood, so be sure to use it first if the directions specify. Some epoxies are stainable, so if your final finish is to be stained, make sure you purchase a product whose specifications indicate it will accept stain.

1 Probe rotted areas with a screwdriver or chisel. Scrape or cut away loose chunks of rotted wood but leave any soft wood that's still attached to good wood.

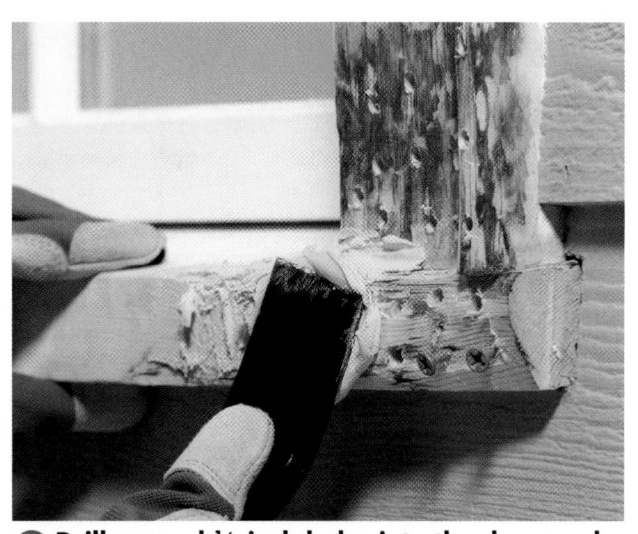

2 Drill several ¼-inch holes into the damaged area and soak the holes and soft wood with the manufacturer's consolidation formulation. Drive deck screws through the rotted material into good wood at angles. These will serve as anchors for the repair. Rebuild one layer of old wood at a time with epoxy filler.

3 After the filler has set up but before it fully cures, smooth its contours with a plastic putty knife. Dip the knife into lacquer thinner to keep the filler from sticking. You don't have to make the contours perfect; just get them close enough so you can finish them with sandpaper.

4 When the filler has completely cured, sand it smooth with 100-grit sandpaper. Dust the surface, then prime and paint it.

Repairing wood siding

Skill level:	Time to complete:	Materials:	Tools:
★★★☆☆	Experienced Variable Handy Variable Novice Variable	Epoxy wood filler, wood spacers, siding material, building paper, siding nails, primer and paint, paintable exterior caulk	Chisel, putty knife, paintbrush, flat pry bar, circular saw, keyhole saw, jigsaw, hammer, shingle puller or hacksaw, circular saw, keyhole saw, jigsaw, hand stapler

Wood siding is subject to deterioration from weather, but some species are more resistant than others. Cedar and redwood for example are less susceptible to rot and are therefore more desirable as siding. Composite materials, such as hardboard, resist rot but are vulnerable to moisture unless treated and sealed. The side of the house will also affect how well the siding stands up to the elements. Sun damage is likely to be greater on the south and west walls.

Siding standards have varied over the years. If you're replacing siding on an older house you may find it difficult to locate a suitable match. A building materials supplier may be able to special order replacement siding or suggest a specialty siding source in your area.

Tips for repairing wood siding

1 Fill small holes in wood siding by cutting out the damaged area with a chisel. Once you've removed all the rotten wood, use a putty knife to fill the area with an epoxy wood filler. Prime and paint to match the existing color.

2 To patch larger holes remove the damaged siding. Start by driving spacers between the damage and the siding above it. Gradually pry up a wide area on either side of the damaged area to avoid splitting or cracking the old wood.

3 Pry out the nails holding the damaged siding in place. If you're worried about damaging a piece of siding close to the damaged area, slip a scrap of wood between the pry bar and siding. Remove the piece of damaged siding.

4 Cut replacement siding boards to fit, leaving an expansion gap of $1/16$ inch at each end. The expansion gap is essential. Without some breathing room the new siding might warp or buckle.

5 Use old siding as a pattern for tracing cutouts around wall openings, fixtures, or obstructions. Prime and seal the cut ends on the house and the replacement boards and let the pieces dry thoroughly before you install them.

6 Replace damaged building paper before attaching the new siding. Cut the replacement paper so it overlaps the repair area by at least 4 inches. Cut and remove the existing building paper. Tuck the top edge of the patch through the cut and staple in place.

7 Nail new siding boards in place using the same nailing pattern as the original boards. If you're replacing more than one board, begin with the lowest boards and work up. Align the bottoms of the replacement boards with the bottoms of existing pieces.

8 Set any spigots in paintable silicone caulk, then paint the new siding. For a color match take a piece of the old siding to a store with a computer color-matching system (or an old pro who's really good). Brush the new paint over the old and dry with a hair dryer to check the color match.

CLOSER LOOK

UGLY IS MORE THAN SKIN DEEP

Wood rot is water damage from a heavy and constant exposure to moisture that encourages the growth of fungi and bacteria. Damp wood is also an inviting home for carpenter ants and termites.

Before you make the repair, find the source of the problem. Sometimes the source is obvious, but it pays to be nosy. Water that damaged the surface of the siding also may have damaged the sheathing. Roll back some of the building paper or moisture barrier and look at what's underneath it. If you see rot poke it with a screwdriver to see how deep it is. If the damage is only skin deep you can probably ignore it, provided you fixed the cause. If it's so deep that it won't hold nails, water will be able to get under the siding again and collect in the sheathing and perhaps in the insulation, which holds water like a sponge.

Unfortunately the source of the water damage may not always be obvious. Your house is a system, and the problem can be anywhere. Roofing keeps the water off the house, gutters collect it, and downspouts direct it away from the foundation. Even something as simple as water from a clogged gutter bouncing back off the sidewalk and onto your deck can cause rot.

If the source of the water causing damage to the siding isn't obvious, work your way up. Are the downspouts connected to the gutter and running freely? Are there loose or damaged shingles? Is the flashing sound, especially around the chimney? Find the problem and fix all the damage. If you have to, remove more siding and cut away some of the sheathing. If possible cut out a section that runs from the middle of one stud to the middle of another so you'll have something to nail your replacement piece to. Nail in the patch, cover it with building paper or moisture barrier, and then fix the siding.

Repairing wood siding (continued)

Replacing shingles or shakes

1 Split damaged shingles or shakes with a hammer and chisel and wiggle them from side to side to remove them. The shingle directly above the one you're removing will hide the existing nails. Remove them by slipping a shingle puller over them or cut them flush with the surface with a hacksaw.

2 Split new shingles or shakes to fit, allowing a ¼-inch expansion gap on the sides. Starting with the lowest row, position the replacements. Nail near the top with aluminum or zinc-coated nails. When you loosely nail the top row in place, slip the top of the replacements under the row above, with the bottom edges ½ inch below the old shingles.

Replacing shingles around windows

To replace a shingle at a window corner, use the old shingle or the window trim to create cutlines in the new shingle. Remove the damaged shingle, retaining the corner cutout if possible. If the shingle splits but you can piece it back together with tape, lay the old shingle atop the new one and mark the cutlines for the corner. Cut the replacement and fasten it in place. If the shingle is damaged beyond repair, line up the bottom of the replacement with the bottom of the one it will abut and mark the horizontal cutline. Line up the top of the replacement shingle with the top of the existing shingle and mark the vertical cutline. Cut the shingle and install.

3 Tap the shingles into alignment, hiding the nails in the process.

Replacing damaged board-and-batten

1 Remove the battens on each side of the damaged panel. Remove the damaged panel. Replace the underlayment if necessary. Select a replacement panel that matches the existing material.

2 Cut a replacement board to fit, leaving a minimum of a ⅛-inch gap on each side between the new board and the old. Prime or finish the edges and back of the new board and let it dry.

Spacing the boards

Board-and-batten siding must allow for the natural expansion of the wood. When you fasten the underboards (the wide ones) each board must have a space of at least ⅛ inch between it and its neighbor. Although this is the minimum requirement, your spacing can be as wide as an inch. No matter what the spacing, it must be consistent along its length. To make spacing easier rip the spacer from a length of 2x stock slightly longer than your boards. Set the spacer against the existing board and slide the new board against it. Make sure it contacts the spacer along its entire length, then nail the new board in place.

3 Nail the replacement board in place. Caulk the joints between the new and old boards, then reattach the battens. Prime and paint or stain to match.

Repairing vinyl and metal siding

Skill level:	Time to complete:	Materials:	Tools:
★★★☆☆	Experienced 1 hr. Handy 2 hrs. Novice 2.5 hrs.	Replacement siding, panel adhesive, caulk, aluminum nails, roofing cement	Siding removal tool, pry bar, slot cutter, hammer, tin snips, roofing knife, file, caulking gun, pliers

Repairs to vinyl and aluminum siding are a bit trickier than those made to wood. The replacement pieces have to match the originals exactly, and finding them sometimes proves harder than the actual repair. Your best option: Once you've removed the damaged panel, take it to a home center or show it to a reputable contractor, who will probably be able to identify the manufacturer. If neither can supply you with the materials you need, contact the manufacturer and ask to be put in touch with a dealer near you.

Patching vinyl siding

1 Remove and install vinyl siding with the help of a siding tool, available at home centers. Find the top of the damaged panel and slip the tool between it and the panel above. Slide the tool along the seam, pulling out and slightly downward.

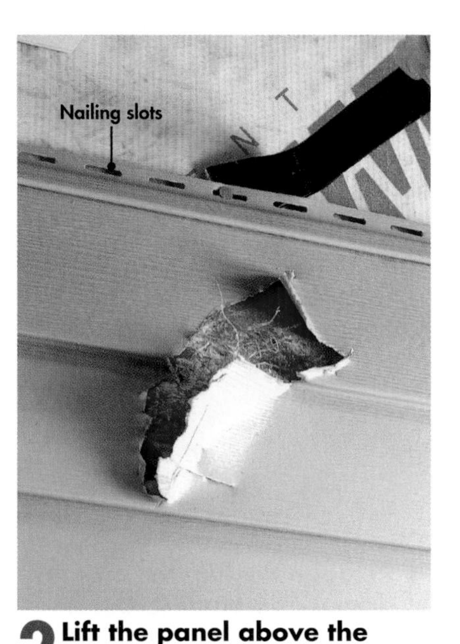

2 Lift the panel above the damaged area out of the way but do not remove it. (The panels are flexible enough to lift away easily.) Use a pry bar to loosen and remove nails securing the damaged panel or panels. Remove the damaged panels.

3 Insert the new panel or panels into the repair area, starting at the bottom. Secure panels with the same type of fasteners used originally. For the last panel force the fastener in with a pry bar slipped under the lap above. Lock the panels together with a siding tool. (See photo, above.)

Let that vinyl breathe

Vinyl siding expands and contracts even more than wood siding. A series of nailing slots runs across the top of the panel. Drive the nail into the center of the slot and let it stick out 1/8 to 1/4 inch so the vinyl can move. Driving the nails tight will cause buckling. Avoid stretching the panel to maximum width when you nail, which will limit its ability to contract and expand. Trimming a piece to fit removes the elongated nail holes; don't nail directly into the paneling, however, even if the trim looks as if it will cover up your work. Use a nail hole slot punch to add holes wherever you need them.

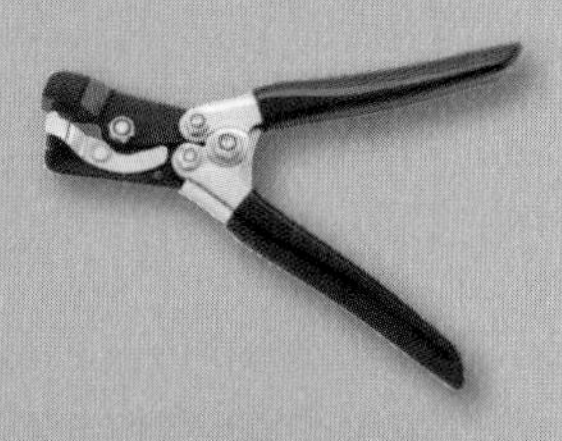

Replacing aluminum siding

1 Cut out the damaged section using a roofing knife and tin snips. Make the top cut about ¼ inch from the top of the damaged piece. Avoid making cuts on the vertical seam between two pieces, as this will deform the seam. Pull downward to remove the piece from the wall.

2 Using an extra piece of siding, cut a patch 1 inch longer than the hole. Trim off the fastener along the top of the piece so it will lie flat, but leave the bottom lip intact. If replacing more than one piece, trim the fastener off the top piece only. File any rough edges smooth.

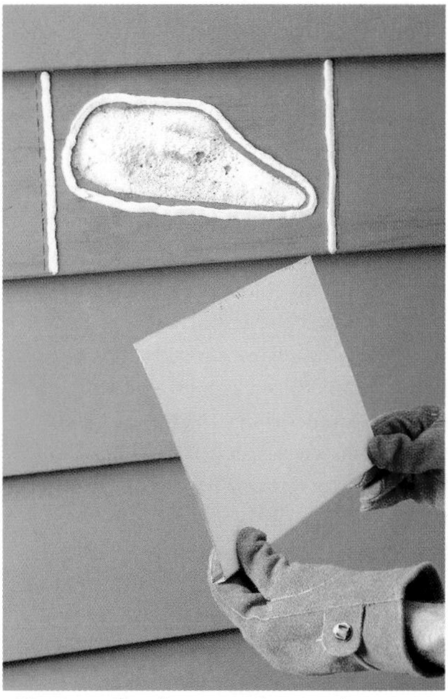

3 Test-fit the patch. Apply construction adhesive to the siding near the edges of the patch and around the damage. Apply the patch over the repair area. Tap the bottom edge with a 2×4 scrap and a hammer to snap the piece into place. Paint to match the existing siding.

Replacing aluminum end caps

1 Sometimes damaged corner caps come off easily. If the cap is pinned tightly under the cap above, however, pry out the bottom of the damaged cap, cut along the top of the cap, and remove it.

2 Locate matching replacement caps and then attach them with aluminum nails. Start at the bottom if replacing more than one cap.

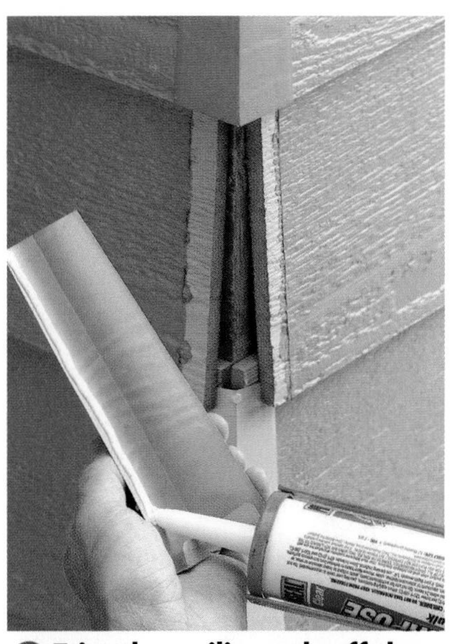

3 Trim the nailing tab off the top replacement cap and then apply panel adhesive to the back. Snap the cap over the bottom lips of joining siding courses. Seat the cap in the construction adhesive, aligning it properly.

Repairing masonry walls

Skill level:	Time to complete:	Materials:	Tools:
★☆☆☆☆	Experienced Variable Handy Variable Novice Variable	Stucco caulk, stucco patch, stucco pigment, stucco mix, masonry anchors, lath nails	Putty knife, wire brush, caulking gun, trowel, whisk broom, hammer, sledge, masonry chisel or drill and masonry disk, stucco trowels, circular saw with masonry blade, jointer, scarifier, mortar raking tool, canned air wheelbarrow

Patching damaged stucco can be difficult because no stucco repair is invisible. It's almost impossible to match the texture and color, but it's important that you try. More important is making a tight seal to adjacent materials. Cracks and holes in stucco let water into the walls, and the problems that result will be far worse than a mismatched patch.

Prior experience with masonry tools will give you a distinct advantage when attempting to match a particular stucco texture. Stucco pigments can be obtained at masonry supply stores and are meant to be mixed with the final coat. When pigmenting stucco keep in mind that the color is likely to change as the stucco dries. For the best match take the time to experiment with stucco and pigment proportions until you find a tint that matches the existing stucco wall when dry.

Make necessary repairs to the underlying structure before you begin. Plan on building up your repair in layers over several days, allowing the stucco to cure between applications.

Repairing stucco

Fill minor cracks with specialty stucco caulk products. These caulks do not harden fully, maintaining a flexible bond between cracks. Stucco caulks are not available in colors, so the repair area will be plainly visible. You can however paint over a caulk line to match the color of your stucco.

1 Use a wire brush to clean out old, loose stucco from the repair area. Inspect the areas around the visible damage, pressing gently on the sides until you find solid wall. A loose wall that gives under hand pressure indicates a more serious repair.

2 Fill the hole with premix stucco patch using a putty knife. Apply the stucco in two or three thin layers, letting each layer dry completely between applications.

3 Smooth out the final coat to match the surrounding texture using a trowel; then dab with the straw ends of a whisk broom to blend in the texture of the repair.

Repairing a large area of damaged stucco

1 Starting in the center of the damaged area, chip out the loose stucco with a masonry chisel and 2-pound sledge. Create a repair area with straight edges by cutting the stucco with a circular saw equipped with a masonry blade. Do not cut the sheathing.

2 Cut new metal lath to fit the cutout area and fasten it to concrete block or brick with masonry anchors or to wood sheathing or siding with lath nails.

3 Apply a smooth layer of stucco mix across the entire area. Make this layer about one-third the depth of the finished stucco, forcing it into the metal lath. When this layer has begun to set up, scratch it with a scarifier or notched trowel.

4 Apply a second coat of stucco, smoothing it and leaving enough space for the finish coat. Let the concrete cure.

5 Apply the finish coat, feathering its edges into the existing stucco. Before this coat cures finish it in the pattern of the original.

Repairing masonry walls (continued)

Repairing mortar joints in brick walls

1 Break up the damaged mortar by chipping it away with a plugging chisel and a 3-pound sledge. Break up only the loose mortar, leaving any solid mortar intact behind it.

2 Rake the loose mortar out of the joints with an old screwdriver or use a mortar raking tool. Blow out the dust with compressed air (use canned air if you don't have a compressor). Wash out the joints with water from a garden hose.

3 While the area is still wet, pack the joints with mortar in ¼-inch layers until the mortar is flush with the face of the brick. Scrape off any excess mortar with a trowel.

4 Tool the mortar by running a jointing tool over the mortar when it sets up firmly enough to hold a thumbprint. Use the type and size of jointer originally used for the rest of the wall so the repair blends in well. Before the mortar dries remove the excess from the face of the brick with a stiff-bristled brush or dry burlap.

Replacing a brick

1 Remove the mortar around the damaged brick by chipping it away with a plugging chisel or a masonry disk attached to a drill. Break up the brick in pieces with the chisel, alternately chipping out more mortar and brick pieces.

2 Remove and discard the brick pieces as you go. Chip off any remaining mortar from the joints and brush or blow out all fragments. Flush the cavity with a spray of water.

3 Spread mortar onto the bottom and sides of the cavity, then apply mortar to the top and back of a replacement brick. Slide the brick into the cavity and tap it gently with the end of the trowel handle until it's flush with the rest of the wall. Hold a 2×4 across the face of the brick to make sure it's flush. Scrape off any excess mortar.

4 Once the mortar is firm enough to hold a thumbprint, shape the joints with the type and size of jointer used on the original bricks so the repair blends in well. When the excess mortar is crumbly, rub it with dry burlap or a stiff-bristle brush to remove the excess from the face of the brick.

Repairing fascia and soffits

Skill level:	**Time to complete:**	**Materials:**	**Tools:**
★★★☆☆	Experienced Variable Handy Variable Novice Variable	Galvanized nails or screws, fascia materials, silicone caulk, primer, paint or stain, soffit materials, 2×2 nailing strips	Pry bar, hammer, ladder, nail set, jigsaw, caulking gun, drill and driver, circular saw, paintbrush

Carpenters originally created fascia and soffits to solve the problems of exposed rafters and open eaves. Fascia are nailed to the cut ends of rafters and prevent water from being drawn back along the overhang and inside the walls. They also provide even surfaces to which you can attach gutters.

Soffits close off the underside of the rafters, preventing birds and other critters from nesting under eaves or getting into the attic. Properly vented, soffits allow air into the attic, helping to solve moisture problems and increase shingle life, thus extending the life of the roof.

Maintenance is essential to the soundness of your fascia and soffits. Solve problems before they affect the structure of your house. Repaint peeling surfaces and replace missing or rotted pieces as soon as you notice them.

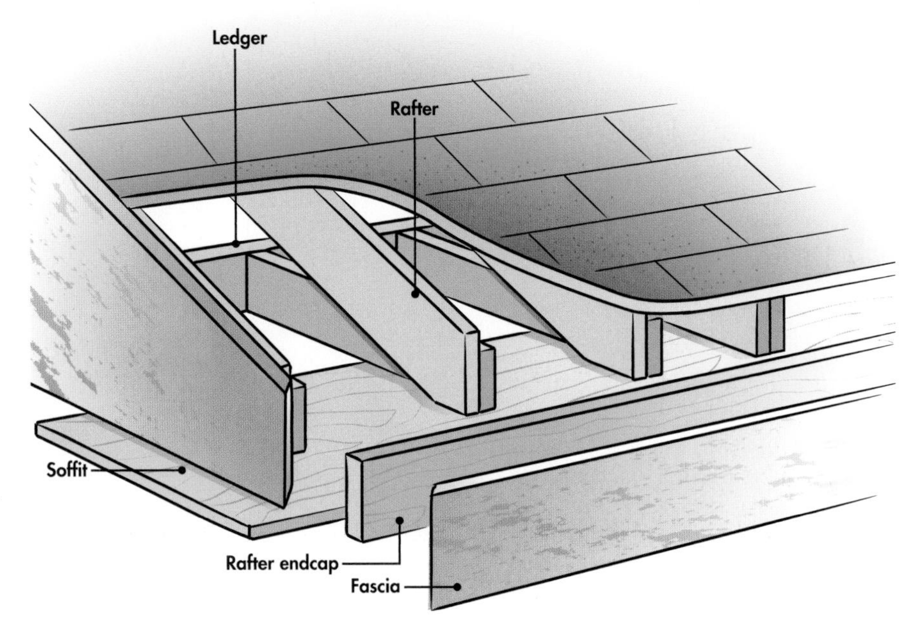

Fascia and soffits work together to close off the area beneath the roof eaves. The fascia covers the rafter ends while providing a surface for attaching gutters. Soffits prevent birds from nesting under your eaves and often have vents to bring fresh air into your attic space. (See pages 494–497.)

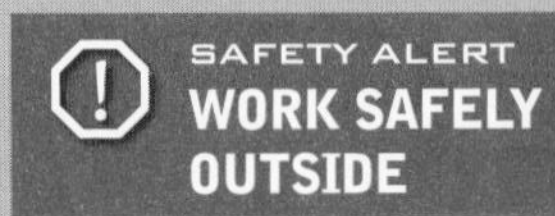

SAFETY ALERT

WORK SAFELY OUTSIDE

Always use a GFCI-protected receptacle and a cord rated for outdoor use if working with power tools outside to minimize the potential for a shock.

Installing fascia covers and soffits

Vinyl or aluminum fascia covers help reduce maintenance on wooden fascia. They are not however a substitute for repairs. Fix any rot or other damage before installing covers. Then nail the covers directly to the fascia. If you have or want soffits, get fascia with a channel designed to hold them.

The quickest way to install soffits is to install fascia covers with channels designed to hold them. Hang matching channels on the house. Cut soffits to fit, angle them up into the opening, and drop them into place. Make sure you've repaired areas covered by the new soffits before you hang them.

Replacing a section of fascia

1 Remove gutters or trim, exposing the entire damaged section of fascia. Be extremely careful when handling gutters and long moldings. If they hit nearby power lines, the shock can kill you. Long pieces also can make you lose your balance. Plan to be near the middle of the piece when you finally pry it loose.

2 Pry the fascia loose with a flat pry bar, then remove. Fascia boards are usually nailed at every rafter end, except when they are attached directly to another fascia at the edge of the roof.

3 Mark off the damaged area of fascia by drawing cutlines that will fall in the middle of the rafters. Set the saw to cut at a 45-degree angle and cut out the damaged area of the fascia.

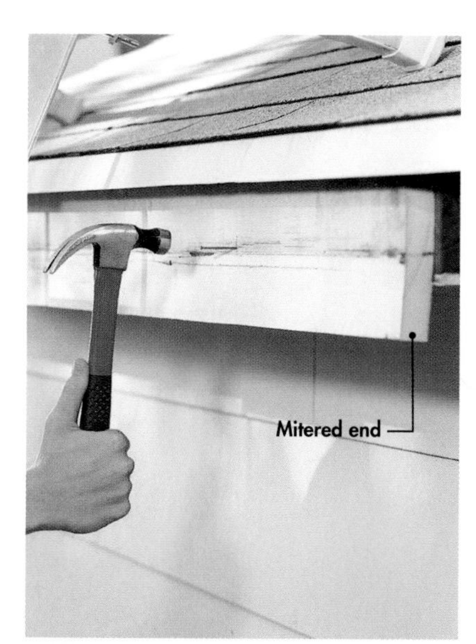

4 Nail or screw the original piece or pieces of fascia in their original positions, leaving a gap where you cut out the damage. Measure the gap, then subtract 1/8 inch to allow for expansion. Cut the new board to this size with the saw still set at 45 degrees. Prime the back and ends of the board.

5 Position the replacement board with an expansion gap of about 1/16 inch at each end. Nail it in place, driving the nail at an angle through the miters.

6 Replace the fascia moldings, then set the nailheads and fill the nail holes with caulk. Prime and paint or stain to match the existing fascia. Reinstall the gutters after the paint or stain dries.

Repairing fascia and soffits (continued)

Repairing plywood soffits

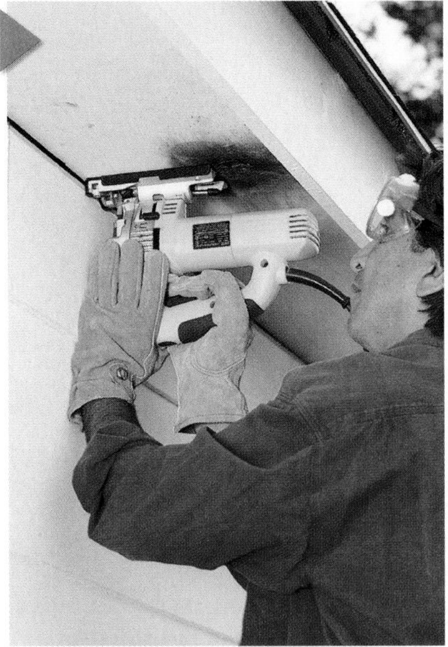

1 Remove any molding holding the soffit in place. To remove the soffit it sometimes helps to cut out the damaged area. Find the rafters on either side of the damaged area and draw a line along the rafter edge closest to the damage. Drill entry holes for a jigsaw and then cut along the lines.

2 Insert a pry bar into the cut you just made and pry to remove the damage. Move slowly and pry gently so you maintain your balance. When you've removed the damage, get a helper on a second ladder. Pull on the soffit with your hands to remove it as your helper supports the far end.

3 Remove any of the damaged soffit that remains on the other side of the cutout. You'll need to remove enough soffit to reveal the seam between the damaged section and its neighbors. Damage is likely to be anyplace where water has been running through a plywood edge.

4 Measure the size of the hole caused by removing the damaged section of soffit. Cut a piece of exterior plywood to fit the opening. (Most home centers will cut a section of plywood for a small fee.) If the damaged section had vents, cut matching ones into the replacement panel. Prime the entire panel and let dry.

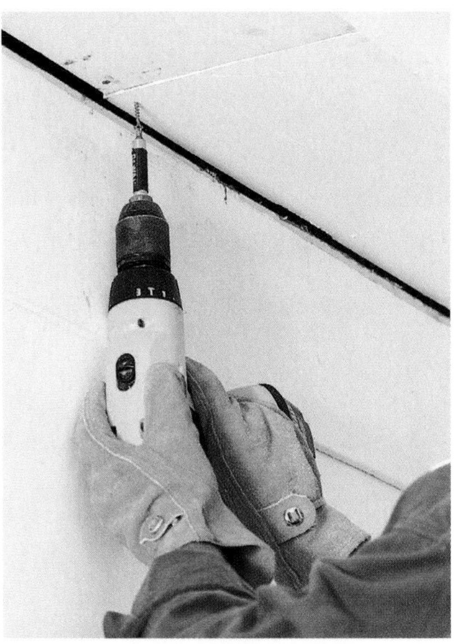

5 Apply the replacement panel over the opening and screw it to the rafters with 1¼-inch galvanized deck screws. Reinstall any molding that helped hold the panel in place.

6 Fill nail holes, screw holes, and joints with paintable silicone caulk. Paint the replacement panel to match the rest of the soffit, then reinstall any vent covers that you removed.

Repairing length-run tongue-and-groove soffits

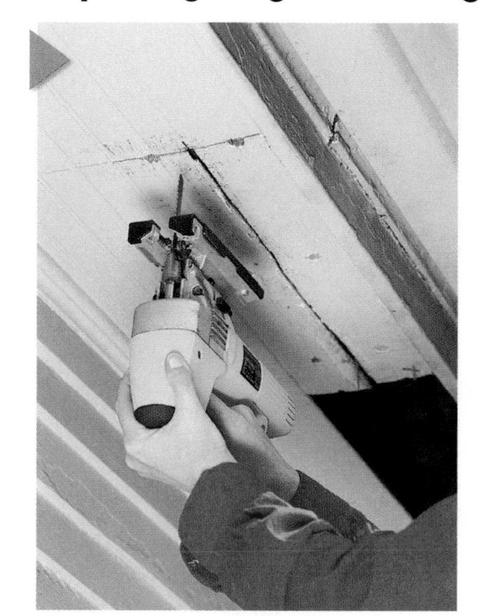

1 Remove any molding over the boards, then locate the rafter on each side of the damage by looking for nails in the fascia. Drill entry holes for a jigsaw, positioning them to avoid the rafter. Insert the jigsaw blade into one of the holes and cut away the damage.

2 Put your finger into one of the holes and pull down any pieces that will come loose. Remove the rest of the scrap. Cut and install 2×2 nailing strips at each edge of the opening in the soffit, screwing them to the rafters.

3 Cut replacement tongue-and-groove boards using boards the same thickness as the originals. Begin installing the new boards next to the siding, nailing them to the nailing strips.

4 Trim the upper lip from the last board, then position it in the opening. Nail it in place, fill the nail holes, and paint the replacement board to match the soffit. Replace the soffit vents if necessary. Prime and paint.

Repairing width-run soffits

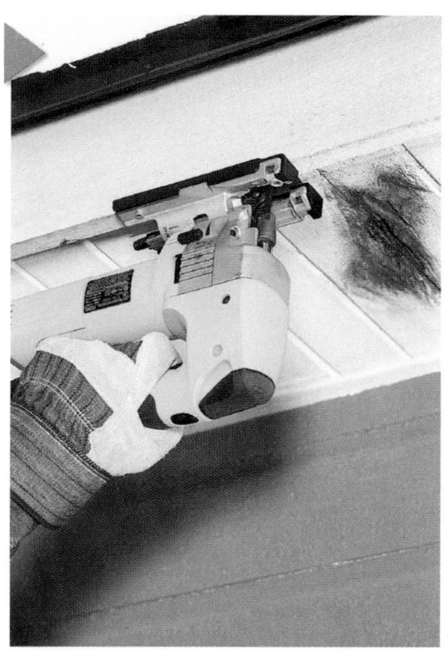

1 Insert a metal cutting blade into a jigsaw and cut along the fascia to free the damaged section. (Width-run soffits are usually inserted into grooves in the fascia and may be nailed through the grooves.) Remove support moldings and pry out the damaged soffit boards.

2 Cut replacement boards to length and prime both sides and ends. Insert the strips into the grooves in the fascia. When you get to the last board, cut off the upper lip so you can install it. Reattach the support molding, caulk the nail holes, and paint the boards to match the existing soffits.

Roofing basics

How you repair your roof (or whether in fact you want to repair it) is a choice that will be affected by a number of factors. The pitch of the roof is a prime consideration. A moderately sloped garage roof is easier to repair than a steeply sloped house roof with lots of valleys, hips, ridges, and rakes. The height of the roof from the ground will also be a factor, and so will its materials. These choices will be even more complicated if you're considering installing a new roof.

Aside from admiring the beauty of a roof from time to time, we don't usually think much about it until it develops problems, and chiefly any problems will be noticed only when the roof begins to leak somewhere. Other than severe damage caused by a fallen tree limb or strong storms, most roof problems are caused by water—and water can come in from anywhere.

The variety of roofing materials is growing. Much of the development of new materials is driven by the decreasing supply of wood and a desire to create long-lasting products that require little maintenance.

What's up on the roof?
Eave: The bottom edge of the roof.
Hip: A line running from the eave to the ridge formed where two sloping sections of roof meet. Found on roofs with more than two main faces.
Rake: The side edge of the roof, which runs from eave to ridge or hip.
Ridge: The line across the top of the roof, formed where two main faces of the roof meet.
Valley: A trough formed by two sections of roof meeting at an angle.

Roofing types

▲ ***Asphalt is by far the most common roofing material in North America.*** *It's one of the least expensive options, and many asphalt shingles are available with guarantees for up to 30 years. The three-tab shingle is the most widely used and is easily installed. Perhaps the only drawback of the common asphalt shingle is its limited effect on the design appearance.*

▲ ***Architectural shingles*** *are asphalt shingles without water lines like those found on three-tab shingles. Architectural shingles have a textured appearance. They are available with longer warranties than three-tab shingles; installation of both types however is the same.*

▲ ***Shakes and shingles*** *are wood products made from a variety of species: western red cedar, Alaskan yellow cedar, and eastern white cedar. Shingles are cut to a uniform thickness of different widths; shakes are split and thicker. Both products have to be installed so air circulates behind them and are nailed not to sheathing but to battens fastened to the rafters. They are expensive and require periodic maintenance, chiefly washing off mildew and moss.*

▲ ***Properly installed, slate roofs*** *are said to last 150 years. In some parts of the country, slate was once standard utilitarian roofing, as likely to be found on a barn as on a fancy Victorian home. Today however slate is hard to get and expensive. If you're in the market for a new slate roof, have a pro install one. (They're very heavy.) To repair a roof find an experienced slate roofer and ask what can be done.*

▲ ***Clay, or terra-cotta,*** *comes in a variety of shapes: flat tiles, shaped tiles, and the Spanish barrel-shaped tiles. Terra-cotta dates from Roman times but became popular in North America in the 19th century. It's available in its natural, red-clay color, as well as yellow, green, and blue glazed tiles. The tiles were originally made by hand. Makers formed the barrel-shaped tiles by spreading clay over their thighs. Original tiles not only bear the shape of the maker's leg but the surface often contains a handprint made hundreds of years ago by a now-anonymous craftsperson.*

▲ ***Metal roofing comes in three broad categories:*** *standing-seam roofing, panel roofing, and look-alikes including tile, cedar, or slate. Traditional standing-seam metal roofing has large ribs that are crimped or soldered together; panel roofing looks somewhat like it but screws down. Metal roofing is durable and long-lasting. But with the exception of screw-down panels, installation requires special training and is usually left to professionals.*

Flat built-up roofs

Flat built-up roofs are installed with a number of techniques—by laying down alternating layers of tar and water-resistant materials covered with gravel, by applying a modified bitumen adhesive product, or by applying a rubber membrane. The chief disadvantage of a flat roof is that it is prone to leaking because of the low angle of its slope.

Roofing basics (continued)

It's a whole lot wiser and more economical to fix your roof before it leaks than to procrastinate. If you do you may find you will then have to fix your roof, ceiling, interior walls, and flooring. The best way to ensure that you won't have to go back up on the roof anytime soon is to buy the highest-quality roofing materials you can afford.

Asphalt shingles are the most common shingle of choice, and installation is well within a homeowner's skill. Asphalt shingles are either tab or architectural. Tab shingles became wildly popular in America during the 1950s. Architectural shingles are essentially tab shingles with a fancier bottom edge.

Top-notch architectural shingles are guaranteed for 40 years, sometimes longer if the manufacturer's installation instructions are strictly followed. They're thicker than low-cost shingles so they resist curling and cupping and generally withstand more abuse from weather extremes.

If you happen to have asbestos roof shingles, hire a professional to do the removal and repair.

If you're doing your own work and you're comfortable working with sheet metal, you can buy galvanized steel or aluminum in bulk rolls and custom-cut it to fit. Otherwise you'll have to spend a little more for prefabricated flashing.

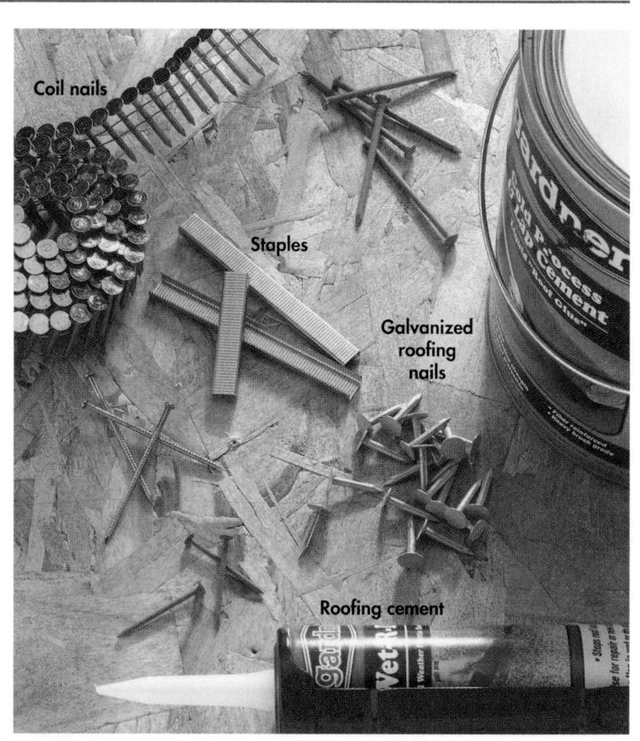

Roofing requires a variety of fasteners. Coil nails fit in a nail gun. Use staples in a hand or hammer stapler. Nail down shingles with hot-dipped galvanized roofing nails. Roofing cement comes in a can and a tube; it seals seams and helps hold down flashing.

The variety of roofing shingles is wide. Cedar shakes are split from wood (cedar shingles are sawn). Three-tab shingles are the most common. The textured look of architectural shingles comes from laminating small pieces of shingle to a solid shingle base. Roll roofing, designed for roofs with low slopes, goes on quickly but is less durable than other materials.

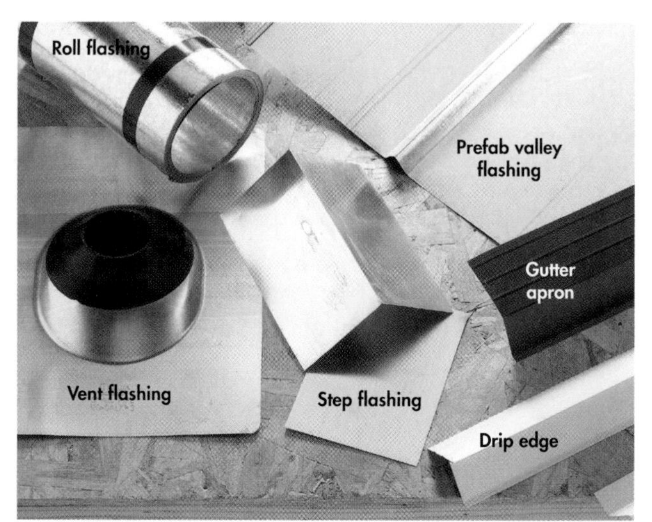

Flashing keeps water from leaking in where two parts of the roof meet. Vent flashing goes around the plumbing stack that comes out of the roof; use step flashing along chimney edges. Prefab valley flashing goes in the valley where two sloping roofs meet. Cut custom replacement flashing from roll flashing. Gutter aprons and drip edges protect the edges of the roof.

SAFETY ALERT

WEAR THE RIGHT GEAR

Roofs are slippery, especially once you've stripped them down to the plywood. Wear the right shoes. Sneakers with flat rubber soles that will grab and hold are great but seem to attracts nails. Steel-toed work boots may not be as comfortable but they prevent injuries.

Put your tools into a tool belt when working on the roof. Tools set on the roof will obey the laws of gravity and quickly end up on the ground—or someone's head.

The roofer's tool kit

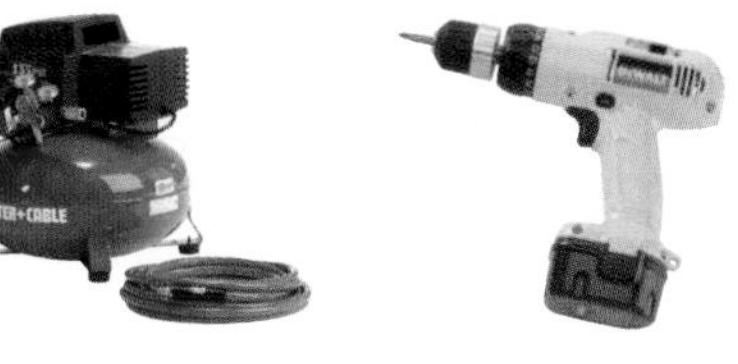
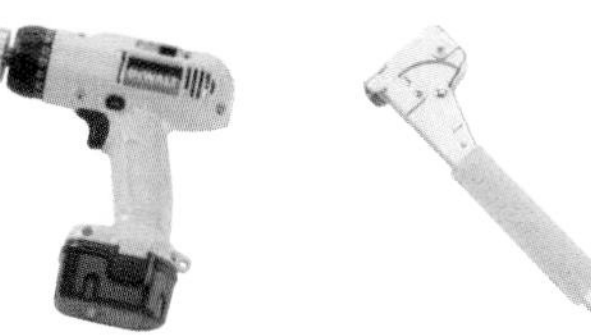

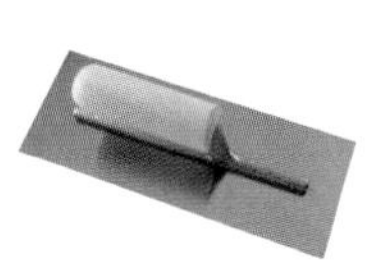

Air compressor

Drill

Hammer stapler

Pry bar

Sawhorse

Trowel

Caulking gun

Drill bits

Knee pads

Push broom

Straightedge

Utility knife

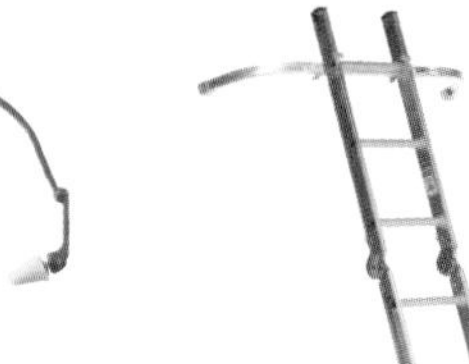

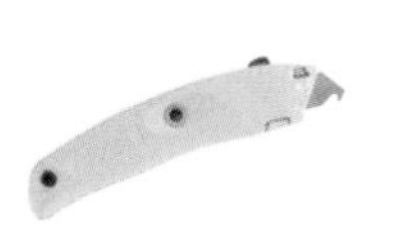

Chalkline

Earplugs

Ladder with stabilizer

Roofing knife

Tape measure

Wheelbarrow

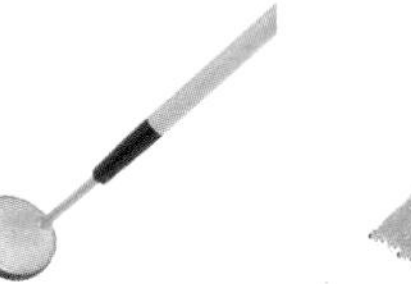

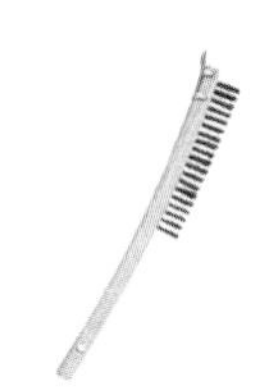

Chisels

Flat pry bar

Magnetic sweep

Roofing shovel

Tarps

Wire brush

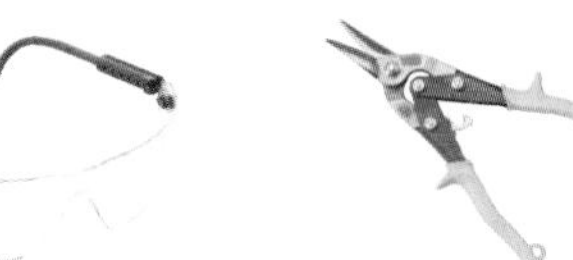

Circular saw

Framing square

Pitchfork

Safety glasses

Tin snips

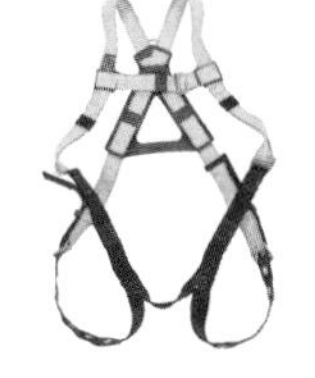

Claw hammer

Gloves

Pneumatic power nailer

Safety harness

Tool belt

Inspecting a roof

A working roof and gutter system usually go unnoticed. If they are working properly, they provide adequate air circulation and venting, protection against the elements, and proper drainage of rain and snow.

If you find problems with the roof, such as leaks, worn sections, missing shingle parts, or cupped or bowed shingles, replacing your roof may be a better idea than trying to repair it. Depending on your location codes will allow either one or two layers of new shingles over the original roof. Beyond that you will need to strip away the old roof and start over.

Flashing around vent pipes often cracks, letting water into the attic and even down into the wall. Look for faulty repairs, such as this one done with roofing cement, as well as actual cracks.

Buckled and cupped shingles generally indicate a moisture problem. Tear off the old shingles, repair the problem, and reroof.

Wear occurs as shingles age. If the majority of shingles are damaged or worn, tear off and replace them.

Damaged or deteriorated shingles are a main cause of roof leaks. These shingles are damaged beyond repair and a new roof is the only solution. In cases of minor or localized problems you need only replace the damaged shingles.

Detached or loose flashing often can be replaced or reattached. Clean out the old caulk or roof cement and replace it with fresh sealant.

Leaks often occur at chimneys when flashing fails. Look for the gaps that occur in other types of flashing, as well as repairs that use lots of roofing cement or patches. Any patch is temporary and is a sure sign that if you don't need a new roof now, you soon will.

Checking for leaks

There are two things certain about a water leak: Its source is never where you think it is, but it's always uphill from its appearance. Water can show up in a ceiling, for example, after traveling long distances down a rafter and across a ceiling joint. Finding the source of a leak takes some patience.

An unfinished attic offers the fewest obstacles in tracking down a leak. You can look for pinholes of light from the inside of the attic on a sunny day, but you're probably better off looking for a leak on a rainy day. Arm yourself with a flashlight and start at any sign of wetness and look for a trail that leads to the source. Pay special attention to the top of the rafters. Water will often course along the top edge for some distance before gravity pulls it down the face of the framing member. Mark the source. You'll need to take some measurements later. If you can't wait for rain, enlist the aid of a partner to hose the roof down. Point the hose at the highest point the water will reach and let it flow downward. Don't shoot the water into the base of the shingles.

If the attic is insulated, wear a respirator and examine the insulation for stains or dark spots that indicate mold. Peel the insulation back from between the rafters or joists and follow a trail to the source. Chimneys are often the sources of leaks, allowing water to travel down the inside until it finds a suitable exit across a ceiling joist. More obvious signs of a leak can often be detected at the juncture of the chimney and the roof. Deteriorated flashing is the likely cause here. Inadequate flashing is the source of more leaks than any other part of the roof.

Water on attic rafters is a sure sign your roof has at least one spot that leaks. If the leak is active, set a bucket under it to catch the water. Mark the location of the source when you find it.

You can stop water from getting to a wall by nailing a small wood block onto the face of the rafter. The block will cause the water to drip down, where you can catch it in a bucket until you find the source and fix it.

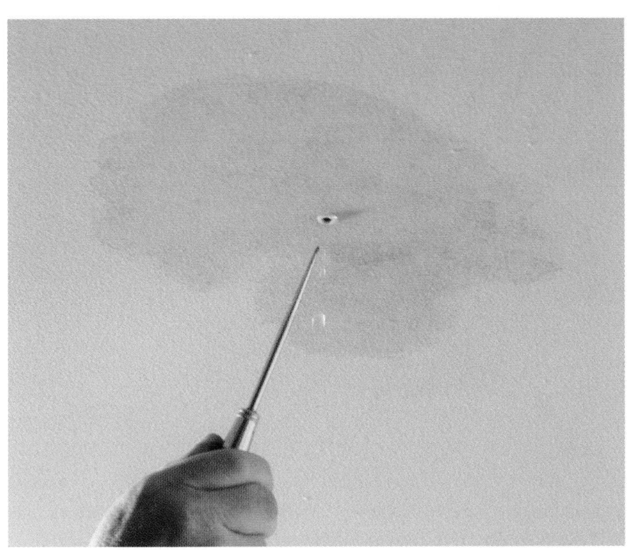

A water mark on ceiling drywall indicates the presence of water. The weight of the water can eventually damage the drywall permanently. Relieve the pressure by driving an awl or screwdriver through the drywall and catch any residual water in a bucket. Fix the leak, then the damaged area, then repaint the drywall.

When you find the source of a leak, measure its distance from a known point on the outside of the roof—the peak or ridge for example. Using the same measurement on the exterior of the roof, mark the spot that needs repair.

Repairing roofs

Skill level:	Time to complete:	Materials:	Tools:
★☆☆☆☆	Experienced 20 min. Handy 25 min. Novice 30 min.	Roofing cement, roofing nails, shingles	Claw hammer, caulking gun, flat pry bar, wood chisel, shingle puller, tool belt

If damage is limited try short-term fixes by replacing shingles and applying roofing cement. Damaged or missing shingles are obvious; cracks or separated joints in the flashing can be harder to locate.

What's insidious about water damage is that it can extend into the neighboring materials. If the area needing repair is large, minimize further damage temporarily by covering the area with a tarp until you can make adequate repairs.

Examine the surrounding material at the source—sheathing, rafters, and joists. Some moisture will be present, but you need to decide whether the water has caused structural damage. Buy an inexpensive moisture meter and check. For any wood showing a moisture content above 18 percent, you'll probably need to shore it up or replace it.

Making repairs with roofing cement

▲ ***Reattach buckled shingles with roofing cement.*** *Also use roofing cement to patch any cracks or other minor shingle problems.*

▲ ***Refresh deteriorated roofing cement around flashing if the seal is bad.*** *Joints around flashing or skylights are the most common places leaks can occur.*

Replacing asphalt shingles

1 Tear off the uppermost shingle needing repair by grasping the sides and wriggling it loose. If you're replacing multiple shingles, start with the highest one. Remove all damaged shingles this way. Be careful not to damage surrounding shingles in good condition.

2 Remove old nails with a pry bar. If you cannot pry them out, drive the nails flat into the sheathing with a hammer. Patch any holes in the building paper with roofing cement.

3 Install new shingles on lower courses following the normal shingle installation procedure shown on the bundle wrapper.

4 Coat the top of the last shingle above the seal line with roofing cement.

5 Slip the last shingle into place under the overlapping shingle. Depending on the arrangement of the shingles, you may be able to drive a couple of nails into the shingle by gently lifting overlapping tabs of other shingles. If not press the shingle down firmly to seat it in roofing cement.

Replacing wood shakes

1 Split the damaged shake with a hammer and chisel and remove the pieces. Use a shingle puller to remove hidden nails. Slip the shingle puller under the shingle above, catch a nail, and hammer on the flat part of the handle to pull or cut the nail. Check the building paper for damage and repair or replace as necessary.

2 Trim a new shake to fit, leaving about 3⁄8-inch clearance on either side for expansion. Push the shingle in place until the lower edge is about an inch below the edge of the neighboring shingles. Drive nails into the top of the replacement shingle.

3 Tap the bottom edge of the shake, as shown, to drive it into place. The nails will bend slightly, hiding them under the shingle above. If the shingle splits when you try this, cut a new one, spread roofing cement onto the upper half, and slide it into place under the shingle above.

Repairing roofs (continued)

Patching valley flashing

1 Using the same gauge flashing material as the original, cut a patch longer than the damaged area and wide enough to slip under the shingles on both sides.

2 Using a high-quality roofing cement, apply a bead around the perimeter of the patch.

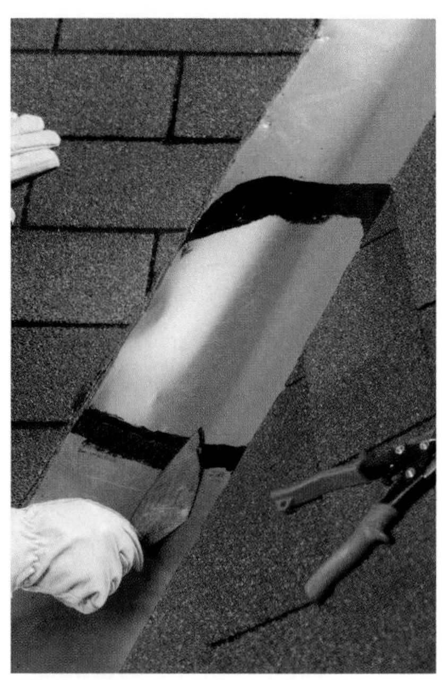

3 Slip the patch under the shingles on one side, then slide it under the shingles on the other. Apply roofing cement to the top and bottom of the patch, smoothing it so the water can flow down without interruption.

Measuring for roofing

The first thing you should consider about new roofing or substantial repairs is getting up on the roof to measure it. It can be done from the ground, and pros do it all the time, but it's much simpler to do it on the roof. It's also the acid test: How willing are you to climb up to the ridge or walk over to the edge and peer over? If you're nervous about climbing up to measure or if you get up to the roof and freeze (as many a good soul has), hire a pro.

Start measuring by drawing a picture of your roof—not necessarily to scale—and then divide it into a series of rectangles and triangles. Climb up on the roof, watching out for loose shingles that could send you tumbling. Measure the height and width of each rectangle and multiply them to get the square footage. Multiply the base and height of the triangles, then divide by 2 to find the area of triangular sections of the roof. Mark your measurements on your sketch and do the math. Add 10 percent for gables and 15 percent for hips.

When you get to the retailer, tell the salesperson how many square feet you need. The experts can convert into the standard roofing measurement of "squares" and tell you how many bundles you need. A "square" is 100 square feet, and a bundle covers about one-third of that, depending on the shingle. A 30×30 roof is 900 square feet, or 9 squares, and requires 27 bundles of shingles. Have them delivered.

Repair vent flashing

Remove the shingles on top of the flashing and any damaged shingles around it. Remove the old flashing and discard it. Apply a bead of roofing cement to the bottom surface and install the new flashing as shown above.

Replace step flashing

1 Using a pry bar remove the old flashing.

2 Pull up the edges of the shingles. Apply roofing cement to the location of the flashing and insert the replacement flashing.

3 Nail the flashing in place with roofing nails and apply a bead of roofing cement to the edge where the shingles will fall. Press the shingles in place.

Hiring a pro?

If you've decided not to do the job yourself, get a reliable roofer. Ask contractors you've worked with for names. Ask the roofers for references and phone numbers, and follow up on the quality of their work.

Verify that the roofer is licensed and bonded and ask for references. Discuss who will handle disposal of the old roof. Have the roofer take out the permit so you won't be responsible for insurance.

Get two or three estimates for time and cost. As a rule it will take two or three workers about a day to strip the average roof and another day or so to apply shingles.

SAFETY ALERT

A SAFETY HARNESS IS A WISE CHOICE

Talk to any roofer and you'll hear tales of falls from high places. Because of the danger involved, OSHA now requires professional roofers to wear harnesses, and if people who walk on roofs every day of their lives need harnesses, so do you.

The kind of harness you want is called a fall-arrest harness as opposed to a rescue, suspension, or positioning harness. You'll need at least a 25-foot lifeline with a shock-absorbing lanyard (strap) and a roof anchor.

The harness slips over your body and legs and has a ring on the back for the lanyard. The lanyard has a shock-absorbing core that stretches to reduce the shock that occurs when the lifeline stops a fall. The lifeline is a heavy-duty rope; one end attaches to the lanyard, the other end to the roof anchor. The roof anchor attaches to the peak of the roof with heavy-duty nails.

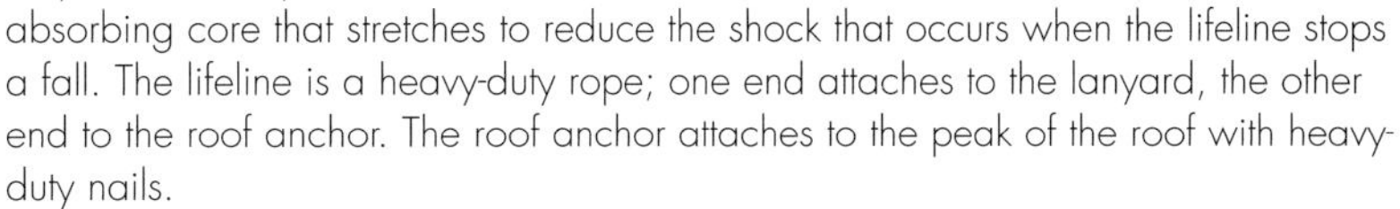

A good harness system will cost you as much as a good nail gun, but unlike a nail gun, it can save your life. Check the Yellow Pages to see whether you can rent a harness. But if you have to buy, do so. If you do rent get printed instructions for using the harness. If your home center doesn't carry harnesses, check with a roofing distributor or look on the Web and in the Yellow Pages. Buy all the components from the same manufacturer to make sure they work as designed. Ask about kits that include everything you need.

Roof tear-off and repair

Skill level:	Time to complete:	Materials:	Tools:
★☆☆☆☆	Experienced Variable Handy Variable Novice Variable	2½-inch galvanized screws, exterior-grade plywood, 8d ringshank nails	Roofing knife, flat pry bar, roofing shovel or pitchfork, circular saw, claw hammer, broom, drill and driver bit

A new roof can go over an old roof. Depending on local code it can even go over two layers of roof. (See page 575 for information about roofing over an old roof.)

Tearing off an old roof is hard work. Roofing materials start out heavy and seem to gain weight as the day goes on. Gathering the torn-up shingles once they hit the ground is even more work, so before you tear off the first shingle, borrow a truck or rent a dumpster and park it under the eaves. Shovel the old shingles off the roof and directly into the truck or container. This method will keep nails out of your lawn mower and your back out of traction.

Find help if you can—this would be an excellent time to call in old favors. Before you let anybody on your roof, though, check your insurance coverage. And if the pitch of your roof is steep, make certain each worker is secured by roofing jacks or safety harnesses. Helpers who discover their fear of heights can still clean up and act as emergency "watchers."

Tearing off an old roof, like all demolition jobs, creates a huge amount of waste material. You can let the old roofing fall to the ground and pick it up later, but that actually makes the job more difficult and creates a safety hazard. Before you start order a 20-cubic-yard dumpster (for an average 1,500-square-foot roof) and have it placed under an eave so the waste material will slide down into it. You might even want to build a temporary plywood chute to direct the old roofing into the container. A pickup truck will also work, but will require making more trips to the landfill.

Don't get rained out

When you are getting ready to tear off your old roof, gather all the equipment you need, round up a couple of friends, and make arrangements for your rented waste container. Then check the weather. If it looks bad reschedule the job. In any case don't get caught by a surprise storm. Have a couple of tarps on hand in case of rain.

1 Start at the top of the roof and remove the old shingles in sections. Keep the roofing shovel (shown) or pitchfork tight against the plywood sheathing or lumber decking so you can peel the shingles off in large chunks instead of individually. If you are saving your gutters, be careful not to ruin them during tear-off.

2 Remove flashing from roof vents, skylights, and dormers. Some flashing, such as that used on skylights, is reusable. Chimneys should have two layers of flashing, some of which may be reusable. The rest, including the boot (a waterproof fitting that goes around vent pipes), valley flashing, and dormer flashing should be removed and replaced.

3 Remove the shingles across the ridge with a pitchfork or roofing shovel last to protect the peak in case of rain.

4 Pry out any remaining nails. A ripping hammer with a flat claw, like the one shown above, is specifically designed for pulling nails. Once you've pulled the nails, sweep the roof completely: It must be free of protruding nails and completely clean before you can move to the next step, which will be sheathing or shingling, depending on the roofing material you choose. Clean up stray nails from the yard using a release magnet, available at most rental centers.

Replacing damaged sheathing

1 Sheathing can be made of plywood or solid wood. Although plywood is shown here, the procedure is the same for solid wood. Use the nail holes to help locate the rafters. Outline an area to cut out that is larger than the damaged area, cutting ends that are directly above the centers of the rafters. Set your circular saw to cut through the sheathing but not into the rafters; then make the cutout.

2 If the rafter is splintered or deteriorated beneath the sheathing, screw or nail a 2×4 cleat to the side to provide a surface to attach the new sheathing. The new sheathing should be the same thickness as the old—generally ½ inch. In some areas 7⁄16-inch material is suitable as a replacement.

3 Cut new sheathing from exterior-grade plywood, matching the thickness of the old sheathing. (Use solid wood to replace solid wood.) Cut the patch to allow a ⅛-inch expansion gap on each side. Nail the patch in place with galvanized 8d ringshank nails driven into the rafters and spaced 6 inches apart.

Installing underlayment

Skill level:	**Time to complete:**	**Materials:** Eave drip cap, underlayment, ice-dam barrier underlayment, hot-dipped galvanized roofing nails, roofing cement, rake drip cap	**Tools:** Safety glasses, claw hammer, tin snips, chalkline, roofing knife, hand roller, tape measure, pry bar
★★★☆☆	Experienced 10 min. Handy 15 min. Novice 20 min.		

In roofing underlayment means rolls of 15- or 30-pound roofing felt (felt soaked in asphalt). Check with the manufacturer of your shingles and use the underlayment specified.

Underlayment is a must—not an option—for a good roof. Using the wrong materials can void the warranty.

Here's why: The roof is a system of layers designed to keep out water. The shingles do the basic job of shedding and channeling rain. The underlayment is a final barrier to moisture penetration.

Application begins at the bottom of the roof and works its way up. Each strip overlaps the previous one by a few inches. Any water flowing down from the top of the roof is directed over the seam instead of into it.

In cold climates heat leaking from the house often melts snow on the upper part of the roof; the water refreezes when it reaches the colder eaves, and the resulting slush and water (called an ice dam) can be forced up under the shingles.

Proper venting (see pages 494-497) and insulation (see pages 516–517) help prevent this, but you should also install an ice-dam barrier underlayment over the section of roof covering the first 2 feet of the attic and in the valleys. It applies much like roofing felt but is heavier and self-adhesive. For more on installation see "Preventing Ice Dams," pages 526–527.

Measure the slope of your roof with a level and tape measure. If the slope is between 2 and 4 inches per foot, apply a double layer of roofing felt at the bottom and overlap courses by 19 inches instead of by the amount shown here. For a roof with a slope of less than 2 inches per foot, use roll roofing (see page 576–577).

Applied correctly, underlayment offers a degree of protection in case it should rain before you shingle. And if the roof has problems, you'll have peace of mind that comes from knowing that its underlayment is solid.

1 Nail a strip of eave drip edge along the bottom of the roof. If you need more than one strip, overlap the ends of neighboring strips by 2 inches. Use tin snips to miter the end that will butt against the drip edge covering the rake, or edge, of the roof. (See "Drip Edges: Getting the Sequence Right," opposite.)

2 Unroll underlayment, also called roofing felt, along the bottom edge of the roof. The felt should overlap the eave drip edge by about ⅜ inch. Staple or nail the felt in place. If you nail use 1-inch hot-dipped galvanized roofing nails, even though they will poke through the sheathing below.

3 Roll out the next course of underlayment, overlapping the existing paper or ice-dam barrier by 4 inches. Fasten the felt with staples or with hot-dipped galvanized roofing nails.

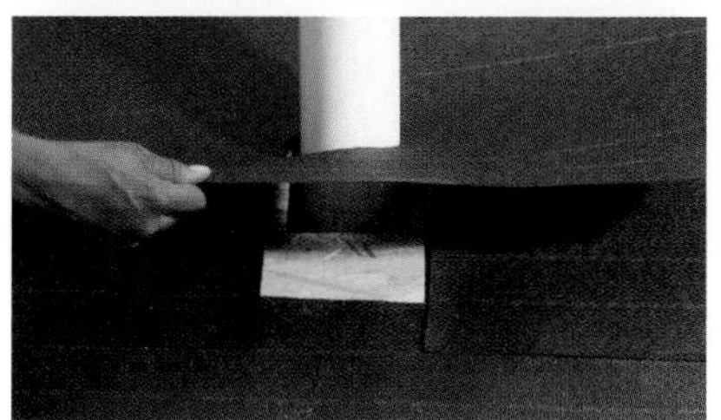

4 Work your way up the roof with roofing felt—overlap courses by 4 inches. When a roll runs out, start a new one, overlapping the ends 12 inches. Roll felt across valleys from both sides, extending it 36 inches on both sides of the valley. At an obstruction cut a hole into the felt that will slip over it if possible. Otherwise roll the felt up to the obstruction, then resume the course on the other side. Cut a patch extending 12 inches on each side of the obstruction, fit it over the obstruction, and nail it in place.

5 At ridges and hips wrap 6 inches over the top and nail or staple in place. Staple every 3 inches along the edge.

Note: If you are installing roll roofing (see pages 576–577): Cut a strip of felt 12 inches wide; snap a chalkline 6 inches on each side of the ridge or hip; spread a 2-inch-wide strip of roofing cement just inside the lines. Set the underlayment so the outside edges anchor in the roofing cement.

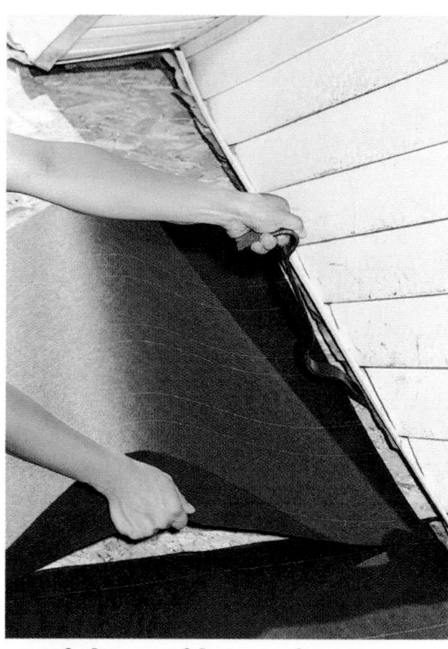

6 If the roof has a dormer or sidewalls, start at the sidewall. Tuck the roofing felt under the siding to create an unbroken seal at the roof and wall joint.

WORK SMART

USE THE RIGHT EDGING

The metal trim along the eave (bottom) of the roof is different from the trim that runs up the side of the roof.

The bottom trim is called the **gutter apron** and directs water into the eave trough. **Drip** or **roof edge** is narrower and runs along the side of the roof to support the ends of the shingles. Underlayment goes over the gutter apron and under the roof or rake edge. (See "Drip edges: Getting the sequence right," right.)

Drip edges: Getting the sequence right

Install the drip edge on the fascia before installing the underlayment. Nail the edge at 12-inch intervals.

Install the edge flashing on the rake fascia after installing the rolled underlayment. Make sure you overlap the ends of the drip edges at least 2 inches.

Installing flashing

See page 591

Skill level:	Time to complete:	Materials:	Tools:
★★★☆☆	Experienced Variable Handy Variable Novice Variable	Flashing, plastic-base asphalt roofing cement in a can and in a tube for a caulking gun, hot-dipped galvanized roofing nails	Tin snips, gloves, scraper, wire brush, claw hammer, caulking gun, nail gun, circular saw, pneumatic nailer

If you have experience working with sheet metal and have the equipment necessary to do so, you can make your own flashing from rolls of metal sold as roll flashing. Avoid using anything less than 26-gauge galvanized steel, even if working with aluminum is easier.

You'll probably get better results with prefabricated flashing, sold in lengths that are already creased and shaped. If necessary trim them to length with a pair of tin snips.

Custom sheet-metal fabricators can also cut and form your flashing to fit. Carefully measure chimneys, dormers, and roof slope to ensure a watertight seal.

Valley flashing is applied before the shingles go up. Other types are applied while you apply the shingles.

Valley flashing options

To make traditional metal flashing, bend your own from rolls of flashing material. Make the bend by folding the metal along a straightedge. Metal flashing provides a sturdy base when laying shingles for a closed valley. (See "Laying a closed-cut valley" on page 572.) Prefab metal flashing is easier and more durable when laying an open valley.

Rolled self-adhesive flashing membranes are guaranteed to last as long as the shingles you put over them. Cut the roll into pieces 6 to 10 feet long. Starting at the bottom of the roof, fold the flashing in half lengthwise. Remove a half-width of the backing covering the adhesive, center the fold in the valley, then stick the membrane to the roof. Remove the rest of the backing and adhere the remainder of the membrane. Install the next piece the same way, overlapping the first piece by at least 6 inches.

Prefabricated metal flashing has a peak that deflects water flow away from the weak spot in the bottom of the valley. It's most commonly used when shingling an open valley and required for shakes or wooden shingles. (See page 573.) Install the flashing from the bottom of the roof up, centering the peak over the valley. Attach the flashing by nailing along the edges but not through them. For extra protection cover the nail with plastic-base asphalt roofing cement. Trim the edge of the flashing flush with the eaves at the bottom of the roof. When you shingle trim the shingles to end short of the peak in the flashing.

Installing flashing around a chimney

Every chimney is different, which makes installing flashing a bit of a custom job. Chimneys generally are not attached to the house framing so the inevitable shifts and settling will not damage them. Consequently the chimney area is a prime place for leaks and water damage. Protecting the chimney requires a two-part flashing solution.

First attach base and step flashing to the roof around the entire base. Then mortar counterflashing (sometimes called cap flashing) into the chimney to protect the base flashing and still allow for movement. Counterflashing must be installed around the entire chimney and overlap at least 3 inches.

If your chimney is not mounted on the peak, install a "cricket" at the high end of the chimney to keep water flowing down and debris from gathering. A cricket is simply a small roof constructed of two triangles of exterior-grade plywood and mounted to the roof deck, creating a small peak. It is flashed and shingled in the same manner as the rest of the roof.

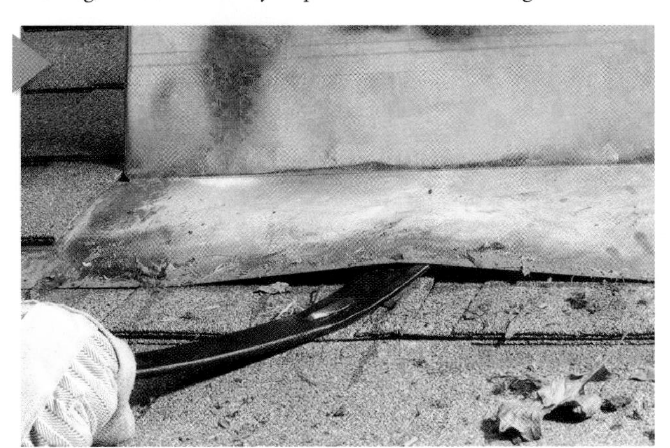

1 Use a pry bar to remove the old flashing. (Save it to use for patterns.) Flashing a chimney involves installing base flashing, step flashing up the sides of the chimney, top flashing, and counterflashing (cap flashing) over the top of the step flashing. First remove all the old flashing around the chimney, then continue shingling and flashing around the chimney, working up the roof. Wear gloves when working with flashing; the edges are sharp.

2 Install the cricket at the top side of the chimney before laying underlayment and shingles. Use the existing cricket if possible. If not, make a new one to fit on the ridge side of the chimney. The edges of the cricket should extend to the edges of the chimney so water and debris will flow cleanly around it. The peak of the cricket should be at least 6 to 8 inches from the deck and should be supported by 2x4 or 2x6 framing underneath. Apply underlayment and staple in place (see inset).

3 Cut a piece of flashing to go around the bottom of the chimney out of 10- or 12-inch galvanized metal. If you can, use the old piece as a pattern. It should wrap around the corners of the chimney as shown. Bend it so it will cover both the chimney and the roof, then cut in from the edges so you can wrap the single piece around the chimney. Nail it to the roof with one nail at each edge and cement it to the chimney with roofing cement.

4 Continue shingling and flashing around the chimney. Before you install the final shingle next to the chimney, insert a piece of 5x7-inch step flashing. Apply roofing cement to the chimney half and align the first piece of the flashing with the bottom edge of the first row of chimney shingles. Nail the flashing to the roof with two nails, one at the top and one at the bottom. Cover with roofing cement and nail the final shingle in place. Continue shingling, lining up the bottom of the flashing with the bottom of the shingle to create the 2-inch overlap.

Installing flashing (continued)

5 You may be able to use the existing grooves in the chimney for counterflashing. If not cut along a mortar joint using a circular saw with a masonry blade to make a groove at least 1 ½ inches deep to hold the counterflashing.

6 Install counterflashing. If possible use the old piece of counterflashing as a pattern. If you cut a new groove, make a cardboard template. The flashing should overlap at least 3 inches. Cut the flashing with tin snips. Bend the edge and put it into the groove. Set it with premix mortar in a caulking gun (see inset). Bend the counterflashing down to cover the step flashing.

7 Shingle and flash the cricket. After installing the underlayment continue shingling up the roof, covering the peak of the cricket as you would the peak of the roof. Finish with hip shingles and add flashing, starting at the peak of the cricket and working down to the base of the chimney. Install the counterflashing around the entire chimney as described next.

8 Cut new counterflashing for the cricket. Use the old piece of counterflashing as a pattern to make the new one if possible. If you cut a new groove, make a cardboard template. Cut out the new flashing with tin snips, put the flashing into the groove, and seal with mortar. Bend the counterflashing in place.

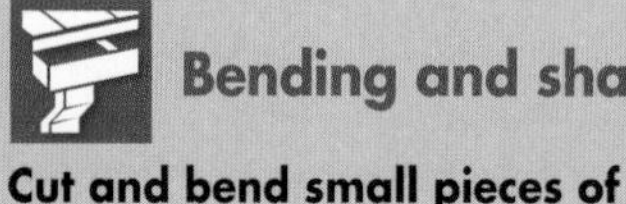

Bending and shaping roll flashing

Cut and bend small pieces of flashing, such as chimney flashing, on a flat surface with a straightedge. A sawhorse or workbench works well. Sometimes you can form the piece freehand, as shown here. Or you can put in a row of nails as a stop. Position the nails to hold the piece so the bend is directly over the straightedge. Clamp the piece in 2x4s or 2x6s.

Use old flashing as a template for replacement flashing. This is especially useful for reproducing complicated flashing such as chimney flashing. Flatten out the old piece, trace around it with a grease pencil or marker, and cut along the lines with tin snips.

Installing flashing around vent pipes

1 Vent pipe flashing goes over the shingles instead of sitting on the underlayment. Shingle until you get to the first shingle that meets the vent pipe. Cut a notch in a shingle, fit it over the pipe, and set the entire shingle in plastic-base asphalt roofing cement.

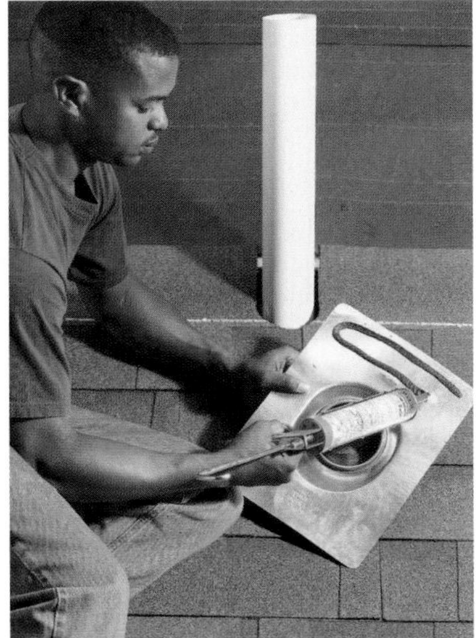

2 Buy a preformed flashing flange designed to fit around the vent pipe. Position the flange so it lies flat on the roof and mark the top of the flange on the underlayment with a pencil. Apply plastic-base asphalt roofing cement to the flange bottom and along the pencil line on the underlayment. Slip the flange over the pipe and press it in place.

3 Continue laying shingles, cutting them to fit around the pipe and setting them in plastic-base asphalt roofing cement (see inset). Apply the shingles to cover the upper edge of the flashing but leave the lower edge exposed so water and debris run off the surface.

Installing step flashing around a dormer

This dormer has yet to be sided. If you're working on a dormer that already has siding, remove the lowest piece of siding. Apply roofing cement to the side of the dormer. Set the flashing in the cement. Work your way up the roof, always positioning the upper piece so it overlaps the piece of flashing below.

1 Flash around a dormer as you're shingling it. Shingle as you normally would, bringing the shingles to a point just below the dormer. Lift the existing counterflashing and slip new flashing underneath it. Nail the lower edge of the flashing in place. This can be done with either a pneumatic nailer or with a regular hammer and nails.

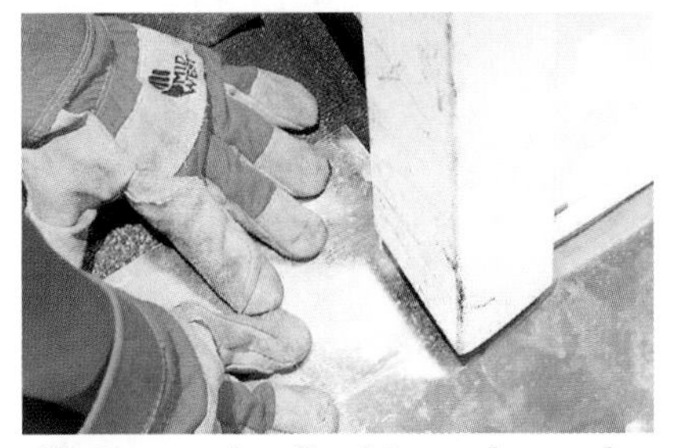

2 Cover the flashing along the front of the dormer with shingles. Apply roofing cement along the lower edge of the flashing. Trim the shingles to fit and set them in the cement. Step-flash the sides starting at the bottom of the dormer and working up the roof. (See "Installing Flashing Around a Chimney" on page 567.)

Installing asphalt shingles

See page 591

Skill level:	Time to complete per square:	Materials:	Tools:
★★★☆☆	Experienced 1 hr. Handy 2 hrs. Novice 3 hrs.	Shingles, galvanized roofing nails, plastic-base asphalt roofing cement, roofing felt	Roofing knife, tape measure, chalkline, claw hammer, roofing hammer, framing square, caulking gun, pneumatic nailer

Shingling begins, not surprisingly, with something called a starter strip, which is immediately covered up completely by the first course of shingles. If you look at a piece of shingling, you'll see why. Each shingle is 36 inches long and 12 inches wide. At the lower end are three tabs coated with a layer of fine stone. Just above the tabs are dabs of black sealant, which softens in warm weather and binds the layers of shingles together. Between the tabs is a space about ⅜ inch wide. If it weren't for the starter strip, water would flow down through these gaps and onto the tar paper, which would quickly wear out. Having a starter strip underneath the first course solves the problem.

Years ago the starter strip was simply a row of shingles installed with the tabs facing the peak of the roof. This method is no longer used. These days the general opinion is that you should cut the tabs off the starter strip and throw them out. Put the rest of the shingle on with the cut edge overlapping the eaves and gutter apron. Although anyone can see that this is a lot more work, it's less obvious that this results in a better roof. The cutting brings the self-sealing adhesive closer to the lower edge of the roof. When you put the first course over the starter strip, the adhesive helps seal the lower edge of the roof.

The roof shown here is a hipped roof. The process is exactly the same on a more traditional shed roof except that on a hipped roof the end shingle is trimmed at an angle. On a shed roof the end shingle is cut in a straight line.

CLOSER LOOK

THREE-TAB VS. ARCHITECTURAL SHINGLES

Three-tab shingles are the shingles that most of us grew up with: Two slots cut through the colored part of the shingle divide it into thirds. The shingles in this project are architectural shingles, which install the same way but look different and last a little longer. Instead of slots they get texture from tabs that are laminated to a solid shingle. The extra thickness helps give the shingle its longer life.

Asphalt shingle basics

1 Begin a starter strip by cutting the tabs off a shingle with a roofing knife. Then cut 6 inches off one end. Position the trimmed shingle on the roof with the cut edges overlapping the rake (edge) and eave (bottom) by ½ to ¾ inch. Nail the shingle onto the roof with four galvanized roofing nails, positioned 3 to 4 inches from the eaves.

2 Cut the tabs off another shingle and put the full length on the roof. Butt it against the first shingle and nail it in place with galvanized roofing nails spaced 12 inches apart. Continue cutting and installing along the roof until you have installed the starter strip from one side to the other.

3 Put a shingle on the roof so the lower edge overlaps the gutter apron at the eaves no more than ¾ inch, as shown in Step 4. Measure from the edge of the roof to the top of the shingle and snap a chalkline this distance from the edge along the entire roof. Do not use red chalk because red pigment will stain roofing materials.

4 Apply the first shingle of the first course. Begin at the edge and start with a full shingle. Position the shingle to overhang the eaves and rake edges by ¾ inch. Nail the shingle in place with four nails.

5 Once the first shingle is on, move to the first shingle of the second course. This helps align the shingles properly and means you don't have to move across the roof for every shingle. Cut 6 inches off the end of a shingle. Align the bottom edge of the shingle with the top of the cutouts in the first shingle. Nail it in place according to the manufacturer's directions.

6 With two shingles in place, start the third course. Cut 12 inches off the end of a shingle. Align the edge with the edge of the roof and align the bottom with the top of the cutouts in the shingle below. Nail the shingle in place. Continue up the roof to the sixth course, trimming each shingle to be 6 inches narrower than the one below it. (After the sixth course you will apply a full-length shingle along the edge of the roof.)

7 Return to the lower edge of the roof to reach the space next to the first shingle you installed. Butt a full-length shingle next to it and nail it in place.

8 Work your way up the roof, nailing a single full-length shingle next to each of the shingles already in place. After you've completed the sixth course, nail a full-length shingle in place to start the seventh course. Measure and snap a chalkline across the top to make sure the row is straight. Snap a line every seven rows so you can correct any errors before they get too serious.

Installing asphalt shingles (continued)

9 Continue working diagonally up and across the roof. All the shingles are full-length except those applied near the edge. Trim these shingles so each is 6 inches narrower than the one below. When the rake shingle is only 6 inches wide, start the pattern over, applying a full shingle above it.

10 When you reach the far edge of the roof, trim the shingles. On a straight-edged roof trim the shingles so they are just long enough to overlap the rake by no more than 3/4 inch. On a roof like the one shown here, trim them using a utility knife. Hooked blades will make cutting easier.

11 Finish shingling all the way up to the ridge, adding flashing as needed. When you reach the top, trim the shingle flush with the ridge. When you shingle the other side of the ridge, overlap the shingle on the ridge and nail it in place.

CLOSER LOOK

LAYING A CLOSED-CUT VALLEY

Lay a closed-cut valley over either metal roll flashing or heavy-duty valley liner, as described on page 566. Then lay the shingles to overlap and cut back the upper layer to create a roof that looks like the one above. Offset the cut 2 inches from the center of the valley so the bulk of the water won't run directly over the seam. Snap a chalkline from top to bottom for the trim. Insert a piece of flashing between the shingles when you trim the top to avoid cutting the layer underneath.

Shingling hips and ridges

1 Cut 12-inch-square hip caps from regular shingles. Then trim them so they taper at one end to 10 inches. Snap a chalkline parallel to the hip and 6 inches away from it on each side of the ridge. Attach each side of each cap with one roofing nail, 1 inch from the edge, just above the sealing tab. Overlap the caps by 1 inch.

2 When two hips meet cut a 4-inch V out of the middle of a hip shingle. Nail it in place and cover the nailheads with roofing cement. Shingle ridges as you would hips, working from each end toward the middle. **At the midpoint of the ridge, butt the neighboring ridge caps.** Cut 1 inch off the narrow end of the final cap shingle and nail over the butted caps. Cover nailheads with roofing cement.

Laying a valley with architectural shingles

1 A valley made with architectural shingles begins like one made with 3-tab shingles. Start on one side of the valley and shingle normally. Continue shingling well across the valley but avoid driving nails into the flashing below.

2 Line the valley with a row of shingles. Lay out the position by snapping a chalkline that runs from the top to the bottom of the valley, positioned so it is about 2 inches above the low point of the valley. Lay a row of shingles up the valley, with the bottom edge of the shingle on the chalkline.

3 Lay shingles for the adjoining roof starting at the valley. Position the first shingle of each row so its lower corner lines up with the lower edge of the shingles going up the valley. Lay the row and then come back to the valley and lay the next row the same way. Continue to the top of the dormer. The completed valley of shingles is shown in the inset above.

Laying a metal open valley

A metal open valley is wider at the bottom than at the top because it channels more water at the bottom of the roof. The heart of the valley is 20-inch-wide noncorroding prefab metal flashing. Make sure you don't drive any nails through the flashing as you lay the roof.

1 Cover the valley with an ice dam barrier, working from the bottom of the roof up and overlapping the ends by 6 inches if you use more than one piece. Center metal flashing in the valley and drive nails along the edges to hold it (see inset). Strike two chalklines to create a space 6 inches wide (3 inches on each side of the center of the flashing) at the peak and tapering ⅛ inch per foot to the eave of the valley on each side.

2 Shingle to the edge of the line. Trim the last shingle of the bottom row so it follows the chalkline. Clip off the top corner. Spread roofing cement from the outer edge of the flashing up to the chalkline (see inset); press the shingle into position. Then nail it in place. Nail the ice-dam barrier, avoiding the metal. Work your way up the roof following the standard roofing pattern.

Installing asphalt shingles (continued)

Roofing a dormer

1 Shingle along the roof in normal pattern, flashing around the dormer and butting shingles against it as you go. For more information see "Installing Step Flashing Around a Dormer," page 569. Snap a chalkline to lay out the first full row of shingles that will cross the roof above the dormer. Apply a row of shingles along this line.

2 Shingle one of the side roofs that form the dormer. Start at the bottom and work your way up as if it were a section of the regular roof. Start near the main roof and shingle it and the valley from the bottom up. (For more information on valleys, see pages 572 and 573.) If the dormer has three roofs like this one, stop the shingles when they touch the corner formed by the front roof. If the dormer has two roofs, shingle to the end. Trim as you would on the main roof.

3 Shingle the other side roof. Use the same technique as in Step 2 but continue shingling so the shingle overlaps the front roof, if any, and the ridge. Fold the shingles over and nail them in place.

4 If the dormer has a front roof, shingle it from the bottom up. Shingle over any shingles from the second side roof (on the right in this photo). Wrap the shingles around onto the first side roof (on the left in the photo). When you have run courses up the peak to the ridge, install cap shingles to cover the hips and top of the dormer. Cap shingles are single tabs (see inset).

5 Cut and install the cap shingles. Cut a group of shingles into single tabs. Starting at the front of the dormer wrap a tab over the peak and nail it as shown. Put a second tab over the first so it covers half the tab. Nail it in place and continue working your way back to the main roof. Tuck the last single tab under the row that you installed in Step 1. If the dormer has a front roof, cover the ridges on each side of it with single tabs and then cover the peak.

6 Make sure the rows on one side of the dormer align with those on the other. Start on the finished section of the main roof and measure the distance from the row you installed in Step 1 to the row you want to install. Transfer the measurement to the unfinished side of the roof, as shown here, and snap a chalkline. Lay a row along the line and repeat until you reach the row from which you're measuring.

Reroofing over an existing roof

Skill level:	Time to complete per square:	Materials:	Tools:
★★★☆☆	Experienced 1 hr. Handy 2 hrs. Novice 3 hrs.	Shingles, roofing nails, plastic-base asphalt roofing cement	Roofing knife, tape measure, pneumatic nailer, chalkline, utility knife, claw hammer, roofing hammer, framing square, caulking gun

Lucky you. If you're reading this your roof has only one or two layers of shingles. They are worn but basically sound and in good repair.

Reroofing differs only slightly from installing a new roof. Think about it: The underlying surface is not smooth. It is in fact shingled. The successive courses of shingles are stacked on top of each other like flat little stairs. Another stairlike layer on top would make for a somewhat ragged roof.

Fortunately the solution is simple: Fill in the first step. Cut shingles lengthwise, making them just wide enough to cover the bottom row of tabs on the existing roof. Nail them over the tabs. This fills in the first step. From here on it's smooth sailing. Shingle as you would a regular roof. Each new shingle fills in the step for the shingle that follows.

Make sure the nails are long enough to go at least ¾ inch into the roofing deck.

1 Trim enough off the top edge of the starter shingles so each shingle fits perfectly over the tabs of the existing first course. Then cut 6 inches off the end of the first shingle so ends won't align with those of the existing shingles. Nail the starter shingles in place along the entire bottom of the roof. **Cover the starter shingles with full-width shingles,** positioning them so they hang no more than ¾ inch over the edge of the roof or gutter apron.

WORK SMART

THREE-TAB SHINGLES

Some shingles applied over an old roof don't last as long as those applied over a roof from which the existing shingles have been removed. Others will and won't void the warranty. To be safe the shingles shown here are three tab instead of thicker, longer-lasting, and more expensive architectural shingles. If you're going to buy the best, strip off the old roof first. If you're going to roof over the existing roof you'll still get a solid roof but the shingles won't last quite as long as advertised.

2 Butt successive courses against the bottom of existing courses. Apply the remaining shingles as you would during a new installation. (See pages 570–574.) Remove damaged flashing as you install shingles and replace it with new flashing, shimming it to the proper height with shingles. Seal seams around flashing with roofing cement.

3 Tear off old hip and ridge caps as you approach the top of the roof. Waiting to remove the old hips and ridges is added protection in case it rains. Replace hip and ridge caps with new shingles after all other shingling has been completed.

Installing roll roofing

Skill level: ★☆☆☆☆

Time to complete: Experienced 1 hr. · Handy 2 hrs. · Novice 3 hrs.

Materials: Eave drip cap, rake drip edge, roofing nails, lap cement, roof cement

Tools: Broom, roofing knife, tape measure, chalkline, hammer or nail gun, trowel, straightedge (for trimming)

Roll roofing is commonly used for garages, outbuildings, storage sheds, and lean-tos that have more gradual roof pitches. Flattened out in precut strips of 18 feet or less, it is fairly easy to install by yourself. Roll roofing is generally made of the same material as asphalt shingles except you can cut it into strips according to your needs.

Roll roofing is generally installed as shown in this project because it is more resistant to wind damage. Another method to install roll roofing is to overlap half of each preceding course with each subsequent course, nail the top edge of each course, and cement the remaining edges. This results in a more appealing roof because there are no exposed nails covered with roof cement. But depending on wind conditions it can be less durable.

1 Sweep the roof deck clean and install gutter apron, rake drip edge, and underlayment (see pages 564–565). Unroll the roofing material on the ground and let it flatten. Cut a full-width strip long enough to overlap the eave and rakes by about ⅜ inch. Reroll the material and take it to the roof.

2 Trowel roofing cement onto the underlayment. Apply the layer no more than ⅛ inch thick. Thicker layers can cause the roof to blister.

3 Put the roll roofing in place, ensuring that it covers the drip cap. Walk along the roofing material to seat it firmly in the roofing cement.

4 Drive nails along the eaves and rake edges every 3 inches. Use hot-dipped galvanized roofing nails long enough to penetrate the deck ¾ inch. On a deck ½ inch thick use nails long enough to go through the deck and extend ¼ inch beyond it. Drive the nails about 1 inch from the edges but stagger them slightly to avoid splitting the wood below.

5 The next course overlaps the first by 2 inches. Snap a chalk guideline marking both the upper and lower edges of the course. Trowel roof cement onto this area and unroll the roofing into it. Seat by walking along the roofing as before. Nail the top edge with nails spaced approximately 18 inches apart.

6 Nail the lower edge and ends of the strip, driving the nails on 3-inch centers. Stagger the nails slightly, placing them at least ¾ inch above the seam. Apply roofing cement, lay subsequent courses, and nail up to the top of the roof.

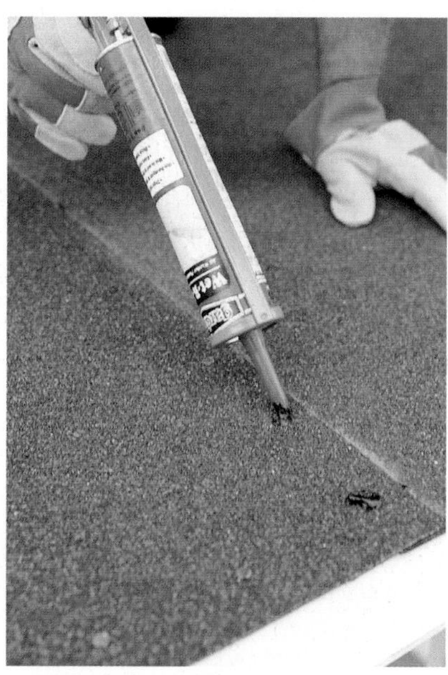

7 Seal the nail holes by covering them with roofing cement. A roof cement caulk, such as that shown here, works well and can be applied with a caulk gun.

8 If a piece of roofing is too short, apply a second piece that overlaps the ends of the first by at least 6 inches. Apply roofing cement to the entire overlap and push the top piece into the one below. Drive a row of nails spaced 4 inches apart through both layers; drive a second row through both layers spaced 4 inches from the first.

Repairing a rolled roof

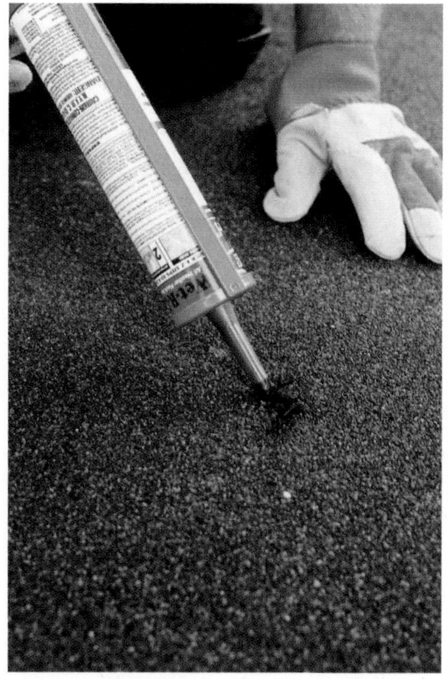

For small holes or punctures clean out the damaged area and fill it with roof sealer or roof tar.

For larger holes cut out the damaged area and replace it with a section of roofing material. Replace the underlayment too if it's damaged. Overlap the existing roof by 2 inches on the top and bottom and 6 inches on the edges. Cement and nail as you would when applying new roofing material.

Repairing walks, drives, and steps

Skill level:	Time to complete:	Materials:	Tools:
★★☆☆☆	Experienced Variable Handy Variable Novice Variable	Mortar, mason's sand, grout, thinset, 2×4, bonding agent, concrete, duplex nails, gravel, expansion joint, wire mesh, burlap, 2x form stock, asphalt repair materials	Tiff-bristle brush, putty knife, rubber mallet, hose, point punch, cold chisel, brick chisel, plugging chisel, pointing trowel, jointer, 3-pound and 7-pound sledgehammers, jackhammer, shovels, mixing tub, mortar bag, carbide scoring tool, straightedge, grout float, metal or wooden float, work gloves, safety glasses, dust mask, knee pads, old driveway broom

In any landscape the hardscape takes a beating. Not only do walks, drives, and outdoor steps get daily foot and equipment traffic, they suffer constant exposure to the elements. Over time something's got to give, and this calls for repairs. Freezing, thawing, and rain attack the most vulnerable spots—the joints. For example watch for small problems with the sand between pavers or the mortar along stones. Fill cracks in asphalt and concrete so freezing water doesn't get under the material and buckle it. On any brick steps check for mortar damage in the treads, where the treads meet the risers, and in joints between the steps and house or walk. Repoint these joints if necessary.

Repairing hardscape surfaces is not usually a large chore—if you attend to them at the first sign of a deteriorating surface. If you put off the repair, however, you may be asking for trouble. Hardscape damage can lead to serious drainage, structural, and safety problems. The best way to avoid catastrophic repair problems is to put your walks, drives, and steps (and yourself) on a regular maintenance schedule.

Whenever you repair masonry surfaces, dress for the repair. Gloves and safety glasses are necessities when chipping mortar. Heavy clothing and knee pads won't make you stylish but will protect you and your joints from bruising and pressure injuries. And whatever you wear when repairing asphalt, don't expect to wear it again. There's almost no way you can avoid spotting your clothing with the repair materials.

Repairing small cracks in concrete

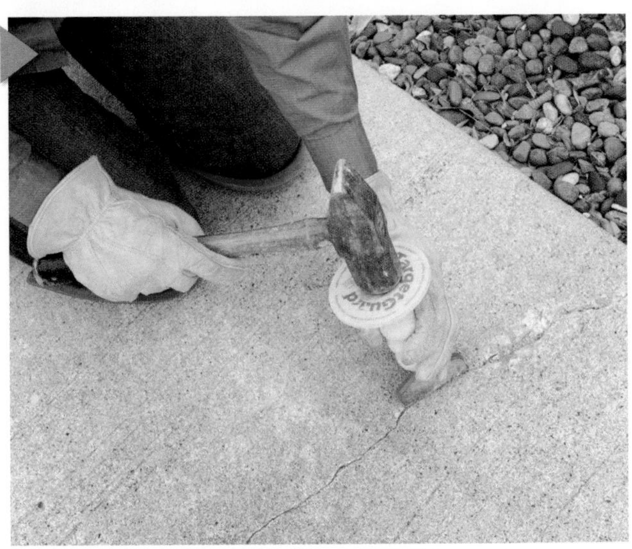

1 Fill cracks less than ⅛ inch wide with latex or epoxy patching compound, following the manufacturer's instructions. Larger cracks need to be undercut with a cold chisel angled slightly outward. Rap it with a 3-pound sledgehammer, widening the crack at the bottom.

2 Sweep the crack clean with a stiff-bristle brush, dampen it, then brush the surface with a concrete bonding agent. Wait 15 minutes before adding mortar to the crack. Prepare mortar by mixing one part portland cement and three parts mason's sand. Add enough water to make a thick paste. For small jobs use premix mortar.

3 Smooth the surface. Trowel on the mortar and smooth the surface with either a metal or wooden float.

Replacing brick, stone, or tile

1 Remove the mortar or grout. Replacing brick, stone, and tile are much the same. Chisel out the mortar around brick or stone with a plugging chisel. Remove the grout around tile with a grout saw.

2 Remove a damaged brick or stone by breaking it into smaller pieces with a hammer and cold chisel. Score a tile repeatedly on the diagonals with a carbide scoring tool and straightedge until the line is 1⁄16 inch deep. Strike in the middle with a point punch and hammer. Break up the rest of it with a cold chisel.

3 Chip away the mortar or thinset with a brick chisel. The resulting surface doesn't need to be perfect; remove enough to make room for a new bed of mortar or thinset.

4 Replace the mortar. Apply a ½-inch layer of mortar for use under brick or stone. For tile apply thinset, combing it out with a trowel that has notches the same size as the tile's thickness.

5 Set the brick, stone, or tile in place. Use a straightedge to make sure it is the same height as the surrounding pavers. Tap with a rubber mallet to set it deeper; add mortar or thinset, if necessary, to raise it.

6 Fill in around bricks or stone with mortar and tool it to match the surrounding mortar. When replacing a tile remove the thinset around the tile while it is still wet. Once the thinset under the tile has dried, apply grout with a grout float. After 15 minutes clean the tile with a scrub pad and water to remove excess grout.

Repairing walks, drives, and steps (continued)

Replacing concrete

1 Break the damaged section of concrete with a sledgehammer. If the area is more than a few square feet you may want to rent a jackhammer. Break up the concrete into small pieces.

2 Replace the existing gravel and tamp the surface. Install form boards against the existing concrete, holding them in place with 2×4 stakes. Nail the forms to the stakes with duplex nails.

TOOL TIP
CURING COMPOUNDS

Curing is the process by which concrete hardens. During this process you must take steps to make sure the concrete does not lose moisture too quickly. Curing products are available at home centers to ensure smooth, even curing of concrete walks and patios. Wax- and resin-base compounds are the most popular. Apply the curing compound with a paintbrush or roller while the concrete is still damp. For larger areas use a sprayer. Apply a second coat, brushing or spraying perpendicular to the first coat.

3 Place wire mesh on wire supports in the repair area at about the midpoint of the concrete's depth. If the concrete abuts a solid structure, such as a house foundation, place an expansion joint along the edge.

4 Empty bagged premix concrete into a wheelbarrow, add water, and mix until the consistency is firm yet workable. Apply a bonding agent to the broken edges of the concrete and pour concrete into the damaged area.

5 Screed the surface of the repaired area with a 2×4 so it is smooth and level with surrounding concrete. Float and finish the surface to match the old concrete. Cover the repaired area with a sheet of plastic and allow the concrete to cure for at least one day.

Repairing concrete steps

1 Scrub the broken area clean with a stiff, wet brush. Apply concrete bonding agent to the exposed concrete with a paintbrush. This helps the patching compound adhere to the old concrete.

2 Wait until the bonding agent gets sticky, then apply patching compound to the damaged area with a mason's trowel. Apply enough compound to replace the missing concrete. If you are using a vinyl concrete-patching mix, no bonding agent is required.

3 Tape together a wood form to fit around the corner. Place pavers against the form so it doesn't move while the compound is hardening. If the area to be patched is large, you may want to create this form before Step 2.

Repairing walks, drives, and steps (continued)

Patching asphalt

It's easy to overlook problems in asphalt that need repair. We drive or walk on these surfaces every day and probably aren't in the habit of paying as much attention to their conditions as we are in getting to where they lead us. In addition the color and texture of asphalt doesn't lend itself to spotting repairs easily. A small crack in a concrete surface, for example, will show up readily as a dark line when the same crack in asphalt might not be perceptible at all. Walk your drive or walk periodically. If you see dents or impressions left by the car after it's been parked overnight, that's an indication of structural damage. Tilted sections or heaving or buckled surfaces mean your drainage is poor. These are major problems that most often require the installation of a new section or a new drive. But there are a host of small problems such as cracks, crumbling, or holes that you can fix easily. The procedures you'll use and the materials you need will vary with the types of repairs you make.

Try to do your asphalt repairs when the temperature is 60°F (16°C) or higher. At colder temperatures asphalt is brittle, crumbles, and becomes difficult to work with. If the weather is cool, store your tools and repair materials indoors in a warm place. Break up any lumps in the bag before opening it.

All asphalt surfaces need sealing about every two years. Whenever the surface looks checked with hairline cracks, buy 5-gallon buckets of sealer and apply it as shown opposite.

1 Clean any loose material from the damaged area with a shop vacuum. Make sure you leave a base of solid material. For deep holes add gravel to conserve your patching material. Then flush out the area with water from a garden hose.

2 Add asphalt patching material to the damaged area, overfilling it slightly. Slice it with a trowel or spade to remove air pockets. Heat the patching material with a heating gun, following the manufacturer's instructions.

3 While the warmed patching material is still soft, tamp it level to the surrounding area with a wooden tamper or concrete block. Add patching material and repeat the process to bring the patched area level with its surroundings.

Sealing asphalt

1 Clean the entire surface with an asphalt cleaner or detergent and water. Scrub away loose material with a stiff brush or garage broom. Flush the area thoroughly.

2 Use a caulking gun to fill all cracks up to ¼ inch wide with patching caulk. Add sand to deep cracks before applying the caulk. For wider cracks clean the area and fill the crack with asphalt patching material.

3 Use a putty knife to press the patching compound into the crack and smooth it.

4 Spread the sealing compound across the surface in sections, working it into the surface and leveling it with a garage broom or squeegee, following the manufacturer's instructions. Always apply two coats, letting the first one cure before applying the second coat.

CANADIAN CODE

Meeting Canadian code

Building codes in the United States (U.S.) and Canada are similar and most of the directions in this book meet code on either side of the border. There are differences, however, and sometimes what meets code in the U.S. doesn't make the grade in Canada, or Canadian codes offer alternatives that wouldn't meet specifications in the U.S.

The biggest differences are in the plumbing and electrical codes. Canadian codes permit the use of ABS plastic pipe for drain and waste lines. U.S. code allows primarily PVC, but ABS is acceptable in certain parts of the country. Canadian electrical code calls for a separate service-panel bus bar for the ground wire and for a ground screw on all receptacles and switchboxes (metal or plastic). U.S. code generally requires neither.

Uniform differences

Neither country has a monopoly on conflicting code authorities. The National Housing Code of Canada (NHC) sets uniform standards, but provinces, cities, and towns can set standards. As a result your local code may vary from what's described here.

You can purchase full-length copies of the relevant codes but they can be expensive and difficult to wade through. Most of the material deals with commercial installations. Smaller, more distilled handbooks are available to buy or borrow from libraries that emphasize residential installations.

In Canada as in the U.S., the only way to be sure you're meeting code is to ask your local building inspector while the job is still in the planning stages. Which begs the question: If it's your house and you're doing the work yourself, why should a city inspector come around and tell you what to do?

Collective wisdom

Codes and inspections are a sort of collective wisdom based on the experience of the construction trades, fire and police departments, and manufacturers. Building codes exist to prevent house fires and injuries from shocks and to keep all the systems in your home running effectively.

Meeting national, provincial, and local codes

Your local building department will often require you to get a permit and have the work approved by one of its inspectors. Inspectors and building departments use the national code references as the basis for most of their regulations. Local standards, however, often supplement or modify these basic rules. You'll find an overview of most common code requirements on the following pages. The list is not complete and you may need other sources of information.

Coordinating the tasks

If you are building an addition to your house or gutting walls to remodel a kitchen or bathroom you'll need to juggle carpentry, plumbing, and wall and floor finishing. Whether you do all or some of the work yourself, it's important that the various jobs are coordinated so workers do not get in the way of each other and inspectors can see what they need to inspect. Here's an example of a properly phased installation:

- Install framing or gut the walls.
- Run the rough plumbing, install electrical cable and boxes, and then call in the inspector.
- Cover the walls with drywall, and paint.
- Install the finish plumbing and electrical and have it inspected.

Working with an inspector

Inspectors usually work with professional electricians who know codes and what is expected at inspections. Inspectors usually have a tight schedule and can't take time to educate you about what is needed. Their job is to inspect, not to help you plan your project. Take these steps to ensure that an inspection goes smoothly:

- **Before scheduling an inspection** ask the building department for printed information about your type of project. Make neat, readable, and complete drawings and provide a list of the materials.
- **When you present your plans, accept criticisms and directives graciously.** It usually does no good to argue—and the inspector does know more than you do. Make it clear you want to do things the right way. Take notes while the inspector talks to you so you can remember every detail of what needs to be done.
- **Be clear on when the inspections will take place and exactly what needs to be done before each inspection.** Before calling for an inspection, double-check that everything required is complete—don't make the inspector come back again. Don't cover up wiring the inspector needs to see. If you install drywall before the inspection, you may have to rip it out and reinstall it after the inspection.
- **Some building departments limit the kinds of work a homeowner can do;** you may have to hire a professional for at least part of a job. Others will let you take on advanced work only if you can pass an oral or written test.

Metrics and you

Most of the world has adopted the metric system—with the exception of the United States and some of the building trades. In Canada you'll find that some trades have converted completely to metric while others still use the old English measurements. When you get right down to it, it doesn't really matter: The guy at the lumberyard is going to hand you exactly the same sheet whether you order 19-mm plywood or ¾-inch plywood. To make it easy to compare sizes, however, we've included both English and metric measurements on these pages where applicable. When you go to the store, use whichever measurement is more commonly used for the items you're buying.

General construction

Basement insulation

In Canada the inside of basement walls must be treated with a damp-proofing product (usually a paint-on product) before insulation is installed. The insulation goes against the damp-proofing and is then covered by a vapor barrier. In the U.S., polyethylene sheeting is attached to the wall instead.

Crawlspace insulation

Insulation must go down the wall but stop no less than 2 inches (51 mm) above the floor. In the U.S., insulation continues to the floor and runs partway across it.

Doorjambs

To help a door withstand forced entry, Canadian code requires solid wood blocking at lock height on both the lock and hinge side of the door.

Floor joists

Replacement joists, generally speaking, should be the same width as the old ones. Canada and the U.S. set standards, however, on how long an unsupported span of joist can be. The span varies based on the width of the joist and how far apart the joists are spaced. Canadian code generally requires shorter spans than those allowed in the U.S. If you suspect the joists supporting your floor aren't wide enough, talk with your local building inspector.

Headers

Although construction of headers is the same in both Canada and the U.S., allowable spans for load-bearing headers are slightly different. Allowable spans also vary with the number of floors the header supports and the amount of snow likely to build up on the roof. In areas with milder weather a header made of two 2×4s (38×89 mm), with ½-inch (12-mm) plywood in between can span a door opening as wide as 40 inches (1.01 meters), considerably more than in the U.S. A 2×8 (38×184 mm) beam built the same way can span an opening of up to 68 inches (1.75 meters) slightly less than in the U.S. Check with your local building authority on how snowfall, number of floors, and the wood species you're using will affect requirements.

Smoke alarms

Smoke alarms must be placed on every floor, must be interconnected, and must be powered by the home's electrical system. Battery-operated smoke alarms are acceptable only in homes with no power.

Wood flooring

Standard wood flooring thicknesses are different in the U.S. and Canada, as are the nailing patterns. In Canada the size and spacing of nails depend on the thickness of the flooring. In the U.S., the nailing pattern also depends on the width of the flooring. Whether in the U.S. or Canada, follow the manufacturer's instructions and check with your local building authority for specifics. Here are the general guidelines for Canadian installations:

- **5⁄16-inch-thick (7.9-mm) floor:** 1½-inch-long (38-mm) nails spaced at a maximum of 8 inches (203 mm).
- **7⁄16-inch-thick (11.1-mm) floor:** 2-inch-long (51-mm) nails spaced at a maximum of 12 inches (305 mm).
- **¾-inch-thick (19-mm) floor:** 2¼-inch-long (57-mm) nails spaced at a maximum of 16 inches (406 mm).

Metric conversions

U.S. Units to Metric Equivalents			Metric Units to U.S. Equivalents		
To convert from	**Multiply by**	**To get**	**To convert from**	**Multiply by**	**To get**
Inches	25.4	Millimeters	Millimeters	0.0394	Inches
Inches	2.54	Centimeters	Centimeters	0.3937	Inches
Feet	30.48	Centimeters	Centimeters	0.0328	Feet
Feet	0.3048	Meters	Meters	3.2808	Feet
Yards	0.9144	Meters	Meters	1.0936	Yards
Square inches	6.4516	Square centimeters	Square centimeters	0.1550	Square inches
Square feet	0.0929	Square meters	Square meters	10.764	Square feet
Square yards	0.8361	Square meters	Square meters	1.1960	Square yards
Acres	0.4047	Hectares	Hectares	2.4711	Acres
Cubic inches	16.387	Cubic centimeters	Cubic centimeters	0.0610	Cubic inches
Cubic feet	0.0283	Cubic meters	Cubic meters	35.315	Cubic feet
Cubic feet	28.316	Liters	Liters	0.0353	Cubic feet
Cubic yards	0.7646	Cubic meters	Cubic meters	1.308	Cubic yards
Cubic yards	764.55	Liters	Liters	0.0013	Cubic yards
To convert from degrees Fahrenheit (F) to degrees Celsius (C), first subtract 32, then multiply by 5⁄9.			To convert from degrees Celsius (C) to degrees Fahrenheit (F), multiply by 9⁄5, then add 32.		

Meeting Canadian code (continued)

Plumbing

Canadian code allows the use of both PVC and ABS pipe in drain and water systems. ABS is the most commonly used in Canada. Procedures for attaching fittings and installing PVC and ABS are similar. They are both easy to cut, lightweight, and rigid; ABS, however, has a slightly shorter lifespan and can become brittle over time. The key difference is the nature of the adhesives, which are not interchangeable. PVC does not require a primer but you must use a specified cleaner before applying the adhesive.

You may find yourself in a situation where you need to join PVC and ABS. If so special transition fittings are available to make the hookup.

▲ ***Double-bowl sinks cannot drain through a center tee in Canada.*** *In Canadian systems the drainpipe from one of the sinks runs straight down, through the trap, and then straight down into the rest of the DVW system. The drainpipe from the second sink connects with the first drain through a vertical tee located above the trap. (On center-tee systems the pipes from the sinks meet midway between the two sinks and then run down through the trap.)*

ABS pipe and fittings

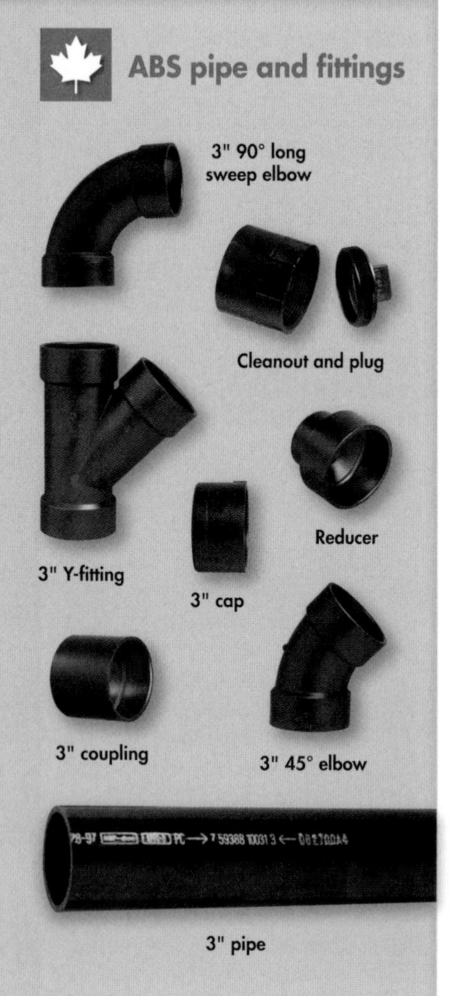

▲ ***P-traps: All drains in Canada must use a P-trap, which keeps sewer gases from backing up into the house.*** *The trap serves as a safety device by preventing noxious gases from backing up the sewer pipe and entering the house. Sewer gases not only pose a health hazard, they can also be explosive. The curved portion of the trap holds standing water. Every time the drain is used, water is flushed through the trap and is replaced with fresh water. Solids will adhere to the trap over time and eventually clog the drain or possibly damage the trap—which means it's time to install a new one.*

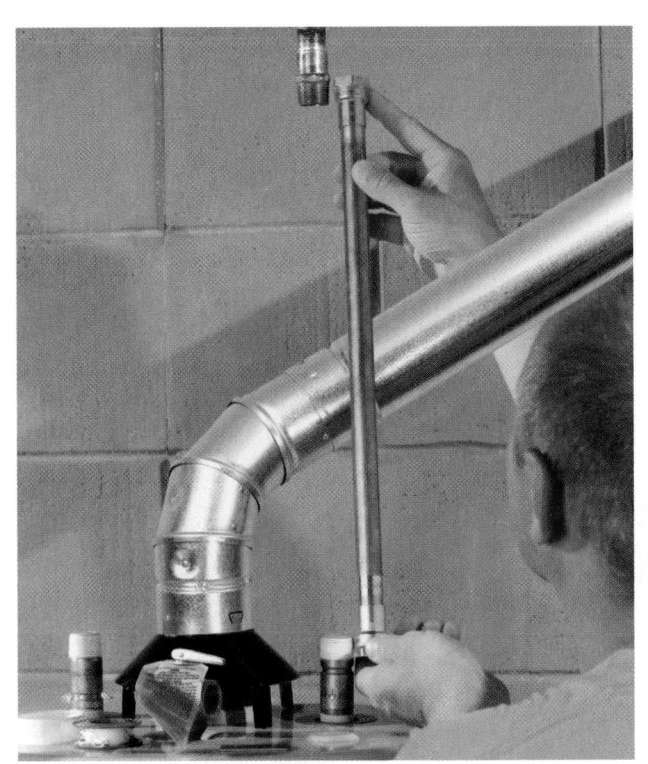

▲ ***Water heaters.*** *Rigid and flexible copper supply pipe, as shown above, can be used to hook up the hot and cold lines in some areas. Check with local provincial codes. Rigid copper pipe remains the most common installation. Flexible gas supply must be used from the gas line to the unit. In areas subject to earthquake, the hot water heater must be attached to the house framing.*

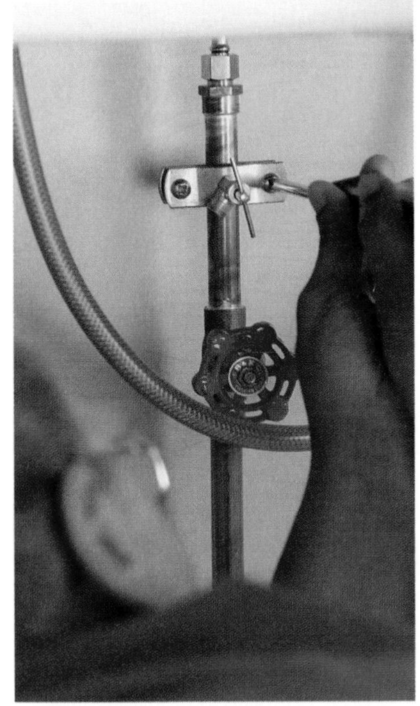

▲ ***The saddle tee shown above cannot be used*** *to tap into an existing pipe in Canada. It does not meet code. You must use a compression tee, as shown at right, for the job.*

Installing a compression fitting

1 Install the valve. The kit may come with a saddle tee, but it may not meet code, so you should use a compression tee instead. Installing the compression tee follows the same steps as installing a shutoff valve. (See page 98.)

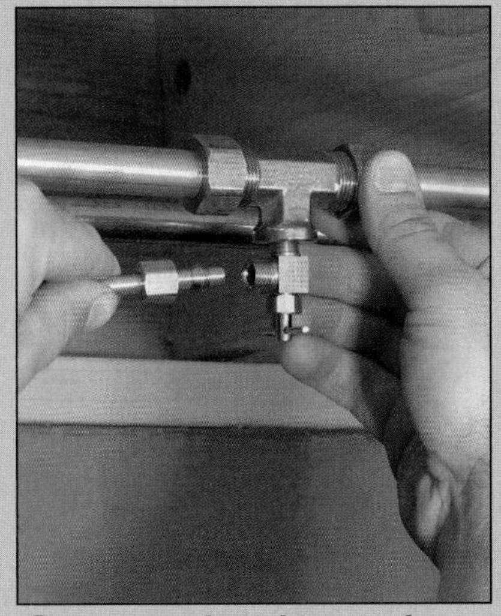

2 Connect the tubing to the valve. Insert the tubing into the valve and tighten the nut. Use an adjustable wrench to connect the compression fitting. (See page 98 for connecting compression fittings.)

Meeting Canadian code (continued)

Electrical

240-volt and 120-/240-volt circuits

The shapes of the plugs and receptacles on these circuits differ in the U.S. and Canada. The wiring is the same. Four-conductor wiring—two hot, a neutral, and a ground—is required by most but not all local codes.

Breakers

Half-size breakers do not meet code in Canada.

Cable Color

Canadian cable is available with a solid red jacket. Red-coded cables are used for wires that run directly from the service panel to an outlet.

GFCI outlets

GFCI outlets are not required along kitchen countertops in Canada. See "Kitchens" (opposite) for other differences.

Grounding metal electrical boxes

Devices such as switches and receptacles, as well as the boxes that house them, must be connected to the service-panel ground bus. There is a screw, generally in the back of the box, for the ground wire. Connect this screw and the screw on the body of the device to pigtails. Attach both pigtails to the circuit's ground wire.

Grounding plastic electrical boxes

Plastic boxes in Canada have a ground screw in them even though plastic is not a conductor. An internal connection in the box connects the screw to the body of the device (a switch or outlet) that the box houses. The connection grounds exposed metal parts of the device, protecting you should they become energized. (The ground screw in a metal box provides the same protection.) When you're wiring connect both the ground screw in the box and the ground screw on the receptacle to a pigtail. Attach the pigtails to the wire running to the service panel's ground bus.

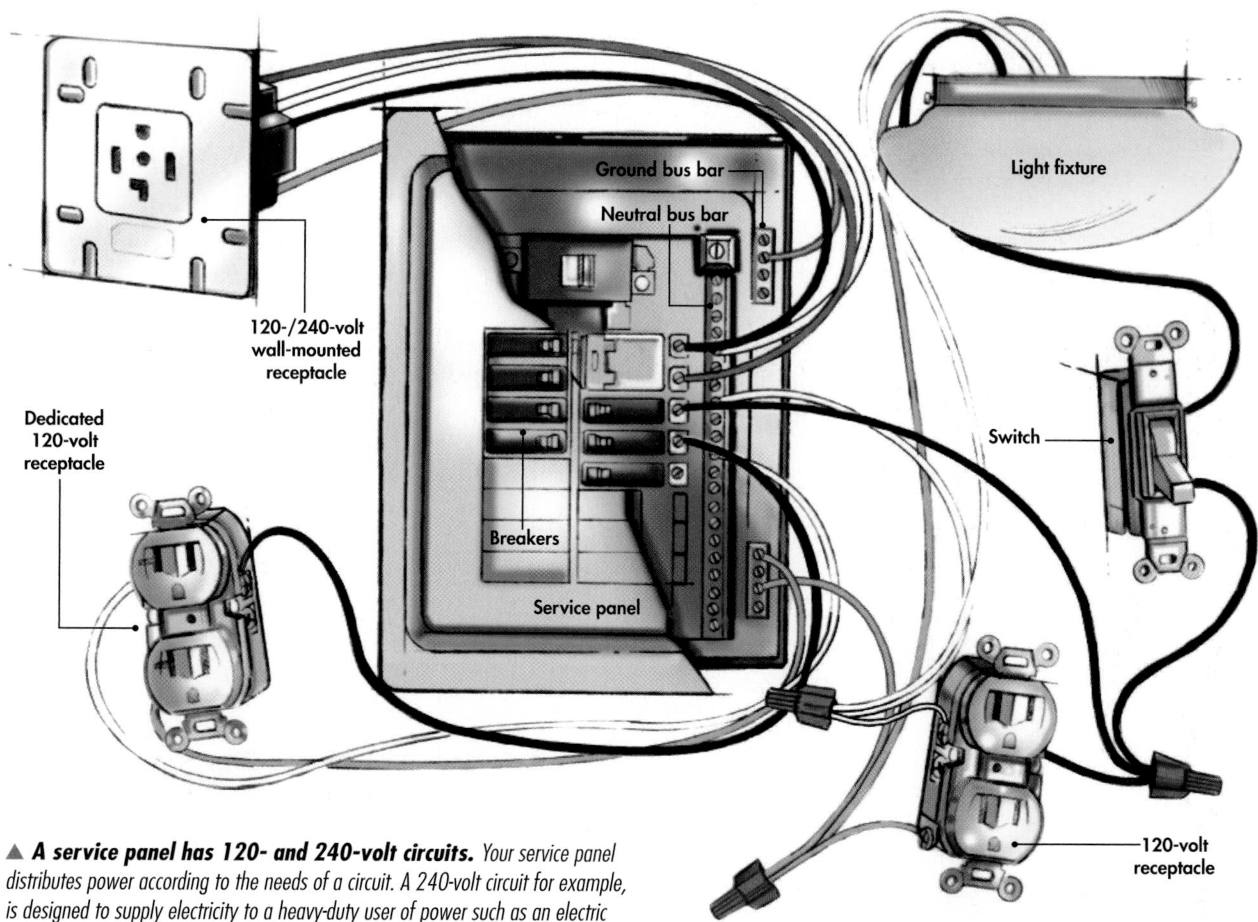

▲ ***A service panel has 120- and 240-volt circuits.*** *Your service panel distributes power according to the needs of a circuit. A 240-volt circuit for example, is designed to supply electricity to a heavy-duty user of power such as an electric range or a dryer. (The 240-volt receptacle has a different shape and configuration than those in the U.S.) The single receptacle on a dedicated 120-volt circuit might feed a refrigerator or a large microwave, while another 120-volt circuit feeds a series of receptacles and switched overhead light fixtures. Depending on local code and the manufacturer, some switches may not have a grounding wire.*

▲ ***Note:*** *In some service panels you may find that the neutral feed wire is not white. If that's the case, strips of white tape may have been added to differentiate between the neutral and hot feeds.*

Grounding light fixtures and ceiling fans

Light fixtures must be grounded in Canada and the U.S. In Canada however the ground wire must run to a separate grounding bus bar in the service panel. (In the U.S., it runs to the common bus bar.) Connect the circuit's ground wire to the fixture's ground wire if it has one. If not connect the circuit's ground wire to a screw on the mounting strap.

Grounding switches and receptacles

Each switch and receptacle has a green ground screw, which should be connected to the circuit's ground wire by a pigtail. A second pigtail should run from the ground wire to the ground screw on the box. The wiring inside the box is the same in the U.S. and Canada. In Canada however the ground wire runs to a ground bus bar in the service panel. In the U.S., it usually runs to the common bus bar.

Grounding service panels

Canadian code requires three separate bus bars in a service panel: a hot bus, neutral bus, and ground bus. (Boxes in the U.S. have only two bus bars: hot and neutral.) All ground wires in the circuit run back to the service panel and are connected to the ground bar.

Kitchens

Canadian code requires at least one 15-amp circuit for lighting. Space those receptacles above countertops no more than 4 feet apart. Receptacles above a countertop must be split-circuit, meaning that the upper outlet must be on one circuit while the lower outlet is on another circuit. (There is no requirement for GFCI receptacles above counters because the outlets on a GFCI cannot be split.) Many local Canadian codes require dedicated circuits for dishwashers and refrigerators. A microwave must have a single 20-amp circuit.

U.S. code requires a 15-amp circuit for lighting, two 20-amp circuits for receptacles, and separate circuits for the dishwasher and refrigerator. Receptacles above counters must be no more than 4 feet apart and must be GFCI.

Electrical codes you may encounter

Here's a quick summary of codes that are typical for household wiring projects. Follow them as you work up your plans and write your materials list.

These guidelines should satisfy most requirements, but keep in mind that your local codes might have different requirements. You probably will want to exceed requirements to provide your family with sufficient and safe electrical service.

The more you communicate your specific plans and techniques to your inspector, the less chance there will be that you will have to tear out and do the job over. It's better to be set straight by your inspector when the job is still on paper.

Cable type

Most locales allow NM (nonmetallic) cable for all installations where the cable runs inside walls or ceilings. Some areas require armored cable or conduit. If the cable will be exposed, many local codes require armored cable or conduit.

Wire gauge

Use #14 wire for 15-amp circuits and #12 wire for 20-amp circuits.

Plastic and metal boxes

Many locales allow plastic boxes for receptacles, switches, and fixtures, but some require metal boxes. Boxes must be flush with the finished drywall, plaster, or paneling. Make sure boxes are large enough for their conductors (page 170).

Running cable

NM and armored cable must be run through holes in the centers of studs or joists so drywall or trim nails cannot reach it. Most codes require metal nail guards as well. Some inspectors want cable for receptacles to be run about 10 inches above the receptacles. NM cable should be stapled to a stud or joist within 8 inches of the box it enters. Once the cable is clamped to a box, at least ¼ inch of sheathing should be visible in the box, and at least 8 inches of wire should be available for connecting to the device or fixture.

Circuit capacity

Make sure usage does not exceed "safe capacity" (pages 362-363). Local codes may be stricter.

Living room, dining room, family room, and bedroom specs

Space receptacles every 12 feet (3.7 meters) along each wall and 6 feet (1.8 meters) from the first opening. If a small section of wall (between two doors, for example) is more than 3 feet (1 meter) wide, it should have a receptacle. For most purposes use 15-amp receptacles. Convenience rooms should have at least one light controlled by a wall switch near the entry door. Pull chains for ceiling lights, however, are acceptable. The switch may control an overhead light or one outlet of a receptacle, into which you can plug a lamp. Make sure the box you attach a ceiling fan to can support the additional weight.

Hallway and stairway specs

A stairway must have an overhead light controlled by three-way switches at the bottom and top of the stairs. If a hallway is longer than 10 feet (3 meters), it must have at least one receptacle.

Kitchen specs

Above countertops space receptacles no more than 4 feet (1.22 meters) apart. Codes call for split-circuit receptacles, which cannot be GFCI, above a countertop. Install one 15-amp circuit for lighting. Many codes require split receptacles on 15-amp circuits in kitchens and dedicated circuits for the dishwasher and refrigerator. A microwave must have a single 20-amp circuit.

Bathroom specs

Any GFCI receptacle should be on its own circuit. Install the lights and fan on a separate 15- or 20-amp circuit.

Garage and workshop specs

Install a 15-amp circuit for lights and a 20-amp circuit for tools. Install two 20-amp circuits if you have many power tools. Many areas require GFCIs in garages. Check your local code.

Meeting Canadian code (continued)

CANADIAN CODE

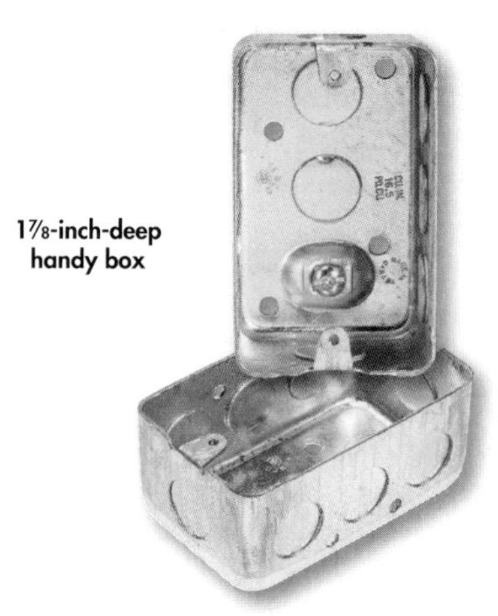

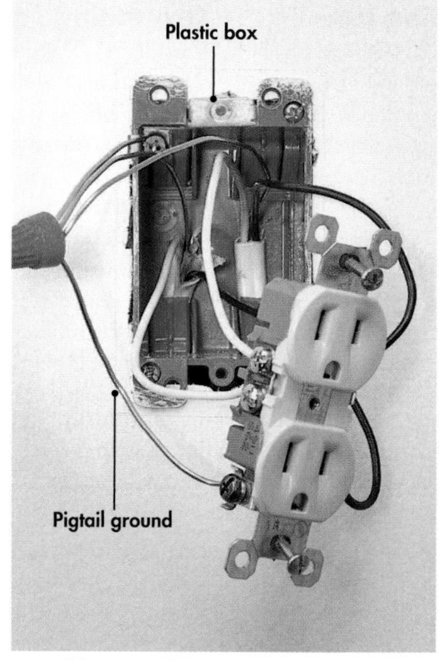

▲ ***Cables in a plastic box.*** *Because plastic boxes do not conduct electricity, the receptacle must be grounded by attaching it to the bare ground wire in the cable. Check that bare copper grounding wires are spliced together and are attached to the grounding screw of the receptacle with a pigtail ground wire.*

▲ ***Conduit in a metal box.*** *If conduit enters the box, it likely acts as the ground for the receptacle. To ground the receptacle connect copper wire to the back of the box and the ground screw on the receptacle. Check the receptacle with an analyzer (see page 370) to make sure it is grounded.*

SAFETY ALERT

GROUND 'EM FIRST

Always connect the ground wires first. Once you are sure all the ground connections are firm, connect the neutral wire, then the hot wire. To ensure a solid connection between the receptacle and the box, remove the cardboard washer from the receptacle's screws. If you forget to ground a device, you may not detect the resulting danger because the ungrounded device or fixture will work just fine.

How a grounded receptacle works

To ground a receptacle, a ground wire (either bare or green) is attached to the receptacle (and to the box) and leads to the ground bus bar in the service panel. The panel itself is grounded (see page 369). This receptacle is also polarized.

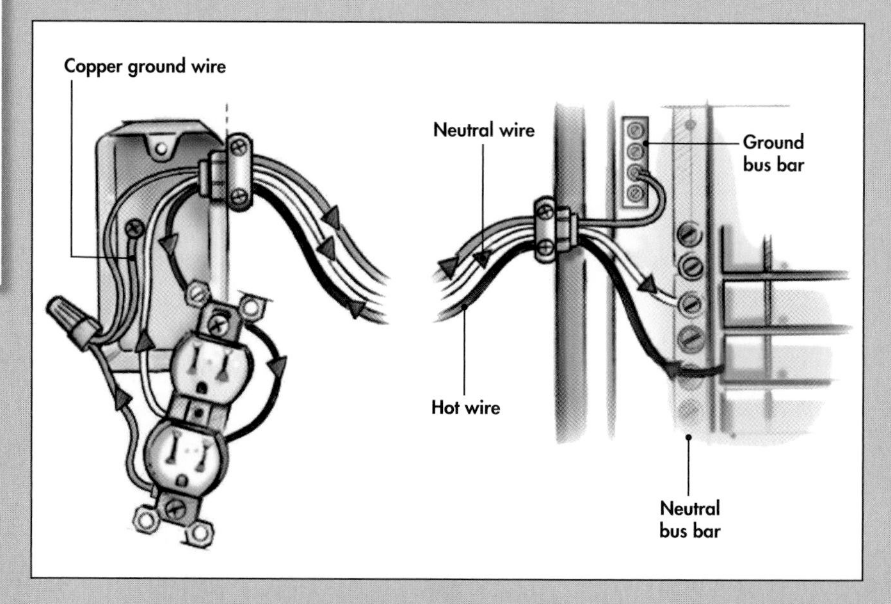

Roofing

Canadian code requires that ice-dam underlayment extend from the eave 36 inches (914 mm) up the roof. U.S. practice is to have underlayment extend 24 inches (610 mm) from the inside face of the exterior wall.

Roofing nails

Canadian code says the nails should go a minimum of ½ inch (13 mm) into the roof deck. U.S. standards call for nails a minimum of ¾ inch long (19 mm), which pass all the way through the deck and protrude a minimum of ¼ inch (6 mm) beyond it.

Roofs with low slopes

In Canada shingles on roofs with a slope less than 1:3 must be set in a band of asphalt cement. The band must be 8 inches (203 mm) wide. When you lay the starter row, the asphalt cement goes directly onto the underlayment. In subsequent rows it's applied to the section of shingles that will be covered by the row above. Space the rows so each shingle overlaps two-thirds of the shingle below instead of the usual half shingle.

The U.S. requires extra underlayment instead of close spacing of the shingles. Start at the bottom of the roof with a 19-inch-wide (483 mm) strip of underlayment. Cover it entirely with a 36-inch-wide (914 mm) strip. Cover the 36-inch strip with another 36-inch strip that starts 17 inches (432 mm) from the bottom of the roof. Subsequent strips are 36 inches wide and overlap the one below by 19 inches. Space shingles normally. Instead of a band of adhesive hold down three-tab shingles with two dabs of asphalt cement. Use three dabs on architectural shingles.

Valleys

In Canada open valleys are required on all but very steep roofs (those with a slope of 1:1.2).

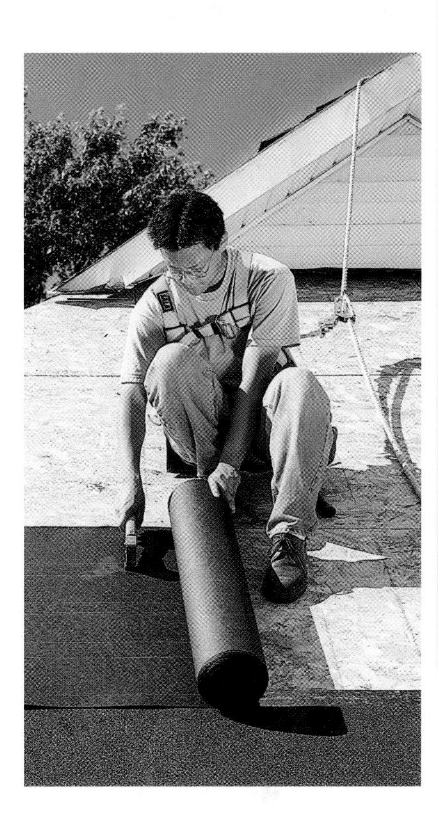

Heating, ventilation, and air-conditioning

Canadian code requires a ventilation system that brings fresh air into the house. Although this can be a separate system it can also be built into the furnace. If so a vent pipe runs from outdoors into the return air plenum. Vent size, the need for a fan, and how the vent is attached vary depending on the size of the house and the furnace. Consult local building authorities for specifics.

Tool glossary

4-in-1 tool

A multipurpose tool for cleaning and deburring copper pipe before soldering.

Abrasive stone file

A file used to finish custom cuts on ceramic tile.

Acid flux brush

Applies flux to copper fittings.

Adjustable wrench

A wrench with an adjustable head to accommodate various sizes of nuts and bolts.

Allen wrenches

Hexagonal wrenches used in conjunction with screws or bolts with recessed hexagonal heads.

Backsaw

Fine-tooth handsaw that cuts on the back stroke. Intended for precise cuts on molding and trim.

Ball peen hammer

A hammer for shaping metal, with a flat face for driving and pounding on one end and a rounded surface on the other.

Bar clamp (hand screw)

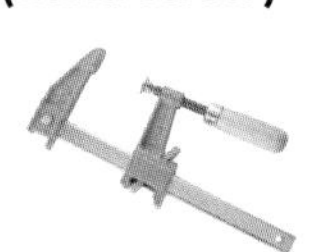

An adjustable clamp. Comes in several lengths.

Basin wrench

A specially designed wrench for removing or installing mounting and coupling nuts on faucets.

Basin wrench (plastic fittings)

A plumbing tool for removing plastic fittings on plumbing fixtures.

Belt sander

A heavy-duty sander that removes grain and thickness on wood.

Bevel gauge

An adjustable measuring tool for copying and marking angles for cutting.

Block plane

A small hand plane that shaves, smooths, and shapes wood.

Brush and roller spinner

Spins excess water out of brushes or roller covers after cleaning.

Brush and tool extender

An extension pole with an adjustable clamp that holds paintbrushes and other tools to get to hard-to-reach places.

C-clamp

A screw-operated clamping device. Comes in several sizes.

Cabinet template

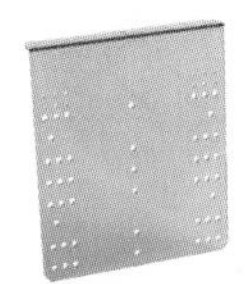

Marks holes for attaching cabinet hardware.

Carbide drill bit (adjustable)

An adjustable carbide drill bit that cuts precise access holes in ceramic tile.

Carbide-grit rod saw

A hand tool for cutting ceramic tile.

Carpenter's level

A straightedge with leveling bubbles for determining horizontal or vertical planes. Available in several lengths.

Carpenter's pencil

A large flat pencil with a wide lead ideal for marking.

Cat's paw (pry bar)

A steel bar to remove nails or pry pieces apart.

Caulking gun

Holds tubes of caulking or adhesives for applications such as sealing seams and bonding materials.

Chalkline

A chalk-filled container that marks long, straight lines for cutting or alignment. Also used as a plumb bob.

Circuit tester (neon)

Determines the presence of electricity in a circuit.

Circular level

Ascertains level on horizontal surfaces.

Circular saw

A hand power tool primarily for crosscutting and ripping wood materials to length and width.

Claw hammer

A hammer that comes in various weights with a face for driving nails and curved tines for prying and nail removal.

Closet auger

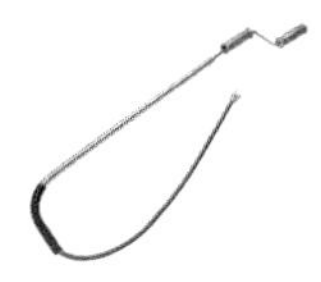

An auger designed specifically to remove clogs in toilets without damaging the toilet.

Cold chisel

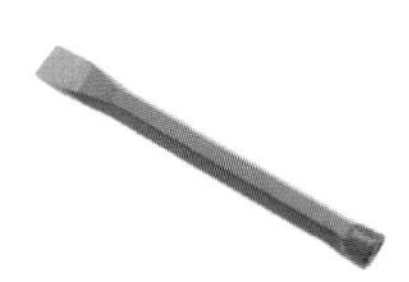

A steel chisel with a tempered edge for cutting steel and removing ceramic tile. Available with rubber safety handles.

Combination square

A layout tool with a sliding handle that marks lines at 90 and 45 degrees.

Combination wrench

A wrench with an open and boxed end. The boxed end provides more control and less slippage.

Combs

Made of plastic or rubber, they apply decorative finishes to surfaces. Fin combs clean fins on air-conditioning units.

Compass (scribing)

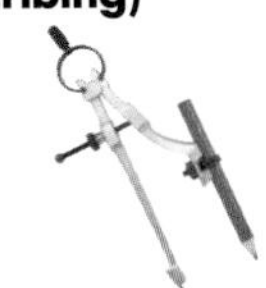

An adjustable tool for marking circles or transferring contours from one surface to another. It has a pin on one leg and pencil on the other.

Continuity tester

An instrument that tells whether a device is capable of carrying electricity.

Coping saw

A fine-tooth, thin-blade saw blade mounted in a C-shape frame, used to cut precise outlines in wood.

Copper fitting brush

Deburrs and cleans debris from the interior surface of copper pipe and fittings.

Copper tube deburrer

Removes burrs and debris from the exterior of copper pipe in preparation for soldering.

Cordless reversible screwdriver

Lightweight, battery-operated screwdriver useful for small assembly projects.

Countersink bit

A combination drill bit that sets screws flush to or below the surface of wood.

Diagonal cutting pliers

Wire-cutting tool with diagonal blades that provide extra leverage; also for removing nails and staples.

Double box-ended ratchet wrench

The box ends allow for more control when removing or installing nuts and bolts. The wrench comes in various sizes.

Double open-ended wrench

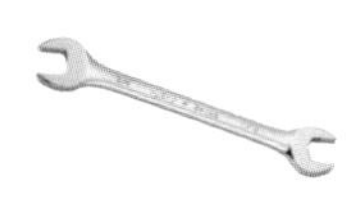

Used to tighten or loosen nuts and bolts. Usually sold in sets with wrenches in graduated sizes.

Drain auger (drill-driven)

A power-driven auger for removing clogs from drain and waste lines; not to be used in toilets or other fragile fixtures.

Drain auger (hand snake)

A manual drain auger that removes clogs in drain and waste pipes; not for use in toilets.

Drain auger (hand spinning)

A hand-turned auger for removing clogs from drain and waste lines; not for toilets.

Drill bit extension

Extends the reach of a standard drill bit.

Drop cloth

Large canvas or paper/plastic sheet that protects surfaces or objects during work sessions.

Drywall hawk

Holds joint compound or plaster on a metal platform with a spindle handle while applying it to surfaces.

Drywall joint knife

A flat-bladed knife for applying joint compound when installing drywall.

Drywall sander

Finely-meshed plastic screen attached to an extension pole, allowing finish sanding of drywall joint compound.

Drywall saw

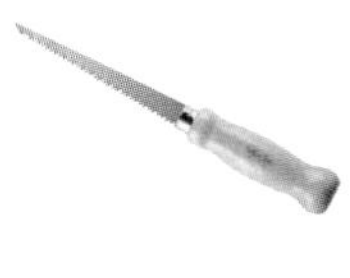

A coarse-bladed handsaw that cuts openings into drywall for fixtures.

Drywall screw bit with depth gauge

A bit with a stop for when you want to set screws the proper depth in drywall without damaging the surface.

Drywall taping knife

A flat-bladed, flexible knife used when finishing and smoothing joint compound on drywall.

Tool glossary (continued)

Dual cartridge respirator

A canister-style respirator with replaceable cartridges that filter particulate matter or solvent vapors.

Dust mask (latex)

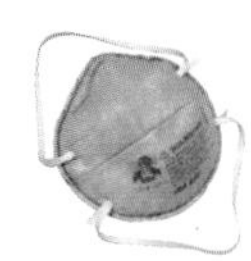

A mask worn to protect from particulate exposure while applying latex paint, usually by spraying.

Dust mask (lead)

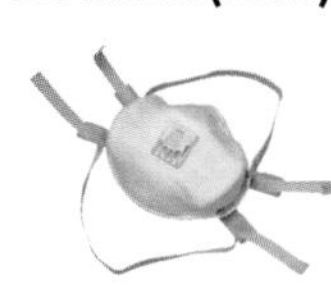

Particle mask with special filters to protect wearer from lead paint particles and fumes.

Dust mask (sanding)

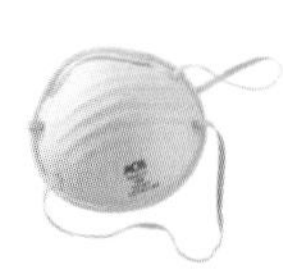

Protects the mouth and nose from particulate matter such as sawdust but will not filter toxic matter or fumes. Use carefully.

Earplugs

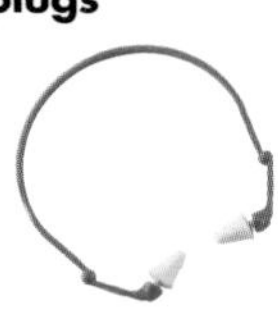

Foam inserts protect hearing by reducing high-frequency and high-decibel noise from power tools and machinery.

Ear protection (muff)

Protects ears and hearing by reducing high-frequency and high-decibel noise from power tools and machinery.

Electric drill (corded)

A general purpose, variable-speed drill with a ⅜-inch chuck for common drilling tasks in wood, metal, and other materials.

Electric drill (cordless)

A battery-operated general-purpose electric drill; generally the higher the battery voltage, the more powerful the drill.

Electrical tape (black)

A plastic tape to insulate and secure wiring connections; used in conjunction with wire nuts.

Electrical tape (colored)

Electricians use various colors to mark and identify wires.

Emery cloth

An abrasive material sold in rolls for cleaning and preparing copper fittings for soldering.

Extension pole

A telescoping rod with a threaded end designed to accept paint rollers or brushes; for ceilings and other hard-to-reach places.

Felt marker

Permanent marking tool for surfaces that resist pencil lines such as tile or metal.

Files

Handheld tools with teeth or ridges for shaping, scraping, and otherwise finishing wood, plastic, and metal.

Fish tape

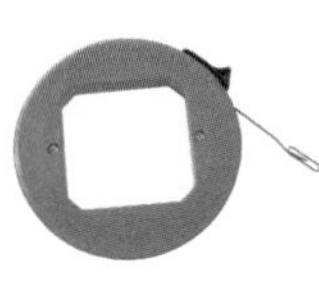

Runs cable through finished walls and pulls wires through conduit.

Flat pry bar

Removes nails and assists in demolition.

Foam brushes

Primarily for single-use applications, economy-level paintbrushes that come in various sizes.

Framing hammers

Long-handled, heavyweight hammers with striking faces and straight tines; used in rough carpentry.

Framing square (carpenter's)

A flat piece of steel with legs at 90 degrees for measuring and layout; essential for general carpentry.

Fuse puller

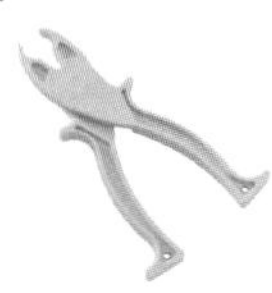

A plastic plier designed specifically to remove fuses from electrical boxes.

GFCI extension cord

An extension cord with a GFCI outlet.

Glass scraper

A hand tool with replaceable blades for removing paint from windows after painting trim.

Glazing tool

To remove and apply glaze to windows, use this multipurpose tool with a flat blade on one end and a notched blade on the other.

Grease pencil

Marking tool for surfaces that resist pencil lines such as tile or metal; mark is removable.

Grout bag

A canvas or plastic tube with a nozzle on the end that holds and applies grout.

Grout float

A masonry tool for applying grout to seams in ceramic tile.

Grout saw

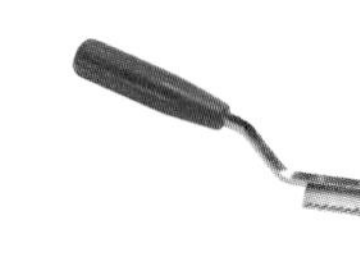

A fine-tooth saw with an offset handle used to remove grout from seams.

Hacksaw
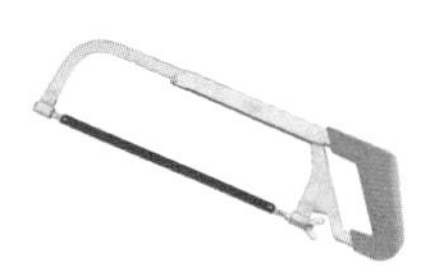
A saw with interchangeable blades designed specifically for cutting metal pipe or tubing.

Hammer drill

An electric drill that pulses the drill bit forward and backward to drill holes into concrete and masonry.

Hammer stapler

A staple gun used like a hammer to set staples, primarily when applying underlayment to decking.

Handsaw

A woodcutting tool designed for crosscutting and ripping lumber.

Hole saw

A cutting bit used with a drill to cut large-diameter holes in wood, plastic, ceramic tile, and a variety of other materials.

Hot-glue gun
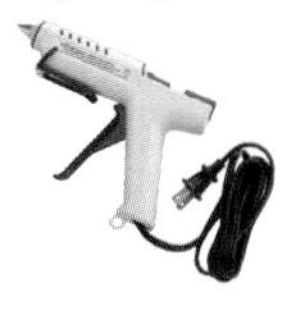
A hand tool that distributes adhesive to surfaces using heat to melt sticks of glue.

Insulation blower

Rental unit with hopper to hold insulation and blower motor. Flexible tubing guides insulation into closed spaces.

Keyhole saw
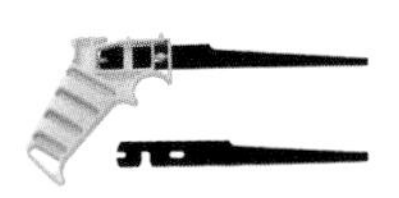
A handsaw with interchangeable blades used for cutting holes into drywall and trimming soft woods such as pine.

Knee pads

Worn to protect the knees while kneeling on hard surfaces.

Laser level

Projects horizontal beams on surfaces to mark level.

Latex gloves

Protect hands while working with paint.

Leather gloves

Protect hands when working with rough-edged materials but will not protect hands from liquids or other solvents.

Line level

A level that attaches to mason's string to set horizontal planes over longer distances.

Locking pliers

Combination pliers and clamp; comes in various sizes.

Mallet hammer

A hammer with a head of hard rubber for applications where a steel hammer might mar the material.

Margin trowel

Masonry tool that spreads adhesive in tight or awkward places such as corners.

Mason's string

Heavy-gauge string woven not to stretch; used to set finish heights and widths for masonry, carpentry, and deck installation.

Masonry drill bits

Designed especially for use with a power drill to bore holes in masonry and brick.

Miter box and backsaw

Tools for cutting simple angles and miters in wood and some plastics.

Mortar mixing paddle
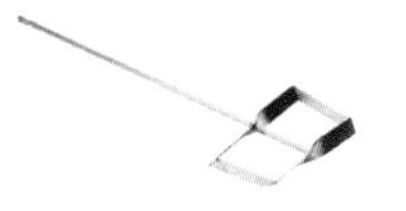
Attaches to an electric drill to mix mortar for tile installation.

Mud pan
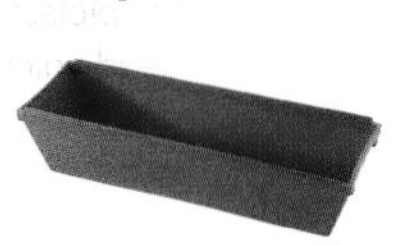
Mixes and holds mortar or other compounds during application.

Multitester (voltage)
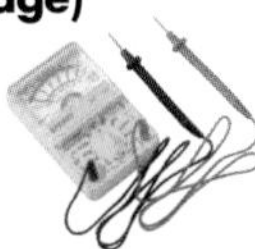
Tests electrical equipment for flow and/or presence of current.

Nail-hole slot punch

Cuts slots in vinyl siding when replacing pieces.

Nail magnet
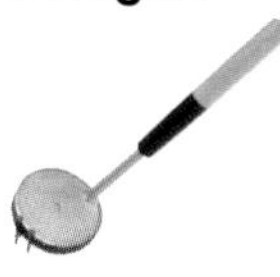
Removes nails and other metal objects from worksites such as lawns and landscaping after a roofing project.

Nail puller

Designed to give extra leverage when removing large nails or fasteners.

Nail set
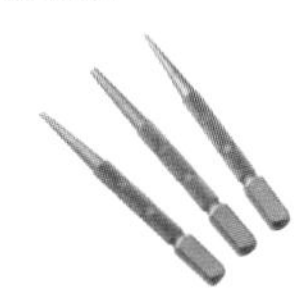
Establishes nailheads below the surface of a material before finishing. Also referred to as nail punches.

Needle-nose pliers

Can reach into enclosed areas and bends or holds wire or small hardware; has cutting blades in the plier joint.

Tool glossary (continued)

Nitrile gloves

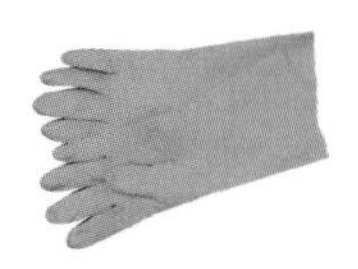

Hand protection for those allergic to latex.

Nonabrasive scouring pad

Used for general cleaning when abrasive materials such as steel wool would damage surfaces.

Offset double box-end wrench

For getting into tight places.

Orbital sander

This power sanding tool has an orbital action that reduces sanding marks on wood; can be used with or against the grain.

Overhead miter box

A hand miter box with the mitersaw mounted in a support bracket for more precise cutting.

Pad sander

A finishing sander with a vibrating action to reduce sanding marks on wood.

Paintbrush comb

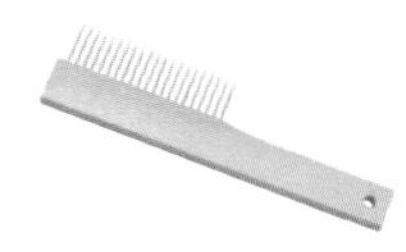

Removes dried or caked paint from the bristles of paintbrushes.

Paintbrush (disposable)

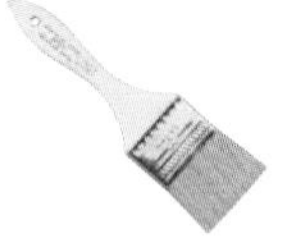

An inexpensive bristle-style brush primarily for one-time use.

Paintbrushes (bristle)

Good quality bristle paintbrushes used for finish painting to guarantee smooth, even surfaces.

Paintbrushes (detail)

Paintbrushes in various shapes and sizes for detail work or decorative painting.

Paint bucket

A plastic or disposable paper paint bucket ranging in size from 1 quart to 5 gallons. Used for holding and mixing paint.

Paint can opener

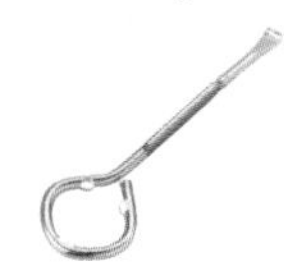

An inexpensive specialty tool designed to open paint cans without damaging the lid.

Paint can pouring spout

Attaches to the lip of a standard paint can to limit spills while pouring paint.

Paint mitt

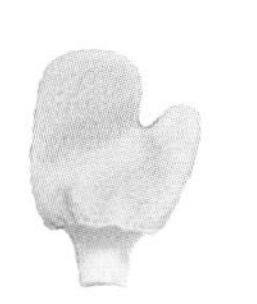

A wool or synthetic glove for applying paint to irregular surfaces such as fences, grillwork, and gates.

Paint mixer

A rod with a paddle on the end, used with an electric drill to thoroughly mix large quantities of paint.

Paint pad

Apply even coats with this foam pad attached to a handle.

Paint roller

Used to apply paint to large surfaces; comes in a variety of materials and thicknesses for different applications.

Paint roller cages

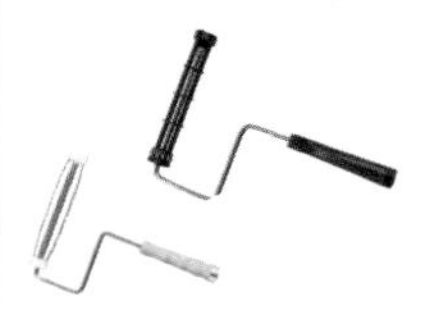

Hold paint rollers for application. A cage with at least five rods has the most reliable tension.

Paint roller grid

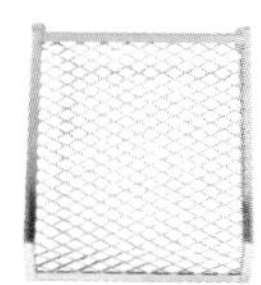

Allows clean and even loading of paint onto the roller when using a five-gallon bucket.

Paint roller (hot dog)

A foam roller for applying smooth, brush-mark-free paint to surfaces such as trim and doors.

Paint scraper

Eases removal of old paint from surfaces in preparation for new applications.

Paint tray liner

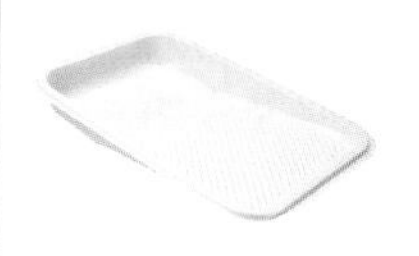

A disposable plastic liner that speeds cleanup by fitting in paint trays.

Paint tray (metal)

A tray with a well at one end to hold paint and a sloped incline designed to apply paint evenly to a paint roller.

Paint tray (plastic)

A tray with a well at one end to hold paint and a sloped incline designed to apply paint evenly to a paint roller.

Painter's masking dispenser

Applies masking tape to masking film or paper for masking surfaces such as baseboards in continuous application.

Painter's tape

A low-tack tape that protects surfaces while painting; removes easily without leaving traces of adhesive.

Painter's tool (5-in-1)

A multipurpose painter's tool: opens paint cans, cleans roller covers, helps with repair and preparation.

Pipe wrench

Used for tightening or loosening large plumbing fittings.

Plastic tubing cutter

Cuts PVC and CPVC plumbing pipe to length.

Plunger

Used to remove clogs from toilets using a suction action. Try a plunger before using a closet auger.

Pneumatic power nailer

Drives nails using compressed air; used for rough carpentry, roofing, and finish work.

Point punch

Punctures and fractures ceramic tile to ease removal.

Pointing trowel

For finishing work in tile and masonry installations.

Power mitersaw (combination)

Makes straight, bevel, and miter cuts.

Power paint sprayer

This tool requires careful masking and the use of respirators and goggles; protective clothing must be worn.

Propane torch
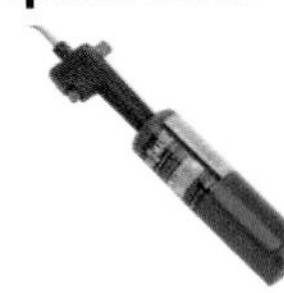
Heats copper pipe in preparation for soldering.

Pry bar

Removes materials or fasteners such as nails. Also called a crowbar.

Putty knives
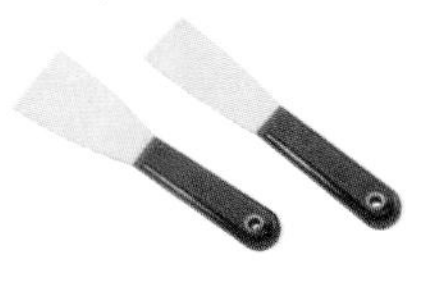
Flat-bladed steel knives for applying wall repair and finish compounds, creating final finishes, scraping, and cleaning.

PVC cutter (ratchet type)

A hand tool used to cut smaller-diameter pieces of PVC and CPVC to length.

Quick grip clamp

A hand clamp with a pistol handle that allows single-handed operation; comes in various lengths.

Ratchet wrench and socket set
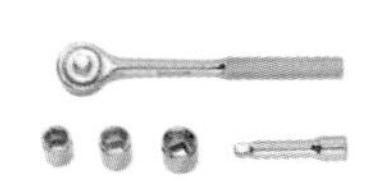
A wrench with a ratcheting head that uses sockets to tighten or loosen nuts. Nominal and metric sockets available.

Reamer (PVC)

Removes debris from the ends of PVC pipe before gluing joints.

Reciprocating saw

Interchangeable blades cut wood and metal for demolition and basic framing and plumbing.

Right-angle power drill
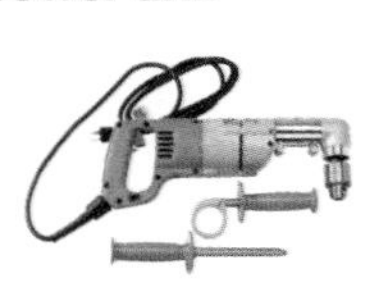
A variable-speed electric drill for hard-to-reach places such as between studs.

Rivet gun

Sets pop rivets in various materials such as sheet metal and flashing.

Roller cover
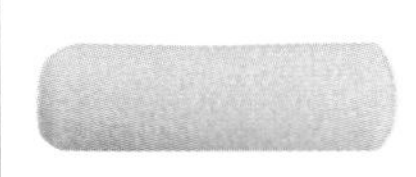
Used with a roller cage to apply paint or stain to surfaces. Available in various thicknesses and textures.

Rotary grinding tool

Grinding and cutting tool for carving, polishing, and finishing wood, tile, glass, plastic, and metal.

Round-cornered sponge

A synthetic sponge to clean excess grout and haze away after application.

Router

A wood shaping, cutting, and finishing tool offering a variety of specialty bits that revolve at high speed to cut and shape edges.

Rubber gloves

Protects hands and lower arms when working with materials that have potentially harmful effects on skin.

Saber saw

A saw with interchangeable blades for cutting curves and outlines in various materials.

Safety glasses

Worn to protect the eyes from flying particles while working with power tools.

Safety goggles

Protects the eyes from flying particles or liquids; can be worn over prescription glasses.

Sanding block

A handheld rubber sanding tool with slots on each end to hold sandpaper.

Tool glossary (continued)

Sanding sponge

A synthetic sponge with coarse and fine surfaces used with water to smooth and finish drywall.

Scratch awl

Scratches cutting marks into various surfaces; also may be used as a hole punch.

Screw gun

A variable-speed hand tool primarily used to set screws when installing drywall, metal stud walls, and sheet metal ductwork.

Screwdrivers (insulated)

Screwdrivers with insulated handles used in electrical work.

Screwdrivers (slotted and phillips)

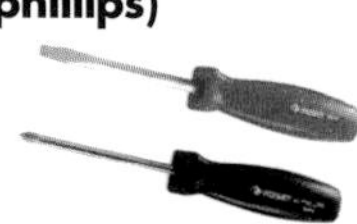

Used to set screws in various materials. Available for various screw heads such as slotted and phillips.

Seat-dressing tool

Resets the valve seat in a compression faucet.

Seat wrench

A specialty wrench for installing the valve seats in compression faucets.

Side-cutting pliers (lineman's)

A heavy-duty square-jawed pliers with insulated handles for cutting and bending wire.

Siding removal tool

Removes vinyl siding for replacement or repair.

Sledgehammer

A hammer with identical striking surfaces used for demolition and to move heavy objects into final position.

Sliding compound power mitersaw

A compound mitersaw that slides on tracks to allow cutting and mitering of larger pieces of material.

Slip-joint pliers

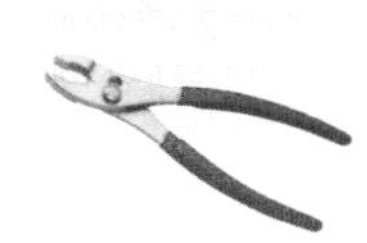

General-purpose pliers with adjustable-grip jaws used to hold and bend objects.

Spade drill bits

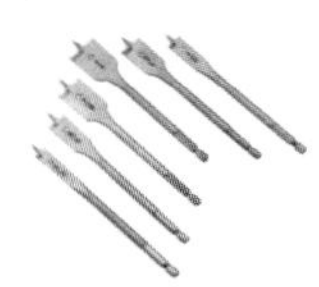

For drilling holes of various diameters, usually up to 1½ inches.

Specialty brushes

Paintbrushes of various sizes and configurations used for finish and decorative painting.

Split foam roller

A foam roller designed to apply paint to acoustical ceilings without damaging the surface.

Spray bottle

Used primarily with water to mist and dampen surfaces for cleaning, preparation, or application of latex paint.

Spud wrench

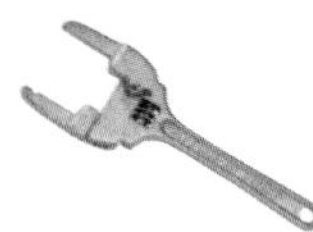

Specially designed plumbing tool to remove or tighten very large nuts by grabbing the lugs on the nut.

Square-notched trowel

A mason's trowel notched on two edges of the blade to apply adhesive to surfaces. Comes in a variety of notch sizes.

Squeegee

Comb with notched rubber edge used in decorative painting to create a combed effect on surfaces.

Stapler (manual)

A hand stapling tool accommodating various lengths of staples.

Stippling brush

Has many long, soft bristles to lift some of the wet glaze off the wall for a decorative painting technique.

Straightedge

A long metal ruler used as a guide for making straight cuts in wallpaper and vinyl tile.

Strainer locknut wrench

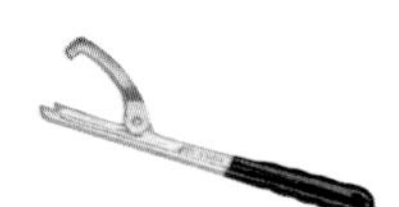

A special tool to ease removal of the locknut on a sink strainer.

Strap wrench

An adjustable wrench that grips larger sizes of pipe for fitting or removal.

Stud driver

A tool powered by a bulletlike cartridge for driving special nails into concrete or other hard surfaces.

Stud finder

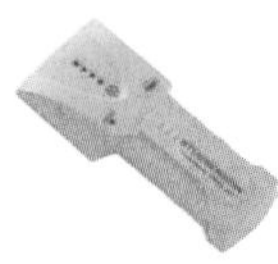

An electronic tool that senses the presence of metal in walls to locate studs.

T-square

Measures drywall sheets and acts as a knife guide when cutting drywall sheets before installation.

Tack hammer

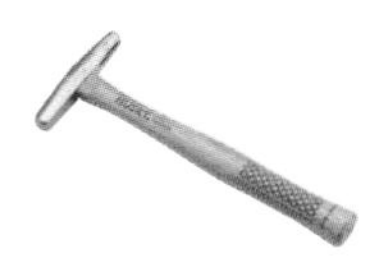

A small hammer for driving small nails with a striking face on one end and a magnetic tip on the other.

Tape measure (retractable)

A handheld measuring tool with a retractable blade used for determining incremental dimensions.

Tile cutter (sliding)

A tool used to cut ceramic tile. The tile is scored and then snapped by pressing down the lever.

Tile nippers

A cutting and shaping tool used to custom-fit ceramic tile around obstacles.

Tile scorer

A knife with two pointed blades for scoring ceramic tile.

Tin snips

Heavy-duty scissorlike tool for cutting metal such as flashing and ducting.

Torpedo level

A level intended for short pieces of material.

Try square

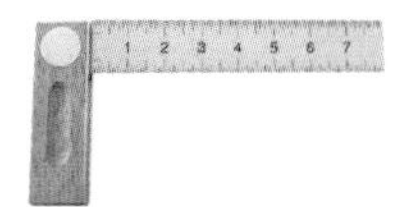

A smaller version of a carpenter's square for checking and/or marking 90-degree angles.

Tubing cutter

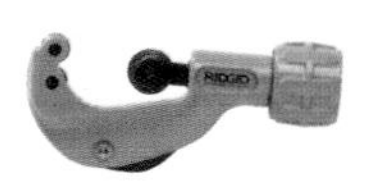

Accurately cuts various kinds of metal tubing, primarily copper, to length while keeping tubing perfectly round.

Utility knife

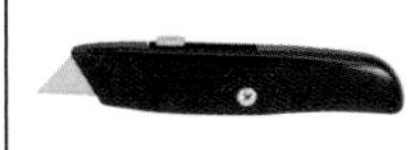

Multipurpose cutting tool with interchangeable razor blades. Used for general cutting, trimming, and fitting.

Utility knife (hooked blade)

A utility knife with a hooked blade to cut flooring and roofing materials; also called a roofing knife.

V-notch trowel

A mason's trowel for applying adhesive to surfaces that will receive tile.

Wallpaper broad knife

Applies and smooths wallpaper.

Wallpaper brushes and roller

Used for wallpaper paste and to smooth and seal seams.

Wallpaper scoring tool

Scores wallpaper to ease removal.

Wallpaper sponge

A synthetic sponge used to clean and smooth wallpaper and to remove excess water or paste.

Wallpaper stripper

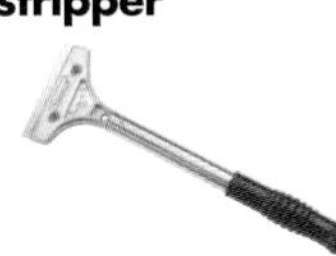

The interchangeable blade removes wallpaper without damaging the wall surface.

Water heater element wrench

Designed specifically for removing the electrical element in a water heater.

Water level

Defines level over long distances with a battery-powered electronic sensor.

Water-pump pliers

Adjustable ridged jaws make for a secure contact. Tape the jaws to prevent damage to fixtures.

Water tray

A long plastic tray holds wallpaper while soaking in preparation for application.

Wet saw

A table-style circular saw for cutting ceramic tile with a special blade and lubricating system using water.

Wire brush

A wooden-handled brush with stiff wire bristles used to clean and prepare surfaces for finishing or bonding.

Wire stripper

Pliers with graduated cutting notches that strip insulation from various gauges of wire without damaging the wire itself.

Wire stripper, combination

A multipurpose tool for cutting and stripping insulation from wire before connecting.

Wood chisels

Wood shaping and finishing tools with angled cutting edges. Used with or without a mallet or hammer to remove precise amounts of wood.

Index

A

ABS pipes, 296, 305
Accent lighting, 400, 401
Access panels, 288
Acoustic texture, 56
Activator, paste, 70, 74, 81, 83, 85
Adhesive. *See also* Mortar
  construction, 99, 102, 121, 128, 144
  engineered flooring, 194
  resilient flooring, 170, 171, 173
  vinyl-to-vinyl, 77, 81, 87, 88
AFCI (Arc Fault Circuit Interrupter), 396
Air-conditioners, 480–485
  evaporative cooler, 486–487
  heat loss from, 509
  thermostat, troubleshooting, 437–438
Aluminum siding
  painting, 63
  repairing, 542, 543
Aluminum wire, 371
Ambient lighting, 398, 399, 400
Ammonia, 26
Amps, 362
Appliances, energy-efficient, 503, 504
Aquastat
  replacing, 464
  testing, 463
Arc Fault Circuit Interrupter (AFCI), 396
Architectural shingles, 552, 570, 573
Archway, wallpapering inside, 81
Armored cable, 365, 391
Artwork, hanging, 147
Asbestos, 20, 56, 163, 536, 554
Asphalt
  patching, 582
  sealing, 583
Asphalt shingles, 552, 554
  application basics, 570–572
  on dormers, 574
  on hips and ridges, 572
  over existing roof, 575
  replacing, 558–559
  in valleys, 572, 573
Attic
  fan installation, 420
  insulation, 516–517
  leaks, 557
  running electrical cable through, 389
  ventilation, 420, 422
Auger, 307, 308, 310, 311

B

Backerboard
  for tile countertops, 276–278
  for tile floor, 174, 175
  for tile walls, 119, 148
  types, 276
Backflow preventor valve, 302
Backsplash, 278
Baffles, 516, 517
Ball valve, 291
Baseboard
  installing, 135–136, 199–202
  removing, 161
  running cable behind, 390
  types, 199
  wainscoting and, 145
Baseboard heater
  electric, 82, 471–472
  hot-water, 460, 473–474
Base cabinets, installing, 269–270
Basement
  insulation, 518–521, 585
  paneling walls, 127
  water infiltration, preventing, 526
  wet walls, 519
Base molding, removing, 183, 186
Basket strainer wrench, 303
Bathroom
  lighting, 399
  tile walls, 148–151
  ventilation, 399, 423–425
Bathtub
  diverter valve repair, 318
  drain assembly, 340
  drains, unclogging, 310
  faucet repair, 315
  freestanding, 339
  installing in an alcove, 338–341
  removing old, 337
  sand mix bed for, 338
  sliding glass door for, 342
  spa tub, 340
  spout, installing, 319
Belt sander, 273
Binder bar, 197
Bleeding baseboard heaters and radiators, 460
Blocking, 102, 138
Blow-in insulation, 500, 504, 516
Board-and-batten siding
  painting, 62
  replacing, 541
Borders
  combining a border with wallpaper, 88–89
  decorative wood floor, 189
  hanging on painted walls, 84–86
  mitering corners, 86
  painted, 85
Brad guns, 265
Brick
  painting interior, 47
  replacing a brick, 547, 579
  wall repair, 546–547
Brushes
  choosing, 17
  cleaning, 68
  stippling, 51
  using, 33
Building codes. *See* Canadian code
Building paper, 186
Butcher-block countertop, 264, 271
BX cable, 365
Bypass valve, 353

C

Cabinets, 256–270
  blind, 269
  codes, 256
  doors and drawers, replacing, 260–261
  framed versus frameless, 256, 265
  hardware, 258–259
  installing, 265–270
  knobs, 43
  materials, 256
  painting, 42–43
  refacing, 261
Cable, electrical
  fishing, 389, 409
  running
    in finished walls, 390
    through attic, 389
    through floor, 390
  structured, 432–434
  types, 365
  upgrading, 365
Cable ripper, 388
Canadian code, 584–591
  electrical, 588–590
  general construction, 585
  heating, ventilation, and air-conditioning, 591
  plumbing, 586–587
  roofing, 591
Can lighting, 401, 408–410
Cap mold, 202
Cap rail, 145
Carbon monoxide, 355
Carpet, 195–198
  indoor/outdoor, 195
  location for, 153
  padding, 195, 198
  removing, 162
  types, 198
Carpet stretcher, 197
Carpet trimmer, 196
Casing, painting exterior, 65, 67
Category 5 (CAT 5) cable, 365, 429–430
Caulk and caulking
  asphalt patching, 583
  bathroom tiling, 151
  concrete repair, 63
  countertops, 274
  deterioration of, 506
  exterior door, 221, 223, 228, 230
  faucets, 334
  glazing compound, 243, 244
  masonry repair, 63
  metal gutters, 531
  moldings, 130, 140
  for painting preparation, 11, 25, 35, 36
  selecting correct, 60
  shower surround, 343, 344
  sinks, 327, 330, 332
  sink strainer, 304
  stucco repair, 544
  tub spout, 319
  types, 511
  wall repair, 97, 100
  weatherproofing, 499, 508, 511
  windows, 249, 251, 252
Ceiling boxes, installing, 385
Ceiling fans, 416–419
Ceiling joists, finding, 105
Ceilings
  balancing, 105
  basics, 94–95
  borders, 84
  drywall, 121
  lighting
    fixtures, 378, 402–403, 406–407
    fluorescent, 412
    installing, 406–414
  repairing plaster, 99
  rosettes, 140
  suspended, installing, 105–108
  tile, installing, 102–103
  tongue-and-groove, 104
  wallpapering, 83
Cellulose insulation, 500, 501, 504, 516
Cement, plastic pipe, 294–296
Ceramic tile. *See* Tile
CFM rating, 426
Chair rails
  custom, 141–142
  height, 84, 135, 136
  installing, 135–136
  multiple, 141–142
  nailing, 133
  wallpaper, 84–86, 88–89
Chandeliers, 402

Chime, door, 435–436
Chimney, flashing around, 561, 567–568
Chlorine, 325
Circuit, electrical, 368, 396–397
Circuit breakers
box, 362
Canadian code, 588
installing, 396–397
types, 396
Circuit finder, 365
Circular saw, cutting paneling with, 128, 129
Clay roofs, 553
Clogs
chemical cleaners, 307, 311
equipment for removal, 307
locating, 307
preventing, 308
unclogging, 308–311
Closets
adding, 279–282
modular storage system, 283–285
Clothing, 21, 363
Club soda, 78
Coaxial cable, 365, 431
Color scheme, 15
Color value, 14
Color wheel, 14
Compression fitting, 299, 302, 348, 587
Concrete
cracks, repairing, 578
curing compounds, 580
floors, leveling uneven, 159
floors, patching, 158–159
painting exterior, 63
painting interior, 48
replacing, 580–581
steps, repairing, 581
test for moisture, 48
Conduit, 365, 392–393
Construction adhesive, 99, 102, 121, 128, 144
Continuity tester, 370
Cope joint
baseboard, 199, 200–201
crown molding, 137–139
for inside corners, 132
Copper pipe
for baseboard heater, 473–474
cleaning, 297, 298
cutting, 297
drying, 298
joining CPVC to, 295
soldering, 297–298
types, 297
Corner bead, 98, 123
Corner block, 130
Corner guard, 90
Corner molding, 90
Counterbalances, window, 240
Countersinking, 267
Countertops
basics, 264, 271
installing, 272–274
linoleum, 264
postform, 272
professional help, 272
removal, 263, 264
sink, installing, 326–327
sink cutout, 274, 275
tiling, 275–278
Cove base, removing, 162
Cover plate
metal, 386
papering, 91
CPVC pipe, 295
Crack repair
in concrete floors, 158–159
in drywall, 97
Crack sealer, 158
Cradle lift, 121
Crawlspace, insulating, 520, 585
Crickets, 567–568
Crimp tool, 301
Crown molding, 99
blocking for, 138
installing no-miter, 137–139
mitering outside corners, 131
tongue-and-groove ceiling, 104

D

Deburring plastic pipe, 294–296
Deglosser, liquid, 25
Dimmer switch, 380, 381, 400
Dishwasher
air gap, installing, 351
cabinet installation and, 262
disposer connection, 350
energy-efficient, 504
replacing, 350
Disposal, of construction wastes, 523
Disposer. *See* Garbage disposer
Disposer wrench, 309, 350
Diverter valve, repairing tub, 318
Door chime, 435–436
Doors, 204–238
cabinet, 42
closet, 281, 282
door-closer, adjusting tension, 513
entry door, installing prehung, 220–221
garage, 231–238
adjusting out-of-balance, 234
components, 231
installing, 231–236
opener, installing and maintaining, 235–238
headers, 215
interior, installing
molding, 218–219
prehung, 216–217
split-jamb, 217
latches, 208, 209
locksets
backset (setback), 208, 211
installing, 211–212, 223
mechanism of action, 208
modular storage system, 284–285
openings, creating, 213–214
painting, 34–35
parts, 205
patio door, hinged, 226–230
prehung versus slab, 206
removing, 210, 216, 226
retrofit, 226
running cable around, 390
selecting, 220
sidelights, 220, 223
sliding glass for tub, 342
sticking, 210
storm door, installing, 224–225
styles, 206
trim, undercutting, 165, 167, 191, 203
wallpapering around, 78–79
weatherproofing, 499, 510, 512–513
Dormer
flashing around, 569
roofing with asphalt shingles, 574
Downrods, 416
Downspouts, 526, 535
Drain lines, fragility of, 307
Drains
Canadian code, 586
pop-up, installing, 335–336
P-trap, installing, 305–306
toilet, 345
tub, installing, 339, 340
unclogging, 307–311
Drip cap, storm door, 224, 225
Drip edge, 227, 564, 565
Drives, repairing asphalt, 582–583
Drop cloths, 21, 28
Drum sander, 182–184
Drywall
dimples, 120–124
dust, 120
installing, 119–126
lifts, 121
nail pops, 98
patching plaster ceilings with, 99
patching plaster walls with, 101
priming, 22
removing, 111, 213
repairing, 96–98
Ductwork, 475–476

E

Edge sander, 184
Efflorescence, 519
Eggshell, paint sheen, 13
Elastomeric stucco patch, 62
Electrical boxes
anchoring cable to, 383
for canister fixture, 409
for ceiling fan, 416–419
choosing, 382
extending, 376
for GFCI, 376
installing, 382–386
surface-mounted wiring, 395
metal cover plate, 386
for outdoor receptacle, 377
size, 382
Electrical system, 360–439. *See also* Electrical boxes
baseboard heater, 471–472
cable
armored, 365, 391
coaxial, 431
nonmetallic (NM), 387, 388
structured, 432–434
types, 365
circuits, 368, 396–397
codes, 361, 588–590
conduit, running, 392–393
fans
attic, 420
bathroom, 343, 423–425
ceiling, 416–419
range hood, 426
roof, 422
whole-house, 421–422
fishing cable, 388, 409
grounding, 369
how the system works, 362
lighting
bathroom, 399
bulbs and tubes, selecting, 404
can, 401, 408–410
ceiling fixtures, choosing, 402–403
fluorescent, installing, 412
halogen, 411
hanging fixture, installing, 406–407
kitchen, 398
living areas, 400
low-voltage landscape, 427–428
motion-sensor, 415
pendent, 402
recessed, 408–410
solar-powered, 427

track, installing, 398, 403, 413–414
wall lights, 405
polarization, 369
receptacles
installing GFCI, 376
installing or replacing, 375
installing outdoor, 377
installing surface-mounted, 395
types, 367
wiring, 373, 374
running cable
in attic, 389
in finished wall, 390
in floor, 390
safety, 362, 363, 371, 373, 388, 396, 397, 416
surface-mounted wiring, 394–395
surge protection, 439
switches
for ceiling fixture, adding, 378
controlling a single outlet with, 379
dimmer, replacing, 381
three-way, replacing, 380
types, 367
wiring, 373, 374
terminology, 362
testers, 370
thermostat, troubleshooting, 437–438
tool kit, 364
water heater, wiring, 357, 359
wire
joining to a terminal, 373
stripping and splicing, 371
telephone and CAT 5, installing, 429–430
types, 365
wiring to receptacles and switches, 373, 374
wire nuts, 366
Electrician's tape, 373
Electrostatic precipitators, 444
Embossed papers, 83, 85
Enamel paint, 12
Energy efficiency, home
evaluating, 506–507
improving, 503–505
Energy Star rating, 240, 504
Engineered flooring, 153, 191, 194
Entropy, 524
Epoxy, plumber's, 291
Epoxy filler, 57, 537, 538
Escutcheon plates, 305
Ethylene glycol, 22
Evaporative cooler, 486–487
Exterior maintenance, 522–583
calendar, 525
fascia and soffit repair, 548–551
gutters, 530–535
masonry wall repair, 544–547
materials, 524
roofing, 552–577
siding, 536–543
trim, patching, 537
walls, drives, and steps, 578–583
water infiltration, preventing, 526–527
Extruded polystyrene (EXPS) insulation, 500, 501
Eyes, protecting, 20

F

Fan-and-limit control, 443, 446, 447
Fans
air-conditioner, 484–485
attic, 420
bathroom, 343, 423–425
ceiling, 416–419
CFM rating, 426
forced-air furnace, 442, 443, 445–448
noise, 424
oil furnace, 455
range hood, 426
roof, 422
whole-house, 421–422
Fascia
covers, 548
painting, 65
repairing, 548–551
Fasteners
for exterior maintenance, 524
roofing, 554
Faucets. *See also* Sinks
anti-scald, 341
avoiding clogged, 334
handle, removing stubborn, 312
installing
center-set, 334
wallmount, 332
widespread, 333
repair
cartridge, 315, 317
ceramic disk, 314
compression, 312, 313
rotary ball, 316
tub and shower, 317
showerhead, cleaning, 319
tub diverter valve, repairing, 318
tub spout, installing, 319
Faux painting techniques
ragging on and ragging off, 54–55
sponging on and sponging off, 52–53
stippling, 51
F-connector, 431
Fiberglass
insulation, 113, 118, 500, 501, 516–517, 520, 521
tape, 124, 276
Fill valve, 322, 323–324
Filter
cleaning, 445
heat pump, 469, 470
oil furnace, 455
types, 444
Finishing
drywall, 124–126
wood floor, 185
Fire block, 110
Fire hazards, 185
Firing assembly, oil furnace, 456–457
Fish tape, 389, 390, 393
Fittings, 288, 296, 299, 304
Flange, toilet, 345, 346
Flapper, replacing toilet, 325
Flashing, 554–569
around chimney, 561, 567–568
around dormer, 569
bending and shaping, 568
counterflashing, 568
damaged, 556
for gutter repair, 531
removing old, 562
step, 561, 567, 569
valleys, 560, 566, 573
vent, 560, 562, 569
Float arm, adjusting toilet, 321
Floating floor, 191
Floating wall, 117
Floor joists
anchoring pipes to, 300
Canadian code, 585
reinforcing, 157
Floor sander, 45, 182–185
Floors and flooring, 152–203
baseboard, installing, 199–202
Canadian code, 585
carpet, 195–198
choosing, 152, 153, 154
concrete, 158–159
drains, unclogging, 310
floating, 191
laminate, 191–193
materials, 154
measuring, 160
painting, 44–47, 48, 64
removing existing, 161–164
running cable through, 390
squeaks, stopping, 156–157, 183
subfloors, 153, 156–157
thresholds, 203
tile, 174–179
underlayment
options for, 164
replacing, 161, 165–166
vinyl sheet, 167–171
vinyl tile, 172–173
wood
acclimating the flooring, 187, 191
border, decorative, 189
engineered, 191, 194
installation tips, 187
laminate, 191–193
parquet tile, 180–181, 185
sanding and refinishing, 182–184
strip-wood, 186–188
wide-plank, 190
Fluorescent lighting
ceiling fixtures, 403
installing, 412
in suspended ceiling, 108
tube types, 404
Flux, 297
Foam insulation, 500, 501, 508–509, 511, 518–519
Forced-air system
fan motor
maintaining, 445
problems with, 446–447
replacing, 448
filter, 444–445
heat run, adding, 475–476
how it works, 443
humidifiers, 442, 490–493
maintaining, 442–448
Framing
closet, 279–282
door or window opening, 213–215
partition wall, 113–117
Frozen pipes, 291
Furnace. *See* Forced-air system; Gas furnace; Oil furnace
Furring strips, 102, 103, 518–519

G

Garage
painting floor, 48
storage in, 255
Garage doors, 231–238
adjusting out-of-balance, 234
components, 231
installing, 231–236
openers
adjusting, 237, 238
choosing, 235
installing, 235–236
maintaining, 237
safety, 231, 234, 236, 237, 238
weatherproofing, 513
Garbage disposer
choosing, 349
dishwasher connection, 350
horsepower of, 349

installing, 349–350
unclogging jammed, 309
Gas furnace. *See also* Forced-air system
air shutter, adjusting, 450
burner, cleaning, 453
cutoff valve, 449
how it works, 442
igniter, 452
leaks, checking for, 450
maintaining, 449–453
pilot, 451
thermocouple, checking, 452
Gas heater
direct-vent, 479
remote controls, 477
types, 477
vented, 478
vent-free, 477–478
Gas leaks, testing for, 358
Gas water heater, installation, 358
GFCI. *See* Ground fault circuit interrupter (GFCI) receptacle
Glass
cutting, 243
masking tape removal, 37
repairing broken window, 243–244
Glaze, 27, 50–55
Glazing compound, 11, 58, 243, 244
Glazing tool, 243, 244
Gloss
paint, 13
removing, 25
Gloves, 20
Goggles, safety, 20
Greenboard, 119
Greenfield conduit, 392
Ground fault circuit interrupter (GFCI) receptacle, 376, 377, 548, 588
Grounding
Canadian code for, 588–590
light fixtures and ceiling fans, 589
to metal cold water pipe, 354
metal electrical boxes, 588
methods, 369
switches and receptacles, 589
Grout, 148, 151, 179, 278
Gumption test, 253
Gutter guards, 533
Gutters
cleaning, 533
evaluating, 530
installing vinyl, 534–535
leaky, 531
replacing a section of, 532

H

Halogen lights, 403, 411
Handle puller, 312
Hangers
picture, 147
for suspended ceiling, 105–107
Hardware
cabinet, 258–259
picture hanging, 147
Harnesses, safety, 561
Headers, 110, 215, 585
Heat gun, 244
Heating
baseboard heater
electric, 82, 471–472
hot-water, 460, 473–474
choosing type, 440, 441
forced-air furnace
heat run, adding, 475–476
humidifiers, online, 442, 490–493
maintaining, 442–448
gas furnace
how it works, 442
maintaining, 449–453
gas heater
direct-vent, 479
types, 477
vented, 478
vent-free, 477–478
heat pump
how it works, 467
ice buildup on coils, 470
maintaining, 467–470
hot-water heat system
maintaining, 458–466
hydronic system, 489
oil furnace, 454–457
radiant system, 488
thermostat, troubleshooting, 437–438
Heating elements, water heater, 356
Heat pump, 467–470
Heat run, insulating, 521
Heat tape, 526, 527
Hinges
cabinet, 256, 260
door, 210, 222
Hips, shingling roof, 572
Hole-cutting saw, 408
Hose bib, 289
Hot-water heat system, 458–466
baseboard heater, 473–474
House, settling, 101
Hue, 14
Humidifiers, 442, 490–493
Humidistat, 442, 491
HVAC, 440–497. *See also* Air-conditioner; Heating; Ventilation
Canadian code, 591
costs of, 504
Hydronic heating system, 489

I

Ice dams, 526–527
Ice-dam underlayment, 591
Icemaker, connecting, 352
Igniter, gas burner, 452
Inspector, working with, 8, 584
Insulation, 498–521. *See also* Weatherproofing
around doors, 230
attic, 516–517
basement walls, 518–519
choosing, 501–502
crawlspace, 520
fiberglass, 113, 118
heat runs, 521
pipe, 291, 300, 521
reflective, 501, 502
R-values, 501
soffit vents, installing, 516
soundproofing, 113, 118
vapor barriers, 516, 520
water heater, 520
Integral stops, 299
Island, kitchen, 370

J

Jack posts, 213
Jack studs, 213, 214, 215
Jamb, door, 216, 217, 222, 585
Joint compound, 70, 96, 97, 98, 124–126
Jointing tool, 47, 546, 547, 579
Junction box, 386, 405

K

Key track stop, 246
King studs, 214, 215
Kitchens
cabinets, 42–43, 265–270
Canadian code, 589
countertop, 264, 271–278
island, installing, 270
lighting, 398
storage in, 255
Knee kicker, 196–197
Knee wall, 148, 151
Knives, drywall, 124–126
Knobs, cabinet, 43, 258
Knockdown texture, 56

L

Lacquer, 38
Ladder, safety, 59, 525, 528
Ladder jacks, 525
Ladder safety, 496
Laminate
countertop, 264, 271, 272–275
flooring, 153, 191–193
tiling over, 278
Laminate trimmer, 273
Landscape lighting, low-voltage, 427–428
Latches, door, 208, 209
Latex portland cement, 276
Latex underlayment, 166
Lauan plywood, 165
Laundry rooms, storage in, 255
Lead, 13, 20, 35
Leaks
gas, 450
gutter, 531
heat loss, 499, 506–507
in pipes, 291
roof, 26, 557
toilet, repairing, 320, 322
Leveling compound, 159
Lifts, for drywall, 121
Lightbulbs, selecting, 404
Light fixture cords, 407
Lighting
accent, 400, 401
bathroom, 399
bulbs and tubes, selecting, 404
can, 401, 408–410
ceiling fixtures, choosing, 402–403
energy-efficient, 404, 505
fluorescent, 108, 412, 505
halogen, 403, 411
hanging fixture, installing, 406–407
kitchen, 398
LED lightbulb, 404
living areas, 400
low-voltage landscape, 427–428
motion-sensor, 415
pendant, 402
recessed, 408–410
rope lights, 400, 411
solar-powered, 427
suspended ceiling, 108
track, installing, 398, 403, 413–414
wall lights, 405
Linoleum countertops, 264
Locks
backset (setback), 208, 211
double-hung window, 247
installing, 211–212, 223
mechanism of action, 208
patio door, 247
sliding window, 246
types, 208
Low-voltage landscape lighting, 427–428

M

Manifold, 301
MAPP gas cylinders, 298
Marble countertop, 271

Masking
  prior to painting, 21, 30–32, 37, 65
  windows, 37, 39, 66
Masonry
  painting, 60
  paneling walls, 127
  repairing walls, 544–547
  venting through wall, 426
Masonry clips, 251
Mastic, duct, 475, 476
Medium density fiberboard (MDF), 199, 256
Metal
  flashing, 566–569
  roofing, 553
Metal-clad (MC) cable, 365
Methylene chloride, 22
Mildew, 24, 26
Miter cuts, 131–134, 136, 139, 142
Mitering
  baseboard, 202
  door trim, 218–219
  outside corners, 131
Mitersaw, tuning, 133
Moisture, test for, 48
Moisture barrier, 192, 221
Molded expanded polystyrene (MEPS) insulation, 500, 501
Molding, 26
  baseboard, 183, 186, 199–202
  built-up, 137, 202
  cap, 202
  chair rails, 135–136
  corner, 90
  crown, 99, 104, 131, 137–139
  custom, creating, 141–142
  exterior door, 230
  hiding nails, 219
  installation skills, 131–134
  for interior doors, 218–219
  layout, 137
  nailing, 133
  no-miter, 130
  picture rails, 134
  polyurethane, 140
  profiles, 137, 141, 142
  quarter-round, 201, 202
  removal, 111
  returns, 134
  shoe, 186, 188
  window, 219
Mortar
  dry-set, 276
  repairing brick joints with, 47
  thinset, 148–151, 174, 175, 177
  for tile countertops, 276–278
  for tile floors, 174, 175, 177
  for tile walls, 148–151
Mortar joint, repairing, 546
Mosaic tile, 175
Motion-sensor lights, 415
Multimeter/multitester, 370, 434, 436, 452, 465

N

Nailer, flooring, 188
Nail guns, 265
Nail hole slot punch, 542
Nailing plates, 387
Nail pops, 98
Nails
  hiding, 219
  predrilling for, 187
  setting, 44
Network, home, 434
Nipper, 178
Nonmetallic (NM) cable, 365, 383, 387, 388
Nut splitter, 345

O

Offset flange, 345
Oil furnace
  fan, cleaning and oiling, 455
  filter replacement, 455
  firing assembly, maintaining, 457
  firing assembly, removing, 456
  how it works, 454
Orange peel texture, 56
Orbital sander, 184, 185
O-ring, 312, 315, 316, 317
Outlets
  controlling a single outlet with a switch, 379
  for garage door opener, 236
  paneling around, 129
  wainscoting installation around, 145
  wallpapering around, 75
  weatherproofing, 499, 509

P

Padding, carpet, 195, 198
Pads, paint, 62
Paint. *See also* Primer
  color, 14
  disposal, 49, 68
  enamel, 12
  environmentally friendly, 22
  gloss, 13
  ingredients, 12
  label, paint can, 12
  latex, 12, 31, 68
  lead, 13, 20, 35
  oil (alkyl), 12, 31, 68
  sheen, 13
  storing, 49
  stripping, 38, 41
  textured, 56
Painting
  borders, 85
  brick, interior, 47
  brush, proper use of, 33
  brushes and rollers, 17
  cabinets, 43
  cleanup, 68
  color scheme, 15
  concrete, interior, 48
  conditions for, 46
  doors and trim, 34–35
  exterior, 57–67
    concrete, 63
    stucco, 62
    techniques, 60
    trim, 64–65
    vinyl or aluminum siding, 63
    walls, 61–62
    windows, 66–67
  floors, 44–47, 48, 64
  garage floor, 48
  over wallpaper, 27
  preparation for, 24–26
  priming, 11, 22–23, 30
  ragging on and ragging off, 54–55
  sponging on and sponging off, 52–53
  spraying paint, 19
  stippling, 51
  textured effects, 56
  walls, 30–32
  windows, 36–37
Paneling
  cutting, 128, 129
  installing, 127–129
  wallpapering, 74
Particleboard, 256
Paste, wallpaper, 27, 70, 74, 83
Paste activator, 70, 74, 81, 83, 85
Patching plaster, 100
Patio door
  installing hinged, 226–230
  locks, 247
Pendent lights, 402
PEX (flexible plastic pipe), 301, 489
Picture rails, 134
Pictures, hanging and arranging, 134
Pigtails, 373, 374
Pilot, gas burner, 451
Pilot holes, 131
Pipe. *See also* Plumbing
  for baseboard heater, 473–474
  Canadian code, 586
  connecting, 294–298
  insulation, 291, 300, 521
  leaking, 291
  noise, reducing, 300, 337
  PEX (flexible plastic), 301, 489
  studs, running through, 300
Plaster
  ceiling, repairing, 99
  dust, 112
  walls, repairing, 100–101
Plaster of Paris, 100
Plaster patching compound, 70
Plastic sheeting, for window insulation, 509
Plinth blocks, 219
Plumb bob, 279, 280
Plumber's putty, 304, 335, 347, 349
Plumbing, 286–359
  access panels, 288
  for baseboard heater, 473–474
  bathtub
    installing in an alcove, 338–341
    removing, 337
    spout installation, 319
  Canadian code, 586–587
  clogs, 307–311
  dishwasher, replacing, 350
  faucets, installing
    center-set, 334
    wallmounted, 332
    widespread, 333
  faucets, repairing, 312–317
    cartridge, 315, 317
    ceramic disk, 314
    compression, 312, 313
    rotary ball, 316
    tub and shower, 317
  garbage disposer, installing, 349–350
  how the system works, 288–289
  icemaker, connecting, 352
  pipe
    Canadian code, 586
    connecting ABS, 296
    connecting copper, 297–298
    connecting CPVC, 295
    connecting CPVC to copper, 295
    connecting PVC, 294
    deburring, 294–296
    frozen, 291
    insulation, 291, 300, 521
    leaking, 291
    noise, reducing, 300, 337
    PEX (flexible plastic), 301, 489
  P-trap, installing PVC, 305–306
  showerhead, cleaning, 319
  shower surround, installing, 343–344
  shutoff valves and supply tubes, installing, 302
  sinks, installing, 326–332
    bowl-type, 331

countertop, 326–327
farmer's/apron, 332
pedestal, 330
pop-up drain, installing, 335
self-rimming, 329
templates, 326, 327
vanity, 328
wall-hung, 330
sink strainer, repairing or replacing, 303–304
supply lines, running new, 299–300
tips, 287
toilets
adjusting tank handle and water level, 321
fill valve, replacing, 323–324
flapper, replacing, 325
installing, 346–348
leaking tank, 322
removing old, 345
repairing, 320–325
troubleshooting, 320
tool kit, 290
water heater, installing, 355–359
basics of installation, 356–357
electric, 357
gas, 358
on-demand, 359
water softener, 353–354
Plumb line, for wallpapering, 73, 77, 89
Plunger, 309, 310, 311
Plywood
cabinets, 256
countertop substrate, 275
lauan, 165
soffits, 550
underlayment, 165–166
Polarization, 369
Pollution, indoor air, 22
Polyisocyanurate insulation, 500, 501
Polystyrene insulation, 500, 501, 518–519
Polyurethane, 38, 140, 185
Polyvinyl acetate (PVA), 23
Popcorn texture, 56
Pop-up drain, installing a, 335–336
Power strip, 439
Pressure relief line, 357
Primer, 11
masonry, 64
purple plumbing, 294–296
stain-blocking, 13, 22, 23, 24, 27, 30, 35, 56, 63
tinting, 23, 30, 73
types of, 23
wallpaper, 70, 73
Priming
borders, 84, 85, 88
cabinets, 43
doors, 34
drywall, 22
exterior surfaces, 58
floors, 45–47
functions of, 22, 30
over wallpaper, 27
spot priming, 30, 35, 45, 63
trim, 35, 64–65
walls, 30
windows, 37
Pry bars, for removing flooring, 161–163, 165
P-trap, 305–306, 339, 350, 586
Puck lighting, 411
Pulling elbow, 393
Pulls, cabinet, 258–259
Purple primer, 294–296
Push fittings, 296
PVC pipe/conduit, 294, 305–306, 392
Pythagoras, 176

Q

Quarter-round molding, 201, 202

R

Raceway, 394–395
Radiant heat, 488
Radiators, 82, 460
Range hood, installing, 426
Receptacle analyzer, 370, 375
Receptacles
end-of-the-run, 379
GFCI, 376, 377, 548, 588
grounding, 369
installing or replacing, 375
middle-of-the-run, 374, 379
outdoor, installing, 377
polarized, 369
split (half-hot), 374
tamper-resistant, 397
types, 367
wiring, 373, 374
Recessed lighting, 408–409
Reciprocating saw, 112
Refacing, cabinet, 261
Refinishing a floor, 182–184
Refrigerator icemaker, 352
Remodeling boxes, 383–384
Renting equipment, 19, 525
Resilient flooring adhesive, 170, 171, 173
Respirators, 20
Rheostat switch, for whole-house fan, 422
Roller, paint
for acoustic ceilings, 56
choosing, 17
cleaning, 68
power, 18
for ragging, 54–55
specialty, 50
for textured finish application, 56
Roller cover, 17
Roof fan, 422
Roofing, 552–577
asphalt shingles, 558–559, 570–575
basics, 552–554
Canadian code, 591
chimney, flashing around, 561, 567–568
dormer, flashing around, 569
dormer, roofing, 574
flashing, 560–561, 566–569
inspecting roof, 556
leaks, 26, 557
measuring for, 560
over existing roof, 575
professional roofer, hiring, 561
repairing, 558–563, 577
roll, 576–577
safety, 554, 561
sheathing, replacing, 563
tear-off, 562–563
types, 552–554
underlayment, 527, 564–565
Roofing cement, 497, 558, 559, 566, 567, 569, 576–577
Roofing felt, 564–565
Roof jacks, 529
Roof vent, 494, 495, 497
Rope lights, 400, 411
Rosettes, 140
Router
drywall, 122, 123
laminate trimmer, 273
R-value, insulation, 501

S

Saber saw
cutting laminate countertop with, 274, 275
cutting laminate flooring with, 193
cutting paneling with, 128, 129
Saddle tee, 587
Saddle valve, 352, 491
Safety
asbestos, 20, 163, 536
carbon monoxide, 355
concrete cleaner, 158
electrical system, 362, 363, 371, 373, 388, 396, 397, 416
fire hazards, 185
garage door, 231, 234, 236, 237, 238
gas, 449, 450
harnesses, 561
ladder use, 59, 496, 525, 528
lead paint, 13, 20, 35
in painting, 20, 26, 57, 59
plaster dust, 112
plumbing primers and cement, 295
roofing, 554, 561
utilities and, 109
Sanding
cabinets, 43
drywall finish, 126
with drywall screen, 25
exterior surfaces, 57, 58
floors, 182–184
between paint coats, 11
windows, 36
Sand texture, 56
Sash brush, 37
Sash cords, replacing broken, 241
Sash knife, 36
Satin paint, 13
Saw. *See specific applications; specific saw types*
Scaffolding, 525, 529
Scarf joints, 132
Sconce, 405
Scraping
exterior surfaces, 57, 63, 66
trim, 35
windows, 36, 66
Screen, replacing window, 245
Screws
driving, 156–157
for drywall, 120
Scribing, 128, 144
Sealer, 70
Seam roller, 75
Seam sealer, 170
Security, window and glass door, 246–247
Security bar, 247
Septic tank, 311
Service panel, 396–397, 588–589
Sewer stack cleanout, 291
Shakes, 540, 553, 559
Shallow well (sump), 291
Sheen, paint, 13
Sheet vinyl. *See* Vinyl, sheet flooring
Shellac, 35, 38, 43, 45
Shimming
base cabinets, 269, 270
doorjamb, 216, 217, 222
patio door, 228, 229–230
subfloor, 156
thresholds, 229
walls, 117
window, 249–251
Shingles. *See also* Roofing
architectural, 552, 570–573
damaged, 556
materials, 554
over existing roof, 575

removing, 562–563
replacing, 540, 558–559
roofing with asphalt, 570–575
three-tab, 552, 570, 575
Shoe molding, 186, 188
Shower
anti-scald faucet, 341
corner, 343
drains, unclogging, 310
faucet repair, 315
surround, installing a, 343–344
Showerhead, 319
Shutoff valve
installing, 302, 348
master, 291
Sidelights, 220, 223
Siding, 524, 536–543
aluminum, 543
asbestos in, 536
materials, 524
painting, 60, 61–63
sheathing, replacing, 536
stucco, 544–545
vinyl, 542
wood, 538–541
Sinks
cutout in countertop, 274, 275
drains, unclogging, 309
installing, 326–332
bowl-type, 331
countertop, 326–327
farmer's/apron, 332
pedestal, 330
self-rimming, 329
templates, 326, 327
vanity, 328
wall-hung, 330
pop-up drain, installing, 335–336
removal, 263, 329
strainer, repairing or replacing, 303–304
Sizing, wallpaper, 70, 84
Skin, protecting, 20
Skylight, installing, 253
Slate roofs, 553
Slip joints, 305
Smoke alarms, 585
Soffit
installing, 548
painting, 60, 65
repairing
length-run tongue-and-groove, 551
plywood, 550
width-run, 551
vent, 494–496, 516
Solar heat gain coefficient, 240
Solar-powered lighting, 427
Soldering copper pipes, 297–298, 474
Solvents, disposing of, 49
Soundproofing, 113, 118, 119
Spacers, tile, 148, 150–151, 177, 276
Spackling paste, 70, 97
Spa tub, 340
Splicing wire, 366, 371, 372
Spline roller, 245
Splitter, signal, 431
Spout, installing a tub, 319
Sprayer, paint, 19, 60
Spud washer, 322
Squeaks, stopping floor, 156–157, 183
Stain-blocking primer, 13, 22, 23, 24, 27, 30, 35, 56, 63
Staining
pine, 41
trim, 40–41
windows, 38–39
wood floors, 185
Stains, treating, 26
Stairs
anchoring treads, 157
repairing concrete, 581
squeaky, 157
Storage. *See also* Cabinets
closets, 279–282
modular storage systems, 283–285
room-by-room solutions, 255
Storm doors, 224–225, 505
Storm window, 252–253
Strike plate, 209, 212, 223
Stripping
trim, 41
windows, 38
wire, 371
Structured cable, 432–434
Stucco
painting, 62
repairing siding, 544–545
Stud finder, 93, 127, 136
Studs, running cable through, 388
Supply lines
braided flexible, 302
icemaker, 352
running new, 299–300
Surface-mounted wiring, 394–395
Surfacing compound, 11, 97, 98
Surge protection, 439
Sweep, door, 225, 510, 512
Switches
for ceiling fixture, adding, 378
controlling a single outlet with, 379
dimmer, replacing, 381
sharing a hot wire, 374
three-way, replacing, 380
types, 367
weatherproofing, 509
wiring, 373, 374
Swivel boxes, 405

T

Tack strips, 195
Tape
blue painter's, 21
drywall, 124–126
electrician's, 373
fiberglass, 124, 276
fish, 389, 390, 393
Teflon, 318, 333, 357
Telephone wiring, 365, 429–430
Temperature, variation within a room, 507
Terminal
joining wire to a, 372–373
traveler, 380
Terra-cotta roofs, 553
Testers, electrical, 370
Thermocouple, 449, 452
Thermostat
baseboard heater, 471–472
forced-air system, 443, 446
gas furnace, 442
hot-water heat system, 459
programmable, 438, 503
troubleshooting, 437–438
vacation setting, 443
Thinset mortar, 148–151, 174, 175, 177
Three-way switch, replacing, 380
Threshold
adjustable, 222
installing a new, 203
removing, 161, 203
replacing door, 513
shimming, 229
for weatherproofing, 510
Tile and tiling
around bathtub, 341
backsplash, 278
bullnose, 151
ceiling, installing, 102–103
countertop, 264, 275–278
cutting, 150, 179, 277
flooring
adhesive, 174
backerboard, 174, 175
cutting, 178
grouting, 179
layout, 174, 176, 177
locations for, 153
removing, 164
setting tiles, 177
mosaics, 175
over plastic laminate, 278
walls, 148–151
Tile spacers, 148, 150–151, 177, 276
Timer, landscape lights, 428
Toenailing, 115
Toggle bolts, 281
Toilets
adjusting tank handle and water level, 321
anatomy, 320
connecting old drains to new toilets, 345
fill valve, replacing, 323–324
flange, 345, 346
flapper, replacing, 325
installing, 346–348
leaks, 320, 322
low-flow, 320
removing, 345
repairing, 320–325
size, 346
troubleshooting, 320
unclogging, 311
upflush, 348
Tongue-and-groove ceiling, 104
Tool glossary, 592–599
Torsion springs, 231
Track lighting
fixtures, choosing, 403
installing, 413–414
in kitchen, 398
Transformer
door chime, 436
low-voltage landscape lighting, 427–428
Trim
color, 37
door, 218–219
painting, 32, 35, 64–65
patching exterior, 537
removing, 111
staining, 40–41
stripping, 41
Trisodium phosphate (TSP)
for cleaning brick, 47
for cleaning concrete, 48
for cleaning exterior surfaces, 58
for cleaning prior to wallpapering, 70, 74
for cleaning walls, 11, 24
for cleaning woodwork, 35
Troffers, 108
Tub. *See* Bathtub
Tuck pointer, 47

U

U-factor, 240
Underground-feed (UF) cable, 365
Underlayment
for laminate flooring, 192
latex, 166
replacing, 161, 165–166
roof, 527, 564–565
Urethane insulation, 518

V

Valley, roof, 560, 566, 572, 573
Valve seat, 313
Vanity light, 405
Vanity sink, 328
Vapor barrier, 516, 520
Varnish, 38, 39, 40–41
Veneer, 261
Ventilation
attic, 420, 422
bathroom, 343, 423–425
Canadian code, 591
Vent pipes, flashing around, 556, 560, 569
Vents
baffles, 516, 517
bathroom, 399, 423–425
roof, 494, 495, 497
soffit, 494–496, 516
through masonry wall, 426
wall, 425
Victorian molding, 219
Vinyl
concrete patch, 159
gutters, 534–535
replacement window, 250
sheet flooring, 153, 167–171
siding, 63, 542
plank flooring, installing, 153, 180–181, 185
tile flooring, 153, 172–173
Vinyl concrete patch, 62
Vinyl-to-vinyl adhesive, 77, 81, 87, 88
Visible transmittance (VT), window, 240
Volatile organic compounds (VOCs), 12, 22
Voltage, 362
Voltage detector, 93, 370
Voltage tester, 370

W

Wainscoting, 135, 143–146
Walks, repairing, 578–581
Wall cabinets, installing, 265–268
Wall lights, installing or replacing, 405
Wallpaper and wallpapering, 69–91
basics, 69–70
booking strips, 74
borders, 84–86, 88–89
bubbles, fixing, 87
ceilings, 83
choosing, 69
combining wallpapers, 88–89
cover plates, 91
cutting, 70, 74–75
double-cutting, 80, 85, 86
dye lots, 70, 73
glazing, 27
measuring and estimating, 72
painting over, 27
patching, 87
preparation for, 70
primer, 73
priming over, 26
removing, 28–29, 69
seams, 77, 87
terminology, 72
textured, 83
transitions, 90
walls, applying to, 73–82
around windows and doors, 78–80
cement block, 74
hanging techniques, 73–75
paneling, 74
washable, scrubbable, 75
Wallpaper liner, 69, 74
Walls, 92–151
basics, 94
contents, 93
corner damage, repairing, 98
drywall
finishing, 124–126
installing, 119–126
repairing, 96–98
fire blocks in, 110
floating, 117
insulating, 504, 518–519
load-bearing, 109, 110, 213–214, 215
molding
built-up, 137
chair rails, 135–136
crown, 99, 131, 137–139
custom, creating, 141–142
installation skills, 131–134
layout, 137
no-miter, 130
picture rails, 134
polyurethane, 140
profiles, 137, 141, 142
removal, 111
non-load-bearing, 213, 214
openings for doors or windows, 110, 213–214
painting exterior, 61–63
paneling, installing, 127–129
partition, 109
attaching new walls to existing joists, 114–115
building, 113–117
framing corners, 115
framing on the floor, 116–117
parts, 109–110
picture rails, installing, 134
plaster, repairing, 100–101
priming and painting, 30–32
removing, 109–112
repairing
masonry, 544–547
prior to painting, 24, 26
prior to wallpapering, 70
soundproofing, 113, 118, 119
tiling, 148–151
tool kit, 95
utilities running in, 93, 111
wainscoting, 143–146
wallpapering, 73–82
Water hammer, 330, 337
Water heaters
Canadian code, 587
components, 355
heating element, 356
installing, 355–359
basics, 356–357
electric, 357
gas, 358
on-demand, 359
insulation, 520
lifespan, 355
removing, 356
size, 355
tankless, 355, 359
thermostat, 338
Water infiltration, preventing, 526
Water softener, 353–354
Water stains, 26
Weatherproofing, 498–521. *See also* Insulation
doors, 499, 512–513
energy efficiency, home
evaluating, 506–507
improving, 503–505
inventory, 499
low-cost solutions, 508
materials, 500
tool kit, 502
windows, 499, 509, 514–515
Weatherstripping
cleaning, 241
deterioration of, 506
types, 500, 510
Weep hole, 252, 499, 514
Wet saw, 150
Whole-house fan, 421–422
Window air-conditioner, 480–483
Window film, 515
Windows, 239–253
broken pane, repairing, 243–244
choosing, 240
cleaning and lubricating, 241
condensation on inner surface, 507
drywalling around, 245–246
energy-efficient construction, 503
energy performance, 240
filling holes, 36, 38
installing
storm window, 252–253
technique, 248–251
vinyl replacement windows, 250
maintenance, 240–241
measuring, 248
openings, creating, 213–214, 233, 336–337
painting exterior, 66–67
painting interior, 36–37
parts, 66
removing, 248
sash cords, replacing broken, 241
sash removal, 37
screen, replacing, 245
security, 246–247
skylights, 253
springs, adjusting, 246
staining, 38–39
sticking, 36, 39, 240
wallpapering around, 78–80
weatherproofing, 499, 509, 514–515
window-well covers, 508
Wire
grounding, 369
joining to a terminal, 372–373
splicing, 366, 371, 372
stripping, 371
surface-mounted wiring, 394–395
types, 365
Wire nuts, 366
Wire nut wrench, 375
Wood
flooring
acclimating the flooring, 187, 191
border, decorative, 189
engineered, 191, 194
installation tips, 187
locations for, 153
materials, 154
painting, 44
parquet tile, 180–181, 185
removing, 163
sanding and refinishing, 182–184
squeaks, 45, 157, 183
strip-wood, 186–188
wide-plank, 190
priming new, 22
shakes and shingles, 540, 559
siding, 538–541
tongue-and-groove ceiling, 104
veneer, 261
Wood conditioner, 40
Wood putty/filler, 36, 38, 45, 57
Wood rot, 539